JANUARY 1, 2005

THE WATCHTOWER

ANNOUNCING JEHOVAH'S KINGDOM

CAN RELIGION UNITE MANKIND?

THE WATCHTOWER®

ANNOUNCING JEHOVAH'S KINGDOM

January 1, 2005   Average Printing Each Issue: 26,439,000   Vol. 126, No. 1

THE PURPOSE OF *THE WATCHTOWER* is to exalt Jehovah God as Sovereign Lord of the universe. It keeps watch on world events as these fulfill Bible prophecy. It comforts all peoples with the good news that God's Kingdom will soon destroy those who oppress their fellowmen and that it will turn the earth into a paradise. It encourages faith in God's now-reigning King, Jesus Christ, whose shed blood opens the way for mankind to gain eternal life. *The Watchtower,* published by Jehovah's Witnesses continuously since 1879, is nonpolitical. It adheres to the Bible as its authority.

IN THIS ISSUE

3   Why Many Doubt That Religion Can Unite Mankind

4   United by Love of God

7   Hold to the Pattern Jesus Set

12   Trained to Give a Thorough Witness

18   We Learned to Trust Completely in Jehovah

23   How to Protect Your Children by Means of Godly Wisdom

27   Beware of Customs That Displease God

31   Questions From Readers

32   Mealtime—More Than Just a Time to Eat!

WATCHTOWER STUDIES

JANUARY 31–FEBRUARY 6:
Hold to the Pattern Jesus Set.
Page 7. Songs to be used: 205, 168.

FEBRUARY 7-13:
Trained to Give a Thorough Witness.
Page 12. Songs to be used: 6, 181.

Publication of *The Watchtower* is part of a worldwide Bible educational work supported by voluntary donations.

Unless otherwise indicated, Scripture quotations are from the modern-language *New World Translation of the Holy Scriptures—With References.*

The Watchtower (ISSN 0043-1087) is published semimonthly by Watchtower Bible and Tract Society of New York, Inc.; M. H. Larson, President; G. F. Simonis, Secretary-Treasurer; 25 Columbia Heights, Brooklyn, NY 11201-2483. Periodicals Postage Paid at Brooklyn, NY, and at additional mailing offices. **POSTMASTER:** Send address changes to Watchtower, **Wallkill, NY 12589.**

Changes of address should reach us 30 days before your moving date. Give us your old and new address (if possible, your old address label).

Semimonthly   ENGLISH

Would you welcome more information or a free home Bible study? Please send your request to Jehovah's Witnesses, using the appropriate address below.

America, United States of: Wallkill, NY 12589. *Antigua:* Box 119, St. Johns. *Australia:* Box 280, Ingleburn, NSW 1890. *Bahamas:* Box N-1247, Nassau, N.P. *Barbados, W.I.:* Crusher Site Road, Prospect, St. James. *Britain:* The Ridgeway, London NW7 1RN. *Canada:* Box 4100, Halton Hills (Georgetown), Ontario L7G 4Y4. *Germany:* Niederselters, Am Steinfels, D-65618 Selters. *Ghana:* P. O. Box GP 760, Accra. *Guyana:* 352-360 Tyrell St., Republic Park Phase 2 EBD. *Hawaii 96819:* 2055 Kam IV Rd., Honolulu. *Hong Kong:* 4 Kent Road, Kowloon Tong. *India:* Post Box 6440, Yelahanka, Bangalore 560 064, KAR. *Ireland:* Newcastle, Greystones, Co. Wicklow. *Jamaica:* P. O. Box 103, Old Harbour, St. Catherine. *Japan:* 1271 Nakashinden, Ebina City, Kanagawa Pref., 243-0496. *Kenya:* P.O. Box 47788, GPO Nairobi 00100. *New Zealand:* P.O. Box 75-142, Manurewa. *Nigeria:* P.M.B. 1090, Benin City 300001, Edo State. *Philippines, Republic of:* P. O. Box 2044, 1060 Manila. *South Africa:* Private Bag X2067, Krugersdorp, 1740. *Trinidad and Tobago, Republic of:* Lower Rapsey Street & Laxmi Lane, Curepe. *Zambia:* Box 33459, Lusaka 10101. *Zimbabwe:* Private Bag WG-5001, Westgate.

NOW PUBLISHED IN 150 LANGUAGES. SEMIMONTHLY: Afrikaans, Albanian,* Amharic, Arabic, Bengali, Bicol, Bislama, Bulgarian, Cebuano,* Chichewa,* Chinese, Chinese (Simplified),* Cibemba,* Croatian,* Czech,*# Danish,*# Dutch,*# East Armenian, Efik,* English*#© (also Braille), Estonian, Ewe, Fijian, Finnish,*# French,*# Ga, Georgian, German,*# Greek,* Gujarati, Gun, Hebrew, Hiligaynon, Hindi, Hungarian,*# Igbo,* Iloko,* Indonesian, Italian,*# Japanese*# (also Braille), Kannada, Kinyarwanda, Kirundi, Korean*# (also Braille), Latvian, Lingala, Lithuanian, Luvale, Macedonian, Malagasy,* Malayalam, Maltese, Marathi, Myanmar, Nepali, New Guinea Pidgin, Norwegian,*# Pangasinan, Papiamento (Aruba), Papiamento (Curaçao), Polish,*# Portuguese*# (also Braille), Punjabi, Rarotongan, Romanian,* Russian,* Samar-Leyte, Samoan, Sango, Sepedi, Serbian, Sesotho, Shona,* Silozi, Sinhala, Slovak,* Slovenian, Solomon Islands Pidgin, Spanish,*# Sranantongo, Swahili,* Swedish,*# Tagalog,* Tamil, Telugu, Thai, Tigrinya, Tongan, Tshiluba, Tsonga, Tswana, Turkish, Twi, Ukrainian,* Urdu, Venda, Vietnamese, Wallisian, Xhosa, Yoruba,* Zulu*

MONTHLY: American Sign Language,△☐ Armenian, Assamese, Azerbaijani (Roman script), Brazilian Sign Language,△ Cambodian, Chitonga, Gilbertese, Greenlandic, Haitian Creole, Hausa, Hiri Motu, Icelandic, Isoko, Kaonde, Kazakh, Kikongo, Kiluba, Kirghiz, Kwanyama/Ndonga, Luganda, Marshallese, Mauritian Creole, Mizo, Monokutuba, Moore, Niuean, Ossetian, Otetela, Palauan, Persian, Ponapean, Seychelles Creole, Tahitian, Tatar, Tiv, Trukese, Tumbuka, Tuvaluan, Umbundu, Yapese, Zande

* Study articles also available in large-print edition.
# Audiocassettes also available.
© CD (MP3 format) also available.
△ Videocassette
☐ DVD

WHY MANY DOUBT
That Religion Can Unite Mankind

Policemen wounded during clash between religious groups in India in 1947

"LOVE your neighbor." (Matthew 22:39) This basic rule of conduct is acclaimed by many religions. If such religions were effective in teaching their members to love their neighbor, their flocks would be drawn together and be united. However, is that what you have observed? Are religions a force for unity? A recent survey in Germany asked the question: "Do religions unite people, or are they more likely to separate them?" Of the respondents, 22 percent felt that religions unite, whereas 52 percent felt that they divide, or separate. Perhaps people in your country feel much the same way.

Why do many have little confidence that religion can unite mankind? Perhaps because of what they know from history. Instead of drawing people together, religion has often pushed them apart. In some instances, religion has been the cover under which the most dreadful atrocities have been committed. Consider some examples from just the last 100 years.

Influenced by Religion

During the second world war, Roman Catholic Croats and Orthodox Serbs in the Balkans were at one another's throats. Both groups claimed to follow Jesus, who taught his followers to love their neighbor. Yet, their conflict led to "one of the most appalling civilian massacres known to history," as one researcher put it. The world was aghast at the death toll of more than 500,000 men, women, and children.

In 1947 the Indian subcontinent was home to some 400 million people—about a fifth of humanity—mainly Hindus, Muslims, and Sikhs. When India was partitioned, the Islamic nation of Pakistan was born. At the time, hundreds of thousands of refugees from both countries were burned, beaten, tortured, and shot in a series of religious massacres.

As if the foregoing examples were not disturbing enough, the turn of the century brought to the fore the threat of terrorism. Today, terrorism has put the whole world on alert, and many terrorist groups claim to have religious ties. Religion is not viewed as a promoter of unity. Instead, it is often associated with violence and disunity. Small wonder, therefore, that the German newsmagazine *FOCUS* compared the world's major religions—Buddhism, Christendom, Confucianism, Hinduism, Islam, Judaism, and Taoism—to gunpowder.

Internal Squabbles

While some religions are at war with one another, others are beset by internal squabbles. For instance, in recent years the church-es of Christendom have been split by ongoing debates on matters of doctrine. Clergy and laity alike ask: Is birth control permitted? What about abortion? Should women be ordained as priests? How ought the church to view homosexuality? Should a religion sanction war? In view of such disunity, many wonder, 'How can a religion unite mankind if it cannot unite even its own members?'

Clearly, religion in general has failed to be a force for unity. But are all religions marked by divisions? Is there a religion that is different—one that can unite mankind?

United by **LOVE OF GOD**

WHEN the Christian congregation was formed in the first century of our Common Era, one of its outstanding characteristics—despite the diversity of its members—was its unity. Those worshipers of the true God came from nations in Asia, Europe, and Africa. They represented a variety of backgrounds—priests, soldiers, slaves, refugees, tradesmen, professionals, and businesspeople. Some were Jews, and others, Gentiles. Many had been adulterers, homosexuals, drunkards, thieves, or extortioners. Nevertheless, when they became Christians, they left their bad practices behind and became closely united in the faith.

What enabled first-century Christianity to bring all these people together in unity? Why were they at peace with one another and with people in general? Why did they not join in uprisings and conflicts? Why was early Christianity so different from today's major religions?

What Drew Congregation Members Close Together?

The foremost factor that united fellow believers in the first century was love of God. Those Christians recognized their primary obligation to love the true God, Jehovah, with all their heart, soul, and mind. For instance, the apostle Peter, a Jew, was instructed to visit the house of a foreign national,

Despite coming from diverse backgrounds, the early Christians were united

someone with whom he would not normally have close association. What moved him to obey was primarily love for Jehovah. Peter and other early Christians enjoyed a close relationship with God that was based on accurate knowledge of His personality, likes, and dislikes. In time, all worshipers understood that it was Jehovah's will for them to be "united in the same mind and in the same line of thought."—1 Corinthians 1:10; Matthew 22:37; Acts 10:1-35.

Believers were further drawn together by their faith in Jesus Christ. They wanted to follow closely in his footsteps. He commanded them: "Love one another; just as I have loved you . . . By this all will know that you are my disciples, if you have love among yourselves." (John 13:34, 35) This was to be, not a superficial emotion, but a self-sacrificing love. What would be the result? Jesus prayed concerning those putting faith in him: "I make request . . . that they may all be one, just as you, Father, are in union with me and I am in union with you, that they also may be in union with us."—John 17:20, 21; 1 Peter 2:21.

Jehovah poured out his holy spirit, or active force, upon his true servants. This spirit promoted unity among them. It opened to them an understanding of Bible teachings that was accepted in all congregations. Worshipers of Jehovah preached the same message—the sanctification of Jehovah's name through God's Messianic Kingdom, a heavenly government that is to rule over all mankind. Early Christians understood their obligation to be "no part of this world." Hence, whenever civil uprisings or military conflicts occurred, Christians remained neutral. They pursued peace with everyone.—John 14:26; 18:36; Matthew 6:9, 10; Acts 2:1-4; Romans 12:17-21.

All believers assumed their responsibility to promote unity. How? By ensuring that their conduct was in harmony with the Bible. Hence, the apostle Paul wrote to Christians: "Put away the old personality which conforms to your former course of conduct," and "put on the new personality."—Ephesians 4:22-32.

Unity Maintained

Of course, believers in the first century were imperfect, and situations developed that challenged their unity. For example, Acts 6:1-6 relates that a difference arose between Jewish Christians who spoke Greek and those who spoke Hebrew. Those speaking Greek felt that they were being discriminated against. Once the apostles were informed about the matter, however, it was attended to swiftly and fairly. Later, a question of doctrine led to controversy regarding the obligations of non-Jews in the Christian congregation. A decision was made based on Bible principles, and this decision was uniformly accepted.—Acts 15:1-29.

These examples show that disagreements did not lead to ethnic divisions or to unyielding doctrinal disunity in the first-century Christian congregation. Why not? Because the unifying factors—love for Jehovah, faith in Jesus Christ, self-sacrificing love for one

another, acceptance of the guidance of the holy spirit, a common understanding of Bible teachings, and a readiness to change one's conduct—were powerful enough to keep the early congregation united and at peace.

United in Worship in Modern Times

Can unity be achieved in the same way today? Can these same factors still draw members of a faith together and enable them to be at peace with all races in all parts of the world? Yes, they can! Jehovah's Witnesses are united in a worldwide brotherhood spanning more than 230 lands, islands, and territories. And they are united by the same factors that united Christians in the first century.

Foremost in contributing to the unity enjoyed by Jehovah's Witnesses is their devotion to Jehovah God. This means that they strive to be loyal to him under all circumstances. Witnesses of Jehovah also exercise faith in Jesus Christ and in his teachings. These Christians show self-sacrificing love for fellow believers and preach the same good news of God's Kingdom in all the lands where they are active. They are happy to talk about this Kingdom with people of all faiths, races, nationalities, and social groups. Jehovah's Witnesses also remain neutral in the affairs of the world, which helps them to withstand the political, cultural, social, and commercial pressures that are so divisive among mankind. All Witnesses accept their obligation to promote unity by conducting themselves in harmony with Bible standards.

Unity Attracts Others

This unity has often aroused the interest of individuals who were not Witnesses. Ilse,* for instance, was once a Catholic nun in a convent in Germany. What attracted her to Jehovah's Witnesses? Ilse said: "They are the best people I have ever met. They do not go to war; they do nothing to harm anyone. They want to help people to live happily on a paradise earth under God's Kingdom."

Then there is Günther, who was a German soldier stationed in France during the second world war. One day a Protestant priest held a religious service for the soldiers in Günther's unit. The priest prayed for blessings, protection, and victory. After the service, Günther took up his position as a lookout. Through his binoculars, he observed enemy troops on the other side of the battle lines also attending a religious service conducted by a priest. Günther later noted: "Likely that priest also prayed for blessings, protection, and victory. I wondered how it was possible for Christian churches to be on opposing sides of the same war." These impressions were etched on Günther's memory. When he later came in contact with Jehovah's Witnesses, who do not participate in war, Günther became part of their worldwide brotherhood.

Ashok and Feema used to belong to an Eastern religion. In their home, they had a shrine to a god. When serious illness struck their family, they reexamined their religion. In conversations with Jehovah's Witnesses, Ashok and Feema were impressed by the teachings of the Bible and by the love existing among the Witnesses. They are now zealous publishers of the good news of Jehovah's Kingdom.

Ilse, Günther, Ashok, and Feema are united with millions of Jehovah's Witnesses in a global brotherhood. They believe the Bible's promise that the same factors that unite them in worship today will soon unite all obedient mankind. Then, there will be no further atrocities, disunity, and division in the name of religion. The whole world will be united in the worship of the true God, Jehovah.—Revelation 21:4, 5.

---

* Some of the names used in this article have been changed.

HOLD TO THE PATTERN JESUS SET

"I set the pattern for you, that, just as I did to you, you should do also."—JOHN 13:15.

IN ALL the history of mankind, only one person has lived his whole life without sinning. That is Jesus. Apart from Jesus, "there is no man that does not sin." (1 Kings 8:46; Romans 3:23) For that reason, genuine Christians view Jesus as a perfect model to be imitated. Indeed, on Nisan 14, 33 C.E., shortly before his death, Jesus himself told his followers to imitate him. He said: "I set the pattern for you, that, just as I did to you, you should do also." (John 13: 15) During that last night, Jesus mentioned a number of ways in which Christians should strive to be like him. In this article, we will consider some of them.

Jesus set the perfect pattern of humility

The Need for Humility

2 When Jesus urged his disciples to follow the pattern he set, he was specifically speaking of humility. On more than one occasion, he had counseled his followers to be humble, and on the night of Nisan 14, he demonstrated his own humility by washing the feet of his apostles. Then Jesus said: "If I, although Lord and Teacher, washed your feet, you also ought to wash the feet of one another." (John 13:14) Thereafter, he told his apostles to follow the pattern he set. And what a fine pattern of humility that was!

3 The apostle Paul tells us that before coming to earth, Jesus was "existing in God's form." Nevertheless, he emptied himself and became a lowly human. More than that, "he humbled himself and became obedient as far as death, yes, death on a torture stake." (Philippians 2:6-8) Think of it. Jesus, the second-highest person in the universe, consented to become lower than the angels, to be born a helpless baby, to grow up subject to imperfect parents, and finally to die like a despised criminal. (Colossians 1:15, 16; Hebrews 2:6, 7) What humility! Is it possible to imitate that "mental attitude" and cultivate such "lowliness of mind"? (Philippians 2: 3-5) Yes, but it is not easy.

---

1. Why is Jesus a model for Christians to imitate?
2, 3. In what ways was Jesus a perfect pattern of humility?

⁴ The opposite of humility is pride. (Proverbs 6:16-19) Pride led to Satan's downfall. (1 Timothy 3:6) It easily takes root in human hearts, and once there, it is hard to remove. People are prideful because of their country, their race, their possessions, their education, their secular achievements, their social standing, their looks, their sporting abilities, and many other things. Yet, none of those things are important to Jehovah. (1 Corinthians 4:7) And if they cause us to be proud, they damage our relationship with him. "Jehovah is high, and yet the humble one he sees; but the lofty one he knows only from a distance."—Psalm 138:6; Proverbs 8:13.

Humble Among Our Brothers

⁵ Even our contributions to and achievements in Jehovah's service should not make us proud; neither should responsibilities in the congregation. (1 Chronicles 29:14; 1 Timothy 6:17, 18) In fact, the weightier our responsibilities, the more humble we need to be. The apostle Peter urged elders not to be "lording it over those who are God's inheritance, but [to become] examples to the flock." (1 Peter 5:3) Elders are appointed to be servants and examples, not lords and masters.—Luke 22:24-26; 2 Corinthians 1:24.

⁶ Elders are not alone in needing humility. To younger men, who may be proud of their quicker minds and stronger bodies compared with those of older ones, Peter wrote: "Gird yourselves with lowliness of mind toward one another, because God opposes the haughty ones, but he gives undeserved kindness to the humble ones." (1 Peter 5:5) Yes, Christlike humility is vital for all. It takes hu-

4. What things make humans proud, but why is pride dangerous?
5. Why is it vital that elders be humble?
6. In what areas of Christian living do we need humility?

mility to preach the good news, especially in the face of indifference or hostility. It takes humility to accept counsel or to simplify our life in order to enlarge our share in the ministry. In addition, we need humility as well as courageous faith when enduring bad publicity, legal attacks, or violent persecution. —1 Peter 5:6.

⁷ How can a person overcome pride and conduct himself "with lowliness of mind considering that the others are superior" to him? (Philippians 2:3) He needs to view himself as Jehovah does. Jesus explained the right attitude when he said: "You, also, when you have done all the things assigned to you, say, 'We are good-for-nothing slaves. What we have done is what we ought to have done.'" (Luke 17:10) Remember, nothing we can do compares with what Jesus did. Yet, Jesus was humble.

⁸ Further, we can ask for Jehovah's help to

7, 8. What are some ways in which we can cultivate humility?

Every aspect of a Christian's life, including preaching, calls for humility

*Satan can make improper entertainment
seem acceptable to a Christian*

cultivate the proper view of ourselves. Like
the psalmist, we can pray: "Teach me goodness, sensibleness and knowledge themselves, for in your commandments I have exercised faith." (Psalm 119:66) Jehovah will
help us to develop a sensible, balanced view
of ourselves, and he will bless us for our
humble attitude. (Proverbs 18:12) Jesus said:
"Whoever exalts himself will be humbled,
and whoever humbles himself will be exalted."—Matthew 23:12.

A Proper View of Right and Wrong

⁹ Despite living for 33 years among imperfect people, Jesus remained "without sin."
(Hebrews 4:15) In fact, when prophesying about the Messiah, the psalmist said:
"You have loved righteousness and you hate
wickedness." (Psalm 45:7; Hebrews 1:9) In
this too Christians strive to imitate Jesus.
Not only do they know right from wrong;
they hate what is wrong and love what is
right. (Amos 5:15) This helps them to battle against their inborn sinful inclinations.
—Genesis 8:21; Romans 7:21-25.

¹⁰ Jesus said to the Pharisee Nicodemus:
"He that practices vile things hates the light

---

9. How did Jesus view right and wrong?
10. If we unrepentantly practice "vile things," what
attitude are we betraying?

and does not come to the light, in order that
his works may not be reproved. But he that
does what is true comes to the light, in order
that his works may be made manifest as having been worked in harmony with God."
(John 3:20, 21) Consider: John identified Jesus as "the true light that gives light to every
sort of man." (John 1:9, 10) Yet, Jesus said
that if we practice "vile things"—things that
are wrong, unacceptable to God—we hate
the light. Can you imagine hating Jesus and
what he stands for? Yet, that is the position
of those who unrepentantly practice sin.
Perhaps they do not view things that way,
but clearly, Jesus does.

How to Cultivate Jesus' View
of Right and Wrong

¹¹ We need a clear understanding of what
is right and what is wrong from Jehovah's
viewpoint. We gain that understanding only
from a study of God's Word, the Bible. As we
pursue such a study, we need to pray as the
psalmist prayed: "Make me know your own
ways, O Jehovah; teach me your own paths."
(Psalm 25:4) Remember, however, that Satan is deceptive. (2 Corinthians 11:14) He
can disguise wrong and make it appear acceptable to an unwary Christian. Hence, we
need to meditate deeply on what we learn
and closely heed the counsel of "the faithful and discreet slave." (Matthew 24:45-47)
Study, prayer, and meditation on what we
learn will help us to grow to maturity and
be among those who "through use have
their perceptive powers trained to distinguish both right and wrong." (Hebrews 5:
14) Then we will be disposed to hate the
wrong and love the right.

¹² If we hate what is wrong, we will not

---

11. What is vital if we are to cultivate Jesus' view of
right and wrong?
12. What Bible counsel helps us not to practice lawlessness?

allow a desire for wrong things to grow in our hearts. Many years after Jesus' death, the apostle John wrote: "Do not be loving either the world or the things in the world. If anyone loves the world, the love of the Father is not in him; because everything in the world—the desire of the flesh and the desire of the eyes and the showy display of one's means of life—does not originate with the Father, but originates with the world."—1 John 2:15, 16.

The love of our brothers will fortify us against opposition

¹³ Some might reason that not everything in the world is wrong. Even so, the world and its attractions can easily distract us from serving Jehovah. And nothing the world provides is designed to draw us closer to God. Hence, if we grow to *love* the things in the world, even things that may not in themselves be wrong, we are on a dangerous course. (1 Timothy 6:9, 10) Besides, much in the world truly is bad and can corrupt us. If we watch movies or television programs that highlight violence, materialism, or sexual immorality, those things can become acceptable—and then tempting. If we mix with people whose main interest is in improving their life-style or cultivating business opportunities, those things can become of chief importance to us too.—Matthew 6:24; 1 Corinthians 15:33.

¹⁴ On the other hand, if we find delight in Jehovah's Word, "the desire of the flesh and the desire of the eyes and the showy display of one's means of life" will lose much of their allure. Further, if we associate with those who put the interests of God's Kingdom first, we will become like them, lov-

ing what they love and avoiding what they avoid.—Psalm 15:4; Proverbs 13:20.

¹⁵ Hating lawlessness and loving righteousness helped Jesus to keep his eyes on "the joy that was set before him." (Hebrews 12:2) The same can be true of us. We know that "the world is passing away and so is its desire." Any gratification that this world affords is only temporary. However, "he that does the will of God remains forever." (1 John 2:17) Because Jesus did God's will, he opened the way for humans to gain everlasting life. (1 John 5:13) May we all imitate him and benefit from his integrity.

Facing Persecution

¹⁶ Jesus indicated another way that his disciples would imitate him, saying: "This is my commandment, that you love one another just as I have loved you." (John 15:12, 13, 17) There are many reasons why Christians love their brothers. On this occasion, Jesus above all had in mind the hatred they would face from the world. He said: "If the world hates you, you know that it has hated me before it hated you. . . . A slave is not greater than his

─────

13, 14. (a) Why is a love of the things of the world dangerous for Christians? (b) How can we avoid cultivating a love of things in the world?

─────

15. As was the case with Jesus, how will loving righteousness and hating lawlessness strengthen us?
16. Why did Jesus urge his followers to love one another?

master. If they have persecuted me, they will persecute you also." (John 15:18, 20) Yes, even in being persecuted, Christians are like Jesus. They need to develop a strong, loving bond to help them withstand that hatred.

[17] Why would the world hate Christians? Because, like Jesus, they are "no part of the world." (John 17:14, 16) They are neutral in military and political matters, and they observe Bible principles, respecting the sanctity of life and keeping to a high moral code. (Acts 15:28, 29; 1 Corinthians 6:9-11) Their primary goals are spiritual, not material. They live in the world, but as Paul wrote, they do not 'use it to the full.' (1 Corinthians 7:31) True, some have expressed admiration for the high standards of Jehovah's Witnesses. But Jehovah's Witnesses do not make compromises to seek admiration or acceptance. As a result, most in the world do not understand them, and many hate them.

[18] Jesus' apostles saw the world's intense hatred when Jesus was arrested and executed, and they saw how Jesus handled that hatred. In the garden of Gethsemane, Jesus' religious opponents came to arrest him. Peter tried to protect him with a sword, but Jesus said to Peter: "Return your sword to its place, for all those who take the sword will perish by the sword." (Matthew 26:52; Luke 22:50, 51) In earlier times, Israelites fought with the sword against their enemies. Now, though, things were different. God's Kingdom was "no part of this world" and had no national boundaries to protect. (John 18:36) Soon Peter would be part of a spiritual nation, whose members would have their citizenship in heaven. (Galatians 6:16; Philippians 3:20, 21) Henceforth, then, Jesus' followers would handle hatred and persecution the way Jesus did—fearlessly but peaceably. They would confidently leave the outcome of matters in Jehovah's hands and rely on him for the strength to endure.—Luke 22:42.

[19] Years later, Peter wrote: "Christ suffered for you, leaving you a model for you to follow his steps closely. . . . When he was being reviled, he did not go reviling in return. When he was suffering, he did not go threatening, but kept on committing himself to the one who judges righteously." (1 Peter 2:21-23) Just as Jesus warned, Christians have experienced harsh persecution over the years. Both in the first century and in our own time, they have followed Jesus' example and built up a wonderful record of faithful endurance, demonstrating that they are peaceful integrity keepers. (Revelation 2:9, 10) May we all individually do likewise when circumstances demand it.—2 Timothy 3:12.

"Put On the Lord Jesus Christ"

[20] Paul wrote to the congregation in Rome: "Put on the Lord Jesus Christ, and do not be planning ahead for the desires of the flesh." (Romans 13:14) Christians wear Jesus, as it were, like a garment. They strive to imitate his qualities and actions to such an extent that they become a reflection—even if imperfect—of their Master.—1 Thessalonians 1:6.

[21] We can successfully "put on the Lord

---

17. Why does the world hate true Christians?
18, 19. Following the pattern of Jesus, how do Christians handle opposition and persecution?

20-22. In what way do Christians "put on the Lord Jesus Christ"?

Can You Explain?

- Why is it vital that a Christian be humble?
- How can we cultivate a proper view of right and wrong?
- In what way do Christians imitate Jesus in handling opposition and persecution?
- How is it possible to "put on the Lord Jesus Christ"?

Jesus Christ" if we become familiar with the Master's life and strive to live as he lived. We imitate his humility, his love of righteousness, his hatred of lawlessness, his love for his brothers, his being no part of the world, and his patient endurance of suffering. We do not 'plan ahead for the desires of the flesh' —that is, we do not make our chief purpose in life the reaching of secular goals or the satisfying of fleshly desires. Rather, when making a decision or handling a problem, we ask: 'What would Jesus do in this situation? What would he want me to do?'

22 Finally, we imitate Jesus in keeping busy "preaching the good news." (Matthew 4:23; 1 Corinthians 15:58) In that way too, Christians follow the pattern that Jesus set, and the following article will discuss how.

TRAINED TO GIVE A THOROUGH WITNESS

"You will be witnesses of me both in Jerusalem and in all Judea and Samaria and to the most distant part of the earth."—ACTS 1:8.

"JESUS who was from Nazareth . . . ordered us to preach to the people and to give a thorough witness that this is the One decreed by God to be judge of the living and the dead." (Acts 10:38, 42) With those words, the apostle Peter explained to Cornelius and his family the commission he had received to be an evangelizer.

2 When did Jesus give that commission? Likely, Peter was thinking of what the resurrected Jesus said just before he ascended to heaven. On that occasion, Jesus told his faithful disciples: "You will be witnesses of me both in Jerusalem and in all Judea and Samaria and to the most distant part of the earth." (Acts 1:8) However, for some time before that, Peter had known that as a disciple of Jesus, he would have to talk to others about his faith in Jesus.

Three Years of Training

3 Several months after his baptism in 29 C.E., Jesus preached where Peter and his brother Andrew worked

---

1, 2. What was Peter's commission, and who gave it to him?
3. What miracle did Jesus perform, and what invitation did he offer to Peter and Andrew?

as fishermen on the Sea of Galilee. They had been working all night but without success. Still, Jesus told them: "Pull out to where it is deep, and you men let down your nets for a catch." When they did what Jesus said, "they enclosed a great multitude of fish. In fact, their nets began ripping apart." On seeing the miracle, Peter was struck with fear, but Jesus calmed him, saying: "Stop being afraid. From now on you will be catching men alive."—Luke 5:4-10.

⁴ Immediately, Peter and Andrew—as well as James and John, the sons of Zebedee—left their boats and followed Jesus. For almost three years, they accompanied Jesus on his preaching tours and received training as evangelizers. (Matthew 10:7; Mark 1:16, 18, 20, 38; Luke 4:43; 10:9) At the end of that time, on Nisan 14, 33 C.E., Jesus told them: "He that exercises faith in me, that one also will do the works that I do; and he will do works greater than these." (John 14:12) Jesus' disciples would give a thorough witness as Jesus did but on a much larger scale. As they soon learned, they and all future disciples would bear witness in "all the nations," right up until "the conclusion of the system of things."—Matthew 28:19, 20.

⁵ We are living in "the conclusion of the system of things." (Matthew 24:3) Unlike those first disciples, we cannot accompany Jesus and observe him preaching to people. Still, we can benefit from his training by reading in the Bible how he preached and what instructions he gave his followers. (Luke 10:1-11) However, this article will discuss something else of vital importance that Jesus demonstrated to his disciples—the right attitude toward the preaching work.

A Concern for People

⁶ Why did Jesus give such an effective witness? One reason was his deep interest in and concern for people. The psalmist foretold that Jesus would "feel sorry for the lowly one and the poor one." (Psalm 72:13) He certainly fulfilled that prophecy. The Bible says about one occasion: "On seeing the crowds he felt pity for them, because they were skinned and thrown about like sheep without a shepherd." (Matthew 9:36) Even gross sinners sensed his concern and were drawn to him.—Matthew 9:9-13; Luke 7:36-38; 19:1-10.

⁷ We today will be effective if we show the same concern for people. Before sharing in the ministry, why not take a moment to reflect on how much people need the information you are taking to them? Think of the problems they may have that only the Kingdom will solve. Be resolved to be positive with everyone, since you do not know who will respond to the message. Perhaps the next person you approach has been praying for someone like you to come and help him!

Motivated by Love

⁸ The good news that Jesus declared had to do with the accomplishment of Jehovah's will, the sanctification of His name, and the vindication of His sovereignty—the most important issues before mankind. (Matthew 6:9, 10) Because he loved his Father, Jesus was moved to keep his integrity to the end and to give a thorough witness about the Kingdom, which will resolve those issues. (John 14:31) Because Jesus' followers today have the same motivation, they are diligent as they share in the ministry. The apostle John said: "This is what the

---

4. (a) How did Jesus prepare his disciples to give a witness? (b) How would the ministry of Jesus' disciples compare with his own?
5. In what ways can we benefit from the training Jesus gave his followers?

6, 7. What quality of Jesus made his ministry effective, and how can we imitate him in this respect?
8. In imitation of Jesus, what motivates his followers to preach the good news?

love of God means, that we observe his commandments," including the commandment to preach the good news and make disciples. —1 John 5:3; Matthew 28:19, 20.

9 Jesus told his followers: "If you love me, you will observe my commandments. He that has my commandments and observes them, that one is he who loves me." (John 14:15, 21) Thus, love of Jesus should motivate us to witness about the truth and observe the other things that Jesus commanded. During one of his postresurrection appearances, Jesus urged Peter: "Feed my lambs. . . . Shepherd my little sheep. . . . Feed my little sheep." What should move Peter to do that? Jesus indicated the answer when he repeatedly asked Peter: "Do you love me? . . . Do you love me? . . . Do you have affection for me?" Yes, Peter's love for Jesus, his affection for him, would motivate him to give a thorough witness, find Jesus' "little sheep," and thereafter be a spiritual shepherd to them.—John 21:15-17.

10 Today, we are not personally acquainted with Jesus as Peter was. Still, we have a deep understanding of what Jesus did for us. Our hearts are moved by the great love that led him to "taste death for every man." (Hebrews 2:9; John 15:13) We feel as Paul felt when he wrote: "The love the Christ has compels us . . . He died for all that those who live might live no longer for themselves, but for him." (2 Corinthians 5:14, 15) We demonstrate that we take Jesus' love for us seriously and that we love him in return by taking seriously the commission to give a *thorough* witness. (1 John 2:3-5) We would never want to adopt a casual approach to the

Starting this year, the Service Year Report of Jehovah's Witnesses Worldwide will not appear in the January 1 issue of *The Watchtower*. It will be published instead in the February 1 issue.

preaching work, as if we esteemed Jesus' sacrifice as of ordinary value.—Hebrews 10:29.

Keeping the Right Focus

11 When Jesus was before Pontius Pilate, he said: "For this I have been born, and for this I have come into the world, that I should bear witness to the truth." (John 18:37) Jesus allowed nothing to distract him from bearing witness to the truth. That was God's will for him.

12 Satan certainly tested Jesus in this regard. Shortly after Jesus' baptism, Satan offered to make him a great man in the world, to give him "all the kingdoms of the world and their glory." (Matthew 4:8, 9) Later, the Jews wanted to make him a king. (John 6:15) Some might ponder the possible benefits of Jesus' accepting those offers, perhaps reasoning that as a human king, Jesus could have done much good for mankind. Jesus, though, rejected that kind of thinking. His focus was on bearing witness to the truth.

13 In addition, Jesus was not distracted by a pursuit of riches. As a result, he did not live a life of wealth. He did not even have his own home. On one occasion, he said: "Foxes have dens and birds of heaven have roosts, but the Son of man has nowhere to lay down his head." (Matthew 8:20) When Jesus died, the only recorded thing of value that he owned was the garment over which the Roman soldiers cast lots. (John 19:23, 24) Was Jesus' life a failure, then? By no means!

_____

9, 10. Apart from love of God, what other love motivates us to give a thorough witness?

11, 12. For what purpose did Jesus come into the world, and how did he keep his focus?

13, 14. (a) What failed to distract Jesus from his focus? (b) Although Jesus was materially poor, what did he accomplish?

[14] Jesus accomplished far more than the wealthiest philanthropist ever could. Paul said: "You know the undeserved kindness of our Lord Jesus Christ, that though he was rich he became poor for your sakes, that you might become rich through his poverty." (2 Corinthians 8:9; Philippians 2:5-8) Although materially poor, Jesus opened the

We will be effective in our ministry if we show the same concern for people that Jesus did

door for humble individuals to enjoy everlasting life in perfection. How grateful we are to him! And how we rejoice in the reward he received because he kept his focus on doing God's will!—Psalm 40:8; Acts 2:32, 33, 36.

[15] Christians who today strive to imitate Jesus also refuse to be distracted by the pursuit

───────────
15. What is more valuable than wealth?

of wealth. (1 Timothy 6:9, 10) They acknowledge that riches can make life comfortable, but they know that wealth does nothing for their everlasting future. When a Christian dies, his material wealth is of no more value to him than Jesus' garment was to him when he died. (Ecclesiastes 2:10, 11, 17-19; 7:12) When a Christian dies, the only thing of real value that he possesses is his relationship with Jehovah and with Jesus Christ.—Matthew 6:19-21; Luke 16:9.

Not Deterred by Opposition

[16] Opposition did not cause Jesus to lose his focus on bearing witness to the truth. Even knowing that his earthly ministry would end in a sacrificial death did not discourage him. Of Jesus, Paul said: "For the joy that was set before him he endured a torture stake, despising shame, and has sat down at the right hand of the throne of God." (Hebrews 12:2) Notice that Jesus 'despised shame.' He was not troubled about what opponents thought of him. His focus was on doing God's will.

[17] Applying the lesson of Jesus' endurance, Paul encourages Christians: "Consider closely the one who has endured such contrary talk by sinners against their own interests, that you may not get tired and give out in your souls." (Hebrews 12:3) True, it can be wearying to face opposition or mockery day after day. It can be tiring to keep resisting the allures of the world, perhaps to the disappointment of relatives who encourage us to "make something" of ourselves. However, like Jesus we look to Jehovah for support as we determinedly put the Kingdom first in our lives.—Matthew 6:33; Romans 15:13; 1 Corinthians 2:4.

[18] Jesus' refusal to be distracted was

───────────
16. How did Jesus face up to opposition?
17. What can we learn from Jesus' endurance?
18. What fine lesson can we learn from Jesus' words to Peter?

demonstrated when he began to tell his disciples about his coming death. Peter encouraged Jesus to "be kind" to himself and assured him that he would "not have this destiny at all." Jesus refused to listen to anything that might weaken his resolve to do Jehovah's will. He turned his back on Peter and said: "Get behind me, Satan! You are a stumbling block to me, because you think, not God's thoughts, but those of men." (Matthew 16:21-23) May we always be equally determined to reject men's thoughts. Rather, let us always be guided by God's thoughts.

Bringing Real Benefits

¹⁹ Jesus performed many miracles to demonstrate that he was the Messiah. He even raised the dead. Those works attracted the crowds, but Jesus did not come to earth merely to do a social work. He came to bear witness to the truth. He knew that any material benefits he provided were temporary. Even the resurrected ones would die again. Only by bearing witness to the truth could he help some to gain everlasting life.—Luke 18:28-30.

²⁰ Today, some individuals try to imitate Jesus' good works by opening hospitals

---

19. Although he was a miracle worker, what was the most important part of Jesus' ministry?
20, 21. What balance do true Christians maintain in the matter of good works?

Jesus came to earth primarily to bear witness to the truth

or performing other services among the world's poor. In some cases, they do this at great personal cost, and their sincerity is commendable; but any relief they supply is temporary at best. Only the Kingdom will bring permanent relief. Hence, Jehovah's Witnesses concentrate, as Jesus did, on bearing witness to the truth about that Kingdom.

²¹ Of course, true Christians do perform good works. Paul wrote: "As long as we have time favorable for it, let us work what is good toward all, but especially toward those related to us in the faith." (Galatians 6:10) In times of crisis or when someone is in need, we do not hesitate to "work what is good" to our neighbors or our Christian brothers. Still, we keep our main focus where it belongs—on bearing witness to the truth.

Learn From Jesus' Example

²² Paul wrote: "Really, woe is me if I did not declare the good news!" (1 Corinthians 9:16) He was not casual about the good news because preaching it meant life for himself

---

22. Why do Christians preach to their neighbors?

Can You Answer?

- How can we benefit from the training Jesus gave his disciples?

- What was Jesus' attitude toward the people he preached to?

- What motivates us to give a thorough witness?

- In what ways can we keep our focus on doing God's will, as Jesus did?

and his hearers. (1 Timothy 4:16) We view our ministry in the same way. We want to help our neighbors. We want to show our love for Jehovah. We want to prove our love for Jesus and our appreciation for his great love for us. Hence, we preach the good news and thus live "no more for the desires of men, but for God's will."—1 Peter 4:1, 2.

23 Like Jesus, we do not lose our focus when others mock us or angrily reject our message. We learn a lesson from the miracle Jesus performed when he called Peter and Andrew to follow him. We see that if we obey Jesus and, so to speak, let down our nets even in seemingly unproductive waters, our fishing might produce results. Many

Christian fishermen have obtained a fine catch after years of work in seemingly barren waters. Others have been able to move to where the fishing is more productive and have obtained a fine catch there. Whatever we do, we will not stop letting down our nets. We know that Jesus has not yet declared the preaching work finished in any part of the earth.—Matthew 24:14.

24 More than six million Witnesses of Jehovah are now busy in over 230 lands. The February 1, 2005, issue of *The Watchtower* will carry the annual worldwide report of their activity during the 2004 service year. That report will demonstrate Jehovah's rich blessing on the preaching work. In the time that remains for this system of things, may we continue to take to heart Paul's stirring words: "Preach the word, be at it urgently." (2 Timothy 4:2) May we continue to give a thorough witness until Jehovah says that the work is finished.

23, 24. (a) What lesson do we learn from the miracle of the fish? (b) Who today are giving a thorough witness?

Jehovah's Witnesses concentrate on giving a thorough witness

We Learned to Trust Completely in Jehovah

AS TOLD BY
NATALIE HOLTORF

It was June 1945. One day that month, a pale-looking man appeared at our house and patiently stood at the front door. Startled, my youngest daughter, Ruth, shouted: "Mama, there is a stranger at the door!" Little did she know that the stranger was her father—my dear husband, Ferdinand. Two years earlier, only three days after Ruth was born, Ferdinand left home, was arrested, and ended up in a Nazi concentration camp. But now, at last, Ruth met her father, and our family was reunited. Ferdinand and I had so much to tell each other!

FERDINAND was born in 1909 in the city of Kiel, in Germany, and I was born in 1907 in the city of Dresden, also in Germany. When I was 12 years old, our family first came in contact with the Bible Students, as Jehovah's Witnesses were then known. At the age of 19, I left the Evangelical Church and dedicated my life to Jehovah.

Meanwhile, Ferdinand graduated from nautical college and became a sailor. During his voyages, he pondered questions about the existence of a Creator. Back in port, Ferdinand visited his brother, who was a Bible Student. This visit was enough to convince him that the Bible had the answers to the questions that were troubling him. He left the Lutheran Church, and he also decided to quit working as a sailor. After spending his first day in the preaching work, he felt a deep desire to do this work for the rest of his life. That same night, Ferdinand dedicated his life to Jehovah. He was baptized in August 1931.

A Sailor and a Preacher

In November 1931, Ferdinand boarded a train for the Netherlands to assist with the preaching work there. When Ferdinand told the brother who organized the work in that country that he had been a sailor, the brother exclaimed: "You are just the man we need!" The brothers had rented a boat so that a group of pioneers (full-time ministers) could preach to those living along the waterways in the northern part of the country. The boat had a crew of five, but none of them could sail it. So Ferdinand became the skipper.

With Ferdinand in October 1932

Six months later Ferdinand was asked to serve as a pioneer in Tilburg, in southern Netherlands. About that time I also arrived in Tilburg to serve as a pioneer, and I met Ferdinand. But right away we were asked to move to Groningen, in the northern part of the country. There, we were married in October 1932, and in a home used by several pioneers, we had our honeymoon while pioneering at the same time!

In 1935 our daughter Esther was born. Although we had little income, we were determined to keep on pioneering. We moved to a village, where we lived in a tiny house.

While I cared for the baby at home, my husband spent a long day in the ministry. The next day we traded places. This went on until Esther was old enough to come with us in the ministry.

Not long thereafter, ominous clouds gathered on Europe's political horizon. We learned about the persecution of the Witnesses in Germany, and we realized that our turn would soon come. We wondered how we would fare under extreme persecution. In 1938 the Dutch authorities issued a decree forbidding foreigners to do colporteur work by distributing religious publications. To help us to continue in our ministry, Dutch Witnesses gave us the names of people who had shown interest in our work, and we were able to study the Bible with some of them.

About that time a convention of Jehovah's Witnesses was coming up. Although we lacked the funds to buy train tickets to travel to the convention site, we wanted to be there. So we set out on a three-day bicycle trip, with little Esther sitting in a handlebar seat. We spent the nights with Witnesses who lived along the route. How glad we were to be present at our first national convention! The program fortified us for the trials ahead. Above all, we were reminded to put our confidence in God. The

The evangelizing boat "Almina" with its crew

words of Psalm 31:6 became our motto: "As for me, in Jehovah I do trust."

Hunted by the Nazis

In May 1940 the Nazis invaded the Netherlands. Shortly thereafter the Gestapo, or secret police, paid us a surprise visit while we were sorting out a shipment of Bible literature. Ferdinand was taken to the Gestapo headquarters. Esther and I regularly visited him there, and sometimes he was interrogated and beaten right in front of us. In December, Ferdinand was suddenly released, but his freedom was short-lived. One evening as we came home, we spotted a Gestapo car near the house. Ferdinand was able to get away while Esther and I entered the house. The Gestapo were waiting for us. They wanted Ferdinand. That same night after the Gestapo left, the Dutch police came and took me along for questioning. The next day Esther and I went into hiding in the home of a newly baptized Witness couple, the Norder family, who provided shelter and protection.

Toward the end of January 1941, a pioneer couple living in a houseboat were arrested. The next day a circuit overseer (traveling minister) and my husband went on board to retrieve some of the couple's belongings, but Gestapo collaborators pounced on them. Ferdinand managed to break loose and to escape on his bike. The circuit overseer, however, was taken to prison.

Ferdinand was asked by the responsible brothers to take the place of the circuit overseer. That meant that he would not be able to come home for more than three days a month. This was a new challenge for us, but I continued to pioneer. The Gestapo had intensified the search for Witnesses, so we had to keep on the move. In 1942 we moved three times. Eventually, we ended up in the city of Rotterdam, far away from where Ferdinand was carrying out his underground ministry. By that time I was expecting my second child. The Kamp family, whose two sons had recently been deported to concentration camps, kindly took us into their home.

The Gestapo Hot on Our Heels

Our second child, Ruth, was born in July 1943. After Ruth's birth, Ferdinand was able to stay with us for three days, but then he had to leave, and that was the last we saw of him for a long time. About three weeks later, Ferdinand was arrested in Amsterdam. He was taken to the Gestapo station, where his identity was confirmed. The Gestapo subjected him to intense interrogation in an effort to force him to give information about our preaching activities. But all that Ferdinand was willing to divulge was that he was one of Jehovah's Witnesses and that he was not involved in any political activity. The Gestapo officers were furious that Ferdinand, a German national, had not reported for military duty, and they threatened to execute him as a traitor.

For the next five months, Ferdinand was kept in a prison cell, where he endured constant threats of being executed by a firing squad. Yet, he did not waver in his loyalty to Jehovah. What helped him to stay spiritually strong? God's Word, the Bible. Of course, as a Witness, Ferdinand was not allowed to have a Bible. However, other prisoners could request one. So Ferdinand convinced his cell mate to ask his family to send a Bible, which the man did. Years later, whenever Ferdinand spoke about this episode, his eyes beamed and he exclaimed: "What comfort that Bible gave me!"

In early January 1944, Ferdinand was suddenly taken to a concentration camp in Vught, in the Netherlands. Unexpectedly, this move proved to be a blessing for him because there he met 46 other Witnesses. When I learned of his relocation, I was so happy to know that he was still alive!

Preaching Without Letup in the Concentration Camp

Life in camp was very rough. Serious malnutrition, lack of warm clothing, and bitter cold were the order of the day. Ferdinand contracted a serious case of tonsillitis. After a long and chilly roll call, he reported to sick bay. Patients with a fever of 104 degrees Fahrenheit or higher were allowed to stay. But no break for Ferdinand, for his temperature was only 102 degrees Fahrenheit! He was told to go back to work. Sympathetic fellow prisoners, however, helped him by hiding him for short periods of time in a warm area. Further relief came when the weather got warmer. Also, when some of the brothers received food packages, they shared the contents with others, so Ferdinand regained some of his strength.

Before my husband was imprisoned, preaching had been his way of life, and inside the camp he continued to share his beliefs. Camp officials often made sneering remarks at him about his purple triangle, the insignia that identified a prisoner as a Witness. But Ferdinand viewed such remarks as an opportunity to start a conversation with them. Initially, the preaching territory of the brothers was confined to the barracks that mainly housed Witnesses. The brothers asked themselves, 'How can we reach more prisoners?' Unwittingly, the camp administration provided a solution. How?

The brothers had a secret supply of Bible literature and also 12 Bibles. One day the guards found some literature, but they could not find out whom it belonged to. So the camp officials decided that the unity of the Witnesses had to be broken. Therefore, as punishment all brothers were relocated to barracks occupied by non-Witness prisoners. Moreover, the brothers had to sit next to non-Witnesses while eating. This arrangement proved to be a blessing. Now the brothers could do what they had wanted to do in the first place—preach to as many of the inmates as possible.

Raising Two Girls Alone

Meanwhile, my two daughters and I were still living in Rotterdam. The winter of 1943/44 was exceptionally harsh. Behind our house was a battery of antiaircraft artillery manned by German soldiers. In front of us was the Waal Harbor, a prime target for Allied bombers. It was not exactly the safest place to hide. Furthermore, food was scarce. More than ever, we learned to put our complete trust in Jehovah.—Proverbs 3:5, 6.

Eight-year-old Esther helped our small family by standing in line at a soup kitchen. However, often when her turn came to collect food, there was nothing left. During one of her trips in search of food, she was caught in the midst of an air raid. I panicked when I heard the explosions, but soon my anxiety gave way to tears of joy when she returned unhurt and even in possession of a few sugar beets. "What happened?" were my first words. Calmly she replied: "When the bombs fell, I did just what Daddy told me to do, 'Fall flat on the ground, keep lying down, and pray.' And it worked!"

Because of my German accent, it was safer that Esther did what little shopping was still possible. This did not escape the attention of the German soldiers, who began to question Esther. But she did not give away any secrets. At home, I gave Esther Bible education, and because she could not attend school, I taught her reading and writing and other skills.

Esther also helped me in the ministry. Before I went out to study the Bible with

With Ferdinand and the children

and thirst—not to mention the stench—they had to endure defies description.

The train ground to a halt at the infamous Sachsenhausen concentration camp. All prisoners were deprived of any personal belongings they still had—except for the 12 small Bibles that the Witnesses had taken along on the journey!

Ferdinand and eight other brothers were sent to a satellite camp in Rathenow to work on the production of war equipment. Although they were often threatened with execution, the brothers refused to do that type of work. To encourage one another to stay firm, in the morning they would share a Bible verse, such as Psalm 18:2, so that they could meditate on it during the day. This helped them to meditate on spiritual matters.

Finally, the roar of artillery announced the approach of Allied and Russian troops. The Russians arrived first at the camp where Ferdinand and his companions were. They gave the prisoners some food and ordered them to leave the camp. By the end of April 1945, the Russian army permitted them to leave for home.

someone, Esther went ahead of me to see if the coast was clear, so to speak. She verified if the signs that I had agreed upon with the Bible student were in place. For example, the person whom I was going to visit would place a flowerpot in a certain position on the windowsill to let me know that I could come in. During the Bible study, Esther stayed outside to watch for signs of danger while she pushed the carriage with little Ruth up and down the street.

To Sachsenhausen

How was Ferdinand faring? In September 1944, he along with many others were marched off to a railway station where groups of 80 prisoners were squeezed into waiting boxcars. Each car had one bucket that served as a toilet and one bucket for drinking water. The journey lasted three days and nights, and there was standing room only! There was hardly any ventilation. The boxcars were closed in with only a peephole here and there. The heat, hunger,

Finally Together as a Family

On June 15, Ferdinand arrived in the Netherlands. The brothers in Groningen gave him a warm welcome. He soon learned that we were alive, living somewhere in the country, and we received word that he had returned. Waiting for his arrival seemed to last for ages. But finally, one day little Ruth called out: "Mama, there is a stranger at the door!" There was our beloved husband and father!

Scores of problems needed to be resolved before we could function as a normal family again. We did not have a place to live, and a major challenge was that of regaining our status as permanent residents. Since we were Germans, for several years the Dutch officials treated us as outcasts. Eventually, though, we were able to settle down and take up the life we so deeply longed for—that of serving Jehovah together as a family.

"In Jehovah I Do Trust"

In later years, whenever Ferdinand and I got together with some of our friends who like us lived through those days of hardship, we recalled Jehovah's loving guidance in those difficult times. (Psalm 7:1) We rejoiced that through the years, Jehovah allowed us to have a share in the furthering of King-dom interests. We also often said how happy we were that we spent our youth in Jehovah's sacred service.—Ecclesiastes 12:1.

After the period of Nazi persecution, Ferdinand and I served Jehovah together for more than 50 years before he finished his earthly course on December 20, 1995. Soon, I will be 98 years old. Daily, I thank Jehovah that our children were so supportive during those difficult years and that I am still able to do what I can in his service to the glory of his name. I am grateful for all that Jehovah has done for me, and it is my heart's desire to continue to live up to my motto: "As for me, in Jehovah I do trust."—Psalm 31:6.

How to Protect Your Children by Means of Godly Wisdom

EVERY day our bodies are at war. They must fight off a host of microbes, parasites, and viruses. Thankfully, most of us have inherited an immune system that protects us against such attacks and saves us from falling prey to numerous infectious diseases.

In a similar way, Christians must fight against unscriptural thinking and values and against the pressures that can destroy our spiritual health. (2 Corinthians 11:3) In order to resist this daily attack on our minds and hearts, we need to develop spiritual defenses.

Such defenses are especially necessary for our children, since they are not born with spiritual defenses that can counter the spirit of the world. (Ephesians 2:2) As children grow up, it is vital for parents to help them develop their own defenses. On what do those defenses depend? The Bible explains: "Jehovah himself gives wisdom; . . . he will guard the very way of his loyal ones." (Proverbs 2:6, 8) Divine wisdom can guard the way of young ones who might otherwise succumb to harmful association, peer pressure, or unwholesome entertainment. How can parents follow Jehovah's guidance and instill godly wisdom?

Seeking Upbuilding Association

Understandably, teenagers like the company of other teenagers, but exclusive companionship with other inexperienced ones will not promote godly wisdom. "Foolishness is tied up with the heart of a boy," warns the proverb. (Proverbs 22:15) How, then, have some parents helped their children apply godly wisdom in this matter of association?

A father named Don* said: "Our boys spent considerable time with friends of their own age-group, but most of that time was spent in our home, in our presence. We kept an open house that was invariably full of young ones, whom we fed and made feel welcome. We were happy to put up with the noise and

---

* Some names in this article have been changed.

commotion in our house for the sake of providing a safe environment in which our children could enjoy themselves."

Brian and Mary have three fine children but freely admit that training them has not always been easy. They related: "In our congregation, there were few young ones in their late teens to associate with our daughter Jane. She did, however, have one friend by the name of Susan, who was an outgoing, cheerful young person. Her parents, though, were more liberal than we were. Susan was allowed to stay out later than Jane, wear shorter skirts, listen to questionable music, and see unsuitable movies. For a long time, Jane had difficulty in seeing our point of view. To her, Susan's parents seemed more understanding, whereas we came across as being too strict. Only when Susan got in trouble did Jane realize that our firmness had served to protect her. We are very glad we didn't weaken in our stand for what we believed was right for our daughter."

Like Jane, many young people have learned the wisdom of seeking their parents' guidance in this matter of association. "The ear that is listening to the reproof of life lodges right in among wise people," says the proverb. (Proverbs 15:31) Godly wisdom leads young ones to seek the company of upbuilding friends.

Coping With the Pressure to Conform

Closely related to association is peer pressure. Day after day, the pressure to conform attacks our children's defenses. Since youths usually seek the approval of those in their own age-group, peer pressure can squeeze them into the mold that the world views as desirable.—Proverbs 29:25.

The Bible reminds us that "the world is passing away and so is its desire." (1 John 2: 17) Thus, parents should not allow their children to be overly influenced by the world's views. How can they help their children to think in a Christian way?

"My daughter always wanted to wear what other young ones were wearing," said Richard. "So we patiently reasoned with her on the merits and demerits of each request. Even with those fashions we judged unobjectionable, we followed the counsel we heard some years ago, 'It is a wise person who is not the first to adopt a new fashion nor the last to leave it.' "

A mother named Pauline counteracted peer pressure in another way. She recalled: "I took an interest in my children's interests and regularly went to their room to talk to them. These long conversations enabled me to shape their ideas and help them to consider other ways of looking at matters."

Peer pressure will not go away, so parents

"We kept an open house that was invariably full of young ones"

will likely face a constant struggle to 'overturn worldly reasonings' and help their children to bring their thoughts 'into captivity, in obedience to the Christ.' (2 Corinthians 10:5) But by 'persevering in prayer,' both parents and children will be strengthened to complete this vital task.—Romans 12:12; Psalm 65:2.

Take an interest in your children's interests

The Powerful Attraction of Entertainment

A third influence that parents may find it hard to deal with is entertainment. Naturally, young children love to play. Many older children also eagerly seek amusement. (2 Timothy 2:22, footnote) But if satisfied in an unwise way, this desire can break down their spiritual defenses. The danger mainly comes in two forms.

First, much entertainment reflects the world's debased moral standards. (Ephesians 4:17-19) Yet, it is invariably presented in an exciting and attractive way. This poses a real danger for young ones, who may not perceive the pitfalls.

Second, the amount of time spent in entertainment can also cause problems. For some, having fun becomes the most important thing in life, absorbing far too much time and energy. The proverb warns that "the eating of too much honey is not good." (Proverbs 25:27) Likewise, too much entertainment will dull the appetite for spiritual sustenance and lead to mental laziness. (Proverbs 21:17; 24:30-34) Enjoying this world to the full will hinder youths from getting "a firm hold on the real life"—everlasting life in God's new world. (1 Timothy 6:12, 19) How have parents coped with the challenge?

Mari Carmen, a mother of three daughters, said: "We wanted our daughters to have wholesome recreation and to enjoy themselves. So we regularly went out as a family, and they also spent time with friends in the congregation. But we kept recreation in its place. We likened it to the dessert at the end of a meal —sweet but not the main course. They learned to become workers at home, at school, and in the congregation."

Don and Ruth did not leave entertainment to chance either. "We made a habit of dedicating Saturday as 'family day,'" they explained. "We would share in the field ministry in the morning, go swimming in the afternoon, and have a special meal in the evening."

The comments of these parents show the value of balance in providing wholesome entertainment and in assigning it to its proper place in a Christian's life.—Ecclesiastes 3:4; Philippians 4:5.

Trust in Jehovah

Spiritual defenses, of course, take many years to develop. There is no miracle drug that will impart godly wisdom, motivating children to trust in their heavenly Father. Rather, parents have to "go on bringing them up in the discipline and mental-regulating of Jehovah." (Ephesians 6:4) This ongoing "mental-regulating" means helping children to view things the way God does. How can parents accomplish that?

A regular family Bible study is a key to success. The study 'uncovers the children's eyes so that they may see the wonderful things out of God's law.' (Psalm 119:18) Diego took

"I prepared thoroughly for the study"

the family study very seriously and thus helped his children draw closer to Jehovah. "I prepared thoroughly for the study," he said. "By doing research in Scriptural publications, I learned to make the Bible characters come to life. I encouraged the children to identify with the faithful ones. This gave my children a vivid reminder of what pleases Jehovah."

Children also learn in informal settings. Moses exhorted parents to speak of Jehovah's reminders 'when they sat in their house and when they walked on the road and when they lay down and when they got up.' (Deu-teronomy 6:7) One father explained: "My son needs time to open his heart and express his feelings. When we go for a walk or do a job together, he eventually gets around to unburdening himself. On these occasions, we have some fine talks that benefit us both."

The prayers said by parents also make a profound impression on their children. To hear their parents humbly approach God to request his help and forgiveness moves children to "believe that he is." (Hebrews 11:6) Many successful parents stress the importance of family prayers, among them prayers that include school matters and other things that are worrying their children. One father said that his wife always prays with the children before they leave for school.—Psalm 62:8; 112:7.

"Let Us Not Give Up in Doing What Is Fine"

All parents make mistakes and may regret the way that they handled certain situations. Nevertheless, the Bible urges us to keep trying, not to "give up in doing what is fine."—Galatians 6:9.

Parents may feel like giving up, however, when they at times just can't understand their children. It would be easy to conclude that the younger generation is different and difficult. But, really, children today have the same weaknesses that earlier generations had, and they face similar temptations, although the pressure to transgress may have increased. Therefore, one father, after correcting his son, softened his words by kindly adding: "Your heart only wants to do what my heart wanted to do when I was your age." Parents might not know much about computers, but they know all about the leanings of the imperfect flesh.—Matthew 26:41; 2 Corinthians 2:11.

Perhaps some children express little en-

IN OUR NEXT ISSUE

Can You Control Your Destiny?

———

Christ—The Focus of Prophecy

———

Saul's Preaching Excites Hostility

thusiasm for their parents' guidance and even rebel against the discipline they receive. Once again, however, endurance is essential. Despite initial reluctance or periods of defiance, many children eventually respond. (Proverbs 22:6; 23:22-25) Matthew, a young Christian now serving at a branch office of Jehovah's Witnesses, related: "When I was a teenager, I felt that my parents' restrictions were unfair. After all, I reasoned, if my friends' parents permitted something, why couldn't mine? And I got really annoyed when they, at times, punished me by not allowing me to go canoeing—something I loved. Looking back, however, I realize that the discipline my parents gave me was both effective and necessary. I am grateful that they gave me the guidance I needed when I needed it."

There is no doubt about it—although our children may sometimes have to be in an unhealthy spiritual environment, they can still grow up to be fine Christians. As the Bible promises, godly wisdom can give them spiritual defenses. "When wisdom enters into your heart and knowledge itself becomes pleasant to your very soul, thinking ability itself will keep guard over you, discernment itself will safeguard you, to deliver you from the bad way."—Proverbs 2:10-12.

Carrying a child in the womb for nine months is not an easy task. And the following 20 years may bring their share of pain along with happiness. But because they love their children, Christian parents strive with all their might to protect them with godly wisdom. They feel about their children as did the aged apostle John regarding his spiritual children: "No greater cause for thankfulness do I have than these things, that I should be hearing that my children go on walking in the truth."—3 John 4.

Beware of Customs That Displease God

IN A small courtyard, a coffin lies open under the hot African sun. As mourners file past it to express their grief, an old man pauses. His eyes filled with sorrow, he leans close to the dead man's face and begins speaking: "Why did you not tell me you were going? Why did you leave me like this? Now that you have returned, will you continue to help me?"

In another part of Africa, a baby is born. Nobody is allowed to see the child. Only after some time has passed is the baby brought out into public view and ceremonially given a name.

To some people, talking to a dead person or hiding a newborn child from the sight of others may seem to be strange behavior. However, in certain cultures and societies, the conduct and views of people toward death and birth are influenced by a very powerful belief that the dead are really not dead but are alive and conscious.

This belief is so strong that it is woven into the fabric of customs and rituals that involve almost all aspects of life. For instance, millions believe that important stages in one's life—such as birth, puberty, marriage, childbearing, and death—are parts of a passage leading into the spirit realm of the ancestors. There, it is believed, the dead person continues to play an active role in the lives of those he left behind. And he can continue the cycle of life through rebirth.

To ensure a smooth transition between all stages of this cycle, numerous customs and rites are performed. These customs are influenced by the belief that something inside us survives death. True Christians avoid any customs associated with this belief. Why?

What Is the Condition of the Dead?

The Bible is clear when it describes the condition of the dead. It simply states: "The living are conscious that they will die; but as for the dead, they are conscious of nothing at all . . . Their love and their hate and their jealousy have already perished . . . There is no work nor devising nor knowledge nor wisdom in Sheol [mankind's common grave], the place to which you are going." (Ecclesiastes 9:5, 6, 10) True worshipers of God have long embraced this basic Bible truth. They have understood that the soul, rather than being immortal, can die and be destroyed. (Ezekiel 18:4) They have also known that spirits of the dead do not exist. (Psalm 146:4) In ancient times, Jehovah strictly commanded his people to separate themselves completely from any custom or ritual that was associated with the belief that the dead are conscious and are able to influence the living.—Deuteronomy 14:1; 18:9-13; Isaiah 8:19, 20.

First-century Christians likewise avoided any traditional custom or rite that was associated with false religious teaching. (2 Corinthians 6:15-17) Today, Jehovah's Witnesses, regardless of race, tribe, or background, shun traditions and customs that are connected with the false teaching that something in man survives death.

What can guide us as Christians in deciding whether to observe a certain custom or not? We must carefully think about its possible connection to any unscriptural teaching, such as the belief that spirits of the dead influence the lives of the living. Further, we need to consider if our sharing in such a custom or ceremony might stumble others who know what Jehovah's Witnesses believe and teach. With those points in mind, let us examine two areas of concern—birth and death.

Birth and Child-Naming Ceremonies

Many customs associated with childbirth are appropriate. However, in places where birth is viewed as a passing over from the realm of the ancestor spirits to that of the human community, true Christians must exercise care. In some parts of Africa, for example, a newborn child is kept indoors and is not given a name until a period of time has passed. While the waiting period may vary according to locality, it ends with a child-naming ceremony, in which the child is brought outdoors and is formally presented to relatives and friends. At that time, the child's name is officially announced to those present.

Explaining the significance of this custom, the book *Ghana—Understanding the People and Their Culture* states: "During the first seven days of its life, a baby is considered to be on a 'visit' and undergoing a transition from the world of spirits to earthly life. . . . The baby is normally kept indoors and people outside the family are not allowed to see it."

Why is there a waiting period before the child is ceremonially named? The book *Ghana in Retrospect* explains: "Before the eighth day, the child is not supposed to be human. He is more or less associated with the other world from which he has come." The book continues: "Since it is the name that, as it were, humanizes a child, when a couple fear that their child will die they will usually defer naming him until they are sure he will live. . . . Therefore this rite of passage, sometimes called outdooring of the child, is thought to be of tremendous consequences for the child and his parents. It is the ceremony that ushers the child into the company or world of human beings."

A senior relative of the family usually officiates during such a child-naming ceremony. Aspects of the occasion vary from place to place, but the ceremony often includes the pouring of a libation, prayers offered to the ancestral spirits expressing appreciation for the child's safe arrival, and other rituals.

The highlight of the ceremony comes when the name of the child is announced. Although the parents are responsible for the naming of their own child, other relatives often have a strong influence on the name chosen. Some names may carry a symbolic meaning in the local language, such as "gone and returned," "Mother has come a second time," or "Father has come again." Other names contain meanings designed to discourage the ancestors from taking the newborn child back into the world of the dead.

Of course, there is nothing wrong with rejoicing over the birth of a child. Naming a child after someone else and giving a name that reflects the circumstances associated with its birth are acceptable customs, and deciding when to give a child its name is a personal decision. However, Christians who want to please God are careful to avoid any customs or ceremonies that give the impression that they are in agreement with the view that the newborn child is a "visitor" passing from the spirit world of the ancestors to the world of the living community.

In addition, while many in the community view the naming ceremony as an important rite of passage, Christians should be sensitive to the consciences of others and consider the impression that is given to unbelievers. What might some conclude, for example, if a Christian family kept their newborn child from the view of others until a naming ceremony was performed? What would be the impression if names that contradicted their claim to be teachers of Bible truth were used?

Hence, when deciding how and when to name their children, Christians strive to "do all things for God's glory" so as not to become a cause for stumbling. (1 Corinthians 10:31-33) They do not 'set aside the commandment of God in order to retain traditions' that are ultimately designed to honor the dead. On the contrary, they give honor and glory to the living God, Jehovah.—Mark 7:9, 13.

Passing From Death to Life

Death, like birth, is considered by many to be a transition; one who dies moves from the visible world into the invisible realm of the spirits of the dead. Many believe that unless certain funeral customs and rites are performed at a person's death, the ancestor spirits, who are believed to have the power to punish or reward the living, will be angered. This belief greatly influences the way funerals are arranged and conducted.

Funerals that are intended to appease the dead often involve a whole range of emotions—from frantic wailing and shouting in the presence of the corpse to joyous festivities after the burial. Unrestrained feasting, drunkenness, and dancing to loud music often characterize such funeral celebrations. So much importance is attached to funerals that even the poorest of families often make great effort to gather enough funds to provide "a fitting burial," though it might bring hardship and debt.

Throughout the years, Jehovah's Witnesses have thoroughly exposed unscriptural funeral customs.* Such customs include wakes, the pouring of libations, talking to and making requests of the dead, ceremonious observances of funeral anniversaries, and other customs based on the belief that something in a person survives death. Such God-dishonoring customs are "unclean," an "empty deception" based on "the tradition of men" and not on God's Word of truth. —Isaiah 52:11; Colossians 2:8.

Pressure to Conform

Avoiding traditional customs has proved to be a challenge for some, especially in lands where honoring the dead is considered extremely important. Because of not following such customs, Jehovah's Witnesses have been viewed with suspicion or have been accused of being antisocial and disrespectful of the dead. Criticism and strong pressure have caused some, despite their correct understanding of Bible truth, to be afraid to stand out as different. (1 Peter 3:14) Others have felt that these customs are part of their culture and cannot be completely avoided. Still others have reasoned that refusing to follow custom may prejudice the community against God's people.

We do not want to offend others needlessly. Still, the Bible warns us that taking a firm stand for truth will result in the disapproval of a world alienated from God. (John 15:18, 19; 2 Timothy 3:12; 1 John 5:19) We willingly take such a stand, knowing that we must be different from those who are in spiritual darkness. (Malachi 3:18; Galatians 6:12) Just as Jesus resisted Satan's temptation to do something that displeased God, so we resist

the pressure to act in a way that displeases God. (Matthew 4:3-7) Rather than being influenced by fear of man, true Christians are primarily concerned with pleasing Jehovah God and honoring him as the God of truth. They do so by not compromising Bible standards of pure worship because of pressure from others.—Proverbs 29:25; Acts 5:29.

Respecting the Dead —Honoring Jehovah

It is normal to feel deep emotional pain and grief when someone we love dies. (John 11:33, 35) Cherishing the memory of a loved one and providing a respectful burial are fitting and appropriate expressions of our love. However, Jehovah's Witnesses cope with the immense sadness of death without being drawn into any traditional practices that displease God. This is not easy for those who have been raised in cultures where there is strong fear of the dead. It can be a challenge to keep our balance when we are emotionally pained by the death of someone close to us. Nevertheless, faithful Christians are strengthened by Jehovah, "the God of all comfort," and benefit from the loving support of fellow believers. (2 Corinthians 1:3, 4) Their strong faith that unconscious dead ones in God's memory will one day live again gives true Christians every reason to separate themselves completely from unchristian funeral customs that deny the reality of the resurrection.

Are we not thrilled that Jehovah has called us "out of darkness into his wonderful light"? (1 Peter 2:9) As we experience the joy of birth and endure the sadness of death, may our strong desire to do what is right and our deep love for Jehovah God always move us to "go on walking as children of light." May we never allow ourselves to be spiritually contaminated by unchristian customs that displease God.—Ephesians 5:8.

---

* Please see the brochures *Spirits of the Dead—Can They Help You or Harm You? Do They Really Exist?* and *The Road to Everlasting Life—Have You Found It?* published by Jehovah's Witnesses.

Questions From Readers

Does Stephen's exclamation at Acts 7:59 indicate that prayers should be directed to Jesus?

Acts 7:59 says: "They went on casting stones at Stephen as he made appeal and said: 'Lord Jesus, receive my spirit.'" Those words have raised questions in the mind of some, since the Bible says that Jehovah is the "Hearer of Prayer." (Psalm 65:2) Did Stephen really pray to Jesus? Would this indicate that Jesus is the same as Jehovah?

The *King James Version* says that Stephen was "calling upon God." Understandably, then, many draw the conclusion reached by Bible commentator Matthew Henry, who said: "Stephen here prays to Christ, and so must we." However, that viewpoint is erroneous. Why?

Barnes' Notes on the New Testament makes this honest admission: "The word *God* is not in the original, and should not have been in the translation. It is in none of the ancient [manuscripts] or versions." How did the word "God" come to be inserted into that verse? Scholar Abiel Abbot Livermore called this "an instance of the sectarian biases of the translators." Most modern translations, therefore, eliminate this spurious reference to God.

Nevertheless, many versions do say that Stephen "prayed" to Jesus. And the footnote in the *New World Translation* shows that the term "made appeal" can also mean "invocation; prayer." Would that not indicate that Jesus is Almighty God? No. *Vine's Expository Dictionary of Old and New Testament Words* explains that in this setting, the original Greek word, *e·pi·ka·le′o*, means: "To call upon, invoke; . . . to appeal to an authority." Paul used this same word when he declared: "I appeal to Caesar!" (Acts 25:11) Appropriately, then, *The New English Bible* says that Stephen "called out" to Jesus.

What prompted Stephen to make such an appeal? According to Acts 7:55, 56, Stephen, "being full of holy spirit, gazed into heaven and caught sight of God's glory and of Jesus standing at God's right hand." Normally, Stephen would have addressed his requests to Jehovah in the name of Jesus. But seeing the resurrected Jesus in vision, Stephen apparently felt free to appeal to him directly, saying: "Lord Jesus, receive my spirit." Stephen knew that Jesus had been given authority to raise the dead. (John 5:27-29) He therefore asked Jesus to safeguard his spirit, or life force, until the day when Jesus would raise him to immortal life in the heavens.

Does Stephen's brief utterance set a precedent for praying to Jesus? Not at all. For one thing, Stephen clearly distinguished Jesus from Jehovah, for the account says that he saw Jesus "standing at God's right hand." Also, these circumstances were exceptional. The only other case of such an utterance being directed to Jesus is that of the apostle John, who similarly addressed Jesus directly when he saw Him in vision.—Revelation 22:16, 20.

Although Christians today properly direct all their prayers to Jehovah God, they too have unshakable faith that Jesus is "the resurrection and the life." (John 11:25) As it did Stephen, so faith in Jesus' ability to raise his followers from the dead can help and sustain us in times of trial.

Mealtime
More Than Just a Time to Eat!

EVERYONE enjoys a fine meal. Add to the meal good conversation and warm association with people you love, and it becomes a delightful event that satisfies more than just our hunger. Many families make it a practice to gather together at least once a day to share a meal. Mealtime gives a family the opportunity to discuss the day's events or plans. Parents who listen to their children's comments and expressions get a glimpse of the thinking and feelings of their young ones. Over time, the happy, relaxed association enjoyed at mealtime builds within a family a sense of security, trust, and love that adds stability to the family unit.

Today, because many family members are busy and always on the move, they find it difficult to meet together for a meal. In some parts of the world, local culture frowns upon a family eating together or even talking during mealtime. Other families have the habit of turning on the TV during the meal, effectively robbing themselves of any meaningful communication.

Christian parents, however, are always alert to opportunities to build up their households. (Proverbs 24:27) Long ago, parents were told that one of the best opportunities to communicate God's word to their children was 'when they sit in their house.' (Deuteronomy 6:7) Regularly sitting down together for a meal offers parents a unique chance to build within their children a deeper love for Jehovah and his righteous principles. By cultivating a happy and relaxed atmosphere, you can make mealtime an enjoyable and upbuilding experience for your family too. Yes, make mealtime more than just a time to eat!

JANUARY 15, 2005

THE WATCHTOWER

ANNOUNCING JEHOVAH'S KINGDOM

CAN YOU CONTROL
YOUR FUTURE?

THE WATCHTOWER®

ANNOUNCING JEHOVAH'S KINGDOM

January 15, 2005   Average Printing Each Issue: 26,439,000   Vol. 126, No. 2

THE PURPOSE OF *THE WATCHTOWER* is to exalt Jehovah God as Sovereign Lord of the universe. It keeps watch on world events as these fulfill Bible prophecy. It comforts all peoples with the good news that God's Kingdom will soon destroy those who oppress their fellowmen and that it will turn the earth into a paradise. It encourages faith in God's now-reigning King, Jesus Christ, whose shed blood opens the way for mankind to gain eternal life. *The Watchtower*, published by Jehovah's Witnesses continuously since 1879, is nonpolitical. It adheres to the Bible as its authority.

IN THIS ISSUE

3   What Controls Your Future?

4   Can You Control Your Destiny?

8   When Old Age Becomes "a Crown of Beauty"

10   Christ—The Focus of Prophecy

15   Foregleams of God's Kingdom Become a Reality

21   "Be Hospitable to One Another"

24   Jehovah's Word Is Alive—Highlights From the Book of Judges

28   Saul's Preaching Excites Hostility

30   Questions From Readers

32   "What Is Your Secret?"

WATCHTOWER STUDIES

FEBRUARY 14-20:
Christ—The Focus of Prophecy.
Page 10. Songs to be used: 105, 53.

FEBRUARY 21-27:
Foregleams of God's Kingdom Become a Reality.
Page 15. Songs to be used: 21, 192.

Publication of *The Watchtower* is part of a worldwide Bible educational work supported by voluntary donations.

Unless otherwise indicated, Scripture quotations are from the modern-language *New World Translation of the Holy Scriptures—With References.*

The Watchtower (ISSN 0043-1087) is published semimonthly by Watchtower Bible and Tract Society of New York, Inc.; M. H. Larson, President; G. F. Simonis, Secretary-Treasurer; 25 Columbia Heights, Brooklyn, NY 11201-2483. Periodicals Postage Paid at Brooklyn, NY, and at additional mailing offices. **POSTMASTER:** Send address changes to Watchtower, **Wallkill, NY 12589.**

Changes of address should reach us 30 days before your moving date. Give us your old and new address (if possible, your old address label).

Semimonthly   ENGLISH

Would you welcome more information or a free home Bible study? Please send your request to Jehovah's Witnesses, using the appropriate address below.

America, United States of: Wallkill, NY 12589. *Antigua:* Box 119, St. Johns. *Australia:* Box 280, Ingleburn, NSW 1890. *Bahamas:* Box N-1247, Nassau, N.P. *Barbados, W.I.:* Crusher Site Road, Prospect, St. James. *Britain:* The Ridgeway, London NW7 1RN. *Canada:* Box 4100, Halton Hills (Georgetown), Ontario L7G 4Y4. *Germany:* Niederselters, Am Steinfels, D-65618 Selters. *Ghana:* P. O. Box GP 760, Accra. *Guyana:* 352-360 Tyrell St., Republic Park Phase 2 EBD. *Hawaii 96819:* 2055 Kam IV Rd., Honolulu. *Hong Kong:* 4 Kent Road, Kowloon Tong. *India:* Post Box 6440, Yelahanka, Bangalore 560 064, KAR. *Ireland:* Newcastle, Greystones, Co. Wicklow. *Jamaica:* P. O. Box 103, Old Harbour, St. Catherine. *Japan:* 1271 Nakashinden, Ebina City, Kanagawa Pref., 243-0496. *Kenya:* P.O. Box 47788, GPO Nairobi 00100. *New Zealand:* P.O. Box 75-142, Manurewa. *Nigeria:* P.M.B. 1090, Benin City 300001, Edo State. *Philippines, Republic of:* P. O. Box 2044, 1060 Manila. *South Africa:* Private Bag X2067, Krugersdorp, 1740. *Trinidad and Tobago, Republic of:* Lower Rapsey Street & Laxmi Lane, Curepe. *Zambia:* Box 33459, Lusaka 10101. *Zimbabwe:* Private Bag WG-5001, Westgate.

NOW PUBLISHED IN 150 LANGUAGES. SEMIMONTHLY: Afrikaans, Albanian,* Amharic, Arabic, Bengali, Bicol, Bislama, Bulgarian, Cebuano,* Chichewa,* Chinese, Chinese (Simplified),* Cibemba,* Croatian,* Czech,*# Danish,*# Dutch,*# East Armenian, Efik,* English*#◎ (also Braille), Estonian, Ewe, Fijian, Finnish,*# French,*# Ga, Georgian, German,*# Greek,* Gujarati, Gun, Hebrew, Hiligaynon, Hindi, Hungarian,*# Igbo,* Iloko,* Indonesian, Italian,*# Japanese*# (also Braille), Kannada, Kinyarwanda, Kirundi, Korean*# (also Braille), Latvian, Lingala, Lithuanian, Luvale, Macedonian, Malagasy,* Malayalam, Maltese, Marathi, Myanmar, Nepali, New Guinea Pidgin, Norwegian,*# Pangasinan, Papiamento (Aruba), Papiamento (Curaçao), Polish,*# Portuguese*# (also Braille), Punjabi, Rarotongan, Romanian,* Russian,* Samar-Leyte, Samoan, Sango, Sepedi, Serbian, Sesotho, Shona,* Silozi, Sinhala, Slovak,* Slovenian, Solomon Islands Pidgin, Spanish,*# Sranantongo, Swahili,* Swedish,*# Tagalog,* Tamil, Telugu, Thai, Tigrinya, Tongan, Tshiluba, Tsonga, Tswana, Turkish, Twi, Ukrainian,* Urdu, Venda, Vietnamese, Wallisian, Xhosa, Yoruba,* Zulu*

MONTHLY: American Sign Language,△▢ Armenian, Assamese, Azerbaijani (Roman script), Brazilian Sign Language,△ Cambodian, Chitonga, Gilbertese, Greenlandic, Haitian Creole, Hausa, Hiri Motu, Icelandic, Isoko, Kaonde, Kazakh, Kikongo, Kiluba, Kirghiz, Kwanyama/Ndonga, Luganda, Marshallese, Mauritian Creole, Mizo, Monokutuba, Moore, Niuean, Ossetian, Otetela, Palauan, Persian, Ponapean, Seychelles Creole, Tahitian, Tatar, Tiv, Trukese, Tumbuka, Tuvaluan, Umbundu, Yapese, Zande

* Study articles also available in large-print edition.
\# Audiocassettes also available.
◎ CD (MP3 format) also available.
△ Videocassette
▢ DVD

WHAT CONTROLS YOUR FUTURE?

"HUMANS can no more be masters of their destiny than any other animal," writes evolutionist John Gray. Author Shmuley Boteach expresses quite the opposite view in his book *An Intelligent Person's Guide to Judaism.* He says: "Man is not an animal, and is therefore always in control of his own destiny."

Many people agree with Gray and believe that blind forces of nature control the destiny of the human family. Others consider man to be a creation of God endowed with the ability to have control over his own future.

Some feel that their future is controlled by powerful human forces. According to writer Roy Weatherford, "the majority of the people in the world—and especially the majority of women in history—have . . . no power or control over their own lives for straightforward reasons of human oppression and exploitation." (*The Implications of Determinism*) Many have seen their dreams of a happy future wrecked by competing political or military powers.

Others throughout history have felt helpless because they thought that supernatural forces controlled their destiny. "The ancient Greeks," says Boteach, "were obsessed with the idea that all hope was futile since man could not overcome predetermined destiny." They felt that the destiny of every person was decided by capricious goddesses. These goddesses, they believed, decided when a person would die as well as how much distress and pain he would have to endure throughout his life.

The belief that a person's destiny is controlled by a superhuman power is common today. For example, many people believe in Kismet, or fate. They say that God has predetermined the outcome of all human actions and the time of one's death. There is also the doctrine of predestination, which promotes the view that "the ultimate salvation or damnation of each human individual has been ordained beforehand" by Almighty God. Many professed Christians adhere to this teaching.

What do you think? Has your destiny already been fixed by forces completely beyond your control? Or is there some truth in the words of English playwright William Shakespeare, who wrote: "Men at some time are masters of their fates"? Consider what the Bible says on this matter.

CAN YOU CONTROL
YOUR DESTINY?

IS OUR ultimate destiny predetermined? Do the choices we make in life have no effect on our future?

Suppose man is master of his own fate. In this case, could any individual be foreordained to perform a specific task or occupy a certain office? And how could God accomplish his will for the earth if humans were free to shape their own destiny? The Bible provides satisfying answers to these questions.

Predestination and Free Will —Reconcilable?

Consider how Jehovah God made us. "In God's image he created [man]; male and female he created them," states the Bible. (Genesis 1:27) Made in God's likeness, we have the ability to reflect his qualities, such as love, justice, wisdom, and power. God has also given us the gift of free will, or freedom of choice. This makes us unique among his earthly creation. We can choose whether we will follow God's moral guidance or not. That is why the prophet Moses could say: "I do take the heavens and the earth as witnesses against you today, that I have put life and death before you, the blessing and the malediction; and you must choose life in order that you may keep alive, you and your offspring, by loving Jehovah your God, by listening to his voice and by sticking to him." —Deuteronomy 30:19, 20.

The gift of freedom of choice, though, does not mean absolute freedom. It does not free us from the physical and moral laws that God made for the stability and peace of the universe. These laws were set up for our good, and any violation of them could lead to serious consequences. Just think of what would happen if we chose to ignore the law of gravity and jumped off the roof of a tall building!—Galatians 6:7.

Freedom of choice also binds us with a restraint that creatures lacking such freedom do not have. The writer Corliss Lamont asks: "How can we attribute ethical responsibility to men, and punish them for wrongdoing, if we accept . . . that their choices and actions

not do this, for "God is love," and "all his ways are justice." (1 John 4:8; Deuteronomy 32:4) Having given us freedom of choice, he did not at the same time 'determine from eternity whom he would save and whom he would damn,' as believers in predestination assert. Freedom of choice precludes predestination.

The Bible clearly shows that the choices we make will alter our destiny. For example, God appeals to wrongdoers, saying: "Turn back, please, every one from his bad way and from the badness of your dealings . . . that I may not cause calamity to you." (Jeremiah 25: 5, 6) This appeal would be pointless if God had already fixed each individual's destiny.

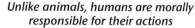

Unlike animals, humans are morally responsible for their actions

Eagle: Foto: Cortesía de GREFA

are predetermined?" Of course, we cannot. Instinct-driven animals are not held morally responsible for what they do, nor are computers deemed accountable for the functions they are programmed to perform. Freedom of choice, then, places upon us a heavy responsibility and makes us accountable for our actions.

How unloving and unjust Jehovah God would be if before we were born, he predetermined the course we would take and then held us responsible for our actions! He does

Moreover, God's Word states: "Repent, therefore, and turn around so as to get your sins blotted out, that seasons of refreshing may come from the person of Jehovah." (Acts 3: 19) Why would Jehovah ask people to repent and turn around if he knew beforehand that they could do absolutely nothing to change their destiny?

The Scriptures speak of some who are invited by God to rule as kings in heaven with Jesus Christ. (Matthew 22:14; Luke 12:32) However, the Bible says that they will lose that privilege if they do not endure to the end. (Revelation 2:10) Why would God invite them at all if he had already decided that they would not be chosen? Consider also the apostle Paul's words to his fellow believers. He wrote: "If we practice sin willfully after having received the accurate knowledge of the truth, there is no longer any sacrifice for sins left." (Hebrews 10:26) Such a warning would be valueless if God had foreordained their destiny. But has not God foreordained at least some individuals to be rulers with Jesus Christ?

Foreordained—Individuals or a Group?

"[God] has blessed us with every spiritual blessing in the heavenly places in union with Christ," wrote the apostle Paul, "just as he chose us in union with him before the founding of the world . . . For he foreordained us to the adoption through Jesus Christ as sons to himself." (Ephesians 1:3-5) What has God foreordained, and what is the meaning of being selected "before the founding of the world"?

This passage states that God has chosen some descendants of the first man, Adam, to rule with Christ in the heavens. (Romans 8:14-17, 28-30; Revelation 5:9, 10) However, the assumption that Jehovah God foreordained thousands of years before they were born specific individuals to receive this privilege conflicts with the fact that humans are endowed with freedom of choice. What God foreordained was a group, or class of people, not individuals.

To illustrate: Suppose that a government decides to set up a particular agency. It predetermines the agency's functions, its powers, and its size. The agency finally goes into operation some time after it was set up, and its members issue a statement saying: "The government determined a number of years ago what our job would be. Now we begin the work assigned to us." Would you conclude that the government must have predetermined some years earlier who the individual members of that agency would be? Surely not. Similarly, Jehovah predetermined that he would set up a special agency to remedy the effects of Adam's sin. He foreordained the class of people who would serve in that agency—but not the individuals. They would be chosen later, and the choices they would make in life would have a bearing on whether they were finally approved or not.

What world did the apostle Paul have in mind when he said: "[God] chose us in union with him before the founding of the world"? The world that Paul refers to here is not the world that God started when he created Adam and Eve. That world was "very good"—absolutely free from sin and corruption. (Genesis 1:31) It did not need a "release" from sin.—Ephesians 1:7.

The particular world that Paul meant is the one that came into existence after Adam and Eve rebelled in Eden—a world very different from the one originally purposed by God. It was the world that began with the children of Adam and Eve. That world consisted of people alienated from God and enslaved to sin and corruption. It was a world of people who, unlike the willful sinners Adam and Eve, were redeemable.—Romans 5:12; 8:18-21.

Jehovah God was instantly able to meet the situation resulting from the rebellion in Eden. As soon as the need arose, he foreordained a special agency—the Messianic Kingdom in the hands of Jesus Christ—that he would use in connection with the redemption of mankind from Adamic sin. (Matthew 6:10) God did this "before the founding of the world" of redeemable mankind, that is, before rebellious Adam and Eve brought forth children.

Humans usually need a plan of action in order to accomplish what they want to do. Predestination is linked with the idea that God must have a detailed plan for the universe wherein everything is predetermined. "It has seemed to many philosophers," writes Roy Weatherford, "that anything less than a complete specification of every event would be incompatible with God's Majesty." Does God really need to specify every event in advance?

Being infinite in power and matchless in wisdom, Jehovah can meet any emergency or contingency that might result as his creatures exercise their free will. (Isaiah 40:25, 26; Romans 11:33) He can do this instantly and without forethought. Unlike fallible men with their limited abilities, Almighty God does not need a detailed, cut-and-dried plan that sets out beforehand the destiny of every individual on the earth. (Proverbs 19:21) In a number of Bible translations, Ephesians 3:11 speaks of God's having an "eternal purpose" rather than a fixed plan.

How You Can Affect Your Future

God has a purpose for the earth, and that purpose is preordained. Revelation 21:3, 4 states: "Look! The tent of God is with mankind, and he will reside with them, and they will be his peoples. And God himself will be with them. And he will wipe out every tear from their eyes, and death will be no more, neither will mourning nor outcry nor pain be anymore. The former things have passed away." Yes, this earth will become a paradise, just as Jehovah originally intended. (Genesis 1:27, 28) The question is, Will you be there? That depends on the choices you make now. Jehovah has not fixed your destiny.

The ransom sacrifice of God's Son, Jesus Christ, makes it possible for anyone who exercises faith in him to receive everlasting life. (John 3:16, 17; Acts 10:34, 35) "He that exercises faith in the Son has everlasting life," says the Bible. "He that disobeys the Son will not see life." (John 3:36) You can choose life by learning about God, his Son, and His will from the pages of the Bible and by applying what you learn. The person acting in accord with true wisdom recorded in God's Word is assured that "he will reside in security and be undisturbed from dread of calamity." —Proverbs 1:20, 33.

When Old Age Becomes "a Crown of Beauty"

"THE best life possible," said 101-year-old Muriel. "Truly a privilege!" is how 70-year-old Theodoros put matters. "I could not have used my life in a better way," stated Maria at the age of 73. All of them had spent a lifetime in service to Jehovah God.

Such older ones are typical of many active worshipers of Jehovah worldwide. Despite advancing age, health concerns, and other adverse circumstances, they still serve God in a whole-souled way. In the Christian congregation, such faithful older ones are respected examples of godly devotion. Jehovah highly esteems the service of elderly ones, even though they may be limited by their circumstances.*—2 Corinthians 8:12.

The book of Psalms makes a fitting observation about the quality of life faithful older ones can expect to have. They can be like an old and stately tree that remains productive. Regarding faithful older ones, the psalmist sang: "They will still keep on thriving during gray-headedness, fat and fresh they will continue to be."—Psalm 92:14.

Some may fear that they will be cast aside and ignored when old age causes their vitality to wane. David beseeched God: "Do not throw me away in the time of old age; just when my power is failing, do not leave me." (Psalm 71:9) What makes the difference between failing and flourishing in old age? The godly quality of righteousness. "The righteous himself will blossom forth as a palm tree does," sang the psalmist.—Psalm 92:12.

Those who have filled their lives with faithful service to God tend to keep bearing good fruit in their senior years. In effect, many of the seeds they have planted in their own life or that of others sprout and mature into a harvest of goodness. (Galatians 6:7-10; Colossians 1:10) Of course, people who have squandered their lives in self-centered pursuits that ignore God's ways usually have little of value to show as they get older.

Righteousness as an adornment of old age is also emphasized in the Bible book of Proverbs. There we read: "Gray-headedness is a crown of beauty when it is found in the way of righteousness." (Proverbs 16:31) Yes, righteousness is a manifestation of inner beauty. Pursuing a righteous course during a long life brings respect. (Leviticus 19:32) Gray hair when accompanied by wisdom and virtue results in honor.—Job 12:12.

To Jehovah, an upright life spent in his service is beautiful. The Scriptures say: "Even to one's old age I [Jehovah] am the same One; and to one's gray-headedness I myself shall keep bearing up. I myself shall certainly act, that I myself may carry and that I myself may bear up and furnish escape." (Isaiah 46:4) How comforting it is to know that our loving

---

*See the *2005 Calendar of Jehovah's Witnesses,* January/February.

> ### JEHOVAH CARES FOR HIS OLDER SERVANTS
>
> *"Before gray hair you should rise up, and you must show consideration for the person of an old man."*
> —Leviticus 19:32.
>
> *"Even to one's old age I am the same One; and to one's gray-headedness I myself shall keep bearing up."*
> —Isaiah 46:4.

> ## "Gray-headedness is a crown of beauty when it is found in the way of righteousness."
> —PROVERBS 16:31

heavenly Father promises to sustain and support his loyal ones in their old age!—Psalm 48:14.

Since a life spent in faithful service to Jehovah is beautiful from his standpoint, does it not also merit the respect of others? Reflecting God's view, we treasure elderly fellow believers. (1 Timothy 5:1, 2) Let us therefore look for practical ways to show Christian love in caring for their needs.

Onto the Path of Righteousness Later in Life

"In the path of righteousness there is life," Solomon assures us. (Proverbs 12:28) Advanced age does not prevent someone from getting on this path later in life. In Moldova, for instance, a 99-year-old man had devoted his youth to promoting Communist ideals. He was proud that he had personally had conversations with renowned Communist leaders, such as V. I. Lenin. With the decline and fall of Communism, however, this elderly man's life lost purpose and direction. But when Jehovah's Witnesses showed him that God's Kingdom is the only real solution to mankind's problems, he embraced Bible truth and became an avid student of the Scriptures. Only death prevented him from becoming a baptized servant of Jehovah.

When learning about God's moral requirements, an 81-year-old woman in Hungary realized that she needed to get married to the man with whom she had been living for several years. The woman summoned all her courage and explained her Bible-based viewpoint to her partner. To her great surprise and joy, he agreed to marry her. After their union was legalized, she made rapid spiritual progress. Within eight months after the start of her Bible study, she became an unbaptized publisher, and she was baptized soon thereafter. How true it is that righteousness can crown older ones with real beauty!

Yes, faithful older Christians can be certain of God's interest in them. Jehovah will not abandon those who remain loyal to him. Rather, he promises to guide, support, and sustain them even into old age. And they attest to the psalmist's words: "My help is from Jehovah."—Psalm 121:2.

CHRIST—THE FOCUS OF PROPHECY

"The bearing witness to Jesus is what inspires prophesying."—REVELATION 19:10.

THE year is 29 C.E. Israel is abuzz with talk about the promised Messiah. The ministry of John the Baptizer has heightened the sense of expectation. (Luke 3:15) John denies being the Christ. Instead, pointing to Jesus of Nazareth, he says: "I have borne witness that this one is the Son of God." (John 1:20, 34) Soon, crowds follow Jesus to listen to his teaching and to be healed by him.

2 In the months that follow, Jehovah provides a mountain of testimony concerning his Son. Those who have studied the Scriptures and who observe Jesus' works have a solid basis for putting their faith in him.

1, 2. (a) Starting in 29 C.E., what decision confronted Israel? (b) What will be considered in this article?

However, God's covenant people in general show a lack of faith. Relatively few acknowledge that Jesus is the Christ, the Son of God. (John 6:60-69) What would you have done if you had lived back then? Would you have been moved to accept Jesus as the Messiah and become his faithful follower? Consider the evidence about his identity that Jesus himself gives when he is accused of breaking the Sabbath, and note subsequent proofs that he gives in order to strengthen the faith of his loyal disciples.

Jesus Himself Gives the Evidence

3 It is Passover time in 31 C.E. Jesus is in Jerusalem. He has just cured a man who had been sick for 38 years. The Jews, though, per-

---

3. What circumstances impelled Jesus to give evidence about his identity?

Jesus pointed to his credentials as the Messiah

secute Jesus for doing this on the Sabbath. They also accuse him of blasphemy and seek to kill him because he calls God his Father. (John 5:1-9, 16-18) The defense that Jesus gives in his own behalf presents three powerful lines of reasoning that would convince any honesthearted Jew of Jesus' true identity.

⁴ First, Jesus points to the witness of his forerunner, John the Baptizer, saying: "You have dispatched men to John, and he has borne witness to the truth. That man was a burning and shining lamp, and you for a short time were willing to rejoice greatly in his light."—John 5:33, 35.

⁵ John the Baptizer was "a burning and shining lamp" in that prior to his unjust imprisonment by Herod, he had fulfilled his divine commission to prepare the way for the Messiah. John said: "The reason why I came baptizing in water was that [the Messiah] might be made manifest to Israel. . . . I viewed the spirit coming down as a dove out of heaven, and it remained upon him. Even I did not know him, but the very One who sent me to baptize in water said to me, 'Whoever it is upon whom you see the spirit coming down and remaining, this is the one that baptizes in holy spirit.' And I have seen it, and I have borne witness that this one is the Son of God."* (John 1:26-37) John specifically identified Jesus as the Son of God—the promised Messiah. So clear was John's witness that some eight months after his death, many honesthearted Jews confessed: "As many things as John said about this man were all true."—John 10:41, 42.

* Evidently, at Jesus' baptism, only John heard God's voice. The Jews whom Jesus is addressing "have neither heard [God's] voice at any time nor seen his figure." —John 5:37.

4, 5. What was the purpose of John's ministry, and how well did he accomplish it?

⁶ Next, Jesus uses another line of reasoning to confirm his credentials as the Messiah. He points to his own fine works as evidence of God's backing. "I have the witness greater than that of John," he says, "for the very works that my Father assigned me to accomplish, the works themselves that I am doing, bear witness about me that the Father dispatched me." (John 5:36) Even Jesus' enemies could not deny this evidence, which included numerous miracles. "What are we to do, because this man performs many signs?" certain ones later ask. (John 11:47) Some, though, respond favorably and say: "When the Christ arrives, he will not perform more signs than this man has performed, will he?" (John 7:31) Jesus' listeners were in an excellent position to discern the Father's qualities in the Son.—John 14:9.

⁷ Finally, Jesus draws attention to an unassailable witness. "The Scriptures . . . are the very ones that bear witness about me," he says, adding: "If you believed Moses you would believe me, for that one wrote about me." (John 5:39, 46) Of course, Moses was just one of the many pre-Christian witnesses who wrote about the Christ. Their writings include hundreds of prophecies and detailed genealogies, all pointing to the Messiah. (Luke 3:23-38; 24:44-46; Acts 10:43) And what about the Mosaic Law? "The Law has become our tutor leading to Christ," wrote the apostle Paul. (Galatians 3:24) Yes, "the bearing witness to Jesus is what inspires [or, is the whole inclination, intent, and purpose of] prophesying."—Revelation 19:10.

⁸ Would not all this evidence—John's explicit witness, Jesus' own powerful works

6. Why should Jesus' works have convinced people that he had God's backing?
7. How do the Hebrew Scriptures bear witness about Jesus?
8. Why did many Jews not put faith in the Messiah?

and godly qualities, and the monumental testimony of the Scriptures—convince you that Jesus was the Messiah? Anyone who had genuine love for God and for his Word would readily see this and exercise faith in Jesus as the promised Messiah. Such love, though, was basically lacking in Israel. To his opposers, Jesus said: "I well know that you do not have the love of God in you." (John 5: 42) Rather than "seeking the glory that is from the only God," they were "accepting glory from one another." No wonder they were at odds with Jesus, who like his Father abhors such thinking!—John 5:43, 44; Acts 12:21-23.

Fortified by a Prophetic Vision

⁹ Over a year has gone by since Jesus gave the aforementioned proof of his Messiahship. The Passover of the year 32 C.E. has come and gone. Many who believed have ceased following him, perhaps because of persecution, materialism, or the anxieties of life. Others may be confused or disappointed because Jesus rejected the people's efforts to make him king. When challenged by the Jewish religious leaders, he refused to provide a self-glorifying sign from heaven. (Matthew 12:38, 39) This refusal may have puzzled some. Furthermore, Jesus has begun to reveal to his disciples something they find very difficult to grasp—"he must go to Jerusalem and suffer many things from the older men and chief priests and scribes, and be killed."—Matthew 16:21-23.

¹⁰ In another nine to ten months, it would be time "for [Jesus] to move out of this world to the Father." (John 13:1) Deeply con-

---

9, 10. (a) Why was the timing of a sign for Jesus' disciples providential? (b) What remarkable promise did Jesus make to his disciples?

cerned about his loyal disciples, Jesus promises some of them the very thing he denied the faithless Jews—a sign from heaven. "Truly I say to you," Jesus says, "there are some of those standing here that will not taste death at all until first they see the Son of man coming in his kingdom." (Matthew 16:28) Obviously, Jesus is not saying that certain ones of his disciples will live until the establishment of the Messianic Kingdom in 1914. Jesus has in mind giving three of his intimate disciples a spectacular foregleam of his glory in Kingdom power. This visionary preview is called the transfiguration.

¹¹ Six days later, Jesus takes Peter, James, and John up into a lofty mountain—likely a ridge of Mount Hermon. There, Jesus is "transfigured before them, and his face shone as the sun, and his outer garments became brilliant as the light." The prophets Moses and Elijah also appear, conversing with Jesus. This awesome event possibly takes place at night, making it especially vivid. In fact, it is so real that Peter offers to erect three tents—one each for Jesus, Moses, and

---

11. Describe the transfiguration vision.

Elijah. While Peter is still speaking, a bright cloud overshadows them and a voice out of the cloud says: "This is my Son, the beloved, whom I have approved; listen to him."—Matthew 17:1-6.

[12] True, Peter had recently testified that Jesus is "the Christ, the Son of the living God." (Matthew 16:16) But imagine hearing God himself give his testimony, confirming the identity and the role of his anointed Son! What a faith-strengthening experience the transfiguration vision is for Peter, James, and John! With their faith thus greatly fortified, they are now better prepared for what lies ahead and for the important role they will play in the future congregation.

[13] The transfiguration makes a lasting impression on the disciples. Over 30 years later, Peter writes: "[Jesus] received from God the Father honor and glory, when words such as these were borne to him by the magnificent glory: 'This is my son, my beloved, whom I myself have approved.' Yes, these words we heard borne from heaven while we were with him in the holy mountain." (2 Peter 1: 17, 18) John is equally moved by the event. More than 60 years after it occurred, he apparently alludes to it with the words: "We had a view of his glory, a glory such as belongs to an only-begotten son from a father." (John 1:14) Yet, the transfiguration is not to be the last of the visions granted to Jesus' followers.

Further Enlightenment for God's Loyal Ones

[14] After his resurrection, Jesus appears to his disciples by the Sea of Galilee. There he tells Peter: "If it is my will for [John] to re-

main until I come, of what concern is that to you?" (John 21:1, 20-22, 24) Do these words indicate that the apostle John would outlive the other apostles? Apparently so, for he serves Jehovah faithfully for almost another 70 years. However, there is more to Jesus' statement.

[15] The expression "until I come" reminds us of Jesus' reference to "the Son of man coming in his kingdom." (Matthew 16:28) John remains until Jesus comes in that John is later given a prophetic vision of Jesus coming in Kingdom power. Near the end of John's life, while in exile on the isle of Patmos, he receives the Revelation with all its amazing prophetic signs of events that are to occur during "the Lord's day." John is so deeply moved by these spectacular visions that when Jesus says: "Yes; I am coming quickly," John exclaims: "Amen! Come, Lord Jesus."—Revelation 1:1, 10; 22:20.

[16] Honesthearted ones living in the first century accept Jesus as the Messiah and put faith in him. In view of the prevailing lack of faith around them, the work that they have to do, and the tests that lie ahead, those who become believers need

---

16. Why is it important that we continue to strengthen our faith?

John was to remain until Jesus' 'coming'

12, 13. What impact did the transfiguration vision have on Jesus' disciples, and why?
14, 15. In what way was the apostle John to remain until Jesus came?

to be strengthened. Jesus has given ample proof of his Messiahship and has provided enlightening prophetic visions for the encouragement of his loyal followers. Today, we are well along in "the Lord's day." Soon, Christ will destroy Satan's entire wicked system of things and deliver God's people. We too must strengthen our faith by taking full advantage of all of Jehovah's provisions for our spiritual welfare.

Preserved Through Darkness and Tribulation

[17] After Jesus' death, the disciples courageously obey his command to bear witness to him "both in Jerusalem and in all Judea and Samaria and to the most distant part of the earth." (Acts 1:8) Despite waves of persecution, Jehovah blesses the fledgling Christian congregation with spiritual enlightenment and with many new disciples.—Acts 2: 47; 4:1-31; 8:1-8.

[18] On the other hand, the prospects of those who oppose the good news grow progressively gloomier. "The way of the wicked

---

17, 18. What sharp contrast existed in the first century between Jesus' followers and those who opposed God's purpose, and how did things turn out for each group?

Do You Recall?

- When Jesus was accused of breaking the Sabbath and of blasphemy, what evidence did he give to show that he was the Messiah?

- How did Jesus' early disciples benefit from the transfiguration?

- What did Jesus mean when he said that John would remain until he came?

- In 1914, what foregleam became a reality?

ones is like the gloom," states Proverbs 4: 19. "They have not known at what they keep stumbling." "The gloom" intensifies in 66 C.E. when Roman forces besiege Jerusalem. After making a temporary withdrawal for no apparent reason, the Romans return in 70 C.E., this time razing the city. According to Jewish historian Josephus, over a million Jews perish. Faithful Christians, however, escape. Why? Because when the first siege is lifted, they obey Jesus' command to flee.—Luke 21:20-22.

[19] Our situation is similar. The upcoming great tribulation will spell the end of Satan's entire wicked system. But God's people need not fear, for Jesus promised: "Look! I am with you all the days until the conclusion of the system of things." (Matthew 28:20) To build up the faith of his early disciples and to prepare them for what lay ahead, Jesus gave them a foregleam of his heavenly glory as Messianic King. What about today? In 1914 that foregleam became a reality. And what a faith-strengthening reality it has been to God's people! It holds promise of a wonderful future, and Jehovah's servants have been granted progressive insight into that reality. In the midst of today's darkening world, "the path of the righteous ones is like the bright light that is getting lighter and lighter until the day is firmly established."—Proverbs 4:18.

[20] Even before 1914, a small band of anointed Christians began to grasp important truths about the Lord's return. For instance, they discerned that it would be invisible, as implied by the two angels who appeared in 33 C.E. to the disciples while Jesus was ascending to heaven. After a cloud

---

19, 20. (a) Why do God's people have no reason to be fearful as the present system nears its end? (b) What remarkable insight did Jehovah give to his people in the decades leading up to 1914?

caught Jesus up from the disciples' vision, the angels said: "This Jesus who was received up from you into the sky will come thus *in the same manner* as you have beheld him going into the sky."—Acts 1:9-11.

²¹ Jesus' departure was observed only by his loyal followers. As with the transfiguration, there was no public display; the world in general was not even aware of what had occurred. The same would be true when Christ returned in Kingdom power. (John 14:19) Only his faithful anointed disciples would discern his royal presence. In the next article, we will see how that insight would have a profound effect on them, culminating in the gathering of millions who would become Jesus' earthly subjects.—Revelation 7:9, 14.

21. What will be discussed in the following article?

FOREGLEAMS OF GOD'S KINGDOM BECOME A REALITY

"You are doing well in paying attention to [the prophetic word] as to a lamp shining in a dark place."—2 PETER 1:19.

CRISIS after crisis—that is a major theme of today's world. From ecological disasters to global terrorism, mankind's problems seem to be raging out of control. Even the world's religions have not been able to help. In fact, they often make matters worse by inflaming the bigotry, hatred, and nationalism that divide people. Yes, as foretold, "thick gloom" has enveloped "the national groups." (Isaiah 60:2) At the same time, however, millions look to the future with confidence. Why? Because they pay attention to God's prophetic word "as to a lamp shining in a dark place." They allow God's "word," or message, now found in the Bible, to guide their steps.—2 Peter 1:19.

² Concerning "the time of the end," the prophet Daniel wrote: "Many will rove about, and the true knowledge will become abundant. Many will cleanse themselves and whiten themselves and will be refined. And the wicked ones will certainly act wickedly, and no wicked ones at all will understand; but the ones having insight will understand." (Daniel 12:4, 10) Spiritual insight is reserved only for those who sincerely "rove about" in, or diligently study, God's Word, submit to his standards, and strive to do his will.—Matthew 13:11-15; 1 John 5:20.

³ As early as the 1870's, before "the last days" commenced, Jehovah God began to shed more light on "the sacred secrets of the kingdom of the heavens." (2 Timothy 3:1-5; Matthew 13:11) At that time a group of Bible students discerned—contrary to popular opinion—that Christ's return was to be invisible. After being enthroned in heaven, Jesus would return in the sense of focusing his royal attention on the earth. A visible,

1. What contrast do we find in the world today?
2. According to Daniel's prophecy about "the time of the end," who only are granted spiritual insight?

3. During the 1870's, what important truth did early Bible students discern?

composite sign would alert his disciples that his invisible presence had begun.—Matthew 24:3-14.

When a Foregleam Becomes a Reality

⁴ The transfiguration vision was a brilliant foregleam of Christ in Kingdom glory. (Matthew 17:1-9) That vision strengthened the faith of Peter, James, and John at a time when many had left off following Jesus because he had not fulfilled their unscriptural expectations. Likewise, in this time of the end, Jehovah has strengthened the faith of his modern-day servants by shedding increased light on the fulfillment of that awesome vision and many related prophecies. Let us now consider some of these faith-strengthening spiritual realities.

⁵ Referring to the transfiguration, the apostle Peter wrote: "Consequently we have the prophetic word made more sure; and you are doing well in paying attention to it as to a lamp shining in a dark place, until day dawns and a daystar rises, in your hearts." (2 Peter 1:19) That figurative Daystar, or "bright morning star," is the glorified Jesus Christ. (Revelation 22:16) He 'rose' in 1914 when God's Kingdom was born in heaven, marking the dawn of a new era. (Revelation 11:15) In the transfiguration vision, Moses and Elijah appeared alongside Jesus, conversing with him. Whom do they foreshadow?

⁶ Since Moses and Elijah shared in Christ's glory, these two faithful witnesses must represent those who rule with Jesus in his Kingdom. The understanding that Jesus has corulers is in harmony with a visionary foregleam of the enthroned Messiah that the prophet Daniel was granted. Daniel saw "someone like a son of man" receiving "an indefinitely lasting rulership" from "the Ancient of Days," Jehovah God. But note what Daniel is shown shortly thereafter. He writes: "The kingdom and the rulership and the grandeur of the kingdoms under all the heavens were given to the people who are the holy ones of the Supreme One." (Daniel 7:13, 14, 27) Yes, more than five centuries before the transfiguration, God revealed that certain "holy ones" would share in Christ's royal grandeur.

⁷ Who are the holy ones in Daniel's vision? It is with reference to such individuals that the apostle Paul says: "The spirit itself bears witness with our spirit that we are God's children. If, then, we are children, we are also heirs: heirs indeed of God, but joint heirs with Christ, provided we suffer together that we may also be glorified together." (Romans 8:16, 17) The holy ones are none other than Jesus' spirit-anointed disciples. In the Revelation, Jesus says: "To the one that conquers I will grant to sit down with me on my throne, even as I conquered and sat down with my Father on his throne." Numbering 144,000, these resurrected 'conquerors,' along with Jesus, will rule over the entire earth.—Revelation 3:21; 5:9, 10; 14:1, 3, 4; 1 Corinthians 15:53.

⁸ Why, though, are anointed Christians represented by Moses and Elijah? The reason

---

4. How has Jehovah strengthened the faith of his modern-day servants?
5. Who proved to be the Daystar, and when and how did he 'rise'?
6, 7. Who are represented by Moses and Elijah in the transfiguration, and what important details do the Scriptures reveal about those represented by them?

---

8. How have Jesus' anointed disciples served in the capacity of Moses and Elijah, and with what results?

A foregleam becomes a reality

is that such Christians, while still in the flesh, do a work similar to that performed by Moses and Elijah. For example, they serve as Jehovah's witnesses, even in the face of persecution. (Isaiah 43:10; Acts 8:1-8; Revelation 11:2-12) Like Moses and Elijah, they courageously expose false religion while exhorting sincere people to give God exclusive devotion. (Exodus 32:19, 20; Deuteronomy 4:22-24; 1 Kings 18:18-40) Has their work borne fruit? Absolutely! Besides helping to gather the full complement of anointed ones, they have helped millions of "other sheep" to show willing submission to Jesus Christ. —John 10:16; Revelation 7:4.

Christ Completes His Conquest

⁹ No longer a mere human mounted on the colt of an ass, Jesus is now a powerful King. He is portrayed as riding on a horse—a Biblical symbol of warfare. (Proverbs 21:31) "Look! a white horse," says Revelation 6:2, "and the one seated upon it had a bow; and a crown was given him, and he went forth conquering and to complete his conquest."

───────

9. How does Revelation 6:2 portray Jesus as he is today?

Moreover, concerning Jesus, the psalmist David wrote: "The rod of your strength Jehovah will send out of Zion, saying: 'Go subduing in the midst of your enemies.'"—Psalm 110:2.

¹⁰ Jesus' first victory was over his most powerful foes—Satan and the demons. Expelling them from heaven, he hurled them down to the earth. Knowing that their time is short, these wicked spirits have vented their violent anger on mankind, causing great woe. This woe is symbolized in Revelation by the ride of three more horsemen. (Revelation 6:3-8; 12:7-12) In line with Jesus' prophecy concerning "the sign of [his] presence and of the conclusion of the system of things," their ride has resulted in warfare, famine, and deadly plague. (Matthew 24:3, 7; Luke 21:7-11) Like literal birth pangs, these "pangs of distress" will no doubt continue to intensify until Christ 'completes his conquest' by destroying every vestige of Satan's visible organization.*—Matthew 24:8.

───────

* In the original Greek, the word rendered "pangs of distress" literally means "pangs of birth." (Matthew 24:8, *Kingdom Interlinear*) This suggests that like birth pangs, the world's problems will increase in frequency, intensity, and duration, climaxing in the great tribulation.

───────

10. (a) How did Jesus' ride of conquest get off to a glorious start? (b) How did Christ's first victory affect the world in general?

Do you know what happened when Christ began his conquest?

¹¹ Jesus' royal authority is also evident in that he has preserved the Christian congregation so that it can fulfill its commission to preach the Kingdom message worldwide. Despite brutal opposition from Babylon the Great—the world empire of false religion—and from hostile governments, the preaching work not only has continued but has attained a scale unprecedented in the history of the world. (Revelation 17:5, 6) What a powerful testimony to Christ's kingship!—Psalm 110:3.

¹² Sadly, though, most people, including millions of professed Christians, fail to discern the invisible realities behind the momentous events occurring on earth. They even ridicule those who announce God's Kingdom. (2 Peter 3:3, 4) Why? Because Satan has blinded their minds. (2 Corinthians 4:3, 4) In fact, he began to cast the veil of spiritual darkness over professed Christians

many centuries ago, even causing them to abandon the precious Kingdom hope.

The Kingdom Hope Abandoned

¹³ Jesus foretold that apostates, like weeds sown among wheat, would infiltrate the Christian congregation and lead many astray. (Matthew 13:24-30, 36-43; Acts 20:29-31; Jude 4) In time, these so-called Christians adopted pagan festivals, practices, and teachings, even labeling them "Christian." For example, Christmas has its origin in rites involving the worship of the pagan deities Mithra and Saturn. But what induced professed Christians to adopt these unchristian celebrations? Says *The New Encyclopædia Britannica* (1974): "Christmas, the festival of the birth of Jesus Christ, was established in connection with a fading of the expectation of Christ's imminent return."

¹⁴ Consider also the distortion of the

---

11. How does the history of the Christian congregation testify to Christ's royal authority?
12. Why do most people not discern Christ's invisible presence?

---

13. To what did the veil of spiritual darkness lead?
14. How did the teachings of Origen and Augustine misrepresent Kingdom truth?

meaning of the word "kingdom." The book *The Kingdom of God in 20th-Century Interpretation* states: "Origen [a third-century theologian] marks the change in Christian usage of 'kingdom' to the interior meaning of the rule of God in the heart." On what did Origen base his teaching? Not on the Scriptures, but on "the framework of a philosophy and world view quite different from the thought world of Jesus and the earliest church." In his work *De Civitate Dei* (The City of God), Augustine of Hippo (354-430 C.E.) stated that the church itself is the Kingdom of God. Such unscriptural thinking gave the churches of Christendom theological grounds to embrace political power. And they wielded such power for many centuries, often with brutality.—Revelation 17: 5, 18.

¹⁵ Today, though, the churches are reaping what they have sown. (Galatians 6:7) Many seem to be losing their power as well as their parishioners. Such a trend is quite noticeable in Europe. According to the journal *Christianity Today,* "now the great cathedrals of Europe [serve] not as houses of worship but as museums, empty of all but tourists." The same trend can be observed in other parts of the world. What does this betoken for false religion? Will it just die from a lack of support? And how will true worship be affected?

Be Prepared for God's Great Day

¹⁶ Just as smoke and ash spewing from a previously dormant volcano may portend an imminent eruption, the simmering hostility toward religion in many parts of the world is an indication that the days of false religion are numbered. Soon, Je-

hovah will move the world's political elements to unite in efforts to expose and devastate the spiritual harlot Babylon the Great. (Revelation 17:15-17; 18:21) Should true Christians fear that event and the other aspects of the "great tribulation" that will follow? (Matthew 24:21) Not at all! They will actually have reasons to rejoice when God acts against the wicked. (Revelation 18: 20; 19:1, 2) Consider the example of first-century Jerusalem and the Christians who lived there.

¹⁷ When Roman forces besieged Jerusalem in 66 C.E., spiritually alert Christians were neither shocked nor terrified. Being good students of God's Word, they knew 'that the desolating of her had drawn near.' (Luke 21: 20) They also knew that God would open the way for them to flee to safety. When that happened, Christians fled. (Daniel 9:26; Matthew 24:15-19; Luke 21:21) Likewise today, those who know God and who obey his Son can face this system's end with confidence. (2 Thessalonians 1:6-9) In fact, when the great tribulation strikes, they will joyfully 'raise themselves erect and lift their heads up, because they know their deliverance is near.'—Luke 21:28.

¹⁸ After the destruction of Babylon the Great, in his role as Gog of Magog, Satan will launch an all-out attack against Jehovah's peaceful Witnesses. Coming up "like clouds to cover the land," Gog's hordes will expect an easy victory. What a shock awaits them! (Ezekiel 38:14-16, 18-23) The apostle John writes: "I saw the heaven opened, and, look! a white horse. And the one seated upon it is called Faithful and True . . . Out of his mouth there protrudes a sharp long sword, that he may strike the nations with

---

15. How has Galatians 6:7 been fulfilled in regard to many of the churches of Christendom?
16. Why is the growing ill will toward Babylon the Great significant?

17. Why can Jehovah's faithful servants face this system's end with confidence?
18. What will be the result of Gog's all-out assault on Jehovah's servants?

it." This invincible "King of kings" will rescue Jehovah's loyal worshipers and annihilate all their enemies. (Revelation 19:11-21) What a culmination that will be of the fulfillment of the transfiguration vision!

[19] Jesus will be "regarded in that day with wonder in connection with all those who exercised faith." (2 Thessalonians 1:10) Do you want to be among those who will stand in awe of the victorious Son of God? Then continue to nourish your faith and to 'prove yourself ready, because at an hour that you do not think to be it, the Son of man is coming.'—Matthew 24:43, 44.

Keep Your Senses

[20] "The faithful and discreet slave" regularly exhorts God's people to stay spiritually vigilant and to keep their senses. (Matthew 24:45, 46; 1 Thessalonians 5:6) Do you appreciate these timely reminders? Do you use them in setting priorities in life? Why not ask yourself: 'Do I have clear spiritual vision that enables me to see the Son of God ruling in heaven? Do I see him poised to execute divine judgment against Babylon the Great and the rest of Satan's system?'

[21] Some now associated with Jehovah's people have allowed their spiritual vision to grow dim. Could it be that they lack patience or endurance, as did some of Jesus' early disciples? Have anxieties of life, materialism, or persecution affected them? (Matthew 13: 3-8, 18-23; Luke 21:34-36) Perhaps some have found certain information published by "the faithful and discreet slave" hard to grasp. If any of this has happened to you, we urge you to study God's Word with renewed zeal and to supplicate Jehovah so that you may regain a strong, close relationship with him.—2 Peter 3:11-15.

[22] The transfiguration vision was given to Jesus' disciples when they needed encouragement. Today, we have something far greater to strengthen us—the fulfillment of that spectacular foregleam and many related prophecies. As we contemplate these glorious realities and their future significance, may we too express with all our heart the sentiments of the apostle John when he said: "Amen! Come, Lord Jesus."—Revelation 22:20.

---

19. How will Christ's total victory affect his loyal disciples, and what should they strive to do now?
20. (a) How can we show our appreciation for God's provision of "the faithful and discreet slave"? (b) What questions should we ask ourselves?
21. Why may some have allowed their spiritual vision to grow dim, and what is it urgent that they do?
22. How has consideration of the transfiguration vision and related prophecies affected you?

Do You Recall?

- In the 1870's, what did a small group of Bible students come to understand about Christ's return?

- How has the transfiguration vision been fulfilled?

- What effect does Jesus' ride of conquest have on the world and on the Christian congregation?

- What must we do to be among those who will survive when Jesus completes his conquest?

"Be Hospitable to One Another"

PHOEBE, a first-century Christian, had a problem. She was journeying from Cenchreae, in Greece, to Rome, but she was unacquainted with fellow believers in that city. (Romans 16:1, 2) "The Roman world [of those days] was a bad and brutal world," says Bible translator Edgar Goodspeed, "and inns were notoriously likely to be no places for a decent woman, particularly a Christian woman." So where was Phoebe to lodge?

People traveled extensively in Bible times. Jesus Christ and his disciples did so to preach the good news throughout Judea and Galilee. Soon thereafter, Christian missionaries like Paul were taking the message to various parts of the Mediterranean basin, including Rome, the capital of the Roman Empire. When first-century Christians traveled, whether inside or outside Jewish territory, where did they stay? In finding accommodations, what difficulties did they face? What can we learn from them about extending hospitality?

"Today I Must Stay in Your House"

Hospitality is defined as the "generous and cordial reception of guests," and it has long been a characteristic of Jehovah's true worshipers. For instance, Abraham, Lot, and Rebekah practiced it. (Genesis 18: 1-8; 19:1-3; 24:17-20) Recounting his attitude toward strangers, the patriarch Job stated: "Outside no alien resident would spend the night; my doors I kept open to the path."—Job 31:32.

For travelers to receive hospitable treatment from their fellow Israelites, it was often sufficient to sit down in the public square of a city and await an invitation. (Judges 19:15-21) Hosts usually washed their guests' feet and offered the visitors food and drink, also providing fodder for their animals. (Genesis 18:4, 5; 19:2; 24:32, 33) Travelers who did not wish to be a burden on their hosts carried with them the needed provisions—bread and wine for themselves and straw and fodder for their asses. They required only shelter for the night.

While the Bible rarely specifies how Jesus found lodging during his preaching tours, he and his disciples had to sleep somewhere. (Luke 9:58) When visiting Jericho, Jesus simply told Zacchaeus: "Today I must stay in your house." Zacchaeus received his guest "with rejoicing." (Luke 19:5, 6) Jesus was often the guest of his friends Martha, Mary, and Lazarus in Bethany. (Luke 10:38; John 11:1, 5, 18) And it seems that in Capernaum,

Jesus stayed with Simon Peter.—Mark 1:21, 29-35.

Jesus' ministerial instruction to his 12 apostles reveals much about what kind of reception they could expect in Israel. Jesus told them: "Do not procure gold or silver or copper for your girdle purses, or a food pouch for the trip, or two undergarments, or sandals or a staff; for the worker deserves his food. Into whatever city or village you enter, search out who in it is deserving, and stay there until you leave." (Matthew 10:9-11) He knew that righthearted individuals would take his disciples in, providing them with food, shelter, and other necessities.

The time was coming, however, when evangelizers on the move would have to provide for themselves and cover their own expenses. In view of future hostility toward his followers and the expansion of the preaching work into territories outside Israel, Jesus said: "Let the one that has a purse take it up, likewise also a food pouch." (Luke 22:36) Travel and lodging would be indispensable to the spreading of the good news.

"Follow the Course of Hospitality"

Relative peace and a great network of paved roads throughout the Roman Empire in the first century resulted in a highly mobile society.* An abundance of travelers generated a great demand for lodging. That demand was met by inns a day's journey apart along the main highways. However, *The Book of Acts in Its Graeco-Roman Setting* states: "What is known of such facilities in the literature presents a rather unhappy picture. The available literary and archaeological sources generally witness to dilapidated and unclean facilities, virtually non-existent furnishings, bed-bugs, poor quality food and drink, untrustworthy pro-

---

* It is estimated that by the year 100 C.E., there were some 50,000 miles of paved Roman roads.

prietors and staff, shady clientele, and generally loose morals." Understandably, a morally upright traveler would avoid staying at such inns whenever possible.

Not surprisingly, then, the Scriptures repeatedly exhort Christians to extend hospitality to others. Paul urged Christians in Rome: "Share with the holy ones according to their needs. Follow the course of hospitality." (Romans 12:13) He reminded the Jewish Christians: "Do not forget hospitality, for through it some, unknown to themselves, entertained angels." (Hebrews 13:2) Peter exhorted his fellow worshipers to "be hospitable to one another without grumbling." —1 Peter 4:9.

Situations did exist, however, in which extending hospitality would be inappropriate. Regarding "everyone that pushes ahead and does not remain in the teaching of the Christ," the apostle John said: "Never receive him into your homes or say a greeting to him. For he that says a greeting to him is a sharer in his wicked works." (2 John 9-11) Concerning unrepentant sinners, Paul wrote: "Quit mixing in company with anyone called a brother that is a fornicator or a greedy person or an idolater or a reviler or a drunkard or an extortioner, not even eating with such a man."—1 Corinthians 5:11.

Impostors and others must have tried to exploit the good nature of true Christians. A second-century C.E. extra-Biblical statement of Christian faith known as *The Didache, or Teaching of the Twelve Apostles,* recommends that an itinerant preacher be entertained for "one day, or if need be a second as well." After that, when he is sent on his way, "let him accept nothing but bread . . . If he ask[s] for money, he is a false prophet." The document continues: "If he wishes to settle among you and has a craft, let him work for his bread. But if he has no craft provide for him according to your understanding, so that no man

Christians "follow the course of hospitality"

shall live among you in idleness because he is a Christian. But if he will not do so, he is making traffic of Christ; beware of such."

The apostle Paul was careful not to impose an expensive burden upon his hosts during his long stays in certain cities. He worked as a tentmaker to support himself. (Acts 18:1-3; 2 Thessalonians 3:7-12) To help deserving travelers among them, early Christians apparently used letters of recommendation, such as Paul's introduction of Phoebe. "I recommend to you Phoebe our sister," wrote Paul, "that you may welcome her in the Lord . . . and that you may assist her in any matter where she may need you." —Romans 16:1, 2.

Blessings From Being Hospitable

First-century Christian missionaries trusted in Jehovah to provide for all their needs. But could they expect to enjoy the hospitality of fellow believers? Lydia opened up her house to Paul and others. The apostle stayed with Aquila and Priscilla in Corinth. A jailer in Philippi set a table before Paul and Silas. Paul was received hospitably by Jason in Thessalonica, by Philip in Caesarea, and by Mnason on the road from Caesarea to Jerusalem. En route to Rome, Paul was entertained by brothers in Puteoli. What spiritually rewarding occasions these must have been for the hosts who received him!—Acts 16:33, 34; 17:7; 18:1-3; 21:8, 16; 28:13, 14.

Scholar Frederick F. Bruce observes: "These friends and co-workers, hosts and hostesses, had no other motive in being so helpful than love of Paul and love of the Master whom he served. They knew that in serving the one they were serving the other." This is an excellent motive for being hospitable.

The need to extend hospitality still exists. Thousands of traveling representatives of Jehovah's Witnesses receive hospitality from fellow believers. Some Kingdom proclaimers travel at their own expense to preach in places seldom reached with the good news. Great benefits result from opening our homes, however humble, to such ones. Warmhearted hospitality that may include no more than a simple meal offers excellent opportunities for "an interchange of encouragement" and for showing love for our brothers and for our God. (Romans 1:11, 12) Such occasions are particularly rewarding for the hosts, for "there is more happiness in giving than there is in receiving."—Acts 20:35.

Jehovah's Word Is Alive

Highlights From the Book of Judges

HOW does Jehovah respond when his own people turn their back on him and begin to worship false gods? What if they repeatedly fall away and call on him for help only when they are in distress? Does Jehovah provide a way of escape for them even then? The book of Judges answers these and other vital questions. Completed by the prophet Samuel about 1100 B.C.E., it covers events that span some 330 years—from the death of Joshua to the enthronement of Israel's first king.

As a part of God's dynamic word, or message, the book of Judges is of great value to us. (Hebrews 4:12) The exciting accounts recorded in it give us insight into God's personality. The lessons that we learn from them strengthen our faith and help us to get a firm hold on "the real life," everlasting life in God's promised new world. (1 Timothy 6:12, 19; 2 Peter 3:13) The deeds of salvation that Jehovah performs in behalf of his people provide a foregleam of the greater deliverance by his Son, Jesus Christ, in the future.

WHY WERE JUDGES NEEDED?
(Judges 1:1–3:6)

After the kings of the land of Canaan are defeated under the leadership of Joshua, the individual tribes of Israel go to their inheritance and take possession of the land. However, the Israelites fail to dispossess the inhabitants of the land. This failure proves to be a real snare for Israel.

The generation that comes after the days of Joshua 'does not know Jehovah or the work that he has done for Israel.' (Judges 2: 10) Moreover, the people proceed to form marriage alliances with the Canaanites and to serve their gods. So Jehovah gives the Israelites into the hands of their enemies. When oppression becomes severe, though, the sons of Israel call upon the true God for help. In this religious, social, and political climate unfolds the account of a line of judges whom Jehovah raises up to save his people from their enemies.

Scriptural Questions Answered:

1:2, 4—Why is Judah designated to be the first tribe to take possession of the land allotted to it? Normally, this privilege would go to the tribe of Reuben, Jacob's firstborn. But in his deathbed prophecy, Jacob foretold that Reuben was not to excel, having forfeited his right as the firstborn. Simeon and Levi, who had acted with cruelty, were to be scattered in Israel. (Genesis 49:3-5, 7) Hence, the next in line was Judah, the fourth son of Jacob. Simeon, who went up with Judah, received small areas of land scattered throughout the large territory of Judah.*—Joshua 19:9.

1:6, 7—Why were the thumbs and the big toes of defeated kings cut off? A person who lost his thumbs and big toes apparently was incapacitated for military action. Without the thumbs, how could a soldier handle a sword or a spear? And the loss of the big toes would result in inability to maintain one's balance properly.

Lessons for Us:

2:10-12. We must have a regular program

---

* The Levites were not given an inheritance in the Promised Land except for 48 cities scattered throughout Israel.

of Bible study so as 'not to forget Jehovah's doings.' (Psalm 103:2) Parents need to sound down the truth of God's Word into the hearts of their children.—Deuteronomy 6:6-9.

2:14, 21, 22. Jehovah allows bad things to happen to his disobedient people for a purpose—to chastise them, to refine them, and to move them to return to him.

JEHOVAH RAISES UP JUDGES
(Judges 3:7–16:31)

The exciting account of the exploits of the judges begins with Othniel's bringing an end to Israel's eight-year subjugation to a Mesopotamian king. Using a courageous strategy, Judge Ehud kills Eglon, the fat Moabite king. Valiant Shamgar single-handedly strikes down 600 Philistines using a cattle goad. With encouragement from Deborah, who serves as a prophetess, and with Jehovah's backing, Barak and his lightly equipped army of ten thousand men rout the powerful army of Sisera. Jehovah raises up Gideon and gives him and his 300 men victory over the Midianites.

Through Jephthah, Jehovah delivers Israel from the Ammonites. Tola, Jair, Ibzan, Elon, and Abdon are also among the 12 men who judge Israel. The period of the Judges ends with Samson, who fights against the Philistines.

Scriptural Questions Answered:

4:8—Why did Barak insist that the prophetess Deborah go with him to the battlefield? Evidently, Barak felt inadequate to go up against Sisera's army by himself. Having the prophetess with him would reassure him and his men that they had God's guidance and would give them confidence. Barak's insistence that Deborah accompany him, then, was not a sign of weakness but of strong faith.

5:20—How did the stars fight from the heavens in behalf of Barak? The Bible does not say whether this involved angelic assistance, meteorite showers that were interpreted ominously by Sisera's wise men, or perhaps astrological predictions for Sisera that proved false. Undoubtedly, however, there was some type of divine intervention.

7:1-3; 8:10—Why did Jehovah say that Gideon's 32,000 men were too many against the enemy force of 135,000? This was because Jehovah was giving Gideon and his men the victory. God did not want them

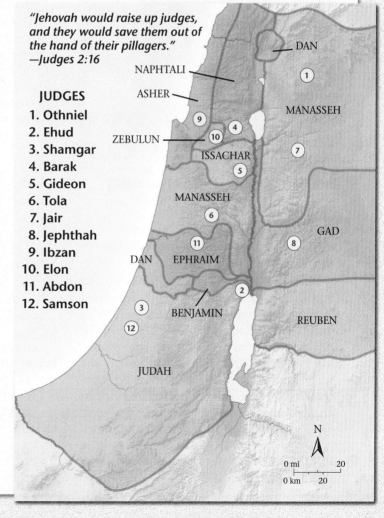

"Jehovah would raise up judges, and they would save them out of the hand of their pillagers." —Judges 2:16

JUDGES

1. Othniel
2. Ehud
3. Shamgar
4. Barak
5. Gideon
6. Tola
7. Jair
8. Jephthah
9. Ibzan
10. Elon
11. Abdon
12. Samson

What lesson did you learn from Barak's insistence that Deborah go to the battlefield?

to think that they defeated the Midianites in their own strength.

11:30, 31—When making his vow, did Jephthah have a human sacrifice in mind? Such a thought would be far from Jephthah's mind, for the Law stipulated: "There should not be found in you anyone who makes his son or his daughter pass through the fire." (Deuteronomy 18:10) However, Jephthah did have in mind a person and not an animal. Animals suitable for sacrifice were not likely kept in Israelite homes. And the of-

fering of an animal would be nothing outstanding. Jephthah was aware that the one coming out of his house to meet him might well be his daughter. This one was to be offered up "as a burnt offering" in that the person would be devoted to Jehovah's exclusive service in connection with the sanctuary.

Lessons for Us:

3:10. Success in spiritual pursuits depends, not on human wisdom, but on Jehovah's spirit.—Psalm 127:1.

3:21. Ehud wielded his sword proficiently and with courage. We must acquire skill in using "the sword of the spirit, that is, God's word." This means that we must use the Scriptures courageously in our ministry. —Ephesians 6:17; 2 Timothy 2:15.

6:11-15; 8:1-3, 22, 23. Gideon's modesty teaches us three important lessons: (1) When a privilege of service is extended to us, we should reflect on the responsibility it entails rather than dwell on the prominence or prestige that may be associated with it. (2) When dealing with those inclined to quarrel, displaying modesty is the course of wisdom. (3) Modesty protects us from being position oriented.

6:17-22, 36-40. We too must be cautious and "not believe every inspired expression." Instead, we need to "test the inspired expressions to see whether they originate with God." (1 John 4:1) To make sure that counsel he plans to give is solidly based on God's Word, a new Christian elder is wise to consult a more experienced elder.

6:25-27. Gideon used discretion so as not to anger his opposers needlessly. When preaching the good news, we must be careful not to offend others unduly by the way we speak.

7:6. When it comes to serving Jehovah, we should be like Gideon's 300 men—alert and vigilant.

9:8-15. How foolish to act proudly and harbor ambition for position or power!

11:35-37. The good example of Jephthah was undoubtedly instrumental in helping his daughter develop strong faith and a self-sacrificing spirit. Parents today can set such an example for their children.

11:40. Offering commendation to someone who displays a willing spirit in Jehovah's service encourages that one.

13:8. In teaching their children, parents should pray to Jehovah for guidance and follow his direction.—2 Timothy 3:16.

14:16, 17; 16:16. Applying pressure by weeping and nagging can damage a relationship.—Proverbs 19:13; 21:19.

OTHER OFFENSES IN ISRAEL
(Judges 17:1–21:25)

The last part of the book of Judges contains two outstanding accounts. The first concerns a man named Micah, who sets up an idol in his house and employs a Levite to act as a priest for him. After destroying the city of Laish, or Leshem, the Danites build their own city and name it Dan. Using Micah's idol and his priest, they set up another form of worship in Dan. Evidently, Laish is captured before Joshua's death.—Joshua 19:47.

The second event takes place not long after the death of Joshua. A mass sex crime committed by some men of the Benjamite city of Gibeah leads to the near annihilation of the entire tribe of Benjamin—only 600 men survive. However, an expedient arrangement allows them to get wives, and their number increases to nearly 60,000 warriors by the time of David's rulership.—1 Chronicles 7:6-11.

Scriptural Questions Answered:

17:6; 21:25—If 'each one was accustomed to do what was right in his own eyes,' did this foster anarchy? Not necessarily, for Jehovah made ample provisions to guide his people. He gave them the Law and the priesthood to educate them in his way. By means of the Urim and the Thummim, the high priest could consult God on important matters. (Exodus 28:30) Every city also had older men capable of providing sound counsel. When an Israelite availed himself of these provisions, he had a sound guide for his conscience. His doing "what was right in his own eyes" in this way resulted in good. On the other hand, if a person ignored the Law and made his own decisions about conduct and worship, the result was bad.

20:17-48—Why did Jehovah let the Benjamites defeat the other tribes twice, even though the former needed to be punished? By allowing the faithful tribes to suffer great losses at first, Jehovah tested their determination to root out evil from Israel.

Lessons for Us:

19:14, 15. The unwillingness on the part of the people of Gibeah to extend hospitality was an indication of a moral shortcoming. Christians are admonished to "follow the course of hospitality."—Romans 12:13.

The Deliverance Ahead

Very soon now, God's Kingdom in the hands of Christ Jesus will destroy the wicked world and provide a great deliverance for the upright and the blameless. (Proverbs 2:21, 22; Daniel 2:44) 'All of Jehovah's enemies will then perish, and his lovers will be as when the sun goes forth in its mightiness.' (Judges 5:31) Let us prove to be among the lovers of Jehovah by applying what we have learned from the book of Judges.

The fundamental truth demonstrated over and over in the accounts of the Judges is this: Obedience to Jehovah leads to rich blessings, disobedience to dire consequences. (Deuteronomy 11:26-28) How vital that we become "obedient from the heart" to the revealed will of God!—Romans 6:17; 1 John 2:17.

Saul's Preaching Excites HOSTILITY

THE Jews in Damascus could not understand it. How could a passionate defender of orthodoxy have become an apostate? Here was Saul, the man who had harassed those calling on Jesus' name in Jerusalem. He had come to Damascus to persecute the disciples there. But now he himself was preaching that the same despised felon impaled for blasphemy was the Messiah! Had Saul gone mad?—Acts 9:1, 2, 20-22.

Perhaps there was an explanation. Others who traveled from Jerusalem in the same caravan as Saul may well have spoken about what transpired on the road. As they approached Damascus, suddenly a bright light flashed around them, and all of them fell to the ground. There was also the sound of a voice. No one except Saul was hurt. He was lying on the road. When he finally got up, other travelers had to lead him into Damascus, for he could not see a thing.—Acts 9:3-8; 26:13, 14.

An Opponent Becomes a Proponent

What had happened to Saul on the road to Damascus? Had the long journey or the heat of the midday sun perhaps debilitated him? Determined to find natural explanations, modern skeptics offer scenarios that include delirium, hallucination, a drastic psychological crisis provoked by the qualms of Saul's tormented conscience, a nervous breakdown, and an assumed predisposition to epilepsy.

The fact was that Jesus Christ appeared to Saul in that blinding light, convincing him that He was the Messiah. Some artistic depictions of this episode show Saul falling from a horse. Though that is possible, the Bible simply says that he "fell to the ground." (Acts 22:6-11) Whatever physical fall Saul experienced was not nearly so great as the fall from the pride of his position. He now had to recognize that what Jesus' followers were preaching was true. The only course open to Saul was to join them. From a militant foe of Jesus' message, Saul became one of its staunchest proponents. After regaining his sight and getting baptized, "Saul kept on acquiring power all the more and was confounding the Jews that dwelt in Damascus as he proved logically that this is the Christ." —Acts 9:22.

Assassination Plot Fails

Where did Saul, later called Paul, go after his conversion? When writing to the Galatians, he said: "I went off into Arabia, and I came back again to Damascus." (Galatians 1:17) The term "Arabia" allows for a journey into any part of the Arabian Peninsula. Some scholars suggest that Paul may have gone into the Syrian Desert or elsewhere in the Nabataean kingdom of Aretas IV. Very likely, Saul

Saul "fell to the ground" when Jesus appeared to him

went to a quiet place for meditation after his baptism, even as Jesus went into the wilderness following his immersion.—Luke 4:1.

When Saul returned to Damascus, "the Jews took counsel together to do away with him." (Acts 9:23) The governor who served as King Aretas' representative in Damascus was guarding the city in order to seize Saul. (2 Corinthians 11:32) But while enemies plotted Saul's death, Jesus' disciples planned his escape.

Among those who helped Saul to escape were Ananias and the disciples whose company the apostle enjoyed immediately after his conversion.* (Acts 9:17-19) Some who had become believers because of Saul's preaching in Damascus may also have helped, for Acts 9:25 states: "His disciples took him and let him down by night through an opening in the wall, lowering him in a basket." The expression "his disciples" may mean those whom Saul taught. In any case, the success of his ministry likely fueled the animosity already harbored against him.

A Lesson to Be Learned

When we examine some of the events surrounding Saul's conversion and baptism, we clearly see that he was not overly concerned about how others judged him; neither did he quit because of severe opposition. What mattered most to Saul was the preaching commission he had received.—Acts 22:14, 15.

Have you recently become convinced of the importance of preaching the good news? If so, you know that all true Christians must be Kingdom preachers. You should not be surprised if your ministry at times provokes hostile re-

---

* Christianity may have arrived in Damascus either following Jesus' preaching in Galilee or after Pentecost 33 C.E.—Matthew 4:24; Acts 2:5.

actions. (Matthew 24:9; Luke 21:12; 1 Peter 2:20) Saul's response to opposition is exemplary. Christians who endure under trials without giving up will have God's favor. Jesus told his disciples: "You will be objects of hatred by all people because of my name." Yet, he assured them: "By endurance on your part you will acquire your souls."—Luke 21:17-19.

Saul escaped an assassination plot in Damascus

Questions From Readers

How could Samson touch dead bodies that he had slain and still remain a Nazirite?

In ancient Israel, an individual could voluntarily make a vow and become a Nazirite for a certain length of time.* One of the restrictions resting upon the one making this vow stipulated: "All the days of his keeping separate to Jehovah he may not come toward any dead soul. Not even for his father or his mother or his brother or his sister may he defile himself when they die." What if someone "should die quite suddenly alongside him"? Such an accidental touching of a dead body would defile his Naziriteship. Thus, it was stated: "The former days will go uncounted." He would need to go through a purification ceremony and start the Nazirite period over again.—Numbers 6:6-12.

Samson, though, was a Nazirite in a different sense. Before Samson's birth, Jehovah's angel told his mother: "Look! you will be pregnant, and you will certainly give birth to a son, and no razor should come upon his head, because a Nazirite of God is what the child will become on leaving the belly; and he it is who will take the lead in saving Israel out of the hand of the Philistines." (Judges 13:5) Samson took no vow of Naziriteship. He was a Nazirite by divine appointment, and

---

* The length of time for Naziriteship was left up to the individual making the vow. According to Jewish tradition, however, the minimum length for the vow was 30 days. It was thought that anything less would make the vow commonplace.

his Naziriteship was for life. The restriction against touching a corpse could not apply in his case. If it did and he accidentally touched a dead body, how could he start over a lifelong Naziriteship that began with his birth? Evidently, then, the requirements for lifetime Nazirites differed in some ways from those for voluntary Nazirites.

Consider Jehovah's commandments to the three lifelong Nazirites—Samson, Samuel, and John the Baptizer—mentioned in the Bible. As noted earlier, Samson was required not to cut the hair of his head. Concerning her yet to be conceived child—Samuel—Hannah made the vow: "I will give him to Jehovah all the days of his life, and no razor will come upon his head." (1 Samuel 1:11) In the case of John the Baptizer, Jehovah's angel said: "He must drink no wine and strong drink at all." (Luke 1:15) Moreover, "John had his clothing of camel's hair and a leather girdle around his loins; his food too was insect locusts and wild honey." (Matthew 3:4) None of these three individuals were commanded not to come near a dead soul.

Though a Nazirite, Samson was among the judges whom Jehovah raised up to save the Israelites out of the hand of their pillagers. (Judges 2:16) And in fulfilling this assignment, he came in contact with dead bodies. On one occasion, Samson struck down 30 Philistines and stripped off their outfits. Later, he went smiting the enemy, "piling legs upon thighs with a great slaughter." He also took a moist jawbone of an ass and killed a thousand men with it. (Judges 14:19; 15:8, 15) Samson did all of this with Jehovah's favor and backing. The Scriptures refer to him as a man of exemplary faith.—Hebrews 11:32; 12:1.

Does the statement that Samson ripped apart a lion "just as someone tears a male kid in two" suggest that the tearing apart of young goats was a common practice in his day?

There is no evidence that in the time of Israel's Judges, it was common for people to tear apart young goats. Judges 14:6 states: "Jehovah's spirit became operative upon [Samson], so that he tore it [a maned young lion] in two, just as someone tears a male kid in two, and there was nothing at all in his hand." This comment likely is an illustration.

The expression "he tore it in two" could have two meanings. Samson either tore apart the jaws of the lion or tore the lion limb from limb in some way. If the former is meant, then doing the same thing to a young goat is conceivably within human power. In this case, the parallel illustrates that conquering a lion with his bare hands was no more difficult for Samson than had the lion been a mere male kid. However, what if Samson killed the lion by tearing it limb from limb? The comment then can hardly be taken as anything more than a simile. The point of the simile

would be that Jehovah's spirit empowered Samson to perform a task that required extraordinary physical strength. In either case, the comparison drawn at Judges 14:6 illustrates that with Jehovah's help, a powerful lion proved to be no more ferocious to Samson than a male kid would be to the average person.

IN OUR NEXT ISSUE

How Precious Is Your Life?

———

"Finding One Pearl of High Value"

———

Is the Truth Bearing Fruit in Those You Teach?

"What Is Your Secret?"

THIS question from an elderly stranger at a fast-food restaurant took Muriel, a mother of three, by surprise. Muriel had been busy with doctors' appointments for her children, and she was running behind schedule. There was not enough time for them to go home and eat supper before attending their Christian meeting. So she took the children to a nearby restaurant so that they could have something to eat.

As they were finishing their meal, a man approached Muriel and said: "I have been observing you ever since you came in here. And I have noticed a big difference between your children and those I normally encounter. You should see the way children treat the tables and chairs. Their feet go on the table. The chairs are bounced around. But your children are so quiet and well behaved. What is your secret?"

Muriel replied: "My husband and I regularly study the Bible with our children, and we try to apply in our lives what we learn. We are Jehovah's Witnesses." At this, the man said: "I am Jewish and a Holocaust survivor. I remember seeing Jehovah's Witnesses being persecuted in Germany. Even then they stood out as being different. The behavior of your children has really impressed me. I must look into your religion."

www.watchtower.org

w05-E 1/15

THE WATCHTOWER

ANNOUNCING JEHOVAH'S KINGDOM

FEBRUARY 1, 2005

What Is Your Life Worth?

THE WATCHTOWER®
ANNOUNCING JEHOVAH'S KINGDOM

February 1, 2005   Average Printing Each Issue: 26,439,000   Vol. 126, No. 3

THE PURPOSE OF *THE WATCHTOWER* is to exalt Jehovah God as Sovereign Lord of the universe. It keeps watch on world events as these fulfill Bible prophecy. It comforts all peoples with the good news that God's Kingdom will soon destroy those who oppress their fellowmen and that it will turn the earth into a paradise. It encourages faith in God's now-reigning King, Jesus Christ, whose shed blood opens the way for mankind to gain eternal life. *The Watchtower,* published by Jehovah's Witnesses continuously since 1879, is nonpolitical. It adheres to the Bible as its authority.

IN THIS ISSUE

3   Life—Precious or Cheap?

4   How Precious Is Your Life?

8   "Finding One Pearl of High Value"

13   Pursuing the "Pearl of High Value" Today

23   Jehovah Always Does What Is Right

28   Is the Truth Bearing Fruit in Those You Teach?

32   "Keep on the Watch"

WATCHTOWER STUDIES

FEBRUARY 28–MARCH 6:
"Finding One Pearl of High Value."
Page 8. Songs to be used: 187, 146.

MARCH 7-13:
Pursuing the "Pearl of High Value" Today.
Page 13. Songs to be used: 211, 43.

MARCH 14-20:
Jehovah Always Does What Is Right.
Page 23. Songs to be used: 136, 131.

Publication of *The Watchtower* is part of a worldwide Bible educational work supported by voluntary donations.

Unless otherwise indicated, Scripture quotations are from the modern-language *New World Translation of the Holy Scriptures—With References.*

The Watchtower (ISSN 0043-1087) is published semimonthly by Watchtower Bible and Tract Society of New York, Inc.; M. H. Larson, President; G. F. Simonis, Secretary-Treasurer; 25 Columbia Heights, Brooklyn, NY 11201-2483. Periodicals Postage Paid at Brooklyn, NY, and at additional mailing offices. **POSTMASTER:** Send address changes to Watchtower, **Wallkill, NY 12589.**

Changes of address should reach us 30 days before your moving date. Give us your old and new address (if possible, your old address label).

Semimonthly   ENGLISH

Would you welcome more information or a free home Bible study? Please send your request to Jehovah's Witnesses, using the appropriate address below.

America, United States of: Wallkill, NY 12589. *Antigua:* Box 119, St. Johns. *Australia:* Box 280, Ingleburn, NSW 1890. *Bahamas:* Box N-1247, Nassau, N.P. *Barbados, W.I.:* Crusher Site Road, Prospect, St. James. *Britain:* The Ridgeway, London NW7 1RN. *Canada:* Box 4100, Halton Hills (Georgetown), Ontario L7G 4Y4. *Germany:* Niederselters, Am Steinfels, D-65618 Selters. *Ghana:* P. O. Box GP 760, Accra. *Guyana:* 352-360 Tyrell St., Republic Park Phase 2 EBD. *Hawaii 96819:* 2055 Kam IV Rd., Honolulu. *Hong Kong:* 4 Kent Road, Kowloon Tong. *India:* Post Box 6440, Yelahanka, Bangalore 560 064, KAR. *Ireland:* Newcastle, Greystones, Co. Wicklow. *Jamaica:* P. O. Box 103, Old Harbour, St. Catherine. *Japan:* 1271 Nakashinden, Ebina City, Kanagawa Pref., 243-0496. *Kenya:* P.O. Box 47788, GPO Nairobi 00100. *New Zealand:* P.O. Box 75-142, Manurewa. *Nigeria:* P.M.B. 1090, Benin City 300001, Edo State. *Philippines, Republic of:* P. O. Box 2044, 1060 Manila. *South Africa:* Private Bag X2067, Krugersdorp, 1740. *Trinidad and Tobago, Republic of:* Lower Rapsey Street & Laxmi Lane, Curepe. *Zambia:* Box 33459, Lusaka 10101. *Zimbabwe:* Private Bag WG-5001, Westgate.

NOW PUBLISHED IN 150 LANGUAGES. SEMIMONTHLY: Afrikaans, Albanian,* Amharic, Arabic, Bengali, Bicol, Bislama, Bulgarian, Cebuano,* Chichewa,* Chinese, Chinese (Simplified),* Cibemba,* Croatian,* Czech,*# Danish,*# Dutch,*# East Armenian, Efik,* English*#◎ (also Braille), Estonian, Ewe, Fijian, Finnish,*# French,*# Ga, Georgian, German,*# Greek,* Gujarati, Gun, Hebrew, Hiligaynon, Hindi, Hungarian,*# Igbo,* Iloko,* Indonesian, Italian,*# Japanese*# (also Braille), Kannada, Kinyarwanda, Kirundi, Korean*# (also Braille), Latvian, Lingala, Lithuanian, Luvale, Macedonian, Malagasy,* Malayalam, Maltese, Marathi, Myanmar, Nepali, New Guinea Pidgin, Norwegian,*# Pangasinan, Papiamento (Aruba), Papiamento (Curaçao), Polish,*# Portuguese*# (also Braille), Punjabi, Rarotongan, Romanian,* Russian,* Samar-Leyte, Samoan, Sango, Sepedi, Serbian, Sesotho, Shona,* Silozi, Sinhala, Slovak,* Slovenian, Solomon Islands Pidgin, Spanish,*# Sranantongo, Swahili,* Swedish,*# Tagalog,* Tamil, Telugu, Thai, Tigrinya, Tongan, Tshiluba, Tsonga, Tswana, Turkish, Twi, Ukrainian,* Urdu, Venda, Vietnamese, Wallisian, Xhosa, Yoruba,* Zulu*

MONTHLY: American Sign Language,△□ Armenian, Assamese, Azerbaijani (Roman script), Brazilian Sign Language,△ Cambodian, Chitonga, Gilbertese, Greenlandic, Haitian Creole, Hausa, Hiri Motu, Icelandic, Isoko, Kaonde, Kazakh, Kikongo, Kiluba, Kirghiz, Kwanyama/Ndonga, Luganda, Marshallese, Mauritian Creole, Mizo, Monokutuba, Moore, Niuean, Ossetian, Otetela, Palauan, Persian, Ponapean, Seychelles Creole, Tahitian, Tatar, Tiv, Trukese, Tumbuka, Tuvaluan, Umbundu, Yapese, Zande

* Study articles also available in large-print edition.
\# Audiocassettes also available.
◎ CD (MP3 format) also available.
△ Videocassette
□ DVD

Life
Precious or Cheap?

**"Since man is made in the image of God,
then the taking of a man's life is the destruction of the
most precious and the most holy thing in the world."**
—*The Plain Man's Guide to Ethics,* by William Barclay.

'THE most precious thing in the world.' Do you share that view of life? From the way people behave, it is obvious that many do not agree with that writer. Millions of lives have been callously snuffed out by violent people who pursued selfish goals without any regard for the well-being of their fellowman.—Ecclesiastes 8:9.

Expendable and Disposable

World War I is a classic example. Time and again during that terrible conflict, "the bodies of men were sacrificed to no purpose," says historian A.J.P. Taylor. In pursuit of prestige and glory, military leaders used soldiers as if they were worthless and totally expendable. In the battle for Verdun in France, there were over half a million casualties. "There was no prize [of any strategic value] to be gained or lost," writes Taylor, "only men to be killed and glory to be won."—*The First World War.*

Such contempt for the value of life is still widespread. Scholar Kevin Bales points out that in recent times, a "population explosion [has] flooded the world's labor markets with millions of poor and vulnerable people." They face a lifelong struggle simply to survive in an oppressive commercial system in which "life becomes cheap." Those who exploit them, says Bales, treat them as little more than slaves—"completely disposable tools for making money."—*Disposable People*.

"A Striving After Wind"

There are many other reasons why millions of people feel totally worthless and desperate—that no one really cares whether they live or die. Besides war and injustice, there are the ravages of drought, famine, disease, bereavement, and countless other things that plague all mankind, making people wonder if life is worth living at all.—Ecclesiastes 1:8, 14.

Not everyone, of course, faces a life of extreme deprivation and anguish. But even those who escape the worst of oppression have often echoed the words of King Solomon of ancient Israel, who asked: "What does a man come to have for all his hard work and for the striving of his heart with which he is working hard under the sun?" On reflection, many come to the realization that much of what they did turned out to be "vanity and a striving after wind."—Ecclesiastes 2:22, 26.

"Is that it?" many ask as they look back on their life. Yes, how many are there who finish their life feeling genuinely 'satisfied with days,' as the patriarch Abraham did? (Genesis 25:8, footnote) Most have an abiding sense of futility. Yet, life need not be futile. God considers every human life precious and wants each one of us to live a truly full, satisfying life. How will that come about? Consider what the next article has to say on this subject.

How Precious Is
Your Life?

WHILE countless lives were being sacrificed in Europe during World War I, amazing efforts were being made to save lives in Antarctica. Anglo-Irish explorer Ernest Shackleton and his companions suffered catastrophe when their ship, *Endurance,* was crushed and sunk by pack ice. Shackleton managed to get his men to a safe haven—of sorts—on Elephant Island in the South Atlantic Ocean. But they still faced extreme danger.

Shackleton realized that their only hope of survival lay in sending for help from a whaling station on the island of South Georgia. That was 700 miles away, and he had only a 22-foot lifeboat that he had salvaged from *Endurance.* Their prospects were not good.

On May 10, 1916, however, after 17 harrowing days, Shackleton and a small party got to South Georgia, but terrible sea conditions forced them to land on the wrong side of the island. They were faced with a 20-mile

trek over uncharted, snow-covered mountains to reach their final destination. Against all odds—in subzero temperatures and without proper climbing equipment—Shackleton and his companions reached their destination, and he eventually rescued all his stranded men. Why did Shackleton put forth such strenuous effort? "His one ambition," writes biographer Roland Huntford, was "to get every one of his men out alive."

"Not One of Them Is Missing"

What saved Shackleton's men from complete despair as they huddled and waited on what was just "a bleak and inaccessible patch of rock and ice twenty miles from end to end"? Their confidence that their leader would keep his promise to rescue them.

Mankind today is much like those men marooned on Elephant Island. Many live under unbelievably adverse conditions and struggle simply to survive. Yet, they can have complete confidence that God will "rescue the afflicted one" from oppression and distress. (Job 36:15) Be assured that God considers everyone's life precious. "Call me in the day of distress," says Jehovah God, the Creator, and "I shall rescue you."—Psalm 50:15.

Do you find it difficult to believe that the Creator considers you—just one individual among earth's billions—personally precious? Then note what the prophet Isaiah wrote about the billions of stars in the billions of galaxies in the vast universe around us. We read: "Raise your eyes high up and see. Who has created these things? It is the One who is bringing forth the army of them even by number, *all of whom he calls even by name.* Due to the abundance of dynamic energy, he also being vigorous in power, not one of them is missing."—Isaiah 40:26.

Do you appreciate what that means? Our Milky Way galaxy—of which our solar system is only a part—contains at least 100 billion stars. And how many other galaxies are there? No one knows for sure, but some estimates put the figure at 125 billion. What a staggering number of stars there must be! Yet, the Bible tells us that the Creator of the universe knows each of the stars by name.

"The Very Hairs of Your Head Are All Numbered"

'But,' someone may object, 'just *knowing* the names of billions of stars—or billions of people—does not necessarily mean *caring* about them individually.' A computer with sufficient memory could register the names of billions of people. Yet, no one would suggest that the computer cares about any of them. The Bible shows, however, that Jehovah God not only *knows the names* of billions of people but also *cares about them as individuals.* "Throw all your anxiety upon him," wrote the apostle Peter, "because he cares for you."—1 Peter 5:7.

Jesus Christ stated: "Do not two sparrows sell for a coin of small value? Yet not one of them will fall to the ground without your Father's knowledge. But the very hairs of your head are all numbered. Therefore have no fear: you are worth more than many sparrows." (Matthew 10:29-31) Notice that Jesus did not say that God would simply be aware of what happened to sparrows and to men. He said: "You are worth more than many sparrows." Why are you worth more? Because you are made "in God's image"—with

The stranded men were confident that Shackleton would keep his promise to rescue them

© CORBIS

"You are worth more than many sparrows"

the potential for cultivating and displaying moral, intellectual, and spiritual qualities that reflect God's own elevated qualities. —Genesis 1:26, 27.

"The Product of Intelligent Activity"

Do not be misled by the assertions of people who deny that there is a Creator. According to them, blind, impersonal forces of nature made you. They claim that far from being made "in God's image," you are no different from all the other animal life on this planet—including the sparrows.

Does it really make sense to you that life got here simply by chance, or blind force? According to molecular biologist Michael J. Behe, the "staggeringly complicated biochemical processes" that govern life make that idea totally unreasonable. The evidence of biochemistry, he says, leads to the inescapable conclusion that "life on earth at its most fundamental level . . . is the product of intelligent activity."—*Darwin's Black Box —The Biochemical Challenge to Evolution.*

The Bible tells us that life on earth at all levels is the product of intelligent activity. And it tells us that the Source of all this intelligent activity is Jehovah God, the Creator of the universe.—Psalm 36:9; Revelation 4:11.

Do not let the fact that we have to endure in a world filled with pain and suffering dissuade you from believing that there is a Creator and Designer of the earth and all life on it. Keep in mind two fundamental truths. One is that God did not design the imperfection that exists all around us. The other is that our Creator has good reasons for temporarily permitting it. As this magazine has often discussed, Jehovah God has permitted evil to exist for a limited time only in order to settle once and for all the moral issues that were raised at the time when humans first rejected his sovereignty.*—Genesis 3: 1-7; Deuteronomy 32:4, 5; Ecclesiastes 7:29; 2 Peter 3:8, 9.

"He Will Deliver the Poor One Crying for Help"

Of course, even with the miserable conditions that many people have to suffer today, life is still a wonderful gift. And we do all we can to preserve it. The future life that God promises is much more than a struggle simply to survive in harsh and painful conditions—like Shackleton's men on Elephant Island. God's purpose is to rescue us from our current existence of pain and futility so that we can "get a firm hold on the real life" that God originally purposed for his human creation.—1 Timothy 6:19.

God will do all of this because each one of us is precious in his eyes. He arranged for his Son, Jesus Christ, to provide the ransom sacrifice needed to free us from the sin, imperfection, and death that we inherited from our original parents, Adam and Eve. (Matthew 20:28) "God loved the world so much," said Jesus Christ, "that he gave his only-begotten Son, in order that everyone exer-

---

* For a detailed discussion of this point, see chapter 8, "Why Does God Permit Suffering?" in the book *Knowledge That Leads to Everlasting Life,* published by Jehovah's Witnesses.

cising faith in him might . . . have everlasting life."—John 3:16.

What will God do for those whose life is now blighted by pain and oppression? Regarding his Son, God's inspired Word tells us: "He will deliver the poor one crying for help, also the afflicted one and whoever has no helper. He will feel sorry for the lowly one and the poor one, and the souls of the poor ones he will save. From oppression and from violence he will redeem their soul." Why will he do this? Because "their blood [or, their life] will be *precious in his eyes.*"—Psalm 72:12-14.

For centuries humanity has been toiling under the burden of sin and imperfection, as if "groaning" in much pain and suffering. God only permitted this with the knowledge that he could remedy any damage that would ensue. (Romans 8:18-22) Very soon now he will bring about the "restoration of all things" through the agency of his Kingdom government in the hands of his Son, Jesus Christ.—Acts 3:21; Matthew 6:9, 10.

That includes the resurrection of people who have suffered and died in the past. They are safe in God's memory. (John 5:28, 29; Acts 24:15) Soon they will receive life "in abundance"—everlasting life in perfection on a paradise earth free from pain and suffering. (John 10:10; Revelation 21:3-5) Everyone living will be able to enjoy life to the full and cultivate the wonderful qualities and abilities that mark those who are made "in God's image."

Will you be on hand to enjoy the life that Jehovah has promised? That is up to you. We urge you to avail yourself of the provisions that God has made to bring about all these blessings. The publishers of this magazine will be happy to help you to do so.

"FINDING ONE PEARL OF HIGH VALUE"

"The kingdom of the heavens is the goal toward which men press, and those pressing forward are seizing it."—MATTHEW 11:12.

IS THERE something that you value so highly that you would give everything you own or sacrifice all that you have in order to gain possession of it? Though people speak about dedication in their pursuit of some goal—money, fame, power, or position—it is rare that a person comes across something so very desirable that he is willing to give up everything for it. Jesus Christ referred to this rare but admirable quality in one of his many thought-provoking parables about the Kingdom of God.

2 It is a parable, or illustration, that Jesus told his disciples in private, one often referred to as the parable of the pearl of great price. This is what Jesus said: "The kingdom of the heavens is like a traveling merchant seeking fine pearls. Upon finding one pearl of high value, away he went and promptly sold all the things he had and bought it." (Matthew 13:36, 45, 46) What did Jesus want his listeners to learn from this illustration? And how can we benefit from Jesus' words?

High Value of Pearls

3 From antiquity, pearls have been valued as ornamental objects. One source observes that according to the Roman scholar Pliny the Elder, pearls occupied the "topmost rank among all things of price." Unlike gold, silver, or many gemstones, pearls are produced by living things. It is well-known that certain types of oysters can turn irritants—small fragments of stone, for instance—into lustrous pearls by enveloping them in layers of a secretion known as nacre. In ancient times, the finest pearls were harvested mainly from the Red Sea, the Persian Gulf, and the Indian Ocean—far from the land of Israel. This is no doubt the reason that Jesus spoke of "a traveling merchant seeking fine pearls." To find truly valuable pearls, a great deal of effort is involved.

4 Even though fine pearls have long commanded high prices, it is evidently not their

---

1, 2. (a) What rare quality did Jesus portray in one of his Kingdom parables? (b) What did Jesus say in the parable of the pearl of great price?
3. Why were fine pearls so valuable in ancient times?

4. What is the central lesson of Jesus' parable of the traveling merchant?

monetary value that constituted the central lesson of Jesus' parable. In this parable, Jesus did not simply liken the Kingdom of God to a pearl of high value; he called attention to "a traveling merchant seeking fine pearls" and to his response upon finding one. Unlike an ordinary shopkeeper, a traveling pearl merchant, or dealer, was what might be called a connoisseur in the trade, one who had the keen eye or the sensibility needed to discern the aesthetic qualities and subtleties that mark a pearl as extraordinary. He would know the genuine article when he saw it and would not be fooled by inferior or counterfeit merchandise.

⁵ Something else about this particular merchant is worthy of note. A common merchant might first figure out the market value of the pearl so as to determine how much he would pay for it in order to make a profit. He might also consider if there was a market for such a pearl so that he could sell it quickly. In other words, he would be interested in making a quick return on his investment, not in owning the pearl. But not so with the merchant in Jesus' parable. His interest was not monetary or material. In fact, he was willing to sacrifice "all the things he had"—possibly all his personal belongings and properties—in order to acquire what he had been searching for.

⁶ In the eyes of most merchants, what that man in Jesus' parable did was probably unwise. An astute businessman would not think of undertaking such a risky venture. But the merchant in Jesus' parable had a different sense of values. His reward was, not any financial advantage, but the joy and satisfaction of possessing something of surpassing value. This point is made clear in a parallel illustration that Jesus gave. He said: "The kingdom of the heavens is like a treasure hidden in the field, which a man found and hid; and for the joy he has he goes and sells what things he has and buys that field." (Matthew 13:44) Yes, the joy that comes from discovering and owning the treasure was enough to move the man to give up everything he had. Are there individuals like that today? Is there a treasure worth such a sacrifice?

Those Who Appreciated the High Value

⁷ In telling his parable, Jesus was talking about "the kingdom of the heavens." He himself certainly appreciated the high value of the Kingdom. The Gospel accounts bear powerful testimony to that fact. After his baptism in 29 C.E., Jesus "commenced preaching and saying: 'Repent, you people, for the kingdom of the heavens has drawn near.'" For three and a half years, he taught multitudes about the Kingdom. He traversed the length and breadth of the land, "journeying from city to city and from village to village, preaching and declaring the good news of the kingdom of God." —Matthew 4:17; Luke 8:1.

⁸ By performing numerous miracles throughout the land—including healing the sick, feeding the hungry, subduing the elements, even raising the dead—Jesus also demonstrated what God's Kingdom will accomplish. (Matthew 14:14-21; Mark 4:37-39; Luke 7:11-17) Finally, he proved his loyalty to God and to the Kingdom by giving his life, dying a martyr's death on a torture stake. Just as that traveling merchant willingly gave everything he had for the "pearl

---

5, 6. (a) What is particularly noteworthy about the merchant in Jesus' parable? (b) The parable of the hidden treasure reveals what about the traveling merchant?

7. How did Jesus show that he keenly appreciated the high value of the Kingdom?
8. What did Jesus do to demonstrate what the Kingdom will accomplish?

of high value," Jesus lived and died for the Kingdom.—John 18:37.

⁹ Not only did Jesus focus his own life on the Kingdom but he also gathered together a small band of followers. These too were individuals who keenly appreciated the high value of the Kingdom. Among them was Andrew, who was originally a disciple of John the Baptizer. Upon hearing John's testimony that Jesus was "the Lamb of God," Andrew and another of John's disciples, most likely one of the sons of Zebedee also named John, were immediately drawn to Jesus and became believers. But matters did not stop there. Right away, Andrew went to his brother Simon and told him: "We have found the Messiah." In quick order, Simon (who became known as Cephas, or Peter) as well as Philip and his friend Nathanael also came to recognize Jesus as the Messiah. In fact, Nathanael was moved to say to Jesus: "You are the Son of God, you are King of Israel."—John 1:35-49.

9. What rare quality was seen among Jesus' early disciples?

Stirred to Action

¹⁰ The excitement experienced by Andrew, Peter, John, and the others when they discovered the Messiah might be compared to that experienced by the traveling merchant when he found the pearl of high value. What would they do now? The Gospels do not tell us much about what they did immediately after this first encounter with Jesus. Apparently, most of them returned to their normal course of life. From about six months to a year later, however, Jesus once again came upon Andrew, Peter, John, and John's brother James at their fishing business by the Sea of Galilee.* Seeing them, Jesus said: "Come after me, and I will make you fishers of men."

---

* John, the son of Zebedee, might have followed Jesus and witnessed some of the things he did after their first meeting, thus enabling John to record them so vividly in his Gospel account. (John, chapters 2-5) Nonetheless, he did return to his family fishing business for some time before Jesus called him.

---

10. How did the disciples respond when Jesus came and called them some time after his first encounter with them?

'They abandoned everything and followed Jesus'

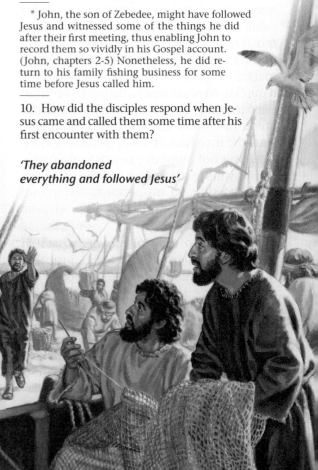

What was their response? About Peter and Andrew, Matthew's account says: "At once abandoning the nets, they followed him." As for James and John, we read: "At once leaving the boat and their father, they followed him." Luke's account adds that they "abandoned everything and followed him."—Matthew 4:18-22; Luke 5:1-11.

11 Was the disciples' prompt response a spur-of-the-moment decision? Hardly! Even though they did return to their family fishing business after their first contact with Jesus, there is no doubt that what they had seen and heard on that occasion left a deep impression on their heart and mind. The passing of nearly a year would have allowed them plenty of time to reflect on such matters. Now the moment of decision had come. Would they be like the traveling merchant whose heart was so stirred by the discovery of the priceless pearl that, as Jesus described it, "away he went and promptly" did what he must to buy that pearl? Yes. What they had seen and heard stirred their heart. They recognized that the time for action had come. Thus, as the accounts tell us, without hesitation they gave up everything and became Jesus' followers.

12 How different these faithful ones were from some others mentioned later in the Gospel accounts! Many were the ones who were cured or fed by Jesus but who simply went about their own business. (Luke 17:17, 18; John 6:26) Some even begged off when Jesus invited them to become his followers. (Luke 9:59-62) In sharp contrast, concerning the faithful ones, Jesus later said: "From the days of John the Baptist until now the kingdom of the heavens is the goal toward which men press, and those pressing forward are seizing it."—Matthew 11:12.

13 "Press" and "pressing forward"—what do these terms imply? With regard to the Greek verb from which these expressions are derived, *Vine's Expository Dictionary of Old and New Testament Words* says: "The verb suggests forceful endeavour." And regarding this verse, Bible scholar Heinrich Meyer states: "In this way is described that eager, irresistible striving and struggling after the approaching Messianic kingdom . . . So eager and energetic (no longer calm and expectant) is the interest in regard to the kingdom." Like the traveling merchant, these few individuals quickly recognized what was truly precious, and they willingly gave up all they had for the sake of the Kingdom.—Matthew 19:27, 28; Philippians 3:8.

Others Joined the Search

14 As Jesus continued in his ministry, he trained and helped others to reach out for the Kingdom. First, he selected 12 from among his disciples and designated them as apostles, or ones sent forth by him. To these, Jesus gave detailed instructions on how they were to carry out their ministry as well as warnings about the challenges and hardships that lay ahead. (Matthew 10:1-42; Luke 6:12-16) For the next two years or so, they accompanied Jesus on his preaching tours throughout the land, enjoying a close relationship with him. They heard his sayings, witnessed his powerful works, and saw his personal example. (Matthew 13:16, 17) All of this no doubt touched them deeply, so much so that like the traveling merchant, they were zealous and wholehearted in their pursuit of the Kingdom.

---

11. What likely accounts for the disciples' prompt response to Jesus' call?
12, 13. (a) In what way did many who heard Jesus respond? (b) What did Jesus say about his faithful disciples, and what do his words imply?

---

14. How did Jesus prepare the apostles for the Kingdom-preaching work, and what was the result?

¹⁵ In addition to the 12 apostles, Jesus "designated seventy others and sent them forth by twos in advance of him into every city and place to which he himself was going to come." He also told them about the trials and hardships ahead and instructed them to tell people: "The kingdom of God has come near to you." (Luke 10:1-12) When the 70 returned, they were overjoyed and gave Jesus this report: "Lord, even the demons are made subject to us by the use of your name." But perhaps to their surprise, Jesus revealed that an even greater joy was in store for them because of their zeal for the Kingdom. He told them: "Do not rejoice over this, that the spirits are made subject to you, but rejoice because your names have been inscribed in the heavens."—Luke 10:17, 20.

¹⁶ Finally, on the last night that Jesus was with the apostles, Nisan 14, 33 C.E., he instituted what came to be known as the Lord's Evening Meal and commanded them to commemorate the event. In the course of the evening, Jesus told the 11 who remained: "You are the ones that have stuck

Before ascending to heaven, Jesus commanded his followers to make disciples

with me in my trials; and I make a covenant with you, just as my Father has made a covenant with me, for a kingdom, that you may eat and drink at my table in my kingdom, and sit on thrones to judge the twelve tribes of Israel."—Luke 22:19, 20, 28-30.

¹⁷ What joy and satisfaction must have filled their heart when the apostles heard those words from Jesus! They were being offered the highest honor and privilege that any human could have. (Matthew 7:13, 14; 1 Peter 2:9) Like that traveling merchant, they had given up much to follow Jesus in pursuit of the Kingdom. Now they were assured that the sacrifices they had made thus far had not been in vain.

¹⁸ The apostles present with Jesus that night were not the only ones to benefit from the Kingdom. It was Jehovah's will that a total of 144,000 be taken into the Kingdom covenant as corulers with Jesus Christ in the glorious heavenly Kingdom. In addition, the apostle John saw in vision "a great crowd, which no man was able to number, . . . standing before the throne and before the Lamb, . . . saying: 'Salvation we owe to

---

15. What did Jesus say was the real reason his followers had for rejoicing?
16, 17. (a) What did Jesus tell his faithful apostles on the last night he was with them? (b) What joy and assurance did Jesus' words bring to the apostles?

---

18. Who besides the 11 apostles would also eventually benefit from the Kingdom?

Can You Explain?

- What is the central lesson of the parable of the traveling merchant?
- How did Jesus show his keen appreciation for the high value of the Kingdom?
- What caused Andrew, Peter, John, and others to respond immediately when Jesus called them?
- What marvelous opportunity lies before people of all the nations?

our God, who is seated on the throne, and to the Lamb.'" These are the earthly subjects of the Kingdom.*—Revelation 7:9, 10; 14:1, 4.

¹⁹ Shortly before Jesus ascended to heaven, he commanded his faithful followers: "Go therefore and make disciples of people of all the nations, baptizing them in the name of the Father and of the Son and of the holy spirit, teaching them to observe all the things I have commanded you. And,

———
* For more details, see chapter 10 of the book *Knowledge That Leads to Everlasting Life,* published by Jehovah's Witnesses.

———
19, 20. (a) What opportunity is open to people of all the nations? (b) What question will be considered in the next article?

look! I am with you all the days until the conclusion of the system of things." (Matthew 28:19, 20) Thus, people out of all nations would come to be disciples of Jesus Christ. These too would set their heart on the Kingdom—whether for a heavenly or for an earthly reward—as the traveling merchant did with regard to the fine pearl.

²⁰ Jesus' words indicated that the task of disciple-making would be extended all the way to "the conclusion of the system of things." So in our day, are there still individuals like the traveling merchant, who are willing to give their all in the pursuit of God's Kingdom? This question will be considered in the next article.

PURSUING THE "PEARL OF HIGH VALUE" TODAY

"This good news of the kingdom will be preached in all the inhabited earth for a witness."—MATTHEW 24:14.

THE Kingdom of God was a subject of intense interest among the Jews when Jesus came to earth. (Matthew 3:1, 2; 4:23-25; John 1:49) At first, however, most of them did not fully comprehend its scope and power; neither did they understand that it would be a heavenly government. (John 3:1-5) Even some who became Jesus' followers did not fully understand what God's Kingdom is or what they must do to receive the blessing of becoming associate rulers with Christ. —Matthew 20:20-22; Luke 19:11; Acts 1:6.

———
1, 2. (a) How did the Jews in Jesus' day feel about God's Kingdom? (b) What did Jesus do to impart proper understanding of the Kingdom, and with what results?

² As time went on, Jesus patiently taught his disciples many lessons, including the parable of the pearl of high value considered in the preceding article, pointing out to them the importance of exerting themselves in the pursuit of the heavenly Kingdom. (Matthew 6:33; 13:45, 46; Luke 13:23, 24) This must have touched their heart deeply because they soon became tireless and courageous proclaimers of the Kingdom good news to distant parts of the earth, to which fact the book of Acts amply testifies. —Acts 1:8; Colossians 1:23.

³ What, then, about today? The blessings

———
3. With reference to our time, what did Jesus say about the Kingdom?

of an earthly paradise under the Kingdom are set out before millions. In his great prophecy about "the conclusion of the system of things," Jesus specifically stated: "This good news of the kingdom will be preached in all the inhabited earth for a witness to all the nations; and then the end will

"Truth . . . attracts all kinds of persons."
—A. H. Macmillan

come." (Matthew 24:3, 14; Mark 13:10) He also explained that this monumental task is to be carried out in spite of formidable obstacles and challenges, even persecution. Nevertheless, he gave this assurance: "He that has endured to the end is the one that will be saved." (Matthew 24:9-13) All of this calls for the kind of self-sacrifice and dedication manifested by the traveling merchant in Jesus' parable. Are there individuals today who demonstrate such faith and zeal in the pursuit of the Kingdom?

The Joy of Discovering the Truth

4 The merchant in Jesus' parable was overjoyed when he found what he perceived to be a "pearl of high value." That joy moved him to do everything within his power to acquire the pearl. (Hebrews 12:1) Today, the truth about God and his Kingdom likewise draws and motivates people. This brings to mind the comments of Brother A. H. Macmillan, who wrote about his personal search for God and His purpose for mankind, in the

---

4. What effect does Kingdom truth have on people today?

book *Faith on the March.* He said: "What I have found thousands of people are still finding every year. And they are people just like you and me, because they come from all nationalities, races, walks of life and are of all ages. Truth is no respecter of persons. It attracts all kinds of persons."

5 The truth of those words is seen as year after year hundreds of thousands of honest-hearted individuals are moved by the good news of God's Kingdom to dedicate their life to Jehovah and to do his will. The 2004 service year, which ran from September 2003 to August 2004, was no exception. In those 12 months, 262,416 people publicly symbolized their dedication to Jehovah by water baptism. This took place in 235 lands, in which Jehovah's Witnesses are conducting 6,085,387 home Bible studies weekly in order to help people from all walks of life and out of many nations, tribes, and tongues to take in the life-giving truth from God's Word.—Revelation 7:9.

6 What made all of this possible? There is no doubt that Jehovah draws these rightly disposed ones to him. (John 6:65; Acts 13: 48) However, not to be minimized are the selfless spirit and tireless efforts on the part of those who have expended themselves in the pursuit of the Kingdom. At age 79, Brother Macmillan wrote: "From my first glimpse of the promises held out to sick and dying mankind my hope in what that message of the Bible has revealed has not faded. Right there I determined to find out more about what the Bible teaches so that I might be able to help others like myself who are seeking knowledge about the Almighty God, Jehovah, and his good purposes toward mankind."

---

5. What fine results are seen in the 2004 service year report?
6. What accounts for the steady increases over the years?

⁷ That eagerness is also seen among Jehovah's servants today. Take, for example, Daniela from Vienna, Austria. She said: "Since my childhood, God has been my very best friend. I always wanted to know his name because for me 'God' was too impersonal. But I had to wait until I was 17 years of age, when Jehovah's Witnesses came to my door. They explained everything that I wanted to know about God. I had finally found the truth, and it was wonderful! I was so excited that I started to preach to everyone." Her enthusiastic approach soon brought ridicule from her schoolmates. "For me, though, it was like seeing Bible prophecy being fulfilled," Daniela continued, "because I had learned that Jesus said that his followers would be hated and persecuted for his name's sake. I was so happy and amazed." Soon, Daniela dedicated her life to Jehovah, was baptized, and started to pursue the goal of missionary service. After she was married, Daniela, together with her husband, Helmut, took up the preaching work among the African, Chinese, Filipino, and Indian populations in Vienna. Daniela and Helmut are now serving as missionaries in southwest Africa.

Daniela and Helmut preached in the foreign-language field in Vienna

They Do Not Give Up

⁸ Indeed, the missionary service is one of the ways in which Jehovah's people today demonstrate their love for God and loyalty to his Kingdom. Like the merchant in Jesus' parable, those who take up this service are willing to travel to faraway places for the sake of the Kingdom. Of course, these missionaries are not traveling to find the Kingdom good news; they are taking it to people living in the far-flung corners of the earth, teaching and helping them to become disciples of Jesus Christ. (Matthew 28:19, 20) In many lands, they have to endure extraordinary hardship. But their endurance is richly rewarded.

⁹ Take, for example, the Central African Republic, where last year the attendance at the Memorial of Christ's death was 16,184, about seven times the number of Kingdom publishers in that land. Since many parts of that country are without electricity, the people usually do their daily chores out-of-doors under the shade of a tree. So it is only

---

7. What experience typifies the joy and eagerness of those finding Bible truth?
8. What is one rewarding way in which many have demonstrated their love for God and loyalty to his Kingdom?

9, 10. What exciting experiences are enjoyed by missionaries in such faraway places as Central African Republic?

Like the traveling merchant, missionaries today are richly blessed

natural for the missionaries to do their work the same way—conduct Bible studies out-of-doors under a shady tree. Not only is it brighter and cooler outside but there is also another advantage. The people have a natural love for the Bible, and discussing religious subjects is as common as talking about sports or the weather in other cultures. Often, passersby take note of what is happening and simply join in the study.

¹⁰ Thus, when one missionary was conducting a Bible study out-of-doors, a young man who lived across the street came over and said that since he had not been called on, the missionary should come over and study the Bible with him too. Of course, the missionary was happy to comply, and the young man is making rapid progress. In that country, the police often flag down the Witnesses on the road, not to give them a summons or a fine, but to ask for the latest issues of the *Watchtower* and *Awake!* magazines or to thank them for an article that they particularly enjoyed.

¹¹ Many of those who entered the missionary service 40 or 50 years ago are still faithfully serving in the field. What an example of faith and perseverance for all of us! Over the past 42 years, one couple has served together as missionaries in three different countries. The husband says: "There have been difficulties. For example, we battled malaria for 35 years. Yet, we never regretted our decision to be missionaries." His wife adds: "There has always been so much to be grateful for. The field ministry is such a joy, and it is easy to start Bible studies. When you see the students come to the meetings and get to know one another, it is like a family get-together each time."

They "Consider All Things to Be Loss"

¹² When the traveling merchant found a pearl of high value, "away he went and promptly sold all the things he had and bought it." (Matthew 13:46) This willingness to give up what may be held as valuable is characteristic of those who truly appreciate the value of the Kingdom. As one who would have a share with Christ in Kingdom glory, the apostle Paul said: "I do indeed also consider all things to be loss on account of

---

11. In spite of trials, how do longtime missionaries feel about their service?

12. How is true appreciation for the value of the Kingdom expressed?

the excelling value of the knowledge of Christ Jesus my Lord. On account of him I have taken the loss of all things and I consider them as a lot of refuse, that I may gain Christ."—Philippians 3:8.

¹³ In the same way, many today are willing to make major changes in their life in order to gain the blessings of the Kingdom. For example, in October 2003, the 60-year-old headmaster of a school in the Czech Republic came across the Bible study aid *Knowledge That Leads to Everlasting Life.* After reading it, he immediately contacted Jehovah's Witnesses in his area to have a Bible study. He made fine spiritual progress and soon started to attend all the meetings. What, though, about his plans to run for the office of mayor and to enter the race for election to be a senator? He chose to enter a different race—the race for life, as a Kingdom proclaimer. He said, "I was able to place a lot of Bible literature with my students." He symbolized his dedication to Jehovah by water immersion at a convention in July 2004.

¹⁴ Millions of others around the world have responded to the Kingdom good news

in a similar way. They have come out of the wicked world, put off their old personality, left their former associates, and given up their worldly pursuits. (John 15:19; Ephesians 4:22-24; James 4:4; 1 John 2:15-17) Why do they do all of this? Because they esteem the blessings of God's Kingdom over and above anything that the present system of things can offer. Do you feel the same way about the Kingdom good news? Are you motivated by it to make the necessary changes to bring your life-style, values, and goals into harmony with what Jehovah requires? Doing so will result in rich blessings for you, now and in the future.

The Harvest Reaching Its Climax

¹⁵ The psalmist wrote: "Your people will offer themselves willingly on the day of your military force." Those who have offered themselves include the "company of young men just like dewdrops" and "a large army" of "women telling the good news." (Psalm 68:11; 110:3) What has been the result of the diligence and self-sacrifice on the part of Jehovah's people—men and women, young and old—in these final days?

¹⁶ A pioneer, or full-time Kingdom proclaimer, in India wondered how the more than two million deaf people in that land might be helped to learn about the Kingdom. (Isaiah 35:5) She decided to enroll in an institute in Bangalore to learn sign language. There she was able to share the Kingdom hope with many deaf ones, and Bible

---

13. How did one individual in the Czech Republic demonstrate his love for the Kingdom?
14. (a) What has the Kingdom good news moved millions to do? (b) What sobering questions could each of us ask himself?

15. What was prophesied that God's people would do in the final days?
16. Give an example of how God's servants are reaching out to help others learn about the Kingdom.

study groups were formed. Within a few weeks, over a dozen people began to come to the meetings at the Kingdom Hall. Later, at a wedding reception, the pioneer met a young deaf man from Calcutta who had many questions and showed a keen interest in knowing more about Jehovah. However, there was a problem. The young man was to return to Calcutta, some 1,000 miles away, to start college, and there were no Witnesses there who knew sign language. With much effort, he persuaded his father to allow him to go to school in Bangalore instead so that he could continue his Bible study. He made fine spiritual progress, and after about a year, he dedicated his life to Jehovah. He, in turn, studied the Bible with a number of deaf individuals, including a childhood friend. The branch office in India is now arranging for pioneers to learn sign language to help in that field.

¹⁷ On pages 19 to 22 of this magazine, you will find the worldwide report of the field activity of Jehovah's Witnesses for the 2004 service year. Take a little time to examine it, and see for yourself the evidence that Jehovah's people around the earth are intensely

---

17. Relate what you find particularly encouraging about the 2004 service year report on pages 19 to 22.

Do You Recall?

- Over the years, what has contributed to the increase among true worshipers?

- What spirit is seen among those serving as missionaries?

- What changes have individuals made because of the Kingdom good news?

- What valuable lesson can we learn from Jesus' parable of the pearl of high value?

---

focused on pursuing the "pearl of high value" today.

Keep "Seeking First the Kingdom"

¹⁸ Coming back once again to Jesus' parable of the traveling merchant, we note that Jesus did not say anything about how the merchant was going to maintain his livelihood after having sold all that he had. Realistically, some might ask: 'How would the merchant find food, clothing, and shelter now that he had nothing to fall back on? What good would that precious pearl be for him?' Those would be reasonable questions from a fleshly point of view. But did Jesus not urge his disciples: "Keep on, then, seeking first the kingdom and his righteousness, and all these other things will be added to you"? (Matthew 6:31-33) The main point of the parable is the need to demonstrate wholehearted devotion to God and zeal for the Kingdom. Is there a lesson in this for us?

¹⁹ Whether we have just learned about the wonderful good news or we have been pursuing the Kingdom and telling others about its blessings for decades, we must continue to make the Kingdom the focus of our interest and attention. These are difficult times, but we have solid reasons for believing that what we are pursuing is real and beyond compare—like the pearl that the merchant came upon. World events and fulfilled Bible prophecies provide convincing proof that we are living in "the conclusion of the system of things." (Matthew 24:3) Let us, like the traveling merchant, demonstrate wholehearted zeal for God's Kingdom and rejoice in the privilege of proclaiming the good news.—Psalm 9:1, 2.

---

18. What information did Jesus not include in the parable of the traveling merchant, and why not?
19. What key lesson can we learn from Jesus' parable of the pearl of high value?

2004 SERVICE YEAR REPORT OF JEHOVAH'S WITNESSES WORLDWIDE

Country or Territory	Population	2004 Peak Pubs.	Ratio, 1 Publisher to	2004 Av. Pubs.	% Inc. Over 2003	2003 Av. Pubs.	2004 No. Bptzd.	Av. Pio. Pubs.	No. of Congs.	Total Hours	Av. Bible Studies	Memorial Attendance
Alaska	660,000	2,309	286	2,225	-1	2,238	69	242	26	361,425	933	4,766
Albania	3,070,000	3,419	898	3,268	12	2,906	359	983	75	1,253,202	6,046	15,412
American Samoa	57,902	202	287	182	0	182	9	23	2	36,272	207	791
Andorra	72,320	175	413	154	11	139	2	20	2	29,191	67	306
Angola	13,000,000	54,652	238	52,218	6	49,475	4,470	5,822	779	11,773,671	136,697	256,072
Anguilla	11,430	35	327	34	3	33		7	1	9,740	63	261
Antigua	75,741	404	187	385	7	360	16	39	5	74,734	393	1,330
Argentina	36,223,947	130,156	278	127,579	1	125,897	5,384	17,431	1,751	26,373,300	99,537	287,887
Armenia	3,312,400	8,690	381	8,343	6	7,870	555	1,753	64	2,342,020	7,891	20,317
Aruba	96,856	720	135	707	2	692	30	60	10	116,279	659	2,356
Australia	20,061,774	62,011	324	60,533	0	60,510	2,176	5,019	768	9,461,142	20,911	114,373
Austria	8,065,166	20,322	397	20,156	0	20,148	428	1,587	298	3,269,452	9,752	34,700
Azerbaijan	8,265,700	452	18,287	423	19	355	55	92	2	132,140	636	983
Azores	243,068	611	398	587	4	564	33	76	15	125,175	609	1,457
Bahamas	304,913	1,511	202	1,435	3	1,400	53	183	27	302,176	1,565	4,043
Bangladesh	141,340,476	106	1,333,401	99	4	95	3	18	2	23,085	128	258
Barbados	277,264	2,362	117	2,327	-1	2,346	42	227	29	374,178	1,778	6,151
Belarus	9,849,100	3,756	2,622	3,637	5	3,449	186	774	38	1,011,121	3,290	8,323
Belau	20,164	98	206	93	0	93		30	1	32,747	197	385
Belgium	10,396,421	24,985	416	23,909	0	24,022	483	1,626	374	3,461,999	8,320	45,991
Belize	270,000	1,628	166	1,538	10	1,400	120	256	35	383,357	2,332	6,986
Benin	6,769,914	7,971	849	7,498	7	7,038	463	1,262	153	1,970,425	14,565	34,522
Bermuda	64,935	482	135	454	3	442	8	72	5	102,340	332	1,135
Bolivia	8,879,600	17,459	509	16,905	1	16,693	1,011	2,658	206	4,313,330	22,407	61,121
Bonaire	12,849	66	195	59	13	52	1	4	1	11,454	69	196
Bosnia & Herzegovina	4,130,000	1,134	3,642	1,093	2	1,069	64	258	14	353,364	641	2,268
Botswana	1,680,863	1,451	1,158	1,333	6	1,253	42	163	36	293,520	2,009	4,374
Brazil	181,586,030	621,541	292	596,355	4	576,069	33,029	67,957	9,415	114,225,153	745,629	1,622,652
Britain	58,081,288	125,546	463	120,514	0	120,478	2,573	10,576	1,492	18,115,252	46,866	219,231
Bulgaria	7,928,901	1,410	5,623	1,383	5	1,316	96	258	21	379,551	1,513	3,724
Burkina Faso	12,202,704	1,137	10,732	1,085	5	1,037	50	155	26	299,158	1,876	3,506
Burundi	7,457,000	5,459	1,366	5,234	11	4,698	476	928	94	1,669,589	13,507	19,612
Cambodia	13,542,410	193	70,168	172	19	145	16	77	3	89,908	494	790
Cameroon	17,211,280	30,059	573	29,249	3	28,435	1,380	2,821	632	5,622,781	43,997	93,341
Canada	31,793,904	110,221	288	108,012	0	108,409	2,210	11,320	1,325	18,849,112	40,157	187,649
Cape Verde	467,680	1,590	294	1,569	0	1,571	75	313	31	421,620	3,317	6,680
Cayman Islands	42,599	182	234	170	4	163	5	16	3	28,938	189	614
Central Afr. Rep.	3,800,000	2,426	1,566	2,350	1	2,338	132	411	53	630,205	4,813	16,184
Chad	8,000,000	637	12,559	586	-3	606	19	90	18	161,400	935	4,787
Chile	15,116,435	70,522	214	64,079	2	62,869	3,294	9,444	743	13,663,764	59,686	168,917
Chuuk	63,525	66	963	61	5	58	4	34	3	38,115	264	701
Colombia	45,888,729	125,922	364	120,175	2	117,774	6,171	15,748	1,812	24,095,560	156,847	414,205
Congo, Dem. Rep. of	53,400,000	126,912	421	122,976	5	117,230	8,260	13,632	2,943	25,386,360	262,707	783,731
Congo, Rep. of	3,800,000	4,615	823	4,252	3	4,130	290	486	78	1,063,406	15,732	24,959
Cook Islands	19,200	186	103	167	5	159	11	22		33,051	189	590
Costa Rica	4,133,001	20,637	200	19,694	1	19,542	865	1,581	267	3,038,624	18,434	53,919
Côte d'Ivoire	18,671,609	6,776	2,756	6,528	4	6,263	447	1,041	157	1,837,116	15,833	27,006
Croatia	4,437,460	5,471	811	5,409	0	5,394	119	655	71	1,129,227	2,327	10,190

Country or Territory	Population	2004 Peak Pubs.	Ratio, 1 Publisher to	2004 Av. Pubs.	% Inc. Over 2003	2003 Av. Pubs.	2004 No. Bptzd.	Av. Pio. Pubs.	No. of Congs.	Total Hours	Av. Bible Studies	Memorial Attendance
Cuba	11,217,100	88,940	126	88,472	1	87,185	3,415	11,298	1,288	16,678,481	140,367	196,869
Curaçao	133,700	1,431	93	1,398	1	1,382	42	141	20	241,474	1,626	4,218
Cyprus	730,400	1,938	377	1,904	2	1,866	66	233	25	351,822	1,019	3,671
Czech Republic	10,210,168	15,779	647	15,649	2	15,657	302	1,171	231	2,331,705	6,576	29,281
Denmark	5,397,640	14,422	374	14,309	-1	14,438	201	1,093	205	2,087,548	4,370	22,539
Dominica	71,794	358	201	337	7	314	19	48	8	82,547	493	1,076
Dominican Rep.	8,949,725	25,635	349	25,055	2	24,535	1,129	4,690	359	6,492,565	45,402	101,819
East Timor	800,000	42	19,048	38	0	38	5	21	1	28,456	124	253
Ecuador	12,842,576	51,007	252	48,560	6	45,997	3,035	8,175	641	11,879,036	80,847	199,149
El Salvador	6,757,408	30,215	224	28,946	6	28,539	1,182	2,393	525	5,000,519	30,036	83,915
Equatorial Guinea	1,085,000	906	1,198	835	6	789	166	179	14	239,825	2,333	3,672
Estonia	1,366,723	4,079	335	4,037	2	3,967	196	555	49	787,259	2,925	8,082
Ethiopia	70,000,000	7,307	9,580	7,191	5	6,867	493	1,484	141	2,178,181	6,151	21,087
Faeroe Islands	47,704	91	524	89	-1	90	2	30	4	28,918	85	133
Falkland Islands	2,967	5	593	5	0				1	460	3	18
Fiji	806,217	2,007	402	1,949	3	1,909	97	244	34	384,059	2,097	8,191
Finland	5,219,732	19,247	271	19,094	0	19,187	339	1,912	300	2,773,374	8,372	27,896
France	60,434,000	118,228	511	113,038	1	112,308	2,483	9,147	1,491	18,062,599	39,793	207,828
French Guiana	172,500	1,680	103	1,621	5	1,549	99	212	27	384,326	3,199	7,437
Gabon	1,318,000	2,725	484	2,356	5	2,254	149	310	36	584,789	6,177	9,750
Gambia, The	1,500,000	165	9,091	159	7	148	1	34	3	52,985	297	469
Georgia	4,371,535	15,689	279	14,863	5	14,742	697	2,261	149	2,996,738	7,578	29,475
Germany	82,488,700	165,201	499	163,092	0	162,943	3,877	12,008	2,196	25,133,391	73,307	284,573
Ghana	20,363,349	75,005	271	72,624	3	70,196	4,110	6,607	1,178	13,656,413	170,008	272,692
Gibraltar	28,605	104	275	91	2	89		8	2	15,019	28	177
Greece	10,539,771	28,044	376	27,959	0	28,036	620	3,349	378	4,952,654	10,477	45,426
Greenland	56,854	137	415	127	-7	137	1	23	7	29,821	103	280
Grenada	89,258	601	149	584	-3	600	13	74	9	116,334	624	1,581
Guadeloupe	422,496	7,673	55	7,508	0	7,477	212	582	112	1,197,030	8,050	19,618
Guam	154,805	635	244	617	0	615	27	154	10	172,002	925	2,071
Guatemala	11,514,755	23,064	499	22,217	2	21,696	1,109	2,349	332	4,266,970	22,019	71,405
Guinea	9,246,462	873	10,592	729	6	685	63	130	20	228,984	1,837	3,554
Guinea-Bissau	1,300,000	103	12,621	94	13	83	12	33	4	53,586	412	566
Guyana	777,648	2,163	360	2,093	0	2,085	100	238	37	375,317	2,385	11,246
Haiti	8,304,062	13,275	626	12,311	2	12,012	845	1,551	213	2,660,789	21,180	78,725
Hawaii	1,257,608	7,897	159	7,698	5	7,691	344	1,244	98	1,672,475	5,526	19,192
Honduras	7,361,931	15,210	484	14,454	0	13,824	834	1,877	221	3,311,721	20,206	51,534
Hong Kong	6,600,000	4,578	1,442	4,507	0	4,506	146	883	48	1,192,386	5,371	9,241
Hungary	10,103,000	21,979	460	20,876	0	20,863	659	1,665	251	3,361,177	11,500	43,298
Iceland	290,570	284	1,023	278	-1	281	6	30	6	49,343	174	543
India	1,070,471,400	25,353	42,223	23,583	3	22,838	1,214	1,735	435	3,319,282	17,227	61,538
Indonesia	215,768,324	18,500	11,663	17,564	5	16,754	1,056	1,712	407	3,616,989	19,407	44,357
Ireland	5,746,428	4,897	1,173	4,757	2	4,666	122	629	114	951,874	2,348	9,196
Israel	10,608,000	1,247	8,507	1,201	-3	1,238	59	92	16	207,412	816	2,438
Italy	57,888,245	233,527	248	230,880	1	229,920	5,107	32,826	3,049	48,254,558	100,684	433,242
Jamaica	2,599,000	11,078	235	10,685	0	10,627	401	1,121	196	1,827,878	11,732	40,987
Japan	126,824,166	217,555	583	217,097	0	217,020	6,055	71,158	3,163	72,574,886	159,434	348,397
Kazakhstan	15,000,000	14,181	1,058	13,606	4	13,075	1,116	2,189	144	3,166,746	12,292	31,699
Kenya	32,000,000	19,314	1,657	18,044	5	17,115	1,450	3,224	453	5,143,040	30,939	53,779
Kiribati	78,300	76	1,030	64	-9	70	3	13	1	23,560	181	319
Korea, Republic of	48,199,277	90,936	530	90,282	1	89,097	2,973	39,314	1,396	38,499,102	60,274	138,323
Kosovo	2,350,000	124	18,952	115	26	91	22	40		52,381	211	534
Kosrae	9,728	30	324	25	4	24		6	1	6,669	66	147
Kyrgyzstan	5,081,429	3,891	1,306	3,622	6	3,415	266	639	36	830,908	4,058	8,669
Latvia	2,311,400	2,345	986	2,281	2	2,233	127	461	38	635,708	2,394	4,643

Country or Territory	Population	2004 Peak Pubs.	Ratio, 1 Publisher to	2004 Av. Pubs.	% Inc. Over 2003	2003 Av. Pubs.	2004 No. Bptzd.	Av. Pio. Pubs.	No. of Congs.	Total Hours	Av. Bible Studies	Memorial Attendance
Lebanon	3,653,000	3,567	1,024	3,535	1	3,493	90	241	70	556,684	1,770	6,635
Lesotho	2,333,846	3,133	745	2,978	2	2,918	151	387	63	676,232	4,172	8,198
Liberia	3,390,635	4,356	778	4,008	12	3,572	408	829	79	1,398,052	15,527	27,926
Liechtenstein	34,294	57	602	49	2	48		2	1	4,544	18	95
Lithuania	3,500,000	2,854	1,226	2,732	2	2,694	142	464	37	679,079	2,159	5,887
Luxembourg	521,719	1,785	292	1,752	0	1,747	28	131	32	276,039	806	3,524
Macao	500,000	109	4,587	107	-2	109	2	20	2	33,826	109	285
Macedonia	2,000,000	1,087	1,840	1,060	3	1,033	35	145	16	251,968	598	3,059
Madagascar	16,681,000	14,716	1,134	14,282	8	13,247	1,343	2,741	311	3,905,598	35,112	78,210
Madeira	246,334	1,113	221	1,089	0	1,091	27	82	18	168,524	718	2,134
Malawi	11,937,934	63,592	188	58,620	6	55,384	4,581	7,161	965	11,689,285	55,562	193,063
Malaysia	24,698,000	2,490	9,919	2,427	3	2,354	136	442	54	631,726	3,740	6,557
Mali	12,400,000	244	50,820	215	8	200	8	53	7	87,347	568	963
Malta	386,350	574	673	545	-1	549	9	52	7	89,099	200	983
Marshall Islands	71,056	212	335	206	1	204	10	62	5	76,390	631	1,278
Martinique	380,460	4,111	93	4,024	0	4,020	105	445	52	772,130	3,984	9,846
Mauritius	1,169,303	1,514	772	1,477	3	1,435	40	134	25	277,284	1,351	3,641
Mayotte	160,265	62	2,585	50	-2	51		5	1	9,397	65	122
Mexico	105,441,657	585,865	180	581,651	5	555,653	22,608	72,392	11,047	113,844,257	659,218	1,753,645
Moldova	4,228,900	18,107	234	17,702	-1	17,836	801	1,764	224	2,631,899	9,045	41,053
Mongolia	2,540,000	91	27,912	84	22	69	11	31	1	43,048	231	460
Montserrat	3,000	11	273	8	14	7		1		962	8	43
Mozambique	18,972,396	40,456	469	38,260	1	37,747	2,845	5,768	901	8,574,383	52,984	179,218
Myanmar	53,490,000	3,086	17,333	2,938	0	2,935	81	240	97	483,364	1,800	7,014
Namibia	1,830,330	1,293	1,416	1,189	4	1,143	66	146	27	267,208	1,605	3,786
Nauru	10,600	3	3,533	3	-33	3				77	2	38
Nepal	25,100,000	663	37,858	630	9	579	68	113	9	161,940	1,179	2,518
Netherlands	16,280,801	31,390	519	29,632	0	29,603	677	1,853	421	3,993,636	9,979	53,830
Nevis	2,601	53	190	49	-6	52	1	3	1	10,124	36	197
New Caledonia	220,000	1,636	134	1,563	1	1,551	65	169	22	299,630	1,844	5,453
New Zealand	4,061,000	13,632	298	12,943	1	12,822	383	1,166	168	2,064,041	6,117	26,850
Nicaragua	5,450,000	18,159	300	16,977	5	16,163	979	2,264	321	3,901,547	29,580	74,275
Niger	11,360,538	243	46,751	227	4	218	22	48	7	73,821	416	1,348
Nigeria	126,635,626	270,608	468	256,024	2	251,031	11,180	33,075	4,676	48,873,898	445,803	637,091
Niue	1,400	29	48	27	4	26	1	4	1	5,855	27	89
Norfolk Island	2,601	13	200	13	0	13			1	1,626	4	20
Norway	4,582,600	10,018	457	9,638	0	9,661	193	643	174	1,244,703	3,506	16,607
Pakistan	159,196,336	826	192,732	692	6	654	65	68	14	118,290	608	2,823
Panama	3,172,380	11,262	282	10,592	3	10,332	519	1,545	230	2,311,495	14,389	36,258
Papua New Guinea	5,774,507	3,579	1,613	3,110	1	3,066	125	349	54	603,108	3,381	19,539
Paraguay	6,100,181	8,412	725	7,667	3	7,458	451	1,173	110	1,753,765	9,560	20,157
Peru	27,545,400	93,145	296	83,755	5	79,498	5,687	22,061	954	25,524,066	138,537	292,575
Philippines	82,000,000	144,738	567	142,313	1	141,420	6,415	27,744	3,419	28,121,517	111,624	438,418
Pohnpei	39,721	82	484	75	10	68	18	18	1	20,907	199	422
Poland	38,632,453	128,616	300	127,377	1	126,573	4,261	8,539	1,794	15,329,731	48,545	237,134
Portugal	9,922,638	48,555	204	47,896	0	47,835	1,266	4,153	653	7,840,354	24,575	99,910
Puerto Rico	3,937,316	25,014	157	24,752	0	24,849	741	2,790	325	4,349,289	14,551	59,818
Réunion	766,214	2,625	292	2,567	-1	2,581	73	254	35	478,662	1,960	5,766
Rodrigues	36,085	38	950	33	10	30		3		6,242	19	74
Romania	21,680,974	38,636	561	38,361	-1	38,595	1,310	3,529	567	5,956,006	19,557	84,201
Rota	2,899	9	322	7	17	6		2	1	2,442	18	37
Russia	143,782,338	138,552	1,038	132,978	5	126,896	7,745	23,771	1,342	33,473,341	120,140	283,110
Rwanda	8,162,715	12,704	643	11,431	8	10,553	1,117	2,611	261	4,361,930	28,982	54,866
Saba	1,600	6	267	4	33	3		1		1,797	14	20

Country or Territory	Population	2004 Peak Pubs.	Ratio, 1 Publisher to	2004 Av. Pubs.	% Inc. Over 2003	2003 Av. Pubs.	2004 No. Bptzd.	Av. Pio. Pubs.	No. of Congs.	Total Hours	Av. Bible Studies	Memorial Attendance
St. Eustatius	2,900	18	161	15	25	12		3	1	2,907	17	68
St. Helena	3,863	136	28	129	4	124		2	3	13,164	82	326
St. Kitts	31,800	171	186	161	5	153	6	21	3	37,520	199	589
St. Lucia	162,157	709	229	662	-3	681	31	102	10	144,901	880	2,066
St. Maarten	40,000	298	134	276	3	268	15	56	3	75,406	400	1,067
St. Pierre & Miquelon	6,316	16	395	16	-6	17		2	1	2,962	8	28
St. Vincent	109,022	311	351	301	4	290	22	44	9	74,590	361	1,035
Saipan	71,400	161	443	157	1	155	7	35	2	44,704	304	562
Samoa	177,714	403	441	370	6	348	13	63	8	89,716	444	1,815
San Marino	26,266	181	145	179	-1	180	6	24	2	41,449	80	334
São Tomé & Príncipe	180,888	404	448	389	6	367	24	93	8	132,820	1,490	1,651
Senegal	10,260,000	1,000	10,260	966	3	937	44	192	25	313,342	1,657	2,787
Serbia & Montenegro	8,129,395	3,999	2,033	3,936	2	3,855	109	584	57	892,978	1,952	8,820
Seychelles	79,879	254	314	230	6	218	17	34	4	57,442	357	758
Sierra Leone	5,883,889	1,422	4,138	1,257	9	1,149	69	163	32	311,038	2,729	7,594
Slovakia	5,380,053	12,100	445	11,933	-1	12,083	261	478	160	1,361,505	3,425	23,146
Slovenia	1,996,370	1,876	1,064	1,853	1	1,835	42	225	29	384,333	777	3,114
Solomon Islands	460,110	1,890	243	1,844	3	1,794	89	332	42	430,107	1,854	7,349
South Africa	46,586,607	76,406	610	73,047	1	72,053	3,088	9,155	1,492	14,936,587	87,972	193,661
Spain	42,717,064	105,255	406	98,922	1	97,806	1,735	11,680	1,362	19,475,008	40,055	178,818
Sri Lanka	19,300,000	3,708	5,205	3,613	1	3,578	222	401	73	640,883	3,288	9,071
Suriname	438,026	2,004	219	1,990	0	1,999	66	272	39	417,843	2,652	7,218
Swaziland	929,718	2,269	410	2,122	3	2,067	96	280	62	485,816	2,845	7,001
Sweden	8,997,335	22,458	401	22,178	-1	22,409	414	2,077	327	3,190,659	8,463	36,609
Switzerland	7,379,200	17,815	414	17,079	0	17,127	348	996	286	2,386,429	7,137	30,564
Tahiti	245,516	1,746	141	1,722	1	1,709	86	154	25	307,423	1,815	5,788
Taiwan	22,653,642	5,281	4,290	5,091	7	4,753	288	1,413	75	1,752,615	6,815	12,548
Tajikistan	6,127,000	468	13,092	422	17	360	105	122	4	146,054	619	1,149
Tanzania	36,510,219	13,416	2,721	12,049	7	11,214	1,143	2,099	366	3,214,684	21,003	51,323
Thailand	64,870,000	2,166	29,949	2,122	3	2,065	76	385	62	518,889	2,482	5,246
Tinian	2,740	15	183	14	-7	15		5	1	6,363	42	50
Togo	5,025,540	13,375	376	12,796	4	12,276	798	1,624	213	2,903,067	31,672	53,884
Tonga	102,371	196	522	181	0	175	14	29	5	46,460	258	621
Trinidad & Tobago	1,289,141	8,185	158	8,069	0	8,059	256	1,273	101	1,600,256	9,196	23,199
Turkey	67,803,927	1,740	38,968	1,697	3	1,653	79	215	32	356,592	934	3,298
Turks & Caicos Isls.	19,956	139	144	125	6	118	5	17	3	30,543	234	486
Tuvalu	9,403	54	174	43	13	38		2	3	5,712	33	117
Uganda	25,000,000	3,743	6,679	3,513	10	3,204	358	604	90	974,493	7,606	13,248
Ukraine	47,441,000	133,152	356	127,761	3	123,798	6,652	17,562	1,401	26,227,508	89,933	279,353
U.S. of America	288,903,351	1,019,696	283	992,809	0	988,236	30,576	125,982	12,078	189,740,398	519,648	2,303,015
Uruguay	3,030,000	11,008	275	10,877	0	10,706	497	846	153	1,524,742	8,727	25,699
Vanuatu	211,000	311	678	289	2	290	6	32	7	58,892	497	1,980
Venezuela	26,011,853	97,022	268	93,979	3	91,512	4,003	15,989	1,294	22,913,682	137,247	341,806
Virgin Isls. (Brit.)	20,647	191	108	180	-2	184	4	31	3	35,542	197	708
Virgin Isls. (U.S.)	109,343	640	171	607	0	607	18	106	9	140,195	631	1,834
Wallis & Futuna Isls.	15,880	77	206	69	19	58		8	1	15,567	98	472
Yap	11,241	27	416	25	-11	28	1	10		9,070	52	134
Zambia	12,476,082	123,579	101	118,068	3	114,757	7,758	12,942	2,136	21,929,242	182,706	570,381
Zimbabwe	11,374,540	31,134	365	29,745	2	29,242	2,160	3,969	888	6,355,158	48,939	78,449
29 Other Lands		12,325		11,376	7.0	10,633	1,376	2,195	262	3,192,626	14,031	28,129
GRAND TOTAL (235 Lands)		6,513,132		6,308,341	2.0	6,184,046	262,416	858,461	96,894	1,282,234,887	6,085,387	16,760,607

MEMORIAL PARTAKERS WORLDWIDE: 8,570

During the 2004 service year, Jehovah's Witnesses spent over $93 million in caring for special pioneers, missionaries, and traveling overseers in their field service assignments.

Jehovah Always Does What Is Right

"Jehovah is righteous in all his ways."—PSALM 145:17.

HAS someone ever drawn the wrong conclusion about you, perhaps questioning your actions or motives, without having all the facts? If so, you likely felt hurt—and understandably so. From this, we can learn an important lesson: It is wise to avoid jumping to conclusions when we do not have the whole picture.

² We do well to keep this lesson in mind when it comes to reaching conclusions about Jehovah God. Why is that? Because there are certain Bible accounts that may at first seem puzzling. These accounts—perhaps about the actions of some of God's worshipers or God's past judgments—may not contain enough details to answer all our questions. Sadly, some take exception to such accounts, even questioning whether God is righteous and just. Yet, the Bible tells us that "Jehovah is righteous in all his ways." (Psalm 145:17) His Word also assures us that he "does not act wickedly." (Job 34:12; Psalm 37:28) Imagine, then, how he must feel when others draw wrong conclusions about him!

³ Let us consider five reasons why we should accept Jehovah's judgments. Then, with those reasons in mind, we will examine two Bible accounts that some may find difficult to understand.

Why Accept Jehovah's Judgments?

⁴ First, because Jehovah knows all the facts involved and we do not, we should be modest when considering God's actions. To illustrate: Imagine that a judge with an outstanding record of making fair-minded decisions has handed down a sentence in a court case. What would you think about someone who without knowing all the facts or really understanding the laws involved criticized the judge's decision? It would be foolish for someone to pass judgment on a matter without being fully informed about it. (Proverbs 18:13) How much more foolish it would be for mere humans to criticize "the Judge of all the earth"!—Genesis 18:25.

⁵ A second reason to accept God's judgments is that unlike humans, God can read hearts. (1 Samuel 16:7) His Word states: "I, Jehovah, am searching the heart, examining the kidneys, even to give to each one according to his ways, according to the fruitage of his dealings." (Jeremiah 17:10) Hence, when we read Bible accounts about God's judgments upon certain individuals, let us not forget that his all-seeing eyes took into account hidden thoughts, motives, and intentions that went unrecorded in his Word.—1 Chronicles 28:9.

---

1. How do you react when someone draws a wrong conclusion about you, and what lesson can we learn from such an experience?
2, 3. How do some react to Bible accounts that do not contain enough details to answer every question, yet what does the Bible tell us about Jehovah?

---

4. Why should we be modest when considering God's actions? Illustrate.
5. What should we not forget when we read Bible accounts about executions of God's judgments upon certain individuals?

⁶ Note a third reason to accept Jehovah's judgments: He holds to his righteous standards even at great personal cost. Consider an example. In giving his Son as a ransom for delivering obedient mankind from sin and death, Jehovah satisfied his just and righteous standards. (Romans 5:18, 19) Yet, seeing his beloved Son suffer and die on a torture stake must have caused Jehovah the greatest possible pain. What does this tell us about God? Regarding "the ransom paid by Christ Jesus," the Bible says: "This was in order to exhibit [God's] own righteousness." (Romans 3:24-26) Another translation of Romans 3:25 reads: "This showed that God always does what is right and fair." (*New Century Version*) Yes, the extent to which Jehovah was willing to go in order to provide the ransom shows that he has the highest regard for "what is right and fair."

⁷ So, then, if we read something in the Bible that causes some to wonder whether God acted in a just or right way, we should remember this: Because of his loyalty to his standards of righteousness and justice, Jehovah did not spare his own Son from undergoing a painful death. Would he compromise those standards in other matters? The truth is, Jehovah *never* violates his righteous and just standards. We thus have ample reason to be convinced that he always does what is right and fair.—Job 37:23.

⁸ Consider a fourth reason why we should accept Jehovah's judgments: Jehovah made man in His image. (Genesis 1:27) Humans are thus endowed with attributes like those of God, including a sense of justice and righteousness. It would be inconsistent if our sense of justice and righteousness caused us to imagine that those same qualities could somehow be lacking in Jehovah. If we become troubled over a particular Bible account, we need to remember that because of our inherited sin, our sense of what is just and right is imperfect. Jehovah God, in whose image we were made, is perfect in justice and righteousness. (Deuteronomy 32:4) It would be absurd even to imagine that humans could be more just and righteous than God!—Romans 3:4, 5; 9:14.

⁹ A fifth reason for accepting Jehovah's judgments is that he is "the Most High over all the earth." (Psalm 83:18) As such, he is not obligated to explain or justify his actions to humans. He is the Great Potter, and we are like clay that has been shaped into vessels, for him to deal with as he pleases. (Romans 9:19-21) Who are we—the pottery of his hand—to question his decisions or actions? When the patriarch Job misunderstood God's dealings with mankind, Jehovah corrected him, asking: "Really, will you invalidate my justice? Will you pronounce me wicked in order that you may be in the right?" Realizing that he had spoken without understanding, Job later repented. (Job 40:8; 42:6) May we never make the mistake of finding fault with God!

¹⁰ Clearly, we have sound reasons to believe that Jehovah always does what is right. With this foundation for understanding Jehovah's ways, let us examine two Bible accounts that some may find puzzling. The first involves the actions of one of God's worshipers, and the other, an execution of judgment by God himself.

6, 7. (a) How has Jehovah demonstrated that he holds to his just and righteous standards even at great personal cost? (b) What should we remember if we read something in the Bible that causes us to wonder whether God acted in a just or right way?
8. Why would it be inconsistent for humans to imagine that justice and righteousness could somehow be lacking in Jehovah?

9, 10. Why is Jehovah not obligated to explain or justify his actions to humans?

Why Did Lot Offer His Daughters to an Angry Mob?

¹¹ In Genesis chapter 19, we find the account of what happened when God sent two materialized angels to Sodom. Lot insisted that the visitors stay in his home. That night, however, a mob of men from the city surrounded the house and demanded that the visitors be brought out to them for immoral purposes. Lot tried to reason with the mob, but to no avail. Seeking to protect his guests, Lot said: "Please, my brothers, do not act badly. Please, here I have two daughters who have never had intercourse with a man. Please, let me bring them out to you. Then do to them as is good in your eyes. Only to these men do not do a thing, because that is why they have come under the shadow of my roof." The mob would not listen and almost broke down the door. Finally, the angelic visitors struck that frenzied crowd with blindness.—Genesis 19:1-11.

¹² Understandably, this account has raised questions in the mind of some. They wonder: 'How could Lot seek to protect his guests by offering his daughters to a lustful mob? Did he not act improperly, even cowardly?'

In view of this account, why would God inspire Peter to call Lot a "righteous man"? Did Lot act with God's approval? (2 Peter 2: 7, 8) Let us reason on this matter so that we do not draw the wrong conclusion.

¹³ To begin with, it should be noted that rather than condoning or condemning Lot's actions, the Bible simply reports what took place. The Bible also does not tell us what Lot was thinking or what motivated him to act as he did. When he comes back in the "resurrection of . . . the righteous," perhaps he will reveal the details.—Acts 24:15.

¹⁴ Lot was hardly a coward. He was placed in a difficult situation. By saying that the visitors had "come under the shadow" of his roof, Lot indicated that he felt compelled to provide protection and refuge for them. But this would not be easy. Jewish historian Josephus reports that the Sodomites were "unjust towards men, and impious towards God . . . They hated strangers, and abused themselves with Sodomitical practices." Yet, Lot did not shrink back from the hateful mob.

11, 12. (a) Relate what happened when God sent two materialized angels to Sodom. (b) This account has raised what questions in the mind of some?

13, 14. (a) What should be noted about the Bible account regarding Lot's actions? (b) What shows that Lot did not act in a cowardly way?

On the contrary, he went out and reasoned with those angry men. He even "shut the door behind him."—Genesis 19:6.

¹⁵ 'Still,' some may ask, 'why would Lot offer his daughters to the mob?' Instead of assuming that his motives were bad, why not consider some possibilities? First of all, Lot may well have acted in faith. How so? No doubt Lot was aware of how Jehovah had protected Sarah, the wife of Abraham, Lot's uncle. Recall that because Sarah was very beautiful, Abraham had asked her to identify him as her brother, lest others kill him in order to take her.* Subsequently, Sarah was taken to the household of Pharaoh. Jehovah, however, intervened, preventing Pharaoh from violating Sarah. (Genesis 12:11-20) It is possible that Lot had faith that his daughters could be similarly protected. Significantly, Jehovah through his angels *did* intervene, and the young women were kept safe.

¹⁶ Consider another possibility. Lot may also have been trying to shock or confuse the men. He may have believed that his daughters would not be desired by the crowd because of the homosexual lust of the Sodomites. (Jude 7) In addition, the young women were engaged to men of the city, so relatives, friends, or business associates of his prospective sons-in-law might well have been in the crowd. (Genesis 19:14) Lot may have hoped that by reason of such ties, some men in that mob would speak up in defense of his daughters. A mob thus divided would not be nearly so dangerous.#

---

* Abraham's fear was valid, for an ancient papyrus tells of a Pharaoh who had armed men seize a beautiful woman and kill her husband.

For additional observations, see *The Watchtower* of December 1, 1979, page 31.

15. Why can it be said that Lot may well have acted in faith?
16, 17. (a) In what way may Lot have been trying to shock or confuse the men of Sodom? (b) Whatever Lot's reasoning, of what can we be sure?

¹⁷ Whatever Lot's reasoning and motives, we can be sure of this: Since Jehovah always does what is right, he must have had good reason to view Lot as a "righteous man." And judging from the actions of the crazed mob of Sodomites, can there be any doubt that Jehovah was fully justified in executing judgment upon the inhabitants of that wicked city?—Genesis 19:23-25.

Why Did Jehovah Strike Uzzah Dead?

¹⁸ Another account that might seem puzzling to some involves David's attempt to bring the ark of the covenant to Jerusalem. The Ark was placed on a wagon, which was led by Uzzah and his brother. The Bible states: "They came gradually as far as the threshing floor of Nacon, and Uzzah now thrust his hand out to the ark of the true God and grabbed hold of it, for the cattle nearly caused an upset. At that Jehovah's anger blazed against Uzzah and the true God struck him down there for the irreverent act, so that he died there close by the ark of the true God." Some months later, a second attempt succeeded when the Ark was transported in the God-appointed way, carried on the shoulders of Kohathite Levites. (2 Samuel 6:6, 7; Numbers 4:15; 7:9; 1 Chronicles 15:1-14) Some may ask: 'Why did Jehovah react so strongly? Uzzah was only trying to save the Ark.' Lest we draw the wrong conclusion, we do well to note some helpful details.

¹⁹ We need to remember that it is impossible for Jehovah to act unjustly. (Job 34:10) For him to do so would be unloving, and we know from our study of the Bible as a whole that "God is love." (1 John 4:8) In addition, the Scriptures tell us that "righteousness

---

18. (a) What happened when David attempted to bring the Ark to Jerusalem? (b) What question does this account raise?
19. Why is it impossible for Jehovah to act unjustly?

and judgment are the established place of [God's] throne." (Psalm 89:14) How, then, could Jehovah ever act unjustly? If he were to do so, he would be undermining the very foundation of his sovereignty.

20 Keep in mind that Uzzah should have known better. The Ark was associated with Jehovah's presence. The Law specified that it was not to be touched by unauthorized individuals, explicitly warning that violators would be punished by death. (Numbers 4: 18-20; 7:89) Therefore, the transfer of that sacred chest was not a task to be treated lightly. Uzzah evidently was a Levite (though not a priest), so he should have been familiar with the Law. Besides, years earlier the Ark had been moved to the house of his father for safekeeping. (1 Samuel 6:20–7:1) It had stayed there for some 70 years, until David chose to move it. So from childhood on, Uzzah had likely been aware of the laws regarding the Ark.

21 As mentioned earlier, Jehovah can read hearts. Since his Word calls Uzzah's deed an "irreverent act," Jehovah may have seen some selfish motive that is not expressly revealed in the account. Was Uzzah perhaps a presumptuous man, prone to overstep due bounds? (Proverbs 11:2) Did leading in public the Ark that his family had guarded in private give him an inflated sense of self-importance? (Proverbs 8:13) Was Uzzah so faithless as to think that Jehovah's hand was too short to steady the sacred chest that symbolized His presence? Whatever the case, we can be sure that Jehovah did what was right. He likely saw something in Uzzah's heart that caused Him to render swift judgment.—Proverbs 21:2.

20. For what reasons should Uzzah have been aware of the regulations regarding the Ark?
21. In the case of Uzzah, why is it important to remember that Jehovah sees the motives of the heart?

A Sound Basis for Confidence

22 Jehovah's incomparable wisdom is seen in that his Word at times omits certain details. Jehovah thereby gives us an opportunity to show that we trust him. From what we have considered, is it not clear that we have sound reasons to accept Jehovah's judgments? Yes, when we study God's Word with a sincere heart and an open mind, we learn more than enough about Jehovah to be convinced that he always does what is just and right. Hence, if some Bible account raises questions to which we cannot find immediate explicit answers, let us have full confidence that Jehovah did what was right.

23 We can have similar confidence regarding Jehovah's future actions. Hence, we may rest assured that when he comes to execute judgment at the approaching great tribulation, he will not "sweep away the righteous with the wicked." (Genesis 18:23) His love of righteousness and justice will never allow him to do that. We can also have full confidence that in the coming new world, he will satisfy all our needs in the best possible way. —Psalm 145:16.

22. How is Jehovah's wisdom seen in that his Word at times omits certain details?
23. What confidence can we have regarding Jehovah's future actions?

Do You Recall?

- For what reasons should we accept Jehovah's judgments?
- What can help us to avoid reaching the wrong conclusion about Lot's offering his daughters to the angry mob?
- What factors can help us to understand why Jehovah struck Uzzah dead?
- What confidence can we have regarding Jehovah's future actions?

Is the Truth **Bearing Fruit** in Those You Teach?

WHEN young Eric announced that he no longer wanted to be known as one of Jehovah's Witnesses, his parents were crushed. They had not seen it coming. As a boy, Eric had shared in the family Bible study, attended Christian meetings, and joined in the preaching work with the congregation. He had seemed to be in the truth, so to speak. But now that he was gone, his parents realized that Bible truth had not been in him. That realization came as both a shock and a disappointment to them.

Others have experienced similar feelings of loss when a Bible student unexpectedly quits studying. At such times, people often ask themselves, 'Why did I not see this coming?' Well, is it possible to determine before spiritual disaster strikes whether the truth is bearing fruit in those we teach? For that matter, how can we be certain that the truth is working in us as well as in those we teach? In his familiar parable of the sower, Jesus provided a clue to the answer to these questions.

The Truth Must Reach the Heart

"The seed is the word of God," Jesus said. "As for that [sown] on the fine soil, these are the ones that, after hearing the word with a fine and good heart, retain it and bear fruit with endurance." (Luke 8:11, 15) So before Kingdom truth can produce any results in our students, it has to take root in their figurative heart. Jesus assures us that like good seed in fine soil, once divine truth has touched a good heart, it immediately goes to work and bears fruit. What should we look for?

We must take note of heart qualities, not just outward show. Merely keeping up a routine of worship does not always reveal what is really going on in someone's heart. (Jeremiah 17:9, 10; Matthew 15:7-9) We need to look deeper. There should be a definite change in the person's desires, motives, and priorities. The individual should be developing the new personality, which conforms to God's will. (Ephesians 4:20-24) To illustrate: When the Thessalonians heard the good news, Paul said that they readily accepted it as the word of God. But it was their subsequent endurance, faithfulness, and love that confirmed to him that the truth was "also at work in [them]."—1 Thessalonians 2:13, 14; 3:6.

Of course, whatever is in a student's heart will sooner or later be revealed in his behavior, as Eric's example illustrates. (Mark 7:21, 22; James 1:14, 15) Unfortunately, by the time certain bad traits become fully evident in a person's actions, it might be too late. The challenge, then, is to try to identify specific weaknesses before they become spiritual stumbling blocks. We need a way to look into the figurative heart. How can we do that?

Learn From Jesus

Jesus, of course, was able to read hearts unerringly. (Matthew 12:25) None of us can do that. Yet, he showed us that we too can discern a person's desires, motives, and priorities. Just as a qualified doctor uses various diagnostic techniques to see what is wrong with a patient's physical heart, Jesus used God's Word to 'draw up' and expose the "thoughts and intentions of the heart," even when they were still hidden from general observation.—Proverbs 20:5; Hebrews 4:12.

For example, on one occasion Jesus helped Peter to become aware of a weakness that later did become a stumbling block. Jesus knew that Peter loved him. In fact, Jesus had just entrusted Peter with "the keys of the kingdom." (Matthew 16:13-19) Jesus also knew, however, that Satan had his eye on the apostles. In the days ahead, they would come under intense

Jesus' words revealed a weakness in Peter

pressure to compromise. Jesus evidently discerned that some of his disciples had weaknesses in their faith. So he did not shy away from pointing out what they needed to work on. Consider how he brought the matter up for discussion.

Matthew 16:21 says: "From that time forward Jesus Christ commenced showing his disciples that he must . . . suffer . . . and be killed." Notice that Jesus *showed* them, not just told them, what would happen to him. Most likely he used Bible verses, such as Psalm 22:14-18 or Isaiah 53:10-12, that indicate that the Messiah would have to suffer and die. At any rate, by reading or quoting directly from the Scriptures, Jesus gave Peter and the others an opportunity to respond

from their hearts. How would they react to the prospect of persecution?

Surprisingly, as bold and zealous as Peter had shown himself to be, his rash response on this occasion revealed a critical flaw in his thinking. "Be kind to yourself, Lord," he said, "you will not have this destiny at all." Peter's way of thinking was clearly misguided, for as Jesus pointed out, Peter was thinking, "not God's thoughts, but those of men"—a serious fault that could lead to grave consequences. What, then, did Jesus do? After rebuking Peter, Jesus told him and the rest of the disciples: "If anyone wants to come after me, let him disown himself and pick up his torture stake and continually follow me." Drawing on thoughts found at Psalm 49:8 and 62:12, he kindly reminded them that their everlasting prospects lay, not with men, who could not provide salvation, but with God. —Matthew 16:22-28.

Though Peter later temporarily succumbed to fear and denied Jesus three times, this discussion and others no doubt helped to prepare him for a rapid spiritual recovery. (John 21:15-19) Just 50 days later, Peter boldly stood up before the crowds in Jerusalem to testify to Jesus' resurrection. In the weeks, months, and years to follow, he courageously faced repeated arrests, beatings, and incarceration, setting an outstanding example of fearless integrity.—Acts 2:14-36; 4:18-21; 5: 29-32, 40-42; 12:3-5.

What do we learn from this? Can you see what Jesus did to draw up and expose what was in Peter's heart? First, he selected appropriate scriptures to focus Peter's attention on the specific area of concern. Next, he gave Peter an opportunity to respond from the heart. Finally, he provided further Scriptural counsel to help Peter adjust his thinking and feelings. You might feel that this level of teaching is beyond your ability, but let us consider two experiences that illustrate how preparation and reliance on Jehovah can help any one of us to follow Jesus' example.

Drawing Up What Is in the Heart

When one Christian father learned that his two sons in the first and second grades had taken candy from the teacher's desk, he sat them down and reasoned with them. Rather than simply dismiss this as a harmless, childish prank, the father relates, "I tried to draw out of their hearts what had motivated them to do this bad thing."

The father asked the boys to recall what happened to Achan, as recounted in Joshua chapter 7. The boys immediately got the point and confessed. Their consciences had already been bothering them. So the father had them read Ephesians 4:28, which says: "Let the stealer steal no more, but rather let him do hard work . . . that he may have something to distribute to someone in need." Having the children make compensation by

buying candy and presenting it to the teacher reinforced the Scriptural counsel.

"We tried to root out any bad motives once these were discerned," the father says, "and replace them with good and pure motives by reasoning with the children." By imitating Jesus when teaching their children, these parents certainly had good results over time. Both sons were eventually invited to become members of the headquarters staff at Brooklyn Bethel, where one still serves after 25 years.

Consider how another Christian was able to help her Bible student. The student was attending meetings and sharing in the ministry and had already expressed a desire to get baptized. However, she appeared to be relying too much on herself rather than on Jehovah. "As a single woman, she had become more independent than she realized," the Witness recalls. "I worried that she was headed for a physical breakdown or a spiritual fall."

So the Witness took the initiative to reason with the student on Matthew 6:33, encouraging her to adjust her priorities, put the Kingdom first, and trust in Jehovah to work matters out for the best. She asked her frankly: "Does living on your own sometimes make it difficult for you to rely on others, including Jehovah?" The student admitted that she had almost quit praying. The publisher then encouraged her to follow the advice found at Psalm 55:22 and throw her burden on Jehovah because, as 1 Peter 5:7 assures us, "he cares for you." Those words touched her heart. The Witness says, "That was one of the few times that I saw her cry."

Keep the Truth Working in You

Seeing those we teach respond to Bible truth brings us great joy. If our efforts to help

IN OUR NEXT ISSUE

Miracles That You Have Seen!

———

Safeguarding Our Christian Identity

———

Do You Measure Yourself Against Others?

Use the Bible to draw up what is in the heart

sessions, one that secures Jehovah's continued blessing. —Malachi 3:10.

This kind of frank self-examination can be sobering. Admitting to specific weaknesses when they are pointed out to us can be hard emotionally. Yet, when you lovingly take the initiative to help your child, your Bible student, or even yourself—no matter how personal or sensitive a matter might be—you may well be taking the first step toward saving his life or your own.—Galatians 6:1.

others are to have success, though, we have to set a good example ourselves. (Jude 22, 23) All of us need to "keep working out [our] own salvation with fear and trembling." (Philippians 2:12) That includes regularly letting the light of the Scriptures shine on our own hearts, searching for attitudes, desires, and affections that might need correction.—2 Peter 1:19.

For instance, has your zeal for Christian activities diminished lately? If so, why? One reason might be that you are relying too much on yourself. How can you tell whether this is so? Read Haggai 1:2-11, and honestly reflect on Jehovah's line of reasoning with the repatriated Jews. Then ask yourself: 'Am I overly concerned with financial security and material comforts? Do I really trust Jehovah to care for my family if I give spiritual things priority? Or do I feel that I have to take care of myself first?' If adjustments in your thinking or feelings are needed, do not hesitate to make them. Scriptural counsel, such as that found at Matthew 6:25-33, Luke 12:13-21, and 1 Timothy 6:6-12, provides the basis for a balanced view of material needs and pos-

What, though, if your efforts do not seem to be producing good results? Do not give up quickly. Adjusting an imperfect heart can be a delicate, time-consuming, and sometimes frustrating endeavor. But it can also be rewarding.

Young Eric, mentioned at the outset, eventually came to his senses and again started "walking in the truth." (2 John 4) "It wasn't until I realized what I had lost that I turned back to Jehovah," he says. With the help of his parents, Eric is now serving God faithfully. Although he once resented his parents' repeated efforts to get him to search his heart, now he deeply appreciates what they did. "My parents are wonderful," he says. "They never stopped loving me."

Shining the light of God's Word on the heart of those we teach is an expression of loving-kindness. (Psalm 141:5) Continue to search the heart of your children and your Bible students for evidence that the new Christian personality is actually taking hold in them. Keep the truth working in others and in yourself by "handling the word of the truth aright."—2 Timothy 2:15.

"Keep on the Watch"

IN ANCIENT times, gatekeepers served at city and temple entrances and, in some instances, at the doorways of private homes. Besides ensuring that the gates were closed at night, gatekeepers also served as watchmen. This was a very responsible assignment, for the safety of the city depended on their calling out to warn the people of any impending danger.

Jesus Christ was acquainted with the role of gatekeepers, also called doorkeepers. On one occasion, he likened his disciples to doorkeepers and encouraged them to keep on the watch with respect to the conclusion of the Jewish system of things. He said: "Keep looking, keep awake, for you do not know when the appointed time is. It is like a man traveling abroad that left his house and . . . commanded the doorkeeper to keep on the watch. Therefore keep on the watch, for you do not know when the master of the house is coming." —Mark 13:33-35.

Likewise, for over 125 years now, this journal, *The Watchtower*, has passed on Jesus' encouragement to "keep on the watch." How? As stated on page 2 of this magazine, "It keeps watch on world events as these fulfill Bible prophecy. It comforts all peoples with the good news that God's Kingdom will soon destroy those who oppress their fellowmen and that it will turn the earth into a paradise." With a worldwide circulation of more than 26,000,000 copies in 150 languages, *The Watchtower* is the most widely distributed religious magazine in the world. By means of it, Jehovah's Witnesses, like the ancient gatekeepers, are urging people everywhere to "keep awake" spiritually because the Master, Jesus Christ, is about to return and execute judgment on this system of things.—Mark 13:26, 37.

FEBRUARY 15, 2005

THE WATCHTOWER

ANNOUNCING JEHOVAH'S KINGDOM

Should You Believe in
Miracles?

THE WATCHTOWER®
ANNOUNCING JEHOVAH'S KINGDOM

February 15, 2005   Average Printing Each Issue: 26,439,000   Vol. 126, No. 4

THE PURPOSE OF *THE WATCHTOWER* is to exalt Jehovah God as Sovereign Lord of the universe. It keeps watch on world events as these fulfill Bible prophecy. It comforts all peoples with the good news that God's Kingdom will soon destroy those who oppress their fellowmen and that it will turn the earth into a paradise. It encourages faith in God's now-reigning King, Jesus Christ, whose shed blood opens the way for mankind to gain eternal life. *The Watchtower,* published by Jehovah's Witnesses continuously since 1879, is nonpolitical. It adheres to the Bible as its authority.

IN THIS ISSUE

3   Miracles—Fact or Fiction?

5   Miracles That You Have Seen!

9   The Berleburg Bible

10   Climbing to The Bottom of Saba

12   Christians—Be Proud of Who You Are!

17   Safeguarding Our Christian Identity

23   'If You Are Impressed Into Service'

27   Questions From Readers

28   Do You Measure Yourself Against Others?

32   Who Will Feed the World?

WATCHTOWER STUDIES

MARCH 21-27:
Christians—Be Proud of Who You Are!
Page 12. Songs to be used: 113, 29.

MARCH 28–APRIL 3:
Safeguarding Our Christian Identity.
Page 17. Songs to be used: 207, 202.

Publication of *The Watchtower* is part of a worldwide Bible educational work supported by voluntary donations.

Unless otherwise indicated, Scripture quotations are from the modern-language *New World Translation of the Holy Scriptures—With References.*

The Watchtower (ISSN 0043-1087) is published semimonthly by Watchtower Bible and Tract Society of New York, Inc.; M. H. Larson, President; G. F. Simonis, Secretary-Treasurer; 25 Columbia Heights, Brooklyn, NY 11201-2483. Periodicals Postage Paid at Brooklyn, NY, and at additional mailing offices. **POSTMASTER:** Send address changes to Watchtower, **Wallkill, NY 12589.**

Changes of address should reach us 30 days before your moving date. Give us your old and new address (if possible, your old address label).

Semimonthly   ENGLISH

Would you welcome more information or a free home Bible study? Please send your request to Jehovah's Witnesses, using the appropriate address below.

America, United States of: Wallkill, NY 12589. *Antigua:* Box 119, St. Johns. *Australia:* Box 280, Ingleburn, NSW 1890. *Bahamas:* Box N-1247, Nassau, N.P. *Barbados, W.I.:* Crusher Site Road, Prospect, St. James. *Britain:* The Ridgeway, London NW7 1RN. *Canada:* Box 4100, Halton Hills (Georgetown), Ontario L7G 4Y4. *Germany:* Niederselters, Am Steinfels, D-65618 Selters. *Ghana:* P. O. Box GP 760, Accra. *Guyana:* 352-360 Tyrell St., Republic Park Phase 2 EBD. *Hawaii 96819:* 2055 Kam IV Rd., Honolulu. *Hong Kong:* 4 Kent Road, Kowloon Tong. *India:* Post Box 6440, Yelahanka, Bangalore 560 064, KAR. *Ireland:* Newcastle, Greystones, Co. Wicklow. *Jamaica:* P. O. Box 103, Old Harbour, St. Catherine. *Japan:* 1271 Nakashinden, Ebina City, Kanagawa Pref., 243-0496. *Kenya:* P.O. Box 47788, GPO Nairobi 00100. *New Zealand:* P.O. Box 75-142, Manurewa. *Nigeria:* P.M.B. 1090, Benin City 300001, Edo State. *Philippines, Republic of:* P. O. Box 2044, 1060 Manila. *South Africa:* Private Bag X2067, Krugersdorp, 1740. *Trinidad and Tobago, Republic of:* Lower Rapsey Street & Laxmi Lane, Curepe. *Zambia:* Box 33459, Lusaka 10101. *Zimbabwe:* Private Bag WG-5001, Westgate.

NOW PUBLISHED IN 150 LANGUAGES. SEMIMONTHLY: Afrikaans, Albanian,* Amharic, Arabic, Bengali, Bicol, Bislama, Bulgarian, Cebuano,* Chichewa,* Chinese, Chinese (Simplified),* Cibemba,* Croatian,* Czech,*# Danish,*# Dutch,*# East Armenian, Efik,* English*#◎ (also Braille), Estonian, Ewe, Fijian, Finnish,*# French,*# Ga, Georgian, German,*# Greek,* Gujarati, Gun, Hebrew, Hiligaynon, Hindi, Hungarian,*# Igbo,* Iloko,* Indonesian, Italian,*# Japanese*# (also Braille), Kannada, Kinyarwanda, Kirundi, Korean*# (also Braille), Latvian, Lingala, Lithuanian, Luvale, Macedonian, Malagasy,* Malayalam, Maltese, Marathi, Myanmar, Nepali, New Guinea Pidgin, Norwegian,*# Pangasinan, Papiamento (Aruba), Papiamento (Curaçao), Polish,*# Portuguese*# (also Braille), Punjabi, Rarotongan, Romanian,* Russian,* Samar-Leyte, Samoan, Sango, Sepedi, Serbian, Sesotho, Shona,* Silozi, Sinhala, Slovak,* Slovenian, Solomon Islands Pidgin, Spanish,*# Sranantongo, Swahili,* Swedish,*# Tagalog,* Tamil, Telugu, Thai, Tigrinya, Tongan, Tshiluba, Tsonga, Tswana, Turkish, Twi, Ukrainian,* Urdu, Venda, Vietnamese, Wallisian, Xhosa, Yoruba,* Zulu*

MONTHLY: American Sign Language,△□ Armenian, Assamese, Azerbaijani (Roman script), Brazilian Sign Language,△ Cambodian, Chitonga, Gilbertese, Greenlandic, Haitian Creole, Hausa, Hiri Motu, Icelandic, Isoko, Kaonde, Kazakh, Kikongo, Kiluba, Kirghiz, Kwanyama/Ndonga, Luganda, Marshallese, Mauritian Creole, Mizo, Monokutuba, Moore, Niuean, Ossetian, Otetela, Palauan, Persian, Ponapean, Seychelles Creole, Tahitian, Tatar, Tiv, Trukese, Tumbuka, Tuvaluan, Umbundu, Yapese, Zande

* Study articles also available in large-print edition.
\# Audiocassettes also available.
◎ CD (MP3 format) also available.
△ Videocassette
□ DVD

Miracles
Fact or Fiction?

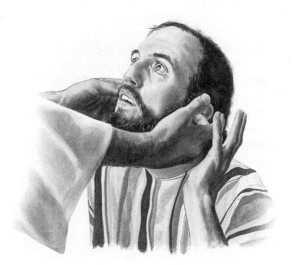

THE gentleman's attention was immediately caught by the bumper sticker on a passing car, "Miracles Happen—Just Ask the Angels." Although he was a religious man himself, he was unsure what this meant. Did the sign mean that the driver believed in miracles? Or was it, rather, a jocular way of indicating lack of belief in both miracles and angels?

You may be interested in what German author Manfred Barthel noted: *"Miracle* is a word that immediately polarizes readers into two warring camps." Those who believe in miracles are convinced that they occur and perhaps occur often.* For example, it is reported that in Greece during the last few years, believers have claimed that miracles take place about once a month. This led a bishop of the Greek Orthodox Church to caution: "The believer tends to humanize God, Mary, and the saints. Believers should not carry things too far."

Belief in miracles is less widespread in some other countries. According to an Allensbach poll published in Germany in 2002, 71 percent of its citizens consider miracles to be fiction, not fact. Among the less than one third who do believe in miracles, however, are three women who claim to have received a message from the Virgin Mary. A few months after Mary allegedly appeared to them—accompanied by angels and

---

* The word "miracles" as used in this article is as defined in a Bible dictionary: "Effects in the physical world that surpass all known human or natural powers and are therefore attributed to supernatural agency."

a dove—the German newspaper *Westfalenpost* reported: "Up until now about 50,000 pilgrims, people in search of healing, as well as the curious have closely followed the visions seen by the women." An additional 10,000 were expected to stream into the village to experience additional appearances. Similar appearances of the Virgin Mary are said to have taken place in Lourdes, France, in 1858, and in Fátima, Portugal, in 1917.

How About Non-Christian Religions?

Belief in miracles is found in almost all religions. *The Encyclopedia of Religion* explains that the founders of Buddhism, Christianity, and Islam held diverse views about miracles, but it notes: "The subsequent history of these religions demonstrates unmistakably that miracles and miracle stories have been an integral part of man's religious life." This reference work says that "the Buddha himself was sometimes led to work miracles." Later, when "Buddhism was transplanted to China, its missionaries often resorted to the display of miraculous powers."

After referring to several such supposed miracles, that encyclopedia concludes: "One may not be prepared to accept all of these miracle stories told by pious biographers, but they were undoubtedly created with the good intention of glorifying the Buddha, who was able to endow his ardent followers with such miraculous powers." The same authority says of Islam: "The majority of the Islamic community has never ceased to expect miracles. Muhammad is presented in the traditions (*hadīths*) as having worked miracles in public on many occasions. . . . Even after their death, saints are believed to work miracles at their own graves on behalf of the faithful, and their intercession is piously invoked."

What of the Miracles in Christianity?

Many of those who have accepted Christianity are divided in their opinions. Some accept as fact the Bible reports about the miracles performed by Jesus Christ or by servants of God in pre-Christian times. Yet, many agree with Protestant Reformer Martin Luther. *The Encyclopedia of Religion* says of him: "Both Luther and Calvin wrote that the age of miracles was over and that their occurrence should not be expected." The Catholic Church held to its belief in miracles "without trying to defend it intellectually," says this reference work. However, "the academic Protestant community came to believe that the practice of Christianity was largely a matter of morality and that neither God nor the spiritual world contacted or influenced practical human life to any great extent."

Other professed Christians, including some clergymen, doubt that the miracles mentioned in the Bible are factual. Take, for example, the burning-bush episode reported in the Bible at Exodus 3:1-5. The book *What the Bible Really Says* explains that a number of German theologians do not take this as

---

WHY CERTAIN MIRACLES NO LONGER OCCUR

Various kinds of miracles are mentioned in the Bible. (Exodus 7:19-21; 1 Kings 17:1-7; 18:22-38; 2 Kings 5:1-14; Matthew 8:24-27; Luke 17:11-19; John 2:1-11; 9:1-7) Many of these miracles served to identify Jesus as the Messiah, and they proved that he had God's backing. Jesus' early followers displayed miraculous gifts, such as speaking in tongues and discernment of inspired utterances. (Acts 2:5-12; 1 Corinthians 12:28-31) Such miraculous gifts were useful for the Christian congregation during its infancy. How so?

Well, copies of the Scriptures were few. Usually, only the rich possessed scrolls or books of any sort. In pagan lands, there was no knowledge of the Bible or of its Author, Jehovah. Christian teaching had to be conveyed by word of mouth. The miraculous gifts were useful in showing that God was using the Christian congregation.

But Paul explained that these gifts would pass away once they were no longer needed. "Whether there are gifts of prophesying, they will be done away with; whether there are tongues, they will cease; whether there is knowledge, it will be done away with. For we have partial knowledge and we prophesy partially; but when that which is complete arrives, that which is partial will be done away with."—1 Corinthians 13:8-10.

Today, people have access to Bibles, as well as concordances and encyclopedias. Over six million trained Christians are assisting others to gain divine knowledge based on the Bible. Thus, miracles are no longer necessary to attest to Jesus Christ as God's appointed Deliverer or to provide proof that Jehovah is backing his servants.

the literal account of a miracle. Instead, they interpret it as "a symbol of Moses' inner struggle with the pricks and burning pangs of conscience." The book adds: "The flames could also be seen as flowers that burst into bloom in the sunlight of the divine presence."

You may find such an explanation less than satisfying. So, what should you believe? Is it realistic to believe that miracles have ever taken place? And what about modern-day miracles? Since we cannot ask the angels, whom can we ask?

The Biblical Position

No one can deny that the Bible reports that God in bygone days at times stepped in to perform humanly impossible acts. Of him, we read: "You proceeded to bring forth your people Israel out of the land of Egypt, with signs and *with miracles* and with a strong hand and with a stretched-out arm and with great fearsomeness." (Jeremiah 32:21) Imagine, the most powerful nation of the day brought to its knees by means of ten divinely sent plagues, including the death of its firstborn. Miracles indeed!—Exodus, chapters 7 to 14.

Centuries later, the four Gospel writers described some 35 miracles performed by Jesus. In fact, their words suggest that he performed even more supernatural feats than those they report. Are these reports fact or fiction?*—Matthew 9:35; Luke 9:11.

If the Bible is what it claims to be—God's Word of truth—then you have clear reason to believe in the miracles about which it speaks. The Bible is explicit in reporting that miracles occurred in bygone days—miraculous healings, resurrections, and the like—yet it is just as explicit in explaining that such miracles no longer take place. (See the box "Why Certain Miracles No Longer Occur," on page 4.) So does this mean that even those who accept the Bible as fact consider belief in modern-day miracles to be unfounded? Let the next article reply.

---

* You can consider evidence that the Bible is worthy of belief. Such is set out in the book *The Bible—God's Word or Man's?* published by Jehovah's Witnesses.

Miracles
That You Have Seen!

THE word "miracle" has the secondary meaning of "an extremely outstanding or unusual event, thing, or accomplishment." We have all seen this kind of miracle, independent of divine intervention.

Gaining increased knowledge of the physical laws of nature, humans have been able to achieve what at one time was commonly viewed as unachievable. For example, a hundred years ago, most people probably thought impossible what computers, television, space technology, and similar modern-day developments have made commonplace now.

Recognizing that they have only partial knowledge of the scientific wonders behind God's creations, some scientists admit that they can no longer state with certainty that

The human body is a marvelous creation

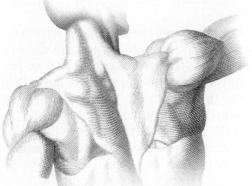

Anatomy Improved and Illustrated, London, 1723, Bernardino Genga

something is impossible. At most, they are willing to say that it is improbable. Thus they leave the way open for future "miracles."

Even if we are using the primary meaning of "miracle," thus referring to things "attributed to supernatural agency," we can say that each of us has seen miracles. For example, we observe the sun, moon, and stars—all products of a "supernatural agency," the Creator himself. Besides, who can fully explain in detail how the human body functions? how the brain works? or how the human embryo develops? The book *The Body Machine* points out: "The human organism, controlled and co-ordinated by the central nervous system, is a sophisticated sensory apparatus, a self-regulating mobile engine, a self-reproducing computer—a marvellous and in many ways mysterious creation." The God who created "the human organism" indeed performed a miracle, one that continues to amaze us. There are also other kinds of miracles that you have seen, though you may not have recognized them as such.

Can a Book Be a Miracle?

No book enjoys such a wide circulation as does the Bible. Do you see in it a miracle? Can we attribute its existence to a "supernat-

ural agency"? True, the Bible is a book written down by humans, but they claimed to have expressed the thoughts of God, not their own. (2 Samuel 23:1, 2; 2 Peter 1:20, 21) Think of it. They were some 40 individuals, living over a span of 1,600 years. They came from backgrounds as varied as those of shepherds, military men, fishermen, civil servants, physicians, priests, and kings. Yet, they were able to convey a unified message of hope that is both truthful and accurate.

Based on a careful study, Jehovah's Witnesses accept the Bible, "not as the word of men, but, just as it truthfully is, as the word of God," as the apostle Paul wrote. (1 Thessalonians 2:13) Their publications have over the years explained how so-called contradictions in the Bible can be harmonized with its overall message. This inner harmony is in itself a proof of divine authorship.*

No other book has been subjected to such vigorous attempts to destroy it as has the Bible. Yet, it still exists and this, at least in part, in over 2,000 languages. Both its physical preservation as a book and the preservation of its integrity manifest divine intervention. The Bible is truly a miracle!

A Miracle That "Is Alive and Exerts Power"

The miracles of bygone days—miraculous healings and resurrections—no longer occur. But we have reason for confidence that in God's upcoming new world, such miracles will take place again, this time on a global scale. They will bring permanent relief and will go beyond our present ability to comprehend.

The miracle of the Bible can even today perform what is tantamount to miracles by

---

* If you desire to investigate more of these so-called contradictions to see how they can be harmonized, many examples are considered in *The Bible—God's Word or Man's?* chapter 7, published by Jehovah's Witnesses.

motivating people to change their personalities for the better. (See an example in the box "The Power of God's Word," on page 8.) Hebrews 4:12 states: "The word of God is alive and exerts power and is sharper than any two-edged sword and pierces even to the dividing of soul and spirit, and of joints and their marrow, and is able to discern thoughts and intentions of the heart." Yes, the Bible has been instrumental in transforming the lives of over six million people who live around the globe, filling their lives with purpose and offering them a marvelous hope for the future.

Why not allow the Bible to work a miracle in your life?

ALREADY DEAD OR STILL ALIVE?

According to John 19:33, 34, Jesus was already dead when "one of the soldiers jabbed his side with a spear, and immediately blood and water came out." However, Matthew 27:49, 50 indicates that Jesus was still alive when this took place. Why the difference?

The Mosaic Law forbade leaving a criminal to hang all night on the execution stake. (Deuteronomy 21:22, 23) Hence, in Jesus' day, if an impaled criminal was still alive late in the day, it was customary to break his legs, thus speeding up the dying process. He would no longer be able to raise himself erect so as to breathe properly. That the soldiers broke the legs of the two evildoers impaled alongside Jesus but did not break his indicates that they thought that he was dead. The soldier possibly pierced his side just to remove all doubt and to eliminate any later revival that might be falsely heralded as a resurrection.

The text at Matthew 27:49, 50 gives a different order of events. It says: *"Another man took a spear and pierced his side, and blood and water came out.* Again Jesus cried out with a loud voice, and yielded up his spirit." The italicized sentence, however, does not appear in all ancient Bible manuscripts. Many authorities believe that it was later interpolated from John's Gospel but was misplaced. Thus, many translations set the sentence off in brackets or parentheses, offer an explanatory footnote, or simply omit the sentence altogether.

The master text by Westcott and Hort, used extensively as a basis for the *New World Translation,* puts the sentence in double brackets. It notes that the sentence "must lie under strong presumption of having been introduced by scribes."

The overwhelming evidence then is that John 19:33, 34 is factual and that Jesus was already dead when the Roman soldier pierced him with the spear.

THE POWER OF GOD'S WORD

As a teenager and victim of a broken home, Detlef drifted into a world of drugs, alcohol, and heavy metal.* He became what is commonly called a skinhead, and his violent behavior soon got him into trouble with the police.

In 1992, 60 skinheads became involved in a massive brawl with about 35 punkers at a restaurant and bar in northeastern Germany. One of the punkers, Thomas, was so badly beaten that he died of his injuries. Several of the ringleaders, including Detlef, were sentenced to prison after a trial that received major media coverage.

Shortly after Detlef was released from prison, a pamphlet was handed to him by Jehovah's Witnesses. The pamphlet was entitled "Why Is Life So Full of Problems?" Detlef immediately recognized the truthfulness of what it said, and he began to study the Bible with the Witnesses. This completely turned his life around. Since 1996 he has been a zealous Witness of Jehovah.

* Names have been changed.

Siegfried, a former punker, was a good friend of Thomas, the young man who was killed; he too later became a Witness and is now a congregation elder. When Siegfried visited Detlef's congregation to deliver a Bible talk (incidentally, Thomas' mother also attends meetings there occasionally), Detlef invited him to lunch. Some ten years ago, their hatred would have been hard to control. Today, their brotherly love is obvious.

Detlef and Siegfried look forward to welcoming Thomas back to life in an earthly paradise. Says Detlef: "Just thinking of this moves me to tears. I am so sorry for what I did." Their common desire is to help Thomas then, as they today help others, to get to know Jehovah and to rejoice in the hope the Bible gives.

Yes, such is the power of God's Word!

The Berleburg Bible

PIETISM was a religious movement that developed within the German Lutheran Church in the 17th and 18th centuries. Some followers of this movement were ridiculed or even persecuted because of their faith. Several Pietist scholars found refuge in Berleburg, some 100 miles north of Frankfurt am Main. They were granted asylum by a local nobleman, Count Casimir von Wittgenstein Berleburg, who held religion in high esteem. The presence of these preachers and academics in Berleburg led to a new translation of the Bible, known today as the Berleburg Bible. How did the translation come about?

One of the asylum seekers was Johann Haug, who was forced to leave his home in Strasbourg because of the intolerance of local theologians. Haug was an erudite scholar and a talented linguist. He told his fellow scholars in Berleburg of his earnest desire "to provide a wholly pure Bible translation, to correct Luther's translation, to render the meaning exactly according to the letter of God's Word and according to its spirit." (*Die Geschichte der Berlenburger Bibel* [The History of the Berleburg Bible]) The goal was to produce a Bible with explanatory notes and comments, and it was to be understandable to the common man. Haug enlisted the support of academics in other European lands, and he worked on the project for 20 years. The Berleburg Bible was published starting in 1726. Because of its extensive notes, it ran to eight volumes.

The Berleburg Bible certainly has some interesting points. For example, Exodus 6: 2, 3 reads: "Further God talked to Moses and spoke to him: I am the LORD! And appeared to Abraham/to Isaac and to Jacob/as an omni-sufficient God: but by my name JEHOVAH I did not become known to them." A note explains: "The name JEHOVAH . . . , the name set apart/or/the declared name." God's own personal name, Jehovah, also appears in comments on Exodus 3:15 and Exodus 34:6.

The Berleburg Bible thus became one in a long line of German Bibles that have used the name Jehovah either in the main text, in footnotes, or in comments. One of the more modern translations giving due honor to God's personal name is the *New World Translation of the Holy Scriptures*, published by Jehovah's Witnesses.

PUERTO RICO

Climbing to
The Bottom
of Saba

T HE Dutch island of Saba once served
as a stronghold for buccaneers who
sailed the waters of the Caribbean Sea
in search of plunder. Today, this tiny island, located 150 miles east of Puerto Rico,
is home to some 1,600 inhabitants, 5 of
whom are Jehovah's Witnesses. These in-
trepid ministers are searching for something
far more valuable than plunder, however.
They are diligently searching for people who
are "rightly disposed for everlasting life."
—Acts 13:48.

The good news of God's Kingdom first
reached the island on June 22, 1952, when
the 59-foot schooner *Sibia,* operated by
Jehovah's Witnesses, anchored off Saba's
coast. (Matthew 24:14) Missionaries Gust
Maki and Stanley Carter climbed The Lad-
der, a pathway of over 500 stone steps up to

Background: www.sabatourism.com

The Bottom, Saba's capital.* For centuries,
this narrow path was the only means to
reach the island's inhabitants.

The first published report of Christian witnessing work on Saba appeared in the *1966
Yearbook of Jehovah's Witnesses.* According
to that report, there was only one active Witness on the island. Later, a family from Canada spent several years preaching the good
news there. Recently, Russel and Kathy, a retired couple from the United States, went to
Saba and shared in the preaching work
there. Consider their story.

---

* It seems that pirates called it The Bottom because
they thought it was at the bottom of a volcanic crater.

Visit to Saba

My wife and I arrive by plane as guests of Ronald, who was the island's only Witness during most of the 1990's. Our host is waiting for us at the airport. He is delighted with the small box of vegetables that we brought as a gift, since no commercial farming is done on the island. Boarding a small truck, we slowly zigzag up the side of Mount Scenery to the peak of this extinct volcano.

We stop at the village of Hell's Gate while Ronald checks the public information board to see if an invitation for Sunday's public talk is still posted. We are glad to see that it is. He hops back in the truck, and we continue our climb to the island's largest hamlet, Windwardside. As its name suggests, this picturesque village is located on the windward side of the island, situated some 1,300 feet above sea level. As we pull into the driveway of Ron's cottage, we see a colorful sign on the front porch identifying it as a Kingdom Hall of Jehovah's Witnesses.

During lunch I raise the question that has prompted our visit, "How did you come to be a Kingdom proclaimer on Saba?"

"When construction on the Puerto Rico branch of Jehovah's Witnesses ended in 1993," says Ron, "my wife and I were interested in remaining in a foreign assignment. Earlier, we had visited Saba with another pioneer couple and had learned that there were 1,400 inhabitants but no Witnesses. So we spoke to the Puerto Rico Branch Committee about our moving here.

"One thing led to another, and we finally received approval to relocate. Sadly, two years later my wife became seriously ill, and we returned to California. Following her death, I came back to Saba. You see, I don't like to start something and not finish it."

House-to-House Witnessing on Saba

The living room of Ron's one-hundred-year-old house doubles as a Kingdom Hall.* As we enjoy breakfast and prepare to go into the ministry, rain from a passing cloud dampens the open-air kitchen. After breakfast, we leave under scattered clouds for a morning of door-to-door witnessing in The Bottom. At each home, Ron greets the householder by name. Our discussion focuses on a recent local news event. Most people are familiar with Ron and his ministry, and many readily accept Bible literature.

Keeping a record of those who are interested in the Kingdom message can be a challenge if you are not acquainted with the villagers. Why? Because "the law requires that all homes are painted the same color," says Ron. Sure enough, I look around and observe that all the houses on Saba are white with red roofs.

After concluding our Bible discussion, we invite the householder to attend the public Bible talk held on Sunday at the Kingdom Hall. When Ron is at home on the island, he gives a public talk every week. Presently, 17 Bible studies are conducted on Saba. Twenty people attended the Memorial of Christ's death in 2004. And while that number may seem quite small, it represents 1 percent of Saba's entire population!

Indeed, Jehovah's Witnesses have spared no effort to reach as many people as possible with God's message of salvation. Whether it is a tiny island like Saba or an entire continent, Jehovah's Witnesses are faithfully carrying out the commission to "make disciples of people of all the nations."—Matthew 28:19.

Sadly, our visit has come to an end. As we board our plane, we wave farewell. We will always remember our visit to Saba and the time we spent climbing to The Bottom!

---

* On September 28, 2003, volunteers from Florida, U.S.A., went to Saba and remodeled a building nearby, which now serves as the Kingdom Hall.

CHRISTIANS—BE PROUD OF WHO YOU ARE!

"He that boasts, let him boast in Jehovah."—1 CORINTHIANS 1:31.

"APATHEISM." A commentator on religious affairs recently used that word to describe the stance many people maintain toward their faith. He explained: "The greatest development in modern religion is not a religion at all—it's an attitude best described as 'apatheism.' " Elaborating, he defined apatheism as "a disinclination to care all that much about one's own religion." Many people, he observed, "believe in God . . . ; they just don't care much about him."

² This slide toward apathy is not surprising to students of the Bible. (Luke 18:8) And when it comes to religion in general, such disinterest is to be expected. False religion has misled and disappointed mankind for so long. (Revelation 17:15, 16) For genuine Christians, however, the pervasive spirit of halfheartedness and lack of zeal presents a danger. We cannot afford to become nonchalant about our faith and lose our zeal for serving God and for Bible truth. Jesus warned against such lukewarmness when he cautioned first-century Christians living in Laodicea: "You are neither cold nor hot. I wish you were cold or else hot. . . . You are lukewarm."—Revelation 3:15-18.

Seeing Who We Are

³ To fight spiritual apathy, Christians need to have a clear view of who they are, and they must take reasonable pride in their distinct identity. As servants of Jehovah and disciples of Christ, we can find in the Bible descriptions of who we are. We are "witnesses" of Jehovah, "God's fellow workers," as we actively share the "good news" with others. (Isaiah 43:10; 1 Corinthians 3:9; Matthew 24:14) We are people who "love one another." (John 13: 34) True Christians are individuals who "through use have their perceptive powers trained to distinguish both right and wrong." (Hebrews 5:14) We are "illuminators in the world." (Philippians 2:15) We strive to "maintain [our] conduct fine among the nations."—1 Peter 2:12; 2 Peter 3:11, 14.

⁴ True worshipers of Jehovah also know what they are not. "They are no part of the world," just as their Leader, Jesus Christ, was no part of the world. (John 17:16) They remain separate from "the nations," which "are in darkness mentally, and alienated

---

1. What trend is evident in the attitude of people toward religion?

2. (a) Why is it not surprising that people have become spiritually apathetic? (b) What danger does indifference pose to true Christians?

3. In what aspects of their identity can Christians take pride?

4. How can a worshiper of Jehovah determine what he is not?

from the life that belongs to God." (Ephesians 4:17, 18) As a result, Jesus' followers "repudiate ungodliness and worldly desires and . . . live with soundness of mind and righteousness and godly devotion amid this present system of things."—Titus 2:12.

5 Our clear view of our identity and our relationship with the Sovereign Ruler of the universe motivates us to "boast in Jehovah." (1 Corinthians 1:31) What kind of boasting is that? As true Christians, we are proud to have Jehovah as our God. We follow the admonition: "Let the one bragging about himself brag about himself because of this very thing, the having of insight and the having of knowledge of me, that I am Jehovah, the One exercising loving-kindness, justice and righteousness in the earth." (Jeremiah 9:24) We "boast" in the privilege of knowing God and of being used by him to assist others.

The Challenge

6 Admittedly, maintaining a sharp perception of our distinct identity as Christians is not always easy. A young man who was raised as a Christian recalled that he for a while had experienced a state of spiritual weakness: "At times, I felt I didn't know why I was one of Jehovah's Witnesses. I had been around the truth since infancy. Sometimes I felt that this was just another mainstream, accepted religion." Others may have let their identity be shaped by the entertainment world, mass media, and the current ungodly outlook on life. (Ephesians 2:2, 3) Some Christians may occasionally go through periods of self-doubt and of a reassessment of their values and goals.

---

5. What is implied by the admonition to "boast in Jehovah"?
6. Why do some find it challenging to maintain a clear perception of their identity as Christians?

7 Is a degree of careful self-examination entirely inappropriate? No. You may recall that the apostle Paul encouraged Christians to keep examining themselves: "Keep testing whether you are in the faith, keep proving what you yourselves are." (2 Corinthians 13:5) The apostle was here promoting a wholesome endeavor to spot any spiritual weaknesses that may have developed, with the objective of taking the necessary steps to rectify them. A Christian, in testing whether he is in the faith, must determine whether his words and deeds harmonize with his profession of faith. However, if misdirected, self-examination that prompts us to look for our "identity" or to search for answers outside our relationship with Jehovah or the Christian congregation will prove to be pointless and can be spiritually fatal.* Never would we want to 'experience shipwreck concerning our faith'!—1 Timothy 1:19.

We Are Not Immune to Challenges

8 Should Christians who occasionally experience self-doubt feel that they have failed? Of course not! Indeed, they can find comfort in knowing that such feelings are not new. Faithful witnesses of God in times past experienced them. Take, for example, Moses, who displayed extraordinary faith, loyalty, and devotion. When assigned a seemingly overwhelming task, Moses diffidently asked: "Who am I?" (Exodus 3:11) Apparently, the answer he had in mind was, 'I am a nobody!' or 'I am incapable!' Several

---

* Here reference is made solely to our spiritual identity. For a few, mental-health issues may necessitate professional treatment.

---

7. (a) What kind of self-examination is fitting for servants of God? (b) Where does danger lurk?
8, 9. (a) How did Moses express his feelings of self-doubt? (b) How did Jehovah respond to Moses' reservations? (c) How are you affected by Jehovah's reassurances?

aspects of Moses' background might have caused him to feel inadequate: He belonged to a nation of slaves. He had been rejected by the Israelites. He was not a fluent speaker. (Exodus 1:13, 14; 2:11-14; 4:10) He was a shepherd, an occupation abhorred by the Egyptians. (Genesis 46:34) No wonder he felt unfit to become the liberator of God's enslaved people!

9 Jehovah reassured Moses by giving him two powerful promises: "I shall prove to be with you, and this is the sign for you that it is I who have sent you: After you have brought the people out of Egypt, you people will serve the true God on this mountain." (Exodus 3:12) God was telling his hesitant servant that He would constantly be with him. In addition, Jehovah was indicating that he would without fail deliver his people. Down through the centuries, God has provided similar promises of support. For instance, through Moses he said to the nation of Israel as they were about to enter the Promised Land: "Be courageous and strong. . . . Jehovah your God is the one marching with you. He will neither desert you nor leave you entirely." (Deuteronomy 31:6) Jehovah also assured Joshua: "Nobody will take a firm stand before you all the days of your life. . . . I shall prove to be with you. I shall neither desert you nor leave you entirely." (Joshua 1:5) And he promises Christians: "I will by no means leave you nor by any means forsake you." (Hebrews 13:5) Having such strong support should make us feel proud to be Christians!

10 About five centuries after Moses, a faithful Levite named Asaph wrote candidly regarding his doubts about the value of pursuing an upright course. While he struggled with serving God despite trials and temptations, Asaph saw some who scoffed at God

For a time, Moses had feelings of self-doubt

grow more powerful and prosperous. How was Asaph affected? "As for me, my feet had almost turned aside," he admitted. "My steps had nearly been made to slip. For I became envious of the boasters, when I would see the very peace of wicked people." He began to doubt the value of being a worshiper of Jehovah. "Surely it is in vain that I have cleansed my heart and that I wash my hands in innocence itself," Asaph thought. "And I came to be plagued all day long."—Psalm 73: 2, 3, 13, 14.

11 How did Asaph deal with these unsettling emotions? Did he deny them? No. He expressed them in prayer to God, as we see in the 73rd Psalm. The turning point for Asaph was a visit to the temple sanctuary. While there, he came to the realization that devotion to God is still the best course. With his spiritual appreciation renewed, he understood that Jehovah hated badness and that in due time the wicked would be punished. (Psalm 73:17-19) In the

10, 11. How was the Levite Asaph helped to maintain the correct attitude toward the value of his service to Jehovah?

process, Asaph strengthened his sense of identity as a privileged servant of Jehovah. He said to God: "I am constantly with you; you have taken hold of my right hand. With your counsel you will lead me, and afterward you will take me even to glory." (Psalm 73:23, 24) Asaph came to take pride in his God again.—Psalm 34:2.

They Had a Strong Sense of Identity

¹² One way to strengthen our sense of Christian identity is to examine and imitate the faith of loyal worshipers, who despite adversity took real pride in their relationship with God. Consider Joseph, the son of Jacob. At a tender age, he was treacherously sold as a slave and taken to Egypt, hundreds of miles away from his God-fearing father and a world away from the warm, supportive atmosphere of his home. While in Egypt, Joseph had no human to turn to for godly

---

12, 13. Give examples of Bible characters who took pride in their relationship with God.

advice, and he had to face challenging situations that tested his morals and reliance on God. However, he clearly made a conscious effort to retain a strong sense of identity as a servant of God, and he remained faithful to what he knew was right. He was proud to be a worshiper of Jehovah even in a hostile environment, and he did not shy away from expressing how he felt.—Genesis 39:7-10.

¹³ Eight centuries later, a captive Israelite girl who became a slave of the Syrian general Naaman did not forget her identity as a worshiper of Jehovah. When the opportunity arose, she boldly gave a fine witness for Jehovah when she identified Elisha as a prophet

Many ancient servants of Jehovah took pride in their distinct identity

of the true God. (2 Kings 5:1-19) Years after that, young King Josiah, despite being in a corrupt environment, enacted long-term religious reforms, repaired God's temple, and led the nation back to Jehovah. He took pride in his faith and worship. (2 Chronicles, chapters 34, 35) Daniel and his three Hebrew companions in Babylon never forgot their identity as servants of Jehovah, and even under pressure and temptation, they kept their integrity. Clearly, they were proud to be servants of Jehovah.—Daniel 1:8-20.

Be Proud of Who You Are

¹⁴ These servants of God were successful because they nurtured a wholesome sense of pride in their standing before God. What about us today? What is involved in boasting in our Christian identity?

¹⁵ Primarily, this includes a deep appreciation for being one of Jehovah's name people, having his blessing and approval. God has no doubts about who belong to him. The apostle Paul, who lived in an era of considerable religious confusion, wrote: "Jehovah knows those who belong to him." (2 Timothy 2:19; Numbers 16:5) Jehovah takes pride in those "who belong to him." He declares: "He that is touching you is touching my eyeball." (Zechariah 2:8) Clear-

---

14, 15. What is involved in boasting in our Christian identity?

ly, Jehovah loves us. In return, our relationship with him should be based on deep love for him. Paul noted: "If anyone loves God, this one is known by him."—1 Corinthians 8:3.

¹⁶ Young people who have been raised as Jehovah's Witnesses do well to examine whether their Christian identity is becoming stronger based on a personal relationship with God. They cannot depend merely on the faith of their parents. Regarding each servant of God, Paul wrote: "To his own master he stands or falls." Thus, Paul continues: "Each of us will render an account for himself to God." (Romans 14:4, 12) Obviously, a halfhearted continuation of family tradition cannot sustain an intimate, long-term relationship with Jehovah.

¹⁷ Throughout history, there has been a succession of witnesses of Jehovah. It extends from the faithful man Abel—about 60 centuries ago—to the "great crowd" of modern Witnesses and on to throngs of worshipers of Jehovah who will enjoy an endless future. (Revelation 7:9; Hebrews 11:4) We are the latest of this long line of faithful worshipers. What a rich spiritual heritage we have!

¹⁸ Our Christian identity also includes the set of values, qualities, standards, and characteristics that identify us as Christians. It is "The Way," the only successful way of life and of pleasing God. (Acts 9:2; Ephesians 4: 22-24) Christians "make sure of all things" and "hold fast to what is fine"! (1 Thessalonians 5:21) We have a clear understanding of the vast difference between Christianity and the world that is alienated from God. Jehovah leaves no room for any ambiguity between true worship and false. Through his

---

16, 17. Why can Christians, young and old, take pride in their spiritual heritage?
18. How do our values and standards set us apart from the world?

prophet Malachi, he declared: "You people will again certainly see the distinction between a righteous one and a wicked one, between one serving God and one who has not served him."—Malachi 3:18.

¹⁹ Since boasting in Jehovah is so important in this confused and disoriented world, what can assist us to maintain a wholesome pride in our God and a strong sense of Christian identity? Helpful suggestions are found in the next article. While considering these, you can be certain of this: True Christians will never become victims of "apatheism."

19. What will true Christians never become?

SAFEGUARDING OUR CHRISTIAN IDENTITY

"'You are my witnesses,' is the utterance of Jehovah."—ISAIAH 43:10.

WHEN you are at a Kingdom Hall, take a good look around you. Whom do you see at this place of worship? You might see earnest young people attentively absorbing Scriptural wisdom. (Psalm 148:12, 13) Likely, you will also observe family heads striving to please God while living in a world that degrades family life. Perhaps you will catch sight of dear older ones, steadfastly living up to their dedication to Jehovah despite the maladies of advanced age. (Proverbs 16:31)

All love Jehovah deeply. And he saw fit to draw them into a relationship with him. "No man can come to me," affirmed the Son of God, "unless the Father, who sent me, draws him."—John 6:37, 44, 65.

² Are we not delighted to be part of a people who have Jehovah's approval and blessing? Yet, maintaining a strong sense of our identity as Christians in these "critical times hard to deal with" is a challenge. (2 Timothy 3:1) This is especially true of young ones who are

1. What kind of people does Jehovah draw to himself?

2, 3. Why can it be challenging to maintain a strong sense of Christian identity?

being raised in Christian families. "Though I was attending Christian meetings," admitted one such youth, "I had no clear spiritual goals and, frankly, no crystallized desire to serve Jehovah."

³ Some, while sincerely desiring to serve Jehovah, might be distracted by intense peer pressure, worldly influences, and sinful tendencies. When pressure is exerted on us, it may gradually cause us to lose our Christian identity. For example, many in the world today view the Bible's standards of morality as old-fashioned or unrealistic in our modern world. (1 Peter 4:4) Some feel that it is not vital to worship God in the way that he directs. (John 4:24) In his letter to the Ephesians, Paul speaks of the world as having a "spirit," or dominant attitude. (Ephesians 2:2) That spirit exerts pressure on people to conform to the thinking of a society that does not know Jehovah.

⁴ However, as dedicated servants of Jehovah, we realize that it would be tragic for any of us—young or old—to lose our Christian identification. A wholesome sense of Christian identity can be based only on Jehovah's standards and his expectations for us. After all, we are created in his image. (Genesis 1:26; Micah 6:8) The Bible likens our clear identification as Christians to outer garments, worn for all to see. Regarding our times, Jesus warned: "Look! I am coming as a thief. Happy is the one that stays awake and keeps his outer garments, that he may not walk naked and people look upon his shamefulness."*

(Revelation 16:15) We do not want to shed our Christian qualities and standards of conduct and allow Satan's world to mold us. If that was to happen, we would lose these "outer garments." Such a situation would be regrettable and shameful.

⁵ A strong sense of Christian identity greatly affects the direction one's life takes. How so? If a worshiper of Jehovah was to lose his clear sense of identity, he might end up unfocused, without well-defined direction or goals. The Bible repeatedly warns against such an indecisive state. "He who doubts," cautioned the disciple James, "is like a wave of the sea driven by the wind and blown about. In fact, let not that man suppose that he will receive anything from Jehovah; he is an indecisive man, unsteady in all his ways." —James 1:6-8; Ephesians 4:14; Hebrews 13:9.

⁶ How can we safeguard our Christian identity? What can help us to enhance our awareness of our great privilege to be worshipers of the Most High? Please consider the following ways.

---

* These words may allude to the duties of the officer of the temple mount in Jerusalem. During the night watches, he went through the temple to see whether its Levite guards were awake or asleep at their posts. Any guard found sleeping was struck with a stick, and his outer garments might be burned as shameful punishment.

---

4. How did Jesus emphasize the need for us to safeguard our clear identification as Christians?

5, 6. Why is spiritual stability vital?

Firmly Establish Your Christian Identity

7 *Continually reaffirm your relationship with Jehovah.* The most precious possession a Christian has is his personal relationship with God. (Psalm 25:14; Proverbs 3:32) If we begin to have disturbing questions about our Christian identity, it is time to examine closely the quality and the depth of this relationship. The psalmist appropriately pleaded: "Examine me, O Jehovah, and put me to the test; refine my kidneys and my heart." (Psalm 26:2) Why is such an examination vital? Because we ourselves cannot be reliable assessors of our own deepest motives and innermost inclinations. Only Jehovah is able to fathom our inner person—our motives, thoughts, and emotions.—Jeremiah 17:9, 10.

8 By asking Jehovah to examine us, we invite him to test us. He may allow situations to develop that reveal our true motives and heart condition. (Hebrews 4:12, 13; James 1: 22-25) We should welcome such tests because they give us an opportunity to demonstrate the depth of our loyalty to Jehovah. Such can show whether we are "complete and sound in all respects, not lacking in anything." (James 1:2-4) And in the process, we can grow spiritually.—Ephesians 4:22-24.

9 *Prove Bible truth to yourself.* Our sense of identity as servants of Jehovah can weaken if it is not solidly based on knowledge of the Scriptures. (Philippians 1:9, 10) Every Christian—young or old—needs to prove to his own satisfaction that what he believes is indeed the truth as found in the Bible. Paul urged fellow believers: "Make sure of all things; hold fast to what is fine." (1 Thessalonians 5:21) Young Christians who belong to

God-fearing families must realize that they cannot live off the faith of their parents. Solomon's own father, David, exhorted him to "*know* the God of your father and serve him with a complete heart." (1 Chronicles 28:9) It would not be enough for young Solomon to watch how his own father built faith in Jehovah. He had to get to know Jehovah for himself, and he did. He beseeched God: "Give me now wisdom and knowledge that I may go out before this people and that I may come in."—2 Chronicles 1:10.

10 Strong faith is built on knowledge. "Faith follows the thing heard," stated Paul. (Romans 10:17) What did he mean by that? He meant that by feeding on God's Word, we build our faith and confidence in Jehovah, his promises, and his organization. Asking honest questions about the Bible can lead to reassuring answers. Furthermore, at Romans 12:2, we find the advice of Paul: "Prove to yourselves the good and acceptable and perfect will of God." Just how can we achieve that? By gaining "the accurate knowledge of the truth." (Titus 1:1) Jehovah's spirit can help us to comprehend even difficult subjects. (1 Corinthians 2:11, 12) We should pray for God's help when we are having problems understanding something. (Psalm 119: 10, 11, 27) Jehovah wants us to understand his Word, believe it, and obey it. He welcomes honest questions asked with the right motive.

Be Determined to Please God

11 *Seek to please God, not man.* It is only natural to define our identity in part by belonging to a group. Everyone needs friends, and being included makes us feel good. During adolescence—as well as later in life—peer

---

7. Why is it profitable to plead with Jehovah to examine us?
8. (a) How can testing by Jehovah benefit us? (b) How have you been helped to make progress as a Christian?
9. Is proving Bible truth to ourselves optional? Explain.

10. Why is there nothing wrong with asking honest questions with the right motive?
11. (a) What natural desire can ensnare us? (b) How can we muster the courage to withstand peer pressure?

pressure can be powerful, generating a desperate desire to imitate or please others. But friends and peers do not always have our best interests at heart. Sometimes they only want company in doing what is wrong. (Proverbs 1:11-19) When a Christian succumbs to negative peer pressure, he usually tries to conceal his identity. (Psalm 26:4) "Do not model yourselves on the behaviour of the world around you," warned the apostle Paul. (Romans 12:2, *The Jerusalem Bible*) Jehovah provides the inner strength we need in order to combat any outside pressure to conform. —Hebrews 13:6.

¹² When outside pressure threatens to damage our sense of Christian identity, it is good to remember that our loyalty to God is far more important than public opinion or the trends of the majority. The words of Exodus 23:2 serve as a safe principle: "You must not follow after the crowd for evil ends." When the majority of fellow Israelites doubted Jehovah's ability to fulfill His promises, Caleb staunchly refused to go along with the majority. He was certain that God's promises were trustworthy, and he was richly rewarded for his stand. (Numbers 13:30; Joshua 14:6-11) Are you similarly willing to resist the pressure of popular opinion in order to safeguard your relationship with God?

¹³ *Make your Christian identity known.* The saying that the best defense is a good offense is true as we stand up for our Christian identity. When confronted with opposition to their efforts to do Jehovah's will in the days of Ezra, faithful Israelites stated: "We are the servants of the God of the heavens and the earth." (Ezra 5:11) If we are affected by the reactions and criticism of hostile people,

we can become paralyzed with fear. A policy of pleasing everyone will undermine our effectiveness. So do not be intimidated. It is always good to make it clearly known to others that you are one of Jehovah's Witnesses. In a respectful but firm way, you can explain to others your values, your beliefs, and your position as a Christian. Let others know that you have resolved to maintain Jehovah's high standards on issues of morality. Make it clear that your Christian integrity is not negotiable. Show that you are proud of your moral standards. (Psalm 64:10) Standing out as a steadfast Christian can fortify you, protect you, and even move some to inquire about Jehovah and his people.

¹⁴ Yes, some might ridicule or oppose you. (Jude 18) If others do not respond favorably

---

12. What principle and what example can fortify us to stand our ground when our trust in God is involved?
13. Why is it the course of wisdom to make known our identity as Christians?

14. Should ridicule or opposition discourage us? Explain.

to your efforts to explain your values to them, do not get discouraged. (Ezekiel 3:7, 8) No matter how determined you are, you are never going to convince people who have no desire to be convinced. Remember Pharaoh. No plague or miracle—not even the personal loss of his firstborn—was able to persuade Pharaoh that Moses was speaking on behalf of Jehovah. Therefore, do not let fear of man paralyze you. Trust and faith in God can help us overcome fear.—Proverbs 3:5, 6; 29:25.

Immersing ourselves in Christian activities can enhance our Christian identity

Look to the Past, Build for the Future

¹⁵ *Cherish your spiritual heritage.* In the light of God's Word, Christians will benefit from pondering their rich spiritual heritage. This inheritance includes the truth of Jehovah's Word, the hope of everlasting life, and the honor to represent God as proclaimers of the good news. Can you see your individual place among his Witnesses, in the privileged group of people who have been commissioned with the lifesaving work of Kingdom preaching? Remember, it is none other than Jehovah who affirms: "You are my witnesses."—Isaiah 43:10.

¹⁶ You can ask yourself such questions as: 'How precious is this spiritual heritage to me? Do I prize it sufficiently to make the doing of God's will the top priority in my life? Is my

15, 16. (a) What is our spiritual heritage? (b) How can we benefit from pondering our spiritual heritage in the light of God's Word?

appreciation of it strong enough to fortify me to resist any temptation that might lead to my forfeiting it?' Our spiritual heritage can also infuse in us a deep sense of spiritual security that can be enjoyed only within Jehovah's organization. (Psalm 91:1, 2) Reviewing remarkable events from the modern-day history of Jehovah's organization can impress upon us that no person or thing can eradicate Jehovah's people from the face of the earth. —Isaiah 54:17; Jeremiah 1:19.

¹⁷ Of course, we cannot depend solely on our spiritual heritage. Each of us must develop an intimate relationship with God. After Paul had worked hard to build the faith of Christians in Philippi, he wrote to them: "Consequently, my beloved ones, in the way that you have always obeyed, not during my presence only, but now much more readily during my absence, keep working out your own salvation with fear and trembling." (Philippians 2:12) We cannot rely on someone else for our salvation.

¹⁸ *Immerse yourself in Christian activities.* It has been observed that "work has been a shaper of personal identity." Christians today have been commissioned to do the vital work of preaching the good news of God's estab-

---

17. What more is needed than merely relying on our spiritual heritage?
18. How can Christian activities enhance our sense of Christian identity?

Do You Recall?

- Why is it vital for Christians to safeguard their spiritual identity?

- How can we firmly establish our Christian identity?

- When faced with the question of whom to please, what factors can help us make the right decision?

- How can a strong sense of identity shape our future as Christians?

lished Kingdom. Paul declared: "Forasmuch as I am, in reality, an apostle to the nations, I glorify my ministry." (Romans 11:13) Our preaching work distinguishes us from the world, and our participation in it enhances our Christian identity. Immersing ourselves in other theocratic activities, such as Christian meetings, programs for building places of worship, efforts to help those in need, and the like, can deepen our sense of identity as Christians.—Galatians 6:9, 10; Hebrews 10: 23, 24.

Clear Identity, Tangible Blessings

¹⁹ Take a moment to contemplate the many benefits and advantages we enjoy because we are true Christians. We have the privilege of being personally recognized by Jehovah. The prophet Malachi said: "Those in fear of Jehovah spoke with one another, each one with his companion, and Jehovah kept paying attention and listening. And a book of remembrance began to be written up before him for those in fear of Jehovah and for those thinking upon his name." (Malachi 3:16) We can be viewed by God as his friends. (James 2:23) Our lives are adorned by a clear sense of purpose, by deep meaning, and by wholesome, productive goals. And we have been given the hope of an eternal future.—Psalm 37:9.

²⁰ Remember that your true identity and value lie in God's estimate of your worth, not in what other people may think of you. Others might appraise us according to inadequate human standards. But God's love and personal interest give us the real basis for our worth—we belong to him. (Matthew 10:29-31) In turn, our own love for God can provide us with the greatest sense of identity and the clearest direction in our lives. "If anyone loves God, this one is known by him." —1 Corinthians 8:3.

19, 20. (a) What benefits have you personally enjoyed by being a Christian? (b) What gives us the basis for our true identity?

'If You Are Impressed Into Service'

"HEY you! Stop what you're doing right now, and get over here to carry this pack for me." How do you think a busy Jew in the first century might have reacted if a Roman soldier had said that to him? In his Sermon on the Mount, Jesus recommended: "If someone under authority impresses you into service for a mile, go with him two miles." (Matthew 5:41) How would Jesus' listeners understand that counsel? And what should it mean for us today?

To get the answers, we need to know about compulsory service in ancient times. That practice was all too familiar to the inhabitants of Israel in Jesus' day.

Compulsory Service

Evidence of compulsory service (or, corvée) in the Near East dates back as far as the 18th century B.C.E. Administrative texts from the ancient Syrian city of Alalakh refer to corvée gangs conscripted by the government for personal service. In Ugarit, on the Syrian coast, tenant farmers were subject to similar duties unless granted immunity by the king.

Of course, conquered or subjugated peoples were frequently set to forced labor. Egyptian taskmasters obliged the Israelites to slave for them in making bricks. Later, the Israelites put Canaanite inhabitants of the Promised Land to slavish labor, and similar practices were continued by David and Solomon. —Exodus 1:13, 14; 2 Samuel 12:31; 1 Kings 9: 20, 21.

When the Israelites asked for a king, Samuel explained what the king's rightful due would be. He would take his subjects to serve as charioteers and horsemen, to do plowing and harvesting, to make weapons, and so on. (1 Samuel 8:4-17) However, during the construction of Jehovah's temple, while foreigners were subjected to slavish forced labor, "there were none of the sons of Israel that Solomon constituted slaves; for they were the warriors and his servants and his princes and his adjutants and chiefs of his charioteers and of his horsemen."—1 Kings 9:22.

As for the Israelites employed in building projects, 1 Kings 5:13, 14 says: "King Solomon kept bringing up those conscripted for forced labor out of all Israel; and those conscripted for forced labor amounted to thirty thousand men. And he would send them to Lebanon in shifts of ten thousand a month. For a month they would continue in Lebanon, for two months at their homes." "There can be no doubt," says one scholar, "that the Israelite and Judean kings made use of the corvée as a means of securing unpaid labor for their building activities as well as for work on the crown-lands."

The burden was heavy under Solomon. So grievous was it that when Rehoboam threatened to increase such loads, all Israel revolted and stoned the official appointed over those conscripted for forced labor. (1 Kings 12:12-18) However, the institution was not abolished. Asa, Rehoboam's grandson, summoned people of Judah to construct the cities of Geba and Mizpah, and "there was none exempt."—1 Kings 15:22.

Under Roman Domination

The Sermon on the Mount shows that first-century Jews were familiar with the possibility of being 'impressed into service.' The expression translates the Greek word *ag·ga·reu′o*, which originally related to the activity of Persian couriers. They had authority to press into service men, horses, ships, or anything else needed to expedite public business.

In Jesus' day, Israel was occupied by the Romans, who had adopted a comparable system. In the Oriental provinces, in addition to normal taxes, compulsory work could be demanded from the population on a regular or an exceptional basis. Such duties would be unpopular at best. Furthermore, unauthorized seizure of animals, drivers, or wagons for State transport was commonplace. According to historian Michael Rostovtzeff, administrators "tried to regulate and to systematize [the institution], but without success, for so long as the practice existed, it was bound to produce evil effects. Edict after edict was issued by the prefects, who honestly endeavoured to stop the arbitrariness and the oppression inherent in the system . . . But the institution remained oppressive."

"Anyone could be impressed to carry the baggage of the army for a certain distance," says one Greek scholar, and "anyone could be compelled to perform any service that the occupiers chose to lay upon him." That happened to Simon of Cyrene, whom Roman soldiers "impressed into service" to carry Jesus' torture stake.—Matthew 27:32.

Simon of Cyrene was impressed into service

Rabbinic texts too refer to this unpopular institution. For example, one rabbi was seized to transport myrtles to a palace. Laborers could be taken from employers and set to other tasks, while employers still had to pay their wages. Pack animals or oxen could be commandeered. If they were returned at all, they were unlikely to be in a condition fit for further work. You can see why seizure was synonymous with confiscation. Thus, a Jewish proverb affirmed: *"Angareia is like death."* Says one historian: "A village could be reduced to ruin by the seizure of ploughing oxen for *angareia* instead of authorized draught animals."

You can just imagine how unpopular such services were, especially since they were often imposed with arrogance and injustice. Given the hatred they nurtured for the Gentile powers that dominated them, the Jews bitterly resented the humiliation of being forced into such vexatious labor. No extant law informs us just how far a citizen could be compelled to carry a load. It is likely that many would not be willing to go one step further than the law required.

Yet, this was the institution Jesus referred to when he said: "If someone under authority impresses you into service for a mile, go with him two miles." (Matthew 5:41) On hearing that, some must have thought him unreasonable. Just what did he mean?

How Christians Should React

Put simply, Jesus was telling his listeners that if an authority compelled them into some kind of legitimate service, they should perform it willingly and without resentment. They were thus to pay "Caesar's things to Caesar" but not overlook the obligation to pay "God's things to God."—Mark 12:17.*

———
* For a full discussion of what it means for Christians to "pay back Caesar's things to Caesar, but God's things to God," see *The Watchtower*, May 1, 1996, pages 15-20.

ANCIENT MISUSE OF IMPRESSMENT

That impressment was often used as a pretext to extort services is seen from regulations to curb such abuses. In 118 B.C.E., Ptolemy Euergetes II of Egypt decreed that his officials "shall not impress any of the inhabitants of the country for private services, nor requisition (*aggareuein*) their cattle for any purpose of their own." Additionally: "No one shall requisition . . . boats for his own use on any pretext whatsoever." In an inscription dated 49 C.E., in the Temple of the Great Oasis, Egypt, Roman prefect Vergilius Capito acknowledged that soldiers had made illegal requisitions, and he established that "no one shall take or requisition . . . anything, unless he has a written authorization from me."

Moreover, the apostle Paul exhorted Christians: "Let every soul be in subjection to the superior authorities, for there is no authority except by God; the existing authorities stand placed in their relative positions by God. Therefore he who opposes the authority has taken a stand against the arrangement of God . . . If you are doing what is bad, be in fear: for it is not without purpose that it bears the sword."—Romans 13:1-4.

Jesus and Paul thus acknowledged the right of a king or a government to mete out punishment to those who violated their demands. What kind of punishment? Greek philosopher Epictetus, of the first and second centuries C.E., provides one answer: "If an unforeseen requisition arises and a soldier takes your young ass, let it go. Do not resist, do not murmur, lest you receive blows as well as lose the ass."

Many Witnesses have spent time in prison for maintaining their Christian stand

Yet, on occasion, both in ancient and in modern times, Christians have felt that they could not in good conscience comply with government demands. Sometimes the consequences have been serious. Some Christians have been sentenced to death. Others have spent many years in prison for refusing to participate in what they considered to be nonneutral activities. (Isaiah 2:4; John 17:16; 18:36) On other occasions, Christians have felt that they could comply with what was asked of them. For example, some Christians feel that they can in good conscience perform services under a civilian administration involving general work useful to the community. That might mean assisting the elderly or disabled, serving as firefighters, cleaning beaches, working in parks, forests, or libraries, and so on.

Naturally, situations vary from land to land. Therefore, in order to decide whether to comply with demands or not, each Christian must follow his Bible-trained conscience.

Going the Second Mile

The principle Jesus taught, that of being willing to carry out legitimate requests, is valid not only for governmental requirements but also in everyday human relations. It may be, for instance, that a person with authority over you asks you to do something that you would prefer not to do but that is not contrary to God's law. How will you react? You may feel that unreasonable demands are being made on your time and energies, and you may therefore react indignantly. The result may be ill will. On the other hand, if you comply sullenly, you may lose your inner peace. The solution? Do as Jesus recommended—go the second mile. Do not only what is asked of you but even more than what is asked. Do it willingly. In that frame of mind, you will no longer feel that you are being taken advantage of, yet you remain free to be master of your own actions.

"Many people go through life doing only those things they are compelled to do," notes one author. "For them life is a hard experience, and they are constantly tired. Others go beyond the call of duty and freely give themselves." In effect, many situations present the choice of going just one mile under compulsion—or two. In the first case, a person may be interested in demanding his rights. In the second, he may have his most rewarding experiences. What kind of person are you? You will probably be much happier and more productive if you can view your activities, not as mere duties or things you have to do, but as things you want to do.

And what if you are a person with authority? Clearly, it is neither loving nor Christian to use authority to force others to do unwillingly what you ask of them. "The rulers of the nations lord it over them and the great men wield authority over them," said Jesus. But that is not the Christian way. (Matthew 20:25, 26) While an authoritarian approach may get results, how much better relations will be among all involved if kind and appropriate requests are met by respectful and cheerful compliance! Yes, a readiness to go two miles instead of just one can truly enrich your life.

Questions From Readers

Did David, a man agreeable to God's own heart, treat his captives savagely, as some conclude from 2 Samuel 12:31 and 1 Chronicles 20:3?

No. David merely consigned the Ammonite captives to forced labor. David's actions have been misunderstood because of the way some Bible translations render these verses.

Describing the treatment meted out to the Ammonites, those Bible versions portray David as barbaric and cruel. For example, 2 Samuel 12:31, according to the *King James Version,* reads: "He brought forth the people that were therein, and put them under saws, and under harrows of iron, and under axes of iron, and made them pass through the brickkiln: and thus did he unto all the cities of the children of Ammon." The account at 1 Chronicles 20:3 is rendered similarly.

However, as noted by Bible scholar Samuel Rolles Driver, cruelty "is alien to all that we know of the personal character and temper of David." Thus, a comment in *The Anchor Bible* states: "David is setting up work crews of captives for the economic exploitation of the conquered territory, evidently standard practice for victorious kings." Along the same line, Adam Clarke comments: "The meaning therefore is, He made the people slaves, and employed them in sawing, making iron harrows, or mining, . . . and in hewing of wood, and making of brick. Sawing asunder, hacking, chopping, and hewing human beings, have no place in this text, no more than they had in David's conduct towards the Ammonites."

Reflecting this more accurate understanding, various modern translations make it clear that David should not be charged with inhumane treatment.* Note the rendering of the *New English Translation* (2003): "He removed the people who were in it and made them do hard labor with saws, iron picks, and iron axes, putting them to work at the brick kiln. This was his policy with all the Ammonite cities." (2 Samuel 12:31) "He took the city's residents and made them work with saws, iron picks, and axes. David did this to all the cities of the Ammonites." (1 Chronicles 20:3) The rendering of the *New World Translation* is also in keeping with the latest scholarship: "The people that were in it, he brought out that he might put them at sawing stones and at sharp instruments of iron and at axes of iron, and he made them serve at brickmaking." (2 Samuel 12:31) "The people that were in it he brought out, and he kept them employed at sawing stones and at sharp instruments of iron and at axes; and that was the way David proceeded to do to all the cities of the sons of Ammon."—1 Chronicles 20:3.

David did not subject the defeated Ammonites to barbarous torture and gruesome massacres. He did not copy the sadistic and brutal war customs of his day.

---

* By a difference of one letter, the Hebrew text can read "he put them into the saw" or "he cut (sawed) them in pieces." Moreover, the word for "brick kiln" can also mean "brick mold." Such a mold would be too narrow for anyone to pass through.

IN OUR NEXT ISSUE

The Benefits of Making Peace

———

Wise Guidance for Married Couples

———

"Faithful Under Trials"

Do You **Measure Yourself** Against Others?

WHO of us has not met a person who is better looking than we are, seems to be more popular, grasps things faster, or gets better grades in school? Maybe others have better health or a more gratifying job, are more successful, or seem to have more friends. They may have more possessions, more money, a newer car, or they may just seem to be happier. In noting such things, do we measure ourselves against others? Are comparisons inevitable? Why might a Christian want to avoid them? And how can we be content without comparing ourselves with anyone?

Why and When We May Compare

One concept of why people may compare themselves with others is that this serves to maintain or enhance their self-esteem. People are often satisfied to find that they are as successful as their peers. Another idea is that comparisons are attempts to reduce uncertainty about ourselves, to understand what we are capable of doing and what our limits are. We observe what others have achieved. If they are like us in many respects and have reached certain objectives, we might feel that we can reach similar goals.

Comparisons are most often made between people who resemble one another —who are of the same sex, of a similar age, and at a similar social level and who know one another. We are less likely to measure ourselves against someone else if the perceived disparity is great. Put another way, the average teenage girl is less likely to compare herself with a top model than with her schoolmates, and the model is unlikely to compare herself with the teenager.

In what areas do comparisons take place? Any possession or attribute considered of value in a community—be it intelligence, beauty, wealth, clothes—may be the basis for comparison. However, we tend to draw comparisons about things that interest us. We will probably not envy the size of the stamp collection of one of our acquaintances, for example, unless we are particularly interested in collecting stamps.

Comparisons elicit a whole spectrum of reactions, ranging from contentment to depression, from admiration and a desire for emulation to uneasiness or antagonism. Some of these emotions are harmful, and they are incompatible with Christian qualities.

Competitive Comparisons

Many who strive to come off "winners" in comparisons display a competitive spirit. They want to be better than others, and they are not content until they feel that they are. It is not pleasant to be around such individuals. Friendships with them are strained, relationships tense. Not only do such people lack humility but they usually fail to apply the Bible's counsel about loving their fellowman, since their attitude can easily arouse in others feelings of inferiority and humiliation.—Matthew 18: 1-5; John 13:34, 35.

Making people feel that they are "losers" injures them in a sense. According to one writer, "our failures are all the more painful when it appears that people who are in the same situation as we are have procured the possessions that we want." A competitive spirit thus provokes envy, resentment, and displeasure toward someone because of his belongings, prosperity, position, reputation, advantages, and so on. This leads to more competition—a vicious circle. The Bible condemns "stirring up competition." —Galatians 5:26.

By degrading the achievements of rivals, envious ones attempt to save their own injured self-esteem. Such reactions may seem petty, but if not recognized and checked, they can lead to malicious wrongdoing.

Consider two Bible accounts in which envy was a factor.

During his residence among the Philistines, Isaac was blessed with "flocks of sheep and herds of cattle and a large body of servants, so that the Philistines began to envy him." They reacted by stopping up the wells dug by Isaac's father, Abraham, and their king asked Isaac to leave the area. (Genesis 26:1-3, 12-16) Their envy was spiteful and destructive. They just could not bear Isaac's enjoyment of prosperity in their midst any longer.

Centuries later, David distinguished himself on the battlefield. His feats were celebrated by the women of Israel, who sang: "Saul has struck down his thousands, and David his tens of thousands." Though he was receiving a measure of praise, Saul considered that comparison to be demeaning, and envy stirred in his heart. From then on, he nurtured ill will toward David. He soon made the first of several attempts to kill David. What wickedness can spring from envy!—1 Samuel 18:6-11.

So if measuring ourselves against others —their feats or advantages—stimulates feelings akin to envy or competitiveness, beware! These are negative emotions, incompatible with God's thinking. But before examining how such attitudes can be resisted, let us consider something else that generates comparisons.

Self-Evaluation and Contentment

'Am I intelligent, attractive, competent, in good physical shape, authoritative, lovable? And to what extent?' We rarely stand in front of a mirror asking things like these. Yet, according to one writer, "implicitly, such questions often cross our mind and tacitly elicit answers that are more or less satisfying." A person who is not sure of what he can achieve might muse about these things without any competitive urge or tinge of envy. He is simply evaluating himself. There is nothing necessarily wrong with that. The right way to do this, however, is not by comparing ourselves with others.

We have different abilities, depending on a variety of factors. There will always be some who seem to be doing better than we are. Hence, rather than observing them enviously, we should gauge our performance in relation to God's righteous standards, which provide a sure guide of what is right and good. Jehovah is interested in what we are individually. He does not need to compare us with anybody. The apostle Paul advises us: "Let each one prove what his own work is, and then he will have cause for exultation in regard to himself alone, and not in comparison with the other person."—Galatians 6:4.

Combating Envy

Because all humans are imperfect, vigorous and protracted efforts may be necessary to combat envy. It is one thing to know that the Scriptures tell us: "In showing honor to one another take the lead," but it is quite another to do it. Paul recognized his own inclination toward sin. To fight it, he had to "pummel [his] body and lead it as a slave." (Romans 12:10; 1 Corinthians 9:27) For us, that may mean resisting competitive thoughts, replacing them with positive ones. We need to pray, asking Jehovah to help us "not to think more of [ourselves] than it is necessary to think."—Romans 12:3.

Bible study and meditation also help. Think, for instance, of the future Paradise God promises. Then all will have peace, good health, abundant food, comfortable homes, and satisfying work. (Psalm 46:8, 9; 72:7, 8, 16; Isaiah 65:21-23) Will anyone feel the urge to compete? Hardly. There will be no reason for doing so. True, Jehovah has not provided every detail of what life will be like then, but we may reasonably suppose that all will be able to pursue interests and skills that appeal to them. One may study astronomy, another design beautiful fabrics. Why would one envy the other? The activities of our fellows will be a stimulus, not a cause for resentment. Such feelings will be things of the past.

If that is the life we desire, should we not strive to nurture the same attitude now? We already enjoy a spiritual paradise, free from many problems of the world around us. Since there will be no competitive spirit in God's new world, there really is reason to avoid it now.

Is it wrong, then, to compare ourselves with others? Or are there times when that may be appropriate?

Appropriate Comparisons

Many comparisons have led to bitter or depressive reactions, but they need not always do so. In this connection, note the apostle Paul's advice: "Be imitators of those who through faith and patience inherit the promises." (Hebrews 6:12) Striving to cultivate qualities like those of Jehovah's faithful servants of ancient times can be productive. Granted, that may involve some comparisons. Yet, it can help us to see examples that we can emulate and areas where we need to improve.

Consider Jonathan. In a sense, he had reason to be envious. As the eldest son of King Saul of Israel, Jonathan may once have expected to become king, but Jehovah chose a man some 30 years his junior, young David. Instead of harboring a grudge, Jonathan distinguished himself in unselfish friendship and support for David as Jehovah's king-designate. Jonathan was a truly spiritual man. (1 Samuel 19:1-4) Unlike his father, who saw David as a rival, Jonathan recognized Jehovah's hand in matters and submitted to His will; he did not compare himself with David, asking, "Why David and not me?"

Among fellow Christians, we should never feel threatened, as if others are trying to outdo us or take our place. Rivalry is inappropriate. Mature Christians are characterized by cooperation, unity, and love, not competition. "Love is envy's great enemy," says sociologist Francesco Alberoni. "If we love someone, we want what is good for him, and we are happy when he is successful and happy." So if someone else in the Christian congregation is chosen for a certain privilege, the loving thing would be to be content with that. That is the way Jonathan was. Like him, we will be blessed if we support those faithfully serving in responsible positions in Jehovah's organization.

The excellent example set by fellow Christians may properly be admired. Balanced comparisons with them can spur us on to healthy imitation of their faith. (He-

Jonathan never viewed the younger David as a rival

brews 13:7) But if we are not careful, emulation can turn into competition. If we feel outdone by someone whom we admire and we try to denigrate or criticize him, emulation would be degraded to envy.

No imperfect human offers an ideal model. Thus, the Scriptures say: "Become imitators of God, as beloved children." Also, "Christ suffered for you, leaving you a model for you to follow his steps closely." (Ephesians 5:1, 2; 1 Peter 2:21) The attributes of Jehovah and Jesus—their love, warmth, empathy, and humility—should be what we strive to imitate. We should take time to measure ourselves against their qualities, purposes, and ways of doing things. Such comparison can enrich our lives, providing sure direction, stability, and security, and can help us to attain to the stature of mature Christian men and women. (Ephesians 4:13) If we concentrate on doing our best to imitate their perfect example, we will surely be less inclined to compare ourselves with fellow humans.

ACCORDING to estimates by the World Food Programme, a United Nations agency for the fight against hunger, 800 million people—many of them children—are at starvation's door. Recently, that agency said that resources and attention that many developed nations could have applied to this situation were monopolized by other problems, such as terrorism. The spread of infectious diseases has intensified the problem. The agency's *Global School Feeding Report* said about African countries where AIDS is rampant: "An entire generation of parents is being wiped out. The children they leave behind are often left to fend for themselves, most lacking the basic farming know-how and life skills that typically pass from one generation to another."

The World Food Programme is promoting an initiative that aims to serve at least one meal a day in schools. The idea is not only to reduce hunger but also to activate through regular education other programs designed to prevent HIV/AIDS among youngsters.

Where the initiative has been implemented, children have received nourishment, training in personal hygiene, and other assistance. It has also been observed that where behavior is modified, HIV/AIDS infection rates decline.

Sadly, the results of human efforts are often only partial and not decisive. But the Bible makes a comforting promise concerning a permanent solution to the problem of hunger. "There will come to be plenty of grain on the earth," says Psalm 72:16. Under God's Kingdom, people will be able to say of Jehovah God: "You have turned your attention to the earth, that you may give it abundance . . . You prepare their grain, for that is the way you prepare the earth."—Psalm 65:9.

WFP/Y. Yuge

Who Will Feed the World?

MARCH 1, 2005

THE WATCHTOWER
ANNOUNCING JEHOVAH'S KINGDOM

How Can You Make Peace With Others?

THE WATCHTOWER®
ANNOUNCING JEHOVAH'S KINGDOM

March 1, 2005   Average Printing Each Issue: 26,439,000   Vol. 126, No. 5

THE PURPOSE OF *THE WATCHTOWER* is to exalt Jehovah God as Sovereign Lord of the universe. It keeps watch on world events as these fulfill Bible prophecy. It comforts all peoples with the good news that God's Kingdom will soon destroy those who oppress their fellowmen and that it will turn the earth into a paradise. It encourages faith in God's now-reigning King, Jesus Christ, whose shed blood opens the way for mankind to gain eternal life. *The Watchtower,* published by Jehovah's Witnesses continuously since 1879, is nonpolitical. It adheres to the Bible as its authority.

IN THIS ISSUE

3   Wars With Words—Why Are They Hurtful?

4   The Benefits of Making Peace

8   "Faithful Under Trials"

10   Marriage Can Succeed in Today's World

15   Wise Guidance for Married Couples

21   We Used Our Changing Circumstances to Witness Far and Wide

26   Jehovah's Word Is Alive—Highlights From the Book of Ruth

30   2005 "Godly Obedience" District Convention Locations

32   Good Conduct 'Adorns the Teaching of God'

WATCHTOWER STUDIES

APRIL 4-10:
Marriage Can Succeed in Today's World.
Page 10. Songs to be used: 173, 89.

APRIL 11-17:
Wise Guidance for Married Couples.
Page 15. Songs to be used: 117, 35.

Publication of *The Watchtower* is part of a worldwide Bible educational work supported by voluntary donations.

Unless otherwise indicated, Scripture quotations are from the modern-language *New World Translation of the Holy Scriptures—With References.*

The Watchtower (ISSN 0043-1087) is published semimonthly by Watchtower Bible and Tract Society of New York, Inc.; M. H. Larson, President; G. F. Simonis, Secretary-Treasurer; 25 Columbia Heights, Brooklyn, NY 11201-2483. Periodicals Postage Paid at Brooklyn, NY, and at additional mailing offices. **POSTMASTER:** Send address changes to Watchtower, **Wallkill, NY 12589.**

Changes of address should reach us 30 days before your moving date. Give us your old and new address (if possible, your old address label).

Semimonthly   ENGLISH

Would you welcome more information or a free home Bible study? Please send your request to Jehovah's Witnesses, using the appropriate address below.

America, United States of: Wallkill, NY 12589. *Antigua:* Box 119, St. Johns. *Australia:* Box 280, Ingleburn, NSW 1890. *Bahamas:* Box N-1247, Nassau, N.P. *Barbados, W.I.:* Crusher Site Road, Prospect, St. James. *Britain:* The Ridgeway, London NW7 1RN. *Canada:* Box 4100, Halton Hills (Georgetown), Ontario L7G 4Y4. *Germany:* Niederselters, Am Steinfels, D-65618 Selters. *Ghana:* P. O. Box GP 760, Accra. *Guyana:* 352-360 Tyrell St., Republic Park Phase 2 EBD. *Hawaii 96819:* 2055 Kam IV Rd., Honolulu. *Hong Kong:* 4 Kent Road, Kowloon Tong. *India:* Post Box 6440, Yelahanka, Bangalore 560 064, KAR. *Ireland:* Newcastle, Greystones, Co. Wicklow. *Jamaica:* P. O. Box 103, Old Harbour, St. Catherine. *Japan:* 1271 Nakashinden, Ebina City, Kanagawa Pref., 243-0496. *Kenya:* P.O. Box 47788, GPO Nairobi 00100. *New Zealand:* P.O. Box 75-142, Manurewa. *Nigeria:* P.M.B. 1090, Benin City 300001, Edo State. *Philippines, Republic of:* P. O. Box 2044, 1060 Manila. *South Africa:* Private Bag X2067, Krugersdorp, 1740. *Trinidad and Tobago, Republic of:* Lower Rapsey Street & Laxmi Lane, Curepe. *Zambia:* Box 33459, Lusaka 10101. *Zimbabwe:* Private Bag WG-5001, Westgate.

NOW PUBLISHED IN 150 LANGUAGES. SEMIMONTHLY: Afrikaans, Albanian,* Amharic, Arabic, Bengali, Bicol, Bislama, Bulgarian, Cebuano,* Chichewa,* Chinese, Chinese (Simplified),* Cibemba,* Croatian,* Czech,*# Danish,*# Dutch,*# East Armenian, Efik,* English*#◎ (also Braille), Estonian, Ewe, Fijian, Finnish,*# French,*# Ga, Georgian, German,*# Greek,* Gujarati, Gun, Hebrew, Hiligaynon, Hindi, Hungarian,*# Igbo,* Iloko,* Indonesian, Italian,*# Japanese*# (also Braille), Kannada, Kinyarwanda, Kirundi, Korean*# (also Braille), Latvian, Lingala, Lithuanian, Luvale, Macedonian, Malagasy,* Malayalam, Maltese, Marathi, Myanmar, Nepali, New Guinea Pidgin, Norwegian,*# Pangasinan, Papiamento (Aruba), Papiamento (Curaçao), Polish,*# Portuguese*# (also Braille), Punjabi, Rarotongan, Romanian,* Russian,* Samar-Leyte, Samoan, Sango, Sepedi, Serbian, Sesotho, Shona,* Silozi, Sinhala, Slovak,* Slovenian, Solomon Islands Pidgin, Spanish,*# Srananntongo, Swahili,* Swedish,*# Tagalog,* Tamil, Telugu, Thai, Tigrinya, Tongan, Tshiluba, Tsonga, Tswana, Turkish, Twi, Ukrainian,* Urdu, Venda, Vietnamese, Wallisian, Xhosa, Yoruba,* Zulu*

MONTHLY: American Sign Language,△□ Armenian, Assamese, Azerbaijani (Roman script), Brazilian Sign Language,△ Cambodian, Chitonga, Gilbertese, Greenlandic, Haitian Creole, Hausa, Hiri Motu, Icelandic, Isoko, Kaonde, Kazakh, Kikongo, Kiluba, Kirghiz, Kwanyama/Ndonga, Luganda, Marshallese, Mauritian Creole, Mizo, Monokutuba, Moore, Niuean, Ossetian, Otetela, Palauan, Persian, Ponapean, Seychelles Creole, Tahitian, Tatar, Tiv, Trukese, Tumbuka, Tuvaluan, Umbundu, Yapese, Zande

* Study articles also available in large-print edition.
# Audiocassettes also available.
◎ CD (MP3 format) also available.
△ Videocassette
□ DVD

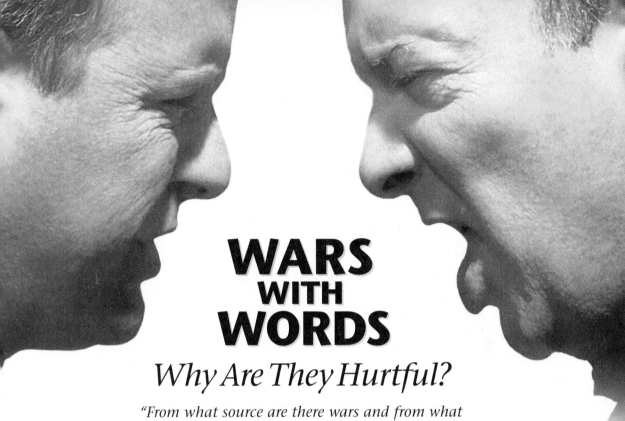

WARS
WITH
WORDS

Why Are They Hurtful?

"From what source are there wars and from what source are there fights among you?"—JAMES 4:1.

THE Bible writer James did not direct this question to the soldiers of Rome's legions, which were then waging wars of conquest; nor was he probing the motives behind the guerrilla fighting of the Jewish Sicarii, or Dagger Men, of the first century C.E. James had in mind disputes that involved as few as two people. Why? Because like wars, personal battles are destructive. Note these Bible accounts.

The sons of the patriarch Jacob hated their brother Joseph so much that they sold him into slavery. (Genesis 37:4-28) Later, Israel's King Saul tried to kill David. Why? Because he was envious of David. (1 Samuel 18:7-11; 23:14, 15) In the first century, two Christian women, Euodia and Syntyche, disturbed the peace of an entire congregation with their arguing.—Philippians 4:2.

In more recent times, men settled their differences in duels, facing off with swords or pistols. Often one of the duelists was killed or was maimed for life. Today, those who feud usually limit their weaponry to bitter, cutting words. Although blood may not be drawn, the verbal attacks injure emotions and reputations. Innocent ones often suffer in these "wars."

Consider what took place some years ago when one Anglican priest accused another of mishandling church finances. Their quarreling became public, and the congregation they served split into factions. Some members refused to attend services if the minister they opposed was presiding. So intense was their mutual contempt that they snubbed each other when they were in church for worship. When the accusing priest himself was accused of sexual misconduct, the dispute heated up.

The Archbishop of Canterbury appealed to the two clerics, calling their fighting "a cancer" and "a scandal dishonouring the name of Our Lord." In 1997 one of the priests agreed to retire. The other held on to his post until he had to leave because he had reached the age of compulsory retirement. However, he stayed on until the last possible moment, retiring on his 70th birthday, on August 7, 2001. *The Church of England Newspaper* mentioned that the day he retired was the feast day of "Saint" Victricius. Who was "Saint" Victricius? A fourth-century bishop who was reportedly flogged because he refused to fight in an army. Noting the contrast in attitudes, the paper said: "Refusing to fight in an ecclesiastical battle was not a trait of [the retiring priest]."

Those priests could have avoided injuring themselves and others had they applied the counsel at Romans 12:17, 18: "Return evil for evil to no one. Provide fine things in the sight of all men. If possible, as far as it depends upon you, be peaceable with all men."

What about you? If someone offends you, does resentment goad you into verbal warfare? Or do you avoid harsh words and keep the door to peace open? If you offend someone, do you avoid that person and hope that time and a short memory will cover over the problem? Or are you prompt to apologize? Whether you ask for forgiveness or extend it to another, trying to make peace will contribute to your well-being. Bible counsel can help us to resolve even long-standing conflicts, as the following article shows.

THE BENEFITS OF
Making Peace

ED WAS dying, and Bill hated him. Two decades earlier, Ed had made a decision that cost Bill his job, and that tore these once close friends apart. Now Ed tried to apologize so that he could die in peace. Bill, however, refused to hear him out.

Almost 30 years later as Bill approached death, he explained why he did not extend forgiveness. "Ed didn't have to do what he did to his best friend. I just didn't want to make up after twenty years. . . . I may have been wrong, but that's the way I felt."*

---

* Based on *The Murrow Boys—Pioneers on the Front Lines of Broadcast Journalism,* by Stanley Cloud and Lynne Olson.

Personal differences do not usually have such a tragic outcome, but they frequently leave people feeling hurt or bitter. Consider someone who feels as Ed did. Realizing that his decision caused damage, such an individual might live with a guilty conscience and an overwhelming sense of loss. Yet, he feels hurt when he thinks of how his offended comrade discarded their friendship like so much trash.

Someone who shares Bill's view, however, sees himself as an unsuspecting victim and might be deeply bitter and resentful. To him, his erstwhile friend knew better and might have caused harm on purpose. Often, when there is a difference between two people, each one is convinced that he is in the right and that the other bears all the blame. Hence, two former friends find themselves at war, as it were.

They carry on a fight with silent weapons —one turns away when the other walks by, and they ignore each other when they meet in a group. From a distance, they watch each other with furtive glances or lock their eyes in cold, hateful stares. When they do speak, they clip their words or offer insults that cut like knives.

Yet, while they seem completely opposed to each other, they likely agree on some matters. They may acknowledge that they have serious problems and that breaking with a close friend is sad. Each one likely feels the pain of the festering wound, and both know that something should be done to heal it. But who will take the first step to fix the damaged relationship and make peace? Neither is willing.

Two thousand years ago, the apostles of Jesus Christ sometimes got into angry arguments. (Mark 10:35-41; Luke 9:46; 22:24) After one of their altercations, Jesus asked: "What were you arguing over on the road?" Silenced by shame, not one of them replied. (Mark 9:33, 34) Jesus' teachings helped them to get back on good terms. His counsel, and that of some of his disciples, continues to help people solve conflicts and repair broken friendships. Let us see how.

Strive to Make Peace

"I do not want to talk to that person. If I ever see her again, it will be too soon." If you have spoken such words about someone, you need to take action, as the following Bible passages show.

Jesus taught: "If, then, you are bringing your gift to the altar and you there remember that your brother has something against you, leave your gift there in front of the altar, and go away; first make your peace with your brother." (Matthew 5:23, 24) He also said: "If your brother commits a sin, go lay bare his fault between you and him alone." (Matthew 18:15) Whether you have offended someone or someone has offended you, Jesus' words emphasize the need for *you* to talk the matter out *promptly* with the other person. You should do this "in a spirit of mildness." (Galatians 6:1) The goal of that conversation is, not to preserve your image by making excuses or to pummel your adversary into apologizing, *but to make peace.* Does this Bible counsel work?

Ernest is a supervisor in a large office.* For many years, his work has required him to handle sensitive matters with all kinds of people and to maintain good working relationships with them. He has seen how easily personal conflicts can develop. He says: "I have had differences with others at times. But when this happens, I sit down with the person and discuss the problem. Go to them directly. Face them, with the goal of making peace. It never fails to work."

Alicia has friends from many different cultures, and she says this: "Sometimes I say something, and then I sense that I may have offended someone. I go and apologize to that person. It may be that I apologize more often than I have to

---

* Some names have been changed.

because even if the other person was not offended, I feel better for it. Then I know that there is no misunderstanding."

Overcoming Obstacles

The way to peace in personal disputes, however, is often blocked by obstacles. Have you ever said: "Why must I be the first one to make peace? He caused the problem." Or have you ever gone to someone to clear up a problem only to hear that person say: "I have *nothing* to say to you"? Some people respond in those ways because of the emotional hurt they have suffered. Proverbs 18:19 says: "A brother who is transgressed against is more than a strong town; and there are contentions that are like the bar of a dwelling tower." So take the other person's feelings into account. If he rebuffs you, wait a short time and try again. Then the "strong town" may be open and the "bar" may be removed from the door to reconciliation.

Another obstacle to peace may involve a person's self-respect. To some people, apologizing or even speaking to an adversary is a humiliation. Concern for self-respect is proper, but does refusing to make peace enhance a person's self-respect or diminish it? Could this concern for self-respect cover up pride?

The Bible writer James shows that there is a connection between a contentious spirit and pride. After exposing the "wars" and "fights" that some Christians wage among themselves, he goes on to say: "God opposes the haughty ones, but he gives undeserved kindness to the humble ones." (James 4: 1-3, 6) How does haughtiness, or pride, hinder peacemaking?

Pride deludes people, making them believe they are better than others. Haughty ones feel that they have the authority to judge the moral value of their fellowman. In what way? When disagreements arise, they often view their antagonists as lost causes, beyond hope of improvement. Pride moves some people to judge those who differ with them as undeserving of attention, let alone a sincere apology. Hence, those driven by personal pride often allow conflicts to continue rather than resolve them properly.

Like a barricade that halts traffic on a highway, pride often halts the steps leading to peace. So if you find yourself resisting efforts to make peace with someone, you may be struggling with pride. How can you overcome pride? By developing its opposite—humility.

Do Just the Opposite

The Bible highly recommends humility. "The result of humility and the fear of Jehovah is riches and glory and life." (Proverbs 22:4) At Psalm 138:6, we read God's view of humble individuals and of proud ones: "Jehovah is high, and yet the humble one he sees; but the lofty one he knows only from a distance."

Many people equate humility with humiliation. World rulers seem to feel this way. Although entire nations submit to their will, political leaders shrink from the challenge of humbly admitting their errors. Hearing a ruler say, "I am sorry" is newsworthy. When a former government official recently apologized for his failure in a fatal disaster, his words made headlines.

Note how one dictionary defines humility: "The quality of being humble or having a lowly opinion of oneself . . . the opposite of pride or haughtiness." So humility describes the view that a person has of himself, not the opinion that others have of him. Humbly admitting his mistakes and sincerely asking for forgiveness does not humiliate a man; rather, it enhances his reputation. The Bible states: "Before a crash the heart of a man is lofty, and before glory there is humility."—Proverbs 18:12.

Apologizing often restores peaceful relations

Regarding politicians who do not apologize for their errors, one observer said: "Unfortunately they seem to think that such an admission is a sign of weakness. Weak and insecure people hardly ever say, 'Sorry.' It is large-hearted and courageous people who are not diminished by saying, 'I made a mistake.'" The same is true for those without political power. If you put forth the effort to replace pride with humility, your prospects for peace in a personal dispute are greatly improved. Note how one family discovered this truth.

A misunderstanding caused tensions between Julie and her brother William. William became so angry with Julie and her husband, Joseph, that he broke off all contact with them. He even returned all the gifts that Julie and Joseph had given him over the years. As the months went by, bitterness replaced the closeness that this brother and sister once enjoyed.

Joseph, however, decided to apply Matthew 5:23, 24. He tried approaching his brother-in-law in a spirit of mildness and sent him personal letters in which he apologized for offending him. Joseph encouraged his wife to forgive her brother. In time, William saw that Julie and Joseph sincerely wished to make peace, and his attitude softened. William and his wife met with Julie and Joseph; they all apologized, embraced, and restored their friendship.

If you long to resolve a personal conflict with someone, patiently apply Bible teachings and strive to make peace with that person. Jehovah will help you. What God said to ancient Israel will prove true in your case: "O if only you would actually pay attention to my commandments! Then your peace would become just like a river."—Isaiah 48:18.

"FAITHFUL UNDER TRIALS"

Stalin: U.S. Army photo

IN EARLY April 1951, the mighty Soviet government descended upon an innocent group of Christians in the western Soviet Union—Jehovah's Witnesses. Thousands of families—including little children, pregnant women, and the elderly—were loaded into boxcars for a grueling 20-day-long train trip to Siberia. They faced permanent exile in harsh, primitive conditions.

In April 2001, the 50th anniversary of this historic event was marked in Moscow with the release of a video that documents the decades-long oppression of Jehovah's Witnesses in the former Soviet Union. In the documentary, historians and eyewitnesses relate how the Witnesses survived and even flourished despite extreme pressure.

This documentary, *Faithful Under Trials—Jehovah's Witnesses in the Soviet Union,* has now been viewed by millions in Russia and elsewhere and has received high acclaim from the public in general and from historians. Following are two comments by Russian scholars who are living in the area to which the majority of Witness families were deported:

"I enjoyed this film very much. I have always liked the representatives of your religion, but after watching the film, my favorable impression of you is even stronger. The film was very professional! I particularly liked the way you presented each person as an individual. Although I am Orthodox and do not intend to change my religion, I am delighted with the Witnesses. I would like our faculty to keep a copy of this film. My colleagues and I have decided to show it to our students and to include it in the curriculum."
—*Professor Sergei Nikolayevich Rubtsov, dean of the faculty of history of the State Pedagogical University, Irkutsk, Russia.*

"I welcome the arrival of this film. When one is making a film about repression, it is always very difficult to develop the story in a logical way. But you managed to do it. Please feel free to bring me more of your films."
—*Professor Sergei Ilyich Kuznetsov, dean of the faculty of history of Irkutsk State University, Russia.*

Jehovah's Witnesses living in Siberia also deeply appreciated the documentary. Following is a sampling of their reactions:

"During the time when the events portrayed in this film were taking place, many in Russia were misinformed about the activities of Jehovah's Witnesses. But after watching the film, they can see that our organization is not merely some sect, as they previously thought. Others who have recently become Witnesses say: 'We couldn't have imagined that we were living and working alongside Christian brothers who had endured so much!' After watching the film, one Witness expressed his desire to become a full-time pioneer minister."—*Anna Vovchuk, who was exiled to Siberia.*

"When the film showed the secret police knocking on the door of a Witness home, I shuddered. It was like the knock on our door, and I remember my mother saying: 'Perhaps there's a fire somewhere.' But the film also reminds me that many Witnesses suffered more than I did. All this information gives us greater strength and enthusiasm to continue serving Jehovah."—*Stepan Vovchuk, who was exiled to Siberia.*

"I am the son of exiled Witnesses. I thought, therefore, that I had already heard a lot about those times. But after watching this film, I realized that I knew practically nothing. As I listened to the interviews, my eyes filled with tears. Now the experiences are not just stories for me but real life. The film has strengthened my relationship with God and helped prepare me to endure all future difficulties."—*Vladimir Kovash, Irkutsk.*

"For me, this film was more powerful than a written account. When I watched and heard the interviews with the brothers, I felt as if I had lived through all their experiences with them. The example of the brother who drew post-cards for his young daughters while

he was in prison motivates me to try to reach my own children's hearts with the Bible's truths. Thank you! This film has made Jehovah's Witnesses in Russia feel more than ever that they are part of Jehovah's worldwide organization."—*Tatyana Kalina, Irkutsk.*

"The saying, 'Seeing once is better than hearing a hundred times' certainly applies to this film. It is so alive, so real, so close to us! After watching it, I needed a lot of time to think. The film allowed me to immerse myself in the lives of those exiled Witnesses. Now when I compare my circumstances with theirs, I am helped to take a different view of our present-day problems."—*Lidia Beda, Irkutsk.*

Faithful Under Trials has thus far been released in 25 languages and is finding a warm reception around the world.* The entire documentary has been broadcast by television stations in St. Petersburg, Omsk, and other cities in Russia, as well as in the Ukrainian cities of Vynnytsya, Kerch, Melitopol and in the Lviv region. It has also earned awards from international film review boards.

The power of the message of this documentary lies in the examples of thousands of ordinary people who displayed extraordinary courage and spiritual strength through long years of persecution. Jehovah's Witnesses in the Soviet Union truly proved themselves faithful under trials. If you would like to see this documentary, Jehovah's Witnesses will be glad to provide it for you. Please contact one of them in your community.

---

* The video is available in Bulgarian, Cantonese, Czech, Danish, Dutch, English, Finnish, French, German, Greek, Hungarian, Indonesian, Italian, Japanese, Korean, Lithuanian, Mandarin, Norwegian, Polish, Romanian, Russian, Slovak, Slovenian, Spanish, and Swedish.

FAITHFUL UNDER TRIALS
JEHOVAH'S WITNESSES IN THE SOVIET UNION

MARRIAGE CAN SUCCEED IN TODAY'S WORLD

"Clothe yourselves with love, for it is a perfect bond of union."
—COLOSSIANS 3:14.

WHEN we look at the Christian congregation, is it not heartwarming to see so many married couples who have been loyal to their mates for 10, 20, 30, or even more years? They have stuck with their mates through thick and thin.—Genesis 2:24.

[2] Most would admit that their marriage has not been without its challenges. One observer wrote: "Happy marriages are not carefree. There are good times and bad times . . . But somehow . . . these people have stayed married despite the [turmoil] of modern life." Successful couples have learned to deal with the inevitable storms and crises that result from the pressures of life, especially if they have raised children. Experience has taught such couples that true love "never fails."—1 Corinthians 13:8.

[3] In contrast, millions of marriages have suffered shipwreck. A report says: "Half of all U.S. marriages today are expected to end in divorce. And half of those [divorces] will happen within the first 7.8 years of marriage . . . Among the 75 percent of people who remarry, 60 percent will divorce again." Even countries that previously had relatively low divorce rates have seen a change. For example, in Japan the divorce rate has nearly doubled in recent years. What are some of the pressures that have led to this situation, pressures that sometimes manifest themselves even within the Christian congregation? What is needed to make a success of marriage in spite of Satan's efforts to undermine that arrangement?

1, 2. (a) What fact is encouraging with regard to the Christian congregation? (b) What is a successful marriage?
3. What do statistics indicate about marriage and divorce, leading to what questions?

Pitfalls to Avoid

4 God's Word helps us to understand the factors that can undermine a marriage. Consider, for example, the words of the apostle Paul concerning conditions that would exist during these last days: "In the last days critical times hard to deal with will be here. For men will be lovers of themselves, lovers of money, self-assuming, haughty, blasphemers, disobedient to parents, unthankful, disloyal, having no natural affection, not open to any agreement, slanderers, without self-control, fierce, without love of goodness, betrayers, headstrong, puffed up with pride, lovers of pleasures rather than lovers of God, having a form of godly devotion but proving false to its power; and from these turn away." —2 Timothy 3:1-5.

5 When we analyze Paul's words, we see that many of the things he listed could contribute to the breakdown of marital relationships. For example, those who are "lovers of themselves" are selfish and lack consideration for others. Husbands or wives who love only themselves are determined to get their own way. They are inflexible, unbending. Would such an attitude contribute to a happy marriage? In no way. The apostle Paul wisely counseled Christians, including married couples: "[You should be] doing nothing out of contentiousness or out of egotism, but with lowliness of mind considering that the others are superior to you, keeping an eye, not in personal interest upon just your own matters, but also in personal interest upon those of the others."—Philippians 2:3, 4.

6 Love of money can drive a wedge between a husband and a wife. Paul warned: "Those who are determined to be rich fall into temptation and a snare and many senseless and hurtful desires, which plunge men into destruction and ruin. For the love of money is a root of all sorts of injurious things, and by reaching out for this love some have been led astray from the faith and have stabbed themselves all over with many pains." (1 Timothy 6:9, 10) Sadly, Paul's warning has come true in many marriages today. In their quest for wealth, many spouses ignore the needs of their mates, including the basic need for emotional support and regular, warm companionship.

7 Paul also said that some in these last days would be "disloyal, having no natural affection, not open to any agreement." The marriage vow is a solemn promise that should lead to a permanent bond, not to treachery. (Malachi 2:14-16) Some, though, have turned their amorous attentions to individuals other than their spouses. One wife in her 30's whose husband left her explained that even before he left, he acted too familiarly, too affectionately, toward other women. He failed to recognize what was inappropriate conduct for a married man. She was deeply hurt when she saw this happening and tactfully tried to warn him of the dangerous path he was treading. Still, he fell into adultery. Even though kind warnings were given, the offending partner did not want to pay attention. He fell headlong into the trap. —Proverbs 6:27-29.

8 How clearly the Bible warns against adultery! "Anyone committing adultery with a woman is in want of heart; he that does it is bringing his own soul to ruin." (Proverbs 6:32) Usually, adultery is not a spontaneous,

---

4. What are some factors that can undermine a marriage?
5. Why is a 'lover of self' endangering his or her marriage, and what is the Bible's counsel in this regard?
6. How can love of money undermine a marital relationship?

---

7. In some cases, what behavior has led to marital disloyalty?
8. What can lead to adultery?

impulsive act. As the Bible writer James pointed out, a sin such as adultery usually takes place only after the thought has been conceived and entertained. (James 1:14, 15) The offending spouse gradually ceases to be loyal to the mate to whom he or she vowed lifelong fidelity. Jesus said: "You heard that it was said, 'You must not commit adultery.' But I say to you that everyone that keeps on looking at a woman so as to have a passion for her has already committed adultery with her in his heart."—Matthew 5:27, 28.

⁹ Therefore, the wise and loyal course is the one encouraged in the book of Proverbs: "Let your water source prove to be blessed, and rejoice with the wife of your youth, a lovable hind and a charming mountain goat. Let her own breasts intoxicate you at all times. With her love may you be in an ecstasy constantly. So why should you, my son, be in an ecstasy with a strange woman or embrace the bosom of a foreign woman?" —Proverbs 5:18-20.

Do Not Rush Into Marriage

¹⁰ Problems in marriage may arise when a couple enter into that relationship prematurely. They may be too young and inexperienced. Or perhaps they do not take the time to get to know each other—their likes and dislikes, their goals in life, their family background. It is wise to exercise patience, taking the time to get to know the prospective mate. Think of Jacob, the son of Isaac. He had to work for his prospective father-in-law for seven years before he was allowed to marry Rachel. He was willing to do that because his feelings were based on real love, not merely physical attraction.—Genesis 29:20-30.

Marriage is more than just a romantic relationship

¹¹ Marriage is more than just a romantic relationship. The marital union yokes together two persons from different family backgrounds and with distinct personalities, emotional makeup, and often disparate educational backgrounds. Sometimes it is a joining of two cultures, even two languages. At the very least, it brings together two voices with the ability to express differing opinions on all kinds of matters. Those two voices are a very real component of a marriage union. They can be constantly critical and complaining, or they can be warmly encouraging and edifying. Yes, with our words we can either hurt or heal our mate. Uncontrolled speech can put a real strain on a marriage. —Proverbs 12:18; 15:1, 2; 16:24; 21:9; 31:26.

¹² Therefore, it is wise to take the time really to get to know a prospective mate. An ex-

9. What wise counsel is found at Proverbs 5:18-20?
10. Why is it wise to take time to get to know a prospective mate?

11. (a) What does the marital union bring together? (b) Why is a wise use of speech vital in marriage?
12, 13. What realistic view of marriage is encouraged?

perienced Christian sister once said: "When you view a prospective marriage partner, think of perhaps ten basic requirements you would like to see in that person. If you can find only seven, ask yourself, 'Am I willing to overlook the three that are missing? Could I on a daily basis tolerate those deficiencies?' If you have doubts, step back and think again." Of course, you need to be realistic. If you want to get married, know that you will never find a perfect mate. But, then, the person you eventually marry will not have found a perfect mate either!—Luke 6:41.

13 Marriage involves sacrifices. Paul highlighted this when he said: "I want you to be free from anxiety. The unmarried man is anxious for the things of the Lord, how he may gain the Lord's approval. But the married man is anxious for the things of the world, how he may gain the approval of his wife, and he is divided. Further, the unmarried woman, and the virgin, is anxious for the things of the Lord, that she may be holy both in her body and in her spirit. However, the married woman is anxious for the things of the world, how she may gain the approval of her husband."—1 Corinthians 7: 32-34.

Why Some Marriages Fail

14 A Christian woman recently experienced the trauma of divorce when her husband left her after 12 years of marriage and began a relationship with another woman. Did she notice any warning signs before the breakup? She explains: "He reached a point where he no longer prayed. He used flimsy excuses for missing Christian meetings and the preaching activity. He claimed to be either too busy or too tired to spend time with me. He would not talk to me. There was a

_____

14, 15. What can contribute to the weakening of the marriage bond?

spiritual alienation. It was such a shame. He was no longer the man I had married."

15 Others report noticing similar signs, including neglect of personal Bible study, prayer, or attendance at Christian meetings. In other words, many individuals who eventually left their mates allowed their relationship with Jehovah to weaken. As a result, their spiritual vision dimmed. Jehovah was no longer a living God to them. The promised new world of righteousness ceased to be a reality. In some cases, this spiritual weakening happened even before the unfaithful spouse formed an attachment outside the marriage.—Hebrews 10:38, 39; 11:6; 2 Peter 3:13, 14.

16 In contrast, one very happy couple attribute the success of their marriage to their strong spiritual bonds. They pray together and study together. The husband says: "We read the Bible together. We go out in the ministry together. We enjoy doing things together." The lesson is clear: Maintaining a good relationship with Jehovah will greatly contribute to the solidity of a marriage.

Be Realistic and Communicate

17 Two other things contribute to a successful marriage: Christian love and communication. When two people are enamored with each other, there is a tendency to ignore each other's faults. The couple may enter marriage with exaggerated expectations, perhaps based on what they have read in romance novels or seen in movies. Eventually, however, the couple have to face reality. Then, minor faults or mildly irritating habits may become major problems. If that happens, Christians need to display the fruitage of the spirit, an aspect of which

_____

16. What strengthens a marriage?
17. (a) What two things contribute to a successful marriage? (b) How does Paul describe Christian love?

A strong relationship with Jehovah helps a couple to make a success of marriage

is love. (Galatians 5:22, 23) Love, indeed, is very powerful—not romantic love but Christian love. Paul described such Christian love, saying: "Love is long-suffering and kind. . . . [It] does not look for its own interests, does not become provoked. It does not keep account of the injury. . . . It bears all things, believes all things, hopes all things, endures all things." (1 Corinthians 13:4-7) Clearly, genuine love makes allowances for human frailties. Realistically, it does not expect perfection.—Proverbs 10:12.

¹⁸ Communication is also vital. Regardless of the years that have passed, spouses should talk with each other and truly listen to each other. Says one husband: "We openly express our feelings but in a friendly way." With experience, a husband or a wife learns to listen not only to what is said but also to what is not said. In other words, as the years go by, a happily married couple learn to discern unspoken thoughts or unexpressed feelings. Some wives have said that their husbands do not really listen to them. Some husbands have complained that their wives seem to want to communicate at the most inconvenient times. Communication involves compassion and understanding. Effective communication is beneficial for both husband and wife. —James 1:19.

¹⁹ Communication sometimes includes apologizing. That is not always easy. It takes humility to admit one's mistakes. Yet, what a difference it makes in a marriage! A sincere apology can remove a possible future cause for conflict and pave the way for real forgiveness and a solution to the problem. Paul stated: "Continue putting up with one another and forgiving one another freely if anyone has a cause for complaint against another. Even as Jehovah freely forgave you, so do you also. But, besides all these things, clothe yourselves with love, for it is a perfect bond of union."—Colossians 3:13, 14.

18. How can communication strengthen a relationship?

19. (a) Why can apologizing be difficult? (b) What will motivate us to apologize?

²⁰ Also vital in a marriage is mutual support. A Christian husband and wife should be able to trust each other, to rely on each other. Neither should undermine the other or in other ways diminish his or her self-confidence. We lovingly commend our marriage partners; we do not harshly criticize them. (Proverbs 31:28b) Certainly, we do not demean them by making them the object of foolish and thoughtless jokes. (Colossians 4:6) Such mutual support is strengthened by regular expressions of affection. A touch or a quiet affectionate word can say: "I still love you. I'm glad you are with me." These are some factors that can influence a relation-

---

20. How should a Christian treat his marriage partner in private and in the presence of others?

Can You Explain?

- What are some factors that can undermine a marriage?
- Why is a hasty marriage unwise?
- How does spirituality affect a marriage?
- What factors help stabilize a marriage?

ship and help marriage to succeed in today's world. There are others, and the following article will offer additional Scriptural guidelines on how to make a success of marriage.*

---

* For more detailed information, see the publication *The Secret of Family Happiness,* published by Jehovah's Witnesses.

WISE GUIDANCE FOR MARRIED COUPLES

"Let wives be in subjection to their husbands as to the Lord. Husbands, continue loving your wives."
—EPHESIANS 5:22, 25.

JESUS said that marriage is the yoking together by God of a man and a woman to be "one flesh." (Matthew 19:5, 6) It involves two people with differing personalities learning to develop common interests and working together toward common goals. Marriage is a lifelong commitment, not a casual agreement that can be lightly abandoned. In many countries, divorce is not difficult to obtain, but in the eyes of a Christian, the marriage relationship is sacred. It is ended only for a very serious reason.—Matthew 19:9.

---

1. What is the correct view of marriage?

² One marriage counselor said: "A good marriage is a process of continual change as it reflects new issues, deals with problems that arise, and uses the resources available at each stage of life." For Christian spouses, those resources include wise counsel from the Bible, support from fellow Christians, and a close, prayerful relationship with Jehovah. A successful marriage endures, and over the years, it brings happiness and

---

2. (a) What help is available to married couples? (b) Why is it important to strive to make a success of marriage?

A Christian husband loves and cares for his wife

A Christian wife respects and honors her husband

contentment to husband and wife. More important, it brings honor to Jehovah God, the Originator of marriage.—Genesis 2:18, 21-24; 1 Corinthians 10:31; Ephesians 3:15; 1 Thessalonians 5:17.

Imitate Jesus and His Congregation

³ Two thousand years ago, the apostle Paul gave wise counsel to Christian couples when he wrote: "As the congregation is in subjection to the Christ, so let wives also be to their husbands in everything. Husbands, continue loving your wives, just as the Christ also loved the congregation and delivered up himself for it." (Ephesians 5:24, 25) What fine comparisons are expressed here! Christian wives who keep in humble submission to their husbands imitate the congregation in recognizing and observing the headship principle. Believing husbands who continue to love their wives, whether in favorable or in trying times, demonstrate that they closely follow Christ's example of loving the congregation and caring for it.

⁴ Christian husbands are the heads of their families, but they too have a head, Jesus. (1 Corinthians 11:3) Hence, as Jesus cared for his congregation, so husbands lovingly care for their families in a spiritual and physical way, even if that takes personal sacrifice. They put the welfare of their families ahead of their own desires and preferences. Jesus said: "All things, therefore, that you want men to do to you, you also must likewise do to them." (Matthew 7:12) That principle applies with special force in marriage. Paul showed this when he said: "Husbands ought to be loving their wives as their own bodies. . . . No man ever hated his own flesh; but he feeds and cherishes it." (Ephesians 5:28, 29) A man should feed and cherish his wife with the same diligence that he feeds and cherishes himself.

⁵ Godly wives look to the Christian congregation as a model. When Jesus was on earth, his followers gladly abandoned their previous pursuits and followed him. After his death, they continued subject to him, and over the past nearly 2,000 years, the true Christian congregation has remained subject to Jesus and followed his leadership in all things. Christian wives similarly do not disdain their husbands or seek to downplay the Scriptural arrangement of headship in marriage. Instead, they support and are submissive to their husbands, cooperate with them, and thus encourage them. When both husband and wife act in such a loving way, their marriage *will* succeed and both will find joy in the relationship.

---

3. (a) Summarize Paul's counsel to married couples. (b) What fine example did Jesus set?
4. How can husbands follow Jesus' example?

5. How can wives imitate the Christian congregation?

Continue Dwelling With Them

⁶ The apostle Peter also had counsel for married couples, and his words to husbands were especially pointed. He said: "Continue dwelling in like manner with [your wives] according to knowledge, assigning them honor as to a weaker vessel, the feminine one, since you are also heirs with them of the undeserved favor of life, in order for your prayers not to be hindered." (1 Peter 3:7) The seriousness of Peter's counsel is seen in the final words of that verse. If a husband fails to honor his wife, his relationship with Jehovah will be affected. His prayers will be hindered.

⁷ How, then, can husbands assign honor to their wives? To honor one's wife means to treat her lovingly, with respect and dignity. Such kindly treatment of a wife would have seemed novel to many. A Greek scholar

_____
6. What counsel did Peter give to husbands, and why is it important?
7. How should a husband honor his wife?

Unlike Roman law, Christian teachings required a husband to honor his wife

writes: "Under Roman law a woman had no rights. In law she remained for ever a child. . . . She was entirely subject to her husband, and completely at his mercy." What a contrast to Christian teachings! The Christian husband honored his wife. His dealings with her were governed by Christian principles, not by personal whim. Moreover, he was considerate of her "according to knowledge," taking into account that she was a weaker vessel.

"A Weaker Vessel" in What Way?

⁸ In saying that the woman is "a weaker vessel," Peter did not mean that women are weaker than men intellectually or spiritually. True, many Christian men have privileges in the congregation that women do not expect to have, and in the family women are subject to their husbands. (1 Corinthians 14: 35; 1 Timothy 2:12) Nevertheless, the same faith, endurance, and high moral standards

_____
8, 9. In what ways are women equal to men?

are required of all, men and women. And as Peter said, both husband and wife are "heirs . . . of the undeserved favor of life." As far as salvation is concerned, they have equal standing before Jehovah God. (Galatians 3: 28) Peter was writing to anointed Christians of the first century. Hence, his words reminded Christian husbands that as "joint heirs with Christ," they and their wives had the same heavenly hope. (Romans 8:17) One day, both would serve as priests and kings in God's heavenly Kingdom!—Revelation 5:10.

⁹ Anointed Christian wives were in no way inferior to their anointed Christian husbands. And in principle, the same is true of those with an earthly hope. Both men and women of the "great crowd" wash their robes and make them white in the blood of the Lamb. Both men and women share "day and night" in the worldwide shout of praise to Jehovah. (Revelation 7:9, 10, 14, 15) Both men and women look forward to enjoying "the glorious freedom of the children of God," when they will delight in "the real life." (Romans 8:21; 1 Timothy 6:19) Whether of the anointed or of the other sheep, all Christians serve Jehovah together as "one flock" under "one shepherd." (John 10:16) What a compelling reason for a Christian husband and wife to show due honor to each other!

¹⁰ In what way, then, are women 'weaker vessels'? Perhaps Peter was referring to the fact that, on average, women are smaller and have less physical strength than men. In addition, in our imperfect state, the wonderful privilege of bearing children exacts a physical toll. Women of childbearing age may be subject to physical discomforts on a regular basis. They certainly need special care and consideration when experiencing such discomforts or enduring the exhausting trials of being pregnant and giving birth. A husband who assigns honor to his wife, recognizing the support that she needs, will contribute greatly to the success of the marriage.

In a Religiously Divided Household

¹¹ What, though, if marriage mates have different religious views because one of them accepted Christian truth some time after they got married and the other did not? Can such a marriage succeed? The experience of many says yes. A husband and wife with different religious views can still have a successful marriage in the sense that it can be enduring and bring happiness to both. Besides, the marriage

10. In what sense are women 'weaker vessels'?
11. In what sense can a marriage succeed even if husband and wife are of different religions?

Both men and women of the "great crowd" look forward to everlasting life in Paradise

is still valid in Jehovah's eyes; they are still "one flesh." Therefore, Christian spouses are counseled to stay with the unbelieving partner if that partner is agreeable. If there are children, they benefit from the faithfulness of the Christian parent.—1 Corinthians 7: 12-14.

¹² Peter addresses kindly words of counsel to Christian women living in religiously divided households. His words can also be applied in principle by Christian husbands in the same situation. Peter writes: "You wives, be in subjection to your own husbands, in order that, if any are not obedient to the word, they may be won without a word through the conduct of their wives, because of having been eyewitnesses of your chaste conduct together with deep respect."—1 Peter 3:1, 2.

¹³ If a wife can tactfully explain her faith to her husband, that is fine. What, though, if he does not want to listen? That is his choice. Still, all is not lost, since Christian conduct also gives a powerful witness. Many husbands who at first were not interested in or who were even opposed to the faith of their wives became "rightly disposed for everlasting life" after seeing the fine conduct of their wives. (Acts 13:48) Even if a husband does not accept Christian truth, he may still be favorably impressed by the conduct of his wife, with good results for the marriage. One husband whose wife is one of Jehovah's Witnesses admitted that he could never live up to their high standards. Still, he called himself "the happy husband of a charming wife" and warmly praised his wife and her fellow Witnesses in a letter to a newspaper.

¹⁴ Christian husbands who have applied the principles of Peter's words have likewise won their wives over by their conduct. Unbelieving wives have seen their husbands gain a sense of responsibility, ceasing to waste money on smoking, drinking, and gambling and no longer using abusive language. Some of those mates have met other members of the Christian congregation. They were impressed with the loving Christian brotherhood, and what they observed among the brothers drew them to Jehovah. —John 13:34, 35.

"The Secret Person of the Heart"

¹⁵ What kind of conduct might win over a husband? Really, it is conduct that is naturally cultivated by Christian women. Peter says: "Do not let your adornment be that of the external braiding of the hair and of the putting on of gold ornaments or the wearing of outer garments, but let it be the secret person of the heart in the incorruptible apparel of the quiet and mild spirit, which is of great value in the eyes of God. For so, too, formerly the holy women who were hoping in God used to adorn themselves, subjecting themselves to their own husbands, as Sarah used to obey Abraham, calling him 'lord.' And you have become her children, provided you keep on doing good and not fearing any cause for terror."—1 Peter 3:3-6.

¹⁶ Peter counsels a Christian woman not to rely on external appearances. Instead, let her husband discern the effect of Bible teachings on her inner person. Let him witness the new personality in operation. Perhaps he will contrast it with the old personality that his wife used to have. (Ephesians 4:22-24) He will surely find her "quiet and mild spirit" refreshing and attractive. Not only is such a spirit pleasing to a husband but it is "of great value in the eyes of God."—Colossians 3:12.

¹⁷ Sarah is pointed to as a model, and she is a worthy example for Christian wives

---

12, 13. Following Peter's counsel, how can Christian wives help unbelieving husbands?
14. How can husbands help unbelieving wives?

15, 16. What kind of conduct by a Christian wife might win over an unbelieving husband?
17. How is Sarah a fine example for Christian wives?

Sarah viewed Abraham as her lord

whether their husbands are believers or not. Sarah unquestionably viewed Abraham as her head. Even in her heart, she called him her "lord." (Genesis 18:12) Yet, that did not diminish her. She was clearly a spiritually strong woman with her own firm faith in Jehovah. Indeed, she is part of the "great cloud of witnesses" whose example of faith should move us to "run with endurance the race that is set before us." (Hebrews 11:11; 12:1) It is not demeaning for a Christian wife to be like Sarah.

[18] In a religiously divided household, the

husband is still the head. If he is the believer, he will be considerate of his wife's beliefs while not compromising his own faith. If the wife is the believer, she too will not compromise her faith. (Acts 5:29) Still, she will not challenge her husband's headship. She will honor his position and remain under "the law of her husband."—Romans 7:2.

The Bible's Wise Guidance

[19] Today, many things can strain the marriage bond. Some men fail to assume their responsibilities. Some women refuse to accept the headship of their husbands. In some marriages, one spouse is abused by the other. For Christians, economic stresses, human imperfection, and the spirit of the world with its immorality and distorted sense of values can test loyalties. Still, Christian men and women who follow Bible principles, whatever their situation, receive Jehovah's blessing. Even if only one partner in a marriage applies Bible principles, things are better than if neither did. Moreover, Jehovah loves and supports his servants who remain faithful to their marriage vows even in difficult situations. He does not forget their loyalty.—Psalm 18:25; Hebrews 6:10; 1 Peter 3:12.

[20] After counseling married men and women, the apostle Peter concluded with warm words of encouragement. He said: "Finally, all of you be like-minded, showing fellow feeling, having brotherly affection, tenderly compassionate, humble in mind, not paying back injury for injury or reviling for reviling, but, to the contrary, bestowing a blessing, because you were called to this course, so that you might inherit a blessing." (1 Peter 3:8, 9) Wise counsel indeed for all, especially for married couples!

---

18. What principles should be borne in mind in a divided household?

---

19. What are some pressures that strain marriage bonds, but how can such pressures be resisted?
20. What counsel does Peter have for all Christians?

Do You Recall?

- How do Christian husbands imitate Jesus?
- How do Christian wives imitate the congregation?
- In what way can husbands honor their wives?
- What is the best course for a Christian wife whose husband is not a believer?

WE USED OUR CHANGING CIRCUMSTANCES TO WITNESS FAR AND WIDE

•

AS TOLD BY
RICARDO MALICSI

When I lost my job because of my stand on Christian neutrality, my family and I asked Jehovah to help us chart our future. In our prayer, we expressed our desire to expand our ministry. Soon thereafter, we embarked on a nomadic journey that took us to eight foreign countries on two continents. As a result, we were able to carry out our ministry in faraway places.

I WAS born in the Philippines in 1933 to a family affiliated with the Philippine Independent Church. All 14 members of our family belonged to that church. When I was about 12 years of age, I asked God in prayer to direct me to the true faith. One of my teachers enrolled me in a religion class, and I became a devout Catholic. I never missed Saturday confession or Sunday Mass. However, skepticism and dissatisfaction set in. Questions about what happens to people when they die and about hellfire and the Trinity bothered me. Answers given by religious leaders were hollow and unsatisfactory.

Getting Satisfying Answers

While studying in college, I joined a fraternity that got me involved in fighting, gambling, smoking, and other unsavory activities. One evening, I met the mother of one of my classmates. She was one of Jehovah's Witnesses. I posed to her the same questions that I had asked my religion teachers. She answered all my questions from the Bible, and I was convinced that what she said was the truth.

I bought a Bible and started to study it with the Witnesses. Soon I was attending all the meetings of Jehovah's Witnesses. Following the wise Bible observation that "bad associations spoil useful habits," I parted company with my immoral friends. (1 Corinthians 15:33) This helped me to make progress in my Bible study and eventually to dedicate myself to Jehovah. After my baptism in 1951, I served as a full-time minister (pioneer) for a while. Then in December 1953, I married Aurea Mendoza Cruz, who became my lifetime partner and faithful coworker in the ministry.

An Answer to Our Prayers

We were really wanting to serve as pioneers. However, our desire to serve Jehovah more fully did not materialize immediately. Even so, we did not stop asking Jehovah to open up opportunities in his service. Yet, our life was hard. Still, we kept our spiritual goals in mind, and at the age of 25, I was appointed congregation servant, the presiding overseer in a congregation of Jehovah's Witnesses.

As I progressed in Bible knowledge and got a better understanding of Jehovah's principles, I realized that my job violated my conscientious position as a neutral Christian. (Isaiah 2:2-4) I decided to quit. This proved to be a test of our faith. How would I care for the needs of my family? Again we approached Jehovah God in prayer. (Psalm 65:2) We told him of our concerns and fears, but we also expressed to him our desire to serve where the need for Kingdom preachers was greater. (Philippians 4:6, 7) Little did we know what a variety of opportunities would open up to us!

Starting Out on Our Journey

In April 1965, I accepted a job as crash fire and rescue supervisor at Vientiane International Airport, in Laos, and we moved there. In the city of Vientiane, there were 24 Witnesses, and we enjoyed the preaching work with the missionaries and the few local brothers. Later, I was transferred to Udon Thani Airport, Thailand. There were no other Witnesses in Udon Thani. As a family, we conducted all the weekly meetings by ourselves. We preached from house to house, made return visits, and started Bible studies.

We remembered Jesus' admonition to his disciples that they should "keep bearing much fruit." (John 15:8) So we determined to follow their example and continued proclaiming the good news. Soon we enjoyed results. A Thai girl accepted the truth and became our spiritual sister. Two North Americans accepted the truth and in time became Christian elders. We continued preaching the good news for more than ten years in northern Thailand. How happy we are to know that there is now a congregation in Udon Thani! Some of the seeds of truth we planted are still yielding results.

Sadly, though, we had to move again, and we prayed that "the Master of the harvest" would help us to continue to have a share in the preaching work. (Matthew 9:38) We were transferred to Tehran, the capital of Iran. This was during the time of the Shah's rule.

Preaching in Challenging Territories

Upon arrival in Tehran, we found our spiritual brothers right away. We associated with a small group of Witnesses made up of 13 different nationalities. We had to make adjustments in order to preach the good news in Iran. Although we experienced no outright opposition, we had to be careful.

With my wife, Aurea

Because of the work schedule of interested ones, we sometimes had to conduct Bible studies at midnight or later—into the early morning. Yet, how happy we were to see the fruitage of that hard work! A number of Filipino and Korean families accepted Christian truth and dedicated themselves to Jehovah.

My next work assignment was in Dhaka, Bangladesh. We arrived there in December 1977. This was another country where our preaching activity was not easy to accomplish. However, we always had in mind that we must keep active. With the guidance of Jehovah's spirit, we were able to find many families of professed Christians. Some of them were thirsting for the refreshing waters of truth found in the Holy Scriptures. (Isaiah 55:1) As a result, we started many Bible studies.

We kept in mind that God's will is that "all sorts of men should be saved." (1 Timothy 2:4) Happily, no one tried to cause problems for us. To overcome any prejudice, we made sure that we used a very friendly approach. Like the apostle Paul, we tried to "become all things to people of all sorts." (1 Corinthians 9:22) When we were asked the reason for our visit, we would kindly explain, and we found that most were quite friendly.

In Dhaka we found a local Witness and encouraged her to join us in our Christian meetings and later in the preaching work. Then, my wife studied the Bible with a family and invited them to our meetings. By Jehovah's loving-kindness, the whole family came into the truth. Later, their two daughters helped with translating Bible literature into Bengali, and many of their relatives also came to know Jehovah. Many other Bible students accepted the truth. Most of them are now serving as elders or pioneers.

Since Dhaka is a very populous city, we invited some of our family members to help us in the preaching work. Several responded and joined us in Bangladesh. How joyful and how thankful to Jehovah we are for the opportunity we had to share in preaching the good news in that country! From the very small beginnings of only one person, there are now two congregations in Bangladesh.

In July 1982, we had to pull up stakes and leave Bangladesh. We left the brothers with tears in our eyes. Not long thereafter, I received employment at Entebbe International Airport, in Uganda, where we would stay for four years and seven months. What would we be able to do in honoring Jehovah's great name in this land?

Serving Jehovah in East Africa

Upon our arrival at Entebbe International Airport, a driver picked up my wife and me to take us to our accommodations. As we were leaving the airport, I started preaching to the driver about God's Kingdom. He asked me: "Are you one of Jehovah's Witnesses?" When I answered in the affirmative, the driver said: "One of your brothers works at the control tower." Right away, I asked him to take me there. We met the brother, who was very happy to see us, and arrangements were made for meetings and field service.

There were only 228 Kingdom publishers in Uganda at that time. Along with a couple of brothers in Entebbe, we spent our first year planting seeds of truth. Since people there are fond of reading, we were able to place much literature, including hundreds of magazines. We invited brothers from Kampala, the capital, to help us preach in Entebbe's territory on weekends. At my first public talk, the attendance was five—including me.

Over the next three years, we experienced some of the happiest moments of our life, seeing those whom we taught respond and make rapid progress. (3 John 4) At one circuit assembly, six of our Bible students were baptized. Many of them said that they were encouraged to pursue the full-time service because they saw us serving as pioneers, even though we had full-time jobs.

We realized that our workplace could also be fruitful territory. On one occasion, I approached an airport fire officer and shared with him the Bible-based hope of life on a paradise earth. I showed him from his own Bible that obedient humankind will live in peace and unity, suffering no more from poverty, lack of housing, war, sickness, or death. (Psalm 46:9; Isaiah 33:24; 65:21, 22; Revelation 21:3, 4) Reading this in his own Bible sparked his interest. A Bible study was started right away. He attended all meetings. Soon he dedicated himself to Jehovah and was baptized. Later he joined us in the full-time ministry.

Civil unrest broke out twice in Uganda while we were there, but that did not bring our spiritual activities to a halt. The dependents of those working for international agencies were transferred to Nairobi, Kenya, for six months. Those of us left in Uganda kept on with our Christian meetings and the

preaching work, although we had to be prudent and cautious.

In April 1988, my job assignment was completed and we moved again. We left the Entebbe Congregation with a feeling of deep satisfaction over the spiritual developments there. In July 1997, we had an opportunity to visit Entebbe again. By then, some of our former Bible students were serving as elders. How thrilled we were to see 106 in attendance at the Public Meeting!

Moving On to Untouched Territory

Would we be able to enter new doors of opportunity? Yes, my next work assignment was at Mogadishu International Airport, in Somalia. We were determined to make good use of this new opportunity to serve in untouched territory.

Our preaching activity was confined mostly to embassy staff, Filipino workers, and other foreigners. Often we met them in the marketplace. We also made friendly visits to their homes. By combining ingenuity, resourcefulness, prudence, and complete reliance on Jehovah, we were able to share Bible truths with others, and this bore fruit among those

BANGLADESH

MYANMAR

LAOS

THAILAND

PHILIPPINES

joy the wonderful privilege of spreading the good news far and wide.

Back Where It All Started

At the age of 58, I decided to take early retirement and return to the Philippines. When we got back, we prayed to Jehovah to direct our steps. We started serving in a congregation in Trece Martires City, in the province of Cavite. When we first arrived, there were only 19 proclaimers of God's Kingdom. Daily preaching activities were organized, and many Bible studies were started. The congregation began to grow. At one time, my wife had as many as 19 home Bible studies, and I had 14.

Soon the Kingdom Hall became too small. We prayed to Jehovah about this. A spiritual brother and his wife decided to donate a piece of land, and the branch office approved a loan for building a new Kingdom Hall. The new building has had a big impact on the preaching work, and the attendance increased week by week. At present, we travel over one hour each way to assist another congregation, of 17 publishers.

My wife and I cherish the privilege we have enjoyed serving in so many different countries. Looking back at our nomadic life, we feel deeply satisfied to know that it was used in the best way possible—to help others to learn about Jehovah!

from different nationalities. After two years, we left Mogadishu—just before war broke out there.

The International Civil Aviation Organization next assigned me to Yangon, Myanmar. Again, fine opportunities opened up for us to help honesthearted ones learn about God's purposes. After Myanmar, we were assigned to Dar es Salaam, Tanzania. Preaching the good news from house to house in Dar es Salaam was much easier because there was an English-speaking community.

In all the countries we worked in, we had very few problems in carrying out our ministry, although in many cases, there were restrictions on the work of Jehovah's Witnesses. Because of the status of my work, which was usually connected with government or international agencies, people did not question our activities.

My secular employment required that my wife and I live as nomads for three decades. However, we viewed my job as only a means to an end. Our first goal was always to promote the interests of God's Kingdom. We thank Jehovah for helping us to make good use of our changing circumstances and to en-

IN OUR NEXT ISSUE

Lessons Jesus Taught—Are They Practical for You?

———

Living No Longer for Ourselves

———

Samson Triumphs in the Strength of Jehovah!

Jehovah's Word Is Alive
Highlights From the Book of Ruth

IT IS a heartwarming drama of loyalty between two women. It is an account of appreciation for Jehovah God and trust in his arrangement. It is a story that underscores Jehovah's keen interest in the Messianic line of descent. It is a touching narrative of the joys and sorrows of a family. The Bible book of Ruth is all that and more.

Do you know why Ruth did not abandon Naomi?

The book of Ruth covers a period of about 11 years "in the days when the judges administered justice" in Israel. (Ruth 1:1) The events recorded must have occurred early in the period of the Judges, since the landowner Boaz, one of the characters in this real-life drama, was the son of Rahab of Joshua's day. (Joshua 2:1, 2; Ruth 2:1; Matthew 1:5) The narrative was likely written by the prophet Samuel in 1090 B.C.E. This is the only book in the Bible that bears the name of a non-Israelite woman. The message contained in it "is alive and exerts power."—Hebrews 4:12.

"WHERE YOU GO I SHALL GO"
(Ruth 1:1–2:23)

When Naomi and Ruth arrive in Bethlehem, they become the center of attention. Pointing to the older of the two, the women of the town keep asking: "Is this Naomi?" To this, Naomi says: "Do not call me Naomi. Call me Mara, for the Almighty has made it very bitter for me. I was full when I went, and it is empty-handed that Jehovah has made me return."—Ruth 1:19-21.

When a famine in Israel causes her family to move from Bethlehem to the land of Moab, Naomi is "full" in that she has a husband and two sons. Some time after they settle in Moab, though, her husband, Elimelech, dies. Later, the two sons marry the Moabite women Orpah and Ruth. About ten years pass, and the two sons die childless, leaving the three women on their own. When the mother-in-law, Naomi, decides to return to Judah, the widows of her sons go with her. Along the way, Naomi urges her daughters-in-law to go back to Moab and find husbands from among their own people. Orpah acquiesces. However, Ruth sticks with Naomi, saying: "Where you go I shall go, and where you spend the night I shall spend the night. Your people will be my people, and your God my God."—Ruth 1:16.

The two widows, Naomi and Ruth, reach Bethlehem at the start of the barley harvest. Taking advantage of a provision made in God's Law, Ruth begins gleaning in a field that happens to belong to a kinsman of Elimelech—an elderly Jew named Boaz. Ruth gains Boaz' favor and continues gleaning in his field "until the harvest of the barley and the harvest of the wheat" come to an end. —Ruth 2:23.

Scriptural Questions Answered:

1:8—Why did Naomi tell her daughters-in-law to return "each one to the house of

her mother" instead of to the house of her **father?** Whether Orpah's father was alive at the time is not stated. However, Ruth's father was. (Ruth 2:11) Still, Naomi spoke of the mother's house, perhaps thinking that the reference to their mothers would bring to their mind the comfort of motherly affection. This would be particularly soothing to daughters overwhelmed by the sorrow of parting from their beloved mother-in-law. The comment may also reflect the thought that unlike Naomi, the mothers of Ruth and Orpah had well-established homes.

1:13, 21—Did Jehovah make life bitter for Naomi and cause her calamity? No, and Naomi did not charge God with any wrongdoing. In view of all that had happened to her, however, she thought that Jehovah was against her. She felt bitter and disillusioned. Moreover, in those days the fruitage of the belly was considered a divine blessing and barrenness, a curse. Lacking grandchildren and with two sons dead, Naomi might have felt justified in thinking that Jehovah had humiliated her.

2:12—What "perfect wage" did Ruth receive from Jehovah? Ruth had a son and received the privilege of becoming a link in history's most important lineage—that of Jesus Christ.—Ruth 4:13-17; Matthew 1:5, 16.

Lessons for Us:

1:8; 2:20. Despite the tragedies she experienced, Naomi maintained her confidence in Jehovah's loving-kindness. We should do the same, particularly when undergoing severe trials.

1:9. A home should be more than just a place where family members eat and sleep. It should be a peaceful place of rest and comfort.

1:14-16. Orpah "returned to her people and her gods." Ruth did not. She left the comfort and security of her native land and remained loyal to Jehovah. Cultivating loyal love for God and manifesting a

What gave Ruth the reputation of being "an excellent woman"?

self-sacrificing spirit will help protect us from succumbing to selfish desires and 'shrinking back to destruction.'—Hebrews 10:39.

2:2. Ruth wanted to take advantage of the provision of gleaning made for the benefit of the foreigners and the afflicted. She was humble at heart. A needy Christian should not be too proud to accept the loving assistance of fellow believers or any governmental aid he or she may qualify for.

2:7. Despite having the right to glean, Ruth asked for permission before doing so. (Leviticus 19:9, 10) This was a sign of meekness on her part. We are wise to "seek meekness," for "the meek ones themselves will possess the earth, and they will indeed find their exquisite delight in the abundance of peace."—Zephaniah 2:3; Psalm 37:11.

2:11. Ruth proved to be more than a relative to Naomi. She was a true friend. (Proverbs 17:17) Their friendship was solid because it was based on such qualities as love, loyalty, empathy, kindness, and a self-sacrificing spirit. More important, it was based on their spirituality—their desire to serve Jehovah and to be among his worshipers. We too have fine opportunities to cultivate genuine friendships with true worshipers.

2:15-17. Even when Boaz made it possible for Ruth to ease her work load, "she continued to glean in the field until the evening." Ruth was a hard worker. A Christian should have a reputation for being a diligent worker.

2:19-22. Naomi and Ruth enjoyed pleasant conversation during the evening hours, the older one taking an interest in the activities of the younger, both freely expressing their thoughts and feelings. Should it be any different in a Christian family?

2:22, 23. Unlike Jacob's daughter Dinah, Ruth sought association with worshipers of Jehovah. What a fine example for us!—Genesis 34:1, 2; 1 Corinthians 15:33.

NAOMI BECOMES "FULL"
(Ruth 3:1–4:22)

Naomi is too old to bring forth children. So she instructs Ruth to substitute for her in a marriage by repurchase, or brother-in-law marriage. Following Naomi's direction, Ruth asks Boaz to act as a repurchaser. Boaz is ready to comply. However, there is a closer relative who should be given the first opportunity.

Boaz loses no time in settling the matter. The very next morning, he gathers ten older men of Bethlehem before the relative and asks him if he is willing to do the repurchasing. The man refuses to do so. Hence, Boaz acts as a repurchaser and marries Ruth. Their marriage produces a son, Obed, the grandfather of King David. The women of Bethlehem now say to Naomi: "Blessed be Jehovah . . . He has become a restorer of your soul and one to nourish your old age, because your daughter-in-law who does love you, who is better to you than seven sons, has given birth to him." (Ruth 4:14, 15) The woman who had returned "empty-handed" to Bethlehem has again become "full"!—Ruth 1:21.

Scriptural Questions Answered:

3:11—What gave Ruth the reputation of being "an excellent woman"? It was not "the external braiding of the hair" or "the putting on of gold ornaments or the wearing of outer garments" that caused others to admire Ruth. Rather, it was "the secret person of the heart"—her loyalty and love, her humility and meekness, her diligence and self-sacrificing spirit. Any God-fearing woman desiring a reputation like that of Ruth must strive to cultivate these qualities.—1 Peter 3:3, 4; Proverbs 31:28-31.

3:14—Why did Ruth and Boaz wake up before daybreak? This was not because something immoral had transpired during the night and they wanted to be secre-

What was the "perfect wage" for Ruth from Jehovah?

tive. Ruth's actions that night were apparently in line with what was customarily done by a woman seeking the right of brother-in-law marriage. She acted in harmony with Naomi's instruction. Moreover, Boaz' response clearly indicates that he did not see anything wrong in what Ruth did. (Ruth 3:2-13) Evidently, Ruth and Boaz got up early so that no one would have a reason for starting groundless rumors.

3:15—What was significant about Boaz' giving Ruth six measures of barley? This act perhaps signified that just as a day of rest followed six days of work, Ruth's day of rest was near. Boaz would see to it that she would have "a resting-place" in the house of her husband. (Ruth 1:9; 3:1) It may also be that six measures of barley is all that Ruth could carry on her head.

3:16—Why did Naomi ask Ruth: "Who are you, my daughter?" Did she not recognize her daughter-in-law? This could very well be, for when Ruth returned to Naomi, it may still have been dark. The question, though, may also mean that Naomi was inquiring about Ruth's possible new identity in connection with her being repurchased.

4:6—In what way could a repurchaser "ruin" his inheritance by doing the repurchasing? First of all, if the one falling into poverty had sold his land inheritance, a repurchaser would have to put out money to buy the land at a price determined by the number of years remaining till the next Jubilee. (Leviticus 25:25-27) Doing so would reduce the value of his own estate. Moreover, should a son be born to Ruth, that son, rather than any of the repurchaser's current near relatives, would inherit the purchased field.

Lessons for Us:

3:12; 4:1-6. Boaz scrupulously followed Jehovah's arrangement. Are we conscientious in following theocratic procedures?—1 Corinthians 14:40.

3:18. Naomi had confidence in Boaz. Should we not have similar confidence in faithful fellow believers? Ruth was willing to perform brother-in-law marriage with a man she hardly knew, a man unnamed in the Bible. (Ruth 4:1) Why? Because she had confidence in God's arrangement. Do we have similar confidence? When it comes to seeking a marriage mate, for example, do we heed the counsel to marry "only in the Lord"? —1 Corinthians 7:39.

4:13-16. Although she was a Moabitess and a former worshiper of the god Chemosh, what a privilege Ruth received! This illustrates the principle that "it depends, not upon the one wishing nor upon the one running, but upon God, who has mercy." —Romans 9:16.

God "May Exalt You in Due Time"

The book of Ruth portrays Jehovah as a God of loving-kindness, who acts in behalf of his loyal servants. (2 Chronicles 16:9) When we reflect on how Ruth was blessed, we see the value of putting our confidence in God with unquestioning faith, fully believing "that he is and that he becomes the rewarder of those earnestly seeking him." —Hebrews 11:6.

Ruth, Naomi, and Boaz placed their complete trust in Jehovah's arrangement, and things worked out well for them. Similarly, "God makes all his works cooperate together for the good of those who love God, those who are the ones called according to his purpose." (Romans 8:28) Let us then take to heart the apostle Peter's counsel: "Humble yourselves, therefore, under the mighty hand of God, that he may exalt you in due time; while you throw all your anxiety upon him, because he cares for you." —1 Peter 5:6, 7.

2005 "GODLY OBEDIENCE" DISTRICT CONVENTION LOCATIONS

MAY 27-29
BAKERSFIELD, CA, Centennial Garden Arena, 1001 Truxtun Ave.
LONG BEACH, CA, Convention Center Arena, 300 E. Ocean Blvd.
PORTLAND, ME, Cumberland County Civic Center, 1 Civic Center Sq.
WEST PALM BEACH, FL, Christian Convention Center of Jehovah's Witnesses, 1610 Palm Beach Lakes Blvd.

JUNE 3-5
BAKERSFIELD, CA (Spanish only), Centennial Garden Arena, 1001 Truxtun Ave.
BILLINGS, MT, MetraPark Arena, 308 6th Ave. N.
FORT WORTH, TX, Convention Center, 1111 Houston St.
PORTLAND, ME, Cumberland County Civic Center, 1 Civic Center Sq.
SAN FRANCISCO, CA, Cow Palace, 2600 Geneva Ave.
WEST PALM BEACH, FL, Christian Convention Center of Jehovah's Witnesses, 1610 Palm Beach Lakes Blvd.

JUNE 10-12
EVANSVILLE, IN, Roberts Stadium, 2600 Division St.
FLORENCE, SC, Civic Center, 3300 W. Radio Dr.
FORT WORTH, TX (Spanish only), Convention Center, 1111 Houston St.
KANSAS CITY, MO, Kemper Arena, 1800 Genessee St.
LONG BEACH, CA (Spanish only), Convention Center Arena, 300 E. Ocean Blvd.
SAN DIEGO, CA, Qualcomm Stadium, 9449 Friars Rd.
SAN FRANCISCO, CA, Cow Palace, 2600 Geneva Ave.
TOLEDO, OH, Seagate Convention Centre Arena, 401 Jefferson Ave.
WEST PALM BEACH, FL, Christian Convention Center of Jehovah's Witnesses, 1610 Palm Beach Lakes Blvd.

JUNE 17-19
AMHERST, MA, The Mullins Center, University of Massachusetts, Commonwealth Ave.
BAKERSFIELD, CA (Spanish only), Centennial Garden Arena, 1001 Truxtun Ave.
COLLEGE STATION, TX, Reed Arena, Texas A&M University, Olsen Blvd.
DAYTON, OH, Ervin J. Nutter Center, Wright State University, 3640 Colonel Glenn Hwy.
DULUTH, GA, The Arena at Gwinnett Center, 6400 Sugarloaf Pkwy.
EVANSVILLE, IN, Roberts Stadium, 2600 Division St.
FLORENCE, SC, Civic Center, 3300 W. Radio Dr.
FORT WORTH, TX, Convention Center, 1111 Houston St.
GREEN BAY, WI, Resch Center, 1901 S. Oneida St.
JACKSON, MS, Mississippi Coliseum, 1207 Mississippi St.
LONG BEACH, CA (Spanish only), Convention Center Arena, 300 E. Ocean Blvd.
LOVELAND, CO (Spanish only), Budweiser Events Center, The Ranch, 5290 Arena Cir.
READING, PA, Sovereign Center Arena, 700 Penn St.
SAN DIEGO, CA (Spanish only), Qualcomm Stadium, 9449 Friars Rd.
SAN FRANCISCO, CA (Spanish only), Cow Palace, 2600 Geneva Ave.
TUCSON, AZ, Convention Center, 260 S. Church St.
WEST PALM BEACH, FL (Spanish only), Christian Convention Center of Jehovah's Witnesses, 1610 Palm Beach Lakes Blvd.

JUNE 24-26
AMHERST, MA, The Mullins Center, University of Massachusetts, Commonwealth Ave.
COLLEGE STATION, TX, Reed Arena, Texas A&M University, Olsen Blvd.
COLUMBIA, SC, The Colonial Center, 801 Lincoln St.
DE KALB, IL, Convocation Center, Northern Illinois University, 1525 W. Lincoln Hwy.
DULUTH, GA, The Arena at Gwinnett Center, 6400 Sugarloaf Pkwy.
GLENDALE, AZ, Glendale Arena, 6520 N. 91st Ave.
HUNTSVILLE, AL, Von Braun Center Arena, 700 Monroe St. SW
LONG BEACH, CA (Spanish only), Convention Center Arena, 300 E. Ocean Blvd.
LOVELAND, CO, Budweiser Events Center, The Ranch, 5290 Arena Cir.
READING, PA, Sovereign Center Arena, 700 Penn St.
RICHMOND, VA, Coliseum, 601 E. Leigh St.
SAN FRANCISCO, CA (Spanish only), Cow Palace, 2600 Geneva Ave.
TUCSON, AZ (Spanish only), Convention Center, 260 S. Church St.
WEST PALM BEACH, FL (Spanish only), Christian Convention Center of Jehovah's Witnesses, 1610 Palm Beach Lakes Blvd.

JULY 1-3
AMHERST, MA, The Mullins Center, University of Massachusetts, Commonwealth Ave.
BAKERSFIELD, CA, Centennial Garden Arena, 1001 Truxtun Ave.
BIRMINGHAM, AL, BJCC Arena, 19th St. & 9th Ave. N.
BISMARCK, ND, Civic Center Arena, 601 E. Sweet Ave.
BOSSIER CITY, LA, CenturyTel Center Arena, 2000 CenturyTel Center Dr.
COLLEGE STATION, TX, Reed Arena, Texas A&M University, Olsen Blvd.
COLUMBIA, SC, The Colonial Center, 801 Lincoln St.
COLUMBUS, GA, Civic Center Arena, 400 4th St.
DAYTON, OH, Ervin J. Nutter Center, Wright State University, 3640 Colonel Glenn Hwy.
DE KALB, IL, Convocation Center, Northern Illinois University, 1525 W. Lincoln Hwy.
FORT WORTH, TX, Convention Center, 1111 Houston St.
FREMONT, CA (Chinese only), Assembly Hall of Jehovah's Witnesses, 43400 Osgood Rd.
GAINESVILLE, FL, Stephen C. O'Connell Center Arena, University of Florida, North South Dr. & University Ave.
GLENDALE, AZ (Spanish only), Glendale Arena, 6520 N. 91st Ave.
HUNTSVILLE, AL, Von Braun Center Arena, 700 Monroe St. SW
JERSEY CITY, NJ (American Sign Language only), Assembly Hall of Jehovah's Witnesses, 2932 Kennedy Blvd.
KENNEWICK, WA (Spanish only), Three Rivers Coliseum, 7100 W. Quinault Ave.
LINCOLN, NE, Bob Devaney Sports Center, University of Nebraska, 16th St. & Military Rd.
LONG BEACH, CA, Convention Center Arena, 300 E. Ocean Blvd.
LOVELAND, CO, Budweiser Events Center, The Ranch, 5290 Arena Cir.
MOBILE, AL, Civic Center Arena, 401 Civic Center Dr.
NEWBURGH, NY (Greek only), Assembly Hall of Jehovah's Witnesses, 23 Unity Pl.
NORMAN, OK, Lloyd Noble Center Arena, University of Oklahoma, 2900 Jenkins Ave.
OGDEN, UT, Dee Events Center, 4450 S. Harrison Blvd.
RICHMOND, VA, Coliseum, 601 E. Leigh St.
ROANOKE, VA (Spanish only), Civic Center Coliseum, 710 Williamson Rd. NE
ROCHESTER, MN, Taylor Arena, Mayo Civic Center, 30 Civic Center Dr. SE
SAN FRANCISCO, CA, Cow Palace, 2600 Geneva Ave.
SPRINGFIELD, IL, Prairie Capital Convention Center Arena, 1 Convention Center Plaza
SUNNYSIDE, NY (Tagalog only), Assembly Hall of Jehovah's Witnesses, 44-17 Greenpoint Ave.
TACOMA, WA, Tacoma Dome, 2727 East D St.
TOPEKA, KS (Spanish only), Landon Arena, Kansas Expocentre, One Expocentre Dr.
TUCSON, AZ (Spanish only), Convention Center, 260 S. Church St.
TULSA, OK, Convention Center, 100 Civic Center
UNIONDALE, NY, Nassau Veterans Memorial Coliseum, 1255 Hempstead Tpk.
WEST PALM BEACH, FL (Spanish only), Christian Convention Center of Jehovah's Witnesses, 1610 Palm Beach Lakes Blvd.
WINSTON-SALEM, NC, Lawrence Joel Veterans Memorial Coliseum, 2825 University Pkwy.

JULY 8-10
AMHERST, MA, The Mullins Center, University of Massachusetts, Commonwealth Ave.
COLLEGE STATION, TX, Reed Arena, Texas A&M University, Olsen Blvd.
COLUMBUS, GA, Civic Center Arena, 400 4th St.
DULUTH, GA (Spanish only), The Arena at Gwinnett Center, 6400 Sugarloaf Pkwy.
FORT WORTH, TX, Convention Center, 1111 Houston St.
FREMONT, CA (Vietnamese only), Assembly Hall of Jehovah's Witnesses, 43400 Osgood Rd.
HAMPTON, VA, Coliseum, 1000 Coliseum Dr.
JERSEY CITY, NJ (French only), Assembly Hall of Jehovah's Witnesses, 2932 Kennedy Blvd.
KENNEWICK, WA (Spanish only), Three Rivers Coliseum, 7100 W. Quinault Ave.
KISSIMMEE, FL, Silver Spurs Arena, 1875 Silver Spur Ln.
LONG BEACH, CA (Spanish only), Convention Center Arena, 300 E. Ocean Blvd.
LOVELAND, CO, Budweiser Events Center, The Ranch, 5290 Arena Cir.
MACON, GA, Centreplex Coliseum, 200 Coliseum Dr.
MIRA LOMA, CA (Tagalog only), Assembly Hall of Jehovah's Witnesses, 3300 Cornerstone Dr.
READING, PA, Sovereign Center Arena, 700 Penn St.

JULY 15-17
AMARILLO, TX, Cal Farley Coliseum, Civic Center, 401 S. Buchanan St.
BEAUMONT, TX (Spanish only), Civic Center Arena, 701 Main St.
BELTON, TX, Bell County Expo Center Arena, 301 W. Loop 121
FORT LAUDERDALE, FL (Portuguese only), Assembly Hall of Jehovah's Witnesses, 20850 Griffin Rd.
GLENDALE, AZ, Glendale Arena, 6520 N. 91st Ave.
HAMPTON, VA, Coliseum, 1000 Coliseum Dr.
JERSEY CITY, NJ (French only), Assembly Hall of Jehovah's Witnesses, 2932 Kennedy Blvd.
JOHNSON CITY, TN, Freedom Hall Civic Center Arena, 1320 Pactolas Rd.
KENNEWICK, WA, Three Rivers Coliseum, 7100 W. Quinault Ave.
KISSIMMEE, FL, Silver Spurs Arena, 1875 Silver Spur Ln.
LITTLE ROCK, AR, Barton Coliseum, Roosevelt Rd. & Dennison St.
LONG BEACH, CA, Convention Center Arena, 300 E. Ocean Blvd.
LONG BEACH, CA (Japanese only), Convention Center Seaside Ballroom, 300 E. Ocean Blvd.
LOVELAND, CO (Spanish only), Budweiser Events Center, The Ranch, 5290 Arena Cir.
MIRA LOMA, CA (American Sign Language only), Assembly Hall of Jehovah's Witnesses, 3300 Cornerstone Dr.
PHILADELPHIA, PA, The Liacouras Center, Temple University, 1776 N. Broad St.
RICHMOND, VA, Coliseum, 601 E. Leigh St.
ROCHESTER, MN, Taylor Arena, Mayo Civic Center, 30 Civic Center Dr. SE
ROCHESTER, NY, Blue Cross Arena, Broad & Exchange Sts.
ST. CHARLES, MO, The Family Arena, 2002 Arena Pkwy.
SAN FRANCISCO, CA (Spanish only), Cow Palace, 2600 Geneva Ave.
TACOMA, WA, Tacoma Dome, 2727 East D St.
TOLEDO, OH, Seagate Convention Centre Arena, 401 Jefferson Ave.
UNIONDALE, NY, Nassau Veterans Memorial Coliseum, 1255 Hempstead Tpk.
WEST PALM BEACH, FL, Christian Convention Center of Jehovah's Witnesses, 1610 Palm Beach Lakes Blvd.
WINSTON-SALEM, NC, Lawrence Joel Veterans Memorial Coliseum, 2825 University Pkwy.

JULY 22-24
AMARILLO, TX, Cal Farley Coliseum, Civic Center, 401 S. Buchanan St.
AMHERST, MA, The Mullins Center, University of Massachusetts, Commonwealth Ave.
BAKERSFIELD, CA, Centennial Garden Arena, 1001 Truxtun Ave.
BELTON, TX, Bell County Expo Center Arena, 301 W. Loop 121
CLEVELAND, OH, Convocation Center Arena, Cleveland State University, Prospect Ave. & E. 21st St.
DAYTON, OH, Ervin J. Nutter Center, Wright State University, 3640 Colonel Glenn Hwy.
DE KALB, IL, Convocation Center, Northern Illinois University, 1525 W. Lincoln Hwy.
JERSEY CITY, NJ (Korean only), Assembly Hall of Jehovah's Witnesses, 2932 Kennedy Blvd.
JOHNSON CITY, TN, Freedom Hall Civic Center Arena, 1320 Pactolas Rd.
KENNEWICK, WA, Three Rivers Coliseum, 7100 W. Quinault Ave.

RICHMOND, VA, Coliseum, 601 E. Leigh St.
(continued)
RICHMOND, VA, Coliseum, 601 E. Leigh St.
ROANOKE, VA, Civic Center Coliseum, 710 Williamson Rd. NE
ROCHESTER, MN, Taylor Arena, Mayo Civic Center, 30 Civic Center Dr. SE
ROCHESTER, NY, Blue Cross Arena, Broad & Exchange Sts.
ST. CHARLES, MO, The Family Arena, 2002 Arena Pkwy.
SAN ANGELO, TX (Spanish only), Convention Center Coliseum, 50 E. 43rd St.
SAN FRANCISCO, CA, Cow Palace, 2600 Geneva Ave.
SUNNYSIDE, NY (Russian only), Assembly Hall of Jehovah's Witnesses, 44-17 Greenpoint Ave.
TACOMA, WA, Tacoma Dome, 2727 East D St.
TOLEDO, OH, Seagate Convention Centre Arena, 401 Jefferson Ave.
TULSA, OK, Convention Center, 100 Civic Center
UNIONDALE, NY, Nassau Veterans Memorial Coliseum, 1255 Hempstead Tpk.
WEST PALM BEACH, FL (French only), Christian Convention Center of Jehovah's Witnesses, 1610 Palm Beach Lakes Blvd.
WINSTON-SALEM, NC, Lawrence Joel Veterans Memorial Coliseum, 2825 University Pkwy.

KISSIMMEE, FL (Spanish only), Silver Spurs Arena, 1875 Silver Spur Ln.
LAKE CHARLES, LA, Burton Coliseum, McNeese State University, 7001 Gulf Hwy.
LITTLE ROCK, AR, Barton Coliseum, Roosevelt Rd. & Dennison St.
MIRA LOMA, CA (Korean only), Assembly Hall of Jehovah's Witnesses, 3300 Cornerstone Dr.
PHILADELPHIA, PA, The Liacouras Center, Temple University, 1776 N. Broad St.
PLANT CITY, FL (American Sign Language only), Assembly Hall of Jehovah's Witnesses, 1904 N. Frontage Rd.
ROCHESTER, MN, Taylor Arena, Mayo Civic Center, 30 Civic Center Dr. SE
ROCKFORD, IL, Metrocentre Arena, 300 Elm St.
SAN FRANCISCO, CA (Portuguese sessions also), Cow Palace, 2600 Geneva Ave.
SUNNYSIDE, NY (Japanese only), Assembly Hall of Jehovah's Witnesses, 44-17 Greenpoint Ave.
TACOMA, WA, Tacoma Dome, 2727 East D St.
TOLEDO, OH (Spanish only), Seagate Convention Centre Arena, 401 Jefferson Ave.
WEST PALM BEACH, FL, Christian Convention Center of Jehovah's Witnesses, 1610 Palm Beach Lakes Blvd.

JULY 29-31
AMARILLO, TX (Spanish only), Cal Farley Coliseum, Civic Center, 401 S. Buchanan St.
AMHERST, MA (Spanish only), The Mullins Center, University of Massachusetts, Commonwealth Ave.
BELTON, TX (Spanish only), Bell County Expo Center Arena, 301 W. Loop 121
CLEVELAND, OH, Convocation Center Arena, Cleveland State University, Prospect Ave. & E. 21st St.
DE KALB, IL, Convocation Center, Northern Illinois University, 1525 W. Lincoln Hwy.
DULUTH, GA, The Arena at Gwinnett Center, 6400 Sugarloaf Pkwy.
JERSEY CITY, NJ (Portuguese only), Assembly Hall of Jehovah's Witnesses, 2932 Kennedy Blvd.
KISSIMMEE, FL (Spanish only), Silver Spurs Arena, 1875 Silver Spur Ln.
LAKE CHARLES, LA, Burton Coliseum, McNeese State University, 7001 Gulf Hwy.
LONG BEACH, CA (Arabic sessions also), Convention Center Arena, 300 E. Ocean Blvd.
NORCO, CA (Armenian only), Assembly Hall of Jehovah's Witnesses, 1001 Parkridge Ave.
PHILADELPHIA, PA, The Liacouras Center, Temple University, 1776 N. Broad St.
ROCKFORD, IL (Spanish only), Metrocentre Arena, 300 Elm St.
SAN FRANCISCO, CA, Cow Palace, 2600 Geneva Ave.
SUNNYSIDE, NY (Polish only), Assembly Hall of Jehovah's Witnesses, 44-17 Greenpoint Ave.
TOLEDO, OH, Seagate Convention Centre Arena, 401 Jefferson Ave.
UNIONDALE, NY, Nassau Veterans Memorial Coliseum, 1255 Hempstead Tpk.
WEST PALM BEACH, FL, Christian Convention Center of Jehovah's Witnesses, 1610 Palm Beach Lakes Blvd.

AUGUST 5-7
AMHERST, MA, The Mullins Center, University of Massachusetts, Commonwealth Ave.
BEAUMONT, TX (Spanish only), Civic Center Arena, 701 Main St.
BELTON, TX (Spanish only), Bell County Expo Center Arena, 301 W. Loop 121
BILOXI, MS, Mississippi Coast Coliseum, 2350 Beach Blvd.
CLEVELAND, OH, Convocation Center Arena, Cleveland State University, Prospect Ave. & E. 21st St.
DAYTON, OH, Ervin J. Nutter Center, Wright State University, 3640 Colonel Glenn Hwy.
DE KALB, IL, Convocation Center, Northern Illinois University, 1525 W. Lincoln Hwy.
HUNTSVILLE, AL (Spanish only), Von Braun Center Arena, 700 Monroe St. SW
KENNEWICK, WA, Three Rivers Coliseum, 7100 W. Quinault Ave.
KISSIMMEE, FL (Spanish only), Silver Spurs Arena, 1875 Silver Spur Ln.
PHILADELPHIA, PA, The Liacouras Center, Temple University, 1776 N. Broad St.
ROCHESTER, NY, Blue Cross Arena, Broad & Exchange Sts.
ROCKFORD, IL (Spanish only), Metrocentre Arena, 300 Elm St.
TOLEDO, OH, Seagate Convention Centre Arena, 401 Jefferson Ave.
WEST PALM BEACH, FL (Spanish only), Christian Convention Center of Jehovah's Witnesses, 1610 Palm Beach Lakes Blvd.

AUGUST 12-14
BEAUMONT, TX (Spanish only), Civic Center Arena, 701 Main St.
BELTON, TX, Bell County Expo Center Arena, 301 W. Loop 121
BILOXI, MS, Mississippi Coast Coliseum, 2350 Beach Blvd.
CLEVELAND, OH, Convocation Center Arena, Cleveland State University, Prospect Ave. & E. 21st St.
KISSIMMEE, FL, Silver Spurs Arena, 1875 Silver Spur Ln.

READING, PA, Sovereign Center Arena, 700 Penn St.
ROCKFORD, IL (Spanish only), Metrocentre Arena, 300 Elm St.
ST. LOUIS, MO (Korean only), Assembly Hall of Jehovah's Witnesses, 953 Laredo Ave.
TOLEDO, OH, Seagate Convention Centre Arena, 401 Jefferson Ave.
UNIONDALE, NY (Spanish only), Nassau Veterans Memorial Coliseum, 1255 Hempstead Tpk.
WEST PALM BEACH, FL (Spanish only), Christian Convention Center of Jehovah's Witnesses, 1610 Palm Beach Lakes Blvd.

AUGUST 19-21
BELTON, TX (Spanish only), Bell County Expo Center Arena, 301 W. Loop 121
KISSIMMEE, FL, Silver Spurs Arena, 1875 Silver Spur Ln.
LONG BEACH, CA (Spanish only), Convention Center Arena, 300 E. Ocean Blvd.
READING, PA, Sovereign Center Arena, 700 Penn St.
ROCKFORD, IL, Metrocentre Arena, 300 Elm St.
UNIONDALE, NY (Spanish only), Nassau Veterans Memorial Coliseum, 1255 Hempstead Tpk.
WEST PALM BEACH, FL (Spanish only), Christian Convention Center of Jehovah's Witnesses, 1610 Palm Beach Lakes Blvd.

AUGUST 26-28
BEAUMONT, TX (Spanish only), Civic Center Arena, 701 Main St.
BELTON, TX (Spanish only), Bell County Expo Center Arena, 301 W. Loop 121
GAINESVILLE, FL, Stephen C. O'Connell Center Arena, University of Florida, North South Dr. & University Ave.
LONG BEACH, CA (Spanish only), Convention Center Arena, 300 E. Ocean Blvd.
LOVELAND, CO, Budweiser Events Center, The Ranch, 5290 Arena Cir.
TOLEDO, OH, Seagate Convention Centre Arena, 401 Jefferson Ave.
UNIONDALE, NY, Nassau Veterans Memorial Coliseum, 1255 Hempstead Tpk.
WEST PALM BEACH, FL (Spanish only), Christian Convention Center of Jehovah's Witnesses, 1610 Palm Beach Lakes Blvd.

SEPTEMBER 2-4
LONG BEACH, CA, Convention Center Arena, 300 E. Ocean Blvd.
UNIONDALE, NY, Nassau Veterans Memorial Coliseum, 1255 Hempstead Tpk.

SEPTEMBER 9-11
LONG BEACH, CA, Convention Center Arena, 300 E. Ocean Blvd.

Britain

JUNE 10-12
GUERNSEY, C.I., Beau Sejour Leisure Centre, St. Peter Port
JUNE 17-19
BOURNEMOUTH, Bournemouth Athletic Football Club, Dean Court Ground
NEWCASTLE-UPON-TYNE, Newcastle Arena, Arena Way
NOTTINGHAM, Nottingham Ice Rink, Lower Parliament St.
JUNE 24-26
COVENTRY, Coventry City Football Club, Highfield Road Stadium, King Richard St.
LEEDS, Leeds United Football Club, Elland Rd.
PLYMOUTH, Plymouth Argyle Football Club, Home Park
JULY 1-3
LONDON (Spanish only), North London Assembly Hall, 174 Bowes Rd.
MANCHESTER, Manchester Arena, Hunts Bank
STOKE, Britannia Stadium, Stanley Matthews Way
JULY 8-10
LONDON (Greek only), North London Assembly Hall, 174 Bowes Rd.
JULY 15-17
CARDIFF, Millennium Stadium, West Gate St.
LONDON (Italian only), North London Assembly Hall, 174 Bowes Rd.
NORWICH, Norwich City Football Club, Carrow Rd.
PERTH, St. Johnstone Football Club, McDiarmid Park, Crieff Rd.
JULY 22-24
BRIGHTON, The Brighton Centre, Kings Rd.
GILLINGHAM, Priestfield Stadium, Redfern Ave., Kent
LONDON (Portuguese only), North London Assembly Hall, 174 Bowes Rd.
JULY 29-31
LONDON (French only), North London Assembly Hall, 174 Bowes Rd.
JULY 30-31
DUDLEY (Mandarin only), Dudley Assembly Hall, 22 Castle Hill
AUGUST 5-7
TWICKENHAM (DATE TENTATIVE), Rugby Football Union, Whitton Rd.

AUGUST 19-21
DUDLEY (Punjabi only), Dudley Assembly Hall, 22 Castle Hill
AUGUST 26-28
DUDLEY (British Sign Language only), Dudley Assembly Hall, 22 Castle Hill

Malta

SEPTEMBER 9-11
ST. PAUL'S BAY, New Dolmen Hotel Conference Centre, Qawra

Ireland

JULY 8-10
SWORDS, National Show Centre, Co. Dublin
JULY 15-17
SWORDS, National Show Centre, Co. Dublin
JULY 22-24
SWORDS, National Show Centre, Co. Dublin

Canada

JUNE 10-12
BELLEVILLE, ON, The Belleville Yardmen Arena, 265 Cannifton Rd.
CALGARY, AB, Pengrowth Saddledome, 555 Saddledome Rise SE
CORNWALL, ON, Ed Lumley Arena, Cornwall Civic Complex, 100 Water St. E.
DARTMOUTH, NS, Dartmouth Sportsplex, 110 Wyse Rd.
NANAIMO, BC, Frank Crane Arena, Beban Park Recreation Centre, 2300 Bowen Rd.
NORTH BAY, ON, Memorial Gardens Sports Arena, 100 Chippewa St. E.
PRINCE GEORGE, BC, Prince George Multi-plex Arena, 2188 Ospika Blvd.
SELKIRK, MB, Selkirk Recreation Complex, 180 Easton Dr.
JUNE 17-19
CORNWALL, ON, Ed Lumley Arena, Cornwall Civic Complex, 100 Water St. E.
GRANDE PRAIRIE, AB, Canada Games Arena, 10017 99th Ave.
KAMLOOPS, BC, Sport Mart Place, 300 Lorne St.
KITCHENER, ON, Kitchener Memorial Auditorium Complex, 400 East Ave.
MONCTON, NB, Coliseum Agrena, 377 Killam Dr.
QUEBEC CITY, QC (French only), Colisée Pepsi, 250, boul. Wilfrid-Hamel
SELKIRK, MB, Selkirk Recreation Complex, 180 Easton Dr.
VICTORIA, BC, Esquimalt's Archie Browning Sports Centre (Arena), 1151 Esquimalt Rd.
JUNE 24-26
CHILLIWACK, BC, Prospera Centre, 45323 Hodgins Ave.
CORNWALL, ON (French only), Ed Lumley Arena, Cornwall Civic Complex, 100 Water St. E.
KAMLOOPS, BC, Sport Mart Place, 300 Lorne St.
KITCHENER, ON, Kitchener Memorial Auditorium Complex, 400 East Ave.
SASKATOON, SK (Sign language also), Credit Union Centre, 3515 Thatcher Ave.
JULY 1-3
CHILLIWACK, BC, Prospera Centre, 45323 Hodgins Ave.
EDMONTON, AB, Rexall Place, Northlands Park, 7424 118th Ave.
HAMILTON, ON, Copps Coliseum, 101 York Blvd.
KITCHENER, ON (Spanish only), Kitchener Memorial Auditorium Complex, 400 East Ave.
MONTREAL, QC (Arabic only), Assembly Hall of Jehovah's Witnesses, 12700, boul. Métropolitain Est, Pointe-aux-Trembles
JULY 8-10
BRAMPTON, ON (Italian only), Assembly Hall of Jehovah's Witnesses, 2594 Highway 7 W.
CHILLIWACK, BC, Prospera Centre, 45323 Hodgins Ave.
HAMILTON, ON, Copps Coliseum, 101 York Blvd.
MOUNT PEARL, NL, Mount Pearl Glacier, Olympic Dr.
SHERBROOKE, QC (French only), Palais des sports, 360, rue du Parc
JULY 15-17
BRAMPTON, ON (Chinese only), Assembly Hall of Jehovah's Witnesses, 2594 Highway 7 W.
CHILLIWACK, BC, Prospera Centre, 45323 Hodgins Ave.
SHERBROOKE, QC (French only), Palais des sports, 360, rue du Parc
JULY 22-24
BRAMPTON, ON (Portuguese only), Assembly Hall of Jehovah's Witnesses, 2594 Highway 7 W.
SHERBROOKE, QC (French only), Palais des sports, 360, rue du Parc
SURREY, BC (Spanish only), Assembly Hall of Jehovah's Witnesses, 15577 82nd Ave.

Letter of appreciation and certificate of merit

БЛАГОДАРСТВЕ
ПИСЬМО

ПОХВАЛЬНАЯ
ГРАМОТА

Maria and her parents after her baptism

Good Conduct 'Adorns the Teaching of God'

YOUNG Maria in Kransnoyarsk, Russia, sings so well that her teacher put her in the school chorus. Soon thereafter, Maria respectfully approached one of her teachers to explain that she could not sing certain songs. Why? Because singing songs with religious connotations conflicted with her Bible-based convictions. Taken aback, the teacher wondered, 'What could be wrong with glorifying God in a song?'

To show why she would decline to sing a song about a Trinitarian God, Maria opened her Bible and explained that God and Jesus

Christ are not one God and that the holy spirit is God's active force. (Matthew 26:39; John 14:28; Acts 4:31) Maria relates: "My relationship with the teacher did not suffer. Overall, we have very good teachers in our school. They want us to be ourselves."

Throughout the school year, Maria's stand earned her the respect of teachers and classmates alike. Maria says: "Bible principles help me in my life. At the end of the school year, I received an award for honesty and orderliness, while my parents received an official thank-you letter from school for giving their daughter a good upbringing."

Maria was baptized on August 18, 2001. She says: "I am happy that I can serve such a wonderful God as Jehovah!" Young Witnesses of Jehovah worldwide live up to the words of Titus 2:10, where we read: "Adorn the teaching of our Savior, God, in all things."

MARCH 15, 2005

THE WATCHTOWER

ANNOUNCING JEHOVAH'S KINGDOM

Lessons Jesus Taught
Are They Practical for You?

THE WATCHTOWER®
ANNOUNCING JEHOVAH'S KINGDOM

March 15, 2005   Average Printing Each Issue: 26,439,000   Vol. 126, No. 6

THE PURPOSE OF *THE WATCHTOWER* is to exalt Jehovah God as Sovereign Lord of the universe. It keeps watch on world events as these fulfill Bible prophecy. It comforts all peoples with the good news that God's Kingdom will soon destroy those who oppress their fellowmen and that it will turn the earth into a paradise. It encourages faith in God's now-reigning King, Jesus Christ, whose shed blood opens the way for mankind to gain eternal life. *The Watchtower*, published by Jehovah's Witnesses continuously since 1879, is nonpolitical. It adheres to the Bible as its authority.

IN THIS ISSUE

3   Jesus' Worldwide Influence

4   What Influence Does Jesus Christ Have on You?

8   Youths Who Praise Jehovah Enrich Their Lives

10   Living No Longer for Ourselves

15   "You Were Bought With a Price"

21   Jehovah's Word Is Alive—Highlights From the Book of First Samuel

25   Samson Triumphs in the Strength of Jehovah!

29   A "Pim" Testifies to the Bible's Historicity

30   Questions From Readers

31   'Like a Precious Red-Colored Stone'

32   An Event to Remember

WATCHTOWER STUDIES

APRIL 18-24:
Living No Longer for Ourselves.
Page 10. Songs to be used: 200, 50.

APRIL 25–MAY 1:
"You Were Bought With a Price."
Page 15. Songs to be used: 2, 156.

Publication of *The Watchtower* is part of a worldwide Bible educational work supported by voluntary donations.

Unless otherwise indicated, Scripture quotations are from the modern-language *New World Translation of the Holy Scriptures—With References.*

The Watchtower (ISSN 0043-1087) is published semimonthly by Watchtower Bible and Tract Society of New York, Inc.; M. H. Larson, President; G. F. Simonis, Secretary-Treasurer; 25 Columbia Heights, Brooklyn, NY 11201-2483. Periodicals Postage Paid at Brooklyn, NY, and at additional mailing offices. **POSTMASTER:** Send address changes to Watchtower, **Wallkill, NY 12589.**

Changes of address should reach us 30 days before your moving date. Give us your old and new address (if possible, your old address label).

Semimonthly   ENGLISH

Would you welcome more information or a free home Bible study? Please send your request to Jehovah's Witnesses, using the appropriate address below.

America, United States of: Wallkill, NY 12589. *Antigua:* Box 119, St. Johns. *Australia:* Box 280, Ingleburn, NSW 1890. *Bahamas:* Box N-1247, Nassau, N.P. *Barbados, W.I.:* Crusher Site Road, Prospect, St. James. *Britain:* The Ridgeway, London NW7 1RN. *Canada:* Box 4100, Halton Hills (Georgetown), Ontario L7G 4Y4. *Germany:* Niederselters, Am Steinfels, D-65618 Selters. *Ghana:* P. O. Box GP 760, Accra. *Guyana:* 352-360 Tyrell St., Republic Park Phase 2 EBD. *Hawaii 96819:* 2055 Kam IV Rd., Honolulu. *Hong Kong:* 4 Kent Road, Kowloon Tong. *India:* Post Box 6440, Yelahanka, Bangalore 560 064, KAR. *Ireland:* Newcastle, Greystones, Co. Wicklow. *Jamaica:* P. O. Box 103, Old Harbour, St. Catherine. *Japan:* 1271 Nakashinden, Ebina City, Kanagawa Pref., 243-0496. *Kenya:* P.O. Box 47788, GPO Nairobi 00100. *New Zealand:* P.O. Box 75-142, Manurewa. *Nigeria:* P.M.B. 1090, Benin City 300001, Edo State. *Philippines, Republic of:* P. O. Box 2044, 1060 Manila. *South Africa:* Private Bag X2067, Krugersdorp, 1740. *Trinidad and Tobago, Republic of:* Lower Rapsey Street & Laxmi Lane, Curepe. *Zambia:* Box 33459, Lusaka 10101. *Zimbabwe:* Private Bag WG-5001, Westgate.

NOW PUBLISHED IN 150 LANGUAGES. SEMIMONTHLY: Afrikaans, Albanian,* Amharic, Arabic, Bengali, Bicol, Bislama, Bulgarian, Cebuano,* Chichewa,* Chinese (Simplified),* Cibemba,* Croatian,* Czech,*# Danish,*# Dutch,*# East Armenian, Efik,* English*#© (also Braille), Estonian, Ewe, Fijian, Finnish,*# French,*# Ga, Georgian, German,*# Greek,* Gujarati, Gun, Hebrew, Hiligaynon, Hindi, Hungarian,*# Igbo,* Iloko,* Indonesian, Italian,*# Japanese*# (also Braille), Kannada, Kinyarwanda, Kirundi, Korean*# (also Braille), Latvian, Lingala, Lithuanian, Luvale, Macedonian, Malagasy,* Malayalam, Maltese, Marathi, Myanmar, Nepali, New Guinea Pidgin, Norwegian,*# Pangasinan, Papiamento (Aruba), Papiamento (Curaçao), Polish,*# Portuguese*# (also Braille), Punjabi, Rarotongan, Romanian,* Russian,* Samar-Leyte, Samoan, Sango, Sepedi, Serbian, Sesotho, Shona,* Silozi, Sinhala, Slovak,* Slovenian, Solomon Islands Pidgin, Spanish,*# Sranantongo, Swahili,* Swedish,*# Tagalog,* Tamil, Telugu, Thai, Tigrinya, Tongan, Tshiluba, Tsonga, Tswana, Turkish, Twi, Ukrainian,* Urdu, Venda, Vietnamese, Wallisian, Xhosa, Yoruba,* Zulu*

MONTHLY: American Sign Language,△□ Armenian, Assamese, Azerbaijani (Roman script), Brazilian Sign Language,△ Cambodian, Chitonga, Gilbertese, Greenlandic, Haitian Creole, Hausa, Hiri Motu, Icelandic, Isoko, Kaonde, Kazakh, Kikongo, Kiluba, Kirghiz, Kwanyama/Ndonga, Luganda, Marshallese, Mauritian Creole, Mizo, Monokutuba, Moore, Niuean, Ossetian, Otetela, Palauan, Persian, Ponapean, Seychelles Creole, Tahitian, Tatar, Tiv, Trukese, Tumbuka, Tuvaluan, Umbundu, Yapese, Zande

* Study articles also available in large-print edition.

\# Audiocassettes also available.

© CD (MP3 format) also available.

△ Videocassette

□ DVD

"I know of no one who has done more for humanity than Jesus."
—Mohandas K. Gandhi

"Nobody else has influenced the world so much."
—Edgar Goodspeed

Culver Pictures

Jesus' Worldwide Influence

"ALL that the gospels report of what Jesus said, in private and in public, he could have uttered in two hours," wrote Bible translator Edgar Goodspeed. "Yet that little was so stirring, so moving and so penetrating that it is safe to say nobody else has influenced the world so much."

When Jesus Christ completed his earthly ministry in the year 33 C.E., his followers numbered at least some 120 men and women. (Acts 1:15) Today, more than two billion people claim to be Christians. Hundreds of millions more recognize Jesus as a prophet. His teachings have indeed had an extraordinary influence on mankind.

Jesus' worldwide influence has been acknowledged even by non-Christian leaders. For example, Jewish rabbi Hyman Enelow wrote: "Jesus has become the most popular, the most studied, the most influential figure in the religious history of mankind." Enelow also stated: "Who can compute all that Jesus has meant to humanity? The love he has inspired, the solace he has given, the good he has engendered, the hope and joy he has kindled—all that is unequalled in human history. Among the great and the good that the human race has produced, none has even approached Jesus in universality of appeal and sway. He has become the most fascinating figure in history." And Hindu leader Mohandas K. Gandhi said: "I know of no one who has done more for humanity than Jesus. In fact, there is nothing wrong with Christianity." However, he added: "The trouble is with you Christians. You do not begin to live up to your own teachings."

Christendom has a long record of failure in living up to Jesus' teachings. Cecil John Cadoux, historian of Christianity, noted that "the gradual and steady growth throughout the Church of a certain moral laxity" had the "attention of Christian leaders as early as . . . 140 A.D." He observed: "This abatement of the primitive moral rigour would naturally assist the process of conformity to the ways of the world."

This process gained momentum in the fourth century, when Roman Emperor Constantine embraced Christianity. "Historians have not failed to notice, and in some cases to deplore," wrote Cadoux, "the immense compromise to which the Church was committed by her alliance with Constantinus." During the centuries since then, professed Christians have carried out many dark deeds that dishonor the name of Christ.

The questions of concern, then, are: What did Jesus actually teach? And what influence should his teachings have on us?

What Influence Does Jesus Christ Have on You?

IN VIEW of what we considered in the preceding article, can there be any doubt that Jesus' teachings have had a worldwide impact? The question of importance, though, is, "What influence do Jesus' teachings have on me personally?"

Jesus' teachings touched on a vast array of subjects. The valuable lessons they convey can affect every aspect of your life. Let us focus on what Jesus taught about setting priorities in life, cultivating friendship with God, establishing good relationships with others, solving problems, and refraining from acts of violence.

Set Priorities in Life

The fast-paced world of today makes so many demands on our time and energies that spiritual considerations often get crowded out. Consider the case of a man in his 20's whom we will call Jerry. While Jerry enjoys conversations on spiritual subjects and values what he learns from them, he laments: "I just do not have the time to engage in them consistently. I work six days a week. Sunday is my only day off. And after I take care of the things I must do, I am too tired." If you find yourself in a similar predicament, you can benefit from what Jesus taught in the Sermon on the Mount.

Jesus said to the crowd who had gathered to hear him: "Stop being anxious about your souls as to what you will eat or what you will drink, or about your bodies as to what you will wear. Does not the soul mean more than food and the body than clothing? Observe intently the birds of heaven, because they do not sow seed or reap or gather into storehouses; still your heavenly Father feeds them. Are you not worth more than they are? . . . So never be anxious and say, 'What are we to eat?' or, 'What are we to drink?' or, 'What are we to put on?' For all these are the things the nations are eagerly pursuing. For your heavenly Father knows you need all these things. Keep on, then, seeking first the kingdom and his righteousness, and all these other things will be added to you." (Matthew 6:25-33) What do we learn from this?

Jesus was not implying that we should neglect taking care of our physical needs and those of our family members. "If anyone does not provide for those who are his own, and especially for those who are members of his household," states the Bible, "he has disowned the faith and is worse than a person without faith." (1 Timothy 5:8) However, Jesus promised that if we put first things first and give priority to spiritual matters, God will make sure that other needs are met. The lesson here is about setting priorities. Following this advice leads to happiness, for "happy are those conscious of their spiritual need." —Matthew 5:3.

"Your heavenly Father feeds them"

Cultivate Friendship With God

Those conscious of their spiritual need see the necessity of cultivating a good relationship with God. How do we establish a good relationship with anyone? Do we not try to get to know that person better? We must take time to learn about his views, attitudes, abilities, accomplishments, likes, and dislikes. The same is true when it comes to building a friendship with God. Accurate knowledge of him is required. When praying to God about his disciples, Jesus said: "This means everlasting life, their taking in knowledge of you, the only true God, and of the one whom you sent forth, Jesus Christ." (John 17:3) Yes, cultivating intimacy with God requires that we come to know him. The only source of that knowledge is God's inspired Word, the Bible. (2 Timothy 3:16) We must set aside time to study the Scriptures.

However, knowledge in itself is not enough. In the same prayer, Jesus said: "They [his disciples] have observed your word." (John 17:6) We must not only take in knowledge of God but also act in harmony with that knowledge. How else could we become God's friend? Can we really expect our friendship with anyone to grow if we willfully act in a manner that goes contrary to that one's ideas and principles? God's views and principles, then, ought to guide all our steps in life. Consider how two of his principles apply to our relationships with other humans.

Establish Good Relationships With Others

On one occasion, Jesus related a short story in order to teach a valuable lesson in human relationships. He spoke of a king who wanted to settle accounts with his servants. One of them, though, had a huge debt and no means to repay it. The master ordered that the man, his wife, and his children be sold and payment made. The debtor fell down and begged: "Be patient with me and I will pay back everything to you." Moved with pity, the master canceled his debt. But that slave went off, found a fellow slave who owed him a modest sum, and demanded repayment. Though this fellow slave begged for mercy, the first slave had him thrown into prison until he paid off all that he owed. When the king heard of this, he became angry. "Ought you not . . . to have had mercy on your fellow slave, as I also had mercy on you?" he demanded. And he had the unforgiving slave imprisoned until he repaid all that he owed. Drawing a lesson from the story, Jesus said: "In like manner my heavenly Father will also deal with you if you do not forgive each one his brother from your hearts."—Matthew 18:23-35.

As imperfect humans, we have many faults. We can never pay back to God the huge debt we have accumulated because of transgressing against him. All we can do is seek his forgiveness. And Jehovah God is ready to forgive all our failings, provided we forgive our brothers for sins they have committed against us. What a forceful lesson that is! Jesus taught his followers to pray: "Forgive us our debts, as we also have forgiven our debtors."—Matthew 6:12.

Get to the Root of the Problem

When it came to understanding human nature, Jesus was an expert. His counsel on solving problems went to their very root. Consider the following two examples.

"You heard that it was said to those of ancient times, 'You must not murder; but whoever commits a murder will be accountable to the court of justice,'" said Jesus. "However, I say to you that everyone who continues wrathful with his brother will be accountable to the court of justice." (Matthew 5:21, 22) Jesus here showed that the root of the problem of murder lies at a level deeper than the violent act itself. It is in the attitude that grows in the murderer's heart. If people did not allow a feeling of resentment or anger to build up, premeditated violence would disappear. How much bloodshed would be avoided if this teaching was applied!

Notice how Jesus gets to the bottom of another problem that causes a great deal of heartache. He told the crowd: "You heard that it was said, 'You must not commit adultery.' But I say to you that everyone that keeps on looking at a woman so as to have a passion for her has already committed adultery with her in his heart. If, now, that right eye of yours is making you stumble, tear it out and throw it away from you." (Matthew 5:27-29) Jesus taught that the problem goes deeper than the immoral behavior itself. It is in what precedes it—immoral desires. If a person refuses to dwell on improper longings and 'tears them out' of his mind, then he will overcome the potential problem of immoral behavior.

"Return Your Sword to Its Place"

On the night of Jesus' betrayal and arrest, one of his disciples drew his sword to defend him. Jesus commanded him: "Return your sword to its place, for all those who take the sword will perish by the sword." (Matthew 26:52) The following morning, Jesus told Pontius Pilate: "My kingdom is no part of this world. If my kingdom were part of this world, my attendants would have fought that I should not be delivered up to the Jews. But, as it is, my kingdom is not from this source." (John 18:36) Is this teaching impractical?

What was the attitude of the early Christians toward what Jesus taught about not resorting to violence? The book *The Early Christian Attitude to War* says: "Inasmuch as they [Jesus' teachings] ruled out as illicit all use of violence and injury against others, clearly implied [was] the illegitimacy of participation in war . . . The early Christians took Jesus at his word, and understood his inculcations of gentleness and nonresistance in their literal sense. They closely identified their religion with peace; they strongly condemned war for the bloodshed which it involved." How

different the course of history would have been had all those who claimed to be Christians actually followed this teaching!

You Can Benefit From All of Jesus' Teachings

The teachings of Jesus that we have considered are beautiful, simple, and powerful. Mankind can benefit from being acquainted with his teachings and putting them into practice.*

Jehovah's Witnesses in your area will be happy to help you to see how you can benefit from the wisest teachings ever uttered by any human. You have our warm invitation to contact them or to write to the address on page 2 of this magazine.

---

* For a systematic consideration of all of Jesus' teachings, see *The Greatest Man Who Ever Lived,* published by Jehovah's Witnesses.

Jesus' teachings can have a fine influence on your life

Youths Who Praise Jehovah Enrich Their Lives

"I WANT the best that life has to offer!" That is how one teenage boy described his expectations. But how can a young person get the very best out of life? The Bible provides a straightforward answer: "Keep your Creator in mind while you are young!" —Ecclesiastes 12:1, *Contemporary English Version.*

Praising and serving Jehovah is not just for grown-ups. Samuel, a son of Elkanah and Hannah, was very young when he ministered to Jehovah at the tabernacle. (1 Samuel 1:19, 20, 24; 2:11) A Hebrew girl of tender age showed implicit faith in Jehovah when she suggested that the Syrian army chief Naaman go to the prophet Elisha in order to be healed of leprosy. (2 Kings 5:2, 3) At Psalm 148:7, 12, both boys and girls are commanded to praise Jehovah.* When he was only 12 years of age, Jesus took a keen interest in the service of his Father. (Luke 2:41-49) Because of their training from the Scriptures, some boys who saw Jesus at the temple cried out: "Save, we pray, the Son of David!"—Matthew 21:15, 16.

Praising Jehovah Today

Today, many youths among Jehovah's Witnesses take pride in their beliefs and courageously speak to others about them in schools and elsewhere. Consider two examples.

In Britain, 18-year-old Stephanie's class was discussing abortion and other ethical issues. The teacher asserted that abortions are now generally accepted and that no young girl would have reason to object to this practice. When everyone in the class agreed with this

_____
* See the *2005 Calendar of Jehovah's Witnesses,* March/April.

viewpoint, Stephanie felt compelled to defend her Bible-based position. The opportunity to do so came when the teacher asked Stephanie for her opinion. Although she was nervous at first, Stephanie used the occasion to present the Scriptural view. She paraphrased Exodus 21:22-24 and explained that if it was wrong to injure an unborn child, then an abortion would obviously be contrary to God's will.

The teacher, a member of the clergy, had never read these verses. Stephanie's bold witness led to many fine discussions with her classmates on various subjects. One girl now regularly accepts the latest copies of *The Watchtower* and *Awake!,* and two others attended a district convention of Jehovah's Witnesses to see Stephanie get baptized in symbol of her dedication to God.

Six-year-old Vareta, living in Suriname, South America, seized the opportunity to praise God when her teacher needed comfort from the Scriptures. Upon returning after a three-day absence, the teacher asked her students if they knew why she was away. They answered, "You were sick, right?" "No,"

> ### JEHOVAH SUPPORTS YOUNG ONES
>
> *"You are my hope, O Sovereign Lord Jehovah, my confidence from my youth."* —Psalm 71:5.
>
> *"[God] is satisfying your lifetime with what is good; your youth keeps renewing itself just like that of an eagle."* —Psalm 103:5.

> ## *"Praise Jehovah from the earth, . . . you young men and also you virgins."*
> —PSALM 148:7, 12

replied the teacher. "My sister died, and I feel very sad. So you have to be quiet."

That afternoon while her mother was taking a nap, Vareta was busy leafing through older magazines, reading the titles. She came upon *The Watchtower* of July 15, 2001, with the title "Is There Life After Death?" Filled with enthusiasm, she awakened her mother and said, "Mommy, Mommy, look! I found a magazine about death for my teacher!" The magazine was sent to the teacher with a letter from Vareta. She wrote: "This is especially for you. In Paradise you are going to see your sister again because Jehovah never lies. He has promised that he will bring a paradise, not in heaven, but on earth." The teacher expressed her deep appreciation for the Bible-based comfort that these articles provided.

Building for the Future

Jehovah is "the happy God," and he wants young ones to be happy. (1 Timothy 1:11) His own Word says: "Enjoy your youth. Be happy while you are still young." (Ecclesiastes 11:9, *Today's English Version*) Jehovah sees beyond the moment and perceives the long-term consequences of both good and bad behavior. That is why his Word admonishes youths: "Remember, now, your Grand Creator in the days of your young manhood, before the calamitous days proceed to come, or the years have arrived when you will say: 'I have no delight in them.'"—Ecclesiastes 12:1.

Yes, Jehovah desires that youths enjoy to the full the precious gift of life. By remembering and praising God, young people can lead a meaningful, rewarding life. Even when faced with challenges, they can confidently say: "My help is from Jehovah." —Psalm 121:2.

LIVING NO LONGER FOR OURSELVES

"[Christ] died for all that those who live might live no longer for themselves."
—2 CORINTHIANS 5:15.

IT WAS Jesus' last night on earth. In just a few hours, he would give his life in behalf of all those who would exercise faith in him. On that night, Jesus told his faithful apostles many important things. Among them was a command regarding a quality that would prove to be an identifying mark of his followers. "I am giving you a new commandment," he said, "that you love one another; just as I have loved you, that you also love one another. By this all will know that you are my disciples, if you have love among yourselves."—John 13:34, 35.

² True Christians are to display self-sacrificing love for one another and put the needs of their fellow believers ahead of their own. They should not hesitate even to 'surrender their soul in behalf of their friends.' (John 15:13) How did the early Christians respond to the new commandment? In his famous work *Apology,* the second-century writer Tertullian quoted others who said of Christians: 'See how they love one another; how they are ready even to die for one another.'

³ We too must "go on carrying the burdens of one another, and thus fulfill the law of the Christ." (Galatians 6:2) However, selfishness is one of the greatest obstacles to obeying the law of the Christ and 'loving Jehovah our God with our whole heart, soul, and mind and loving our neighbors as ourselves.' (Matthew 22:37-39) Being imperfect, we are inclined to be self-centered. Add

1, 2. What Scriptural command moved Jesus' first-century followers to overcome selfishness?

3, 4. (a) Why should we counteract selfishness? (b) What will we consider in this article?

to this the stress of everyday life, the competitive atmosphere at school or in the workplace, and the struggle to make ends meet, and this natural tendency is intensified. This inclination toward selfishness is not on the wane. The apostle Paul warned: "In the last days . . . men will become utterly self-centred." —2 Timothy 3:1, 2, *Phillips.*

"Be kind to yourself, Lord"

⁴ Toward the last part of his earthly ministry, Jesus gave his disciples a three-step process that could help them to overcome selfishness. What was it, and how can we benefit from his instructions?

A Sure Antidote!

⁵ Jesus was preaching near Caesarea Philippi in northern Galilee. This peaceful, picturesque area may have seemed more suitable for leisure than for self-denial. While there, however, Jesus began to show his disciples that "he must go to Jerusalem and suffer many things from the older men and chief priests and scribes, and be killed, and on the third day be raised up." (Matthew 16: 21) How shocking this disclosure must have been to Jesus' disciples, for up to then they had expected their Leader to establish his Kingdom on the earth!—Luke 19:11; Acts 1:6.

⁶ Peter immediately "took [Jesus] aside and commenced rebuking him, saying: 'Be kind to yourself, Lord; you will not have this destiny at all.'" How did Jesus respond? "Turning his back, he said to Peter: 'Get behind me, Satan! You are a stumbling block to me, because you think, not

God's thoughts, but those of men.'" What a contrast there was between the two outlooks! Jesus willingly accepted the self-sacrificing course God had assigned him—one that would lead to his death on a torture stake within a few months. Peter recommended a comfortable course. "Be kind to yourself," he said. Peter undoubtedly had good intentions. Still, Jesus rebuked him because Peter had on that occasion allowed himself to be influenced by Satan. Peter had "not God's mind, but that of men." —Matthew 16:22, 23; footnote.

⁷ Echoes of Peter's words to Jesus can be heard today. The world commonly urges a person to 'be good to yourself' or 'follow the course of least resistance.' On the other hand, Jesus recommended a completely different mental attitude. He told his disciples: "If anyone wants to come after me, let him disown himself and pick up his torture stake and continually follow me." (Matthew 16: 24) "These words are not an invitation to discipleship for outsiders," states *The New Interpreter's Bible,* "but reflection on the meaning of discipleship for those who have already responded to the call of Christ." The three steps that Jesus outlined, as recorded in that scripture, are to be taken by believers. Let us consider each step separately.

⁸ First, we must *disown ourselves.* The Greek word for "to disown oneself" indicates a willingness to say no to selfish desires or personal convenience. Disowning ourselves is not just a matter of our occasionally forgoing certain pleasures; neither

---

5. While preaching in northern Galilee, what did Jesus disclose to his disciples, and why was that shocking to them?
6. Why did Jesus strongly rebuke Peter?

7. As recorded at Matthew 16:24, what course did Jesus outline for his followers to take?
8. Explain what it means to disown yourself.

does it mean that we become ascetic or self-destructive. We no longer 'belong to ourselves' in that we willingly surrender our whole life and everything in it to Jehovah. (1 Corinthians 6:19, 20) Rather than being self-oriented, our life becomes God-oriented. Disowning ourselves implies a determination to do the will of God, even though this may go against our own imperfect inclinations. We show that we are exclusively devoted to God when we make a dedication to him and get baptized. We then strive to live up to our dedication for the rest of our life.

9 The second step is that we must *pick up our torture stake.* In the first century, a torture stake represented suffering, shame, and death. Normally, only criminals were executed on a torture stake or had their dead bodies hung on a stake. By this expression, Jesus showed that a Christian must be prepared to accept persecution, contempt, or even death, since he is no part of the world. (John 15:18-20) Our Christian standards set us apart, so the world may 'speak abusively of us.' (1 Peter 4:4) This could happen at school, at our place of work, or even within the family. (Luke 9:23) Nevertheless, we are willing to endure the world's contempt because we no longer live for ourselves. Jesus said: "Happy are you when people reproach you and persecute you and lyingly say every sort of wicked thing against you for my sake. Rejoice and leap for joy, since your reward is great in the heavens." (Matthew 5:11, 12) Indeed, having God's favor is what matters.

10 Third, Jesus Christ said that we must *continually follow him.* According to *An Expository Dictionary of New Testament Words,*

by W. E. Vine, to follow means to be a companion—"one going in the same way." First John 2:6 states: "He that says he remains in union with [God] is under obligation himself also to go on walking just as that one [Christ] walked." How did Jesus walk? Jesus' love for his heavenly Father and for his disciples left no room for selfishness. "The Christ did not please himself," wrote Paul. (Romans 15:3) Even when he felt tired or hungry, Jesus put the needs of others before his own. (Mark 6:31-34) Jesus also exerted himself vigorously in the Kingdom preaching and teaching work. Should we not imitate him as we zealously fulfill our commission to 'make disciples of people of all the nations, teaching them to observe all the things Jesus has commanded'? (Matthew 28:19, 20) In all of this, Christ left a model for us, and we must "follow his steps closely."—1 Peter 2:21.

11 It is vital that we disown ourselves, pick up our torture stake, and continually follow our Exemplar. Our doing so counteracts selfishness—a sure obstacle to displaying self-sacrificing love. Moreover, Jesus said: "Whoever wants to save his soul will lose it; but whoever loses his soul for my sake will find it. For what benefit will it be to a man if he gains the whole world but forfeits his soul? or what will a man give in exchange for his soul?"—Matthew 16:25, 26.

We Cannot Serve Two Masters

12 Some months after Jesus emphasized the need for his disciples to disown themselves, a rich young ruler came up to him and said: "Teacher, what good must I do in

---

9. (a) When Jesus was on earth, what did a torture stake represent? (b) In what way do we pick up our torture stake?
10. What is involved in following Jesus continually?

11. Why is it important that we disown ourselves, pick up our torture stake, and continually follow Jesus Christ?
12, 13. (a) What was a matter of concern to the young ruler who asked for Jesus' advice? (b) What counsel did Jesus give the young man, and why?

What prevented the young ruler from following Jesus?

order to get everlasting life?" Jesus told him to "observe the commandments continually" and then cited some of them. The young man said: "I have kept all these." The man was apparently sincere and had done his best to obey the commandments of the Law. So he asked: "What yet am I lacking?" In response, Jesus extended to the young man a unique invitation, saying: "If you want to be perfect ["complete," *New American Standard Bible*], go sell your belongings and give to the poor and you will have treasure in heaven, and come be my follower." —Matthew 19:16-21.

¹³ Jesus saw that for the young man to serve Jehovah whole-souled, he needed to get rid of the big distraction in his life—his material wealth. A true disciple of Christ cannot serve two masters. He "cannot slave for God and for Riches." (Matthew 6:24) He needs a 'simple eye' that is focused on spiritual matters. (Matthew 6:22) Getting rid of one's belongings and giving them to the poor is an act of self-sacrifice. In exchange for this material sacrifice, Jesus offered the

young ruler the priceless privilege of amassing treasure in heaven—a treasure that would mean everlasting life for him and would lead to the prospect of eventually ruling with Christ in heaven. The young man was not ready to disown himself. "He went away grieved, for he was holding many possessions." (Matthew 19:22) Other followers of Jesus, however, responded differently.

¹⁴ Some two years earlier, Jesus had extended a similar invitation to four fishermen named Peter, Andrew, James, and John. Two of them were fishing at the time, and the other two were busy mending their nets. Jesus said to them: "Come after me, and I will make you fishers of men." All four ultimately abandoned their fishing business and followed Jesus for the rest of their life.—Matthew 4:18-22.

¹⁵ Many Christians today have imitated the example of the four fishermen rather than that of the rich young ruler. They have sacrificed wealth and opportunity in this world in order to serve Jehovah. "When I was 22, I had to make a big decision," says Deborah. She explains: "I had studied the Bible for about six months, and I wanted to dedicate my life to Jehovah, but my family were very much opposed. They were multimillionaires, and they felt that my becoming a Witness would bring them social disgrace. They gave me 24 hours to decide which I preferred—a life of luxury or the truth. If I didn't cut off all contact with the Witnesses, my family would disinherit me.

---

14. How did four fishermen respond to Jesus' invitation to follow him?
15. How did one modern-day Witness of Jehovah make sacrifices to follow Jesus?

Jehovah helped me make the right decision and gave me the strength to carry it out. I have spent the last 42 years in full-time service, and I have no regrets whatsoever. By turning my back on a selfish, pleasure-oriented life-style, I escaped the emptiness and unhappiness I see among my family members. Along with my husband, I have helped over a hundred people to learn the truth. These spiritual children are much more precious to me than any material riches." Millions of other Witnesses of Jehovah share her sentiments. What about you?

¹⁶ The desire to live no longer for themselves has moved thousands of Jehovah's Witnesses to serve as pioneers, or full-time Kingdom proclaimers. Others, whose circumstances do not allow them to share in the full-time ministry, cultivate the pioneer spirit and support the Kingdom-preaching work to the best of their ability. Parents show a similar spirit when they devote much of their time and they sacrifice personal interests in order to give spiritual training to their children. In one way or another, all of us can show that Kingdom interests come first in our lives.—Matthew 6:33.

Whose Love Compels Us?

¹⁷ Displaying self-sacrificing love is not the easiest course to follow. But think of what it is that compels us. Paul wrote: "The love the Christ has compels us, because this is what we have judged, that one man died for all . . . And he died for all that those who live might live no longer for themselves, but for him who died for them and was raised up." (2 Corinthians 5:14, 15) It is the love of the Christ that compels us to live no longer for ourselves. What a powerful motivation that is! Since Christ died for us, do we not

sense the moral obligation to live for him? After all, gratitude for the depth of the love that God and Christ have shown us compelled us to dedicate our lives to God and become disciples of Christ.—John 3:16; 1 John 4:10, 11.

¹⁸ Is living no longer for ourselves worthwhile? After the rich young ruler rejected Christ's invitation and went away, Peter said to Jesus: "Look! We have left all things and followed you; what actually will there be for us?" (Matthew 19:27) Peter and the other apostles had truly disowned themselves. What would be their reward? Jesus first spoke of the privilege they would have of ruling with him in heaven. (Matthew 19:28) On the same occasion, Jesus referred to blessings that every one of his followers could enjoy. He said: "No one has left house or brothers or sisters or mother or father or children or fields for my sake and for the sake of the good news who will not get a hundredfold now in this period of time . . . and in the coming system of things everlasting life." (Mark 10:29, 30) We receive much more than what we have sacrificed. Are not our spiritual fathers, mothers, brothers, sisters, and children much more valuable than anything we have renounced for the sake of

18. Why is a self-sacrificing course worthwhile?

Do You Recall?

- Why should we counteract our selfish tendencies?
- What does it mean to disown ourselves, pick up our torture stake, and follow Jesus continually?
- What motivates us to live no longer for ourselves?
- Why is living a life of self-sacrifice worthwhile?

16. How can we show that we no longer live for ourselves?
17. What motivates us to make sacrifices?

*Love compels
Jehovah's Witnesses
to serve as zealous
Kingdom proclaimers*

the Kingdom? Who had the most rewarding life—Peter or the rich young ruler?

¹⁹ By his words and deeds, Jesus showed that happiness comes from giving and from serving, not from selfishness. (Matthew 20: 28; Acts 20:35) When we no longer live for

ourselves but follow Christ continually, we find great satisfaction in life now and have the prospect of eternal life in the future. Of course, when we disown ourselves, Jehovah becomes our Owner. We thus become slaves of God. Why is this slavery rewarding? How does it affect the decisions we make in life? The next article will discuss these questions.

---

19. (a) On what does true happiness depend? (b) What will we consider in the following article?

"YOU WERE BOUGHT WITH A PRICE"

"You were bought with a price. By all means, glorify God."—1 CORINTHIANS 6:20.

"SLAVERY was prevalent and widely accepted in the ancient world," states the *Holman Illustrated Bible Dictionary*. It adds: "The economy of Egypt, Greece, and Rome was based on slave labor. In the first Christian century, one out of three persons in Italy and one out of five elsewhere was a slave."

² Although slavery also existed in ancient Israel, the Mosaic Law ensured that Hebrew slaves received protection. For instance, the

Law required that an Israelite could serve as a slave for no more than six years. In the seventh year, he was to "go out as one set free without charge." But the regulations concerning the treatment of slaves were so fair and humane that the Law of Moses made the following provision: "If the slave should insistently say, 'I really love my master, my wife and my sons; I do not want to go out as one set free,' then his master must bring him near to the true God and must bring him up against the door or the doorpost; and his master must pierce his ear through with an awl, and he must be his slave to time

---

1, 2. (a) According to the Mosaic Law, how were Israelite slaves to be treated? (b) What choice did the slave who loved his master have?

The provision of voluntary slavery in Israel was a foregleam of Christian servitude

indefinite."—Exodus 21:2-6; Leviticus 25:42, 43; Deuteronomy 15:12-18.

³ The provision of voluntary servitude provided a foregleam of the type of slavery that true Christians are under. For example, the Bible writers Paul, James, Peter, and Jude identified themselves as slaves of God and of Christ. (Titus 1:1; James 1:1; 2 Peter 1:1; Jude 1) Paul reminded the Thessalonian Christians that they had "turned to God from [their] idols to slave for a living and true God." (1 Thessalonians 1:9) What moved those Christians to become willing slaves of God? Well, what was the motivating force in the case of the Israelite slave who renounced his personal freedom? Was it not love for his master? Christian slavery is based on love for God. When we come to know and love the true and living God, we are moved to serve him "with all [our] heart and all [our] soul." (Deuteronomy 10:12, 13) What, though, does becoming slaves of God and of Christ involve? How does this affect our daily lives?

---

3. (a) What type of slavery did first-century Christians accept? (b) What moves us to serve God?

"Do All Things for God's Glory"

⁴ A slave has been defined as "a person who is the legal property of another or others and is bound to absolute obedience." We become Jehovah's legal property when we dedicate our lives to him and get baptized. "You do not belong to yourselves, for you were bought with a price," explains the apostle Paul. (1 Corinthians 6:19, 20) That price, of course, is Jesus Christ's ransom sacrifice, since on that basis God accepts us as his servants, whether we are anointed Christians or we are their companions with an earthly hope. (Ephesians 1:7; 2:13; Revelation 5:9) Thus, from the time of our baptism, "we belong to Jehovah." (Romans 14:8) Since we have been bought with the precious blood of Jesus Christ, we also become his slaves and are under obligation to keep his commandments.—1 Peter 1:18, 19.

⁵ Slaves must obey their master. Our servitude is voluntary and stems from our love

---

4. How do we become slaves of God and of Christ?
5. As slaves of Jehovah, what primary obligation do we have, and how can we fulfill it?

We become God's slaves when we get baptized

Christians put God's will first

for the Master. "This is what the love of God means," states 1 John 5:3, "that we observe his commandments; and yet his commandments are not burdensome." For us, then, our obedience is proof of our love as well as our submission. It is evident in everything we do. "Whether you are eating or drinking or doing anything else," said Paul, "do all things for God's glory." (1 Corinthians 10:31) In everyday life, even in small ways, we want to show that we "slave for Jehovah." —Romans 12:11.

⁶ When making decisions, for example, we want to be careful to take into account the will of our heavenly Master, Jehovah. (Malachi 1:6) Difficult decisions may test our obedience to God. Will we then heed his counsel rather than follow the inclinations of our "treacherous" and "desperate" heart? (Jeremiah 17:9) Melisa, a single Christian, had been baptized for only a short time when a young man began to take an interest in her. He seemed to be a nice person, and

he was already studying the Bible with Jehovah's Witnesses. Nevertheless, an elder spoke to Melisa about the wisdom of following Jehovah's command to marry "only in the Lord." (1 Corinthians 7:39; 2 Corinthians 6:14) "It was not easy for me to follow this advice," Melisa admits. "But I decided that since I had made a dedication to God to do his will, I would obey his clear instructions." Reflecting on what transpired, she says: "I am so glad that I followed the advice. The man soon stopped studying. If I had pursued that relationship, I would now be married to an unbeliever."

⁷ As slaves of God, we must not become slaves of men. (1 Corinthians 7:23) True, none of us like to be unpopular, but we must bear in mind that Christians have standards that are different from those in the world. Paul asked: "Am I seeking to please men?" His conclusion was: "If I were yet pleasing men, I would not be Christ's slave."

6. How does being slaves of God affect the decisions we make in life? Illustrate this with an example.

7, 8. (a) Why should we not be overly concerned about pleasing men? (b) Illustrate how fear of man can be overcome.

Moses was reluctant to accept his assignment

(Galatians 1:10) We simply cannot give in to peer pressure and become men pleasers. What, then, can we do when confronted with pressures to conform?

8 Consider the example of Elena, a young Christian in Spain. She had several classmates who were blood donors. They knew that Elena, one of Jehovah's Witnesses, would not donate blood or accept blood transfusions. When an opportunity arose to explain her position to the whole class, Elena volunteered to give a presentation. "Frankly, I felt very nervous about doing this," Elena explains. "But I prepared well, and the results were surprising. I won the respect of many of my fellow students, and the teacher told me that he admired the work I was doing. Above all, I felt satisfied that I had defended the name of Jehovah and had been able to explain clearly the reasons for my Scriptural stand." (Genesis 9:3, 4; Acts 15:28, 29) Yes, as slaves of God and of Christ, we stand out as different. However, we may well win people's respect if we are prepared to defend our beliefs respectfully.—1 Peter 3:15.

9 Remembering that we are slaves of God can also help to keep us humble. On one occasion, the apostle John felt so impressed by a magnificent vision of heavenly Jerusalem that he fell down to worship before the feet of the angel who had served as God's spokesman. "Be careful!" the angel told him. "Do not do that! All I am is a fellow slave of you and of your brothers who are prophets and of those who are observing the words of this scroll. Worship God." (Revelation 22:8, 9) What a fine example the angel set for all of God's slaves! Certain Christians may be in positions of special responsibility in the congregation. Nevertheless, Jesus said: "Whoever wants to become great among you must be your minister, and whoever wants to be first among you must be your slave." (Matthew 20:26, 27) As Jesus' followers, all of us are slaves.

"What We Have Done Is What We Ought to Have Done"

10 Doing God's will is not always easy for imperfect humans. The prophet Moses was reluctant to obey when Jehovah asked him to go and bring the sons of Israel out of Egyptian bondage. (Exodus 3:10, 11; 4:1, 10) Upon receiving an assignment to proclaim a judgment message to the people of Nineveh, Jonah "proceeded to get up and run away to Tarshish from before Jehovah." (Jonah 1:2, 3) Baruch, the scribal secretary of the prophet Jeremiah, complained of growing weary. (Jeremiah 45:2, 3) How should we respond when our personal desire or preference conflicts with the doing of God's will? An illustration that Jesus gave provides the answer.

11 Jesus spoke of a slave who had been caring for his master's flock all day in the field.

9. What do we learn from an angel who appeared to the apostle John?

10. Give Scriptural examples to show that faithful servants of God did not always find it easy to do his will.

11, 12. (a) Briefly relate Jesus' illustration recorded at Luke 17:7-10. (b) What lesson do we derive from Jesus' illustration?

When the slave arrived home, weary from some 12 hours of hard work, his master did not invite him to sit down and enjoy a good supper. Instead, the master said: "Get something ready for me to have my evening meal, and put on an apron and minister to me until I am through eating and drinking, and afterward you can eat and drink." The slave could attend to his own needs only after he had served his master. Jesus concluded the illustration by saying: "So you, also, when you have done all the things assigned to you, say, 'We are good-for-nothing slaves. What we have done is what we ought to have done.'"—Luke 17:7-10.

¹² Jesus did not give this illustration to show that Jehovah does not appreciate what we do in his service. The Bible clearly states: "God is not unrighteous so as to forget your work and the love you showed for his name." (Hebrews 6:10) Rather, the point of Jesus' parable is that a slave cannot please himself or concentrate on his own comforts. When we dedicated ourselves to God and chose to be his slaves, we agreed to put his will ahead of our own. We must subject our own will to the will of God.

¹³ Regularly studying God's Word and the publications of "the faithful and discreet slave" may require great effort on our part. (Matthew 24:45) This may be the case especially if reading has always been difficult for us or if a publication is discussing "the deep things of God." (1 Corinthians 2:10) Should we not, though, make time for personal study? We may have to discipline ourselves to sit down and spend time with the study material. Yet, without doing so, how would we acquire a taste for "solid food [that] belongs to mature people"?—Hebrews 5:14.

¹⁴ What about the times when we come home tired after a long day's work? We might have to push ourselves to attend Christian meetings. Or preaching to strangers may go against our natural inclination. Paul himself recognized that there could be times when we declare the good news 'against our will.' (1 Corinthians 9:17) However, we do these things because Jehovah —our heavenly Master, whom we love—tells us that we should. And do we not invariably feel satisfied and refreshed after we have put forth the effort to study, to attend meetings, and to preach?—Psalm 1:1, 2; 122:1; 145:10-13.

Do Not Look at "the Things Behind"

¹⁵ Jesus Christ demonstrated his submission to his heavenly Father in a superlative way. "I have come down from heaven to do, not my will, but the will of him that sent me," Jesus told his disciples. (John 6:38) When in anguish in the garden of Gethsemane, he prayed: "My Father, if it is possible, let this cup pass away from me. Yet, not as I will, but as you will."—Matthew 26:39.

¹⁶ Jesus Christ wants us to keep faithful to our decision to be slaves of God. He said: "No man that has put his hand to a plow and looks at the things behind is well fitted for the kingdom of God." (Luke 9:62) Dwelling on what we have left behind is definitely not the right thing to do when slaving for God. Instead, we should treasure what we have gained by choosing to be God's slaves. To the Philippians, Paul wrote: "I do indeed also consider all things to be loss on account of the excelling value of the knowledge of Christ Jesus my Lord. On account of him

---

13, 14. (a) In what circumstances may we have to override our own inclinations? (b) Why should we let God's will prevail?

15. How did Jesus set an example of submission to God?

16, 17. (a) How should we view the things we have left behind? (b) Show how Paul was realistic in assessing his worldly prospects as "a lot of refuse."

I have taken the loss of all things and I consider them as a lot of refuse, that I may gain Christ."—Philippians 3:8.

¹⁷ Think of all that Paul considered a lot of refuse and abandoned in favor of the spiritual rewards as a slave of God. He left behind not only the comforts of the world but also the possibility of becoming a future leader of Judaism. If Paul had continued to practice Judaism, he may well have risen to a position similar to that of Simeon, the son of Paul's educator, Gamaliel. (Acts 22:3; Galatians 1:14) Simeon became a leader of the Pharisees and played a prominent role—despite some reservations—in the Jewish rebellion against Rome in 66-70 C.E. He died in that conflagration, at the hands of either Jewish extremists or the Roman army.

¹⁸ Many of Jehovah's Witnesses have followed Paul's example. "Within a few years after leaving school, I got a job as an executive secretary for a prominent London solicitor," says Jean. "I enjoyed my work and earned good money, but in my heart I knew that I could do more to serve Jehovah. Finally, I handed in my resignation and started pioneering. I am so thankful that I took that step nearly 20 years ago! My full-time service has enriched my life more than any secretarial job ever could have. Nothing gives greater satisfaction than seeing how Jehovah's Word can change a person's life. To have a part in that process is wonderful. What we give to Jehovah is nothing compared with what we receive."

¹⁹ Our circumstances may change with time. However, our dedication to God remains the same. We are still Jehovah's slaves, and he leaves it up to us to decide how we can best use our time, energy, talents, and other assets. Hence, the decisions we make in this regard can reflect our love for God. They also show the extent to which we are willing to make personal sacrifices. (Matthew 6:33) Regardless of our circumstances, should we not be determined to give Jehovah our best? Paul wrote: "If the readiness is there first, it is especially acceptable according to what a person has, not according to what a person does not have."—2 Corinthians 8:12.

"You Are Having Your Fruit"

²⁰ Being slaves of God is not oppressive. On the contrary, it provides an escape from a pernicious form of slavery that robs us of happiness. "Because you were set free from sin but became slaves to God," wrote Paul, "you are having your fruit in the way of holiness, and the end everlasting life." (Romans 6:22) Our slaving for God bears fruit in the way of holiness in that we reap the benefits of holy, or morally clean, conduct. Moreover, it leads to everlasting life in the future.

²¹ Jehovah is generous to his slaves. When we do our best in his service, he opens to us "the floodgates of the heavens" and pours out upon us "a blessing until there is no more want." (Malachi 3:10) What a delight it will be to continue to serve as Jehovah's slaves for all eternity!

20, 21. (a) What fruitage is produced by slaves of God? (b) How does Jehovah reward those who give him their best?

18. Give an example to show how spiritual achievements bring rewards.
19. What should be our resolve, and why?

Jehovah's Word Is Alive
Highlights From the Book of First Samuel

THE year is 1117 B.C.E. Some three hundred years have elapsed since Joshua completed the conquest of the Promised Land. The older men of Israel come to Jehovah's prophet with a remarkable request. The prophet takes the matter up in prayer, and Jehovah allows them to have their way. This marks the end of the period of the Judges and the beginning of the era of human kings. The Bible book of First Samuel narrates exciting events surrounding that turning point in the history of the nation of Israel.

Written by Samuel, Nathan, and Gad, First Samuel covers a period of 102 years —from 1180 to 1078 B.C.E. (1 Chronicles 29:29) It is an account of four leaders of Israel. Two serve as judges, two as kings; two are obedient to Jehovah, two are not. We also meet two exemplary women and a valiant but gentle warrior. Such examples provide valuable lessons about attitudes and actions to imitate and to avoid. The contents of First Samuel can thus exert power on our thoughts and deeds.—Hebrews 4:12.

ELI'S JUDGESHIP GIVES WAY TO SAMUEL'S
(1 Samuel 1:1–7:17)

It is time for the Festival of Ingathering, and Hannah, who lives in Ramah, is beside herself with joy.* Jehovah has answered her prayers, and she has given birth to a son. To fulfill her vow, Hannah presents her son Samuel for service at "the house of Jehovah." There the boy becomes "a minister of Jeho-

---

* For locations of various places mentioned in the book of First Samuel, see pages 18-19 of the brochure *"See the Good Land,"* published by Jehovah's Witnesses.

vah before Eli the priest." (1 Samuel 1:24; 2:11) When Samuel is still of tender age, Jehovah speaks to him, pronouncing judgment against the house of Eli. As Samuel grows older, all the people of Israel come to recognize him as a prophet of Jehovah.

In time, the Philistines come up against Israel. They capture the Ark and slay Eli's two sons. Upon hearing the news, aged Eli dies, having "judged Israel forty years." (1 Samuel 4:18) Possession of the Ark proves to be disastrous for the Philistines, so they return it to the Israelites. Samuel now judges Israel, and there is peace in the land.

Scriptural Questions Answered:

2:10—Why did Hannah pray that Jehovah "give strength to his king" when there was no human king over Israel? That the Israelites would have a human king was foretold in the Mosaic Law. (Deuteronomy 17:14-18) In his deathbed prophecy, Jacob said: "The scepter [a symbol of royal authority] will not turn aside from Judah." (Genesis 49:10) Moreover, concerning Sarah—the ancestress of the Israelites—Jehovah said: "Kings of peoples will come from her." (Genesis 17:16) Hannah, then, was praying about a future king.

3:3—Did Samuel actually sleep in the Most Holy? No, he did not. Samuel was a Levite of the nonpriestly family of the Kohathites. (1 Chronicles 6:33-38) As such, he was not permitted to "come in to see the holy things." (Numbers 4:17-20) The only part of the sanctuary that Samuel had access to was the tabernacle courtyard. That is where he must have slept. Apparently, Eli also slept somewhere in the courtyard. The expression "where the ark of God was" evidently refers to the tabernacle area.

7:7-9, 17—Why did Samuel offer up a burnt offering at Mizpah and set up an altar in Ramah, since sacrifices were to be offered on a regular basis only at the place of Jehovah's choosing? (Deuteronomy 12:4-7, 13, 14; Joshua 22:19) After the removal of the sacred Ark from the tabernacle at Shiloh, Jehovah's presence was no longer evident there. So as God's representative, Samuel offered a burnt offering at Mizpah and also set up an altar in Ramah. These actions were apparently approved by Jehovah.

Lessons for Us:

1:11, 12, 21-23; 2:19. Hannah's prayerful attitude, her humility, her appreciation for Jehovah's kindness, and her lasting motherly affection are exemplary for all God-fearing women.

1:8. What an example Elkanah set in strengthening others with words! (Job 16:5) He first asked depressed Hannah the unaccusing question: "Why does your heart feel bad?" This encouraged her to talk about her feelings. Then Elkanah reassured her of his affection, saying: "Am I not better to you than ten sons?"

2:26; 3:5-8, 15, 19. By sticking to our God-assigned work, by taking advantage of spiritual training, and by being polite and respectful, we become "more likable" both to God and to men.

4:3, 4, 10. Even an object as holy as the ark of the covenant did not prove to be a charm for protection. We must 'guard ourselves from idols.'—1 John 5:21.

ISRAEL'S FIRST KING
—A SUCCESS OR A FAILURE?
(1 Samuel 8:1–15:35)

Samuel is faithful to Jehovah all his life, but his sons do not walk in godly ways. When the older men of Israel request a human king, Jehovah permits them to have one. Samuel follows Jehovah's direction and anoints Saul, a handsome Benjamite, as king. Saul strengthens his position as king by defeating the Ammonites.

Saul's valiant son Jonathan strikes down a Philistine garrison. The Philistines come up against Israel with a huge army. Saul panics and disobediently offers a burnt sacrifice himself. Taking along only his armor-bearer, courageous Jonathan attacks another Philistine outpost. Saul's rash oath, however, weakens the force of the victory. Saul goes "warring round about" against all his enemies. (1 Samuel 14:47) Upon defeating the Amalekites, though, he disobeys Jehovah by sparing what had been "devoted to destruction." (Leviticus 27:28, 29) Consequently, Jehovah rejects Saul as king.

Scriptural Questions Answered:

9:9—What is significant about the expression "the prophet of today used to be called a seer in former times"? These words may indicate that as the prophets became more prominent in the days of Samuel and during the era of the kings in Israel, the word "seer" came to be replaced by the term "prophet." Samuel is considered the first of the line of the prophets.—Acts 3:24.

14:24-32, 44, 45—Did Jonathan lose God's favor for eating honey in violation of Saul's oath? This act does not seem to have placed Jonathan in God's disfavor. First of all, Jonathan did not know about his father's oath. Moreover, the oath, prompted either by false zeal or by a wrong view of kingly power, caused problems for the people. How could such an oath have God's approval? Although Jonathan was willing to accept the consequences of breaking the oath, his life was spared.

15:6—Why did the Kenites receive special consideration from Saul? The Kenites were

Israel's first king changed from a humble and modest ruler to a proud and presumptuous monarch

the sons of Moses' father-in-law. They assisted the Israelites after these pulled away from Mount Sinai. (Numbers 10:29-32) In the land of Canaan, the Kenites also took up dwelling with the sons of Judah for a time. (Judges 1: 16) Even though they later resided among the Amalekites and various other peoples, the Kenites remained on friendly terms with Israel. For good reason, then, Saul spared the Kenites.

Lessons for Us:

9:21; 10:22, 27. The modesty and humility that Saul had when he first became king safeguarded him from acting rashly when some "good-for-nothing men" did not accept his kingship. What a protection such a mindset is against irrational actions!

12:20, 21. Never allow "the unrealities," such as trust in men, confidence in the military might of nations, or idolatry, to turn you aside from serving Jehovah.

12:24. A key to maintaining reverential fear of Jehovah and serving him with all our heart is to "see what great things he has done" for his people in ancient as well as modern times.

13:10-14; 15:22-25, 30. Be on guard against presumptuousness—whether expressed through disobedient acts or a proud attitude.—Proverbs 11:2.

A SHEPHERD BOY IS CHOSEN FOR THE KINGSHIP
(1 Samuel 16:1–31:13)

Samuel anoints David of the tribe of Judah to be the future king. Shortly thereafter, David slays the Philistine giant Goliath with a single slingstone. A bond of friendship develops between David and Jonathan. Saul places David over his warriors. In response to David's many victories, the women of Israel sing: "Saul has struck down his thousands, and David his tens of thousands." (1 Samuel 18:7) Consumed with envy, Saul seeks to kill David. After three attacks by Saul, David flees and becomes a fugitive.

During his years as a runaway, David spares Saul's life twice. He also meets and eventually marries beautiful Abigail. As the Philistines come up against Israel, Saul inquires of Jehovah. But Jehovah has left him. Samuel has died. Desperate, Saul consults a spirit medium, only to hear that he will be killed in the battle against the Philistines. During that battle, Saul is severely wounded, and his sons are killed. The account closes with Saul dying as a failure. David is still in hiding.

Scriptural Questions Answered:

16:14—What bad spirit terrorized Saul? The bad spirit that deprived Saul of his peace of mind was the bad inclination of his mind and heart—his inward urge to do wrong. When Jehovah withdrew his holy spirit, Saul lost its protection and came to be dominated by his own bad spirit. Since God permitted that spirit to replace His holy spirit, this bad spirit is termed "a bad spirit from Jehovah."

17:55-58—In view of 1 Samuel 16:17-23, why did Saul ask whose son David was?

Saul's inquiry was not just about the name of David's father. Very likely, he wanted to know what kind of man fathered a boy who had just accomplished the amazing feat of slaying a giant.

Lessons for Us:

16:6, 7. Rather than being impressed by the outward appearance of others or judging them hastily, we must try to see them as Jehovah sees them.

17:47-50. We can courageously face opposition or persecution from Goliathlike enemies because "to Jehovah belongs the battle."

18:1, 3; 20:41, 42. True friends can be found among those who love Jehovah.

21:12, 13. Jehovah expects us to use our mental faculties and abilities to deal with difficult situations in life. He has given us his inspired Word, which imparts prudence, knowledge, and thinking ability. (Proverbs 1:4) We also have the help of appointed Christian elders.

24:6; 26:11. What a fine example David provides of genuine respect for the anointed of Jehovah!

25:23-33. Abigail's sensibleness is exemplary.

28:8-19. In their efforts to misguide or harm people, wicked spirits can pretend to be certain dead individuals. We must keep free from all forms of spiritism.—Deuteronomy 18:10-12.

30:23, 24. This decision, based on Numbers 31:27, shows that Jehovah values those who serve in supportive roles in the congregation. Whatever we are doing, then, let us "work at it whole-souled as to Jehovah, and not to men."—Colossians 3:23.

What Is "Better Than a Sacrifice"?

What fundamental truth is emphasized by the experiences of Eli, Samuel, Saul, and David? It is this: "To obey is better than a sacrifice, to pay attention than the fat of rams; for rebelliousness is the same as the sin of divination, and pushing ahead presumptuously the same as using uncanny power and teraphim."—1 Samuel 15:22, 23.

What a privilege we have to share in the worldwide Kingdom-preaching and disciple-making work! As we offer to Jehovah "the young bulls of our lips," we must do our best to obey the direction he gives through his written Word and the earthly part of his organization. —Hosea 14:2; Hebrews 13:15.

Of what can we be confident when we face opposition from Goliathlike enemies?

SAMSON TRIUMPHS IN THE STRENGTH OF JEHOVAH!

VINDICTIVE captors bore out his eyes and consign him to hard labor. Then they bring him out of the prison house into a pagan temple to provide amusement for the crowd. They parade him before thousands of onlookers and make sport of him. The prisoner is neither a criminal nor a commander of an enemy army. He is a worshiper of Jehovah and has served as judge in Israel for 20 years.

How did Samson—physically the strongest man who ever lived—end up in such a humiliating situation? Would his extraordinary strength save him? What was the secret of Samson's strength? What, if anything, can we learn from his life story?

He Will "Take the Lead in Saving Israel"

The sons of Israel had a history of turning away from true worship. So when they "engaged again in doing what was bad in Jehovah's eyes, . . . Jehovah gave them into the hand of the Philistines for forty years." —Judges 13:1.

Samson's story began when Jehovah's angel appeared to the barren wife of an Israelite named Manoah and informed her that she would give birth to a son. "No razor should come upon his head," the angel instructed her, "because a Nazirite of God is what the child will become on leaving the belly; and

he it is who will take the lead in saving Israel out of the hand of the Philistines." (Judges 13:2-5) Before Samson was conceived, Jehovah determined that Samson was to have a specific task. From the moment of his birth, he was to be a Nazirite—one singled out for a special kind of sacred service.

She Is "Just Right in My Eyes"

As Samson kept growing, "Jehovah continued to bless him." (Judges 13:24) One day Samson came to his father and mother and said: "There is a woman that I have seen in Timnah of the daughters of the Philistines, and now get her for me as a wife." (Judges 14:2) Imagine their surprise. Instead of freeing Israel from the hands of the oppressors, their son wanted to form a marriage alliance with them. Taking a wife from among worshipers of pagan gods was against God's Law. (Exodus 34:11-16) Hence, the parents objected: "Is there not among the daughters of your brothers and among all my people a woman, so that you are going to take a wife from the uncircumcised Philistines?" Still, Samson insisted: "Get just her for me, because she is the one just right in my eyes."—Judges 14:3.

In what way was this particular Philistine woman "just right" for Samson? Not in the sense that she was "beautiful, engaging, attractive," suggests McClintock and Strong's *Cyclopedia,* "but right relative to an end, purpose, or object." Relative to what end? Judges 14:4 explains that Samson "was looking for an opportunity against the Philistines." Samson was interested in the woman for that purpose. As Samson grew to adulthood, "Jehovah's spirit started to impel him," or stir him to action. (Judges 13:25) So the spirit of Jehovah was the driving force behind Samson's unusual request for a wife as well as his entire career as judge over Israel. Did Samson get the opportunity he was seeking? Let us first consider how Jehovah assured him of divine backing.

Samson was en route to his future bride's city, Timnah. "When he got as far as the vineyards of Timnah," the Scriptural account relates, "why, look! a maned young lion roaring upon meeting him. Then Jehovah's spirit became operative upon him, so that he tore it in two." This remarkable manifestation of strength came when Samson was alone. There were no eyewitnesses. Was this Jehovah's way of assuring Samson that he as a Nazirite was capable of fulfilling his God-given commission? The Bible does not say, but Samson surely realized that such unusual power was not his. It must have come from

What was the secret of Samson's strength?

God. He could rely upon Jehovah to assist him in the work ahead. Fortified by the incident with the lion, Samson "continued on his way down and began to speak to the woman; and she was still right in [his] eyes." —Judges 14:5-7.

When Samson later went back to take the woman home, "he turned aside to look at the carcass of the lion, and there there was a swarm of bees in the lion's corpse, and honey." Noting this, Samson posed this riddle to 30 Philistine groomsmen at his wedding: "Out of the eater something to eat came forth, and out of the strong something sweet came forth." If they guessed the meaning of the riddle, Samson would give them 30 undergarments and outfits of clothes. If not, they would have to give the same to him. The Philistines were baffled by the riddle for three days. On the fourth day, they resorted to threatening the woman. They told her: "Fool your husband that he may tell us the riddle. Otherwise we shall burn you and the house of your father with fire." How cruel! If the Philistines treated their own people this way, imagine the plight of the oppressed Israelites!—Judges 14:8-15.

The terrified woman pressured Samson into disclosing the answer. Displaying lack of love and loyalty to Samson, she promptly informed the groomsmen. They solved the riddle, and Samson knew why. He said to them: "If you had not plowed with my young cow, you would not have solved my riddle." The opportunity that Samson had been waiting for now presented itself. "Jehovah's spirit became operative upon him, so that he went down to Ashkelon and struck down thirty men of theirs and took what he stripped off them and gave the outfits to the tellers of the riddle."—Judges 14:18, 19.

Was Samson's action at Ashkelon prompted by a desire for revenge on his part? No. It was an act of God through his chosen deliverer. Through Samson, Jehovah initiated a fight against the cruel oppressors of his people. This campaign was to continue. The next opportunity arose when Samson came to visit his wife.

Single-Handed Warfare

Upon returning to Timnah, Samson discovered that his wife's father had married the woman off to another man, believing that Samson hated her. Samson was outwardly offended. He caught 300 foxes and tied them in twos with a torch between their tails. When freed, they set ablaze fields, vineyards, and olive groves, destroying Philistia's three main crops for the year. The irate Philistines displayed cruelty. They considered Samson's wife and her father responsible and burned them. Their barbaric revenge

served Samson's purpose. He, in turn, went smiting them with a great slaughter.—Judges 15:1-8.

Did the Israelites see that Jehovah God was blessing Samson and therefore unite with him to bring an end to the Philistine domination? Hardly. To avoid trouble, the men of Judah sent 3,000 men to arrest God's chosen leader and surrender him to his enemies. This Israelite disloyalty, however, offered Samson an occasion to inflict further losses on his enemies. As he was about to be delivered to the Philistines, "Jehovah's spirit became operative upon him, and the ropes that were upon his arms came to be like linen threads that have been scorched with fire, so that his fetters melted off his hands." He then picked up the jawbone of an ass and struck down a thousand foes with it.—Judges 15:10-15.

Calling on Jehovah, Samson said: "It was you that gave this great salvation into the hand of your servant, and now shall I die of thirst and must I fall into the hand of the uncircumcised?" Jehovah heard Samson's prayer and answered it. "God split open a mortar-shaped hollow . . . , and water began to come out of it, and he proceeded to drink, after which his spirit returned and he revived."—Judges 15:18, 19.

Samson was single-minded in the pursuit of his objective, his fight against the Philistines. His staying at the house of a prostitute at Gaza was for the purpose of fighting against God's enemies. Samson needed a lodging place for the night in an enemy city, and it could be found in the house of a prostitute. Samson had no immoral purpose in mind. He left the woman's house at midnight, grabbed the city gates and the two side posts, and carried them to the top of a mountain near Hebron, which was some 37 miles away. This was done with divine approval and God-given strength.—Judges 16:1-3.

The way the holy spirit operated in Samson's case was unique because of the unusual circumstances. Faithful servants of God today can rely on the same spirit to empower them. Jesus assured his followers that Jehovah will "give holy spirit to those asking him."—Luke 11:13.

Why Did Jehovah 'Depart From Samson'?

It came about that Samson fell in love with a woman named Delilah. The five axis lords of the Philistines were so eager to eliminate Samson that they enlisted her help. They approached Delilah and said to her: "Fool him and see in what his great power is and with what we can prevail over him." As a bribe, each of the five axis lords offered her "one thousand one hundred silver pieces."—Judges 16:4, 5.

If the silver pieces were shekels, the offer of 5,500 shekels was a huge bribe. Abraham paid 400 shekels for a burial place for his wife, and a slave sold for just 30. (Genesis 23:14-20; Exodus 21:32) The fact that the axis lords—rulers of five Philistine cities—appealed to Delilah's greed and not to her ethnic loyalty suggests that she was perhaps an Israelite woman. In any case, Delilah accepted the offer.

Three times Samson gave Delilah misleading answers to her inquiry, and three times she betrayed him by trying to deliver him to his enemies. But "it came about that because she pressured him with her words all the time and kept urging him, his soul got to be impatient to the point of dying." Samson finally revealed the truth—his hair had never been cut. Were it to be cut, he would grow weak and become like all other men.—Judges 16:6-17.

That was Samson's downfall. Delilah maneuvered him into a situation to have his head shaved. Samson's power, however, was not literally in his hair. His hair merely represented his special relationship with God as a Nazirite. When Samson allowed himself to get into a situation that affected his Naziriteship because of the shaving of his head, 'Jehovah departed from him.' Philistines now overpowered Samson, blinded him, and put him in prison.—Judges 16:18-21.

What a powerful lesson this teaches us! Should we not value our relationship with Jehovah as something very precious? If we compromise our Christian dedication in any way, how can we expect God to go on blessing us?

"Let My Soul Die With the Philistines"

Exultant Philistines thanked their god Dagon for Samson's defeat. In celebration of their victory, they led their captive to the temple of Dagon. But Samson knew the real reason for his downfall. He knew why Jehovah had left him, and Samson repented of his having failed. While Samson was in the prison house, his hair had begun to grow luxuriantly. Now that he was in front of thousands of Philistines, what action would he take?

"Sovereign Lord Jehovah," prayed Samson, "remember me, please, and strengthen me, please, just this once, O you the true God, and let me avenge myself upon the Philistines with vengeance for one of my two eyes." Then he braced himself against the two center columns of the building, and "he bent himself with power." The result? "The house went falling upon the axis lords and upon all the people that were in it, so that the dead that he put to death in his own death came to be more than those he had put to death during his lifetime."—Judges 16:22-30.

For physical strength, Samson was without equal among men. His mighty acts were notable indeed. But most important, Jehovah's Word counts Samson among those strong in faith.—Hebrews 11:32-34.

A "Pim" Testifies to the Bible's Historicity

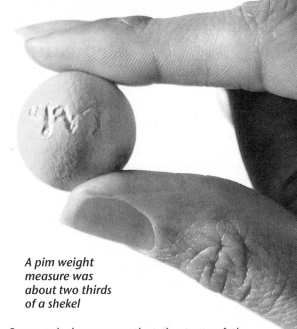

A pim weight measure was about two thirds of a shekel

THE word "pim" occurs only once in the Bible. In the days of King Saul, the Israelites had to get their metal tools sharpened by Philistine smiths. "The price for sharpening proved to be a pim for the plowshares and for the mattocks and for the three-toothed instruments and for the axes and for fixing fast the oxgoad," states the Bible. —1 Samuel 13:21.

What was a pim? The answer to that question remained a mystery until 1907 C.E. when the first pim weight stone was excavated at the ancient city of Gezer. Bible translators of earlier dates had difficulty translating the word "pim." The *King James Version,* for example, rendered 1 Samuel 13:21: "Yet they had a file for the mattocks, and for the coulters, and for the forks, and for the axes, and to sharpen the goads."

Scholars today know that a pim was a weight measure averaging 7.82 grams, or approximately two thirds of a shekel, the basic Hebrew unit of weight. A pim measure of silver scrap was the price the Philistines charged the Israelites for sharpening their tools. The shekel weight system went out of use with the fall of the kingdom of Judah and its capital, Jerusalem, in 607 B.C.E. So how does the pim measure testify to the historicity of the Hebrew text?

Some scholars argue that the texts of the Hebrew Scriptures, including the book of First Samuel, date to the Hellenistic-Roman era, even as late as from the second to the first century B.C.E. It is claimed, therefore, that "they are . . . 'unhistorical,' of little or no value for reconstructing a 'biblical' or an 'ancient Israel,' both of which are simply modern Jewish and Christian literary constructs."

Referring to the pim measure mentioned at 1 Samuel 13:21, however, William G. Dever, professor of Near Eastern archaeology and anthropology, says: "[It] cannot possibly have been 'invented' by writers living in the Hellenistic-Roman period several centuries after these weights had disappeared and had been forgotten. In fact, this bit of biblical text . . . would not be understood until the early 20th century A.D., when the first actual archaeological examples turned up, reading *pîm* in Hebrew." The professor continues: "If the biblical stories are all 'literary inventions' of the Hellenistic-Roman era, how did this particular story come to be in the Hebrew Bible? One may object, of course, that the *pîm* incident is 'only a detail.' To be sure; but as is well known, 'history is in the details.'"

Questions From Readers

Does the eating of the loaves of presentation by David and his men indicate that God's law can be broken with impunity under difficult circumstances?—1 Samuel 21: 1-6.

According to Leviticus 24:5-9, the loaves of presentation that were replaced on each Sabbath were reserved for the priests to eat. The principle behind this use was that the loaves were holy and were to serve as food for the men engaged in God's service—the priests. Giving them to a common laborer or eating them just for pleasure would definitely be wrong. However, the priest Ahimelech did nothing sinful when he shared the showbread with David and his men.

New loaves of presentation were placed inside the tabernacle each Sabbath

David appeared to be on a special assignment from King Saul. David and his men were hungry. Ahimelech determined that they were ceremonially clean. While their eating of the loaves of presentation was technically unlawful, it was in harmony with the basic designated use of the showbread. This consideration permitted Ahimelech to make an exception to the rule. Jesus Christ himself used this incident to illustrate the impropriety of the unduly rigid application of the Sabbath law demanded by the Pharisaic interpretation of it.—Matthew 12:1-8.

The foregoing, however, does not mean that God's law can be violated when circumstances become difficult. For example, a seemingly critical situation developed when Israelite warriors were fighting the Philistines. King Saul had said: "Cursed is the man that eats bread before the evening and until I have taken vengeance upon my enemies!" The Bible says: "On that day they kept striking down the Philistines." The soldiers were battle-weary and hungry, 'and the people began slaughtering animals on the earth and fell to eating along with the blood.' (1 Samuel 14:24, 31-33) They sinned against Jehovah by violating his law on blood. Their actions were not in accord with the only God-designated use of blood, namely "to make atonement" for sins. (Leviticus 17:10-12; Genesis 9:3, 4) Mercifully, Jehovah accepted special sacrifices in behalf of those who had sinned.—1 Samuel 14: 34, 35.

Yes, Jehovah expects us to obey his laws under all circumstances. "This is what the love of God means," says the apostle John, "that we observe his commandments."—1 John 5:3.

IN OUR NEXT ISSUE

Science and the Bible—Do They Really Contradict Each Other?

———

Parents, Protect Your Precious Inheritance

———

Making Jehovah Your God

'Like a Precious Red-Colored Stone'

THE apostle John had a vision of a glorious throne in heaven. The One seated upon the throne looked "like a jasper stone." He was also like "a precious red-colored stone." (Revelation 4:2, 3) What stones were these?

These were not opaque stones that shine from their surface. In ancient times, the Greek word translated "jasper" was used to denote stones of different colors, including precious gems that were transparent. The "jasper stone" of Revelation 4:3 "certainly [was] not our cheap modern jasper," states A. T. Robertson in *Word Pictures in the New Testament.* Moreover, later in the book of Revelation, John describes the heavenly city, Jerusalem, saying: "Its radiance was like a most precious stone, as a jasper stone shining crystal-clear." (Revelation 21:10, 11) The stones John refers to were apparently translucent, allowing light to pass through them.

The one represented as being seated upon the throne in John's vision is the most glorious Person in the universe, Jehovah God. He is pure and holy to a superlative degree. In harmony with that, the apostle John wrote: "God is light and there is no darkness at all in union with him." (1 John 1:5) Hence, John urged his fellow believers to 'purify themselves just as Jehovah is pure.'—1 John 3:3.

What must we do to be viewed by God as pure? Our having faith in Christ's shed blood for forgiveness of our sins is absolutely essential. We must also keep "walking in the light" by regularly studying the Bible and living in harmony with its teachings.—1 John 1:7.

An EVENT to REMEMBER

WHAT event is this? It is the death of a man who died nearly 2,000 years ago. "I surrender my soul, in order that I may receive it again," he said. "No man has taken it away from me, but I surrender it of my own initiative." (John 10:17, 18) That man was Jesus Christ.

Jesus instructed his followers to observe the Memorial of his sacrificial death. The occasion is also called "the Lord's evening meal," or "the Lord's supper." (1 Corinthians 11:20; *King James Version*) The Memorial that Jesus instituted to commemorate his death will be observed by Jehovah's Witnesses and their friends on Thursday, March 24, 2005, after sunset.

A Bible-based talk will explain the meaning of the unleavened bread and the red wine used for the occasion. (Matthew 26:26-28) The discourse will also answer such questions as these: How often should Christians commemorate this event? Who should rightly partake of the emblems of bread and wine? Who benefit from Jesus' death? This important observance will help all to appreciate the purpose of Jesus' life and death.

APRIL 1, 2005

THE WATCHTOWER
ANNOUNCING JEHOVAH'S KINGDOM

SCIENCE AND THE BIBLE
Do They Contradict Each Other?

THE WATCHTOWER®

ANNOUNCING JEHOVAH'S KINGDOM

April 1, 2005   Average Printing Each Issue: 26,439,000   Vol. 126, No. 7

THE PURPOSE OF *THE WATCHTOWER* is to exalt Jehovah God as Sovereign Lord of the universe. It keeps watch on world events as these fulfill Bible prophecy. It comforts all peoples with the good news that God's Kingdom will soon destroy those who oppress their fellowmen and that it will turn the earth into a paradise. It encourages faith in God's now-reigning King, Jesus Christ, whose shed blood opens the way for mankind to gain eternal life. *The Watchtower,* published by Jehovah's Witnesses continuously since 1879, is nonpolitical. It adheres to the Bible as its authority.

IN THIS ISSUE

3   Science and Religion—The Birth of a Conflict

4   Science and the Bible—Do They Really Contradict Each Other?

8   Our Children—A Precious Inheritance

13   Parents, Protect Your Precious Inheritance

20   A Forsaken Orphan Finds a Loving Father

25   Making Jehovah Your God

29   Questions From Readers

30   Kingdom Proclaimers Report

32   A Humble African Who Loved God's Word

WATCHTOWER STUDIES

MAY 2-8:
Our Children—A Precious Inheritance.
Page 8. Songs to be used: 164, 183.

MAY 9-15:
Parents, Protect Your Precious Inheritance.
Page 13. Songs to be used: 157, 191.

Publication of *The Watchtower* is part of a worldwide Bible educational work supported by voluntary donations.

Unless otherwise indicated, Scripture quotations are from the modern-language *New World Translation of the Holy Scriptures—With References.*

The Watchtower (ISSN 0043-1087) is published semimonthly by Watchtower Bible and Tract Society of New York, Inc.; M. H. Larson, President; G. F. Simonis, Secretary-Treasurer; 25 Columbia Heights, Brooklyn, NY 11201-2483. Periodicals Postage Paid at Brooklyn, NY, and at additional mailing offices. POSTMASTER: Send address changes to Watchtower, **Wallkill, NY 12589.**

Changes of address should reach us 30 days before your moving date. Give us your old and new address (if possible, your old address label).

Semimonthly   ENGLISH

Would you welcome more information or a free home Bible study? Please send your request to Jehovah's Witnesses, using the appropriate address below.

America, United States of: Wallkill, NY 12589. *Antigua:* Box 119, St. Johns. *Australia:* Box 280, Ingleburn, NSW 1890. *Bahamas:* Box N-1247, Nassau, N.P. *Barbados, W.I.:* Crusher Site Road, Prospect, St. James. *Britain:* The Ridgeway, London NW7 1RN. *Canada:* Box 4100, Halton Hills (Georgetown), Ontario L7G 4Y4. *Germany:* Niederselters, Am Steinfels, D-65618 Selters. *Ghana:* P. O. Box GP 760, Accra. *Guyana:* 352-360 Tyrell St., Republic Park Phase 2 EBD. *Hawaii 96819:* 2055 Kam IV Rd., Honolulu. *Hong Kong:* 4 Kent Road, Kowloon Tong. *India:* Post Box 6440, Yelahanka, Bangalore 560 064, KAR. *Ireland:* Newcastle, Greystones, Co. Wicklow. *Jamaica:* P. O. Box 103, Old Harbour, St. Catherine. *Japan:* 1271 Nakashinden, Ebina City, Kanagawa Pref., 243-0496. *Kenya:* P.O. Box 47788, GPO Nairobi 00100. *New Zealand:* P.O. Box 75-142, Manurewa. *Nigeria:* P.M.B. 1090, Benin City 300001, Edo State. *Philippines, Republic of:* P. O. Box 2044, 1060 Manila. *South Africa:* Private Bag X2067, Krugersdorp, 1740. *Trinidad and Tobago, Republic of:* Lower Rapsey Street & Laxmi Lane, Curepe. *Zambia:* Box 33459, Lusaka 10101. *Zimbabwe:* Private Bag WG-5001, Westgate.

NOW PUBLISHED IN 150 LANGUAGES. SEMIMONTHLY: Afrikaans, Albanian,* Amharic, Arabic, Bengali, Bicol, Bislama, Bulgarian, Cebuano,* Chichewa,* Chinese, Chinese (Simplified),* Cibemba,* Croatian,* Czech,*# Danish,*# Dutch,*# East Armenian, Efik,* English*#+◎ (also Braille), Estonian, Ewe, Fijian, Finnish,*# French,*# Ga, Georgian, German,*# Greek,* Gujarati, Gun, Hebrew, Hiligaynon, Hindi, Hungarian,*# Igbo,* Iloko,* Indonesian, Italian,*# Japanese*# (also Braille), Kannada, Kinyarwanda, Kirundi, Korean*# (also Braille), Latvian, Lingala, Lithuanian, Luvale, Macedonian, Malagasy,* Malayalam, Maltese, Myanmar, Nepali, New Guinea Pidgin, Norwegian,*# Pangasinan, Papiamento (Aruba), Papiamento (Curaçao), Polish,*# Portuguese*# (also Braille), Punjabi, Rarotongan, Romanian,* Russian,* Samar-Leyte, Samoan, Sango, Sepedi, Serbian, Sesotho, Shona,* Silozi, Sinhala, Slovak,* Slovenian, Solomon Islands Pidgin, Spanish*# (also Braille), Sranantongo, Swahili,* Swedish,*# Tagalog,* Tamil, Telugu, Thai, Tigrinya, Tongan, Tshiluba, Tsonga, Tswana, Turkish, Twi, Ukrainian,* Urdu, Vietnamese, Wallisian, Xhosa, Yoruba,* Zulu*

MONTHLY: American Sign Language,△□ Armenian, Assamese, Azerbaijani (roman script), Brazilian Sign Language,△ Cambodian, Chitonga, Gilbertese, Greenlandic, Haitian Creole, Hausa, Hiri Motu, Icelandic, Isoko, Kaonde, Kazakh, Kikongo, Kiluba, Kirghiz, Kosraean, Kwanyama/Ndonga, Luganda, Marathi, Marshallese, Mauritian Creole, Maya, Mizo, Monokutuba, Moore, Niuean, Ossetian, Otetela, Palauan, Persian, Ponapean, Seychelles Creole, Tahitian, Tatar, Tiv, Trukese, Tumbuka, Tuvaluan, Umbundu, Venda, Yapese, Zande

* Study articles also available in large-print edition.
\# Audiocassettes also available.
+ CD also available.
◎ MP3 CD-ROM also available.
△ Videocassette
□ DVD

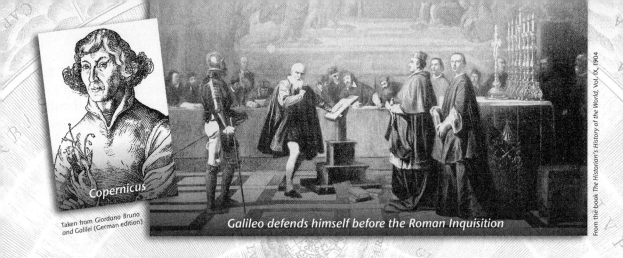

Copernicus

Taken from *Giordano Bruno and Galilei* (German edition)

Galileo defends himself before the Roman Inquisition

From the book *The Historian's History of the World, Vol. IX*, 1904

SCIENCE AND RELIGION
The Birth of a Conflict

THE 70-year-old astronomer was on his deathbed, struggling to read. In his hands were the proofs of a document of his, ready for publication. Whether he knew it or not, his work would revolutionize mankind's view of the universe. It would also trigger a heated controversy within Christendom, the effects of which are still being felt today.

The dying man was Nicolaus Copernicus, a Polish Catholic, and the year was 1543. Copernicus' work, entitled *On the Revolutions of the Heavenly Spheres,* put the sun, not the earth, at the center of the solar system. In one stroke Copernicus replaced the extremely complex, earth-centered system with one of elegant simplicity.

At first, there was little indication of the clash that was to come. For one thing, Copernicus had been discreet when sharing his ideas. Additionally, the Catholic Church, which had adopted the earth-centered view, seemed to be more tolerant of scientific speculation at the time. Even the pope himself urged Copernicus to publish his work. When Copernicus finally did publish it, a fearful editor wrote his own preface, presenting the sun-centered, or heliocentric, concept as a mathematical ideal, not necessarily an astronomical truth.

The Conflict Becomes Heated

Next on the scene was Italian astronomer, mathematician, and physicist Galileo Galilei (1564-1642), also a Catholic. Using telescopes that he built incorporating the newly invented lens, Galileo saw the heavens in unprecedented detail. His observations convinced him that Copernicus was correct. Galileo also saw spots on the sun, today called sunspots, thus challenging another cherished philosophical and religious tenet—that the sun is not subject to change or decay.

Unlike Copernicus, Galileo was bold and zealous in promoting his ideas. And he did so in a more hostile religious environment,

Background: Chart depicting Copernicus' concept of the solar system

for the Catholic Church had by then become openly opposed to the Copernican theory. Hence, when Galileo argued that not only was the heliocentric concept correct but it harmonized with Scripture, the church smelled heresy.*

Galileo went to Rome to defend himself but to no avail. In 1616 the church ordered him to stop advocating Copernicus. Galileo

_____

* Galileo unnecessarily made powerful enemies for himself by his quick wit and cutting sarcasm. Also, by arguing that the heliocentric concept harmonized with Scripture, he presented himself as an authority on religion, which further provoked the church.

was silenced for a time. Then in 1632 he published another work in support of Copernicus. The very next year, the Inquisition sentenced Galileo to life imprisonment. Out of consideration for his age, however, they quickly commuted the sentence to house arrest.

Many view Galileo's conflict with the church as a great triumph of science over religion and, by extension, over the Bible. However, as we shall see in the next article, this simplistic conclusion ignores many facts.

SCIENCE AND THE BIBLE
Do They Really Contradict Each Other?

THE seeds of the clash between Galileo and the Catholic Church were sown centuries before Copernicus and Galileo were born. The earth-centered, or geocentric, view of the universe was adopted by the ancient Greeks and made famous by the philosopher Aristotle (384-322 B.C.E.) and the astronomer-astrologer Ptolemy (second century C.E.).*

Aristotle's concept of the universe was influenced by the thinking of Greek mathematician and philosopher Pythagoras (sixth century B.C.E.). Adopting Pythagoras'

_____

* In the third century B.C.E., a Greek named Aristarchus of Samos put forth the hypothesis that the sun is at the center of the cosmos, but his ideas were dismissed in favor of Aristotle's.

view that the circle and sphere were perfect shapes, Aristotle believed that the heavens were a series of spheres within spheres, like layers of an onion. Each layer was made of crystal, with the earth at the center. Stars moved in circles, deriving their motion from the outermost sphere, the seat of divine power. Aristotle also held that the sun and other celestial objects were perfect, free of any marks or blemishes and not subject to change.

Aristotle's great scheme was a child of philosophy, not science. A moving earth, he felt, would violate common sense. He also rejected the idea of a void, or space, believing that a moving earth would be

Aristotle

◄ From the book *A General History for Colleges and High Schools*, 1900

subject to friction and would grind to a halt without the application of constant force. Because Aristotle's concept seemed logical within the framework of existing knowledge, it endured in its basic form for almost 2,000 years. Even as late as the 16th century, French philosopher Jean Bodin expressed that popular view, stating: "No one in his senses, or imbued with the slightest knowledge of physics, will ever think that the earth, heavy and unwieldy . . . , staggers . . . around its own center and that of the sun; for at the slightest jar of the earth, we would see cities and fortresses, towns and mountains thrown down."

Aristotle Adopted by the Church

A further step leading to the confrontation between Galileo and the church occurred in the 13th century and involved Catholic authority Thomas Aquinas (1225-74). Aquinas had a profound respect for Aristotle, whom he referred to as The Philosopher. Aquinas struggled for five years to fuse Aristotle's philosophy with church teaching. By the time of Galileo, says Wade Rowland in his book *Galileo's Mistake,* "the hybridized Aristotle in the theology of Aquinas had become bedrock dogma of the Church of Rome." Keep in mind, too, that in those days there was no scientific community as such. Education was largely in the hands of the church. The authority on religion and science was often one and the same.

The stage was now set for the confrontation between the church and Galileo. Even before his involvement with astronomy, Galileo had written a treatise on motion. It challenged many assumptions made by the revered Aristotle. However, it was Galileo's steadfast promotion of the heliocentric concept and his assertion

Thomas Aquinas
From the book *Encyclopedia of Religious Knowledge,* 1855

that it harmonizes with Scripture that led to his trial by the Inquisition in 1633.

In his defense, Galileo affirmed his strong faith in the Bible as the inspired Word of God. He also argued that the Scriptures were written for ordinary people and that Biblical references to the apparent movement of the sun were not to be interpreted literally. His arguments were futile. Because Galileo rejected an interpretation of Scripture based on Greek philosophy, he stood condemned! Not until 1992 did the Catholic Church officially admit to error in its judgment of Galileo.

Lessons to Be Learned

What can we learn from these events? For one thing, Galileo had no quarrel with the Bible. Instead, he questioned the teachings of the church. One religion writer observed: "The lesson to be learned from Galileo, it appears, is not that the Church held too tightly to biblical truths; but rather that it did not hold tightly enough." By allowing Greek philosophy to influence its theology, the church bowed to tradition rather than follow the teachings of the Bible.

All of this calls to mind the Biblical warning: "Look out: perhaps there may be someone who will carry you off as his prey through the philosophy and empty deception according to the tradition of men, according to the elementary things of the world and not according to Christ."—Colossians 2:8.

Even today, many in Christendom continue to embrace theories and philosophies that contradict the Bible. One example is Darwin's theory of evolution, which they have accepted in place of the Genesis account of creation. In making this substitution, the churches have, in effect, made Darwin a modern-day Aristotle and evolution an article of faith.*

True Science Harmonizes With the Bible

The foregoing should in no way discourage an interest in science. To be sure, the Bible itself invites us to learn from God's handiwork and to discern God's amazing qualities in what we see. (Isaiah 40:26; Romans 1:20) Of course, the Bible does not claim to teach science. Rather, it reveals God's standards, aspects of his personality that creation alone cannot teach, and his purpose for humans. (Psalm 19:7-11; 2 Timothy 3:16) Yet, when the Bible does refer to natural phenomena, it is consistently accurate. Galileo himself said: "Both the Holy Scriptures and nature proceed from the Divine Word . . . Two

Isaac Newton

truths can never contradict one another." Consider the following examples.

Even more fundamental than the movement of stars and planets is that all matter in the universe is governed by laws, such as the law of gravity. The earliest known non-Biblical reference to physical laws was made by Pythagoras, who believed that the universe could be explained by numbers. Two thousand years later, Galileo, Kepler, and Newton finally proved that matter is governed by rational laws.

The earliest Biblical reference to natural law is contained in the book of Job. About 1600 B.C.E., God asked Job: "Have you come to know the *statutes* [or, laws] of the heavens?" (Job 38:33) Recorded in the seventh century B.C.E., the book of Jeremiah refers to Jehovah as the Creator of "the *statutes* of the moon and the stars" and "the *statutes* of heaven and earth." (Jeremiah 31:35; 33:25) In view of these statements, Bible commen-

---

* For an in-depth discussion on this topic, see chapter 15, "Why Do Many Accept Evolution?" in the book *Life—How Did It Get Here? By Evolution or by Creation?* published by Jehovah's Witnesses.

THE PROTESTANTS' ATTITUDE

Luther

Calvin

▲ From the book *Servetus and Calvin*, 1877

Leaders of the Protestant Reformation also railed against the sun-centered concept. They included Martin Luther (1483-1546), Philipp Melanchthon (1497-1560), and John Calvin (1509-64). Luther said of Copernicus: "This fool wishes to reverse the entire science of astronomy."

The Reformers based their argument on a literal interpretation of certain scriptures, such as the account in Joshua chapter 10 that mentions that the sun and the moon "kept motionless."* Why did the Reformers take this stand? The book *Galileo's Mistake* explains that while the Protestant Reformation broke the papal yoke, it failed to "shake the essential authority" of Aristotle and Thomas Aquinas, whose views were "accepted by Catholic and Protestant alike."

---

* Scientifically speaking, we use incorrect terms when we refer to "sunrise" and "sunset." But in everyday speech, these words are both acceptable and accurate, when we keep in mind our terrestrial perspective. Likewise, Joshua was not discussing astronomy; he was simply reporting events as he saw them.

Over 3,000 years ago, the Bible described the earth's water cycle

tator G. Rawlinson observed: "The general prevalence of law in the material world is quite as strongly asserted by the sacred writers as by modern science."

If we use Pythagoras as a point of reference, the statement in Job was about a thousand years ahead of its time. Keep in mind that the Bible's objective is not simply to reveal physical facts but primarily to impress upon us that Jehovah is the Creator of all things—the one who can *create* physical laws.—Job 38:4, 12; 42:1, 2.

Another example we can consider is that the earth's waters undergo a cyclic motion called the water cycle, or the hydrologic cycle. Put simply, water evaporates from the sea, forms clouds, precipitates onto the land, and eventually returns to the sea. The oldest surviving non-Biblical references to this cycle are from the fourth century B.C.E. However, Biblical statements predate that by hundreds of years. For example, in the 11th century B.C.E., King Solomon of Israel wrote: "All the rivers run into the sea, yet the sea is not full. To the place from which the rivers come, to there and from there they return again."—Ecclesiastes 1:7, *The Amplified Bible.*

Likewise, about 800 B.C.E. the prophet Amos, a humble shepherd and farmworker,

wrote that Jehovah is "the One calling for the waters of the sea, that he may pour them out upon the surface of the earth." (Amos 5:8) Without using complex, technical language, both Solomon and Amos accurately described the water cycle, each from a slightly different perspective.

The Bible also speaks of God as "hanging the earth upon nothing," or he "suspends earth in the void," according to *The New English Bible.* (Job 26:7) In view of the knowledge available in 1600 B.C.E., roughly when those words were spoken, it would have taken a remarkable man to assert that a solid object can remain suspended in space without any physical support. As previously mentioned, Aristotle himself rejected the concept of a void, and he lived over 1,200 years later!

Does it not strike you as amazing that the Bible makes such accurate statements —even in the face of the erroneous yet seemingly commonsense perceptions of the day? To thinking people, this is one more evidence of the Bible's divine inspiration. We are wise, therefore, not to be easily swayed by any teaching or theory that contradicts God's Word. As history has repeatedly shown, human philosophies, even those of towering intellects, come and go, whereas "the saying of Jehovah endures forever." —1 Peter 1:25.

OUR CHILDREN —A PRECIOUS INHERITANCE

"Look! Sons are an inheritance from Jehovah; the fruitage of the belly is a reward."—PSALM 127:3.

CONSIDER the miraculous events that Jehovah God made possible by the way he created the first man and woman. Both the father, Adam, and the mother, Eve, contributed a part of themselves that developed within Eve's womb into a fully formed new person—the first human baby. (Genesis 4:1) Down till today, the conception and birth of a child fill us with wonder and are described by many as nothing short of a miracle.

2 Within some 270 days, the original cell that was created within the mother as a result of her union with the father grows into a baby made up of trillions of cells. That original cell has within it the instructions needed to produce more than 200 kinds of cells. Following those marvelous instructions, which are beyond human understanding, these cells of stunning complexity develop in just the right order and manner to form a new living person!

3 Who, would you say, is the real maker of the baby? It is surely the One who created life in the first place. The Bible psalmist sang: "Know that Jehovah is God. It is he that has made us, and not we ourselves." (Psalm 100:3) Parents, you well know that it is not because of any brilliance on your part that you have produced such a precious little bundle of life. Only a God of infinite wisdom could be responsible for the miraculous formation of a new living human. For thousands of years, reasoning people have credited the formation of a child inside its mother's womb to the Grand Creator. Do you?—Psalm 139:13-16.

4 Is Jehovah, though, an unfeeling Creator who simply instituted a biological process whereby men and women could produce offspring? Some humans are unfeeling, but Jehovah is never like that. (Psalm 78:38-40) The Bible says at Psalm 127:3: "Look! Sons [and daughters as well] are an inheritance from Jehovah; the fruitage of the belly is a reward." Let us now consider what an inheritance is and what it gives evidence of.

An Inheritance and a Reward

5 An inheritance is like a gift. Parents often work long and hard to leave their children an inheritance. It may consist of money, property, or perhaps some treasured possession. In any case, it is evidence of a parent's love. The Bible says that God has given parents their children as an inheritance. They are a loving gift from him. If you are a parent, would you say that your actions show that you view your little ones as a gift

---

1. How did the first human baby come to be born?
2. Why would you say that what occurs inside the womb of a pregnant woman is a miracle?
3. Why do many reasoning people agree that God must be responsible for the birth of a new living human?

---

4. What human fault could never be ascribed to Jehovah?
5. Why are children an inheritance?

that the Creator of the universe has entrusted to you?

⁶ Jehovah's purpose in granting this gift was to have the earth populated with the descendants of Adam and Eve. (Genesis 1:27, 28; Isaiah 45:18) Jehovah did not individually create every human, as he did the millions of angels. (Psalm 104:4; Revelation 4:11) Instead, God chose to create humans with the ability to produce children who would resemble their parents in identifiable ways. What a marvelous privilege it is for a mother and father to bring forth and care for such a new person! As parents, do you thank Jehovah for making it possible for you to enjoy this precious inheritance?

Learn From Jesus' Example

⁷ Sad to say, not all parents consider children a reward. Many show little compassion for their offspring. Such parents do not reflect the attitude of Jehovah or of his Son. (Psalm 27:10; Isaiah 49:15) In contrast, consider Jesus' interest in young ones. Even before Jesus came to earth as a human—when he was a mighty spirit person in heaven—the Bible says that his "fulness of delight was with the sons of men." (Proverbs 8: 31, *Rotherham*) His love for humans was so great that he willingly gave his life as a ransom so that we might receive everlasting life. —Matthew 20:28; John 10:18.

⁸ While on earth, Jesus set an especially fine example for parents. Consider what he did. He took time for children, even when he was very busy and under stress. He watched them at play in the marketplace and used aspects of their behavior in his teaching. (Matthew 11:16, 17) During his final trip to Jerusalem, Jesus knew that he would suffer and be killed. So when people brought little ones to see him, Jesus' disciples, perhaps in an effort to protect Jesus from further stress, tried to turn the children away. But Jesus reprimanded his disciples. Showing his "fulness of delight" with little ones, he said: "Let the young children come to me; do not try to stop them."—Mark 10:13, 14.

⁹ We can learn from Jesus' example. When young ones come to us, how do we respond —even when we are busy? As Jesus did? What children need, especially from their parents, is what Jesus was willing to give them—his time and attention. True, such words as "I love you" are important. Yet, actions speak louder than words. Your love is manifest not only by what you say but even more so by what you do. It is shown by the time, attention, and care that you provide your little ones. Doing all of that, however, may not produce tangible results, at least not as quickly as you would hope. Patience is required. We can learn patience if we imitate the way Jesus dealt with his disciples.

Jesus' Patience and Affection

¹⁰ Jesus was aware of the ongoing competition for prominence among his disciples. One day, after arriving in Capernaum with

---

6. What was God's purpose for enabling humans to have children?

7. In contrast with what some parents do, how did Jesus show interest in and compassion for "the sons of men"?

8. How did Jesus set a good example for parents?

9. Why may what we do be even more important than what we say?

10. How did Jesus teach his disciples a lesson on humility, and with what success at first?

his disciples, he asked them: "'What were you arguing over on the road?' They kept silent, for on the road they had argued among themselves who is greater." Instead of harshly reprimanding them, Jesus patiently provided an object lesson in an effort to teach them humility. (Mark 9:33-37) Did it produce the desired results? Not immediately. Some six months later, James and John put their mother up to requesting from Jesus prominent positions in the Kingdom. Again, Jesus patiently corrected their thinking.—Matthew 20:20-28.

What can parents learn from Jesus' way of teaching?

¹¹ Soon the Passover of 33 C.E. arrived, and Jesus met privately with his apostles to celebrate it. On arriving in the upper room, not one of the 12 apostles took the initiative to perform the customary service of washing the dusty feet of the others—the menial task of a servant or of a woman in the household. (1 Samuel 25:41; 1 Timothy 5:10) How it must have grieved Jesus to see that his disciples continued to show evidence of aspiring to rank and position! So Jesus washed the feet of each one and then earnestly appealed to them to follow his example of serving others. (John 13:4-17) Did they? The Bible says that later that evening "there also arose a heated dispute among them over which one of them seemed to be greatest." —Luke 22:24.

¹² When your children fail to respond to your counsel, do you parents appreciate how Jesus must have felt? Note that Jesus did not give up on his apostles, though they were slow in correcting their shortcomings. His patience eventually bore fruit. (1 John 3:14, 18) Parents, you do well to imitate Jesus' love and patience, never giving up in your efforts to train your children.

¹³ Young ones need to sense that their parents love them and are interested in them. Jesus wanted to know what his disciples were thinking, so he listened when they had questions. He asked them what they thought about certain matters. (Matthew 17:25-27) Yes, good teaching includes attentive listening and genuine interest. A parent should resist any inclination to put off an inquiring child with a gruff: "Go away! Can't you see that I am busy?" If a parent really is busy, the child should be told that the matter will be discussed later. Parents must then make sure that it is discussed. In this way the child will sense that the parent really is interested in him, and he will more readily confide in the parent.

¹⁴ Can parents appropriately show their affection by putting their arms around their

11. (a) What customary task did Jesus' apostles fail to perform after arriving in an upper room with Jesus? (b) What did Jesus do, and were his efforts successful at that time?
12. How might parents imitate Jesus in their efforts to train their children?

13. Why should a parent not gruffly dismiss a child's inquiry?
14. What can parents learn from Jesus about showing affection to their children?

children and hugging them? Again, parents can learn from Jesus. The Bible says that he "took the children into his arms and began blessing them, laying his hands upon them." (Mark 10:16) How do you think the young ones responded? Surely their hearts were warmed, and they were drawn to Jesus! If there is genuine affection and love between you parents and your young ones, they will respond more readily to your efforts to discipline and teach them.

The Question of How Much Time

15 Some have questioned whether children really need much of their parents' time and

15, 16. What has been a popular child-rearing concept, and what apparently prompted it?

When and how were Israelite parents to teach their children?

loving attention. A child-rearing concept that has been skillfully promoted is called *quality time.* Advocates claim that children do not need a lot of their parents' time as long as the limited time spent with them is meaningful, well-thought-out, and planned. Is the quality-time concept a good one, conceived with the welfare of young ones in mind?

16 One writer who had spoken with many children said that what they "wanted most from their parents was more time," along with "undivided attention." Significantly, one college professor observed: "The term [quality time] has grown out of parental guilt. People were giving themselves permission to spend less time with their children." How much time should parents spend with their children?

17 The Bible does not say. However, Israelite parents were urged to speak with their children when they were in their house, when they walked on the road, when they lay down, and when they got up. (Deuteronomy 6:7) This clearly means that parents need to interact with children and to teach them constantly each day.

18 Jesus successfully trained his disciples as he ate with them, traveled with them, and even relaxed with them. He thus took advantage of every opportunity to teach them. (Mark 6:31, 32; Luke 8:1; 22:14) Similarly, Christian parents should be alert to use every opportunity to establish and maintain good communication with their children and to train them in Jehovah's ways.

What to Teach and How to Do It

19 Simply spending time with children and

17. What do children need from their parents?
18. How did Jesus take advantage of opportunities to train his disciples, and what can parents learn from this?
19. (a) What is needed besides spending time with children? (b) What do parents primarily need to teach young ones?

even teaching them is not all there is to rearing them successfully. Vital, too, is *what* is taught. Notice how the Bible emphasizes what this should be. "These words that I am commanding you today," it says, "you must inculcate . . . in your son." What are "these words" that children need to be taught? Evidently, they are the words that had just been mentioned, namely: "You must love Jehovah your God with all your heart and all your soul and all your vital force." (Deuteronomy 6: 5-7) Jesus said that this is the most important of all God's commandments. (Mark 12:28-30) Parents primarily need to teach young ones about Jehovah, explaining why he alone is worthy of our whole-souled love and devotion.

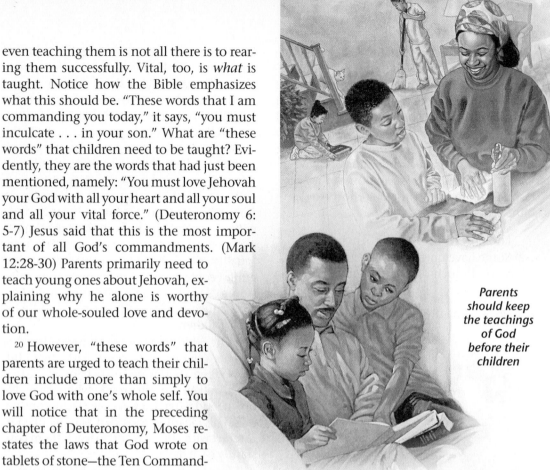

Parents should keep the teachings of God before their children

²⁰ However, "these words" that parents are urged to teach their children include more than simply to love God with one's whole self. You will notice that in the preceding chapter of Deuteronomy, Moses restates the laws that God wrote on tablets of stone—the Ten Commandments. These laws include commands not to lie, not to steal, not to murder, and not to commit adultery. (Deuteronomy

5:11-22) So the need to impart moral values to their children was impressed upon parents of old. Christian parents today need to provide their children with similar instruction if they are to help them to have a secure, happy future.

²¹ Note that parents are told *how* they are to teach "these words," or commandments, to their young ones: "You must inculcate them in your son." The word "inculcate" means "to teach and impress by frequent repetitions or admonitions: urge on or fix in the mind." So God is, in effect, telling parents to institute a planned program of Bible instruction that

---

20. What were parents of old commanded by God to teach their children?

21. What was meant by the instruction to "inculcate" God's word in young ones?

has the express purpose of impressing spiritual matters on the minds of their children.

22 Such a planned program takes parental initiative. The Bible says: "You must tie them ["these words," or commandments of God] as a sign upon your hand, and they must serve as a frontlet band between your eyes; and you must write them upon the doorposts of your house and on your gates." (Deuteronomy 6:8, 9) This does not mean that parents should literally write God's laws on doorposts and gates, tie a copy of them on the hands of their children, and place one between their eyes. Rather, the point is that

_____
22. What were Israelite parents told to do to instruct their children, and what did that mean?

parents should constantly keep the teachings of God before their children. Teaching their children should be done in such a regular, constant way that it is as though God's teachings are right there before the children all the time.

23 What are some especially important things that parents need to teach their children? Why is it vital today that children be both taught and trained to protect themselves? What assistance is now available to parents to help them teach their children effectively? These and other questions that concern many parents will be considered in the following article.

_____
23. What will be considered in next week's lesson?

PARENTS, PROTECT YOUR PRECIOUS INHERITANCE

"Wisdom is for a protection . . . [It] preserves alive its owners."
—ECCLESIASTES 7:12.

PARENTS bring into the world a new living person who has physical characteristics and personality traits similar to their own. The Bible calls such little ones "an inheritance from Jehovah." (Psalm 127:3) Since he is the true Life-Giver, Jehovah is really entrusting parents with what ultimately belongs to him. (Psalm 36:9) Parents, how do you view receiving such a precious gift from God?

2 Surely such a gift should be received with humility and appreciation. Over 3,000 years

_____
1. Why should parents view their children as gifts?
2. What was Manoah's response upon learning that he was to become a father?

ago, the Israelite Manoah responded in this way when his wife was informed by an angel that she was to bear a child. Upon hearing the good news, Manoah prayed: "Excuse me, Jehovah. The man of the true God that you just sent, let him, please, come again to us and instruct us as to what we ought to do to the child that will be born." (Judges 13:8) Parents, what can you learn from Manoah's example?

Why Divine Help Is Needed Now

3 Now more than ever before, parents need Jehovah's help in rearing their children. The

_____
3. Why is God's help in rearing children especially needed today?

reason? Satan the Devil and his angels have been hurled from heaven down to earth. "Woe for the earth," the Bible warns, "because the Devil has come down to you, having great anger, knowing he has a short period of time." (Revelation 12:7-9, 12) "Like a roaring lion," the Bible explains, Satan is "seeking to devour someone." (1 Peter 5:8) Lions usually prey on the most vulnerable, often the young. Wisely, then, Christian parents look to Jehovah for direction to protect their children. How much effort are you making to do so?

⁴ If you knew that a lion was loose in the neighborhood, protecting your children would surely be a primary concern. Satan is a predator. He seeks to corrupt God's people, thus making them unworthy of God's approval. (Job 2:1-7; 1 John 5:19) Children are an easy target. To escape the snares of the Devil, children must come to know and obey Jehovah. Bible knowledge is essential. "This means everlasting life," Jesus said, "their taking in knowledge of you, the only true God, and of the one whom you sent forth, Jesus Christ." (John 17:3) Furthermore, young ones need wisdom—the ability to understand and to apply what they learn. Since "wisdom itself preserves alive its owners," you parents need to instill the truth in the hearts of your children. (Ecclesiastes 7:12) How might you do this?

⁵ You can—and should—read to your children from God's Word. But helping them to love and obey Jehovah requires more than that—it requires understanding on their part. To illustrate: A child may be told not to cross the street before looking both ways. Yet, some children do not obey. Why not? The consequences of being hit by a car may not

have been explained often enough or in a manner that impresses the danger upon the child, overcoming the "foolishness" that could lead to an accident. Imparting wisdom takes time, as well as much patience. But how valuable wisdom is! "Its ways are ways of pleasantness," the Bible says, "and all its roadways are peace. It is a tree of life to those taking hold of it, and those keeping fast hold of it are to be called happy."—Proverbs 3:13-18; 22:15.

Teaching That Imparts Wisdom

⁶ Often young ones act improperly, not because they have not been taught what is right, but because the teaching has not reached their heart—their inner self. The Devil is waging a battle for the heart of young ones. He schemes to see that they are exposed to ungodly influences of his world. He also tries to exploit their inherited sinful inclination to do bad things. (Genesis 8:21; Psalm 51:5) Parents need to recognize that a real war is being waged for the heart of their children.

⁷ Parents usually *tell* a child what is right or wrong, believing that they have taught him a certain moral principle. They may say to the child that it is wrong to lie, to steal, or to have sexual relations with anyone to whom one is not married. However, the child needs to have a stronger motivation for obeying than simply because his parents say so. These are Jehovah's laws. The child should learn that the course of wisdom is to obey God's commandments.—Proverbs 6:16-19; Hebrews 13:4.

⁸ The complexity of the universe, the diversity of living things, the change of the sea-

---

4. (a) Knowing that a lion is roaming in the neighborhood should prompt what reaction from parents? (b) What do children need for protection?
5. (a) How can wisdom be imparted? (b) How does Proverbs describe the value of wisdom?

6. (a) Why do children often act unwisely? (b) What battle is going on?
7. Why is telling a child what is right or wrong not sufficient?
8. What kind of teaching can help children act wisely?

*Parents, what can you learn
from Manoah's example?*

regulating," in the original Greek, conveys the idea of "putting mind in." So fathers are, in effect, urged to put the mind of Jehovah in their children. What a protection that will be for the young ones! If children have God's thoughts, his way of thinking, inculcated in their mind, they are safeguarded against wrongdoing.

Desire Motivated by Love

¹⁰ In order for you to fulfill your desire to bring your child up properly, however, your efforts need to be prompted by love. An important factor is good communication. Find out what is happening in your youngster's life and what his or her views are. In a comfortable setting, tactfully draw out your child. At times, you may be shocked by what he says. Be very careful not to overreact. Rather, listen with sympathetic concern.

¹¹ True, you may have read to your child from the Bible about God's laws prohibiting sexual immorality, even doing so a number of times. (1 Corinthians 6:18; Ephesians 5:5) This may have impressed upon your young ones what is pleasing and not pleasing to Jehovah. However, putting his mind in a child requires more. Children need help to reason on the value of Jehovah's laws. They need to be convinced that his laws are right and good and that obeying them is the proper and loving thing to do. Only if you reason with your children from the Scriptures so that they accept God's viewpoint can it be said that you have put his mind in them.

¹² When talking about sex, you might ask, "Do you think that obeying Jehovah's law

sons—all such things can help a young child appreciate the existence of an all-wise Creator. (Romans 1:20; Hebrews 3:4) Further, the child should be taught that God loves him and has made provision through the sacrifice of His Son to give him eternal life and that he can make God happy by obeying what He says. Then likely the child will come to want to serve Jehovah, despite attempts of the Devil to stop him.—Proverbs 22:6; 27:11; John 3:16.

⁹ The kind of teaching that protects a child and motivates him to do what is right takes time, attention, and planning. It requires that parents accept direction from God. The Bible says: "You, fathers, . . . go on bringing [your children] up in the discipline and mental-regulating of Jehovah." (Ephesians 6:4) What does that mean? "Mental-

---

9. (a) What does lifesaving teaching require? (b) What are fathers instructed to do, and what does this involve?

10. To instruct your child effectively, what is it important for you to know?
11. How can a parent put God's mind in a child?
12. How can a parent help his child to get the proper view of sexual relations?

Young ones, what can you learn from the example of the three Hebrews?

not to have sexual relations before marriage will rob a person of happiness?" Encourage your child to explain his answer. After reviewing God's marvelous provision for producing a child, you might ask: "Do you think our loving God would make laws to rob us of enjoyment of life? Or do you think his laws are there to make us happy and to protect us?" (Psalm 119:1, 2; Isaiah 48:17) Get your child's thinking on this matter. Then you might draw attention to examples of how sexual immorality has led to heartache and trouble. (2 Samuel 13:1-33) By reasoning with your child so that he understands and accepts God's view, you will have gone a long way toward putting God's mind in him. However, there is something else you can do.

¹³ Wisely, you will not only teach your child the consequences of disobeying Jehovah but also explain how Jehovah is personally affected by the way we live. Show your child from the Bible that we can cause Jehovah pain when we fail to do his will. (Psalm 78:41) You might ask, "Why do you not want to hurt Jehovah?" and explain: "God's enemy Satan claims that we serve Jehovah for selfish reasons and not because we love him." Then explain that by keeping integri-

ty, Job made God's heart rejoice, thus providing an answer to Satan's lying charge. (Job 1: 9-11; 27:5) Your child needs to understand that depending on how he behaves, he can make Jehovah either sad or happy. (Proverbs 27:11) This and many other vital lessons can be taught to children by using the book *Learn From the Great Teacher.**

Gratifying Results

¹⁴ A grandfather in Croatia who reads the *Teacher* book with his seven-year-old grandson writes that the boy told him the following: "Mum said to do something, but I didn't want to do it. Then I remembered the chapter 'Obedience Protects You,' so I went back and told her I would be obedient to her." Regarding the chapter "Why We Should Not Lie," a couple in Florida, U.S.A., said: "It provides questions that invite children to open their hearts and admit errors they would otherwise not admit."

---

* Published by Jehovah's Witnesses. See chapter 40, "How to Make God Happy."

---

13. Understanding what can especially motivate a child to obey Jehovah?

14, 15. (a) Which lessons in the *Teacher* book have motivated children? (b) What good results have you had from using the book? (See also box on pages 18-19.)

What lie is Ananias telling Peter?

The pictures and captions in the "Teacher" book are powerful teaching tools

Yet, talking about this is not always easy. A newspaper columnist observed that she grew up in an era in which using words that refer to the sexual organs was considered rude. Concerning the teaching of her children, she wrote: "I'm going to have to get over my embarrassment." Truly, when out of embarrassment parents avoid the subject of sex, it does not protect a child. Sexual molesters exploit a child's ignorance. *Learn From the Great Teacher* addresses the subject in a wholesome, dignified manner. Informing children about sex does not take away their

Who can see everything we do?

¹⁵ The *Teacher* book has more than 230 pictures, and there is a caption, or description, for each picture or group of pictures. "Often my son will fix his eyes on a picture and not want the page turned," noted one appreciative mother. "Not only are the pictures appealing but they teach lessons on their own, or at least cause children to ask questions. Regarding a picture in which a child is watching television in a darkened room, my son asked, 'Mommy, what is that boy doing?' in a tone that indicated that he knew that something was wrong." The caption to the picture reads: "Who can see everything we do?"

Vital Education for Today

¹⁶ Children need to know the proper and the improper use of their private body parts.

innocence, whereas failing to do so can lead to their being robbed of it.

¹⁷ In chapter 10, when discussing the wicked angels who came to earth and fathered children, the child is asked, "What do you know about sex relations?" The book gives a simple, dignified answer. Later, chapter 32 explains how children can be protected from sexual predators. Many letters have reported that such teaching is vital. One observed: "Last week when my son Javan saw his pediatrician, she asked if we had discussed with him the proper use of private parts of the

---

16. What is it vital that children be taught today, and why?

17. How does the *Teacher* book help parents to teach their children about sex?

body. She was very impressed that we had done this using our new book."

¹⁸ Another chapter deals with the Bible account of the three Hebrew youths Shadrach, Meshach, and Abednego, who refused to bow to an image representing the Babylonian State. (Daniel 3:1-30) Some may not relate paying homage to an image to saluting the flag, as the *Teacher* book does. However, note what author Edward Gaffney had to say in an interview by *U.S. Catholic.* He mentioned that when his daughter told him after her first day at public school that she had learned a "new prayer at school," he asked her to repeat it to him. "She put her hand on her heart," said Gaffney, "and proudly began, 'I pledge allegiance to the flag . . .'" He continued: "All of a sudden, it kicked in. The Jehovah's Witnesses were right. There is an aspect of national spirituality that's being shaped in our schools at a very early stage—an unquestioning transcendent loyalty."

Worth All the Effort

¹⁹ Really, teaching your children is worth all your effort. A mother in Kansas, U.S.A., was moved to tears upon receiving a letter from her son. He wrote: "I feel very fortu-

---

18. How does the *Teacher* book discuss paying homage to national emblems?
19. What rewards are there for teaching children?

How Would You Answer?

- Why do parents especially now need to protect their children?
- What kind of teaching imparts wisdom?
- What are vital issues to discuss with your children today?
- How has the *Teacher* book helped parents teach their children?

A Book for Everyone

Learn From the Great Teacher was prepared to help parents or other adults read and discuss the teachings of Jesus Christ with children. Yet, adults who have read the book by themselves have expressed sincere appreciation for what they have learned.

A man in Texas, U.S.A., said: *"Learn From the Great Teacher* is eloquent in its simplicity, motivating us at any age—even at 76, as I am. Thank you very much, from one who has served Jehovah since youth."

A reader from London, England, reports: "The beautiful illustrations are bound to capture the hearts of parents and children alike. The questions and format are wonderful, and how fantastic to see sensitive issues dealt with, as in chapter 32, 'How Jesus Was Protected.'" She concluded: "Even though this book is no doubt primarily designed

nate to have had an upbringing that left me relatively emotionally stable and whole. You and Daddy certainly deserve commendation." (Proverbs 31:28) *Learn From the Great Teacher* can help many more parents to teach children so as to protect this precious heritage.

20 Our children deserve all the time, atten-

---

20. What should parents always remember, and what effect should that have on them?

tion, and effort we can give them. They are young for such a short time. Take advantage of every opportunity to be with them and to help them. You will never regret it. They will come to love you. Always remember, your children are God's gift to you. What a precious inheritance they are! (Psalm 127:3-5) So treat them as such, as though you are answerable to God for how you rear them because the fact is, you are.

---

with the children of Jehovah's Witnesses in mind, I imagine that teachers and others will be more than glad to have a copy too. I look forward to using it in the months and years to come."

A woman from Massachusetts, U.S.A., commented about the many "well-thought-out pictures." She observed: "I noticed that even though the book is meant for children, the subjects discussed can also help us adults think about our personal relationship with Jehovah."

"Wow! What a wonderful book!" exclaimed a woman from Maine, U.S.A. "It is not just for young ones but for all of us as God's children. It has reached into places I didn't know were there and has stirred emotions and then soothed them, so that there was peace. I feel so close to Jehovah as my Father. He has taken away all the hurt that has happened over the years and has made his purpose so clear." She concluded: "I'm telling everyone, 'Please read it.'"

A woman from Kyoto, Japan, reported that when she was reading to her grandchildren, they asked such questions as: "'What

is that boy doing? Why is this little girl being scolded? What about this mother? What about this lion?' It teaches things we are interested in, so I love it much more than any book I could find in a library."

A father in Calgary, Canada, says that as soon as he received the book, he began to read it to his six-year-old daughter and his nine-year-old son. "Immediately the response was wonderful," he reports. "My children were following along and answering the questions from their heart. They felt a part of the study, and it gave them a chance to express themselves. They have come alive, and my daughter says she wants to study from the new book every night."

After one study, the father said: "My son and I talked for hours about Jehovah and his purposes. He had so many questions that came from the book. Tears came to my eyes when he said good night to me and asked: 'Can we do this again, Dad? I have so many questions, and I want to know everything about Jehovah.'"

A FORSAKEN ORPHAN FINDS A LOVING FATHER

AS TOLD BY
DIMITRIS SIDIROPOULOS

"Go ahead, pick up that weapon and shoot," snarled the officer, thrusting a rifle in front of me. I calmly refused. To the horror of the onlooking soldiers, bullets from the officer's gun began to whiz over my shoulder. Death seemed imminent. Happily, I survived. But this was not the first time my life was in danger.

MY FAMILY belonged to an ethnic minority living near Kayseri, in Cappadocia, Turkey. Some individuals from this area apparently embraced Christianity in the first century C.E. (Acts 2:9) By the beginning of the 20th century, however, things had changed drastically.

From Refugee to Orphan

A few months after I was born in 1922, ethnic conflict caused my family to flee to Greece as refugees. My panic-stricken parents left with nothing but their months-old baby,

me. After suffering untold hardships, they arrived in a wretched condition in the village of Kiria, near Drama, in northern Greece.

When I was four years old and after my younger brother was born, my father died. He was only 27 years of age, but the misery of those harrowing times had worn him down. Mother suffered terrible deprivations, and soon she too died. My brother and I were left completely destitute. We were sent from orphanage to orphanage, and at the age of 12, I ended up in one in Thessalonica, where I served an apprenticeship as a mechanic.

As I was growing up inside the cold and inhospitable walls of orphanages, I wondered why certain people experience so much suffering and injustice. I asked myself why God allows such sad conditions to exist. In our religious education classes, we were taught that God is omnipotent, but no reasonable explanation was given about the existence and prevalence of evil. A popular mantra said that the Greek Orthodox Church is the best religion. When I asked, "If Orthodoxy is the best religion, why isn't everybody Orthodox?" I received no satisfactory answer.

Our teacher, nevertheless, had deep respect for the Bible, and he impressed on us that it is a sacred book. The director of the orphanage displayed the same attitude, but he inexplicably refrained from participating in religious services. When I inquired about this, I was told that he had once studied with Jehovah's Witnesses, a religion unknown to me.

When my education at the Thessalonica orphanage was completed, I was 17 years old. World War II had begun, and Greece was under Nazi occupation. People were dying in the streets from hunger. In order to survive, I fled to the countryside to work for meager wages as a field hand.

The Bible Provides Answers

When I returned to Thessalonica in April 1945, I received a visit from the sister of one of my childhood friends with whom I had lived in a number of orphanages. Paschalia told me that her brother had disappeared and asked me if I knew anything of his whereabouts. During the conversation, she said that she was one of Jehovah's Witnesses and mentioned God's interest in humans.

Bitterly, I raised many objections. Why had I been suffering since early childhood?

Why had I been left an orphan? Where is God when we need him the most? She replied, "Are you sure that God is to blame for these conditions?" Using her Bible, she showed me that God does not make people suffer. I was helped to see that the Creator loves humans and will shortly improve things. Using such scriptures as Isaiah 35:5-7 and Revelation 21:3, 4, she showed me that soon war, strife, sickness, and death will be removed, and faithful people will live forever on earth.

Finding a Supportive Family

I learned that Paschalia's brother had been killed in a skirmish of the guerrilla forces. I visited her family to comfort them, but instead they provided Scriptural comfort to me. I went back for more consoling thoughts from the Bible, and soon I became part of a small group of Jehovah's Witnesses who met secretly to study and worship. Despite the ostracism brought upon the Witnesses, I was determined to continue associating with them.

In that group of humble Christians, I found the warm, loving family atmosphere that I missed. They provided the spiritual support and assistance that I desperately needed. In them, I found selfless and concerned friends, who were ready and willing to help and comfort me. (2 Corinthians 7: 5-7) More important, I was helped to draw closer to Jehovah, whom I now thought of as my loving heavenly Father. His qualities of love, compassion, and deep concern were very appealing. (Psalm 23:1-6) At last I had found a spiritual family and a loving Father! My heart was touched. Soon I was moved to dedicate myself to Jehovah, and I was baptized in September 1945.

Attending Christian meetings not only increased my knowledge but also deepened my faith. Since there was no other means of transportation, a number of us often walked the three miles between our village and the meeting place, engaging in unforgettable spiritual discussions. In late 1945, when I learned of the opportunity to participate in the full-time evangelizing work, I started pioneering. A strong relationship with Jehovah was vital, as my faith and integrity would soon be tested to the limit.

Opposition Backfires

The police often raided our meeting place at gunpoint. The country was under martial law, since civil war was raging in Greece. Opposing groups turned on one another with savage hatred. Taking advantage of the situation, the clergy led the authorities to believe that we were Communists and to persecute us viciously.

During a two-year period, we were arrested numerous times, and six times we received sentences of up to four months. However, the prisons were already full of political prisoners, so we were set free. We used our unexpected freedom to continue preaching, but after a while we were again arrested —three times in the same week. We knew that many of our brothers had been exiled to barren islands. Would my faith be strong enough for me to face such a test?

Conditions became extremely difficult when I was put on police probation. In order to keep an eye on me, the authorities sent me to Evosmos, near Thessalonica, where there was a police station. I rented a room nearby, and to support myself, I started working as an itinerant craftsman, polishing copper pots and pans. While I pioneered in the surrounding villages, this trade enabled me to get easy access to homes without arousing the suspicion of the police. As a result, several people heard the good news and responded favorably. More than ten of them eventually became dedicated worshipers of Jehovah.

Ten Years, Eight Prisons

I remained under police surveillance until the end of 1949, and then I returned to Thessalonica, eager to continue in the full-time ministry. Just when I thought that my travails were over, in 1950, I was unexpectedly ordered to join the army. Because of my Christian neutrality, I was determined not to "learn war." (Isaiah 2:4) Thus started a long, tormenting journey that would take me to some of the most infamous prisons in Greece.

I worked as a cook in the Drama prison

It all started in the city of Drama. During the first weeks of my incarceration there, the newly conscripted soldiers began their target practice. One day, I was taken to the shooting range. One of the officers thrust a rifle in front of me and ordered me to shoot. When I refused, he started shooting at me. When other officers saw that I would not compromise, they began to punch me savagely. They lit cigarettes and stubbed them out in the palms of my hands. Afterward, they threw me into solitary confinement. This went on for three days. The pain from the cigarette burns was excruciating, and for many years I bore the scars on my hands.

Before I was court-martialed, I was transferred to a military camp at Iráklion, Crete. There, in an effort to break my integrity, they beat me severely. Afraid that I might give in, I prayed fervently, asking my heavenly Father to strengthen me. The words of Jeremiah 1:19 came to mind: "They will be certain to fight against you, but they will not prevail against you, for 'I am with you,' is the utterance of Jehovah, 'to deliver you.'" The soothing "peace of God" brought calmness and tranquillity. I understood the wisdom of putting implicit trust in Jehovah.—Philippians 4:6, 7; Proverbs 3:5.

At the trial that followed, I was sentenced to life imprisonment. Jehovah's Witnesses were considered the worst "enemies of the State." The life term began at the Itsedin criminal prison, outside Canea, where I was put in solitary confinement. Itsedin was an old fort, and my cell was full of rats. I used to wrap a ragged, old blanket around me from head to toe so that the rats would not have direct contact with my body when they crawled all over me. I fell very sick with pneumonia. The doctor said that I had to sit in the sunshine, and thus I was able to have discussions with many of the prisoners in the courtyard. However, my condition worsened, and after a massive pulmonary hemorrhage, I was transferred to the Iráklion hospital.

Again, my spiritual family of fellow Christians were there when I needed them. (Colos-

With Katina on our wedding day, 1959

sians 4:11) The brothers in Iráklion visited me regularly, providing comfort and encouragement. I told them that I needed literature in order to witness to interested ones. They brought me a suitcase with a double bottom in which I could safely hide the literature. How happy I was that during my stay in those prisons, at least six fellow inmates were helped to become true Christians!

In the meantime the civil war had ended, and my sentence was commuted to ten years in prison. I served the remainder of my sentence in prisons in Rethimno, Genti Koule, and Cassandra. After spending almost ten years in eight prisons, I was discharged, and I returned to Thessalonica, where I was warmly received into the arms of my beloved Christian brothers.

Thriving in the Christian Brotherhood

By now the Witnesses in Greece could worship in relative freedom. I immediately seized the opportunity to continue in the

An assembly in a forest near Thessalonica, late 1960's

full-time ministry. Soon another blessing was added, as I got to know a faithful Christian sister, Katina, who loved Jehovah and was very active in the preaching work. We were married in October 1959. The birth of our daughter, Agape, and having my own Christian family further healed the wounds of my orphanhood. Above all, our family was content to serve under the protective care of our loving heavenly Father, Jehovah.—Psalm 5:11.

With our daughter, 1967

Because of circumstances beyond my control, I was forced to stop pioneering, but I supported my wife as she continued in the full-time service. A real milestone in my Christian life came in 1969 when an international convention of Jehovah's Witnesses was held in Nuremberg, Germany. As I prepared to travel there, I applied for a passport. When my wife went to the police station to ask why more than two months had passed without my getting the passport, an officer pulled a thick file out of his drawer and said: "Are you asking for a passport for this person so that he can proselytize people in Germany? No way! He is dangerous."

With Jehovah's help and the assistance of some brothers, I was included in a group passport and was thus able to attend that wonderful convention. The attendance reached a peak of over 150,000, and I could clearly see Jehovah's spirit directing and unifying this international spiritual family. Later in life, I would appreciate even more the value of the Christian brotherhood.

In 1977 my beloved wife and faithful companion passed away. I tried my best to raise my daughter according to Bible principles, but I was not left alone. Again, my spiritual family came to the rescue. I will always be grateful for the support of the brothers during that difficult time. Some of them even moved into our home for a while to look after my daughter. I will never forget their self-sacrificing love.—John 13: 34, 35.

Agape grew up and married a brother, Elias. They have four sons, all in the truth. In recent years, I have had a number of strokes and my health has deteriorated. My daughter and her family take good care of me. Despite poor health, I still have many reasons to rejoice. I remember the time when there were only about one hundred brothers in all of Thessalonica, meeting secretly in private homes. Now there are about five thousand zealous Witnesses in that area. (Isaiah 60:22) At conventions, young brothers approach me, asking: "Do you remember when you used to bring the magazines to our home?" Although the parents might not have been reading those magazines, their children did, and they progressed spiritually!

As I observe the growth of Jehovah's organization, I feel that it was worth all the trials I endured. I always tell my grandchildren and other young ones to remember their heavenly Father in their youth, and he will never abandon them. (Ecclesiastes 12:1) Jehovah proved true to his word, becoming for me "a father of fatherless boys." (Psalm 68:5) Although I was a forsaken orphan early in life, eventually I found a caring Father!

Making Jehovah Your God

IN Bible times, certain individuals enjoyed such a close relationship with Jehovah that he was spoken of as their God. For example, in the Scriptures, Jehovah is described as "the God of Abraham," "the God of David," and "the God of Elijah."—Genesis 31:42; 2 Kings 2:14; 20:5.

How did each of these men come to have a close attachment to God? What can we learn from them so that we too can build and maintain a strong personal relationship with the Creator?

Abraham Put "Faith in Jehovah"

Abraham was the first person about whom the Bible speaks about putting faith in Jehovah. Faith was the preeminent quality of Abraham that gained him God's approval. In fact, Abraham enjoyed such favor with Jehovah that the Creator later introduced himself to Moses as "the God of Abraham" and of his son and grandson, Isaac and Jacob.—Genesis 15:6; Exodus 3:6.

How did Abraham come to have this kind of faith in God? First of all, Abraham built his faith on a solid foundation. He may have been instructed in Jehovah's ways by Noah's son Shem, who was an eyewitness of God's saving acts. Shem was a living testimony that Jehovah "kept Noah, a preacher of righteousness, safe with seven others when he brought a deluge upon a world of ungodly people." (2 Peter 2:5) Abraham might have learned from Shem that once Jehovah promised something, the fulfillment was certain. In any case, when Abraham himself received a promise from God, he rejoiced and based his course of life on the sure knowledge that the promise would be fulfilled.

Having a solid foundation, Abraham's faith was then strengthened by works. The apostle Paul wrote: "By faith Abraham, when he was called, obeyed in going out into a place he was destined to receive as an inheritance; and he went out, although not knowing where he was going." (Hebrews 11:8) That act of obedience enhanced Abraham's faith, regarding which the disciple James wrote: "You behold that his faith worked along with his works and by his works his faith was perfected."—James 2:22.

Furthermore, Jehovah allowed Abraham's faith to be tested, making it more robust. Paul went on to say: "By faith Abraham, when he was tested, as good as offered

Acts of obedience enhanced Abraham's faith

Like David, we should repent when we sin

up Isaac." Testing refines and strengthens faith, making it "of much greater value than gold."—Hebrews 11:17; 1 Peter 1:7.

Although Abraham did not live to see the fulfillment of all that God had promised, he had the joy of seeing others follow his example. His wife Sarah and three other members of his family—Isaac, Jacob, and Joseph—are also commended in the Bible for their outstanding faith.—Hebrews 11:11, 20-22.

Faith Like Abraham's Today

Faith is essential for anyone who desires to make Jehovah his God. "Without faith it is impossible to please [God] well," wrote Paul. (Hebrews 11:6) How can a servant of God today develop strong faith like that of Abraham?

As with Abraham, our faith must be established on a solid foundation. That can best be done by regular study of the Bible and Bible-based publications. Reading the Bible and meditating on what is read can assure us that God's promises will come true. We are then moved to fashion our way of life on the basis of that assured expectation. Our faith is further enhanced by acts of obedience, which include participation in the public ministry and attendance at Christian meetings.—Matthew 24:14; 28:19, 20; Hebrews 10:24, 25.

Our faith will certainly be tested, perhaps by opposition, serious illness, the death of a loved one, or something else. Remaining loyal to Jehovah under test enriches our faith, making it more valuable than gold. Whether we live to see the fulfillment of all of God's promises or not, our faith will draw us closer to Jehovah. Moreover, our example will encourage others to imitate our faith. (Hebrews 13:7) This was the case with Ralph, who observed and imitated the faith of his parents. He explains:

"When I was living at home, my parents encouraged the whole family to get up early in the morning so that we could read the Bible together. We read the entire Bible that way." Ralph still reads the Bible each morning, and this gives him a fine start to the day. Ralph used to go in the public ministry with his father every week. "That is when I learned to make return visits and to conduct home Bible studies." Ralph now serves as a volunteer at one of the branch offices of Jehovah's Witnesses in Europe. What a fine reward for his parents' faith!

A Man Agreeable to Jehovah's Heart

David, born about 900 years after Abraham, is an outstanding figure among Jehovah's servants mentioned in the Scriptures. Concerning Jehovah's choice of David as future king, the prophet Samuel said: "Jehovah will certainly find for himself a man agreeable to his heart." So close was the attachment between Jehovah and David that the prophet Isaiah later spoke to King Hezekiah of "Jehovah the God of David your forefather."—1 Samuel 13:14; 2 Kings 20:5; Isaiah 38:5.

Though David was agreeable to Jehovah's heart, there were occasions when he let his desires run away with him. Three times he made serious mistakes: He allowed the ark of the covenant to be transported improperly on its way to Jerusalem; he committed adultery with Bath-sheba and plotted the death of her husband, Uriah; and he conducted a census of the people of Israel and Judah that Jehovah had not commanded. On each occasion, David overstepped the Law of God. —2 Samuel 6:2-10; 11:2-27; 24:1-9.

When David was confronted with his sins, however, he accepted responsibility for them and did not shift the blame to others. He admitted that the transporting of the Ark had not been properly arranged, adding that "we did not search after [Jehovah] according to the custom." When Nathan the prophet uncovered David's adultery, David replied by saying: "I have sinned against Jehovah." And once David became aware of the foolishness of counting the people, he admitted: "I have sinned very much in what I have done." David repented of his sins and remained close to Jehovah.—1 Chronicles 15:13; 2 Samuel 12:13; 24:10.

When We Err

In our efforts to make Jehovah our God, David's example is encouraging. If a man so agreeable to Jehovah's heart was capable of such serious sins, we need not despair if, despite our best efforts, we at times err or even make big mistakes. (Ecclesiastes 7:20) We can take heart from the fact that when David repented, his sins were forgiven. That is what happened to Uwe* some years ago.

Uwe was serving as an elder in a congregation of Jehovah's Witnesses. On one occasion, he succumbed to wrong desires and committed immorality. At first Uwe, like King David, tried to keep the matter to himself, hoping that Jehovah would turn a blind eye to his transgression. Eventually, Uwe's conscience bothered him so much that he confessed to a fellow elder and action was taken to help Uwe recover from his spiritual disaster.

---

* Name has been changed.

Uwe repented of his sins and stayed close to Jehovah and the congregation. He was so grateful for the help he received that some weeks later he wrote to the elders expressing his sincere and deeply felt gratitude for the assistance. "You helped me to clear the name of Jehovah of reproach," he wrote. Uwe was able to retain his relationship with Jehovah and in time was reappointed as a servant in the same congregation.

"A Man With Feelings Like Ours"

Elijah, who lived in the century after David, was one of Israel's foremost prophets. Elijah was a champion of true worship at a time when corruption and immorality were widespread, and he never wavered in his devotion to Jehovah. No wonder that his successor, Elisha, once called Jehovah "the God of Elijah"!—2 Kings 2:14.

Nonetheless, Elijah was not superhuman. James wrote: "Elijah was a man with feelings like ours." (James 5:17) For instance, after he had dealt Baal worshipers in Israel a painful defeat, Queen Jezebel threatened to kill him. How did he react? He became afraid and fled into the wilderness. There, sitting under a broom tree, Elijah lamented: "It is enough! Now, O Jehovah, take my soul away, for I am no better than my forefathers." Elijah no longer wanted to be a prophet but preferred to die instead.—1 Kings 19:4.

Jehovah, however, showed understanding of Elijah's feelings. God strengthened him, reassuring Elijah that he was not alone, since there were others who were loyal to true worship. Moreover, Jehovah still trusted Elijah and had work for him to do.—1 Kings 19: 5-18.

Elijah's emotional turmoil was not a sign that he had lost God's favor. About 1,000 years later, when Christ Jesus was transfigured before Peter, James, and John, whom did Jehovah choose to appear in the vision alongside Jesus? Moses and Elijah. (Matthew 17:1-9) Clearly, Jehovah regarded Elijah as an exemplary prophet. Although Elijah was just "a man with feelings like ours," God appreciated his hard work in restoring pure worship and sanctifying His name.

Our Emotional Struggle

Servants of Jehovah today may at times feel discouraged or anxious. What a comfort to know that Elijah experienced the same emotions! And how reassuring that just as Jehovah understood Elijah's feelings, He also understands our emotional struggle.—Psalm 103:14.

On the one hand, we love God and our fellowman and desire to do Jehovah's work of proclaiming the Kingdom good news. On the other hand, we may be disappointed at the lack of response to our preaching or even anxious over threats from enemies of true worship. However, just as Jehovah equipped Elijah to carry on, He also equips his servants today. Take, for example, the case of Herbert and Gertrud.

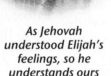

As Jehovah understood Elijah's feelings, so he understands ours

Herbert and Gertrud were baptized as Jehovah's Witnesses in Leipzig, in the former German Democratic Republic, in 1952. Life then was difficult for servants of God, since their public ministry was under ban. How did Herbert feel about preaching from house to house?

"We were very anxious at times. When we went from house to house, we did not know whether the authorities would suddenly appear and arrest us." What helped Herbert and others to overcome their fear? "We did a great deal of personal Bible study. And Jehovah gave us the strength to carry on our preaching work." In his public ministry, Herbert had a number of experiences that fortified—even amused—him.

Herbert met a middle-aged woman who showed interest in the Bible. When Herbert called back on her some days later, a young man was present and listened to the conversation. After several minutes Herbert caught sight of something that made him shudder. On a chair in the corner of the room was a police officer's hat. It belonged to the young man, who was clearly a policeman determined to arrest Herbert.

"You are one of Jehovah's Witnesses!" the young man exclaimed. "Let me see your ID." Herbert handed over his identification card. Then the unexpected happened. The woman turned to the policeman and warned him: "If anything happens to this man of God, you are no longer welcome in this house."

The young man paused for a moment, handed the ID to Herbert, and let him go. Herbert later learned that the policeman was courting the woman's daughter. Obviously, he felt that he would do better to continue to court the girl than to turn Herbert in.

Make Jehovah Our God

What can we learn from these events? Like Abraham, we must have a robust faith in Jehovah's promises. Like David, we should turn to Jehovah in true repentance whenever we err. And like Elijah, we need to lean on Jehovah for strength in times of anxiety. Doing so, we can make Jehovah our God now and for all eternity, since he is "a living God, who is a Savior of all sorts of men, especially of faithful ones."—1 Timothy 4:10.

Questions From Readers

Should a Christian give a government employee a tip or a gift for his services, or would that be viewed as bribery?

Wherever they live, Christians seek to exercise practical wisdom in dealing with local situations, remembering that what is acceptable and legal in one land may be totally unacceptable and illegal in another. (Proverbs 2:6-9) Of course, a Christian should always bear in mind that anyone who wants to be "a guest in [Jehovah's] tent" must shun bribery. —Psalm 15:1, 5; Proverbs 17:23.

What is bribery? According to *The World Book Encyclopedia*, "bribery means giving or offering something of value to a . . . person in a position of public trust, who in return violates his or her duty or the law in order to benefit the giver." Thus, regardless of where one lives, it is bribery to give money or a gift to a judge or a police officer to pervert justice or to an inspector to turn a blind eye to a defect or a violation. It is also bribery to use a gift to receive preferential treatment, such as getting moved forward on a waiting list or bypassing others in line. Such a course would also betray a lack of love.—Matthew 7:12; 22:39.

But is it bribery to give a gift or a tip to, say, a public servant in order to obtain a legitimate service or to avoid unfair treatment? For example, in some lands officials may be unwilling to enroll children in school, admit a person into a hospital, or stamp immigration documents until they receive a tip. Or they may procrastinate in processing applications to renew licenses and permits.

Tipping practices and the general attitude toward them vary from one place to another. Where such payments are customary or ex-

pected, some Christians may feel that within the law, they are not violating Bible principles when they tip an official to perform his duty. In some lands people may even view such payments as a gift to supplement a public employee's otherwise low income. Keep in mind that there is a difference between extending a gift for a legitimate service and offering a bribe for an unlawful favor.

On the other hand, when making legitimate requests, some of Jehovah's Witnesses have declined to give tips to inspectors, customs officials, or others even where such gift-giving is routine. Because the Witnesses are known locally both for taking this conscientious stand and for their honesty, they sometimes receive treatment that most people get only through a payment.—Proverbs 10:9; Matthew 5:16.

In summary, each servant of Jehovah must decide for himself whether he will extend a tip to receive a legitimate service or to avoid unfair treatment. Above all, he should pursue a course that leaves him with a good conscience, that brings no reproach on Jehovah's name, and that does not stumble others. —Matthew 6:9; 1 Corinthians 10:31-33; 2 Corinthians 6:3; 1 Timothy 1:5.

IN OUR NEXT ISSUE

Taking in Knowledge Now and Forever

———

A Useful Translation Aid

———

Does Your Faith Move You to Action?

Searching for Deserving Ones in Australia's Outback

A VAST inland section of Australia is affectionately known as the outback. Some parts of this remote area had not received a witness in 12 years. So Jehovah's Witnesses in Darwin, the Northern Territory's capital city, organized an intensive nine-day preaching campaign to search out deserving ones. —Matthew 10:11.

Careful planning began 12 months ahead of the campaign, including the mapping of more than 300,000 square miles—an area three times the size of New Zealand. To get some idea of how isolated this vast territory is, consider that the average driveway in a cattle station (ranch) stretches more than 20 miles from the front gate to the house! Moreover, some stations are 180 miles or more apart.

A total of 145 Witness volunteers shared in the campaign. Some came from as far away as Tasmania. Some arrived in four-wheel-drive vehicles packed with camping gear, spare parts, and fuel. Others hauled their gear in trailers. In addition, two 22-seat buses were hired to carry those who did not have suitable four-wheel-drive vehicles. Those traveling by bus concentrated on witnessing to the inhabitants of small towns in the selected territory.

Before setting out, the brothers arranged talks and demonstrations to provide guidelines on how to present the good news in this unusual territory. For example, to preach effectively in Aboriginal communities usually requires following certain protocol and being aware of Aboriginal customs. Environmental concerns were also discussed to help protect the wildlife.

Many outstanding experiences were enjoyed. For instance, in one Aboriginal settlement, the brothers arranged to deliver

a Bible-based public talk. The headlady in the community personally went to inform people about it. Afterward, 5 books and 41 brochures were placed with those in attendance. In another settlement an Aborigine was contacted. He even had his own Bible, a *King James Version,* but it was old and tattered. When asked if he knew God's name, he said yes and then proceeded to pull out of his jacket an old issue of *The Watchtower.* He read from the magazine, quoting Mark 12: 30, which says: "You must love Jehovah your God with your whole heart." He said, "I really like that scripture." After an extensive Bible discussion, he accepted a new Bible and other Bible-based literature.

Near the Gulf of Carpentaria, the headman of a million-acre cattle station showed some interest in the Kingdom message. When he was shown the publications *My Book of Bible Stories* and *Knowledge That Leads to Everlasting Life,** he asked if there was any literature available in the Kriol language. This was unusual because even though many Aborigines speak Kriol, few can read it. It turned out that all 50 of the workers on that station were able to read Kriol. The headman was delighted to obtain Bible literature in Kriol, and he gladly provided his telephone number so that he could be contacted.

During the nine days of intensive witnessing, a total of 120 Bibles, 770 books, 705 magazines, and 1,965 brochures were placed. Additionally, 720 return visits were made, and 215 Bible studies were started.

Indeed, the spiritual hunger of many deserving ones scattered across this vast area was at last being satisfied.—Matthew 5:6.

---

* Published by Jehovah's Witnesses.

A Humble African
Who Loved God's Word

VISITORS to Africa are often surprised to find how easy it is to start a conversation on Bible topics with the local people. Such questions as, "What is the Kingdom of God?" or "Is there a lasting solution to problems like food shortage, disease, war, and crime?" easily find listening ears. Many will gladly allow a stranger to show them the answers from the Bible. This often leads to a regular study of the Bible. And as the students make spiritual progress, they become baptized Christians.

One of the first Africans to respond in that way is mentioned in the Bible at Acts 8:26-40. He was an Ethiopian man who had traveled to Jerusalem to worship the true God, Jehovah.

As shown in the picture below, the Ethiopian man is returning home in his chariot, reading from an open scroll. A stranger approaches him and asks: "Do you actually know what you are reading?" Humbly, the Ethiopian acknowledges his need for help and entreats the stranger, the Christian evangelizer Philip, to get into the chariot. Then he asks Philip to explain the meaning of the Scripture passage he has just read. Philip explains that it is a prophecy pointing to the recent death of the Messiah, Jesus Christ. Philip also relates other matters concerning "the good news about Jesus," undoubtedly including Jesus' resurrection.

Having heard these wonderful truths, the Ethiopian wants to become a disciple of Jesus and asks: "What prevents me from getting baptized?" Following his baptism, this humble African man happily gets back on the road home, and the Bible speaks no more about him.

Today, Jehovah's Witnesses are helping millions of people around the world to learn about the same "good news." About six million free home Bible studies are currently being conducted.

*w*05-E 4/1

APRIL 15, 2005

THE WATCHTOWER

ANNOUNCING JEHOVAH'S KINGDOM

TAKING IN KNOWLEDGE

Will It Ever End?

THE WATCHTOWER®
ANNOUNCING JEHOVAH'S KINGDOM

April 15, 2005   Average Printing Each Issue: 26,439,000   Vol. 126, No. 8

THE PURPOSE OF *THE WATCHTOWER* is to exalt Jehovah God as Sovereign Lord of the universe. It keeps watch on world events as these fulfill Bible prophecy. It comforts all peoples with the good news that God's Kingdom will soon destroy those who oppress their fellowmen and that it will turn the earth into a paradise. It encourages faith in God's now-reigning King, Jesus Christ, whose shed blood opens the way for mankind to gain eternal life. *The Watchtower,* published by Jehovah's Witnesses continuously since 1879, is nonpolitical. It adheres to the Bible as its authority.

IN THIS ISSUE

3   Too Much Knowledge for Us?

4   Taking in Knowledge—Now and Forever

8   Filling a Need in Macedonia

10   Trust in Jehovah's Word

15   Let God's Word Light Your Roadway

21   A Useful Translation Aid

22   Hope Amid Despair—An Assembly in a Refugee Camp

25   Does Your Faith Move You to Action?

30   Do You Remember?

31   Questions From Readers

32   Bible History—How Accurate?

WATCHTOWER STUDIES

MAY 16-22:
Trust in Jehovah's Word.
Page 10. Songs to be used: 59, 180.

MAY 23-29:
Let God's Word Light Your Roadway.
Page 15. Songs to be used: 46, 203.

Publication of *The Watchtower* is part of a worldwide Bible educational work supported by voluntary donations.

Unless otherwise indicated, Scripture quotations are from the modern-language *New World Translation of the Holy Scriptures—With References.*

The Watchtower (ISSN 0043-1087) is published semimonthly by Watchtower Bible and Tract Society of New York, Inc.; M. H. Larson, President; G. F. Simonis, Secretary-Treasurer; 25 Columbia Heights, Brooklyn, NY 11201-2483. Periodicals Postage Paid at Brooklyn, NY, and at additional mailing offices. POSTMASTER: Send address changes to Watchtower, **Wallkill, NY 12589.**

Changes of address should reach us 30 days before your moving date. Give us your old and new address (if possible, your old address label).

Semimonthly   ENGLISH

Would you welcome more information or a free home Bible study? Please send your request to Jehovah's Witnesses, using the appropriate address below.

America, United States of: Wallkill, NY 12589. *Antigua:* Box 119, St. Johns. *Australia:* Box 280, Ingleburn, NSW 1890. *Bahamas:* Box N-1247, Nassau, N.P. *Barbados, W.I.:* Crusher Site Road, Prospect, St. James. *Britain:* The Ridgeway, London NW7 1RN. *Canada:* Box 4100, Halton Hills (Georgetown), Ontario L7G 4Y4. *Germany:* Niederselters, Am Steinfels, D-65618 Selters. *Ghana:* P. O. Box GP 760, Accra. *Guyana:* 352-360 Tyrell St., Republic Park Phase 2 EBD. *Hawaii 96819:* 2055 Kam IV Rd., Honolulu. *Hong Kong:* 4 Kent Road, Kowloon Tong. *India:* Post Box 6440, Yelahanka, Bangalore 560 064, KAR. *Ireland:* Newcastle, Greystones, Co. Wicklow. *Jamaica:* P. O. Box 103, Old Harbour, St. Catherine. *Japan:* 1271 Nakashinden, Ebina City, Kanagawa Pref., 243-0496. *Kenya:* P.O. Box 47788, GPO Nairobi 00100. *New Zealand:* P.O. Box 75-142, Manurewa. *Nigeria:* P.M.B. 1090, Benin City 300001, Edo State. *Philippines, Republic of:* P. O. Box 2044, 1060 Manila. *South Africa:* Private Bag X2067, Krugersdorp, 1740. *Trinidad and Tobago, Republic of:* Lower Rapsey Street & Laxmi Lane, Curepe. *Zambia:* Box 33459, Lusaka 10101. *Zimbabwe:* Private Bag WG-5001, Westgate.

NOW PUBLISHED IN 150 LANGUAGES. SEMIMONTHLY: Afrikaans, Albanian,* Amharic, Arabic, Bengali, Bicol, Bislama, Bulgarian, Cebuano,* Chichewa,* Chinese, Chinese (Simplified),* Cibemba,* Croatian,* Czech,*# Danish,*# Dutch,*# East Armenian, Efik,* English*#+© (also Braille), Estonian, Ewe, Fijian, Finnish,*# French,*# Ga, Georgian, German,*# Greek,* Gujarati, Gun, Hebrew, Hiligaynon, Hindi, Hungarian,*# Igbo,* Iloko,* Indonesian, Italian,*# Japanese*# (also Braille), Kannada, Kinyarwanda, Kirundi, Korean*# (also Braille), Latvian, Lingala, Lithuanian, Luvale, Macedonian, Malagasy,* Malayalam, Maltese, Myanmar, Nepali, New Guinea Pidgin, Norwegian,*# Pangasinan, Papiamento (Aruba), Papiamento (Curaçao), Polish,*# Portuguese*# (also Braille), Punjabi, Rarotongan, Romanian,* Russian,* Samar-Leyte, Samoan, Sango, Sepedi, Serbian, Sesotho, Shona,* Silozi, Sinhala, Slovak,* Slovenian, Solomon Islands Pidgin, Spanish*# (also Braille), Sranantongo, Swahili,* Swedish,*# Tagalog,* Tamil, Telugu, Thai, Tigrinya, Tongan, Tshiluba, Tsonga, Tswana, Turkish, Twi, Ukrainian,* Urdu, Vietnamese, Wallisian, Xhosa, Yoruba,* Zulu*

MONTHLY: American Sign Language,△□ Armenian, Assamese, Azerbaijani (roman script), Brazilian Sign Language,△ Cambodian, Chitonga, Gilbertese, Greenlandic, Haitian Creole, Hausa, Hiri Motu, Icelandic, Isoko, Kaonde, Kazakh, Kikongo, Kiluba, Kirghiz, Kosraean, Kwanyama/Ndonga, Luganda, Marathi, Marshallese, Mauritian Creole, Maya, Mizo, Monokutuba, Moore, Niuean, Ossetian, Otetela, Palauan, Persian, Ponapean, Seychelles Creole, Tahitian, Tatar, Tiv, Trukese, Tumbuka, Tuvaluan, Umbundu, Venda, Yapese, Zande

* Study articles also available in large-print edition.
\# Audiocassettes also available.
+ CD also available.
© MP3 CD-ROM also available.
△ Videocassette
□ DVD

Too Much Knowledge for Us?

A missionary couple sitting on a beach in West Africa were watching the silvery moon above. "How much does man know about the moon, and how much is there to know?" reflected the husband.

His wife responded: "Imagine that we could observe the earth drifting by like this—how much knowledge is there already on earth, and how much more is there to learn? And just think! Not only is the earth rotating around the sun but our whole solar system is in motion. This means that we will probably never again be here at this exact point in the universe. In fact, we know our present location only in relation to familiar heavenly bodies. We possess so much knowledge about some things, but in a sense, we don't even know where we are!"

THOSE thoughts touch on some basic truths. There seems to be so much to learn. Of course, each of us learns new things every day. Regardless of how much we do learn, however, we do not seem to be able to keep up with what we would like to know.

Granted, in addition to the ability to take in new information, the capacity to store knowledge has increased greatly. The collective memory of mankind has taken on immense proportions by means of technology. Computer hard disks now have such large capacities that new mathematical terms had to be coined to describe them. A simple CD-ROM can store a wealth of information; its capacity is described as 680 megabytes or more. A standard DVD can hold almost seven times that much, and some with even greater capacity are becoming available.

Modern man's means to communicate information are almost beyond our comprehension. Rotary presses run at incredible speeds, turning out newspapers, magazines, and books. For someone using the Internet, endless amounts of information are just a click away. In these and many other ways, dissemination of information is increasing faster than anyone can assimilate it. This quantity of information has sometimes been likened to a sea, being of such proportions that we must learn to swim in it, as it were, but try not to drink it all in. The sheer quantity of it forces us to be selective.

Another reason to be selective is that much available information is not particularly useful. Indeed, some of it is even undesirable, not worth knowing. Remember that knowledge refers to information —whether good or bad, positive or negative. To make matters more confusing, some things considered by many to be facts are just not accurate. How often the statements of even esteemed authorities have later proved to be erroneous, or false! Think, for instance, of the city recorder of ancient Ephesus, certainly viewed there as a knowledgeable official. He claimed: "Who really is there of mankind that does not know that the city of the Ephesians is the temple keeper of the great Artemis and of the image that fell from heaven?" (Acts 19:35, 36) Although this seems to have been common knowledge—even indisputable, many would say—it was not true that the image had fallen from heaven. With good reason, the Holy Bible warns Christians to guard against that which is "falsely called 'knowledge.' "—1 Timothy 6:20.

A compelling reason to be selective about knowledge is that our present life span is so short. Regardless of how old you may be, there are undoubtedly many fields of knowledge that you would like to investigate, but you realize that you will simply not live long enough to do so.

Will this basic problem ever change? Could a field of knowledge be available that will prolong life significantly, even forever? Could such knowledge already exist? If so, will it be made available to all? Will the day come when all knowledge will consist of what we expect—the truth? The missionary couple mentioned above have found satisfying answers to those questions, and you can too. Please read the next article, which will offer you the prospect of taking in knowledge forever.

Taking in Knowledge NOW AND FOREVER

GERMAN physician Ulrich Strunz wrote a series of books entitled *Forever Young.* In these he argued that exercise, nutrition, and a wholesome life-style can promote better health and possibly lead to a longer life. Still, he does not promise his readers that they could literally live forever by following his counsel.

However, there is one kind of knowledge that does promise everlasting life. Conversely, if you did live forever, you could take in useful knowledge forever. Jesus said in prayer to God: "This means everlasting life, their taking in knowledge of you, the only true God, and of the one whom you sent forth, Jesus Christ." (John 17:3) Let us first define the term "everlasting life" and then establish what the knowledge entails and how you can obtain it.

According to the Bible, the Creator will soon transform the earth into a literal paradise, which will favor long life. Bringing about that Paradise will involve drastic action, similar to that of the Flood of Noah's day. Matthew chapter 24, verses 37 to 39, shows that Jesus compared our time with "the *days* of Noah," in which people "took no note" of their critical situation. They also ignored the message that Noah preached. Then came *"the day* that Noah entered into the ark" and the Flood destroyed all who had rejected this knowledge. Noah and those with him in the ark remained alive.

Jesus indicated that a similar "day" is coming in our time. Those heeding the knowledge associated with this event will have the prospect of not only surviving but also living forever. In addition, the dead who are in God's memory will be raised to life with the prospect of never having to die again. (John 5:28, 29) Notice how Jesus expressed these two thoughts. When speaking to Martha about the resurrection of the dead, he said: "He that exercises faith in me, even though he dies, will come to life; and everyone that is living and exercises faith in me will never die at all." All evidence shows that this "day" is very near, which means that you may "never die at all."—John 11:25-27.

Jesus then asked Martha: "Do you believe this?" She answered: "Yes, Lord." If Jesus were to ask you the same question today, what would your answer be? Perhaps you would find it difficult to believe in the possibility of never dying. But even if that was your reaction, undoubtedly you would *like* to be able to believe it. Imagine how much you could learn if you would "never die at all"! Picture yourself enjoying all the things that you now wish you could learn and do but never have time for. And just think of being reunited with your loved ones who have been lost in death! What is the knowledge that might make such things possible, and how can you acquire it?

Acquiring Life-Giving Knowledge —Within Our Capacity

Is taking in knowledge of God and Christ beyond our capacity? No. It is true that knowledge of the Creator's works is endless. Yet, Jesus was not referring to astronomy or one of the other sciences when he linked "knowledge" and "everlasting life." Proverbs chapter 2, verses 1 and 5, indicates that the "sayings" and "commandments" found in the Bible are fundamental to "the very knowledge of God." And concerning Jesus, John 20:30, 31 indicates that the things written down are sufficient that we "may have life."

Hence, the knowledge of Jehovah and Jesus Christ as found in the Bible is sufficient to show you how to gain everlasting life. The Bible is a unique book. The Creator kindly inspired it in such a way that even unlettered men with limited opportunities can take in enough knowledge to gain everlasting life. Likewise, someone with a quick mind and with much time and means at his disposal

"This means everlasting life, their taking in knowledge . . ."

will always be able to learn something new from the inspired Scriptures. The fact that you can read this article is proof that you have the capacity to learn, but how should you use that capacity?

Around the globe, experience has shown that the most efficient way to acquire this knowledge is by means of a personal Bible study guided by someone who has already grasped the material. Just as Noah endeavored to impart knowledge to his contemporaries, Jehovah's Witnesses are willing to come to your home to consider the Bible with you. They might use the brochure *What Does God Require of Us?* or the handbook appropriately entitled *Knowledge That Leads to Everlasting Life.** Even if you find the

------

* Both published by Jehovah's Witnesses.

concept that in the earthly Paradise, faithful ones will "never die at all" difficult to believe, you can learn to put confidence in this promise by means of these Bible discussions. So if you would like to live forever or just want to see if it is reasonable to believe that you could, what should you do? Accept this opportunity to study the Bible.

How long will it take? The 32-page brochure just mentioned, available in hundreds of languages, contains just 16 short lessons. Or if you can reserve about an hour a week, you will need only a few months to study key Bible subjects, using the book *Knowledge That Leads to Everlasting Life*. These publications have helped many to acquire much knowledge and to develop a deep love for God. The Creator will reward those who truly love him, enabling them to have everlasting life.

Life-giving knowledge is indeed within our reach, and it is readily available. The Bible has been translated, at least in part, into over 2,000 languages. Jehovah's Witnesses in 235 lands are pleased to render personal assistance and to provide Bible-based publications so that you can increase your knowledge further.

Personal Study

Your relationship with God is a personal matter between you and the Creator. Only you can maintain and strengthen it, and only he can grant you everlasting life. Therefore, you should continue a personal study of his written Word. By having someone come to your home on a regular basis, you may find it easier to reserve time for study.

Since the Bible and Bible study aids contain "the very knowledge of God," it is most appropriate to take good care of them. (Proverbs 2:5) You will thus have them for years. If you live in a developing country, you may not have used many textbooks at school,

having learned mainly by listening and observing. In Benin, for example, over 50 languages are spoken. It is not unusual for individuals to speak four or five languages fluently, although they have never had a textbook in these languages in their hands. Your ability to learn by listening, observing, and concentrating is a blessing. Still, you will find that books can greatly aid you in your study.

Even if your living quarters are cramped, try to have a suitable place for your Bible and related publications. Keep them where they are readily available and where they will not be damaged.

Family Study

If you are a parent, you should be interested in helping your children gain the same knowledge that you are acquiring. In developing countries, parents are often accustomed to teaching their children many of life's necessary skills. This may include cooking, gathering wood, fetching water, farming, fishing, and bartering at the market. This is truly education for life. However, many parents do not include in this education the knowledge that can lead to everlasting life.

Whatever your situation may be, you probably feel that you do not have much time to spare. The Creator realizes this too. Regarding how to teach children his ways, note what he said a long time ago: "You must inculcate them in your son [or daughter] and speak of them when you sit in your house and when you walk on the road and when you lie down and when you get up." (Deuteronomy 6:7) Based on these thoughts, why not try to develop your own teaching program, such as the following:

1. "When you sit in your house": Endeavor to have regular discussions, perhaps weekly, with your children at home, just as

someone may have had with you. Jehovah's Witnesses provide Bible-based publications suitable for teaching children of all ages.

2. "When you walk on the road": Speak to your children informally about Jehovah, just as you teach them about life's necessities or give them guidelines in an informal manner.

3. "When you lie down": Pray with your children each evening.

4. "When you get up": Many families have experienced rewarding results from considering one Bible text every morning. Jehovah's Witnesses use the booklet *Examining the Scriptures Daily** as a basis for this.

In developing countries, many parents go to great

* Published by Jehovah's Witnesses.

lengths to make sure that one of their children gets a good secular education. In that way the child will be able to care for the parents when they get older. However, if you study the Bible and help all your children to do likewise, you will gain the knowledge that will enable you and your whole family to live forever.

Will the day ever come when we know everything? No. As our earth continues on its journey through the endless universe, we will continue to take in knowledge. Indeed, Ecclesiastes 3:11 states: "Everything [God] has made pretty in its time. Even time indefinite he has put in their heart, that mankind may never find out the work that the true God has made from the start to the finish." Taking in knowledge is a pleasure that will never end.

Help your family take in knowledge now and forever

FILLING A NEED
IN MACEDONIA

BULGARIA

Skopje

MACEDONIA

ALBANIA

GREECE

"**S**TEP over into Macedonia and help us." (Acts 16:9) These words of a man who appeared in a vision to the apostle Paul revealed the need to declare the good news of God's Kingdom in a new territory, in cities that now are in Greece.

In the present nation of Macedonia, there is only 1 of Jehovah's Witnesses to every 1,840 inhabitants. Many people have never heard about Jehovah God. Yes, there is a dire need for people of this nation to hear the message of peace. —Matthew 24:14.

God has opened the way to help satisfy that need. One day in November 2003, the Macedonia office of Jehovah's Witnesses in Skopje received an unexpected phone call. It was from the Macedonian Center for International Cooperation, inviting the Witnesses to set up a booth to explain their beliefs at a three-day fair that was to start on November 20. What a grand opportunity to reach thousands of people who had never heard the Kingdom good news!

Volunteers scrambled to prepare and set up a display of various publications of Jehovah's Witnesses in the Macedonian language. Samples of this literature were laid out so that visitors could take copies if they so desired. The display gave many the opportunity to get refreshing spiritual water free.—Revelation 22:17.

Visitors particularly sought publications that touched their lives, such as *Questions Young People Ask—Answers That Work* and *The Secret of Family Happiness.** Ninety-eight people turned in their addresses, asking to have Jehovah's Witnesses call on them. Many made favorable comments on the fine work of Jehovah's Witnesses and the quality of the literature.

One man came to the booth holding his little boy's hand. The father asked whether there was literature for children. The Witnesses showed him the publication *My Book of Bi-*

Skopje, Macedonia

*ble Stories.** He leafed through it and excitedly asked how much it cost. When he heard that the educational work of Jehovah's Witnesses is fully supported by voluntary donations, he got even more excited. (Matthew 10:8) He showed the book to his son and said: "What a nice book! Daddy will read one story to you every day!"

A professor of philosophy approached the booth. He was very much interested in religion in general but particularly in the beliefs of Jehovah's Witnesses. Looking through the book *Mankind's Search for God,** the professor said: "Logically presented material indeed! Exactly the way I imagined matters should be presented." Later, some students from his school came to the booth and asked for their own copies of the book that the professor had obtained. They wanted to study the same book. They thought that he would use the material in his lessons.

The exhibit provided some people with their very first exposure to Scriptural truths. A group of deaf teenagers came to look around. One of the Witnesses gave them a short talk, with help from a girl who interpreted it into sign language. Using illustrations from the book *The Greatest Man Who Ever Lived,** he explained that Jesus healed the sick, including the deaf. They were pleased to "hear" the Bible's promise that Jesus would soon do the same for people living on earth in our day. A number of them happily accepted Bible-based literature, and arrangements were made for a Witness who knows sign language to visit them.

Besides Macedonian, literature was also available in Albanian, English, and Turkish. One man who did not speak Macedonian asked for some literature in English. After receiving issues of the *Watchtower* and *Awake!* magazines, he mentioned that he spoke Turkish. When he was shown literature in his own language, he could hardly believe his eyes! He saw that Jehovah's Witnesses want to help everyone.

What a fine witness was given on that occasion, and how encouraging it was to see so many people showing interest in Bible truth! Yes, Jehovah opened the way to spread the Kingdom good news further in Macedonia.

---

* All published by Jehovah's Witnesses.

A MILESTONE!

Efforts to spread the good news of God's Kingdom took a major step forward on May 17, 2003. An office of Jehovah's Witnesses was dedicated in Skopje. Construction work had proceeded for two years, expanding the former facilities fourfold.

There are three separate buildings that house administration and translation offices as well as living quarters, a kitchen, and a laundry. Guy Pierce, a member of the Governing Body of Jehovah's Witnesses, was present to give the dedication talk. Visitors from ten different countries attended the dedication program. All were thrilled to see the beautiful new buildings.

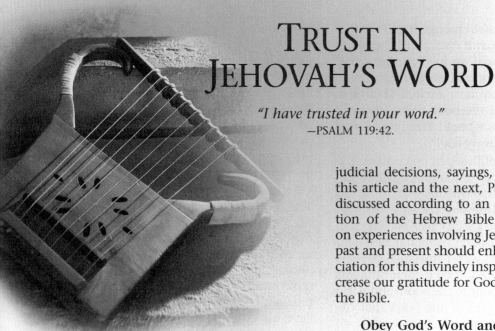

TRUST IN JEHOVAH'S WORD

"I have trusted in your word."
—PSALM 119:42.

judicial decisions, sayings, and statutes. In this article and the next, Psalm 119 will be discussed according to an accurate translation of the Hebrew Bible text. Reflecting on experiences involving Jehovah's servants past and present should enhance our appreciation for this divinely inspired song and increase our gratitude for God's written Word, the Bible.

Obey God's Word and Be Happy

³ True happiness depends on our walking in God's law. (Psalm 119:1-8) If we do this, Jehovah will consider us 'faultless in our way.' (Psalm 119:1) Being faultless does not mean that we are perfect, but it does indicate that we strive to do Jehovah God's will. Noah "proved himself faultless among his contemporaries" as a man who "walked with the true God." That faithful patriarch and his family survived the Flood because he pursued the life course outlined by Jehovah. (Genesis 6:9; 1 Peter 3:20) Similarly, our survival of this world's end depends on our 'carefully keeping God's orders,' thus doing his will.—Psalm 119:4.

⁴ Jehovah will never leave us if we 'laud him with uprightness of heart and continue to keep his regulations.' (Psalm 119:7, 8) God did not abandon the Israelite leader Joshua, who applied the counsel to 'read in the book of the law day and night so that he might do all that was written in it.' That made him suc-

JEHOVAH'S word was cherished by the composer of Psalm 119. He may have been Prince Hezekiah of Judah. Sentiments expressed in this inspired song fit the spirit of Hezekiah, who "kept sticking to Jehovah" while serving as king of Judah. (2 Kings 18:3-7) One thing is certain: The composer was conscious of his spiritual need.—Matthew 5:3.

² A key point of Psalm 119 is the value of God's word, or message.* Likely as a memory aid, the writer made this an alphabetic song. Its 176 verses are based on successive letters of the Hebrew alphabet. In the original Hebrew, each of the psalm's 22 stanzas has 8 lines that begin with the same letter. This psalm refers to God's word, law, reminders, ways, orders, regulations, commandments,

---

* Reference is here made to Jehovah's message, not to the entire content of the Bible—God's Word.

---

1. What can you say about the identity and spirit of the writer of Psalm 119?
2. What is the theme of Psalm 119, and how is this song designed?

---

3. Explain and illustrate what it means to be faultless.
4. Our happiness and success depend on what?

cessful and enabled him to act wisely. (Joshua 1:8) Near the end of his life, Joshua was still lauding God and could remind the Israelites: "You well know with all your hearts and with all your souls that not one word out of all the good words that Jehovah your God has spoken to you has failed." (Joshua 23:14) Like Joshua and the writer of Psalm 119, we can find happiness and success by praising Jehovah and trusting in his word.

Jehovah's Word Keeps Us Clean

⁵ We can be spiritually clean if we keep on guard according to God's word. (Psalm 119:9-16) This is so even if our parents have not set a good example. Although Hezekiah's father was an idolater, Hezekiah 'cleansed his path,' possibly of pagan influences. Suppose a young person serving God today sins seriously. Repentance, prayer, parental help, and the loving assistance of Christian elders can help him to be like Hezekiah and 'cleanse his path and keep on guard.'—James 5:13-15.

⁶ Although Rahab and Ruth lived long before Psalm 119 was composed, they 'cleansed their path.' Rahab was a Canaanite prostitute, but she became known for her faith as a worshiper of Jehovah. (Hebrews 11:30, 31) The Moabitess Ruth left her own gods, served Jehovah, and complied with his Law to Israel. (Ruth 1:14-17; 4:9-13) Both of these non-Israelite women 'kept on guard according to God's word' and had the wonderful privilege of becoming ancestresses of Jesus Christ.—Matthew 1:1, 4-6.

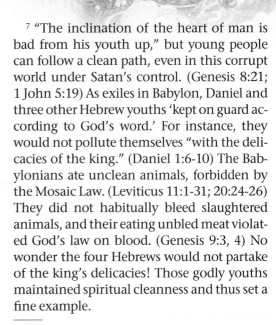

Ruth, Rahab, and the Hebrew youths exiled in Babylon 'kept on guard according to God's word'

⁷ "The inclination of the heart of man is bad from his youth up," but young people can follow a clean path, even in this corrupt world under Satan's control. (Genesis 8:21; 1 John 5:19) As exiles in Babylon, Daniel and three other Hebrew youths 'kept on guard according to God's word.' For instance, they would not pollute themselves "with the delicacies of the king." (Daniel 1:6-10) The Babylonians ate unclean animals, forbidden by the Mosaic Law. (Leviticus 11:1-31; 20:24-26) They did not habitually bleed slaughtered animals, and their eating unbled meat violated God's law on blood. (Genesis 9:3, 4) No wonder the four Hebrews would not partake of the king's delicacies! Those godly youths maintained spiritual cleanness and thus set a fine example.

---

5. (a) Show how it is possible to keep spiritually clean. (b) What help is there for a young person who has sinned seriously?
6. What women 'cleansed their path and kept on guard according to God's word'?

---

7. How did Daniel and three other Hebrew youths set a fine example in maintaining spiritual cleanness?

Paul courageously 'spoke about God's reminders in front of kings'

God's Word an Aid to Faithfulness

8 Fondness for God's word is an important factor in keeping us faithful to Jehovah. (Psalm 119:17-24) If we are like the inspired songwriter, we will yearn to understand "the wonderful things" of God's law. We will constantly 'long for Jehovah's judicial decisions' and show a 'fondness for his reminders.' (Psalm 119:18, 20, 24) If we have been dedicated to Jehovah for even a short time, have we 'formed a longing for the unadulterated milk belonging to the word'? (1 Peter 2:1, 2) We need to understand elementary Bible teachings so that we can be in a better position to comprehend and apply God's law.

9 We may be fond of God's reminders, but what if "princes" speak against us for some reason? (Psalm 119:23, 24) Today, people in authority often try to force us to put human laws above the law of God. When there is a conflict between the demands of man and the will of God, what will we do? Our fondness for God's word will help us to remain faithful to Jehovah. Like Jesus Christ's persecuted apostles, we will say: "We must obey God as ruler rather than men."—Acts 5:29.

10 We can remain faithful to Jehovah even under the most trialsome circumstances. (Psalm 119:25-32) If we are going to succeed in maintaining our integrity to God, we must be teachable and pray earnestly for his instruction. We must also choose "the way of faithfulness."—Psalm 119:26, 30.

11 Hezekiah, who may have written Psalm 119, chose "the way of faithfulness." He did so even though he was surrounded by false worshipers and may have been ridiculed by members of the royal court. Very likely, 'his soul was sleepless from grief' because of such circumstances. (Psalm 119:28) But Hezekiah trusted in God, was a good king, and did "what was right in Jehovah's eyes." (2 Kings 18:1-5) With reliance on God, we too can endure trials as integrity keepers. —James 1:5-8.

Jehovah's Word Imparts Courage

12 Following the guidance of God's word gives us the courage needed to cope with

---

8. What attitude and knowledge do we need if we are to comprehend and apply God's law?
9. How should we react when there is a conflict between God's law and human demands?

10, 11. Illustrate how we can maintain integrity to Jehovah under the most trialsome circumstances.
12. How can we personally apply Psalm 119:36, 37?

life's trials. (Psalm 119:33-40) We humbly seek Jehovah's instruction so that we can keep his law "with the whole heart." (Psalm 119:33, 34) Like the psalmist, we ask of God: "Incline my heart to your reminders, and not to profits," or "unjust profit." (Psalm 119:36; footnote) Like the apostle Paul, we "conduct ourselves honestly in all things." (Hebrews 13:18) If an employer wants us to do something dishonest, we muster up courage to adhere to God's directions—and Jehovah always blesses such a course. In fact, he helps us to keep all bad inclinations under control. Let us therefore pray: "Make my eyes pass on from seeing what is worthless." (Psalm 119:37) Never would we want to view as desirable any worthless thing hated by God. (Psalm 97:10) Among other things, this moves us to avoid pornography and spiritistic practices.—1 Corinthians 6:9, 10; Revelation 21:8.

13 Accurate knowledge of God's word gives us confidence to witness courageously. (Psalm 119:41-48) And we do need courage to 'answer the one reproaching us.' (Psalm 119:42) At times, we may be like Jesus' persecuted disciples, who prayed: "Jehovah, . . . grant your slaves to keep speaking your word with all boldness." The result? "They were one and all filled with the holy spirit and were speaking the word of God with boldness." The same Sovereign Lord gives us the courage to speak his word with boldness. —Acts 4:24-31.

14 We will have the courage needed to give a witness without any fear of shame if we cherish "the word of truth" and 'keep God's law constantly.' (Psalm 119:43, 44) Diligent study of God's written Word equips us to 'speak about his reminders in front of kings.'

(Psalm 119:46) Prayer and Jehovah's spirit will also help us to say the right things in a proper way. (Matthew 10:16-20; Colossians 4:6) Paul courageously spoke about God's reminders to first-century rulers. For example, he witnessed to Roman Governor Felix, who "listened to him on the belief in Christ Jesus." (Acts 24:24, 25) Paul also gave a witness before Governor Festus and King Agrippa. (Acts 25:22–26:32) With Jehovah's backing, we too can be courageous witnesses, never "ashamed of the good news."—Romans 1:16.

God's Word Gives Us Comfort

15 Jehovah's Word provides unfailing comfort. (Psalm 119:49-56) There are times when we especially need to be comforted. Although we courageously speak out as Witnesses of Jehovah, "presumptuous ones"—those acting presumptuously toward God—sometimes 'deride us in the extreme.' (Psalm 119:51) While praying, however, we may recall positive things said in God's Word, and we thus 'find comfort for ourselves.' (Psalm 119:52) During our supplications, we may remember a Scriptural law or principle that gives us the comfort and courage needed in a stressful situation.

16 The presumptuous ones who derided the psalmist were Israelites—members of a nation dedicated to God. What a shame! Unlike them, however, let us be determined never to deviate from God's law. (Psalm 119: 51) In the face of Nazi persecution and similar treatment through the years, thousands of God's servants have refused to deviate from the laws and principles found in God's Word. (John 15:18-21) And it is no burden to obey Jehovah, for his regulations are like

13. How did Jesus' persecuted disciples get the courage needed to witness boldly?
14. What helps us to witness courageously, as Paul did?

15. How can God's Word bring comfort when others deride us?
16. What have God's servants not done despite persecution?

comforting melodies to us.—Psalm 119:54; 1 John 5:3.

Be Grateful for Jehovah's Word

[17] We prove our gratitude for God's word by observing it. (Psalm 119:57-64) The psalmist 'promised to keep Jehovah's words,' and even 'at midnight he got up to thank God for His righteous judicial decisions.' If we awaken at night, what a fine opportunity we have to express gratitude to God in prayer! (Psalm 119:57, 62) Our appreciation for God's word moves us to seek divine teaching and makes us the joyful 'partners of those fearing Jehovah'—individuals having reverential awe for God. (Psalm 119:63, 64) Who could find better company on earth?

[18] When we pray with all our heart and humbly ask Jehovah to teach us, we are 'softening his face' with the thought of enjoying his favor. We especially need to pray when 'the very ropes of the wicked ones surround us.' (Psalm 119:58, 61) Jehovah can cut enemy ropes of restraint and free us for the Kingdom-preaching and disciple-making work. (Matthew 24:14; 28:19, 20) This has been demonstrated repeatedly in lands where our work has been banned.

---

17. Appreciation for God's word moves us to do what?
18. How does Jehovah answer our prayers when 'the ropes of the wicked surround us'?

How Would You Answer?

- On what does true happiness depend?
- How does Jehovah's word keep us spiritually clean?
- In what ways does God's word impart courage and comfort?
- Why should we have faith in Jehovah and his word?

Have Faith in God's Word

[19] Faith in God and his word helps us to endure affliction and to do his will. (Psalm 119:65-72) Although presumptuous ones had 'smeared him with falsehood,' the psalmist sang: "It is good for me that I have been afflicted." (Psalm 119:66, 69, 71) How could it be good for any of Jehovah's servants to suffer affliction?

[20] When we suffer affliction, we undoubtedly supplicate Jehovah earnestly, and that draws us closer to him. We may spend more time studying God's written Word and may make greater effort to apply it. This results in a happier life. But what if we react to affliction in a way that shows up undesirable traits, such as impatience and pride? With earnest prayer and the help of God's Word and spirit, we can overcome such flaws and more fully 'clothe ourselves with the new personality.' (Colossians 3:9-14) Moreover, our faith is strengthened when we endure adversity. (1 Peter 1:6, 7) Paul benefited from his tribulations because they made him more dependent on Jehovah. (2 Corinthians 1:8-10) Do we allow suffering to have a good effect on us?

Always Trust in Jehovah

[21] God's word gives us a sound basis for trust in Jehovah. (Psalm 119:73-80) If we really trust in our Creator, we will have no reason for shame. Because of what others do, however, we need comfort and may feel like praying: "Let the presumptuous ones be ashamed." (Psalm 119:76-78) When Jehovah puts such ones to shame, this results in the exposure of their evil ways and in the sanctification of his holy name. We can be sure that persecutors of God's people really do not gain anything. For example, they never have —and never will—put an end to Jehovah's

---

19, 20. How can it be good to be afflicted?
21. What happens when God puts presumptuous ones to shame?

Witnesses, who trust in God with all their heart.—Proverbs 3:5, 6.

22 God's word strengthens our trust in him when we are persecuted. (Psalm 119:81-88) Because presumptuous ones were persecuting him, the psalmist felt "like a skin bottle in the smoke." (Psalm 119:83, 86) In Bible times, bottles made of animal hide were used to hold water, wine, and other liquids. When not in use, these bottles might shrivel up if hung near a fire in a room lacking a chimney. Does hardship or persecution ever make you feel "like a skin bottle in the smoke"? If so, trust in Jehovah, and pray: "According to your loving-kindness preserve me alive, that I may keep the reminder of your mouth." —Psalm 119:88.

23 What we have considered in the first half of Psalm 119 shows that Jehovah exercises loving-kindness toward his servants because they trust in his word and are fond of his statutes, reminders, commandments, and laws. (Psalm 119:16, 47, 64, 70, 77, 88) He is pleased that those devoted to him keep on guard according to his word. (Psalm 119:9, 17, 41, 42) As you look forward to a study of the rest of this beautiful psalm, you might well ask yourself, 'Do I really let Jehovah's word light my roadway?'

22. In what sense was the psalmist "like a skin bottle in the smoke"?

23. What have we considered in reviewing Psalm 119:1-88, and what might we ask ourselves as we look forward to studying Psalm 119:89-176?

LET GOD'S WORD LIGHT YOUR ROADWAY

"Your word is . . . a light to my roadway."—PSALM 119:105.

JEHOVAH'S word will light our roadway if we allow that to happen. To enjoy such spiritual light, we must be diligent students of God's written Word and apply its counsel. Only then can we share the psalmist's sentiments: "Your word is a lamp to my foot, and a light to my roadway."—Psalm 119:105.

2 Let us now consider Psalm 119:89-176. What a wealth of information is contained in these verses, arranged in 11 stanzas! They can help us to stay on the road to everlasting life.—Matthew 7:13, 14.

Why Be Fond of God's Word?

3 Fondness for Jehovah's word results in spiritual stability. (Psalm 119:89-96) The psalmist sang: "To time indefinite, O Jehovah, your word is stationed in the heavens. . . . You have solidly fixed the earth, that it may keep standing." (Psalm 119:89, 90)

1, 2. Under what circumstances will Jehovah's word light our roadway?

3. How does Psalm 119:89, 90 show that we can depend on God's word?

By God's word—his "statutes of the heavens"—the celestial bodies move flawlessly in their orbits and the earth is solidly fixed forever. (Job 38:31-33; Psalm 104:5) We can depend on every word going forth from Jehovah's mouth; what God says will have "certain success" in the fulfillment of his purpose.—Isaiah 55:8-11.

⁴ The psalmist would have 'perished in his affliction if he had not been fond of God's law.' (Psalm 119:92) He was not being afflicted by foreigners; it was Israelite lawbreakers who hated him. (Leviticus 19:17) But this did not overwhelm him, for he loved God's sustaining law. At Corinth, the apostle Paul was "in dangers among false brothers," perhaps including "superfine apostles" seeking an accusation against him. (2 Corinthians 11:5, 12-14, 26) Yet, Paul survived spiritually because he was fond of God's word. Since we are fond of Jehovah's written Word and apply what it says, we love our brothers.

4. What does fondness for God's word do for his servants who suffer affliction?

God's word is a source of spiritual light

(1 John 3:15) Even the world's hatred does not make us forget any of God's instructions. We keep doing his will in loving unity with our brothers as we look forward to an eternity of joyous service to Jehovah.—Psalm 119:93.

⁵ Expressing our devotion to Jehovah, we might pray: "I am yours. O save me, because I have searched for your own orders." (Psalm 119:94) King Asa searched for God and rooted out apostasy in Judah. At a great assembly in the 15th year of Asa's reign (963 B.C.E.), Judah's inhabitants "entered into a covenant to search for Jehovah." God "let himself be found by them" and "continued to give them rest all around." (2 Chronicles 15:10-15) This example should encourage a renewed search for God by any who have drifted away from the Christian congregation. He will bless and protect those who resume active association with his people.

⁶ Jehovah's word imparts wisdom that can protect us from spiritual harm. (Psalm 119:97-104) God's commandments make us wiser than our enemies. Heeding his reminders gives us insight, and 'observing his orders enables us to behave with more understanding than older men.' (Psalm 119:98-100) If Jehovah's sayings are 'smoother to our palate than honey to our mouth,' we will hate and avoid "every false path." (Psalm 119:103, 104) This will serve as a protection from spiritual harm as we encounter haughty, fierce, ungodly people in these last days.—2 Timothy 3:1-5.

A Lamp to Our Foot

⁷ God's word is a source of unfailing spiritual light. (Psalm 119:105-112)

5. How did King Asa search for Jehovah?
6. What course will protect us from spiritual harm?
7, 8. In keeping with Psalm 119:105, what do we need to do?

Whether we are anointed Christians or we are their companions of the "other sheep," we declare: "Your word is a lamp to my foot, and a light to my roadway." (John 10:16; Psalm 119:105) God's word is like a lamp lighting our way, so that we do not stumble and fall spiritually. (Proverbs 6:23) Yet, we must personally let Jehovah's word be a lamp to our foot.

⁸ We need to be as resolute as the composer of Psalm 119. He was determined not to wander from God's orders. "I have made a sworn statement," he said, "and I will carry it out, to keep your [Jehovah's] righteous judicial decisions." (Psalm 119:106) Let us never underestimate the value of regular Bible study and participation in Christian meetings.

⁹ The psalmist did not 'wander from God's orders,' but that can happen to a person dedicated to Jehovah. (Psalm 119:110) King Solomon wandered, although he was a member of a nation dedicated to Jehovah and had originally acted in harmony with God-given wisdom. "Even him the foreign wives caused to sin" by inducing him to worship false gods.—Nehemiah 13:26; 1 Kings 11:1-6.

¹⁰ "The birdcatcher," Satan, sets many traps. (Psalm 91:3) For instance, a former associate may try to induce us to wander off the pathway of spiritual light into the darkness of apostasy. Among Christians at Thyatira, there was "that woman Jezebel," possibly a group of women teaching others to practice idolatry and commit fornication. Jesus did not tolerate such evils, and neither should we. (Revelation 2:18-22; Jude 3, 4) Let us therefore pray for Jehovah's help so that we do not wander from his orders but remain in divine light.—Psalm 119:111, 112.

If we love Jehovah's reminders, he will never regard us as "scummy dross"

Sustained by God's Word

¹¹ If we never stray from his regulations, God will sustain us. (Psalm 119:113-120) We do not approve of "halfhearted ones," even as Jesus disapproves of lukewarm professing Christians today. (Psalm 119:113; Revelation 3:16) Because we wholeheartedly serve Jehovah, he is 'our place of concealment' and will sustain us. He will 'toss away all those straying from his regulations' by resorting to trickiness and falsehood. (Psalm 119:114, 117, 118; Proverbs 3:32) He views such wicked ones as "scummy dross"—impurities removed from such valuable metals as silver and gold. (Psalm 119:119; Proverbs 17:3) May we always display love for God's reminders, for we surely do not want to join the wicked on the slag heap of destruction!

¹² "From the dread of you [Jehovah] my flesh has had a creepy feeling," said the psalmist. (Psalm 119:120) Our having a wholesome dread of God, manifested by avoiding what he disapproves, is vital if he is to sustain us as his servants. Reverential fear

---

9, 10. How do we know that individuals dedicated to Jehovah can 'wander from his orders,' but how can this be avoided?

11. According to Psalm 119:119, how does God view the wicked?

12. Why is fear of Jehovah important?

If we read the Bible daily, helpful passages may readily come to mind when we pray

of Jehovah caused Job to live a righteous life. (Job 1:1; 23:15) Godly fear can enable us to persevere in a divinely favored course regardless of what we must endure. Endurance, though, calls for earnest prayers said in faith.—James 5:15.

Pray in Faith

13 We can pray in faith that God will act in our behalf. (Psalm 119:121-128) Like the psalmist, we are sure that our prayers will be answered. Why? Because we love divine commandments "more than gold, even refined gold." Moreover, 'we consider all of God's orders regarding all things to be right.'—Psalm 119:127, 128.

14 Jehovah hears our petitions because we pray in faith and also carefully comply with

his orders. (Psalm 65:2) But what if we sometimes have such bewildering problems that we do not know what to say in prayer? Then "the spirit itself pleads for us with groanings unuttered." (Romans 8:26, 27) At such times, God accepts expressions found in his Word as prayers covering our needs.

15 The Scriptures are full of prayers and thoughts that would tie in with our 'unuttered groanings.' For example, consider Psalm 119:121-128. The way things are expressed here may fit our circumstances. If we fear being defrauded, for instance, we might ask for God's help in the way the psalmist did. (Verses 121-123) Suppose we need to make a very difficult decision. Then we might pray that Jehovah's spirit help us to recall and apply his reminders. (Verses 124, 125) Although we 'hate every false path,' we may need to ask God to act in our behalf so that we do not succumb to some temptation to break his law. (Verses 126-

13-15. (a) Why can we have faith that our prayers will be answered? (b) What can happen if we do not know what to say in prayer? (c) Illustrate how Psalm 119:121-128 might tie in with our 'unuttered groanings' in prayer.

128) If we read the Bible daily, such helpful passages may come to mind when we supplicate Jehovah.

Helped by Jehovah's Reminders

16 To be heard in prayer and to enjoy divine favor, we must heed God's reminders. (Psalm 119:129-136) Since we are forgetful, we need Jehovah's wonderful reminders that bring his instruction and commandments back to our minds. Of course, we appreciate the spiritual light shed by every new disclosure of God's words. (Psalm 119:129, 130) We are also grateful that Jehovah has 'made his face shine upon us' in approval, although 'streams of water run from our eyes' because others violate his law.—Psalm 119: 135, 136; Numbers 6:25.

17 We are sure to have God's continued favor if we comply with his righteous reminders. (Psalm 119:137-144) As Jehovah's servants, we acknowledge that it is right for him to bring his righteous reminders to our attention and place them upon us as commandments that we should obey. (Psalm 119:138) Since the psalmist obeyed God's commandments, why did he say: "I am insignificant and contemptible"? (Psalm 119: 141) Apparently, he was alluding to the way his enemies viewed him. If we maintain an uncompromising stand for righteousness, others may look down on us. Yet, what really matters is that Jehovah looks on us with favor because we live in accord with his righteous reminders.

Secure and at Peace

18 Observing God's reminders keeps us close to him. (Psalm 119:145-152) Because we pay attention to Jehovah's reminders, we feel free to call upon him with our whole heart, and we can expect to be heard. We may awaken "early in the morning twilight" and cry for help. What a fine time to pray! (Psalm 119:145-147) God is also near us because we avoid loose conduct and view his word as truth, even as Jesus did. (Psalm 119: 150, 151; John 17:17) Our relationship with Jehovah sustains us in this troubled world and will carry us through his great war of Armageddon.—Revelation 7:9, 14; 16:13-16.

19 Because of our deep regard for God's word, we enjoy true security. (Psalm 119:153-160) Unlike the wicked, we 'have not deviated from Jehovah's reminders.' We love God's orders and therefore are secure in his loving-kindness. (Psalm 119:157-159) Jehovah's reminders stimulate our memory so that we remember what he requires of us in specific situations. God's orders, on the other hand, are directives, and we readily acknowledge our Creator's right to direct us. Aware that 'the substance of God's word is truth' and that we cannot direct our own steps independently, we gladly accept divine direction.—Psalm 119:160; Jeremiah 10:23.

20 Our love for Jehovah's law brings us abundant peace. (Psalm 119:161-168) Persecution does not rob us of the incomparable "peace of God." (Philippians 4:6, 7) So much do we appreciate Jehovah's judicial decisions that we praise him for them often —"seven times in the day." (Psalm 119:161-164) "Abundant peace belongs to those loving your law," sang the psalmist, "and for them there is no stumbling block." (Psalm 119:165) If we as individuals love and keep Jehovah's law, we will not be stumbled spiritually by what someone else does or by any other matter.

16, 17. (a) Why do we need God's reminders, and how should we view them? (b) How may others look upon us, but what really matters?
18, 19. What results from our observing God's reminders?

---

20. Why do we have "abundant peace"?

²¹ Many individuals of Bible record did not let anything be a lasting stumbling block for them. For instance, the Christian man Gaius was not stumbled but 'went on walking in the truth' despite the ungodly conduct of Diotrephes. (3 John 1-3, 9, 10) Paul exhorted the Christian women Euodia and Syntyche "to be of the same mind in the Lord," likely because difficulties had arisen between them. Apparently, they were helped to resolve their problem, and they continued to serve Jehovah faithfully. (Philippians 4:2, 3) So we need not stumble if difficulties of some sort arise in the congregation. Let us concentrate on keeping Jehovah's orders, remembering that 'all our ways are in front of him.' (Psalm 119:168; Proverbs 15:3) Then nothing will permanently rob us of "abundant peace."

²² If we always obey Jehovah, we will be privileged to keep on praising him. (Psalm 119:169-176) By living in harmony with God's regulations, not only do we enjoy spiritual security but 'our lips continue to bubble forth Jehovah's praise.' (Psalm 119:169-171, 174) This is the greatest privilege we could have in these last days. The psalmist wanted to keep living and praising Jehovah,

---

21. What Scriptural examples show that we need not stumble if difficulties arise in the congregation?
22. (a) If we obey God, what privilege can we enjoy? (b) How should we view some who have wandered away from the Christian congregation?

How Would You Answer?
- Why should we be fond of God's word?
- How are we sustained by God's word?
- In what ways are we helped by Jehovah's reminders?
- Why are Jehovah's people secure and at peace?

but in some undisclosed way, he had 'wandered like a lost sheep.' (Psalm 119:175, 176) Some who have wandered away from the Christian congregation may still love God and may want to praise him. Let us therefore do all we can to help them so that they may again find spiritual security and experience the joy of praising Jehovah with his people. —Hebrews 13:15; 1 Peter 5:6, 7.

Lasting Light for Our Roadway

²³ Psalm 119 can benefit us in various ways. For instance, it can make us more reliant on God, for it shows that true happiness results from "walking in the law of Jehovah." (Psalm 119:1) The psalmist reminds us that 'the substance of God's word is truth.' (Psalm 119:160) This surely ought to enhance our appreciation for the entire written Word of God. Meditating on Psalm 119 should move us to study the Scriptures diligently. The psalmist repeatedly petitioned God: "Teach me your regulations." (Psalm 119:12, 68, 135) He also pleaded: "Teach me goodness, sensibleness and knowledge themselves, for in your commandments I have exercised faith." (Psalm 119:66) We do well to pray in a similar way.

²⁴ Divine teaching makes possible a close relationship with Jehovah. The psalmist repeatedly calls himself God's servant. In fact, he addresses Jehovah with the touching words: "I am yours." (Psalm 119:17, 65, 94, 122, 125; Romans 14:8) What a privilege it is to serve and praise Jehovah as one of his Witnesses! (Psalm 119:7) Are you serving God joyfully as a Kingdom proclaimer? If so, be assured that Jehovah will continue to support and bless you in this privileged activity if you always trust in his word and let it light your roadway.

23, 24. What benefits have you drawn from Psalm 119?

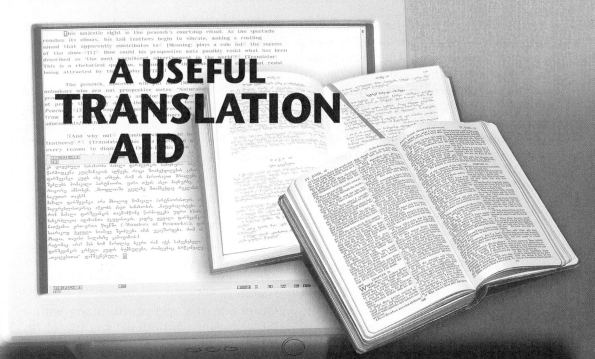

A USEFUL TRANSLATION AID

T HE Author of the Bible, Jehovah God, desires that the good news of his Kingdom be declared "to every nation and tribe and tongue and people." (Revelation 14:6) He wants his written Word to be readily available to all mankind. To that end, the Bible has been translated into more languages than any other book in the world. Thousands of translators have spared no time or effort to render God's thoughts into another tongue.

But the Bible is not simply the object of translation. Time and again, it itself has been used as an aid in translating other texts. Many a translator has compared the renderings of Bible terms in different languages to come up with a good translation for certain words. The Bible's qualities as a translation aid have now been put to use in computer translation as well.

It is really difficult for a computer to translate. Some experts have even felt that translation is beyond what a computer can do. Why? A language is not just a set of words. Each language has its own word combinations, rules, exceptions to these rules, idioms, and allusions. Efforts to teach a computer all of this have met with very little success. Most of the resulting computer translations have been barely understandable.

Now, however, computer scientists are exploring new ways. "Our approach uses statistical models to find the most likely translation," says Franz Josef Och, a leading specialist in computer translation. Let us say that you want to translate Hindi into English. First, take some existing text that is available in both languages. Then feed it into a computer. The computer compares the texts. When, for example, the computer finds the same Hindi word in several places and each time in the corresponding phrase it finds the English word "house," the computer concludes that the Hindi word must be the word for "house." And chances are that nearby words are adjectives, such as "big," "small," "old," or "new." Hence, the computer builds a list of corresponding terms and word combinations. After such "training," which might take just a few days or weeks, the computer can apply what it has "learned" to new text. While the resulting translation might be poor as to grammar and style, it is usually readable enough to convey the meaning and the important details.

The quality of the translation depends to a large degree on the quantity and quality of the text that was initially fed into the computer. And here is where the Bible comes into its own. It has been carefully translated into scores of languages, is readily available, and contains a sizable amount of text. So the Bible was the researcher's first choice when training the computer for a new language.

HOPE AMID DESPAIR
An Assembly in a Refugee Camp

KAKUMA refugee camp is situated in the northern part of Kenya, close to the Sudan border. It is home to over 86,000 people. The area is arid, with daytime temperatures reaching 120°F. Violence between the displaced communities is common. For many, the camp is a place of despair. Others, however, have hope.

Among the refugees are a number of Jehovah's Witnesses, who are zealously declaring the Kingdom good news. They are part of a small congregation in Lodwar, 75 miles to the south. The next congregation is an eight-hour drive away.

Since the refugees cannot freely travel out of the camp, many are not able to attend the assemblies and conventions held by Jehovah's Witnesses. For this reason, arrangements were made to hold a special assembly day inside the camp.

Traveling North

To support the assembly, 15 Witnesses in the town of Eldoret, 300 miles south of the camp, volunteered to make the arduous journey to the arid north, along with a Bible student who offered the use of his minibus and driver. Their heartfelt desire was to encourage and strengthen their brothers.

The journey started on a cold early morning in the Kenyan western highlands. The bumpy road climbed through farmland and forests before descending into the heat of desert scrub. Flocks of goats and camels grazed on the inhospitable land. Tribesmen walked along in traditional clothes, many carrying clubs, bows, and arrows. After traveling for 11 hours, the Witnesses reached Lodwar, a hot and dusty community of nearly 20,000 people. Warmly greeted by their Witness hosts, the travelers went to get some rest so that they would be ready for a full weekend of activity.

The next morning, the visitors went to see some of the area's sights. Lake Turkana, Kenya's largest, was a must. Surrounded by miles and miles of desert bush, it is home to the world's largest crocodile population. The alkaline waters help support the few people who live along its shore. The evening was enjoyably spent attending the Theocratic Ministry School and Service Meeting with the local congregation. They have a beautiful Kingdom Hall, built in 2003 through the Witnesses' building program for countries with limited resources.

The Special Assembly Day

Sunday was set aside for the special assembly day. The Lodwar Congregation and the visiting brothers had been granted permission to enter the camp by 8:00 a.m., so the Witnesses were eager to get an early start. The road wound its way through the barren landscape toward the Sudan border.

Jagged mountains towered above the road. The vista opened up at Kakuma village. It had been raining, and the dirt road into the camp was flooded in places. Most homes were mud brick with roofs made of tin or tarpaulin. Groups of Ethiopians, Somali, Sudanese, and others each live in their own areas. The travelers were enthusiastically greeted by the refugees.

The assembly was held in a training center. Drawings on the walls spoke of the horrors of refugee life, but the spirit in the hall that day was one of hope. Every talk was given in English and Swahili. Some speakers

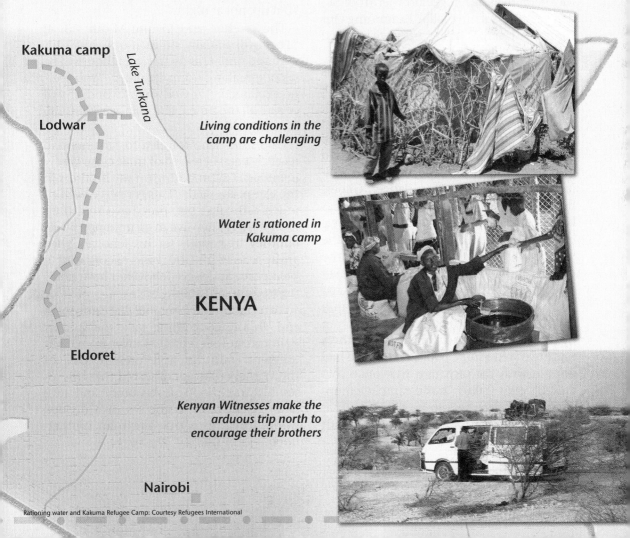

Kakuma camp

Lake Turkana

Lodwar

Living conditions in the camp are challenging

Water is rationed in Kakuma camp

KENYA

Eldoret

Kenyan Witnesses make the arduous trip north to encourage their brothers

Nairobi

Rationing water and Kakuma Refugee Camp: Courtesy Refugees International

A missionary interpreting a talk given by a local special pioneer

Baptism pool

fluent in both languages even interpreted for themselves. A refugee brother from Sudan gave the opening talk, "Examining Our Figurative Heart." Other parts were handled by visiting elders.

A special highlight of every assembly is the baptism. At the conclusion of the baptism discourse, all eyes were on the one candidate as he rose. Gilbert had fled with his father from their native land during the genocide of 1994. At first, they had hoped to find safety in Burundi, but they soon realized that they were still in danger. Gilbert fled to Zaire, then to Tanzania—at times hiding in the forest—and finally to Kenya. Many eyes were filled with tears as the speaker welcomed him as a brother in the congregation. Standing before the small assembly of 95 people, Gilbert answered with a clear, confident *"Ndiyo!"*—Swahili for "Yes!"—to the two questions put to him by the speaker. He and some other brothers had excavated a small pool by hand and had lined it with the tarpaulin that once covered his own shelter in the camp. Demonstrating his eagerness to be baptized, that very morning he had filled the pool with water, bucket by bucket, all by himself!

One of the highlights of the afternoon session was the relating of experiences about the unique situation of the refugee Witnesses. One brother explained how he approached a man resting under a tree.

"Tell me, is it safe *all* the time to sit under a tree?"

"Yes," the man replied. Then he added, "But no, not at night."

The brother read to him Micah 4:3, 4: "They will actually sit, each one under his vine and under his fig tree, and there will be no one making them tremble." "You see," he explained, "in God's new world, it will be safe *all* the time." The man accepted a Bible study aid.

One sister who traveled to Kakuma had recently been bereaved of three close family members. Commenting on the brothers in the camp, she said: "This is a place with so much difficulty; yet, they have kept their faith strong. They live in an unhappy place, but they are happily serving Jehovah. They are at peace with God. I was encouraged to keep peace and serve Jehovah. I have nothing to complain about!"

All too soon the assembly day came to an end. In the concluding talk, the speaker pointed out that representatives from eight different countries were present. One of the Witness refugees observed that this assembly was proof of the unity and love among Jehovah's Witnesses in a divided world. Theirs is a true Christian brotherhood.—John 13:35.

Since the beginning of the civil war in Sudan in 1983, five million people have been driven from their homes. Among them were some 26,000 children, separated from their families. Thousands of them fled to refugee camps in Ethiopia, where they remained for about three years. Forced to move again, they trekked for a year back through Sudan to northern Kenya, ravaged by soldiers, bandits, diseases, and wild animals. Only half the children survived these arduous journeys, eventually becoming the nucleus of the Kakuma camp. To relief agencies, they have come to be known as the lost boys of Sudan.

Courtesy Refugees International

The Kakuma refugee camp is now a multinational home for refugees from Sudan, Somalia, Ethiopia, and other countries. On arrival at the camp, a refugee is given some basic material for building a home and a tarpaulin for roofing. Twice a month, each refugee is given about 13 pounds of flour, 2 pounds of beans, and some oil and salt. Many refugees trade some of their allotment to obtain other provisions.

Some of these lost boys have been reunited with their families or resettled in other countries. But according to the Office of Refugee Resettlement, "thousands more have remained in the dusty, fly-ridden refugee camp at Kakuma, where they have had to scrape for food and struggle for education."

Does Your Faith
Move You to Action?

THE army officer was convinced that Jesus could cure the paralysis of the officer's slave. But the army officer did not invite Jesus into his home, perhaps because he felt unworthy or because he was a Gentile. Instead, the officer had some older men of the Jews approach Jesus and say: "Sir, I am not a fit man for you to enter under my roof, but just say the word and my manservant will be healed." Noting that the army officer believed that Jesus could heal even from a distance, Jesus told the crowd following him: "I tell you the truth, With no one in Israel have I found so great a faith."—Matthew 8:5-10; Luke 7:1-10.

This experience can help us focus on an essential element of faith. True faith is not passive belief; it is backed up by action. The Bible writer James explained: "Faith, if it does not have works, is dead in itself." (James 2:17) This fact becomes even clearer when we consider a real example of what can happen when faith becomes inactive.

In 1513 B.C.E., the nation of Israel was joined to Jehovah God by means of the Law covenant. As mediator of that covenant, Moses conveyed God's word to the sons of Israel: "If you will strictly obey my voice and will indeed keep my covenant, then you will certainly become . . . a holy

Was studying the Law enough?

nation." (Exodus 19:3-6) Yes, Israel's holiness was dependent on obedience.

Many centuries later, the Jews began to attach more importance to a study of the Law than to the application of its principles. In his book *The Life and Times of Jesus the Messiah,* Alfred Edersheim wrote: "The [rabbis]—the 'great ones of the world' had long settled it, that study was before works."

Granted, the ancient Israelites were commanded to study God's requirements diligently. God himself said: "These words that I am commanding you today must prove to be on your heart; and you must inculcate them in your son and speak of them when you sit in your house and when you walk on the road and when you lie down and when you get up." (Deuteronomy 6:6, 7) But did Jehovah ever mean for a study of the Law to take precedence over actions in harmony with it or indicated by it? Let us see.

Scholarly Works

Placing extreme emphasis on a study of the Law might have made sense to the Israelites, since a certain Jewish tradition held that God himself spent three hours every day studying the Law. You can see why some Jews might reason, 'If God regularly studies the Law, should not his earthly creatures be consumed with doing the same?'

By the first century C.E., the rabbis' obsession with dissecting and interpreting the Law had completely distorted their thinking. "The scribes and the Pharisees . . . say but do not perform," said Jesus. "They bind up heavy loads and put them upon the shoulders of men, but they themselves are not willing to budge them with their finger." (Matthew 23:2-4) Those religious leaders weighed the common people down with innumerable rules and regulations, but they themselves hypocritically created loopholes that would exclude them from observing those same laws. Moreover, those men who concentrated on scholarly efforts "disregarded the weightier matters of the Law, namely, justice and mercy and faithfulness."—Matthew 23:16-24.

How ironic that in seeking to establish their own righteousness, the scribes and the Pharisees ended up violating the very Law that they claimed to uphold! All the centuries of debates over words and other minutiae of the Law did not bring them closer to God. The effect was similar to the deviation caused by what the apostle Paul called "empty speeches," "contradictions," and false "knowledge." (1 Timothy 6:20, 21) Another serious problem, though, was the impact that endless research had on them. They did not come to have the sort of faith that moved them to right action.

Intelligent Minds, Faithless Hearts

How different the thinking of the Jewish religious leaders was from that of God! Shortly before the Israelites entered the Promised Land, Moses told them: "Apply your hearts to all the words that I am speaking in warning to you today, that you may command your sons to take care to do all the words of this law." (Deuteronomy 32: 46) Clearly, God's people were to be not just scholars of the Law but doers of the Law.

Time and again, however, the nation of Israel proved unfaithful to Jehovah. Instead of doing the right sort of works, the sons of Israel "did not exercise faith toward him and did not listen to his voice." (Deuteronomy 9:23; Judges 2:15, 16; 2 Chronicles 24: 18, 19; Jeremiah 25:4-7) Finally, the Jews committed their ultimate act of unfaithfulness when they rejected Jesus as the Messiah. (John 19:14-16) Accordingly, Jehovah God rejected Israel and turned his attention to the nations.—Acts 13:46.

We certainly need to be careful not to fall into the same trap—thinking that we can worship God with intelligent minds but faithless hearts. To put it another way, our study of the Bible needs to be more than an academic exercise. Accurate knowledge must reach our hearts to affect our lives for the good. Would it make sense to study vegetable gardening but never plant any seeds? Granted, we might gain a certain amount of knowledge about how to cultivate a garden, but we would never harvest anything! Similarly, people who learn God's requirements through a study of the Bible must allow seeds of truth to reach the heart in order for those seeds to sprout and move them to action.—Matthew 13:3-9, 19-23.

"Become Doers of the Word"

The apostle Paul said that "faith follows the thing heard." (Romans 10:17) This natural progression from hearing the Word of God to exercising faith in his Son, Jesus Christ, puts us in line for everlasting life. Yes, something more is required than simply saying, 'I believe in God and Christ.'

Jesus urged his followers to have the kind of faith that would move them to action: "My Father is glorified in this, that you keep bearing much fruit and prove yourselves my disciples." (John 15:8) Later, Jesus' half brother James wrote: "Become doers of the word, and not hearers only." (James 1:22) How, though, can we know what to do? By word and example, Jesus indicated what we need to do to please God.

While on earth, Jesus worked hard to promote Kingdom interests and to glorify his Father's name. (John 17:4-8) In what way? Many people may call to mind Jesus' miracles of healing the sick and the crippled. But Matthew's Gospel makes clear the principal way: "Jesus set out on a tour of all the cities and villages, teaching in their synagogues and preaching the good news of the kingdom." Notably, Jesus did not limit his ministry to speaking casually to a few friends and acquaintances or to those he came in contact with locally. He exerted himself vigorously, using whatever means were available to him to visit people "throughout the whole of Galilee."—Matthew 4:23, 24; 9:35.

Jesus directed his followers to share in the disciple-making work as well. Indeed, he provided a perfect example for them to imitate. (1 Peter 2:21) Jesus told his faithful disciples: "Go therefore and make disciples of people of all the nations, baptizing them in the name of the Father and of the Son and of the holy spirit, teaching them to observe all the things I have commanded you." —Matthew 28:19, 20.

Admittedly, sharing in the preaching activity presents a real challenge. Jesus himself said: "Look! I am sending you forth as lambs in among wolves." (Luke 10:3) When we are faced with opposition, a natural tendency is to shrink back in order to spare ourselves unnecessary grief or anxiety. That is what happened on the evening of Jesus' arrest. The apostles fled after being overcome by fear. Later that evening, Peter three times denied knowing Jesus.—Matthew 26:56, 69-75.

Furthermore, you may be surprised to learn that even the apostle Paul said that he struggled to preach the good news. He wrote to the congregation in Thessalonica: "We mustered up boldness by means of our God to speak to you the good news of God with a great deal of struggling."—1 Thessalonians 2:1, 2.

Paul and his fellow apostles were able to overcome any fear of speaking to others about God's Kingdom, and so can you. How? The most important step is to lean on Jehovah. If we put full faith in Jehovah, that faith will move us to action, and we will be able to do his will.—Acts 4:17-20; 5:18, 27-29.

There Exists a Reward for Your Activity

Jehovah is well-aware of the effort we put forth to serve him. He knows, for example, when we are sick or weary. He is aware of our insecurities and self-doubts. When financial burdens weigh us down or when our health or our emotions seem to betray us, Jehovah is ever mindful of our situation. —2 Chronicles 16:9; 1 Peter 3:12.

How delighted Jehovah must be when despite our imperfections and difficulties, our faith moves us to action! The tender regard that Jehovah has for his faithful servants is not just a vague feeling—it is backed up with a promise. Under divine inspiration, the apostle Paul wrote: "God is not unrighteous so as to forget your work and the love you showed for his name, in that you have ministered to the holy ones and continue ministering."—Hebrews 6:10.

You can trust the Bible's description of Jehovah as "a God of faithfulness, with whom there is no injustice," and as "the rewarder of those earnestly seeking him." (Deuteronomy 32:4; Hebrews 11:6) For example, a woman in California, U.S.A., recalls: "My father served as a full-time minister for ten years before he began raising a family. He delighted me with stories of how Jehovah sustained him in the ministry. Many a time he spent his last dollar for gas in order to go out in the ministry. When he got home from the ministry, there would

Our faith needs to be backed up by works

often be unexpected provisions waiting for him at the door."

In addition to material support, "the Father of tender mercies and the God of all comfort" gives us emotional and spiritual support. (2 Corinthians 1:3) "Relying on Jehovah is a comfortable feeling," says one Witness who has endured many trials over the years. "It gives you the opportunity to trust in Jehovah and see him in action as he helps you." You can humbly approach the "Hearer of prayer," assured that he will give attention to your personal concerns. —Psalm 65:2.

The blessings and rewards that spiritual harvest workers receive are many. (Matthew 9:37, 38) Sharing in the public ministry has brought health benefits to many, and it may do so for you. More important, though, witnessing to others helps us to strengthen a good relationship with God. —James 2:23.

Keep Doing Good

It would be a mistake for one of God's servants to conclude that Jehovah is disappointed if infirmities or old age somehow prevents him from doing all that he would like to do in the ministry. The same holds true regarding those who are limited by poor health, family responsibilities, or other circumstances.

Recall that when the apostle Paul felt hampered by an infirmity or obstacle, he "three times entreated the Lord that it might depart" from him. Rather than cure Paul so that he might accomplish more in Jehovah's service, God said: "My undeserved kindness is sufficient for you; for my power is being made perfect in weakness." (2 Corinthians 12:7-10) Therefore, rest assured that despite any difficult circumstances you may be enduring, your heavenly Father appreciates whatever you may be able to do to advance his interests. —Hebrews 13:15, 16.

Our loving Creator does not require more of us than we can give. He simply asks that we have the kind of faith that moves us to action.

Do You Remember?

Have you appreciated reading the recent issues of *The Watchtower?*
Well, see if you can answer the following questions:

● **What was behind the choice of December 25 as a date for celebrating Jesus' birth?**

God's Word provides no date for Jesus' birth. The *Enciclopedia Hispánica* notes: "The date of December 25 for the celebration of Christmas is not the result of a strict chronological anniversary but, rather, of the Christianization of the festivals of the winter solstice." The ancient Romans celebrated the rise of the sun in the winter sky by feasting, revelry, and the exchanging of presents. —12/15, pages 4-5.

● **Does Acts 7:59 mean that Stephen prayed to Jesus?**

No. The Bible shows that prayer is to be directed only to Jehovah God. Seeing Jesus in vision, Stephen apparently felt free to appeal to him directly, saying: "Lord Jesus, receive my spirit." Stephen knew that Jesus had been given authority to raise the dead. (John 5:27-29) So Stephen asked, or appealed to, Jesus to safeguard his life force until the resurrection.—1/1, page 31.

● **How do we know that a person's destiny is not predetermined?**

God has given man freedom of choice, which precludes predestination. It would have been unloving and unjust for Jehovah to have predetermined the course we would take and then hold us responsible for our actions. (Deuteronomy 32:4; 1 John 4:8) —1/15, pages 4-5.

● **Why would it be immodest to say that miracles are impossible?**

Recognizing that they have only partial knowledge of the scientific wonders behind God's creations, some scientists admit that they can no longer state with certainty that something is impossible. At most, they are willing to say that it is improbable.—2/15, pages 5-6.

● **Why did Judge Samson tell his parents that he wanted a daughter of the Philistines as a wife? (Judges 14:2)**

It was against God's law to marry a false worshiper. (Exodus 34:11-16) Yet, the Philistine woman was "just right" in Samson's eyes. Samson "was looking for an opportunity against the Philistines," and the woman was just right for that purpose. God backed Samson by means of His spirit. (Judges 13: 25; 14:3, 4, 6)—3/15, page 26.

● **Should a Christian give a government employee a tip or some type of gift for his services?**

It is wrong to bribe an official, to give him something valuable so that he will do something illegal, pervert justice, or give preferential treatment. But it is not bribery to give a tip or a gift to a public servant when he performs his duty or to obtain a legitimate service or to avoid unfair treatment.—4/1, page 29.

IN OUR NEXT ISSUE

The Resurrection—A Glorious Prospect

———

Who Will Be Resurrected?

———

The Resurrection Hope—What Does It Mean for You?

Questions From Readers

Did not the apostle Paul compromise his Christian faith when he said before the Sanhedrin: "I am a Pharisee"?

To understand Paul's statement, found at Acts 23:6, we need to consider its context.

After being mobbed by Jews in Jerusalem, Paul addressed the crowd. He mentioned that he was "educated in [Jerusalem] at the feet of Gamaliel, instructed according to the strictness of the ancestral Law." Although the crowd listened to his defense for a while, when they eventually grew wrathful, the escorting military commander took Paul to the soldiers' quarters. When he was about to be whipped, Paul said: "Is it lawful for you men to scourge a man that is a Roman and uncondemned?"—Acts 21:27–22:29.

The following day, the commander took Paul before the Jewish high court, the Sanhedrin. Paul looked intently at them and saw that the Sanhedrin was made up of Sadducees and Pharisees. He then said: "Men, brothers, I am a Pharisee, a son of Pharisees. Over the hope of resurrection of the dead I am being judged." As a result, a dissension arose between the Pharisees and the Sadducees, "for Sadducees say there is neither resurrection nor angel nor spirit, but the Pharisees publicly declare them all." Some who belonged to the party of the Pharisees contended fiercely: "We find nothing wrong in this man."—Acts 23:6-10.

Being known as a very zealous Christian, Paul could not have convinced the Sanhedrin that he was a practicing Pharisee. The Pharisees present would have accepted no compromise or misrepresentation. So Paul's statement about being a Pharisee must have had limitations, and the Pharisees present must have understood Paul's words in that context.

In saying that he was being judged over the hope of the resurrection of the dead, Paul clearly meant that *in this respect* he was like the Pharisees. In any controversy on this topic, Paul was to be identified with the Pharisees rather than the Sadducees, who did not believe in the resurrection.

What Paul believed as a Christian was not in conflict with the beliefs of the Pharisees on such matters as the resurrection, angels, and some points of the Law. (Philippians 3:5) So within these limits, Paul could link himself with the Pharisees, and it was within this restricted meaning that those present of the Sanhedrin understood his words. He was thus using his background to deal with the biased Jewish supreme court.

However, the greatest evidence that Paul did not compromise his faith is seen in his continuing to have Jehovah's approval. The night after Paul made the statement in question, Jesus said: "Be of good courage! For as you have been giving a thorough witness on the things about me in Jerusalem, so you must also bear witness in Rome." Since Paul had God's approval, we must conclude that Paul did not compromise his Christian faith.—Acts 23:11.

BIBLE HISTORY
How Accurate?

IN THEIR book *Battles of the Bible*, Chaim Herzog, former president of the State of Israel, and Mordechai Gichon, emeritus professor of archaeology at Tel Aviv University, make this point:

"The tactical description of the battles of the Bible . . . cannot be explained by mere inventiveness. It suffices, for example, to compare the campaign of Gideon against the Midianites and their allies, as related in Judges, 6-8, with the battles of the Trojan War, described by Homer in his *Iliad*. For the latter, any accessible sea shore and a not-far-away fortified town will do nicely as geographic setting . . . Not so the biblical account of Gideon's campaign. The detailed tactical movements and encounters based on the interaction between specific topographical features and the actions of both friend or foe—over a theatre of war covering some forty miles in length—simply cannot be reproduced anywhere . . . We are thus virtually forced to accept the veracity of the tactical narrative of the battles as described in the Bible."

You might study Gideon's campaign by using the map on pages 18 and 19 of the atlaslike brochure *"See the Good Land."**

* Published by Jehovah's Witnesses.

The story began when "all Midian and Amalek and the Easterners gathered together as one and proceeded to cross over and camp in the low plain of Jezreel." Gideon called nearby tribes to help. Events moved from the well of Harod to the hill of Moreh, then down the Jordan Valley. After pursuing the enemies across the Jordan River, Gideon subdued them.—Judges 6:33–8:12.

That map in *"See the Good Land"* shows the major places mentioned and the land features involved. Another map (page 15) identifies the territories of Israel's tribes. The two maps can help you to appreciate the accuracy of the Bible account.

This illustrates an observation made by the late Professor Yohanan Aharoni: "In the land of the Bible, geography and history are so deeply interwoven that neither can be really understood without the help of the other."

THE WATCHTOWER

ANNOUNCING JEHOVAH'S KINGDOM

MAY 1, 2005

Will the Dead Live Again?

THE WATCHTOWER®
ANNOUNCING JEHOVAH'S KINGDOM

May 1, 2005   Average Printing Each Issue: 26,439,000   Vol. 126, No. 9

THE PURPOSE OF *THE WATCHTOWER* is to exalt Jehovah God as Sovereign Lord of the universe. It keeps watch on world events as these fulfill Bible prophecy. It comforts all peoples with the good news that God's Kingdom will soon destroy those who oppress their fellowmen and that it will turn the earth into a paradise. It encourages faith in God's now-reigning King, Jesus Christ, whose shed blood opens the way for mankind to gain eternal life. *The Watchtower,* published by Jehovah's Witnesses continuously since 1879, is nonpolitical. It adheres to the Bible as its authority.

IN THIS ISSUE

3 A Tragedy Strikes

4 The Resurrection—A Glorious Prospect

8 The Resurrection—A Teaching That Affects You

13 Who Will Be Resurrected?

18 The Resurrection Hope—What Does It Mean for You?

23 Though Weak, I Am Powerful

29 Questions From Readers

30 Courage in the Face of Opposition

31 Triumphant in a Special Way

32 How to Make Each Day Count

WATCHTOWER STUDIES

MAY 30–JUNE 5:
The Resurrection—A Teaching That Affects You.
Page 8. Songs to be used: 185, 23.

JUNE 6-12:
Who Will Be Resurrected?
Page 13. Songs to be used: 218, 135.

JUNE 13-19:
The Resurrection Hope—What Does It Mean for You?
Page 18. Songs to be used: 102, 71.

Publication of *The Watchtower* is part of a worldwide Bible educational work supported by voluntary donations.

Unless otherwise indicated, Scripture quotations are from the modern-language *New World Translation of the Holy Scriptures—With References.*

The Watchtower (ISSN 0043-1087) is published semimonthly by Watchtower Bible and Tract Society of New York, Inc.; M. H. Larson, President; G. F. Simonis, Secretary-Treasurer; 25 Columbia Heights, Brooklyn, NY 11201-2483. Periodicals Postage Paid at Brooklyn, NY, and at additional mailing offices. **POSTMASTER:** Send address changes to Watchtower, **Wallkill, NY 12589.**

Changes of address should reach us 30 days before your moving date. Give us your old and new address (if possible, your old address label).

Semimonthly   ENGLISH

Would you welcome more information or a free home Bible study? Please send your request to Jehovah's Witnesses, using the appropriate address below.

America, United States of: Wallkill, NY 12589. *Antigua:* Box 119, St. Johns. *Australia:* Box 280, Ingleburn, NSW 1890. *Bahamas:* Box N-1247, Nassau, N.P. *Barbados, W.I.:* Crusher Site Road, Prospect, St. James. *Britain:* The Ridgeway, London NW7 1RN. *Canada:* Box 4100, Halton Hills (Georgetown), Ontario L7G 4Y4. *Germany:* Niederselters, Am Steinfels, D-65618 Selters. *Ghana:* P. O. Box GP 760, Accra. *Guyana:* 352-360 Tyrell St., Republic Park Phase 2 EBD. *Hawaii 96819:* 2055 Kam IV Rd., Honolulu. *Hong Kong:* 4 Kent Road, Kowloon Tong. *India:* Post Box 6440, Yelahanka, Bangalore 560 064, KAR. *Ireland:* Newcastle, Greystones, Co. Wicklow. *Jamaica:* P. O. Box 103, Old Harbour, St. Catherine. *Japan:* 1271 Nakashinden, Ebina City, Kanagawa Pref., 243-0496. *Kenya:* P.O. Box 47788, GPO Nairobi 00100. *New Zealand:* P.O. Box 75-142, Manurewa. *Nigeria:* P.M.B. 1090, Benin City 300001, Edo State. *Philippines, Republic of:* P. O. Box 2044, 1060 Manila. *South Africa:* Private Bag X2067, Krugersdorp, 1740. *Trinidad and Tobago, Republic of:* Lower Rapsey Street & Laxmi Lane, Curepe. *Zambia:* Box 33459, Lusaka 10101. *Zimbabwe:* Private Bag WG-5001, Westgate.

NOW PUBLISHED IN 150 LANGUAGES. SEMIMONTHLY: Afrikaans, Albanian,* Amharic, Arabic, Bengali, Bicol, Bislama, Bulgarian, Cebuano,* Chichewa,* Chinese, Chinese (Simplified),* Cibemba,* Croatian,* Czech,*# Danish,*# Dutch,*# East Armenian, Efik,* English*#+☉ (also Braille), Estonian, Ewe, Fijian, Finnish,*# French,*# Ga, Georgian, German,*# Greek,* Gujarati, Gun, Hebrew, Hiligaynon, Hindi, Hungarian,*# Igbo,* Iloko,* Indonesian, Italian,*# Japanese*# (also Braille), Kannada, Kinyarwanda, Kirundi, Korean*# (also Braille), Latvian, Lingala, Lithuanian, Luvale, Macedonian, Malagasy,* Malayalam, Maltese, Myanmar, Nepali, New Guinea Pidgin, Norwegian,*# Pangasinan, Papiamento (Aruba), Papiamento (Curaçao), Polish,*# Portuguese*# (also Braille), Punjabi, Rarotongan, Romanian,* Russian,* Samar-Leyte, Samoan, Sango, Sepedi, Serbian, Sesotho, Shona,* Silozi, Sinhala, Slovak,* Slovenian, Solomon Islands Pidgin, Spanish*# (also Braille), Sranantongo, Swahili,* Swedish,*# Tagalog,* Tamil, Telugu, Thai, Tigrinya, Tongan, Tshiluba, Tsonga, Tswana, Turkish, Twi, Ukrainian,* Urdu, Vietnamese, Wallisian, Xhosa, Yoruba,* Zulu*

MONTHLY: American Sign Language,△□ Armenian, Assamese, Azerbaijani (roman script), Brazilian Sign Language,△ Cambodian, Chitonga, Gilbertese, Greenlandic, Haitian Creole, Hausa, Hiri Motu, Icelandic, Isoko, Kaonde, Kazakh, Kikongo, Kiluba, Kirghiz, Kosraean, Kwanyama/Ndonga, Luganda, Marathi, Marshallese, Mauritian Creole, Maya, Mizo, Monokutuba, Moore, Niuean, Ossetian, Otetela, Palauan, Persian, Ponapean, Seychelles Creole, Tahitian, Tatar, Tiv, Trukese, Tumbuka, Tuvaluan, Umbundu, Venda, Yapese, Zande

* Study articles also available in large-print edition.
# Audiocassettes also available.
+ CD also available.
☉ MP3 CD-ROM also available.
△ Videocassette
□ DVD

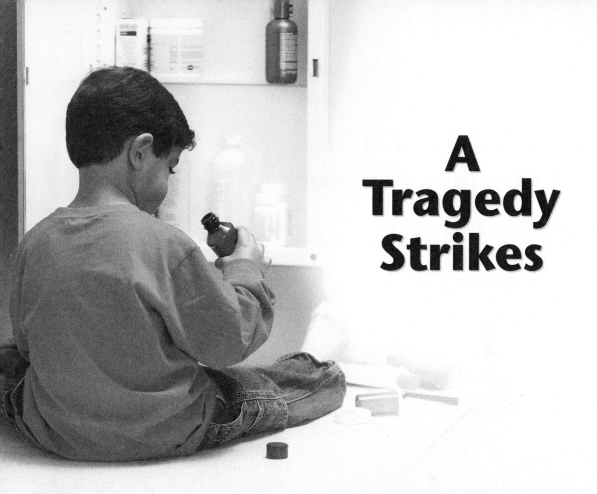

A Tragedy Strikes

OWEN, a two-and-a-half-year-old boy, was playing in the bathroom of his home. He managed to climb up to a medicine cabinet that his parents believed was beyond his reach. Among its contents, he discovered a bottle that caught his attention. He opened it and drank the liquid inside. Tragedy struck.

The bottle contained a corrosive acid, and sadly, young Owen died. His parents were heartbroken. His father, Percy, sought comfort from his church. "Why did this happen?" he asked. The clergyman answered, "God wanted another little angel in heaven." Devastated, the bereaved parent felt that this was completely unjust. Had God really intended that such a tragedy occur?

Disillusioned, Percy decided to have nothing more to do with his church.

Reflecting on what had happened, Percy wondered: 'Is my little boy still in pain? Will I ever see him again?'

You too may have wondered what happens at death and whether it will be possible to be reunited with dead loved ones in the future. God's Word, the Bible, sheds light on these questions. Its pages contain clear and comforting answers for all who have faced similar tragedies. More than that, it reveals a glorious prospect that God has promised—the resurrection.

Please read the following article to learn more about this marvelous hope.

The Resurrection
A Glorious Prospect

BELIEF in a resurrection is widespread. The holy book of Islam, the Koran, devotes a whole chapter to the resurrection. Surah 75 says in part: "I do swear by the Resurrection Day . . . Does man think that We cannot assemble his bones? . . . He questions: 'When is the Day of Resurrection?' Has not He, (the same), the power to give life to the dead?"—Surah 75:1-6, 40.

"Zoroastrianism," observes *The New Encyclopædia Britannica,* "holds a belief in a final overthrow of Evil, a general resurrection, a Last Judgment, and the restoration of a cleansed world to the righteous."

The *Encyclopaedia Judaica* defines the resurrection as "the belief that ultimately the dead will be revived in their bodies and live again on earth." The same reference work also comments that the belief adopted into Judaism that man has an immortal soul presents a dilemma. It admits: "Basically the two beliefs of resurrection and the soul's immortality are contradictory."

Hinduism teaches that man undergoes a series of rebirths, or reincarnations. For this to be true, man must have a soul that lives on after death. The Hindu holy book *Bhagavad Gita* states: "That which pervades the entire body is indestructible. No one is able to destroy the imperishable soul."

Buddhism differs from Hinduism in that it denies the existence of an immortal soul. Nevertheless, today many Buddhists in the Far East believe in the transmigration of an immortal soul.*

Confusion About the Teaching of the Resurrection

Funeral services conducted in Christendom often refer both to the soul as living on after death and to the resurrection. For example, Anglican clergymen usually recite the words: "Forasmuch as it hath pleased Almighty God of his great mercy to take unto himself the soul of our dear brother here departed, we therefore commit his body to the ground; earth to earth, ashes to ashes, dust to dust; in sure and certain hope of the Resurrection to eternal life, through our Lord Jesus Christ."—*The Book of Common Prayer.*

This statement may make one wonder whether the Bible teaches the resurrection or the doctrine of an immortal soul. Note, however, the comment made by French Protestant Professor Oscar Cullmann. He writes in his book *Immortality of the Soul or Resurrection of the Dead?:* "There is a radical

---

* See the book *Mankind's Search for God,* pages 150-4, published by Jehovah's Witnesses.

difference between the Christian expectation of the resurrection of the dead and the Greek belief in the immortality of the soul. . . . Although Christianity later established a link between these two beliefs, and today the average Christian confuses them completely, I see no reason to hide what I and the majority of scholars consider to be the truth. . . . The life and thought of the New Testament are entirely dominated by faith in the resurrection. . . . The whole man, who is really dead, is brought back to life by a new creative act of God."

It is little wonder that people in general are confused about death and the resurrection. To resolve the confusion, we need to look to the Bible, which presents truths revealed by man's Creator, Jehovah God. The Bible documents a number of resurrections. Let us examine four of these accounts and consider what they reveal.

"Women Received Their Dead by Resurrection"

In his letter to Jews who had become Christians, the apostle Paul said that women of faith had "received their dead by resurrection." (Hebrews 11:35) One of those women lived in Zarephath, a Phoenician town near Sidon on the Mediterranean Coast. She was a widow who hospitably received God's prophet Elijah and gave him food even during a time of extreme famine. Sadly, this woman's son fell sick and died. Elijah immediately carried him up

Jehovah used Elisha to resurrect the Shunammite's son

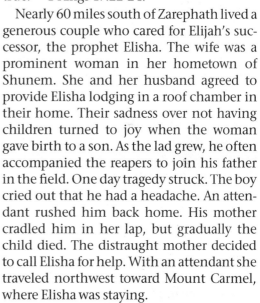

Elijah petitioned Jehovah to restore a boy's life

to the roof chamber where the prophet lodged and petitioned Jehovah to restore the boy's life. A miracle occurred, and the boy "came to life." Elijah returned him to his mother and said: "See, your son is alive." How did she react? She happily said: "Now, indeed, I do know that you are a man of God and that Jehovah's word in your mouth is true."—1 Kings 17:22-24.

Nearly 60 miles south of Zarephath lived a generous couple who cared for Elijah's successor, the prophet Elisha. The wife was a prominent woman in her hometown of Shunem. She and her husband agreed to provide Elisha lodging in a roof chamber in their home. Their sadness over not having children turned to joy when the woman gave birth to a son. As the lad grew, he often accompanied the reapers to join his father in the field. One day tragedy struck. The boy cried out that he had a headache. An attendant rushed him back home. His mother cradled him in her lap, but gradually the child died. The distraught mother decided to call Elisha for help. With an attendant she traveled northwest toward Mount Carmel, where Elisha was staying.

Responding, the prophet sent his attendant, Gehazi, ahead, and he found that the boy was indeed dead. Elisha and the woman followed, but what happened when they finally arrived in Shunem? The account at 2 Kings 4:32-37 relates: "At last Elisha came into the house, and there the boy was dead, being laid upon his couch. Then he came in and closed the door behind them both and began to pray to Jehovah. Finally he went up and lay down upon the child and put his own mouth upon his mouth and his own eyes upon his eyes and his own palms upon his palms and kept bent over him, and gradually the child's flesh grew warm. Then he began walking again in the house, once this way and once that way, after which he went up and bent over him. And the boy began to sneeze as many as seven times, after which the boy opened his eyes. He now called Gehazi and said: 'Call this Shunammite woman.' So he called her and she came in to him. Then he said: 'Lift up your son.' And she proceeded to come in and fall at his feet and bow down to him to the earth, after which she lifted up her son and went out."

Like the widow of Zarephath, the woman from Shunem knew that what had happened was as a result of God's power. Both these women experienced great joy as God restored their beloved offspring to life.

Resurrections During Jesus' Ministry

Some 900 years later, a resurrection occurred a short distance north of Shunem outside the village of Nain. As Jesus Christ and his disciples traveled from Capernaum and neared the gate of Nain, they met a burial procession, and Jesus caught sight of a widow who had lost her only son. Jesus told her to stop weeping. Luke, a physician, described what happened next: "With that [Jesus] approached and touched the bier, and the bearers stood still, and he said: 'Young man, I say to you, Get up!' And the dead man sat up and started to speak, and he gave him to his mother." (Luke 7:14, 15) Those who witnessed this miracle glorified God. News of the resurrection spread southward into Judea and the surrounding district. Interestingly, the disciples of John the Baptizer heard of it and reported the miracle to John. He, in turn, dispatched them to find Jesus and ask him whether He was the expected Messiah. Jesus told them: "Go your way, report to John what you saw and heard: the blind are receiving sight, the lame are walking, the lepers are being cleansed and the deaf are hearing, the dead are being raised up, the poor are being told the good news."—Luke 7:22.

The best known of Jesus' resurrection miracles was that performed in behalf of his close friend Lazarus. In this case, there was a delay between Lazarus' death and Jesus' ar-

Jesus resurrected the son of the widow of Nain

rival at the family home. When Jesus finally reached Bethany, Lazarus had been dead for four days. When Jesus instructed that the stone covering the entrance to the burial chamber be removed, Martha objected, saying: "Lord, by now he must smell, for it is four days." (John 11:39) Yet, any deterioration of Lazarus' body did not prevent the resurrection. At Jesus' command, "the man that had been dead came out with his feet and hands bound with wrappings, and his countenance was bound about with a cloth." The subsequent actions of Jesus' enemies prove that it was indeed Lazarus who had come back to life.—John 11:43, 44; 12:1, 9-11.

What do we conclude from these four resurrection accounts? Each resurrected individual returned to life as the same person. All were recognized, even by their closest relatives. None of the resurrected spoke of what had occurred during the short time they were dead. None spoke of traveling to another world. Apparently, they all returned in good health. For them, it was as though they slept for a while and then woke up, even as Jesus intimated. (John 11:11) Nevertheless, after some time each of these died again.

Reunion With Loved Ones
—A Glorious Prospect

A short time after the tragic death of Owen, mentioned in the preceding article, his father visited a neighbor's home. There on a table, he found a handbill advertising a public talk organized by Jehovah's Witnesses. Its title, "Where Are the Dead?," appealed to him. That was exactly the question he had on his mind. He attended the discourse and found true comfort from the Bible. He learned that the dead do not suffer. Rather than experiencing torment in a hellfire or being taken by God to become angels in heaven, the dead, including Owen, wait in the grave until it is time to be awakened in the resurrection.—Ecclesiastes 9:5, 10; Ezekiel 18:4.

Has tragedy struck your family? Do you, like Owen's father, wonder where your deceased loved ones are now and what possibility there is of seeing them again? If so, we invite you to consider what the Bible further teaches about the resurrection. Perhaps you wonder: 'When will the resurrection occur? Who exactly will benefit from it?' Please read the following articles for a discussion of these and other questions.

The resurrection will reunite relatives with their loved ones

THE RESURRECTION
—A TEACHING THAT AFFECTS YOU

"I have hope toward God . . . that there is going to be a resurrection of both the righteous and the unrighteous."—ACTS 24:15.

AT THE end of his third missionary tour in 56 C.E., the apostle Paul was in Jerusalem. After being arrested by the Romans, he was permitted to appear before the Jewish high court, the Sanhedrin. (Acts 22:29, 30) As Paul observed the members of that court, he noted that some were Sadducees and others were Pharisees. These two groups differed in one outstanding way. The Sadducees denied the resurrection; the Pharisees accepted it. To show where he stood on that issue, Paul declared: "Men, brothers, I am a Pharisee, a son of Pharisees. Over the hope of resurrection of the dead I am being judged." In so doing, he threw the assembly into confusion!—Acts 23:6-9.

2 Years earlier, when he was on the road to Damascus, Paul saw a vision in which he heard Jesus' voice. Paul even asked Jesus: "What shall I do, Lord?" Jesus answered: "Rise, go your way into Damascus, and there you will be told about everything it is appointed for you to do." On arrival in Damascus, Paul was found by a helpful Christian disciple, Ananias, who explained: "The God of our forefathers has chosen you to come to know his will and to see the righteous One [the resurrected Jesus] and to hear the voice of his mouth." (Acts 22:6-16) Little wonder, then, that Paul was prepared to make a de-

---

1. How did the resurrection become an issue before the Sanhedrin?
2. Why was Paul prepared to make a defense of his belief in the resurrection?

fense of his belief in the resurrection.—1 Peter 3:15.

Publicly Declaring the Resurrection Hope

3 Paul later appeared before Governor Felix. On that occasion, Tertullus, "a public speaker" who presented the Jews' case against Paul, accused him of being the leader of a sect and guilty of sedition. In answer Paul forthrightly declared: "I do admit this to you, that, according to the way that they call a 'sect,' in this manner I am rendering sacred service to the God of my forefathers." Then, coming to the main issue, he continued: "I have hope toward God, which hope these men themselves also entertain, that there is going to be a resurrection of both the righteous and the unrighteous."—Acts 23:23, 24; 24:1-8, 14, 15.

4 About two years later, Felix' successor, Porcius Festus, invited King Herod Agrippa to join him in examining the prisoner Paul. Festus explained that the accusers disputed Paul's assertion that "a certain Jesus who

---

3, 4. How did Paul prove to be a staunch advocate of the resurrection, and what can we learn from his example?

was dead . . . was alive." In his defense Paul asked: "Why is it judged unbelievable among you men that God raises up the dead?" Then he declared: "Because I have obtained the help that is from God I continue to this day bearing witness to both small and great, but saying nothing except things the Prophets as well as Moses stated were going to take place, that the Christ was to suffer and, as the first to be resurrected from the dead, he was going to publish light both to this people and to the nations." (Acts 24:27; 25:13-22; 26:8, 22, 23) What a staunch advocate of the resurrection Paul was! Like Paul, we too can proclaim with conviction that there will be a resurrection. But what reaction can we expect? Likely the same as Paul received.

5 Consider what occurred earlier during Paul's second missionary tour (about 49-52 C.E.) when he visited Athens. He reasoned with people who believed in many deities, and he urged them to note God's purpose to judge the inhabited earth in righteousness by a man whom He had appointed. This was none other than Jesus. Paul explained that God had furnished a guarantee of this by resurrecting Jesus. What was the reaction? We read: "Well, when they heard of a resurrection of the dead, some began to mock, while others said: 'We will hear you about this even another time.' "—Acts 17:29-32.

6 That reaction mirrored what Peter and John had experienced shortly after Pentecost 33 C.E. Again the Sadducees figured prominently in the controversy. Acts 4:1-4 relates what happened: "Now while the two were speaking to the people, the chief priests and the captain of the temple and the Sadducees came upon them, being annoyed because they were teaching the people and were plainly declaring the resurrection from the dead in the case of Jesus." Others, however, reacted favorably. "Many of those who had listened to the speech believed, and the number of the men became about five thousand." Evidently, we can expect varied reactions when we speak about the resurrection hope. In view of that, it is vital that we strengthen our faith in this teaching.

Faith and the Resurrection

7 Not all who became Christians in the first century C.E. found it easy to accept the resurrection hope. Some who found it difficult were associated with the congregation in Corinth. To them Paul wrote: "I handed on to you, among the first things, that which I also received, that Christ died for our sins according to the Scriptures; and that he was buried, yes, that he has been raised up the third day according to the Scriptures." Paul then attested to this truth by stating that the resurrected Christ had "appeared to upward of five hundred brothers," most of whom, added Paul, were still alive. (1 Corinthians 15:3-8) He further reasoned: "If Christ is being preached that he has been raised up from the dead, how is it some among you say there is no resurrection of the dead? If, indeed, there is no resurrection of the dead, neither has Christ been raised up. But if Christ has not been raised up, our preaching is certainly in vain, and our faith is in vain." —1 Corinthians 15:12-14.

8 Yes, so fundamental is the teaching of the resurrection that the Christian faith is in vain if the resurrection is not accepted as

_____
5, 6. (a) The apostles' advocating the resurrection prompted what reaction? (b) As we express our hope in the resurrection, what is vital?

_____
7, 8. (a) As shown in a letter to the first-century Corinthian congregation, how can faith be in vain? (b) How does a correct understanding of the resurrection hope set true Christians apart?

Paul, appearing before Governor Felix, proclaimed with conviction the resurrection hope

a reality. Indeed, the correct understanding of the resurrection sets true Christians apart from the false. (Genesis 3:4; Ezekiel 18:4) Thus, Paul includes the teaching of the resurrection in "the primary doctrine" of Christianity. May our determination be to "press on to maturity." "And this we will do," exhorts Paul, "if God indeed permits." —Hebrews 6:1-3.

The Resurrection Hope

9 To strengthen our faith in the resurrection further, let us review such questions as: What does the Bible mean when it refers to the resurrection? How does the teaching of the resurrection magnify Jehovah's love? Answers to these questions will draw us closer to God and at the same time help us to teach others.—2 Timothy 2:2; James 4:8.

10 "Resurrection" is the translation of a Greek word that literally means "a standing up again." What does that expression involve? According to the Bible, the resurrection hope is the conviction that a dead person can live again. The Bible further shows that the person is restored in either a human or a spirit body, depending on whether he has an earthly or a heavenly hope. We marvel at Jehovah's love, wisdom, and power manifest in this wonderful resurrection prospect.

11 The resurrection of Jesus and his anointed brothers provides them with a spirit body fit for service in heaven. (1 Corinthians 15:35-38, 42-53) Together they will serve as rulers of the Messianic Kingdom, which will bring Paradise conditions to the earth. Under Jesus as High Priest, the anointed constitute a royal priesthood. They will apply the benefits of Christ's ran-

Why did Abraham have faith in the resurrection?

som sacrifice to mankind in the new world of righteousness. (Hebrews 7:25, 26; 9:24; 1 Peter 2:9; Revelation 22:1, 2) In the meantime, those of the anointed still alive on earth desire to remain acceptable to God. At their death, they will receive their "award" through resurrection to immortal spirit life in heaven. (2 Corinthians 5:1-3, 6-8, 10; 1 Corinthians 15:51, 52; Revelation 14:13) "If we have become united with him in the likeness of his death," wrote Paul, "we shall certainly also be united with him in the likeness of his resurrection." (Romans 6:5) But what about those for whom the resurrection will mean life on earth again as humans? How can the resurrection hope draw them closer to God? We can learn much from the example of Abraham.

The Resurrection and
Friendship With Jehovah

12 Abraham, who was described as "Jehovah's friend," was a man of outstanding faith. (James 2:23) Paul referred to Abraham's faith three times in his listing of faithful men and women recorded in the

---

9, 10. What does the Bible mean when it refers to the resurrection?

11. What resurrection prospects are offered to God's anointed servants?

12, 13. What powerful basis for faith in the resurrection did Abraham have?

11th chapter of Hebrews. (Hebrews 11:8, 9, 17) His third reference focuses on the faith Abraham displayed when he obediently prepared to offer up his son Isaac as a sacrifice. Abraham was convinced that the promise of a seed through Isaac was guaranteed by Jehovah. Even if Isaac were to die as a sacrifice, Abraham "reckoned that God was able to raise him up even from the dead."

¹³ As events turned out, when Jehovah saw the strength of Abraham's faith, he arranged for an animal to substitute as a sacrifice. Still, Isaac's experience served as an illustration of the resurrection, as Paul explained: "From there he [Abraham] did receive him [Isaac] also in an illustrative way." (Hebrews 11:19) More than that, Abraham already had a powerful basis for his belief in the resurrection. Had not Jehovah brought back to life Abraham's reproductive powers when he and his wife, Sarah, came together in their old age and produced their son, Isaac?—Genesis 18:10-14; 21:1-3; Romans 4:19-21.

¹⁴ Paul described Abraham as an alien resident and a tent dweller who was "awaiting the city having real foundations, the builder and maker of which city is God." (Hebrews 11:9, 10) This was not a literal city like Jerusalem, which was the location of God's temple. No, this was a symbolic city. It was God's heavenly Kingdom made up of Christ Jesus and his 144,000 corulers. The 144,000 in their heavenly glory are also spoken of as "the holy city, New Jerusalem," the "bride" of Christ. (Revelation 21:2) In 1914, Jehovah enthroned Jesus as Messianic King of the heavenly Kingdom and commanded him to rule in the midst of his enemies. (Psalm 110: 1, 2; Revelation 11:15) To receive the blessings of Kingdom rule, Abraham, "Jehovah's

---

14. (a) According to Hebrews 11:9, 10, what did Abraham await? (b) To receive Kingdom blessings in the new world, what must yet happen to Abraham? (c) How can we receive Kingdom blessings?

friend," will have to live again. Likewise, for us to receive Kingdom blessings, we must be alive in God's new world, either as members of the great crowd of Armageddon survivors or as those resurrected from the dead. (Revelation 7:9, 14) What, though, is the basis of the resurrection hope?

God's Love—The Basis of the Resurrection Hope

¹⁵ Our close relationship with our loving heavenly Father, our strong faith like that of Abraham, and our obedience to God's commands allow us to be declared righteous and to be viewed by Jehovah as his friends. This brings us in line to benefit from Kingdom rule. Indeed, the very first prophecy recorded in God's Word, at Genesis 3:15, lays the basis for the resurrection hope and friendship with God. It foretells not only the crushing of Satan's head but also, by contrast, the bruising in the heel of the Seed of God's woman. Jesus' death on the stake was a figurative bruising in the heel. His resurrection on the third day healed that wound and paved the way for decisive action against "the one having the means to cause death, that is, the Devil."—Hebrews 2:14.

15, 16. (a) How does the first prophecy in the Bible lay the basis for our resurrection hope? (b) How can belief in the resurrection draw us closer to Jehovah?

Do You Recall?

- What reaction did Paul encounter when he declared his hope in the resurrection?

- Why does the resurrection hope set true Christians apart from the false?

- How do we know that Abraham, Job, and Daniel had faith in the resurrection?

¹⁶ Paul reminds us that "God recommends his own love to us in that, while we were yet sinners, Christ died for us." (Romans 5:8) Appreciation for this undeserved kindness truly brings us closer to Jesus and to our loving heavenly Father.—2 Corinthians 5:14, 15.

¹⁷ Job, a faithful man from pre-Christian times, also looked forward to a resurrection. He suffered greatly at Satan's hands. Unlike his false companions, who never mentioned the resurrection, Job drew comfort from this hope and asked: "If an able-bodied man dies can he live again?" In answer Job himself declared: "All the days of my compulsory service I shall wait, until my relief comes." Addressing his God, Jehovah, he acknowledged: "You will call, and I myself shall answer you." Concerning the feelings of our loving Creator, Job noted: "For the work of your hands you will have a yearning." (Job 14:14, 15) Yes, Jehovah eagerly anticipates the time when faithful ones return to life in the resurrection. How this draws us closer to him as we meditate on the love and undeserved kindness that he shows us even though we are imperfect! —Romans 5:21; James 4:8.

¹⁸ The prophet Daniel, described by God's angel as a "very desirable man," lived a long life of faithful service. (Daniel 10:11, 19) His integrity to Jehovah re-

Job drew comfort from the resurrection hope

mained intact from his exile in 617 B.C.E. until his death some time after he received a vision in 536 B.C.E., the third year of Cyrus, king of Persia. (Daniel 1:1; 10:1) Some time during that third year of Cyrus, Daniel received a vision of the march of world powers that culminates in the coming great tribulation. (Daniel 11:1–12:13) As he could not fully understand the vision, Daniel asked the angelic messenger who delivered it: "O my lord, what will be the final part of these things?" In answer the angel called attention to "the time of the end," during which "the ones having insight will understand." As for Daniel himself, what were his prospects? The angel acknowledged: "You will rest, but you will stand up for your lot at the end of the days." (Daniel 12:8-10, 13) Dan-

Daniel will return in the resurrection of the righteous ones

17. (a) What hope did Job express? (b) What does Job 14:15 reveal about Jehovah, and how does this make you feel?
18, 19. (a) What prospect does Daniel have for living again? (b) What will we review in the next article?

12   THE WATCHTOWER • MAY 1, 2005

iel will return "in the resurrection of the righteous ones," during Christ's Millennial Reign.—Luke 14:14.

¹⁹ We live deep in the time of the end and nearer the start of Christ's Millennial Rule than when we first became believers. Therefore, we must ask ourselves, 'Will I be there in the new world to associate with Abraham, Job, Daniel, and other faithful men and women?' We shall be, provided we stay close to Jehovah and obey his commands. In our next article, we will review the resurrection hope in further detail so as to identify who will be resurrected.

WHO WILL BE RESURRECTED?

"Do not marvel at this, because the hour is coming in which all those in the memorial tombs will hear his voice and come out."—JOHN 5:28, 29.

SOMETHING very unusual occurred more than 3,500 years ago. Moses was caring for the sheep that belonged to the patriarch Jethro. Near Mount Horeb, Jehovah's angel appeared to Moses in a flame of fire in the midst of a thornbush. "As he kept looking, why, here the thornbush was burning with the fire and yet the thornbush was not consumed," relates the Exodus account. Then a voice called to him from the thornbush. "I am the God of your father," the voice declared, "the God of Abraham, the God of Isaac and the God of Jacob." (Exodus 3:1-6) Later, in the first century C.E., those words were recalled by none other than God's own Son, Jesus.

² Jesus was having a discussion with some Sadducees, who did not believe in the resurrection. Jesus declared: "That the dead are raised up even Moses disclosed, in the account about the thornbush, when he calls Jehovah 'the God of Abraham and God of Isaac and God of Jacob.' He is a God, not of the dead, but of the living, for they are all living to him." (Luke 20:27, 37, 38) By saying these words, Jesus confirmed that from God's viewpoint the long-dead Abraham, Isaac, and Jacob still lived in God's memory. Like Job, they await the end of their "compulsory service," their sleep in death. (Job 14:14) In God's new world, they will be resurrected.

³ What, though, about the billions of others who have died throughout human history? Will they too receive a resurrection? Before we can obtain a satisfying answer to that question, let us find out from God's Word where people go when they die.

Where Are the Dead?

⁴ The Bible declares that the dead are "conscious of nothing at all." At death there is no torment in hellfire, no agonizing wait

---

1. What outstanding declaration did Moses hear at the burning thornbush, and who later recalled those words?

2, 3. (a) What prospect awaits Abraham, Isaac, and Jacob? (b) What questions arise?

4. (a) Where do people go when they die? (b) What is Sheol?

in Limbo, but simply a return to the dust. Therefore, God's Word advises the living: "All that your hand finds to do, do with your very power, for there is no work nor devising nor knowledge nor wisdom in Sheol, the place to which you are going." (Ecclesiastes 9:5, 10; Genesis 3:19) "Sheol" is an unfamiliar term to many. It is a Hebrew word of uncertain derivation. Many religions teach that the dead are still alive, but as the inspired Word of God shows, those in Sheol are dead, without consciousness. Sheol is the common grave of mankind.

5 In the Bible, we find the first occurrence of the word "Sheol" at Genesis 37:35. Following the apparent loss of his beloved son Joseph, the patriarch Jacob refused to take comfort, declaring: "I shall go down mourning to my son into Sheol!" Believing that his son was dead, Jacob desired to die and be in Sheol. Later, nine of Jacob's older children wanted to take his youngest son, Benjamin, down to Egypt to find relief from the famine. However, Jacob refused, saying: "My son will not go down with you men, because his brother is dead and he has been left by himself. If a fatal accident should befall him on the way on which you would go, then you would certainly bring down my gray hairs with grief to Sheol." (Genesis 42:36, 38) These two references link death, not some kind of afterlife, with Sheol.

6 The Genesis account reveals that Joseph had become the food administrator in Egypt. Consequently, Jacob was able to journey there for a joyous reunion with Joseph. After that, Jacob resided in that land until his death at the very advanced age of 147. According to his dying wishes, his sons took his remains and buried them in the cave of Machpelah in the land of Canaan. (Gene-

---

5, 6. At his death, where did Jacob go, and whom did he join there?

sis 47:28; 49:29-31; 50:12, 13) Thus, Jacob joined Isaac, his father, and Abraham, his grandfather.

'Gathered to Their Forefathers'

7 Earlier, when Jehovah confirmed his covenant with Abraham and promised that his seed would become many, he indicated what would happen to Abraham. "As for you," Jehovah said, "you will go to your forefathers in peace; you will be buried at a good old age." (Genesis 15:15) And this is exactly what happened. Genesis 25:8 states: "Then Abraham expired and died in a good old age, old and satisfied, and was gathered to his people." Who were these people? Genesis 11:10-26 lists his ancestors as far back as Noah's son Shem. So it was to these already sleeping in Sheol that Abraham was gathered at death.

8 The expression "gathered to his people" occurs frequently in the Hebrew Scriptures. Thus, it is logical to conclude that Abraham's son Ishmael and Moses' brother, Aaron, both went to Sheol at their death, there to await a resurrection. (Genesis 25:17; Numbers 20:23-29) Accordingly, Moses too went to Sheol, although no one knew where his grave was. (Numbers 27:13; Deuteronomy 34:5, 6) Similarly, Joshua, Moses' successor as leader of Israel, along with a whole generation of people also descended to Sheol at death.—Judges 2:8-10.

9 Centuries later, David became king of the 12 tribes of Israel. At his death, he "lay down with his forefathers." (1 Kings 2:10) Was he too in Sheol? Interestingly, on the day of Pentecost 33 C.E., the apostle Peter re-

---

7, 8. (a) Where did Abraham go at his death? Explain. (b) What shows that others entered Sheol at their death?

9. (a) How does the Bible show that the Hebrew word "Sheol" and the Greek word "Hades" refer to the same place? (b) What prospect do those in Sheol, or Hades, have?

ferred to David's death and quoted Psalm 16: 10: "You will not leave my soul in Sheol." After mentioning that David was still in his tomb, Peter applied those words to Jesus and indicated that David "saw beforehand and spoke concerning the resurrection of the Christ, that neither was he forsaken in Hades nor did his flesh see corruption. This Jesus God resurrected, of which fact we are all witnesses." (Acts 2: 29-32) Peter here used the word "Hades," the Greek counterpart of the Hebrew word "Sheol." Thus, those said to be in Hades are in the same situation as those said to be in Sheol. They are sleeping, awaiting a resurrection.

Like Abraham, those who go to Sheol are in line for a resurrection

Are There Unrighteous Ones in Sheol?

¹⁰ After Moses led the nation of Israel out of Egypt, a rebellion broke out in the wilderness. Moses told the people to separate themselves from the ringleaders—Korah, Dathan, and Abiram. They would die violently. Moses explained: "If it is according to the death of all mankind that these people will die and with the punishment of all mankind that punishment will be brought upon them, then it is not Jehovah that has sent me. But if it is something created that Jehovah will create, and the ground has to open its mouth and swallow up them and everything that belongs to them and they have to go down alive into Sheol, you will then know for certain that these men have treated Jehovah disrespectfully." (Numbers 16:29, 30) So whether by the earth opening and swallowing them or by fire consuming them as in the case of Korah and the 250 Levites who sided with him, all these rebels ended up in Sheol, or Hades. —Numbers 26:10.

¹¹ Shimei, who had called down evil on King David, met his punishment at the hands of David's successor, Solomon. "Do not leave him unpunished," David commanded, "for you are a wise man and you well know what you ought to do to him, and you must bring his gray hairs down to Sheol with blood." Solomon had Benaiah execute the sentence. (1 Kings 2:8, 9, 44-46) Another victim of Benaiah's executional sword was Israel's former army chief Joab. His gray hairs did not "go down in peace to Sheol." (1 Kings 2:5, 6, 28-34) Both these examples testify to the truthfulness of David's inspired song: "Wicked people will turn back to Sheol, even all the nations forgetting God." —Psalm 9:17.

¹² Ahithophel was personal adviser to David. His counsel was valued as though it was from Jehovah himself. (2 Samuel 16:23) Sadly, this trusted servant turned traitor and joined in a coup led by David's son Absalom. Apparently, David alluded to this defection when he wrote: "It was not an

---

10, 11. Why can we say that some unrighteous ones go to Sheol, or Hades, at their death?

12. Who was Ahithophel, and where did he go at his death?

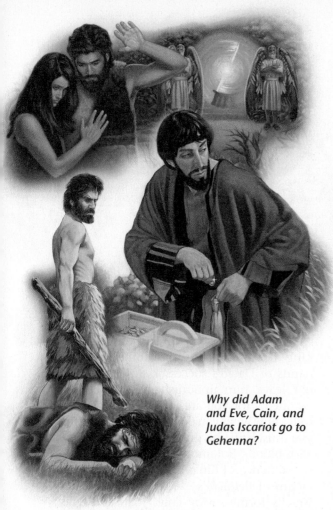

Why did Adam and Eve, Cain, and Judas Iscariot go to Gehenna?

Christ's 12 apostles, Judas Iscariot, turned traitor like Ahithophel. Judas' treacherous act was far more serious than that of Ahithophel. Judas acted against God's only-begotten Son. In a prayer at the end of his earthly ministry, God's Son reported about his followers: "When I was with them I used to watch over them on account of your own name which you have given me; and I have kept them, and not one of them is destroyed except the son of destruction, in order that the scripture might be fulfilled." (John 17: 12) By here referring to Judas as "the son of destruction," Jesus indicated that when Judas died, there was no hope of a return for him. He did not live on in God's memory. He went, not to Sheol, but to Gehenna. What is Gehenna?

¹⁴ Jesus condemned the religious leaders of his day because they made each of their disciples "a subject for Gehenna." (Matthew 23:15) Back at that time, people were familiar with the Valley of Hinnom, an area used as a garbage dump where bodies of executed criminals who were deemed unworthy of a proper burial were deposited. Earlier, Jesus himself had made mention of Gehenna in his Sermon on the Mount. (Matthew 5:29, 30) Its symbolic meaning was clear to his listeners. Gehenna represented complete destruction without hope of a resurrection. Apart from Judas Iscariot of Jesus' day, have others gone to Gehenna rather than to Sheol, or Hades, at their death?

¹⁵ The first humans, Adam and Eve, were created perfect. Their fall into sin was deliberate. Before them was either everlasting life or death. They disobeyed God and sided with Satan. When they died, they had no prospect of benefiting from Christ's ransom sacrifice. Rather, they went to Gehenna.

enemy that proceeded to reproach me; otherwise I could put up with it. It was not an intense hater of me that assumed great airs against me; otherwise I could conceal myself from him." David continued: "Desolations be upon them! Let them go down into Sheol alive; for during their alien residence bad things have been within them." (Psalm 55: 12-15) At their death, Ahithophel and his companions went to Sheol.

Who Are in Gehenna?

¹³ Compare David's situation with that experienced by the Greater David, Jesus. One of

---

13. Why is Judas called "the son of destruction"?

14. What does Gehenna represent?
15, 16. Who at death went to Gehenna, and why did they go there?

¹⁶ Adam's firstborn son, Cain, murdered his brother Abel and thereafter lived as a fugitive. The apostle John described Cain as one "who originated with the wicked one." (1 John 3:12) It is reasonable to conclude that like his parents, he went to Gehenna when he died. (Matthew 23:33, 35) What a contrast this is with the situation of righteous Abel! "By faith Abel offered God a sacrifice of greater worth than Cain, through which faith he had witness borne to him that he was righteous, God bearing witness respecting his gifts," explained Paul, adding, "and through it he, although he died, yet speaks." (Hebrews 11:4) Yes, Abel is presently in Sheol awaiting a resurrection.

A "First" and a "Better" Resurrection

¹⁷ Many who read this will wonder about the situation of those who die during this "time of the end." (Daniel 8:19) Revelation chapter 6 describes the ride of four horsemen during that time. Interestingly, the last of these is named Death, and he is followed by Hades. Thus, many who die an untimely death from the activity of the preceding horsemen end up in Hades, there to await a resurrection in God's new world. (Revelation 6:8) What, then, are the prospects for those in Sheol (Hades) and those in Gehenna? Simply put, resurrection for the former; eternal destruction—nonexistence—for the latter.

¹⁸ The apostle John wrote: "Happy and holy is anyone having part in the first resurrection; over these the second death has no authority, but they will be priests of God and of the Christ, and will rule as kings with him for the thousand years." Those who will be corulers with Christ share in "the first resurrection," but what hope is there for the rest of mankind?—Revelation 20:6.

¹⁹ From the days of God's servants Elijah and Elisha, the miracle of the resurrection brought people back to life. "Women received their dead by resurrection," recounted Paul, "but other men were tortured because they would not accept release by some ransom, in order that they might attain a better resurrection." Yes, these faithful integrity-keepers looked forward to a resurrection that would offer them, not just a few more years followed by death, but the prospect of *everlasting life!* That will indeed be "a better resurrection."—Hebrews 11:35.

²⁰ If we die faithful before Jehovah brings an end to this wicked system, we have the sure hope of "a better resurrection," better in the sense that it is one with everlasting life in view. Jesus promised: "Do not marvel at this, because the hour is coming in which all those in the memorial tombs will hear his voice and come out." (John 5:28, 29) Our next article further considers the purpose of the resurrection. It will show how the resurrection hope strengthens us to be integrity-keepers and helps us to develop the spirit of self-sacrifice.

---

17. (a) During this "time of the end," who go to Sheol? (b) What are the prospects for those in Sheol and for those in Gehenna?
18. What prospect does "the first resurrection" offer?
19. How do some benefit from "a better resurrection"?
20. What will the next article consider?

Do You Recall?

- Why is Jehovah described as the God "of the living"?
- What is the condition of those in Sheol?
- What are the prospects for those in Gehenna?
- How will some benefit from "a better resurrection"?

THE RESURRECTION HOPE —WHAT DOES IT MEAN FOR YOU?

"You are opening your hand and satisfying the desire of every living thing."
—PSALM 145:16.

NINE-YEAR-OLD Christopher and his brother had spent the morning, along with their uncle, aunt, and two cousins, calling from house to house in their Christian ministry near Manchester, England. Our companion magazine, *Awake!*, explained what happened. "In the afternoon, they set out together on a sight-seeing trip to Blackpool, a nearby seaside resort. All 6 were among 12 people killed instantly in a motorway crash, described by the police as 'an absolute holocaust.'"

2 The night before the tragedy, the family had attended the Congregation Book Study, where the subject of death had been discussed. "Christopher was always a very thoughtful boy," related his father. "That night, he spoke clearly about a new world and his hope for the future. Then, as our discussion continued, Christopher suddenly said: 'The thing about being one of Jehovah's Witnesses is that while death hurts, we know we will see each other again on earth one day.' Little did any of us present realize how memorable those words were going to be."*

3 Years earlier, in 1940, an Austrian Witness named Franz was faced with the prospect of execution by guillotine for his refusal to be disloyal to Jehovah. Franz wrote to his mother from a Berlin detention center: "With what I knew, if I had taken the [military] oath, I would have committed a sin deserving death. That would be evil to me. I would have no resurrection. . . . And now, my dear Mother and all my brothers and sisters, today I was told my sentence, and don't be terrified, it is death, and I will be executed tomorrow morning. I have my strength from God, the same as it always was with all true Christians away back in the past. . . . If you will stand firm until death, we shall meet again in the resurrection. . . . Until we meet again."*

4 The resurrection hope meant much to both Christopher and Franz. It was real to them. Surely these accounts touch our heart! To deepen our appreciation for Jehovah and to strengthen our hope in the resurrection, let us consider why the resurrection will occur and how this should affect us personally.

Vision of the Earthly Resurrection

5 In a vision of events during the Millennial Reign of Christ Jesus, the apostle John saw the earthly resurrection taking place. "I saw the dead, the great and the small," he report-

---

* See *Awake!* July 8, 1988, page 10, published by Jehovah's Witnesses.

1-3. What hope do some entertain for the future? Illustrate.

---

* *Jehovah's Witnesses—Proclaimers of God's Kingdom*, page 662, published by Jehovah's Witnesses.

---

4. What effect do the experiences related here have on you, and what will we next consider?
5, 6. What does the vision recorded by the apostle John at Revelation 20:12, 13 reveal?

ed. "And the sea gave up those dead in it, and death and Hades gave up those dead in them." (Revelation 20:12, 13) Of whatever rank or station—whether "great" or "small"—all those held captive within Hades (Sheol), the common grave of mankind, will be released. Those who lost their lives at sea will also return to life at that time. This wonderful occurrence is part of Jehovah's purpose.

6 Christ's reign of a thousand years begins with the binding of Satan and his abyssing. None of those resurrected nor any of the survivors of the great tribulation will be misled by Satan during that reign, for he will be inactive. (Revelation 20:1-3) A thousand years may appear to you to be a long time, but in fact, Jehovah views it "as one day." —2 Peter 3:8.

7 According to the vision, Christ's Millennial Reign will be a time for judgment. The apostle John wrote: "I saw the dead, the great and the small, standing before the throne, and scrolls were opened. But another scroll was opened; it is the scroll of life. And the dead were judged out of those things written in the scrolls according to their deeds. . . . And they were judged individually according to their deeds." (Revelation 20:12, 13) Notice that the basis for this judging is not what the person had or had not done before he died. (Romans 6:7) Rather, it relates to "scrolls" that are to be opened. A person's deeds performed after he learns the contents of the scrolls will furnish the basis for determining whether his name is written in "the scroll of life."

"Resurrection of Life" or "Resurrection of Judgment"

8 Earlier in John's vision, Jesus is described as having "the keys of death and of Hades." (Revelation 1:18) He serves as Jehovah's "Chief Agent of life," empowered to judge "the living and the dead." (Acts 3:15; 2 Timothy 4:1) How will he do this? By bringing back to life those who sleep in death. "Do not marvel at this," Jesus said to the crowds to whom he preached, "because the hour is coming in which all those in the memorial tombs will hear his voice and come out." He then added: "Those who did good things to a resurrection of life, those who practiced vile things to a resurrection of judgment." (John 5:28-30) So, what future awaits faithful men and women of old?

9 When these ancient faithful ones return in the resurrection, they will soon find out that the promises they trusted in are now a reality. How interested they will be to learn the identity of the Seed of God's woman, mentioned in the first prophecy in the Bible, at Genesis 3:15! How happy they will be to hear that this promised Messiah, Jesus, proved faithful to death, thereby giving his life as a ransom sacrifice! (Matthew 20:28) Those welcoming them back to life will find great joy in helping them to appreciate that this ransom provision is an expression of Jehovah's undeserved kindness and mercy. When resurrected ones discover what God's Kingdom is accomplishing in fulfilling Jehovah's purpose for the earth, their hearts will no doubt overflow with expressions of praise to Jehovah. They will have ample opportunity to demonstrate their attachment to their loving heavenly Father and his Son. Everyone living will delight in sharing in the vast educational work needed to teach the billions returning from the grave, who will also need to accept God's ransom provision.

---

7. What will be the basis for judgment during Christ's Millennial Reign?
8. What two possible outcomes will there be for the resurrected ones?

---

9. (a) On returning in the resurrection, what will many no doubt learn? (b) What vast educational work will be undertaken?

¹⁰ The resurrected Abraham will find great comfort in experiencing the reality of life under the rule of that "city" to which he looked forward. (Hebrews 11:10) What a thrill faithful Job of old will have when he learns that his life course strengthened other servants of Jehovah who faced tests of their integrity! And how much Daniel will want to know about the fulfillment of the prophecies he was inspired to write!

¹¹ Indeed, all who gain life in the righteous new world, whether by resurrection or by surviving the great tribulation, will have much to learn about Jehovah's purpose for the earth and its inhabitants. The prospect of living forever and praising Jehovah for all eternity will surely make the Millennial education program a real delight. However, it will be what we do individually as we learn the contents of the scrolls that will count the most. Will we apply what we learn? Will we meditate on and take to heart the vital information that will strengthen us to resist Satan's final attempt to divert us from the truth?

¹² Not to be forgotten are the wonderful blessings that will result from the application of the benefits of Christ's ransom sacrifice. Those restored to life in the resurrection will not have the kind of infirmities or disabilities presently experienced. (Isaiah 33:24) A sound body and the prospect of perfect health will allow all inhabitants of the new world to share fully in the educational work of instructing those billions resurrected in the way of life. Those inhabitants will also share in the greatest undertaking ever attempted on earth—that of transforming the whole planet into a paradise to Jehovah's praise.

¹³ When Satan is released from the abyss for the final test, he will try to mislead humans once again. According to Revelation 20:7-9, all the 'misled nations,' or groups of people, who fall under Satan's wicked influence will meet their judgment of destruction: 'Fire will come down out of heaven and devour them.' For those among them who experienced a resurrection during the Millennium, this destruction will make theirs a resurrection of condemnatory judgment. By contrast, resurrected integrity-keepers will receive the gift of everlasting life. Truly, theirs will be "a resurrection of life."—John 5:29.

¹⁴ How can the hope of the resurrection comfort us even now? Indeed, what must we do to ensure that we will receive its benefits in the future?

Lessons to Learn Now

¹⁵ You may recently have lost a loved one in death and may be coping with the big adjustment that such a great loss brings. The resurrection hope helps you to gain an inner calm and strength that those who do not know the truth fail to obtain. "We do not want you to be ignorant concerning those who are sleeping in death," Paul consoled the Thessalonians, "that you may not sorrow just as the rest also do who have no hope." (1 Thessalonians 4:13) Do you see yourself in the new world, witnessing the resurrection? Find comfort now by meditating on the prospect of meeting your loved ones again.

¹⁶ You may at present be suffering the

10, 11. (a) The Millennium will afford what opportunities to all on earth? (b) How should this affect us?
12. What will help each one to have a full share in both the educational work and the transformation of the earth into a paradise?

13, 14. What is the purpose of Satan's release at the final test, and what outcome will be possible for us individually?
15. How can belief in the resurrection be of help now?
16. What may well be your feelings when the resurrection occurs?

How can belief in the resurrection help us now?

physical consequences of Adam's rebellion, perhaps in the form of ill health. Do not let the distress this brings cause you to forget the joyful prospect of personally experiencing the resurrection and coming to life again with renewed health and vigor in the new world. Then when your eyes open and you see welcoming faces eager to share with you their joy at your resurrection, you will not fail to thank God for his loving-kindness.

¹⁷ In the meantime, consider two lessons that we should take to heart. One is the importance of whole-souled service to Jehovah right now. In imitation of our Master, Christ Jesus, our life of self-sacrifice demonstrates love for Jehovah and our neighbors. If opposition or persecution rob us of our livelihood or our freedom, we resolve to remain firm in the faith whatever trials we may face. Should opposers threaten us with death, then the resurrection hope

---

17, 18. What two important lessons should we take to heart?

comforts and strengthens us to remain loyal to Jehovah and his Kingdom. Yes, our zeal for the Kingdom-preaching and disciple-making work keeps us in line for the eternal blessings Jehovah has in store for the righteous.

¹⁸ A second lesson relates to how we face temptations caused by the fallen flesh. Our knowledge of the resurrection hope and our appreciation for Jehovah's undeserved kindness strengthen our resolve to remain firm in the faith. "Do not be loving either the world or the things in the world," warned the apostle John. "If anyone loves the world, the love of the Father is not in him; because everything in the world—the desire of the flesh and the desire of the eyes and the showy display of one's means of life—does not originate with the Father, but originates with the world. Furthermore, the world is passing away and so is its desire, but he that does the will of God remains forever." (1 John 2:15-17) The world's allure in the form of materialism will hold little attraction for us when we compare it to "the real life." (1 Timothy 6:

17-19) If tempted to commit immorality, we will firmly resist. We realize that should we die before Armageddon, a continued course of conduct displeasing to Jehovah could put us in the same position as those who have no prospect of a resurrection.

¹⁹ Above all, we should never forget the inestimable privilege of making Jehovah's heart glad now and forever. (Proverbs 27:11) Our faithfulness until death or our continued integrity-keeping until the end of this wicked system shows Jehovah on whose side of the issue of universal sovereignty we stand. Then what joy it will be to live in the earthly Paradise either by surviving the great tribulation or by experiencing a miraculous resurrection!

Satisfying Our Desires

²⁰ Our discussion of the resurrection leaves some questions unanswered. How will Jehovah arrange matters for those who were married when they died? (Luke 20:34, 35) Will resurrections take place in the area where people died? Will the resurrected come back to life close to their families? A host of other questions about the arrangements for the resurrection remain. Nevertheless, we have to keep in mind the words of Jeremiah: "Good is Jehovah to the one hoping in him, to the soul that keeps seeking for him. Good it is that one should wait, even silently, for the salvation of Jehovah." (Lamentations 3:25, 26) In Jehovah's due time, all will be revealed to our fullest satisfaction. Why can we be sure of this?

²¹ Reflect on the psalmist's inspired words when he sang of Jehovah: "You are opening your hand and satisfying the desire of every

_____
19. What inestimable privilege should we not forget?
20, 21. What will help us to remain faithful even if we have unanswered questions about the resurrection? Explain.

living thing." (Psalm 145:16) As we age, our desires change. What we hoped for when we were children is not our desire today. How we look at life is affected by what we experience as well as by our hopes. Still, whatever our proper desires will be in the new world, Jehovah will certainly satisfy them.

²² What concerns each of us now is to be faithful. "What is looked for in stewards is for a man to be found faithful." (1 Corinthians 4:2) We are stewards of the glorious good news of God's Kingdom. Our diligence in proclaiming this good news to all we meet helps keep us in line for life. Never overlook the fact that "time and unforeseen occurrence" befall us all. (Ecclesiastes 9:11) To counteract any unnecessary anxiety caused by life's uncertainties, hold fast to the glorious hope of the resurrection. Know that if it appears that you are going to die before the start of Christ's Millennial Reign, you can take comfort in the certainty that relief will come. At Jehovah's time you will be able to echo Job's words addressed to the Creator: "You will call, and I myself shall answer you." Praise be to Jehovah, who yearns to bring back to life all those who are in his memory!—Job 14:15.

_____
22. Why do we have good reason for praising Jehovah?

Do You Recall?

- On what basis will people be judged during the Millennium?

- Why will some have "a resurrection of life" and others "a resurrection of judgment"?

- How can the resurrection hope comfort us now?

- How do the words of Psalm 145:16 help us to deal with unanswered questions about the resurrection?

THOUGH WEAK,
I AM POWERFUL

AS TOLD BY
LEOPOLD ENGLEITNER

Foto Hofer, Bad Ischl, Austria

The SS officer drew his pistol, held it to my head, and asked: "Are you ready to die? I'm going to pull the trigger because you're really a hopeless case." "I'm ready," I said, trying to keep my voice steady. I braced myself, closed my eyes, and waited for him to pull the trigger, but nothing happened. "You're even too stupid to die!" he shouted, removing the gun from my temple. How did I end up in such a desperate situation?

I WAS born on July 23, 1905, in the town of Aigen-Voglhub, nestled in the Austrian Alps. I was the eldest son of a sawmill worker and a local farmer's daughter. My parents were poor but hardworking people. My early years were spent in Bad Ischl, near Salzburg, amid scenic lakes and breathtaking summits.

As a child, I would often muse about life's injustices, not only because my family was poor but also because I suffered from congenital curvature of the spine. The backache caused by this disorder made it almost impossible for me to stand erect. At school, I was barred from gymnastics and thus became a target of ridicule among my classmates.

At the end of World War I, just shy of the age of 14, I decided that it was time to look for a job in order to escape poverty. Gnawing hunger was my constant companion, and I was weakened by bouts of high fever caused by the Spanish flu, which had sent millions to the grave. "What use could we possibly have for a weakling like you?" is how most farmers reacted to my request for work. However, one kind farmer did hire me.

Thrilled by God's Love

Even though Mother was a devout Catholic, I rarely went to church, mainly because my father had liberal views on the matter. As for me, I was disturbed by the worship of images, so widely practiced in the Roman Catholic Church.

One day in October 1931, a friend asked me to accompany him to a religious meeting sponsored by the Bible Students, as Jehovah's Witnesses were then known. There, I was given Bible answers to important questions, such as: Is image worship pleasing to God? (Exodus 20:4, 5) Is there a fiery hell? (Ecclesiastes 9:5) Will the dead be resurrected?—John 5:28, 29.

What most impressed me was the fact that God does not condone man's bloodthirsty wars, even if they are said to be fought in His name. I learned that "God is love" and that he has an exalted name, Jehovah. (1 John 4:8; Psalm 83:18) I was thrilled to find out that by means of Jehovah's Kingdom, humans will be able to live forever in happiness in an earth-wide paradise. I also learned of the marvelous prospect open to some imperfect humans who have been called by God to share with Jesus in God's heavenly Kingdom. I was prepared to give my all for that Kingdom. So in May 1932, I was baptized and became one of Jehovah's Witnesses. That step required courage, considering the religious intolerance prevailing in the strictly Catholic Austria of the time.

Facing Contempt and Opposition

My parents were horrified when I quit the church, and the priest was quick to spread the news from the pulpit. Neighbors would spit on the ground in front of me to show their contempt. Nevertheless, I was determined to join the ranks of full-time ministers, and I started pioneering in January 1934.

The political situation became increasingly tense because of the strong influence the Nazi party was gaining in our province. During my pioneer days in the Styrian Valley of Enns, the police were hot on my heels, and I had to be 'cautious as a serpent.' (Matthew 10:16) From 1934 to 1938, persecution was an inseparable part of my daily life. Though I was unemployed, I was denied unemployment compensation, and I was sentenced to several short and four longer prison terms because of my preaching activity.

Hitler's Troops Occupy Austria

In March 1938, Hitler's troops marched into Austria. Within a few days, over 90,000 people—about 2 percent of the adult population—were arrested and sent to prisons and concentration camps, accused of opposing the Nazi regime. Jehovah's Witnesses were somewhat prepared for what was in store. In the summer of 1937, several members of my home congregation made the 220-mile trip to Prague by bicycle to attend an international convention. There they heard of the atrocities perpetrated against our fellow believers in Germany. Clearly, now it was our turn.

From the day Hitler's troops set foot in Austria, the meetings and the preaching activity of Jehovah's Witnesses were forced underground. Though Bible literature was being smuggled across the Swiss border, there was not enough to go around. So fellow Christians in Vienna would secretly produce literature. I often served as a courier, delivering literature to the Witnesses.

To a Concentration Camp

On April 4, 1939, three fellow Christians

Arrested by the Gestapo, April 1939

and I were arrested by the Gestapo while we were observing the Memorial of Christ's death in Bad Ischl. We were all taken by car to State police headquarters in Linz. That was my very first car ride, but I was too troubled to enjoy it. In Linz, I was submitted to a series of excruciating interrogations, but I did not renounce my faith. Five months later, I was brought before the examining justice in Upper Austria. Unexpectedly, criminal proceedings against me were dropped; yet that was not the end of my ordeal. In the meantime, the other three were sent to concentration camps, where they died, remaining faithful to the end.

I was kept in custody, and on October 5, 1939, I was notified that I would be taken to the Buchenwald concentration camp in Germany. A special train awaited us prisoners at the Linz train station. The boxcars were equipped with two-man cells. The man who shared the cell with me was none other than the former governor of Upper Austria, Dr. Heinrich Gleissner.

Dr. Gleissner and I struck up an interesting conversation. He was sincerely interested in my plight and was appalled that even

Gestapo document with charges, May 1939

Both images: Privatarchiv; B. Rammerstorfer

during his time in office, Jehovah's Witnesses faced countless legal problems in his province. He stated regretfully: "Mr. Engleitner, I cannot undo the wrong, but I do want to apologize. It seems that our government was guilty of a miscarriage of justice. Should you ever need any help, I would be more than willing to do what I can." Our paths crossed again after the war. He helped me to receive government retirement pay for Nazi victims.

"I'm Going to Shoot You"

On October 9, 1939, I arrived at the Buchenwald concentration camp. Shortly thereafter, the bunker attendant was informed that a Witness was among the newcomers, and I became his target. He ruthlessly beat me. Then, after realizing that he could not make me renounce my faith, he said: "I'm going to shoot you, Engleitner. But before I do, I'm going to let you write a farewell card to your parents." I thought of words of comfort I could write to my folks, but every time I put the pen to the paper, he knocked my right elbow, causing me to scribble. He jeered: "Such an idiot! He can't even write two straight lines. But that doesn't keep him from reading the Bible, does it?"

Next the attendant drew his pistol, held it to my head, and made me believe that he was going to pull the trigger, as I related at the outset of this account. Then he crammed me into a small, overcrowded cell. I had to spend the night standing. But

I could not have slept anyway, since my whole body was aching. "Dying for some stupid religion is really such a waste!" was the only "comfort" my cell mates had to offer. Dr. Gleissner was in the adjacent cell. He heard what had happened and pensively said, "The persecution of Christians is once again rearing its ugly head!"

In the summer of 1940, all prisoners were ordered to report for quarry duty on a Sunday, even though we usually had Sundays off. This was a retaliatory measure for some inmates' "misdemeanors." We were ordered to carry large stones from the quarry into the camp. Two prisoners were trying to place a huge stone on my back, and I nearly collapsed under the weight. However, Arthur Rödl, the feared *Lagerführer* (camp supervisor), unexpectedly came to the rescue. Seeing my agonizing efforts to carry the stone, he said to me: "You'll never make it back to the camp with that stone on your back! Put it down immediately!" That was an order I was relieved to obey. Then Rödl pointed to a much smaller stone, saying: "Pick that one up, and bring it into the camp. It's easier to carry!" Afterward, turning to our supervisor, he ordered: "Let the Bible Students return to their barracks. They've worked enough for one day!"

At the end of each workday, I was always happy to associate with my spiritual family. We had arrangements for distributing spiritual food. A brother would write a Bible verse on a scrap of paper and pass it on to the others. A Bible had also been smuggled into the camp. It was taken apart and divided into individual books. For three months I was entrusted with the book of Job. I hid it in my socks. The account of Job helped me to remain steadfast.

Finally, on March 7, 1941, I joined a large convoy that was transferred to the Niederhagen concentration camp. My condition was getting worse by the day. One day, two brothers and I were ordered to pack tools into crates. After doing that, we accompanied another group of inmates back to the barracks. An SS man noticed that I was lagging behind. He got so furious that he brutally kicked me from behind without warning, causing serious injury. The pain was excruciating, but despite the pain I went to work the next day.

Unexpected Release

In April of 1943, the Niederhagen camp was finally evacuated. Following that, I was transferred to the death camp at Ravensbrück. Then, in June 1943, I was unexpect-

Nearby mountains provided refuge

edly offered the opportunity of a discharge from the concentration camp. This time, release was not conditional on my abjuring my faith. I just had to agree to do forced labor on a farm for the rest of my life. I was willing to do that to escape the horrors of the camp. I went to the camp doctor for a final checkup. The doctor was surprised to see me. "Why, you're still one of Jehovah's Witnesses!" he exclaimed. "You're right, Herr Doctor," I answered. "Well, in that case I don't see why we should give you a discharge. On the other hand, it would be such a relief to get rid of a wretched creature like you."

His description was no exaggeration. My state of health was truly wretched. My skin had been partly eaten away by lice, beatings had left me deaf in one ear, and my whole body was covered with festering sores. After 46 months of deprivation, endless hunger, and forced labor, I weighed only 54 pounds. In that condition, I was discharged from Ravensbrück on July 15, 1943.

I was sent back to my hometown by train without a guard to escort me, and I reported to Gestapo headquarters in Linz. The Gestapo officer gave me my discharge papers and warned me: "If you think that we are releasing you so that you can persist in your underground activity, you are sadly mistaken! God help you if we ever catch you preaching."

I was home at last! My mother had not changed a thing in my room since I was first arrested, on April 4, 1939. Even my Bible lay open on my bedside table! I got on my knees and said a heartfelt prayer of thanks.

I was soon assigned to work on a mountain farm. The farmer, a childhood friend, even paid me a small salary, though he was not obliged to do so. Before the war, this friend had given me permission to hide some Bible literature on his premises. I was happy to make good use of that small literature depot to gain strength spiritually. All my needs were satisfied, and I was determined to wait out the war on the farm.

Hiding in the Mountains

Those calm days of freedom were short-lived, however. In mid-August 1943, I was ordered to report to a military doctor for a medical examination. First, he declared that I was unfit for active service because of my bad back. However, a week later the same doctor revised his findings to read: "Fit for active service on the front lines." The army lost track of me for a while, but on April 17, 1945, shortly before the end of the war, it finally caught up with me. I was drafted for service on the front lines.

Equipped with a few provisions and a Bible, I sought refuge in the nearby mountains. At first, I was able to sleep outdoors, but the weather took a turn for the worse, and two feet of snow fell. I got soaked to the skin. I made it to a mountain cabin located at nearly 4,000 feet above sea level. Shivering, I got a fire going in the fireplace, and I was able to warm myself and dry my clothing. Exhausted, I fell asleep on a bench in front of the fireplace. Before long, I was abruptly awakened by intense pain. I had caught fire! I rolled around on the floor to

IN OUR NEXT ISSUE

A World Without Poverty Is Near

———

Mari—Ancient Queen of the Desert

———

'Keep Yourself Restrained Under Evil'

extinguish the flames. My whole back was covered with blisters.

At great risk, I sneaked back to the mountain farm before daybreak, but the farmer's wife was so scared that she sent me away, telling me that a manhunt was on to find me. So I went to my parents. At first, even my parents hesitated to take me in, but they finally let me sleep in the hayloft, and Mother tended to my wounds. After two days, however, my parents were so uneasy that I decided it would be best to hide in the mountains again.

On May 5, 1945, I was awakened by a loud noise. I caught sight of Allied airplanes flying low. At that moment, I knew that Hitler's regime had been overthrown! Jehovah's spirit had strengthened me to endure an unbelievable ordeal. I had experienced the truth of the words recorded at Psalm 55:22, which had comforted me so much at the outset of my trials. I had 'thrown my burden upon Jehovah,' and though I was physically weak, he had sustained me as I walked through "the valley of deep shadow."—Psalm 23:4.

Jehovah's Power "Made Perfect in Weakness"

After the war, life slowly got back to normal. At first, I worked as a hired hand on my farmer friend's mountain farm. It was only after the U.S. occupation army intervened in April 1946 that I was released from my obligation to perform forced agricultural labor for the rest of my life.

At the end of the war, Christian brothers in Bad Ischl and the surrounding district started holding meetings regularly. They began preaching with renewed vigor. I was offered employment as a night watchman in a factory and was thus able to continue pioneering. Eventually, I settled down in the St. Wolfgang area, and in 1949, I married Theresia Kurz, who had a daughter by a former marriage. We were together for 32 years until my dear wife died in 1981. I had cared for her for over seven years.

After Theresia's death, I resumed the pioneer service, which helped me get over the great sense of loss. I am presently serving as a pioneer and an elder in my congregation in Bad Ischl. Since I am confined to a wheelchair, I offer Bible literature and talk to people about the Kingdom hope in the Bad Ischl park or in front of my own home. The fine Bible discussions I have are a source of great joy to me.

In retrospect, I can attest that the dreadful experiences I was forced to endure did not embitter me. Of course, there were times when I felt downcast because of the trials. However, my warm relationship with Jehovah God helped me get over such negative periods. The Lord's admonition to Paul, "My power is being made perfect in weakness" proved true in my life too. Now, at the age of nearly 100, I can join the apostle Paul in saying: "I take pleasure in weaknesses, in insults, in cases of need, in persecutions and difficulties, for Christ. For when I am weak, then I am powerful."—2 Corinthians 12: 9, 10.

Questions From Readers

Why did Paul write regarding a Christian wife: "She will be kept safe through childbearing"?—1 Timothy 2:15.

What does the context of this verse reveal about what Paul meant? Under inspiration he was giving counsel on the role of the Christian woman in the congregation. He wrote: "I desire the women to adorn themselves in well-arranged dress, with modesty and soundness of mind, not with styles of hair braiding and gold or pearls or very expensive garb, but in the way that befits women professing to reverence God, namely, through good works." (1 Timothy 2:9, 10) Paul was urging his Christian sisters to be modest, to be balanced in choosing personal adornment, and to be 'adorned' with good works.

Next, Paul explained the headship arrangement in the congregation, saying: "I do not permit a woman to teach, or to exercise authority over a man, but to be in silence." (1 Timothy 2:12; 1 Corinthians 11:3) He explains the basis for this arrangement by showing that while Adam was not deceived by Satan, Eve "was thoroughly deceived and came to be in transgression." How could a Christian woman be protected against Eve's error? Paul answers: "However, she will be kept safe through childbearing, provided they continue in faith and love and sanctification along with soundness of mind." (1 Timothy 2:14, 15) What did Paul mean by these words?

Some translators seem to imply that a woman's salvation depends on her having children. For example, *Today's English Version* says: "A woman will be saved through having children." However, this interpretation of Paul's words is not accurate. Many scriptures show that to be saved, a person must come to know Jehovah, believe in Jesus, and exercise faith, demonstrating that faith by works. (John 17:3; Acts 16:30, 31; Romans 10:10; James 2:26) In addition, Paul did not mean that safe childbirth is guaranteed to believing women. Women have come safely through the experience of giving birth whether they were believers or not. And sadly, some have died giving birth, whether they were believers or not.—Genesis 35:16-18.

Paul's additional counsel regarding women later in this same letter helps us to understand what he meant. He warns of some younger widows who were "unoccupied, gadding about to the houses; yes, not only unoccupied, but also gossipers and meddlers in other people's affairs, talking of things they ought not." What was Paul's advice? He continues: "Therefore I desire the younger widows to marry, to bear children, to manage a household, to give no inducement to the opposer to revile."—1 Timothy 5:13, 14.

Paul highlights the positive role of women in the family arrangement. Occupied with such activities as 'bearing children and managing a household,' a woman who continued "in faith and love and sanctification along with soundness of mind" would not gravitate toward conduct that is not upbuilding. Her spirituality would be preserved, or "kept safe." (1 Timothy 2:15) Following such a course would help many young women to avoid Satan's snares.

Paul's words to Timothy remind all of us, men and women, to be profitably occupied. God's Word advises all Christians: "Keep strict watch that how you walk is not as unwise but as wise persons."—Ephesians 5:15.

COURAGE IN THE FACE OF OPPOSITION

A FANATIC mob had forced Gaius and Aristarchus, two companions of the apostle Paul, to enter the theater of Ephesus. There, the enraged crowd shouted for two hours: "Great is Artemis of the Ephesians!" (Acts 19:28, 29, 34) Did Paul's companions stand firm in the face of this opposition? And what had caused this situation in the first place?

Paul had successfully preached in the city of Ephesus for about three years. As a result, many Ephesians had stopped worshiping idols. (Acts 19:26; 20:31) The typical idol of Ephesus was a small silver shrine of Artemis, the goddess of fertility, whose magnificent temple overlooked the city. These small representations of the temple were worn as amulets or were set up in homes. Christians, of course, would not buy these idols.—1 John 5:21.

Demetrius, one of the silversmiths, believed that Paul's ministry threatened their lucrative business. By means of half-truths and exaggerations, he convinced fellow craftsmen that people throughout Asia Minor would stop worshiping Artemis. Once the angry silversmiths began shouting the praises of Artemis, a veritable riot broke out and the whole city was thrown into confusion.—Acts 19:24-29.

Thousands of people converged on the theater, which could seat 25,000 spectators. Paul offered to address the unruly mob, but friendly officials convinced him otherwise. Finally, the city recorder succeeded in calming the crowd, and Gaius and Aristarchus escaped unharmed.—Acts 19:35-41.

Today, God's people may also face opposers and even riots as they carry on their ministry. They often preach the good news in cities where an atmosphere of idolatry, immorality, and delinquency prevails. Nevertheless, they courageously imitate the apostle Paul, who 'did not hold back from teaching publicly and from house to house' in the city of Ephesus. (Acts 20:20) And they likewise rejoice when they see that 'the word of Jehovah keeps growing and prevailing.'—Acts 19:20.

Ruins of the theater at Ephesus

Erna Ludolph (seated) with members of the Holtz family

Triumphant
in a Special Way

D O YOU encounter opposition to your faith—perhaps at work, at school, in the family, or because of restrictions imposed by the State? Then do not lose heart. Many of Jehovah's Witnesses have faced similar trials, yet they came off triumphant. Consider the example of Erna Ludolph.

Erna was born in Lübeck, Germany, in 1908. She was the only member of her family who served Jehovah. When the Hitler regime came to power in 1933, life became difficult for Jehovah's Witnesses. Erna's colleagues at work denounced her for refusing to give the Hitler salute, and this led to her arrest by the Nazis. She spent eight years in various prisons and in the concentration camps at Hamburg-Fuhlsbüttel, Moringen, Lichtenburg, and Ravensbrück. While Erna was in Ravensbrück, something happened that led to her coming off triumphant.

Housekeeper With a Difference

Professor Friedrich Holtz and his wife, Alice, lived in Berlin. They were not members of the Nazi party and did not support its ideology. However, they were related to a senior SS official who was responsible for certain concentration camp inmates. So when the professor and his wife were looking for a housekeeper, this SS officer allowed them to choose a female prisoner. Thus, in March 1943, Alice visited Ravensbrück to select a housekeeper. Whom did she choose? Erna Ludolph. Erna moved in with the Holtz family, who treated her well. After the war ended, she moved with the same family to Halle on the Saale. There, once again Erna met with opposition, this time from the Socialist authorities in East Germany. In 1957 the family was deported to West Germany, and Erna moved with them. At last Erna was free to practice her faith.

How did Erna come off triumphant in a special way? As a result of Erna's fine conduct and skillful preaching of the Bible's message, Alice Holtz and her five children all became baptized Witnesses of Jehovah. Furthermore, 11 of Alice's grandchildren are also Witnesses. Two of them currently serve in the branch office of Jehovah's Witnesses in Selters, Germany. "Our family is in the truth largely because of Erna's example," says Susanne, one of Alice's daughters. Erna's endurance was richly rewarded. What about your situation? Your faithful endurance under difficult circumstances may have similar rewarding results. Yes, fine conduct and skillful preaching might help you to come off triumphant in a special way.*

---

* While this article was being prepared for publication, Erna Ludolph passed away at age 96. She was faithful to the end.

How to Make Each Day Count

"SHOW us just how to count our days in such a way that we may bring a heart of wisdom in." (Psalm 90:12) This was the humble prayer of the Bible writer Moses. What specifically was he asking for? Should we make a similar worshipful request?

In verse 10, Moses lamented the shortness of the human life span. On another occasion, he recorded the testimony of Job, who said: "Man, born of woman, is short-lived and glutted with agitation." (Job 14:1) It is evident that Moses was painfully aware of the transitory nature of imperfect human life. Therefore, he viewed each day of life as a precious resource. In directing this plea to God, Moses expressed his desire to live his remaining days wisely, in a way that would please his Creator. Should not we too seek to spend our days meaningfully? That will be our endeavor if we want God's approval now.

There was an additional factor that motivated both Moses and Job, a factor that should also motivate us. Both of these godly men looked forward to a future reward—life on earth under better conditions. (Job 14:14, 15; Hebrews 11:26) At that time, no one's good works will be cut short by death. Our Creator purposes that faithful ones will live forever on a paradise earth. (Isaiah 65:21-24; Revelation 21: 3, 4) This can be *your* prospect too if you 'count your days in such a way that you may bring a heart of wisdom in.'

THE WATCHTOWER

ANNOUNCING JEHOVAH'S KINGDOM

MAY 15, 2005

A WORLD WITHOUT POVERTY IS NEAR

THE WATCHTOWER®
ANNOUNCING JEHOVAH'S KINGDOM

May 15, 2005   Average Printing Each Issue: 26,439,000   Vol. 126, No. 10

THE PURPOSE OF *THE WATCHTOWER* is to exalt Jehovah God as Sovereign Lord of the universe. It keeps watch on world events as these fulfill Bible prophecy. It comforts all peoples with the good news that God's Kingdom will soon destroy those who oppress their fellowmen and that it will turn the earth into a paradise. It encourages faith in God's now-reigning King, Jesus Christ, whose shed blood opens the way for mankind to gain eternal life. *The Watchtower,* published by Jehovah's Witnesses continuously since 1879, is nonpolitical. It adheres to the Bible as its authority.

IN THIS ISSUE

3   Can Man Bring an End to Poverty?

4   A World Without Poverty Is Near

8   Families Fortified by the Knowledge of God

10   Mari—Ancient Queen of the Desert

14   Common Sense—Why So Uncommon?

16   Jehovah's Word Is Alive—Highlights From the Book of Second Samuel

20   Coming to Know Jehovah's Ways

25   'Keep Yourself Restrained Under Evil'

31   Questions From Readers

32   On What Foundation Are You Building?

WATCHTOWER STUDIES

JUNE 20-26:
Coming to Know Jehovah's Ways.
Page 20. Songs to be used: 61, 48.

JUNE 27–JULY 3:
'Keep Yourself Restrained Under Evil.'
Page 25. Songs to be used: 36, 124.

Publication of *The Watchtower* is part of a worldwide Bible educational work supported by voluntary donations.

Unless otherwise indicated, Scripture quotations are from the modern-language *New World Translation of the Holy Scriptures—With References.*

The Watchtower (ISSN 0043-1087) is published semimonthly by Watchtower Bible and Tract Society of New York, Inc.; M. H. Larson, President; G. F. Simonis, Secretary-Treasurer; 25 Columbia Heights, Brooklyn, NY 11201-2483. Periodicals Postage Paid at Brooklyn, NY, and at additional mailing offices. POSTMASTER: Send address changes to Watchtower, **Wallkill, NY 12589.**

Changes of address should reach us 30 days before your moving date. Give us your old and new address (if possible, your old address label).

Semimonthly   ENGLISH

Would you welcome more information or a free home Bible study? Please send your request to Jehovah's Witnesses, using the appropriate address below.

America, United States of: Wallkill, NY 12589. **Antigua:** Box 119, St. Johns. **Australia:** Box 280, Ingleburn, NSW 1890. **Bahamas:** Box N-1247, Nassau, N.P. **Barbados, W.I.:** Crusher Site Road, Prospect, St. James. **Britain:** The Ridgeway, London NW7 1RN. **Canada:** Box 4100, Halton Hills (Georgetown), Ontario L7G 4Y4. **Germany:** Niederselters, Am Steinfels, D-65618 Selters. **Ghana:** P. O. Box GP 760, Accra. **Guyana:** 352-360 Tyrell St., Republic Park Phase 2 EBD. **Hawaii 96819:** 2055 Kam IV Rd., Honolulu. **Hong Kong:** 4 Kent Road, Kowloon Tong. **India:** Post Box 6440, Yelahanka, Bangalore 560 064, KAR. **Ireland:** Newcastle, Greystones, Co. Wicklow. **Jamaica:** P. O. Box 103, Old Harbour, St. Catherine. **Japan:** 1271 Nakashinden, Ebina City, Kanagawa Pref., 243-0496. **Kenya:** P.O. Box 47788, GPO Nairobi 00100. **New Zealand:** P.O. Box 75-142, Manurewa. **Nigeria:** P.M.B. 1090, Benin City 300001, Edo State. **Philippines, Republic of:** P. O. Box 2044, 1060 Manila. **South Africa:** Private Bag X2067, Krugersdorp, 1740. **Trinidad and Tobago, Republic of:** Lower Rapsey Street & Laxmi Lane, Curepe. **Zambia:** Box 33459, Lusaka 10101. **Zimbabwe:** Private Bag WG-5001, Westgate.

NOW PUBLISHED IN 150 LANGUAGES. SEMIMONTHLY: Afrikaans, Albanian,* Amharic, Arabic, Bengali, Bicol, Bislama, Bulgarian, Cebuano,* Chichewa,* Chinese, Chinese (Simplified),* Cibemba,* Croatian,* Czech,*# Danish,*# Dutch,*# East Armenian, Efik,* English*#+◎ (also Braille), Estonian, Ewe, Fijian, Finnish,*# French,*# Ga, Georgian, German,*# Greek,* Gujarati, Gun, Hebrew, Hiligaynon, Hindi, Hungarian,*# Igbo,* Iloko,* Indonesian, Italian,*# Japanese*# (also Braille), Kannada, Kinyarwanda, Kirundi, Korean*# (also Braille), Latvian, Lingala, Lithuanian, Luvale, Macedonian, Malagasy,* Malayalam, Maltese, Myanmar, Nepali, New Guinea Pidgin, Norwegian,*# Pangasinan, Papiamento (Aruba), Papiamento (Curaçao), Polish,*# Portuguese*# (also Braille), Punjabi, Rarotongan, Romanian,* Russian,* Samar-Leyte, Samoan, Sango, Sepedi, Serbian, Sesotho, Shona,* Silozi, Sinhala, Slovak,* Slovenian, Solomon Islands Pidgin, Spanish*# (also Braille), Sranantongo, Swahili,* Swedish,*# Tagalog,* Tamil, Telugu, Thai, Tigrinya, Tongan, Tshiluba, Tsonga, Tswana, Turkish, Twi, Ukrainian,* Urdu, Vietnamese, Wallisian, Xhosa, Yoruba,* Zulu*

MONTHLY: American Sign Language,△□ Armenian, Assamese, Azerbaijani (roman script), Brazilian Sign Language,△ Cambodian, Chitonga, Gilbertese, Greenlandic, Haitian Creole, Hausa, Hiri Motu, Icelandic, Isoko, Kaonde, Kazakh, Kikongo, Kiluba, Kirghiz, Kosraean, Kwanyama/Ndonga, Luganda, Marathi, Marshallese, Mauritian Creole, Maya, Mizo, Monokutuba, Moore, Niuean, Ossetian, Otetela, Palauan, Persian, Ponapean, Seychelles Creole, Tahitian, Tatar, Tiv, Trukese, Tumbuka, Tuvaluan, Umbundu, Venda, Yapese, Zande

* Study articles also available in large-print edition.
# Audiocassettes also available.
+ CD also available.
◎ MP3 CD-ROM also available.
△ Videocassette
□ DVD

Can **Man** Bring an
END TO POVERTY?

MILLIONS have grown up without experiencing poverty. They have never had to go to bed hungry or fall asleep shivering from the cold. Still, many of those individuals feel sorry for the poor and go out of their way to help them.

Poverty, however, remains a harsh reality for people who are plagued by civil war, floods, droughts, and other problems. These factors are a nightmare to African subsistence farmers. Some have been forced to leave their homes and move to big cities or to live as refugees in a new country. Other rural dwellers move to cities because they are enticed by promises of a better life.

Overcrowded cities often become breeding grounds for poverty. There is very little space, if any at all, to plant crops. Employment is usually hard to find. Out of sheer desperation, many turn to a life of crime. City dwellers cry out for help, but human governments are unable to solve the growing problem of poverty. Referring to a United Nations report released in November 2003, *The Independent* of London stated: "The world is getting hungrier." It added: "Across the world an estimated 842 million people are today undernourished—and that figure is again climbing, with an additional 5 million hungry people every year."

The South Africa branch office of Jehovah's Witnesses at times receives letters from poverty-stricken people. For example, a man from Bloemfontein wrote: "I'm unemployed, and I steal in the city whenever there's a chance. If I don't, we are hungry for days—not to mention the bitter cold. There's absolutely no work. Many are roaming the streets in search of work and something to eat. I know of others who search the dustbins for food. Some commit suicide. Many like me are depressed and hopeless. It seems that there's no hope for the future. Does God, who created us with the need to eat and clothe ourselves, not see this?"

There are comforting answers to this man's concerns. As the following article will show, these answers are found in the pages of God's Word, the Bible.

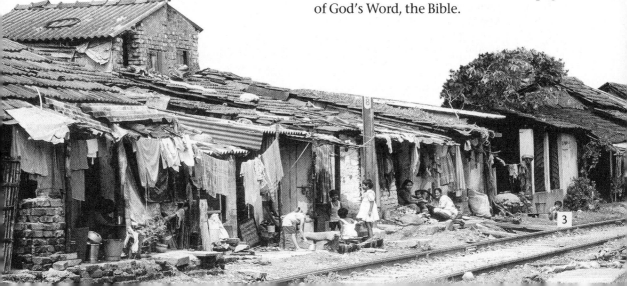

A World
WITHOUT POVERTY
Is Near

PICTURES of Paradise, such as the one on the cover of this magazine, appeal to people who live in poverty. A paradise was a reality for the first human couple, Adam and Eve. Their home was the garden of Eden. (Genesis 2:7-23) Although that Paradise was lost, belief in a future paradise—in a new world without poverty—is not just a dream. It is solidly based on the promises contained in the Bible.

Consider the promise that Jesus Christ made on the last day of his life on earth. One of the evildoers who died with Jesus showed faith in God's ability to solve man's problems. He said: "Jesus, remember me when you get into your kingdom." These words show that the evildoer believed that Jesus would rule as King and that the dead would be brought back to life. Jesus answered: "Truly I tell you today, You will be with me in Paradise."—Luke 23:42, 43.

Speaking of those who will live in Paradise, the Bible states: "They will certainly build houses and have occupancy; and they will certainly plant vineyards and eat their fruitage." (Isaiah 65:21) Yes, "they will actually sit, each one under his vine and under his fig tree, and there will be no one making them tremble; for the very mouth of Jehovah of armies has spoken it."—Micah 4:4.

Why, though, is poverty permitted to exist now? What help does God give to the poverty-stricken? When will poverty finally end?

Why Has Poverty Been Permitted?

The Paradise that Adam and Eve were placed in was lost as a result of the rebellion initiated by a wicked angel, Satan the Devil. Using a serpent as his mouthpiece, Satan seduced Eve into breaking God's law against eating the fruit of a certain tree. He deceived her into believing that independence from God would bring her a better life. When Eve offered the forbidden fruit to Adam, he too ate, turning his back on God in favor of his wife.—Genesis 3:1-6; 1 Timothy 2:14.

The rebellious couple were rightly driven out of Paradise and from then on had to struggle to survive. Until today, Jehovah has allowed Satan to rule over sinful mankind, making evident the results of disobedience to God. Human history has proved that mankind cannot bring about Paradise on earth. (Jeremiah 10:23) Rather, independence from God has resulted in

Tukiso and Maseiso with the missionary who studied the Bible with Tukiso

Maseiso at the door of her home with the missionary who studied the Bible with her

disastrous problems, including poverty.—Ecclesiastes 8:9.

However, the poor are not left helpless in this trouble-filled world. God's inspired Word, the Bible, contains sound guidance for them.

"Never Be Anxious"

When speaking to a large audience that included many poor people, Jesus said: "Observe intently the birds of heaven, because they do not sow seed or reap or gather into storehouses; still your heavenly Father feeds them. Are you not worth more than they are? . . . So never be anxious and say, 'What are we to eat?' or, 'What are we to drink?' or, 'What are we to put on?' For all these are the things the nations are eagerly pursuing. For your heavenly Father knows you need all these things. Keep on, then, seeking first the kingdom and his righteousness, and all these other things will be added to you."—Matthew 6:26-33.

A poor person does not need to steal. (Proverbs 6:30, 31) He will be provided for if he puts God first in his life. Consider the case of Tukiso, a man in Lesotho, southern Africa. In 1998, foreign troops entered Lesotho to quell an uprising against the government. As a result of that war, shops were looted, people lost their jobs, and there were dire food shortages.

Tukiso lived in the poorest part of the capital. Many of his neighbors had looted shops in order to survive. When Tukiso came back to his one-room dwelling place, he found that Maseiso, the woman with whom he was living, had many goods that she had looted. "Take these things outside," Tukiso said, explaining that it was against God's law to steal. Maseiso obeyed. The neighbors mocked them and helped themselves to the stolen food.

Tukiso took this stand because of what he had learned in his study of the Bible with Jehovah's Witnesses. Did his obedience to God's law result in starvation? No. Some time later, the elders in the congregation of Jehovah's Witnesses that he attended made contact with Tukiso and brought him some food. In fact, Jehovah's Witnesses in neighboring South Africa had sent more than two tons of relief aid for their Christian brothers and sisters in Lesotho. Maseiso was moved by Tukiso's obedience to God and by the loving aid of the congregation. She too began to study the Bible. Eventually, the two of them got legally married and thus qualified to be baptized as Jehovah's Witnesses. They are still serving God faithfully.

Jehovah God cares for the poor. (See the box entitled "How Does God View the Poor?") He has lovingly made provision to help others like Tukiso and Maseiso to learn more about him. And in his Word, he has provided practical advice for day-to-day living.

A Fine Provision

Jehovah's Witnesses have always tried to reflect God's concern for the poor. (Galatians 2:10) Often when disaster strikes a land and true Christians are affected, arrangements are made for necessary help to be given. More important, the Witnesses show concern for the spiritual needs of all, including the poor. (Matthew 9:36-38) During the past 60 years, thousands of trained ministers have volunteered to serve as missionaries in foreign lands. For example, it was a missionary couple from Finland who by learning the Sesotho language were able to teach Tukiso and Maseiso to become disciples of Jesus. (Matthew 28:19, 20) Such missionary work often involves sacrificing a comfortable life in an affluent country and moving to a poor land.

Stealing to survive is not an option for true Christians. Instead, they have faith in Jehovah God's ability to provide. (Hebrews 13:5, 6) One way that Jehovah provides for his people is through the worldwide organization of his worshipers, who care for one another.

Another way that Jehovah helps the poor is by giving them practical advice on daily living. For example, the Bible commands:

HOW DOES GOD VIEW THE POOR?

The Bible describes the Creator of mankind as "the One giving bread to the hungry ones." (Psalm 146:7) It contains over one hundred verses that highlight God's concern for the poor.

For instance, when Jehovah gave his Law to the ancient nation of Israel, he commanded Israelite farmers not to harvest the edges of their fields completely. They were not to collect leftover fruit by going over an olive tree or a vine a second time. These laws were a loving provision for aliens, orphans, widows, and other afflicted ones.—Leviticus 19:9, 10; Deuteronomy 24:19-21.

Moreover, God commanded the Israelites: "You people must not afflict any widow or fatherless boy. If you should afflict him at all, then if he cries out to me at all, I shall unfailingly hear his outcry; and my anger will indeed blaze, and I shall certainly kill you with the sword, and your wives must become widows and your sons fatherless boys." (Exodus 22:22-24) Sadly, many wealthy Israelites ignored those words. For this and other wrongdoing, Jehovah God gave the Israelites various warnings through his prophets. (Isaiah 10:1, 2; Jeremiah 5:28; Amos 4:1-3) Eventually, God caused the Assyrians and later the Babylonians to conquer Israelite territory. Many Israelites were killed, and the survivors were taken captive to foreign lands.

God's beloved Son, Jesus Christ, reflected his Father's loving concern for the poor. Explaining the purpose of his ministry, Jesus said: "Jehovah's spirit is upon me, because he anointed me to declare good news to the poor." (Luke 4:18) This does not mean that Jesus limited his ministry to the poor. He lovingly helped rich people too. However, when doing so, Jesus often expressed his concern for the poor. For example, he gave this advice to one rich ruler: "Sell all the things you have and distribute to poor people, and you will have treasure in the heavens; and come be my follower."—Luke 14:1, 12-14; 18:18, 22; 19:1-10.

"Let the stealer steal no more, but rather let him do hard work, doing with his hands what is good work, that he may have something to distribute to someone in need." (Ephesians 4:28) Many unemployed people have been able to create jobs for themselves, doing hard work, such as planting and caring for a vegetable garden. The Bible also helps poor people to save money by teaching them to avoid bad habits, such as the abuse of alcohol.—Ephesians 5:18.

A World Without Poverty—When?

The Bible indicates that we are living in "the last days" of Satan's rule. (2 Timothy 3:1) Soon, Jehovah God will send Jesus Christ to judge mankind. What will happen at that time? Jesus gave the answer in one of his illustrations. He said: "When the Son of man arrives in his glory, and all the angels with him, then he will sit down on his glorious throne. And all the nations will be gathered before him, and he will separate people one from another, just as a shepherd separates the sheep from the goats."—Matthew 25:31-33.

The sheep of this illustration are those who submit to Jesus' kingship. Jesus likened them to sheep because they follow him as their Shepherd. (John 10:16) These sheeplike ones will gain life under Jesus' perfect rulership. It will be a happy life in a new world free of poverty. Goatlike humans, who reject Jesus' rule, will be destroyed forever. —Matthew 25:46.

God's Kingdom will bring an end to wickedness. Then poverty will be a thing of the past. Instead, the earth will be inhabited by people who love and care for one another. That such a new world is possible can be seen in the loving international brotherhood of Jehovah's Witnesses, for Jesus said: "By this all will know that you are my disciples, if you have love among yourselves."—John 13:35.

Jehovah God and his Son care deeply about the poor. (Mark 12:41-44; James 2:1-6) Reflecting his concern for the poor, Jehovah holds within his memory millions of poor people who have died. All such ones will be resurrected into a new world free from poverty.—Acts 24:15.

The international brotherhood of Jehovah's Witnesses shows that the new world is possible

DIAMO GLORIA A DIO

Families Fortified by the Knowledge of God

THE "Berlin Wall." That is what a married couple in Argentina called an actual wall that they had built to divide their house in two! They had irreconcilable differences; they simply could not stand each other.

Sadly, the situation of that couple is not unique. Many families are plagued by strife, infidelity, and outright hostility. This is regrettable, since the family is an institution established by God himself. (Genesis 1:27, 28; 2:23, 24) This divine gift is an ideal setting for showing deep love. (Ruth 1:9) By meeting their God-given obligations, family members can honor Jehovah and be a blessing to one another.*

Inasmuch as God instituted the family arrangement, we need to let his perspective shape our understanding of how families should function. His Word provides much practical counsel designed to help families succeed, especially when challenges arise. As to the role of husbands, the Bible says: "Husbands ought to be loving their wives as their own bodies." When the husband fulfills this requirement, it is a pleasure for his wife to have "deep respect for her husband."—Ephesians 5: 25-29, 33.

Concerning the relationship between parents and their children, the apostle Paul wrote: "Fathers, do not be irritating your children, but go on bringing them up in the discipline and mental-regulating of Jehovah." (Ephesians 6:4) This, in turn, creates a warm family atmosphere, which makes it easier for children to obey their parents.—Ephesians 6:1.

The foregoing points illustrate the Bible's

---

* See 2005 Calendar of Jehovah's Witnesses, May/ June.

sound advice on family life. By applying divine principles, many enjoy happiness in the home. Take, for example, the couple in Argentina mentioned at the outset. After they studied the Bible with Jehovah's Witnesses for three months, they both began to apply its wise counsel on marriage. They worked hard to improve communication, to be sympathetic to the needs of each other, and to become forgiving. (Proverbs 15:22; 1 Peter 3:7; 4:8) They learned to control their anger and to turn to God for help when things seemed to be getting out of control. (Colossians 3:19) Soon, the "Berlin Wall" came down!

God Can Build a Family

Knowledge and application of God's standards can fortify a family to withstand pressures. This is vital, for it was prophesied that the family arrangement would experience a vicious attack in our day. Paul foretold the current breakdown of morality and human society. He said that "the last days" would be characterized by disloyalty, the absence of "natural affection," and disobedience to parents, even among those "having a form of godly devotion."—2 Timothy 3:1-5.

JEHOVAH CHERISHES THE FAMILY ARRANGEMENT

"God blessed them and God said to them: 'Be fruitful and become many and fill the earth.'"—Genesis 1:28.

"Happy is everyone fearing Jehovah . . . Your wife will be like a fruit-bearing vine in the innermost parts of your house."
—Psalm 128:1, 3.

To God "every family in heaven and on earth owes its name."

—EPHESIANS 3:15

Trying to please God can help counteract such detrimental effects on the family. Many families have found that a spiritual solution is required to help them meet many of the challenges they face. If family members desire to maintain a good relationship with God, they above all need to apply Bible principles and realize that "unless Jehovah himself builds the house, it is to no avail that its builders have worked hard on it." (Psalm 127:1) The greatest success in promoting domestic happiness comes from putting God first in family life.—Ephesians 3:14, 15.

In Hawaii a man named Dennis discovered how true that is. Although he was a professed Christian, abusive speech and fights became a way of life for him. After serving in the army, he became even more aggressive and hateful. "I was always in conflict," he recalls. "I didn't care what happened to me, and I wasn't afraid to die. The profanity and fighting continued. My wife, who was one of Jehovah's Witnesses, encouraged me to study the Bible."

Dennis resisted his wife's efforts. However, her Christian conduct softened his negative attitude. Dennis eventually went to a Christian meeting with his wife and children. Thereafter, a Bible study was started with Dennis, and he made fine progress. He gave up a 28-year-long smoking habit and stopped associating with friends who engaged in all the things he was trying to overcome. Thankful to Jehovah, Dennis commented: "My family life got better. We went to the meetings and in the ministry as a family. My two children were no longer afraid of me, for I learned to control my temper and stopped using abusive speech. We could talk and enjoy having Bible discussions. If it were not for Bible truth, I wouldn't be here today; I was so temperamental."

Families can attain happiness when they work hard to do Jehovah's will. Experience has shown that even if one member of a family applies Bible principles, things are better than if no one does. Building a Christian household is hard work, requiring skill and time. But members of such families have the assurance that Jehovah will crown their building efforts with success. They can echo the psalmist's words: "My help is from Jehovah."—Psalm 121:2.

Mari

Ancient Queen of the Desert

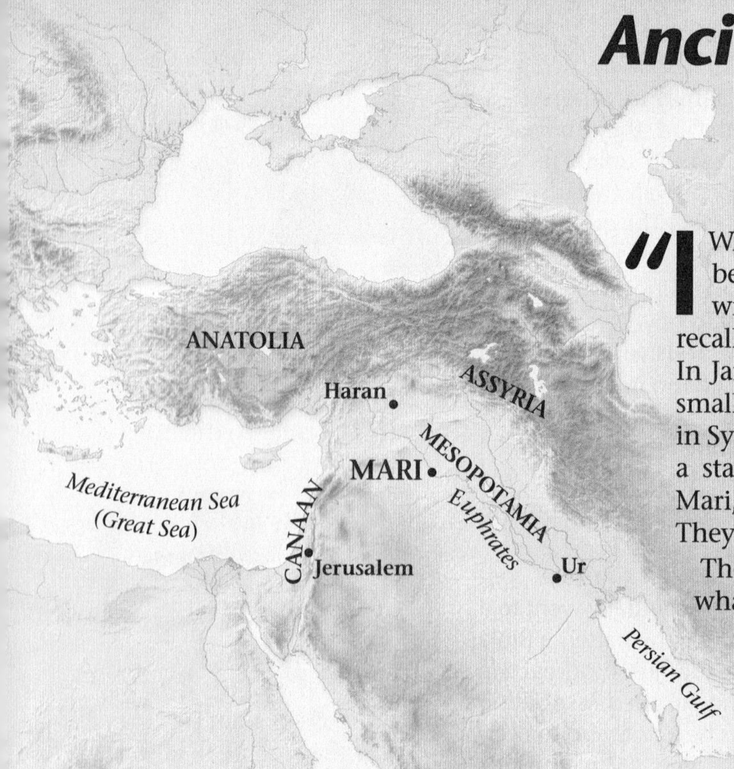

ANATOLIA

Haran

ASSYRIA

MARI

MESOPOTAMIA

Mediterranean Sea (Great Sea)

CANAAN

Jerusalem

Euphrates

Ur

Persian Gulf

"I WAS a little giddy upon arriving in my bedroom that night after celebrating with my companions our good fortune," recalled French archaeologist André Parrot. In January of 1934, at Tell Hariri, near the small town of Abu Kemal on the Euphrates in Syria, Parrot and his team had unearthed a statue bearing the inscription: "Lamgi-Mari, king of Mari, high priest of Enlil." They were thrilled at the discovery.

The city of Mari had at last been found! Of what interest is this discovery to students of the Bible?

Why of Interest?

Though the existence of Mari was known from ancient texts, its exact location long remained a mystery. According to Sumerian scribes, Mari was the seat of a dynasty that may at one time have held sway over all of Mesopotamia. Built on the banks of the Euphrates, Mari was strategically situated at the crossroads of trade routes linking the Persian Gulf with Assyria, Mesopotamia, Anatolia, and the Mediterranean Coast. Goods including wood, metal, and stone—all sorely lacking in Mesopotamia—transited the city. Taxes on them greatly enriched Mari, enabling her to assert her authority over the re-

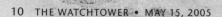

gion. This predominance ended, however, when Syria was conquered by Sargon of Akkad.

For some 300 years after Sargon's conquest, Mari was ruled by a series of military governors. Under them, the city regained a measure of prosperity. By the time of her last ruler, Zimri-Lim, however, Mari was on the decline. Zimri-Lim attempted to consolidate his empire through a series of military conquests, treaties, and marriage alliances. But about 1760 B.C.E., King Hammurabi of Babylon conquered and destroyed the city, putting an end to what Parrot called "a civilization that was one of the lights of the ancient world."

When Hammurabi's troops razed Mari, they inadvertently rendered a huge service to modern-day archaeologists and historians. In toppling the unbaked mud-brick walls, they buried certain buildings up to a height of 15 feet in some places, thus preserving them from the ravages of time. Archaeologists have unearthed the ruins of temples and palaces, along with a host of artifacts and thousands of inscriptions that shed light on ancient civilization.

Why are the ruins of Mari of interest to us? Consider the time when the patriarch Abraham walked the earth. Abraham was born in the year 2018 B.C.E., 352 years after the great Flood. His was the tenth generation from Noah. At God's command, Abraham left his native city, Ur, and went to Haran. In the year 1943 B.C.E., when Abraham was 75 years of age, he left Haran for the land of Canaan. "The migrations of Abraham from Ur to Jerusalem [in Canaan] are situated historically at the time of Mari," says Italian archaeologist Paolo Matthiae. The discovery of Mari, therefore, has value

In this document King Iahdun-Lim of Mari boasted about his construction work

The discovery of this statue of Lamgi-Mari resulted in the positive identification of Mari

in that it can help us to envisage the world in which God's faithful servant Abraham lived.*—Genesis 11:10–12:4.

What Do the Ruins Reveal?

Religion flourished in Mari as it did elsewhere in Mesopotamia. It was considered man's duty to serve the gods. The will of the gods was always sought before making any important decision. Archaeologists have found the vestiges of six temples. Included among them are the Temple of Lions (considered by some to be a temple of Dagan, Biblical Dagon) and the sanctuaries of Ishtar, the goddess of fertility, as well as of the sun-god Shamash. These temples originally contained a statue of the deity to whom offerings and supplications were made. Devotees placed smiling effigies of themselves in prayer on benches in the sanctuary, in the belief that their image prolonged the act of worship. Parrot noted:

---

* It is also quite likely that the Jewish exiles taken to Babylon after the destruction of Jerusalem in 607 B.C.E. skirted the ruins of Mari.

Podium in the palace, where the statue of a goddess may have stood

Ebih-Il, the superintendent of Mari, in prayer

Ruins of Mari, showing unbaked mud-brick construction

"The statue, like the candle in Catholic worship today but to an even greater degree, was in actual fact a substitute for the believer."

The most spectacular discovery in the ruins of Tell Hariri was the remains of a huge palace complex, known by the name of its last occupant, King Zimri-Lim. French archaeologist Louis-Hugues Vincent described it as "the jewel of archaic Oriental architecture." Covering over six acres, it contained some 300 rooms and courtyards. Even in antiquity, this palace was considered one of the marvels of the world. "Such

A palace bathroom

was its fame," comments Georges Roux in his book *Ancient Iraq,* "that the King of Ugarit, on the Syrian coast, did not hesitate to send his son 600 kilometres [370 miles] inland for the sole purpose of visiting 'the house of Zimri-Lim.'"

Before reaching a spacious courtyard, visitors gained access to the fortified palace via a single entrance flanked by towers. Seated on a throne placed on a dais, Mari's last king, Zimri-Lim, handled military, commercial, and diplomatic affairs; handed down judgments; and received visitors and embassies. Accommodations were available for guests, who were regularly wined and dined by the king during sumptuous banquets. Dishes included roasted, grilled, or boiled beef, mutton, gazelle, fish, and poultry—all served with spicy garlic sauces and an assortment of vegetables and cheeses. Dessert consisted of fresh, dried, or crystallized fruit and cakes baked in intricate molds. To quench their thirst, guests were served beer or wine.

Sanitation was not absent from the palace. Bathrooms were discovered that had terra-cotta tubs and seat-less toilets. The floors and lower part of the walls of these rooms were protected with a coating of bitumen. Wastewater was drained via brick gutters, and clay pipes waterproofed with bitumen are still operational after some 3,500 years. When three women from the royal harem were struck with a fatal disease, the instructions were strict. Such a sickly woman was to be isolated and kept in quarantine. "None should drink from her cup, eat at her table, sit on her seat."

What Can We Learn From the Archives?

Parrot and his team discovered some 20,000 cuneiform tablets written in Akkadian. The tablets consisted of letters and administrative and economic texts. Of these archives, only one third have been published. Nevertheless, they consist of 28 volumes. Of what value are they? "Before the discovery of the Mari archives," says Jean-Claude Margueron, director of the Mari Archaeological Mission, "we knew almost nothing of the history, institutions, and daily life in Mesopotamia and Syria

The victory stele of Naram-Sin, conqueror of Mari

at the beginning of the second millennium. Thanks to them, it has been possible to write whole chapters of history." As Parrot commented, the archives "reveal surprising similarities between the peoples that they mention and what the Old Testament tells us of the period of the Patriarchs."

The tablets found at Mari also shed light on certain Bible passages. For example, the tablets indicate that taking possession of an enemy's harem was "a fundamental fact of royal conduct at the time." The counsel of the traitor Ahithophel to King David's son Absalom to have relations with his father's concubines was by no means original.—2 Samuel 16:21, 22.

There have been 41 archaeological campaigns to Tell Hariri since 1933. So far, however, only 20 of Mari's 270 acres have been examined. Likely, many fascinating discoveries will yet be made in Mari, the ancient queen of the desert.

About 20,000 cuneiform tablets were found in the ruins of the palace

COMMON SENSE
Why So Uncommon?

"**W**HAT is the matter with him? He should know better," remarks an observer. Shaking his head in disbelief, another walks away muttering, "If he had a little common sense, he would never have done that." Have you perhaps heard similar comments? What, though, is "common sense"?

The word "sense" is defined as "accurate appreciation," "understanding," and "practical wisdom or judgement." It implies that a person has the ability to judge and decide with intelligence. Common sense evidently requires that we use thinking ability. Many people would rather let others do their thinking for them. They allow the media, their peers, or popular opinion to make decisions for them.

Common sense seems to be so lacking in today's world that an observant man once noted, 'Common sense, in truth, is very uncommon.' How can we acquire common

A wealth of sound advice is found in the Bible

sense? What are its benefits?

How Acquired?

While it takes time, sustained thought, and consistent effort to develop good sense and fine judgment, common sense is certainly attainable. Consider three factors that can help us to acquire common sense.

Study the Bible, and follow its advice. The Bible, written in the finest language and with clear logic, is an excellent aid in gaining wisdom and good sense. (Ephesians 1:8) For example, the apostle Paul admonishes fellow Christians: "Whatever things are true, whatever things are of serious concern, whatever things are righteous, whatever things are chaste, whatever things are lovable, whatever things are well spoken of, whatever virtue there is and whatever praiseworthy thing there is, continue considering these things." (Philippians 4:8) If we consistently follow this advice, sound judgment and prudent behavior will result.

Learn from experience. Associating common sense with experience in life, a Swiss poet stated: "Common sense is . . . composed of experience and prevision [foresight]." Indeed, "anyone inexperienced puts faith in every word, but the shrewd one considers his steps." (Proverbs 14:15) Common sense may be developed through observation, training, and experience. We can

---

IN OUR NEXT ISSUE

Whatever Happened to World Unity?

———

Jehovah Safeguards Those Who Hope in Him

———

When Marital Disagreements Arise

learn to do things better over a period of time. Learning from our mistakes, however, calls for humility and meekness. The self-assuming, haughty, and headstrong spirit of people in these last days is not a manifestation of common sense.—2 Timothy 3:1-5.

Choose associates wisely. In using wisdom and common sense, we are also helped or hindered by our associates. Proverbs 13:20 states: "He that is walking with wise persons will become wise, but he that is having dealings with the stupid ones will fare badly." We do not have to accept the mentality or ideas of those who disobey God and ignore his Word. Proverbs 17:12 puts the matter this way: "Let there be an encountering by a man of a bear bereaved of its cubs rather than anyone stupid in his foolishness."

Of What Benefit?

Developing common sense is advantageous. It makes life more interesting and can save us time. Common sense may even reduce the frustration that often comes from doing things thoughtlessly. Those lacking good judgment make life harder for themselves. "The hard work of the stupid ones makes them weary," states the Bible. (Ecclesiastes 10:15) Such individuals may toil endlessly and tire themselves out; yet, they accomplish virtually nothing truly worthwhile.

The Bible provides a wealth of practical advice on cleanliness, communication, industriousness, coping with poverty, and many other aspects of life. Millions can testify that the difference between success and failure in their lives has depended on the degree to which they have applied Bible principles, helping them to manifest wisdom.

Common sense enables us to do more than simply follow a set of detailed instructions or rules. It helps us to fulfill our responsibilities. However, common sense is not a substitute for taking in knowledge. "A wise person will listen and take in more instruction," says Proverbs 1:5. We must also learn to analyze the information we gather, drawing proper conclusions from it. This helps us to 'walk in wisdom.'—Proverbs 28:26.

Modesty goes hand in hand with common sense. Although we may want to care for many responsibilities, we need to use good judgment and stay within the limits of our strength. True, the apostle Paul tells us to have "plenty to do in the work of the Lord." (1 Corinthians 15:58) Yet, this admonition must be balanced with the principle recorded at Ecclesiastes 9:4: "A live dog is better off than a dead lion." Taking proper care of our health as we serve Jehovah may allow us to live longer and to continue to be active. Common sense can help us to find a reasonable balance that permits us to get necessary things accomplished without losing our joy. Yes, common sense brings many benefits.

Jehovah's Word Is Alive
Highlights From the Book of Second Samuel

DOES recognizing Jehovah's sovereignty require our perfect obedience? Does a man of integrity always do what is right in God's eyes? What kind of individual does the true God find "agreeable to his heart"? (1 Samuel 13:14) The Bible book of Second Samuel gives satisfying answers to these questions.

Second Samuel was written by Gad and Nathan, two prophets who were close to King David of ancient Israel.* Completed in about 1040 B.C.E., toward the end of David's 40-year kingship, the book is primarily about David and his relationship with Jehovah. This thrilling narrative relates how a strife-torn nation becomes a prosperous united kingdom under a valiant king. The gripping drama is packed with human emotions expressed with deep intensity.

----

* Even though Samuel did not have a part in writing it, the book bears his name because the two books of Samuel were initially one roll in the Hebrew canon. Samuel wrote a major part of First Samuel.

Remembering who had firmly established him as king helped David to remain humble

DAVID BECOMES "GREATER AND GREATER"
(2 Samuel 1:1–10:19)

David's response to the news of the death of Saul and Jonathan reveals his feelings for them and for Jehovah. In Hebron, David is appointed king over the tribe of Judah. Saul's son Ish-bosheth is made king over the rest of Israel. David goes on "getting greater and greater," and some seven and a half years later, he is made king over all Israel.—2 Samuel 5:10.

David captures Jerusalem from the Jebusites and makes it the capital of his kingdom. His first attempt to transfer the ark of the covenant to Jerusalem results in disaster. However, the second attempt succeeds, and David dances for joy. Jehovah makes a covenant with David for a kingdom. David subdues his enemies as God continues to be with him.

Scriptural Questions Answered:

2:18—Why were Joab and his two brothers identified as the three sons of Zeruiah, their mother? In the Hebrew Scriptures, genealogies were usually reckoned through the father. Zeruiah's husband may have died prematurely, or he could have been considered unsuitable for inclusion in the Sacred Record. It is possible that Zeruiah was listed because she was David's sister or half sister. (1 Chronicles 2:15, 16) The only reference to the father of the three brothers is in connection with his burial place at Bethlehem. —2 Samuel 2:32.

3:29—What is meant by "a man taking hold of the twirling spindle"? Women customarily did the weaving of cloth. Therefore, this expression may refer to men who were unfit for such activities as warfare and who were thus obliged to do the work usually done by a woman.

5:1, 2—How long after Ish-bosheth's assassination was David made king over all Israel? It seems reasonable to conclude that Ish-bosheth began his two-year-long kingship shortly after Saul's death, about the same time David began his in Hebron. David ruled over Judah from Hebron for seven and a half years. Soon after being made king over all Israel, he shifted his capital to Jerusalem. Hence, about five years elapsed after Ish-bosheth's death before David became king over all Israel.—2 Samuel 2:3, 4, 8-11; 5:4, 5.

8:2—How many Moabites were executed after Israel's conflict with them? The number may have been determined by measuring rather than by counting. It seems that David had the Moabites lie down side by side on the ground in a row. Next, he had the row measured with the length of a line, or a cord. Apparently, two line measures, or two thirds of the Moabites, were put to death, and one line measure, or one third of them, were spared.

Lessons for Us:

2:1; 5:19, 23. David inquired of Jehovah before taking up residence in Hebron and prior to going up against his enemies. We too should seek Jehovah's guidance before making decisions that affect our spirituality.

3:26-30. Revenge reaps sad consequences. —Romans 12:17-19.

3:31-34; 4:9-12. David's lack of vindictiveness and ill will is exemplary.

5:12. We should never forget that Jehovah has educated us in his ways and made a good relationship with him possible.

6:1-7. Though David was well-meaning, his attempt to move the Ark in a wagon was in violation of God's command and resulted in failure. (Exodus 25:13, 14; Numbers 4: 15, 19; 7:7-9) Uzzah's grabbing hold of the Ark also shows that good intentions do not change what God requires.

6:8, 9. In a trialsome situation, David first became angry, then afraid—perhaps even blaming Jehovah for the tragedy. We must guard against blaming Jehovah for problems that result from ignoring his commands.

7:18, 22, 23, 26. David's humility, exclusive devotion to Jehovah, and interest in exalting God's name are qualities for us to imitate.

8:2. A prophecy uttered some 400 years earlier is fulfilled. (Numbers 24:17) Jehovah's word always comes true.

9:1, 6, 7. David kept his promise. We too must endeavor to keep our word.

JEHOVAH RAISES UP CALAMITY AGAINST HIS ANOINTED
(2 Samuel 11:1–20:26)

"Here I am raising up against you calamity out of your own house," Jehovah says to David, "and I will take your wives under your own eyes and give them to your fellowman, and he will certainly lie down with your wives under the eyes of this sun." (2 Samuel 12:11) What is the reason for this pronouncement? It is David's sin with Bathsheba. Though repentant David is forgiven, he is not spared the consequences of his sin.

First the child that Bath-sheba gives birth to dies. Then David's virgin daughter Tamar is raped by her half brother Amnon. Her full brother Absalom murders Amnon in revenge. Absalom conspires against his own father and proclaims himself king in Hebron. David is forced to flee Jerusalem. Absalom has relations with ten of his father's concubines left behind to take care of the house.

David returns to his kingship only after Absalom is killed. A revolt by the Benjaminite Sheba ends in Sheba's death.

Scriptural Questions Answered:

14:7—What is symbolized by "the glow of my charcoals"? The glow of slow-burning charcoal is used to denote a living offspring.

19:29—Why did David respond the way he did to Mephibosheth's explanation? Upon hearing Mephibosheth, David must have realized that he erred when he took Ziba's words at face value. (2 Samuel 16:1-4; 19:24-28) Very likely, this irritated David, and he did not want to hear anything further about the matter.

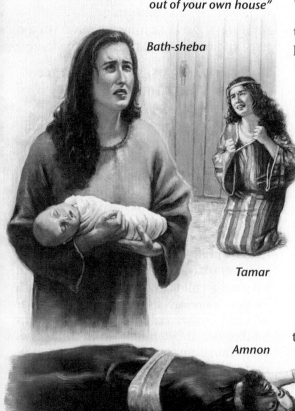

"Here I am raising up against you calamity out of your own house"

Bath-sheba

Tamar

Amnon

Lessons for Us:

11:2-15. The candid account of David's shortcomings testifies to the fact that the Bible is the inspired Word of God.

11:16-27. When we commit a serious sin, we should not try to cover it over as David did. Rather, we should confess our sin to Jehovah and seek help from the elders in the congregation.—Proverbs 28:13; James 5: 13-16.

12:1-14. Nathan set a fine example for appointed elders in the congregation. They are to help those who fall into sin to correct their course. The elders must discharge this responsibility skillfully.

12:15-23. Having the correct view of what befell him helped David to respond properly to adversity.

15:12; 16:15, 21, 23. When it appeared that Absalom would ascend to the throne, pride and ambition led the brilliant counselor Ahithophel to become a traitor. Having intelligence without humility and loyalty can be a snare.

19:24, 30. Mephibosheth was truly appreciative of David's loving-kindness. He willingly submitted to the king's decision about Ziba. Appreciation for Jehovah and his organization should move us to be submissive.

20:21, 22. The wisdom of one person can avert a disaster for many.—Ecclesiastes 9:14, 15.

LET US FALL "INTO THE HAND OF JEHOVAH" (2 Samuel 21:1–24:25)

There is a famine for three years because of the bloodguilt that Saul incurred by putting the Gibeonites to death. (Joshua 9:15) In order to avenge that bloodguilt, the Gibeonites ask for seven sons of Saul for execution. David gives them into the Gibeonites' hands, and the drought ends with a downpour of rain. Four Philistine giants come to "fall by the hand of David and by the hand of his servants." —2 Samuel 21:22.

David commits a serious sin by ordering an illegal census. He repents and chooses to fall "into the hand of Jehovah." (2 Samuel 24:14) As a result, 70,000 die from pestilence. David follows Jehovah's command, and the scourge is halted.

Scriptural Questions Answered:

21:8—How can it be said that Saul's daughter Michal had five sons, when 2 Samuel 6:23 states that she died childless? The most widely accepted explanation is that these were the sons of Michal's sister Merab, who married Adriel. Likely, Merab died early, and childless Michal brought up the boys.

21:9, 10—For how long did Rizpah keep up a vigil for her two sons and the five grandsons of Saul who were put to death by the Gibeonites? These seven were hanged "in the first days of harvest"—March or April. Their dead bodies were left exposed on a mountain. Rizpah guarded the seven bodies by day and by night until Jehovah showed by ending the drought that his anger had subsided. Any heavy downpour of rain would have been very unlikely before the completion of the harvest season in October. Hence, Rizpah may have kept up the vigil for as long as five or six months. Thereafter, David had the bones of the men buried.

24:1—Why did taking a count of people constitute a serious sin for David? The taking of a census was not in itself forbidden in the Law. (Numbers 1:1-3; 26:1-4) The Bible does not say what objective moved David to number the people. However, 1 Chronicles 21:1 indicates that Satan incited him to do so. In any event, his military chief, Joab, knew that David's decision to register the people was wrong, and he tried to dissuade David from doing it.

Lessons for Us:

22:2-51. How beautifully David's song portrays Jehovah as the true God, worthy of our implicit trust!

23:15-17. David had such a deep respect for God's law on life and blood that on this occasion, he refrained from doing what even resembled a violation of that law. We must cultivate such an attitude toward all of God's commands.

24:10. David's conscience moved him to repentance. Is our conscience sensitive enough to respond in that way?

24:14. David well knew that Jehovah is more merciful than humans are. Do we have such conviction?

24:17. David felt regret that his sin brought suffering upon the entire nation. A repentant wrongdoer should feel remorse over the reproach his action may have brought upon the congregation.

Being 'Agreeable to God's Heart' Is Within Our Reach

The second king of Israel proved to be 'a man agreeable to Jehovah's heart.' (1 Samuel 13:14) David never questioned Jehovah's righteous standards, and he did not seek to pursue a course of independence from God. Each time David erred, he acknowledged his sin, accepted discipline, and corrected his ways. David was a man of integrity. Are we not wise to be like him, particularly when we err?

The life story of David vividly illustrates that recognizing Jehovah's sovereignty is a matter of accepting His standards of good and bad and striving to abide by them as integrity keepers. This is within our reach. How grateful we can be for the lessons we learn from the book of Second Samuel! The inspired message contained in its pages is, indeed, alive and exerts power.—Hebrews 4:12.

COMING TO KNOW JEHOVAH'S WAYS

"Make me know . . . your ways, that I may know you."—EXODUS 33:13.

MOSES had been reared in the household of Pharaoh and had been educated in the wisdom esteemed by the nobility of Egypt. Yet, Moses realized that he was not an Egyptian. He was born to Hebrew parents. In his 40th year, he went out to make an inspection of his brothers, the sons of Israel. When he saw an Egyptian mistreat one of the Hebrews, Moses was not indifferent. He struck down the Egyptian. Moses chose to side with Jehovah's people and thought that God was using him to provide deliverance for his brothers. (Acts 7:21-25; Hebrews 11:24, 25) When this incident became known, Egypt's royal house viewed Moses as an outlaw, and he had to flee for his life. (Exodus 2:11-15) If Moses was to be used by God, he had to become better acquainted with Jehovah's ways. Would Moses be teachable?—Psalm 25:9.

² For the next 40 years, Moses lived as an exile and a shepherd. Instead of letting himself be consumed with bitterness because his Hebrew brothers apparently did not appreciate him, Moses submitted to what God permitted. Although many years passed during which he received no apparent recognition, Moses allowed Jehovah to shape him. Not as a personal estimate, but under the influence of God's holy spirit, he láter wrote: "The man Moses was by far the meekest of all the men who were upon the surface of the ground." (Numbers 12:3) Jehovah used Moses in outstanding ways. If we too seek meekness, Jehovah will bless us.—Zephaniah 2:3.

Given a Commission

³ One day an angel representing Jehovah spoke to Moses near Mount Horeb on the Sinai Peninsula. Moses was told: "Unquestionably I have seen the affliction of my people who are in Egypt, and I have heard their outcry as a result of those who drive them to work; because I well know the pains they suffer. And I am proceeding to go down to deliver them out of the hand of the Egyptians and to bring them up out of that land to a land good and spacious, to a land flowing with milk and honey." (Exodus 3:2, 7, 8) In this regard, God had work for Moses to do, but it had to be done Jehovah's way.

⁴ Jehovah's angel continued: "Now come and let me send you to Pharaoh, and you bring my people the sons of Israel out of Egypt." Moses hesitated. He did not feel qualified, and in himself, he was not. However, Jehovah assured Moses: "I shall prove to be with you." (Exodus 3:10-12) Jehovah empowered Moses to perform miraculous signs that would serve as credentials proving that he had truly been sent by God. Moses' brother, Aaron, was to go along as spokesman. Jehovah would teach them what should be said and done. (Exodus 4:1-17) Would Moses faithfully fulfill that assignment?

⁵ Israel's older men initially believed Mo-

1, 2. (a) Why did Moses react as he did when he saw an Egyptian mistreat a Hebrew? (b) To be suitable for Jehovah's service, what did Moses need to learn?

3, 4. (a) What commission did Jehovah give Moses? (b) What support was provided for Moses?
5. Why did Israel's attitude present a challenge to Moses?

Moses faithfully delivered Jehovah's word to Pharaoh

ses and Aaron. (Exodus 4:29-31) Soon, however, "the officers of the sons of Israel" blamed Moses and his brother for making them "smell offensive" before Pharaoh and his servants. (Exodus 5:19-21; 6:9) When the Israelites were leaving Egypt, they were alarmed to see Egyptian chariots in pursuit. With the Red Sea before them and war chariots behind them, the Israelites felt trapped, and they blamed Moses. How would you have reacted? Though the Israelites had no boats, at Jehovah's direction Moses urged the people to break camp. Then God pushed back the waters of the Red Sea, and the seabed became dry land so that Israel could pass through.—Exodus 14:1-22.

An Issue Greater Than Deliverance

6 On commissioning Moses, Jehovah emphasized the importance of the divine name. Respect for that name and the One whom it represents was vital. When asked about his name, Jehovah told Moses: "I shall prove to be what I shall prove to be." Further, Moses was to tell the sons of Israel: "Jehovah the God of your forefathers, the God of Abraham, the God of Isaac and the God of Jacob,

has sent me to you." Jehovah added: "This is my name to time indefinite, and this is the memorial of me to generation after generation." (Exodus 3:13-15) Jehovah is still the name by which God is known to his servants around the earth.—Isaiah 12:4, 5; 43:10-12.

7 Appearing before Pharaoh, Moses and Aaron delivered their message in the name of Jehovah. But Pharaoh arrogantly said: "Who is Jehovah, so that I should obey his voice to send Israel away? I do not know Jehovah at all and, what is more, I am not going to send Israel away." (Exodus 5:1, 2) Pharaoh proved to be both hardhearted and deceitful, yet Jehovah urged Moses to deliver messages to him again and again. (Exodus 7:14-16, 20-23; 8:1, 2, 20) Moses could see that Pharaoh was irritated. Would any good come from confronting him again? Israel was eager for deliverance. Pharaoh was adamant in his refusal. What would you have done?

8 Moses delivered yet another message, saying: "This is what *Jehovah* the God of the Hebrews has said: 'Send my people away that they may serve me.'" God also said: "By now I could have thrust my hand out that I might strike you and your people with pestilence and that you might be effaced from the earth. But, in fact, for this cause I have kept you in existence, for the sake of showing you my power and in order to have my name declared in all the earth." (Exodus 9:13-16) Because of what would be done with hardhearted Pharaoh, Jehovah purposed to demonstrate his power in a way that would serve notice on all who defy him. This would include Satan the Devil, the one whom Jesus Christ later called "the ruler of the world." (John 14:30; Romans 9:17-24) As foretold,

___

6. What did Jehovah emphasize when commissioning Moses?

7. What did God urge Moses to do despite Pharaoh's arrogance?

8. What benefit came from the way that Jehovah dealt with the situation involving Pharaoh, and how should those events affect us?

Jehovah's name was declared around the earth. His long-suffering led to preservation for the Israelites and a vast mixed multitude that joined them in worshiping him. (Exodus 9:20, 21; 12:37, 38) Since then, the declaration of Jehovah's name has benefited millions more who have taken up true worship.

Dealing With a Difficult People

⁹ The Hebrews knew the divine name. Moses used that name when speaking to them, but they did not always show proper respect for the One to whom it belongs. Soon after Jehovah miraculously delivered the Israelites from Egypt, what happened when they did not quickly find suitable drinking water? They murmured against Moses. Next they complained about the food. Moses cautioned them that their murmuring was not merely against him and Aaron but against Jehovah. (Exodus 15:22-24; 16:2-12) At Mount Sinai, Jehovah gave the Israelites the Law, and this was accompanied by supernatural displays. The people, however, disobediently made a golden calf for worship and claimed that they were having "a festival to Jehovah."—Exodus 32:1-9.

¹⁰ How was Moses to deal with a people whom Jehovah himself described as stiff-necked? Moses petitioned Jehovah: "If, please, I have found favor in your eyes, make me know, please, your ways, that I may know you, in order that I may find favor in your eyes." (Exodus 33:13) In caring for Jehovah's modern-day Witnesses, Christian overseers shepherd a far more humble flock. Yet, they similarly pray: "Make me know your own ways, O Jehovah; teach me your own paths." (Psalm 25:4) Knowledge of Jehovah's ways enables overseers to deal with situations in a manner that is in harmony with God's Word and that is consistent with his personality.

What Jehovah Expects of His People

¹¹ What Jehovah expected of his people was disclosed orally at Mount Sinai. Moses later received two tablets containing the Ten Commandments in written form. Upon descending from the mountain, he saw the Israelites worshiping the molten calf and angrily threw down the tablets, shattering them. Jehovah again inscribed the Ten Commandments on stone tablets that Moses had carved out. (Exodus 32:19; 34:1) These commandments had not changed since they were first given. Moses was to act in harmony with them. God also impressed upon Moses the sort of person that He is, thus showing Moses how to conduct himself as Jehovah's representative. Christians are not under the Mosaic Law, but what Jehovah told Moses embodies many basic principles that have not changed and that continue to apply to all who worship Jehovah. (Romans 6:14; 13:8-10) Let us consider a few of these.

¹² *Give Jehovah exclusive devotion.* The nation of Israel was present when Jehovah declared that he requires exclusive devotion. (Exodus 20:2-5) The Israelites had seen abundant evidence that Jehovah is the true God. (Deuteronomy 4:33-35) Jehovah made it clear that regardless of what other nations were doing, he would not tolerate any form of idolatry or spiritism among his people. Their devotion to him was to be no mere formality. All of them were to love Jehovah with their whole heart, their whole soul, and all their vital force. (Deuteronomy 6:5, 6) This would involve their speech, their conduct —indeed, every aspect of their lives. (Leviticus 20:27; 24:15, 16; 26:1) Jesus Christ also

---

9. How did Moses' own people show disrespect for Jehovah?

10. Why is Moses' request recorded at Exodus 33:13 of special interest to Christian overseers today?

11. What guidelines did Jehovah provide for Moses, and why are we interested in them?

12. How should Jehovah's exacting exclusive devotion have affected Israel?

Jehovah disclosed his requirements to Moses

made it clear that Jehovah requires exclusive devotion.—Mark 12:28-30; Luke 4:8.

¹³ *Strictly obey Jehovah's commandments.* The people of Israel needed to be reminded that when they entered into a covenant relationship with Jehovah, they vowed to obey him strictly. They enjoyed much personal freedom, but in matters on which Jehovah had given them commandments, they had to be strictly obedient. Doing so would give evidence of their love for God and would benefit them and their offspring because all of Jehovah's requirements were for their good.—Exodus 19:5-8; Deuteronomy 5:27-33; 11:22, 23.

¹⁴ *Give priority to spiritual matters.* The nation of Israel was not to allow caring for physical needs to crowd out attention given to

spiritual activities. The Israelites' lives were not to be devoted solely to mundane pursuits. Jehovah set aside time each week that he designated as sacred, time used exclusively for activity related to worship of the true God. (Exodus 35:1-3; Numbers 15:32-36) Each year, additional time was to be set aside for specified holy conventions. (Leviticus 23:4-44) These would provide opportunities to recount Jehovah's mighty acts, to be reminded of his ways, and to express gratitude to him for all of his goodness. As the people expressed their devotion to Jehovah, they would grow in godly fear and love and would be helped to walk in his ways. (Deuteronomy 10:12, 13) The wholesome principles embodied in those instructions benefit Jehovah's servants today.—Hebrews 10:24, 25.

Appreciating Jehovah's Qualities

¹⁵ Appreciation for Jehovah's qualities would also help Moses in dealing with the people. Exodus 34:5-7 states that God passed by before Moses' face and declared: "Jehovah, Jehovah, a God merciful and gracious, slow to anger and abundant in loving-kindness and truth, preserving loving-kindness for thousands, pardoning error and transgression and sin, but by no means will he give exemption from punishment, bringing punishment for the error of fathers upon sons and upon grandsons, upon the third generation and upon the fourth generation." Take time to meditate on those words. Ask yourself: 'What does each quality mean? How did Jehovah demonstrate it? How can Christian overseers display this quality? How should the particular quality influence what each one of us does?' Consider just a few examples.

---

13. Why did Israel owe God strict obedience, and what should motivate us to obey him? (Ecclesiastes 12:13)
14. How did God emphasize to Israel the importance of giving priority to spiritual pursuits?

---

15. (a) Why was appreciation for Jehovah's qualities beneficial to Moses? (b) What questions might help us to think deeply about each of Jehovah's qualities?

Meditate on Jehovah's qualities

¹⁶ Jehovah is "a God merciful and gracious." If you have the reference work *Insight on the Scriptures,* why not read what it says under "Mercy"? Or do research on that subject with the use of the *Watch Tower Publications Index* or the computer program *Watchtower Library* (CD-ROM).* Use a concordance to find scriptures referring to mercy. You will see that in addition to allowing for a lightening of punishment at times, Jehovah's mercy includes tender compassion. It moves God to take action to bring his people relief. As evidence of this, God provided for the Israelites both physically and spiritually during their trek to the Promised Land. (Deuteronomy 1:30-33; 8:4) Jehovah mercifully allowed for forgiveness when mistakes were made. He showed mercy toward his ancient people. How much more so should his present-day servants show compassion to one another! —Matthew 9:13; 18:21-35.

¹⁷ Jehovah's mercy is coupled with graciousness. If you have a dictionary, read what it says under "gracious." Compare this with scriptures that speak of Jehovah as being gra-

---
* All published by Jehovah's Witnesses.
---

16. How might we deepen our appreciation for God's mercy, and why is doing this important?
17. How can our understanding of Jehovah's graciousness promote true worship?

What Did You Learn?

- Why was meekness important for Moses, and why is it vital for us?

- What good was accomplished by repeatedly confronting Pharaoh with Jehovah's word?

- What are some outstanding principles that Moses was taught and that also apply to us?

- How can we deepen our understanding of Jehovah's qualities?

---

cious. The Bible shows that graciousness on Jehovah's part includes loving concern for disadvantaged ones among his people. (Exodus 22:26, 27) In any country, aliens as well as others may find themselves at a disadvantage. When teaching his people to be impartial and to show kindness toward such ones, Jehovah reminded them that they too had been aliens—in Egypt. (Deuteronomy 24:17-22) What about us as God's people today? Graciousness on our part helps to unite us and to attract others to the worship of Jehovah.—Acts 10:34, 35; Revelation 7:9, 10.

¹⁸ Kind concern for people of other nations, however, was not to override Israel's love for Jehovah and his moral standards. Thus, the Israelites were taught not to take up the ways of the surrounding nations, not to adopt their religious customs and immoral life-styles. (Exodus 34:11-16; Deuteronomy 7:1-4) That also applies to us today. We are to be a holy people, even as our God, Jehovah, is holy.—1 Peter 1:15, 16.

¹⁹ So that Moses would understand His

---
18. What do we learn from the limitations that Jehovah taught Israel regarding the ways of people of other nations?
19. How can understanding Jehovah's view of wrongdoing safeguard his people?

ways, Jehovah made it clear that although he does not approve of sin, he is slow to anger. He allows time for people to learn his requirements and comply with them. When there is repentance, Jehovah pardons sin, but he does not give exemption from deserved punishment for serious wrongs. He cautioned Moses that future generations could be affected, for good or for bad, by what the Israelites did. Having appreciation for Jehovah's ways can safeguard God's people from blaming God for situations that they have brought on themselves or from concluding that he is slow.

[20] If you desire to deepen your own knowledge of Jehovah and his ways, continue to do research and to meditate when you read the Bible. Carefully examine the various fascinating aspects of Jehovah's personality. Prayerfully consider how you might imitate God and conform your life more fully to his purpose. This will help you to avoid pitfalls, to deal appropriately with fellow believers, and to aid others in coming to know and love our magnificent God.

---

20. What can help us to deal appropriately with fellow believers and with those we meet in our ministry? (Psalm 86:11)

'KEEP YOURSELF RESTRAINED UNDER EVIL'

"A slave of the Lord does not need to fight, but needs to be gentle toward all, . . . keeping himself restrained under evil."—2 TIMOTHY 2:24.

HOW do you react when you are confronted by those who are not favorably disposed toward you or toward what you represent? In his description of the last days, the apostle Paul foretold that people would be "blasphemers, . . . slanderers, without self-control, fierce." (2 Timothy 3:1-5, 12) You may encounter such individuals in your ministry or in other activities.

[2] Not everyone who indulges in verbal abuse lacks all interest in what is right. Extreme hardship or frustration may cause people to lash out at whoever is around them. (Ecclesiastes 7:7) Many act this way because they live and work in an environment where rough speech is common. This does not make such speech acceptable for us as Christians, but it does help us to understand why other people use it. How should we react to harsh speech? Proverbs 19:11 states: "The insight of a man certainly slows down his anger." And Romans 12:17, 18 advises us: "Return evil for evil to no one. . . . If possible, as far as it depends upon you, be peaceable with all men."

[3] If we truly are peaceable, this will be

---

1. When engaged in Christian activity, why do we occasionally encounter people who speak harshly?
2. What scriptures can help us to deal wisely with people who speak harshly to us?

3. How is peaceableness involved in the message we preach?

evident in the spirit that we show. It will be reflected in what we say and do, perhaps also in our facial expression and in our tone of voice. (Proverbs 17:27) When sending his apostles out to preach, Jesus counseled them: "When you are entering into the house, greet the household ["wish the house peace," *The New English Bible*]; and if the house is deserving, let the peace you wish it come upon it; but if it is not deserving, let the peace from you return upon you." (Matthew 10:12, 13) The message that we bear is good news. The Bible calls it "the good news of peace," "the good news of the undeserved kindness of God," and "this good news of the kingdom." (Ephesians 6:15; Acts 20:24; Matthew 24:14) Our objective is, not to criticize the other person's beliefs or to argue with him about his viewpoints, but to share with him good news from God's Word.

4 Without really listening, a householder may abruptly state, "I am not interested." In many cases, it is possible to say, "I was hoping to read just this one brief text from the Bible." He may not object to that. In other cases, it may be appropriate to say: "I was hoping to tell you about a time when there will be no injustice and all people will learn to love one another." If that does not promptly elicit a request for an explanation, you might add: "But evidently this is not a convenient time for you." Even if the householder's response is not peaceable, should we conclude that he is "not deserving"? Regardless of the reaction, remember the Bible's counsel to be "gentle to-

---

4. What might you say when told "I am not interested" before you even have an opportunity to state the reason for your visit?

ward all, . . . restrained under evil."—2 Timothy 2:24.

Insolent but Misguided

5 In the first century, a man named Saul was well-known for his disrespectful speech, even for his violent behavior. The Bible says that he was "breathing threat and murder against the disciples of the Lord." (Acts 9: 1, 2) He later acknowledged that he had been "a blasphemer and a persecutor and an inso-

---

5, 6. How did Saul deal with Jesus' followers, and why did he act that way?

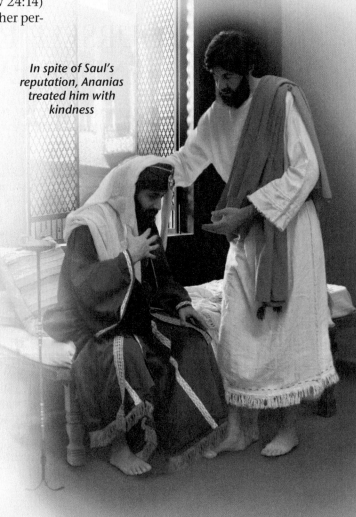

In spite of Saul's reputation, Ananias treated him with kindness

lent man." (1 Timothy 1:13) Although some of his relatives may already have become Christians, he said of his own attitude toward Christ's followers: "Since I was extremely mad against them, I went so far as to persecuting them even in outside cities." (Acts 23: 16; 26:11; Romans 16:7, 11) There is no evidence that the disciples tried to engage Saul in public debate while he was conducting himself in that manner.

⁶ Why did Saul act like that? Years later, he wrote: "I was ignorant and acted with a lack of faith." (1 Timothy 1:13) He was a Pharisee, educated "according to the strictness of the ancestral Law." (Acts 22:3) Though Saul's teacher Gamaliel was evidently somewhat broad-minded, high priest Caiaphas, with whom Saul came to be associated, proved to be fanatic. Caiaphas had been a ringleader in the plot that led to the execution of Jesus Christ. (Matthew 26:3, 4, 63-66; Acts 5:34-39) After that, Caiaphas saw to it that the apostles of Jesus were flogged, and he sternly ordered them to quit preaching on the basis of Jesus' name. Caiaphas presided over the Sanhedrin at the emotionally charged session during which Stephen was taken away to be stoned. (Acts 5:27, 28, 40; 7:1-60) Saul observed the stoning, and Caiaphas authorized him to follow through on further efforts to suppress the followers of Jesus by arresting them in Damascus. (Acts 8:1; 9:1, 2) Under this influence, Saul thought that his conduct gave evidence of zeal for God, but he actually lacked real faith. (Acts 22:3-5) As a result, Saul failed to realize that Jesus was the true Messiah. But Saul came to his senses when the resurrected Jesus miraculously spoke to him on the road to Damascus.—Acts 9:3-6.

⁷ Shortly after this, the disciple Ananias was dispatched to witness to Saul. Would you have been eager to make that call? Ananias

was apprehensive, but he spoke to Saul in a kind way. Saul's attitude had changed as a result of his miraculous encounter with Jesus on the road to Damascus. (Acts 9:10-22) He came to be known as the apostle Paul, a zealous Christian missionary.

Mild-Tempered but Courageous

⁸ Jesus was a zealous Kingdom proclaimer who was mild-tempered but courageous in dealing with people. (Matthew 11:29) He reflected the spirit of his heavenly Father, who urges the wicked to turn from their bad ways. (Isaiah 55:6, 7) In dealing with sinners, Jesus took note when there was evidence of a change for the better, and he encouraged such individuals. (Luke 7:37-50; 19:2-10) Rather than judging others on the basis of outward appearances, Jesus imitated his Father's kindness, forbearance, and long-suffering with a view to leading them to repentance. (Romans 2:4) It is Jehovah's will that people of all sorts should repent and be saved.—1 Timothy 2:3, 4.

⁹ Giving Jehovah's view of Jesus Christ, the Gospel writer Matthew quotes these prophetic words: "Look! My servant whom I chose, my beloved, whom my soul approved! I will put my spirit upon him, and what justice is he will make clear to the nations. He will not wrangle, nor cry aloud, nor will anyone hear his voice in the broad ways. No bruised reed will he crush, and no smoldering flaxen wick will he extinguish, until he sends out justice with success. Indeed, in his name nations will hope." (Matthew 12:17-21; Isaiah 42:1-4) Consistent with those prophetic words, Jesus did not indulge in noisy arguments. Even when under pressure, he spoke the truth in a manner that appealed to honesthearted ones.—John 7:32, 40, 45, 46.

---

7. What happened to Saul as a result of his encounter with Jesus on the road to Damascus?

8. How did Jesus reflect his Father's attitude toward people who had done bad things?
9. What can we learn from the way that Isaiah 42:1-4 was fulfilled in Jesus?

¹⁰ During his ministry, Jesus spoke to many Pharisees. Though some of them endeavored to trap him in his speech, Jesus did not conclude that all of them had bad motives. Simon, a Pharisee who was somewhat critical, evidently wanted to get a closer look at Jesus and invited him for a meal. Jesus accepted the invitation and witnessed to those present. (Luke 7: 36-50) On another occasion, a prominent Pharisee named Nicodemus came to Jesus under cover of night. Jesus did not reproach him for waiting until it was dark. Instead, he witnessed to Nicodemus about the love shown by God in sending his Son in order to open the way of salvation to those who would exercise faith. Jesus also kindly pointed out the importance of obedience to God's arrangement. (John 3:1-21) Nicodemus later spoke up in behalf of Jesus when a favorable report about Jesus was belittled by other Pharisees.—John 7:46-51.

¹¹ Jesus was not blind to the hypocrisy of those who were trying to entrap him. He did not allow opposers to lead him into fruitless debates. When appropriate, however, he did give brief, powerful replies by stating a principle, using an illustration, or quoting a scripture. (Matthew 12:38-42; 15:1-9; 16:1-4) At other times, Jesus simply did not answer when it was evident that no good would be accomplished by doing so.—Mark 15:2-5; Luke 22:67-70.

¹² Occasionally, Jesus was shouted at by people under the control of unclean spirits. When that happened, he exercised restraint and even used his God-given power to bring relief. (Mark 1:23-28; 5:2-8, 15) If some peo-ple become angry and shout at us when we are engaging in the ministry, we similarly need to exercise restraint, and we should endeavor to handle such a situation in a kind and tactful manner.—Colossians 4:6.

Within the Family

¹³ The need for Jesus' followers to exercise restraint often becomes most evident within the family. A person whose heart is deeply touched by Bible truth longs for his family to respond in the same way. But as Jesus said, family members may show hostility. (Matthew 10:32-37; John 15:20, 21) There are various reasons for this. For instance, while Bible teachings can help us to become honest, responsible, and respectful, the Scriptures also teach that in any situation our higher responsibility is to our Creator. (Ecclesiastes 12: 1, 13; Acts 5:29) A family member who feels that his influence in the family is somehow being diminished because of our loyalty to Jehovah may take offense. When dealing with such a situation, how important it is

---

10, 11. (a) Although Pharisees were among Jesus' most vocal opposers, why did he witness to some of them? (b) What sort of replies did Jesus occasionally give to opposers, but what did he not do?

12. Even when he was shouted at, how was Jesus able to help people?

---

13. Why do people sometimes oppose a family member who begins to study the Bible with Jehovah's Witnesses?

that we follow Jesus' example of showing restraint!—1 Peter 2:21-23; 3:1, 2.

¹⁴ Many now serving Jehovah had a marriage mate or other family member who was opposed to the changes they were making when they began studying the Bible. The opposers may have heard negative comments about Jehovah's Witnesses, and perhaps they feared that there would be an undesirable influence on the household. What caused them to change their attitude? In many cases, good example was a big factor. Because the believer steadfastly applied Bible counsel—regularly attending Christian meetings and participating in the ministry while also caring for family responsibilities and showing restraint in the face of any verbal abuse—family opposition sometimes softened.—1 Peter 2:12.

¹⁵ An opposer may also have refused to listen to any explanation from the Bible because of prejudice or pride. That was true of a man in the United States who said that he was very patriotic. One time, when his wife was at a convention, he took all his clothes and moved out. Another time, he left home with a gun and threatened to kill himself. He blamed her religion for any unreasonable conduct on his part. But she endeavored to keep applying Bible counsel. Twenty years after she became one of Jehovah's Witnesses, he did too. In Albania a woman became angry because her daughter studied the Bible with Jehovah's Witnesses and then got baptized. On 12 occasions the mother destroyed her daughter's copy of the Bible. Then one day she opened a new Bible that her daughter had left on a table. By chance, it opened to Matthew 10:36, and the mother realized that what was said there applied to her. Still, concerned about the daughter's welfare, the mother accompanied her to the boat when she was going to depart with other Witnesses for a convention in Italy. When the mother saw the love, hugs, and smiles of the group and heard their happy laughter, her feelings began to change. Soon after this, she agreed to study the Bible. Today she endeavors to help others who initially oppose.

¹⁶ In one instance, a knife-wielding husband confronted his wife, hurling bitter accusations at her as she approached the Kingdom Hall. She gently replied: "Come into the Kingdom Hall, and see for yourself." He did, and in time he became a Christian elder.

¹⁷ Even if everyone in your household is a Christian, there may be times when the family situation becomes tense and words even become harsh because of human imperfection. It is noteworthy that Christians in ancient Ephesus were counseled: "Let all malicious bitterness and anger and wrath and screaming and abusive speech be taken away from you along with all badness." (Ephesians 4:31) Evidently, the environment

---

14-16. What brought about changes in some who formerly opposed their family members?

A Christian's faithfully caring for responsibilities can soften family opposition

---

17. If the situation sometimes gets tense in a Christian home, what Scriptural counsel can help?

that surrounded Christians in Ephesus, their own imperfection and, in some cases, their former way of life influenced them. What would help them to change? They needed to "be made new in the force actuating [their] mind." (Ephesians 4:23) As they studied God's Word, meditated on how it should influence their lives, associated with fellow Christians, and earnestly prayed, the fruitage of God's spirit would be more fully manifest in their lives. They would learn to "become kind to one another, tenderly compassionate, freely forgiving one another just as God also by Christ freely forgave [them]." (Ephesians 4:32) Regardless of what others may do, we need to exercise restraint, being kind, compassionate, forgiving. Indeed, we must "return evil for evil to no one." (Romans 12:17, 18) Showing genuine love in imitation of God is always the right thing to do. —1 John 4:8.

Counsel for All Christians

18 Counsel to keep ourselves "restrained under evil" applies to all Christians. (2 Timothy 2:24) But it was first directed to Timothy, who needed it when he served as an elder in

_____

18. Why was the counsel found at 2 Timothy 2:24 appropriate for an elder in ancient Ephesus, and how can it benefit all Christians?

Christians promote love and unity

Ephesus. Some in the congregation there were quite vocal in making known their views and were teaching wrong doctrine. Because they did not fully discern the objective of the Mosaic Law, they failed to appreciate the importance of faith, love, and a good conscience. Pride created strife as they engaged in debates over words, while missing the point of Christ's teachings and the importance of godly devotion. To handle this situation, Timothy was to be firm for Scriptural truth yet gentle in dealing with his brothers. Like present-day elders, he knew that the flock did not belong to him and that he was to deal with others in a way that would promote Christian love and unity. —Ephesians 4:1-3; 1 Timothy 1:3-11; 5:1, 2; 6:3-5.

19 God urges his people to "seek meekness." (Zephaniah 2:3) The Hebrew expression for "meekness" denotes a disposition that enables a person to endure injury patiently, without irritation and without retaliation. May we earnestly petition Jehovah for help so that we can exercise restraint and represent him properly, even under difficult circumstances.

_____

19. Why is it important for all of us to "seek meekness"?

What Did You Learn?

- When you are confronted with insolent speech, what scriptures can help you?
- Why did Saul act in an insolent manner?
- How does Jesus' example help us to deal appropriately with all sorts of people?
- What benefits may come from exercising restraint in our speech at home?

Questions From Readers

Why were David and Bath-sheba not put to death for committing adultery, whereas their newborn son died?

The Mosaic Law stipulated: "In case a man is found lying down with a woman owned by an owner, both of them must then die together, the man lying down with the woman and the woman. So you must clear away what is bad out of Israel." (Deuteronomy 22:22) If Jehovah God had allowed the judicial case of David and Bath-sheba's sin to be handled by human judges under the Law, the adulterous couple would have been executed. Since the human judges could not read hearts, they were to render judgment on the basis of the conduct of the wrongdoers as established by the facts. An act of adultery called for the death sentence. The Israelite judges were not authorized to pardon that sin.

On the other hand, the true God can read hearts and forgive sins if he sees a basis for doing so. Since the case involved David, with whom He had made the Kingdom covenant, Jehovah chose to make an exception and deal with the matter himself. (2 Samuel 7:12-16) "The Judge of all the earth" has the right to make such a choice.—Genesis 18:25.

What did Jehovah see as he examined David's heart? The superscription to Psalm 51 says that this psalm reveals David's feelings "when Nathan the prophet came in to him after he had had relations with Bath-sheba." Psalm 51:1-4 states: "Show me favor, O God, according to your loving-kindness. According to the abundance of your mercies wipe out my transgressions. Thoroughly wash me from my error, and cleanse me even from my sin. For my transgressions I myself know, and my sin is in front of me constantly. Against you, you alone, I have sinned, and what is bad in your eyes I have done." Jehovah must have viewed this intense remorse in David's heart as an evidence of genuine repentance and decided that there was a basis for showing mercy to the wrongdoers. Moreover, David himself was a merciful person, and Jehovah shows mercy to the merciful. (1 Samuel 24:4-7; Matthew 5:7; James 2:13) Hence, when David acknowledged his sin, Nathan told him: "Jehovah, in turn, does let your sin pass by. You will not die."—2 Samuel 12:13.

David and Bath-sheba were not to escape all consequences of their sin. "Because you have unquestionably treated Jehovah with disrespect by this thing," Nathan told David, "also the son himself, just born to you, will positively die." Their child grew sick and died despite the fasting and mourning that David carried on for seven days.—2 Samuel 12:14-18.

Some find it difficult to understand why the son had to die, since Deuteronomy 24:16 states: "Children should not be put to death on account of fathers." But we must remember that if the case had been handled by human judges, the parents as well as the unborn child in the womb would have lost their lives. The loss of the son might also have helped David to realize more keenly how displeased Jehovah was with his sin with Bath-sheba. We can be confident that Jehovah dealt with the matter justly, for "perfect is his way."—2 Samuel 22:31.

David manifested true repentance

ON WHAT FOUNDATION ARE YOU BUILDING?

THE durability of a building depends largely on the strength of its substructure, or foundation. The Bible sometimes uses this principle in a figurative sense.

The prophet Isaiah, for example, refers to Jehovah God as the one "laying the foundation of the earth." (Isaiah 51:13) This foundation consists of the unchangeable laws of God that control the movement of the earth and hold it in its place. (Psalm 104:5) God's Word, the Bible, also speaks of "the foundations" on which human society rests. These are justice, law, and order. When they are "torn down," or undermined, by injustice, corruption, and violence, there is a breakdown in social order. —Psalm 11:2-6; Proverbs 29:4.

This principle also applies on a personal level. Concluding his famous Sermon on the Mount, Jesus Christ said: "Everyone that hears these sayings of mine and does them will be likened to a discreet man, who built his house upon the rock-mass. And the rain poured down and the floods came and the winds blew and lashed against that house, but it did not cave in, for it had been founded upon the rock-mass. Furthermore, everyone hearing these sayings of mine and not doing them will be likened to a foolish man, who built his house upon the sand. And the rain poured down and the floods came and the winds blew and struck against that house and it caved in, and its collapse was great."—Matthew 7:24-27.

On what foundation are you building your life? Is it on the unstable sands of godless human philosophy, which will result in structural collapse? Or are you building on the solid rock-mass of obedience to the sayings of Jesus Christ, which will help you to weather the figurative storms in life?

THE **WATCHTOWER**

ANNOUNCING JEHOVAH'S KINGDOM

JUNE 1, 2005

WORLD UNITY

NOT JUST A DREAM

THE WATCHTOWER®
ANNOUNCING JEHOVAH'S KINGDOM

June 1, 2005   Average Printing Each Issue: 26,439,000   Vol. 126, No. 11

THE PURPOSE OF *THE WATCHTOWER* is to exalt Jehovah God as Sovereign Lord of the universe. It keeps watch on world events as these fulfill Bible prophecy. It comforts all peoples with the good news that God's Kingdom will soon destroy those who oppress their fellowmen and that it will turn the earth into a paradise. It encourages faith in God's now-reigning King, Jesus Christ, whose shed blood opens the way for mankind to gain eternal life. *The Watchtower,* published by Jehovah's Witnesses continuously since 1879, is nonpolitical. It adheres to the Bible as its authority.

IN THIS ISSUE

3   Whatever Happened to World Unity?

4   Where Is the World Heading?

8   Kingdom Proclaimers Report

9   Jehovah Safeguards Those Who Hope in Him

14   Saved, Not by Works Alone, But by Undeserved Kindness

20   When Marital Disagreements Arise

24   "The Life Now"—Enjoying It to the Full!

29   Do Not Give Up in Doing What Is Fine

31   Questions From Readers

32   Do You Converse With Those You Love?

WATCHTOWER STUDIES

JULY 4-10:
Jehovah Safeguards Those Who Hope in Him.
Page 9. Songs to be used: 77, 76.

JULY 11-17:
Saved, Not by Works Alone, But by Undeserved Kindness.
Page 14. Songs to be used: 213, 30.

Publication of *The Watchtower* is part of a worldwide Bible educational work supported by voluntary donations.

Unless otherwise indicated, Scripture quotations are from the modern-language *New World Translation of the Holy Scriptures—With References.*

The Watchtower (ISSN 0043-1087) is published semimonthly by Watchtower Bible and Tract Society of New York, Inc.; M. H. Larson, President; G. F. Simonis, Secretary-Treasurer; 25 Columbia Heights, Brooklyn, NY 11201-2483. Periodicals Postage Paid at Brooklyn, NY, and at additional mailing offices. **POSTMASTER:** Send address changes to Watchtower, **Wallkill, NY 12589.**

Changes of address should reach us 30 days before your moving date. Give us your old and new address (if possible, your old address label).

Semimonthly   ENGLISH

Would you welcome more information or a free home Bible study? Please send your request to Jehovah's Witnesses, using the appropriate address below.

America, United States of: Wallkill, NY 12589. **Antigua:** Box 119, St. Johns. **Australia:** Box 280, Ingleburn, NSW 1890. **Bahamas:** Box N-1247, Nassau, N.P. **Barbados, W.I.:** Crusher Site Road, Prospect, St. James. **Britain:** The Ridgeway, London NW7 1RN. **Canada:** Box 4100, Halton Hills (Georgetown), Ontario L7G 4Y4. **Germany:** Niederselters, Am Steinfels, D-65618 Selters. **Ghana:** P. O. Box GP 760, Accra. **Guyana:** 352-360 Tyrell St., Republic Park Phase 2 EBD. **Hawaii 96819:** 2055 Kam IV Rd., Honolulu. **Hong Kong:** 4 Kent Road, Kowloon Tong. **India:** Post Box 6440, Yelahanka, Bangalore 560 064, KAR. **Ireland:** Newcastle, Greystones, Co. Wicklow. **Jamaica:** P. O. Box 103, Old Harbour, St. Catherine. **Japan:** 1271 Nakashinden, Ebina City, Kanagawa Pref., 243-0496. **Kenya:** P.O. Box 47788, GPO Nairobi 00100. **New Zealand:** P.O. Box 75-142, Manurewa. **Nigeria:** P.M.B. 1090, Benin City 300001, Edo State. **Philippines, Republic of:** P. O. Box 2044, 1060 Manila. **South Africa:** Private Bag X2067, Krugersdorp, 1740. **Trinidad and Tobago, Republic of:** Lower Rapsey Street & Laxmi Lane, Curepe. **Zambia:** Box 33459, Lusaka 10101. **Zimbabwe:** Private Bag WG-5001, Westgate.

NOW PUBLISHED IN 150 LANGUAGES. SEMIMONTHLY: Afrikaans, Albanian,* Amharic, Arabic, Bengali, Bicol, Bislama, Bulgarian, Cebuano,* Chichewa,* Chinese, Chinese (Simplified),* Cibemba,* Croatian,* Czech,*# Danish,*# Dutch,*# East Armenian, Efik,* English*#+⊙ (also Braille), Estonian, Ewe, Fijian, Finnish,*# French,*# Ga, Georgian, German,*# Greek,* Gujarati, Gun, Hebrew, Hiligaynon, Hindi, Hungarian,*# Igbo,* Iloko,* Indonesian, Italian,*# Japanese*# (also Braille), Kannada, Kinyarwanda, Kirundi, Korean*# (also Braille), Latvian, Lingala, Lithuanian, Luvale, Macedonian, Malagasy,* Malayalam, Maltese, Myanmar, Nepali, New Guinea Pidgin, Norwegian,*# Pangasinan, Papiamento (Aruba), Papiamento (Curaçao), Polish,*# Portuguese*# (also Braille), Punjabi, Rarotongan, Romanian,* Russian,* Samar-Leyte, Samoan, Sango, Sepedi, Serbian, Sesotho, Shona,* Silozi, Sinhala, Slovak,* Slovenian, Solomon Islands Pidgin, Spanish*# (also Braille), Sranantongo, Swahili,* Swedish,*# Tagalog,* Tamil, Telugu, Thai, Tigrinya, Tongan, Tshiluba, Tsonga, Tswana, Turkish, Twi, Ukrainian,* Urdu, Vietnamese, Wallisian, Xhosa, Yoruba,* Zulu*

MONTHLY: American Sign Language,△▢ Armenian, Assamese, Azerbaijani (roman script), Brazilian Sign Language,△ Cambodian, Chitonga, Gilbertese, Greenlandic, Haitian Creole, Hausa, Hiri Motu, Icelandic, Isoko, Kaonde, Kazakh, Kikongo, Kiluba, Kirghiz, Kosraean, Kwanyama/Ndonga, Luganda, Marathi, Marshallese, Mauritian Creole, Maya, Mizo, Monokutuba, Moore, Niuean, Ossetian, Otetela, Palauan, Persian, Ponapean, Seychelles Creole, Tahitian, Tatar, Tiv, Trukese, Tumbuka, Tuvaluan, Umbundu, Venda, Yapese, Zande

* Study articles also available in large-print edition.
\# Audiocassettes also available.
+ CD also available.
⊙ MP3 CD-ROM also available.
△ Videocassette
▢ DVD

WHATEVER HAPPENED TO WORLD UNITY?

Arlo K. Abrahamson/AFP/ Getty Images

AP Photo/Lionel Cironneau

"For the first time since World War II the international community is united. . . . The world can therefore seize this opportunity to fulfill the long-held promise of a new world order."

SO SAID a president of the United States in the last decade of the 20th century. At that time, international events seemed to suggest that world unity was on the horizon. Totalitarian governments fell one after another. The Berlin Wall came down, signaling a new era for Europe. The Soviet Union, viewed by many in the West as an instigator of global conflicts, disappeared before the eyes of an astonished world. The Cold War came to an end, and there was optimistic talk about disarmament, including nuclear disarmament. Granted, war broke out in the Persian Gulf, but that seemed to be just a momentary blip that left much of the world more determined to pursue a peaceful order.

Positive signs could be seen not only on the political front but also in other areas of life.

The standard of living was improving in many parts of the world. Advancements in the medical field made it possible for doctors to do things that would have been called miracles just a few decades earlier. Economic growth in many countries moved ahead at a pace that appeared to be leading to global prosperity. It looked as though things were heading in the right direction.

Today, not many years later, we cannot help but ask: 'What happened? Where is the promised world unity?' If anything, the world seems to be moving in the opposite direction. Suicide bombings, terrorist attacks, the reported proliferation of weapons of mass destruction, and other disturbing developments have become regular features of published news. Such events appear to be pushing the world further and further away from unity. One prominent financier recently said: "We are becoming enmeshed in a vicious circle of escalating violence."

World Unity or Global Fragmentation?

When the United Nations was formed, one of the stated purposes was "to develop friendly relations among nations based on respect for the principle of equal rights and self-determination of peoples." After nearly 60 years, has that noble objective been reached? Far from it! Rather than "friendly relations," the expression "self-determination" appears to be more on the mind of the nations. Peoples and ethnic groups struggling to establish their own identity and sovereignty have increasingly divided the world. When the United Nations was formed, it had 51 member nations. Today, there are 191.

As we have seen, toward the end of the 20th century, hope for a united world was in the air. Since then, that hope has turned to dismay as mankind has witnessed the progressive fragmentation of the world community. The violent disintegration of Yugoslavia, the clashes between Chechnya and Russia, the war in Iraq, and the continued carnage in the Middle East —all of this has been evidence of ever greater disunity.

There is no doubt that many of the efforts for peace have been sincere and well-meant. In spite of this, world unity seems unattainable. Many are left wondering: 'Why does world unity remain so elusive? Where is the world heading?'

WHERE IS THE WORLD HEADING?

WORLD UNITY. It sounds so good. Does not everyone want it? Yes, there has been much talk about unity. Again and again, meetings of world leaders have focused on the subject. In August 2000, more than 1,000 religious leaders met at the United Nations in New York for the Millennium World Peace Summit. They discussed solutions to world conflicts. However, the conference itself was a reflection of the world's simmering controversies. A mufti from Jerusalem refused to come because of the presence of a Jewish rabbi. Others were offended because the Dalai Lama was not invited to the first two days for fear of antagonizing China.

In October 2003, world security issues were discussed by Pacific Rim nations at the Asia-Pacific Economic Cooperation (APEC) summit held in Thailand. The 21 nations present pledged to dismantle terrorist groups and agreed on ways to increase global security. Yet, during the conference several representatives grumbled about one prime minister's remarks, which were said to be a hate-filled attack on the Jews.

Why No Unity?

Though there is a lot of talk about unifying the world, we see few concrete results. Despite the sincere efforts of many, why has world unity continued to elude mankind into the 21st century?

Part of the answer is reflected in the comments of one of the prime ministers who attended the APEC conference. He said, "There is this thing called national pride." Yes, human society is steeped in nationalism. Each nation and ethnic group is driven by the desire for self-determination. National sovereignty combined with the spirit of competition and greed has produced a volatile mix. In one case after another, when national interests conflict with global interests, national interests win out.

Nationalism is well described by the psalmist's expression, "the pestilence causing adversities." (Psalm 91:3) It has been like a plague on humanity, leading to untold suffering. Nationalism with its resultant ha-tred of other peoples has existed for centuries. Today, nationalism continues to fan the flames of divisiveness, and human rulers have not been able to stop it.

Many authorities recognize that nationalism and self-interest are the root of the world's problems. For example, former United Nations Secretary-General U Thant observed: "So many of the problems that we face today are due to, or the result of, false attitudes . . . Among these is the concept of narrow nationalism—'my country, right or wrong.'" Still, nations today, engrossed in self-interest, are clamoring more and more for their own sovereignty. Those who have the advantage do not wish to give up even a little of it. For example, the *International Herald Tribune* made this observation about the European Union: "Rivalry and mistrust remain basic patterns of European politics. For most EU member states, it is still unacceptable for one of their peers to gain greater influence and take the lead."

God's Word, the Bible, correctly describes the result of all human rule, saying: "Man has dominated man to his injury." (Ecclesiastes 8:9) By breaking the world up into their own separate dominions, groups of men as well as individuals have experienced the fulfillment of this Bible principle: "One isolating himself will seek his own selfish longing; against all practical wisdom he will break forth."—Proverbs 18:1.

Our Creator, who knows what is best for us, never purposed for humans to set up their own governments and rule themselves. By doing so, men have ignored God's purpose and the fact that everything belongs to him. Psalm 95:3-5 says: "Jehovah is a great God and a great King over all other gods, he in whose hand are the inmost depths of the earth and to whom the peaks of the mountains belong; to whom the sea, which he himself made, belongs and whose own hands formed the dry land itself." God is the rightful Sovereign to whom all should look for rulership. By pursuing their own sovereignties, the nations are working against his will.—Psalm 2:2.

What Is Needed?

The only way the world will become united is by having one world authority that works in the interests of all people. Many thinking people recognize this need. Those who do, however, often look in the wrong place. For example, many commentators, including religious leaders, have urged people to look to the United Nations for world unity. However, human organizations, no matter how noble their ideals, have *never* been able to solve mankind's international problems. Rather, most of these organizations have simply become a reflection of the disunity that exists among various nations.

The Bible warns against looking to human institutions for the solution when it says: "Do not put your trust in nobles, nor in the son of earthling man, to whom no salvation belongs." (Psalm 146:3) Does this leave us at a dead end as far as world unity is concerned? Not at all. There is another way.

Many are unaware that God has already set up a government that is capable of uniting the world. The Bible says about Jehovah God: "I, even I, have installed my king upon Zion, my holy mountain. Ask of me, that I may give nations as your inheritance and the ends of the earth as your own possession." (Psalm 2:6, 8) Note that the scripture refers to Jehovah God as having 'installed his king,' whom he refers to as "my son" in verse 7. This is none other than God's foremost spirit Son, Jesus Christ, who has been given authority over all nations.

How World Unity Will Come About

Most people do not recognize this heavenly rulership that God has set up. The nations tenaciously hang on to their own perceived right to sovereignty. However, God will not tolerate those who refuse to recognize his sovereignty and the government that he has set up. Concerning those who refuse to accept this arrangement, Psalm 2:9 says: "You [the Son, Jesus Christ] will break them with an iron scepter, as though a potter's vessel you will dash them to pieces." Whether they realize it or not, the nations are now on a march that will lead to a collision with God. The last book of the Bible speaks of "the kings of the entire inhabited earth" being gathered together "to the war of the great day of God the Almighty." (Revelation 16:14) The nations and their divisive ways will be put out of existence. This will pave the way for God's government to go about its work unhindered.

As the Universal Sovereign, Jehovah God through his Son will wisely exert the power to make the changes necessary for a united world. God's government will bring about true unity and will bless all lovers of righteousness. Why not take a few minutes to read Psalm 72 in your Bible? There, a prophetic picture is given of what rulership under God's Son will do for mankind. People will experience true world unity, and all their problems—oppression, violence, poverty, and so forth—will be gone.

In today's divided world, many think that such a hope is unrealistic. But it would be a mistake to think so. God's promises have never failed, and they never will. (Isaiah 55: 10, 11) Would you like to see this change? You can. In fact, there is already a people who are preparing for that time. They come from all nations, but instead of fighting, they are now unitedly submitting to God's sovereignty. (Isaiah 2:2-4) Who are they? They are known as Jehovah's Witnesses. Why not accept the invitation to visit their meeting places? Likely, you will enjoy refreshing association with a people who can help you to submit to God's sovereignty and enjoy unity that will never end.

People from all nations are preparing for life in a united world

An Honest People Brings Praise to Jehovah

THROUGHOUT the earth, Jehovah's Witnesses—young and old—are known for their honesty. Consider examples from three continents.

Seventeen-year-old Olusola, who lives in Nigeria, was going home from school one day when she found a purse on the ground. She took it to the principal, who counted the money, and it came to ₦6,200 (about $45, U.S.). The principal returned the purse to the teacher who had lost it. In appreciation, the teacher gave Olusola ₦1,000 (about $7, U.S.) and told her to pay her school fees with it. When other students heard what had happened, they ridiculed Olusola. Some weeks later, a student reported his money stolen, so the teachers were asked to search all the students. "You stand here," the teacher told Olusola. "I know that as one of Jehovah's Witnesses, you cannot steal." The money was found with two of the boys who had ridiculed Olusola, and they were severely punished. Olusola wrote: "I am very happy that I am known as one of Jehovah's Witnesses, who will never steal, thus giving glory to Jehovah."

Upon leaving home one day, Marcelo, a native of Argentina, found a briefcase on the ground a few yards from his back door. Taking the briefcase inside the house, he and his wife carefully opened it. Much to their surprise, they found a huge sum of money in cash, credit cards, and several signed checks, one of which was for a million pesos. On an invoice, they found a phone number. They called the owner and arranged to return the briefcase with its contents at the place where Marcelo works. When the owner arrived, he seemed nervous. The employer told him to calm down, for Marcelo was one of Jehovah's Witnesses. As a reward for finding the briefcase, the owner gave Marcelo only 20 pesos (about $6, U.S.). This infuriated the employer because he was very much impressed by Marcelo's honesty. This gave Marcelo the opportunity to explain that as one of Jehovah's Witnesses, he wants to be honest at all times.

From Kyrgyzstan comes the following experience. Rinat, a six-year-old boy, found a purse belonging to a lady who lived nearby. The purse contained 1,100 som (about $25, U.S.). When Rinat returned the lost purse to the lady, she counted the money and then told Rinat's mother that 200 som was missing. Rinat said that he had not taken the money. Then all went out to search for the missing money and found it near the place where the purse had been found. The woman was astonished. She expressed her gratitude to Rinat and his mother, first for returning the lost money and second, for his Christian upbringing.

JEHOVAH SAFEGUARDS THOSE WHO HOPE IN HIM

"Let your loving-kindness and your trueness themselves constantly safeguard me."
—PSALM 40:11.

KING DAVID of ancient Israel "earnestly hoped in Jehovah" and was moved to say that Jehovah "inclined his ear to [him] and heard [his] cry for help." (Psalm 40:1) He repeatedly saw firsthand how Jehovah safeguarded those who loved Him. David, therefore, could ask to be *constantly* safeguarded by Jehovah. (Psalm 40:11) Counted among the faithful men and women to whom "a better resurrection" is promised, David is presently secure in Jehovah's memory as one who will receive that reward. (Hebrews 11:32-35) His future is thus assured in the best possible way. His name is inscribed in Jehovah's "book of remembrance."—Malachi 3:16.

2 Although the faithful ones mentioned in Hebrews chapter 11 lived before the earthly sojourn of Jesus Christ, they nevertheless lived in harmony with what Jesus taught when he said: "He that is fond of his soul destroys it, but he that hates his soul in this world will safeguard it for everlasting life." (John 12:25) Thus, being safeguarded by Jehovah clearly does not mean immunity from suffering or persecution. It does mean that one is protected in a spiritual way so as to be able to maintain a fine standing before God.

1. What did King David request of Jehovah, and how is that request presently being granted?
2. How do the Scriptures help us to understand what is meant by being safeguarded by Jehovah?

3 Jesus himself was the object of cruel persecution and reproach, and his enemies finally succeeded in putting him to a most disgraceful and painful death. Yet, this is no contradiction of God's promise to safeguard the Messiah. (Isaiah 42:1-6) Jesus' resurrection on the third day after his ignominious death proves that Jehovah heard his cry for help—just as Jehovah had heard David's. In response, Jehovah gave Jesus the strength to maintain integrity. (Matthew 26:39) Thus safeguarded, Jesus gained immortality in the heavens, and millions of humans who have exercised faith in the ransom have come in line for everlasting life.

3. What evidence do we have that Christ Jesus was safeguarded by Jehovah, and what was the outcome?

How did Jehovah safeguard David and Jesus?

⁴ We can be confident that Jehovah is just as willing and able to safeguard his servants now as he was in the days of David and of Jesus. (James 1:17) The relatively few remaining anointed brothers of Jesus still on earth can rely on Jehovah's promise: "An incorruptible and undefiled and unfading inheritance . . . is reserved in the heavens for you, who are being safeguarded by God's power through faith for a salvation ready to be revealed in the last period of time." (1 Peter 1: 4, 5) The "other sheep," who have an earthly hope, can likewise put their trust in God and his promise through the psalmist: "O love Jehovah, all you loyal ones of his. The faithful ones Jehovah is safeguarding."—John 10:16; Psalm 31:23.

Safeguarded Spiritually

⁵ In modern times, Jehovah has made provisions for safeguarding his people in a spiritual way. While not shielding them from persecution or from difficulties and tragedies common to life, he has loyally given them the help and incentive needed to safeguard their intimate relationship with him. The foundation upon which they have built this relationship is their faith in God's loving ransom provision. Some of these faithful Christians have been anointed by God's spirit to become joint rulers with Christ in heaven. They have been declared righteous as spiritual sons of God, and to them these words apply: "He delivered us from the authority of the darkness and transferred us into the kingdom of the Son of his love, by means of whom we have our release by ransom, the forgiveness of our sins."—Colossians 1:13, 14.

⁶ Millions of other faithful Christians are assured that they too can benefit from God's provision of the ransom. We read: "The Son of man came, not to be ministered to, but to minister and to give his soul a ransom in exchange for many." (Mark 10:45) Those Christians look forward to enjoying in due time "the glorious freedom of the children of God." (Romans 8:21) Meanwhile, they treasure their personal friendship with God and sincerely strive to strengthen that relationship.

⁷ One way in which Jehovah safeguards the spiritual welfare of his people is by providing a program of progressive training. This allows them to come to an ever more ac-

4. What assurance is given to anointed Christians and to the "other sheep"?
5, 6. (a) How have God's people been safeguarded in modern times? (b) What relationship do the anointed have with Jehovah, and what about those with an earthly hope?

7. By what means does Jehovah today safeguard the spiritual welfare of his people?

In what ways are God's people safeguarded spiritually today?

inite they will certainly be guarded." —Psalm 37:28.

Safeguarded by Loving-Kindness and Trueness

9 In his prayer recorded in Psalm 40, David asked to be safeguarded by Jehovah's loving-kindness and trueness. Jehovah's trueness and his love for righteousness require that he clearly set out what his standards are. Those who live by these standards are to a great degree safeguarded from the distresses, fears, and problems experienced by those who ignore them. For example, we can protect ourselves and our loved ones from many heartbreaking problems if we avoid drug and alcohol abuse, sexual promiscuity, and a violent life-style. And even those who wander from Jehovah's way of trueness—as did David at times—have the assurance that God is still "a place of concealment" for repentant wrongdoers. Such can joyfully cry out: "You will safeguard me from distress itself." (Psalm 32:7) What an expression of God's loving-kindness!

10 Another example of divine loving-kindness is that God warns his servants to remain separate from the wicked world, which he will soon destroy. We read: "Do not be loving either the world or the things in the world. If anyone loves the world, the love of the Father is not in him; because everything in the world—the desire of the flesh and the desire of the eyes and the showy display of one's means of life—does not originate with the Father, but originates with the world." By giving heed to this warning and acting accordingly, we can literally safeguard our life

curate knowledge of truth. Jehovah also provides ongoing guidance through his Word, his organization, and his holy spirit. Under the direction of "the faithful and discreet slave," God's people around the world are like an international family. The slave class looks after the spiritual needs and when necessary even the physical needs of the family of Jehovah's servants—irrespective of their national origin or social standing.—Matthew 24:45.

8 As Jehovah did not physically shield Jesus from the onslaughts of his enemies, He does not shield Christians that way today. But this is no indication of God's displeasure. Far from it! Rather, it underscores his confidence that they will uphold his side of the great universal issue. (Job 1:8-12; Proverbs 27:11) Jehovah will never forsake those loyal to him, "for Jehovah is a lover of justice, and he will not leave his loyal ones. To time indef-

_____
8. What confidence does Jehovah place in his loyal ones, assuring them of what?

_____
9, 10. (a) How does Jehovah's trueness safeguard his people? (b) How does the Bible show that Jehovah safeguards his loyal ones by means of his loving-kindness?

Although we are proud to be serving Jehovah, we must always remain humble

for all eternity, for the text continues: "Furthermore, the world is passing away and so is its desire, but he that does the will of God remains forever."—1 John 2:15-17.

Safeguarded by Thinking Ability, Discernment, and Wisdom

11 To those hoping to gain God's approval, David's son Solomon was inspired to write: "Thinking ability itself will keep guard over you, discernment itself will safeguard you." He also urged: "Acquire wisdom . . . Do not leave it, and it will keep you. Love it, and it will safeguard you."—Proverbs 2:11; 4:5, 6.

12 We exercise thinking ability if we meditate on what we learn from God's Word. Doing so enables us to develop greater discernment so that we can set proper priorities. This is vital, since most of us know—possibly through personal experience—that problems arise when people either purposely or unintentionally set unwise priorities. Satan's world puts before us as goals material riches, prominence, and power, while Jehovah stresses the more important spiritual values. A failure to give the latter priority over the

former can cause families to disintegrate, friendships to collapse, and spiritual goals to fade. As a result, a person can be left with nothing more than the sad reality indicated by Jesus' words: "Of what benefit is it for a man to gain the whole world and to forfeit his soul?" (Mark 8:36) Wisdom dictates that we heed Jesus' counsel: "Keep on, then, seeking first the kingdom and his righteousness, and all these other things will be added to you."—Matthew 6:33.

The Danger of Becoming Self-Centered

13 Humans are by nature interested in themselves. When personal desires and interests become paramount in life, however, trouble results. Therefore, to safeguard our friendship with him, Jehovah instructs us to avoid being self-centered. This term means being "concerned solely with one's own desires, needs, or interests." Does that not accurately describe many people today? Significantly, the Bible foretells that "in the last days" of Satan's wicked system, "men will be lovers of themselves," or will become self-centered.—2 Timothy 3:1, 2.

11, 12. Explain how thinking ability, discernment, and wisdom safeguard us.

13, 14. What does it mean to be self-centered, and why is it unwise to become so?

14 Christians appreciate the wisdom of observing the Bible command to take an interest in others, loving them as one loves oneself. (Luke 10:27; Philippians 2:4) People in general may view this as impractical, yet it is vital if we are to enjoy successful marriages, happy family relationships, and satisfying friendships. Thus, a true servant of Jehovah must never allow the natural interest in self to dominate his life to the exclusion of more important interests. First and foremost, this means the interests of Jehovah, the God he worships.

15 A self-centered attitude can lead to one's being self-righteous, which, in turn, can cause a person to become narrow-minded, presumptuous. The Bible aptly says: "You are inexcusable, O man, whoever you are, if you judge; for in the thing in which you judge another, you condemn yourself, inasmuch as you that judge practice the same things." (Romans 2:1; 14:4, 10) The religious leaders in Jesus' day became so convinced of their own righteousness that they felt qualified to censure Jesus and his followers. By so doing, they set themselves up as judges. Being blind to their own shortcomings, they actually brought condemnation upon themselves.

16 Judas, the follower of Jesus who betrayed him, allowed himself to become a person judging others. On the occasion at Bethany when Mary, Lazarus' sister, anointed Jesus with perfumed oil, Judas strongly objected. He voiced his indignation by arguing: "Why was it this perfumed oil was not sold for three hundred denarii and given to the poor people?" But the report continues in explanation: "He said this, though, not because he was concerned about the poor, but because he was a thief and had the money box and used to carry off the monies put in it." (John 12:1-6) Let us never become like Judas or the religious leaders, who were quick to judge others, only to condemn themselves.

17 Regrettably, some early Christians, while they were not thieves like Judas, did fall victim to pride, becoming self-assuming. Of them, James wrote: "You take pride in your self-assuming brags." Then he added: "All such taking of pride is wicked." (James 4:16) Boasting about what we have done or about our privileges in Jehovah's service is self-defeating. (Proverbs 14:16) We recall what happened to the apostle Peter, who in a moment of excessive self-confidence boasted: "Although all the others are stumbled in connection with you, never will I be stumbled! . . . Even if I should have to die with you, I will by no means disown you." In reality, we have nothing to boast about in ourselves. Everything we enjoy is only because of Jehovah's loving-kindness. Remembering this will keep us from being self-assuming.—Matthew 26:33-35, 69-75.

18 "Pride is before a crash, and a haughty spirit before stumbling," we are told. Why? Jehovah answers: "Self-exaltation and pride . . . I have hated." (Proverbs 8:13; 16:18) No wonder Jehovah was incensed at "the insolence of the heart of the king of Assyria and for the self-importance of his loftiness of

15, 16. (a) To what can a self-centered attitude lead, as exemplified by whom? (b) In reality, what does a person do when he is quick to judge others?

17. Illustrate the danger inherent in being self-assuming or in becoming excessively self-confident.
18. How does Jehovah feel about pride?

Do You Recall?

- How were King David and Jesus Christ safeguarded?
- How are Jehovah's people today safeguarded?
- Why should we avoid overemphasizing self?
- Why can we be proud and yet humble?

eyes"! (Isaiah 10:12) Jehovah called him to account. Soon all of Satan's world, together with its proud, self-important leaders, visible and invisible, will also be called to account. May we never mirror the self-willed attitude of Jehovah's adversaries!

19 True Christians have every reason to be proud of being servants of Jehovah. (Jeremiah 9:24) At the same time, they have every reason to remain humble. Why? Because "all have sinned and fall short of the glory of God." (Romans 3:23) So to safeguard our position as Jehovah's servants, we must have the attitude of the apostle Paul, who said that "Christ Jesus came into the world to save sin-

19. In what respect are God's people proud and yet humble?

ners," and then he added: "Of these I am foremost."—1 Timothy 1:15.

20 Since Jehovah's people gladly push self into the background in order to place divine interests in the foreground, we can be assured that Jehovah will continue to safeguard them spiritually. We can also be assured that when the great tribulation strikes, Jehovah will safeguard his people not only spiritually but also physically. Upon entering into God's new world, they will be able to cry out: "Look! This is our God. We have hoped in him, and he will save us. This is Jehovah. We have hoped in him. Let us be joyful and rejoice in the salvation by him."—Isaiah 25:9.

20. How does Jehovah safeguard his people now, and how will he safeguard them in the future?

SAVED, NOT BY WORKS ALONE, BUT BY UNDESERVED KINDNESS

"You have been saved through faith . . . It is not owing to works, in order that no man should have ground for boasting."—EPHESIANS 2:8, 9.

PEOPLE today take great pride in personal accomplishments, and they are often quick to boast about them. Christians are different. They refrain from overemphasizing their own accomplishments, even those having to do with true worship. While they rejoice over what Jehovah's people accomplish as a whole, they keep their individual contribution in the background. They realize that in Jehovah's service, right motives are more important than personal accomplishments. Anyone who is eventually given the gift of

1. How do Christians differ from people in general as regards personal accomplishments, and why?

eternal life will have gained it, not by personal accomplishments, but through faith and by God's undeserved kindness.—Luke 17:10; John 3:16.

2 The apostle Paul was well-aware of this fact. After having prayed three times for relief from "a thorn in the flesh," he received Jehovah's reply: "My undeserved kindness is sufficient for you; for my power is being made perfect in weakness." Humbly accepting Jehovah's decision, Paul said: "Most gladly, therefore, will I rather boast as respects my weaknesses, that the power of the Christ may

2, 3. Of what did Paul boast, and why?

like a tent remain over me." Paul's humble attitude is one that we should want to imitate.—2 Corinthians 12:7-9.

3 Even though Paul was outstanding in performing Christian works, he recognized that his achievements were not owing to any particular abilities of his own. With modesty, he noted: "To me, a man less than the least of all holy ones, this undeserved kindness was given, that I should declare to the nations the good news about the unfathomable riches of the Christ." (Ephesians 3:8) No boastful attitude here nor holier-than-thou haughtiness. "God opposes the haughty ones, but he gives undeserved kindness to the humble ones." (James 4:6; 1 Peter 5:5) Do we follow Paul's example, humbly considering ourselves to be less than the least of our brothers?

"Considering That the Others Are Superior"

4 The apostle Paul counseled Christians:

---

4. Why may we sometimes find it difficult to consider others to be superior to us?

"My undeserved kindness is sufficient for you"

"[Do] nothing out of contentiousness or out of egotism, but with lowliness of mind considering that the others are superior to you." (Philippians 2:3) This may be a challenge, especially if we happen to be in a position of responsibility. Perhaps the difficulty arises because we have been influenced, to a certain extent, by the spirit of competition so prevalent in the world today. Possibly, as children we were taught to compete, either with our siblings at home or with our classmates at school. We were perhaps constantly urged to reach out for the honor of being the school's star athlete or its top student. Of course, giving our best in any proper undertaking is commendable. However, Christians do so, not to call undue attention to themselves, but to benefit fully from the activity and perhaps to benefit others as well. However, aspiring always to be praised as number one can be dangerous. How so?

5 If left unchecked, a competitive or egotistical spirit can cause a person to become disrespectful and arrogant. He may become envious of the abilities and privileges of others. Proverbs 28:22 says: "A man of envious eye is bestirring himself after valuable things, but he does not know that want itself will come upon him." He might even presumptuously reach out for positions to which he is not entitled. To justify his actions, he may start to murmur and become critical of others—tendencies that Christians should shun. (James 3:14-16) At any rate, he is running the risk of developing a me-first attitude.

6 The Bible, therefore, urges Christians: "Let us not become egotistical, stirring up competition with one another, envying one

---

5. If left unchecked, to what can a competitive spirit lead?
6. How does the Bible warn against a competitive spirit?

another." (Galatians 5:26) The apostle John spoke of a fellow Christian who evidently fell victim to this kind of spirit. "I wrote something to the congregation," said John, "but Diotrephes, who likes to have the first place among them, does not receive anything from us with respect. That is why, if I come, I will call to remembrance his works which he goes on doing, chattering about us with wicked words." What a sad situation for a Christian to fall into! —3 John 9, 10.

⁷ Of course, it is unrealistic to think that a Christian can completely avoid all competitive pursuits. His secular work, for example, may involve economic competition with other individuals or businesses producing similar products or offering similar services. Even in such instances, however, a Christian will want to carry on his business in a spirit of respect, love, and consideration. He will rule out illegal or unchristian practices and avoid becoming a person known primarily for a competitive, dog-eat-dog attitude. He will not feel that being number one—in whatever pursuit—is the most important thing in life. If that is true of secular pursuits, how much more it is true in the realm of worship!

"Not in Comparison With the Other Person"

⁸ The attitude Christians should have in their worship is set out in these inspired words: "Let each one prove what his own

---

7. What will a Christian want to avoid in today's competitive workplace?
8, 9. (a) Why do Christian elders have no reason to compete with one another? (b) Why does 1 Peter 4:10 apply to all of God's servants?

work is, and then he will have cause for exultation in regard to himself alone, and not in comparison with the other person." (Galatians 6:4) Elders in the congregation, knowing that they are not in competition with one another, cooperate and work closely together as a body. They rejoice in the contribution each one can make to the overall welfare of the congregation. They thus ward off disruptive competition and set a fine example in unity for the rest of the congregation.

⁹ Because of age, experience, or natural abilities, some elders may be more efficient than others, or they may be endowed with greater insight. As a result, elders have different responsibilities in Jehovah's organization. Instead of making comparisons, they bear in mind the counsel: "In proportion as each one has received a gift, use it in ministering to one another as fine stewards of God's undeserved kindness expressed in various ways." (1 Peter 4:10) In reality, this text applies to all of Jehovah's servants, for to some extent all have received the

Elders rejoice in the contribution each one can make to the welfare of the congregation

gift of accurate knowledge and all enjoy the privilege of sharing in the Christian ministry.

¹⁰ Our sacred service is pleasing to Jehovah only when it is rendered out of love and devotion, not for the sake of elevating ourselves over others. It is therefore vital to have a balanced view of our activity in support of true worship. While no one can accurately judge another's motives, Jehovah "is making an estimate of hearts." (Proverbs 24:12; 1 Samuel 16:7) Thus, we do well to ask ourselves from time to time, 'What is my motive for performing works of faith?'—Psalm 24:3, 4; Matthew 5:8.

Proper View of Our Work

¹¹ If motive is all-important in gaining Jehovah's approval, then to what extent should we be concerned about our works of faith? As long as we perform our ministry with the right motive, is it really necessary to keep account of what we do or how much? These are reasonable questions, since we do not want to put numbers ahead of acts of faith or let having a good report become a major concern regarding our Christian activity.

¹² Notice what the book *Organized to Do Jehovah's Will* says: "Early followers of Jesus Christ took an interest in reports of progress in the preaching work. (Mark 6:30) The Bible book of Acts tells us that there were about 120 persons present when holy spirit was poured out on the disciples at Pentecost. Soon the number of disciples grew to 3,000 and then to 5,000. . . . (Acts 1:15; 2:5-11, 41, 47; 4:4; 6:7) What fine encouragement the news of these increases must have brought to the disciples!" For the same reason, Jehovah's Witnesses today endeavor to keep accurate records of what is accomplished worldwide in fulfillment of Jesus' words: "This good news of the kingdom will be preached in all the inhabited earth for a

10. In what way only will our sacred service be acceptable to Jehovah?
11. What questions about our activity in the ministry can reasonably be considered?

12, 13. (a) What are some reasons why we keep a record of our field service? (b) What reasons do we have for joy when viewing the overall report of our preaching activity?

witness to all the nations; and then the end will come." (Matthew 24:14) Such reports provide a realistic picture of what is done in the world field. They show where help is needed and which kind of literature and how much of it is required to advance the preaching work.

¹³ Thus, reporting our preaching activity enables us to carry out our commission to preach the Kingdom good news more effectively. Besides, are we not encouraged when we hear about the work that our brothers are doing in other parts of the world? News of growth and expansion earth wide fills us with joy, moves us to greater activity, and assures us of Jehovah's blessing. And how gratifying to know that *our personal* report is included in that worldwide report! Ours is small in comparison with the grand total, but it does not go unnoticed by Jehovah. (Mark 12:42, 43) Remember, without *your* report, the overall report would be incomplete.

¹⁴ Of course, much of what every Witness does in fulfilling his responsibility as a dedicated servant of Jehovah does not appear on his report. For instance, the report does not include regular personal Bible study, attendance and participation at Christian meetings, congregational duties, assistance to fellow believers as needed, financial support of the worldwide Kingdom work, and so on. Thus, while our field service report plays its part, helping us to maintain our zeal in preaching and to avoid slacking off, we must keep it in proper perspective. It is not to be viewed as a spiritual license or passport, determining our eligibility for everlasting life.

---

14. Besides preaching and teaching, what is included in our worship of Jehovah?

"Zealous for Fine Works"

¹⁵ Clearly, even though works alone cannot save us, they are necessary. That is why Christians are called "a people peculiarly his own, zealous for fine works" and why they are encouraged to "consider one another to incite to love and fine works." (Titus 2:14; Hebrews 10:24) More to the point, another Bible writer, James, simply says: "As the body without spirit is dead, so also faith without works is dead."—James 2:26.

¹⁶ Important though the good works themselves may be, the motives for doing them are even more important. It is therefore wise for us to check our motives from time to time. Since no human can accurately know the motives of others, however, we must beware of judging others. "Who are you to judge the house servant of another?" we are asked, with the obvious answer: "To his own master he stands or falls." (Romans 14:4) Jehovah, the Master of all, and his appointed Judge, Christ Jesus, will judge us,

---

15. Though works alone cannot save us, why are they necessary?
16. What is even more important than works, but of what should we beware?

Without your report, the overall report would be incomplete

not on the basis of our works alone but also on the basis of our motives, our opportunities, our love, and our devotion. Only Jehovah and Christ Jesus can accurately judge whether we have done what Christians are admonished to do, in the words of the apostle Paul: *"Do your utmost* to present yourself approved to God, a workman with nothing to be ashamed of, handling the word of the truth aright."—2 Timothy 2:15; 2 Peter 1:10; 3:14.

¹⁷ Jehovah is reasonable in what he expects of us. According to James 3:17, "the wisdom from above is," among other things, *"reasonable."* Would it not be the course of wisdom, as well as a true accomplishment, for us to imitate Jehovah in this regard? Thus, we should not try to set unreasonable and unreachable expectations for ourselves or for our brothers.

¹⁸ As long as we keep a balanced view of our works of faith and Jehovah's un-

deserved kindness, we will maintain the joy that is a distinguishing mark of true servants of Jehovah. (Isaiah 65:13, 14) We can rejoice in the blessings that Jehovah is pouring out on his people as a whole, regardless of how much we personally may be able to do. Continuing in "prayer and supplication along with thanksgiving," we will petition God to help us do our utmost. Then, beyond all doubt, "the peace of God that excels all thought will guard [our] hearts and [our] mental powers by means of Christ Jesus." (Philippians 4:4-7) Yes, we can draw comfort and encouragement from knowing that we can be saved, not by works alone, but by Jehovah's undeserved kindness!

Can You Explain Why Christians

- refrain from boasting about personal accomplishments?
- avoid showing a competitive spirit?
- report their Christian activity in the field ministry?
- avoid judging fellow Christians?

---

17. While striving to do our utmost, why should we keep James 3:17 in mind?
18. What can we look forward to when we have a balanced view of our works and Jehovah's undeserved kindness?

When MARITAL DISAGREEMENTS Arise

NO HUSBAND or wife of sound mind enjoys marital conflict, but it is all too common. Typically, one spouse says something that irritates the other. Voices are raised, and tempers flare, igniting an emotionally charged argument with caustic remarks. Then comes icy silence, with both mates stubbornly refusing to talk. In time, the anger subsides and apologies are exchanged. Peace is restored—at least until the next disagreement.

Marital spats are the topic of an endless stream of jokes and story lines of television programs, but the reality is far from amusing. Indeed, a Bible proverb says: "Thoughtless words can wound as deeply as any sword." (Proverbs 12:18, *Today's English Version*) Yes, harsh speech may leave emotional scars that linger long after the dispute has ended. Arguing may even lead to violence. —Exodus 21:18.

Of course, because of human imperfection, problems in marriage are sometimes unavoidable. (Genesis 3:16; 1 Corinthians 7:28) Still, frequent and intense disputes should not be dismissed as normal. Experts have noted that a pattern of quarreling increases the likelihood that a couple will eventually divorce. Hence, it is vital that you and your spouse learn to handle disagreements in a peaceful manner.

Assessing the Situation

If your marriage is plagued by arguments, try to determine if there is a pattern to your disputes. Typically, what happens when you and your spouse disagree on a matter? Does the discussion quickly veer off course and deteriorate into a volley of insults and accusations? If so, what can you do?

First, take an honest look at how you as an individual might be contributing to the problem. Are you easily provoked? Are you argumentative by nature? What would your spouse say about you in this regard? This last question is important to consider, for you and your mate may have different views about what constitutes being argumentative.

For example, suppose that your spouse tends to be somewhat reserved, while you are candid and highly intense when expressing yourself. You might say: "When I was growing up, that's the way *everyone* in my family communicated. It's not arguing!" And perhaps to you it is not. Possibly, though, what you see as uninhibited straight talk is perceived by your mate as hurtful and combative arguing. Simply being aware that you and your mate have different communication styles can help prevent misunderstandings.

Remember, too, that arguing does not always involve shouting. Paul wrote to Christians: "Let . . . screaming and abusive speech be taken away from you." (Ephesians 4: 31) "Screaming" alludes to a raised voice, whereas "abusive speech" refers to the content of the message. Viewed in that light, even whispered words can be argumentative if they are irritating or demeaning.

With the foregoing in mind, look again at how you handle disagreements with your mate. Are you argumentative? As we have seen, the real answer to that question largely depends on the perception of your spouse. Rather than dismissing your mate's view as oversensitive, try to see yourself as that one sees you, and make adjustments where they are needed. Paul wrote: "Let each one keep seeking, not his own advantage, but that of the other person."—1 Corinthians 10:24.

"Pay Attention to How You Listen"

Another aspect of handling disagreements is found in Jesus' words: "Pay attention to how you listen." (Luke 8:18) True, Jesus was not talking about communication in marriage. Nevertheless, the principle applies. How well do you listen to your spouse? Do you listen at all? Or do you abruptly interrupt with pat solutions to problems that you have not completely understood? "When anyone is replying to a matter before he hears it, that is foolishness on his part and a humiliation," the Bible says. (Proverbs 18:13) When a disagreement arises, then, you and your spouse need to talk the matter out and truly listen to each other.

Rather than downplay your spouse's viewpoint, strive to show "fellow feeling." (1 Peter 3:8) In the original Greek, this term basically denotes suffering with another person. If your mate is distressed over something, you should share the feeling. Endeavor to look at the matter from his or her perspective.

Evidently, the godly man Isaac did that. The Bible tells us that his wife, Rebekah, was deeply disturbed over a family issue involving her son Jacob. "I have come to abhor this life of mine because of the daughters of Heth," she said to Isaac. "If Jacob ever takes a wife from the daughters of Heth like these from the daughters of the land, of what good is life to me?"—Genesis 27:46.

Granted, out of anxiety, Rebekah likely overstated matters. After all, did she really abhor her life? Would she literally prefer to die if her son married one of the daughters of Heth? Probably not. Still, Isaac did not minimize Rebekah's feelings. Instead, Isaac saw that Rebekah's concern had merit, and he took action accordingly. (Genesis 28:1) Do the same the next time your mate is anxious over a matter. Instead of dismissing it as something trivial, *listen* to your mate, *respect* his or her view, and *respond* in a compassionate manner.

Listening and Insight

A Bible proverb states: "The insight of a man certainly slows down his anger." (Proverbs 19:11) In the heat of a disagreement, it is so easy to react impulsively to every sharp word that is uttered by your spouse. Usually, though, this only serves to escalate the argument. Hence, when listening to your

spouse, make it your determination to hear not only the words being said but also the feelings behind the words. Such insight will help you to see past personal annoyances and get to the root of the problem.

For instance, suppose your wife says to you, "You never spend any time with me!" You could be inclined to get irritated and deny the charge with cold facts. "I spent a whole day with you last month!" you might reply. But if you listen attentively, you might find that your wife is not really asking for more minutes or hours. Instead, she may be asking for reassurances, telling you that she feels neglected and unloved.

Suppose that you are a wife and your husband expresses his concern over a recent purchase. "How could you spend that much money?" he asks in utter disbelief. Your impulse might be to defend yourself with facts regarding the family finances or by comparing your purchase with one of his own. Insight, however, will help you to see that your husband may not be talking about dollars and cents. Instead, he may be troubled because he was left out of the decision-making process when it came to a major purchase.

Of course, each couple may have a different way to address how much time they spend together and how purchasing decisions are made. The point is that when matters become subjects of contention, insight will slow down your anger and enable you to perceive the real issues at hand. Rather than impulsively reacting, follow the Bible writer James' admonition to be "swift about hearing, slow about speaking, slow about wrath."—James 1:19.

When you do speak, remember that how you speak to your mate is important. The Bible says that "the tongue of the wise ones is a healing." (Proverbs 12:18) When you and your spouse are caught up in a disagreement, do your words hurt or do they heal? Do they build roadblocks, or do they pave the way for reconciliation? As we have already seen, angry or impulsive responses only stir up contention.—Proverbs 29:22.

If a disagreement deteriorates into a verbal boxing match, put forth more effort to stick to the point. Focus on the cause, not

"I feel neglected and unloved"

"You never spend any time with me!"

"I spent a whole day with you last month!"

the person. Be more concerned with *what* is right than *who* is right. Be careful that your words do not fan the flames of the argument. The Bible says: "A word causing pain makes anger to come up." (Proverbs 15:1) Yes, what you say and how you say it may make a difference in whether you elicit your mate's cooperation or not.

Aim to Resolve, Not to Win

In our dealing with disagreements, the goal is a solution rather than a victory. How can you reach a solution? The surest way is to search out and apply the Bible's counsel, and husbands especially should take the initiative to do so. Rather than being quick to express strong opinions on the issues or problems at hand, why not look at them from Jehovah's viewpoint? Pray to him, and seek the peace of God that will guard your hearts and mental powers. (Ephesians 6:18; Philippians 4:6, 7) Make an earnest effort to look out for the personal interest of not just you but also your mate.—Philippians 2:4.

What often makes a bad situation worse is letting hurt feelings and uncontrolled emotions dominate your thoughts and actions. On the other hand, being willing to be readjusted by the counsel of God's Word leads to peace, agreement, and Jehovah's blessing. (2 Corinthians 13:11) Therefore, be guided by "the wisdom from above," manifest godly qualities, and reap benefits as "those who are making peace."—James 3:17, 18.

Really, all should learn to handle disagreements peacefully, even if this means sacrificing personal preferences. (1 Corinthians 6:7) Indeed, apply Paul's admonition to put away "wrath, anger, badness, abusive speech, and obscene talk out of your mouth. . . . Strip off the old personality with its practices, and clothe yourselves with the new personality."—Colossians 3:8-10.

At times, of course, you will say things that you later regret. (James 3:8) When this happens, apologize to your spouse. Continue to put forth effort. In time, you and your spouse will likely see great improvement in how you handle disagreements.

"THE LIFE NOW"
—ENJOYING IT TO THE FULL!

AS TOLD BY
TED BUCKINGHAM

I had been a full-time minister for six years and married for six months when I was suddenly stricken with poliomyelitis. It was 1950, and I was just 24 years old. Nine months in the hospital gave me plenty of time to reflect on my life. With my new disabilities, what would the future hold for my wife, Joyce, and me?

IN 1938 my father, never a religious man, obtained a copy of the book *Government.** The political turmoil and prospect of war probably prompted him to get the book. To my knowledge, he never read it, but my deeply religious mother did. Her reaction to its message was immediate. She left the Church of England, and despite opposition from my father, she became a faithful Witness of Jehovah and remained such until her death in 1990.

Mother took me to my first Christian meeting at a Kingdom Hall in Epsom, south of London. The congregation met in a former store, and we listened to a recording of a talk by J. F. Rutherford, who was overseeing the work of Jehovah's Witnesses at that time. It left a deep impression on me.

The heavy bombing during the blitz on London posed increasing dangers. So in 1940 my father decided to move the family to a safer location—Maidenhead, a small town 30 miles west of London. This was beneficial, as the 30 members of the congrega-

---

* Published in 1928 by Jehovah's Witnesses, but no longer in print.

tion there proved to be a fine source of encouragement. Fred Smith, a spiritual stalwart baptized in 1917, took me under his wing and trained me to become a more effective preacher. I remain greatly indebted to him for his example and loving help.

Entering Full-Time Service

In 1941, at age 15, I was baptized in the river Thames on a cold March day. By then, my elder brother, Jim, had enrolled as a full-time evangelizer. Today, he and his wife, Madge, live in Birmingham, after spending a lifetime in Jehovah's service in circuit and district assignments throughout Britain. My younger sister, Robina, and her husband, Frank, also remain faithful servants of Jehovah.

I was working as an accountant for a dress manufacturer. One day the managing director called me to his office to offer me the prospect of a promising career as a buyer for the firm. For some time, however, I had been thinking of following my brother's example, so I politely declined my employer's offer, explaining why. To my surprise, he warmly commended me for wanting to pursue such worthwhile Christian activity. So after a district convention in Northampton in 1944, I became a full-time evangelizer.

My first assignment was to Exeter, in the county of Devon. This city was by then slowly recovering from wartime bombing. I shared an apartment already occupied by two pioneers, Frank and Ruth Middleton, who were very kind to me. I was just 18 with little experience in laundry and cooking, but things improved as I developed my skills.

My preaching companion was 50-year-old Victor Gurd, an Irishman who had been

With my mother in 1946

witnessing since the 1920's. He taught me to schedule my time profitably, to develop a deeper interest in Bible reading, and to appreciate the value of different Bible translations. During those formative years, Victor's steadfast example was just what I needed.

The Challenge of Neutrality

The war was drawing to a close, but the authorities were still pursuing young men for military service. I had appeared before a tribunal in 1943 at Maidenhead, where I clearly stated my case for exemption as a minister of the Gospel. Although my appeal was refused, I decided to move to Exeter to take up my assignment. So it was at Exeter that I was eventually summoned to appear before the local court. Sentencing me to six months of hard labor in prison, the magistrate told me that he was sorry it could not be for longer. After serving those six months, I was sent back to prison for an additional four months.

As I was the only Witness in the prison, the warders called me Jehovah. It was rather strange responding to that name at roll call, as I had to, but what a privilege to hear God's name heralded day after day! It let the other prisoners know that it was my conscientious stand as one of Jehovah's Witnesses that had put me among them. Later, Norman Castro was sent to the same prison, and there was a name change. We then became Moses and Aaron.

I was moved from Exeter to Bristol and finally to Winchester prison. Conditions were not always pleasant, but it helped to have a sense of humor. Norman and I were happy to observe the Memorial together while at Winchester. Francis Cooke, who visited us in prison, gave a fine talk for us.

Changes in the Postwar Years

At the Bristol convention in 1946, where the Bible study aid *"Let God Be True"* was

With Joyce on our wedding day, in 1950

At a Bristol convention in 1953

released, I met a pretty lass, Joyce Moore, who was also pioneering in Devon. Our friendship blossomed, and we were married four years later at Tiverton, where I had been since 1947. We made our home in a rented room for which we paid 15 shillings ($1.10, U.S.) a week. It was a great life!

During our first year of marriage, another move took us south to Brixham, a delightful port town where the technique of trawling for fish was first developed. We had not been there long, however, when I was stricken with polio while traveling to a London convention. I fell into a coma. I was eventually discharged from the hospital—after nine months, as mentioned earlier. My right hand and both legs were badly affected, as they still are, and I had to use a walking stick. My dear wife was my constant cheerful companion and source of encouragement, especially as she managed to continue in the fulltime ministry. But what would we do now? I was soon to learn that Jehovah's hand is never short.

The following year we attended an assembly at Wimbledon, London. By this time I was walking without my stick. There we met Pryce Hughes, who was overseeing the work in Britain. He immediately greeted me: "Hey! We want you in the circuit work!" I could have received no greater encouragement! Was I fit enough? Joyce and I both wondered about that, but with a week's training and full trust in Jehovah, we were on our way back to the southwest of England, where I had been assigned to serve as a circuit overseer. I was by then just 25 years of age, but I still recall with deep appreciation the kindness and patience of those Witnesses who were so helpful to me.

Of all our different fields of theocratic activity, Joyce and I found that visiting the congregations brought us closest to our Christian brothers and sisters. We had no car, so we traveled either by train or by bus.

Although I was still adapting to the restrictions brought about by my illness, we enjoyed our privileges right up to 1957. It was a fulfilling life, but that year a further challenge presented itself.

To Missionary Service

Receiving an invitation to attend the 30th class of Gilead was thrilling for us. I was coping well with my paralysis, so Joyce and I gladly accepted the call. From experience, we knew that Jehovah always provides the strength if we seek to do his will. Five months of intensive training at the Watchtower Bible School of Gilead, located in beautiful South Lansing, New York, U.S.A., quickly passed. The students were mainly married couples in the traveling work. When the class was asked if any would like to volunteer for the foreign missionary field, we were among those who readily did so. Where would we go? To Uganda, East Africa!

Since the work of Jehovah's Witnesses was banned in Uganda at that time, I was advised to settle in the country and find secular employment. After a long journey by train and boat, we arrived at Kampala, Uganda. The immigration officials were not pleased to see us and allowed us to stay for just a few months. We were then ordered to leave. On instructions from headquarters, we traveled to Northern Rhodesia (now Zambia). There it was a great joy to meet four of our Gilead classmates—Frank and Carrie Lewis and Hayes and Harriet Hoskins. From there, we were reassigned shortly afterward to Southern Rhodesia (now Zimbabwe).

We traveled by train and had our first glimpse of the magnificent Victoria Falls before arriving in Bulawayo. We stayed for a while with the McLuckie family, who had been among the first Witnesses to settle there. It was our privilege to get to know them well during the next 16 years.

Serving an isolated group (above) and a congregation (left) in Southern Rhodesia, now Zimbabwe

Adapting to Changes

After two weeks' training to become acquainted with the African field, I was appointed to serve as district overseer. Witnessing in the African bush meant carrying water, food, bedding, personal clothing, a film projector and electric generator, a large screen, and other necessities. All of this was packed into a truck sturdy enough to carry us over the rough terrain.

I worked with the African circuit overseers while Joyce happily helped their wives and children who came along too. Walking in the African veld can be tiring, especially during the heat of the day, but I soon found that in this climate, my physical limitations were easier to cope with, and for that I was grateful.

The people were generally poor. Many were steeped in tradition and superstition and practiced polygamy; yet they showed a deep respect for the Bible. In some areas, congregation meetings were held under large, shady trees, and during the evenings, illumination came from suspended oil lamps. We always experienced a sense of awe when studying God's Word directly under the starry heavens, such a magnificent part of his creation.

Showing the Watch Tower Society's films on African reserves was another unforgettable experience. A congregation might number 30 Witnesses, but on those occasions, we knew we could often expect an attendance of 1,000 or more people!

In the tropics, ill health can be a problem, of course, but at all times it is essential to keep a positive outlook. Joyce and I learned to manage quite well—I dealt with my occasional bouts of malaria, and Joyce coped with sickness caused by amoebas.

We were later assigned to the branch office in Salisbury (now Harare), where it was a privilege to work alongside other faithful servants of Jehovah, among them Lester Davey and George and Ruby Bradley. The government appointed me to serve as a marriage officer, which enabled me to conduct weddings for the African brothers, thereby strengthening the bond of Christian marriage within the congregations. A few years later, another privilege came my way. I was to visit all the non-Bantu congregations in the country. For more than a decade, Joyce and I enjoyed getting to know our brothers in this way, and we rejoiced at their spiritual progress. During that time we also visited our brothers in Botswana and Mozambique.

Moving On Again

After many happy years in southern Africa, we were reassigned in 1975 to Sierra Leone, West Africa. We soon settled in at the branch office to enjoy our new field of activity, but this was not to last. I became sick and weak because of a severe attack of malaria, and eventually I had to be treated in London, where I was advised not to return to Africa. We were saddened by this, but Joyce and I were warmly welcomed into the London Bethel family. The numerous African brothers in many of the London congregations made us feel right at home too. As my health improved, we adapted to yet another routine, and I was asked to care for the Purchasing Department. With all the expansion we have seen over the ensuing years, this has been absorbing work.

In the early 1990's, my dear Joyce became ill with motor neuron disease, and she died in 1994. She had proved to be a loving, loyal, and faithful wife, always willing to adjust to the varying circumstances we faced together. To deal with a loss such as this, I have found that it is important to maintain a clear spiritual outlook and keep looking forward. Prayerfully holding to a good theocratic schedule, including preaching, also helps me to keep my mind fully occupied.—Proverbs 3:5, 6.

Serving at Bethel is a privilege and a fine way of life. There are so many young folk to work with and many joys to be shared. One blessing is the number of visitors we receive here in London. Sometimes I see dear friends from my African assignments, and happy memories come flooding back. All of this helps me to continue to enjoy fully "the life now" and to contemplate with confidence and hope the life "which is to come." —1 Timothy 4:8.

Do Not Give Up in *Doing What Is Fine*

"MAINTAIN your conduct fine among the nations," exhorted the apostle Peter. (1 Peter 2:12) The Greek word translated "fine" refers to something that is "beautiful, noble, honorable, excellent." In this day and age, it may seem hopelessly unrealistic to expect noble or honorable conduct from people in general. By and large, however, Jehovah's people today have succeeded in following Peter's exhortation. In fact, they are known the world over for their fine conduct.

This is particularly noteworthy when we consider the stresses and strains we face during these "critical times hard to deal with." (2 Timothy 3:1) Trials are part of our daily life, and opposition to the Christian way of life is common. In addition, while some trials are short-lived, others persist without letup, even increasing in intensity. Nevertheless, the apostle Paul admonished: "Let us not give up in doing what is fine, for in due season we shall reap if we do not tire out." (Galatians 6:9) Just how is it possible to do—and continue to do—what is fine in the face of heartrending trials and unrelenting hostilities?

Help in Doing What Is Fine

Being "noble, honorable, excellent" is clearly a state of the inner person, a quality of the heart. Therefore, maintaining fine conduct in the face of trials and hardships is,

> *We must have implicit trust that Jehovah will not allow any test 'beyond what we can bear,' that he will always "make the way out"*

not a spur-of-the-moment reaction, but the result of daily following and practicing Bible principles in all aspects of life. What are some things that can help in this regard? Consider the following.

Cultivate the mental attitude of Christ. It takes humility to endure what may seem unjust. A person who thinks highly of himself is unlikely to tolerate mistreatment. Jesus, however, "humbled himself and became obedient as far as death." (Philippians 2:5, 8) By imitating him, we will not 'get tired or give out' in our sacred service. (Hebrews 12:2, 3) Practice humble obedience by cooperating willingly with those taking the lead in your local congregation. (Hebrews 13:17) Learn to view others as "superior" to you, putting their interests ahead of your own. —Philippians 2:3, 4.

Remember that Jehovah loves you. We must be convinced that Jehovah "is and that he becomes the rewarder of those earnestly seeking him." (Hebrews 11:6) He genuinely cares for us and wants us to get everlasting life. (1 Timothy 2:4; 1 Peter 5:7) Remembering that nothing can nullify God's love for us will help us not to give up under trial. —Romans 8:38, 39.

Put full trust in Jehovah. Trust in Jehovah is essential, especially when trials seem to be unending or life threatening. We must have implicit trust that Jehovah will not

that we ask . . . , he hears us." (1 John 5:14) If Jehovah allows our trial to continue as a test of our integrity, we pray for his help to endure. (Luke 22:41-43) Prayer teaches us that we are never alone, that with Jehovah on our side, we will always come off victorious.—Romans 8:31, 37.

Fine Works—'Cause for Praise and Honor'

From time to time, all Christians are "grieved by various trials." Yet, we must "not give up in doing what is fine." When under stress, draw strength from the knowledge that your faithfulness will ultimately be "a cause for praise and glory and honor." (1 Peter 1:6, 7) Take full advantage of all spiritual provisions from Jehovah to build you up. When you need personal attention, go to those who serve as shepherds, teachers, and counselors in the Christian congregation. (Acts 20:28) Be regular in attending all congregation meetings, which 'incite us to love and fine works.' (Hebrews 10:24) A program of daily Bible reading and personal study will help keep you alert and spiritually strong; so will having a regular share in the Christian ministry. —Psalm 1:1-3; Matthew 24:14.

The more you taste of Jehovah's love and care, the greater will be your desire to be "zealous for fine works." (Titus 2:14) Remember, "he that has endured to the end is the one that will be saved." (Matthew 24:13) Yes, be determined 'not to give up in doing what is fine'!

Keeping busy in theocratic activities can help prepare us to face trials

allow any test 'beyond what we can bear,' that he will always "make the way out." (1 Corinthians 10:13) Even the threat of death can be faced courageously when our trust is in Jehovah. —2 Corinthians 1:8, 9.

Persevere in prayer. Heartfelt prayer is vital. (Romans 12:12) Sincere prayer is one of the ways that we draw close to Jehovah. (James 4:8) Through personal experience, we learn that "no matter what it is

---

IN OUR NEXT ISSUE

Work—A Blessing or a Curse?

———

Parents, Provide for the Needs of Your Family

———

Praising Jehovah at School

Questions From Readers

Upon hearing that the imprisoned Peter was at the door, why did the disciples say: "It is his angel"?—Acts 12:15.

The disciples may erroneously have assumed that an angelic messenger representing Peter stood at the gate. Consider the context of this passage.

Peter had been arrested by Herod, who had put James to death. So the disciples had good reason to believe that Peter would meet a similar end. Bound by chains, the imprisoned Peter was guarded by four shifts of four soldiers each. Then, one night he was miraculously freed and led out of the prison by an angel. When Peter finally realized what was happening, he said: "Now I actually know that Jehovah sent his angel forth and delivered me out of Herod's hand."—Acts 12:1-11.

Peter immediately went to the house of Mary the mother of John Mark, where a number of the disciples were gathered. When he knocked on the door of the gateway, a servant girl named Rhoda went to answer. Upon recognizing Peter's voice, she ran to tell the others without even letting him in! At first, the disciples could not believe that Peter was at the gate. Instead, they erroneously assumed: "It is his angel."—Acts 12:12-15.

Did the disciples believe that Peter had already been put to death and that his disembodied spirit was at the gate? This could hardly be the case, for Jesus' followers knew the Scriptural truth about the dead—that they are "conscious of nothing at all." (Ecclesiastes 9:5, 10) What, then, could the disciples have meant when they said: "It is his angel"?

Jesus' disciples knew that throughout history, angels rendered personal assistance to God's people. For example, Jacob spoke of "the angel who has been recovering me from all calamity." (Genesis 48:16) And regarding a young child in their midst, Jesus told his followers: "See to it that you men do not despise one of these little ones; for I tell you that their angels in heaven always behold the face of my Father who is in heaven." —Matthew 18:10.

Interestingly, *Young's Literal Translation of the Holy Bible* renders the word *ag'ge·los* ("angel") as "messenger." It appears that there was a belief among some Jews that each servant of God had his own angel—in effect, a "guardian angel." Of course, this view is not directly taught in God's Word. Still, it is possible that when the disciples said, "It is his angel," they were assuming that an angelic messenger representing Peter stood at the gate.

Do You Converse With Those You Love?

"**O**UR ability to communicate with loved ones is decreasing dramatically," reports the Polish weekly *Polityka*. In the United States, it is estimated that marriage mates spend only six minutes a day conversing with each other in a meaningful way. Some authorities think that half of all separations and divorces are the result of this decline.

How about conversation between parents and children? In most instances, "it turns out to be, not a conversation, but an interrogation: How was school? How about your friends?" observes the above report. "How are our children to learn to develop emotional relationships?" it asks.

Since good communication skills do not just happen, how can we improve our ability to converse? The Christian disciple James gave us important advice: "Every man must be swift about hearing, slow about speaking, slow about wrath." (James 1:19) Yes, to have an upbuilding conversation, we need to listen attentively and not interrupt impatiently or jump to conclusions. Avoid criticism because it can easily smother a conversation. Moreover, Jesus used tactful questions, not to interrogate, but to draw out what was in the heart of his listener and to strengthen the bond between them.—Proverbs 20:5; Matthew 16:13-17; 17:24-27.

Applying the fine principles found in the Bible, take the initiative to converse and communicate with those dear to you. That may result in a warm relationship that will be cherished for many years—even a lifetime.

JUNE 15, 2005

THE WATCHTOWER

ANNOUNCING JEHOVAH'S KINGDOM

WORK A Blessing or a Curse?

THE WATCHTOWER®

ANNOUNCING JEHOVAH'S KINGDOM

June 15, 2005   Average Printing Each Issue: 26,439,000   Vol. 126, No. 12

THE PURPOSE OF *THE WATCHTOWER* is to exalt Jehovah God as Sovereign Lord of the universe. It keeps watch on world events as these fulfill Bible prophecy. It comforts all peoples with the good news that God's Kingdom will soon destroy those who oppress their fellowmen and that it will turn the earth into a paradise. It encourages faith in God's now-reigning King, Jesus Christ, whose shed blood opens the way for mankind to gain eternal life. *The Watchtower,* published by Jehovah's Witnesses continuously since 1879, is nonpolitical. It adheres to the Bible as its authority.

IN THIS ISSUE

3   The Work Paradox

4   Work—A Blessing or a Curse?

9   Philo of Alexandria—Mixing Scripture With Speculation

13   Expanding Where Early Christianity Once Flourished

18   Parents, Provide for the Needs of Your Family

23   Young People, Praise Jehovah!

29   Praising Jehovah at School

30   We Can Cope With Any Trial!

32   "Persecuted for His Faith"

WATCHTOWER STUDIES

JULY 18-24:
Parents, Provide for the Needs of Your Family.
Page 18. Songs to be used: 164, 152.

JULY 25-31:
Young People, Praise Jehovah!
Page 23. Songs to be used: 221, 165.

Publication of *The Watchtower* is part of a worldwide Bible educational work supported by voluntary donations.

Unless otherwise indicated, Scripture quotations are from the modern-language *New World Translation of the Holy Scriptures—With References.*

The Watchtower (ISSN 0043-1087) is published semimonthly by Watchtower Bible and Tract Society of New York, Inc.; M. H. Larson, President; G. F. Simonis, Secretary-Treasurer; 25 Columbia Heights, Brooklyn, NY 11201-2483. Periodicals Postage Paid at Brooklyn, NY, and at additional mailing offices. POSTMASTER: Send address changes to Watchtower, **Wallkill, NY 12589.**

Changes of address should reach us 30 days before your moving date. Give us your old and new address (if possible, your old address label).

Semimonthly   ENGLISH

Would you welcome more information or a free home Bible study? Please send your request to Jehovah's Witnesses, using the appropriate address below.

America, United States of: Wallkill, NY 12589. *Antigua:* Box 119, St. Johns. *Australia:* Box 280, Ingleburn, NSW 1890. *Bahamas:* Box N-1247, Nassau, N.P. *Barbados, W.I.:* Crusher Site Road, Prospect, St. James. *Britain:* The Ridgeway, London NW7 1RN. *Canada:* Box 4100, Halton Hills (Georgetown), Ontario L7G 4Y4. *Germany:* Niederselters, Am Steinfels, D-65618 Selters. *Ghana:* P. O. Box GP 760, Accra. *Guyana:* 352-360 Tyrell St., Republic Park Phase 2 EBD. *Hawaii 96819:* 2055 Kam IV Rd., Honolulu. *Hong Kong:* 4 Kent Road, Kowloon Tong. *India:* Post Box 6440, Yelahanka, Bangalore 560 064, KAR. *Ireland:* Newcastle, Greystones, Co. Wicklow. *Jamaica:* P. O. Box 103, Old Harbour, St. Catherine. *Japan:* 1271 Nakashinden, Ebina City, Kanagawa Pref., 243-0496. *Kenya:* P.O. Box 47788, GPO Nairobi 00100. *New Zealand:* P.O. Box 75-142, Manurewa. *Nigeria:* P.M.B. 1090, Benin City 300001, Edo State. *Philippines, Republic of:* P. O. Box 2044, 1060 Manila. *South Africa:* Private Bag X2067, Krugersdorp, 1740. *Trinidad and Tobago, Republic of:* Lower Rapsey Street & Laxmi Lane, Curepe. *Zambia:* Box 33459, Lusaka 10101. *Zimbabwe:* Private Bag WG-5001, Westgate.

NOW PUBLISHED IN 150 LANGUAGES. SEMIMONTHLY: Afrikaans, Albanian,* Amharic, Arabic, Bengali, Bicol, Bislama, Bulgarian, Cebuano,* Chichewa,* Chinese, Chinese (Simplified),* Cibemba,* Croatian,* Czech,*# Danish,*# Dutch,*# East Armenian, Efik,* English*#+☉ (also Braille), Estonian, Ewe, Fijian, Finnish,*# French,*# Ga, Georgian, German,*# Greek,* Gujarati, Gun, Hebrew, Hiligaynon, Hindi, Hungarian,*# Igbo,* Iloko,* Indonesian, Italian,*# Japanese*# (also Braille), Kannada, Kinyarwanda, Kirundi, Korean*# (also Braille), Latvian, Lingala, Lithuanian, Luvale, Macedonian, Malagasy,* Malayalam, Maltese, Myanmar, Nepali, New Guinea Pidgin, Norwegian,*# Pangasinan, Papiamento (Aruba), Papiamento (Curaçao), Polish,*# Portuguese*# (also Braille), Punjabi, Rarotongan, Romanian,* Russian,* Samar-Leyte, Samoan, Sango, Sepedi, Serbian, Sesotho, Shona,* Silozi, Sinhala, Slovak,* Slovenian, Solomon Islands Pidgin, Spanish*# (also Braille), Sranantongo, Swahili,* Swedish,*# Tagalog,* Tamil, Telugu, Thai, Tigrinya, Tongan, Tshiluba, Tsonga, Tswana, Turkish, Twi, Ukrainian,* Urdu, Vietnamese, Wallisian, Xhosa, Yoruba,* Zulu*

MONTHLY: American Sign Language,△▢ Armenian, Assamese, Azerbaijani (roman script), Brazilian Sign Language,△ Cambodian, Chitonga, Gilbertese, Greenlandic, Haitian Creole, Hausa, Hiri Motu, Icelandic, Isoko, Kaonde, Kazakh, Kikongo, Kiluba, Kirghiz, Kosraean, Kwanyama/Ndonga, Luganda, Marathi, Marshallese, Mauritian Creole, Maya, Mizo, Monokutuba, Moore, Niuean, Ossetian, Otetela, Palauan, Persian, Ponapean, Seychelles Creole, Tahitian, Tatar, Tiv, Trukese, Tumbuka, Tuvaluan, Umbundu, Venda, Yapese, Zande

* Study articles also available in large-print edition.
\# Audiocassettes also available.
+ CD also available.
☉ MP3 CD-ROM also available.
△ Videocassette
▢ DVD

The Work Paradox

**"To work—to work! It is such infinite delight to know that we still have the best things to do."
—Katherine Mansfield, author (1888-1923).**

DO YOU share the idealistic notion of work expressed in the statement above? How do you personally view work? Do you perhaps feel that work is a long, dark tunnel between leisurely weekends? Or has your work become a passion bordering on addiction?

For most people, the largest segment of their waking hours is devoted to work. Work may determine where we live and what kind of life-style we have. From young adulthood to retirement, many find that work is the single pursuit that most dominates their lives. Some of us get great personal satisfaction from our labor. Others measure the value of work by income or prestige, while still others see work as no more than a time filler or even a time waster.

There are those who work to live and those who live to work; others die at or because of their work. For instance, according to a recent United Nations report, work causes more pain and death "than wars or drug and alcohol abuse combined." Commenting on this, *The Guardian* newspaper of London reported: "More than two million people die from work-related accidents or disease every year . . . Exposure to dust, chemicals, noise and radiation [is] causing cancer, heart disease and strokes." Child labor and forced labor are just two other ugly realities of current working conditions.

In addition, there is what psychologist Steven Berglas calls "supernova burnout." He describes the diligent worker who has reached the pinnacle of his career only to feel "chronic trepidation, distress, despondency or depression attributable to the belief that he is trapped in a job, or on a career path, from which he can neither escape nor derive psychological gratification."

Hard Work Versus Workaholism

In a world where many toil for long hours, it is useful to distinguish between hard workers and workaholics. Many workaholics see the workplace as a haven in a dangerous,

unpredictable world; the industrious experience work as an essential and sometimes fulfilling obligation. Workaholics allow work to crowd out all other aspects of life; hard workers know when to turn off the computer, to switch gears mentally, and to be present when celebrating their wedding anniversary, for example. Workaholics find an emotional payoff in overwork and get an adrenaline high from it; hard workers do not.

Modern society blurs the line between the two as it glamorizes overwork. Modems, cell phones, and pagers may blur the boundary between workplace and home. When any place can be the workplace and any time can be work time, some will work themselves to death.

How do some people react to such an unwholesome attitude? Sociologists have discerned a trend of overworked and overstressed people toward bringing spirituality into the workplace and integrating religious and professional lives. The *San Francisco Examiner* reported that "the melding of spirituality and work has become something of a public phenomenon."

Regarding Silicon Valley, a high-tech mecca in the United States, a recent report stated: "As executives count the empty workplace parking slots as layoffs persist, parking spots at evening Bible studies are in short supply." Whatever the significance of that might be, many around the globe have found that the Bible has a positive influence on their outlook on work, resulting in a more balanced approach to life.

How can the Bible help us gain a balanced view of work? Are there any Scriptural principles that can help us face the challenges of the modern workplace successfully? The following article will deal with these questions.

Work
A Blessing or a Curse?

"With a man there is nothing better than that he should . . . see good because of his hard work."—Ecclesiastes 2:24.

"USED up at the end of the workday." In a recent survey, that is how 1 in 3 employees described the way they very often feel. This comes as no surprise in an environment where people suffer from stress; they work longer and take more work home —all the while having bosses who seldom offer a word of appreciation.

The advent of mass production has made many workers feel like little more than cogs in the wheels of a massive, impersonal machine. Inspiration and creativity are often squelched. Naturally, this affects people's attitudes toward work. Motivation to take a personal interest in one's work is easily dampened. The desire for excellence in craftsmanship might be quenched. Such consequences could breed dislike for the work itself, perhaps making a person hate his job.

Examining Our Attitude

Granted, we cannot always change our circumstances. Do you not agree, however, that we can adjust our attitude? If you find that you have to some extent been influenced by negative attitudes toward work, you do well to consider God's viewpoint and principles relating to this subject. (Ecclesiastes 5:18) Many have found that considering these has given them a measure of happiness and contentment in their work.

God is the Supreme Worker. God is a worker. Perhaps we have not thought of him in that way, but that is how he first introduces himself in the Bible. The Genesis account opens with Jehovah's creating the heavens and the earth. (Genesis 1:1) Think of the array of roles that God assumed when he thus started creating—designer, organizer, engineer, artist, materials specialist, project developer, chemist, biologist, zoologist, programmer, linguist, to name just a few. —Proverbs 8:12, 22-31.

What was the quality of God's work? The Bible record says that it was "good," "very good." (Genesis 1:4, 31) Indeed, the creation is "declaring the glory of God," and we too should praise him! —Psalm 19:1; 148:1.

Many workers feel like cogs in an impersonal machine

However, God's work did not end with the creation of the physical heavens and earth and the first human pair. Jehovah's Son, Jesus Christ, said: "My Father has kept working until now." (John 5: 17) Yes, Jehovah continues to work by providing for his creatures, sustaining his creation, and saving his faithful worshipers. (Nehemiah 9:6; Psalm 36:6; 145:15, 16) He even uses people, "God's fellow workers," to assist with accomplishing certain tasks. —1 Corinthians 3:9.

Work can be a blessing. Does the Bible not say that work is a curse? Genesis 3:17-19 might seem to imply that God punished Adam and Eve for their rebellion by putting the burden of work on them. When condemning those first humans, God said to Adam: "In the sweat of your face you will eat bread until you return to the ground." Was that a blanket condemnation of work?

No. Rather, because of Adam and Eve's unfaithfulness, extension of the Edenic Paradise would not happen then and there. The ground came under God's curse. Sweat and toil were required for a person to eke out a living from the soil.—Romans 8:20, 21.

Instead of presenting work as a curse, the Bible shows that it is a blessing to be cherished. As noted above, God himself is a hard worker. Having created humans in his image, Jehovah has bestowed on them the ability and the authority to manage his earthly creation. (Genesis 1:26, 28; 2:15) That work assignment was given *before* God pronounced the words recorded at Genesis 3:19. If work were a curse and an evil, Jehovah would never have encouraged people to engage in it. Noah and his family had much work to do before and after the Flood. In the Christian era, Jesus' disciples were also urged to work. —1 Thessalonians 4:11.

Still, we all know that work can be burdensome nowadays. Stress, hazards, boredom, disappointment, competition, deception, and injustice are just some of the "thorns and thistles" now associated with it. But work in itself is not a curse. At Ecclesiastes 3: 13, the Bible calls work and its fruitage a gift from God.—See the box "Dealing With Work-Related Stress."

You can glorify God with your work. Quality and excellence in the workplace have always been praised. Quality is one of the keys to a Biblical view of work. God himself does his work with excellence. He has given us talents and abilities, and he wants us to use our skills to a good end. For example, during the construction of the tabernacle in ancient Israel, Jehovah filled people like Bezalel and Oholiab with wisdom, understanding, and knowledge, enabling them to carry out specific artistic and practical tasks. (Exodus 31:1-11) This shows that God took a special interest in the function, craftsmanship, design, and other details of their work.

This has profound implications for our perception of personal abilities and work habits. It helps us see them in a sense as gifts from God, which are not to be taken for granted. Thus, Christians are admonished to do their work as if God himself were reviewing their performance: "Whatever you are doing, work at it whole-souled as to Jehovah, and not to men." (Colossians 3:23) God's servants are commanded to do good work,

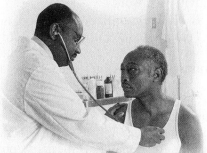

only to increase the sense of pressure.—Matthew 6:25-34.

It is essential that Christians rely on God's strength, not their own. When we feel that we are at the breaking point, God can give us peace and joy in our hearts and provide us with wisdom to deal with any hardship. "Go on acquiring power in the Lord and in the mightiness of his strength," wrote the apostle Paul.—Ephesians 6:10; Philippians 4:7.

Finally, even stressful circumstances can produce positive results. Trials can make us turn to Jehovah, seeking him and trusting in him. They can also prompt us to continue cultivating a Christian personality and the ability to persevere under pressure. Paul admonishes us: "Let us exult while in tribulations, since we know that tribulation produces endurance; endurance, in turn, an approved condition; the approved condition, in turn, hope."—Romans 5:3, 4.

Thus, even stress can become a catalyst for spiritual growth rather than the source of despair and grief.

DEALING WITH WORK-RELATED STRESS

Medical professionals have classified job stress as an occupational hazard. It can cause ulcers and depression and can even lead to suicide. The Japanese have a term for it—*karoshi,* "death from overwork."

Various work-related factors can contribute to stress. These include a change in working hours or conditions, trouble with supervision, a change in responsibilities or kind of work, retirement, and dismissal. Reacting to such stress, some try to escape by changing jobs or environment. Others seek to suppress such stress, only to find that it spills over into other areas of life, most commonly the family. Some people even suffer emotionally, giving way to depression and despair.

Christians are well-equipped to deal with work-generated stress. The Bible provides numerous fundamental principles that can carry us through difficult times with a positive effect on our spiritual and emotional well-being. For example, Jesus said: "Never be anxious about the next day, for the next day will have its own anxieties. Sufficient for each day is its own badness." The encouragement here is to focus on today's problems, not tomorrow's. Thus we avoid blowing our troubles out of proportion, thus making the Christian message more attractive to coworkers and others.—See the box "Applying Bible Principles in the Workplace."

In the light of this, we do well to ask ourselves what kind of quality and diligence we put into our work. Would God be pleased with our performance? Are we fully satisfied with the way we carry out our assigned tasks? If not, there is room for improvement.—Proverbs 10:4; 22:29.

Balance work with spirituality. Although working hard is commendable, there is yet another key element to finding satisfaction in work and in life. It is spirituality. King Solomon, who worked hard and enjoyed all the riches and comforts that life had to offer, came to this conclusion: "Fear the true God and keep his commandments. For this is the whole obligation of man."—Ecclesiastes 12:13.

Clearly, we must consider God's will in whatever we do. Are we working in harmony with his will, or might we be working against it? Are we endeavoring to please God, or are we just trying to please ourselves? If we do

APPLYING BIBLE PRINCIPLES IN THE WORKPLACE

A Christian's attitude and behavior on the job can make the message of the Bible attractive to coworkers and others. In his letter to Titus, the apostle Paul admonishes those in a situation like employees to "be in subjection to their [supervisors] in all things, and please them well, not talking back, not committing theft, but exhibiting good fidelity to the full, so that they may adorn the teaching of our Savior, God, in all things."—Titus 2:9, 10.

For example, consider what one businessman wrote to the world headquarters of Jehovah's Witnesses: "I am writing to ask permission to hire Jehovah's Witnesses. I want to hire them because I know for a fact that they are honest, sincere, and trustworthy, and they will not cheat you. The only people I really trust are Jehovah's Witnesses. Please help me."

Kyle is a Christian who works as a receptionist at a private school. As a result of a misunderstanding, a coworker cursed at her in front of some students. "I had to be careful not to bring shame on Jehovah's name," recalls Kyle. For the next five days, Kyle gave thought to how she could apply Bible principles. One is found at Romans 12:18: "If possible, as far as it depends upon you, be peaceable with all men." She e-mailed her coworker and apologized for the tension between them. Kyle invited her coworker to stay after work to talk and clear the air. When they did that, Kyle's colleague softened and acknowledged the wisdom of Kyle's approach. She said to Kyle, "This must have something to do with your religion" and gave her a warm embrace as they said good night. Kyle's conclusion? "We can never go wrong if we apply Bible principles."

not do God's will, we will eventually suffer the pain of despair, loneliness, and emptiness.

Steven Berglas suggested that burned-out executives 'find a cause they feel passion for and work it into their life.' There is no cause more worthwhile than serving the One who gave us the skills and abilities to do meaningful work. Doing work that pleases our Creator will not leave us dissatisfied. To Jesus, the work he was assigned by Jehovah was as nourishing, satisfying, and refreshing as food. (John 4:34; 5:36) And recall that God,

world can alert us to areas where we need to grow in faith.—1 Corinthians 16:13, 14.

When Work Will Be a Blessing

Those who are now working hard to serve God can look forward to the time when he will restore Paradise and the whole earth will be filled with worthwhile work. Isaiah, a prophet of Jehovah, foretold regarding life then: "They will certainly build houses and have occupancy; and they will certainly plant vineyards and eat their fruitage. They will not build and someone else have

God is the Supreme Worker:
Genesis 1:1, 4, 31;
John 5:17

You can glorify God with your work:
Exodus 31:1-11;
Colossians 3:23

Work can be a blessing:
Genesis 1:28; 2:15;
1 Thessalonians 4:11

Balance work with spirituality:
Ecclesiastes 12:13;
1 Corinthians 3:9

the Supreme Worker, invites us to become his "fellow workers."—1 Corinthians 3:9.

Worshiping God and growing spiritually prepare us for rewarding work and responsibility. Since the workplace is often filled with pressures, conflicts, and demands, our deep-rooted faith and spirituality can supply much-needed strength as we strive to be better employees or employers. On the other hand, the realities of life in this ungodly

occupancy; they will not plant and someone else do the eating. . . . The work of their own hands my chosen ones will use to the full." —Isaiah 65:21-23.

What a blessing work will then be! By learning what God's will is for you and working in harmony with it, may you be among the blessed ones of Jehovah and always 'see good for all your hard work.'—Ecclesiastes 3:13.

PHILO OF ALEXANDRIA
Mixing Scripture With Speculation

IN 332 B.C.E., Alexander the Great advanced into Egypt. Before marching eastward on the road to world conquest, he founded a city that he called Alexandria. It became a center of Greek culture. There, about 20 B.C.E., another conqueror was born, one whose weapons were, not swords and lances, but philosophical reasonings. He is known as Philo of Alexandria, or Philo Judaeus because of his Jewish background.

The Diaspora, which occurred after Jerusalem's destruction in 607 B.C.E., resulted in many Jews living in Egypt. Thousands lived in Alexandria. There were problems, however, between the Jews and their Greek neighbors. The Jews refused to worship the Greek gods, while the Greeks ridiculed the Hebrew Scriptures. With his Greek education and Jewish upbringing, Philo was familiar with the controversy. He believed that Judaism was the true religion. But unlike many, Philo looked for a peaceful way to lead the Gentiles to God. He wanted to make Judaism acceptable to them.

The great lighthouse of Alexandria

Archives Charmet/Bridgeman Art Library

New Meaning to Old Writings

Philo's first language was Greek, as was true of many Jews in Alexandria. So the Greek Septuagint version of the Hebrew Scriptures was the basis of his study. As he examined the *Septuagint* text, he became convinced that it contained elements of philosophy and that Moses possessed "the genius of the philosopher."

Centuries earlier, Greek intellectuals had found stories of gods and goddesses—giants and demons of their ancient Greek mythology—hard to accept. They started reinterpreting those old stories. Classical scholar James Drummond said this about their method: "The philosopher would begin to look for subtle meanings hidden beneath the surface of the mythological tales, and to infer from their very grossness and absurdity that their authors must have intended to exhibit through their sensuous imagery some profound or edifying truth." This process is called allegorical interpretation, and Philo tried to use it to explain the Scriptures.

As an example, think about Genesis 3:22 in Bagster's version of the *Septuagint,* which says: "The Lord God made for Adam and his wife garments of skin, and clothed them." The Greeks felt that making clothes was beneath the dignity of the Supreme God. So Philo found symbolism in that verse and stated: "The garment of skins is a figurative expression for the natural skin, that is to say, our body; for God, when first of all he made the intellect, called it Adam; after that he created the outward sense, to which he gave the name of Life. In the third place, he of necessity also made a body, calling that by a figurative expression, a garment of skins." Thus Philo attempted to make God's act of clothing Adam and Eve a philosophical point to ponder.

Consider also Genesis 2:10-14, which describes the water source for the garden in Eden and mentions four rivers that flowed out of the garden. Philo attempted to penetrate the words and look far beyond the landscape. After commenting on the land itself, he said: "Perhaps this passage also contains an allegorical meaning; for the four rivers are the signs of four virtues." He spec-ulated that the river Pishon represents prudence, the river Gihon is the symbol of sobriety, the Tigris symbolizes fortitude, and the Euphrates denotes justice. Thus allegory supplants geography.

Philo used allegorical interpretation to analyze the creation account, the record of Cain murdering Abel, the Flood of Noah's day, the confusion of languages at Babel, and many precepts of the Mosaic Law. As the example in the preceding paragraph shows, he often acknowledged the literal point of a Bible verse and then introduced his symbolic understanding with such words as: "Perhaps we ought to look on these things as spoken in an allegorical sense." In Philo's

THE CITY OF PHILO

Philo lived and worked in Egyptian Alexandria. For centuries, that city was the world capital of books and scholarly discussions.

Students learned from famous scholars who taught in the schools of the city. Alexandria's library became world renowned. Its holdings grew to hundreds of thousands of items as the librarians sought to obtain copies of every written document.

Later, the worldwide esteem for Alexandria and its stores of knowledge gradually diminished. Emperors in Rome gave preeminence to their own city, and the cultural center shifted to Europe. The decline of Alexandria climaxed in the seventh century C.E. when invaders conquered the city. To this day, historians lament the loss of the famous library, with some claiming that civilization was set back 1,000 years.

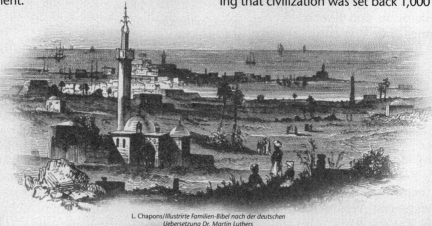

L. Chapons/*Illustrirte Familien-Bibel nach der deutschen Uebersetzung Dr. Martin Luthers*

writings, symbolisms stand out while, sadly, the obvious meaning of the Scriptures fades away.

Who Is God?

Philo argued for the existence of God with a powerful illustration. After describing the land, rivers, planets, and stars, he concluded: "The world is the most artificial and skilfully made of all works, as if it had been put together by some one who was altogether accomplished and most perfect in knowledge. It is in this way that we have received an idea of the existence of God." This was sound reasoning.—Romans 1:20.

But when Philo expounded on the nature of Almighty God, he strayed far from the truth. Philo claimed that God "has no distinctive qualities" and that God "is incomprehensible." Philo discouraged efforts to come to know God, saying that "to attempt to proceed further, so as to pursue investigations into the essence or distinctive qualities of God, is an absolute piece of folly." This thinking came, not from the Bible, but from the pagan philosopher Plato.

Philo said that God is so far beyond comprehension that calling him by a personal name is impossible. Said Philo: "It was, therefore, quite consistent with reason that no proper name could with propriety be assigned to him who is in truth the living God." How contrary to fact!

The Bible leaves no doubt that God has a personal name. Psalm 83:18 says: "You, whose name is Jehovah, you alone are the Most High over all the earth." Isaiah 42:8 quotes God as saying: "I am Jehovah. That is my name." Why did Philo, a Jew with knowledge of these Bible texts, teach that God was nameless? Because he was describing, not the personal God of the Bible, but a nameless, inaccessible god of Greek philosophy.

What Is the Soul?

Philo taught that the soul is separate from the body. He speaks of man as "consisting of body and soul." Can the soul die? Notice Philo's explanation: "When we are alive, we are so though our soul is dead and buried in our body, as if in a tomb. But if it [the body] were to die, then our soul would live according to its proper life, being released from the evil and dead body to which it is bound." To Philo, the soul's death was symbolic. It never really dies. It is immortal.

Yet, what does the Bible teach regarding the soul? Genesis 2:7 says: "Jehovah God proceeded to form the man out of dust from the ground and to blow into his nostrils the breath of life, and the man came to be a living soul." According to the Bible, humans do not *have* souls; rather, they *are* souls.

The Bible also teaches that the soul is not immortal. Ezekiel 18:4 states: "The soul that is sinning—it itself will die." From these scriptures we can properly draw a conclusion: A human is a soul. Therefore, when a human dies, a soul dies.—Genesis 19:19.*

After Philo died, the Jews paid little heed to him. Christendom, however, embraced him. Eusebius and other church leaders believed that Philo had converted to Christianity. Jerome listed him as one of the Church Fathers. Apostate Christians, rather than the Jews, preserved the writings of Philo.

Philo's writings led to a religious revolution. His influence led nominal Christians to adopt the unscriptural doctrine of the immortality of the soul. And Philo's teaching about the Logos (or, Word)

---

* Regarding the soul, *The Jewish Encyclopedia* of 1910 comments: "The belief that the soul continues its existence after the dissolution of the body is a matter of philosophical or theological speculation rather than of simple faith, and is accordingly nowhere expressly taught in Holy Scripture."

contributed to the development of the Trinity, a non-Biblical dogma of apostate Christianity.

Do Not Be Misled

In his study of the Hebrew Scriptures, Philo made sure that he was "not omitting any allegorical meaning which may perchance be concealed beneath the plain language." However, as found at Deuteronomy 4:2, Moses said regarding God's Law: "You must not add to the word that I am commanding you, neither must you take away from it, so as to keep the commandments of Jehovah your God that I am commanding you." With all his apparently good intentions, Philo added layers of speculation that, like a thick haze, obscured the clear instruction of God's inspired Word.

"It was not by following artfully contrived false stories that we acquainted you with the power and presence of our Lord Jesus Christ," said the apostle Peter. (2 Peter 1:16) Unlike the writings of Philo, Peter's instruction to the early Christian congregation was based on fact and on direction by God's spirit, "the spirit of the truth," which guided them into all the truth.—John 16:13.

If you are interested in worshiping the God of the Bible, you need truthful guidance, not interpretations based on human thinking. You need accurate knowledge of Jehovah and his will, and you need the humility to be a sincere student. If you study the Bible with that wholesome attitude, you will get to know "the holy writings, which are able to make you wise for salvation through the faith in connection with Christ Jesus." You will see that the Word of God can make you "fully competent, completely equipped for every good work."—2 Timothy 3:15-17.

ALLEGORICAL INTERPRETATION TODAY

Allegory usually is "the expression by means of symbolic fictional figures and actions of truths or generalizations about human existence." Accounts that employ allegory are said to be symbolic of more important things that are hidden. Like Philo of Alexandria, some modern-day religious teachers use allegorical interpretation to explain the Bible.

Consider Genesis chapters 1-11, in which human history from creation to the scattering of peoples at the tower of Babel is recorded. *The New American Bible,* a Catholic translation, says regarding that part of the Bible: "To make the truths contained in these chapters intelligible to the Israelite people destined to preserve them, they needed to be expressed through elements prevailing among that people at that time. For this reason, the truths themselves must therefore be clearly distinguished from their literary garb." This is saying that Genesis chapters 1-11 are not to be taken literally. Rather, just as garb (clothing) covers the body, so the words cover a deeper meaning.

Jesus, however, taught that those early chapters of Genesis were literally true. (Matthew 19:4-6; 24:37-39) The apostles Paul and Peter did likewise. (Acts 17:24-26; 2 Peter 2:5; 3:6, 7) Sincere Bible students reject explanations that do not agree with the entire Word of God.

Expanding Where Early Christianity Once Flourished

ITALY, the boot-shaped peninsula extending into the Mediterranean Sea, has been a place where religious and cultural events have influenced world history. It is a magnet for millions of tourists attracted by the beauty of its diverse landscape, its famous works of art, and its delicious cuisine. This is also a country where Bible education thrives.

True Christianity may first have reached Rome—capital of the then world power—when Jews and proselytes who became Christians at Pentecost 33 C.E. returned home from Jerusalem. About 59 C.E., the apostle Paul visited Italy for the first time. In seaside Puteoli he "found brothers" in the faith.—Acts 2:5-11; 28:11-16.

As predicted by Jesus and the apostles, before the end of the first century C.E., apostate elements gradually fell away from true Christianity. However, prior to the end of this wicked system of things, true disciples of Jesus have spearheaded the preaching of the good news worldwide—including in Italy.—Matthew 13:36-43; Acts 20:29, 30; 2 Thessalonians 2:3-8; 2 Peter 2:1-3.

A Less Than Promising Beginning

In 1891, Charles Taze Russell, who was taking the lead in the worldwide preaching work of the Bible Students (as Jehovah's Witnesses were then known), visited some Italian cities for the first time. He had to admit that the result of his ministry there was not very promising: "We saw nothing to encourage us to hope for any harvest in Italy." In the spring of 1910, Brother Russell returned to Italy and delivered a Bible lecture in a gymnasium in the center of Rome. What

was the result? "On the whole," he reported, "the meeting was quite a disappointment."

In fact, for some decades the progress of the preaching of the good news in Italy was slow, partly because Jehovah's Witnesses were persecuted by the Fascist dictatorship. During that period, there were no more than 150 Witnesses of Jehovah in the country, the majority of whom had learned Bible truths from relatives or friends who lived abroad.

Spectacular Progress

Following World War II, a number of missionaries were sent to Italy. But as shown by correspondence found in State archives, high-ranking individuals in the Vatican hierarchy asked the government to expel the missionaries. With a few exceptions, the missionaries were forced to leave the country.

Despite the obstacles, crowds in Italy began streaming to "the mountain" of Jehovah's worship. (Isaiah 2:2-4) The increase in

Witnesses has been remarkable. In 2004 there was a peak of 233,527 publishers of the good news, 1 for every 248 inhabitants, and 433,242 attended the Memorial of Christ's death. There were 3,049 congregations of Jehovah's Witnesses meeting in comfortable Kingdom Halls. In recent times, certain segments of the population in particular have been enjoying considerable growth.

Preaching in Scores of Languages

Many immigrants from Africa, Asia, and Eastern Europe come to Italy to find work or a better life or, in some cases, to escape tragic situations. How can these millions be helped spiritually?

Many Witnesses in Italy have accepted the challenge of learning difficult languages, such as Albanian, Amharic, Arabic, Bengali, Chinese, Punjabi, Sinhala, and Tagalog. Starting in 2001, language courses were held to teach these willing ones to give a witness in foreign languages. During the past three years, 3,711 Witnesses attended 79 courses held in 17 different languages. This has made it possible to form and strengthen 146 congregations and 274 groups in 25 different languages. Many sincere ones have thus heard the good news and have started to study the Bible. Often the results are extraordinary.

IN OUR NEXT ISSUE

"Happy Are Those Conscious of Their Spiritual Need"

———

"Bringing Good News of Something Better"

———

Good News for People of All Nations

A minister of Jehovah's Witnesses spoke about the Bible to George, a Malayalam-speaking man from India. Despite having major problems with work, George happily accepted a Bible study. A few days later, George's friend Gil, a Punjabi-speaking Indian man, went to the Kingdom Hall, and a Bible study was started with him. Gil introduced David, a Telugu-speaking Indian, to the Witnesses. David was soon studying the Bible. Two other Indians, Sonny and Shubash, were living in the same house as David. Both of them joined in the Bible study.

Some weeks later, the Witnesses received a telephone call from Dalip, a Marathi-speaking man. He said: "I am George's friend. Can you teach me the Bible?" Then came Sumit, a Tamil-speaking man. Finally, another of George's friends telephoned, asking for a Bible study. George then brought another young man, Max, to the Kingdom Hall. He too asked for a study. To date, six Bible studies are being conducted, and arrangements are being made for four more. They are held in English, although publications in Hindi, Malayalam, Marathi, Punjabi, Tamil, Telugu, and Urdu are also being used.

The Deaf "Hear" the Good News

There are more than 90,000 deaf people in Italy. In the mid-1970's, the Witnesses began to give attention to teaching Bible truth to them. Initially, some deaf Witnesses taught Italian Sign Language (ISL) to fellow ministers who were willing to assist in that field. Then more and more deaf people started to show interest in the Bible. Today, more than 1,400 who use ISL are attending Christian meetings. Fifteen congregations and 52 groups hold meetings in ISL.

At first, preaching to deaf people depended mainly on the initiative of individual Witnesses. But in 1978, the Italy branch office of Jehovah's Witnesses began to organize conventions for the deaf. In May of that year, it was announced that at the forthcoming international convention in Milan, there would be sessions for the deaf. The first circuit assembly for the deaf was held at the Assembly Hall in Milan in February 1979.

The branch office has since paid close attention to the spiritual nourishment of deaf ones by encouraging a growing number of evangelizers to improve in their skill with this language. Since 1995, special pioneers (full-time evangelizers) have been sent to some groups to train deaf Witnesses in the ministry and to organize Christian meetings. Three Assembly Halls are equipped with state-of-the-art video systems to improve program viewing. And videocassettes of Christian publications are available to provide spiritual food to deaf people.

Observers have noticed that the Witnesses care well for the spiritual needs of deaf people. *P@role & Segni,* a magazine published by the Italian Deaf Society, quoted from a letter sent by a Catholic monsignor: "Being deaf is awkward in the sense that the deaf person needs constant attention. For example, he arrives at the church alone without any difficulty, but he needs the aid of an interpreter to follow everything that is being read, declared, or sung during the services." The magazine added that the prelate "reckons that unfortunately, the church is not yet prepared to deal with the disability, and he points out that many deaf people are better cared for in Kingdom Halls of Jehovah's Witnesses than in the parish church."

Good News Preached to Prisoners

Can one be free yet still be in prison? Yes, because God's Word has the power to 'set free' those who accept it and apply it in their

The Bitonto Assembly Hall and an Italian Sign Language congregation in Rome

lives. The message that Jesus proclaimed "to the captives" was freedom from sin and false religion. (John 8:32; Luke 4: 16-19) In Italy excellent results are being obtained by preaching in prisons. Almost 400 ministers of Jehovah's Witnesses have been authorized by the State to visit prisoners in order to provide spiritual assistance. Jehovah's Witnesses were the first non-Catholic organization to ask for and obtain such permission.

Prisoners are being 'set free' by Bible truth

The Bible's message may be spread in unpredictable ways. Prisoners talk to fellow inmates about the Bible education work of Jehovah's Witnesses. Some of those inmates have, in turn, requested a visit by a Witness minister. Or family members who have started studying the Bible encourage the prisoners to request a visit by the Witnesses. Some prisoners who are serving life sentences for homicide or other serious crimes have repented and drastically changed their lives. This prepares them for dedication to Jehovah God and for baptism.

In a number of prisons, arrangements have been made to give public discourses on Bible subjects, to commemorate the Memorial of Jesus' death, and to show videocassettes of Bible programs produced by Jehovah's Witnesses. Often scores of prisoners attend these meetings.

To help the prison population in practical ways, the Witnesses have widely distributed magazines that deal with subjects the inmates will find helpful. One such magazine was the May 8, 2001, *Awake!*, which discussed the subject "Can Prisoners Be Reformed?" The April 8, 2003, issue was on the topic "Drug Abuse in the Family—What Can You Do?" Thousands of copies have been placed with prisoners. As a result, several hundred Bible studies are being conducted.

Some prison guards have also shown interest in the Bible's message.

After obtaining a special permit from the authorities, a prisoner named Costantino was baptized in a Kingdom Hall in San Remo, with 138 local Witnesses present. "I felt that I was showered with affection," said a visibly moved Costantino after the event. A local newspaper reported the words of the prison warden: "It was with great joy . . . that we granted this permission. Everything that can further the social, personal, and spiritual rehabilitation of a prisoner should be considered." Costantino's wife and daughter were impressed with the way accurate knowledge of the Bible had affected Costantino's life: "We are proud of him for the changes he has made. He has become peaceable, and his concern for us keeps growing. We have renewed trust in and respect for him." They too have started to study the Bible and to attend Christian meetings.

Sergio, who was convicted of theft, armed robbery, drug smuggling, and homicide, was sentenced to imprisonment until 2024. After examining the Scriptures for three years and turning his life around, Sergio decided to get baptized. He is the 15th prisoner in the Porto Azzurro prison, on the isle of Elba, to get baptized as one of Jehovah's Witnesses. With several fellow inmates in attendance, his baptism was held in a portable pool set up on the prison's sporting grounds.

Leonardo, who is serving a 20-year prison sentence, obtained special permission to get baptized in a Kingdom Hall in Parma. Interviewed by the local newspaper, Leonardo stated that he wanted to "make it clear that he had decided to become one of Jehovah's Witnesses, not to find a way out of the darkness of prison, but to fill a deeply felt spiritual need." Leonardo said: "My life has been one of errors, but I have left that behind. I have changed, though not overnight. I will need to continue being upright."

Salvatore, who was convicted of homicide, is in the Spoleto maximum-security prison. His baptism, held within prison walls, impressed many. The prison warden there said: "The social importance of a choice that leads to better behavior toward all should be encouraged, both for the benefit of the prison community and for all society." As a result of the changes Salvatore has made, his wife and a daughter are now attending the meetings of Jehovah's Witnesses. A prisoner to whom Salvatore had witnessed was baptized as a dedicated servant of Jehovah.

Some of early Christianity's expansion and increase took place in Italy. (Acts 2:10; Romans 1:7) In this time of harvest, spiritual growth and expansion continue in the same areas where Paul and his fellow Christians toiled to preach the good news.—Acts 23:11; 28:14-16.

Spiritual growth continues where early Christianity once flourished

17

PARENTS, PROVIDE FOR THE NEEDS OF YOUR FAMILY

"If anyone does not provide for those who are his own,
. . . he has disowned the faith."—1 TIMOTHY 5:8.

WHEN you look around in the Christian congregation before a meeting begins, you may see clean and well-dressed children settling into their seats alongside their parents. Is it not pleasant to see the love evident in such families—the love for Jehovah and for one another? It is easy to forget, though, how much effort goes into getting a family to the meetings on time.

² In most cases, parents are very busy all day long, and on meeting nights, family life becomes even busier. There is a meal to prepare, chores to do, homework to complete. The parents carry the heaviest load, making sure that everyone is clean, fed, and ready on time. Of course, with children the unexpected may happen at the most inopportune moments. The oldest tears his pants while playing. The youngest spills his food. The children begin to bicker. (Proverbs 22:15) The result? Even careful parental planning may go awry. Yet, the family is nearly always at the Kingdom Hall well before the meeting starts. How encouraging it is to see them there week after week, year af-

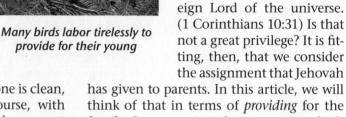

Many birds labor tirelessly to provide for their young

ter year, as the children grow up to serve Jehovah!

³ Though your work as a parent is at times difficult, even exhausting, you may be assured that Jehovah greatly values your efforts. Jehovah is the Originator of the family arrangement. His Word thus says that every family "owes its name"—its very existence—to Jehovah. (Ephesians 3:14, 15) So when you parents seek to fulfill your family roles in the right way, you honor the Sovereign Lord of the universe. (1 Corinthians 10:31) Is that not a great privilege? It is fitting, then, that we consider the assignment that Jehovah has given to parents. In this article, we will think of that in terms of *providing* for the family. Let us review three ways in which God expects parents to provide.

Providing Materially

⁴ The apostle Paul wrote: "Certainly if anyone does not provide for those who are his own, and especially for those who are members of his household, he has disowned the faith and is worse than a person without

---

1, 2. (a) Why is it encouraging to see families attending Christian meetings together? (b) What are some challenges that families face in order to get to meetings on time?

3. How do we know that Jehovah greatly values families?
4. In the family, what arrangements has Jehovah made to provide for the needs of the children?

faith." (1 Timothy 5:8) When Paul spoke of "anyone" here, whom did he have in mind? It was the family head, usually the father. God also gives the woman a dignified role as helper to her husband. (Genesis 2:18) Women in Bible times often helped their husbands to provide for the family. (Proverbs 31: 13, 14, 16) Today, single-parent families are ever more common.* Many single Christian parents are doing an admirable job of providing for their household. Of course, it is ideal for a family to have both parents, with the father taking the lead.

5 At 1 Timothy 5:8, what kind of providing did Paul have in mind? The context suggests that he was speaking directly about the material needs of the family. In today's world, there are many obstacles a family head may face in order to provide in that way. Economic hardships are common worldwide, as are layoffs, high unemployment rates, and a rising cost of living. What can help a provider to persevere in the face of such challenges?

6 A provider does well to remember that he is carrying out an assignment from Jehovah. Paul's inspired words show that a man who is able to obey this command yet refuses to do so is comparable to one who has "disowned the faith." A Christian would do his utmost to avoid such a standing before his God. Sadly, though, many people in today's world have "no natural affection." (2 Timothy 3:1, 3) Indeed, countless fathers shirk their responsibility, leaving their family in the lurch. Christian husbands do not share that hardhearted, casual view of providing for their own. Unlike many of their coworkers, Christian providers see even the most menial of jobs as being dignified and important, a means of pleasing Jehovah God, since it enables them to provide for their loved ones.

7 Family heads may also find it helpful to contemplate Jesus' perfect example. Remember, the Bible prophetically refers to Jesus as our "Eternal Father." (Isaiah 9:6, 7) As "the last Adam," Jesus effectively replaces "the first man Adam" as the father of those of mankind who exercise faith. (1 Corinthians 15:45) Unlike Adam, who turned out to be a selfish, self-serving father, Jesus is the ideal father. The Bible says of him: "By this we have come to know love, because that one surrendered his soul for us." (1 John 3:16) Yes, Jesus willingly offered up his own life for others. However, he also on a day-to-day basis put the needs of others ahead of his own in smaller ways. You parents do well to imitate that self-sacrificing spirit.

8 Parents can learn much about selfless love from Jesus' words to God's wayward people: "How often I wanted to gather your children together, the way a hen gathers her chicks together under her wings!" (Matthew 23:37) Jesus here painted a vivid word picture of a mother hen sheltering her young with her wings. Truly, parents may learn much from the protective instincts of a mother bird, who will readily put herself at risk to protect her chicks from harm. What parent birds do on a day-to-day basis, though, is also remarkable to see. They fly to and fro incessantly in their search for food. Even when near exhaustion, they drop the food into the gaping beaks of their hatchlings, who

---

* In this discussion, the provider will generally be referred to in the male gender. However, the principles are also applicable to Christian women who serve as primary providers.

5, 6. (a) What are some of the challenges facing those trying to provide materially for their own? (b) Maintaining what viewpoint toward secular work will help Christian providers to persevere?

7. Why is it fitting that parents contemplate Jesus' example?

8, 9. (a) What may parents learn from birds about providing selflessly for their young? (b) How are many Christian parents showing a self-sacrificing spirit?

swallow it and usually clamor for more. Many of Jehovah's creatures are "instinctively wise" in the way they care for the needs of their young.—Proverbs 30:24.

⁹ In a comparable way, Christian parents around the world are showing an admirably self-sacrificing spirit. You would rather suffer harm yourself than allow any harm to come to your children. Further, you willingly make daily sacrifices in order to provide for your own. Many of you rise early to work at exhausting or tedious jobs. You labor to put nutritious food on the table. You struggle to make sure that your children have clean clothing, suitable shelter, and an adequate education. And you keep at it day after day, year after year. Surely such self-sacrifice and endurance please Jehovah! (Hebrews 13:16) At the same time, though, you remember that there are more important ways in which to provide for your own.

Providing Spiritually

¹⁰ Even more essential than providing materially is providing spiritually. Jesus said: "Man must live, not on bread alone, but on every utterance coming forth through Jehovah's mouth." (Matthew 4:4; 5:3) What can you parents do to provide spiritually?

10, 11. What is the most important of human needs, and what must Christian parents do first in order to fill this need in their children?

Parents must first cultivate their own spirituality

¹¹ On this subject, perhaps no passage of Scripture is quoted more often than Deuteronomy 6:5-7. Please open your Bible and read those verses. Note that parents are first told to cultivate their own spirituality, building love for Jehovah and taking his words to heart. Yes, you need to be a serious student of God's Word, reading the Bible regularly and meditating on it so that you develop a real understanding of and love for Jehovah's ways, principles, and laws. As a result, your heart will be full of fascinating Bible truths that will move you to feel joy, awe, and love for Jehovah. You will have an abundance of good things to impart to your children. —Luke 6:45.

¹² Spiritually strong parents are prepared to apply the counsel found at Deuteronomy 6:7, to "inculcate" Jehovah's words in their offspring at every opportunity. To "inculcate" means to teach and impress by means of repetition. Jehovah well knows that all of us—children in particular—need repetition in order to learn. Thus, Jesus used repetition

---

12. How may parents imitate Jesus' example when it comes to inculcating Bible truths in their children?

Parents can find many occasions to teach their children about the Creator

in his ministry. For example, when teaching his disciples to be humble instead of proud and competitive, he found a variety of ways to repeat the same principle. He taught by reasoning, by illustrating, even by demonstrating. (Matthew 18:1-4; 20:25-27; John 13:12-15) Remarkably, though, Jesus never showed impatience. Similarly, parents need to find ways to teach basic truths to their children, patiently repeating Jehovah's principles until the children absorb and apply them.

[13] Family study sessions are ideal occasions for such teaching. Indeed, a regular, upbuilding, happy family Bible study is a mainstay of family spirituality. Christian families around the world delight in such studies, making use of the literature provided through Jehovah's organization and tailoring the study to the needs of the children. The book *Learn From the Great Teacher* has been an outstanding blessing in this regard, as has the book *Questions Young People Ask—Answers That Work.** How-

———
* Published by Jehovah's Witnesses.
———

13, 14. What are some occasions when parents can inculcate Bible truths in their children, using what aids?

ever, the family study is not the only time to teach children.

[14] As Deuteronomy 6:7 shows, there are many occasions when you parents can discuss spiritual things with your children. Whether traveling together, doing chores together, or relaxing together, you may find opportunities to provide for your children's spiritual needs. Of course, you need not incessantly "lecture" your children about Bible truths. Rather, try to keep family conversation on an upbuilding, spiritual level. For example, the *Awake!* magazine contains many articles on a wide variety of subjects. Such articles may pave the way for conversations about Jehovah's animal creation, places of natural beauty around the world, and the wonderful variety among human cultures and ways of life. Such conversations may move young ones to read more of the literature provided by the faithful and discreet slave class.—Matthew 24:45-47.

[15] Engaging in upbuilding conversations with your children will help you to satisfy another spiritual need. Christian children need to learn to share their faith effectively with others. In the course of talking about some point of interest in *The Watchtower* or *Awake!* you may look for opportunities to relate the

———
15. How might parents help their children to view the Christian ministry as interesting and rewarding?

material to the ministry. For example, you might ask: "Wouldn't it be wonderful if more people knew this about Jehovah? How do you think we could get someone interested in this subject?" Such discussions may help young ones to develop greater interest in sharing with others what they are learning. Then, when your children accompany you in the ministry, they see a living example of putting such conversations into practice. They may also learn that the ministry is an interesting and happy work, producing great satisfaction and joy.—Acts 20:35.

Children draw strength and courage from parental approval

¹⁶ Parents also provide for their children's spiritual needs when praying. Jesus taught his disciples how to pray, and he prayed with them on many occasions. (Luke 11:1-13) Just think of how much they learned by joining in prayer with Jehovah's own Son! Similarly, your children can learn a lot from your prayers. They may learn, for example, that Jehovah wants us to speak to him freely from the heart, approaching him with any concern that we might have. Yes, your prayers can help your children to learn a vital spiritual truth: They can have a relationship with their heavenly Father.—1 Peter 5:7.

Providing Emotionally

¹⁷ Of course, children also have pressing emotional needs. God's Word tells parents

---

16. What may children learn from listening to their parents' prayers?
17, 18. (a) How does the Bible reveal the importance of showing love to children? (b) How should fathers imitate Jehovah in expressing love for their children?

how important it is to provide in this respect. For example, younger women are exhorted "to love their children." Their doing so is related to young mothers' being recalled to their senses, or being "mentally sound." (Titus 2:4, footnote) Indeed, it is sensible to show a child love. This teaches a child to love and brings lifelong benefits. On the other hand, a failure to show a child love is senseless. It causes great pain and represents a failure to imitate Jehovah, who shows us immense love despite our imperfections.—Psalm 103:8-14.

¹⁸ Jehovah even takes the initiative in loving his earthly children. As 1 John 4:19 says, "he first loved us." You fathers in particular should imitate Jehovah's example, taking the initiative to build a loving bond with your children. The Bible urges fathers to avoid exasperating their children, "that they do not become downhearted." (Colossians 3:21) Few things are more exasperating for children than the impression that a parent does not love or value them. Fathers who are reluctant to express their feelings do well to remember Jehovah's example. Jehovah even spoke from heaven to express approval and love for his Son. (Matthew 3:17; 17:5) How encouraging that must have been for Jesus! Likewise, children draw much strength and courage from their parents' honest expressions of love and approval.

¹⁹ Of course, parental love is more than just words. Love is expressed primarily in action. Providing materially and spiritually can be

---

19. Why is discipline important, and what balance do Christian parents strive to find?

an expression of parental love, especially when parents do so in a way that conveys that love is the primary motivation. Additionally, discipline is a vital expression of parental love. Indeed, "whom Jehovah loves he disciplines." (Hebrews 12:6) On the other hand, a failure to discipline is an expression of parental hatred! (Proverbs 13:24) Jehovah always finds the right balance, disciplining "to the proper degree." (Jeremiah 46:28) Such balance is not always easy for imperfect parents to find. Still, it is worth your every effort to strive for that balance. Firm, loving discipline helps a child grow up to live a happy, productive life. (Proverbs 22:6) Is that not what every Christian parent wants for his child?

[20] When you parents do the important work Jehovah has assigned you—providing

---

20. How can parents give their children the best possible opportunity to "choose life"?

for your children's material, spiritual, and emotional needs—the rewards are great. You thereby give your children the best possible opportunity to "choose life" and thereafter to "keep alive." (Deuteronomy 30:19) Those children who choose to serve Jehovah and stay on the path to life as they mature bring their parents tremendous joy. (Psalm 127:3-5) Such joy will last forever! How, though, can young people praise Jehovah now? The following article will take up that subject.

How Would You Answer?

What can parents do in order to provide for their children

- materially?
- spiritually?
- emotionally?

YOUNG PEOPLE, PRAISE JEHOVAH!

"Praise Jehovah from the earth, . . .
you young men and also you virgins."—PSALM 148:7, 12.

YOUNG people are often keenly aware of what they are not yet allowed to do. Many of them can readily tell you how old they will have to be before they are allowed to cross a street alone or stay up until a certain hour of the evening or drive a car. At times, a youth may feel that too many of

---

1, 2. (a) Many young people are aware of what sort of restrictions? (b) Why do young ones not need to resent the restrictions that their parents place upon them?

his or her eager requests meet with the same answer, "Wait until you are older."

[2] You young people know that your parents feel that it is wise to make such restrictions, perhaps for your own protection. You surely know, too, that Jehovah is pleased when you obey your parents. (Colossians 3: 20) Do you ever feel, though, as if you were waiting for your life to start? Are all the important things off limits until you are older? Nothing could be further from the truth!

There is a work going on today that is far more important than any other privilege you might be waiting for. Are you young people *allowed* to join in this work? Better than that—you are actually *invited* to do so by the Most High God himself!

³ What work are we talking about? Note the words of our theme text for this article: "Praise Jehovah from the earth, . . . you young men and also you virgins, you old men together with boys." (Psalm 148:7, 12) There is your great privilege: You can praise Jehovah. As a young person, are you thrilled to take part in that work? Many are. To see why it is worth feeling that way, let us consider three questions. First, *why* should you praise Jehovah? Second, *how* can you praise him effectively? Third, *when* is it a good time to start praising Jehovah?

Why Praise Jehovah?

⁴ An outstanding reason for praising Jehovah is that he is the Creator. The 148th Psalm helps us to focus on this truth. Just imagine: If you approached a large group of people who in unison were singing a beautiful, moving song, how would you feel? What if the song's lyrics were words that you knew to be true, expressing thoughts that you knew to be important, joyful, and uplifting? Would you feel a desire to learn the words and join in? Most of us would. Well, the 148th Psalm shows that you are in a situation that is similar but far more wonderful. That psalm describes an immense crowd, all praising Jehovah in unison. As you read the psalm, though, you may notice something unusual. What is that?

⁵ Many of the praisers described in Psalm 148 can neither speak nor reason. For example, we read of the sun, moon, stars, snow, wind, mountains, and hills praising Jehovah. How can these inanimate creations do such a thing? (Verses 3, 8, 9) Really, in the same way that the trees, sea creatures, and animals do. (Verses 7, 9, 10) Have you ever watched a beautiful sunset or looked up at a full moon sailing across a sea of stars or laughed in delight at animals playing or gasped in awe at a gorgeous landscape? Then you have "heard" the song of praise coming from creation. All that Jehovah has made reminds us that he is the almighty Creator, that there is no one in all the universe so powerful, so wise, or so loving.—Romans 1: 20; Revelation 4:11.

⁶ The 148th Psalm also describes intelligent creation as praising Jehovah. In verse 2, we find Jehovah's celestial "army," the angels, praising God. In verse 11, powerful and influential humans, such as kings and judges, are invited to join in the praise. If the mighty angels find delight in praising Jehovah, what mere human could rightly say that he is too important to do so? Then, in verses 12 and 13, you young people are invited to join in and praise Jehovah as well. Are you moved to want to do that?

⁷ Consider an illustration. If you had a close friend with an amazing skill—perhaps in sports, art, or music—would you talk about him to your family and other friends? No doubt. Well, learning about all that Jehovah has done can have a similar effect on us. For example, Psalm 19:1, 2 says that the starry heavens cause "speech to bubble forth." As for us, when we think about the amazing things that Jehovah has accomplished, we can hardly hold back from talking to others about our God.

_____

3. Jehovah invites young ones to have what privilege, and what questions will we now consider?

4, 5. (a) According to the 148th Psalm, we are in what wondrous situation? (b) How can creations that neither speak nor reason still praise Jehovah?

_____

6, 7. (a) The 148th Psalm describes what intelligent creatures as praising Jehovah? (b) Why might we be moved to praise Jehovah? Illustrate.

If your friend had an outstanding skill, would you not mention this to others?

16) Yes, when you teach others about Jehovah God, praising him, they may come to know Jehovah too. Such knowledge can lead to their everlasting salvation!—John 17:3.

¹⁰ There is yet another reason for praising Jehovah. Remember the illustration about your remarkable friend. If you heard others telling lies about him, slandering his good name, would you not be even more determined to praise him? Well, Jehovah is widely slandered in this world. (John 8:44; Revelation 12:9) Those who love him thus feel impelled to tell the truth about him, setting the record straight. Would you too like to express your love and appreciation to Jehovah and show that you want him as your Ruler instead of his chief enemy, Satan? You can do all of that by praising Jehovah. The next question, then, is how.

How Some Young Ones Praised Jehovah

¹¹ The Bible shows that young people are often very effective in praising Jehovah. For example, there was an Israelite girl who was taken captive by the Syrians. She boldly witnessed to her mistress about Jehovah's prophet Elisha. Her words led to a miracle, and a powerful witness was given. (2 Kings 5:1-17) Jesus too witnessed boldly as a child. Of all the events of his youth that could have been recorded in the Scriptures, Jehovah chose one, the occasion when 12-year-old Jesus courageously questioned the religious teachers at the temple in Jerusalem and left them astounded at his understanding of Jehovah's ways.—Luke 2:46-49.

¹² As a grown man, Jesus also inspired children to praise Jehovah. For example, just

⁸ Another outstanding reason for praising Jehovah is that he wants us to do so. Why? Is it because he needs praise from humans? No. We humans may need praise at times, but Jehovah is far higher than we are. (Isaiah 55:8) He has no uncertainties about himself or his qualities. (Isaiah 45:5) Yet, he wants us to praise him and is pleased when we do. Why? Consider two reasons. First, he knows that we need to praise him. He designed us with a spiritual need, a need to worship. (Matthew 5:3) To see us filling that need pleases Jehovah, much the way it pleases your parents to see you eating food that they know is good for you.—John 4:34.

⁹ Second, Jehovah knows that other people need to hear us praising him. The apostle Paul wrote these words to the younger man Timothy: "Pay constant attention to yourself and to your teaching. Stay by these things, for by doing this you will save both yourself and those who listen to you." (1 Timothy 4:

8, 9. For what reasons does Jehovah want us to praise him?

10. Why do we feel impelled to praise our God?
11. What Bible examples show that young people can be very effective in praising Jehovah?
12, 13. (a) What did Jesus do in the temple shortly before his death, with what effect on the people there? (b) How did Jesus feel about the praise uttered by young boys?

children were doing what all the adults there should have been doing. In their youthful minds, it all must have seemed so clear. They saw this man do marvelous things, speak with courage and faith, and show intense love for God and his people. He was who he claimed to be—the promised "Son of David," the Messiah. Blessed for their faith, the boys even had the privilege of fulfilling prophecy.—Psalm 8:2.

a few days before his death, Jesus spent time at the temple in Jerusalem. He did "marvelous things" there, the Bible says. He threw out those who were making that sacred place a den of thieves. He also cured blind and lame people. Everyone there, especially the religious leaders, should have been moved to praise Jehovah and his Son, the Messiah. Sadly, though, many in those days uttered no such praises. They knew that Jesus was sent by God, but they were afraid of the religious leaders. One group of people, however, did speak up boldly. Do you know who they were? The Bible says: "When the chief priests and the scribes saw the marvelous things [Jesus] did and the boys that were crying out in the temple and saying: 'Save, we pray, the Son of David!' they became indignant and said to [Jesus]: 'Do you hear what these are saying?' "—Matthew 21:15, 16; John 12:42.

¹³ Those priests were hoping that Jesus would silence the boys who were praising him. Did he? Far from it! Jesus answered the priests: "Yes. Did you never read this, 'Out of the mouth of babes and sucklings you have furnished praise'?" Clearly, Jesus and his Father were pleased with the praise of the young boys. Those

¹⁴ What can we learn from such examples? That young ones can be very effective praisers of Jehovah. They often have the gift of seeing the truth clearly and simply, expressing their faith with earnestness and zeal. They also have the gift mentioned at Proverbs 20:29: "The beauty of young men is their power." Yes, you young ones are blessed with strength and energy—real assets in praising Jehovah. How, specifically, can you put such gifts to work?

How Can You Praise Jehovah?

¹⁵ Being effective starts in the heart. You cannot praise Jehovah effectively if you are doing it only because others want you to. Remember, the greatest of all the commandments is this: "You must love Jehovah your God with your whole heart and with your whole soul and with your whole mind." (Matthew 22:37) Have you come to know Jehovah personally through your own study of his Word? The proper result of such learning is a feeling of love for Jehovah. The natural way to express that love is

14. How do the gifts young ones possess lend themselves to praising God?
15. To praise Jehovah effectively, what motive is needed?

Fellow students may be interested in your beliefs

by praising him. Once your motive is clear and strong, you are ready to praise Jehovah enthusiastically.

¹⁶ Now, even before considering what you will *say,* consider how you will *act.* If that Israelite girl of Elisha's day had been habitually rude, disrespectful, or dishonest, do you think that her Syrian captors would have listened to her words about Jehovah's prophet? Probably not. Similarly, people are more likely to listen to you if they see that you are respectful, honest, and well behaved. (Romans 2: 21) Consider an example.

¹⁷ An 11-year-old girl in Portugal faced pressure in school to celebrate holidays that were in violation of her Bible-trained conscience. She respectfully explained to her teacher why she must refuse, but the teacher ridiculed her. As time passed, the teacher tried again and again to shame her, making fun of her religion. However, the young girl remained respectful. Years later, that young sister was serving as a regular pioneer, a full-time minister. At a convention, she watched people being baptized and recognized one of them. It was her former teacher! After a tearful embrace, the older woman told the younger that she had never forgotten her student's respectful conduct. A Witness had called on her, and the teacher had spoken about her former student's behavior. As a result, a Bible study was started, and this woman embraced Bible truth. Yes, your conduct can be a very powerful way to praise Jehovah!

¹⁸ Do you at times find it hard to start con-

versations in school about your faith? You are not alone in feeling that way. However, you can make it more likely that others will ask you about your faith. For example, if it is legal and permissible to do so, why not bring Bible-based publications with you and read them during lunchtime or other periods when it is allowable to do so? Your fellow students may ask you about what you are reading. By answering them and telling them what you find interesting about the article or book in your hands, you may find that a good conversation is under way before you know it. Remember to ask questions, finding out what your fellow students believe. Listen respectfully, sharing what you have learned from the Bible. As the experiences on page 29 show, many young people are praising God in school. This brings them great joy and helps many to come to know Jehovah.

¹⁹ The door-to-door ministry is a most effective way to praise Jehovah. If you are not yet taking part, why not set it as a goal? If you are taking part, are there further goals that you may set for yourself? For example, rather than saying essentially the same thing at each door, look for ways to improve, asking your parents and other

---

16, 17. What role does conduct play in praising Jehovah? Illustrate.

18. What might a young person do if he is hesitant to strike up conversations about the Bible and Jehovah God?

19. How can young people become more effective in the door-to-door ministry?

If you want to improve in your ministry, ask a more experienced Witness for pointers

experienced ones for pointers. Learn how to use the Bible more, to make effective return visits, and to start a Bible study. (1 Timothy 4:15) The more you praise Jehovah in such ways, the more effective you will become, and the more you will enjoy your ministry.

When Should You Begin Praising Jehovah?

[20] Of the three questions in this discussion, the answer to this last one is the simplest. Notice the Bible's direct answer: "Remember, now, your Grand Creator in the days of your young manhood." (Ecclesiastes 12:1) Yes, the time to start praising Jehovah is *now*. It is all too easy to say: "I am too young to praise Jehovah. I am inexperienced. I should wait until I am older." You would not be the first to feel that way. Young Jeremiah, for instance, told Jehovah: "Alas, O Sovereign Lord Jehovah! Here I actually do not know how to speak, for I am but a boy." Jehovah reassured him that there was no reason to fear. (Jeremiah 1:6, 7) Likewise, we have nothing to fear when we praise Jehovah. There is no harm that might come to

---

20. Why is there no need for youths to feel that they are too young to praise Jehovah?

How Would You Answer?

- What are some important reasons for praising Jehovah?
- What Bible examples show that young people can be very effective in praising Jehovah?
- How can young people praise Jehovah today?
- When should young ones begin praising Jehovah, and why?

---

us that Jehovah cannot completely undo. —Psalm 118:6.

[21] We urge you young ones, then: Do not hesitate to praise Jehovah! Now while you are young is the best time to join in the most important work being done on earth today. When you do, you become part of something wonderful—the universal family of those praising Jehovah. Jehovah is delighted that this family includes you. Note these inspired words that the psalmist addressed to Jehovah: "Your people will offer themselves willingly on the day of your military force. In the splendors of holiness, from the womb of the dawn, you have your company of young men just like dewdrops."—Psalm 110:3.

[22] Dewdrops glistening in the morning light present a beautiful picture, do they not? They are refreshing, bright, and virtually beyond counting for multitude. That is how Jehovah sees you young ones who are faithfully praising him in these critical times. Clearly, your choice to praise Jehovah makes his heart rejoice. (Proverbs 27:11) By all means, then, you young ones, praise Jehovah!

21, 22. Why are young praisers of Jehovah likened to dewdrops, and why is that comparison encouraging?

PRAISING JEHOVAH at School

AROUND the world, young Witnesses of Jehovah are finding ways to praise God at school—by means of both their speech and their conduct. Note some experiences that illustrate their youthful zeal.

A young Witness in Greece was assigned to write a report on the pollution of the earth's atmosphere. After looking in the *Watch Tower Publications Index,* she found useful material in the *Awake!* magazine, crediting it as her source at the conclusion of her essay. Her teacher told her that it was one of the best essays she had ever read. The teacher later used the information at a seminar, with good results. The young sister thus decided to offer the teacher more issues of *Awake!* including one featuring the series "Teachers —What Would We Do Without Them?" The teacher later praised the *Awake!* magazine in class, and some other students began asking for copies. The sister had to bring copies of the magazine to school so that they could read other issues.

In Benin, Africa, a teenage Christian faced an unusual type of pressure. According to custom, the parents of a number of students in her school got together to hire tutors for difficult subjects in order to prepare the youths for exams. However, the tutors chose Saturday mornings for the sessions. The young Witness objected: "Saturday morning is the time when the whole congregation preaches together. It is the happiest time of the week for me, and I would not trade it for anything!" Her father, a single parent and a Witness himself, agreed and tried to get one group of parents and tutors to change the schedule. However, they all refused. The young girl decided to do without the tutoring. She engaged in preaching with her congregation instead. Her classmates ridiculed her, urging her to give up her witnessing case and her God as well. They were quite sure that she would fail the exams. As it turned out, though, that group of tutored students failed, whereas our young sister passed. Needless to say, the mockery ceased. Now the students are telling her, "You should continue to serve your God."

In the Czech Republic, a 12-year-old girl had to prepare a book report. Her mother urged her to use the book *The Greatest Man Who Ever Lived.* She began her report with the questions: "What do you think? Who could be the greatest man who ever lived?" She described Jesus, his life on earth, and his teachings. Then she discussed the chapter entitled "A Lesson in Forgiveness." Her teacher exclaimed, "That is the best report I have ever heard from you!" and gratefully accepted a copy of the book. Some fellow students also wanted a copy. The next day, the girl was thrilled to distribute 18 copies.

Such young ones are finding great joy in praising Jehovah at school. All of us do well to imitate their youthful zeal.

We Can Cope
With Any Trial!

ARE you presently facing a trial in your life? Do you feel at a loss, unable to cope with it? Do you even at times fear that your problem is unique and that there is no solution to it? If so, take heart! Whatever trials we may face, the Bible assures us that God can enable us to deal with them.

The Bible acknowledges that God's servants will "meet with various trials." (James 1:2) Note the word "various" (Greek *poi·ki'-los*). According to ancient usage, the original word means "manifold" or "many-tinted" and emphasizes "the diversity of the trials." In fact, in everyday speech, that basically means "many-colored." Thus, "various trials" are trials that come in many colors, so to speak. Nevertheless, Jehovah supports us so that we can cope with each one of them. Why can we be sure of that?

"God's Undeserved Kindness Expressed in Various Ways"

The apostle Peter notes that Christians are "grieved by various trials." (1 Peter 1:6) Later in his inspired letter, he states that "God's undeserved kindness" is "expressed in various ways." (1 Peter 4:10) The phrase "in various ways" contains a form of the same original Greek word. In commenting on this expression, one Bible scholar notes: "This is a tremendous thought. . . . To speak of the grace [or, undeserved kindness] of God as *poikilos* means that there is no colour in the human situation which the grace of God cannot match." He further notes: "There is no possible set of circumstances, no possible crisis, emergency or demand through which the grace of God cannot find a way, and which the grace of God cannot triumphantly deal with and overcome. There is nothing in life with which the grace of God cannot cope. This vivid word *poikilos* leads our thoughts straight to that many-coloured grace of God which is indeed sufficient for all things."

Trials Matched by Kindness

According to Peter, one way that God's undeserved kindness is expressed is through the various ones who make up the Christian congregation. (1 Peter 4:11) Each servant of God has spiritual gifts, or abilities, that may serve as a source of encouragement to those facing trials. (Romans 12: 6-8) For instance, some members of the congregation are outstanding Bible teachers. Their insightful words inspire and motivate others to endure. (Nehemiah 8:1-4, 8, 12) Others make regular shepherding visits at the homes of those in need of support. Such visits are occasions for encouragement, a 'comforting of hearts.' (Colossians 2:2) When overseers make such faith-strengthening visits, they impart a spiritual gift. (John 21:16) Still others in the congregation are known for warmth, compassion, and tenderness in dealing with fellow believers who are saddened by trials. (Acts 4:36; Romans 12:10; Colossians 3:10) The empathy and active assistance shown by such loving brothers and sisters is a significant expression, or "color," of God's undeserved kindness.—Proverbs 12:25; 17:17.

"The God of All Comfort"

Above all, Jehovah provides comfort. He is "the God of all comfort, who comforts us in all our tribulation." (2 Corinthians 1:3, 4) The wisdom found in God's inspired Word and the strength provided by his holy spirit are principal means by which Jehovah answers our prayers for help. (Isaiah 30:18, 21; Luke 11:13; John 14:16) We can be heartened by the inspired promise made by the apostle Paul. He said: "God is faithful, and he will not let you be tempted beyond what you can bear, but along with the temptation he will also make the way out in order for you to be able to endure it."—1 Corinthians 10:13.

Yes, whatever is the "color," or nature, of our trial, there will always be a "color," or expression, of God's undeserved kindness that will match it. (James 1:17) Jehovah's timely and appropriate support provided for his servants—no matter how diverse their temptations or challenges may be—is but one evidence of "the greatly diversified wisdom of God." (Ephesians 3:10) Do you not agree?

Jehovah helps us to cope with our trials

"Persecuted for His Faith"

THE town of Cernobbio in northern Italy established a memorial site in a local park to remember victims of human rights violations. One of the plaques unveiled in their memory is dedicated to Narciso Riet. Born in Germany of Italian parents, Riet became one of Jehovah's Witnesses in the 1930's. During the Hitler regime, Jehovah's Witnesses were persecuted because they refused to put Hitler above the true God, Jehovah.

When the Gestapo discovered that Riet was involved in bringing copies of *The Watchtower* into the concentration camps, he fled to Cernobbio. There he was asked to translate *The Watchtower* into Italian and to distribute it to his fellow believers nearby. His energetic activities did not go unnoticed. An SS officer and his men burst into Riet's home, arrested him, and seized the "criminal" evidence—two Bibles and a few letters! Riet was deported to Germany, incarcerated in the Dachau concentration camp, and executed shortly before the end of World War II. He was "persecuted for his faith," says the Cernobbio plaque.

The faith of Narciso Riet and hundreds of other Witnesses who fell victim to Nazi persecution is an encouragement to Christians today to remain faithful to Jehovah, the only Personage in the universe worthy of their worship. (Revelation 4:11) Jesus said: "Happy are those who have been persecuted for righteousness' sake." God will remember their deeds and bless them for their courageous course.—Matthew 5:10; Hebrews 6:10.

JULY 1, 2005

THE WATCHTOWER

ANNOUNCING JEHOVAH'S KINGDOM

HOW CAN YOU FIND INNER PEACE?

THE WATCHTOWER®
ANNOUNCING JEHOVAH'S KINGDOM

July 1, 2005   Average Printing Each Issue: 26,439,000   Vol. 126, No. 13

THE PURPOSE OF *THE WATCHTOWER* is to exalt Jehovah God as Sovereign Lord of the universe. It keeps watch on world events as these fulfill Bible prophecy. It comforts all peoples with the good news that God's Kingdom will soon destroy those who oppress their fellowmen and that it will turn the earth into a paradise. It encourages faith in God's now-reigning King, Jesus Christ, whose shed blood opens the way for mankind to gain eternal life. *The Watchtower*, published by Jehovah's Witnesses continuously since 1879, is nonpolitical. It adheres to the Bible as its authority.

IN THIS ISSUE

3   The Search for Inner Peace

4   "Happy Are Those Conscious of Their Spiritual Need"

8   Happy for My Share in Global Bible Education

13   They Are Making Themselves Available

16   "Bringing Good News of Something Better"

21   Good News for People of All Nations

27   Questions From Readers

28   Jehovah's Word Is Alive—Highlights From the Book of First Kings

32   "It Is Finished"

WATCHTOWER STUDIES

AUGUST 1-7:
"Bringing Good News of Something Better."
Page 16. Songs to be used: 151, 193.

AUGUST 8-14:
Good News for People of All Nations.
Page 21. Songs to be used: 215, 92.

Publication of *The Watchtower* is part of a worldwide Bible educational work supported by voluntary donations.

Unless otherwise indicated, Scripture quotations are from the modern-language *New World Translation of the Holy Scriptures—With References.*

The Watchtower (ISSN 0043-1087) is published semimonthly by Watchtower Bible and Tract Society of New York, Inc.; M. H. Larson, President; G. F. Simonis, Secretary-Treasurer; 25 Columbia Heights, Brooklyn, NY 11201-2483. Periodicals Postage Paid at Brooklyn, NY, and at additional mailing offices. **POSTMASTER:** Send address changes to Watchtower, **Wallkill, NY 12589.**

Changes of address should reach us 30 days before your moving date. Give us your old and new address (if possible, your old address label).

Semimonthly   ENGLISH

Would you welcome more information or a free home Bible study? Please send your request to Jehovah's Witnesses, using the appropriate address below.

America, United States of: Wallkill, NY 12589. **Antigua:** Box 119, St. Johns. **Australia:** Box 280, Ingleburn, NSW 1890. **Bahamas:** Box N-1247, Nassau, N.P. **Barbados, W.I.:** Crusher Site Road, Prospect, St. James. **Britain:** The Ridgeway, London NW7 1RN. **Canada:** Box 4100, Halton Hills (Georgetown), Ontario L7G 4Y4. **Germany:** Niederselters, Am Steinfels, D-65618 Selters. **Ghana:** P. O. Box GP 760, Accra. **Guyana:** 352-360 Tyrell St., Republic Park Phase 2 EBD. **Hawaii 96819:** 2055 Kam IV Rd., Honolulu. **Hong Kong:** 4 Kent Road, Kowloon Tong. **India:** Post Box 6440, Yelahanka, Bangalore 560 064, KAR. **Ireland:** Newcastle, Greystones, Co. Wicklow. **Jamaica:** P. O. Box 103, Old Harbour, St. Catherine. **Japan:** 1271 Nakashinden, Ebina City, Kanagawa Pref., 243-0496. **Kenya:** P.O. Box 47788, GPO Nairobi 00100. **New Zealand:** P.O. Box 75-142, Manurewa. **Nigeria:** P.M.B. 1090, Benin City 300001, Edo State. **Philippines, Republic of:** P. O. Box 2044, 1060 Manila. **South Africa:** Private Bag X2067, Krugersdorp, 1740. **Trinidad and Tobago, Republic of:** Lower Rapsey Street & Laxmi Lane, Curepe. **Zambia:** Box 33459, Lusaka 10101. **Zimbabwe:** Private Bag WG-5001, Westgate.

NOW PUBLISHED IN 150 LANGUAGES. SEMIMONTHLY: Afrikaans, Albanian,* Amharic, Arabic, Bengali, Bicol, Bislama, Bulgarian, Cebuano,* Chichewa,* Chinese, Chinese (Simplified),* Cibemba,* Croatian,* Czech,*# Danish,*# Dutch,*# East Armenian, Efik,* English*#+⊙ (also Braille), Estonian, Ewe, Fijian, Finnish,*# French,*# Ga, Georgian,* German,*# Greek,* Gujarati, Gun, Hebrew, Hiligaynon, Hindi, Hungarian,*# Igbo,* Iloko,* Indonesian, Italian,*# Japanese*# (also Braille), Kannada, Kinyarwanda, Kirundi, Korean*# (also Braille), Latvian, Lingala, Lithuanian, Luvale, Macedonian, Malagasy,* Malayalam, Maltese, Myanmar, Nepali, Norwegian,*# Pangasinan, Papiamento (Aruba), Papiamento (Curaçao), Polish,*# Portuguese*# (also Braille), Punjabi, Rarotongan, Romanian,* Russian,* Samar-Leyte, Samoan, Sango, Sepedi, Serbian, Sesotho, Shona,* Silozi, Sinhala, Slovak,* Slovenian, Solomon Islands Pidgin, Spanish*# (also Braille), Sranantongo, Swahili,* Swedish,*# Tagalog,* Tamil, Telugu, Thai, Tigrinya, Tok Pisin, Tongan, Tshiluba, Tsonga, Tswana, Turkish, Twi, Ukrainian,* Urdu, Vietnamese, Wallisian, Xhosa, Yoruba,* Zulu*

MONTHLY: American Sign Language,△⊡ Armenian, Assamese, Azerbaijani (roman script), Brazilian Sign Language,△ Cambodian, Chitonga, Gilbertese, Greenlandic, Haitian Creole, Hausa, Hiri Motu, Icelandic, Isoko, Kaonde, Kazakh, Kikongo, Kiluba, Kirghiz, Kosraean, Kwanyama/Ndonga, Luganda, Marathi, Marshallese, Mauritian Creole, Maya, Mizo, Monokutuba, Moore, Niuean, Ossetian, Otetela, Palauan, Persian, Ponapean, Seychelles Creole, Tahitian, Tatar, Tiv, Trukese, Tumbuka, Tuvaluan, Umbundu, Venda, Yapese, Zande

* Study articles also available in large-print edition.
# Audiocassettes also available.
+ CD also available.
⊙ MP3 CD-ROM also available.
△ Videocassette
⊡ DVD

Will pursuing wealth, power, or education help you to find inner peace?

The Search for
Inner Peace

ALBERT was a happily married man with two delightful children. But he felt that something was missing in his life. During a time when he had to struggle to find work, he became involved in politics and adopted socialism. He even became an active member of the local Communist party.

Before long, however, Albert became disillusioned with Communism. He severed his ties with politics and devoted himself wholly to his family. Seeing to their happiness became his purpose in life. Nevertheless, Albert still felt a nagging void inside; true inner peace continued to elude him.

Albert's story is by no means unique. In order to find a meaningful purpose in life, millions have experimented with various ideologies, philosophies, and religions. In the Western world, the hippie movement of the 1960's was a rebellion against traditional moral and social values. Young people in particular searched for happiness and the meaning of life through mind-altering drugs and the philosophies of the movement's so-called gurus and high priests. Nevertheless, the hippie movement failed to bring genuine happiness. Instead, it helped to produce drug addicts and promiscuous youths, accelerating society's downward slide into moral confusion.

For centuries, many have sought happiness through wealth, power, or education. These paths ultimately lead to disappointment. "Even when a person has an abundance," Jesus said, "his life does not result from the things he possesses." (Luke 12:15) Rather, the determined pursuit of wealth usually brings unhappiness. The Bible says: "Those who are determined to be rich fall into temptation and a snare and many senseless and hurtful desires, which plunge men into destruction and ruin. For the love of money is a root of all sorts of injurious things, and by reaching out for this love some . . . have stabbed themselves all over with many pains."—1 Timothy 6:9, 10.

How, then, can one find inner peace and a purpose in life? Is it a matter of trial and error, like shooting an arrow at an elusive target in the dark? Thankfully, no. As we shall see in the following article, the solution lies in satisfying a very important and, indeed, uniquely human need.

"Happy Are Those Conscious of
Their Spiritual Need"

WHEN birds wake up in the morning, they often chirp for a while and then fly off in search of food. In the evening, they return to their roosts, chirp a little more, and go to sleep. In certain seasons they mate, lay eggs, and raise their young. Other animals follow a similarly predictable pattern.

We humans are different. True, we eat, sleep, and reproduce, but most of us are not content with just those things. We want to know why we are here. We seek meaning in our lives. We also desire a hope for the future. These deeper needs point to a quality that is unique to humankind—spirituality, or the need and capacity for spiritual things.

Unlike animals, humans have a spiritual need

Made in God's Image

The Bible explains the reason for the spiritual side of man's nature, saying: "God proceeded to create the man in his image, in God's image he created him; male and female he created them." (Genesis 1:27) Our being formed "in God's image" means that even though we have been tarnished by sin and imperfection, we have the ability to mirror certain qualities of God. (Romans 5:12) For example, we can be creative. We also have a measure of wisdom, a sense of justice, and the ability to show self-sacrificing love for one another. Furthermore, we can reflect on the past and plan for the future.—Proverbs 4:7; Ecclesiastes 3:1, 11; Micah 6:8; John 13:34; 1 John 4:8.

Our spiritual capacity is most clearly demonstrated in our innate desire to worship God. Unless we properly satisfy the need to be in touch with our Creator, we cannot find true and lasting happiness. "Happy are those conscious of their spiritual need," Jesus said. (Matthew 5:3) We must be careful, however, to satisfy that need with spiritual truth—facts about God, his standards, and his purpose for mankind. Where can we find spiritual truth? In the Bible.

"Your Word Is Truth"

The apostle Paul wrote: "All Scripture is inspired of God and beneficial for teaching, for reproving, for setting things straight." (2 Timothy 3:16) Paul's words harmonize with those of Jesus, who said in prayer to God: "Your word is truth." Today, we know that Word as the Holy Bible, and we are wise to check that our beliefs and standards measure up to it.—John 17:17.

By comparing our beliefs with God's Word, we imitate the people of ancient Beroea, who made sure that Paul's teachings harmonized with the Scriptures. Rather than criticize the Beroeans, Luke commended them for their attitude. They "received the word with the greatest eagerness of mind," he wrote, "carefully examining the Scriptures daily as to whether these things were so." (Acts 17:11) In view of the contradictory religious and moral teachings that abound today, it is important that we imitate the example of the noble-minded Beroeans.

Another way to identify spiritual truth is to see how it influences people's lives. (Matthew 7:17) For example, living according to Bible truth should make one a bet-

"They will accumulate teachers for themselves to have their ears tickled."—2 Timothy 4:3

ter husband, a better father, a better wife, or a better mother, thus adding to family happiness and enhancing one's contentment. "Happy are those hearing the word of God and keeping it," said Jesus.—Luke 11:28.

Jesus' words remind us of those of his heavenly Father, who said to the ancient Israelites: "I, Jehovah, am your God, the One teaching you to benefit yourself, the One causing you to tread in the way in which you should walk. O if only you would actually pay attention to my commandments! Then your peace would become just like a river, and your righteousness like the waves of the sea." (Isaiah 48:17, 18) All who love goodness and righteousness would surely be moved by such a warm appeal!

Some Prefer to Have Their "Ears Tickled"

God made that heartfelt appeal to the Israelites because they were being misled by religious lies. (Psalm 106:35-40) We too must be on guard against falsehoods. Concerning professed Christians, Paul wrote: "There will be a period of time when they will not put up with the healthful teaching, but, in accord with their own desires, they will accumulate teachers for themselves to have their ears tickled; and they will turn their ears away from the truth."—2 Timothy 4:3, 4.

Religious leaders tickle people's ears by condoning practices that appeal to wrong desires, such as sex outside of marriage, homosexuality, and drunkenness.

IS YOUR SPIRITUAL NEED BEING SATISFIED?

Are you satisfied with the spiritual food you are receiving? We invite you to read the following questions and check those you can answer correctly.

☐ Who is God, and what is his name?

☐ Who is Jesus Christ? Why did he have to die? How can his death benefit you?

☐ Is there a Devil? If so, where did he come from?

☐ What happens to us when we die?

☐ What is God's purpose for the earth and for mankind?

☐ What is the Kingdom of God?

☐ What are God's standards of morality?

☐ In the family, what are the God-assigned roles of the husband and of the wife? What are some Bible principles that promote family happiness?

If you are unsure of the answers to any of these questions, you may request a copy of the brochure *What Does God Require of Us?* Published by Jehovah's Witnesses in nearly 300 languages, this brochure discusses 16 basic Bible topics and provides a Scriptural answer to all the questions listed above.

The Bible clearly states that those who approve of such things and those who practice them "will not inherit God's kingdom." —1 Corinthians 6:9, 10; Romans 1:24-32.

To be sure, it takes courage to live by Bible standards, especially in the face of ridicule, but it can be done. Among Jehovah's Witnesses are many individuals who used to be drug addicts, drunkards, fornicators, street fighters, thieves, and liars. Yet, they took God's Word to heart and with the help of holy spirit made changes in their lives so as to "walk worthily of Jehovah." (Colossians 1: 9, 10; 1 Corinthians 6:11) Having made peace with God, they also gained inner peace and, as we shall see, a genuine hope for the future.

The Kingdom Hope

The Bible hope of lasting peace for obedient humans will be fulfilled through the Kingdom of God. "Let your kingdom come. Let your will take place, as in heaven, also upon earth," said Jesus in his model prayer. (Matthew 6:10) Yes, only God's Kingdom can ensure that God's will is done on earth. Why? Because that heavenly Kingdom—a government in the hands of Jesus Christ—is God's means of expressing His rightful sovereignty over the earth.—Psalm 2: 7-12; Daniel 7:13, 14.

As King of that heavenly Kingdom, Jesus Christ will liberate obedient humans from every form of bondage, including the vise-like grip of Adamic sin and its legacy of sickness and death. Says Revelation 21:3, 4: "Look! The tent of God is with mankind ... And he [Jehovah God] will wipe out every tear from their eyes, and death will be no more, neither will mourning nor outcry nor pain be anymore. The former things have passed away."

Lasting peace will prevail earth wide. Why can we be sure of that? The reason is revealed at Isaiah 11:9, which says: "They [the Kingdom's subjects] will not do any harm or cause any ruin in all my holy mountain; because the earth will certainly be filled with the knowledge of Jehovah as the waters are covering the very sea." Yes, every human on earth will have accurate knowledge of God and be obedient to him. Does that prospect warm your heart? If so, now is the time to begin taking in the precious "knowledge of Jehovah."

Will You Listen to the Kingdom Message?

By means of the Kingdom, God will undo all the works of Satan and educate people in His righteous ways. Hence, it comes as no surprise that the Kingdom was the focus of Jesus' teaching. "I must declare the good news of the kingdom of God," he said, "because for this I was sent forth." (Luke 4:43) Christ commanded his disciples to share that same message with others. (Matthew 28:19, 20) "This good news of the kingdom," he foretold, "will be preached in all the inhabited earth for a witness to all the nations; and then the end will come." (Matthew 24:14) That end is fast approaching. How important, then, that honesthearted people listen to the lifesaving good news!

Albert, mentioned in the preceding article, heard the Kingdom message when his wife and son began to study the Bible with Jehovah's Witnesses. At first, Albert was skeptical. He even asked a local clergyman to visit his wife and son in order to expose the Witnesses. But the clergyman did not want to get involved. So Albert decided to listen in on a Bible discussion to point out any errors. After just one session, he joined in the study, eager to learn more. He later explained why his attitude had changed. "This was what I had always been looking for," he said.

At last, Albert began to satisfy his spiritual need, and he never looked back. Bible truth gave him what he had been searching for all his life—the solution to the injustice and corruption that permeate society and a hope for the future. Bible truth gave him inner peace. Is your spiritual need being satisfied? Why not take a moment to read through the questions listed in the box on page 6? If you desire additional information, Jehovah's Witnesses will be delighted to help you.

Lasting peace will be brought about through the Messianic Kingdom of God

HAPPY FOR MY SHARE IN GLOBAL BIBLE EDUCATION

AS TOLD BY
ANNA MATHEAKIS

The ferryboat was on fire. If it sank, the 561-foot-long hulk would drag me into a watery grave. I frantically swam to safety, fighting violent waves. The only way to stay afloat was to hold tight to a life jacket worn by another woman. I prayed to God for strength and courage. It was all I could do.

THE year was 1971, and I was returning to my third missionary assignment, Italy. In that shipwreck, I lost almost everything I owned. But I did not lose the most important things—my life, the loving Christian brotherhood, and the privilege of serving Jehovah. That service had already taken me to three continents, and the shipwreck was just one incident in an eventful life.

I was born in 1922. My family lived in Rām Allāh, about ten miles north of Jerusalem. My parents were both from the island of Crete, but my father was raised in Nazareth. I was the youngest of three boys and two girls. Our family was shattered by the death of my second-eldest brother, who drowned in the Jordan River while on a school excursion. After this tragedy my mother refused to stay in Rām Allāh, and we moved to Athens, Greece, when I was three years old.

Bible Truth Reaches Our Family

Shortly after we arrived in Greece, my eldest brother, Nikos, who at the time was 22 years old, came in contact with the Bible Students, as Jehovah's Witnesses were then known. Taking in Bible knowledge gave him great joy and a burning zeal for the Christian ministry. This enraged my father, and he put Nikos out of the house. However, when my father would travel to Palestine, my mother, my sister, and I would accompany Nikos to Christian meetings. I can still hear my mother speaking enthusiastically about the things she heard at those meetings. But shortly thereafter, she succumbed to cancer and died at age 42. During that difficult time, my sister, Ariadne, lovingly took charge of our family. Despite her youth, she was like a mother to me for years to come.

My father always took me to the Orthodox Church when he was in Athens, and after he died, I continued going to church, though less frequently. Since I saw no sign of godly devotion being practiced at church, I eventually stopped attending.

After my father died, I was able to get a secure job with the ministry of finance. My brother, however, had devoted his life to the Kingdom-preaching work, serving for many years in Greece. In 1934 he moved to Cyprus. At the time, there were no baptized Witnesses of Jehovah on that island, so he had the privilege of advancing the preaching work there. After he married, his wife, Galatia, also served as a full-time minister for many years.* Nikos frequently sent us Bible-based books and magazines, but we hardly ever opened them. He remained in Cyprus until his death.

Making Bible Truth My Own

In 1940, George Douras, a zealous Witness in Athens and a friend of Nikos, visited us and invited us to join a small group for a Bible study in his home. We gladly accepted the invitation. Soon we started sharing with

---

* See pages 73-89 of the *1995 Yearbook of Jehovah's Witnesses,* published by Jehovah's Witnesses.

With my sister, Ariadne, and her husband, Michalis, as I was leaving for Gilead

others what we were learning. Taking in knowledge from the Bible led my sister and me to dedicate our lives to Jehovah. Ariadne was baptized in 1942, and I, in 1943.

When World War II ended, Nikos invited us to come to Cyprus, so in 1945 we moved to Nicosia. Unlike in Greece, in Cyprus the preaching work was unhindered. We shared not only in the house-to-house ministry but also in street witnessing.

Two years later, Ariadne had to return to Greece. There she met her future husband, a fellow worshipper of Jehovah, so she remained in Athens. Soon my brother-in-law and my sister encouraged me to return to Greece and take up the full-time ministry in the capital. Since pioneering had always been my goal, I returned to Athens, where the need was greater.

New Doors of Opportunity Are Opened

On November 1, 1947, I started pioneering, spending 150 hours every month in the preaching work. Our congregation territory was vast, and I had to walk a lot. Still, I enjoyed many blessings. The police often arrested any Witnesses they found engaging in the preaching work or attending Christian meetings, so it was not long before I was arrested.

I was charged with proselytism, a serious offense at the time. I was sentenced to two months in the Averof Women's Prison in Athens. Another female Witness was already there, and the two of us enjoyed delightful

and upbuilding Christian fellowship despite being locked up. After I had served my sentence, I happily continued pioneering. Many of those with whom I then studied the Bible are still faithful servants of Jehovah, and that gives me great joy.

In 1949, I received an invitation to attend the 16th class of the Watchtower Bible School of Gilead in the United States, where full-time servants are trained for missionary work. My relatives and I were thrilled. I planned to attend an international convention in New York City in the summer of 1950 and then to enter Gilead.

After arriving in the United States, I had the privilege of serving for a few months as a housekeeper at the world headquarters of Jehovah's Witnesses in New York City. The environment there was clean, pleasant, and upbuilding, and I was surrounded by smiling brothers and sisters. I will always remember with fondness the six months I spent there. Then it was time to attend Gilead School, where five months of intensive study and instruction flew by. We students came to realize how rich and beautiful Scriptural knowledge is, and that increased our joy and our desire to share with others the life-giving knowledge of the truth.

My First Missionary Assignment

At Gilead School, we were allowed to choose our future partners before receiving our missionary assignments. Ruth Hemmig (now Bosshard), an exceptional sister, was my partner. Ruth and I were overjoyed when we received our assignment to Istanbul, Turkey—a crossroads between Asia and Europe! We knew that the preaching work was not yet recognized in that country, but we had no doubt that Jehovah would support us.

Istanbul is a beautiful cosmopolitan city. There we found overflowing bazaars, a blend of the world's finest cuisines, interesting museums, charming neighborhoods, and an always fascinating waterfront. More important, we found sincere people who wanted to learn about God. The small group of Witnesses in Istanbul consisted mainly of Armenians, Greeks, and Jews. However, there were many other nationalities, and it was useful to be conversant with a variety of languages, including Turkish. We thoroughly enjoyed meeting people of different nationalities who were thirsting for the truth. Many of these continue to serve Jehovah faithfully.

Unfortunately, it was impossible for Ruth to renew her residence permit, and she was obliged to leave the country. She continues in the full-time service in Switzerland. After all these years, I still miss her pleasant, upbuilding companionship.

Moving to Another Hemisphere

In 1963 my residence permit in Turkey was not renewed. It was difficult to leave behind fellow Christians whom I had seen progressing spiritually while they struggled to overcome many hardships. In order to cheer me up, my relatives graciously paid my way to New York City so that I could attend a convention there. I had not yet received my next assignment.

After the convention, I was assigned to Lima, Peru. Along with a young sister who

Ruth Hemmig and I were assigned to Istanbul, Turkey

was to be my partner, I went straight from New York to my new assignment. I learned Spanish and lived in the missionary home that was situated above the branch office of Jehovah's Witnesses. It was very pleasant to preach there and get to know the local brothers and sisters.

Another Assignment, Another Language

In time, my relatives back in Greece began to experience the effects of old age and deteriorating health. They never encouraged me to discontinue my full-time service and return to a so-called normal life in order to assist them. However, after much thought and prayer, I realized that it would be better for me to serve closer to my family. The responsible brothers lovingly agreed and assigned me to Italy, and my relatives offered to cover the expenses for the transfer. As it turned out, there was a great need for evangelizers in Italy.

Once again, I had to learn a new language —Italian. My first assignment was in the city of Foggia. Later, I was transferred to Naples, where the need was greater. My territory was Posilipo, one of the most beautiful parts of Naples. It covered a large area, and there was only one Kingdom publisher. I enjoyed the work very much, and Jehovah helped me to start many Bible studies. In time, a large congregation developed in that area.

Among the first local people with whom I studied the Bible were a mother and her four children. She and her two daughters are still Witnesses of Jehovah. I also studied with a married couple who had a little girl. The whole family progressed in the truth and symbolized their dedication by water baptism. Now the daughter is married to a faithful servant of Jehovah, and together they are serving God zealously. While studying the Bible with one large family, I was impressed with the power of God's Word. When we read several scriptures that show that God does not approve of worship through images, the mother did not even wait for the study to finish. Right then and there, she disposed of all the images in her house!

In Dangers at Sea

When shuttling between Italy and Greece, I always traveled by ship. The voyage was usually very pleasant. But one trip, in the summer of 1971, was different. I was traveling back to Italy on the ferryboat *Heleanna.* Early on the morning of August 28, a fire broke out in the ship's kitchen. The fire spread and so did panic among the passengers. Women were fainting, children were crying, and men were protesting and shouting threats. People ran to the lifeboats on each side of the deck. However, there were too few life jackets, and the mechanism that lowers the lifeboats into the sea did not work properly. I had no life jacket, but the flames were rising higher, so the only sensible thing to do was to jump into the sea.

As soon as I found myself in the water, I saw floating near me a woman who was wearing a life jacket. It seemed that she could not swim, so I grabbed her by the arm to pull her away from the sinking ship.

In Italy, early 1970's

The sea was getting rougher, and the fight to stay afloat made me very tired. The situation seemed hopeless, but I kept beseeching Jehovah for courage, and this gave me strength. I could not help but remember the shipwreck experienced by the apostle Paul.—Acts, chapter 27.

Holding on to my companion, I struggled with the waves for four hours, swimming when I had the strength for it and calling on Jehovah for help. Finally, I spotted a dinghy approaching. I was rescued, but my companion had already died. When we reached the town of Bari, Italy, I was taken to a hospital, where I received first aid. I had to stay in the hospital for a few days, and many Witnesses visited me, kindly providing all that I needed. The Christian love they showed deeply impressed others who were in the hospital ward.*

Today, with my sister, Ariadne

After I had recuperated fully, I was assigned to Rome. I was asked to work the business territory in the center of the city, which I did for five years, with Jehovah's help. For a total of 20 years, I enjoyed the ministry in Italy, and I came to love the Italian people.

Back to Where I Started

In time, the health of Ariadne and her husband took a turn for the worse. I realized that if I lived closer to them, I would be able to repay in some measure all that they had so lovingly done for me. I must admit that it was heartbreaking to leave Italy. However, the responsible brothers gave their permission, and since the summer of 1985, I have

---

* For more details, see *Awake!* February 8, 1972, pages 12-16.

been pioneering in Athens, where I began the full-time service back in 1947.

I preached in the territory assigned to my own congregation, and I asked the brothers at the branch office if I could also preach in the business territory in the city center. This I did for three years with a pioneer partner. We were able to give a thorough witness to people who are rarely found at home.

As time passes, though, my desire to serve is constantly being renewed but my physical strength is not. Now my brother-in-law has fallen asleep in death. Ariadne, who has been like a mother to me, has lost her eyesight. As for me, my health was good during the years I spent in full-time service. Recently, however, I tumbled down a marble staircase and broke my right arm. Then I fell and broke my pelvis. I had to undergo surgery and was in bed for a long time. Now I can no longer move about freely. I use a walking stick and can go out only if someone accompanies me. Still, I do my best, hoping that my physical condition will improve. Sharing in the Bible education work, even in a limited way, continues to be my main source of happiness and satisfaction.

When I recall the happy years that I have spent in the full-time ministry, my heart overflows with gratitude to Jehovah. He and the earthly part of his organization have consistently provided sound direction and precious assistance, enabling me to reach my full potential as I have spent my life serving him. My heartfelt desire is that Jehovah strengthen me to continue in his service. I am happy for my modest share in the global Bible education work that he directs.—Malachi 3:10.

They Are Making Themselves Available

"**Y**OUR people will offer themselves willingly." (Psalm 110:3) Those words have special meaning for the 46 students of the 118th class of the Watchtower Bible School of Gilead. How did they prepare themselves to attend this school, which trains prospective missionaries to serve the spiritual needs of people in foreign lands? Mike and Stacie, members of the 118th class, explained: "Our decision to live a simple life helped us to minimize distractions and to keep our spiritual focus. We were determined not to allow our success in the business world to push aside spiritual goals." Like Mike and Stacie, the other students of this class willingly made themselves available and now serve as Kingdom proclaimers on four different continents.

On Saturday, March 12, 2005, an audience of 6,843 listened with obvious delight to the graduation program. Theodore Jaracz, a member of the Governing Body of Jehovah's Witnesses, served as chairman. After giving a warm welcome to the guests, present from 28 different lands, he focused attention on the value of Bible education. Quoting William Lyon Phelps, an American educator, the speaker declared: "Everyone who has a thorough knowledge of the Bible may truly be called educated." As useful as secular education may be, Bible education is superior. It helps people to take in knowledge of God, which leads to everlasting life. (John 17:3) Brother Jaracz commended the graduates for their willingness to have a greater share in the global Bible educational program that is carried out in over 98,000 congregations of Jehovah's Witnesses worldwide.

Timely Encouragement for the Graduates

After the chairman's opening remarks, William Samuelson spoke on the subject "How You Can Be Like a Luxuriant Olive Tree in God's House," based on Psalm 52:8. He point-ed out that the olive tree is figuratively used in the Bible as a symbol of fruitfulness, beauty, and dignity. (Jeremiah 11:16) Comparing the students to olive trees, the speaker said: "Jehovah will credit you with beauty and dignity as you faithfully carry out your work of Kingdom preaching in your missionary assignments." Just as the olive tree needs extensive roots to survive a period of drought, the students need to fortify their spiritual roots in order to endure indifference, opposition, or

CLASS STATISTICS

Number of countries represented: 8

Number of countries assigned to: 19

Number of students: 46

Average age: 33.0

Average years in truth: 16.5

Average years in full-time ministry: 12.9

other trials that they may encounter in their foreign service.—Matthew 13:21; Colossians 2:6, 7.

John E. Barr, one of the three members of the Governing Body who shared in the program, spoke on the theme "You Are the Salt of the Earth." (Matthew 5:13) He pointed out that just as literal salt preserves food from decay, so the missionaries' preaching about God's Kingdom will have a lifesaving effect on those who listen, protecting them from moral and spiritual decay. Then in a fatherly tone, Brother Barr urged the graduates to "keep peace" with others. (Mark 9:50) "Cultivate the fruitage of the spirit, and make sure that your conduct and speech are always gracious and considerate," admonished the speaker.

"Stay on Board in Deep Waters" was the theme highlighted by Wallace Liverance, one of the Gilead instructors. Just as a ship sailing in deep waters can move in the right direction, so an understanding of "the deep things of God"—truths concerning God's purpose and how it will be carried out—can help one to make spiritual progress. (1 Corinthians 2:10) Simply staying in shallow spiritual waters by being content with "the elementary things of the sacred pronouncements of God" hinders our advancement and may even invite "shipwreck concerning [our] faith." (Hebrews 5:12, 13; 1 Timothy 1: 19) "Let 'the depth of God's riches and wisdom and knowledge' sustain you in your missionary assignments," concluded Brother Liverance.—Romans 11:33.

Mark Noumair, another Gilead instructor, spoke on the subject "Will You Live Up to Your Heritage?" For over 60 years, the Watchtower Bible School of Gilead has acquired credibility and a sterling reputation because of the 'heap of good witness' given by the school's graduates. (Genesis 31:48) This Gilead heritage has been passed on to the students of the 118th class. Brother Noumair encouraged the students to imitate the ancient Tekoites of Nehemiah's day and humbly cooperate with the local congregation and fellow missionaries. They were admonished to avoid the attitude of the proud "majestic ones" spoken of by Nehemiah and instead be willing to work quietly in the background.—Nehemiah 3:5.

Instructive Experiences and Interviews

The next part on the program was entitled "The Word of God Went On Growing." (Acts 6:7) Under the direction of Gilead instructor Lawrence Bowen, the students reenacted experiences that they had enjoyed in the field ministry while attending school. The experiences demonstrated that the students had proclaimed God's Word with zeal and that Jehovah had richly blessed their efforts.

Richard Ashe conducted interviews with Bethel family members who work closely with the school. Their comments gave insight into the support the Bethel family gives to help Gilead students to get the most out of their schooling. Then, Geoffrey Jackson spoke with some past graduates of Gilead. They highlighted the numerous opportunities that missionary life offers to bring praise and honor to Jehovah. One commented: "People observe everything you do as a missionary. They listen, they watch, and they remember." Hence, the students were encouraged to be conscious of setting a good example at all times. This sound advice will no doubt prove invaluable in the days to come.

Stephen Lett, a member of the Governing Body, gave the concluding talk, entitled "Go Forth as Bearers of 'Living Water.' " (John 7:38) He noted that for the past five months, the students benefited immeasurably by drinking deeply from God's Word of

118th Graduating Class of the Watchtower Bible School of Gilead

In the list below, rows are numbered from front to back, and names are listed from left to right in each row.

(1) Brockmeyer, A.; Moloney, S.; Symonds, N.; Lopez, Y.; Howard, C. (2) Jastrzebski, T.; Brown, D.; Hernandez, H.; Malagón, I.; Jones, A.; Connell, L. (3) Howard, J.; Lareau, E.; Shams, B.; Hayes, S.; Brown, O. (4) Burrell, J.; Hammer, M.; Mayer, A.; Kim, K.; Stanley, R.; Rainey, R. (5) Jastrzebski, P.; Zilavetz, K.; Ferris, S.; Torres, B.; Torres, F. (6) Connell, J.; Hernandez, R.; Moloney, M.; Malagón, J.; Shams, R.; Hayes, J. (7) Ferris, A.; Hammer, J.; Stanley, G.; Kim, C.; Symonds, S.; Lopez, D.; Burrell, D. (8) Brockmeyer, D.; Mayer, J.; Rainey, S.; Zilavetz, S.; Jones, R.; Lareau, J.

truth. But what will the new missionaries do with the information they have taken in? Brother Lett urged the graduates to share these spiritual waters unselfishly so that others will come to have within themselves "a fountain of water bubbling up to impart everlasting life." (John 4:14) The speaker added: "Never forget to give Jehovah, 'the source of living water,' the honor and glory that he deserves. Be patient when teaching those who have come out of drought-stricken Babylon the Great." (Jeremiah 2:13) Brother Lett concluded by encouraging the graduates to imitate enthusiastically the spirit and the bride and keep on saying: " 'Come!' And let anyone

thirsting come; let anyone that wishes take life's water free."—Revelation 22:17.

Brother Jaracz concluded the program by sharing greetings received from various lands. This was followed by the reading of a letter of gratitude by a member of the graduating class.

Can you make yourself available to serve where the need is greater? If so, then pursue spiritual goals, as these graduating students have done. Reap the joy and satisfaction that are found when a person cheerfully offers himself willingly in God's service—whether as a missionary in a foreign country or as a minister closer to home.

"BRINGING GOOD NEWS OF SOMETHING BETTER"

"How comely upon the mountains are the feet of the one . . . bringing good news of something better."—ISAIAH 52:7.

TODAY people the world over feel that they are drowning in bad news. They turn on the radio and hear frightening reports about deadly diseases stalking the earth. They watch the news on television and see haunting images of starving children crying for help. They pick up a newspaper and read about bomb blasts that rip through buildings, killing scores of innocent people.

² Yes, dreadful things are happening every day. The scene of this world is definitely changing—for the worse. (1 Corinthians 7:31) A newsmagazine in Western Europe noted that at times it seems as though the entire world were "about to go up in flames." No wonder that a growing number of people are distressed! One person who was quoted in a survey about television news in the United States no doubt echoed the feelings of millions when he said: 'After I watch the news, I'm thoroughly depressed. It's all bad news. It's overwhelming.'

News That Everyone Needs to Hear

³ In such a gloomy world, can better news be found? Indeed it can! It is comforting to know that the Bible proclaims *good* news. It is the news that sickness, hunger, crime, war, and all sorts of oppression will be brought to an end by God's Kingdom. (Psalm 46:9; 72:12) Is that not news that everyone needs to hear? Jehovah's Witnesses certainly think so. Therefore, they are known everywhere for their ongoing effort to share the good news of God's Kingdom with people of all nations.—Matthew 24:14.

⁴ What, though, can we do in order to continue to have a satisfying and meaningful share in the preaching of this good news —even in less responsive territories? (Luke 8:15) A brief review of three important aspects of our preaching work will no doubt help. We can examine (1) our motives, or *why* we preach; (2) our message, or *what* we preach; and (3) our methods, or *how* we preach. By keeping our motives pure, our message clear, and our methods effective, we will give to a wide range of people the opportunity to hear the best of good news—the good news of God's Kingdom.*

1, 2. (a) What dreadful things are happening every day? (b) How do many people react to hearing bad news constantly?

3. (a) What good news does the Bible proclaim? (b) Why do you value the good news of the Kingdom?

---

* This article will consider the first two aspects. The second article will consider the third.

---

4. Which aspects of our ministry will we consider in this and the following article?

Why We Share in Preaching the Good News

⁵ Let us consider the first aspect—our motives. *Why* do we preach the good news? For the same reason Jesus did. He said: "I love the Father." (John 14:31; Psalm 40:8) Above all, we are motivated by our love for God. (Matthew 22:37, 38) The Bible makes a connection between love for God and the ministry, for it states: "This is what the love of God means, that we observe his commandments." (1 John 5:3; John 14:21) Do God's commandments include the one to 'go and make disciples'? (Matthew 28:19) Yes. True, those words were spoken by Jesus, but ultimately they originated with Jehovah. How so? Jesus explained: "I do nothing of my own initiative; but just as the Father taught me I speak these things." (John 8:28; Matthew 17:5) Hence, by observing the command to preach, we show Jehovah that we love him.

⁶ In addition, love for Jehovah motivates us to preach because we want to counteract the lies that Satan is promoting against him. (2 Corinthians 4:4) Satan has brought into question the righteousness of God's rule. (Genesis 3:1-5) As Jehovah's Witnesses, we yearn to share in exposing Satan's slanders and in sanctifying God's name before mankind. (Isaiah 43:10-12) Moreover, we share in the ministry because we have come to know Jehovah's qualities and ways. We feel close to him and feel a strong desire to tell others about our God. In fact, Jehovah's goodness and his righteous ways bring us such joy that we cannot stop talking about him. (Psalm 145:7-12) We feel impelled to tell forth his praise and speak about his "excellencies" to those who will listen.—1 Peter 2:9; Isaiah 43:21.

⁷ There is another important reason for continuing to share in the ministry: We sincerely want to bring relief to individuals who are overwhelmed by the relentless onslaught of bad news and to those who suffer for one reason or another. In this, we strive to imitate Jesus. Look, for example, at what is described in Mark chapter 6.

⁸ The apostles return from a preaching campaign and relate to Jesus all that they have done and taught. Jesus notices that the apostles are tired, and he tells them to come with him to "rest up a bit." So they get into a boat and travel to a quiet place. People follow them, running along the shoreline, and soon catch up with them. What does Jesus do? "He saw a great crowd," the record says, "but he was *moved with pity* for them, because they were as sheep without a shepherd.

---

5. (a) Above all, what motivates us to share in the ministry? (b) Why can it be said that our obedience to the Biblical command to preach is an expression of love for God?

6. In what ways does love for God motivate us to preach?

7. Besides love for God, for what other important reason do we share in the preaching work?

8. What does the account in Mark chapter 6 show about Jesus' feelings for people?

And he started to teach them many things." (Mark 6:31-34) Pity moves Jesus to continue sharing the good news in spite of his tiredness. Clearly, Jesus' heart goes out to these people. He feels compassion for them.

[9] What do we learn from this account? As Christians, we feel an obligation to preach the good news and to make disciples. We recognize our responsibility to declare the good news, since it is God's will that "all sorts of men should be saved." (1 Timothy 2:4) However, we perform our ministry not only out of a sense of duty but also out of compassion. If we feel deeply for people as Jesus did, our heart will move us to do all we can to continue sharing the good news with them. (Matthew 22:39) Having such fine motives for engaging in the ministry will move us to preach the good news without letup.

Our Message—The Good News of God's Kingdom

[10] What of the second aspect of our ministry—our message? *What* do we preach? The prophet Isaiah gave this beautiful description of the message we publish: "How comely upon the mountains are the feet of the one bringing good news, the one publishing peace, the one bringing good news of something better, the one publishing salvation, the one saying to Zion: 'Your God has become king!'"—Isaiah 52:7.

[11] The key expression in that scripture, "your God has become king," reminds us of the message that we must proclaim, namely, the good news of God's Kingdom. (Mark 13:10) Note, too, that this verse reveals the positive tenor of our message. Isaiah uses such terms as "salvation," "good news," "peace," and "something better." Centuries after Isaiah, in the first century C.E., Jesus Christ fulfilled this prophecy in an outstanding way by setting a zealous example in publishing news of something better—the coming Kingdom of God. (Luke 4:43) In modern times, especially since 1919, Jehovah's Witnesses have followed Jesus' example by zealously proclaiming the good news of God's established Kingdom and the blessings it will bring.

[12] What effect does the Kingdom good news have on those who respond to it? Today as in Jesus' day, the good news gives hope and comfort. (Romans 12:12; 15:4) It gives honesthearted ones hope because they learn that there are solid reasons for believing that better times are ahead. (Matthew 6:9, 10;

The Kingdom message gives strength to the brokenhearted

---

12. What effect does the Kingdom good news have on those who accept it?

---

9. What do we learn from the account in Mark chapter 6 regarding the right motive for preaching?
10, 11. (a) How does Isaiah describe the message that we preach? (b) How did Jesus bring good news of something better, and how have God's servants in modern times followed Jesus' example?

2 Peter 3:13) Such hope greatly helps God-fearing ones to maintain a positive outlook. The psalmist states that they "will not be afraid even of bad news."—Psalm 112:1, 7.

A Message That Will "Bind Up the Brokenhearted"

[13] In addition, the good news we preach brings immediate relief and blessings to those who listen to it. How? Some of the blessings were indicated by the prophet Isaiah when he foretold: "The spirit of the Sovereign Lord Jehovah is upon me, for the reason that Jehovah has anointed me to tell good news to the meek ones. He has sent me to bind up the brokenhearted, to proclaim liberty to those taken captive and the wide opening of the eyes even to the prisoners; to proclaim the year of goodwill on the part of Jehovah and the day of vengeance on the part of our God; to comfort all the mourning ones."—Isaiah 61:1, 2; Luke 4:16-21.

[14] According to that prophecy, by preaching the good news, Jesus would "bind up the brokenhearted." What a telling word picture Isaiah used! According to one Bible dictionary, the Hebrew word translated "bind up" "is often used of 'binding' on a bandage, and thus of medicating and healing the wounded." A caring nurse may wrap a bandage or a compress around a victim's injured body part to give it support. In the same way, when preaching the Kingdom message, caring publishers give support to all responsive ones who are suffering in some way. And by supporting those in need, they reflect Jehovah's concern. (Ezekiel 34:15, 16) The psalmist states concerning God: "He is healing the

brokenhearted ones, and is binding up their painful spots."—Psalm 147:3.

How the Kingdom Message Makes a Difference

[15] Numerous real-life examples illustrate how the Kingdom message does indeed support and strengthen those who are brokenhearted. Consider Oreanna, an elderly woman in South America, who had given up on life. A Witness of Jehovah began visiting Oreanna and reading to her the Bible and the publication My Book of Bible Stories.* At first, the depressed woman listened to the reading while lying in bed with her eyes closed, from time to time heaving sighs. Before long, though, she began to make an effort to sit up in her bed during the reading. Some time later, she was sitting in a chair in the living room, waiting for her Bible teacher to come. Next, the woman began attending Christian meetings at the Kingdom Hall. Encouraged by what she learned at those gatherings, she began to offer Bible literature to anyone passing by her house. Then, at age 93, Oreanna was baptized as one of Jehovah's Witnesses. The Kingdom message had renewed her desire to live.—Proverbs 15:30; 16:24.

[16] The Kingdom message gives crucial support even to those who know that their life is about to be cut short by illness. Take as an example Maria from Western Europe. She was suffering from a terminal disease and had lost all hope. She was deeply depressed when she was contacted by Jehovah's Witnesses. However, when she learned about God's purposes, her life became meaningful again. She was baptized and became very active in the preaching work. During the final two years of her life, her eyes radiated hope and joy. Maria

---

13. How does the prophet Isaiah describe the immediate blessings that come to those who accept the good news?
14. (a) What does the expression "bind up the brokenhearted" indicate about the Kingdom message? (b) How do we reflect Jehovah's concern for brokenhearted ones?

---

* Published by Jehovah's Witnesses.

15, 16. What real-life examples illustrate how the Kingdom message gives support and strength to those in need?

died with a firm hope in the resurrection.—Romans 8:38, 39.

¹⁷ Such reports testify to the difference the Kingdom message can make in the lives of ones who long for Bible truths. Individuals who mourn the death of a loved one gain new strength when they learn about the resurrection hope. (1 Thessalonians 4:13) People who live in poverty and struggle to feed their family find new dignity and courage when they learn that Jehovah will never forsake them if they are loyal to him. (Psalm 37:28) With Jehovah's help, many who are overwhelmed by depression gradually develop the strength needed to cope and in some cases are even enabled to overcome that illness. (Psalm 40:1, 2) Indeed, by means of the power supplied through his Word, Jehovah is right now "raising up all who are bowed down." (Psalm 145:14) By observing how the Kingdom good news brings comfort to brokenhearted ones in our territory and in the Christian congregation, we are time and again reminded that we have the *best* news available today! —Psalm 51:17.

17. (a) How is the Kingdom message making a difference in the lives of those who accept it? (b) In what ways have you personally experienced that Jehovah is "raising up all who are bowed down"?

Prayer helps us to endure in our ministry

What Have You Learned?

- For what reasons do we share in the ministry?
- What is the main message that we preach?
- What blessings are experienced by those who accept the Kingdom message?
- What will help us to continue in our ministry?

"My Supplication to God for Them"

¹⁸ Although our message contains the best news, many reject it. How might this affect us? In the same way that it did the apostle Paul. He often preached to Jews, but most of them rejected the message of salvation. Their refusal affected Paul deeply. He admitted: "I have great grief and unceasing pain in my heart." (Romans 9:2) Paul felt compassion for the Jews to whom he preached. It saddened him that they rejected the good news.

¹⁹ We too preach the good news out of compassion. Hence, it is understandable that we may feel discouraged when many people reject the Kingdom message. Such a reaction shows that we have genuine concern for the spiritual welfare of those to whom we preach. However, we do well to remember the example of the apostle Paul. What helped him to continue in his preaching work? Although the Jews' refusal to accept the good news caused him grief and pain, Paul did not give up on all Jews, thinking that they were beyond help. His hope was that there were still

---

18. How was Paul affected by the Jews' rejection of the good news, and why?
19. (a) Why is it understandable that we may feel discouraged at times? (b) What helped Paul to continue in his preaching work?

some who would accept Christ. Hence, concerning his feelings toward individual Jews, Paul wrote: "The goodwill of my heart and my supplication to God for them are, indeed, for their salvation."—Romans 10:1.

[20] Notice the two things that Paul highlighted. It was his heart's desire that some individuals would find salvation, and he supplicated God to that end. Today, we follow Paul's example. We maintain a heartfelt de-

sire to locate any who might still be rightly disposed toward the good news. We keep on praying to Jehovah that we may find such individuals so that we may help them to follow the course that will lead to their salvation.—Proverbs 11:30; Ezekiel 33:11; John 6:44.

[21] However, to reach as many individuals as possible with the Kingdom message, we need to pay attention not only to *why* and *what* we preach but also to *how* we preach. This subject will be considered in the following article.

20, 21. (a) Regarding our ministry, how can we follow Paul's example? (b) What aspect of our ministry will be considered in the following article?

GOOD NEWS FOR PEOPLE OF ALL NATIONS

"You will be witnesses of me . . . to the most distant part of the earth."—ACTS 1:8.

CAPABLE teachers pay attention not only to what they tell their students but also to how they tell it. As teachers of Bible truth, we do the same. We give attention to both the message we preach and the methods we use. Our message, the good news of God's Kingdom, does not change, but we do adapt our methods. Why? To reach as many people as possible.

[2] By adapting our preaching methods, we imitate God's servants of old. Consider, for example, the apostle Paul. He said: "To the Jews I became as a Jew . . . To those without law I became as without law . . . To the weak I became weak, that I might gain the weak. I have become all things to people of all

sorts, that I might by all means save some." (1 Corinthians 9:19-23) Paul's adaptable approach was effective. We too will be effective if we considerately adjust our presentations to fit the individuals we are talking to.

To "the Ends of the Earth"

[3] A major challenge faced by those preaching the good news is the extent of the territory—"all the inhabited earth." (Matthew 24:14) During the last century, many servants of Jehovah worked hard to reach new lands in order to spread the good news. What was the result? Breathtaking worldwide expansion. At the dawn of the 20th century, preaching was reported in only a few lands, but at present, Jehovah's Witnesses are active in 235

---

1. As Bible teachers, to what do we pay attention, and why?
2. When we adapt our preaching methods, whom are we imitating?

3. (a) What challenge do we face in our preaching work? (b) How are the words of Isaiah 45:22 being fulfilled today?

lands! Truly, the Kingdom good news is being proclaimed even to "the ends of the earth."—Isaiah 45:22.

4 What accounts for such progress? Many things. Missionaries trained at the Watchtower Bible School of Gilead and, more recently, upwards of 20,000 graduates of the Ministerial Training School have made a huge contribution. So have the many Witnesses who at their own expense have moved to lands where the need for Kingdom publishers is greater. Such self-sacrificing Christians—men and women, young and old, single and married—play a significant role in preaching the Kingdom message throughout the earth. (Psalm 110:3; Romans

_____

4, 5. (a) Who have played a significant role in spreading the good news? (b) What did some branch offices say about those from abroad who serve in the branch territory?

10:18) They are greatly appreciated. Note what some branch offices wrote about those from abroad who serve where the need is greater in the branch territory.

5 "These dear Witnesses take the lead in preaching in isolated areas, help to form new congregations, and contribute to the spiritual growth of the local brothers and sisters." (Ecuador) "If the hundreds of foreigners who serve here were to leave, the stability of the congregations would be affected. It is a blessing to have them with us." (Dominican Republic) "In many of our congregations, there is a high percentage of sisters, at times up to 70 percent. (Psalm 68:11) Most of them are new in the truth, but single pioneer sisters who have come from other lands provide invaluable assistance by training such new ones. These sisters from abroad are a true gift to us!" (An Eastern European

A Deep Sense of Fulfillment

"Happy and enjoying their united service to Jehovah." That describes a family who moved from Spain to Bolivia. A son of the family had gone there to support an isolated group. His evident joy so impressed his parents that soon the whole family—including four boys from 14 to 25 years of age—was serving there. Three of the boys are now pioneering, and the one who led the way recently attended Ministerial Training School.

"The challenges are many," says Angelica, aged 30 from Canada, who serves in Eastern Europe, "but I get satisfaction from helping people in the ministry. I am also touched by the many expressions of gratitude from local Witnesses who often thank me for coming to help them."

"There were so many different customs to get used to," say two fleshly sisters in their late 20's from the United States, who serve in the Dominican Republic. "However, we persevered in our assignment, and seven of our Bible students now attend the meetings." These two sisters were instrumental in organizing a group of

Kingdom publishers in a town where there is no congregation.

Laura, a sister in her late 20's, has been serving abroad for over four years. She says: "I deliberately keep my life simple. This helps the publishers to see that modest living is a matter of choice and of soundness of mind, not of poverty. Being able to help others, especially youths, has been a source of joy for me that offsets the real hardships of serving in a foreign field. I would not trade my service here for any other life, and I will stay as long as Jehovah permits."

LAPLAND (SWEDEN)

GHANA

*Our Bible
publications are
now available in over
400 languages*

PHILIPPINES

fulfillment of this important detail of the prophecy? Yes, indeed.

7 Consider some statistics. Fifty years ago our literature was published in 90 languages. Today, that number has risen to over 400. "The faithful and discreet slave" has spared no effort in providing literature even for some whose language is spoken by relatively few people. (Matthew 24:45) For example, Bible literature is now available in Greenlandic (spoken by 47,000 people), Palauan (spoken by 15,000), and Yapese (spoken by fewer than 7,000 people).

land) Have you ever considered serving in another country?*—Acts 16:9, 10.

"Ten Men Out of All the Languages"

6 Another major challenge is the great diversity of languages spoken on earth. God's Word foretold: "It will be in those days that ten men out of all the languages of the nations will take hold, yes, they will actually take hold of the skirt of a man who is a Jew, saying: 'We will go with you people, for we have heard that God is with you people.'" (Zechariah 8:23) In the modern fulfillment of this prophecy, the ten men represent the great crowd, prophesied about at Revelation 7:9. Note, however, that according to Zechariah's prophecy, the "ten men" would come not only out of all nations but also "out of *all the languages* of the nations." Have we seen a

"A Large Door" Leading to New Opportunities

8 Nowadays, though, we may not need to go abroad to share the good news with people of all tongues. In recent years, the arrival of millions of immigrants and refugees in economically developed lands has created numerous immigrant communities speaking many tongues. For instance, in Paris, France, some 100 different languages are spoken. In Toronto, Canada, the number is 125; and in London, England, more than 300 foreign languages are spoken! This presence of people from other lands in many congregation territories opens "a large door" leading to new opportunities to share the good news with people of all nations.—1 Corinthians 16:9.

9 Thousands of Witnesses are responding to the challenge by learning another language. For most of them, it is difficult; yet the struggle is more than balanced by the joy of helping immigrants and refugees to

---

* See the box "A Deep Sense of Fulfillment," on page 22.

6. How does Zechariah 8:23 point to the linguistic challenge in our preaching work?

7. What statistics show that people "out of all the languages" are being reached with the good news?
8, 9. What development has opened "a large door" for us, and how have thousands of Witnesses responded?

learn the truth found in God's Word. In a recent year, nearly 40 percent of all those baptized at the district conventions in one Western European country had come from another land.

¹⁰ True, most of us are not in a position to learn a foreign language. Even so, we can have a share in helping immigrants by making good use of the newly released booklet *Good News for People of All Nations,** which contains an appealing Bible message in many different languages. (John 4:37) Are you using this booklet in the ministry?

When People Are Unresponsive

¹¹ As Satan's influence grows in the earth, another challenge is more frequently faced —there is little response in some territories. Of course, this situation does not surprise us, since Jesus foretold that such a condition would exist. Speaking about our day, he said: "The love of the greater number will cool off." (Matthew 24:12) Indeed, belief in God and respect for the Bible have waned among many. (2 Peter 3:3, 4) Consequently, in some parts of the world, relatively few individuals become new disciples of Christ. That does not mean, however, that the labors of our dear Christian brothers and sisters who faithfully preach in such unresponsive territories are in vain. (Hebrews 6:10) Why not? Consider the following.

¹² The Gospel of Matthew highlights two main objectives of our preaching activities. One is that we "make disciples of people of all the nations." (Matthew 28:19) The other

---

* Published by Jehovah's Witnesses.

---

10. How have you used the booklet *Good News for People of All Nations?* (See the box "Features of the Booklet *Good News for People of All Nations,*" on page 26.)
11. What additional challenge is faced in some territories?
12. What are two objectives of our preaching work?

ECUADOR

Can you serve where there is a greater need for Kingdom proclaimers?

is that the Kingdom message serves as "a witness." (Matthew 24:14) Both objectives are important, but the latter is especially significant. Why?

¹³ Bible writer Matthew recorded that the apostles asked Jesus: "What will be the sign of your presence and of the conclusion of the system of things?" (Matthew 24:3) In response, Jesus said that one outstanding feature of that sign would be a global preaching work. Was he speaking about disciple making? No. He said: "This good news of the kingdom will be *preached* in all the inhabited earth for a witness to all the nations." (Matthew 24:14) Thus Jesus showed that the Kingdom-preaching work itself would be an important feature of the sign.

¹⁴ Hence, as we preach the good news of the Kingdom, we remember that even if we do not always succeed in making disciples, we do succeed in giving "a witness." Regardless of how people respond, they know what we are doing, and thus we share in fulfilling

---

13, 14. (a) What is an outstanding feature of the sign of Christ's presence? (b) What should we keep in mind, especially when preaching in less responsive territories?

DOMINICAN REPUBLIC

Jesus' prophecy. (Isaiah 52:7; Revelation 14: 6, 7) Jordy, a young Witness in Western Europe, noted: "To know that I am used by Jehovah to play a part in fulfilling Matthew 24: 14 makes me very happy." (2 Corinthians 2: 15-17) No doubt you feel the same way.

When Our Message Is Opposed

[15] Adverse circumstances pose another challenge to preaching the Kingdom good news. Jesus forewarned his followers: "You will be objects of hatred by all the nations on account of my name." (Matthew 24:9) Like the early Christians, Jesus' followers today have been hated, opposed, and persecuted. (Acts 5:17, 18, 40; 2 Timothy 3:12; Revelation 12:12, 17) In some lands, they are at present the target of governmental bans. Still, in obedience to God, true Christians in such lands continue preaching the Kingdom good news. (Amos 3:8; Acts 5:29; 1 Peter 2: 21) What enables them, as well as all other Witnesses worldwide, to do so? Jehovah em-

---

15. (a) About what did Jesus forewarn his followers? (b) What enables us to preach despite opposition?

powers them by means of his holy spirit. —Zechariah 4:6; Ephesians 3:16; 2 Timothy 4:17.

[16] Jesus underlined the close link between God's spirit and the preaching work when he told his followers: "You will receive power when the holy spirit arrives upon you, *and* you will be witnesses of me . . . to the most distant part of the earth." (Acts 1:8; Revelation 22:17) The order of events in this scripture is significant. First, the disciples received the holy spirit, and then they undertook the global witnessing work. Only with the support of God's spirit would they have the strength to endure in giving "a witness to all the nations." (Matthew 24:13, 14; Isaiah 61:1, 2) Appropriately, therefore, Jesus referred to the holy spirit as "the helper." (John 15:26) He said that God's spirit would teach and guide his disciples.—John 14:16, 26; 16:13.

[17] In what ways does God's spirit help us today when we are faced with fierce opposition to the preaching of the good news? God's spirit strengthens us, and it opposes those who persecute us. To illustrate this, consider an event in the life of King Saul.

---

16. How did Jesus show the link between the preaching work and God's spirit?
17. When we are faced with fierce opposition, how does the holy spirit help us?

Can You Recall?

- Why do we adapt our methods of preaching?
- "A large door" leading to what new opportunities has been opened?
- What is accomplished by our preaching work, even in less responsive territories?
- Why can no opposer stop the preaching of the Kingdom good news?

Features of the Booklet
Good News for People of All Nations

The booklet *Good News for People of All Nations* contains a one-page message presented in up to 92 different languages. The message is written in the first person. So when the householder reads the message, it sounds as if you were talking to him.

The inside cover features a world map. Use this map as a means to establish a rapport with the householder. Perhaps you can point to the country where you are living and indicate that you would like to know where he is from. In that way, you may draw him out and create a friendly and relaxed atmosphere.

The foreword of the booklet lists several steps that we should take in order to give effective help to those who speak a language that we do not understand. Please read these steps carefully and apply them conscientiously.

The table of contents lists

Are you using this booklet in the ministry?

not only the languages but also the corresponding language symbols. This feature helps you to identify the language symbols printed on our tracts and other publications in different languages.

Confronted by God's Spirit

¹⁸ Saul had a good start as Israel's first king, but later he became disobedient to Jehovah. (1 Samuel 10:1, 24; 11:14, 15; 15:17-23) As a result, God's spirit no longer supported the king. Saul became violently angry at David, who had been anointed as the next king and now enjoyed the support of God's spirit. (1 Samuel 16:1, 13, 14) David seemed to be easy prey. After all, he held only a harp, whereas Saul wielded a spear. So one day while David was playing the harp, "Saul proceeded to hurl the spear and say: 'I will pin David even to the wall!' but David turned aside from before him, twice." (1 Samuel 18:10, 11) Afterward, Saul listened to his son Jonathan, David's friend, and swore: "As Jehovah is living, [David] will

not be put to death." But then, Saul again "sought to pin David to the wall with the spear." However, David "dodged from before Saul, so that he struck the spear into the wall." David fled, but Saul came after him. At that critical time, God's spirit became Saul's opposer. In what way?—1 Samuel 19:6, 10.

¹⁹ David fled to the prophet Samuel, but Saul sent his men to seize David. When they arrived at David's hiding place, however, "the spirit of God came to be upon Saul's messengers, and they began behaving like prophets." They were so overwhelmed by God's spirit that they completely forgot the purpose of their mission. Two more times Saul sent men to bring David back, and the same thing happened each time. Finally, King Saul himself went to David, but Saul too was unable to withstand God's spirit. In fact, the holy spirit immobilized

---

18. (a) What dramatic change for the worse did Saul undergo? (b) What methods did Saul use to persecute David?

19. How did God's spirit protect David?

him "all that day and all that night"—giving David sufficient time to flee.—1 Samuel 19:20-24.

20 This account of Saul and David contains a strengthening lesson: Persecutors of God's servants cannot succeed when opposed by God's spirit. (Psalm 46:11; 125:2) Jehovah purposed that David would be king over Israel. No one could change that. For our day, Jehovah has determined that the "good news of the kingdom *will* be preached." No one can stop that from taking place.—Acts 5: 40, 42.

------

20. What lesson can we learn from the account of Saul's persecution of David?

21 Some religious and political leaders use lies and even violence to try to hinder us. However, just as Jehovah protected David spiritually, so He will protect His people today. (Malachi 3:6) Therefore, like David, we say with confidence: "In God I have put my trust. I shall not be afraid. What can earthling man do to me?" (Psalm 56:11; 121:1-8; Romans 8:31) With Jehovah's help, may we continue to meet all challenges as we carry out the God-given commission to preach the good news of the Kingdom to people of all nations.

------

21. (a) How do some opposers today act? (b) Of what are we confident?

Questions From Readers

Deuteronomy 14:21 reads: "You must not eat any body already dead." Does that contradict Leviticus 11:40, which reads: "He who eats any of its dead body will wash his garments, and he must be unclean until the evening"?

There is no contradiction between these two verses. The first text repeats the prohibition against eating an animal found dead, perhaps one that was killed by wild beasts. (Exodus 22: 31; Leviticus 22:8) The second explains what an Israelite might have done if he violated that prohibition, possibly by accident.

The fact that something was prohibited by the Law did not mean that the prohibition would not at some time be ignored. For example, there were laws against stealing, murder, bearing false witness, and so forth. At the same time, there were penalties for breaking those divinely given laws. Such penalties gave

force to the laws and showed how serious they were.

A person who transgressed the prohibition against eating the flesh of an animal found dead would be unclean in Jehovah's eyes and would have to undergo the proper procedure for cleansing. If he failed to cleanse himself properly, he would have to "answer for his error."—Leviticus 17:15, 16.

IN OUR NEXT ISSUE

True Teachings—Where Can You Find Them?

"Jehovah's Sword and Gideon's!"

Are You Faithful in All Things?

Jehovah's Word Is Alive
Highlights From the Book of First Kings

"WHEN the righteous become many, the people rejoice; but when anyone wicked bears rule, the people sigh." (Proverbs 29:2) The Bible book of First Kings vividly demonstrates the truth of this proverb. It relates the life story of Solomon, during whose kingship ancient Israel enjoys a time of security and great prosperity. First Kings also includes an account of the dividing of the nation after Solomon's death and of 14 kings who followed him, some in Israel and some in Judah. Only two of these kings were consistently faithful to Jehovah. In addition, the book recounts the activities of six prophets, including Elijah.

Written in Jerusalem and Judah by the prophet Jeremiah, the narrative covers a period of some 129 years—from 1040 B.C.E. to 911 B.C.E. While compiling the book, Jeremiah evidently consulted such ancient records as "the book of the affairs of Solomon." Those separate records are no longer extant. —1 Kings 11:41; 14:19; 15:7.

A WISE KING PROMOTES PEACE AND PROSPERITY
(1 Kings 1:1–11:43)

First Kings begins with an intriguing account of an attempt by King David's son Adonijah to usurp his father's kingship. The prophet Nathan's prompt action foils the plan, and David's son Solomon is made king. Jehovah is pleased with the request of the newly enthroned king and gives him "a wise and understanding heart" along with "riches and glory." (1 Kings 3:12, 13) The king's wisdom is without equal, his wealth beyond compare. Israel enjoys a period of peace and prosperity.

Among the building projects Solomon completes are Jehovah's temple and various government buildings. Jehovah assures Solomon: "I [will] establish the throne of your kingdom over Israel to time indefinite," provided the king remains obedient. (1 Kings 9:4, 5) The true God also warns him of the consequences of disobedience. Solomon, though, comes to have many foreign wives. Under their influence, he turns to false worship in his old age. Jehovah foretells that his kingdom will be divided. In 997 B.C.E., Solomon dies, bringing an end to his 40-year reign. His son Rehoboam ascends the throne.

Scriptural Questions Answered:

1:5—Why did Adonijah try to seize the throne while David was still alive? The Bible does not say. However, it is reasonable to conclude that since Adonijah's older brothers Amnon and Absalom were already dead, as was probably David's son Chileab, Adonijah thought that he had the right to the throne as the eldest of David's remaining sons. (2 Samuel 3:2-4; 13:28, 29; 18:14-17) Having elicited the support of the powerful army chief Joab and the influential high priest Abiathar, Adonijah likely felt confident that his attempt would succeed. The Bible does not say whether he knew of David's intent to have Solomon inherit the throne. However, Adonijah did not invite Solomon and others loyal to David to "a sacrifice." (1 Kings 1:9, 10) This suggests that he viewed Solomon as a rival.

1:49-53; 2:13-25—Why did Solomon put Adonijah to death after granting him a pardon? Even though Bath-sheba had failed to recognize it, Solomon discerned the true intention behind Adonijah's request that she ask the king to give him Abishag as a wife. Though David had not had relations with her, beautiful Abishag was considered David's concubine. According to the custom of the times, she would become the property only of David's legal heir. Adonijah might have thought that by taking Abishag as his wife, he could again make a bid for the throne. Interpreting Adonijah's request as a manifestation of ambition for the kingship, Solomon revoked the pardon.

6:37–8:2—When was the temple inaugurated? The temple was completed in the eighth month of 1027 B.C.E., the 11th year of Solomon's reign. It seems that bringing in the furnishings and making other preparations took 11 months. The inauguration must have taken place in the seventh month of the year 1026 B.C.E. The narrative describes other construction projects after the temple's completion and before mentioning its inauguration, evidently to round out the discussion about the building operations. —2 Chronicles 5:1-3.

9:10-13—Was Solomon's gift of 20 cities in the land of Galilee to King Hiram of Tyre in harmony with the Mosaic Law? The Law as stated at Leviticus 25:23, 24 could have been regarded as applying only to an area occupied by the Israelites. It is possible that the cities Solomon gave to Hiram were inhabited by non-Israelites, although lying within the boundary of the Promised Land. (Exodus 23:31) Solomon's action could also have been an indication of his failure to comply completely with the Law, as when he 'increased horses for himself' and took many wives. (Deuteronomy 17:16, 17) Whatever the case, Hiram was dissatisfied with the gift. Perhaps the cities were not well-kept by their pagan inhabitants, or it may be that they were not ideally located.

11:4—Did senility cause Solomon to become unfaithful in his old age? This does not seem to be the case. Solomon was quite young when he began ruling, and although he reigned for 40 years, he did not reach an advanced old age. Moreover, he did not completely leave off following Jehovah. He apparently tried to practice some form of interfaith.

Lessons for Us:

2:26, 27, 35. What Jehovah foretells always comes true. The removal of Abiathar, a descendant of Eli, fulfilled "Jehovah's word that he had spoken against the house of Eli." Replacing Abiathar with Zadok from the line of Phinehas was in fulfillment of Numbers

The temple and other buildings constructed by Solomon

25:10-13.—Exodus 6:25; 1 Samuel 2:31; 3:12; 1 Chronicles 24:3.

2:37, 41-46. How dangerous it is to think that one can step out of bounds with impunity! Those who deliberately deviate from following 'the cramped road leading off into life' will suffer the consequences of that unwise decision.—Matthew 7:14.

3:9, 12-14. Jehovah answers his servants' sincere prayers for wisdom, understanding, and guidance in carrying out his service. —James 1:5.

8:22-53. What heartfelt appreciation Solomon expressed for Jehovah—a God of loving-kindness, the Fulfiller of promises, and the Hearer of prayer! Meditating on the words of Solomon's inauguration prayer will enhance our appreciation for these and other aspects of God's personality.

11:9-14, 23, 26. When Solomon became disobedient in his later years, Jehovah raised up resisters. "God opposes the haughty ones, but he gives undeserved kindness to the humble ones," says the apostle Peter.—1 Peter 5:5.

After Jehovah demonstrated his power, the people exclaimed: "Jehovah is the true God!"

11:30-40. King Solomon sought to kill Jeroboam because of what Ahijah had prophesied concerning Jeroboam. How different the king's response was some 40 years earlier when he refused to seek revenge against Adonijah and other conspirators! (1 Kings 1:50-53) This change of attitude was a result of his drawing away from Jehovah.

A UNITED KINGDOM IS RIPPED APART
(1 Kings 12:1–22:53)

Jeroboam and the people come to King Rehoboam and ask him to lighten the burden imposed by his father, Solomon. Instead of granting their request, Rehoboam threatens to place an even heavier load on them. Ten tribes revolt and make Jeroboam king over them. The kingdom stands divided. Rehoboam rules over the southern kingdom, made up of the tribes of Judah and Benjamin, and Jeroboam reigns over the northern ten-tribe kingdom of Israel.

To discourage the people from going to Jerusalem to worship, Jeroboam sets up two golden calves—one at Dan and the other at Bethel. Among the kings who rule in Israel after Jeroboam are Nadab, Baasha, Elah, Zimri, Tibni, Omri, Ahab, and Ahaziah. Abijam, Asa, Jehoshaphat, and Jehoram succeed Rehoboam in Judah. Prophets active in the days of these kings include Ahijah, Shemaiah, and an unnamed man of God, as well as Jehu, Elijah, and Micaiah.

Scriptural Questions Answered:

18:21—Why were the people silent when Elijah asked them to follow either Jehovah or Baal? It could be that they recognized their failure to give Jehovah the exclusive devotion that he exacts and therefore felt guilty. Or perhaps their consciences were hardened to the extent that they saw nothing wrong with worshipping Baal while claiming to be worshippers of Jehovah. It was only after Jehovah demonstrated his power that they said: "Jehovah is the true God! Jehovah is the true God!" —1 Kings 18:39.

20:34—After Jehovah gave Ahab victory over the Syrians, why did Ahab spare their king, Ben-hadad? Instead of striking Ben-hadad down, Ahab concluded a covenant with him by which streets in the Syrian capital, Damascus, would be assigned to Ahab, evidently for the establishment of bazaars, or markets. Earlier, Ben-hadad's father had similarly assigned himself streets in Samaria for commercial purposes. Hence, Ben-hadad was released so that Ahab could establish commercial interests in Damascus.

Lessons for Us:

12:13, 14. When making vital decisions in life, we should seek the advice of wise and mature individuals who are knowledgeable in the Scriptures and have high regard for godly principles.

13:11-24. Advice or a suggestion that seems questionable, even if it comes from a well-meaning fellow believer, should be measured against the sound guidance of God's Word.—1 John 4:1.

14:13. Jehovah searches through us to look for the good in us. Regardless of how insignificant that good may be, he can make it grow as we do our best to serve him.

15:10-13. We must courageously reject apostasy and instead promote true worship.

17:10-16. The widow of Zarephath recognized Elijah as a prophet and received him as such, and Jehovah blessed her acts of faith. Today, Jehovah also notices our acts of faith, and he rewards those who support the Kingdom work in various ways.—Matthew 6:33; 10:41, 42; Hebrews 6:10.

19:1-8. When facing intense opposition, we can be confident of Jehovah's support. —2 Corinthians 4:7-9.

19:10, 14, 18. True worshippers are never alone. They have Jehovah and their worldwide brotherhood.

19:11-13. Jehovah is not a nature god or a mere personification of natural forces.

20:11. When Ben-hadad bragged about destroying Samaria, Israel's king answered: "Do not let one girding on [his armor in preparation for battle] boast about himself like one unfastening" his armor after returning victorious from battle. When faced with a new task, we must avoid the overconfidence of a braggart.—Proverbs 27:1; James 4:13-16.

Of Great Value to Us

When recounting the giving of the Law at Mount Sinai, Moses told the sons of Israel: "See, I am putting before you today blessing and malediction: the blessing, provided you will obey the commandments of Jehovah your God that I am commanding you today; and the malediction, if you will not obey the commandments of Jehovah your God and you do turn aside from the way about which I am commanding you today." —Deuteronomy 11:26-28.

How clearly this vital truth is brought to our attention in the book of First Kings! As we have seen, this book also teaches other valuable lessons. Its message is indeed alive and exerts power.—Hebrews 4:12.

"It Is Finished"

IN THE year 2002, Jehovah's Witnesses held a district convention in the city of Mbandaka, in the northwestern part of the Democratic Republic of Congo. When the *New World Translation of the Christian Greek Scriptures* in Lingala was released at the convention, those in the audience literally jumped for joy, and some shed tears. Later, people rushed to the platform to have a closer look at the new Bible, crying: *"Basuki, Basambwe,"* which means: "It is finished! They are confounded!"

Why were the audience so excited, and what did they mean by those words? In some parts of Mbandaka, Jehovah's Witnesses had been unable to obtain Lingala Bibles. Why? Because the churches refused to sell them to Jehovah's Witnesses. The Witnesses had to ask a third party to obtain copies. Now they were extremely happy because the churches could no longer prevent them from getting Bibles.

The new translation will benefit not only Jehovah's Witnesses but also the general public. A man who could hear the program in his home over the loudspeakers from the assembly site wrote to the branch office of Jehovah's Witnesses: "I am very happy about the release of this Bible. It will enlighten us about many things. I am not one of Jehovah's Witnesses, but I am eagerly awaiting this Bible that you have just published."

JULY 15, 2005

THE WATCHTOWER

ANNOUNCING JEHOVAH'S KINGDOM

TRUE TEACHINGS
Where Can You Find Them?

THE WATCHTOWER®
ANNOUNCING JEHOVAH'S KINGDOM

July 15, 2005   Average Printing Each Issue: 26,439,000   Vol. 126, No. 14

THE PURPOSE OF *THE WATCHTOWER* is to exalt Jehovah God as Sovereign Lord of the universe. It keeps watch on world events as these fulfill Bible prophecy. It comforts all peoples with the good news that God's Kingdom will soon destroy those who oppress their fellowmen and that it will turn the earth into a paradise. It encourages faith in God's now-reigning King, Jesus Christ, whose shed blood opens the way for mankind to gain eternal life. *The Watchtower,* published by Jehovah's Witnesses continuously since 1879, is nonpolitical. It adheres to the Bible as its authority.

IN THIS ISSUE

3   True Teachings—Where Can You Find Them?

4   True Teachings That Please God

8   Single and Contented in Jehovah's Service

10   "Clear Light" on the Bible From Russia's Oldest Library

14   "Jehovah's Sword and Gideon's!"

17   "The Shrewd One Considers His Steps"

21   "Keep Proving What You Yourselves Are"

26   Are You Faithful in All Things?

31   Questions From Readers

32   "They Did Not Compromise"

WATCHTOWER STUDIES

AUGUST 15-21:
"Keep Proving What You Yourselves Are."
Page 21. Songs to be used: 177, 98.

AUGUST 22-28:
Are You Faithful in All Things?
Page 26. Songs to be used: 10, 34.

Publication of *The Watchtower* is part of a worldwide Bible educational work supported by voluntary donations.

Unless otherwise indicated, Scripture quotations are from the modern-language *New World Translation of the Holy Scriptures—With References.*

The Watchtower (ISSN 0043-1087) is published semimonthly by Watchtower Bible and Tract Society of New York, Inc.; M. H. Larson, President; G. F. Simonis, Secretary-Treasurer; 25 Columbia Heights, Brooklyn, NY 11201-2483. Periodicals Postage Paid at Brooklyn, NY, and at additional mailing offices. POSTMASTER: Send address changes to Watchtower, **Wallkill, NY 12589.**

Changes of address should reach us 30 days before your moving date. Give us your old and new address (if possible, your old address label).

Semimonthly   ENGLISH

Would you welcome more information or a free home Bible study? Please send your request to Jehovah's Witnesses, using the appropriate address below.

America, United States of: Wallkill, NY 12589. *Antigua:* Box 119, St. Johns. *Australia:* Box 280, Ingleburn, NSW 1890. *Bahamas:* Box N-1247, Nassau, N.P. *Barbados, W.I.:* Crusher Site Road, Prospect, St. James. *Britain:* The Ridgeway, London NW7 1RN. *Canada:* Box 4100, Halton Hills (Georgetown), Ontario L7G 4Y4. *Germany:* Niederselters, Am Steinfels, D-65618 Selters. *Ghana:* P. O. Box GP 760, Accra. *Guyana:* 352-360 Tyrell St., Republic Park Phase 2 EBD. *Hawaii 96819:* 2055 Kam IV Rd., Honolulu. *Hong Kong:* 4 Kent Road, Kowloon Tong. *India:* Post Box 6440, Yelahanka, Bangalore 560 064, KAR. *Ireland:* Newcastle, Greystones, Co. Wicklow. *Jamaica:* P. O. Box 103, Old Harbour, St. Catherine. *Japan:* 1271 Nakashinden, Ebina City, Kanagawa Pref., 243-0496. *Kenya:* P.O. Box 47788, GPO Nairobi 00100. *New Zealand:* P.O. Box 75-142, Manurewa. *Nigeria:* P.M.B. 1090, Benin City 300001, Edo State. *Philippines, Republic of:* P. O. Box 2044, 1060 Manila. *South Africa:* Private Bag X2067, Krugersdorp, 1740. *Trinidad and Tobago, Republic of:* Lower Rapsey Street & Laxmi Lane, Curepe. *Zambia:* Box 33459, Lusaka 10101. *Zimbabwe:* Private Bag WG-5001, Westgate.

NOW PUBLISHED IN 150 LANGUAGES. SEMIMONTHLY: Afrikaans, Albanian,* Amharic, Arabic, Bengali, Bicol, Bislama, Bulgarian, Cebuano,* Chichewa,* Chinese, Chinese (Simplified),* Cibemba,* Croatian,* Czech,*# Danish,*# Dutch,*# East Armenian, Efik,* English*#+☉ (also Braille), Estonian, Ewe, Fijian, Finnish,*# French,*# Ga, Georgian,* German,*# Greek,* Gujarati, Gun, Hebrew, Hiligaynon, Hindi, Hungarian,*# Igbo,* Iloko,* Indonesian, Italian,*# Japanese*# (also Braille), Kannada, Kinyarwanda, Kirundi, Korean*# (also Braille), Latvian, Lingala, Lithuanian, Luvale, Macedonian, Malagasy,* Malayalam, Maltese, Myanmar, Nepali, Norwegian,*# Pangasinan, Papiamento (Aruba), Papiamento (Curaçao), Polish,*# Portuguese*# (also Braille), Punjabi, Rarotongan, Romanian,* Russian,* Samar-Leyte, Samoan, Sango, Sepedi, Serbian, Sesotho, Shona,* Silozi, Sinhala, Slovak,* Slovenian, Solomon Islands Pidgin, Spanish*# (also Braille), Sranantongo, Swahili,* Swedish,*# Tagalog,* Tamil, Telugu, Thai, Tigrinya, Tok Pisin, Tongan, Tshiluba, Tsonga, Tswana, Turkish, Twi, Ukrainian,* Urdu, Vietnamese, Wallisian, Xhosa, Yoruba,* Zulu*

MONTHLY: American Sign Language,△□ Armenian, Assamese, Azerbaijani (roman script), Brazilian Sign Language,△ Cambodian, Chitonga, Gilbertese, Greenlandic, Haitian Creole, Hausa, Hiri Motu, Icelandic, Isoko, Kaonde, Kazakh, Kikongo, Kiluba, Kirghiz, Kosraean, Kwanyama/Ndonga, Luganda, Marathi, Marshallese, Mauritian Creole, Maya, Mizo, Monokutuba, Moore, Niuean, Ossetian, Otetela, Palauan, Persian, Ponapean, Seychelles Creole, Tahitian, Tatar, Tiv, Trukese, Tumbuka, Tuvaluan, Umbundu, Venda, Yapese, Zande

* Study articles also available in large-print edition.
# Audiocassettes also available.
+ CD also available.
☉ MP3 CD-ROM also available.
△ Videocassette
□ DVD

TRUE TEACHINGS
Where Can You Find Them?

A MAN in Tibet spins a prayer wheel, a drum containing written prayers. He believes that his petitions are repeated with each turn of the wheel. In a spacious home in India, a small room is set aside for doing puja—worship that may include making offerings of incense, flowers, and other things to images of various gods and goddesses. Thousands of miles away in Italy, a woman in an ornate church kneels before an image of Mary, the mother of Jesus, and prays while holding a string of rosary beads.

Perhaps you have seen for yourself the influence of religion on the lives of people. "Religion . . . has been and continues to be the lifeblood of societies all over the world," states the book *The World's Religions—Under-standing the Living Faiths.* In the book *God —A Brief History,* author John Bowker observes: "There has never been any human society in which God has not been a part, usually a controlling and creative part. That is true even of those societies that set out to be deliberately secular."

Indeed, religion has influenced the lives of millions of people. Is this not strong evidence that man has a spiritual need and yearning? In his book *The Undiscovered Self,* the eminent psychologist Dr. Carl G. Jung refers to man's need to worship a higher power and says that "its manifestations can be followed all through human history."

Yet, many people neither profess belief in God nor have any interest in religion. Some who doubt or deny that God exists do so primarily because the religions that they are familiar with have failed to meet their spiritual need. Religion has been defined as "devotion to some principle; strict fidelity or faithfulness; conscientiousness; pious affection or attachment." By this definition, nearly everyone displays some form of religious devotion in his life. That even includes atheists.

During the thousands of years of human history, man's attempts to satisfy his spiritual need have led him down many pathways. The result is the enormous diversity of religious views found worldwide. For example, though nearly all religions promote a belief in a higher power, they have different concepts of who or what that is. Most faiths also stress the importance of salvation or liberation. But their teachings differ as to what salvation is and how it is attained. Out of the vast array of beliefs, how can we identify true teachings that please God?

True Teachings That Please God

FOR earth's inhabitants to know what teachings are true and pleasing to God, he must reveal his thoughts to humans. He must also make that revelation available to all. How else could mankind know what God approves of in the way of doctrine, worship, and conduct? Has God supplied such information? If so, in what form?

Can any human with a life span of a few decades personally reach all mankind and serve as a channel of communication from God? No. But a permanent written record can. Therefore, would it not be appropriate that the revelation from God be made available in the form of a book? One of the ancient books claiming inspiration by God is the Bible. "All Scripture is inspired of God and beneficial for teaching, for reproving, for setting things straight, for disciplining in righteousness," states one of its writers. (2 Timothy 3:16) Let us take a closer look at the Bible and see if it is the source of true teachings.

How Old?

Among the major books of religion, the Bible is one of the very oldest. Its first parts were written some 3,500 years ago. This book was completed in 98 C.E.* Though some 40 men were its writers over a period of 1,600 years, the Bible is a harmonious body of writings. That is so because its real Author is God.

The Bible is the most widely circulated and translated book in all history. Each year, some 60 million copies of the entire Bible or portions of it are distributed. The complete Bible or parts of it have been translated into more than 2,300 languages and dialects. Over 90 percent of the human family have access to the Bible, or at least part of it, in their native language. This book has transcended national boundaries, racial divisions, and ethnic barriers.

---

* C.E. denotes "Common Era," often called A.D., for Anno Domini, meaning "in the year of the Lord." B.C.E. means "Before the Common Era."

How Organized?

If you have a Bible, why not open it and see how it is organized?* First, turn to the table of contents. Most Bibles have one at the beginning, listing the name of each book and the page number where it can be found. You will note that the Bible is actually a large collection of individual books, each having a unique name. The very first book is Genesis, and the last is Revelation, or Apocalypse. The books are grouped into two sections. The first 39 books are called the Hebrew Scriptures, since they were written mostly in the Hebrew language. The last 27 books were written in the Greek language and make up the Greek Scriptures. Some refer to these two sections as the Old Testament and the New Testament.

The books of the Bible have chapters and verses for easy reference. When scriptures are cited in this magazine, after the name of the Bible book, the first number indicates the chapter of that book and the next denotes the verse. For example, the citation "2 Timothy 3:16" means the book of Second Timothy, chapter 3, verse 16. See if you can find that verse in the Bible.

Would you not agree that the best way to become familiar with the Bible is to read it regularly? Some have found it helpful to read the Greek Scriptures first, starting with the book of Matthew. By reading from three to five chapters a day, you can read the entire Bible in a year. But how can you be sure that what you read in the Bible is actually inspired of God?

Can You Trust the Bible?

Should not a divinely inspired book for all

NASA photo

people contain timeless advice for living? The Bible reflects an understanding of human nature that applies to every generation of mankind, and its principles are just as practical today as they were when first stated. This can easily be seen in a famous discourse given by Jesus Christ, the Founder of Christianity. It is recorded in Matthew chapters 5 to 7. This address, known as the Sermon on the Mount, shows us not only how to find true happiness but also how to settle disputes, how to pray, how to view material needs, and much more. In this discourse, and throughout the rest of its pages, the Bible clearly tells us what to do and what to avoid in order to please God and improve our lot in life.

Another reason why you can put your trust in the Bible is that when it comes to scientific matters, what this ancient book states is accurate. For example, at a time when most people believed that the earth was flat, the Bible spoke of "the circle [or, sphere] of the earth."* (Isaiah 40:22) And over 3,000 years before the famous scientist Sir Isaac Newton explained that the planets are held in empty space by gravity, the Bible poetically stated that 'the earth is hanging upon nothing.' (Job 26:7) Consider also this poetic description of the earth's water cycle, recorded some 3,000 years ago: "All streams flow into the sea, yet the sea is never full. To the place the streams come from, there they return again." (Ecclesiastes 1:7, *New International Version*) Yes, the Creator of the universe is also the Author of the Bible.

The historical accuracy of the Bible agrees with the fact that it is inspired of God. Events

---

* If you do not have a personal copy of the Bible, Jehovah's Witnesses will be happy to supply you with one.

* The original-language word translated "circle" at Isaiah 40:22 may also be rendered "sphere." Certain Bible translations read, "the globe of the earth" (*Douay Version*) and "the round earth."—*Moffatt.*

covered in the Bible are not mere myths. They are related to specific dates, people, and places. For example, Luke 3:1 factually refers to "the fifteenth year of the reign of Tiberius Caesar, when Pontius Pilate was governor of Judea, and Herod was district ruler of Galilee."

Although ancient historians almost always reported only the successes and virtues of rulers, the Bible writers were honest, openly admitting even their own mistakes. For instance, King David of Israel confessed: "I have sinned very much in what I have done. . . . I have acted very foolishly." That statement is candidly documented in the Bible. (2 Samuel 24:10) And the Bible writer Moses himself recorded the incident in which he did not demonstrate reliance on the true God.—Numbers 20:12.

The Bible has yet another mark of divine inspiration. That mark is its fulfilled prophecies—history written in advance. Some of these are prophecies concerning Jesus Christ. For example, over 700 years before Jesus' birth, the Hebrew Scriptures accurately foretold that this Promised One would be born "in Bethlehem of Judea."—Matthew 2: 1-6; Micah 5:2.

Consider another example. At 2 Timothy 3:1-5, the Bible states: "In the last days critical times hard to deal with will be here. For men will be lovers of themselves, lovers of money, self-assuming, haughty, blasphemers, disobedient to parents, unthankful, disloyal, having no natural affection, not open to any agreement, slanderers, without self-control, fierce, without love of goodness, betrayers, headstrong, puffed up with pride, lovers of pleasures rather than lovers of God, having a form of godly devotion but proving false to its power." Does this not describe the attitude of people in general today? These words were penned in the year 65 C.E., over 1,900 years ago!

What Does the Bible Teach Us?

As its message unfolds before your eyes, you will be able to see that the Bible is a source of higher wisdom. It provides satisfying answers to such questions as these: Who is God? Is the Devil real? Who is Jesus Christ? Why does suffering exist? What happens to us when we die? The answers you may hear from others are as diverse as the beliefs and customs of the people giving them. But the Bible reveals the truth about these and many other subjects. Furthermore, in the matter of conduct and attitude toward other humans and higher authorities, the Bible's guidance cannot be surpassed.*

What does the Bible reveal about God's purpose for the earth and mankind? It promises: "Just a little while longer, and the wicked one will be no more . . . But the meek ones themselves will possess the earth, and they will indeed find their exquisite delight in the abundance of peace." (Psalm 37:10, 11) "God himself will be with [mankind]. And he will wipe out every tear from their eyes, and death will be no more, neither will mourning nor outcry nor pain be anymore. The former things have passed away." (Revelation 21:3, 4) "The righteous themselves will possess the earth, and they will reside forever upon it."—Psalm 37:29.

The Bible also foretells that war, crime, violence, and wickedness will soon end. Sickness, old age, and death will be no more. Everlasting life on a paradise earth will become a reality. What delightful prospects! And how all of this demonstrates God's love for mankind!

What Will You Do?

The Bible is a marvelous gift from the Creator. How should you respond to this book? A man of Hindu background believed that

---

* These subjects are discussed in the book *Knowledge That Leads to Everlasting Life,* published by Jehovah's Witnesses.

for a revelation from God to be of benefit to all mankind, it has to date back to the dawn of civilization. Upon realizing that parts of the Bible are older than the most ancient Hindu writings, the Vedas, he decided to read the Bible and examine its contents.* A university professor in the United States also came to see the need to read this most widely circulated book in the world before forming an opinion about it.

Reading the Bible and applying what it teaches will bring you rich blessings. The Bible states: "Happy is the man . . . [whose] delight is in the law of Jehovah, and in his law he reads in an undertone day and night. And he will certainly become like a tree planted by streams of water, that gives its own fruit in its season and the foliage of which does not wither, and everything he does will succeed."# (Psalm 1:1-3) Studying

---

* The earliest hymns of the Vedas are believed to have been composed nearly 3,000 years ago and transmitted orally. "It was only in the fourteenth century A.D. that the Veda was written down," says P. K. Saratkumar in his book *A History of India.*

Jehovah is the name of the God of the Bible. In many Bible translations, it can be found at Psalm 83:18.

the Bible and reflecting upon what it says will bring you happiness because your spiritual need will thus be satisfied. (Matthew 5:3) The Bible will show you how to live a fruitful life and how to cope with problems successfully. Yes, "in the keeping of [God's laws set out in the Bible] there is a large reward." (Psalm 19:11) Moreover, putting confidence in God's promises will bring you blessings now and will give you a bright hope for the future.

The Bible urges us: "As newborn infants, form a longing for the unadulterated milk belonging to the word." (1 Peter 2:2) An infant depends on nourishment and insists on having that need met. Likewise, we really are dependent on knowledge from God. So "form a longing," or a strong desire, for his Word. The Bible is a book of true teachings from God. Make it a goal to study it regularly. Jehovah's Witnesses in your community will be happy to help you to get the most out of your study. You have our warm invitation to contact them. Or you may write to the publishers of this magazine.

"Form a longing" for God's Word. Study the Bible regularly

Single and Contented in Jehovah's Service

"SO MANY of us are completely happy even though we are not married," noted a Christian woman in Spain. What is the reason for her contentment? "We love being free from many anxieties so that we can serve our God, Jehovah, more fully."

Such feelings harmonize with what God's Word observes about singleness. When the apostle Paul discussed matters involving marriage, he offered this inspired insight: "I say to the unmarried persons and the widows, it is well for them that they remain even as I am." Paul himself was not married. But what reason did he give for recommending singleness? He pointed out that the married person is divided, whereas the unmarried man or woman is "anxious for the things of the Lord." (1 Corinthians 7:8, 32-34) Serving Jehovah is the principal factor that makes a single person happy and contented.

Singleness With a Noble Purpose

Paul's comments may be puzzling in cultures that place a premium on marriage and the raising of a family. However, Jesus Christ —himself unmarried but happy and contented—mentioned a noble purpose for Christians who are single. He said: "There are eunuchs that have made themselves eunuchs on account of the kingdom of the heavens. Let him that can make room for it make room for it."—Matthew 19:12.

True to those words, many have found that singleness allows them to serve God without the distraction common to married life. (1 Corinthians 7:35) Thousands of Christians are happily worshipping Jehovah without a marriage mate, and they find joy in actively assisting others.*

Many unmarried Christians realize that happiness is not the prerogative of married people and that unhappiness is not the experience of all single individuals. In both groups, some at times experience happiness as well as grief. Actually, the Bible realistically observes that marriage itself brings 'tribulation in the flesh.'—1 Corinthians 7:28.

Single by Circumstance

Many are single not by choice but because of circumstances. They may desire the warmth, companionship, and affection that can be found within the marital arrangement. For some, however, financial or other considerations may at present preclude marriage. Some Christians—many of them dear spiritual sisters—have remained single because they are determined to obey the Bible counsel to

---

* See *2005 Calendar of Jehovah's Witnesses*, July/ August.

> ### MAKING SINGLENESS REWARDING
>
> Jesus, who never married, stated: *"My food is for me to do the will of him that sent me and to finish his work."*
> —John 4:34.
>
> Philip's four unmarried daughters kept busy 'prophesying.'
> —Acts 21:8, 9.
>
> Single Christian sisters who declare the Kingdom message are part of the 'large army of women telling the good news.'
> —Psalm 68:11.

> ## "The unmarried man is anxious for the things of the Lord, how he may gain the Lord's approval."
> —1 CORINTHIANS 7:32

marry "only in the Lord." (1 Corinthians 7:39) They loyally seek a marriage mate only among dedicated, baptized worshippers of Jehovah.

At times, some of these individuals are lonely. After admitting that she feels this way, one single Christian states: "We know Jehovah's law and would not want to displease Jehovah in any way. We may want the companionship of a mate, but no matter how many times people in the world try to 'fix us up,' we're standing firm. We don't even want to be in the company of unbelieving men or women." Such Christians are to be commended for applying Bible counsel and maintaining high moral standards so as to please Jehovah despite any emotional distress they may experience.

Generous Divine Help

Jehovah is loyal to those showing their loyalty to him in such matters as refusing to marry individuals who do not serve him. From personal experience, King David could testify: "With someone loyal you [Jehovah] will act in loyalty." (Psalm 18:25) And to those who faithfully obey him, God promises: "I will by no means leave you nor by any means forsake you." (Hebrews 13:5) Imitating Jehovah, we can give generous commendation to single Christians of all ages who faithfully stick to God's Word. We can also pray that Jehovah strengthen them to meet their challenges.—Judges 11:30-40.

Many single Christians find that engaging fully in Bible educational work fills their lives with meaning. For example, consider Patricia, an unmarried woman in her mid-30's who is a pioneer, or full-time evangelizer. She says: "Although trials come with singleness, it has afforded me the opportunity to become a regular pioneer. Since I am a single person, my schedule is more flexible, which allows more time for study. I have also learned to lean more heavily on Jehovah, especially through trying times."

Such sentiments are based on the Bible's reassuring promise: "Roll upon Jehovah your way, and rely upon him, and he himself will act." (Psalm 37:5) Indeed, all faithful worshippers of Jehovah, married or single, can find comfort and strength in the inspired words: "My help is from Jehovah."—Psalm 121:2.

"CLEAR LIGHT" on the Bible From RUSSIA'S OLDEST LIBRARY

Both images: National Library of Russia, St. Petersburg

Manuscript room of The National Library

TWO scholars are on the hunt for ancient Bible manuscripts. They individually travel through deserts and search caves, monasteries, and ancient cliff dwellings. Years later, their paths cross in Russia's oldest public library, where some of the most exciting Bible discoveries the world has ever known come together. Who were these men? How did the treasures they discovered end up in Russia?

Ancient Manuscripts —Champions of God's Word

To meet one of these two scholars, we must go back to the beginning of the 19th century when Europe was being swept by the winds of an intellectual revolution. It was a time of scientific progress and cultural achievement, which promoted a skeptical view of traditional beliefs. Higher critics sought to undermine the Bible's authority. In fact, scholars were voicing doubts about the authenticity of the Bible text itself.

Certain sincere defenders of the Bible discerned that new champions—as yet undiscovered ancient Bible manuscripts—would undoubtedly uphold the integrity of God's Word. If manuscripts older than those then extant could be found, they would serve as silent witnesses to the purity of the Bible text, even though repeated attempts had long been made to destroy or distort its message. Such manuscripts could also expose the few places where erroneous renderings had crept into the text.

Some of the hottest debates on the authenticity of the Bible raged in Germany. There a young professor slipped away from his comfortable academic life to go on a journey that would lead him to one of the biggest Bible discoveries of all time. His name was Konstantin von Tischendorf, a Bible scholar whose rejection of higher criticism led to notable success in defending the authenticity of Bible text. His first journey to the wilderness of Sinai in 1844 met with unbelievable success. A casual look into a monastery wastebasket revealed an ancient copy of the *Septuagint,* or Greek translation of the Hebrew Scriptures—the oldest one that had ever been discovered!

Exultant, Tischendorf managed to take away 43 sheets. Although he was convinced that there were more, a return visit in 1853 produced only a fragment. Where were the rest? His funds exhausted, Tischendorf sought the patronage of a wealthy sponsor, and he decided to leave his homeland again in search of ancient manuscripts. Before going on this mission, though, he would appeal to the czar of Russia.

The Czar Takes an Interest

Tischendorf may well have wondered what kind of reception that he, a Protestant scholar, would get in Russia, a vast land espousing the Russian Orthodox religion. Happily, Russia had entered a favorable era of change and reform. An emphasis on education had led to the founding of St. Petersburg's Imperial Library in 1795 by Empress Catherine II (also known as Catherine the Great). As Russia's first public library, it had made a wealth of printed information accessible to millions.

Hailed as one of the finest libraries in Europe, The Imperial Library did have one drawback. Fifty years after it was founded, the library contained only six Hebrew manuscripts. It could not keep up with Russia's rising interest in the study of Bible languages and translations. Catherine II had sent scholars to European universities to study Hebrew. After the scholars returned, Hebrew courses sprang up in major Russian Orthodox semi-

Empress Catherine II

Konstantin von Tischendorf (center) and Alexander II, czar of Russia

Catherine II: National Library of Russia, St. Petersburg; Alexander II: From the book *Spamers Illustrierte Weltgeschichte*, Leipzig, 1898

naries, and for the first time, Russian scholars started work on an accurate translation of the Bible from ancient Hebrew into Russian. But they faced a lack of resources and even opposition from conservative church leaders. True enlightenment had yet to begin for those seeking Bible knowledge.

The czar, Alexander II, was quick to appreciate Tischendorf's mission and extended his patronage. Despite "jealous and fanatical opposition" from some, Tischendorf returned from his mission to Sinai with the rest of the copy of the *Septuagint.** Later named the Codex Sinaiticus, it is still one of the oldest Bible manuscripts in existence. Back in St. Petersburg, Tischendorf hastened to the czar's residence, the Imperial Winter Palace. He proposed that the czar support "one of the greatest undertakings in critical and Biblical study"—a published edition of the newly found manuscript, which was later placed in The Imperial Library. The czar readily agreed, and an elated Tischendorf later wrote: "Providence has given to our age . . . the Sinaitic Bible, to be to us a full and clear light as to what is the real text of God's Word written, and to assist us in defending the truth by establishing its authentic form."

Bible Treasures From the Crimea

Another scholar searching for Bible treasures was mentioned at the outset. Who was

---

* He also brought a complete copy of the Christian Greek Scriptures dating back to the fourth century C.E.

he? A few years before Tischendorf returned to Russia, The Imperial Library received a proposal so unbelievable that it drew the czar's interest and brought scholars to Russia from all over Europe. They could hardly believe their eyes. Before them was an enormous collection of manuscripts and other material. It numbered

Abraham Firkovich

a staggering 2,412 items, including 975 manuscripts and scrolls. Among these were 45 Bible manuscripts dating earlier than the tenth century. As incredible as it seemed, all these manuscripts had been collected almost single-handedly by a man named Abraham Firkovich, a Karaite scholar who was then more than 70 years old! But who were the Karaites?*

This question was of great interest to the czar. Russia had extended its borders to encompass territory previously held by other states. This had brought new ethnic groups into the empire. The picturesque Crimea region, on the shores of the Black Sea, was populated by a people who seemed to be Jewish but who had Turkish customs and spoke a language related to Tatar. These Karaites traced their de-

* For more information on the Karaites, see the article "The Karaites and Their Quest for Truth," in the July 15, 1995, issue of *The Watchtower.*

IN OUR NEXT ISSUE

The Bible Can Help You Find Joy

When Is There a Basis for Taking Offense?

Jehovah Has Numbered "the Very Hairs of Your Head"

scent from Jews exiled to Babylon after the destruction of Jerusalem in 607 B.C.E. Unlike rabbinic Jews, however, they rejected the Talmud and emphasized the reading of the Scriptures. The Crimean Karaites were eager to present to the czar evidence of their distinctness from rabbinic Jews, thereby giving them a separate status. By presenting ancient manuscripts owned by Karaites, they hoped to prove that they had descended from Jews who had immigrated to the Crimea after the Babylonian exile.

When Firkovich undertook his search for ancient records and manuscripts, he started with the Crimean cliff dwellings of Chufut-Kale. Generations of Karaites had lived and worshipped in these small houses built from the stones carved out of cliffs. The Karaites never destroyed worn-out copies of the Scriptures where the divine name, Jehovah, appeared because they considered such action sacrilege. The manuscripts were carefully placed in a small storehouse called a genizah, meaning "hiding place" in Hebrew. Because the Karaites had deep respect for the divine name, such parchments were seldom disturbed.

Undeterred by the dust of centuries, Firkovich searched the genizah sites carefully. In one, he found the famous manuscript of 916 C.E. Called the Petersburg Codex of the Latter Prophets, it is one of the oldest copies of the Hebrew Scriptures in existence.

Firkovich managed to amass great numbers of manuscripts, and in 1859 he decided to offer his vast collection to The Imperial Library. In 1862, Alexander II helped to purchase the collection for the library for the then enormous sum of 125,000 rubles. At that time, the entire library budget was no more than 10,000 rubles a year! This acquisition included the renowned Leningrad Codex (B 19ᴬ). It dates from 1008 and is the world's oldest complete copy of the Hebrew Scriptures. One scholar noted that it is "probably the single most important manuscript of the Bible, for it established the text of most modern critical editions of the Hebrew Bible." (See the accompanying box.) That same year, 1862, Tischendorf's Codex Sinaiticus was published, to worldwide acclaim.

Spiritual Enlightenment in Modern Times

The library now known as The National Library of Russia houses one of the world's largest collections of ancient manuscripts.* Reflecting Russian history, the name of the library has been changed seven times over the course of two centuries. One well-known name is The State Saltykov-Shchedrin Public Library. Though the turmoil of the 20th century did not leave the library unscathed, its manuscripts survived intact through both world wars and the siege of Leningrad. How do we benefit from such manuscripts?

Ancient manuscripts are the reliable basis for many modern Bible translations. They allow sincere truth-seekers to enjoy a clear version of the Holy Scriptures. Both the Sinaiticus and the Leningrad codices have made valuable contributions to the *New World Translation of the Holy Scriptures,* published by Jehovah's Witnesses and released in its complete form in 1961. For example, *Biblia Hebraica Stuttgartensia* and Kittel's *Biblia Hebraica,* used by the New World Bible Translation Committee, are based on the Leningrad Codex and use the Tetragrammaton, or divine name, 6,828 times in the original text.

---

* Most of the Codex Sinaiticus was sold to the British Museum. Only fragments remain in The National Library of Russia.

THE DIVINE NAME KNOWN AND USED

In his wisdom, Jehovah has seen to it that his Word, the Bible, has been preserved until modern times. The diligent work of scribes throughout the ages has been involved in its preservation. The most meticulous of these were the Masoretes, professional Hebrew scribes who worked from the sixth to the tenth century C.E. Ancient Hebrew was written without vowels. Over time, this increased the danger of losing the proper pronunciation as Aramaic replaced Hebrew. The Masoretes developed a system of vowel points to add to the Bible text in order to indicate the correct pronunciation of Hebrew words.

Significantly, the Masoretic vowel points in the Leningrad Codex allow for the pronunciation of the Tetragrammaton—the four Hebrew consonants making up the divine name—as *Yehwah', Yehwih',* and *Yeho·wah'.* "Jehovah" is now the most widely known pronunciation of the name. The divine name was a living, familiar term to Bible writers and others of ancient times. Today, God's name is known and used by millions who acknowledge that 'Jehovah alone is the Most High over all the earth.'—Psalm 83:18.

Relatively few Bible readers are aware of their indebtedness to the quiet library in St. Petersburg and its manuscripts, some bearing the city's former name, Leningrad. Yet, our greatest debt is to the Bible's Author, Jehovah, who gives spiritual light. The psalmist therefore petitioned him: "Send out your light and your truth. May these themselves lead me."—Psalm 43:3.

"JEHOVAH'S SWORD AND GIDEON'S!"

THEY are as numerous as locusts, reducing fertile fields to a wasteland. It is sometime during the period when judges rule in Israel, and the Israelites are in despair. For seven years, just as sown seed has begun to sprout, plundering hordes of camel-riding Midianites, Amalekites, and Easterners descend upon the land. The marauders' flocks spread out in search of pasturage, devouring everything green. But the people of Israel have neither ass nor bull nor sheep. So severe is Midian's reign of terror that the poverty-stricken Israelites resort to underground storage in the mountains, the caves, and places difficult to approach.

Why such a plight? Apostate Israel is serving false gods. In turn, Jehovah has abandoned them to oppressors. When the sons of Israel can stand it no longer, they call to Jehovah for aid. Will he listen? What can Israel's experience teach us?—Judges 6:1-6.

Cautious Farmer or "Valiant, Mighty One"?

Israelite farmers normally thresh wheat with an ox and a sledge in an exposed, airy location so that the breeze can catch the chaff and separate it from the grain in the winnowing process. But the threat posed by marauders intent on stripping the land makes that far too conspicuous. Out of sight of the Midianites, Gideon threshes wheat in a winepress—likely a large, sheltered vat carved out of rock. (Judges 6:11) There the grain can likely be beaten with a stick in small quantities only. Under the circumstances, Gideon is improvising.

Imagine Gideon's surprise when Jehovah's angel appears to him and says: "Jehovah is with you, you valiant, mighty one." (Judges 6:12) As a man secretly threshing grain in a winepress, Gideon must feel anything but valiant. Yet, those words indicate divine confidence that Gideon can be a valiant leader in Israel. Even so, he himself needs to be convinced.

When Jehovah commissions him to "save Israel out of Midian's palm," Gideon modestly states: "Excuse me, Jehovah. With what shall I save Israel? Look! My thousand is the least in Manasseh, and I am the smallest in my father's house." Cautious Gideon requests a sign that God would be with him in striking down Midian, and Jehovah is willing to accommodate Gideon's reasonable need for assurance. So Gideon presents a gift of food to his angelic visitor, and fire ascends out of a rock, consuming the offering. After Jehovah has allayed Gideon's fright, Gideon builds an altar at that location.—Judges 6:12-24.

"Let Baal Make a Legal Defense"

Israel's biggest problem is not Midianite oppression. It is bondage to Baal worship. Jehovah is "a jealous God," and no one can serve him acceptably while revering other gods. (Exodus 34:14) Therefore, Jehovah commands Gideon to destroy his father's altar to Baal and to cut down the sacred pole. Fearing his father's reaction and that of others if he does this during the day, Gideon acts at night, with the help of ten servants.

Gideon's caution is justified, for on discovering his "sacrilege," local Baal worshippers demand his life. With unassailable logic, however, Gideon's father, Joash, reasons with the people that if Baal were God, he would be able to defend himself. At that, Joash aptly calls his son Jerubbaal, meaning "Let Baal Make a Legal Defense Against Him."—Judges 6:25-32, footnote.

God always blesses his servants for taking a bold stand for true worship. When the Midianites and their allies again invade Israelite territory, 'Jehovah's spirit envelops Gideon.' (Judges 6:34) Under the influence of God's spirit, or active force, Gideon musters troops from the tribes of Manasseh, Asher, Zebulun, and Naphtali.—Judges 6:35.

Preparing for Action

Although Gideon now has an army of 32,-000, he asks God for a sign. If a fleece left on the threshing floor becomes wet with dew while the ground remains dry, this will indicate that God will save Israel through him. Jehovah performs this miracle, and Gideon seeks and receives confirmation when the sign is reversed—wet ground and a dry fleece. Is Gideon being overly cautious? Apparently not, for Jehovah grants his request for reassurance. (Judges 6:36-40) We do not expect such miracles today. Yet, we can receive Jehovah's guidance and reassurance from his Word.

God now raises the point that Gideon's army is too big. If they prevail over their enemies with such a large force, the Israelites might brag that they have saved themselves. But Jehovah must receive credit for the coming victory. The solution? Gideon is to apply a provision of the Mosaic Law by inviting the fearful to withdraw. At that, 22,000 of his men do so, leaving only 10,000.—Deuteronomy 20:8; Judges 7:2, 3.

From God's standpoint, there are still too many men. Gideon is told to have them go down to the water. Jewish historian Josephus says that God had Gideon march his troops to a river in the heat of the day. Be that as it may, Gideon observes how the men drink. Just 300 dip one hand in the water and lap from it while watching for a possible enemy attack. Only the vigilant 300 will go with Gideon. (Judges 7:4-8) Imagine yourself in their shoes. Since your enemies number 135,000, you must surely conclude that a victory could come about only by Jehovah's power, not your own!

God invites Gideon to take along an attendant and scout the Midianite camp. While there, Gideon overhears a man relating a dream to a companion who unhesitatingly interprets it to mean that God has determined to give Midian into Gideon's hand. That is just what Gideon needs to hear. He is certain that Jehovah will grant him and his 300 men victory over the Midianites. —Judges 7:9-15.

Battle Strategy

The 300 are divided into three bands of 100 each. Every man is given a horn and a large empty jar. A torch is hidden in the jar. Gideon's first order is this: 'Watch me, and do just as I do. When I blow the horn, you blow yours and shout "Jehovah's sword and Gideon's!" '—Judges 7:16-18, 20.

The 300 Israelite warriors stealthily move to the edge of the enemy camp. It is about ten o'clock in the evening—just after the changing of the guard. This seems to be the opportune time to strike, for it will take a while before the eyes of the new sentries adjust to the darkness.

What terror the Midianites now experience! Suddenly, the stillness is broken by the shattering of 300 jars, the blare of 300 horns, and the shouts of 300 men. Stunned, especially by the cry "Jehovah's sword and Gideon's!," the Midianites add their own cries to the din. In the chaos, it is impossible for them to tell friend from foe. The 300 stand still in their assigned positions as God causes the enemies to use their own swords to slaughter one another. The camp is routed, escape is cut off, and mop-up operations involving an arduous pursuit permanently remove the Midianite threat. The long and murderous occupation has finally come to an end.—Judges 7:19-25; 8:10-12, 28.

Even after this victory, Gideon is modest. When the Ephraimites, who apparently feel slighted at not being called for the fight, pick a quarrel with him, he responds mildly. His mild answer turns away their rage and calms their spirit.—Judges 8:1-3; Proverbs 15:1.

Now that peace has been established, the Israelites urge Gideon to become their king. What a temptation! But Gideon rejects it. He has not lost sight of who won the victory over Midian. "I myself shall not rule over you, nor will my son rule over you," he declares. "Jehovah is the one who will rule over you." —Judges 8:23.

Being imperfect, however, Gideon does not always exercise good judgment. For some unstated reason, he makes an ephod with the spoils of war and exhibits it in his city. The record says that all Israel begins to have "immoral intercourse" with the ephod. They worship it, and it becomes a snare even to Gideon and his household. Yet, he has not become a rank idolater, for the Scriptures reckon him a man with faith in Jehovah. —Judges 8:27; Hebrews 11:32-34.

Lessons for Us

Gideon's story provides lessons of both warning and encouragement. It warns us that if Jehovah should remove from us his spirit and blessing because of our wayward conduct, our spiritual condition would become like that of poverty-stricken residents of a land ravaged by locusts. We live in critical times and should never forget that Jehovah's blessing "is what makes rich, and he adds no pain with it." (Proverbs 10:22) We enjoy God's blessing because we "serve him with a complete heart and with a delightful soul." Otherwise, he would cast us off. —1 Chronicles 28:9.

We can draw encouragement from the account about Gideon, for it proves that Jehovah can deliver his people from any menace, even by using those who appear weak or helpless. That Gideon and his 300 men were able to vanquish 135,000 Midianites attests to God's infinite power. We may find ourselves in desperate straits and may seem to be hopelessly outnumbered by our enemies. Yet, the Bible account involving Gideon encourages us to trust in Jehovah, who will bless and deliver all of those exercising faith in Him.

"THE SHREWD ONE
Considers His Steps"

A SHREWD person is practical and clever, sound in judgment and sharp in perception, judicious and prudent, discerning and wise. He is neither devious nor manipulative. "Everyone shrewd will act with knowledge," states Proverbs 13:16. Yes, shrewdness, or prudence, is a desirable trait.

How can we display shrewdness in our day-to-day life? How is this quality made evident by the choices we make, the way we treat others, and the way we respond to various situations? What rewards do the prudent reap? What calamities do they avoid? King Solomon of ancient Israel gives practical answers to these questions, as we read at Proverbs 14:12-25.*

Choose Your Course Wisely

Making wise choices and being successful in life certainly require the ability to distinguish what is right from what is wrong. However, the Bible warns: *"There exists a way that is upright before a man, but the ways of death are the end of it afterward."* (Proverbs 14:12) Hence, we must learn to differentiate what is truly right from what appears to be right. The expression "the ways of death" indicates that there are many such deceptive paths. Consider some areas that we should be aware of and avoid.

The rich and famous of the world are generally viewed as respectable people to be admired. Their social and financial success

---

* For a discussion of Proverbs 14:1-11, see pages 26-9 of the November 15, 2004, issue of *The Watchtower.*

may make it seem that their way of doing things is right. What, though, about the means that many of such individuals use to gain wealth or fame? Are their ways always upright and moral? Then there are some individuals who display admirable zeal for their religious beliefs. But does their sincerity really prove that their beliefs are right? —Romans 10:2, 3.

A way may also appear upright because of self-deception. To base our decisions on what we personally feel is right is to depend upon the heart, a treacherous guide. (Jeremiah 17:9) An unenlightened and untrained conscience can lead us into thinking that the wrong way is the right way. What, then, will help us to choose a proper course?

Diligent personal study of the deeper truths of God's Word is a must if we are to acquire "perceptive powers trained to distinguish both right and wrong." Moreover, we must train these powers "through use" in applying Bible principles. (Hebrews 5:14) We must be careful not to allow a way that merely seems to be right to cause us to veer off 'the cramped road leading into life.' —Matthew 7:13, 14.

When "the Heart May Be in Pain"

Can we be happy when we are not at peace inside? Does laughter and merriment alleviate deep-rooted pain? Is it shrewd to drown feelings of depression in alcohol, to abuse drugs, or to try to eliminate those feelings by adopting a promiscuous lifestyle?

Diligent study of deeper truths is a must if we are to distinguish both right and wrong

A faithless person is not concerned about rendering an account to God. Therefore, doing what is right in Jehovah's eyes is of no consequence to a man without faith. (1 Peter 4:3-5) Such a person is satisfied with the results of his materialistic lifestyle. (Psalm 144:11-15a) The good person, on the other hand, has spiritual interests at heart. In all his dealings, he adheres to God's righteous standards. Such an individual is satisfied with the results because Jehovah is his God and he derives incomparable joy from serving the Most High.—Psalm 144:15b.

Do Not 'Put Faith in Every Word'

Contrasting the ways of the inexperienced with those of the prudent, Solomon says: *"Anyone inexperienced puts faith in every word, but the shrewd one considers his steps."* (Proverbs 14:15) The shrewd one is not gullible. Rather than believing everything he hears or letting others do his thinking for him, he considers his steps wisely.

Is a materialistic lifestyle truly satisfying?

The answer is no. *"In laughter the heart may be in pain,"* says the wise king.—Proverbs 14:13a.

Laughter may mask the pain, but it fails to remove it. "For everything there is an appointed time," states the Bible. Indeed, there is "a time to weep and a time to laugh; a time to wail and a time to skip about." (Ecclesiastes 3:1, 4) When depression persists, we must take steps to overcome it, seeking "skillful direction" when necessary. (Proverbs 24:6)* Laughter and amusement are of some value, but their relative worth is small. Warning against improper forms of amusement and excesses in entertainment, Solomon says: *"Grief is what rejoicing ends up in."*—Proverbs 14:13b.

The Faithless and the Good —Satisfied How?

"The one faithless at heart will be satisfied with the results of his own ways," continues the king of Israel, *"but the good man with the results of his dealings."* (Proverbs 14:14) How do the faithless and the good get satisfied with the results of their dealings?

* See pages 11-16 of the October 22, 1987, issue of *Awake!*

Gathering all available facts, he acts with knowledge.

Take, for example, the question, "Is there a God?" The inexperienced one is inclined to go along with what is popular or with what prominent people believe. The shrewd one, on the other hand, takes time to examine the facts. He reflects on such scriptures as Romans 1:20 and Hebrews 3:4. In spiritual matters, a prudent person does not just accept the word of religious leaders. He 'tests the inspired expressions to see whether they originate with God.'—1 John 4:1.

How wise it is to heed the advice not to 'put faith in every word'! Those entrusted with the responsibility to counsel others in the Christian congregation must especially take this to heart. The counselor must have the complete picture of what has transpired. He must listen well and gather facts from all sides so that his counsel is not unsound or one-sided.—Proverbs 18:13; 29:20.

"The Man of Thinking Abilities Is Hated"

Pointing to yet another difference between the wise and the foolish, the king of Israel says: *"The wise one fears and is turning away from badness, but the stupid is becoming furious and self-confident. He that is quick to anger will commit foolishness, but the man of thinking abilities is hated."*—Proverbs 14: 16, 17.

The wise person fears the consequences of following a wrong course. Therefore, he is cautious and appreciates any counsel that helps him to avoid badness. The stupid one does not have such fear. Being self-confident, he arrogantly ignores the counsel of others. Prone to becoming furious, such a person acts foolishly. But how is it that a man of thinking abilities becomes an object of hostility?

The original-language expression translated "thinking abilities" has two meanings. In a positive sense, it can denote discernment or cleverness. (Proverbs 1:4; 2:11; 3:21) Or negatively, the phrase can refer to wicked ideas or malicious thinking.—Psalm 37:7; Proverbs 12:2; 24:8.

If the expression "the man of thinking abilities" refers to a malicious schemer, it is not difficult to see why such a person is hated. However, is it not true that a man of discernment may also be hated by those lacking this quality? For example, those who exercise their mental faculties and choose to be "no part of the world" are hated by the world. (John 15:19) Christian youths who exercise their thinking abilities and stand up to unwholesome peer pressure in order to avoid improper behavior are ridiculed. The fact is that true worshippers are hated by the world, which is lying in the power of Satan the Devil.—1 John 5:19.

"Bad People Will Have to Bow Down"

The prudent, or the shrewd, differ from inexperienced ones in yet another way. *"The inexperienced ones will certainly take possession of foolishness, but the shrewd ones will bear knowledge as a headdress."* (Proverbs 14: 18) Lacking discernment, the inexperienced ones choose what is foolish. This becomes their lot in life. On the other hand, knowledge adorns the shrewd just as a crown honors a king.

"Bad people will have to bow down before the good ones," says the wise king, *"and the wicked people at the gates of the righteous one."* (Proverbs 14:19) In other words, the good will ultimately triumph over the wicked. Consider the increase in numbers and the superior way of life that God's people enjoy today. Seeing these blessings bestowed upon Jehovah's servants will force some opposers to "bow down" to Jehovah's figurative heavenly woman, represented by the

spirit-anointed remnant on earth. At Armageddon at the latest, those opposers will be compelled to acknowledge that the earthly part of God's organization truly represents the heavenly part.—Isaiah 60:1, 14; Galatians 6:16; Revelation 16:14, 16.

"Showing Favor to the Afflicted Ones"

Making an observation about human nature, Solomon says: *"Even to his fellowman one who is of little means is an object of hatred, but many are the friends of the rich person."* (Proverbs 14:20) How true this is of imperfect humans! Being selfishly inclined, they tend to favor the rich over the poor. While the friends of the rich person are many, they are as transitory as his wealth. Should we not then avoid making friends by means of money or flattery?

What if an honest self-examination reveals that we curry the favor of the rich and look down on those of little means? We must realize that showing such favoritism is condemned in the Bible. It states: *"The one despising his own fellowman is sinning, but happy is he who is showing favor to the afflicted ones."*—Proverbs 14:21.

We should show consideration to those in difficult circumstances. (James 1:27) How can we do this? By providing "this world's means for supporting life," which can include money, food, shelter, clothing, and personal attention. (1 John 3:17) Happy is he who is showing favor to such ones, since "there is more happiness in giving than there is in receiving."—Acts 20:35.

How Do They Fare?

The principle "whatever a man is sowing, this he will also reap" applies to the shrewd person as well as to the foolish one. (Galatians 6:7) The former does what is good; the latter devises mischief. *"Will not those devising mischief go wandering about?"* asks the wise king. The answer is yes; they do "go astray." (*An American Translation*) *"But there are loving-kindness and trueness as regards those devising good."* (Proverbs 14:22) Those who do good enjoy the goodwill of others as well as God's loving-kindness.

Associating success with hard work and linking failure with much talk and little action, Solomon says: *"By every kind of toil there comes to be an advantage, but merely the word of the lips tends to want."* (Proverbs 14:23) This principle certainly applies to our spiritual endeavors. When we work hard in the Christian ministry, we reap the rewards of introducing the lifesaving truth of God's Word to many others. Faithfully carrying out any theocratic assignment we may receive leads to joy and satisfaction.

"The crown of the wise is their riches; the foolishness of the stupid ones is foolishness," says Proverbs 14:24. This could mean that the wisdom that the wise strive to attain is their riches, and it crowns, or adorns, them. The stupid, on the other hand, gain merely foolishness. According to one reference work, this proverb could also suggest that "wealth is an ornament to those who use it well . . . [whereas] fools only have their folly." Whatever the case, the wise one fares better than the foolish one.

"A true witness is delivering souls," says the king of Israel, *"but a deceitful one launches forth mere lies."* (Proverbs 14:25) While this certainly is true in a judicial context, consider its implications for our ministry. Our Kingdom-preaching and disciple-making work involves bearing witness to the truth of God's Word. That witness delivers righthearted individuals from false religion and saves lives. By paying constant attention to ourselves and to our teaching, we will save both ourselves and those who listen to us. (1 Timothy 4:16) As we continue to do this, let us be alert to display shrewdness in all aspects of life.

"KEEP PROVING WHAT YOU YOURSELVES ARE"

"Keep testing whether you are in the faith, keep proving what you yourselves are."
—2 CORINTHIANS 13:5.

A MAN traveling through the countryside comes to a fork in the road. Uncertain about which way will lead him to his destination, he asks passersby for directions but receives conflicting information. Confused, he is unable to go on. Having doubts about our beliefs can have a similar effect on us. Such uncertainty can interfere with our ability to make decisions, causing us to be unsure of the way in which to walk.

² A situation arose that could have had such an effect on some people in the Christian congregation in first-century Corinth, Greece. "Superfine apostles" were challenging the authority of the apostle Paul, saying: "His letters are weighty and forceful, but his presence in person is weak and his speech contemptible." (2 Corinthians 10:7-12; 11:5, 6) Such a viewpoint may have caused some in the Corinthian congregation to be unsure of how to walk.

³ Paul founded the congregation in Corinth during his visit there in 50 C.E. He stayed in Corinth "a year and six months, teaching among them the word of God." Indeed, "many of the Corinthians that heard began to believe and be baptized." (Acts 18:5-11) Paul was keenly interested in the spiritual welfare of his fellow believers in Corinth. Moreover, the Corinthians had written Paul for advice on certain matters. (1 Corinthians 7:1) So he gave them very fine admonition.

⁴ "Keep testing whether you are in the faith," Paul wrote, "keep proving what you yourselves are." (2 Corinthians 13:5) Applying this counsel would have protected those brothers in Corinth from being uncertain about the way in which to walk. It can do the same for us today. How, then, can we follow Paul's advice? How can we test whether we are in the faith? And what is involved in proving what we ourselves are?

"Keep Testing Whether You Are in the Faith"

⁵ In a test, usually a subject or an object is tested, and there is a measure or a standard according to which the test is performed. In this case, the test subject is not the faith —the body of beliefs we have embraced. We as individuals are the subject. To perform the test, we have a perfect standard. A melody composed by the psalmist David states: "The law of Jehovah is perfect, bringing back the soul. The reminder of Jehovah is trustworthy, making the inexperienced one wise. The orders from Jehovah

1, 2. (a) How can uncertainty about our beliefs affect us? (b) What situation in first-century Corinth may have caused some to be unsure of the way in which to walk?

3, 4. Why should Paul's admonition to the Corinthians be of interest to us?

5, 6. What standard do we have for testing whether we are in the faith, and why is that the ideal standard?

are upright, causing the heart to rejoice; the commandment of Jehovah is clean, making the eyes shine." (Psalm 19:7, 8) The Bible contains Jehovah's perfect laws and upright orders, his trustworthy reminders and clean commandments. The message found therein is the ideal standard for testing.

⁶ Concerning that God-inspired message, the apostle Paul says: "The word of God is alive and exerts power and is sharper than any two-edged sword and pierces even to the dividing of soul and spirit, and of joints and their marrow, and is able to discern thoughts and intentions of the heart." (Hebrews 4:12) Yes, God's word can test our heart—what we really are on the inside. How can we make this sharp and powerful message come to life for us? The psalmist leaves no doubt as to what this entails. He sang: "Happy is the man . . . [whose] delight is in the law of Jehovah, and in his law he reads in an undertone day and night." (Psalm 1:1, 2) "The law of Jehovah" is found in God's written Word, the Bible. We must take pleasure in reading Jehovah's Word. Indeed, we must take time to read in it in an undertone, or to meditate on it. As we do this, we need to expose ourselves —the test subjects—to what is written there.

⁷ The foremost way of testing whether we are in the faith, then, is to read and meditate on God's Word and examine how our conduct measures up to what we learn. We can be glad that we have much help to understand God's Word.

⁸ Jehovah has provided teachings and instruction through the publications of "the faithful and discreet slave," which explain the Scriptures. (Matthew 24:45) For example, consider the box entitled "Questions for Meditation" at the end of most chapters in the book *Draw Close to Jehovah.** What fine opportunities for personal reflection this feature of the book provides! Numerous subjects discussed in our journals, *The Watchtower* and *Awake!,* also help us to test whether we are in the faith. Regarding the articles on the book of Proverbs in recent issues of *The Watchtower,* one Christian woman said: "I find these articles very practical. They help me examine whether my speech, conduct, and attitude really measure up to Jehovah's righteous standards."

⁹ We also receive abundant direction and encouragement at congregation meetings, assemblies, and conventions. These are among the spiritual provisions that God has made for those concerning whom Isaiah prophesied: "It must occur in the final part of the days that the mountain of the house of Jehovah will become firmly established above the top of the mountains, and it will certainly be lifted up above the hills; and to it all the nations must stream. And many peoples will certainly go and say: 'Come, you people, and let us go up to the mountain of Jehovah, . . . and he will instruct us about his ways, and we will walk in his paths.'" (Isaiah 2:2, 3) It certainly is a blessing to have such instruction about Jehovah's ways.

¹⁰ Not to be overlooked is the counsel from those who have spiritual qualifications, including Christian elders. Concerning them, the Bible says: "Brothers, even though a man takes some false step before

---

7. What is the foremost way of testing whether we are in the faith?

8. How can the publications of "the faithful and discreet slave" help us to test whether we are in the faith?

---

* Published by Jehovah's Witnesses.

9, 10. What provisions of Jehovah help us to keep testing whether we are in the faith?

he is aware of it, you who have spiritual qualifications try to readjust such a man in a spirit of mildness, as you each keep an eye on yourself, for fear you also may be tempted." (Galatians 6:1) How grateful we can be for this provision for our readjustment!

¹¹ Our publications, Christian meetings, appointed men—these are wonderful provisions from Jehovah. Testing whether we are in the faith, though, requires self-examination. So when we are reading our publications or listening to Scriptural admonition, we need to ask ourselves: 'Does this describe me? Do I do this? Am I adhering to the body of Christian beliefs?' Our attitude toward the information we receive by means of these provisions also has a bearing on our spiritual condition. "A physical man does not receive the things of the spirit of God, for they are foolishness to him," says the Bible. "However, the spiritual man examines indeed all things." (1 Corinthians 2:14, 15) Should we not strive to maintain a positive, spiritual view of what we read in our books, magazines, and other publications and of what we hear at our meetings and from the elders?

"Keep Proving What You Yourselves Are"

¹² Proving what we ourselves are involves self-evaluation. Yes, we can be in the truth, but what is the level of our spirituality? Proving what we are involves giving proof of maturity and of genuine appreciation for spiritual provisions.

¹³ What proof of Christian maturity can we look for in ourselves? The apostle Paul

Do you know the foremost way of testing whether you are in the faith?

wrote: "Solid food belongs to mature people, to those who through use have their perceptive powers trained to distinguish both right and wrong." (Hebrews 5:14) We give proof of maturity by training our perceptive powers. Just as certain muscles in the body of an athlete need to be trained through repeated use before he can excel at his sport, our perceptive powers have to be trained through use in applying Bible principles.

¹⁴ Before we can train our perceptive powers, though, we must acquire knowledge. For this, diligent personal study is essential. When we regularly engage in personal study—especially of the deeper things of God's Word—our perceptive powers are improved. Over the years, many deep subjects have been discussed in *The Watchtower.* How do we respond when we come across articles that discuss deeper truths? Do we tend to shy away from them just because they contain "some things hard to understand"? (2 Peter 3:16) On the

---

11. Testing whether we are in the faith calls for what?
12. What does proving what we ourselves are involve?
13. According to Hebrews 5:14, what serves as proof of our maturity?

14, 15. Why should we put forth diligent effort to study the deeper things of God's Word?

We give proof of our Christian maturity by exercising our perceptive powers

contrary, we put forth extra effort to understand what is being said.—Ephesians 3:18.

¹⁵ What if personal study is difficult for us? It is vital that we endeavor to acquire or cultivate a taste for it.* (1 Peter 2:2) Growing to maturity requires that we learn to draw nourishment from solid food, the deeper truths of God's Word. Otherwise, our perceptive powers will necessarily remain limited. Giving proof of maturity, however, involves more than acquiring perceptive powers. In daily life we must put to use the knowledge that we gain through diligent personal study.

¹⁶ The proof of what we ourselves are is also found in our expressions of appreciation for the truth—our works of faith. Using a powerful illustration to describe this area of self-evaluation, the disciple

---

* For helpful suggestions on how to study, see pages 27-32 of the book *Benefit From Theocratic Ministry School Education,* published by Jehovah's Witnesses.

16, 17. What admonition does the disciple James give about becoming "doers of the word"?

James says: "Become doers of the word, and not hearers only, deceiving yourselves with false reasoning. For if anyone is a hearer of the word, and not a doer, this one is like a man looking at his natural face in a mirror. For he looks at himself, and off he goes and immediately forgets what sort of man he is. But he who peers into the perfect law that belongs to freedom and who persists in it, this man, because he has become, not a forgetful hearer, but a doer of the work, will be happy in his doing it."
—James 1:22-25.

¹⁷ James is saying: 'Peer into the mirror of God's word, and evaluate yourself. Persist in doing this, and scrutinize yourself in the light of what you find in God's word. Then, do not quickly forget what you have seen. Make the needed corrections.' Following this advice may at times present a challenge.

¹⁸ Take, for example, the requirement to share in the Kingdom-preaching work. "With the heart one exercises faith for righteousness," wrote Paul, "but with the mouth one makes public declaration for salvation." (Romans 10:10) Making public declaration for salvation with our mouth requires a number of adjustments. Participating in the preaching work does not come naturally to most of us. Being zealous at it and giving the work the place that it deserves in our lives requires even more changes and sacrifices. (Matthew 6:33) But once we become doers of this God-given work, we are happy because of the praise that it brings to Jehovah. Are we, then, zealous Kingdom proclaimers?

¹⁹ How inclusive should our works of

---

18. Why does following James' counsel present a challenge?
19. What should our works of faith include?

We prove what we are by becoming 'not forgetful hearers, but doers of the word'

faith be? Paul states: "The things that you learned as well as accepted and heard and saw in connection with me, practice these; and the God of peace will be with you." (Philippians 4:9) Proof of what we are is given by our practicing what we have learned, accepted, heard, and seen—the full scope of Christian dedication and discipleship. "This is the way. Walk in it," instructs Jehovah through the prophet Isaiah.—Isaiah 30:21.

20 Men and women who are diligent students of God's Word, who are zealous preachers of the good news, who are flawless in their integrity, and who are loyal supporters of the Kingdom are a great blessing to the congregation. Their presence adds stability to the congregation they associate with. They prove to be very helpful, especially because there are so many new ones to care for. When we take to heart Paul's advice to 'keep testing whether we are in the faith, keep proving what we ourselves are,' we too become a good influence on others.

---

20. What type of individuals are a great blessing to the congregation?

Take Delight in Doing God's Will

21 "To do your will, O my God, I have delighted," sang King David of ancient Israel, "and your law is within my inward parts." (Psalm 40:8) David took pleasure in doing God's will. Why? Because Jehovah's law was in David's heart. David was not uncertain about the way in which to walk.

22 When God's law is within our inward parts, we are not unsure of the way in which to walk. We take delight in doing God's will. By all means, then, let us 'exert ourselves vigorously' as we serve Jehovah from the heart.—Luke 13:24.

21, 22. How can we take delight in doing God's will?

Do You Recall?

- How can we test whether we are in the faith?
- What is involved in proving what we ourselves are?
- What proof can we give of Christian maturity?
- How do our works of faith help us to evaluate what we are?

ARE YOU FAITHFUL IN ALL THINGS?

"The person faithful in what is least is faithful also in much."—LUKE 16:10.

A S THE day progresses, have you ever noticed what happens to a shadow that a tree casts on the ground? Why, the shadow keeps changing in size and direction! Human endeavors and promises are often as unsteady as a shadow. Jehovah God, on the other hand, does not change with time. Referring to him as "the Father of the celestial lights," the disciple James says: "With him there is not a variation of the turning of the shadow [or, "variation or shadow caused by a turning," footnote]." (James 1:17) Jehovah is constant and dependable, even in the minutest details. He is "a God of faithfulness." —Deuteronomy 32:4.

___
1. What is one of the ways that Jehovah is faithful?

² How does God view the dependability of his worshippers? In the same way as did David, who said of them: "My eyes are upon the faithful ones of the earth, that they may dwell with me. The one walking in a faultless way, he it is who will minister to me." (Psalm 101:6) Yes, Jehovah takes delight in the faithfulness of his servants. With good reason, the apostle Paul wrote: "What is looked for in stewards is for a man to be found faithful." (1 Corinthians 4:2) What does being faithful entail? In what areas of life should we act in faithfulness? What are the blessings of "walking in a faultless way"?

___
2. (a) Why should we examine ourselves to determine whether we are faithful? (b) What questions about faithfulness will we consider?

Faithful in what is least, faithful also in much

What It Means to Be Faithful

3 "Moses as an attendant was faithful," states Hebrews 3:5. What made the prophet Moses faithful? In the construction and setting up of the tabernacle, "Moses proceeded to do according to all that Jehovah had commanded him. He did just so." (Exodus 40:16) As worshippers of Jehovah, we show faithfulness by obediently serving him. This certainly includes our remaining loyal to Jehovah while facing difficult tests or severe trials. However, success in dealing with big tests is not the sole factor that determines our faithfulness. "The person faithful in what is least is faithful also in much," stated Jesus, "and the person unrighteous in what is least is unrighteous also in much." (Luke 16:10) We must remain faithful even in seemingly small matters.

4 Obedience each day in "what is least" is important for two reasons. First, it reveals how we feel about Jehovah's sovereignty. Think of the test of loyalty placed before the first human pair, Adam and Eve. It was a requirement that imposed no hardship whatsoever on them. While having access to all sorts of food in the garden of Eden, they were merely to refrain from eating the fruit of just one tree—"the tree of the knowledge of good and bad." (Genesis 2:16, 17) Their faithfulness in obeying that simple command would have demonstrated that the first human couple were for Jehovah's rulership. Following Jehovah's instructions in our day-to-day life shows that we are on the side of Jehovah's sovereignty.

5 Second, our conduct in "what is least" has a bearing on how we will respond "also in much," that is, when we face bigger issues in life. In this regard, consider what happened to Daniel and his three faithful Hebrew companions—Hananiah, Mishael, and Azariah. They were taken into exile in Babylon in 617 B.C.E. While still young, likely in their teens, these four found themselves in the royal court of King Nebuchadnezzar. There they were "appointed a daily allowance from the delicacies of the king and from his drinking wine, even to nourish them for three years, that at the end of these they might stand before the king."—Daniel 1:3-5.

6 The provisions of the Babylonian king, however, presented a challenge to the four Hebrew youths. Foods prohibited by the Mosaic Law were likely included in the delicacies of the king. (Deuteronomy 14:3-20) The slaughtered animals may not have been bled properly, and partaking of such meat would have violated God's Law. (Deuteronomy 12:23-25) The food may also have been offered to idols, as was the custom among Babylonian worshippers before eating a communion meal.

7 Dietary restrictions undoubtedly were not of high concern to the royal household of the Babylonian king. However, Daniel and his friends were determined in their hearts not to pollute themselves by eating food forbidden in God's Law to Israel. This was an issue that touched on their loyalty and faithfulness to God. So they requested a diet of vegetables and water, and it was granted to them. (Daniel 1:9-14) To some people today, what those four young men did may seem insignificant. However, their obedience to God showed where they stood on the issue of Jehovah's sovereignty.

8 Proving faithful in what might have seemed less significant prepared Daniel's

---

3. What determines whether we are faithful?
4, 5. What does our faithfulness in "what is least" reveal?

6. What test did Daniel and his three Hebrew companions face in the Babylonian royal court?
7. What did the obedience of Daniel and his three friends show?
8. (a) What critical test of loyalty did the three Hebrews face? (b) What was the outcome of the test, and what does this illustrate?

three friends to cope with a greater trial. Turn to chapter 3 of the Bible book of Daniel, and read for yourself how the three Hebrews faced the death penalty for refusing to worship the golden image that King Nebuchadnezzar had set up. When brought before the king, they declared their determination with confidence: "If it is to be, our God whom we are serving is able to rescue us. Out of the burning fiery furnace and out of your hand, O king, he will rescue us. But if not, let it become known to you, O king, that your gods are not the ones we are serving, and the image of gold that you have set up we will not worship." (Daniel 3:17, 18) Did Jehovah rescue them? The guards who threw the young men into the fiery furnace perished, but the three faithful Hebrews stepped out alive—not even scorched by the heat of the furnace! Their well-established pattern of faithfulness helped prepare them to be faithful during that critical test. Does this not illustrate the importance of being faithful in small things?

Faithfulness Regarding "Unrighteous Riches"

9 Before stating the principle that one who is faithful in seemingly small things is also faithful in important matters, Jesus advised his listeners: "Make friends for yourselves by means of the unrighteous riches, so that, when such fail, they may receive you into the everlasting dwelling places." He followed up with the statement about faithfulness in what is least. Then Jesus said: "Therefore, if you have not proved yourselves faithful in connection with the unrighteous riches, who will entrust you with what is true? . . . No house servant can be a slave to two masters; for, either he will hate the one and love the other, or he will stick to the one and despise the other. You cannot be slaves to God and to riches."—Luke 16:9-13.

---

9. What is the context of Jesus' words recorded at Luke 16:10?

10 According to the context, the original application of Jesus' words found at Luke 16: 10 has to do with the use of "unrighteous riches," our material resources or possessions. They are called unrighteous because material riches—particularly money—are under the control of sinful humans. Moreover, a desire for acquiring riches can lead to unrighteous acts. We show faithfulness by exercising wisdom in the way we use our material possessions. Rather than using them for selfish purposes, we want to use them in furthering Kingdom interests and in helping those in need. By being faithful in this way, we make friends with Jehovah God and Jesus Christ, the possessors of "the everlasting dwelling places." They will receive us into these places, granting us eternal life either in heaven or in Paradise on earth.

11 Consider, too, what we extend to people with whom we place Bibles or Bible-based literature when we proclaim the Kingdom message and explain to them that we accept contributions to the worldwide work done by Jehovah's people. Are we not extending to them an opportunity to make wise use of their material resources? Though the original application of Luke 16:10 concerns the use of material resources, the principle stated there also applies in other areas of life.

Honesty Really Matters

12 The apostle Paul wrote: "We trust we have an honest conscience, as we wish to conduct ourselves honestly in all things." (Hebrews 13:18) "All things" certainly include all matters that involve the handling of finances. We pay our debts and our taxes promptly and honestly. Why? We do so be-

---

10. How can we demonstrate faithfulness in our use of "unrighteous riches"?
11. Why should we not hold back from explaining to householders that we accept contributions to the worldwide work done by Jehovah's Witnesses?
12, 13. In what areas can we demonstrate honesty?

'Conduct yourselves honestly in all things'

cause of our conscience and primarily out of love for God and in obedience to his instructions. (Romans 13:5, 6) How do we respond when we find something that does not belong to us? We seek to return it to its rightful owner. What a fine witness this results in when we explain what prompted us to return the individual's possession!

¹³ Being faithful and honest in all things calls for honesty at our place of employment. Honesty in our work habits draws attention to the kind of God we represent. We do not "steal" time by being lazy. Rather, we work hard, as to Jehovah. (Ephesians 4:28; Colossians 3:23) It is estimated that in one European land, one third of the employees who request a doctor's letter authorizing sick leave do so fraudulently. True servants of God do not fabricate excuses to avoid going to work. At times, Jehovah's Witnesses are offered promotions because employers observe their honesty and hard work.—Proverbs 10:4.

Faithfulness in Our Christian Ministry

¹⁴ How do we show faithfulness in the ministry that is entrusted to us? "Let us always offer to God a sacrifice of praise," says

14, 15. What are some ways that we can prove ourselves faithful in the Christian ministry?

A fine way to show faithfulness is to prepare well for the field ministry

the Bible, "that is, the fruit of lips which make public declaration to his name." (Hebrews 13:15) The foremost way to show faithfulness in the field ministry is to participate in it regularly. Why should we allow a month to pass without witnessing about Jehovah and his purpose? A regular share in the preaching work also helps us to improve our skills and our effectiveness.

¹⁵ Another fine way to show faithfulness in the field service is to apply the suggestions found in *The Watchtower* and *Our Kingdom Ministry.* When we prepare and use the suggested presentations or others that are realistic, do we not find that our ministry is more productive? When we meet someone who shows interest in the Kingdom message, do we promptly follow up on the interest? And what about home Bible studies that we may start with interested people? Are we dependable and faithful in caring for them? Our proving faithful in the ministry can lead to life for us and for those who listen to us. —1 Timothy 4:15, 16.

Keeping Separate From the World

¹⁶ In prayer to God, Jesus said of his

16, 17. In what ways can we show that we are separate from the world?

Be modest in dress and grooming

followers: "I have given your word to them, but the world has hated them, because they are no part of the world, just as I am no part of the world. I request you, not to take them out of the world, but to watch over them because of the wicked one. They are no part of the world, just as I am no part of the world." (John 17:14-16) We may be firm and determined to keep separate from the world on large issues, such as neutrality, religious holidays and customs, and immorality. What, though, about smaller things? Could it be that even without realizing it, we may be influenced by the ways of the world? If we are not careful, for instance, how easily our manner of dress can become undignified and inappropriate! Being faithful calls for "modesty and soundness of mind" in the matter of dress and grooming. (1 Timothy 2:9, 10) Yes, "in no way are we giving any cause for stumbling, that our ministry might not be found fault with; but in every way we recommend ourselves as God's ministers."—2 Corinthians 6:3, 4.

¹⁷ Out of a desire to honor Jehovah, we dress in a dignified way for our congregation meetings. The same is true when we meet in large numbers at our assemblies and conventions. Our dress needs to be practical and presentable. This serves as a witness to others who observe us. Even the angels take note of our activity, as they did of that of Paul and his Christian associates. (1 Corinthians 4:9) In fact, we should always be appropriately attired. To some, faithfulness in the choice of clothing may seem to be a small matter, but in God's eyes it is important.

Blessings for Faithfulness

¹⁸ True Christians are spoken of as "fine stewards of God's undeserved kindness expressed in various ways." As such, they are "dependent on the strength that God supplies." (1 Peter 4:10, 11) Moreover, as stewards, we are entrusted with what does not personally belong to us—expressions of God's undeserved kindness, including the ministry. In proving ourselves fine stewards, we rely on the strength that God supplies, "the power beyond what is normal." (2 Corinthians 4:7) What fine training to help us face whatever trials the future may bring!

¹⁹ The psalmist sang: "O love Jehovah, all you loyal ones of his. The faithful ones Jehovah is safeguarding." (Psalm 31:23) Let us be determined to prove ourselves faithful, fully confident that Jehovah is "a Savior of all sorts of men, especially of faithful ones." —1 Timothy 4:10.

———

18, 19. What blessings result from faithfulness?

Do You Recall?

- Why should we be "faithful in what is least"?
- How can we prove faithful
    in regard to honesty?
    in the ministry?
    in keeping separate from the world?

Questions From Readers

Since King Solomon of ancient Israel in his old age turned unfaithful to God, can we conclude that he will not be resurrected?—1 Kings 11:3-9.

While the Bible lists by name some men and women of faith who will no doubt be resurrected, it does not specifically comment on the resurrection prospects of every single individual it names. (Hebrews 11:1-40) In the case of Solomon, however, we can get an idea of God's judgment by comparing what happened to him at death with what happened to certain faithful ones when they died.

The Scriptures speak of only two possibilities for the dead—the temporary state of nonexistence and the state of eternal death. Those who are judged unworthy of a resurrection are pitched into "Gehenna," or "the lake of fire." (Matthew 5:22; Mark 9:47, 48; Revelation 20:14) Among these would be the first human pair, Adam and Eve, the betrayer Judas Iscariot, and certain ones who died when God executed judgment upon them, such as the people in Noah's day and the inhabitants of Sodom and Gomorrah.* At death, those who will be favored with a resurrection go to the common grave of mankind—Sheol, or Hades. Speaking of their future, the Bible states: "The sea gave up those dead in it, and death and Hades gave up those dead in them, and they were judged individually according to their deeds."—Revelation 20:13.

The faithful ones referred to in Hebrews chapter 11, then, are in Sheol, or Hades, awaiting the resurrection. Among these are God's loyal servants

---

* See pages 30-1 of the June 1, 1988, issue of *The Watchtower*.

Abraham, Moses, and David. Now consider how the Bible speaks of them with regard to their dying. "As for you," Jehovah told Abraham, "you will go to your forefathers in peace; you will be buried at a good old age." (Genesis 15:15) Jehovah said to Moses: "Look! You are lying down with your forefathers." (Deuteronomy 31:16) Concerning Solomon's father, David, the Bible says: "David lay down with his forefathers and was buried in the City of David." (1 Kings 2:10) Thus, the expression 'lying down with one's forefathers' is another way of saying that the person went to Sheol.

What happened to Solomon when he died? The Bible answers: "The days that Solomon had reigned in Jerusalem over all Israel were forty years. Then Solomon lay down with his forefathers, and was buried in the City of David his father." (1 Kings 11:42, 43) Hence, it seems reasonable to conclude that Solomon is in Sheol, or Hades, from which he will be resurrected.

This conclusion implies that the possibility of being resurrected is open to others concerning whom the Scriptures specifically say, 'they lay down with their forefathers.' In fact, many of the kings who succeeded Solomon, though unfaithful, are spoken of in this way. This is not inconceivable, since "there is going to be a resurrection of both the righteous and the unrighteous." (Acts 24:15) Of course, only after "all those in the memorial tombs" are raised will we know for a certainty who has been favored with a resurrection. (John 5: 28, 29) So rather than be dogmatic about the resurrection of any particular individual of old, we wait, trusting in Jehovah's perfect decision.

"THEY DID NOT COMPROMISE"

"**H**APPY are you when people reproach you and persecute you and lyingly say every sort of wicked thing against you for my sake," Jesus Christ told his disciples. (Matthew 5:11) Jehovah's Witnesses today are happy because, in harmony with Christ's teaching and example, they remain "no part of the world" and maintain strict political neutrality and integrity to God under all kinds of circumstances.—John 17:14; Matthew 4:8-10.

Concerning the uncompromising stand that Jehovah's Witnesses took in the former Soviet Union, including those in Estonia, Lutheran theologian and Bible translator Toomas Paul writes in his book *Kirik keset küla* (The Church in the Middle of the Village): "Very few have heard of what happened in the early hours of April 1, 1951. A campaign was planned to dispose of Jehovah's Witnesses and all their supporters—279 persons in all were captured and deported to Siberia . . . They were given an opportunity to sign a standard form renouncing their faith in order to avoid deportation or imprisonment. . . . Together with the ones arrested earlier, there were 353 interned, including at least 171 persons only associating with their congregations. They did not compromise—even in Siberia. . . . Not many members of the [Estonian Lutheran] Church had a faith similar to that of Jehovah's Witnesses."

Jehovah's Witnesses around the world trust in God to help them remain faithful and obedient to him despite persecution. They rejoice in knowing that the reward for their faithfulness is great.—Matthew 5:12.

AUGUST 1, 2005

THE WATCHTOWER

ANNOUNCING JEHOVAH'S KINGDOM

The Bible Can Help You Find True Joy

THE WATCHTOWER®
ANNOUNCING JEHOVAH'S KINGDOM

August 1, 2005   Average Printing Each Issue: 26,439,000   Vol. 126, No. 15

THE PURPOSE OF *THE WATCHTOWER* is to exalt Jehovah God as Sovereign Lord of the universe. It keeps watch on world events as these fulfill Bible prophecy. It comforts all peoples with the good news that God's Kingdom will soon destroy those who oppress their fellowmen and that it will turn the earth into a paradise. It encourages faith in God's now-reigning King, Jesus Christ, whose shed blood opens the way for mankind to gain eternal life. *The Watchtower,* published by Jehovah's Witnesses continuously since 1879, is nonpolitical. It adheres to the Bible as its authority.

IN THIS ISSUE

3   Do You Struggle With Your Feelings?

4   The Bible Can Help You Find Joy

8   Jehovah's Word Is Alive—Highlights From the Book of Second Kings

13   When Is There a Basis for Taking Offense?

16   Jehovah Richly Rewards Those Who Keep His Way

21   Jehovah Has Numbered "the Very Hairs of Your Head"

26   Jehovah Is "the Rewarder of Those Earnestly Seeking Him"

31   Questions From Readers

32   A Long Journey Rewarded

WATCHTOWER STUDIES

AUGUST 29–SEPTEMBER 4:
Jehovah Has Numbered "the Very Hairs of Your Head."
Page 21. Songs to be used: 44, 58.

SEPTEMBER 5-11:
Jehovah Is "the Rewarder of Those Earnestly Seeking Him."
Page 26. Songs to be used: 114, 125.

Publication of *The Watchtower* is part of a worldwide Bible educational work supported by voluntary donations.

Unless otherwise indicated, Scripture quotations are from the modern-language *New World Translation of the Holy Scriptures—With References.*

The Watchtower (ISSN 0043-1087) is published semimonthly by Watchtower Bible and Tract Society of New York, Inc.; M. H. Larson, President; G. F. Simonis, Secretary-Treasurer; 25 Columbia Heights, Brooklyn, NY 11201-2483. Periodicals Postage Paid at Brooklyn, NY, and at additional mailing offices. POSTMASTER: Send address changes to Watchtower, **Wallkill, NY 12589.**

Changes of address should reach us 30 days before your moving date. Give us your old and new address (if possible, your old address label).

© 2005 Watch Tower Bible and Tract Society of Pennsylvania. All rights reserved. Printed in U.S.A.

Semimonthly   ENGLISH

Would you welcome more information or a free home Bible study? Please send your request to Jehovah's Witnesses, using the appropriate address below.

America, United States of: Wallkill, NY 12589. *Antigua:* Box 119, St. Johns. *Australia:* Box 280, Ingleburn, NSW 1890. *Bahamas:* Box N-1247, Nassau, N.P. *Barbados, W.I.:* Crusher Site Road, Prospect, St. James. *Britain:* The Ridgeway, London NW7 1RN. *Canada:* Box 4100, Halton Hills (Georgetown), Ontario L7G 4Y4. *Germany:* Niederselters, Am Steinfels, D-65618 Selters. *Ghana:* P. O. Box GP 760, Accra. *Guyana:* 352-360 Tyrell St., Republic Park Phase 2 EBD. *Hawaii 96819:* 2055 Kam IV Rd., Honolulu. *Hong Kong:* 4 Kent Road, Kowloon Tong. *India:* Post Box 6440, Yelahanka, Bangalore 560 064, KAR. *Ireland:* Newcastle, Greystones, Co. Wicklow. *Jamaica:* P. O. Box 103, Old Harbour, St. Catherine. *Japan:* 1271 Nakashinden, Ebina City, Kanagawa Pref., 243-0496. *Kenya:* P.O. Box 47788, GPO Nairobi 00100. *New Zealand:* P.O. Box 75-142, Manurewa. *Nigeria:* P.M.B. 1090, Benin City 300001, Edo State. *Philippines, Republic of:* P. O. Box 2044, 1060 Manila. *South Africa:* Private Bag X2067, Krugersdorp, 1740. *Trinidad and Tobago, Republic of:* Lower Rapsey Street & Laxmi Lane, Curepe. *Zambia:* Box 33459, Lusaka 10101. *Zimbabwe:* Private Bag WG-5001, Westgate.

NOW PUBLISHED IN 150 LANGUAGES. SEMIMONTHLY: Afrikaans, Albanian,* Amharic, Arabic, Bengali, Bicol, Bislama, Bulgarian, Cebuano,* Chichewa,* Chinese, Chinese (Simplified),* Cibemba,* Croatian,* Czech,*# Danish,*# Dutch,*# East Armenian, Efik,* English*#+⊚ (also Braille), Estonian, Ewe, Fijian, Finnish,*# French,*# Ga, Georgian,* German,*# Greek,* Gujarati, Gun, Hebrew, Hiligaynon, Hindi, Hungarian,*# Igbo,* Iloko,* Indonesian, Italian,*# Japanese*# (also Braille), Kannada, Kinyarwanda, Kirundi, Korean*# (also Braille), Latvian, Lingala, Lithuanian, Luvale, Macedonian, Malagasy,* Malayalam, Maltese, Myanmar, Nepali, Norwegian,*# Pangasinan, Papiamento (Aruba), Papiamento (Curaçao), Polish,*# Portuguese*# (also Braille), Punjabi, Rarotongan, Romanian,* Russian,* Samar-Leyte, Samoan, Sango, Sepedi, Serbian, Sesotho, Shona,* Silozi, Sinhala, Slovak,* Slovenian, Solomon Islands Pidgin, Spanish*# (also Braille), Sranantongo, Swahili,* Swedish,*# Tagalog,* Tamil, Telugu, Thai, Tigrinya, Tok Pisin, Tongan, Tshiluba, Tsonga, Tswana, Turkish, Twi, Ukrainian,* Urdu, Vietnamese, Wallisian, Xhosa, Yoruba,* Zulu*

MONTHLY: American Sign Language,△□ Armenian, Assamese, Azerbaijani (roman script), Brazilian Sign Language,△ Cambodian, Chitonga, Gilbertese, Greenlandic, Haitian Creole, Hausa, Hiri Motu, Icelandic, Isoko, Kaonde, Kazakh, Kikongo, Kiluba, Kirghiz, Kosraean, Kwanyama/Ndonga, Luganda, Marathi, Marshallese, Mauritian Creole, Maya, Mizo, Monokutuba, Moore, Niuean, Ossetian, Otetela, Palauan, Persian, Ponapean, Seychelles Creole, Tahitian, Tatar, Tiv, Trukese, Tumbuka, Tuvaluan, Umbundu, Venda, Yapese, Zande

* Study articles also available in large-print edition.
# Audiocassettes also available.
+ CD also available.
⊚ MP3 CD-ROM also available.
△ Videocassette
□ DVD

Do You Struggle With Your Feelings?

FOR much of her life, Lena has struggled with negative feelings about herself. "Years of sexual abuse during my childhood killed a big part of my self-respect," she said. "I felt that I was completely useless." Simone too looks back on her youth and says, "Deep within me there was a void and the belief that I wasn't worth much." The profound unhappiness that results from such feelings seems to be widespread today. One telephone counseling service for teenagers says that almost half of their callers express "persistent feelings of low self-value."

According to some experts, feelings of inadequacy emerge when people are made to feel worthless by others. Such a state of mind may develop when one is subjected to constant berating, excessive and harsh criticism, or abusive exploitation. Whatever the reason, the consequences can be debilitating and even destructive. A recent medical study found that individuals with negative feelings about themselves tend to distrust themselves and others, thus unwittingly sabotaging close relationships and friendships. "In a sense," says the report on the study, "they 'create' the very situations they fear most."

People who feel that way are often victims of what the Bible calls their own "disquieting thoughts." (Psalm 94:19) They feel that they are never good enough. When something goes wrong, they instinctively blame themselves. Though others may praise them for their achievements, deep down inside they feel like a fraud who will be exposed sooner or later. Believing that they are unworthy of happiness, many fall into self-destructive behavior that they feel powerless to correct. Lena, mentioned earlier, developed a serious eating disorder because of her lack of self-respect, and she admits, "I felt unable to change anything."

Are those who struggle with such "disquieting thoughts" doomed to feel this way for the rest of their life? Can anything be done to combat such feelings? The Bible sets out principles and practical advice that have helped many to succeed in the struggle. What are some of these principles, and how have they helped sufferers find joy in life? The next article will explain.

The Bible Can Help You Find Joy

THOUGH not a medical manual, the Bible does comment on the effect that emotions—positive or negative—can have on a person's mental and physical health. "A heart that is joyful does good as a curer," says the Bible, "but a spirit that is stricken makes the bones dry." Further, we read: "Have you shown yourself discouraged in the day of distress? Your power will be scanty." (Proverbs 17:22; 24:10) Feelings of discouragement can sap our energy, making us feel weak and vulnerable with no desire to change or to seek help.

Discouragement can also affect a person spiritually. People who feel worthless often feel that they can never enjoy a good relationship with God and be blessed by him. Simone, mentioned in the preceding article, doubted that she was "the kind of person God would approve of." However, when we look into God's Word, the Bible, we find that God takes a positive view of those who endeavor to please him.

God Does Care

The Bible tells us that "Jehovah is near to those that are broken at heart; and those who are crushed in spirit he saves." God does not despise "a heart broken and crushed," but he promises "to revive the spirit of the lowly ones and to revive the heart of the ones being crushed."—Psalm 34:18; 51:17; Isaiah 57:15.

On one occasion God's Son, Jesus, found it necessary to draw to the attention of his disciples the fact that God sees the good in His servants. By way of an illustration, he related that God notices when a sparrow falls to the ground—something that most humans would consider of little importance.

He also highlighted that God knows the smallest detail about humans, even the number of the hairs on their head. Jesus concluded his illustration by saying: "Therefore have no fear: you are worth more than many sparrows." (Matthew 10: 29-31)* Jesus indicated that despite what individuals may feel about themselves, humans with faith do have value in God's eyes. In fact, the apostle Peter reminds us that "God is not partial, but in every nation the man that fears him and works righteousness is acceptable to him."—Acts 10: 34, 35.

Maintain a Sense of Balance

God's Word urges us to cultivate balance in the way we view ourselves. The apostle Paul wrote under inspiration: "Through the undeserved kindness given to me I tell everyone there among you not to think more of himself than it is necessary to think; but to think so as to have a sound mind, each one as God has distributed to him a measure of faith."—Romans 12:3.

Certainly, we would not want to think too highly of ourselves to the point of becoming conceited; nor would we want to go to the other extreme and think nothing of ourselves. Rather, our aim should be to cultivate a reasonable view of ourselves, one that takes into consideration our strengths as well as our limitations. A Christian woman put it this way: "I'm not the epitome of evil; nor am I God's gift to others. I have both good points and bad points, and so does everyone else."

Of course, to attain such a balanced perspective is easier said than done. It may take a great deal of effort to undo an overly negative view of ourselves that we may have

developed over many years. Nevertheless, with God's help we can change our personality as well as our outlook on life. Actually, this is what God's Word urges us to do. We read: "Put away the old personality which conforms to your former course of conduct and which is being corrupted according to his deceptive desires; but . . . you should be made new in the force actuating your mind, and should put on the new personality which was created according to God's will in true righteousness and loyalty."—Ephesians 4:22-24.

By making the effort to transform 'the force actuating our mind,' that is, the dominant inclination of our mind, we can change our personality from one that is overly negative to one that is positive. Lena, mentioned in the preceding article, came to appreciate that until she put away the thought that no one could love her or help her, nothing would or could change her

---

* This portion of Scripture is discussed in detail on pages 22 and 23.

feelings about herself. What practical counsel found in the Bible helped Lena, Simone, and others to make such a transformation?

Bible Principles That Promote Joy

"Throw your burden upon Jehovah himself, and he himself will sustain you." (Psalm 55:22) First and foremost, prayer can help us find true joy. Simone says: "Whenever I feel discouraged, I turn to Jehovah and ask for his help. I have never been in a situation where I have not felt his strength and his guidance." When the psalmist urges us to throw our burden on Jehovah, he is in effect reminding us that Jehovah not only cares about us but also views us as individuals worthy of his help and support. On the night of the Passover 33 C.E., Jesus' disciples were grieved because of what Jesus said about his impending departure. Jesus urged them to pray to the Father, and then he added: "Ask and you will receive, that your joy may be made full."—John 16: 23, 24.

"There is more happiness in giving than there is in receiving." (Acts 20:35) As Jesus taught, giving is a key to finding true joy in life. Applying this Bible truth enables us to focus on the needs of others rather than on our own inadequacies. When we help others and see their appreciative response, we feel better about ourselves. Lena is

convinced that regularly sharing the good news from the Bible with her neighbors helps her in two ways. "First, it gives me the kind of happiness and satisfaction Jesus spoke of," she says. "Second, I receive much positive feedback from others, which helps me to find joy." By generously giving of ourselves, we will experience the truthfulness of Proverbs 11:25: "The one freely watering others will himself also be freely watered."

"All the days of the afflicted one are bad; but the one that is good at heart has a feast constantly." (Proverbs 15:15) All of us have a choice as to how we view ourselves and our circumstances. We can be like the one who sees everything negatively and feels afflicted, or we can choose to think positively, feel "good at heart," and be joyful as if we were at a feast. Says Simone: "I try to remain as positive as possible. I keep busy in personal study and in the ministry, and I persevere in prayer. I also try to surround myself with positive people, and I try to be there for others." Such a heart attitude leads to true joy, even as the Bible urges us: "Rejoice in Jehovah and be joyful, you righteous ones; and cry out joyfully, all you who are upright in heart."—Psalm 32:11.

"A true companion is loving all the time, and is a brother that is born for when there is distress." (Proverbs 17:17) Confiding in a loved one or in a trusted counselor can help

us get a grip on negative feelings and put them out of the way before they overwhelm us. Speaking with others can help us to see things from a balanced, positive viewpoint. "Talking things out helps a lot," admits Simone. "You need to tell someone how you're feeling. Often just getting it out is all that's needed." Doing so will help you experience the truthfulness of the proverb that says: "Anxious care in the heart of a man is what will cause it to bow down, but the good word is what makes it rejoice."—Proverbs 12:25.

Living by Bible principles promotes joy

What You Can Do

We have considered but a few of the many wonderful and practical principles from the Bible that can help us overcome negative feelings and find true joy. If you are among those who are struggling with feelings of inadequacy, we encourage you to make a closer examination of God's Word, the Bible. Learn to cultivate a realistic and healthy feeling about yourself and about your relationship with God. It is our sincere hope that with guidance from God's Word, you will be able to find true joy in all that you do.

Jehovah's Word Is Alive
Highlights From the Book of Second Kings

THE Bible book of Second Kings takes up where the book of First Kings leaves off. It is an account of 29 kings—12 from the northern kingdom of Israel and 17 from the southern kingdom of Judah. Second Kings also relates activities of the prophets Elijah, Elisha, and Isaiah. Though not strictly in chronological order, the record reaches down to the time of the destruction of Samaria and Jerusalem. Altogether, Second Kings covers a period of 340 years—from 920 B.C.E. to 580 B.C.E. when the prophet Jeremiah completed the writing of this book.

Of what value is Second Kings to us? What does it teach us about Jehovah and his dealings? What lessons can we draw from the actions of the kings, the prophets, and others mentioned in the book? Let us see what we can learn from Second Kings.

ELISHA SUCCEEDS ELIJAH
(2 Kings 1:1–8:29)

King Ahaziah of Israel suffers a fall in his home and is sick. He receives a notice of death from the prophet Elijah. Ahaziah dies, and his brother Jehoram ascends to the throne. Meanwhile, Jehoshaphat is king over Judah. Elijah is taken up in a windstorm, and his assistant, Elisha, succeeds him as a prophet. During some 60 years of his ministry that follows, Elisha performs many miracles.—See the box "Elisha's Miracles."

When a Moabite king rebels against Israel, Jehoram, Jehoshaphat, and the king of Edom go out to meet him in battle. They are given victory because of the faithfulness of Jehoshaphat. Later, the king of Syria plans a surprise attack against Israel. However, Elisha foils the plan. The Syrian king is enraged and sends "horses and war chariots and a heavy military force" to capture Elisha. (2 Kings 6:14) Elisha performs two miracles and turns back the Syrians in peace. In time, Syrian King Ben-hadad lays siege against Samaria. This results in a severe famine, but Elisha foretells that the famine will end.

Some time later, Elisha goes to Damascus. King Ben-hadad, now sick, sends Hazael to inquire if he will recover from his sickness. Elisha foretells that the king will die and that Hazael will rule in his place. The very next day, Hazael suffocates the king under a wet "netted cloth" and assumes the kingship. (2 Kings 8:15, footnote) In Judah, Jehoshaphat's son Jehoram becomes king, and he is succeeded by his son Ahaziah.—See the box "Kings of Judah and of Israel."

Scriptural Questions Answered:

2:9—Why did Elisha ask for 'two parts in Elijah's spirit'? To carry out the responsibility as a prophet to Israel, Elisha would need the same spirit that Elijah had shown, that of courage and fearlessness. Realizing this, Elisha asked for a double portion of Elijah's spir-

Naaman humbled himself and was healed by Jehovah's power

What happened to Elijah as he "went ascending in the windstorm"?

it. Elisha was appointed by Elijah as his successor and had been his attendant for six years, so Elisha viewed Elijah as his spiritual father; Elisha was like the firstborn spiritual son of Elijah. (1 Kings 19:19-21; 2 Kings 2:12) Hence, just as the literal firstborn received two parts of his father's inheritance, Elisha asked for and received two parts of spiritual inheritance from Elijah.

2:11—What were "the heavens" to which "Elijah went ascending in the windstorm"? These were neither the distant parts of the physical universe nor the spiritual place where God and his angelic sons dwell. (Deuteronomy 4:19; Psalm 11:4; Matthew 6:9; 18:10) "The heavens" to which Elijah ascended were the atmospheric heavens. (Psalm 78:26; Matthew 6:26) Racing through earth's atmosphere, the fiery chariot evidently transferred Elijah to another part of the earth, where he continued living for a time. Years later, in fact, Elijah wrote a letter to Jehoram, the king of Judah.—2 Chronicles 21:1, 12-15.

5:15, 16—Why did Elisha not accept Naaman's gift? Elisha refused the gift because he recognized that the miracle of healing Naaman was performed by Jehovah's power, not his own. It would have been unthinkable on his part to profit from his God-appointed of-

fice. True worshippers today do not reach out for personal gain from Jehovah's service. They take to heart Jesus' admonition: "You received free, give free."—Matthew 10:8.

5:18, 19—Was Naaman requesting forgiveness for having to participate in a religious act? The Syrian king evidently was old and weak and had to lean upon Naaman for support. When the king bowed down in worship to Rimmon, Naaman did also. For Naaman, though, it was a purely mechanical act, strictly for the purpose of supporting the body of the king and not for rendering worship. Naaman was asking Jehovah to forgive him for performing this civil duty. Believing Naaman, Elisha said to him: "Go in peace."

Lessons for Us:

1:13, 14. Learning from observation and acting with humility can save lives.

2:2, 4, 6. Even though Elisha had been Elijah's attendant for perhaps six years, he insisted on not leaving him. What a fine example of loyalty and friendship!—Proverbs 18:24.

2:23, 24. The main reason for this mocking of Elisha appears to be that a bald man was wearing Elijah's official garment. The children recognized Elisha as Jehovah's representative and simply did not want him around. They told him to "go up," that is, keep going up to Bethel or be taken up as Elijah had been. The children evidently reflected the antagonistic attitude of their parents. How vital that parents teach their children to respect God's representatives!

3:14, 18, 24. Jehovah's word always comes true.

3:22. The reflection of the early morning light created the illusion that the water was blood, perhaps because the soil in the freshly made ditches contained red clay. Jehovah may choose to use natural phenomena to accomplish his purposes.

4:8-11. Recognizing Elisha to be "a holy man of God," a woman in Shunem extended hospitality to him. Should we not do the same to faithful worshippers of Jehovah?

5:3. The little Israelite girl had faith in God's ability to perform miracles. She also had the courage to speak about her faith. Do you young ones strive to fortify your faith in God's promises and muster up courage to share the truth with your teachers and fellow students?

5:9-19. Does not Naaman's example show that a proud person can learn humility? —1 Peter 5:5.

5:20-27. What a price to pay for trying to live a lie! Giving thought to the personal heartache and tragedy that living a double life can bring will help us avoid such a course.

ISRAEL AND JUDAH GO INTO EXILE
(2 Kings 9:1–25:30)

Jehu is anointed king over Israel. He loses no time in carrying out the campaign to strike down the house of Ahab. Jehu skillful-

ELISHA'S MIRACLES

1. **The waters of the Jordan are made to divide.**—2 Kings 2:14

2. **The bad water supply of Jericho is made healthful.** —2 Kings 2:19-22

3. **Juvenile delinquents are attacked by bears.**—2 Kings 2:23, 24

4. **Water is supplied to armies.**—2 Kings 3:16-26

5. **A widow receives edible oil.**—2 Kings 4:1-7

6. **A barren Shunammite woman conceives a child.** —2 Kings 4:8-17

7. **A child is raised from the dead.**—2 Kings 4:18-37

8. **A poisonous stew becomes edible.**—2 Kings 4:38-41

9. **One hundred men are fed with 20 loaves.**—2 Kings 4:42-44

10. **Naaman is healed of his leprosy.**—2 Kings 5:1-14

11. **Gehazi receives Naaman's leprosy.**—2 Kings 5:24-27

12. **An axhead is made to float.**—2 Kings 6:5-7

13. **A servant sees angelic chariots.**—2 Kings 6:15-17

14. **The Syrian army is struck with blindness.**—2 Kings 6:18

15. **The sight of the Syrian army is restored.**—2 Kings 6:19-23

16. **A dead man comes to life.** —2 Kings 13:20, 21

ly 'annihilates Baal worship out of Israel.' (2 Kings 10:28) Upon learning that her son has been killed by Jehu, Ahaziah's mother, Athaliah, 'rises up to destroy all the offspring of the kingdom of Judah' and usurps the throne. (2 Kings 11:1) Only Ahaziah's baby son, Jehoash, is rescued and after six years in hiding is appointed king over Judah. Instructed by Jehoiada the priest, Jehoash continues to do what is right in Jehovah's eyes.

After Jehu, all the kings who rule Israel do what is bad in Jehovah's eyes. Elisha dies a natural death in the time of Jehu's grandson. The fourth Judean king following Jehoash is Ahaz, and he 'does not do what is right in the eyes of Jehovah.' (2 Kings 16:1, 2) His son Hezekiah, however, proves to be a king who 'keeps sticking to Jehovah.' (2 Kings 17:20; 18:6) In 740 B.C.E., when Hezekiah is king over Judah and Hoshea rules over Israel, Assyrian King Shalmaneser 'captures Samaria and leads Israel into exile in Assyria.' (2 Kings 17:6) Subsequently, foreigners are brought into the territory of Israel, and the Samaritan religion is born.

Of the seven kings who follow Hezekiah in Judah, only Josiah takes steps to rid the land of false worship. Finally, in 607 B.C.E., the Babylonians capture Jerusalem and 'Judah goes into exile from its soil.'—2 Kings 25:21.

Scriptural Questions Answered:

13:20, 21—Does this miracle support the veneration of religious relics? No, it does not. The Bible does not show that the bones of Elisha were ever venerated. It was God's power that made this miracle possible, as was the case with all the miracles Elisha performed when he was still alive.

15:1-6—Why did Jehovah plague Azariah (Uzziah, 15:6, footnote) with leprosy? "As soon as [Uzziah] was strong, his heart became haughty . . . , so that he acted unfaithfully against Jehovah his God and came into the temple of Jehovah to burn incense upon the altar of incense." When the priests "stood up against Uzziah" and told him to "go out from the sanctuary," he became enraged against the priests and was struck with leprosy.—2 Chronicles 26:16-20.

18:19-21, 25—Had Hezekiah made an alliance with Egypt? No. Rabshakeh's accusation was false, as was his claim to have come with "authorization from Jehovah." Faithful King Hezekiah relied solely on Jehovah.

Lessons for Us:

9:7, 26. The heavy judgment against the house of Ahab shows that false worship and the shedding of innocent blood are detestable to Jehovah.

9:20. Jehu's reputation as a furious chariot driver gave evidence of his zeal in carrying out his commission. Are you personally known as a zealous Kingdom proclaimer? —2 Timothy 4:2.

9:36, 37; 10:17; 13:18, 19, 25; 14:25; 19:20, 32-36; 20:16, 17; 24:13. We can be confident that 'the word that goes forth from Jehovah's mouth always has certain success.'—Isaiah 55:10, 11.

10:15. Just as Jehonadab wholeheartedly accepted Jehu's invitation to get up into the chariot with him, the "great crowd" willingly support Jesus Christ, the modern-day Jehu, and his anointed followers.—Revelation 7:9.

10:30, 31. Though Jehu's record was not flawless, Jehovah showed appreciation for all that he did. Indeed, 'God is not unrighteous so as to forget our work.'—Hebrews 6:10.

13:14-19. Since Jehu's grandson Jehoash did not exert himself but struck the earth with arrows only three times, he had limited success in defeating the Syrians. Jehovah expects us to do his assigned work wholeheartedly and with zeal.

20:2-6. Jehovah is the "Hearer of prayer." —Psalm 65:2.

24:3, 4. On account of Manasseh's blood-guilt, Jehovah "did not consent to grant forgiveness" to Judah. God respects the blood of the innocent. We can be confident that Jehovah will avenge innocent blood by destroying those responsible for shedding it.—Psalm 37:9-11; 145:20.

Valuable to Us

The book of Second Kings portrays Jehovah as the Fulfiller of promises. The exile of residents of the two kingdoms, first of Israel and then of Judah, forcefully brings to our attention how the prophetic judgment recorded at Deuteronomy 28:15-29:28 came true. Second Kings describes Elisha as a prophet with great zeal for Jehovah's name and for true worship. Hezekiah and Josiah are depicted as humble kings who respect God's Law.

As we reflect on the attitude and actions of the kings, prophets, and others referred to in Second Kings, do we not learn valuable lessons in what to strive for and what to avoid? (Romans 15:4; 1 Corinthians 10:11) Yes, "the word of God is alive and exerts power."—Hebrews 4:12.

KINGS OF JUDAH AND OF ISRAEL

Saul/David/Solomon: 1117/1077/1037 B.C.E.*

KINGDOM OF JUDAH	DATE (B.C.E.)	KINGDOM OF ISRAEL
Rehoboam	997	Jeroboam
Abijah/Asa	980/978	
	976/975/952	Nadab/Baasha/Elah
	951/951/951	Zimri/Omri/Tibni
	940	Ahab
Jehoshaphat	937	
	920/917	Ahaziah/Jehoram
Jehoram	913	
Ahaziah	906	
(Athaliah)	905	Jehu
Jehoash	898	
	876/859	Jehoahaz/Jehoash
Amaziah	858	
	844	Jeroboam II
Azariah (Uzziah)	829	
	803/791/791	Zechariah/Shallum/Menahem
	780/778	Pekahiah/Pekah
Jotham/Ahaz	777/762	
	758	Hoshea
Hezekiah	746	
	740	Samaria captured
Manasseh/Amon/Josiah	716/661/659	
Jehoahaz/Jehoiakim	628/628	
Jehoiachin/Zedekiah	618/617	
Jerusalem destroyed	607	

* Some dates are the approximate beginning year of the reign.

When Is There a Basis for Taking Offense?

AT ECCLESIASTES 7:9, the Bible states: "The *taking* of offense is what rests in the bosom of the stupid ones." This verse shows that we should not be overly sensitive when someone offends us; rather, we should be forgiving.

However, is Ecclesiastes 7:9 saying that we should never be offended by anything or anyone, that we are to forgive all offenses regardless of how severe or how frequent they are and not do anything about them? Should we be unconcerned about our *giving* offense by word or action because we know that the one offended should be forgiving? This cannot be the case.

Jehovah God is the epitome of love, mercy, forgiveness, and long-suffering. Yet, in the Bible, he is many times spoken of as being offended. When the offense was severe, he took action against the offenders. Consider some examples.

Offenses Against Jehovah

The account at 1 Kings 15:30 speaks of the sins of Jeroboam "with which he caused Israel to sin and by his offensiveness with which he offended Jehovah." At 2 Chronicles 28:25, the Bible says regarding King Ahaz of Judah: "He made high places for making sacrificial smoke to other gods, so that he offended Jehovah the God of his forefathers." Another example is found at Judges 2:11-14: "Israel fell to doing what was bad in the eyes of Jehovah and serving the Baals . . . , so that they offended Jehovah. . . . At this Jehovah's anger blazed against Israel, so that he gave them into the hands of the pillagers."

There are other things that offended Jehovah and that called for strong action. For example, at Exodus 22:18-20, we read: "You must not preserve a sorceress alive. Anyone lying down with a beast is positively to be put to death. One who sacrifices to any gods but Jehovah alone is to be devoted to destruction."

Jehovah did not continually forgive the major offenses of ancient Israel when they kept offending him and did not show true repentance. Where there was no true repentance and no actions to indicate that there was a turning around to obey Jehovah, God eventually gave the perpetrators up to destruction. This happened on a national scale in 607 B.C.E., at the hands of the Babylonians, and again in 70 C.E., at the hands of the Romans.

Yes, Jehovah takes offense at the bad things that people say and do, and he even executes unrepentant offenders whose sins are gross. But does this put him in the category of those of whom Ecclesiastes 7:9 speaks? Not at all. He is justified in taking offense at gross sins and always judges fairly. The Bible says of Jehovah: "Perfect is his activity, for all his ways are justice. A God of faithfulness, with whom there is no injustice; righteous and upright is he."—Deuteronomy 32:4.

Major Offenses Against Individuals

Under the Law that God gave to ancient

Jehovah gave unrepentant Israel up to destruction by the Romans in 70 C.E.

Israel, there were serious consequences for major offenses against individuals. For instance, if a thief came into a house at night and the householder killed him, there was no bloodguilt on the part of the householder. He was an innocent victim of a major crime. Hence, we read: "If a thief should be found in the act of breaking in and he does get struck and die, there is no bloodguilt for [the householder]."—Exodus 22:2.

A woman who has been raped has a right to be highly offended, as this is a major crime in God's eyes. Under the Mosaic Law, a man who raped a woman was to die "just as when a man rises up against his fellowman and indeed murders him." (Deuteronomy 22:25, 26) While we are no longer under that Law, it gives us insight into how Jehovah feels about rape—a horrible wrong.

In our time, rape is also a major crime with severe penalties. The victim has every right to report the matter to the police. In this way the proper authorities can punish the offender. And if the victim is a minor, the parents may want to initiate these actions.

Lesser Offenses

However, not all offenses require action by the authorities. Thus, we should not want to take undue offense at the relatively

---

IN OUR NEXT ISSUE

"Death Is Swallowed Up Forever"

———

The Royal Bible—A Milestone in Scholarship

———

Will You Reflect God's Glory?

---

minor mistakes that others make, but we should be forgiving. How often should we forgive? The apostle Peter asked Jesus: "Lord, how many times is my brother to sin against me and am I to forgive him? Up to seven times?" Jesus answered: "I say to you, not, Up to seven times, but, Up to seventy-seven times."—Matthew 18:21, 22.

On the other hand, there is a continuing need for us to work on our Christian personality to try to minimize giving offense. For instance, when you deal with others, are you at times blunt, tactless, insulting? Such ways are likely to offend. Rather than blaming the victim for taking offense and feeling that the burden of forgiveness is on him, the offender needs to realize that he is the reason that the person took offense. The of-

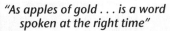

"As apples of gold . . . is a word spoken at the right time"

fender needs to work on controlling his actions and speech so as not to give offense in the first place. This effort will reduce the number of times we hurt the feelings of others. The Bible reminds us: "There exists the one speaking thoughtlessly as with the stabs of a sword, but the tongue of the wise ones is a healing." (Proverbs 12:18) When we offend others, even if we did not intend to do so, our making an apology goes a long way toward remedying the situation.

God's Word shows that we should "pursue the things making for peace and the things that are upbuilding to one another." (Romans 14:19) When we are tactful and kind, the proverb applies: "As apples of gold in silver carvings is a word spoken at the right time for it." (Proverbs 25:11) What a pleasant and delightful impression that leaves! Mild, tactful speech can even change the rigid attitudes of others: "A mild tongue itself can break a bone."—Proverbs 25:15.

Hence, God's Word counsels us: "Let your utterance be always with graciousness, seasoned with salt, so as to know how you ought to give an answer to each one." (Colossians 4:6) "Seasoned with salt" means that we make our expressions tasteful to others, thereby reducing the possibility of giving offense. In both word and deed, Christians strive to apply the Bible's admonition: "Seek peace and pursue it."—1 Peter 3:11.

Thus, Ecclesiastes 7:9 must mean that we should refrain from taking offense at the relatively minor sins of others. These may be the result of human imperfection or may even be deliberate yet not gross. But when an offense is a major sin, it is understandable that the victim may be offended and may choose to initiate appropriate action. —Matthew 18:15-17.

JEHOVAH RICHLY REWARDS THOSE WHO KEEP HIS WAY

● ● ●

AS TOLD BY
ROMUALD STAWSKI

When the second world war started in September 1939, northern Poland was the site of heavy fighting. As a curious nine-year-old boy, I went to a nearby battlefield to have a look. What I saw was horrifying—corpses littered the ground, and choking smoke filled the air. Although I was mainly thinking of how to get home safely, some questions came to my mind: "Why does God allow such terrible things to happen? Whose side is he on?"

NEAR the end of the war, youngsters were forced to work for the German regime. Anyone who dared to refuse was hanged on a tree or a bridge with the sign "traitor" or "saboteur" on his chest. Our town, Gdynia, was located between opposing armies. When we went outside the town to fetch water, bullets and bombs whizzed over our heads, and my younger brother Henryk was mortally wounded. Because of the terrible conditions, my mother moved us four children to a basement for safety. There my two-year-old brother, Eugeniusz, died of diphtheria.

Again I asked myself: "Where is God? Why does he allow all this suffering?" Even though I was a zealous Catholic and attended church regularly, I did not find the answers.

I Embraced Bible Truth

Answers to my questions came from an unexpected source. The war ended in 1945, and early in 1947, one of Jehovah's Witnesses called at our home in Gdynia. My mother talked to the Witness, and I heard some of what was said. It seemed logical, so we accepted an invitation to a Christian meeting. Just a month later, though not yet firmly established in Bible truth, I joined a group of local Witnesses and preached to others about a better world, free from wars and atrocities. This gave me a lot of joy.

In September 1947, I was baptized at a circuit assembly in Sopot. The following May, I started in the regular pioneer service, devoting most of my time to preaching the Bible's message to others. The local clergy bitterly opposed our work and incited violence against us. Once, an angry mob attacked us, hurled stones at us, and beat us severely. On another occasion local nuns and clergymen urged a group of people to attack us. We took refuge in a police station, but the mob surrounded the building, threatening to beat us. Finally, police reinforcements came, and we were taken away with a strong escort.

At that time, there was no congregation in our area. Sometimes we stayed overnight in the forest under the sky. We were happy that we could carry out the preaching work in spite of the conditions. Today, there are strong congregations in that area.

Bethel Service and Arrest

In 1949, I was invited to the Bethel Home in Łódź. What a privilege it was to serve at such a place! Sadly, my stay there did not last very long. In June 1950, a month before our work was officially banned, I was arrested along with other brothers at Bethel. I was taken to prison, and as it turned out, I was to face a cruel interrogation.

Because my father worked on a ship that regularly sailed to New York, the officers conducting the investigation tried to make me admit that he spied for the United States. I was subjected to merciless interrogation. In addition, four officers simultaneously tried to make me testify against Brother Wilhelm Scheider, who was then supervising our activity in Poland. They beat me on my heels with thick sticks. As I lay on the floor bleeding, feeling that I could not bear it anymore, I cried, "Jehovah, help me!" My persecutors were surprised and stopped beating me. Within a few minutes, they fell asleep. I felt

At an assembly held in a brother's garden in Kraków, 1964

relieved and regained my strength. This convinced me that Jehovah lovingly responds to his dedicated servants when they cry out to him. It strengthened my faith and taught me to place my full confidence in God.

The final report of the investigation included false testimony supposedly given by me. When I protested, an officer told me, "You will explain it in court!" A friendly cell mate advised me not to worry, since the final report had to be verified by a military prosecutor, which would give me a chance to refute the false testimony. That turned out to be so.

Circuit Work and Another Imprisonment

I was released in January 1951. A month later, I started to serve as a traveling overseer.

Despite the ban, I worked with other brothers to strengthen the congregations and help fellow Witnesses who were dispersed because of the activity of the security services. We encouraged the brothers to continue in the ministry. In later years, these brothers courageously supported the traveling overseers and carried out the work of printing and distributing Bible literature underground.

One day in April 1951, after attending a Christian meeting, I was arrested in the street by security officers who had been watching me carefully. Because I refused to answer their questions, they took me to a prison in Bydgoszcz and started interrogating me that same night. I was ordered to stand against a wall for six days and six nights, with no food or drink and in dense tobacco smoke from the officers' cigarettes. I was beaten with a club and burned with cigarettes. When I fainted, they poured water on me and resumed the interrogation. I begged Jehovah for strength to endure, and he supported me.

Staying in Bydgoszcz prison had its good side. There I was able to share Bible truth with people who could not otherwise be reached. And truly, there were many opportunities to give a witness. Because of their sad, often hopeless, situation, the prisoners readily opened their ears and hearts to the good news.

Two Important Changes

Soon after I was released in 1952, I met Nela, a zealous pioneer sister. She had been pioneering in the south of Poland. Later she worked in a "bakery," a secret place where our literature was printed. That was hard work, requiring alertness and self-sacrifice. We were married in 1954, and we continued in the full-time service until our daughter, Lidia, was born. Then we decided that in order to allow me to continue in the traveling work, Nela would stop her full-time service, return home, and take care of our daughter.

That same year, we faced another important decision. I was asked to serve as a district overseer in an area that covered one third of Poland. We considered the matter prayerfully. I knew how important it

With my wife, Nela, and our daughter, Lidia, 1968

was to strengthen our brothers under ban. There were many arrests, so there was a great need for spiritual encouragement. With Nela's support, I accepted the assignment. Jehovah helped me to serve in this capacity for 38 years.

In Charge of "Bakeries"

In those days, the district overseer was responsible for the "bakeries," located in secluded places. The police were constantly on our heels, trying to find and shut down our printing operations. Sometimes they succeeded, but we never lacked the necessary spiritual food. It was clearly evident that Jehovah was taking care of us.

To be invited to do the hard and dangerous work of printing, a person had to be loyal, alert, self-sacrificing, and obedient. It was those qualities that made it possible for a "bakery" to continue to function safely. Finding a good location for underground printing was also difficult. Some locations seemed suitable, but the brothers there were not very discreet. In other locations, the situation was the other way around. The brothers were willing to make exceptional sacrifices. I really appreciated all the brothers and sisters with whom I had the privilege to work.

Defending the Good News

During those difficult years, we were constantly accused of engaging in illegal, subversive activity and taken to court. This was a problem because we did not have lawyers to defend us. Some lawyers were sympathetic, but most were afraid of the publicity and did not want to risk displeasing the authorities. However, Jehovah was aware of our needs, and in due time he maneuvered matters accordingly.

Alojzy Prostak, a traveling overseer from Kraków, was so brutally treated during interrogation that he had to be taken to the prison hospital. His firm stand in the face of mental and physical torture earned him the respect and admiration of the other prisoners in the hospital. One of them was a lawyer named Witold Lis-Olszewski, who was impressed with the courage of Brother Prostak. He talked to him several times and promised, "As soon as I am released and allowed to resume my practice, I will be willing to defend Jehovah's Witnesses." He meant what he said.

Mr. Olszewski had his own team of attorneys, whose commitment was truly admirable. During the time when opposition was most intense, they defended the brothers in about 30 trials per month—one a day! Because Mr. Olszewski needed to be well-informed about all the cases, I was assigned to keep in touch with him. I worked with him for seven years in the 1960's and 1970's.

I learned a lot about legal work during those days. I often observed the trials, the lawyers' comments—both positive and negative—the methods of legal defense, and the testimony of accused fellow believers. It all became very useful in helping our brothers, especially those called as witnesses, to know what to say and when to keep silent before the court.

When a trial was on, Mr. Olszewski often stayed overnight in the homes of Jehovah's Witnesses. It was not because he could not afford a hotel room, but as he once said, "Before the trial, I want to breathe in some of your spirit." Thanks to his assistance, many trials ended favorably. He defended me several times, and he never accepted any money from me. On another occasion, he refused payment for 30 cases. Why? He said, "I want to contribute even a little bit to your work." And it was no little sum of money. The activity of Mr. Olszewski's team did not go unnoticed by the authorities, but that did not discourage him from assisting us.

It is difficult to describe the fine witness given by our brothers during those trials. Many came to the courts to observe the trials and to strengthen the accused brothers. During the time of the peak number of trials, I counted as many as 30,000 such supporters in one year. That surely was a great crowd of Witnesses!

A New Assignment

By 1989 the ban on our work had been lifted. Three years later a new branch office was built and dedicated. I was invited there to work with Hospital Information Services, which assignment I gladly accepted. Working as a three-person team, we supported our brothers facing the blood issue and helped

With Dr. Wites, chief surgeon of bloodless heart surgery for children, at a Katowice hospital

With a Witness boy before his bloodless heart surgery

them to defend their stand, based on their Christian conscience.—Acts 15:29.

My wife and I have been very grateful for the privilege of serving Jehovah in the public ministry. Nela has always supported and encouraged me. I am always thankful that whenever I was busy with theocratic assignments or was sent to prison, she never complained about my absence from home. In difficult times, she comforted others instead of breaking down herself.

For example, in 1974, I was arrested along with other traveling overseers. Some brothers who knew about it wanted to inform my wife in a gentle way. When they saw her, they asked, "Sister Nela, are you ready for the worst?" At first, she froze with fear, as she thought I had died. When she learned what had really happened, she said with relief: "He is alive! This is not his first imprisonment." The brothers told me later

With Nela, 2002

that they were deeply impressed with her positive attitude.

Even though we have had some painful experiences in the past, Jehovah has always richly rewarded us for keeping his way. How glad we are that our daughter, Lidia, and her husband, Alfred De-Rusha, have proved to be an exemplary Christian couple. They have brought up their sons, Christopher and Jonathan, to be dedicated servants of God, which adds to our happiness. My brother, Ryszard, and my sister, Urszula, have also been faithful Christians for many years.

Jehovah has never left us, and we want to continue serving him wholeheartedly. We have personally experienced the truthfulness of the words of Psalm 37:34: "Hope in Jehovah and keep his way, and he will exalt you to take possession of the earth." We look forward to that time with all our heart.

Jehovah Has Numbered "The Very Hairs of Your Head"

"Not one [sparrow] will fall to the ground without your Father's knowledge. But the very hairs of your head are all numbered."—MATTHEW 10:29, 30.

"I CALL to you, O God, but you never answer; and when I pray, you pay no attention. You are treating me cruelly; you persecute me with all your power." The man who spoke those words was in great anguish, and no wonder! He had lost his livelihood, a freakish disaster had claimed the lives of his children, and now he was beset by a debilitating illness. The man's name was Job, and his harrowing ordeal is recorded in the Bible for our benefit.—Job 30:20, 21, *Today's English Version.*

2 Job's expressions might make it appear that he had turned against God, but that was not the case. Job simply spoke from the depths of his distressed heart. (Job 6:2, 3) He did not know that Satan was the cause of his trials, so he mistakenly concluded that God had left him. At one point, Job even said to Jehovah: "Why do you conceal your very face and regard me as an enemy of yours?"* —Job 13:24.

3 Today, many of Jehovah's people suffer unrelenting hardships as a result of wars, political or social upheavals, natural disasters, old age, sickness, dire poverty, and governmental bans. Likely you too are undergoing trials of one kind or another. At times, you may think that Jehovah is concealing his face from you. You well know the words of John 3:16: "God loved the world so much that he gave his only-begotten Son." Still, when you are suffering with no relief in sight, you may wonder: 'Does God really love *me?* Does he notice what I am going through? Does he care about me as an individual?'

4 Consider what happened to the apostle Paul. "There was given me a thorn in the flesh, an angel of Satan, to keep slapping me," he wrote, adding: "I three times entreated the Lord that it might depart from me." Jehovah heard his entreaties. Nevertheless, he indicated to Paul that he would not intervene by means of a miraculous solution. Instead, Paul would have to rely on God's power to help him cope with his "thorn in the flesh."* (2 Corinthians 12:7-9) Like Paul, you may be experiencing a certain ongoing trial. Perhaps you wonder, 'Does the fact that Jehovah appears not to have done anything about my trial mean that he is unaware of my situation or that he does not care about me?' The answer is a resounding no! Jehovah's deep concern for each of

---

* Similar statements were made by righteous David and by the faithful sons of Korah.—Psalm 10:1; 44:24.

1, 2. (a) Why did Job feel abandoned by God? (b) Did Job's expressions mean that he had turned against Jehovah? Explain.
3. When adversities strike, what might come to our mind?

---

* The Bible does not state just what Paul's "thorn in the flesh" was. It might have been a physical affliction, such as poor eyesight. Or the expression "thorn in the flesh" might refer to false apostles and others who challenged Paul's apostleship and ministry.—2 Corinthians 11:6, 13-15; Galatians 4:15; 6:11.

4. What ongoing situation did Paul have to endure, and in what ways might such a situation affect us?

his faithful servants is underscored by what Jesus told his apostles shortly after he selected them. Let us see how his words can encourage us today.

"Have No Fear"—Why?

5 The apostles received extraordinary powers from Jesus, including "authority over unclean spirits, in order to expel these and to cure every sort of disease and every sort of infirmity." Yet, this did not mean that their course would be free from trials and hardships. On the contrary, Jesus described in detail some of the things that were to befall them. However, he urged them: "Do not become fearful of those who kill the body but cannot kill the soul; but rather be in fear of him that can destroy both soul and body in Gehenna."—Matthew 10:1, 16-22, 28.

6 To help his apostles understand why

5, 6. (a) How did Jesus help the apostles not to be fearful of what lay ahead? (b) How did Paul show confidence in Jehovah's care for him?

Why did Jehovah not remove Paul's "thorn in the flesh"?

they need not be fearful, Jesus went on to give two illustrations. He said to them: "Do not two sparrows sell for a coin of small value? Yet not one of them will fall to the ground without your Father's knowledge. But the very hairs of your head are all numbered. Therefore have no fear: you are worth more than many sparrows." (Matthew 10:29-31) Note that Jesus linked not being fearful in the face of adversity with being confident that Jehovah cares for us personally. Evidently, the apostle Paul had such confidence. He wrote: "If God is for us, who will be against us? He who did not even spare his own Son but delivered him up for us all, why will he not also with him kindly give us all other things?" (Romans 8:31, 32) No matter what challenges you face, you too can be sure that Jehovah cares for you personally as long as you remain loyal to him. This will become even more evident as we take a closer look at Jesus' admonition to his apostles.

The Value of a Sparrow

7 Jesus' word pictures effectively describe Jehovah's concern for each of His servants. Consider first the matter of the sparrows. In Jesus' day, sparrows were used for food, but because they were a threat to crops, they were largely viewed as pests. Sparrows were so abundant and cheap that two could be purchased for less than the equivalent of five cents in modern values. Twice that amount would buy not four but five sparrows—the

7, 8. (a) How were sparrows viewed in Jesus' day? (b) Why, evidently, does Matthew 10:29 use the diminutive form of the Greek word for "sparrows"?

© J. Heidecker/VIREO

extra bird being thrown in, as if it had no value at all!—Luke 12:6.

⁸ Think, too, about the size of this common bird. Compared to many other birds, even a full-grown sparrow is quite small. Yet, the Greek word translated "sparrows" at Matthew 10:29 specifically refers to *little* sparrows. Jesus evidently wanted his apostles to imagine a bird of the very least significance. As one reference work says, "Jesus cites a very small bird and uses a diminutive even of that!"

⁹ Jesus' analogy of the sparrows makes a powerful point: What seems valueless to humans is important to Jehovah God. Jesus further emphasized this truth by adding that a little sparrow would not "fall to the ground" without Jehovah's notice.* The lesson is clear. If Jehovah God takes note of the smallest and most insignificant bird, how much more will he be concerned about the plight of a human who has chosen to serve him!

¹⁰ In addition to his illustration about the sparrows, Jesus said: "The very hairs of your head are all numbered." (Matthew 10:30) This brief but profound statement amplifies the point of Jesus' illustration about the sparrows. Consider: The average human head has about 100,000 strands of hair. For the most part, one hair seems just like the next, and no single hair seems to deserve our particular scrutiny. Yet, each hair is noticed

---

* Some scholars suggest that the sparrow's falling to the ground may allude to more than its dying. They say that the original-language phrase may refer to a bird's alighting on the ground for food. If this is the case, it would imply that God notices and cares for the bird in its daily activities, not just when it dies.—Matthew 6:26.

---

9. What powerful point is made by Jesus' illustration of the sparrows?
10. What is the significance of the statement: "The very hairs of your head are all numbered"?

and numbered by Jehovah God. Since this is the case, is there any detail of our life that Jehovah cannot know? Surely Jehovah understands the unique makeup of each of his servants. Indeed, he "sees what the heart is." —1 Samuel 16:7.

¹¹ David, who was no stranger to hardship, was confident that Jehovah noticed him. "O Jehovah, you have searched through me, and you know me," he wrote. "You yourself have come to know my sitting down and my rising up. You have considered my thought from far off." (Psalm 139:1, 2) You too can be certain that Jehovah knows you personally. (Jeremiah 17:10) Do not be quick to assume that you are too insignificant to be noticed by Jehovah's all-seeing eyes!

"Put My Tears in Your Skin Bottle"

¹² Jehovah not only knows his servants individually but is also fully aware of the adversities each one suffers. For example, when the Israelites were being oppressed as slaves, Jehovah said to Moses: "Unquestionably I have seen the affliction of my people who are in Egypt, and I have heard their outcry as a result of those who drive them to work; because I well know the pains they suffer." (Exodus 3:7) How comforting it is to realize that when we are enduring a trial,

---

11. How did David express his confidence in Jehovah's concern for him personally?
12. How do we know that Jehovah is fully aware of the adversities that his people suffer?

Jehovah sees what is happening and hears our outcries! He is certainly not indifferent to our suffering.

¹³ Jehovah's care for those who have entered into a relationship with him is further seen in his feelings for the Israelites. Even though their suffering was often a result of their own stubbornness, Isaiah wrote concerning Jehovah: "During all their distress it was distressing to him." (Isaiah 63:9) As a faithful servant of Jehovah, you can be sure, then, that when you are pained, Jehovah is pained. Does that not impel you to face up to adversity fearlessly and to continue doing your best to serve him?—1 Peter 5:6, 7.

¹⁴ King David's conviction that Jehovah cared for him and felt for him is made evident in Psalm 56, which David composed while running from murderous King Saul. David escaped to Gath, but he feared capture when he was recognized by the Philistines. He wrote: "My foes have kept snapping all day long, for there are many warring against me high-mindedly." Because of his perilous situation, David turned to Jehovah. "All day long they keep hurting my personal affairs," he said. "All their thoughts are against me for bad."—Psalm 56:2, 5.

¹⁵ Then, as recorded at Psalm 56:8, David makes these intriguing statements: "My being a fugitive you yourself have reported. Do put my tears in your skin bottle. Are they not in your book?" What a touching description of Jehovah's tender care! When we are under stress, we may cry out to Jehovah with tears. Even the perfect man Jesus did so. (Hebrews 5:7) David was convinced that Jehovah observed him and would remember his agony, as if preserving his tears in a skin bottle or inscribing them in a book.* Perhaps you feel that your tears would fill a good part of that skin bottle or many pages of such a book. If that is the case, you can take comfort. The Bible assures us: "Jehovah is near to those that are broken at heart; and those who are crushed in spirit he saves."—Psalm 34:18.

Becoming an Intimate Companion of God

¹⁶ The fact that Jehovah has numbered 'the very hairs of our head' gives us some idea of the kind of observant and caring God we are privileged to worship. Though we will have to wait until the promised new world for all pain and suffering to vanish, Jehovah is doing something marvelous for his people right now. David wrote: "The intimacy with Jehovah belongs to those fearful of him, also his covenant, to cause them to know it." —Psalm 25:14.

¹⁷ "Intimacy with Jehovah." Why, the very idea seems beyond comprehension for imperfect humans! Yet, Jehovah invites those who fear him to be guests in his tent. (Psalm 15:1-5) And what does Jehovah do for his guests? He causes them to know his covenant, according to David. Jehovah confides in them, revealing his "confidential matter" to the prophets, so that they could know what his purposes are and what they must do to live in harmony with them. —Amos 3:7.

---

* In ancient times, skin bottles were made from the tanned hides of sheep, goats, and cattle. Such bottles were used to hold milk, butter, cheese, or water. Those that were subjected to a more thorough tanning process could hold oil or wine.

---

13. What shows that Jehovah truly feels for his servants?
14. What were the circumstances surrounding the composing of Psalm 56?
15. (a) What did David mean when he asked Jehovah to put his tears in a skin bottle or in a book? (b) When we are enduring a faith-challenging situation, of what can we be certain?

16, 17. (a) How do we know that Jehovah is not indifferent to the problems his people face? (b) What has Jehovah done to allow people to enjoy intimacy with him?

By reading the Bible regularly, we can find assurance that God cares for us personally

[18] Truly, it is heartwarming to know that we imperfect humans can become intimate companions of the Most High, Jehovah God. In fact, he urges us to do just that. "Draw close to God, and he will draw close to you," says the Bible. (James 4:8) Jehovah wants us to have a close relationship with him. Actually, he has already taken steps to make such a relationship possible. The ransom sacrifice of Jesus has opened the door for us so that we can have a friendship with Almighty God. The Bible states: "As for us, we love, because he first loved us."—1 John 4:19.

[19] That close relationship is enhanced when we endure under adverse circumstances. The disciple James wrote: "Let endurance have its work complete, that you may be complete and sound in all respects, not lacking in anything." (James 1:4) What "work" is accomplished by enduring hardship? Recall Paul's "thorn in the flesh." What did endurance accomplish in his case? Paul said this about his trials: "Most gladly, therefore, will I rather boast as respects my weaknesses, that the power of the Christ may like a tent remain over me. Therefore I take pleasure in weaknesses, in insults, in cases of need, in persecutions and difficulties, for Christ. For when I am weak, then I am powerful." (2 Corinthians 12:9, 10) Paul's experience was that Jehovah would supply the power needed—"the power beyond what is normal" if necessary—so that he could endure. That, in turn, drew him closer to Christ and to Jehovah God.—2 Corinthians 4:7; Philippians 4:11-13.

18. How do we know that Jehovah wants us to have a close relationship with him?
19. How can endurance enhance our relationship with Jehovah?

[20] Perhaps Jehovah has allowed your trials to continue. If so, take to heart his promise to those who fear him: "I will by no means leave you nor by any means forsake you." (Hebrews 13:5) You can experience such support and comfort. Jehovah has numbered "the very hairs of your head." He sees your endurance. He feels your pain. He genuinely cares for you. And he will never "forget your work and the love you showed for his name."—Hebrews 6:10.

20. How can we be sure that Jehovah will support and comfort us in the face of adversity?

Do You Recall?

- What factors can cause a person to feel abandoned by God?

- What lesson do we learn from Jesus' illustrations of the sparrows and of the numbering of the hairs of our head?

- What does it mean to have one's tears put in Jehovah's "skin bottle" or in his "book"?

- How can we come to enjoy "intimacy with Jehovah"?

JEHOVAH IS "THE REWARDER OF THOSE EARNESTLY SEEKING HIM"

"He that approaches God must believe that he is and that he becomes the rewarder of those earnestly seeking him."—HEBREWS 11:6.

"I HAVE been a Witness of Jehovah for nearly 30 years, but I have never felt worthy to be called that," confides Barbara.* "Even though I have pioneered and have had many other privileges, none of them seem enough to make me believe in my heart that I belong." Keith expresses similar thoughts. "I have at times felt unworthy because Jehovah's servants have many reasons to be happy, but I was not," he says. "This led to feelings of guilt, which only made matters worse."

———
* Some names have been changed.
———

1, 2. Why might some of Jehovah's servants struggle with negative feelings?

2 Many of Jehovah's faithful servants, both past and present, have struggled with similar feelings. Have you at times? You might be overwhelmed by one problem after another, while your fellow believers seem to be enjoying life, carefree and happy. As a result, you might feel that you neither have Jehovah's approval nor merit his attention. Do not hastily conclude that this is the case. The Bible assures us: "[Jehovah] has neither despised nor loathed the affliction of the afflicted one; and he has not concealed his face from him, and when he cried to him for help he heard." (Psalm 22:24) Those prophetic words about the Messiah show that

Paul

Elijah

Hannah

Jehovah not only hears his faithful ones but also rewards them.

3 No one is immune to the pressures of this system of things—not even Jehovah's people. We live in a world that is ruled by Jehovah's archenemy, Satan the Devil. (2 Corinthians 4:4; 1 John 5:19) Rather than being miraculously protected, Jehovah's servants are, in fact, the prime target of Satan. (Job 1:7-12; Revelation 2:10) Until God's appointed time, therefore, we need to "endure under tribulation" and "persevere in prayer," confident that Jehovah cares for us. (Romans 12:12) We should not give in to the thought that we are unloved by our God, Jehovah!

Ancient Examples of Endurance

4 Many ancient servants of Jehovah had to endure distressing situations. Hannah, for example, was "bitter of soul" because she was childless—a condition that she considered tantamount to being forgotten by God. (1 Samuel 1:9-11) When Elijah was being pursued by murderous Queen Jezebel, he became fearful and prayed to Jehovah: "It is enough! Now, O Jehovah, take my soul away, for I am no better than my forefathers." (1 Kings 19:4) And the apostle Paul must have felt the full burden of his imperfection when he admitted: "When I wish to do what is right, what is bad is present with me." He added: "Miserable man that I am!" —Romans 7:21-24.

5 Of course, we know that Hannah, Elijah, and Paul all endured in Jehovah's service, and He rewarded them richly. (1 Samuel 1:

20; 2:21; 1 Kings 19:5-18; 2 Timothy 4:8) Still, they struggled with the full range of human emotions, including grief, despair, and fear. It should not surprise us, then, if at times we have negative feelings. What can you do, though, when life's anxieties cause you to wonder if you are really loved by Jehovah? You can draw comfort from God's Word. For example, in the preceding article, we discussed Jesus' statement that Jehovah has numbered "the very hairs of your head." (Matthew 10:30) Those encouraging words indicate that Jehovah is deeply interested in each of his servants. Recall, too, Jesus' illustration of the sparrows. If not one of those small birds falls to the ground without Jehovah's notice, why would he turn a blind eye to your plight?

6 Is it really possible that we imperfect humans can be precious in the eyes of the all-powerful Creator, Jehovah God? Yes! In fact, there are numerous Bible passages that assure us of this. By taking these to heart, we can echo the words of the psalmist who stated: "When my disquieting thoughts became many inside of me, your own consolations began to fondle my soul." (Psalm 94:19) Let us consider some of these consoling statements from God's Word that will help us to appreciate more fully that we are valued by God and that he will reward us as we continue to do his will.

Jehovah's "Special Property"

7 A deplorable situation existed among the Jews during the fifth century B.C.E. The priests were accepting unfit animals and were offering these as sacrifices on Jehovah's altar. Judges were showing partiality. Sorcery, lying, fraud, and adultery

---

3. Why are we not immune to the pressures of this system of things?
4. Give some examples of faithful servants of Jehovah who endured distressing situations.
5. (a) How were Hannah, Elijah, and Paul rewarded? (b) What comfort can we draw from God's Word if we struggle with negative emotions?

---

6. How can the Bible be a source of comfort to those who battle negative feelings?
7. What encouraging prophecy did Jehovah give through Malachi to the corrupt nation?

were rampant. (Malachi 1:8; 2:9; 3:5) To this blatantly corrupt nation, Malachi uttered an astonishing prophecy. In time, Jehovah would bring his people back into an approved condition. We read: " 'They will certainly become mine,' Jehovah of armies has said, 'at the day when I am producing a special property. And I will show compassion upon them, just as a man shows compassion upon his son who is serving him.' "—Malachi 3:17.

⁸ Malachi's prophecy has a modern-day fulfillment in connection with spirit-anointed Christians, who make up a spiritual nation of 144,000. That nation is indeed "a special property," or "a people for special possession," to Jehovah. (1 Peter 2:9) Malachi's prophecy can also be encouraging to the "great crowd," who are "standing before the throne and before the Lamb, dressed in white robes." (Revelation 7:4, 9) These become one flock with the anointed, under one Shepherd, Jesus Christ.—John 10:16.

⁹ How does Jehovah view those who choose to serve him? As noted at Malachi 3:17, he views them in the way that a loving father views his son. And note the glowing terms in which he describes his people—"a special property." Other translations render that phrase "my very own," "my most prized possession," and "my jewels." Why would Jehovah view those who serve him as being that special? For one thing, he is an appreciative God. (Hebrews 6:10) He draws close to

God's Word contains an abundance of consoling thoughts

and views as special those who serve him from the heart.

¹⁰ Can you think of a valued personal possession that you view as special property? Do you not take steps to protect it? Jehovah does the same with his "special property." True, he does not shield his people from all of life's trials and tragedies. (Ecclesiastes 9:11) But Jehovah can and will protect his faithful servants spiritually. He gives them the strength they need to endure any trial. (1 Corinthians 10:13) Hence, Moses told God's ancient people, the Israelites: "Be courageous and strong. . . . Jehovah your God is the one marching with you. He will neither desert you nor leave you entirely." (Deuteronomy 31:6) Jehovah deals rewardingly with his people. To him, they are "a special property."

Jehovah "the Rewarder"

¹¹ Another evidence that Jehovah values his servants is that he rewards them. He told the Israelites: " 'Test me out, please, in this respect,' Jehovah of armies has said, 'whether I shall not open to you people the floodgates of the heavens and actually empty out upon you a blessing until there is no more want.' " (Malachi 3:10) Ultimately, of course, Jehovah will reward his servants with everlasting life. (John 5:24; Revelation 21:4) This priceless reward reveals the magnitude of Jehovah's love and generosity. It also shows that he truly values those who choose to

8. Why can Malachi 3:17 be applied in principle to the great crowd?
9. Why are Jehovah's people "a special property" to him?

10. How does Jehovah provide protection for his people?
11, 12. How can appreciating Jehovah in his role as our Rewarder help us fight feelings of doubt?

serve him. Learning to view Jehovah as a generous Rewarder can help us to battle any doubts about our standing with God. In fact, Jehovah urges us to view him as a Rewarder! Paul wrote: "He that approaches God must believe that he is and that he becomes the rewarder of those earnestly seeking him." —Hebrews 11:6.

¹² Of course, we serve Jehovah because we love him—not just because he promises to reward us. Still, keeping close in our heart the hope of a reward is not improper or selfish. (Colossians 3:23, 24) Out of his love for them and the high value he places upon them, Jehovah takes the initiative and rewards those earnestly seeking him.

¹³ The greatest indication of mankind's potential value in Jehovah's eyes is the provision of the ransom. The apostle John wrote: "God loved the world so much that he gave his only-begotten Son, in order that everyone exercising faith in him might not be destroyed but have everlasting life." (John 3:16) The provision of the ransom sacrifice of Jesus Christ runs counter to the very notion that we are worthless or unlovable in Jehovah's eyes. Indeed, if Jehovah paid so high a price for us—offering his only-begotten Son—he must surely love us deeply.

¹⁴ Hence, should negative feelings well up in you, meditate on the ransom. Yes, view this gift as a personal provision from Jehovah. That is what the apostle Paul did. Recall that he said: "Miserable man that I am!" But then he went on to say: "Thanks to God through Jesus Christ our Lord," who, said Paul, "loved *me* and handed himself over for *me*." (Romans 7:24, 25; Galatians 2:20) In saying this, Paul was not being egotistical. He simply had confidence that Jehovah val-

ued him as an individual. Like Paul, you too should learn to view the ransom as a personal gift from God. Jehovah is not only a powerful Savior but also a loving Rewarder.

Beware of Satan's 'Crafty Acts'

¹⁵ Still, you might find it hard to believe that the inspired consolations found in God's Word really apply to you. You may feel that the reward of living forever in God's new world is something that others can attain, but you are simply not worthy of it. If this is how you feel, what can you do?

¹⁶ You are no doubt familiar with Paul's admonition to the Ephesians: "Put on the complete suit of armor from God that you may be able to stand firm against the machinations ["crafty acts," footnote] of the Devil." (Ephesians 6:11) When we think of Satan's devices, such things as materialism and immorality might immediately come to mind and rightly so. These temptations have ensnared many of God's people both in ancient times and in our day. However, we should not overlook another crafty act of Satan—his effort to convince people that they are unloved by Jehovah God.

¹⁷ The Devil is skilled at exploiting such feelings in his attempt to turn people away from God. Recall Bildad's words to Job: "How can mortal man be in the right before God, or how can one born of a woman be clean? Look! There is even the moon, and it is not bright; and the stars themselves have not proved clean in his eyes. How much less so mortal man, who is a maggot, and a son of man, who is a worm!" (Job 25:4-6; John 8:44) Can you imagine how demoralizing those words must have been? So do not let Satan dishearten you. On the other hand, be

---

13. Why is the provision of the ransom the greatest evidence of Jehovah's love for us?
14. What shows how Paul viewed the ransom?

15-17. (a) How does the Devil exploit negative feelings? (b) What encouragement can we draw from the experience of Job?

aware of Satan's designs so that you will have the courage and stamina to fight all the harder to do what is right. (2 Corinthians 2: 11) As for Job, even though he had to be corrected, Jehovah rewarded his endurance by restoring to him in double measure all that he had lost.—Job 42:10.

Jehovah "Is Greater Than Our Hearts"

[18] Admittedly, it can be difficult to quell feelings of discouragement if these are deeply ingrained. Yet, Jehovah's spirit can help you progressively to overturn "strongly entrenched things . . . raised up against the knowledge of God." (2 Corinthians 10: 4, 5) When negative thoughts threaten to overwhelm you, ponder the apostle John's words: "By this we shall know that we originate with the truth, and we shall assure our hearts before him as regards whatever our hearts may condemn us in, because God is greater than our hearts and knows all things."—1 John 3:19, 20.

[19] What is meant by the phrase "God is greater than our hearts"? At times, our heart may condemn us, especially when we become painfully aware of our imperfections and shortcomings. Or it may be that because of our background, we have an inordinate tendency to think negatively of ourselves, as

18, 19. How is God "greater than our hearts," and in what way does he 'know all things'?

Do You Remember?

- How are we "a special property" to Jehovah?
- Why is it important to view Jehovah as the Rewarder?
- What 'crafty acts' of Satan must we be on guard against?
- In what way is God "greater than our hearts"?

if nothing we do could be acceptable to Jehovah. The apostle John's words assure us that Jehovah is greater than that! He sees past our mistakes and perceives our real potential. He also knows our motives and intentions. David wrote: "He himself well knows the formation of us, remembering that we are dust." (Psalm 103:14) Yes, Jehovah knows us better than we know ourselves!

"A Crown of Beauty" and "a Kingly Turban"

[20] Through the prophet Isaiah, Jehovah gave his ancient people the hope of the restoration. Exiled as they would be in Babylon, this comfort and reassurance was just what these despondent ones would need! Looking ahead to the time when they would be returned to their homeland, Jehovah stated: "You must become a crown of beauty in the hand of Jehovah, and a kingly turban in the palm of your God." (Isaiah 62:3) With these words, Jehovah clothed his people with dignity and splendor. He has done the same with his nation of spiritual Israel today. It is as though he held them up high for all to admire.

[21] While this prophecy finds its primary fulfillment in the anointed, it illustrates the dignity Jehovah bestows upon all who serve him. Hence, when beset by feelings of doubt, remember that even though imperfect, you can be as valuable as "a crown of beauty" and "a kingly turban" to Jehovah. So continue to make his heart rejoice by earnestly seeking to do his will. (Proverbs 27: 11) By doing so, you can be confident that Jehovah will reward your faithful endurance!

20. What does Isaiah's restoration prophecy reveal about how Jehovah views his servants?
21. How can you gain confidence that Jehovah will reward your faithful endurance?

Questions From Readers

Does the word "probably" at Zephaniah 2:3 mean that servants of God cannot be sure of receiving eternal life?

This scripture reads: "Seek Jehovah, all you meek ones of the earth, who have practiced His own judicial decision. Seek righteousness, seek meekness. Probably you may be concealed in the day of Jehovah's anger." Why does this verse say "probably"?

To understand how Jehovah will deal with his faithful ones at Armageddon, it is helpful to recall what the Bible teaches concerning what God will do for those who die before that time of judgment. Some will experience a resurrection to immortal life as spirit creatures in the heavens, while others will be res-urrected to the earth with the prospect of living forever in Paradise. (John 5:28, 29; 1 Corinthians 15:53, 54) If Jehovah remembers and rewards his loyal ones who die before Armageddon, he will surely deal similarly with his servants who are alive on the day of his anger.

The inspired words of the apostle Peter are also encouraging. He wrote: "[God] kept Noah, a preacher of righteousness, safe with seven others when he brought a deluge upon a world of ungodly people; and by reducing the cities Sodom and Gomorrah to ashes he condemned them, . . . and he delivered righteous Lot . . . Jehovah knows how to deliver people of godly devotion out of trial, but to reserve unrighteous people for the day of judgment to be cut off." (2 Peter 2:5-9) Though Jehovah brought destruction on the wicked in times past, he preserved alive both Noah and Lot, who served him faithfully. Jehovah will also deliver people of godly devotion when he brings destruction on the wicked at Armageddon. "A great crowd" of righteous ones will survive.—Revelation 7:9, 14.

"Jehovah knows how to deliver people of godly devotion out of trial"

It seems, then, that "probably" is not used at Zephaniah 2:3 because of any uncertainty about God's ability to preserve those who have his approval. Rather, a person's being concealed in the day of Jehovah's anger is only a probability when he begins to seek righteousness and meekness. Preservation will depend on an individual's *continuing* to seek meekness and righteousness. —Zephaniah 2:3.

A Long Journey Rewarded

FROM the Democratic Republic of Congo comes the report of two fleshly sisters who decided to make a long trip in a war-torn zone to attend the "Give God Glory" District Convention in Lisala. Apart from the spiritual instruction and Christian association that they hoped to enjoy at the convention, they looked forward to meeting representatives from the branch office of Jehovah's Witnesses in Kinshasa. Because of the civil war in the country, they had not seen anyone from the branch for years, and they wanted to take this opportunity to do so.

Traveling by pirogue, or dugout, the two sisters went from their native Basankusu to Lisala, a trip of some 200 miles through forest and along two rivers. It took them three weeks to make the trip. Since both of them are in the full-time ministry, having served 3 and 19 years respectively, they took advantage of their trip to spread the Kingdom good news. They spent some 110 hours preaching to those they met along the way, placing 200 tracts and 30 magazines.

Along the river, they had to navigate between the hippos and the crocodiles that are common to that region. They could not travel the river at night—no navigation after dark! They also passed through many military checkpoints.

Although this was a very long and tiring trip, the sisters were happy to make the effort. Both were full of appreciation and joy at being present for the convention in Lisala. Their hearts were burning with enthusiasm for the truth, and they were encouraged by the company of the 7,000 brothers and sisters present. After the convention, they met the same challenges on their trip home, where they found their families safe and sound.

AUGUST 15, 2005

THE WATCHTOWER

ANNOUNCING JEHOVAH'S KINGDOM

DEATH
CAN WE UNDERSTAND IT?

THE WATCHTOWER®
ANNOUNCING JEHOVAH'S KINGDOM

August 15, 2005   Average Printing Each Issue: 26,439,000   Vol. 126, No. 16

THE PURPOSE OF *THE WATCHTOWER* is to exalt Jehovah God as Sovereign Lord of the universe. It keeps watch on world events as these fulfill Bible prophecy. It comforts all peoples with the good news that God's Kingdom will soon destroy those who oppress their fellowmen and that it will turn the earth into a paradise. It encourages faith in God's now-reigning King, Jesus Christ, whose shed blood opens the way for mankind to gain eternal life. *The Watchtower*, published by Jehovah's Witnesses continuously since 1879, is nonpolitical. It adheres to the Bible as its authority.

IN THIS ISSUE

3   Death's Devastating Effect

4   "Death Is Swallowed Up Forever"

8   On the Sea of Galilee

9   The Royal Bible—A Milestone in Scholarship

14   Will You Reflect God's Glory?

19   Christians Reflect the Glory of Jehovah

24   A Law of Love in Hearts

30   "They Could Have Been Immediately Freed"

31   Questions From Readers

32   Interest in the Bible Appreciated

WATCHTOWER STUDIES

SEPTEMBER 12-18:
Will You Reflect God's Glory?
Page 14. Songs to be used: 63, 187.

SEPTEMBER 19-25:
Christians Reflect the Glory of Jehovah.
Page 19. Songs to be used: 96, 190.

SEPTEMBER 26–OCTOBER 2:
A Law of Love in Hearts.
Page 24. Songs to be used: 132, 40.

Publication of *The Watchtower* is part of a worldwide Bible educational work supported by voluntary donations.

Unless otherwise indicated, Scripture quotations are from the modern-language *New World Translation of the Holy Scriptures—With References*.

The Watchtower (ISSN 0043-1087) is published semimonthly by Watchtower Bible and Tract Society of New York, Inc.; M. H. Larson, President; G. F. Simonis, Secretary-Treasurer; 25 Columbia Heights, Brooklyn, NY 11201-2483. Periodicals Postage Paid at Brooklyn, NY, and at additional mailing offices. **POSTMASTER:** Send address changes to Watchtower, **Wallkill, NY 12589.**

Changes of address should reach us 30 days before your moving date. Give us your old and new address (if possible, your old address label).

Semimonthly   ENGLISH

Would you welcome more information or a free home Bible study? Please send your request to Jehovah's Witnesses, using the appropriate address below.

America, United States of: Wallkill, NY 12589. *Antigua:* Box 119, St. Johns. *Australia:* Box 280, Ingleburn, NSW 1890. *Bahamas:* Box N-1247, Nassau, N.P. *Barbados, W.I.:* Crusher Site Road, Prospect, St. James. *Britain:* The Ridgeway, London NW7 1RN. *Canada:* Box 4100, Halton Hills (Georgetown), Ontario L7G 4Y4. *Germany:* Niederselters, Am Steinfels, D-65618 Selters. *Ghana:* P. O. Box GP 760, Accra. *Guyana:* 352-360 Tyrell St., Republic Park Phase 2 EBD. *Hawaii 96819:* 2055 Kam IV Rd., Honolulu. *Hong Kong:* 4 Kent Road, Kowloon Tong. *India:* Post Box 6440, Yelahanka, Bangalore 560 064, KAR. *Ireland:* Newcastle, Greystones, Co. Wicklow. *Jamaica:* P. O. Box 103, Old Harbour, St. Catherine. *Japan:* 1271 Nakashinden, Ebina City, Kanagawa Pref., 243-0496. *Kenya:* P.O. Box 47788, GPO Nairobi 00100. *New Zealand:* P.O. Box 75-142, Manurewa. *Nigeria:* P.M.B. 1090, Benin City 300001, Edo State. *Philippines, Republic of:* P. O. Box 2044, 1060 Manila. *South Africa:* Private Bag X2067, Krugersdorp, 1740. *Trinidad and Tobago, Republic of:* Lower Rapsey Street & Laxmi Lane, Curepe. *Zambia:* Box 33459, Lusaka 10101. *Zimbabwe:* Private Bag WG-5001, Westgate.

NOW PUBLISHED IN 150 LANGUAGES. SEMIMONTHLY: Afrikaans, Albanian,* Amharic, Arabic, Bengali, Bicol, Bislama, Bulgarian, Cebuano,* Chichewa,* Chinese, Chinese (Simplified),* Cibemba,* Croatian,* Czech,*# Danish,*# Dutch,*# East Armenian, Efik,* English*#+◎ (also Braille), Estonian, Ewe, Fijian, Finnish,*# French,*# Ga, Georgian,* German,*# Greek,* Gujarati, Gun, Hebrew, Hiligaynon, Hindi, Hungarian,*# Igbo,* Iloko,* Indonesian, Italian,*# Japanese*# (also Braille), Kannada, Kinyarwanda, Kirundi, Korean*# (also Braille), Latvian, Lingala, Lithuanian, Luvale, Macedonian, Malagasy,* Malayalam, Maltese, Myanmar, Nepali, Norwegian,*# Pangasinan, Papiamento (Aruba), Papiamento (Curaçao), Polish,*# Portuguese*# (also Braille), Punjabi, Rarotongan, Romanian,* Russian,* Samar-Leyte, Samoan, Sango, Sepedi, Serbian, Sesotho, Shona,* Silozi, Sinhala, Slovak,* Slovenian, Solomon Islands Pidgin, Spanish*# (also Braille), Sranantongo, Swahili,* Swedish,*# Tagalog,* Tamil, Telugu, Thai, Tigrinya, Tok Pisin, Tongan, Tshiluba, Tsonga, Tswana, Turkish, Twi, Ukrainian,* Urdu, Vietnamese, Wallisian, Xhosa, Yoruba,* Zulu*

MONTHLY: American Sign Language,△□ Armenian, Assamese, Azerbaijani (roman script), Brazilian Sign Language,△ Cambodian, Chitonga, Gilbertese, Greenlandic, Haitian Creole, Hausa, Hiri Motu, Icelandic, Isoko, Kaonde, Kazakh, Kikongo, Kiluba, Kirghiz, Kosraean, Kwanyama/Ndonga, Luganda, Marathi, Marshallese, Mauritian Creole, Maya, Mizo, Monokutuba, Moore, Niuean, Ossetian, Otetela, Palauan, Persian, Ponapean, Seychelles Creole, Tahitian, Tatar, Tiv, Trukese, Tumbuka, Tuvaluan, Umbundu, Venda, Yapese, Zande

* Study articles also available in large-print edition.
\# Audiocassettes also available.
+ CD also available.
◎ MP3 CD-ROM also available.
△ Videocassette
□ DVD

Death's Devastating Effect

"SIX-YEAR-OLD COMMITS SUICIDE." This shocking headline referred to the tragic death of a little girl named Jackie. Her mother had recently died of a terminal illness. Before Jackie stepped in front of a train, she told her siblings that she wanted 'to become an angel and be with her mother.'

Ian was 18 when he pleaded with his priest to explain why Ian's father had died of cancer. The priest claimed that since Ian's father was a good man, God wanted him in heaven. After hearing that explanation, Ian concluded that he did not want to know such a cruel God. Since life appeared to be so meaningless, Ian decided to pursue a life of pleasure. To that end, he turned to alcohol, drugs, and immorality. His life was spinning out of control.

"The Living Are Conscious That They Will Die"

These two distressing incidents illustrate how death can devastate people's lives, especially if it strikes unexpectedly. Admittedly, all are aware of this fact stated in the Bible: "The living are conscious that they will die." (Ecclesiastes 9:5) But many prefer to ignore that harsh reality. What about you? Life makes so many demands on our time and attention that we may push to the back of our minds the seemingly distant prospect of death.

"Most people fear death and try to avoid thinking about it," notes *The World Book Encyclopedia*. Nevertheless, a serious accident or a life-threatening illness may suddenly force us to look death in the face. Or perhaps the funeral of a friend or a relative provides us with a harsh reminder of the outcome that awaits all mankind.

Still, at funerals mourners often say something like, "Life must go on." And indeed it does. In fact, life may seem to pass by so quickly that all too soon the problems of old age must be faced. At that point, death is no longer such a remote prospect. There are too many funerals to attend, the loss of too many lifelong friends to endure. For many of the elderly, the disturbing question, "When will it be me?" often dominates.

The Great Question Mark

Although nobody denies the certainty of death, what occurs after death can be like a great question mark. The many contradictory explanations may lead the skeptic to see the whole matter as a futile debate about the unknown. The pragmatist may conclude that since "you live only once," you should enjoy the good things of life as best you can.

In contrast, others refuse to believe that death is the end of everything. Nevertheless, they have no clear idea about what comes afterward. Some assume that life will continue in a place of eternal bliss, while others think that they will live again at some future time, perhaps as a different person.

Bereaved relatives invariably ask themselves, "Where are the dead?" Several years ago, members of a football club were en route to a sporting event when a truck suddenly plowed into their minibus, sending the bus cartwheeling off the road. Five members of the team died. Since the day her son was killed in that accident, the life of one mother has almost come to a halt. She grapples with the issue of where her son is.

She regularly visits his grave and talks to him out loud for hours. "I just can't believe that there is nothing after death," she laments, "but I am not sure."

Clearly, our attitude toward death can affect our lives now. In view of people's reactions to the tragedy of death, several questions arise. Consider how you would respond to them. Should we just forget about death and concentrate on living? Should we allow the menacing presence of death to spoil our life? Must a grieving relative be forever left to ponder the whereabouts of a dead loved one? Must death remain an enigma?

"Death Is Swallowed Up Forever"

IMAGINE reading a newspaper with the above headline instead of reading about a young girl who has taken her own life. Of course, no newspaper has ever been able to make such a statement. But the above words do appear in a book that is thousands of years old—the Bible.

In the Scriptures, death is clearly explained. Furthermore, the Bible not only reveals why we die but also explains the condition of the dead and offers hope for our deceased loved ones. Finally, it speaks of a momentous time when it will be possible to report: "Death is swallowed up forever." —1 Corinthians 15:54.

The Bible explains death in familiar rather than mysterious terms. For example, it re-

peatedly likens dying to 'falling asleep,' and it describes dead people as "sleeping in death." (Psalm 13:3; 1 Thessalonians 4:13; John 11:11-14) Death is also identified as an "enemy." (1 Corinthians 15:26) More important, the Bible enables us to understand why death is like a sleep, why death afflicts mankind, and how this enemy will finally be defeated.

Why Do We Die?

The first book of the Bible relates how God made the first man, Adam, and settled him into a paradise home. (Genesis 2:7, 15) When starting out in life, Adam received work assignments, along with one strict prohibition. Regarding a certain tree in the garden of Eden, God told him: "You must not eat from it, for in the day you eat from it you will positively die."* (Genesis 2:17) Hence, Adam understood that death was not inevitable. It was the direct result of violating a divine law.

Tragically, Adam and his wife, Eve, disobeyed. They chose to ignore the will of their Creator, and they reaped the consequences. "Dust you are and to dust you will return," God told them when he outlined the results of their sin. (Genesis 3:19) They became seriously defective—imperfect. Their imperfection, or sinfulness, would lead to their death.

This defect—sin—was also passed on to Adam and Eve's offspring, the entire human race. In a sense, it was like a hereditary disease. Not only did Adam lose the opportunity to live a life free from the scourge of death but he also transmitted imperfection to his offspring. The human family was taken hostage to sin. The Bible states: "That is why, just as through one man sin entered into the world and death through sin, and thus death spread to all men because they had all sinned."—Romans 5:12.

Adam and Eve's disobedience led to death

"Sin Entered Into the World"

This hereditary defect, or sin, cannot be seen under a microscope. "Sin" refers to a moral and spiritual deficiency that has been transmitted to us from our first parents, and it has physical consequences. However, the Bible reveals that God has provided a remedy. The apostle Paul ex-

---

* This is the first Bible reference to death.

plains: "The wages sin pays is death, but the gift God gives is everlasting life by Christ Jesus our Lord." (Romans 6:23) In his first letter to the Corinthians, Paul added an assurance that was very meaningful for him: "Just as in Adam all are dying, so also in the Christ all will be made alive."—1 Corinthians 15:22.

Clearly, Jesus Christ plays a key role in eliminating sin and death. He said that he came to earth "to give his soul a ransom in exchange for many." (Matthew 20:28) The situation is comparable to a kidnapping, in which release of the hostage can be obtained only by a specified payment. In this case, the ransom that can free us from sin and death is Jesus' perfect human life.* —Acts 10:39-43.

To provide the ransom, God sent Jesus to the earth to sacrifice his life. "God loved the world so much that he gave his only-begotten Son, in order that everyone exercising faith in him might . . . have everlasting life." (John 3:16) Before dying a sacrificial death, Christ 'bore witness to the truth.' (John 18:37) And during his public ministry, he took advantage of certain events to reveal the truth about death.

"The Little Girl . . . Is Sleeping"

Jesus was no stranger to death while he was on earth. He felt the grief of losing people around him, and he was fully aware that

---

* The ransom price was a perfect human life because that was what Adam had lost. Sin contaminated all humans, so no imperfect human could serve as a ransom. Thus, God sent his Son from heaven for that purpose. (Psalm 49:7-9) For more information on this subject, see chapter 7 of the book *Knowledge That Leads to Everlasting Life,* published by Jehovah's Witnesses.

Jesus took the dead girl's hand, and she got up

he himself would die prematurely. (Matthew 17:22, 23) Evidently some months before Jesus was executed, his close friend Lazarus died. That event provides us with an insight into Jesus' view of death.

Soon after receiving word of Lazarus' death, Jesus said: "Lazarus our friend has gone to rest, but I am journeying there to awaken him from sleep." The disciples assumed that if Lazarus was merely resting, he would get better. So Jesus said plainly: "Lazarus has died." (John 11:11-14) Obviously, Jesus understood death to be like sleep. While death may be difficult for us to comprehend, we do understand sleep. During a good night's rest, we are unaware of the passage of time and what is going on around us because we are in a state of temporary unconsciousness. This is exactly how the Bible explains the condition of the dead. Ecclesiastes 9:5 states: "As for the dead, they are conscious of nothing at all."

Jesus also compared death to a sleep because people can be awakened from death, thanks to the power of God. On one occasion, Jesus visited the home of a distraught family whose little girl had just expired. "The little girl did not die, but she is sleeping," Jesus said. Then he approached the dead girl and took hold of her hand, and she "got up." In other words, she rose from the dead.—Matthew 9:24, 25.

Jesus likewise raised his friend Lazarus from death. But before performing that miracle, he consoled Martha, Lazarus' sister, by saying: "Your brother will rise." She confidently replied: "I know he will rise in the resurrection on the last day." (John 11:23, 24) She evidently expected all of God's servants to be resurrected at some point in the future.

What exactly does a resurrection imply? The Greek word for "resurrection" (*a·na'sta-sis*) literally means "standing up." It denotes a rising from the dead. This may sound incredible to some, yet after saying that the dead would hear his voice, Jesus said: "Do not marvel at this." (John 5:28) The resurrections that Jesus himself performed on earth give us confidence in the Bible's promise that the dead in God's memory will awake from their long "sleep." Revelation 20:13 prophesies: "The sea gave up those dead in it, and death and Hades [mankind's common grave] gave up those dead in them."

Will these dead ones be resurrected back to life only to grow old and die again, somewhat like Lazarus? That is not God's purpose. The Bible assures us that the time will come when "death will be no more," so no one will be growing old and then dying. —Revelation 21:4.

Death is an enemy. The human race has many other common enemies, such as sickness and old age, which likewise cause much suffering. God promises to vanquish them all, finally passing sentence on mankind's greatest foe. "As the last enemy, death is to be brought to nothing."—1 Corinthians 15:26.

With that promise fulfilled, humans will enjoy perfect life, unmarred by sin and death. Meanwhile, we can take comfort in knowing that our dead loved ones are resting, and if they are in God's memory, they will be resurrected in his due time.

Understanding Death Helps Give Meaning to Life

A clear understanding of death and the hope for the dead can change our outlook on life. Ian, mentioned in the preceding article, was in his 20's when he learned about the Bible's explanation of death. "I always had a vague hope that my father was somewhere," he says. "So when I learned that he was just asleep in death, I felt dejected at first." Nevertheless, when Ian read of God's promise to resurrect the dead, he was overjoyed to know that he could see his father again. "For the first time in my life, I felt at peace," he recalls. A proper understanding of death brought him a peace of mind that calmed his spirit.

Clive and Brenda lost their 21-year-old son, Steven, in the fatal crash mentioned in the preceding article. Although they knew what the Bible says about death, they were still heartbroken by their sudden loss. After all, death is an enemy, and its sting is painful. Their Scriptural knowledge about the condition of the dead gradually cushioned their grief. Brenda says: "Our understanding of death has allowed us to pick up the pieces of our lives and move on. Mind you, not a day goes by when we don't think about the time when Steven will wake up from his deep sleep."

"Death, Where Is Your Sting?"

Clearly, comprehending the condition of the dead can help us have a balanced view of life. Death does not need to be an enigma. We can enjoy life without a morbid fear of this enemy hovering in the background. And realizing that death need not extinguish our lives forever eliminates any urge to live for pleasure, in the belief that "life is so short." Knowing that our deceased loved ones in God's memory are asleep in death and awaiting a resurrection can give us solace and kindle our desire to carry on with life.

Yes, we can confidently look to the future when Jehovah God, the Giver of life, will bury death forever. What a blessing it will be when we can rightly ask: "Death, where is your victory? Death, where is your sting?" —1 Corinthians 15:55.

Many await the time when their dead loved ones will awaken from sleep, as Lazarus did

On the Sea of Galilee

AN ACCOUNT recorded at Mark 4:35-41 reports that Jesus and his disciples boarded a boat to cross the Sea of Galilee. We read: "Now a great violent windstorm broke out, and the waves kept dashing into the boat, so that the boat was close to being swamped. But he [Jesus] was in the stern, sleeping upon [the] pillow."

This is the only place that the Greek word for "pillow" occurs in the Bible. Scholars therefore do not know the exact meaning of the word as used here. Most Bibles translate the word "pillow" or "cushion." Yet, what was the nature of it? Mark's use of the definite article, *the* pillow, suggests that it was part of the boat's equipment. A boat discovered near the Sea of Galilee in 1986 has brought to light a possible understanding of this Greek word as used by Mark.

Research reveals that the 26-foot-long boat was powered by sail and oars. It was used for fishing and had a stern deck to hold the large and heavy seine net. The remains of the boat are dated to between 100 B.C.E. and 70 C.E. and may represent the type of boat used by Jesus and his disciples. Shelley Wachsmann, involved in the excavation of the boat, authored the book *The Sea of Galilee Boat—An Extraordinary 2000 Year Old Discovery.* He suggests that the "pillow" Je-

sus slept on was a sandbag used for ballast. A veteran fisherman from Jaffa experienced in seine-net fishing said: "When I was young, the boats that I worked on in the Mediterranean always carried a sandbag or two. . . . The bags were kept on board for ballasting the boat. But when they were not in use, we stored them under the stern deck. Then, if someone was tired, he would crawl in beneath the stern deck, use the sandbag as a pillow, and go to sleep."

Many scholars believe that Mark's description meant that Jesus slept on a sack of ballast sand beneath the stern deck, the most protected part of the boat during a storm. Whatever the exact form of that pillow, the more significant point is what happened thereafter. With God's backing and power, Jesus calmed the storm-tossed sea. Even the disciples asked: "Who really is this, because even the wind and the sea obey him?"

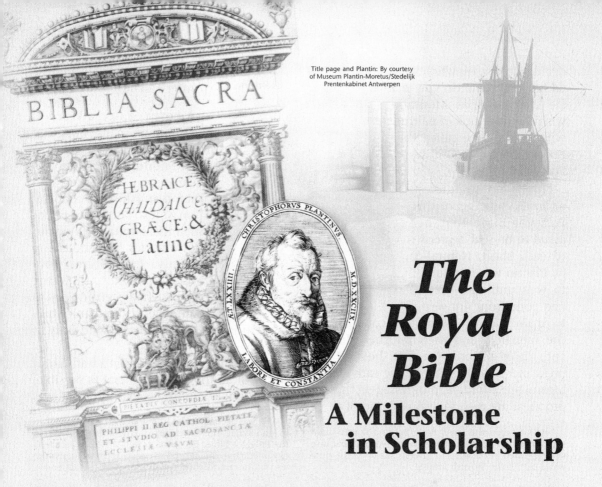

The Royal Bible

A Milestone in Scholarship

THE ship left Spain en route to the Italian peninsula in the early 16th century. Stored in its hold was a cargo of immense value—the bulk of the total production of the Complutensian Polyglot Bible printed between 1514 and 1517. Suddenly, a violent storm came up. The crew fought to save the ship, but their efforts proved futile. The ship sank with its priceless cargo.

That disaster led to the demand for a new edition of the Polyglot Bible. Finally, the master printer Christophe Plantin accepted the challenge. He needed a rich

Philip II, king of Spain

sponsor to finance this monumental work, so he asked Philip II, king of Spain, to be the official patron. Before making his decision, the king consulted various Spanish scholars, among others the renowned Bible scholar Benito Arias Montano. He told King Philip: "Apart from rendering a service to God and benefiting the universal church, it will also bring great glory to the royal name of Your Majesty and esteem to your personal reputation."

A revised edition of the Complutensian Polyglot would be a notable cultural achievement, so Philip

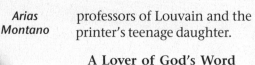

Arias Montano

decided to give his wholehearted support to Plantin's project. He charged Arias Montano with the huge task of editing what came to be called the Royal Bible, or the Antwerp Polyglot.*

Philip was so interested in the progress of this Polyglot Bible that he asked to be sent a proof of each sheet. Naturally, Plantin was reluctant to wait until the sheet had gone from Antwerp to Spain, had been read and corrected by the monarch, and then returned. In the end, Philip got only the first sheet off the press and possibly some of the early pages. Meanwhile, Montano progressed on the real proofreading with the valuable aid of three professors of Louvain and the printer's teenage daughter.

A Lover of God's Word

Arias Montano made himself at home among Antwerp's scholars. His broad-minded approach endeared him to Plantin, and their friendship and cooperation were to last for the rest of their life. Montano stood out not only for his scholarship but also for his great love for God's Word.* As a young man, he had been anxious to complete his academic studies in order to devote himself exclusively to the study of the Scriptures.

Arias Montano believed that a translation of the Bible should be as literal as possible. He sought to translate exactly what was

---

* It was called the Royal Bible because it was sponsored by King Philip, and the Antwerp Polyglot because it was printed in the city of Antwerp, which at the time was a part of the Spanish Empire.

* He was accomplished in Arabic, Greek, Hebrew, Latin, and Syriac, the five principal languages employed in the Polyglot Bible. He was also well-versed in archaeology, medicine, the natural sciences, and theology, studies that he put to good use in preparing the appendix.

Original printing presses in Antwerp, Belgium

Title page and Plantin: By courtesy of Museum Plantin-Moretus/Stedelijk Prentenkabinet Antwerpen

Left: Christophe Plantin and the title page of the Antwerp Polyglot

Above: Exodus chapter 15 in four columns of text

written in the original text, thus allowing the reader access to the true Word of God. Montano followed the motto of Erasmus, who urged scholars "to preach about Christ from the original." The sense of the original languages of the Scriptures had been hidden from the people for centuries because of the difficulty of understanding the Latin translations.

Composition of the Work

All the manuscripts that Alfonso de Zamora had prepared and revised for printing the Complutensian Polyglot came into the hands of Arias Montano, who used them for the Royal Bible.*

The Royal Bible was at first conceived as a second edition of the Complutensian Polyglot, but it became much more than a simple revision. The Hebrew text and the Greek

text of the *Septuagint* were taken from the Complutensian Bible; then new texts were added along with an extensive appendix. The new Polyglot finally had eight volumes. The printing took five years, from 1568 until 1572—a very short time in view of the complex nature of the work. Finally, 1,213 copies were printed.

Whereas the Complutensian Polyglot of 1517 proved to be a "monument to typographical art," the new Antwerp Polyglot surpassed its predecessor in technical merit and in content. It was another milestone in the history of printing and, more important, in the preparation of refined master texts of the Bible.

Attacks From Enemies of God's Word

Not surprisingly, enemies of faithful Bible translation soon appeared on the scene. Although the Antwerp Polyglot had papal approval and Arias Montano had a well-deserved reputation as an honorable

---

* For an explanation of the significance of the Complutensian Polyglot Bible, see *The Watchtower,* April 15, 2004.

scholar, he was denounced to the Inquisition. Opposers said that his work portrayed the new revised Latin text of Santes Pagninus as a more accurate translation of the Hebrew and Greek originals than the *Vulgate,* translated centuries earlier. They also accused Montano of consulting the original languages in his desire to produce an accurate translation of the Bible—a procedure they viewed as heretical.

The Inquisition even asserted that "the King had not gained much honor by having put his royal name to the work." They expressed regret that Montano had not given

THE POLYGLOT BIBLES

"A Polyglot Bible is one that contains the text in various languages," explains Spanish scholar Federico Pérez Castro. "Traditionally, however, the term refers to Bibles that have the Scriptural text in the original languages. In this restricted sense of the term, the number of polyglot Bibles is very small."

1. *The Complutensian Polyglot (1514-17)*, sponsored by Cardinal Cisneros, was printed in Alcalá de Henares, Spain. Its six volumes contained the Bible text in four languages: Hebrew, Greek, Aramaic, and Latin. It provided 16th-century translators with a master text of the Hebrew-Aramaic Scriptures.

2. *The Antwerp Polyglot (1568-72)*, edited by Benito Arias Montano, added to the Complutensian text the Syriac Peshitta version of the Christian Greek Scriptures and the Aramaic Targum of Jonathan. The Hebrew text, which contained vowel points and accent marks, was revised according to the received Hebrew text of Jacob ben Hayyim. It thus became a standard text of the Hebrew Scriptures for Bible translators.

3. *The Paris Polyglot (1629-45)* was sponsored by French lawyer Guy Michel le Jay. It was inspired by the Antwerp Polyglot, although it also contained some Samaritan and Arabic texts.

4. *The London Polyglot (1655-57)*, edited by Brian Walton, was also based on the Antwerp Polyglot. This Polyglot included ancient translations of the Bible into Ethiopian and Persian, although these versions did not significantly add clarity to the Bible text.

sufficient authority to the official *Vulgate.* Despite these accusations, they could not find sufficient proof to condemn either Montano or his Polyglot Bible. In the end, the Royal Bible was well received, and it became a standard work in various universities.

A Useful Tool for Bible Translation

Though the Antwerp Polyglot was not a work conceived for the public at large, it soon became a useful tool for Bible translators. Like its predecessor, the Complutensian Polyglot, it contributed to the refining of the texts that were available of the Scriptures. It also helped translators to improve their understanding of the original languages. Translations of the Bible into several major European languages benefited from this work. For example, *The Cambridge History of the Bible* reports that translators of the famous *King James Version,* or *Authorized Version,* of 1611 used the Antwerp Polyglot as a valuable aid for translating the ancient languages. The Royal Bible also exercised a considerable influence on two important Polyglot Bibles published in the 17th century.—See the box "The Polyglot Bibles."

One of the many merits of the Antwerp Polyglot was the fact that it made available to European scholars the Syriac version of the Greek Scriptures for the first time. That Syriac text was set alongside a literal Latin translation. This was a very useful addition, since the Syriac was one of the oldest translations of the Christian Greek Scriptures. Dating from the fifth century C.E., the Syriac version was based on manuscripts dating back to the second century C.E. According to *The International Standard Bible Encyclopedia,* "the value of the [Syriac] Peshitta for textual criticism is generally acknowledged.

"As for the word of our God, it will last to time indefinite"

Biblioteca Histórica. Universidad Complutense de Madrid

It is one of the oldest and most important witnesses to the ancient traditions."

Neither the raging sea nor the attacks of the Spanish Inquisition prevented an improved and amplified version of the Complutensian Polyglot from resurfacing in 1572 in the form of the Royal Bible. The history of the Polyglot Bible of Antwerp is another example of the efforts sincere men have made to defend the Word of God.

Whether they knew it or not, by their selfless labor, these dedicated men reflected the truth of the prophetic words of Isaiah. Almost three thousand years ago, he wrote: "The green grass has dried up, the blossom has withered; but as for the word of our God, it will last to time indefinite."—Isaiah 40:8.

IN OUR NEXT ISSUE

Does It Pay to Be Loyal?

———

Mennonites Search for Bible Truth

———

Let Jehovah's "Saying" Safeguard You

WILL YOU REFLECT GOD'S GLORY?

"We . . . reflect like mirrors the glory of Jehovah."—2 CORINTHIANS 3:18.

IT WAS one of the most awe-inspiring visions any man had ever experienced. Alone, high up on Mount Sinai, Moses was granted an unusual request. He was allowed to see what no human had ever seen—the glory of Jehovah. Of course, Moses did not see Jehovah directly. So splendid is the appearance of God that no man may behold him and yet live. Instead, Jehovah put his "palm" over Moses as a protective screen until He had passed by, evidently using an angelic representative. Then Jehovah allowed Moses to see the afterglow of this divine manifestation of glory. Jehovah also spoke with Moses through an angel. The Bible describes what happened afterward: "Now it came about when Moses came down from Mount Sinai . . . that the skin of his face emitted rays because of his having spoken with [Jehovah]."—Exodus 33:18–34:7, 29.

² Imagine yourself on that mountain with Moses. How thrilling it would be to behold the dazzling splendor of the Almighty and to listen to his words! What a privilege it would be to walk down Mount Sinai alongside Moses, the mediator of the Law covenant! Did you know, though, that in some ways true Christians reflect God's glory in a way that surpasses even the way Moses reflected it? That thought-provoking fact is found in a letter written by the apostle Paul. He wrote that anointed Christians "reflect like mirrors the glory of Jehovah." (2 Corinthians 3:7, 8, 18)

In a sense, Christians with an earthly hope also reflect God's glory.

How Christians Reflect God's Glory

³ How could we possibly reflect God's glory? We have not beheld or heard Jehovah in the way that Moses did. We have, however, come to know Jehovah in ways that Moses could not. Jesus did not appear as the Messiah until nearly 1,500 years after Moses died. Consequently, Moses could not have known how the Law would be fulfilled in Jesus, who died to redeem humans from the terrible oppression of sin and death. (Romans 5:20, 21; Galatians 3:19) Moreover, Moses could perceive only in a limited way the magnificence of Jehovah's purpose, centered on the Messianic Kingdom and the earthly Paradise it will bring. We thus perceive Jehovah's glory, not with our literal eyes, but with eyes of faith based on Bible teachings. Furthermore, we have heard Jehovah's voice, not by means of an angel, but through the Bible, particularly the Gospels, which so beautifully describe the teachings and the ministry of Jesus.

⁴ Though Christians do not reflect God's glory by means of rays that beam from their faces, their faces fairly beam as they tell others about Jehovah's glorious personality and purposes. Concerning our day, the prophet Isaiah foretold that God's people would "for certain tell about [Jehovah's] glory among

---

1. What did Moses behold, and what happened afterward?
2. What did the apostle Paul write about the glory that Christians reflect?

3. How have we come to know Jehovah in ways that Moses could not?
4. (a) How do anointed Christians reflect God's glory? (b) In what ways can those who have the earthly hope reflect God's glory?

Moses' face reflected glory

the nations." (Isaiah 66:19) Furthermore, at 2 Corinthians 4:1, 2, we read: "Since we have this ministry . . . , we have renounced the underhanded things of which to be ashamed, not walking with cunning, neither adulterating the word of God, but by making the truth manifest recommending ourselves to every human conscience in the sight of God." Paul was referring in particular to anointed Christians, who are "ministers of a new covenant." (2 Corinthians 3:6) But their ministry has had an effect on countless numbers who have gained the hope of everlasting life on earth. The ministry of both groups involves reflecting the glory of Jehovah not only in what they teach but also in how they live. It is our responsibility and our privilege to mirror the glory of the Most High God!

⁵ Today, the glorious good news of God's Kingdom is being preached in all the inhabited earth, as Jesus foretold. (Matthew 24:14) Individuals of all nations, tribes, peoples, and tongues have enthusiastically responded to the good news and have transformed their

---

5. Of what does our spiritual prosperity give evidence?

lives in order to do the will of God. (Romans 12:2; Revelation 7:9) Like the early Christians, they cannot stop speaking about the things they have seen and heard. (Acts 4:20) Over six million people, more than at any other time in human history, are reflecting God's glory today. Are you among them? The spiritual prosperity of God's people gives convincing evidence of Jehovah's blessing and protection. That Jehovah's spirit is upon us is all the more evident in view of the powerful forces arrayed against us. Let us now see why that is so.

God's People Will Not Be Silenced

⁶ Suppose you were called to testify in court against a ruthless criminal. You know that the criminal has a powerful organization and will use every means to prevent you from exposing him. For you to bear witness against such a criminal would require courage as well as confidence that the authorities would protect you from him. We are in a similar situation. In bearing witness to Jehovah and his purposes, we testify against Satan the Devil, exposing him as a manslayer and a liar who is misleading the entire inhabited earth. (John 8:44; Revelation 12:9) To take your stand for Jehovah and against the Devil requires both faith and courage.

⁷ Jehovah is, of course, the Supreme One. His power is infinitely superior to that of Satan. We may be sure that Jehovah is not only able but also eager to protect us as we serve him loyally. (2 Chronicles 16:9) Nevertheless, Satan is ruler of both the demons and the world of mankind alienated from God. (Matthew 12:24, 26; John 14:30) Confined to the vicinity of the earth and filled with "great anger," Satan bitterly opposes Jehovah's servants and uses the world under

---

6. Why are faith and courage required in order to take a stand for Jehovah?
7. How influential is Satan, and what does he try to do?

his control to try to shut the mouths of all who preach the good news. (Revelation 12: 7-9, 12, 17) How does he do this? In at least three ways.

[8] One way in which Satan tries to distract us is through the cares of life. People in these last days are lovers of money, lovers of themselves, and lovers of pleasures. They are not lovers of God. (2 Timothy 3:1-4) Preoccupied with the everyday affairs of life, most people 'take no note' of the good news we bring to them. They are simply not interested in learning Bible truth. (Matthew 24:37-39) Such an attitude can be contagious, lulling us into a state of spiritual lethargy. If we allow ourselves to cultivate love for material things and the pleasures of life, our love of God will grow cold.—Matthew 24:12.

[9] For this reason, Christians carefully choose those with whom they associate. "He that is walking with wise persons will become wise," wrote King Solomon, "but he that is having dealings with the stupid ones will fare badly." (Proverbs 13:20) May we 'walk' with those who reflect God's glory. How pleasant it is to do so! As we gather together with our spiritual brothers and sisters at our meetings and at other times, we find encouragement in their love, their faith, their joy, and their wisdom. Such wholesome association strengthens our determination to persevere in our ministry.

[10] A second way that Satan tries to stop all Christians from reflecting God's glory is by ridicule. This tactic should come as no surprise. During his ministry on earth, Jesus Christ was ridiculed—laughed at, sneered at, made fun of, treated insolently, and even spit upon. (Mark 5:40; Luke 16:14; 18:32) Early Christians were also objects of mockery. (Acts 2:13; 17:32) Modern-day servants of Jehovah

We reflect the glory of God in our ministry

face similar abuse. According to the apostle Peter, they would, in effect, be labeled "false prophets." "In the last days," foretold Peter, "there will come ridiculers with their ridicule, proceeding according to their own desires and saying: 'Where is this promised presence of his? Why, . . . all things are continuing exactly as from creation's beginning.'" (2 Peter 3:3, 4) God's people are ridiculed as being out of touch with reality. The Bible's moral standards are viewed as oldfashioned. To many, the message that we preach is foolishness. (1 Corinthians 1:18, 19) As Christians, we may face ridicule at school, at work, and at times even in the family circle. Undeterred, we continue to reflect God's glory through our preaching, knowing as did Jesus that God's Word is truth.—John 17:17.

[11] A third tactic that the Devil uses in an attempt to silence us is opposition or persecu-

8, 9. How does Satan use misguided love, and why should we choose our associates carefully?
10. In what ways has Satan used ridicule against those who reflect God's glory?

11. How has Satan used persecution to try to silence Christians?

tion. Jesus said to his followers: "People will deliver you up to tribulation and will kill you, and you will be objects of hatred by all the nations on account of my name." (Matthew 24:9) Indeed, as Jehovah's Witnesses, we have faced vicious persecution in many parts of the earth. We are aware that Jehovah long ago foretold that hatred, or enmity, would develop between those who serve God and those who serve Satan the Devil. (Genesis 3:15) We also know that by maintaining integrity under trial, we testify to the rightfulness of Jehovah's universal sovereignty. Knowing this can make us strong even under the most extreme circumstances. No persecution will ever permanently silence us if we remain determined to reflect the glory of God.

¹² Do you resist the allure of the world and prove faithful despite ridicule and opposition? Then you have reason to rejoice. Jesus assured those who would follow him: "Happy are you when people reproach you and persecute you and lyingly say every sort of wicked thing against you for my sake. Rejoice

---

12. Why should we rejoice as we remain faithful in the face of Satan's opposition?

and leap for joy, since your reward is great in the heavens; for in that way they persecuted the prophets prior to you." (Matthew 5:11, 12) Your endurance gives evidence that Jehovah's powerful holy spirit is upon you, empowering you to reflect his glory.—2 Corinthians 12:9.

Endurance Comes From Jehovah

¹³ A key reason why we endure in the ministry is that we love Jehovah and delight to reflect his glory. Humans tend to imitate those whom they love and respect, and no one is more worthy of imitation than Jehovah God. Because of his own great love, he sent his Son to the earth to bear witness to the truth and to redeem obedient mankind. (John 3:16; 18:37) Like God, we desire that people of all sorts attain to repentance and salvation; that is why we preach to them. (2 Peter 3:9) This desire, along with our determination to imitate God, moves us to persevere in reflecting his glory through our ministry.

¹⁴ Ultimately, though, our strength to endure in the Christian ministry comes from Jehovah. He sustains and fortifies us by means of his spirit, his organization, and his Word, the Bible. Jehovah "supplies endurance" to those who are willing to reflect his glory. He

---

13. What is a key reason why we endure in our Christian ministry?
14. How does Jehovah strengthen us to endure in our ministry?

answers our prayers and gives us the wisdom to deal with trials. (Romans 15:5; James 1:5) What is more, Jehovah does not allow us to be subjected to any trial that is impossible to bear. If we trust in Jehovah, he will make the way out so that we can continue to reflect his glory.—1 Corinthians 10:13.

¹⁵ Endurance in our ministry gives evidence that God's spirit is upon us. To illustrate: Suppose someone asked you to distribute a certain type of bread from door to door, free of charge. You are instructed to do this at your own expense and on your own time. Further, you soon learn that only a very few people actually want your bread; some will even oppose your efforts to distribute it. Do you think you would continue working at that task month after month, year after year? Probably not. Yet, you may have exerted yourself in declaring the good news on your own time and at your own expense for years, even decades. Why? Is it not because you love Jehovah and through his spirit he has blessed your efforts by helping you to endure? By all means!

A Work to Be Remembered

¹⁶ The ministry of the new covenant is a gift beyond compare. (2 Corinthians 4:7) Similarly, the Christian ministry carried on by the other sheep around the globe is a trea-

---

15. What helps us to endure?
16. Endurance in our ministry means what for us and for those who listen to us?

Can You Explain?

- How do Christians reflect the glory of God?
- What are some tactics that Satan uses in his attempt to silence God's people?
- What evidence is there that God's spirit is upon us?

---

sure. As you continue to endure in your ministry, you can, as Paul wrote to Timothy, "save both yourself and those who listen to you." (1 Timothy 4:16) Think of what that means. The good news that you preach offers to others the opportunity to live forever. You can forge a strong bond of friendship with those whom you help spiritually. Imagine what a joy it will be to live eternally in Paradise with those whom you have helped to learn about God! Surely they will never forget your efforts to help them. What a cause for satisfaction!

¹⁷ You live in a unique period in human history. Never again will the good news be preached amid a world alienated from God. Noah lived in such a world, and he saw it pass away. How he must have rejoiced to know that he faithfully carried out God's will in building an ark, which led to the preservation of him and his family! (Hebrews 11:7) You too can have such joy. Think of how you will feel in the new world as you look back on your activity during these last days, knowing that you did what you could to promote Kingdom interests.

¹⁸ Let us keep on, then, reflecting God's glory. Our doing so will be something that we will remember forever. Jehovah remembers our works too. The Bible provides this encouragement: "God is not unrighteous so as to forget your work and the love you showed for his name, in that you have ministered to the holy ones and continue ministering. But we desire each one of you to show the same industriousness so as to have the full assurance of the hope down to the end, in order that you may not become sluggish, but be imitators of those who through faith and patience inherit the promises." —Hebrews 6:10-12.

---

17. Why is ours a unique period in human history?
18. What assurance and encouragement does Jehovah give his servants?

CHRISTIANS REFLECT THE GLORY OF JEHOVAH

"Happy are your eyes because they behold, and your ears because they hear."
—MATTHEW 13:16.

THE Israelites gathered at Mount Sinai had every reason to draw close to Jehovah. After all, he had delivered them from Egypt with a mighty hand. He cared for their needs, providing food and water in the wilderness. Next, he gave them victory over an attacking Amalekite army. (Exodus 14:26-31; 16:2–17:13) As they camped in the wilderness before Mount Sinai, the people were so frightened by thunders and lightnings that they trembled. Later, they saw Moses descend from Mount Sinai, his face reflecting the glory of Jehovah. Yet, instead of responding with wonderment and appreciation, they withdrew. "They grew afraid of

1. What question comes to mind concerning the Israelites' reaction to Moses at Mount Sinai?

coming near to [Moses]." (Exodus 19:10-19; 34:30) Why were they fearful of beholding a reflection of the glory of Jehovah, the one who had done so much for them?

² Likely, much of the Israelites' fear on this occasion had to do with what had happened earlier. When they deliberately disobeyed Jehovah by making a golden calf, he disciplined them. (Exodus 32:4, 35) Did

2. Why might the Israelites have been fearful at seeing the glory of God that Moses reflected?

The Israelites could not gaze at Moses' face

they learn from Jehovah's discipline and appreciate it? No, most did not. Toward the end of his life, Moses recalled the incident of the golden calf along with other instances of Israelite disobedience. He said to the people: "You behaved rebelliously against the order of Jehovah your God, and you did not exercise faith toward him and did not listen to his voice. You have proved yourselves rebellious in behavior with Jehovah from the day of my knowing you."—Deuteronomy 9:15-24.

³ Consider how Moses reacted to the fear shown by the Israelites. The account reads: "When Moses would finish speaking with them, he would put a veil over his face. But when Moses would go in [to the tabernacle] before Jehovah to speak with him, he would take away the veil until his going out. And he went out and spoke to the sons of Israel what he would be commanded. And the sons of Israel saw Moses' face, that the skin of Moses' face emitted rays; and Moses put the veil back over his face until he went in to speak with [Jehovah]." (Exodus 34:33-35) Why did Moses veil his face at times? What can we learn from this? The answers to these questions can help us to evaluate our own relationship with Jehovah.

Missed Opportunities

⁴ The apostle Paul explained that Moses' wearing of the veil had to do with the minds and the heart condition of the Israelites themselves. Paul wrote: "The sons of Israel could not gaze intently at the face of Moses because of the glory of his face . . . Their mental powers were dulled." (2 Corinthians 3:7, 14) What a sad situation! The

Israelites were Jehovah's chosen people, and he wanted them to draw close to him. (Exodus 19:4-6) Yet, they were reluctant to gaze intently on the reflection of God's glory. Instead of turning their hearts and minds toward Jehovah in loving devotion, they in a sense turned away from him.

⁵ In this, we find a parallel in the first century C.E. By the time of Paul's conversion to Christianity, the Law covenant had been replaced by the new covenant, mediated by Jesus Christ, the Greater Moses. In both word and deed, Jesus perfectly reflected the glory of Jehovah. Paul wrote concerning the resurrected Jesus: "He is the reflection of [God's] glory and the exact representation of his very being." (Hebrews 1:3) What a magnificent opportunity the Jews had! They could listen to the sayings of everlasting life from the Son of God himself! Sadly, most of those to whom Jesus preached did not listen. Concerning them, Jesus quoted Jehovah's prophecy through Isaiah: "The heart of this people has grown unreceptive, and with their ears they have heard without response, and they have shut their eyes; that they might never see with their eyes and hear with their ears and get the sense of it with their hearts and turn back, and I heal them."—Matthew 13:15; Isaiah 6:9, 10.

⁶ There was a sharp contrast between the Jews and Jesus' disciples, of whom Jesus said: "Happy are your eyes because they behold, and your ears because they hear." (Matthew 13:16) True Christians yearn to know and serve Jehovah. They delight to carry out his will, as it is revealed in the

---

3. What did Moses do as to veiling his face?
4. What meaning did the apostle Paul reveal about Moses' wearing of the veil?

5, 6. (a) What first-century parallel was there to the Israelites of Moses' day? (b) What contrast was there between those who listened to Jesus and those who did not?

pages of the Bible. In turn, anointed Christians reflect Jehovah's glory in their ministry of the new covenant, and those of the other sheep do similarly.—2 Corinthians 3: 6, 18.

Why the Good News Is Veiled

7 As we have seen, both in Jesus' day and in Moses' day, most Israelites rejected the unique opportunity open to them. It is similar in our time. Most people reject the good news that we preach. This does not surprise us. Paul wrote: "If, now, the good news we declare is in fact veiled, it is veiled among those who are perishing, among whom the god of this system of things has blinded the minds of the unbelievers." (2 Corinthians 4:3, 4) In addition to Satan's efforts to conceal the good news, many people veil their own faces because they do not want to see.

8 The figurative eyes of many are blinded by ignorance. The Bible speaks of the nations as being "in darkness mentally, and alienated from the life that belongs to God, because of the ignorance that is in them." (Ephesians 4:18) Before he became a Christian, Paul, a man versed in the Law, was so blinded by ignorance that he persecuted the congregation of God. (1 Corinthians 15:9) Yet, Jehovah revealed the truth to him. Explains Paul: "The reason why I was shown mercy was that by means of me as the foremost case Christ Jesus might demonstrate all his long-suffering for a sample of those who are going to rest their faith on him for everlasting life." (1 Timothy 1:16) Like Paul, many who once opposed God's

truth are now serving Him. This is a good reason for continuing to bear witness even to those who oppose us. Meanwhile, by regularly studying God's Word and getting the sense of it, we are protected from acting in ignorance in a way that brings Jehovah's displeasure.

9 For many, spiritual vision is obstructed because they are unteachable and rigid in their views. Many Jews rejected Jesus and his teachings because they doggedly clung

Like Paul, many who once opposed God's truth are now serving Him

to the Mosaic Law. There were, of course, exceptions. For example, after Jesus was resurrected, "a great crowd of priests began to be obedient to the faith." (Acts 6:7) Nevertheless, concerning the majority of the Jews, Paul wrote: "Down till today whenever Moses is read, a veil lies upon their hearts." (2 Corinthians 3:15) Paul

___

7. Why is it not surprising that most reject the good news?

8. In what way are many blinded by ignorance, and how can we avoid being similarly affected?

9, 10. (a) How did first-century Jews show themselves unteachable and rigid in their views? (b) Is there a parallel in Christendom today? Explain.

likely knew what Jesus had previously said to the Jewish religious leaders: "You are searching the Scriptures, because you think that by means of them you will have everlasting life; and these are the very ones that bear witness about me." (John 5:39) The Scriptures they so carefully searched should have helped them discern that Jesus was the Messiah. However, the Jews had their own ideas, and not even the miracle-working Son of God could persuade them otherwise.

10 The same is true of many in Christendom today. Like the first-century Jews, "they have a zeal for God; but not according to accurate knowledge." (Romans 10:2) Though some study the Bible, they do not want to believe what it says. They refuse to accept that Jehovah teaches his people through his faithful and discreet slave class of anointed Christians. (Matthew 24:45) We, though, understand that Jehovah is teaching his people and that the understanding of divine truth has always been progressive. (Proverbs 4:18) By allowing ourselves to be taught by Jehovah, we are blessed with the knowledge of his will and purpose.

11 Others are blinded by wishful thinking. It was foretold that some would ridicule God's people and the message they proclaim concerning Jesus' presence. The apostle Peter wrote: "According to their wish, this fact escapes their notice," namely that God brought a deluge upon the world of Noah's time. (2 Peter 3:3-6) Similarly, many professed Christians readily acknowledge that Jehovah displays mercy, kindness, and forgiveness; yet they ignore or reject the fact that he does not give exemption from punishment. (Exodus 34: 6, 7) True Christians take care to understand what the Bible really teaches.

12 Many churchgoers are blinded by tradition. To religious leaders in his day, Jesus said: "You have made the word of God invalid because of your tradition." (Matthew 15:6) The Jews zealously restored pure worship after returning from exile in Babylon, yet the priests themselves became proud and self-righteous. Religious festivals became formalistic, devoid of genuine reverence for God. (Malachi 1:6-8) By Jesus' time, the scribes and the Pharisees had added countless traditions to the Mosaic Law. Jesus exposed those men as hypocrites because they had lost sight of the righteous principles on which the Law was based. (Matthew 23:23, 24) True Christians must take care not to allow man-made religious traditions to sidetrack them from pure worship.

"Seeing the One Who Is Invisible"

13 Moses asked to see God's glory in the mountain, and he did see the afterglow of Jehovah's glory. When he went into the tabernacle, he did not wear a veil. Moses was a man of deep faith who desired to do God's will. Though he was blessed with

---

11. What role has wishful thinking played in hiding the truth?

12. How have people been blinded by tradition?
13. In what two ways did Moses behold some of God's glory?

Do You Remember?

- Why were the Israelites afraid to behold the glory of God that Moses reflected?

- In what ways was the good news "veiled" in the first century? in our day?

- How do we reflect God's glory?

Jehovah's servants delight to reflect God's glory

seeing some of Jehovah's glory in vision, in a sense he had already beheld God with eyes of faith. The Bible says that Moses "continued steadfast as seeing the One who is invisible." (Hebrews 11:27; Exodus 34:5-7) And he reflected God's glory not merely by those rays that emanated from his face for a time but also through his efforts to assist the Israelites to come to know and serve Jehovah.

¹⁴ In heaven, Jesus directly beheld the glory of God for untold ages, even since before the universe was created. (Proverbs 8: 22, 30) During all that time, a deeply loving and affectionate relationship developed. Jehovah God expressed the most tender love and affection for this firstborn of all creation. Jesus reciprocated in expressing his deep love and affection for his divine Life-Giver. (John 14:31; 17:24) Theirs was a perfect love between Father and Son. Jesus, like Moses, delighted in reflecting Jehovah's glory in the things he taught.

_____

14. How did Jesus behold God's glory, and in what did he delight?

¹⁵ Like Moses and Jesus, God's present-day Witnesses on earth are eager to contemplate Jehovah's glory. They have not turned away from the glorious good news. The apostle Paul wrote: "When there is a turning to Jehovah [to do his will], the veil is taken away." (2 Corinthians 3:16) We study the Scriptures because we want to do God's will. We admire the glory reflected in the face of Jehovah's Son and anointed King, Jesus Christ, and we imitate his example. Like Moses and like Jesus, we have been blessed with a ministry, teaching others about the glorious God whom we worship.

¹⁶ Jesus prayed: "I publicly praise you, Father, . . . because you have hidden these things from the wise and intellectual ones and have revealed them to babes." (Matthew 11:25) Jehovah gives an understanding of his purposes and personality to those who are sincere and humble in heart. (1 Corinthians 1:26-28) We have come

_____

15. In what way do Christians contemplate God's glory?
16. Why are we blessed to know the truth?

under his protective care, and he teaches us to benefit ourselves—to get the most out of life. May we take advantage of every opportunity to draw close to Jehovah, appreciating his many provisions to come to know him more intimately.

[17] Paul wrote to anointed Christians: "We with unveiled faces reflect like mirrors the glory of Jehovah [and] are transformed

---

17. How do we come to know Jehovah's qualities more fully?

into the same image from glory to glory." (2 Corinthians 3:18) Whether our hope is heavenly or earthly, the more we come to know Jehovah—his qualities and personality as revealed in the Bible—the more we become like him. If we appreciatively contemplate the life, the ministry, and the teachings of Jesus Christ, we will reflect Jehovah's qualities more fully. What a joy to know that we bring praise to our God, whose glory we seek to reflect!

A LAW OF LOVE IN HEARTS

"I will put my law within them, and in their heart I shall write it."—JEREMIAH 31:33.

IN THE preceding two articles, we learned that when Moses came down from Mount Sinai, his face emanated rays that reflected Jehovah's glory. We also discussed the veil Moses wore. Let us now consider a related matter that has meaning for Christians today.

[2] When Moses was up on the mountain, he received instructions from Jehovah. Assembled before Mount Sinai, the Israelites witnessed a stunning manifestation of God himself. "Thunders and lightnings began occurring, and a heavy cloud upon the mountain and a very loud sound of a horn, so that all the people who were in the camp began to tremble. . . . And Mount Sinai smoked all over, due to the fact that Jehovah came down upon it in fire; and its smoke kept ascending like the

---

1, 2. (a) What will we now consider? (b) How did Jehovah manifest himself at Mount Sinai?

smoke of a kiln, and the whole mountain was trembling very much."—Exodus 19:16-18.

[3] Jehovah spoke to the people through an angel, providing what has come to be known as the Ten Commandments. (Exodus 20:1-17) Hence, there could be no doubt that these laws were from the Almighty. Jehovah wrote those commandments upon stone tablets—tablets that Moses shattered when he saw the Israelites worshipping a golden calf. Jehovah again wrote the commandments upon stone. This time, when Moses came down carrying the tablets, his face emitted rays. By then, all would understand that those laws had enormous significance.—Exodus 32:15-19; 34:1, 4, 29, 30.

---

3. By what means did Jehovah give the Ten Commandments to Israel, and what did that nation come to understand?

⁴ The two tablets on which the Ten Commandments were written were placed inside the ark of the covenant within the Most Holy compartment of the tabernacle and later the temple. The laws they bore set out the core principles of the Mosaic Law covenant and formed the basis for the theocratic administration of a national government. They gave evidence that Jehovah was dealing with a specific people, a chosen people.

The Israelites had laws written on tablets of stone

⁵ Those laws revealed much about Jehovah, particularly his love for his people. What a precious gift they proved to be to those who obeyed them! One scholar wrote: "No moral system ever humanly formulated before or since . . . can approach, much less equal, or excel, these ten words of God." Concerning the Mosaic Law as a whole, Jehovah said: "If you will strictly obey my voice and will indeed keep my covenant, then you will certainly become my special property out of all other peoples, because the whole earth belongs to me. And you yourselves will become to me a kingdom of priests and a holy nation."—Exodus 19:5, 6.

A Law Written in the Heart

⁶ Yes, those divine laws had great value. Did you know, though, that anointed Christians possess something far more valuable than laws written on stone? Jehovah foretold the making of a new covenant unlike the Law covenant made with the nation of Israel. "I will put my law within them, and in their heart I shall write it." (Jeremiah 31:31-34) Jesus, the Mediator of the new covenant, did not personally impart a written code of law to his followers. He sounded down Jehovah's law into the minds and hearts of his disciples by the things he said and did.

⁷ This law is called "the law of the Christ." It was first given, not to the nation of natural Israel, who were the descendants of Jacob, but to a spiritual nation, "the Israel of God." (Galatians 6:2, 16; Romans 2:28, 29) The Israel of God is made up of spirit-anointed Christians. In time, they were joined by "a great crowd" from all nations who also seek to worship Jehovah. (Revelation 7:9, 10; Zechariah 8:23) As "one flock" under "one shepherd," both groups embrace "the law of the Christ," allowing it to govern all that they do.—John 10:16.

---

4. Why were the Ten Commandments of great importance?
5. In what ways did God's laws to Israel reflect his love?

6. What law has proved to be of more value than laws written on stone?
7. To whom was "the law of the Christ" first given, and who later embraced it?

⁸ Unlike the natural Israelites, who were bound to the Mosaic Law by birth, Christians remain under the law of the Christ by choice, factors such as race and place of birth being irrelevant. They learn about Jehovah and his ways and yearn to do his will. Having God's law "within them," written, as it were, "in their heart," anointed Christians do not obey God merely because he can punish those who disobey; nor do they obey him solely out of a sense of duty. Their obedience is rooted in something more fundamental and vastly more powerful, and those of the other sheep are similarly obedient because of having God's law in their hearts.

---

8. What was a difference between the Mosaic Law and the law of the Christ?

Laws Based on Love

⁹ The essence of all of Jehovah's laws and regulations can be summed up in a single word: love. That has always been and will always be an essential part of pure worship. When asked which was the greatest commandment in the Law, Jesus answered: "Love Jehovah your God with your whole heart and with your whole soul and with your whole mind." The second was: "Love your neighbor as yourself." He then said: "On these two commandments the whole Law hangs, and the Prophets." (Matthew 22:35-40) Jesus thus indicated that, not just the Law with the Ten Commandments, but the entire Hebrew Scriptures were based on love.

---

9. How did Jesus indicate that love was the essence of Jehovah's laws?

Christians have God's law in their hearts

¹⁰ Is love of God and neighbor also central to the law in the hearts of Christians? Absolutely! The law of the Christ involves a heartfelt love of God and includes a new command—Christians are to have self-sacrificing love for one another. They are to love as Jesus did, and he willingly laid down his life in behalf of his friends. He taught his disciples to love God and to love one another, just as he loved them. The outstanding love they show toward one another is the main identifying quality by which true Christians can be recognized. (John 13:34, 35; 15:12, 13) Jesus even instructed them to love their enemies.—Matthew 5:44.

¹¹ Jesus set the perfect example in showing love. As a mighty spirit creature in heaven, he welcomed the opportunity to advance his Father's interests on earth. Apart from giving his human life that others might live eternally, he showed people how they should live. He was humble, kind, and considerate, helping those burdened down and oppressed. He also imparted "sayings of everlasting life," tirelessly helping others to come to know Jehovah.—John 6:68.

¹² Love of God and neighbor, in fact, are inextricably linked. The apostle John stated: "Love is from God . . . If anyone makes the statement: 'I love God,' and yet is hating his brother, he is a liar. For he who does not love his brother, whom he has seen, cannot be loving God, whom he has not seen." (1 John 4:7, 20) Jehovah is both the source and the very personification of love. Everything he does is influenced by love. We love because we are made in his image. (Genesis 1:27) By showing love to our neighbor, we demonstrate our love of God.

To Love Means to Obey

¹³ How can we love God, whom we cannot see? The crucial first step is to get to know him. We cannot truly love or trust a stranger. Thus, God's Word encourages us to get to know God by reading the Bible, by praying, and by associating with those who already know and love him. (Psalm 1:1, 2; Philippians 4:6; Hebrews 10:25) The four Gospels are especially valuable, for they reveal the personality of Jehovah as reflected in the life and ministry of Jesus Christ. Our desire to obey God and to imitate his personality grows ever stronger as we come to know him and appreciate the love he showed for us. Yes, love of God involves obedience.

¹⁴ When we love individuals, we are in tune with what they like and dislike, and we conduct ourselves accordingly. We do not wish to displease those whom we love. "This is what the love of God means," wrote the apostle John, "that we observe his commandments; and yet his commandments are not burdensome." (1 John 5:3) They are not burdensome, nor are they numerous. Love guides our way. We do not need to memorize an extensive code of rules to direct our every act; our love for God guides us. If we love God, it is a pleasure to do his will. We thus gain God's approval, and we benefit ourselves, his direction always working for our good.—Isaiah 48:17.

¹⁵ Love of God moves us to imitate his qualities. When we love a person, we admire his qualities and seek to be like him.

---

10. How do we know that love is central to the law of the Christ?
11. How did Jesus demonstrate love for both God and mankind?
12. Why can it be said that love of God and neighbor are inextricably linked?

---

13. If we are to love God, what must we first do?
14. Why can it be said that God's laws are not burdensome?
15. What will move us to imitate Jehovah? Explain.

Consider the relationship between Jehovah and Jesus. They were together in heaven for perhaps billions of years. Deep, pure love existed between them. So perfectly did Jesus resemble his heavenly Father that he could say to his disciples: "He that has seen me has seen the Father." (John 14:9) As we gain knowledge and appreciation for Jehovah and his Son, we are moved to be like them. Our love for Jehovah, along with the help of his holy spirit, will enable us to "strip off the old personality with its practices, and clothe [ourselves] with the new personality."—Colossians 3:9, 10; Galatians 5:22, 23.

Love in Action

¹⁶ As Christians, we allow our love for God and neighbor to motivate us to share in the Kingdom-preaching and disciple-making work. In so doing, we please Jehovah God, "whose will is that all sorts of men should be saved and come to an accurate

16. How is love for God and neighbor demonstrated by our preaching and teaching activity?

knowledge of truth." (1 Timothy 2:3, 4) We can thus find joy in helping others to have the law of the Christ written in their hearts. And we delight to observe as their personalities are transformed to reflect the divine qualities of Jehovah. (2 Corinthians 3:18) Really, to help others to come to know God is the most precious gift we can give them. Those who accept Jehovah's friendship can enjoy it throughout eternity.

¹⁷ We live in a world where material things are greatly valued, even loved. Yet, material things are not everlasting. They

17. Why is it wise to cultivate love for God and neighbor rather than for material things?

Sonia with a Senegalese girl at the 2004 district convention

can be stolen or consumed by decay. (Matthew 6:19) The Bible warns us: "The world is passing away and so is its desire, but he that does the will of God remains forever." (1 John 2:16, 17) Yes, Jehovah will remain forever, and so will those who love and serve him. Consequently, does it not make more sense to cultivate love for God and for people than it does to pursue the things of the world, which are at best only temporary?

[18] Those who pursue love bring praise to Jehovah. Consider Sonia, a missionary in Senegal. She studied the Bible with a woman named Heidi, who contracted HIV from her unbelieving husband. After her husband died, Heidi was baptized, but soon her health failed, and she was hospitalized with AIDS. Sonia relates: "The hospital staff did their best, but they were few in number. Volunteers from the congregation were called on to take care of her needs at the hospital. The second night, I stayed on a mat next to her bed and helped to care for her until her death. The doctor in charge said: 'Our biggest problem is that even relatives often abandon family members when they know they have AIDS. Why do you, who are not related, not from the same country, not even the same color, agree to put yourself at risk?' I explained that to me, Heidi was really my sister, as close as if we had the same mother and father. Having come to know this new sister of mine, I found it a pleasure to take care of her." Incidentally, Sonia suffered no ill effects from her loving efforts to care for Heidi.

[19] Many examples of self-sacrificing love may be found among Jehovah's servants.

No written law code identifies God's people today. Instead, we see the fulfillment of what is written at Hebrews 8:10: "'This is the covenant that I shall covenant with the house of Israel after those days,' says Jehovah. 'I will put my laws in their mind, and in their hearts I shall write them. And I will become their God, and they themselves will become my people.'" May we ever cherish the law of love that Jehovah has written in our hearts, taking advantage of every opportunity to demonstrate love.

[20] What a joy it is to serve God along with a worldwide brotherhood that displays such love! Those who have the law of the Christ in their heart enjoy a priceless possession in this loveless world. Not only do they enjoy Jehovah's love but they also delight in the strong bond of love in the brotherhood. "Look! How good and how pleasant it is for brothers to dwell together in unity!" Though Jehovah's Witnesses reside in many nations, speak many tongues, and represent many cultures, they enjoy religious unity that is without equal. This unity brings Jehovah's favor. Wrote the psalmist: "There [amid a people united in love] Jehovah commanded the blessing to be, even life to time indefinite."—Psalm 133:1-3.

20. Why is the law of the Christ a priceless possession?

---

18. How did one missionary demonstrate self-sacrificing love?
19. Having God's law in our hearts, of what should we take advantage?

Can You Answer?

- How important were the Ten Commandments?
- What is the law written in hearts?
- What role does love play in "the law of the Christ"?
- In what ways may we display our love for God and neighbor?

"They Could Have Been Immediately Freed"

GENEVIÈVE DE GAULLE, niece of Charles de Gaulle, former president of France, got to know Jehovah's Witnesses personally in the Nazi concentration camp at Ravensbrück, northern Germany. She wrote the above words in a letter in August 1945.

The concentration camp at Auschwitz, Poland, was liberated on January 27, 1945. Ever since 1996, this date has been a memorial day in Germany for victims of Hitler's Third Reich.

During an official memorial speech on January 27, 2003, the president of the State Parliament of Baden-Württemberg, Peter Straub, commented: "All those who suffered persecution because of their religious or political beliefs and who were willing to accept death rather than submit deserve our great respect, such respect as is hard to express in words. Jehovah's Witnesses were the only religion that completely refused to accede to the demands of the Hitler regime: They did not raise their hand to give the Hitler salute. They refused to swear allegiance to 'Führer and State,' just as they refused to perform military and labor service. And their children did not join the Hitler Youth Movement."

Jesus Christ said of his followers: "They are no part of the world, just as I am no part of the world." (John 17:16) Hence, the stand of Jehovah's Witnesses was purely on religious grounds. Straub continued: "Jehovah's Witnesses, who had to wear a purple triangle on their clothes as concentration camp prisoners, were the only ones who could themselves have put an end to their own martyrdom. Signing a declaration denying their faith would have been sufficient."

For the vast majority of the Witnesses, denying their faith was out of the question. Thus, about 1,200 of them died during the Nazi period. Two hundred and seventy were executed as conscientious objectors. They paid much more than just lip service to the statement: "We must obey God as ruler rather than men."—Acts 5:29.

Jehovah's Witnesses were not extraordinary people, as noted by Ulrich Schmidt, president of the State Parliament of North Rhine-Westphalia. Referring to his speech, the brochure *Landtag Intern* called them "ordinary people who, following their conscience, stood firm for their religious beliefs, showed civil courage, and offered ideological opposition out of Christian conviction." We can be sure that Jehovah God rejoices over all who stick loyally to him under difficult circumstances. At Proverbs 27:11, we read: "Be wise, my son, and make my heart rejoice, that I may make a reply to him that is taunting me."

Questions From Readers

In ancient Israel, what was signified by the miraculous light sometimes called Shechinah that appeared in the Most Holy of the tabernacle and the temple?

Jehovah, the loving Father and Protector of his people, made his presence distinctly felt in Israel. One way he accomplished that was through a resplendent cloud that was intimately related to his place of worship.

That striking light represented Jehovah's invisible presence. It appeared in the Most Holy both of the tabernacle and of the temple that Solomon built. That miraculous light did not signify that Jehovah was physically present there. God cannot be confined in any building made by humans. (2 Chronicles 6:18; Acts 17:24) This supernatural effulgence in God's sanctuary could give confidence to the high priest and through him to all the Israelites that Jehovah's protective presence attended to them and their needs.

In postbiblical Aramaic, this light was called Shechinah (*shekhi·nah'*), a word meaning "that which dwells" or "the dwelling." This term does not occur in the Bible but is found in Aramaic translations of the Hebrew Scriptures, also known as the Targums.

When giving instructions for constructing the tabernacle, Jehovah said to Moses: "You must place the cover above upon the Ark, and in the Ark you will place the testimony that I shall give you. And I will present myself to you there and speak with you from above the cover, from between the two cherubs that are upon the ark." (Exodus 25:21, 22) The Ark mentioned was a gold-covered chest in the Most Holy. There were two golden cherubs on the lid of the Ark.

From where would Jehovah speak? He provided the answer when he said to Moses: "In a cloud I shall appear over the cover." (Leviticus 16:2) This cloud hovered over the sacred Ark between the two golden cherubs. The Bible does not reveal how high that cloud was or how far above the cherubs it extended.

This luminous cloud lit up the Most Holy. In fact, it was the only source of illumination in that compartment. The high priest would benefit from such lighting when he entered that innermost chamber on Atonement Day. He was standing in the presence of Jehovah.

Does this miraculous light have any significance for Christians? The apostle John saw in vision a city in which "night will not exist." The city is New Jerusalem, made up of anointed Christians resurrected to rule with Jesus. The light of this symbolic city is not from the sun or the moon. Jehovah God's glory directly lights up this organization, just as the Shechinah cloud illuminated the Most Holy. Also, the Lamb, Jesus Christ, is the city's "lamp." In turn, this "city" sheds its spiritual light and favor down upon redeemed people out of all the nations for their guidance.—Revelation 21:22-25.

Because they receive such abundant blessings from above, Jehovah's worshippers can be certain that Jehovah is their protective Shepherd and affectionate Father.

Interest in the Bible Appreciated

MARIANNA, one of Jehovah's Witnesses in the south of Italy, is 18 years old and in her last year of high school. She attends the same school as some other young Witnesses.

"For a few years now," writes Marianna, "some of us have been reading the Bible text for the day from *Examining the Scriptures Daily* during our break. The only place we could do so was in one of the corridors near the staff room. It was not very quiet. Most of the teachers saw us as they passed, and some stopped to see what we were doing. This has often given us the opportunity to answer their questions. On an average, one teacher stopped every day. Several have stayed to listen to our discussion of the Bible text and have expressed appreciation for the interest we Witnesses have in spiritual things. Once, the assistant principal invited us to have our conversation in the staff room.

"After seeing where we were considering the text, my teacher asked the principal if we could discuss it in one of the classrooms, where it would be quieter. The principal gave permission, and my teacher praised us before the whole class for the good example we set. We are all very happy for the great privilege Jehovah has granted us."

SEPTEMBER 1, 2005

THE WATCHTOWER
ANNOUNCING JEHOVAH'S KINGDOM

Why It Pays to Be Loyal

THE WATCHTOWER®

ANNOUNCING JEHOVAH'S KINGDOM

September 1, 2005   Average Printing Each Issue: 26,439,000   Vol. 126, No. 17

THE PURPOSE OF *THE WATCHTOWER* is to exalt Jehovah God as Sovereign Lord of the universe. It keeps watch on world events as these fulfill Bible prophecy. It comforts all peoples with the good news that God's Kingdom will soon destroy those who oppress their fellowmen and that it will turn the earth into a paradise. It encourages faith in God's now-reigning King, Jesus Christ, whose shed blood opens the way for mankind to gain eternal life. *The Watchtower*, published by Jehovah's Witnesses continuously since 1879, is nonpolitical. It adheres to the Bible as its authority.

IN THIS ISSUE

3   Does It Pay to Be Loyal?

4   There Are Benefits to Being Loyal

8   Enduring as a Soldier of Christ

13   Walk With God in These Turbulent Times

18   We Shall Walk in the Name of Jehovah Our God

23   Mennonites Search for Bible Truth

27   Questions From Readers

28   Let Jehovah's "Saying" Safeguard You

32   Early German Bible Uses God's Name

WATCHTOWER STUDIES

OCTOBER 3-9:
Walk With God in These Turbulent Times.
Page 13. Songs to be used: 138, 106.

OCTOBER 10-16:
We Shall Walk in the Name of Jehovah Our God.
Page 18. Songs to be used: 80, 55.

Publication of *The Watchtower* is part of a worldwide Bible educational work supported by voluntary donations.

Unless otherwise indicated, Scripture quotations are from the modern-language *New World Translation of the Holy Scriptures—With References*.

The Watchtower (ISSN 0043-1087) is published semimonthly by Watchtower Bible and Tract Society of New York, Inc.; M. H. Larson, President; G. F. Simonis, Secretary-Treasurer; 25 Columbia Heights, Brooklyn, NY 11201-2483. Periodicals Postage Paid at Brooklyn, NY, and at additional mailing offices. **POSTMASTER:** Send address changes to Watchtower, **Wallkill, NY 12589.**

Changes of address should reach us 30 days before your moving date. Give us your old and new address (if possible, your old address label).

Would you welcome more information or a free home Bible study? Please send your request to Jehovah's Witnesses, using the appropriate address below.

America, United States of: Wallkill, NY 12589. *Antigua:* Box 119, St. Johns. *Australia:* Box 280, Ingleburn, NSW 1890. *Bahamas:* Box N-1247, Nassau, N.P. *Barbados, W.I.:* Crusher Site Road, Prospect, St. James. *Britain:* The Ridgeway, London NW7 1RN. *Canada:* Box 4100, Halton Hills (Georgetown), Ontario L7G 4Y4. *Germany:* Niederselters, Am Steinfels, D-65618 Selters. *Ghana:* P. O. Box GP 760, Accra. *Guyana:* 352-360 Tyrell St., Republic Park Phase 2 EBD. *Hawaii 96819:* 2055 Kam IV Rd., Honolulu. *Hong Kong:* 4 Kent Road, Kowloon Tong. *India:* Post Box 6440, Yelahanka, Bangalore 560 064, KAR. *Ireland:* Newcastle, Greystones, Co. Wicklow. *Jamaica:* P. O. Box 103, Old Harbour, St. Catherine. *Japan:* 1271 Nakashinden, Ebina City, Kanagawa Pref., 243-0496. *Kenya:* P.O. Box 47788, GPO Nairobi 00100. *New Zealand:* P.O. Box 75-142, Manurewa. *Nigeria:* P.M.B. 1090, Benin City 300001, Edo State. *Philippines, Republic of:* P. O. Box 2044, 1060 Manila. *South Africa:* Private Bag X2067, Krugersdorp, 1740. *Trinidad and Tobago, Republic of:* Lower Rapsey Street & Laxmi Lane, Curepe. *Zambia:* Box 33459, Lusaka 10101. *Zimbabwe:* Private Bag WG-5001, Westgate.

NOW PUBLISHED IN 151 LANGUAGES. SEMIMONTHLY: Afrikaans, Albanian,* Amharic, Arabic, Bengali, Bicol, Bislama, Bulgarian, Cebuano,* Chichewa,* Chinese, Chinese (Simplified),* Cibemba,* Croatian,* Czech,*# Danish,*# Dutch,*# East Armenian, Efik,* English*#+◎ (also Braille), Estonian, Ewe, Fijian, Finnish,*# French*# (also Braille), Ga, Georgian,* German,*# Greek,* Gujarati, Gun, Hebrew, Hiligaynon, Hindi, Hungarian,*# Igbo,* Iloko,* Indonesian, Italian,*# Japanese*# (also Braille), Kannada, Kinyarwanda, Kirundi, Korean*# (also Braille), Latvian, Lingala, Lithuanian, Luvale, Macedonian, Malagasy,* Malayalam, Maltese, Myanmar, Nepali, Norwegian,*# Pangasinan, Papiamento (Aruba), Papiamento (Curaçao), Polish,*# Portuguese*# (also Braille), Punjabi, Rarotongan, Romanian,* Russian,* Samar-Leyte, Samoan, Sango, Sepedi, Serbian, Sesotho, Shona,* Silozi, Sinhala, Slovak,* Slovenian, Solomon Islands Pidgin, Spanish*# (also Braille), Sranantongo, Swahili,* Swedish,*# Tagalog,* Tamil, Telugu, Thai, Tigrinya, Tok Pisin, Tongan, Tshiluba, Tsonga, Tswana, Turkish, Twi, Ukrainian,* Urdu, Vietnamese, Wallisian, Xhosa, Yoruba,* Zulu*

MONTHLY: American Sign Language,△□ Armenian, Assamese, Azerbaijani (roman script), Brazilian Sign Language,△ Cambodian, Chitonga, Gilbertese, Greenlandic, Haitian Creole, Hausa, Hiri Motu, Icelandic, Isoko, Kaonde, Kazakh, Kikongo, Kiluba, Kirghiz, Kosraean, Kwanyama/Ndonga, Luganda, Marathi, Marshallese, Mauritian Creole, Maya, Mizo, Monokutuba, Moore, Niuean, Ossetian, Otetela, Palauan, Persian, Ponapean, Seychelles Creole, Tahitian, Tatar, Tiv, Trukese, Tumbuka, Tuvaluan, Umbundu, Uruund, Venda, Yapese, Zande

* Study articles also available in large-print edition.
\# Audiocassettes also available.
\+ CD also available.
◎ MP3 CD-ROM also available.
△ Videocassette
□ DVD

Does It Pay to Be
Loyal?

"**Y**OU are paying far too much for health insurance," said Karl, an insurance representative.* "If you switch to my company, you will save 15 euros a month, which is a lot."

"That might be true," replied Jens. "But I have had my health insurance with the same company for several years. They were very helpful in the past, and I want to stay loyal to them."

"Loyalty is a fine quality," answered Karl. "Still, being loyal is costing you money!"

Karl was right. Often, being loyal, or faithful, to someone else may cost money.# It also demands time, energy, and emotional commitment. Is loyalty worth it?

More Widely Praised Than Practiced

In a survey carried out in Germany by the Allensbach Opinion Research Institute, 96 percent of those who responded viewed faithfulness as a desirable quality. A second Allensbach survey carried out among 18- to 24-year-olds showed that 2 out of 3 respondents regarded faithfulness as being "in," that is, they viewed it favorably.

Although loyalty, or faithfulness, is widely praised, things are different when it comes to actually *being* loyal, or *being* faithful. In several European lands, for example, married couples or family members frequently show little loyalty to one another. Friends are often disloyal to one another. And the loyalty that in times past bonded employer and employee

or a business and its customers has basically disappeared. Why?

Sometimes the hectic pace of life leaves little time or emotional stamina for commitments that demand loyalty. People who have been disappointed and let down in human relationships perhaps now shy away from being faithful to anyone. Others may prefer a here-today-and-gone-tomorrow kind of life that does not demand loyalty.

Whatever the reason, loyalty is a virtue more often praised than practiced. Hence, the questions: Does it pay to be loyal? If so, to whom do we owe loyalty, and in what ways? What are the benefits of being loyal?

Loyalty is a virtue more often praised than practiced

---

* Some names have been changed in this and in the next article.
# While "loyalty" and "faithfulness" are not always used in the same context, they are sometimes used interchangeably in these articles.

There Are Benefits to
Being Loyal

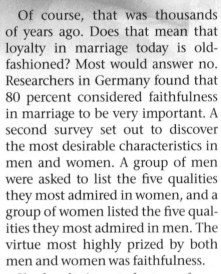

IN SOME countries, children love to tease a playmate by sticking burs onto his woolen pullover. The burs attach themselves to the wool, and whatever the playmate does—whether he walks, runs, shakes, or jumps—the burs cling. The only way to get rid of them is to pull them off one by one. To youngsters, that is all great fun.

Of course, not everyone appreciates burs on his clothes, but everyone is amazed at their ability to stick. A person who is loyal has a similar quality. The loyal one stays close to someone in an enduring relationship. He sticks faithfully to the duties and obligations of that relationship even when circumstances make it difficult. The word "loyalty" brings to mind virtues like trueness, allegiance, and devotion. However, while you might appreciate it when people are loyal to you, do you have the strength of character to be loyal to others? If so, to whom should you be loyal?

Faithfulness in Marriage—A Basic Need

Marriage is one area where loyalty is vital but where, sadly, it is frequently lacking. A husband and wife who remain faithful to their marriage vows —that is, who stay together and each work for the good of the other—have taken an important step toward finding happiness and security. Why? Because humans were created with a need both to show and to receive loyalty. When the marriage of Adam and Eve was performed in the garden of Eden, God declared: "A man will leave his father and his mother and he must stick to his wife." The same was to apply to a wife; she was to stick to her husband. Husband and wife were to be faithful to and cooperate with each other.—Genesis 2:24; Matthew 19:3-9.

Of course, that was thousands of years ago. Does that mean that loyalty in marriage today is old-fashioned? Most would answer no. Researchers in Germany found that 80 percent considered faithfulness in marriage to be very important. A second survey set out to discover the most desirable characteristics in men and women. A group of men were asked to list the five qualities they most admired in women, and a group of women listed the five qualities they most admired in men. The virtue most highly prized by both men and women was faithfulness.

Yes, loyalty is part of a strong foundation for a successful marriage. Yet, as we saw in the preceding article, loyalty is more often praised than practiced. For example, the high divorce rate in many lands gives evidence of widespread disloyalty. How can marriage partners counteract this trend and stay loyal to each other?

Loyalty Makes Marriage Durable

Loyalty is shown when marriage mates look for opportunities to confirm their devotion to each other. For example, it is usually better to say "our" rather than "my" —"our friends," "our children," "our home," "our experiences," and so on. When making plans and decisions—whether regarding housing, employment, child rearing, entertainment, vacations, or religious activities—husband and wife do well to take into account the feelings and opinions of the other mate.—Proverbs 11:14; 15:22.

Loyalty is shown when each mate makes the other feel needed and wanted. A married person feels insecure when the mate acts in a too friendly manner with someone of the opposite sex. The Bible counsels men to stick "with the wife of [their] youth." A husband ought not to allow his heart to desire the ad-

Loyal family members care for one another's needs

miring attention of a woman other than his wife. Surely he should avoid becoming physically involved with another woman. The Bible warns: "Anyone committing adultery with a woman is in want of heart; he that does it is bringing his own soul to ruin." That same high standard of faithfulness is expected of a wife.—Proverbs 5:18; 6:32.

Is faithfulness in marriage worth the effort? Of course it is. It makes the marriage more stable and lasting, and each of the partners benefits as an individual. For instance, when a husband is faithfully committed to the well-being of his wife, she has a feeling of security that brings out the best in her. The same is true of the husband. His resolve to be loyal to his wife helps him to develop a commitment to righteous principles in all areas of his life.

If a husband and wife go through a difficult period, loyalty will make both feel secure. On the other hand, in a marriage lacking loyalty, a frequent reaction to problems is to separate or seek a divorce. Such a step, far from solving problems, often means a transition to other problems. Back in the 1980's, a well-known fashion consultant parted from his wife and family. Did he find happiness as a single man? Twenty years later, he admitted that the parting left him "lonely and disturbed and lying awake at night wanting to say good night to [his] children."

Loyalty Between Parents and Children

When parents are loyal to each other, there is a good possibility that this quality will rub off on their children. Later in life, children raised in a loyal, loving family will find it easier to act responsibly toward their mates as well as toward their parents as these suffer the disabilities of old age.—1 Timothy 5:4, 8.

Of course, it is not always the parents who become infirm first. Sometimes a child needs faithful care. This was the situation of Herbert and Gertrud—both Jehovah's Witnesses—for over 40 years. Their son, Dietmar, suffered all his life from muscular dystrophy. For the last seven years before his death in November 2002, Dietmar needed care and attention around the clock. His parents lovingly cared for his needs. They even installed medical equipment in their home and underwent medical training. A fine example of family loyalty!

Loyalty Is Vital for Friendship

"A person can be happy without a marriage mate, but it's difficult to be happy without a friend," observes Birgit. Perhaps you agree. Whether you are married or single, the loyalty of a good friend will warm your heart and enrich your life. Of course, if you are married, your closest friend should be your marriage mate.

A friend is not just an acquaintance. We may have many acquaintances—neighbors, colleagues, and people we meet now and again. True friendship requires an investment of time, energy, and emotional commitment. It is an honor to be someone's friend. Friendship brings privileges, but it also involves responsibilities.

Having good communication with our friends is a must. Such communication might be dictated partly by need. "If one of us has a problem, my girlfriend and I telephone once or twice a week. It's great to know she's there and is willing to listen," explains Birgit. Distance need not be a barrier to friendship. Gerda and Helga live thousands of miles apart, but they have been good friends for over 35 years. "We write regularly," explains Gerda, "relating experiences and describing our innermost feel-

ings, be they joyful or sad. Mail from Helga makes me extremely happy. We are simply on the same wavelength."

Loyalty is vital for friendship. An act of disloyalty can shatter even long-term relationships. It is common for friends to advise each other even on confidential matters. Friends will speak from the heart without fear of being belittled or having their confidences betrayed. The Bible states: "A true companion is loving all the time, and is a brother that is born for when there is distress."—Proverbs 17:17.

Since our friends influence how we think, feel, and act, it is important that we make friends with people whose way of life is compatible with our own. For example, be careful to cultivate friendship with individuals who have the same beliefs, the same moral viewpoint, and the same standards of right and wrong as you do. Such friends will help you to reach your goals. Besides, why would you want to be close to someone

The loyalty of a good friend will warm your heart

whose standards and morals you do not share? The Bible shows the importance of choosing the right friends when it says: "He that is walking with wise persons will become wise, but he that is having dealings with the stupid ones will fare badly."—Proverbs 13:20.

Loyalty Can Be Learned

When a child learns to stick burs on someone's clothing, he will likely want to play the game over and over again. The same can be said of a person who is loyal. Why? Be-

cause the more we practice showing loyalty, the easier it becomes. If a person learns early in life to be loyal within the family, he will later find it easier to develop friendships based on loyalty. In due course, such strong and durable friendships may pave the way for loyalty in marriage. This will also help him to be loyal in the most important friendship of all.

Jesus said that the greatest commandment is to love Jehovah God with our whole heart, soul, mind, and strength. (Mark 12: 30) This means that we owe God total loyalty. Being loyal to Jehovah God brings rich rewards. He will never let us down or disappoint us, for he says of himself: "I am loyal." (Jeremiah 3:12) Indeed, loyalty, or faithfulness, to God brings everlasting rewards. —1 John 2:17.

ENDURING AS A SOLDIER OF CHRIST

AS TOLD BY
YURII KAPTOLA

"Now I am convinced that you really do have faith!"
Those words came from an unlikely source—an officer in the Soviet army—
and they gave me a boost at just the right time. I was facing a long
prison sentence and had fervently implored Jehovah for support.
I was facing a long struggle that would require endurance and resolve.

I WAS born on October 19, 1962, and grew up in the western part of Ukraine. In that same year, my father, who was also named Yurii, came in contact with Jehovah's Witnesses. Soon he became the first worshipper of Jehovah in our village. His activity did not go unnoticed by officials who opposed Jehovah's Witnesses.

Most of our neighbors, however, respected my parents for their Christian qualities and concern for others. My parents took every opportunity to instill in my three sisters and me a love of God from an early age,

and this helped me to face the many challenges I encountered at school. One such challenge arose when each student was required to wear a badge identifying him as one of Lenin's October Children. Because of my Christian neutrality, I did not put the badge on and therefore stood out as being different.—John 6:15; 17:16.

Later, when I was in the third grade, all students were required to join a Communist youth organization called the Young Pioneers. One day our class was taken out to the school yard for the enrollment ceremony. I dreaded it, expecting to be ridiculed and berated. Everyone except me had brought his new red Pioneer scarf from home, and the students stood in a long row in front of the school principal, the teachers, and senior class members. When the senior class members were told to tie the scarves around our necks, I lowered my head and looked down, hoping that no one would pay any attention to me.

Taken to Faraway Prisons

When I was 18, I was sentenced to three years' imprisonment for maintaining Christian neutrality. (Isaiah 2:4) I served the first year in the town of Trudovoye, in the Vinnitskaya District of Ukraine. While there, I met about 30 other Witnesses of Jehovah. We were assigned by twos to separate work detachments, as the authorities wanted to prevent us from associating with one another.

In August 1982, Eduard—another Witness—and I were sent by train in prison cars to the northern Ural Mountains along with a group of other prisoners. For eight days we endured extremely hot and cramped conditions until we arrived at Solikamsk Prison, in the Permskaya District. Eduard and I were assigned to different cells. Two weeks later, I was taken farther north to Vels, in the Krasnovishersky region.

Our transport arrived in the middle of the night, and it was pitch-black. Despite the darkness, an officer ordered our group to cross a river by boat. We could see neither the river nor the boat! Still, we groped around until we stumbled upon a boat and, although frightened, managed to make our way across the river. Once on the other shore, we headed for a light that was visible on a nearby hill, where we found a few tents. This was to be our new home. I lived in a comparatively large tent with about 30 other prisoners. During the winter, we endured temperatures that sometimes plunged to minus 40 degrees Fahrenheit, and the tent offered little comfort. The inmates' primary job was to chop down trees, but I worked at building huts for prisoners.

Spiritual Food Reaches Our Isolated Settlement

I was the only Witness in that settlement; yet Jehovah did not abandon me. One day a package arrived from my mother, who still lived in western Ukraine. When a guard opened the parcel, the first thing he saw was a small Bible. He picked it up and began flipping through the pages. I tried to think of something to say that would prevent this spiritual treasure from being confiscated. "What is this?" the guard asked abruptly. Before I could think of an answer, an inspector standing nearby responded: "Oh! That's a dictionary." I said nothing. (Ecclesiastes 3:7) The inspector searched through the rest of the package and then handed it to me along with the precious Bible. I was so happy that I offered him some nuts from my parcel. When I received this package, I knew that Jehovah had not forgotten me. He generously reached out and cared for my spiritual needs.—Hebrews 13:5.

Preaching Without Letup

A few months later, I was surprised to receive a letter from a Christian brother who was imprisoned about 250 miles away. He asked me to seek out a man who had shown interest and might now be in my camp. Writing such an open letter was unwise, for our letters were censored. Not surprisingly, one of the officers summoned me to his office and strongly warned me not to preach. He then ordered me to sign

a document stating that I would stop sharing my beliefs with others. I replied that I did not understand why I should sign such a statement, since everybody already knew that I was one of Jehovah's Witnesses. I mentioned that other prisoners wanted to know why I had been imprisoned. What should I say to them? (Acts 4:20) The officer realized that he could not intimidate me, so he decided to get rid of me. I was sent to another camp.

I was transferred to the village of Vaya, 125 miles away. There the supervisors respected my Christian stand and assigned me to nonmilitary work—first as a carpenter, then as an electrician. But these jobs presented their own challenges. On one occasion, I was told to get my tools and go to the village club. When I arrived, the soldiers in the club were glad to see me. They were having problems getting the lights adorning various military emblems to work properly. They wanted me to help them fix things because they were preparing for the annual Red Army Day celebration. After prayerfully thinking about what to do, I told them that I could not do that kind of work. I gave them my tools and left. I was reported to the deputy director, and to my surprise he listened to the complaints against me and replied: "I respect him for that. He is a man of principle."

Encouragement From an Unlikely Source

On June 8, 1984, after exactly three years of confinement, I was released. Upon my return to Ukraine, I had to register with the militia as a former prisoner. The officials told me that I would be tried again in six months and that it would be better for me to leave the district entirely. So I left Ukraine and eventually found work in Latvia. For a while I was able to preach and associate with the small group of Witnesses who lived in and around Riga, the capital. However, after only one year, I was again called up for military service. At the enlistment office, I told the officer that I had previously refused military service. In reply, he screamed: "Do you really know what you are doing? Let's see what you will say to the lieutenant colonel!"

He escorted me to a room on the second floor where the lieutenant colonel sat behind a long table. He carefully listened to me as I explained my position and then told me that I still had time to reconsider my decision before facing the enlistment committee. As we left the lieutenant colonel's office, the officer who had initially scolded me confessed: "Now I am convinced that you really do have faith!" When I appeared before a military committee, I repeated my neutral stand, and for the time being, they let me go.

During that time, I lived in a hostel. One evening, I heard a soft knock at the door. I

I was sentenced to forced labor for four years and imprisoned in Riga Central Prison

opened it and found a man dressed in a suit and carrying a briefcase. He introduced himself, saying: "I am from State Security. I know that you are having difficulties and that you are going to be tried in court." "Yes, that is right," I replied. The man went on: "We can help you if you agree to work for us." "No, that is not possible," I said. "I will remain loyal to my Christian beliefs." With no further effort to persuade me, he left.

Back to Prison, Back to Preaching

On August 26, 1986, the National Court of Riga sentenced me to four years' forced labor, and I was taken to the Riga Central Prison. They put me in a large cell together with 40 other prisoners, and I tried to preach to every inmate in that cell. Some claimed to believe in God; others just laughed. I had noticed that the men were gathered in groups, and after two weeks the leaders of these groups told me that I was not allowed to preach, since I did not go along with their unwritten rules. I explained that I was imprisoned for that very reason—I lived by different laws.

I continued to preach discreetly, and when I found some who were spiritually inclined, I was able to study the Bible with four of them. During our discussions, they wrote down basic Bible teachings in a notebook. A few months later, I was sent to a high-security camp in Valmiera, where I worked as an electrician. There I was able to study the Bible with another electrician who four years later became one of Jehovah's Witnesses.

On March 24, 1988, I was moved from the high-security camp to a nearby settlement camp. This was a real blessing, since it allowed me more freedom. I was assigned to work on various construction sites, and I constantly looked for opportunities to preach. Frequently, I was away from the camp, preaching until late in the evening, but I never had any difficulties when I returned to the settlement.

Jehovah blessed my efforts. A few Witnesses lived in the area, but in the town itself there was only one, Vilma Krūmiņa—an elderly sister. Sister Krūmiņa and I began to conduct many Bible studies with young people. Occasionally, brothers and sisters traveled from Riga to share in the ministry, and some regular pioneers even came from Leningrad (now St. Petersburg). With Jehovah's help, we started several Bible studies, and soon I enrolled in the pioneer service, devoting 90 hours a month to the preaching work.

On April 7, 1990, my case came up for review at the People's Court in Valmiera. When the hearing began, I recognized the prosecutor. He was a young man with whom I had previously discussed the Bible! He recognized me and smiled but said nothing. I still recall what the judge said to me at the trial that day: "Yurii, the decision to imprison you four years ago was illegal. They should not have convicted you." All of a sudden, I was free!

A Soldier of Christ

In June 1990, I once again needed to register at the enlistment office in order to obtain a residency permit in Riga. I entered the same office with the same long table where four years earlier I had told the lieutenant colonel that I would not serve in the military. This time, he rose to greet me, shook my hand, and said: "It is a shame you had to go through all of this. I am sorry that it turned out that way."

With Karina in the ministry

the Russian congregation. The growth was so rapid that the following year our congregation was divided into three! When I look back, it is clear that Jehovah himself was directing his sheep to his organization.

In 1998, I was appointed to serve as a special pioneer in Jelgava, a town 25 miles southwest of Riga. That same year, I became one of the first from Latvia to be invited to attend the Ministerial Training School conducted in the Russian language at Solnechnoye, near St. Petersburg, Russia. While at school, I came to appreciate how important it is to have a loving attitude toward people in order to be successful in the ministry. What especially impressed me, above and beyond the things we were taught in the school, was the love and attention that we were shown by the Bethel family and the school instructors.

I reached another milestone in my life in 2001 when I married Karina, a lovely Christian woman. Karina joined me in special full-time service, and every day I am encouraged when I see my wife returning from field service looking so happy. Indeed, it is a great joy to serve Jehovah. The harsh experiences under the Communist regime taught me to trust in him completely. No sacrifice is too great for one who wishes to keep Jehovah's friendship and support his sovereignty. Helping others learn about Jehovah has given my life purpose. It has been a wondrous honor for me to serve Jehovah "as a fine soldier of Christ."—2 Timothy 2:3.

I replied: "I am a soldier of Christ, and I must live up to my commission. With help from the Bible, you too can enjoy what Christ has promised his followers—a happy life and an eternal future." (2 Timothy 2: 3, 4) The colonel answered: "Not long ago I bought a Bible, and I am now reading it." I had with me the book *You Can Live Forever in Paradise on Earth.** I opened it to the chapter discussing the sign of the last days and showed him how Bible prophecy is related to our time. With deep appreciation the colonel shook my hand again and wished me success in my work.

By this time the field was really white for harvesting in Latvia. (John 4:35) In 1991, I began to serve as a congregation elder. There were only two appointed elders in the entire country! A year later, the only congregation in Latvia was divided into two —one Latvian-speaking and one Russian-speaking. I was privileged to serve with

---

* Published by Jehovah's Witnesses but now out of print.

WALK WITH GOD IN THESE TURBULENT TIMES

"Enoch kept walking with the true God.
Then he was no more, for God took him."—GENESIS 5:24.

TURBULENT times! Those words well describe the years of unrest and violence that mankind has lived through since the birth of the Messianic Kingdom in 1914. During all that time, humans have been in "the last days." Such calamities as famines, diseases, earthquakes, and wars have plagued them on an unprecedented scale. (2 Timothy 3:1; Revelation 6:1-8) Those who worship Jehovah have not been exempt. To a greater or lesser degree, we all have to cope with the hardships and uncertainties of the times. Economic pressures, political unrest, crime, and sickness are among the things that make life very difficult.

² In addition, many of Jehovah's servants have endured wave after wave of intense persecution as Satan has kept waging war against those "who observe the commandments of God and have the work of bearing witness to Jesus." (Revelation 12:17) And while we have not all suffered direct persecution, all true Christians have to struggle against Satan the Devil and the spirit that he engenders among mankind. (Ephesians 2:2; 6:12) It takes constant vigilance not to be influenced by that spirit, since we encounter it at work, at school, and in any other place where we have to rub shoulders with those who have no interest in pure worship.

Walk With God, Not With the Nations

³ Back in the first century, Christians likewise fought hard against the spirit of this world, and that made them very different from those outside the Christian congregation. Paul described the difference when he

---

1. What are some features of our times that make them calamitous?
2. What challenges have Jehovah's servants faced?

3, 4. In what way are Christians different from the world?

wrote: "This, therefore, I say and bear witness to in the Lord, that you no longer go on walking just as the nations also walk in the unprofitableness of their minds, while they are in darkness mentally, and alienated from the life that belongs to God, because of the ignorance that is in them, because of the insensibility of their hearts. Having come to be past all moral sense, they gave themselves over to loose conduct to work uncleanness of every sort with greediness."—Ephesians 4: 17-19.

⁴ How eloquently those words describe the deep spiritual and moral darkness of this world—both in Paul's day and in ours! As in the first century, Christians today do not 'go on walking as the nations do.' Rather, they enjoy the wonderful privilege of walking with God. True, some people may question whether it is reasonable to say that lowly, imperfect humans walk with Jehovah. However, the Bible shows that they can. Moreover, Jehovah expects them to do so. In the eighth century before our Common Era, the prophet Micah wrote the following inspired words: "What is Jehovah asking back from you but to exercise justice and to love kindness and to be modest *in walking with your God?*"—Micah 6:8.

How and Why Walk With God?

⁵ How can we walk with the all-powerful, invisible God? Clearly, not in the way that we walk with fellow humans. In the Bible the expression "to walk" can mean "to follow a certain course of action."* With this in mind, we understand that one who walks with God follows a life course outlined by God and pleasing to him. Pursuing such a course makes us different from most of the

---

* See Volume 1, page 220, paragraph 6, of *Insight on the Scriptures,* published by Jehovah's Witnesses.

---

5. How can an imperfect human walk with God?

people around us. Yet, it is the only proper choice for a Christian. Why? There are many reasons.

⁶ First, Jehovah is our Creator, the Source of our life, and the Provider of all that we need to sustain life. (Revelation 4:11) As a result, only he has the right to tell us how to walk. In addition, walking with God is the most beneficial course possible. For those who walk with him, Jehovah has made provision for the forgiveness of sin, and he offers the sure hope of everlasting life. Our all-loving heavenly Father also provides wise counsel that helps those who walk with him to make a success of life now, despite their being imperfect and living in a world that is lying in Satan's power. (John 3:16; 2 Timothy 3:15, 16; 1 John 1:8; 2:25; 5:19) A further reason for walking with God is that our willingness to do so contributes to the peace and unity of the congregation.—Colossians 3: 15, 16.

⁷ Finally, and most important, when we walk with God, we show where we stand on the great issue that was raised back in the garden of Eden—the issue of sovereignty. (Genesis 3:1-6) We demonstrate by our life course that we stand squarely on Jehovah's side, and we fearlessly proclaim that he alone is the rightful Sovereign. (Psalm 83: 18) We thus act in harmony with our prayer that God's name be sanctified and his will be done. (Matthew 6:9, 10) How wise are those who choose to walk with God! They can be sure that they are going in the right direction, since Jehovah is "wise alone." He never makes a mistake.—Romans 16:27.

⁸ How, though, is it possible to live as Christians should when times are so turbu-

---

6, 7. Why is walking with God the very best course?
8. How were the times of Enoch and Noah similar to our time?

lent and most people have no interest in serving Jehovah? We see the answer when we consider faithful men of old who kept their integrity during very difficult times. Two of these were Enoch and Noah. Both of them lived in times quite similar to our own. Wickedness was rampant. In Noah's day the earth was filled with violence and immorality. Yet, Enoch and Noah resisted the spirit of the world of their time and walked with Jehovah. How were they able to do so? To answer that question, we will in this article discuss the example of Enoch. In the following article, we will consider Noah.

Enoch Walked With God in Turbulent Times

9 Enoch was the first person described in the Scriptures as walking with God. The Bible record says: "After his fathering Methuselah Enoch went on walking with the true God." (Genesis 5:22) Then, after reporting the length of Enoch's life—which, while long compared with our life span, was short for those days—the record says: "Enoch kept walking with the true God. Then he was no

—————
9. What information do we have about Enoch?

more, for God took him." (Genesis 5:24) Evidently, Jehovah transferred Enoch from the land of the living to the sleep of death before opposers could lay hold of him. (Hebrews 11:5, 13) Apart from those brief verses, there are few references to Enoch in the Bible. Nevertheless, from the information that we have and from other indications, we have good reason to say that Enoch's times were turbulent.

10 Consider, for example, how quickly corruption spread in the human race after Adam sinned. The Bible tells us that Adam's firstborn son, Cain, became the first human murderer when he killed his brother Abel. (Genesis 4:8-10) After Abel's violent death, another son was born to Adam and Eve, and they named him Seth. Of him, we read: "To Seth also there was born a son and he proceeded to call his name Enosh. At that time a start was made of calling on the name of Jehovah." (Genesis 4:25, 26) Sadly, that "calling on the name of Jehovah" was in an

—————
10, 11. (a) How did corruption spread after the rebellion of Adam and Eve? (b) What prophetic message did Enoch preach, and what response did he surely meet up with?

By faith, "Enoch kept walking with the true God"

apostate way.* Many years after the birth of Enosh, a descendant of Cain named Lamech composed a song for his two wives proclaiming that he had killed a young man who wounded him. He also warned: "If seven times Cain is to be avenged, then Lamech seventy times and seven."—Genesis 4:10, 19, 23, 24.

¹¹ Such brief facts as the foregoing indicate that the corruption introduced by Satan in the garden of Eden quickly led to the spread of wickedness among Adam's descendants. In such a world, Enoch was a prophet of Jehovah whose powerful inspired words resonate even today. Jude reports that Enoch prophesied: "Look! Jehovah came with his holy myriads, to execute judgment against all, and to convict all the ungodly concerning all their ungodly deeds that they did in an ungodly way, and concerning all the shocking things that ungodly sinners spoke against him." (Jude 14, 15) Those words will find their final fulfillment at Armageddon. (Revelation 16:14, 16) Still, we can be sure that even in Enoch's day, there were many "ungodly sinners" who heard Enoch's prophecy with annoyance. How loving that Jehovah took the prophet out of their reach!

---

* Before the days of Enosh, Jehovah spoke with Adam. Abel made an acceptable offering to Jehovah. God even communicated with Cain before jealous anger drove Cain to commit murder. Hence, this beginning of "calling on the name of Jehovah" must have been in a new way, not in pure worship.

How Would You Answer?

- What does it mean to walk with God?
- Why is walking with God the best course?
- What enabled Enoch to walk with God despite turbulent times?
- How can we imitate Enoch?

What Strengthened Enoch to Walk With God?

¹² Back in the garden of Eden, Adam and Eve listened to Satan, and Adam rebelled against Jehovah. (Genesis 3:1-6) Their son Abel followed a different course, and Jehovah looked with favor upon him. (Genesis 4: 3, 4) Unhappily, the majority of Adam's offspring were not like Abel. However, Enoch, born hundreds of years later, was. What was the difference between Enoch and so many other descendants of Adam? The apostle Paul answered that question when he wrote: "By faith Enoch was transferred so as not to see death, and he was nowhere to be found because God had transferred him; for before his transference he had the witness that he had pleased God well." (Hebrews 11:5) Enoch was part of a great "cloud of [pre-Christian] witnesses," who were sterling examples of faith. (Hebrews 12:1) It was faith that enabled Enoch to endure in right conduct throughout a lifetime of over 300 years—more than three lifetimes for most of us today!

¹³ Paul described the faith of Enoch and other witnesses when he wrote: "Faith is the assured expectation of things hoped for, the evident demonstration of realities though not beheld." (Hebrews 11:1) Yes, faith is the confident expectation, based on assurances, that the things we hope for will come true. It involves an expectation so strong that it affects the focus of our life. That kind of faith enabled Enoch to walk with God even though the world around him did not.

¹⁴ True faith is based on accurate knowledge. What knowledge did Enoch have? (Romans 10:14, 17; 1 Timothy 2:4) Undoubtedly, he knew about the events

---

12. What made Enoch different from his contemporaries?
13. What kind of faith did Enoch have?
14. Upon what accurate knowledge might Enoch's faith have been based?

in Eden. Probably, he also heard about what life had been like in the garden in Eden—which was perhaps still in existence, although barred to humans. (Genesis 3:23, 24) And he knew of God's purpose that Adam's offspring would fill the earth and make the whole planet like that original Paradise. (Genesis 1:28) In addition, Enoch surely cherished Jehovah's promise to produce a Seed that would crush Satan's head and undo the ill effects of Satan's deception. (Genesis 3:15) Indeed, Enoch's own inspired prophecy, preserved in the book of Jude, has to do with the destruction of Satan's seed. Since Enoch had faith, we know that he worshipped Jehovah as the one who "becomes the rewarder of those earnestly seeking him." (Hebrews 11:6) Hence, while Enoch did not possess all the knowledge that we do, he had enough to form the foundation of a firm faith. With such a faith, he kept his integrity during turbulent times.

We firmly believe that Jehovah's promises will come true

Imitate Enoch's Example

¹⁵ Since, like Enoch, we want to please Jehovah during the turbulent times that exist today, we do well to follow Enoch's example. We need to gain and retain accurate knowledge of Jehovah and his purpose. But we need more. We need to allow that accurate knowledge to direct our course. (Psalm 119: 101; 2 Peter 1:19) We need to be guided by God's thinking, always striving to please him with our every thought and action.

¹⁶ We have no record of who else in Enoch's time was serving Jehovah, but clearly he was either alone or part of a small minority. We too are a minority in the world, but that does not dismay us. Jehovah will support us no matter who may be against us. (Romans 8: 31) Enoch courageously warned about the coming destruction of ungodly men. We too are courageous as we preach "this good news of the kingdom" despite mockery, opposition, and persecution. (Matthew 24:14) Enoch did not live as long as many of his contemporaries. Still, his hope was not in that world. He had his eye fixed on something far grander. (Hebrews 11:10, 35) We too have our eye fixed on the fulfillment of Jehovah's purpose. Hence, we do not use this world to the full. (1 Corinthians 7:31) Instead, we use our strength and resources primarily in Jehovah's service.

¹⁷ Enoch had faith that the Seed promised by God would appear in Jehovah's due time. It has now been almost 2,000 years since that Seed—Jesus Christ—appeared, provided the ransom, and opened the way for us, as well as for such faithful ancient witnesses as Enoch, to inherit everlasting life. That Seed, now enthroned as King of God's Kingdom, cast Satan out of heaven down to this earth, and we see the resulting tribulation all around us. (Revelation 12:12) Yes, there is far more knowledge available to us than was available to Enoch. May we, then, have firm faith as he did. May our confidence in the fulfillment of God's promises influence everything we do. May we, like Enoch, walk with God, although we live in turbulent times.

15, 16. How can we follow Enoch's course?

17. What knowledge do we have that Enoch did not have, so what should we do?

WE SHALL WALK IN THE NAME OF JEHOVAH OUR GOD

"We, for our part, shall walk in the name of Jehovah our God to time indefinite, even forever."—MICAH 4:5.

THE first man mentioned in the Bible as walking with God was Enoch. The second was Noah. The record tells us: "Noah was a righteous man. He proved himself faultless among his contemporaries. Noah walked with the true God." (Genesis 6:9) By Noah's time, mankind in general had deviated from pure worship. The bad situation was made worse by unfaithful angels who formed unnatural unions with women and produced offspring called Nephilim, "the mighty ones," or "the men of fame," of those days. No wonder the earth became filled with violence! (Genesis 6:2, 4, 11) Still, Noah proved himself faultless and was "a preacher of righteousness." (2 Peter 2:5) When God commanded him to build an ark for the preservation of life, Noah obediently "proceeded to do according to all that God had commanded him. He did just so." (Genesis 6:22) Truly, Noah walked with God.

² Paul included Noah in his list of faithful witnesses when he wrote: "By faith Noah, after being given divine warning of things not yet beheld, showed godly fear and constructed an ark for the saving of his household; and through this faith he condemned the world, and he became an heir of the righteousness that is according to faith." (He-brews 11:7) What a splendid example! Certain that Jehovah's words would come true, Noah expended time, energy, and resources in order to fulfill God's commands. In a similar way, many today turn their backs on secular opportunities in this world and expend their time, energy, and resources in obeying Jehovah's commands. Their faith is noteworthy and will result in their own salvation as well as that of others.—Luke 16:9; 1 Timothy 4:16.

³ Exercising faith must have been as difficult for Noah and his family as it was for Enoch, Noah's great-grandfather, who was discussed in the preceding article. In Noah's day as in Enoch's, true worshippers were a small minority—just eight people proved faithful and survived the Flood. Noah preached righteousness in a violent and immoral world. Moreover, he and his family were building a huge wooden ark in preparation for a worldwide flood, although no one had seen such a flood before. That must have seemed very strange to those observing them.

⁴ Interestingly, when Jesus referred to the days of Noah, he did not speak of the violence, the false religion, or the immorality —grievous as those were. The error that Jesus highlighted was the refusal of people to

---

1. As regards morality, what was the situation in Noah's day, and how was Noah different?
2, 3. What fine example did Noah provide for us today?

4. What failing of Noah's contemporaries did Jesus highlight?

system of things—the faith of Noah led to his salvation through the Flood. However, Jehovah executed judgment on all those who were living "normal" lives and taking no note of the meaning of the times they were living in.

Violence Again Plagues Mankind

⁶ After the waters of the Flood receded, mankind had a fresh start. However, humans were still imperfect, and "the inclination of the heart of man" continued to be "bad from his youth up." (Genesis 8:21) Besides, although the demons could no longer materialize human bodies, they were still very active. The world of ungodly mankind quickly showed that it was "lying in the power of the wicked one," and just as today, true worshippers had to fight against "the machinations of the Devil."—1 John 5:19; Ephesians 6:11, 12.

⁷ At least from the time of Nimrod, the post-Flood earth once again became the scene of human violence. As a result of increasing population and the progress of technology, that violence has escalated over time. In earlier years, there were the sword, the spear, the bow and arrow, and the chariot. In more recent times came the musket and the cannon, then the rifle and the sophisticated artillery of the early 20th century. World War I brought to the fore more frightening weapons, such as the airplane, the tank, the submarine, and poison gas. In that war, these weapons took millions of lives. Was that unexpected? No.

⁸ In the year 1914, Jesus was enthroned as King of God's heavenly Kingdom, and "the Lord's day" began. (Revelation 1:10) In a vision reported in the book of Revelation,

heed the warning being given. He said that they were "eating and drinking, men marrying and women being given in marriage, until the day that Noah entered into the ark." Eating, drinking, marrying, being given in marriage—what was wrong with that? They were just living "normal" lives! But a flood was coming, and Noah was preaching righteousness. His words and his conduct should have been a warning to them. Still, they "took no note until the flood came and swept them all away."—Matthew 24:38, 39.

⁵ Looking back on those times, we see the wisdom of Noah's course. However, in the days before the Flood, it took courage to be different from everyone else. It took strong conviction for Noah and his family to build the huge ark and fill it with representatives of the animal kinds. Did some among those few faithful souls sometimes wish that they could be less conspicuous and just live "normal" lives? Even if such thoughts crossed their minds, they did not weaken in their integrity. After a great many years—longer than any one of us will have to endure in this

---

5. What qualities did Noah and his family need?

6. After the Flood, what situation still existed?
7. How did violence escalate in the post-Flood world?
8. How has Revelation 6:1-4 been fulfilled?

Just as in Noah's day, people today are consumed with their daily activities

Jesus is seen as a King riding forth victoriously on a white horse. Other horsemen follow him, each representing a different plague on mankind. One of them rides a fiery-colored horse, and to him it was granted "to take peace away from the earth so that they should slaughter one another; and a great sword was given him." (Revelation 6:1-4) This horse and its rider picture warfare, and the great sword represents the unprecedented destructiveness of modern warfare with its powerful weapons. Those weapons today include nuclear devices, each one capable of destroying tens of thousands of people; rockets able to deliver those devices to targets thousands of miles away; as well as sophisticated chemical and biological weapons of mass destruction.

We Take Note of Jehovah's Warnings

⁹ In the days of Noah, Jehovah brought mankind to ruin because of the extreme violence of wicked humans abetted by the Nephilim. What of today? Is the earth any less violent than it was then? Hardly! Moreover, just as in Noah's day, people today are going about their business, trying to live a "normal" life, refusing to heed the warnings being sounded. (Luke 17:26, 27) Is there any

reason, then, to doubt that Jehovah will once again bring mankind to ruin? No.

¹⁰ Hundreds of years before the Flood, Enoch prophesied the destruction that must come in our day. (Jude 14, 15) Jesus too spoke of the coming "great tribulation." (Matthew 24:21) Other prophets warned of that time. (Ezekiel 38:18-23; Daniel 12:1; Joel 2:31, 32) And in the book of Revelation, we read a graphic description of that final destruction. (Revelation 19:11-21) As individuals, we imitate Noah and are active as preachers of righteousness. We take note of Jehovah's warnings and lovingly help our neighbors to do the same. Hence, like Noah, we walk with God. Indeed, it is vital that any who desire life keep on walking with God. How can we do that in view of the pressures that we face each day? We need to cultivate strong faith in the outworking of God's purpose.—Hebrews 11:6.

Keep Walking With God in Troublous Times

¹¹ In the first century, anointed Christians were spoken of as belonging to "The Way." (Acts 9:2) Their whole way of life centered on faith in Jehovah and Jesus Christ. They

---

9. How does today's world compare with that existing before the Flood?

10. (a) What warning is repeatedly given in Bible prophecy? (b) What is the only wise course today?
11. In what way do we imitate first-century Christians?

walked in the path their Master had trod. Today, faithful Christians do likewise.

¹² The importance of faith is seen in an event that took place during Jesus' ministry. On one occasion, Jesus miraculously fed a crowd of about 5,000 men. The people were amazed and delighted. Notice, though, what happened next. We read: "When the men saw the signs he performed, they began to say: 'This is for a certainty the prophet that was to come into the world.' Therefore Jesus, knowing they were about to come and seize him to make him king, withdrew again into the mountain all alone." (John 6:10-15) That night he traveled to another location. Jesus' refusal to accept the kingship likely disappointed many. After all, he had shown that he was wise enough to be king and that he had the power to satisfy the people's physical needs. However, it was not yet Jehovah's time for him to rule as King. Besides, Jesus' Kingdom was to be heavenly, not earthly.

¹³ Nevertheless, the crowds determinedly followed Jesus and found him, as John says, "across the sea." Why did they follow him after he avoided their efforts to make him a king? Many betrayed a fleshly viewpoint, speaking pointedly of the material provisions that Jehovah had made in the wilderness in Moses' day. The implication was that Jesus should continue to make material provisions for them. Jesus, perceiving their wrong motives, began to teach them spiritual truths that could help adjust their thinking. (John 6:17, 24, 25, 30, 31, 35-40) In response, some murmured against him, especially when he spoke this illustration: "Most truly I say to you, Unless you eat the flesh of the Son of man and drink his blood,

As Kingdom preachers, "we are not the sort that shrink back"

you have no life in yourselves. He that feeds on my flesh and drinks my blood has everlasting life, and I shall resurrect him at the last day."—John 6:53, 54.

¹⁴ Jesus' illustrations often moved people to show whether they truly desired to walk with God. This one was no exception. It provoked strong reactions. We read: "Many of his disciples, when they heard this, said: 'This speech is shocking; who can listen to it?'" Jesus went on to explain that they should look for the spiritual meaning of his words. He said: "It is the spirit that is life-giving; the flesh is of no use at all. The sayings that I have spoken to you are spirit and are life." Still, many would not listen, and the account reports: "Owing to this many of his disciples went off to the things behind and would no longer walk with him."—John 6:60, 63, 66.

¹⁵ Nevertheless, not all of Jesus' disciples reacted that way. Admittedly, the loyal disciples did not fully understand what Jesus had said. Still, their confidence in him remained very firm. Peter, one of those loyal disciples, expressed the feelings of all who remained

---

12. What happened after Jesus miraculously fed a crowd?
13, 14. What viewpoint did many betray, and how was their faith tested?

15. What right viewpoint did some of Jesus' followers have?

when he said: "Lord, whom shall we go away to? You have sayings of everlasting life." (John 6:68) What an excellent attitude, and what a fine example!

16 We today could be tested as those early disciples were. In our case, we might be disappointed that Jehovah's promises are not being fulfilled as quickly as we personally would like. We might feel that explanations of the Scriptures in our Bible-based publications are difficult to understand. The conduct of a fellow Christian might disappoint us. Would it be right to stop walking with God for these or similar reasons? Of course not! The disciples who abandoned Jesus betrayed a fleshly way of thinking. We must avoid doing the same.

"We Are Not the Sort That Shrink Back"

17 The apostle Paul wrote: "All Scripture is inspired of God." (2 Timothy 3:16) Through the pages of the Bible, Jehovah tells us clearly: "This is the way. Walk in it." (Isaiah 30:21) Obeying God's Word helps us to 'keep strict watch on how we walk.' (Ephesians 5:15) Studying the Bible and meditating on what we learn enable us to "go on walking in the truth." (3 John 3) Truly, as Jesus said, "the spirit . . . is life-giving; the flesh is of no use at all." The only reliable guidance by which to direct our steps is spiritual guidance, which comes through Jehovah's Word, his spirit, and his organization.

18 Today, those who become disgruntled because of fleshly thinking or unfulfilled expectations often turn to making the most of what this world has to offer. Losing their sense of urgency, they see no need to "keep on the watch," and they choose to pursue selfish goals instead of putting Kingdom interests first. (Matthew 24:42) Walking in that way is most unwise. Notice the apostle Paul's words: "We are not the sort that shrink back to destruction, but the sort that have faith to the preserving alive of the soul." (Hebrews 10:39) Like Enoch and Noah, we live in turbulent times, but like them, we have the privilege of walking with God. Doing so, we have the assured expectation that we will see Jehovah's promises fulfilled, wickedness destroyed, and a righteous new world brought to pass. What a wonderful prospect!

19 The inspired prophet Micah said of the nations of the world that they would "walk each one in the name of its god." Then he spoke of himself and other faithful worshippers and said: "We, for our part, shall walk in the name of Jehovah our God to time indefinite, even forever." (Micah 4:5) If your determination is the same as Micah's, stay close to Jehovah however turbulent the times become. (James 4:8) May it be the heartfelt desire of each one of us to walk with Jehovah our God now and to time indefinite, even forever!

19. How does Micah describe the course of true worshippers?

16. How might we be tested, and what proper viewpoint should we cultivate?
17. How can we be helped to keep walking with God?
18. (a) What do some unwisely do? (b) What kind of faith do we cultivate?

How Would You Answer?

- What similarities are there between Noah's day and today?

- What course did Noah and his family follow, and how can we imitate their faith?

- What wrong viewpoint was betrayed by some of Jesus' followers?

- What are true Christians determined to do?

MENNONITES
Search for Bible Truth

ONE morning in November 2000, some missionaries of Jehovah's Witnesses in Bolivia glanced out the window of their small home and saw a group of plainly dressed men and women standing nervously at the gate. When the missionaries opened the gate, the visitors' first words were, "We want to find the truth from the Bible." The visitors were Mennonites. The men wore overalls, the women dark aprons, and they spoke among themselves in a German dialect. There was fear in their eyes. They kept looking to see if they had been followed. Nevertheless, even while climbing the steps to enter the house, one of the young men said, "I want to know the people who use God's name."

Inside, the visitors began to relax when they were served some refreshments. They had come from a distant, isolated farming colony. There, they had been receiving the *Watchtower* magazine by mail for six years. "We have read that there will be a paradise on earth. Is that true?" they asked. The Witnesses showed them the Bible's answer. (Isaiah 11:9; Luke 23:43; 2 Peter 3:7, 13; Revelation 21:3, 4) "You see!" said one farmer to the others. "It *is* true. There *will* be a paradise on earth." Others kept saying: "I think we have found the truth."

Who are the Mennonites? What do they believe? To answer these questions, we must go back to the 16th century.

Who Are the Mennonites?

In the 1500's, the upsurge in Bible translation and printing in the common languages of Europe sparked renewed interest in Bible study there. Martin Luther and other Reformers rejected many teachings of the Catholic Church. Yet, the newly formed Protestant churches retained many non-Biblical practices. For instance, most expected every newborn infant to be baptized into the church. However, some searchers for Bible truth realized that a person becomes a member of the Christian congregation only by making an informed decision *before* being baptized. (Matthew 28:19, 20) Zealous preachers who held this belief began traveling through towns and villages teaching the Bible and baptizing adults. Thus, they were called Anabaptists, meaning "rebaptizers."

One who looked to the Anabaptists in his search for truth was Menno Simons, a Catholic priest in the village of Witmarsum in the northern part of the Netherlands. By 1536 he had severed all ties with the church and had become a hunted man. In 1542 the Holy Roman Emperor Charles V himself promised 100 guilders as a reward for Menno's arrest. Nevertheless, Menno gathered some of the Anabaptists into congregations. He and his followers soon came to be called Mennonites.

Mennonites Today

In the course of time, persecution drove thousands of Mennonites from Western Europe to North America. There they had the opportunity to continue their search for truth and to spread their message to many others. But the burning zeal of their forebears for progressive Bible study and public preaching had largely been lost. Most clung to certain unbiblical teachings, such as the Trinity, the immortality of the human soul, and hellfire. (Ecclesiastes 9:5; Ezekiel 18:4;

IN OUR NEXT ISSUE

Who Is Jesus Christ?

———

"The Fear of Jehovah—That Is Wisdom"

———

What Others Think of Us—Does It Matter?

Mark 12:29) Today, Mennonite missionary efforts tend to focus more on medical and social services than on evangelism.

It is estimated that there are now about 1,300,000 Mennonites living in 65 countries. Yet, present-day Mennonites lament their lack of unity, as Menno Simons did centuries ago. During World War I, differences of opinion about the world's conflicts caused major divisions. Many in North America refused military service on Biblical grounds. But *An Introduction to Mennonite History* says: "By 1914 non-resistance was largely a historical memory for the Mennonite churches in Western Europe." Today, some Mennonite groups have adopted modern ways to a greater or lesser extent. Others still fasten their clothes with hooks and eyes rather than with buttons and believe that men should not shave their beards.

Some Mennonite groups, determined to keep separate from the modern world, have moved their communities to places where local governments allow them to live without interference. In Bolivia, for instance, an estimated 38,000 Mennonites live in numerous remote colonies, each with different rules of conduct. Some colonies forbid motor vehicles, permitting only horses and buggies. Certain colonies forbid radio, TV, and music. Some even forbid learning the language of the country they live in. "So as to keep us under their control, the preachers don't let us learn Spanish," commented one colony resident. Many feel oppressed and live in dread of being expelled from the community—a terrible prospect for one who has never experienced life outside.

How a Seed of Truth Was Sown

It was under these circumstances that a Mennonite farmer named Johann saw a copy of the *Watchtower* magazine in his neighbor's home. Johann's family had emigrated from Canada to Mexico and later to Bolivia. But Johann had always desired help in his search for Bible truth. He asked to borrow the magazine.

Later, while in the city to sell his farm products, Johann approached a Witness who was offering *The Watchtower* in the market. She directed him to a German-speaking missionary, and soon Johann was receiving *The Watchtower* by mail in German. Each issue was carefully studied and passed from family to family in his colony until the magazine was worn-out. Sometimes families would get together and study a *Watchtower* magazine until midnight, looking up the cited Bible texts. Johann became convinced that Jehovah's Witnesses must be the ones who are unitedly doing God's will earth wide. Before he died, Johann told his wife and children: "You must always read *The Watchtower*. It will help you to understand the Bible."

Some of Johann's family began talking to their neighbors about the things they were learning from the Bible. "The earth will not be destroyed. Rather, God will make it a paradise," they said. "And God doesn't torment people in hell." Word of these conversations soon reached the church preachers, who threatened Johann's family with expulsion if they did not stop. Later, during a family discussion about the pressure the Mennonite elders were putting on them, one young man spoke up. "I don't know why we complain about our church elders," he said. "We all know which is the true religion, and we haven't done anything about it." These words touched the heart of the young man's father. Soon, ten of the family set out on a secret trip in search of Jehovah's Witnesses and ended up at the home of the missionaries, as mentioned at the outset.

The next day, the missionaries went to visit their new friends in the colony. The missionaries' motor vehicle was the only one on

Happy response to receiving Bible literature in German

the road. As they slowly drove past horse-drawn buggies, they exchanged glances with the equally intrigued local residents. Soon they sat at a table with ten Mennonites, representing two families.

That day, it took four hours to study chapter 1 of the book *Knowledge That Leads to Everlasting Life.** For each paragraph, the farmers had looked up additional Bible texts and wanted to know if they were applying the texts correctly. Each study question was followed by a pause of several minutes while the farmers consulted in Low German before a spokesman finally answered for the group in Spanish. It was a memorable day, but a storm of trouble was brewing. They were about to face trials, just as Menno Simons had when he began his search for Bible truth nearly five centuries ago.

Facing Trials for the Truth

A few days later, the church elders came to the home of Johann's family with an ultimatum for the interested ones: "We heard that Jehovah's Witnesses visited you. You must forbid them to return, and unless you hand over their literature to be burned, you face expulsion." They had had just one Bible study with the Witnesses, so this presented a formidable test.

_____

* Published by Jehovah's Witnesses.

"We cannot do as you ask," replied one of the family heads. "Those people came to teach us the Bible." How did the elders react? They expelled them for studying the Bible! This was a cruel blow indeed. The cart belonging to the colony cheese factory passed by the home of one family without collecting their milk, denying them their only source of income. One family head was dismissed from his job. Another was turned away from buying supplies at the colony store, and his ten-year-old daughter was expelled from school. Neighbors surrounded one home to take away the wife of one of the young men, asserting that she could not live with her expelled husband. Despite all of this, the families who studied the Bible did not give up their search for the truth.

The missionaries continued to make the long weekly drive to conduct the Bible study. How strengthening the families found those studies to be! Some family members traveled two hours by horse and buggy to be present. It was a moving occasion when the families first invited one of the missionaries to pray. In these colonies Mennonites never pray aloud, so they had never before heard anyone pray in their behalf. The men had tears in their eyes. And can you imagine their curiosity when the missionaries brought along a tape recorder? Music had never been allowed in their colony. They were so delighted with the beautiful *Kingdom Melodies* that they decided to sing Kingdom songs after each study! Nevertheless, the question remained, How could they survive in their new circumstances?

Finding a Loving Brotherhood

Cut off from their community, the families began making their own cheese. The missionaries helped them to find buyers. A longtime Witness in North America who grew up in a South American Mennonite colony heard about the families' plight. He had a special desire to help. Within a week, he flew down to Bolivia to visit them. In addition to providing much spiritual encouragement, he helped the families to buy their own pickup truck so that they could get to meetings at the Kingdom Hall and also get their farm products to market.

"It was difficult after we were expelled from the community. We would travel to the Kingdom Hall with sad faces," recalls one family member, "but we returned joyful." Indeed, local Witnesses rose to the occasion and offered support. Some learned German, and several German-speaking Witnesses came from Europe to Bolivia to help conduct Christian meetings in German. Soon, 14 from the Mennonite community were preaching the good news of the Kingdom to others.

On October 12, 2001, less than a year after that first visit to the missionary home, 11 of these former Anabaptists were baptized again, this time in symbol of their dedication to Jehovah. Since then, more have taken this step. One later commented: "Since we have learned the truth from the Bible, we feel like slaves who have been set free." Another said: "Many Mennonites complain about a lack of love in their community. But Jehovah's Witnesses take an interest in one another. I feel safe among them." If you are searching for a better understanding of the truth from the Bible, you too may face difficulties. But if you seek Jehovah's help and show faith and courage as these families did, you too will be successful and find happiness.

Though music had always been forbidden, now they sing after each Bible study

Questions From Readers

What basis is there for saying that such phrases as "the one alone having immortality" and the one "whom not one of men has seen or can see" refer to Jesus rather than to Jehovah God?

The apostle Paul wrote: "This manifestation the happy and only Potentate will show in its own appointed times, he the King of those who rule as kings and Lord of those who rule as lords, the one alone having immortality, who dwells in unapproachable light, whom not one of men has seen or can see."—1 Timothy 6:15, 16.

Bible commentators generally reason: 'How could such phrases as "the one alone having immortality," the "only Potentate," and the one "whom not one of men has seen or can see" point to anyone *other* than the Almighty?' Admittedly, such terms could be used to describe Jehovah. However, the context indicates that at 1 Timothy 6:15, 16, Paul was specifically referring to Jesus.

At the end of verse 14, Paul mentions "the manifestation of our Lord Jesus Christ." (1 Timothy 6:14) Hence, when Paul writes in verse 15 that *"this* manifestation the happy and only Potentate will show in its own appointed times," he is referring to a manifestation of Jesus, not of Jehovah God. Who, then, is the "only Potentate"? It seems reasonable to conclude that Jesus is the Potentate referred to by Paul. Why? The context makes it evident that Paul is comparing Jesus with human rulers. Jesus truly is, as Paul wrote, "King of those [humans] who rule as kings and Lord of those [humans] who rule as lords."* Yes, compared to them, Jesus is the *"only* Potentate." Jesus has been given "rulership and

---

* Similar expressions are applied to Jesus at 1 Corinthians 8:5, 6; Revelation 17:12, 14; 19:16.

dignity and kingdom, that the peoples, national groups and languages should all serve even him." (Daniel 7:14) No human potentate can make that claim!

What about the phrase "the one alone having immortality"? Again, a comparison is being drawn between Jesus and *human* kings. No earthly rulers can claim to have been granted immortality, but Jesus can. Paul wrote: "We know that Christ, now that he has been raised up from the dead, dies no more; death is master over him no more." (Romans 6:9) Thus, Jesus is the first one to be described in the Bible as receiving the gift of immortality. Indeed, at the time of Paul's writing, Jesus was the *only* one who had attained indestructible life.

It should also be kept in mind that it would have been wrong for Paul to say that Jehovah God *alone* had immortality, since Jesus too was immortal when Paul wrote those words. But Paul could say that Jesus alone was immortal in comparison with earthly rulers.

Further, it is certainly true that after Jesus' resurrection and ascension to heaven, he can be described as one "whom not one of men has seen or can see." Granted, his anointed disciples would behold Jesus after their own death and subsequent resurrection to heaven as spirit creatures. (John 17:24) But no man on earth would see Jesus in his glorified state. Hence, it can truthfully be stated that since Jesus' resurrection and ascension, "not one of men" has actually seen Jesus.

True, at first glance, it may seem as if the descriptions found at 1 Timothy 6:15, 16 could apply to God. But the context of Paul's words—along with the corroboration of other scriptures—shows that Paul was referring to Jesus.

LET JEHOVAH'S "SAYING" SAFEGUARD YOU

IN 490 B.C.E. at the historic battle of Marathon, from 10 thousand to 20 thousand Athenians faced a greatly superior Persian army. A key factor in the Greek tactics was the phalanx—a block of soldiers marching in tight formation. Their shields presented an almost unbroken wall of armor, one bristling with spears. The phalanx gave the Athenians a famous victory over the vastly superior forces of the Persians.

True Christians are engaged in spiritual warfare. They contend with powerful foes —the invisible rulers of the present wicked system, who are described in the Bible as "the world rulers of this darkness, . . . the wicked spirit forces in the heavenly places." (Ephesians 6:12; 1 John 5:19) God's people continue to be victorious—but not in their own strength. All credit goes to Jehovah, who safeguards and instructs them, as stated at Psalm 18:30: "The saying of Jehovah is a refined one. A shield he is to all those taking refuge in him."

Yes, by means of his refined "saying," which is contained in the Sacred Scriptures, Jehovah shields his loyal servants from spiritual harm. (Psalm 19:7-11; 119:93) Concerning the wisdom manifest in God's Word, Solomon wrote: "Do not leave it, and it will keep you. Love it, and it will safeguard you." (Proverbs 4:6; Ecclesiastes 7:12) How does divine wisdom safeguard us against harm? Consider the example of ancient Israel.

A People Shielded by Godly Wisdom

Jehovah's Law protected and guided the Israelites in every facet of life. For example, the regulations on diet, hygiene, and quarantine spared them from many of the diseases that ravaged other nations. Only after the discovery of bacteria in the 19th century did science

begin to catch up with God's Law. The laws on land ownership, repurchase, debt release, and usury brought social benefits in Israel by promoting a stable society and a just economy. (Deuteronomy 7:12, 15; 15:4, 5) Jehovah's Law even helped to preserve the health of Israel's soil! (Exodus 23:10, 11) Commandments against false worship safeguarded the people spiritually, shielding them from demon oppression, child sacrifice, and many other evils, besides the demeaning practice of humans' bowing down before lifeless idols.—Exodus 20:3-5; Psalm 115:4-8.

Clearly, Jehovah's "saying" proved to be "no valueless word" for Israel; rather, it meant life and length of days to all who heeded it. (Deuteronomy 32:47) The same is true today of those who observe Jehovah's wise sayings, even though Christians are no longer under the Law covenant. (Galatians 3:24, 25; Hebrews 8:8) In fact, instead of a code of laws, Christians have a broad range of Bible principles to guide and safeguard them.

A People Protected by Principles

Laws may have a limited application and may be just temporary. However, Bible principles, being fundamental truths, usually have a broad and permanent application. Consider, for instance, the principle stated at James 3:17, which says in part: "The wisdom from above is first of all chaste, then peaceable." How can that fundamental truth serve as a shield to God's people today?

To be chaste means to be morally clean. Hence, those who value chastity strive to avoid not just immorality but even things that lead up to it, including sexual fantasizing and pornography. (Matthew 5:28) Likewise, courting couples who have taken the principle at James 3:17 to heart avoid intimacies that may lead to a loss of self-control. As lovers of principle, they are not lured

away from chastity, perhaps thinking that as long as they do not break the letter of the law, their conduct has Jehovah's approval. They know that Jehovah "sees what the heart is" and responds accordingly. (1 Samuel 16:7; 2 Chronicles 16:9) Such wise ones safeguard their flesh against the many sexually transmitted diseases rampant today as well as preserve their mental and emotional well-being.

Godly wisdom is also "peaceable," says James 3:17. Satan, we know, tries to estrange us from Jehovah by sowing a spirit of violence in our hearts, in part by way of questionable literature, movies, music, and computer games—some of which incite players to simulate unimaginable brutality and slaughter! (Psalm 11:5) That Satan is succeeding is evident in the growing wave of violent crime. Concerning such crime, some years ago the Australian newspaper *The Sydney Morning Herald* quoted Robert Ressler, coiner of the term "serial killer." Ressler said that the killers he interviewed in the 1970's were inflamed by soft-core material that "pales by today's standards." Hence, Ressler expressed "a bleak outlook for the future—a new century in which multiple murderers multiply."

Indeed, just months after that news item appeared, a gunman killed 16 infants and their teacher at a kindergarten in Dunblane, Scotland, before killing himself. The following month another crazed gunman massacred 32 people in the quiet Tasmanian town of Port Arthur, Australia. In recent years the United States has been rocked by a number of school massacres, causing Americans to ask, Why? In June 2001, Japan made world headlines when a deranged man entered a school and knifed 8 children in the first and second grades to death and slashed 15 other people. To be sure, the reasons behind such evils are complex, but media violence is increasingly seen as a contributing factor. "If a 60-second commercial can move mountains in the marketplace," wrote Australian columnist Phillip Adams, "don't tell me that a two-hour, mega-million movie doesn't modify attitudes." Interestingly, in the home of the Port Arthur gunman, police confiscated 2,000 violent and pornographic videos.

Those who cleave to Bible principles shield their mind and heart from all forms of entertainment that nurture a lust for violence. Hence, "the spirit of the world" finds no welcome mat in their thinking and desires. Instead, they are "taught by the spirit [of God]," and they strive to cultivate a love for its fruitage, which includes peace. (1 Corinthians 2:12, 13; Galatians 5: 22, 23) This they do through regular Bible study, prayer, and upbuilding meditation. They also avoid fraternizing with individuals of violent bent, choosing instead to associate with those who, like them, yearn for Jehovah's peaceful new world. (Psalm 1:1-3; Proverbs 16:29) Yes, what protection godly wisdom affords!

Let Jehovah's "Saying" Guard Your Heart

When tempted in the wilderness, Jesus refuted Satan by accurately quoting God's Word. (Luke 4:1-13) However, he did not engage the Devil in a mere battle of wits. In resting his defense on the Scriptures, Jesus spoke from his heart, and that is why the Devil's strategy, which had worked so well in Eden, failed in Jesus' case. Satan's machinations will also fail with us if we fill our heart with Jehovah's sayings. Nothing could be more important, for "out of [the heart] are the sources of life."—Proverbs 4:23.

Furthermore, we must *continue* to guard our heart, never letting up. Satan, having failed in the wilderness, did not cease to test

Jesus. (Luke 4:13) He will also persist with us, trying a variety of strategies to break our integrity. (Revelation 12:17) Hence, let us imitate Jesus by cultivating a deep love for God's Word, at the same time praying incessantly for holy spirit and wisdom. (1 Thessalonians 5:17; Hebrews 5:7) For his part, Jehovah promises all who take refuge in him that they will come to no spiritual harm.—Psalm 91:1-10; Proverbs 1:33.

God's Word Safeguards the Congregation

Satan cannot prevent the foretold "great crowd" from surviving the great tribulation. (Revelation 7:9, 14) Nevertheless, he still feverishly tries to corrupt Christians so that at least some individuals will lose Jehovah's favor. That strategy worked in ancient Israel and led to the death of 24,000 on the very portals of the Promised Land. (Numbers 25: 1-9) Of course, erring Christians who show true repentance receive loving help so as to be restored spiritually. But unrepentant sinners, like Zimri of old, endanger the moral and spiritual welfare of others. (Numbers 25: 14) Like soldiers in a phalanx who have thrown away their shields, they expose not just themselves to harm but their companions as well.

Hence, the Bible commands: "Quit mixing in company with anyone called a brother that is a fornicator or a greedy person or an idolater or a reviler or a drunkard or an extortioner, not even eating with such a man. . . . Remove the wicked man from among yourselves." (1 Corinthians 5:11, 13) Do you not agree that this wise "saying" helps to safeguard the moral and spiritual purity of the Christian congregation?

In sharp contrast, many of Christendom's churches as well as apostates regard as obsolete those parts of the Bible that contradict modern, liberal views of morality. Hence,

'The wisdom from above is chaste, then peaceable'

they excuse all forms of gross sin, even among the clergy. (2 Timothy 4:3, 4) Note, however, that Proverbs 30:5, which also refers to Jehovah's shieldlike "saying," is followed by the command in verse 6: "Add nothing to [God's] words, that he may not reprove you, and that you may not have to be proved a liar." Yes, those who tamper with the Bible are really spiritual liars—the most reprehensible liars of all! (Matthew 15: 6-9) Let us be truly grateful, then, to be part of an organization that deeply respects God's Word.

Shielded by "a Sweet Odor"

Because God's people cleave to the Bible and share its comforting message with others, they diffuse an incenselike "sweet odor" of life that gives pleasure to Jehovah. But to unrighteous individuals, the bearers of that message emit, according to the J. B. Phillips' translation, "the deathly smell of doom." Yes, the figurative sense of smell of the wicked has been so distorted by Satan's system of things that they feel uncomfortable or even hostile in the presence of those diffusing the "sweet odor of Christ." On the other hand,

those zealously spreading the good news become "a sweet odor of Christ among those who are being saved." (2 Corinthians 2:14-16) Such honesthearted ones are often disgusted with the hypocrisy and religious lies that characterize false religion. Thus, when we open God's Word and share with them the Kingdom message, they feel drawn to Christ and want to learn more.—John 6:44.

So do not feel discouraged when some react negatively to the Kingdom message. Rather, view the "sweet odor of Christ" as a form of spiritual protection that repels many potentially harmful individuals from the spiritual estate inhabited by God's people, while attracting those of good heart.—Isaiah 35:8, 9.

Because the Greek soldiers at Marathon closed ranks and held on to their shields with all their might, they won despite overwhelming odds. Likewise, Jehovah's loyal Witnesses are assured of complete victory in their spiritual warfare, for that is their "hereditary possession." (Isaiah 54:17) Hence, let each of us continue to take refuge in Jehovah by maintaining "a tight grip on the word of life."—Philippians 2:16.

EARLY GERMAN BIBLE USES GOD'S NAME

A 1558 edition of Eck's Bible, with marginal reference to the name Jehovah at Exodus 6:3

GOD'S personal name, Jehovah, appears thousands of times in the *New World Translation of the Holy Scriptures,* published in the German language in 1971.* However, this was not the first German Bible to use the divine name. It seems likely that the first German Bible in which the name Jehovah appeared was published almost 500 years ago by Johann Eck, a prominent Roman Catholic theologian.

Johann Eck was born in 1486 in southern Germany. By the age of 24, he was professor of theology at the university of Ingolstadt, a position he held until his death in 1543. Eck was a contemporary of Martin Luther, and the two were friends for a time. However, Luther went on to become a leading figure of the Reformation, whereas Eck was a defender of the Catholic Church.

The duke of Bavaria commissioned Eck to translate the Bible into German, and the translation was published in 1537. According to the *Kirchliches Handlexikon,* his translation stuck faithfully to the original text and "deserves more recognition than it has received so far." Eck's translation of Exodus 6:3 reads: "I am the Lord, who appeared to Abraam, Isaac, and Jacob in the Almighty God: and my name Adonai, I have not revealed to them." Eck added a marginal comment to the verse: "The name Adonai Jehoua." Many Bible scholars believe that this was the first time God's personal name was used in a German Bible.

However, God's personal name has been known and used for thousands of years. Its earliest recorded use is in the Hebrew language, in which "Jehovah" is used to identify the only true God. (Deuteronomy 6:4) Almost 2,000 years ago, Jesus' statement that he had made God's name known was recorded in the Greek language. (John 17:6) Since then, the name has been published in countless tongues, and soon, in fulfillment of Psalm 83:18, all will know that the one whose name is Jehovah is the Most High over all the earth.

* Published by Jehovah's Witnesses, initially in English in 1961. Now available in whole or in part in over 50 languages.

SEPTEMBER 15, 2005

THE WATCHTOWER

ANNOUNCING JEHOVAH'S KINGDOM

Who Is Jesus Christ?

THE WATCHTOWER®
ANNOUNCING JEHOVAH'S KINGDOM

September 15, 2005   Average Printing Each Issue: 26,439,000   Vol. 126, No. 18

THE PURPOSE OF *THE WATCHTOWER* is to exalt Jehovah God as Sovereign Lord of the universe. It keeps watch on world events as these fulfill Bible prophecy. It comforts all peoples with the good news that God's Kingdom will soon destroy those who oppress their fellowmen and that it will turn the earth into a paradise. It encourages faith in God's now-reigning King, Jesus Christ, whose shed blood opens the way for mankind to gain eternal life. *The Watchtower,* published by Jehovah's Witnesses continuously since 1879, is nonpolitical. It adheres to the Bible as its authority.

IN THIS ISSUE

3   A God or a Man?

4   Who Is Jesus Christ?

8   Multitudes Embrace Jehovah's Worship

10   Who Was Pontius Pilate?

13   "The Fear of Jehovah—That Is Wisdom"

16   Walk by Faith, Not by Sight!

21   Go On Walking as Jesus Christ Walked

26   Resist Wrong Thinking!

29   Questions From Readers

30   What Others Think of Us—Does It Matter?

32   Help With Our Emotions

WATCHTOWER STUDIES

OCTOBER 17-23:
Walk by Faith, Not by Sight!
Page 16. Songs to be used: 56, 160.

OCTOBER 24-30:
Go On Walking as Jesus Christ Walked.
Page 21. Songs to be used: 168, 134.

Publication of *The Watchtower* is part of a worldwide Bible educational work supported by voluntary donations.

Unless otherwise indicated, Scripture quotations are from the modern-language *New World Translation of the Holy Scriptures—With References.*

The Watchtower (ISSN 0043-1087) is published semimonthly by Watchtower Bible and Tract Society of New York, Inc.; M. H. Larson, President; G. F. Simonis, Secretary-Treasurer; 25 Columbia Heights, Brooklyn, NY 11201-2483. Periodicals Postage Paid at Brooklyn, NY, and at additional mailing offices. POSTMASTER: Send address changes to Watchtower, **Wallkill, NY 12589.**

Changes of address should reach us 30 days before your moving date. Give us your old and new address (if possible, your old address label).

Semimonthly   ENGLISH

Would you welcome more information or a free home Bible study? Please send your request to Jehovah's Witnesses, using the appropriate address below.

America, United States of: Wallkill, NY 12589. *Antigua:* Box 119, St. Johns. *Australia:* Box 280, Ingleburn, NSW 1890. *Bahamas:* Box N-1247, Nassau, N.P. *Barbados, W.I.:* Crusher Site Road, Prospect, St. James. *Britain:* The Ridgeway, London NW7 1RN. *Canada:* Box 4100, Halton Hills (Georgetown), Ontario L7G 4Y4. *Germany:* Niederselters, Am Steinfels, D-65618 Selters. *Ghana:* P. O. Box GP 760, Accra. *Guyana:* 352-360 Tyrell St., Republic Park Phase 2 EBD. *Hawaii 96819:* 2055 Kam IV Rd., Honolulu. *Hong Kong:* 4 Kent Road, Kowloon Tong. *India:* Post Box 6440, Yelahanka, Bangalore 560 064, KAR. *Ireland:* Newcastle, Greystones, Co. Wicklow. *Jamaica:* P. O. Box 103, Old Harbour, St. Catherine. *Japan:* 1271 Nakashinden, Ebina City, Kanagawa Pref., 243-0496. *Kenya:* P.O. Box 47788, GPO Nairobi 00100. *New Zealand:* P.O. Box 75-142, Manurewa. *Nigeria:* P.M.B. 1090, Benin City 300001, Edo State. *Philippines, Republic of:* P. O. Box 2044, 1060 Manila. *South Africa:* Private Bag X2067, Krugersdorp, 1740. *Trinidad and Tobago, Republic of:* Lower Rapsey Street & Laxmi Lane, Curepe. *Zambia:* Box 33459, Lusaka 10101. *Zimbabwe:* Private Bag WG-5001, Westgate.

NOW PUBLISHED IN 151 LANGUAGES. SEMIMONTHLY: Afrikaans, Albanian,* Amharic, Arabic, Bengali, Bicol, Bislama, Bulgarian, Cebuano,* Chichewa,* Chinese, Chinese (Simplified),* Cibemba,* Croatian,* Czech,*# Danish,*# Dutch,*# East Armenian, Efik,* English*#+◉ (also Braille), Estonian, Ewe, Fijian, Finnish,*# French*# (also Braille), Ga, Georgian,* German,*# Greek,* Gujarati, Gun, Hebrew, Hiligaynon, Hindi, Hungarian,*# Igbo,* Iloko,* Indonesian, Italian,*# Japanese*# (also Braille), Kannada, Kinyarwanda, Kirundi, Korean*# (also Braille), Latvian, Lingala, Lithuanian, Luvale, Macedonian, Malagasy,* Malayalam, Maltese, Myanmar, Nepali, Norwegian,*# Pangasinan, Papiamento (Aruba), Papiamento (Curaçao), Polish,*# Portuguese*# (also Braille), Punjabi, Rarotongan, Romanian,* Russian,* Samar-Leyte, Samoan, Sango, Sepedi, Serbian, Sesotho, Shona,* Silozi, Sinhala, Slovak,* Slovenian, Solomon Islands Pidgin, Spanish*# (also Braille), Sranantongo, Swahili,* Swedish,*# Tagalog,* Tamil, Telugu, Thai, Tigrinya, Tok Pisin, Tongan, Tshiluba, Tsonga, Tswana, Turkish, Twi, Ukrainian,* Urdu, Vietnamese, Wallisian, Xhosa, Yoruba,* Zulu*

MONTHLY: American Sign Language,△□ Armenian, Assamese, Azerbaijani (roman script), Brazilian Sign Language,△ Cambodian, Chitonga, Gilbertese, Greenlandic, Haitian Creole, Hausa, Hiri Motu, Icelandic, Isoko, Kaonde, Kazakh, Kikongo, Kiluba, Kirghiz, Kosraean, Kwanyama/Ndonga, Luganda, Marathi, Marshallese, Mauritian Creole, Maya, Mizo, Monokutuba, Moore, Niuean, Ossetian, Otetela, Palauan, Persian, Ponapean, Seychelles Creole, Tahitian, Tatar, Tiv, Trukese, Tumbuka, Tuvaluan, Umbundu, Uruund, Venda, Yapese, Zande

* Study articles also available in large-print edition.
\# Audiocassettes also available.
+ CD also available.
◉ MP3 CD-ROM also available.
△ Videocassette
□ DVD

A God or a Man?

"I AM the light of the world. He that follows me will by no means walk in darkness, but will possess the light of life." (John 8:12) These words were spoken by Jesus Christ. A learned man of the first century wrote about him: "Carefully concealed in him are all the treasures of wisdom and of knowledge." (Colossians 2:3) Moreover, the Bible says: "This means everlasting life, their taking in knowledge of you, the only true God, and of the one whom you sent forth, Jesus Christ." (John 17:3) Accurate knowledge about Jesus is essential in order to satisfy our spiritual need.

People around the earth have heard of Jesus Christ. His influence on the history of mankind is beyond question. In fact, the calendar used in most parts of the world is based on the year he is thought to have been born. "Many people refer to dates before that year as B.C., or *before Christ*," explains *The World Book Encyclopedia*. "They use A.D., or *anno Domini* (in the year of our Lord), for dates after that year."

Yet, there are conflicting ideas about who Jesus was. To some, he was no more than an outstanding man who left his mark on history. Others, though, worship him as God Almighty. Some Hindu thinkers have likened Jesus Christ to the Hindu god Krishna, said by many to be a god incarnate. Was Jesus merely a man, or was he someone to be worshipped? Exactly who was he? Where did he come from? What was he like? And where is he now? As we will see in the following article, the book that has a great deal to say about Jesus gives truthful answers to these questions.

Who Is Jesus Christ?

IMAGINE how excited a young Jew named Andrew must have been when he first listened to the words of Jesus of Nazareth! The Bible states that Andrew rushed to his brother and said: "We have found the Messiah [or, Christ]." (John 1:41) In the Hebrew and Greek languages, the words usually translated "Messiah" and "Christ" mean "Anointed One." Jesus was the Anointed One, or the Chosen One of God—the promised Leader. (Isaiah 55:4) The Scriptures contained prophecies concerning him, and the Jews at the time were in expectation of him.—Luke 3:15.

How do we know that Jesus really was God's Chosen One? Well, consider what happened in the year 29 C.E. when Jesus was 30 years of age. He went to John the Baptizer to be baptized by him in the waters of the Jordan River. The Bible states: "After being baptized Jesus immediately came up from the water; and, look! the heavens were opened up, and he saw descending like a dove God's spirit coming upon him. Look! Also, there was a voice from the heavens that said: 'This is my Son, the beloved, whom I have approved.'" (Matthew 3:16, 17) After hearing those words of approval, could John have had any doubt that Jesus was God's Chosen One? By pouring out His holy spirit on Jesus, Jehovah God anointed him, or appointed him, to be the King of His coming Kingdom. Thus, Jesus became Jesus Christ, or Jesus the Anointed One. In what way, though, was Jesus God's Son? What was his origin?

His Origin Was "From Early Times"

Jesus' life course might be divided into three stages. The first began long before his human birth. His origin was "from early times, from the days of time indefinite," says Micah 5:2. Jesus himself said: "I am from the realms above"—that is, from heaven. (John 8:23) He had been in heaven as a mighty spirit person.

Since all created things had a beginning, there was a time when God was alone. Countless ages ago, however, God became a Creator. Who was his first creation? The last book of the Bible identifies Jesus as "the beginning of the creation by God." (Revelation 3:14) Jesus is "the firstborn of all creation." That is so "because by means of him all other things were created in the heavens and upon the earth, the things visible and the things invisible." (Colossians 1:15, 16) Yes, Jesus was the only one directly created by God himself. Therefore, he is called God's "only-begotten Son." (John 3:16) The firstborn Son also bears the title "the Word." (John 1:14) Why? Because before being born as a human, he served in heaven as one who spoke for God.

"The Word" was with Jehovah God "in the beginning," when "the heavens and the earth" were created. He was the one to whom God said: "Let us make man in our image." (John 1:1; Genesis 1:1, 26) Jehovah's firstborn Son was there at his Father's side, actively working with him. At Proverbs 8:22-31, he is represented as saying: "I came to be beside [the Creator] as a master worker, and I came to be the one he was specially fond of day by day, I being glad before him all the time."

How intimately Jehovah God and his only-begotten Son must have come to know each other as they worked side by side! That close association with Jehovah for untold ages deeply affected God's Son. This obedient Son came to be just like his Father, Jehovah. In fact, Colossians 1:15 calls Jesus "the image of the invisible God." This is one reason why knowledge about Jesus is vital in satisfying our spiritual need and our natural desire to know God. Everything Jesus did while on earth is exactly what Jehovah expected him to do. Hence, getting to know Jesus also means increasing our knowledge of Jehovah. (John 8:28; 14:8-10) But how did Jesus come to be on earth?

His Life as a Man

The second stage of Jesus' life course began when God sent his Son to the earth. Jehovah did this by miraculously transferring the life of Jesus from heaven to the womb of a faithful Jewish virgin named Mary. Jesus inherited no imperfections because he did not have a human father. Jehovah's holy spirit, or active force, came upon Mary, and his power 'overshadowed' her, miraculously causing her to become pregnant. (Luke 1:34, 35) Mary therefore gave birth to a perfect child. As the adopted son of the carpenter Joseph, he was brought up in a humble home and was the first of several children in the family.—Isaiah 7:14; Matthew 1:22, 23; Mark 6:3.

Little is known about Jesus' childhood, but one incident is noteworthy. When Jesus was 12 years old, his parents took him on their annual visit to Jerusalem for the Passover. While there, he spent quite some time at the temple, "sitting in the midst of the teachers and listening to them and questioning them." Moreover, "all those listening to him were in constant amazement at his understanding and his answers." Yes, young Jesus could not only ask thought-provoking, spiritually oriented questions but also give intelligent answers that amazed others. (Luke 2:41-50) As he grew up in the city of Nazareth, he learned to be a carpenter, undoubtedly from his adoptive father, Joseph. —Matthew 13:55.

Jesus lived in Nazareth until he was 30 years old. Then he went to John to be baptized. Following his baptism, Jesus embarked on his dynamic ministry. For three and a half years, he traveled throughout his homeland declaring the good news of God's Kingdom. He gave evidence that he had been sent by God. How? By performing many miracles—powerful works that were beyond human ability.—Matthew 4:17; Luke 19:37, 38.

Jesus was also a man of tender warmth and deep feelings. His tenderness was especially evident in the way he viewed and

At his baptism, Jesus became God's Anointed One

treated others. Because Jesus was approachable and kind, people were attracted to him. Even children felt at ease in his presence. (Mark 10:13-16) Jesus treated women with respect, even though some in his day looked down on them. (John 4:9, 27) He helped the poor and oppressed to 'find refreshment for their souls.' (Matthew 11:28-30) His manner of teaching was clear, simple, and practical. And what he taught reflected his heartfelt desire to acquaint his listeners with the true God, Jehovah.—John 17:6-8.

Using God's holy spirit to perform miracles, Jesus compassionately healed the sick and the afflicted. (Matthew 15:30, 31) For example, a person with leprosy came to him and said: "If you just want to, you can make me clean." What did Jesus do? He stretched out his hand and touched the man, saying to him: "I want to. Be made clean." And the sick man was healed!—Matthew 8:2-4.

Consider, too, an occasion when a crowd who came to Jesus stayed with him for three days with nothing to eat. He felt pity for the people and miraculously fed the "four thousand men, besides women and young children." (Matthew 15:32-38) On another occasion, Jesus calmed a storm that threatened the safety of his friends. (Mark 4:37-39) He resurrected, or brought back to life, those who had died.* (Luke 7:22; John 11:43, 44) Jesus even willingly gave his perfect human life so that imperfect mankind would have a hope for the future. What profound love Jesus had for people!

Where Is Jesus Today?

Jesus died on a torture stake at the age of 33 1/2.# But death was not the end of his life course. The third stage of his life began about three days later when Jehovah God resurrected his Son as a spirit person. After his resurrection, Jesus appeared to hundreds of people living in the first century C.E. (1 Corinthians 15:3-8) Thereafter, he "sat down at the right hand of God" and waited to receive kingly power. (Hebrews 10:12, 13) When that time came, Jesus began ruling as King. So how should we imagine Jesus today? Should we think of him as a suffering man being put to death? Or should we view him as someone to be worshipped? Jesus today is neither a man nor God Almighty. Rather, he is a mighty spirit creature, a reigning King. Very soon now, he will manifest his rulership over our troubled earth.

Using symbolic language, Revelation 19:11-16 describes Jesus Christ as a king seated upon a white horse and coming to judge and carry on war in righteousness. He has "a sharp long sword, that he may strike the nations with it." Yes, Jesus will use his great power to destroy the wicked. And what about those who strive to follow the example he set while on earth? (1 Peter 2:21) He and his Father will preserve them through the upcoming "war of the great day of God the Almighty"—often called Armageddon—so that they can live forever as earthly subjects of God's heavenly Kingdom.—Revelation 7:9, 14; 16:14, 16; 21:3, 4.

During his reign of peace, what miracles Jesus will perform in behalf of all mankind! (Isaiah 9:6, 7; 11:1-10) He will cure sickness and bring an end to death. Jesus will be used by God to resurrect billions, giving them an opportunity to live forever on earth. (John 5:28, 29) We cannot even imagine how wonderful our lives will be under Kingdom rule. It is important, then, that we continue to take in Bible knowledge and become better acquainted with Jesus Christ.

---

* The miracles that Jesus performed were common knowledge. Even Jesus' enemies acknowledged that he 'performed many signs.'—John 11:47, 48.

For an explanation of whether Christ died on a stake or on a cross, see pages 89-90 of the book *Reasoning From the Scriptures,* published by Jehovah's Witnesses.

Today, Jesus is a mighty King

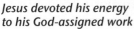

Jesus devoted his energy to his God-assigned work

IS JESUS GOD ALMIGHTY?

Many religious people say that Jesus is God. Some claim that God is a Trinity. According to this teaching, "the Father is God, the Son is God, and the Holy Spirit is God, and yet there are not three Gods but one God." It is held that the three "are co-eternal and co-equal." (*The Catholic Encyclopedia*) Are such views correct?

Jehovah God is the Creator. (Revelation 4: 11) He is without beginning or end, and he is almighty. (Psalm 90:2) Jesus, on the other hand, had a beginning. (Colossians 1:15, 16) Referring to God as his Father, Jesus said: "The Father is greater than I am." (John 14:28) Jesus also explained that there were some things neither he nor the angels knew but that were known only by his Father.—Mark 13:32.

Moreover, Jesus prayed to his Father: "Let, not my will, but yours take place." (Luke 22: 42) To whom was Jesus praying if not to a superior Personage? Furthermore, it was God who resurrected Jesus from the dead, not Jesus himself. (Acts 2:32) Obviously, the Father and the Son were not equal before Jesus came

to the earth or during his earthly life. What about after Jesus' resurrection to heaven? First Corinthians 11:3 states: "The head of the Christ is God." In fact, the Son will always be in subjection to God. (1 Corinthians 15:28) The Scriptures therefore show that Jesus is not God Almighty. Instead, he is God's Son.

The so-called third person of the Trinity —the holy spirit—is not a person. Addressing God in prayer, the psalmist said: "If you send forth your spirit, they are created." (Psalm 104:30) This spirit is not God himself; it is an active force that he sends forth or uses to accomplish whatever he wishes. By means of it, God created the physical heavens, the earth, and all living things. (Genesis 1:2; Psalm 33:6) God used his holy spirit to inspire the men who wrote the Bible. (2 Peter 1:20, 21) The Trinity, then, is not a Scriptural teaching.* "Jehovah our God is one Jehovah," says the Bible.—Deuteronomy 6:4.

---

* For further information, see the brochure *Should You Believe in the Trinity?* published by Jehovah's Witnesses.

Multitudes Embrace Jehovah's Worship

BIBLE prophecies pointing to our day foretold that people from all nations would flock to Jehovah's elevated worship. For example, through the prophet Haggai, Jehovah God declared: "I will rock all the nations, and the desirable things of all the nations must come in; and I will fill this house with glory." (Haggai 2:7) Both Isaiah and Micah prophesied that during our time—"the final part of the days"—nations and peoples would worship Jehovah in an acceptable way.—Isaiah 2:2-4; Micah 4:1-4.

Are such prophecies really being fulfilled today? Let the facts speak for themselves. During the past ten years alone, more than 3,110,000 new ones have dedicated themselves to Jehovah in more than 230 lands. Indeed, 6 out of every 10 Witnesses of Jehovah currently serving worldwide were baptized during the last decade. In 2004, on average, a newly dedicated servant of God was added to the Christian congregation every two minutes!*

As in the first century, today 'a great number have become believers and have turned to the Lord.' Although numerical increase is not in itself proof of God's blessing, it does provide evidence that "the hand of Jehovah" is with his people. (Acts 11:21) What leads millions to Jehovah's worship? And how are you personally affected by this development?

Righthearted People Are Attracted

In very direct terms, Jesus stated: "No man can come to me unless the Father, who sent me, draws him." (John 6:44) Ultimately, therefore, Jehovah is responsible for drawing

---

* See *2005 Calendar of Jehovah's Witnesses*, September/October.

people who are "rightly disposed for everlasting life." (Acts 13:48) God's spirit can awaken people to their spiritual need. (Matthew 5:3) A disturbed conscience, a desperate quest for hope, or a gripping crisis may lead some to search for God and thus learn about his purpose for mankind.—Mark 7:26-30; Luke 19:2-10.

Many individuals are attracted to Jehovah's worship because the Bible educational program of the Christian congregation helps them to get answers to questions that perplex them.

"If there is a God, why do people continue to suffer injustice?" That was the question that tormented Davide, a drug dealer in Italy. He was not particularly interested in religious matters, so he posed this challenging question more as a provocation than anything else. "I didn't think I was going to receive a reasonable and convincing answer," he says. "But the Witness who spoke with me was very patient and backed up with passages from the Bible what he was saying. That conversation had

---

WHO IS BEHIND THIS INCREASE?

"Unless Jehovah himself builds the house, it is to no avail that its builders have worked hard on it."
—Psalm 127:1.

"God kept making it grow; so that neither is he that plants anything nor is he that waters, but God who makes it grow."
—1 Corinthians 3:6, 7.

"No man can come to me unless the Father, who sent me, draws him."
—JOHN 6:44

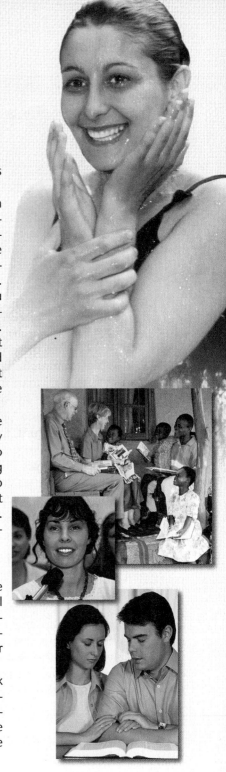

a profound effect on me." Today, Davide has straightened out his life and serves Jehovah.

Others are led to the earthly part of Jehovah's organization as a result of their quest for meaning and purpose. Seeking therapy for her own emotional problems, a psychiatrist in Zagreb, Croatia, visited a famous colleague. To her surprise, the doctor gave her the phone number of the branch office of Jehovah's Witnesses in Zagreb, as well as the name of a Witness he knew. "Look," he said, "I think these people can help you. If I send you to the church, you will find only lifeless statues—nobody is speaking, and everything is dark. I don't think the church can help you. I have sent other patients to Jehovah's Witnesses, and I think it would be the best for you too." Obligingly, the Witnesses visited her and soon started a Bible study with her. In a few weeks, that psychiatrist joyfully declared that knowledge of God's purpose had given meaning to her life.—Ecclesiastes 12:13.

When a personal crisis strikes, many have found that only Bible truth can provide real comfort. In Greece, a seven-year-old boy fell from the roof of his school and died. A few months later, two Witnesses met his mother and tried to comfort her by discussing the resurrection hope. (John 5:28, 29) At that, the lady burst into tears. The sisters asked: "If you would like to know more about the Bible, when can we visit you?" "Right now," she answered. The woman took them to her home, and a Bible study was started. Today, her whole family is serving Jehovah.

Are You Having a Part?

Such experiences are typical of what is happening around the world. Jehovah is gathering and training a great multinational crowd of true worshippers. This international group has the happy prospect of surviving the approaching end of this wicked system of things and living on into a righteous new world.—2 Peter 3:13.

As a result of Jehovah's blessing, this unprecedented work of ingathering is moving irresistibly toward its successful completion. (Isaiah 55:10, 11; Matthew 24:3, 14) Are you zealously engaging in this Kingdom-preaching activity? If you are, you can be confident of divine support and can echo these words of the psalmist: "My help is from Jehovah."—Psalm 121:2.

Who Was
PONTIUS
PILATE?

"**M**OCKING, skeptical Pilate is a historical figure who haunts our imagination. For some he is a saint, for others the embodiment of human weakness, an archetypal politician willing to sacrifice one man for the sake of stability."—*Pontius Pilate,* by Ann Wroe.

Whether you share any of those views or not, Pontius Pilate did make a name for himself because of the way he treated Jesus Christ. Who was Pilate? What is known about him? A better grasp of his position will enhance our understanding of the most important events ever to unfold on the earth.

Position, Duties, and Power

Roman Emperor Tiberius appointed Pilate governor of the province of Judaea in 26 C.E. Such prefects were men of the so-called equestrian order—the lower nobility, as opposed to aristocrats of senatorial status. Pilate likely joined the army as a military tribune, or junior commander; passed through the ranks during successive tours of duty; and was appointed governor before he was 30 years old.

When in uniform, Pilate would have worn a leather tunic and metal breastplate. His public clothing was a white toga with a purple border. He would have had short hair and have been clean-shaven. Although some believe that he came from Spain, his name suggests that he belonged to the tribe of the Pontii—Samnite nobles from southern Italy.

Prefects of Pilate's rank were usually sent to barbarous territories. The Romans considered Judaea to be such a place. In addition to maintaining order, Pilate oversaw the collection of indirect taxes and the poll tax. Day-to-day administration of justice was a concern of the Jewish courts, but cases requiring the death penalty were evidently referred to the governor, who was the supreme judicial authority.

With a small staff of scribes, companions, and messengers, Pilate and his wife lived in the port city of Caesarea. Pilate commanded five infantry cohorts of from 500 to 1,000 men each as well as a cavalry regiment likely consisting of 500. His soldiers routinely impaled lawbreakers. In peacetime, executions followed summary hearings, but during an uprising, rebels were put to death on the spot and en masse. For example, the Romans impaled 6,000 slaves to crush the revolt led by Spartacus. If trouble threatened in Judaea, the governor could normally turn to the imperial legate in Syria, who commanded legions. During much of Pilate's tenure, however, the legate was absent, and Pilate had to end disorders quickly.

Governors regularly communicated with the emperor. Matters involving his dignity or any threats to Roman authority required reports and resulted in imperial orders. A governor might be anxious to give the emperor his own version of events in his province before others could complain. With trouble brewing in Judaea, such concerns were very real to Pilate.

Aside from the Gospel accounts, the historians Flavius Josephus and Philo are the main sources of information on Pilate. Roman historian Tacitus also states that Pilate executed Christus, from whom Christians took their name.

Jewish Outrage Provoked

Josephus says that out of regard for Jewish scruples over the making of images, Roman governors had avoided taking into Jerusalem military standards bearing effigies of the emperor. Because Pilate showed no such restraint, outraged Jews rushed to Caesarea to complain. Pilate did nothing for five days. On the sixth day, he ordered his soldiers to surround the protesters and threaten to execute them if they did not disperse. When the Jews said that they would rather die than see their Law transgressed, Pilate relented and ordered that the images be removed.

Pilate was capable of using force. In an incident recorded by Josephus, the prefect began work on an aqueduct to bring water into Jerusalem and used funds from the temple treasury to finance the project. Pilate did not simply seize the money, for he knew that plundering the temple was sacrilege and would have caused angry Jews to ask Tiberius to recall him. So it seems that Pilate had the

This inscription identifying Pontius Pilate as prefect of Judaea was found at Caesarea

cooperation of the temple authorities. Dedicated funds, termed "corban," could legitimately be used for public works to benefit the city. But thousands of Jews gathered to express their indignation.

Pilate had troops mingle with the crowd with orders not to use swords but to beat the protesters with clubs. He apparently wanted to control the mob without provoking a massacre. This seems to have paid off, though some did die. Certain ones who reported to Jesus that Pilate had mixed the blood of Galileans with their sacrifices may have been referring to this incident.—Luke 13:1.

"What Is Truth?"

What makes Pilate infamous is his investigation of charges made by the Jewish chief priests and older men that Jesus was presenting himself as King. On hearing of Jesus' mission to bear witness to the truth, Pilate saw that the prisoner presented no threat to Rome. "What is truth?" he asked, evidently thinking that truth was too elusive a concept to merit much attention. His conclusion? "I find no crime in this man." —John 18:37, 38; Luke 23:4.

That should have been the end of Jesus' trial, but the Jews insisted that he was subverting the nation. Envy was the chief priests' reason for turning Jesus over, and Pilate knew it. He also knew that releasing Jesus would cause trouble, something he wanted to avoid. There had been enough of that already, for Barabbas and others were in custody for sedition and murder. (Mark 15: 7, 10; Luke 23:2) Moreover, previous disputes with the Jews had tarnished Pilate's reputation with Tiberius, who was notorious for dealing severely with bad governors. Yet, to give in to the Jews would be a sign of weakness. So Pilate faced a dilemma.

On hearing where Jesus was from, Pilate tried to pass the case on to Herod Antipas, district ruler of Galilee. When that failed, Pilate attempted to get those gathered outside his palace to ask for Jesus' release, in accord with the custom of freeing a prisoner at Passover. The crowd clamored for Barabbas. —Luke 23:5-19.

Pilate may have wanted to do what was right, but he also desired to save himself and please the crowd. Finally, he put his career ahead of conscience and justice. Calling for water, he washed his hands and claimed innocence in the death he now sanctioned.* Though he believed that Jesus was innocent, Pilate had him scourged and allowed soldiers to mock, strike, and spit upon him. —Matthew 27:24-31.

Pilate made a final attempt to free Jesus, but the crowd shouted that if he did so, he was no friend of Caesar. (John 19:12) At that, Pilate caved in. One scholar said this about Pilate's decision: "The solution was easy: execute the man. All that was to be lost was the life of one apparently insignificant Jew; it would be foolish to let trouble develop over him."

---

* Hand washing was a Jewish, not a Roman, way of expressing nonparticipation in bloodshed.—Deuteronomy 21:6, 7.

What Happened to Pilate?

The last recorded incident in Pilate's career was another conflict. Josephus says that a multitude of armed Samaritans gathered on Mount Gerizim in hopes of uncovering treasures that Moses had supposedly buried there. Pilate intervened, and his troops slew a number of the crowd. The Samaritans complained to Pilate's superior, Lucius Vitellius, governor of Syria. Whether Vitellius thought that Pilate had gone too far is not stated. In any case, he ordered Pilate to Rome to answer to the emperor for his actions. Before he arrived, however, Tiberius died.

"At that point," says one source, "Pilate passes out of history into legend." But many have tried to supply missing details. It has been claimed that Pilate became a Christian. Ethiopian "Christians" made him a "saint." Eusebius, who wrote in the late third and early fourth centuries, was the first of many to say that Pilate, like Judas Iscariot, committed suicide. However, just what became of Pilate is a matter of speculation.

Pilate could be obstinate, flippant, and heavy-handed. But he remained in office for ten years, whereas most prefects of Judaea had much shorter tenures. From a Roman viewpoint, therefore, Pilate was competent. He has been called a coward who reprehensibly had Jesus tortured and killed to protect himself. Others argue that Pilate's duty was not so much to uphold justice as it was to promote peace and Roman interests.

Pilate's times were very different from our own. Yet, no judge could justly condemn a man he considered innocent. Had it not been for his encounter with Jesus, Pontius Pilate might be just another name in the history books.

"THE FEAR OF JEHOVAH

That Is Wisdom"

"THE conclusion of the matter, everything having been heard, is: Fear the true God and keep his commandments. For this is the whole obligation of man." (Ecclesiastes 12:13) What a profound conclusion King Solomon of ancient Israel drew under divine inspiration! The patriarch Job also appreciated the value of the fear of God, for he said: "Look! The fear of Jehovah—that is wisdom, and to turn away from bad is understanding."—Job 28:28.

The Bible places great importance on fearing Jehovah. Why is our cultivating reverential fear of God the course of wisdom? In what way does having godly fear benefit us —individually and as a group of true worshippers? Verses 26 to 35 of Proverbs chapter 14 answer these questions.*

Source of "Strong Confidence"

"In the fear of Jehovah there is strong confidence," states Solomon, *"and for his sons there will come to be a refuge."* (Proverbs 14: 26) A God-fearing man's source of trust is none other than the loyal and almighty God, Jehovah. No wonder such a man faces what lies ahead with strong confidence! His future is long and blessed.

What, though, can be said about the future of those who put their confidence in the world—its schemes, its organizations, its

---

* For a discussion of Proverbs 14:1-25, see *The Watchtower* of November 15, 2004, pages 26-9, and July 15, 2005, pages 17-20.

ideologies, and its goods? Whatever future they hope to have is short, for the Bible states: "The world is passing away and so is its desire, but he that does the will of God remains forever." (1 John 2:17) Is there any reason for us, then, to "be loving either the world or the things in the world"?—1 John 2:15.

What measures can God-fearing parents take to ensure that "there will come to be a refuge" for their children? "Come, you sons, listen to me," sang the psalmist, "the fear of Jehovah is what I shall teach you." (Psalm 34:11) When children by parental example and instruction are taught to fear God, they are more likely to grow up to be men and women who have strong confidence in Jehovah.—Proverbs 22:6.

"The fear of Jehovah is a well of life," continues Solomon, *"to turn away from the snares of death."* (Proverbs 14:27) The fear of Jehovah is "a well of life" because the true God is "the source of living water." (Jeremiah 2:13) Taking in knowledge of Jehovah and of Jesus Christ can mean everlasting life for us. (John 17:3) Godly fear also turns us away from the snares of death. How? Proverbs 13:14 states: "The law of the wise one is a source of life, to turn one away from the snares of death." When we fear Jehovah, obey his law, and allow his Word to guide our steps, are we not protected from harmful practices and emotions that can lead to early death?

"Adornment of a King"

During most of his reign, Solomon was a God-fearing king who obeyed Jehovah. This contributed to a successful rulership. What determines how well a king rules? Proverbs 14:28 answers: *"In the multitude of people there is an adornment of a king, but in the lack of population is the ruin of a high official."* The success of a king is measured by the welfare of his subjects. If a great multitude of people desire to remain under his rulership, that recommends him as a good ruler. Solomon had "subjects from [the Red] sea to [the Mediterranean] sea and from the River [Euphrates] to the ends of the earth." (Psalm 72:6-8) His rulership was marked by unprecedented peace and prosperity. (1 Kings 4:24, 25) Solomon's reign was a success. On the other hand, a lack of approval by the populace spells disgrace for a high official.

In this regard, what can be said about the glory of the Greater Solomon, the Messianic King, Jesus Christ? Think of the subjects he has even today. From one end of the earth to the other, over six million God-fearing men and women have already chosen to live under Christ's rulership. They exercise faith in Jesus and are united in true worship of the living God. (John 14:1) By the end of the Millennial Rule, all those in God's memory will have been resurrected. A paradise earth will then be full of happy, righteous people who have manifested appreciation for their King. What a testimony that will be to the success of Christ's rulership! Let us hold fast to our wonderful Kingdom hope.

Spiritual and Physical Benefits

Reverential fear of God can give us calmness of heart and tranquillity of spirit. This is so because wisdom's many facets include good judgment and discernment. Proverbs 14:29 states: *"He that is slow to anger is abundant in discernment, but one that is impatient is exalting foolishness."* Discernment helps us to realize that uncontrolled anger has a damaging effect on our spirituality. "Enmities, strife, jealousy, fits of anger, contentions" are listed among the works that could prevent us from 'inheriting God's kingdom.' (Galatians 5:19-21) We are counseled against harboring even justifiable anger. (Ephesians 4:26, 27) And impatience can lead to foolish speech and action that we later regret.

Pointing to the adverse physical effects of anger, the king of Israel says: *"A calm heart is the life of the fleshly organism, but jealousy is rottenness to the bones."* (Proverbs 14:30) Ailments resulting from anger and rage include respiratory troubles, increased blood pressure, liver disorders, and ill effects on the pancreas. Physicians also list anger and rage as emotions that aggravate, or even cause, such illnesses as ulcers, hives, asthma, skin diseases, and digestive problems. On the other hand, "a heart at peace gives life to the body." (Proverbs 14:30, *New International Version*) We are wise, then, to "pursue the things making for peace and the things that are upbuilding to one another." —Romans 14:19.

Fear of God Helps Us to Be Impartial

"He that is defrauding the lowly one has reproached his Maker," says Solomon, *"but the one showing favor to the poor one is glorifying Him."* (Proverbs 14:31) A God-fearing man realizes that all humans have the same Maker, Jehovah God. Therefore, the lowly one is a fellow human, and how he is treated reflects on the Creator of mankind. To glorify God, we must deal fairly and impartially with others. The Christian of little means should receive spiritual attention without

partiality. We must reach the poor and the rich alike with the good news of God's Kingdom.

Referring to another benefit of godly fear, the wise king says: *"Because of his badness the wicked will be pushed down, but the righteous will be finding refuge in his integrity."* (Proverbs 14:32) How is the wicked one pushed down? It has been suggested that this means that he lacks any possibility of recovery when he experiences a calamity. On the other hand, when adversity strikes, the God-fearing man takes refuge in his integrity to God. Having implicit trust in Jehovah even to death, he displays the same determination as did Job, who said: "Until I expire I shall not take away my integrity from myself!"—Job 27:5.

Maintaining integrity calls for godly fear and wisdom. And where can wisdom be found? *"In the heart of the understanding one there rests wisdom,"* answers Proverbs 14:33, *"and in the midst of stupid ones it becomes known."* Yes, wisdom can be found in the heart of a man with understanding. In what way, though, does it become known in the midst of fools? According to one reference work, "the fool, anxious to appear wise, blurts out what he thinks is wisdom but in the process turns it to folly."

"Exalts a Nation"

Shifting our attention from how an individual is affected by the fear of God to how it affects an entire nation, the king of Israel says: *"Righteousness is what exalts a nation, but sin is something disgraceful to national groups."* (Proverbs 14:34) How clearly this principle was demonstrated in the case of the nation of Israel! Adhering to God's high standards resulted in Israel's being exalted over the surrounding nations. However, repeated acts of disobedience led to the disgrace and eventual rejection of Israel by Jehovah. This principle applies to God's people today. The Christian congregation is different from the world because it adheres to God's righteous principles. To maintain that elevated position, though, we must individually live a chaste life. Practicing sin only brings disgrace to us personally as well as reproach on the congregation and on God.

Expressing what brings delight to a king, Solomon says: *"The pleasure of a king is in the servant who is acting with insight, but his fury comes to be toward one acting shamefully."* (Proverbs 14:35) And Proverbs 16:13 states: "The lips of righteousness are a pleasure to a grand king; and the speaker of upright things he loves." Yes, our Leader and King, Jesus Christ, is well-pleased when we act righteously and with insight and use our lips in the Kingdom-preaching and disciple-making activity. By all means, then, let us keep busy in that work as we enjoy the blessings that come from fearing the true God.

Godly fear can be taught

WALK BY FAITH, NOT BY SIGHT!

"We are walking by faith, not by sight."—2 CORINTHIANS 5:7.

THE year is 55 C.E. Some 20 years have passed since a man then named Saul, a persecutor of Christians, embraced Christianity. He has not allowed the passing of time to diminish or weaken his faith in God. Even though he has not beheld heavenly realities with his physical eyes, he is firm in faith. When writing to anointed Christians, who had the heavenly hope, the apostle Paul therefore said: "We are walking by faith, not by sight."—2 Corinthians 5:7.

2 Walking by faith requires implicit trust in God's ability to direct our lives. We must be fully convinced that he really knows what is in our best interests. (Psalm 119:66) As we make decisions in life and act on them, we take into account "realities we do not see." (Hebrews 11:1, *The New English Bible*) These include the promised "new heavens and a new earth." (2 Peter 3:13) Walking by sight, on the other hand, means that we pursue a life course governed solely by what we perceive with our physical senses. This is dangerous because it can lead to our ignoring God's will altogether.—Psalm 81:12; Ecclesiastes 11:9.

3 Whether we are of the "little flock," with the heavenly calling, or of the "other sheep," with the earthly hope, each one of us should take to heart the admonition to walk by faith and not by sight. (Luke 12:32;

John 10:16) Let us see how following this inspired advice will protect us from falling victim to "the temporary enjoyment of sin," from the snare of materialism, and from losing sight of the end of this system of things. We will also examine the dangers of walking by sight.—Hebrews 11:25.

Rejecting "the Temporary Enjoyment of Sin"

4 Imagine the life that Moses, a son of Amram, could have had. Raised among the royal offspring in ancient Egypt, Moses had within his grasp power, wealth, and influence. Moses could have reasoned: 'I have been well-educated in the vaunted wisdom of Egypt, and I am powerful in word and deed. If I stay attached to the royal household, I can use my position to benefit my oppressed Hebrew brothers!' (Acts 7:22) Instead, Moses chose to be "ill-treated with the people of God." Why? What moved Moses to turn his back on all that Egypt had to offer? The Bible answers: "By faith [Moses] left Egypt, but not fearing the anger of the king, for he continued steadfast as seeing the One who is invisible." (Hebrews 11:24-27) Moses' faith in Jehovah's sure reward for righteousness helped him to resist sin and indulgence and its fleeting pleasure.

5 We too are often faced with the need to make difficult decisions on such issues as these: 'Should I give up certain practices

1. What shows that the apostle Paul walked by faith, not by sight?
2, 3. (a) How do we demonstrate that we are walking by faith? (b) What does it mean to walk by sight?

4. What choice did Moses make, and why?
5. How does Moses' example encourage us?

Moses walked by faith

or habits that are not fully in line with Bible principles? Should I accept employment that has apparent material advantages but that would hinder my spiritual progress?' Moses' example encourages us not to make choices that reflect the shortsightedness of this world; rather, we should exercise faith in the farsighted wisdom of "the One who is invisible"—Jehovah God. Like Moses, may we cherish Jehovah's friendship more than anything that this world has to offer.

⁶ Contrast Moses with Esau, a son of the patriarch Isaac. Esau preferred instant gratification. (Genesis 25:30-34) "Not appreciating sacred things," Esau gave away his rights as firstborn "in exchange for one meal." (Hebrews 12:16) He failed to consider how his decision to sell his birthright would affect his relationship with Jehovah or what influence his action would have on his offspring. He lacked spiritual vision. Esau

closed his eyes to God's precious promises, viewing them as of little value. He walked by sight, not by faith.

⁷ Esau provides a warning example for us today. (1 Corinthians 10:11) When we face decisions, whether great or small, we must not be seduced by the propaganda of Satan's world, which says that you must have what you want right now. We do well to ask ourselves: 'Are Esaulike tendencies showing up in the decisions I make? Would pursuing what I want now mean putting spiritual interests in the background? Are my choices endangering my friendship with God and my future reward? What kind of example am I setting for others?' If our choices reflect appreciation for sacred things, Jehovah will bless us.—Proverbs 10:22.

Avoiding the Snare of Materialism

⁸ In a revelation to the apostle John toward the close of the first century, the glorified Jesus Christ delivered a message to the congregation located in Laodicea, Asia Minor. It was a warning message against materialism. Though materially rich, Laodicean Christians were bankrupt spiritually. Instead of continuing to walk by faith, they allowed material possessions to blind their spiritual vision. (Revelation 3:14-18) Materialism has a similar effect today. It weakens our faith and causes us to stop 'running with endurance the race' for life. (Hebrews 12:1) If we are not careful, the "pleasures of this life" can smother spiritual activities to the point that they are "completely choked."—Luke 8:14.

⁹ A key to spiritual protection is contentment rather than the use of this world to

---

6, 7. (a) How did Esau show that he preferred to walk by sight? (b) What warning example do we find in Esau?

---

8. What warning did the Laodicean Christians receive, and why is that of interest to us?
9. How do contentment and appreciation for spiritual food protect us?

Does recreation often keep you from theocratic activities?

the full and the enrichment of ourselves materially. (1 Corinthians 7:31; 1 Timothy 6:6-8) When we walk by faith and not by sight, we find joy in the present spiritual paradise. As we partake of nourishing spiritual food, are we not moved to "cry out joyfully because of the good condition of the heart"? (Isaiah 65:13, 14) Moreover, we take delight in our association with those who manifest the fruitage of God's spirit. (Galatians 5:22, 23) How vital that we find satisfaction and refreshment in what Jehovah provides in a spiritual way!

¹⁰ Some questions we do well to ask ourselves are: 'What place do material things occupy in my life? Am I using the material possessions I have to live a life of pleasure or to promote true worship? What brings me the greatest satisfaction? Is it Bible study and fellowship at Christian meetings, or is it weekends away from Christian responsibilities? Do I reserve many weekends for recreation instead of using such time for the field ministry and other activities in connection with pure worship?' Walking by faith means that we keep busy in the Kingdom work, with full trust in Jehovah's promises. —1 Corinthians 15:58.

Keeping the End in Sight

¹¹ Walking by faith helps us to shun fleshly views that the end is far off or is not coming at all. Unlike skeptics who make light of Bible prophecy, we discern how world events line up with what God's Word foretold for our day. (2 Peter 3:3, 4) For example, do not the attitude and the behavior of people in general give evidence that we are living in "the last days"? (2 Timothy 3:1-5) With the eyes of faith, we see that current world events are not just history repeating itself. Rather, they form "the sign of [Christ's] presence and of the conclusion of the system of things."—Matthew 24:1-14.

¹² Consider an event in the first century of our Common Era that has a parallel in our day. When on earth, Jesus Christ warned his followers: "When you see Jerusalem surrounded by encamped armies, then know that the desolating of her has drawn near. Then let those in Judea begin fleeing to the mountains, and let those in the midst of her withdraw." (Luke 21:20, 21) In fulfillment of this prophecy, Roman armies under the command of Cestius Gallus laid siege to Je-

10. What questions do we do well to ask ourselves?

11. How does walking by faith help us to keep the end in sight?

12. How were Jesus' words recorded at Luke 21:20, 21 fulfilled in the first century?

rusalem in 66 C.E. But the armies withdrew abruptly, furnishing the signal and the opportunity for the Christians there 'to flee to the mountains.' In 70 C.E., the Roman armies returned, attacked the city of Jerusalem, and destroyed its temple. Josephus reports that over a million Jews died, and 97,000 were taken captive. Divine judgment was executed upon that Jewish system of things. Those who walked by faith and heeded Jesus' warning escaped the calamity.

¹³ Something similar is about to take place in our day. Elements within the United Nations will be involved in the execution of divine judgment. Just as the Roman armies of the first century were designed to maintain the *Pax Romana* (Roman Peace), the United Nations of today is intended to be a peacekeeping instrument. Although the Roman armies tried to ensure relative safety throughout the then known world, they became the desolater of Jerusalem. Likewise today, Bible prophecy indicates that militarized powers within the United Nations will see religion as a disturbing element and will act to destroy modern-day Jerusalem —Christendom—as well as the rest of Babylon the Great. (Revelation 17:12-17) Yes, the entire world empire of false religion stands on the brink of destruction.

¹⁴ The desolation of false religion will mark the beginning of the great tribulation. In the final part of the great tribulation, the remaining elements of this wicked system of things will be destroyed. (Matthew 24:29, 30; Revelation 16:14, 16) Walking by faith keeps us alert to the fulfillment of Bible prophecy. We are not duped into thinking that any man-made agency like the United Nations is God's means of bringing true peace and security. So, then, should not our

---

13, 14. (a) What events lie ahead? (b) Why should we stay alert to the fulfillment of Bible prophecy?

way of life demonstrate our conviction that "the great day of Jehovah is near"?—Zephaniah 1:14.

Walking by Sight—How Dangerous?

¹⁵ The experiences of ancient Israel illustrate the dangers of allowing walking by sight to weaken one's faith. In spite of witnessing the ten plagues that humiliated the false gods of Egypt and then experiencing the spectacular deliverance through the Red Sea, the Israelites disobediently made a golden calf and began to worship it. They became restless and grew weary of waiting for Moses, who "was taking a long time about coming down from the mountain." (Exodus 32:1-4) Impatience moved them to worship an idol visible to the natural eye. Their walking by sight insulted Jehovah and led to the execution of "about three thousand men." (Exodus 32:25-29) How sad it is when a worshipper of Jehovah today makes decisions that indicate distrust of Jehovah and a lack of confidence in his ability to fulfill his promises!

¹⁶ Outward appearances affected the Israelites negatively in other ways. Walking by sight made them tremble in fear of

---

15. In spite of their experiencing God's blessing, what snare did the nation of Israel fall into?
16. How were the Israelites affected by outward appearances?

Do You Recall?

- What did you learn from the examples of Moses and Esau about walking by faith, not by sight?
- What is a key to avoiding materialism?
- How does walking by faith help us to avoid the view that the end is far off?
- Why is walking by sight dangerous?

their enemies. (Numbers 13:28, 32; Deuteronomy 1:28) It caused them to challenge Moses' God-given authority and complain about their lot in life. This lack of faith led to their preferring demon-controlled Egypt to the Promised Land. (Numbers 14:1-4; Psalm 106:24) How hurt Jehovah must have been as he witnessed the gross disrespect his people showed for their invisible King!

How does paying attention to God's Word protect you?

¹⁷ Again in the prophet Samuel's day, the favored nation of Israel was caught in the snare of walking by sight. The people began to desire a king whom they could see. Even though Jehovah had demonstrated that he was their King, this was not enough to make them walk by faith. (1 Samuel 8:4-9) To their own harm, they foolishly rejected the flawless guidance of Jehovah, preferring instead to be like the surrounding nations. —1 Samuel 8:19, 20.

¹⁸ As Jehovah's modern-day servants, we cherish our good relationship with God. We are eager to learn and apply in our lives valuable lessons from past events. (Romans

---

17. What caused the Israelites to reject Jehovah's guidance in Samuel's day?
18. What lessons can we learn about the dangers of walking by sight?

15:4) When the Israelites walked by sight, they forgot that God through Moses was directing them. If we are not careful, we too can forget that Jehovah God and the Greater Moses, Jesus Christ, are directing the Christian congregation today. (Revelation 1:12-16) We must be on guard against taking a human view of the earthly part of Jehovah's organization. Our doing so can lead to a complaining spirit and a loss of appreciation for Jehovah's representatives as well as for the spiritual food provided by "the faithful and discreet slave."—Matthew 24:45.

Be Resolved to Walk by Faith

¹⁹ "We have a wrestling," states the Bible, "not against blood and flesh, but against the governments, against the authorities, against the world rulers of this darkness, against the wicked spirit forces in the heavenly places." (Ephesians 6:12) Our chief enemy is Satan the Devil. His aim is to destroy our faith in Jehovah. He will not overlook any type of persuasion that might sway us from our decision to serve God. (1 Peter 5:8) What will protect us from being deceived by the outward appearance of Satan's system? Walking by faith, not by sight! Trust and confidence in Jehovah's promises will safeguard us from experiencing 'shipwreck concerning our faith.' (1 Timothy 1:19) By all means, then, let us be determined to continue walking by faith, fully confident in Jehovah's blessing. And may we keep on praying that we may escape all the things destined to occur in the near future.—Luke 21:36.

²⁰ As we walk by faith, not by sight, we have a superb Exemplar. "Christ suffered for you," states the Bible, "leaving you a model for you to follow his steps closely." (1 Peter 2:21) The next article will discuss how we can go on walking as he walked.

19, 20. What are you resolved to do, and why?

GO ON WALKING AS JESUS CHRIST WALKED

"He that says he remains in union with [God] is under obligation himself also to go on walking just as that one [Jesus] walked."—1 JOHN 2:6.

"LET us run with endurance the race that is set before us," wrote the apostle Paul, "as we look intently at the Chief Agent and Perfecter of our faith, Jesus." (Hebrews 12: 1, 2) Following the course of faithfulness requires that we look intently at Jesus Christ.

2 The original-language word for "look intently," as used in the Christian Greek Scriptures, means "to direct one's attention without distraction," "to look away from one thing so as to see another," "to concentrate the gaze upon." One reference work observes: "The minute the Greek runner in the stadium takes his attention away from the race course and the goal to which he is speeding, and turns it upon the onlooking crowds, his speed is slackened. It is so with the Christian." Distractions can hinder our spiritual progress. We must look intently at Jesus Christ. And what are we looking for in the Chief Agent? The Greek term rendered "chief agent" means "chief leader, one that takes the lead in anything and thus furnishes the

example." Looking intently at Jesus calls for following his example.

3 "He that says he remains in union with [God] is under obligation himself also to go on walking just as that one [Jesus] walked," states the Bible. (1 John 2:6) We must remain in union with God by observing Jesus' commandments as he observed those of his Father. —John 15:10.

4 Hence, walking as Jesus walked requires that we closely observe him as the Chief Leader and that we follow his steps closely. The important questions to consider in this regard are: How does Christ lead us today? How should imitating his manner of walking affect us? What are the benefits of adhering to the pattern set by Jesus Christ?

How Christ Leads His Followers

5 Before ascending to heaven, the resurrected Jesus Christ appeared to his disciples and assigned them an important work. He said: "Go therefore and make disciples of people of all the nations."

1, 2. What is involved in looking intently at Jesus?

3, 4. (a) Walking as Jesus Christ walked requires what on our part? (b) What questions deserve our attention?
5. Before his ascension to heaven, what promise did Jesus make to his followers?

On that occasion the Chief Leader also promised to be with them as they fulfill this assignment, saying: "Look! I am with you all the days until the conclusion of the system of things." (Matthew 28:19, 20) How is Jesus Christ with his followers in this time of the conclusion of the system of things?

⁶ "The helper, the holy spirit, which the Father will send in my name," said Jesus, "that one will teach you all things and bring back to your minds all the things I told you." (John 14:26) The holy spirit, sent in Jesus' name, guides and strengthens us today. It enlightens us spiritually and helps us to understand "even the deep things of God." (1 Corinthians 2:10) Moreover, the godly qualities of "love, joy, peace, long-suffering, kindness, goodness, faith, mildness, self-control" are "the fruitage of the spirit." (Galatians 5:22, 23) With the help of the holy spirit, we can cultivate these qualities.

⁷ As we study the Scriptures and endeavor to apply what we learn, Jehovah's spirit helps us to grow in wisdom, discernment, understanding, knowledge, judgment, and thinking ability. (Proverbs 2:1-11) Holy spirit also helps us to endure temptations and trials. (1 Corinthians 10:13; 2 Corinthians 4:7; Philippians 4:13) Christians are exhorted to 'cleanse themselves of every defilement of flesh and spirit, perfecting holiness.' (2 Corinthians 7:1) Can we really measure up to God's requirement of holiness, or cleanness, without the help of the holy spirit? One of the means Jesus uses to lead us today is the holy spirit, which Jehovah God has authorized his Son to employ.—Matthew 28:18.

⁸ Consider another means by which Christ leads the congregation today. Commenting on his presence and the conclusion of the system of things, Jesus said: "Who really is the faithful and discreet slave whom his master appointed over his domestics, to give them their food at the proper time? Happy is that slave if his master on arriving finds him doing so. Truly I say to you, He will appoint him over all his belongings."—Matthew 24:3, 45-47.

⁹ The "master" is Jesus Christ. The "slave" is the group of anointed Christians on earth. This slave class is entrusted with caring for Jesus' earthly interests and with providing timely spiritual food. A small group of qualified overseers from among the composite "faithful and discreet slave" form the Governing Body, serving as the representative of the slave class. They direct the worldwide Kingdom-preaching work and the supplying of spiritual nourishment at the right time. Christ thus leads the congregation by means of the spirit-anointed "faithful and discreet slave" and its Governing Body.

¹⁰ Still another manifestation of Christ's leadership are the "gifts in men"—Christian elders, or overseers. They have been given "with a view to the readjustment of the holy ones, for ministerial work, for the building up of the body of the Christ." (Ephesians 4: 8, 11, 12) Concerning them, Hebrews 13:7 states: "Remember those who are taking the lead among you, who have spoken the word of God to you, and as you contemplate how their conduct turns out imitate their faith." The elders take the lead in the congregation. Since they imitate Christ Jesus, their faith becomes worthy of imitation. (1 Corinthians 11:1) We can show our gratitude for the elder arrangement by being obedient and submissive to these "gifts in men."—Hebrews 13:17.

6, 7. How does Jesus lead us by means of the holy spirit?

8, 9. How does Christ use "the faithful and discreet slave" to provide leadership?

---

10. What should be our attitude toward the elders, and why?

Christian elders help us to follow Christ's leadership

[11] Yes, Jesus Christ leads his followers today through the holy spirit, "the faithful and discreet slave," and the congregation elders. Our walking as Christ walked involves understanding his way of leading and submitting to it. It also requires that we imitate his manner of walking. "To this course you were called," wrote the apostle Peter, "because even Christ suffered for you, leaving you a model for you to follow his steps closely." (1 Peter 2:21) In what way should following Jesus' perfect model affect us?

Be Reasonable When Exercising Authority

[12] Though Jesus had received unmatched authority from his Father, he was reasonable in the way he wielded it. All in the congregation—particularly the overseers—should let their "reasonableness become known to all men." (Philippians 4:5; 1 Timothy 3:2, 3) Since elders have a measure of authority in the congregation, it is essential that they follow Christ's footsteps in exercising it.

[13] Jesus took into consideration the limitations of his disciples. He did not demand of them more than they were capable of giving. (John 16:12) Without pressuring them, Jesus encouraged his followers to 'exert themselves vigorously' in doing God's will. (Luke 13:24) He did this by taking the lead and by appealing to their hearts. Similarly, Christian elders today do not intimidate others into serving God through shame or guilt. Rather, they encourage them to serve Jehovah out of love for him and for Jesus, as well as for their fellow man.—Matthew 22:37-39.

[14] Jesus did not abuse the authority entrusted to him by controlling people's lives. He neither set unreachable standards nor laid down countless rules. His approach was to motivate others by reaching their hearts with the principles behind the laws given through Moses. (Matthew 5:27, 28) In imitation of Jesus Christ, the elders refrain from making arbitrary rules or insisting on their personal viewpoints. In matters of dress and grooming or recreation and entertainment, elders try to reach hearts using godly principles, such as those outlined at Micah 6: 8; 1 Corinthians 10:31-33; and 1 Timothy 2: 9, 10.

Be Sympathetic and Forgiving

[15] Christ left a model for us to follow in the way he treated his disciples' failures and errors. Consider two events from his last night on earth as a human. After arriving at Gethsemane, Jesus "took Peter and James and John along with him" and told them to "keep on the watch." Then, "going a little way forward he proceeded to fall on the ground and began praying." Upon returning, he "found them sleeping." How did Jesus respond? He said: "The spirit, of course,

---

11. By what means does Christ lead his followers today, and what is involved in walking as he did?
12. What aspect of Christ's example is of particular interest to the elders in the congregation?
13, 14. In what way can elders imitate Christ as they encourage others to serve God?

---

15. How did Jesus respond to the failures of his disciples?

is eager, but the flesh is weak." (Mark 14:32-38) Instead of sharply rebuking Peter, James, and John, he expressed sympathy! On that same night, Peter denied Jesus three times. (Mark 14:66-72) How did Jesus treat Peter thereafter? "The Lord was raised up and he appeared to Simon [Peter]." (Luke 24:34) "He appeared to Cephas," says the Bible, "then to the twelve." (1 Corinthians 15:5) Instead of feeling resentment, Jesus forgave the repentant apostle and strengthened him. Later, Jesus entrusted Peter with great responsibilities.—Acts 2:14; 8:14-17; 10:44, 45.

¹⁶ When our fellow believers fail us or wrong us in some way because of human imperfection, should we not also be sympathetic and forgiving as Jesus was? Peter urged his fellow believers: "All of you be like-minded, showing fellow feeling, having brotherly affection, tenderly compassionate, humble in mind, not paying back injury for injury or reviling for reviling, but, to the contrary, bestowing a blessing." (1 Peter 3:8, 9) What if another person fails to treat us as Jesus would have, refusing to be sympathetic or forgiving? Even then we are under obligation to try to imitate Jesus and respond as he would have.—1 John 3:16.

Put Kingdom Interests First

¹⁷ In yet another way, we need to walk as Jesus Christ walked. Declaring the good news of God's Kingdom occupied the central place in Jesus' life. After preaching to the Samaritan woman near the city of Sychar in Samaria, Jesus told his disciples: "My food is for me to do the will of him that sent me and to finish his work." (John 4:34) The doing

Young people, what plans are you making for a rewarding Christian life?

of his Father's will sustained Jesus; it was as nourishing, satisfying, and refreshing to him as food. Would imitating Jesus by remaining focused on doing God's will lead to anything less than a truly meaningful and satisfying life?

¹⁸ When parents encourage their children to take up full-time service, they as well as their offspring receive many blessings. A father of twin sons held pioneer service before them as a goal from their early childhood. After finishing their secular education, the twins did become pioneers. Reflecting on the joys he has experienced as a result, this father writes: "Our boys have not disappointed us. Gratefully we can say, 'Sons are an inheritance from Jehovah.'" (Psalm 127:3) And how do children benefit from pursuing full-time service? A mother of five says: "Pioneering has helped all my children to develop a much closer relationship with Jehovah, has improved their personal study habits, has helped them learn how to manage their time wisely, and has helped them learn to put spiritual things first in their lives. Although all of them had to make many adjustments, none of them regret the path they have chosen to follow."

---

16. How can we walk as Jesus walked when our fellow believers fail us or wrong us in some way?
17. What shows that Jesus gave the doing of God's will the first place in his life?

18. What blessings result from encouraging children to take up the full-time service?

¹⁹ Youths, what are your plans for the future? Are you seeking to excel in some professional field? Or are you working toward a career in the full-time service? "Keep strict watch that how you walk is not as unwise but as wise persons," admonished Paul, "buying out the opportune time for yourselves, because the days are wicked." He adds: "On this account cease becoming unreasonable, but go on perceiving what the will of Jehovah is."—Ephesians 5:15-17.

Be Loyal

²⁰ Walking as Jesus walked calls for imitating his loyalty. Concerning Jesus' loyalty, the Bible states: "Although he was existing in God's form, [he] gave no consideration to a seizure, namely, that he should be equal to God. No, but he emptied himself and took a slave's form and came to be in the likeness of men. More than that, when he found himself in fashion as a man, he humbled himself and became obedient as far as death, yes, death on a torture stake." Jesus loyally upheld Jehovah's sovereignty by submitting to God's will for him. He became obedient as far as suffering death on a torture stake. We

---

19. What plans for the future should youths wisely consider?
20, 21. In what way was Jesus loyal, and how can we imitate his loyalty?

must "keep this mental attitude" and loyally submit to doing God's will.—Philippians 2:5-8.

²¹ Jesus also showed loyalty to his faithful apostles. Despite their weaknesses and imperfections, Jesus loved them "to the end." (John 13:1) Similarly, we should not let the imperfections of our brothers cause us to adopt a critical attitude.

Adhere to the Pattern Set by Jesus

²² Of course, as imperfect humans, we cannot walk precisely in the footsteps of our perfect Exemplar. However, we can strive to follow his steps closely. Doing so requires that we understand and submit to Christ's way of leading and stick to the pattern he set.

²³ Becoming imitators of Christ leads to many blessings. Our life becomes more meaningful and satisfying because we are focused on doing God's will rather than our own. (John 5:30; 6:38) We have a good conscience. Our way of walking becomes exemplary. Jesus invited all who were toiling and loaded down to come to him and find refreshment for their souls. (Matthew 11:28-30) When we follow Jesus' example, we too can refresh others by our association. Let us, then, continue to walk as Jesus walked.

22, 23. What are the benefits of adhering to the pattern set by Jesus?

Do You Recall?

- How does Christ lead his followers today?

- How can elders follow Christ's lead in exercising their God-given authority?

- How can we follow Jesus' example when dealing with the shortcomings of others?

- How can youths put Kingdom interests first?

Resist Wrong Thinking!

WHEN experiencing calamity, the patriarch Job received a visit from his three friends Eliphaz, Bildad, and Zophar. They came to sympathize with him and to comfort him. (Job 2:11) The most influential and perhaps the oldest of the three was Eliphaz. He was the first one to speak and had the most to say. What type of thinking did Eliphaz reflect in his three speeches?

Recalling a supernatural experience he once had, Eliphaz said: "A spirit itself went passing over my face; the hair of my flesh began to bristle. It began to stand still, but I did not recognize its appearance; a form was in front of my eyes; there was a calm, and I now heard a voice." (Job 4:15, 16) What kind of spirit had influenced the thinking of Eliphaz? The critical tone of the words that followed shows that the spirit certainly was not one of God's righteous angels. (Job 4:17, 18) It was a wicked spirit creature. Otherwise, why would Jehovah have reproved Eliphaz and his two associates for having spoken lies? (Job 42:7) Yes, Eliphaz had come under demon influence. His comments reflected ungodly thinking.

What ideas can be identified from the statements of Eliphaz? Why is it important that we guard against wrong thinking? And what measures can we take to resist it?

"In His Servants He Has No Faith"

In all three speeches, Eliphaz presented the idea that God is so exacting that nothing his servants do is good enough for him. "Look! In his servants he has no faith," Eliphaz told Job, "and his angels he charges with faultiness." (Job 4:18, footnote) Eliphaz later said of God: "In his holy ones he has no faith, and the heavens themselves are actually not clean in his eyes." (Job 15:15) And he asked: "Does the Almighty have any delight in that you are righteous?" (Job 22:3) Bildad was in agreement with this viewpoint, for he stated: "There is even the moon, and it is not bright; and the stars themselves have not proved clean in [God's] eyes."—Job 25:5.

We must be on guard against being influenced by such thinking. It can lead us to feel that God requires too much of us. This view attacks our very relationship with Jehovah. Moreover, if we succumb to this type of reasoning, how would we respond when we are given needed discipline? Rather than humbly accepting the correction, our heart may become "enraged against Jehovah himself," and we may harbor resentment toward him. (Proverbs 19:3) How spiritually disastrous that would be!

*Job resisted
negative thinking*

26

"Can an Able-Bodied Man Be of Use to God?"

Closely related to the idea that God is too exacting is the view that he regards humans as useless. Eliphaz' third speech contains the question: "Can an able-bodied man be of use to God himself, that anyone having insight should be of use toward him?" (Job 22:2) Eliphaz was implying that man is useless to God. In a similar vein, Bildad argued: "How can mortal man be in the right before God, or how can one born of a woman be clean?" (Job 25:4) According to that line of reasoning, how could Job, a mere mortal, ever presume to have a righteous standing before God?

Some people today are plagued with negative feelings about themselves. Such factors as family upbringing, exposure to the pressures of life, or being victims of racial or ethnic hatred may have contributed to this. But Satan and his demons also take delight in crushing a person. If they can influence an individual to feel that nothing he does is good enough for Almighty God, he is more vulnerable to despondency. In time, such a person could drift away, even draw away, from the living God.—Hebrews 2:1; 3:12.

Advancing age and health problems put limitations on us. The share we have in Kingdom service may seem quite small in comparison with what we did when we were younger, healthier, and stronger. How important it is to recognize that Satan and his demons want us to feel that what we do is not good enough for God! We must resist such thinking.

How to Resist Negative Thinking

Despite the suffering brought upon him by Satan the Devil, Job said: "Until I expire I shall not take away my integrity from myself!" (Job 27:5) Because he loved God, Job was determined to maintain his integrity no matter what happened, and nothing was going to change that. Herein lies a key to resisting negative thinking. We must acquire a good understanding of God's love and cultivate heartfelt appreciation for it. We also need to deepen our love for him. This is achieved by means of a regular study of God's Word and prayerful meditation on what we learn.

For example, John 3:16 states: "God loved the world so much that he gave his only-begotten Son." Jehovah has deep love for the world of mankind, and his dealings with humans over time show that love. Meditating on examples from the past ought to build up our appreciation for Jehovah and deepen our love for him, thus helping us to resist wrong or negative thinking.

Consider the way Jehovah treated Abraham at the time of the impending destruction of Sodom and Gomorrah. Abraham inquired of Jehovah eight times respecting His judgment. At no point did Jehovah show irritation or frustration. Instead, his replies reassured and comforted Abraham. (Genesis 18:22-33) When God later rescued Lot and his family from Sodom, Lot asked to escape to a nearby city rather than to the mountains. Jehovah replied: "Here I do show you consideration to this extent also, by my not overthrowing the city of which you have spoken." (Genesis 19:18-22) Do these accounts portray Jehovah as an exacting, unloving, authoritarian ruler? No. They show him to be what he really is—a loving, kind, merciful, and understanding Sovereign.

Disproving the idea that God is a faultfinder and that no one can be good enough for him are the examples of Aaron, David, and Manasseh of ancient Israel. Aaron was guilty of three serious wrongs. He made the golden calf, joined his sister Miriam in criticizing Moses, and failed to sanctify and honor God at Meribah. Nevertheless, Jehovah saw good in him and allowed him to continue serving as high priest right up to his death.—Exodus 32:3, 4; Numbers 12:1, 2; 20:9-13.

King David committed grave sins during his reign. These included adultery, plotting an innocent man's death, and taking an illegal census. However, Jehovah noted David's repentance and loyally stuck to the Kingdom covenant by allowing him to serve as king until his death.—2 Samuel 12:9; 1 Chronicles 21:1-7.

Judaean King Manasseh set up altars to Baal, made his sons pass through fire, promoted spiritistic practices, and built false religious altars in the temple courtyards. After he showed heartfelt repentance, however, Jehovah forgave him, released him from captivity, and gave him back the kingship. (2 Chronicles 33:1-13) Are these the actions of a God for whom no one is good enough? Hardly!

Lot learned that Jehovah is an understanding Sovereign

The False Accuser Himself Is Guilty

It should not surprise us that Satan is the chief embodiment of the very characteristics he accuses Jehovah of having. Satan is harsh and exacting. This can clearly be seen from the practice of child sacrifice connected with false worship in times past. The apostate Israelites burned their sons and daughters in the fire—a thing that had not even come up into Jehovah's heart.—Jeremiah 7:31.

It is Satan, not Jehovah, who is a faultfinder. Revelation 12:10 refers to Satan as "the accuser of our brothers . . . , who accuses them day and night before our God!" On the other hand, concerning Jehovah, the psalmist sang: "If errors were what you watch, O Jah, O Jehovah, who could stand? For there is the true forgiveness with you." —Psalm 130:3, 4.

When Wrong Thinking Will Be No More

What relief the angelic spirit creatures must have felt when Satan the Devil and his demons were cast out of the heavens! (Revelation 12:7-9) Thereafter, these wicked spirits could no longer have any effect on the activities of Jehovah's angelic family in heaven. —Daniel 10:13.

The inhabitants of the earth will rejoice in the near future. Soon, an angel coming down out of heaven with the key of the abyss and a great chain in his hand will bind Satan and his demons and hurl them into the abyss of inactivity. (Revelation 20:1-3) What relief we will experience when that happens!

Meanwhile, we must be on guard against wrong thinking. Whenever we find that wrong or negative thoughts are creeping into our mind, we need to resist them by focusing our minds on Jehovah's love. Then 'the peace of God that excels all thought will guard our hearts and our mental powers.' —Philippians 4:6, 7.

Questions From Readers

Could playing violent computer games affect one's relationship with Jehovah?

"Jehovah himself examines the righteous one as well as the wicked one," wrote King David of ancient Israel, "and anyone loving violence His soul certainly hates." (Psalm 11:5) The original-language word for "hate" can carry the thought of being "one who is an enemy." Therefore, anyone loving violence is making himself an enemy of God. The question that we need to consider, then, is: Could playing certain computer games nurture a love of violence?

Violent computer games glorify the use of weapons. They often train the user in the art of war. The magazine *The Economist* stated: "America's military is relying more heavily on computer games as training tools. Some games which the military uses are off-the-shelf products."

True, those who play violent computer games are not doing harm to real people. But what does this choice of entertainment indicate about what may be happening to their hearts? (Matthew 5:21, 22; Luke 6:45) What would you conclude about a person who enjoyed stabbing, shooting, maiming, and killing imaginary people? What if this person spent many hours each week indulging those violent fantasies, becoming almost addicted to such games? At the very least, you would conclude that he was fostering a love of violence, just as a person who watches pornography is cultivating immoral desires.—Matthew 5:27-29.

How intensely does Jehovah hate someone who loves violence? David said that Jehovah "certainly hates" him. In Noah's day, Jehovah demonstrated the intensity of his hatred for those who love violence. Jehovah said to Noah: "The end of all flesh has come before me, because the earth is full of violence as a result of them; and here I am bringing them to ruin together with the earth." (Genesis 6:13) The true God destroyed an entire world of mankind because of their violent ways. He preserved only Noah and his family—eight individuals who did not love violence.—2 Peter 2:5.

People who want to be Jehovah's friends "beat their swords into plowshares and their spears into pruning shears." Instead of learning to love violence, they do not "learn war anymore." (Isaiah 2:4) To remain God's friend rather than become his enemy, we must "turn away from what is bad and do what is good." We need to "seek peace and pursue it."—1 Peter 3:11.

What if we have already been involved in playing violent video games? Then we need to be firmly resolved to please Jehovah by desisting from practicing what he hates. Surely we should pray for the help of God's holy spirit to end this spiritually detrimental practice. We can stop if we allow such qualities as peace, goodness, and self-control to exercise a godly influence in our lives.—Luke 11:13; Galatians 5:22, 23.

IN OUR NEXT ISSUE

Do You Recognize the Sign of Jesus' Presence?

———

Is Your Conscience Well Trained?

———

Parents—What Future Do You Want for Your Children?

What Others Think of Us
Does It Matter?

ALMOST everyone likes to be praised. Compliments can make us feel good, giving us a sense of accomplishment. Approval can even make us want to improve our performance. The opposite is true when we perceive that some people disapprove of us. A cold response or a critical remark may crush our spirit. What others think of us may have a profound effect on what we think of ourselves.

It would be a mistake to ignore how others view us. We can actually benefit by having others scrutinize our conduct. When based on high moral principles, the opinions of others can act as a force for good, motivating us to be upright. (1 Corinthians 10:31-33) However, public opinion is often very unfair. Think of the distorted view the chief priests and others had of Jesus Christ when "they began to yell, saying: 'Impale! Impale him!'" (Luke 23:13, 21-25) Viewpoints based on false information or influenced by envy or prejudice may just have to be dismissed. Hence, we need to exercise good judgment and react sensibly to the opinions of others.

Whose Opinion Matters?

We want the approval of those close to us in true worship. These include family members who are in the faith and our Christian brothers and sisters. (Romans 15:2; Colossians 3:18-21) The love and respect of fellow believers and the "interchange of encouragement" among them mean a great deal to us. (Romans 1:11, 12) With 'lowliness of mind, we consider that others are superior to us.'

"Praise shames me, for I secretly beg for it."

—INDIAN POET RABINDRANATH TAGORE

(Philippians 2:2-4) Moreover, we seek and value the approval of "those who are taking the lead" among us—the elders in the congregation.—Hebrews 13:17.

Also desirable is "a fine testimony from people on the outside." (1 Timothy 3:7) How good it is when unbelieving relatives, workmates, and neighbors respect us! And do we not try to leave a good impression with the people to whom we preach so that they will be favorably inclined toward the Kingdom message? Our having a reputation in the community as being morally clean, upright, and honest people brings glory to God. (1 Peter 2:12) However, we can never compromise Bible principles to win the favor of others; neither can we put on a false front to impress them. We must recognize that it is impossible to please everyone. Jesus said: "If you were part of the world, the world would be fond of what is its own. Now because you are no part of the world, but I have chosen you out of the world, on this account the world hates you." (John 15:19) Can we do anything to gain the respect of those who oppose us?

Gaining the Respect of Opposers

"You will be objects of hatred by all people on account of my name," warned Jesus, "but he that has endured to the end is the one that will be saved." (Matthew 10:22) This hatred sometimes brings forth vicious accusations. Biased government officials may label us as "seditious" or "subversive." Outspoken opposers may allege that we are a troublesome sect that must be suppressed. (Acts 28:22) These false accusations can sometimes be counteracted. How? By following the apostle Peter's counsel: "[Be] ready to make a defense before everyone that demands of you a reason for the hope in you, but doing so together with a mild temper and deep respect." (1 Peter 3:15) Moreover, we should use "wholesome speech which cannot be condemned; so that the man on the opposing side may get ashamed, having nothing vile to say about us."—Titus 2:8.

While we try to clear our name of reproach, we need not be discouraged or overwhelmed when we are unfairly maligned. Jesus, the perfect Son of God, was accused of blasphemy, sedition, and even spiritism. (Matthew 9:3; Mark 3:22; John 19:12) The apostle Paul was defamed. (1 Corinthians 4:13) Both Jesus and Paul ignored such criticism and kept busy in their work. (Matthew 15:14) They knew that they could never win the approval of their enemies, since "the whole world is lying in the power of the wicked one." (1 John 5:19) Today, we face the same challenge. We do not have to be intimidated when hateful opposers spread lies about us.—Matthew 5:11.

Opinions That Really Count

What people think of us varies a great deal, depending on their motives and what they have heard about us. We are praised and honored by some, reviled and hated by others. As long as we are being guided by Bible principles, however, we have every reason to be happy and at peace.

The apostle Paul wrote: "All Scripture is inspired of God and beneficial for teaching, for reproving, for setting things straight, for disciplining in righteousness, that the man of God may be fully competent, completely equipped for every good work." (2 Timothy 3:16, 17) We gain the favor of Jehovah God and of his Son, Jesus Christ, by gratefully accepting God's Word as our guide in all things. In the end, the opinions that matter the most are those of Jehovah and his Son. What they think of us reflects our true worth. Ultimately, our life depends on their approval.—John 5:27; James 1:12.

The opinions of our fellow believers matter

Help
With Our
Emotions

DO NEGATIVE emotions at times seem to take over your life? Do you easily become upset, angry, or frustrated? Do anxieties of life tend to overwhelm you? What will help?

Emotional reactions are part and parcel of human experience. When properly controlled, they add spice to life. The Bible acknowledges, though, that "mere oppression may make a wise one act crazy." (Ecclesiastes 7:7) In a world where violence and accidents are all too common, who is not affected emotionally by what happens around him? However, the Scriptures also state: "There is nothing better than that . . . man should rejoice in his works." (Ecclesiastes 3:22) To make life more enjoyable, we therefore need to learn to rejoice by cultivating positive emotions. How can we nurture beneficial emotions and curb harmful ones?

Taking practical measures often alleviates the intensity of our negative emotions. For example, when we feel anxious over matters that we have no control over, is it not better to change our routine or environment rather than occupy our mind with worry? Taking a leisurely walk, listening to soothing music, engaging in vigorous exercise, or doing a kind deed for someone in need may provide some relief and bring us a measure of happiness.—Acts 20:35.

The best way to dispel negative thoughts, however, is by putting our confidence in the Creator. When negative thinking persists, we need to 'throw all our anxiety upon God' by means of prayer. (1 Peter 5:6, 7) The Bible assures us: "Jehovah is near to those that are broken at heart . . . Many are the calamities of the righteous one, but out of them all Jehovah delivers him." (Psalm 34:18, 19) How can we be confident that God can be our "assistance and the Provider of escape"? (Psalm 40:17) We can do so by studying the Bible and reflecting on its vivid examples of God's personal interest in the well-being of his servants.

OCTOBER 1, 2005

THE WATCHTOWER

ANNOUNCING JEHOVAH'S KINGDOM

Do You RECOGNIZE THE SIGN?

THE WATCHTOWER®
ANNOUNCING JEHOVAH'S KINGDOM

October 1, 2005   Average Printing Each Issue: 26,439,000   Vol. 126, No. 19

THE PURPOSE OF *THE WATCHTOWER* is to exalt Jehovah God as Sovereign Lord of the universe. It keeps watch on world events as these fulfill Bible prophecy. It comforts all peoples with the good news that God's Kingdom will soon destroy those who oppress their fellowmen and that it will turn the earth into a paradise. It encourages faith in God's now-reigning King, Jesus Christ, whose shed blood opens the way for mankind to gain eternal life. *The Watchtower,* published by Jehovah's Witnesses continuously since 1879, is nonpolitical. It adheres to the Bible as its authority.

IN THIS ISSUE

3   Interpreting Signs Is a Serious Matter!

4   Do You Recognize the Sign of Jesus' Presence?

8   Jehovah's Word Is Alive—Highlights From the Book of First Chronicles

12   Is Your Conscience Well Trained?

16   My Parents' Example Strengthened Me

21   "Keep on the Watch"—The Hour of Judgment Has Arrived!

26   Parents—What Future Do You Want for Your Children?

32   Are You "Rich Toward God"?

WATCHTOWER STUDIES

OCTOBER 31–NOVEMBER 6:
"Keep on the Watch"—The Hour of Judgment Has Arrived!
Page 21. Songs to be used: 174, 60.

NOVEMBER 7–13:
Parents—What Future Do You Want for Your Children?
Page 26. Songs to be used: 157, 123.

Publication of *The Watchtower* is part of a worldwide Bible educational work supported by voluntary donations.

Unless otherwise indicated, Scripture quotations are from the modern-language *New World Translation of the Holy Scriptures—With References.*

The Watchtower (ISSN 0043-1087) is published semimonthly by Watchtower Bible and Tract Society of New York, Inc.; M. H. Larson, President; G. F. Simonis, Secretary-Treasurer; 25 Columbia Heights, Brooklyn, NY 11201-2483. Periodicals Postage Paid at Brooklyn, NY, and at additional mailing offices. POSTMASTER: Send address changes to Watchtower, **Wallkill, NY 12589.**

Changes of address should reach us 30 days before your moving date. Give us your old and new address (if possible, your old address label).

Semimonthly   ENGLISH

Would you welcome more information or a free home Bible study? Please send your request to Jehovah's Witnesses, using the appropriate address below.

America, United States of: Wallkill, NY 12589. *Antigua:* Box 119, St. Johns. *Australia:* Box 280, Ingleburn, NSW 1890. *Bahamas:* Box N-1247, Nassau, N.P. *Barbados, W.I.:* Crusher Site Road, Prospect, St. James. *Britain:* The Ridgeway, London NW7 1RN. *Canada:* Box 4100, Halton Hills (Georgetown), Ontario L7G 4Y4. *Germany:* Niederselters, Am Steinfels, D-65618 Selters. *Ghana:* P. O. Box GP 760, Accra. *Guyana:* 352-360 Tyrell St., Republic Park Phase 2 EBD. *Hawaii 96819:* 2055 Kam IV Rd., Honolulu. *Hong Kong:* 4 Kent Road, Kowloon Tong. *India:* Post Box 6440, Yelahanka, Bangalore 560 064, KAR. *Ireland:* Newcastle, Greystones, Co. Wicklow. *Jamaica:* P. O. Box 103, Old Harbour, St. Catherine. *Japan:* 1271 Nakashinden, Ebina City, Kanagawa Pref., 243-0496. *Kenya:* P.O. Box 47788, GPO Nairobi 00100. *New Zealand:* P.O. Box 75-142, Manurewa. *Nigeria:* P.M.B. 1090, Benin City 300001, Edo State. *Philippines, Republic of:* P. O. Box 2044, 1060 Manila. *South Africa:* Private Bag X2067, Krugersdorp, 1740. *Trinidad and Tobago, Republic of:* Lower Rapsey Street & Laxmi Lane, Curepe. *Zambia:* Box 33459, Lusaka 10101. *Zimbabwe:* Private Bag WG-5001, Westgate.

NOW PUBLISHED IN 151 LANGUAGES. SEMIMONTHLY: Afrikaans, Albanian,* Amharic, Arabic, Bengali, Bicol, Bislama, Bulgarian, Cebuano,* Chichewa,* Chinese, Chinese (Simplified),* Cibemba,* Croatian,* Czech,*# Danish,*# Dutch,*# East Armenian, Efik,* English*#+© (also Braille), Estonian, Ewe, Fijian, Finnish,*# French*# (also Braille), Ga, Georgian,* German,*# Greek,* Gujarati, Gun, Hebrew, Hiligaynon, Hindi, Hungarian,*# Igbo,* Iloko,* Indonesian, Italian,*# Japanese*# (also Braille), Kannada, Kinyarwanda, Kirundi, Korean*# (also Braille), Latvian, Lingala, Lithuanian, Luvale, Macedonian, Malagasy,* Malayalam, Maltese, Myanmar, Nepali, Norwegian,*# Pangasinan, Papiamento (Aruba), Papiamento (Curaçao), Polish,*# Portuguese*# (also Braille), Punjabi, Rarotongan, Romanian,* Russian,* Samar-Leyte, Samoan, Sango, Sepedi, Serbian, Sesotho, Shona,* Silozi, Sinhala, Slovak,* Slovenian, Solomon Islands Pidgin, Spanish*# (also Braille), Sranantongo, Swahili,* Swedish,*# Tagalog,* Tamil, Telugu, Thai, Tigrinya, Tok Pisin, Tongan, Tshiluba, Tsonga, Tswana, Turkish, Twi, Ukrainian,* Urdu, Vietnamese, Wallisian, Xhosa, Yoruba,* Zulu*

MONTHLY: American Sign Language,△□ Armenian, Assamese, Azerbaijani (roman script), Brazilian Sign Language,△ Cambodian, Chitonga, Gilbertese, Greenlandic, Haitian Creole, Hausa, Hiri Motu, Icelandic, Isoko, Kaonde, Kazakh, Kikongo, Kiluba,* Kirghiz, Kosraean, Kwanyama/Ndonga, Luganda, Marathi, Marshallese, Mauritian Creole, Maya, Mizo, Monokutuba, Moore, Niuean, Ossetian, Otetela, Palauan, Persian, Ponapean, Seychelles Creole, Tahitian, Tatar, Tiv, Trukese, Tumbuka, Tuvaluan, Umbundu, Uruund, Venda, Yapese, Zande

* Study articles also available in large-print edition.
# Audiocassettes also available.
+ CD also available.
© MP3 CD-ROM also available.
△ Videocassette
□ DVD

Interpreting Signs Is a Serious Matter!

"At first I thought that our son Andreas just had a headache. But he lost his appetite and had a high fever. The headache got worse, and I became worried. When my husband came home, we took Andreas to the doctor. He checked the symptoms and sent Andreas straight to the hospital. The problem was more serious than a headache. Andreas had meningitis. He was treated and was soon well again."—Gertrud, a mother in Germany.

GERTRUD'S experience is probably familiar to many parents. They observe signs indicating that their child might be ill. Though not every illness is serious, parents cannot afford to ignore symptoms of ill health in their children. Observing the signs and taking appropriate action may make a big difference. It is a serious matter.

This is true in matters other than health. A case in point is the tsunami disaster in December 2004 in areas surrounding the Indian Ocean. Agencies in such places as Australia and Hawaii detected the massive earthquake in northern Sumatra and foresaw the potential danger of the aftereffect. Yet, there were no means in place for the people in the endangered areas to receive or respond to any warning. As a result, more than 220,000 lives were lost.

Signs of Much Greater Importance

When Jesus Christ was on earth, he gave his listeners a lesson in observing signs and acting accordingly. He was talking about something of far-reaching importance. The Bible reports: "The Pharisees and Sadducees approached him and, to tempt him, they asked him to display to them a sign from heaven. In reply he said to them: 'When evening falls you are accustomed to say, "It will be fair weather, for the sky is fire-red"; and at morning, "It will be wintry, rainy weather today, for the sky is fire-red, but gloomy-looking." You know how to interpret the appearance of the sky, but the signs of the times you cannot interpret.' " —Matthew 16:1-3.

In mentioning "the signs of the times," Jesus indicated that his first-century Jewish listeners should have been aware of the urgency of the times in which they were living. The Jewish system of things was about to experience a cataclysm that would affect all of them. A few days before his death, Jesus spoke to his disciples about another sign —the sign of his presence. What he said on that occasion is of vital importance to everyone today.

Do You Recognize the Sign of Jesus' Presence?

NO ONE wants to be seriously ill or to be caught in a disaster. In order to avoid such calamities, a wise person takes note of the signs pointing to danger and acts accordingly. Jesus Christ described a particular sign that we need to recognize. What he was pointing to would have global impact and would affect all mankind. That includes you and your family.

Jesus spoke about the Kingdom of God, which will remove wickedness and make the earth into a paradise. His disciples were curious about this and wanted to know when that Kingdom would come. They asked: "What will be the sign of your presence and of the conclusion of the system of things?"—Matthew 24:3.

Jesus knew that following his execution and resurrection, centuries would pass before he would be enthroned in heaven as the Messianic King to rule over mankind. Since his enthronement would be invisible to humans, Jesus gave a sign that would enable his followers to recognize his "presence" as well as "the conclusion of the system of things." This sign is composed of several facets, which together make up a composite identifying mark, or signal —the sign of Jesus' presence.

Gospel writers Matthew, Mark, and Luke each carefully recorded Jesus' answer. (Matthew, chapters 24 and 25; Mark, chapter 13; Luke, chapter 21) Other Bible writers added details to the sign. (2 Timothy 3:1-5; 2 Peter 3:3, 4; Revelation 6:1-8; 11:18) Space does not permit a close look at all the details, but we will consider five key elements that make up the sign mentioned by Jesus. You will find that this is relevant and important to you personally.—See box on page 6.

Jesus foretold a multitude of events that together would constitute a sign that would be identifiable from anywhere on earth

"An Epoch-Making Breach"
"Nation will rise against nation and kingdom against kingdom." (Matthew 24:7) Ger-

man newsmagazine *Der Spiegel* reports that prior to 1914, people "believed in a golden future with more freedom, progress, and prosperity." Then everything changed. "The war that began in August 1914 and came to an end in November 1918 was a dramatic event. It made a historic break, separating the old from the new," states the magazine *GEO*. More than 60 million soldiers from five continents engaged in savage conflict. On average, some 6,000 soldiers were killed *each day*. Since then, historians of each generation and of all political persuasions have viewed "the years 1914 to 1918 as being an epoch-making breach."

World War I forced irreversible changes on human society and thrust mankind into the last days of this system of things. The rest of that century was characterized by more wars, armed conflicts, and terrorism. Things have not changed for the better in the early years of the present century. Besides war, other facets of the sign are visible.

Famine, Pestilence, and Earthquakes
"There will be food shortages." (Matthew 24:7) Hunger hit Europe during the first world war, and famine

WWI soldiers: From the book *The World War —A Pictorial History*, 1919; poor family: AP Photo/Aijaz Rahi; polio victim: © WHO/P. Virot

has haunted mankind ever since. Historian Alan Bullock wrote that in Russia and Ukraine in 1933, "hordes of the starving wandered across the countryside . . . Corpses were piled by the sides of the roads." In 1943 journalist T. H. White witnessed famine in the Chinese province of Henan. He wrote: "In a famine, almost anything becomes edible and can be ground, consumed and converted to energy by the human body. But it requires the terror of death to provoke the imagination to eat what, hitherto, is unedible." Sad to say, famine in Africa has become almost commonplace during recent decades. Although the earth produces enough food for everyone, the UN Food and Agriculture Organization estimates that 840 million people worldwide have too little to eat.

"In one place after another pestilences." (Luke 21:11) "The Spanish influenza is estimated to have killed between 20 million and 50 million people in 1918, more than the plague or the first world war," reports the *Süddeutsche Zeitung*. Since then, untold numbers have been stricken by such diseases as malaria, smallpox, tuberculosis, polio, and cholera. And the world looks on aghast as AIDS spreads unabated.

5

We now have the baffling situation that persistent disease exists alongside astonishing medical progress. This paradox, hitherto unknown to mankind, helps identify our extraordinary times.

"*Earthquakes.*" (Matthew 24:7) During the past 100 years, earthquakes have snuffed out the lives of hundreds of thousands of people. According to one source, earthquakes with the power to ruin buildings and split open the ground have averaged 18 per year since 1914. Deadlier quakes strong enough to level buildings have occurred about once a year. Despite advances in technology, the death toll remains high because many rapidly growing cities are located on earthquake fault lines.

Welcome News!

Most facets of the sign of the last days are distressing. But Jesus also told of welcome news.

> Do you see a pattern, a composite sign of global importance?

"This good news of the kingdom will be preached in all the inhabited earth for a witness to all the nations." (Matthew 24:14) The work that Jesus himself started —preaching the good news of the Kingdom—would reach a climax during the last days. This has truly been the case. Jehovah's Witnesses are preaching the Bible's message and are teaching willing people to apply what they learn in everyday life. Currently, over six million Witnesses preach in 235 lands and in over 400 languages.

Note that Jesus did not say that life would come to a standstill because of the distressing world conditions. He also did not say that the whole world would be engulfed by one facet of the sign. But he did foretell a multitude of events that together would constitute a sign that would be identifiable from anywhere on earth.

Looking beyond single events or isolated incidents, do you see a pattern, a composite

IDENTIFYING MARKS OF THE LAST DAYS

Unprecedented warfare.—Matthew 24:7; Revelation 6:4
Famine.—Matthew 24:7; Revelation 6:5, 6, 8
Pestilences.—Luke 21:11; Revelation 6:8
Increasing lawlessness.—Matthew 24:12
Earthquakes.—Matthew 24:7
Critical times hard to deal with.—2 Timothy 3:1
Inordinate love of money.—2 Timothy 3:2
Disobedience to parents.—2 Timothy 3:2
A lack of natural affection.—2 Timothy 3:3
Loving pleasures rather than God.—2 Timothy 3:4
A lack of self-control.—2 Timothy 3:3
Without love of goodness.—2 Timothy 3:3
Taking no note of the impending danger.—Matthew 24:39
Ridiculers rejecting proof of the last days.—2 Peter 3:3, 4
Global preaching of God's Kingdom.—Matthew 24:14

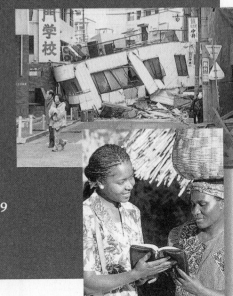

sign of global importance? What is happening affects you and your family. But why, we might ask, do so few people take notice?

Own Interests Come First

"No Swimming," "High Voltage," "Reduce Speed." These are some of the signs and warnings that we see but that are often ignored. Why? We are easily swayed by what we consider to be in our own best interests. For example, we may feel the need to drive faster than the law permits, or we may have a strong desire to swim where it is forbidden. But ignoring signs is unwise.

For instance, avalanches in the Alpine mountains of Austria, France, Italy, and Switzerland sometimes claim the lives of tourists who ignore warnings that urge them to ski or snowboard only on secure routes. According to the *Süddeutsche Zeitung,* many tourists who ignore such warnings live by the maxim, No risk, no fun. Sadly, ignoring warnings can have tragic results.

What reasons do people have for disregarding the sign described by Jesus? They may be blinded by avarice, numbed by apathy, paralyzed by indecision, bogged down by routine, or gripped by fear of losing prestige. Could

any of these be causing you to ignore the sign of Jesus' presence? Would it not be wiser to recognize the sign and act accordingly?

Life on a Paradise Earth

A growing number of people are heeding the sign of Jesus' presence. Kristian, a young married man in Germany, writes: "These are gloomy times. We are undoubtedly living in 'the last days.'" He and his wife spend much time talking to others about the Messianic Kingdom. Frank lives in the same country. He and his wife encourage others with good news from the Bible. Frank says: "Because of the situation in the world, many people today are anxious about the future. We try to encourage them with Bible prophecies of a paradise earth." Kristian and Frank thus help fulfill one facet of Jesus' sign—the preaching of the good news of the Kingdom.—Matthew 24:14.

As the last days reach their climax, Jesus will wipe out this old system and the people who support it. The Messianic Kingdom will then administer affairs on earth, which will be brought to its foretold Paradise condition. Mankind will be freed from sickness and death, and the dead will be resurrected to life on earth. These are the delightful prospects awaiting those who recognize the sign of the times. Would it not be the wise course to learn more about the sign and what one must do to survive the end of this system? Surely this ought to be a matter of great urgency for everyone.—John 17:3.

7

Jehovah's Word Is Alive
Highlights From the Book of First Chronicles

SOME 77 years have passed since the Jews returned to their homeland from Babylonian exile. The temple that was rebuilt by Governor Zerubbabel has now stood for 55 years. The prime reason for the Jews' return was the restoration of true worship in Jerusalem. However, the people lack zeal for Jehovah's worship. There is an urgent need for encouragement, and that is exactly what the Bible book of First Chronicles provides.

Aside from the genealogical records, First Chronicles covers a period of some 40 years, from the death of King Saul to the death of King David. The priest Ezra is credited with the writing of this book in the year 460 B.C.E. First Chronicles is of interest to us because it gives insight into worship at the temple and provides details about the lineage of the Messiah. As a part of the inspired Word of God, its message strengthens our faith and enhances our understanding of the Bible.—Hebrews 4:12.

A MEANINGFUL RECORD OF NAMES
(1 Chronicles 1:1–9:44)

The detailed genealogical listing that Ezra compiles is necessary for at least three reasons: to ensure that only authorized men serve in the priesthood, to help determine tribal inheritance, and to preserve the record of the lineage leading up to the Messiah. The record links the Jews with their past all the way back to the first man. Ten generations take us from Adam to Noah, and another ten take us to Abraham. After listing the sons of Ishmael, the sons of Abraham's concubine Keturah, and the sons of Esau, the account focuses on the line of descent of the 12 sons of Israel.—1 Chronicles 2:1.

The descendants of Judah are given extensive coverage because they provide the royal line of King David. There are 14 generations from Abraham to David and another 14 to the deportation to Babylon. (1 Chronicles 1: 27, 34; 2:1-15; 3:1-17; Matthew 1:17) Ezra then lists descendants of the tribes on the east side of the Jordan, followed by the genealogy of the sons of Levi. (1 Chronicles 5:1-24; 6:1) Then comes a summary of some of the other tribes to the west of the Jordan River and of the line of Benjamin in detail. (1 Chronicles 8:1) The names of the first inhabitants of Jerusalem after the Babylonian captivity are also listed.—1 Chronicles 9: 1-16.

Scriptural Questions Answered:

1:18—Who was Shelah's father—Cainan or Arpachshad? (Luke 3:35, 36) Arpachshad was the father of Shelah. (Genesis 10: 24; 11:12) The term "Cainan" at Luke 3:36 may well be a corruption of the term "Chal-

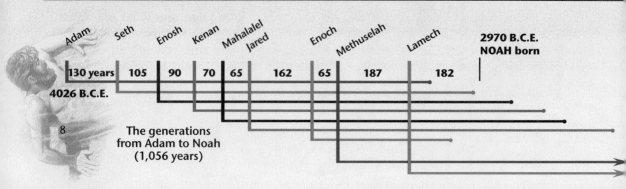

Adam	Seth	Enosh	Kenan	Mahalalel	Jared	Enoch	Methuselah	Lamech	2970 B.C.E. NOAH born
130 years	105	90	70	65	162	65	187	182	

4026 B.C.E.

8

The generations from Adam to Noah (1,056 years)

deans." If this is so, the original text may have read, "the son of Chaldean Arpachshad." Or it may be that the names Cainan and Arpachshad refer to one and the same person. Not to be overlooked is the fact that the expression "son of Cainan" is not found in some manuscripts.—Luke 3:36, footnote.

2:15—Was David the seventh son of Jesse? No. Jesse had eight sons, and David was the youngest. (1 Samuel 16:10, 11; 17:12) One of the sons of Jesse evidently died without having any children. Since that son would have no bearing on genealogical records, Ezra omitted his name.

3:17—Why does Luke 3:27 refer to Jeconiah's son Shealtiel as the son of Neri? Jeconiah was the father of Shealtiel. However, Neri apparently gave his daughter to Shealtiel as a wife. Luke referred to Neri's son-in-law as Neri's son just as he did in the case of Joseph, calling him the son of Mary's father, Heli.—Luke 3:23.

3:17-19—How were Zerubbabel, Pedaiah, and Shealtiel related? Zerubbabel was a son of Pedaiah, who was a brother of Shealtiel. Yet, the Bible at times calls Zerubbabel the son of Shealtiel. (Matthew 1:12; Luke 3: 27) This could be because Pedaiah died and Shealtiel raised Zerubbabel. Or perhaps since Shealtiel died without having a child, Pedaiah performed brother-in-law marriage, and Zerubbabel was the firstborn of that union.—Deuteronomy 25:5-10.

5:1, 2—What did receiving the right of the firstborn mean for Joseph? It meant that Joseph received a double portion of the inheritance. (Deuteronomy 21:17) He thus became the father of two tribes—Ephraim and Manasseh. The other sons of Israel fathered only one tribe each.

Lessons for Us:

1:1–9:44. The genealogies of real people prove that the entire arrangement of true worship is based, not on myth, but on fact.

4:9, 10. Jehovah answered the fervent prayer of Jabez for a peaceful enlargement of his territory so that it might accommodate more God-fearing people. We too need to offer heartfelt prayers for an increase as we zealously share in the disciple-making work.

5:10, 18-22. In the days of King Saul, the tribes east of the Jordan defeated the Hagrites even though these tribes were outnumbered more than 2 to 1. This was because the valiant men of these tribes trusted in Jehovah and looked to him for help. Let us have complete confidence in Jehovah as we carry on our spiritual warfare against formidable odds.—Ephesians 6:10-17.

9:26, 27. The Levite gatekeepers occupied an office of great trust. They were given the key to the entrance to the holy areas of the temple. They proved to be reliable in opening the gates each day. We have been entrusted with the responsibility of reaching out to the people in our territory and helping them to come to worship Jehovah. Should we not prove to be just as dependable and trustworthy as the Levite gatekeepers?

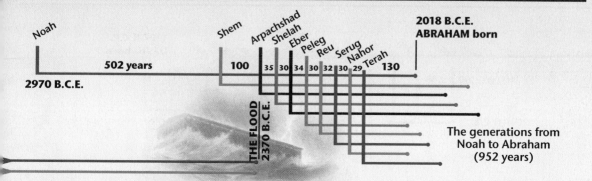

Noah

502 years

2970 B.C.E.

Shem 100

Arpachshad 35
Shelah 30
Eber 34
Peleg 30
Reu 32
Serug 30
Nahor 29
Terah 130

2018 B.C.E.
ABRAHAM born

THE FLOOD
2370 B.C.E.

The generations from
Noah to Abraham
(952 years)

DAVID RULES AS KING
(1 Chronicles 10:1–29:30)

The narrative opens with the account of King Saul and his three sons dying in battle against the Philistines at Mount Gilboa. David, the son of Jesse, is made king over the tribe of Judah. Men from all tribes come to Hebron and make him king over all Israel. (1 Chronicles 11:1-3) Soon thereafter, he captures Jerusalem. Later, the Israelites bring the ark of the covenant to Jerusalem "with joyful shouting and with the sounding of the horn and with . . . playing aloud on stringed instruments and harps." —1 Chronicles 15:28.

David expresses a desire to build a house for the true God. Reserving that privilege for Solomon, Jehovah makes a covenant with David for a Kingdom. As David carries on his campaign against Israel's enemies, Jehovah gives him one victory after another. An illegal census results in 70,000 deaths. After receiving angelic direction to erect an altar to Jehovah, David purchases a place from Ornan the Jebusite. David begins making "preparation in great quantities" for building a "surpassingly magnificent" house to Jehovah at that site. (1 Chronicles 22:5) David organizes Levitical services, described here in greater detail than anywhere else in the Scriptures. The king and the people make generous contributions for the temple. After a 40-year reign, David dies "satisfied with days, riches and glory; and Solomon his son [begins] to reign in place of him."—1 Chronicles 29:28.

Scriptural Questions Answered:

11:11—Why is the number of slain 300 and not 800 as in the parallel account at 2 Samuel 23:8? The head of David's three most valiant men was Jashobeam, or Josheb-basshebeth. The other two mighty men were Eleazar and Shammah. (2 Samuel 23:8-11) The reason for the difference in the two accounts may well be that they refer to different deeds performed by the same man.

11:20, 21—What was Abishai's standing with respect to the three principal mighty men of David? Abishai was not one of the three mightiest men who served David. However, as stated at 2 Samuel 23:18, 19, he was the head of 30 warriors and was more distinguished than any of them. Abishai's reputation rivaled that of the three principal mighty ones because he performed a mighty act similar to that of Jashobeam.

12:8—In what way were the faces of the Gadite warriors like "the faces of lions"? These valiant men were at David's side in the wilderness. Their hair had grown long. Having a hairy mane gave them a fierce, lionlike appearance.

13:5—What is "the river of Egypt"? Some have thought that this expression refers to a branch of the Nile River. However, it is generally understood that the reference is to "the torrent valley of Egypt"—a long ravine marking the southwest boundary of the Promised Land.—Numbers 34:2, 5; Genesis 15:18.

16:30—What is the meaning of "severe pains" on account of Jehovah? The expression "pains" is here used figuratively to de-

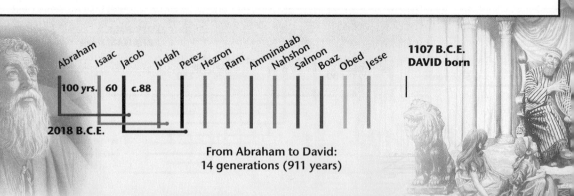

Abraham Isaac Jacob Judah Perez Hezron Ram Amminadab Nahshon Salmon Boaz Obed Jesse

1107 B.C.E. DAVID born

100 yrs. 60 c.88

2018 B.C.E.

From Abraham to David:
14 generations (911 years)

note reverential fear of and high regard for Jehovah.

16:1, 37-40; 21:29, 30; 22:19—What arrangement for worship remained operative in Israel from the time the Ark was brought to Jerusalem until the temple was built? When David brought the Ark to Jerusalem and placed it inside the tent he had made, the Ark had not been in the tabernacle for many years. After the move, the Ark remained in that tent in Jerusalem. The tabernacle was in Gibeon, where High Priest Zadok and his brothers carried out sacrifices prescribed in the Law. This arrangement continued until the completion of the temple in Jerusalem. When the temple was ready, the tabernacle was brought from Gibeon to Jerusalem, and the Ark was housed in the Most Holy of the temple.—1 Kings 8:4, 6.

Lessons for Us:

13:11. Rather than becoming angry and blaming Jehovah when our efforts fail, we must analyze the situation and try to see what caused the failure. Undoubtedly, David did that. He learned from his mistake and later successfully brought the Ark to Jerusalem, using the proper method.*

14:10, 13-16; 22:17-19. We should always approach Jehovah in prayer and seek his direction before undertaking any endeavor that will affect us spiritually.

16:23-29. Jehovah's worship should be our first concern in life.

18:3. Jehovah is the Fulfiller of his promises. Through David, he carried out his promise to give Abraham's seed the entire land of Canaan, extending "from the river of Egypt to the great river, the river Euphrates."—Genesis 15:18; 1 Chronicles 13:5.

21:13-15. Jehovah commanded the angel

---

* For other lessons from David's attempt to transport the Ark to Jerusalem, see *The Watchtower,* May 15, 2005, pages 16-19.

to halt the plague because He is sensitive to the suffering of His people. Indeed, "very many are his mercies."*

22:5, 9; 29:3-5, 14-16. Although he was not commissioned to build Jehovah's temple, David exhibited a generous spirit. Why? Because he appreciated that all he had acquired was due to Jehovah's goodness. Similar feelings of gratitude should move us to have a spirit of generosity.

24:7-18. The arrangement of 24 priestly divisions that David instituted was in effect when Jehovah's angel appeared to Zechariah, the father of John the Baptizer, and announced the coming birth of John. As a member of "the division of Abijah," Zechariah was then serving his turn at the temple. (Luke 1:5, 8, 9) True worship revolves around historical—not mythological—figures. Blessings result from our loyal cooperation with "the faithful and discreet slave" in connection with the well-organized worship of Jehovah today.—Matthew 24:45.

Serve Jehovah "With a Delightful Soul"

First Chronicles is not all about genealogies. It is also a narrative of David's bringing the ark of the covenant to Jerusalem, of his great victories, of the preparation for building the temple, and of the setting up of the Levitical priestly divisions of service. All that Ezra relates in First Chronicles must surely have benefited the Israelites, helping them to renew their zeal for Jehovah's worship at the temple.

What an example David set in keeping Jehovah's worship foremost in his life! Instead of seeking special privileges for himself, David sought to do God's will. We are encouraged to apply his advice to serve Jehovah "with a complete heart and with a delightful soul."—1 Chronicles 28:9.

---

* For other lessons related to David's illegal census, see *The Watchtower,* May 15, 2005, pages 16-19.

IS YOUR
Conscience
WELL TRAINED?

HAVE you ever said, "I know in my heart that it is not right," or, "I cannot do what you ask me to do. Something inside tells me it is wrong"? That was the "voice" of your conscience, that inward recognition, or sense, of right and wrong, which excuses or accuses a person. Yes, conscience is inherent in us.

Even in his state of alienation from God, man still has the general ability to distinguish right from wrong. This is because he was made in God's image, so that he to some degree reflects the godly qualities of wisdom and righteousness. (Genesis 1:26, 27) Regarding this, the apostle Paul wrote under divine inspiration: "Whenever people of the nations that do not have law do *by nature* the things of the law, these people, although not having law, are a law to themselves. They are the very ones who demonstrate the matter of the law to be written in their hearts, while their conscience is bearing witness with them and, between their own thoughts, they are being accused or even excused."*—Romans 2:14, 15.

This moral nature, inherited from the first man, Adam, works as a "law," or a rule of conduct, in people of all races and nationalities. It is the ability to look at ourselves and

---

* The Greek word for conscience here used means "the inward faculty of moral judgment" (*The Analytical Greek Lexicon Revised,* by Harold K. Moulton); "distinguishing between what is morally good and bad." —*Greek-English Lexicon,* by J. H. Thayer.

render judgment about ourselves. (Romans 9:1) Adam and Eve manifested this faculty as soon as they broke God's law—they hid themselves. (Genesis 3:7, 8) Another example of how the conscience operates is the way King David reacted when he discerned that he had sinned by taking a census. The Bible says that "David's heart began to beat him."—2 Samuel 24:1-10.

The ability to look back and judge one's moral conduct can produce the very important effect of godly repentance. David wrote: "When I kept silent my bones wore out through my groaning all day long. My sin I finally confessed to you, and my error I did not cover. I said: 'I shall make confession over my transgressions to Jehovah.' And you yourself pardoned the error of my sins." (Psalm 32:3, 5) Thus, a functioning conscience can bring the sinner back to God, helping him to recognize the need to have God's forgiveness and to follow His ways. —Psalm 51:1-4, 9, 13-15.

The conscience also provides warnings or gives guidance when we have to make a choice or a moral decision. It was this aspect of conscience that may have helped Joseph to sense beforehand that adultery was wrong and bad—a sin against God. A specific law against adultery was later included in the Ten Commandments given to Israel. (Genesis 39:1-9; Exodus 20:14) Clearly, we stand to benefit far more when our con-

Is your conscience trained to guide you rather than just judge you?

customs, beliefs, and environment. Surely the degraded morals and the falling standards of the world cannot be the standard of a good conscience.

A Christian, therefore, must have the additional assistance of the firm and righteous standards found in God's Word, the Bible. These can guide our conscience to assess matters correctly and set them straight. (2 Timothy 3:16) When our conscience is enlightened according to God's standards, it can better serve as a moral safety device, enabling us "to distinguish both right and wrong." (Hebrews 5:14) Without God's standards, our conscience may give us no warning when we stray into a bad course. "There exists a way that is upright before a man," says the Bible, "but the ways of death are the end of it afterward."—Proverbs 16:25; 17:20.

In some areas of life, God's Word sets out explicit guidelines and directions, and we do well to follow them. On the other hand, there are many situations for which there are no specific instructions in the Bible. These may involve choices in employment, health matters, recreation, dress and grooming, and other areas. It is not easy to know what to do in each case and make the right decision. For that reason we should have the attitude of David, who prayed: "Make me know your own ways, O Jehovah; teach me your own paths. Make me walk in your truth and teach me, for you are my God of salvation." (Psalm 25:4, 5) The better we understand God's views and ways, the more we will be able to evaluate our circumstances accurately and make decisions with a clean conscience.

Hence, when faced with a question or a decision, we should first reflect on Bible principles that may apply. Some of these may be: respect for headship (Colossians

science is trained to guide us rather than just judge us. Does your conscience work in such a manner?

Training the Conscience to Make Right Decisions

Although we inherit the faculty of conscience, that endowment is unfortunately flawed. Though mankind was given a perfect start, "all have sinned and fall short of the glory of God." (Romans 3:23) Because we are marred by sin and imperfection, our conscience may be warped and may no longer function fully in the ways originally intended. (Romans 7:18-23) In addition, external factors can affect our conscience. It can be influenced by our upbringing or by local

3:18, 20); honesty in all things (Hebrews 13:18); hatred of what is bad (Psalm 97:10); pursuing peace (Romans 14:19); obedience to established authorities (Matthew 22:21; Romans 13:1-7); exclusive devotion to God (Matthew 4:10); being no part of the world (John 17:14); avoiding bad associations (1 Corinthians 15:33); modesty in dress and grooming (1 Timothy 2:9, 10); and not causing others to stumble (Philippians 1:10). Identifying the relevant Bible principle can thus strengthen our conscience and help us make the right decision.

Listen to Your Conscience

In order for our conscience to help us, we must heed it. Only when we respond promptly to the proddings of our Bible-trained conscience do we benefit from it. We can compare the trained conscience to the warning lights on an automobile's instrument panel. Suppose a light comes on warning us that the oil pressure is low. What would happen if we did not

A well-trained conscience results from our learning and applying Bible principles

give prompt attention to the matter and continued to drive the vehicle? We could cause serious damage to the motor. In a similar way, our conscience, or inner voice, can alert us that a certain course of action is wrong. Comparing our Scriptural standards and values with the course of action being taken or contemplated, it flashes a warning, as the light on the instrument panel does. Heeding the warning will help us not only to avoid the bad consequences of the wrong action but also to preserve the proper operation of our conscience.

What would happen if we chose to ignore the warning? In time, the conscience could become insensitive. The effect of persistently ignoring or suppressing the conscience can be likened to that of searing the flesh with a branding iron. The scar tissue, devoid of nerve endings, has no more sense of feeling. (1 Timothy 4:2) Such a conscience no longer reacts to the commission of sin, nor does it give warnings to prevent a repetition of the sin. A scarred conscience ignores Bible standards of right and wrong and thus is a bad conscience. It is a defiled conscience, its possessor being "past all moral sense" and alienated from God. (Ephesians 4:17-19; Titus 1:15) What a tragic outcome!

"Hold a Good Conscience"

To maintain a good conscience requires constant effort. The apostle Paul stated: "I am exercising myself continually to have a consciousness of committing no offense against God and men." (Acts 24:16) As a

---

IN OUR NEXT ISSUE

Benefit From the Best Education Available!

———

Jehovah's Word Soars in "the Land of the Eagle"

———

Cultivate Genuine Humility

Do not ignore the warnings of your conscience

Christian, Paul continually checked and corrected his course of action to make sure that he committed no offense against God. Paul knew that in the final analysis, it is God who will determine the rightness or wrongness of what we do. (Romans 14:10-12; 1 Corinthians 4:4) Paul said: "All things are naked and openly exposed to the eyes of him with whom we have an accounting."—Hebrews 4:13.

Paul also made mention of committing no offense against men. A case in point is his counsel to the Corinthian Christians concerning "the eating of foods offered to idols." His point was that even when a certain course may not be objectionable in itself from the standpoint of God's Word, it is vital to take into account the conscience of others. Failing to do so can cause spiritual 'ruin to our brothers for whose sake Christ died.' We could also ruin our own relation-ship with God.—1 Corinthians 8:4, 11-13; 10: 23, 24.

Thus, continue to train your conscience and to keep a good conscience. When making decisions, seek God's guidance. (James 1:5) Study God's Word, and allow its principles to mold your mind and heart. (Proverbs 2:3-5) When serious issues arise, consult with mature Christians to be sure that you have the correct understanding of the Bible principles involved. (Proverbs 12:15; Romans 14:1; Galatians 6:5) Consider how your decision will affect your conscience, how it will affect others and, above all, how it will affect your relationship with Jehovah. —1 Timothy 1:5, 18, 19.

Our conscience is a marvelous gift from our loving heavenly Father, Jehovah God. By using it in harmony with the will of its Giver, we will draw closer to our Creator. As we endeavor to "hold a good conscience" in all that we do, we come that much closer to showing that we are made in God's image. —1 Peter 3:16; Colossians 3:10.

My Parents' Example Strengthened Me

AS TOLD BY
JANEZ REKELJ

The year was 1958. My wife, Stanka, and I were high in the Karawanken Alps on the Yugoslav-Austrian border, attempting to flee to Austria. This was dangerous, as armed Yugoslav border patrols were determined to prevent anyone from crossing. As we moved on, we were confronted by a sheer cliff dropping away beneath us. Stanka and I had never seen the Austrian side of the mountains before. We headed east until we came to a rough slope of rock and gravel. Tying ourselves to a tarpaulin we were carrying, we slid down the mountainside to an uncertain future.

L ET me relate how we came to be in this situation and how my parents' faithful example motivated me to remain loyal to Jehovah in times of difficulty.

I grew up in Slovenia, which today is a small Central European country. It is nestled in the European Alps, with Austria to the north, Italy to the west, Croatia to the south, and Hungary to the east. However, when my parents, Franc and Rozalija Rekelj, were born, Slovenia was part of the Austro-Hungarian Empire. At the end of World War I, Slovenia became part of a new state called the Kingdom of the Serbs, Croats, and Slovenes. In 1929 the name of the country was changed to Yugoslavia, literally "South Slavia." I was born on January 9 of that same year, on the outskirts of the village of Podhom, near picturesque Lake Bled.

My parents in the late 1920's

Mother had a strict Catholic upbringing. One of her uncles was a priest, and three of her aunts were nuns. She had a burning desire to own a Bible, to read it, and to understand it. Father, however, took a dim view of religion. He was disgusted by religion's role in the Great War of 1914-18.

Learning the Truth

Sometime after the war, my mother's cousin, Janez Brajec, and his wife, Ančka, became Bible Students, as Jehovah's Witnesses were then known. At the time, they lived in Austria. From about 1936 onward, Ančka came to visit Mother on a number of occasions. She provided a Bible, which Mother quickly read, along with copies of *The Watchtower* and other Bible publications in Slovenian. Finally, because of Hitler's annexation of Austria in 1938, Janez and Ančka moved back to Slovenia. I recall that they were an educated, discerning couple with a real love for Jehovah.

They often discussed Bible truths with Mother, which moved her to dedicate her life to Jehovah. She was baptized in 1938.

Mother caused a stir in the area when she stopped observing unscriptural customs, such as the celebrating of Christmas; when she would no longer eat blood sausage; and particularly when she took all the images in our possession and burned them. Opposition was not slow in coming. Mother's aunts, the nuns, made it a point to write to her, trying to convince her to return to Mary and the church. However, when Mother wrote and asked them for answers to specific Bible questions, she received no reply. My grandfather also strongly opposed her. He was not a bad man, but he was put under a great deal of pressure by our relatives and the community. As a result, he destroyed Mother's Bible literature on a number of occasions, but he never touched her Bible. He begged her on his knees to return to the church. He even went so far as to threaten her with a knife. My father, though, let him know in no uncertain terms that such behavior would not be tolerated.

Father continued to support Mother's right to read the Bible and to make her own choices as to her beliefs. In 1946 he too was baptized. Seeing how Jehovah strengthened my mother to stand up fearlessly for the truth despite opposition and how Jehovah rewarded her for her faith motivated me to develop

My mother, far right, with Ančka, who taught her the truth

With my wife, Stanka, shortly after we were married

my own relationship with God. I also benefited greatly from Mother's habit of reading aloud to me from the Bible and from Bible-based publications.

Mother also had long discussions with her sister, Marija Repe, and eventually Aunt Marija and I were baptized on the same day in the middle of July 1942. A brother came to give a short talk, and we were baptized at our home in a large wooden tub.

Forced Labor During World War II

In 1942, in the midst of World War II, Germany and Italy invaded Slovenia and divided it among themselves and Hungary. My parents refused to join the *Volksbund*, the Nazi people's organization. I refused to say "Heil Hitler" in school. Apparently, my teacher informed the authorities of the situation.

We were put on a train bound for a castle near the village of Hüttenbach, Bavaria, that was used as a forced labor camp. Father arranged for me to work and live with the local baker and his family. During this time, I learned to be a baker, which later proved very useful. In time, all the rest of my family (including Aunt Marija and her family) were transferred to the camp in Gunzenhausen.

At the end of the war, I was going to join a group to travel to where my parents were. On the evening before I was to leave, Father turned up. I do not know where I would have ended up if I had gone with the group, as it was of questionable character. Once more, I felt Jehovah's loving care as he used my parents to protect and train me. Father and I walked for three days to meet up with the family. By June 1945 we all arrived back home.

After the war, the Communists under the leadership of President Josip Broz Tito came to power in Yugoslavia. Consequently, conditions for Jehovah's Witnesses remained difficult.

In 1948 a brother came from Austria and accepted a meal from us. Everywhere he went, the police followed him and arrested the brothers he visited. Father too was arrested for offering him hospitality and not reporting him to the police, and Father spent two years in prison as a result. This was a very difficult time for Mother not only because Father was absent but also because she knew that my younger brother and I would soon face the test of neutrality.

Prison Term in Macedonia

In November 1949, I received my call for military service. I went to report and to explain my conscientious refusal to serve. The authorities would not listen to me and put me on a train with the recruits headed for Macedonia, at the other end of Yugoslavia.

For three years I was cut off from my family and the brotherhood and was left without any literature or even a Bible. It was very difficult. I was sustained by meditating on Jehovah and the example of his Son, Jesus Christ. My parents' example also strengthened me. In addition, constant prayer for strength enabled me to avoid despair.

In time, I was sent to a prison in Idrizovo, near Skopje. In this prison, inmates worked at various tasks and trades. Initially, I worked as a cleaner and as a courier between offices. Although often bullied by one prisoner who was formerly a member of the secret police, I had a good working relationship with everyone else—guards, prisoners, even the manager of the prison factory.

Later, I learned that a baker was needed in the prison bakery. A few days thereafter, the manager came to the roll call. He walked up the line, stopped in front of me, and asked, "Are you a baker?" "Yes, sir," I said. "Tomorrow morning report to the bakery," was his reply. The prisoner who had mistreated me passed by the bakery often but could do nothing about it. I worked there from February to July in 1950.

I was then transferred to the barracks called Volkoderi, in the south of Macedonia, near Lake Prespa. From nearby Otešovo I was able to write letters home. I worked on a road gang, but most of the time, I worked in a bakery, which made things easier for me. I was released in November of 1952.

During the time I was absent from Podhom, a congregation was formed in the area. At first, the congregation met in a guesthouse in Spodnje Gorje. Later, Father made a room available in our house for the congregation to meet in. I was happy to join them when I returned from Macedonia. I also renewed my acquaintance with Stanka, whom I met before I went to prison. On April 24, 1954, we were married. My respite, however, was coming to a close.

Prison Term in Maribor

In September 1954, I received another call-up. This time, I was sentenced to more than three and a half years in a prison in Maribor, which is located at the eastern end of Slovenia. As soon as I was able to, I purchased some paper and pencils. I started to write down everything I could remember—scriptures, quotes from *The Watchtower*,

and thoughts from other Christian publications. I read my notes and added more to my book as I remembered more. In the end, the book was full, and this enabled me to stay focused on the truth and remain spiritually strong. Prayer and meditation were also invaluable aids to my spiritual strength, enabling me to be more courageous in sharing the truth with others.

At that time, I was allowed to receive one letter a month and one 15-minute visit a month. Stanka traveled all night on the train in order to be at the prison early to visit me, and then she could travel back the same day. I found these visits to be very encouraging. Then I put into action a plan to get a Bible. Stanka and I were seated opposite each other at a table, with a guard assigned to watch us. When the guard was not looking, I slipped a letter into her handbag, asking her to put a Bible in her bag the next time she visited.

Stanka and my parents thought that this was too dangerous, so they took apart a copy of the Christian Greek Scriptures and put pages of it inside some buns. In this way I received the Bible I needed. In the same manner, I also received copies of *The Watchtower*, handwritten by Stanka. I would immediately make another copy in my own handwriting and destroy the original so that no one

The congregation that met in our family home in 1955

finding the articles would be able to discover where I had obtained them.

Because of my persistent witnessing, fellow prisoners commented that I would surely get in trouble. On one occasion, I was engaged in quite an animated Bible discussion with a fellow prisoner. We heard the key being inserted in the lock, and in walked a guard. I immediately thought that I would receive solitary confinement. But that was not the guard's intention. He had heard the discussion and wanted to join in. Satisfied with the answers to his questions, he left and locked the cell door behind him.

During the last month of my sentence, the commissioner in charge of reforming the prisoners commended me for my determined stand for the truth. I felt that this was a fine reward for my efforts to make known Jehovah's name. In May 1958, I was again released from jail.

Escape to Austria, Then Australia

In August 1958 my mother died. She had been ill for some time. Then in September of 1958, I received my third call-up. That evening Stanka and I made the momentous decision that led us to the dramatic border crossing mentioned earlier. Without telling anyone, we packed a couple of backpacks and a tarpaulin and left through the window, bound for the Austrian border just west of Mount Stol. It seemed that Jehovah made the way out for us when he knew that we needed some relief.

The Austrian authorities sent us to a refugee camp near Salzburg. During our six months there, we were always with the local Witnesses, so we spent very little time in the camp. Others in the camp were amazed at how quickly we had made friends. It was during this time that we attended our first assembly. Another first was being able to preach freely from house to house. It was very difficult for us to leave these dear friends when it was time to depart.

The Austrian authorities offered us the chance to immigrate to Australia. Never did we even dream that we would go so far. We traveled by train to Genoa, Italy, and then boarded a ship bound for Australia. We finally settled in the city of Wollongong, New South Wales. Here our son, Philip, was born on March 30, 1965.

Living in Australia has opened up many avenues of service, including the opportunity to preach to others who have migrated from the areas formerly known as Yugoslavia. We are thankful for Jehovah's blessings, including our being able to serve him as a united family. Philip and his wife, Susie, have the privilege of serving in the Australia branch office of Jehovah's Witnesses, and they even had the opportunity to spend two years at the branch office in Slovenia.

Despite the challenges brought on by advancing years and health problems, my wife and I continue to enjoy our service to Jehovah. I am so grateful for my parents' fine example! It continues to strengthen me, helping me to do what the apostle Paul said: "Rejoice in the hope. Endure under tribulation. Persevere in prayer."—Romans 12:12.

With my wife, our son, Philip, and his wife, Susie

"KEEP ON THE WATCH" —THE HOUR OF JUDGMENT HAS ARRIVED!

"Keep on the watch . . . because you do not know on what day your Lord is coming."—MATTHEW 24:42.

WHAT would you do if you knew that a thief was on the prowl, burglarizing homes in your neighborhood? To protect your loved ones and your valuables, you would keep alert, watchful. After all, a thief does not send a letter announcing when he is coming. On the contrary, he comes stealthily and unexpectedly.

² On more than one occasion, Jesus used the ways of a thief as an illustration. (Luke 10: 30; John 10:10) Regarding events that would occur during the time of the end and that would lead up to his coming to execute judgment, Jesus gave this warning: "Keep on the watch, therefore, because you do not know on what day your Lord is coming. But know one thing, that if the householder had known in what watch the thief was coming, he would have kept awake and not allowed his house to be broken into." (Matthew 24: 42, 43) So Jesus likened his coming to the arrival of a thief—unexpected.

³ The illustration was fitting, for the precise date of Jesus' coming would not be known. Earlier, in the same prophecy, Jesus said: "Concerning that day and hour nobody knows, neither the angels of the heavens nor the Son, but only the Father." (Matthew 24:36) Jesus, therefore, urged his listeners: "Prove yourselves ready." (Matthew 24: 44) Those heeding Jesus' warning would be ready, conducting themselves properly, *whenever* he would come as Jehovah's Executional Agent.

⁴ Some important questions arise: Is Jesus' warning only for people of the world, or do true Christians also need to "keep on the watch"? Why is it urgent to "keep on the watch," and what does this involve?

A Warning for Whom?

⁵ It is certainly true that the Lord's coming will be thieflike to people of the world, who shut their ears to the warning of impending calamity. (2 Peter 3:3-7) However, what about true Christians? The apostle Paul wrote to fellow believers: "You yourselves know quite well that Jehovah's day is coming exactly as a thief in the night." (1 Thessalonians 5:2) There is no doubt in our minds that "Jehovah's day is coming." But does that minimize the need for us to keep on the watch? Notice that it was to his disciples that Jesus said: "At an hour that *you* do not think to be it, the Son of man is coming."

1, 2. To what did Jesus fittingly liken his coming?
3, 4. (a) What is involved in heeding Jesus' warning about his coming? (b) What questions arise?

The information in this study article is based on the brochure *Keep on the Watch!* released at the district conventions that were held around the world during 2004/05.

5. How do we know that the warning to "keep on the watch" applies to true Christians?

(Matthew 24:44) Earlier, when urging his disciples to seek continually the Kingdom, Jesus cautioned: "Keep ready, because at an hour that *you* do not think likely the Son of man is coming." (Luke 12:31, 40) Is it not clear that Jesus had his followers in mind when he warned: "Keep on the watch"?

⁶ Why do we need to "keep on the watch" and "keep ready"? Jesus explained: "Two men will be in the field: one will be taken along and the other be abandoned; two women will be grinding at the hand mill: one will be taken along and the other be abandoned." (Matthew 24:40, 41) Those who prove themselves ready will be "taken along," or saved, when the ungodly world is destroyed. Others will be "abandoned" to destruction because they have been selfishly pursuing their own way of life. These may well include individuals who were once enlightened but who did not keep on the watch.

⁷ Not knowing the exact day of the end of this old system gives us the opportunity to demonstrate that we serve God out of a pure motive. How so? It may be that the end seems to be a long time in arriving. Sad to say, some Christians who feel this way have allowed their zeal for Jehovah's service to cool off. Yet, by our dedication, we have without reservation presented ourselves to Jehovah to serve him. Those who know Jehovah realize that a last-minute display of zeal will not impress him. He sees what is in the heart. —1 Samuel 16:7.

⁸ Because we truly love Jehovah, we find the greatest delight in doing his will. (Psalm 40:8; Matthew 26:39) And we want to serve Jehovah forever. That prospect is not less precious just because we must wait a little longer than we may have expected. Above all, we keep on the watch because we eagerly anticipate what Jehovah's day will mean for the accomplishment of his purpose. Our earnest desire to please God moves us to apply the counsel of his Word and give his Kingdom first place in our life. (Matthew 6:33; 1 John 5:3) Let us consider how keeping on the watch should influence the decisions we make and the way we live our life each day.

Where Is Your Life Heading?

⁹ Many people today recognize that serious problems and shocking events have become everyday occurrences, and they may not be pleased with the direction that their own life is taking. However, do they know the real meaning of world conditions? Do they realize that we are living in "the conclusion of the system of things"? (Matthew 24:3) Do they recognize that the prevalence of selfish, violent, even ungodly attitudes marks these times as "the last days"? (2 Timothy 3:1-5) There is an urgent need for them to wake up to the significance of all of this and to consider the way their life is heading.

¹⁰ What about us? Every day we face decisions that involve our employment, our health, our family, and our worship. We know what the Bible says, and we endeavor to apply it. Therefore, we do well to ask ourselves: 'Have I allowed the anxieties of life to push me off course? Am I letting the world's philosophies, its thinking, determine the choices I make?' (Luke 21:34-36; Colossians 2:8) We need to continue to demonstrate that we trust in Jehovah with all our heart and not lean upon our own understanding. (Proverbs 3:5) In that way, we will keep "a

6. Why do we need to "keep on the watch"?
7. What does not knowing when the end will come allow us to do?
8. How does love for Jehovah move us to keep on the watch?

9. Why is there an urgent need for people of the world to wake up to the significance of our times?
10. What must we do to be sure that we are keeping on the watch?

Jesus likened his coming to the arrival of a thief

firm hold on the real life"—eternal life in God's new world.—1 Timothy 6:12, 19.

[11] The Bible contains many warning examples that can help us to keep on the watch. Consider what happened in Noah's day. Well in advance, God saw to it that warning was given. But apart from Noah and his household, people took no note. (2 Peter 2:5) Regarding this, Jesus said: "Just as the days of Noah were, so the presence of the Son of man will be. For as they were in those days before the flood, eating and drinking, men marrying and women being given in marriage, until the day that Noah entered into the ark; and they took no note until the flood came and swept them all away, so the presence of the Son of man will be." (Matthew 24:37-39) What can we learn from that? If any of us are allowing mundane concerns —even the normal activities of life—to crowd out the spiritual activities that God urges us to keep in first place, we need to think seriously about our situation.—Romans 14:17.

[12] Think, too, about the days of Lot. The city of Sodom, where Lot and his family lived, was materially prosperous but morally bankrupt. Jehovah sent his angels to bring the place to ruin. The angels urged Lot and his family to flee from Sodom and

not to look back. Encouraged by the angels, they did leave the city. Lot's wife, however, evidently could not let go of her feelings for her home in Sodom. Disobediently, she looked back, and for this she paid with her life. (Genesis 19:15-26) Prophetically, Jesus warned: "Remember the wife of Lot." Are we acting on that warning? —Luke 17:32.

[13] Those who heeded divine warnings were spared. That was true of Noah and his family and of Lot and his daughters. (2 Peter 2:9) As we take to heart the warning in these examples, we are also encouraged by the message of deliverance contained therein for lovers of righteousness. That fills our heart with confident expectation of the fulfillment of God's promise of "new heavens and a new earth" in which "righteousness is to dwell."—2 Peter 3:13.

'The Hour of the Judgment Has Arrived'!

[14] As we keep on the watch, what can we expect? The book of Revelation outlines progressive steps in the fulfillment of God's purpose. Acting on what it says is vital if we are to prove ourselves ready. The prophecy vividly describes events that would occur in "the Lord's day," which began when Christ was enthroned in heaven in 1914. (Revelation 1: 10) Revelation alerts us to an angel who has been entrusted with "everlasting good news to declare." He proclaims in a loud voice: "Fear God and give him glory, because the hour of the judgment by him has arrived." (Revelation 14:6, 7) That "hour" of judgment is a brief period; it includes both the

___
11-13. What can we learn from the examples of what happened (a) in the days of Noah? (b) in the days of Lot?

___
14, 15. (a) What does "the hour" of judgment include? (b) What is involved in 'fearing God and giving him glory'?

pronouncement and the execution of the judgments that are depicted in that prophecy. We are now living in that period.

15 Now, before the hour of judgment concludes, we are urged: "Fear God and give him glory." What does this involve? Proper fear of God should cause us to turn away from badness. (Proverbs 8:13) If we honor God, we will listen to him with deep respect. We will not be too busy to read his Word, the Bible, regularly. We will not minimize his counsel to attend Christian meetings. (Hebrews 10:24, 25) We will cherish the privilege of proclaiming the good news of God's Messianic Kingdom and will do so zealously. We will trust in Jehovah at all times and with our whole heart. (Psalm 62:8) Recognizing that Jehovah is the Universal Sovereign, we honor him by willingly submitting to him as the Sovereign of our life. Do you truly fear God and give him glory in all such ways?

16 Revelation chapter 14 goes on to describe further events that are to take place in the hour of judgment. Babylon the Great,

_____
16. Why can we say that the judgment against Babylon the Great stated at Revelation 14:8 has already been fulfilled?

the world empire of false religion, is mentioned first: "Another, a second angel, followed, saying: 'She has fallen! Babylon the Great has fallen!'" (Revelation 14:8) Yes, from God's viewpoint, Babylon the Great has already fallen. In 1919, Jehovah's anointed servants were set free from the bondage of Babylonish doctrines and practices, which have dominated peoples and nations for millenniums. (Revelation 17:1, 15) They could henceforth devote themselves to promoting true worship. Global preaching of the good news of God's Kingdom has taken place since then.—Matthew 24:14.

17 That is not all there is to God's judgment against Babylon the Great. Her final destruction is soon to come. (Revelation 18:21) With good reason, the Bible urges people everywhere: "Get out of her [Babylon the Great] . . . if you do not want to share with her in her sins." (Revelation 18:4, 5) How do we get out of Babylon the Great? This involves more than just severing any ties with false religion. Babylonish influence is present in many popular celebrations and customs, in the world's permissive attitude toward sex, in the promoting of entertainment involving spiritism, and much more. To keep on the watch, it is vital that both in our actions and in the desires of our heart, we give evidence that we are truly separate from Babylon the Great in every way.

18 At Revelation 14:9, 10, a further aspect of 'the hour of judgment' is described. Another angel says: "If anyone worships the wild beast and its image, and receives a mark on his forehead or upon his hand, he will also drink of the wine of the anger of God." Why? "The wild beast and its image" are symbols of hu-

_____
17. What is involved in getting out of Babylon the Great?
18. In view of what is described at Revelation 14:9, 10, what are alert Christians careful to avoid?

The destruction of Babylon the Great is near

Let us be resolved to preach with ever greater zeal and determination

man rulership, which does not acknowledge Jehovah's sovereignty. Alert Christians are careful not to allow themselves to be influenced or to be marked, in either attitude or action, as being in servitude to those who refuse to acknowledge the supreme sovereignty of the true God, Jehovah. Christians know that God's Kingdom has already been set up in heaven, that it will put an end to all human rulerships, and that it will stand forever. —Daniel 2:44.

Do Not Lose Your Sense of Urgency!

[19] As we get deeper into the last days, pressures and temptations will only intensify. As long as we are living in this old system and are plagued by our own imperfection, we are affected by such things as poor health, old age, the loss of loved ones, hurt feelings, disappointment in the face of apathy toward our efforts to preach God's Word, and much more. Never forget that Satan would like nothing better than to exploit the pressures we face to induce us to give up—to stop preaching the good news or to quit living by God's standards. (Ephesians 6:11-13) This is

—————
19, 20. (a) As we get deeper into the last days, what can we be certain that Satan will try to do? (b) What should we be determined to do?

not the time to lose our sense of urgency regarding the times in which we live!

[20] Jesus knew that we would be under much pressure to give up, so he counseled us: "Keep on the watch . . . because you do not know on what day your Lord is coming." (Matthew 24:42) Let us, then, keep ever alert to where we are in the stream of time. Let us be on guard against Satan's ploys that could cause us to slow down or quit. Let us be resolved to preach the good news of God's Kingdom with ever greater zeal and determination. By all means, let us keep our sense of urgency as we heed Jesus' warning: "Keep on the watch." Doing so, we will bring honor to Jehovah and will be among those in line for his eternal blessings.

How Would You Answer?

- How do we know that Jesus' warning to "keep on the watch" applies to true Christians?

- What warning examples in the Bible can help us to "keep on the watch"?

- What is the hour of judgment, and what are we urged to do before it concludes?

PARENTS—WHAT FUTURE DO YOU WANT FOR YOUR CHILDREN?

"You young men and also you virgins . . . Let them praise the name of Jehovah."
—PSALM 148:12, 13.

WHAT parents are not anxiously concerned about the future of their children? From the moment an infant is born —or even before—the parents start worrying about his welfare. Will he be healthy? Will he develop normally? As the child grows older, there are additional concerns. By and large, parents want only what is best for their offspring.—1 Samuel 1:11, 27, 28; Psalm 127:3-5.

² In today's world, however, it is a challenge for parents to provide what is best for their children. Many parents have gone through hard times—wars, political upheavals, economic hardships, physical or emotional traumas, and so on. Naturally, it is their heartfelt desire that their children not

go through the same things. In affluent lands, parents may see the sons and daughters of their friends and relatives move ahead in professional careers and enjoy seemingly successful lives. Thus, they feel compelled to do everything they can to ensure that their children too will be able to enjoy a reasonably comfortable and secure life—a good life—when they grow up.—Ecclesiastes 3:13.

Choosing a Good Life

³ As followers of Jesus Christ, Christians have chosen to dedicate their life to Jehovah. They have taken to heart Jesus' words: "If anyone wants to come after me, let him disown himself and pick up his torture stake day after day and follow me continually." (Luke

---

1. What concerns do parents have for their children?
2. Why do many parents today feel strongly about having their children enjoy a good life when they grow up?

3. What choice have Christians made?

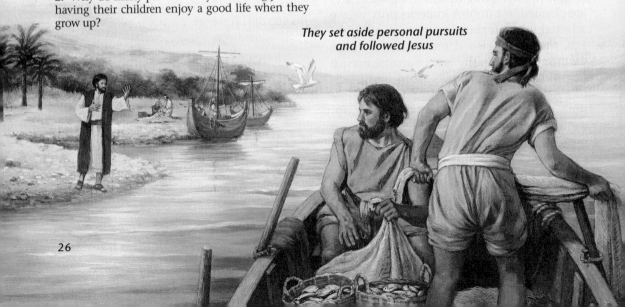

They set aside personal pursuits and followed Jesus

9:23; 14:27) Yes, a Christian's life does involve self-sacrifice. Yet, it is not a life of deprivation and misery. On the contrary, it is a happy and satisfying life—a good life—because it involves giving, and as Jesus said, "there is more happiness in giving than there is in receiving."—Acts 20:35.

⁴ People in Jesus' day were living under very difficult circumstances. In addition to making a living, they had to bear the harsh rule of the Romans and the oppressive burden of the formalistic religionists of the day. (Matthew 23:2-4) Still, many who heard about Jesus gladly set aside personal pursuits —even careers—and became his followers. (Matthew 4:18-22; 9:9; Colossians 4:14) Were those disciples taking a risk and endangering their future? Note Jesus' words: "Everyone that has left houses or brothers or sisters or father or mother or children or lands for the sake of my name will receive many times more and will inherit everlasting life." (Matthew 19:29) Jesus assured his followers that the heavenly Father knew their needs. He therefore urged them: "Keep on, then, seeking first the kingdom and his righteousness, and all these other things will be added to you."—Matthew 6:31-33.

⁵ Things are not very different today. Jehovah knows our needs, and those who put Kingdom interests first in their life, especially those pursuing the full-time ministry, have the same assurance that he will care for them. (Malachi 3:6, 16; 1 Peter 5:7) Some parents, however, are ambivalent in this regard. On the one hand, they would like to see their children make advancement in Jehovah's service, perhaps in time entering the full-time ministry. On the other hand, considering the economic and employment situation in the world today, they feel that it is impor-

tant for young ones to get a good education first so that they will have the necessary qualifications for a desirable job or at least have something to fall back on if needed. To such parents, a good education often means higher education.

Preparing for the Future

⁶ The educational system varies from country to country. In the United States, for example, public schools offer 12 years of basic education. Thereafter, students may choose to attend university or college for four or more years, leading to a bachelor's degree or to postgraduate studies for careers in medicine, law, engineering, and so forth. Such university education is what is meant when the term "higher education" is used in this article. On the other hand, there are technical and vocational schools, offering short-term courses that result in a certificate or diploma in some trade or service.

⁷ The trend today is for secondary schools or high schools to groom their students for higher education. To this end, most high schools focus on academic subjects that enable the students to score well in university entrance examinations rather than on courses that will equip the students for the workplace. High school students today are under tremendous pressure from teachers, counselors, and fellow students to aim for enrollment in the best universities, where they will hopefully earn the degrees that can open for them doors to promising and well-paying jobs.

⁸ What, then, are Christian parents to do? Of course, they want their children to do well in school and learn the necessary skills for

---

4. What did Jesus urge his followers to pursue?
5. How do some parents feel about Jesus' assurance that God will care for his servants?

6. In what way is the term "higher education" used in this article?
7. What pressures are students exposed to in high schools?
8. What choices are Christian parents confronted with?

maintaining themselves in the days ahead. (Proverbs 22:29) But should they simply let their children be swept along by the spirit of competition for material advancement and success? What sort of goals do they put before their children, either by word or by personal example? Some parents work very hard and save so as to be able to send their children to institutions of higher learning when the time comes. Others are willing to go into debt for this purpose. The cost of such a decision, however, cannot be measured merely in dollars and cents. What is the cost of pursuing higher education today?—Luke 14:28-33.

The Cost of Pursuing Higher Education

9 When we think of cost, we usually think of financial expenditures. In some countries, higher education is government sponsored and qualified students do not have to pay fees or tuition. In most places, however, higher education is expensive and is getting more so. A *New York Times* Op-Ed article observes: "Higher education used to be regarded as an engine of opportunity. Now it's certifying the gap between the haves and the have-lesses." In other words, quality higher education is fast becoming the domain of the rich and influential, who put their children through it to ensure that they too become the rich and influential of this system. Should Christian parents choose such a goal for their children?—Philippians 3:7, 8; James 4:4.

10 Even where higher education is free, there may be strings attached. For example, *The Wall Street Journal* reports that in one Southeast Asian country, the government runs a "pyramid-style school structure that unabashedly pushes the cream to

---

9. What can be said about the financial cost of higher education today?
10. How is higher education closely linked to advancing the present system?

the top." "The top" ultimately means placement in the world's elite institutions—Oxford and Cambridge in England, the Ivy League schools in the United States, and others. Why does the government provide such a far-reaching program? "To fuel the national economy," says the report. The education may be practically free, but the price that the students pay is a life engrossed in advancing the present system. Though such a way of life is highly sought-after in the world, is it what Christian parents want for their children? —John 15:19; 1 John 2:15-17.

11 Then there is the environment. University and college campuses are notorious for bad behavior—drug and alcohol abuse, immorality, cheating, hazing, and the list goes on. Consider alcohol abuse. Reporting on binge drinking, that is, drinking for the sole purpose of getting drunk, *New Scientist* magazine says: "About 44 per cent of [university students in the United States] binge at least once in a typical two-week period." The same problem is common among young people in Australia, Britain, Russia, and elsewhere. When it comes to sexual immorality, the talk

---

11. What do reports show regarding alcohol abuse and sexual immorality among university students?

among students today is about "hooking up," which according to a *Newsweek* report "describes one-time sexual encounters—anything from kissing to intercourse—between acquaintances who've no plans to even talk afterward." Studies show that from 60 to 80 percent of students engage in this kind of activity. "If you're a normal college student," says one researcher, "you do it."—1 Corinthians 5:11; 6:9, 10.

¹² In addition to the bad environment, there is the pressure of schoolwork and examinations. Naturally, students need to

—————

12. What pressures are college students exposed to?

study and do their homework to pass the exams. Some may also need to hold at least a part-time job while going to school. All of this takes a great deal of their time and energy. What, then, will be left for spiritual activities? When pressures mount, what will be let go? Will Kingdom interests still come first, or will they be put aside? (Matthew 6:33) The Bible urges Christians: "Keep strict watch that how you walk is not as unwise but as wise persons, buying out the opportune time for yourselves, because the days are wicked." (Ephesians 5:15, 16) How sad that some have fallen away from the faith as a result of succumbing to the demands on their time and

· ·

What Is the Value of Higher Education?

Most people who enroll in a university look forward to earning a degree that will open doors for them to well-paying and secure jobs. Government reports show, however, that only about one quarter of those who go to college earn a degree within six years—a dismal success rate. Even so, does that degree translate into a good job? Note what current research and studies have to say.

"Going to Harvard or Duke [universities] won't automatically produce a better job and higher pay. . . . Companies don't know much about young employment candidates. A shiny credential (an Ivy League degree) may impress. But after that, what people can or can't do counts for more."—*Newsweek,* November 1, 1999.

"While today's typical job requires higher skills than in the past . . . , the skills required for these jobs are strong high school-level skills—math, reading, and writing at a ninth-grade level . . . , not college-level skills. . . . Students do not need to go to college to get a good job, but they do need to master high school-level skills."—*American Educator,* Spring 2004.

"Most colleges are seriously out of step with the real world in getting students ready to become workers in the postcollege world. Vocational schools . . . are seeing a mini-boom. Their enrollment grew 48% from 1996 to 2000. . . . Meanwhile, those expensive, time-sucking college diplomas have become worth less than ever."—*Time,* January 24, 2005.

"Projections from the U.S. Department of Labor through 2005 paint the chilling scenario that at least one-third of all four-year college graduates will not find employment that matches their degrees."—*The Futurist,* July/August 2000.

In view of all of this, more and more educators are seriously doubting the value of higher education today. "We are educating people for the wrong futures," laments the *Futurist* report. In contrast, note what the Bible says about God: "I, Jehovah, am your God, the One teaching you to benefit yourself, the One causing you to tread in the way in which you should walk. O if only you would actually pay attention to my commandments! Then your peace would become just like a river, and your righteousness like the waves of the sea."—Isaiah 48:17, 18.

energy or of getting entangled in unscriptural conduct at college!

13 Of course, immorality, bad behavior, and pressures are by no means limited to the college or university campus. However, many worldly youths view all such things merely as part of the education, and they think nothing of it. Should Christian parents knowingly expose their children to that kind of environment for four or perhaps more years? (Proverbs 22:3; 2 Timothy 2:22) Is the risk involved worth whatever benefit the young ones may receive? And most important, what are the young ones learning about things that should come first in their life?* (Philippians 1:10; 1 Thessalonians 5:21) Parents must give serious and prayerful consideration to these questions, as well as to the danger of sending their children away to school in another city or another country.

What Are the Alternatives?

14 Today, the popular opinion is that for young people to succeed, the only option is to get a university education. However, instead of following what is popular, Christians heed the Bible's admonition: "Quit being fashioned after this system of things, but be transformed by making your mind over, that you may prove to yourselves the good and acceptable and perfect will of God." (Romans 12:2) What is God's will for his people, young and old, in this final stage of the time of the end? Paul urged Timothy: "Keep your senses in all things, suffer evil, do the work of

an evangelizer, fully accomplish your ministry." Those words are surely applicable to all of us today.—2 Timothy 4:5.

15 Rather than be caught up by the materialistic spirit of the world, all of us need to 'keep our senses'—our spiritual bearings. If you are a young person, ask yourself: 'Am I putting forth my best effort to "accomplish my ministry," to make myself a qualified minister of God's Word? What are my plans for pursuing my ministry "fully"? Have I considered taking up full-time service as a career?' These are challenging questions, especially when you see other youths indulging in selfish pursuits, "seeking great things" that they think will lead to a bright future. (Jeremiah 45:5) Christian parents, therefore, wisely provide their children from infancy with the right kind of spiritual environment and training.—Proverbs 22:6; Ecclesiastes 12:1; 2 Timothy 3:14, 15.

16 "Mother watched our association very closely," recalls the eldest of three boys in one family in which the mother has been a full-time minister over the years. "We did not associate with our schoolmates but only with those in the congregation who had good spiritual habits. She also regularly invited those in full-time service—missionaries, traveling overseers, Bethelites, and pioneers—to our home for association. Listening to their experiences and seeing their joy helped to implant in our hearts the desire for full-time service." What a joy to see today all three sons in the full-time ministry—one serving at Bethel, one having attended the Ministerial Training School, and one pioneering!

17 Besides providing a strong spiritual environment, parents must also offer their chil-

---

* For accounts of those who valued theocratic education more than university education, see *The Watchtower,* May 1, 1982, pages 3-6; April 15, 1979, pages 5-10; *Awake!* June 8, 1978, page 15; and August 8, 1974, pages 3-7.

---

13. What questions must Christian parents consider?
14, 15. (a) In spite of popular opinion, what Bible counsel applies today? (b) What questions can young ones ask themselves?

16. How can Christian parents wisely provide the right kind of spiritual environment for their children?
17. What guidance can parents provide young ones in their choice of school subjects and vocation goals? (See box on page 29.)

Christian parents wisely provide their children from infancy with a strong spiritual environment

icate." Many such institutions offer short courses in office skills, auto repair, computer repair, plumbing, hairdressing, and a host of other trades. Are these desirable jobs? Certainly! Perhaps they are not as glamorous as some might envision, but they do offer the means and the flexibility needed by those whose true vocation is service to Jehovah. —2 Thessalonians 3:8.

19 "You young men and also you virgins," entreats the Bible, "let them praise the name of Jehovah, for his name alone is unreachably high. His dignity is above earth and heaven." (Psalm 148:12, 13) Compared with the positions and rewards that the world offers, a career in full-time service to Jehovah is without doubt the surest way to a life of joy and contentment. Take to heart the Bible's assurance: "The blessing of Jehovah—that is what makes rich, and he adds no pain with it."—Proverbs 10:22.

dren, as early as possible, proper guidance in their choice of school subjects and vocation goals. Another young man, now in Bethel service, says: "Both of my parents pioneered before and after they got married and did their best to pass on the pioneer spirit to the whole family. Whenever we were choosing subjects at school or making decisions that would affect our future, they always encouraged us to make a choice that would give us the best opportunity to find part-time work and pioneer." Rather than choose academic subjects that are geared toward a university education, parents and children need to consider courses that are useful in pursuing a theocratic career.*

18 Studies show that in many countries, there is an acute need, not for university graduates, but for people to work in the trades and services. *USA Today* reports that "70% of the workers in the coming decades will not need a four-year college degree, but, rather, an associate degree from a community college or some type of technical certif-

---

* See *Awake!* October 8, 1998, "In Search of a Secure Life," pages 4-6, and May 8, 1989, "What Career Should I Choose?" pages 12-14.

---

18. What job opportunities might young ones consider?

19. What is the surest way to a life of joy and contentment?

Can You Explain?

- In what do Christians put their trust for a secure future?

- What challenges do Christian parents face regarding their children's future?

- What must be considered when counting the cost of pursuing higher education?

- How can parents help their children to pursue a career in Jehovah's service?

Are You "Rich Toward God"?

A MONG the many thought-provoking parables given by Jesus Christ, there is one about a wealthy landowner. In an effort to make a secure future sure for himself, the landowner made plans to build bigger storehouses. Yet, in Jesus' illustration, the man is called an "unreasonable one." (Luke 12:16-21) A number of Bible translations even use the word "fool." Why the harsh assessment?

Evidently, this wealthy man's plans did not include God; nor did he give any credit to God for the land's productiveness. (Matthew 5:45) Rather, he boasted: "Soul, you have many good things laid up for many years; take your ease, eat, drink, enjoy yourself." Yes, he imagined that the fruitage of his endeavors would serve as "a protective wall."—Proverbs 18:11.

In warning against such a haughty spirit, the disciple James wrote: "Come, now, you who say: 'Today or tomorrow we will journey to this city and will spend a year there, and we will engage in business and make profits,' whereas you do not know what your life will be tomorrow. For you are a mist appearing for a little while and then disappearing."—James 4:13, 14.

True to those words, the rich man in Jesus' parable was told: "Unreasonable one, this night they are demanding your soul from you. Who, then, is to have the things you stored up?" Like a disappearing mist, the rich man would pass away before he could see his dreams fulfilled. Do we discern the lesson? Said Jesus: "So it goes with the man that lays up treasure for himself but is not rich toward God." Are you "rich toward God"?

w05-E 10/1

OCTOBER 15, 2005

THE WATCHTOWER

ANNOUNCING JEHOVAH'S KINGDOM

What Is the Best Education?

THE WATCHTOWER®

ANNOUNCING JEHOVAH'S KINGDOM

October 15, 2005 · Average Printing Each Issue: 26,439,000 · Vol. 126, No. 20

THE PURPOSE OF *THE WATCHTOWER* is to exalt Jehovah God as Sovereign Lord of the universe. It keeps watch on world events as these fulfill Bible prophecy. It comforts all peoples with the good news that God's Kingdom will soon destroy those who oppress their fellowmen and that it will turn the earth into a paradise. It encourages faith in God's now-reigning King, Jesus Christ, whose shed blood opens the way for mankind to gain eternal life. *The Watchtower*, published by Jehovah's Witnesses continuously since 1879, is nonpolitical. It adheres to the Bible as its authority.

IN THIS ISSUE

3　What Kind of Education Can Make Your Life a Success?

4　Benefit From the Best Education Available!

8　Jehovah Will By No Means Leave You

12　Christianity Spreads Among First-Century Jews

16　Jehovah's Word Soars in "the Land of the Eagle"

21　Beware of Developing a Haughty Heart

26　Cultivate Genuine Humility

32　"They That Go Down to the Sea in Ships"

WATCHTOWER STUDIES

NOVEMBER 14-20:
Beware of Developing a Haughty Heart.
Page 21. Songs to be used: 132, 212.

NOVEMBER 21-27:
Cultivate Genuine Humility.
Page 26. Songs to be used: 122, 1.

Publication of *The Watchtower* is part of a worldwide Bible educational work supported by voluntary donations.

Unless otherwise indicated, Scripture quotations are from the modern-language *New World Translation of the Holy Scriptures—With References.*

The Watchtower (ISSN 0043-1087) is published semimonthly by Watchtower Bible and Tract Society of New York, Inc.; M. H. Larson, President; G. F. Simonis, Secretary-Treasurer; 25 Columbia Heights, Brooklyn, NY 11201-2483. Periodicals Postage Paid at Brooklyn, NY, and at additional mailing offices. POSTMASTER: Send address changes to Watchtower, **Wallkill, NY 12589.**

Changes of address should reach us 30 days before your moving date. Give us your old and new address (if possible, your old address label).

Semimonthly　　　　　　　　　ENGLISH

Would you welcome more information or a free home Bible study? Please send your request to Jehovah's Witnesses, using the appropriate address below.

America, United States of: Wallkill, NY 12589. *Antigua:* Box 119, St. Johns. *Australia:* Box 280, Ingleburn, NSW 1890. *Bahamas:* Box N-1247, Nassau, N.P. *Barbados, W.I.:* Crusher Site Road, Prospect, St. James. *Britain:* The Ridgeway, London NW7 1RN. *Canada:* Box 4100, Halton Hills (Georgetown), Ontario L7G 4Y4. *Germany:* Niederselters, Am Steinfels, D-65618 Selters. *Ghana:* P. O. Box GP 760, Accra. *Guyana:* 352-360 Tyrell St., Republic Park Phase 2 EBD. *Hawaii 96819:* 2055 Kam IV Rd., Honolulu. *Hong Kong:* 4 Kent Road, Kowloon Tong. *India:* Post Box 6440, Yelahanka, Bangalore 560 064, KAR. *Ireland:* Newcastle, Greystones, Co. Wicklow. *Jamaica:* P. O. Box 103, Old Harbour, St. Catherine. *Japan:* 1271 Nakashinden, Ebina City, Kanagawa Pref., 243-0496. *Kenya:* P.O. Box 47788, GPO Nairobi 00100. *New Zealand:* P.O. Box 75-142, Manurewa. *Nigeria:* P.M.B. 1090, Benin City 300001, Edo State. *Philippines, Republic of:* P. O. Box 2044, 1060 Manila. *South Africa:* Private Bag X2067, Krugersdorp, 1740. *Trinidad and Tobago, Republic of:* Lower Rapsey Street & Laxmi Lane, Curepe. *Zambia:* Box 33459, Lusaka 10101. *Zimbabwe:* Private Bag WG-5001, Westgate.

NOW PUBLISHED IN 151 LANGUAGES. SEMIMONTHLY: Afrikaans, Albanian,* Amharic, Arabic, Bengali, Bicol, Bislama, Bulgarian, Cebuano,* Chichewa,* Chinese, Chinese (Simplified),* Cibemba,* Croatian,* Czech,*# Danish,*# Dutch,*# East Armenian, Efik,* English*#+☺ (also Braille), Estonian, Ewe, Fijian, Finnish,*# French*# (also Braille), Ga, Georgian,* German,*# Greek,* Gujarati, Gun, Hebrew, Hiligaynon, Hindi, Hungarian,*# Igbo,* Iloko,* Indonesian, Italian,*# Japanese*# (also Braille), Kannada, Kinyarwanda, Kirundi, Korean*# (also Braille), Latvian, Lingala, Lithuanian, Luvale, Macedonian, Malagasy,* Malayalam, Maltese, Myanmar, Nepali, Norwegian,*# Pangasinan, Papiamento (Aruba), Papiamento (Curaçao), Polish,*# Portuguese*# (also Braille), Punjabi, Rarotongan, Romanian,* Russian,* Samar-Leyte, Samoan, Sango, Sepedi, Serbian, Sesotho, Shona,* Silozi, Sinhala, Slovak,* Slovenian, Solomon Islands Pidgin, Spanish*# (also Braille), Sranantongo, Swahili,* Swedish,*# Tagalog,* Tamil, Telugu, Thai, Tigrinya, Tok Pisin, Tongan, Tshiluba, Tsonga, Tswana, Turkish, Twi, Ukrainian,* Urdu, Vietnamese, Wallisian, Xhosa, Yoruba,* Zulu*

MONTHLY: American Sign Language,△◎ Armenian, Assamese, Azerbaijani (roman script), Brazilian Sign Language,△ Cambodian, Chitonga, Gilbertese, Greenlandic, Haitian Creole, Hausa, Hiri Motu, Icelandic, Isoko, Kaonde, Kazakh, Kikongo, Kiluba, Kirghiz, Kosraean, Kwanyama/Ndonga, Luganda, Marathi, Marshallese, Mauritian Creole, Maya, Mizo, Monokutuba, Moore, Niuean, Ossetian, Otetela, Palauan, Persian, Ponapean, Seychelles Creole, Tahitian, Tatar, Tiv, Trukese, Tumbuka, Tuvaluan, Umbundu, Uruund, Venda, Yapese, Zande

* Study articles also available in large-print edition.
\# Audiocassettes also available.
+ CD also available.
◎ MP3 CD-ROM also available.
△ Videocassette
□ DVD

What Kind of **Education** Can Make Your Life a **Success?**

HAVE you ever been so overwhelmed by problems that you felt as though you were drowning in a whirlpool? Just imagine how much suffering could result if you made a mistake in coping with one or more of those problems! No one is born with the ability to solve all problems successfully, making good decisions every time. This is where education comes in. Where can you get education to prepare yourself to cope with life's problems?

Many, both young and old, extol the importance of an academic education. Some experts even say that they "fully believe that you will never be able to find a [decent] job without a college degree." Yet, there are a number of human needs that go beyond material achievements. For instance, does higher learning help you to be a good parent, mate, or friend? For that matter, people admired for their intellectual achievements may develop undesirable personality traits, fail in their family life, or even end up committing suicide.

Some look to religion for guidance, a source of education, but become disappointed because of not receiving practical help to face life's difficulties. Illustrating this, Emilia* from Mexico says: "It was 15 years ago that I felt that my husband and I simply could not be together any longer. We argued all the time. I couldn't get him to stop drinking. I frequently had to leave our small children by themselves while I went looking for my husband. I was emotionally worn out. Several times I went to church seeking something that might help me find a solution. Although the Bible was occasionally used, I never heard any counsel that directly dealt with my situation; neither did anyone approach me to tell me what to do. Sitting in church for a while and repeating some prayers did not satisfy me." Others may become disillusioned when they see how far their own spiritual leaders are from living an exemplary life. As a result, many lose confidence in religion as a source of training or education for a successful life.

Therefore, you might ask yourself, 'What kind of education should I obtain in order to make my life a success?' Does true Christianity have the answer to this important question? This will be discussed in the following article.

---

* Name has been changed.

3

Benefit
From the
Best Education
Available!

THE Bible identifies Jehovah God as the Creator of all things, including humans. (Genesis 1:27; Revelation 4:11) As the Grand Instructor, he educated the first human couple, Adam and Eve, and prepared them for life in the beautiful garden in Eden. It was his purpose to continue educating them and caring for them eternally. (Genesis 1:28, 29; 2:15-17; Isaiah 30:20, 21) Just think of that prospect!

Sadly, however, the first pair threw everything away. Their disobedient course opened the way for moral and physical degradation of the human race. (Genesis 3:17-19; Romans 5:12) Referring to those who lived just a few generations after the founding of mankind, the Bible says: "Jehovah saw that the badness of man was abundant in the earth and every inclination of the thoughts of his heart was only bad all the time."—Genesis 6:5.

Almost 4,500 years have gone by since Jehovah concluded that man was constantly inclined toward badness, and mankind's situation is now worse than ever. Many lie shamelessly, steal, or attack others. Problems increase every day, while concern for one's fellow man decreases. Are not most personal relationships, including those within families, in real crisis? Yet, God is not to be blamed for the present conditions, nor has he ceased to be concerned about today's problems. Jehovah has always been interested in man's welfare, and he is ready to educate those who look to him for guidance to

attain a happy life. Some 2,000 years ago, he sent his Son, Jesus Christ, to the earth and demonstrated His interest in educating people who want to make a success of their life. Jesus left a model for education that was perfect because he had been taught by the Grand Instructor for untold aeons of time.

True Christianity—An Education

Jesus Christ instituted true Christianity, a way of life based on love. In it, all thoughts and actions are to harmonize with God's will, for the purpose of bringing honor and glory to his name. (Matthew 22:37-39; Hebrews 10:7) Behind Jesus' teachings on this way of life was his Father, Jehovah. We read at John 8:29 about the support Jesus received from God: "He that sent me is with me; *he did not abandon me to myself,* because I always do the things pleasing to him." Yes, Jesus had his Father's support and guidance throughout his ministry. Jesus' early followers did not have to face life's challenges without guidance. Jehovah educated them by means of his Son. Their following Jesus' teachings and example made them better people. This is true of his disciples today. —See the box "The Influence of Jesus and His Teachings," on page 6.

A distinctive feature of true Christianity is that it includes education that affects mind and heart so as to transform people from within. (Ephesians 4:23, 24) To cite just one example, consider what Jesus taught about

being faithful to one's mate: "You heard that it was said, 'You must not commit adultery.' But I say to you that everyone that keeps on looking at a woman so as to have a passion for her has already committed adultery with her in his heart." (Matthew 5:27, 28) With these words, Jesus was teaching his disciples that the heart should be kept clean and that improper thoughts and desires, though not yet carried out, may have grave consequences. Is it not true that bad thoughts can lead to acts that offend God and hurt others?

Therefore, the Bible offers this counsel: "Quit being fashioned after this system of things, but be transformed by making your mind over, that you may prove to yourselves the good and acceptable and perfect will of God." (Romans 12:2) 'Is it really possible to make the mind over through education?' you may ask. Making the mind over involves motivating it in a different direction by filling it with the principles and instruction given in God's Word. This can be accomplished by accepting education that God provides through his Word.

Motivated to Change

"The word of God is alive and exerts power." (Hebrews 4:12) It is still exerting a powerful influence on individuals, thus proving that it does not become outdated. It can give a person the motivation to change his course, embrace true Christianity, and become a better person. The following examples illustrate the value of Bible education.

Emilia, mentioned in the preceding article, states: "Just making an effort by myself was not enough to improve the situation in my home. When I started to study the Bible with Jehovah's Witnesses, I realized that there was hope and began to change my attitude. I learned to be more patient and not to indulge in fits of anger. In time, my husband joined me in the study. It was not easy for him to stop drinking, but he was able to quit. This gave our marriage a fresh start. Now we are happy Christians and are inculcating in our children the fine principles of the Bible." —Deuteronomy 6:7.

The education that true Christianity provides can free a person from vices and an immoral lifestyle. Manuel* found this to be true. At the age of 13, he ran away from home and began to use marijuana. In time, he turned to heroin. He had sexual encounters with men and women in exchange for shelter and money. At times, Manuel also supported himself by mugging people. He was almost always under the influence of drugs.

---

* Some names have been changed.

His violent conduct often landed him in prison. Once he spent four years behind bars, and there he became involved in trafficking in weapons. After he got married, Manuel's life course continued to cost him dearly. He says: "We ended up living in what was once a henhouse. I still remember my wife cooking on some bricks. Our circumstances were so precarious that my own family encouraged my wife to abandon me."

What changed his life? Manuel answers: "An acquaintance came to our house talking about the Bible. I accepted his visits just to show him that a God who was interested in people did not exist. I considered myself living proof of that. I was surprised that the Witness was patient and polite, so I agreed to attend the meetings at the Kingdom Hall. Although some there knew my background, they greeted me in a friendly manner. They made me feel like one of them. This was a great comfort. I was moved to the point of deciding to leave the world of drugs to get an honest job. Four months after beginning my Bible study, I qualified to join in the preaching work, and four months after that, I was baptized as one of Jehovah's Witnesses."

What has true Christianity meant for Manuel and his family? "Without Bible education I would surely have been dead years ago. The way of life that Jesus taught gave my family back to me. My two children do not have to go through what I went through as a youth. I feel proud and very grateful to Jehovah for the good relationship I now have with my wife. Some of my former acquaintances have congratulated me and told me that they think that the course I am now following is the best one."

In the Christian way of life, moral cleanness is accompanied by physical cleanness. John, who lives in a poverty-stricken area

The Influence of Jesus and His Teachings

Using his position as chief tax collector, Zacchaeus had become rich by extorting money and robbing common people. But he changed his way of life by applying Jesus' teachings.—Luke 19:1-10.

Saul of Tarsus stopped persecuting Christians and converted to Christianity, becoming the apostle Paul.—Acts 22:6-21; Philippians 3:4-9.

Some of the Christians in Corinth had been 'fornicators, idolaters, adulterers, homosexuals, thieves, greedy persons, drunkards, revilers, and extortioners.' Yet, upon learning true Christianity, they 'were washed clean, sanctified, and declared righteous in the name of their Lord Jesus Christ.'—1 Corinthians 6:9-11.

in South Africa, came to understand that. He explains: "Our daughter would sometimes not wash for a week, and none of us seemed to care." His wife acknowledges that their home had a terrible appearance. But with Christian education, things changed. John stopped associating with a gang of car thieves and began to give more attention to his family. "We learned that as Christians, we should keep our bodies and clothing clean. I like the words at 1 Peter 1:16, which exhort us to be holy because Jehovah God is holy. Now we also try to make our simple home look nice."

You Can Find the Best Education

The experiences mentioned above are not isolated cases. As a result of education based on the Bible, thousands of people have learned to live better lives. By being honest and industrious, they are appreciated by their employers. They have become good neighbors and friends, taking an interest in the well-being of their fellow man. They are determined to avoid vices and fleshly tendencies, so they take better care of their own health physically, mentally, and emotionally. Instead of wasting their resources on vices, they use them for their own good and for the good of their family. (1 Corinthians 6:9-11; Colossians 3:18-23) Without a doubt, the results of putting into practice what Je-

hovah sets forth in the Bible demonstrate that living by true Christianity is the best course in life, providing the best education available. With respect to a person who lives in harmony with God's laws, the Bible states: "Everything he does will succeed."—Psalm 1:3.

It is encouraging to know that Almighty God, Jehovah, is willing to educate us. He says of himself: "I, Jehovah, am your God, the One teaching you to benefit yourself, the One causing you to tread in the way in which you should walk." (Isaiah 48:17) Yes, Jehovah has shown the way through the example and teachings of his Son, Jesus Christ. His teachings made a difference in the life of many who knew him when he was on earth, and the same is true of many others who live by his teachings today. Why not take the time to learn more about these teachings? Jehovah's Witnesses in your neighborhood will be happy to help you to receive such valuable education.

The Bible can show you how to succeed

Jehovah Will
By No Means Leave You

CHRISTIANS in Judaea were experiencing vicious opposition, and they had to contend with the materialistic view of people around them. To encourage them, the apostle Paul quoted the words of Jehovah to the Israelites as they were entering the Promised Land. Paul wrote: "I will by no means leave you nor by any means forsake you." (Hebrews 13:5; Deuteronomy 31:6) This promise undoubtedly strengthened the first-century Hebrew Christians.

The same promise should fortify us to cope with anxieties that come from living in "critical times hard to deal with." (2 Timothy 3:1) If we trust in Jehovah and act accordingly, he will sustain us even in the most difficult circumstances. To see how Jehovah can act on this promise, let us consider the example of a sudden loss of one's livelihood.

Facing the Unexpected

The number of unemployed is growing worldwide. According to a Polish magazine, unemployment is considered to be "one of the most difficult socioeconomic problems."

Industrialized nations are no exception. For example, even among the members of the Organization for Economic Cooperation and Development, by 2004 unemployment had "risen to above 32 million, reaching a higher level than during the Great Depression of the 1930's." In Poland, the Central Statistical Office listed three million unemployed as of December 2003, which "constituted 18 percent of civilians of working age." One source said that the unemployment rate among the African population in South Africa reached 47.8 percent in 2002!

Sudden unemployment and unexpected layoffs are real threats to many, including Jehovah's servants. "Time and unforeseen occurrence" befall anyone. (Ecclesiastes 9:11) We may find ourselves uttering the words of the psalmist David: "Distresses of my heart have multiplied." (Psalm 25:17) Would you be able to cope with such unfavorable circumstances? They could affect your emotional, spiritual, and material well-being. If unemployed, could you manage to get back on your feet?

Coping With Emotional Strain

"The loss of employment hurts men more," since they are traditionally viewed as the breadwinner of the family, explains psychologist Janusz Wietrzyński. He said that it can start a man on "a roller coaster of emotions," from anger to resignation. A father who has been laid off may lose his self-esteem and start "quarreling with his family."

Adam, a Christian father of two, explains how he felt when he lost his job: "I easily became agitated; everything irritated me. Even at night my dreams were all about work and how to provide for my children and my wife, who had also been laid off unexpectedly." When Ryszard and Mariola, a married couple with a child, lost their means of income, they had a large, outstanding bank loan. The wife relates: "I was constantly troubled, my conscience telling me that it was a mistake to have taken out that loan. I kept thinking that it was all my fault." Faced with such situations, we may easily feel angry, anxious, or bitter, and our emotions can get the better of us. How, then, can we control the negative emotions that may well up in us?

The Bible gives effective advice on how to maintain a positive attitude. "Do not be anxious over anything," the apostle Paul admonished, "but in everything by prayer and supplication along with thanksgiving let your petitions be made known to God; and the peace of God that excels all thought will guard your hearts and your mental powers by means of Christ Jesus." (Philippians 4: 6, 7) Approaching Jehovah in prayer will give us "the peace of God," a calm state of mind based on our faith in him. Adam's wife, Irena, says: "In our prayers, we told Jehovah about our situation and how we would simplify our lives even more. My husband, who has usually been quick to find

Use the time for spiritual activities

reasons to be anxious, began to feel that a solution would present itself."

If you are faced with the unexpected loss of your job, you are in a good position to apply Jesus Christ's admonition in the Sermon on the Mount: "Stop being anxious about your souls as to what you will eat or what you will drink, or about your bodies as to what you will wear. . . . Keep on, then, seeking first the kingdom and his righteousness, and all these other things will be added to you." (Matthew 6:25, 33) Ryszard and Mariola applied this counsel in coping with their emotions. "My husband always comforted me and emphasized that Jehovah would not abandon us," recalls Mariola. Her husband adds: "Through persistent prayers together, we have drawn closer to God and to each other, and that has provided the needed comfort."

God's holy spirit will also help us to cope. Self-control, which the spirit can produce in us, can help us to keep ourselves and our feelings intact. (Galatians 5:22, 23) It may not be easy, but it is possible, for Jesus promised that "the Father in heaven [will] give holy spirit to

those asking him."—Luke 11:13; 1 John 5: 14, 15.

Do Not Neglect Your Spiritual Needs

Unexpected dismissal from a job may at first unnerve even the most balanced Christian, but we should not neglect our spiritual needs. Take, for example, 40-year-old Moses, whose whole life changed when he lost his position within the aristocracy and had to become a shepherd, a job the Egyptians despised. (Genesis 46:34) Moses had to adjust to his new circumstances. For the following 40 years, he allowed Jehovah to mold and prepare him for new tasks ahead. (Exodus 2: 11-22; Acts 7:29, 30; Hebrews 11:24-26) Despite facing difficulties, Moses was spiritually focused, willing to accept Jehovah's training. May we never allow unfavorable circumstances to overshadow our spiritual values!

Although suddenly losing a job can be traumatic, that is a good time to strengthen

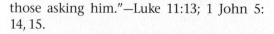

Learn to be thrifty, and do not be too choosy when you are looking for a job

our bonds with Jehovah God and his people. Adam, mentioned earlier, felt that way. He says: "When my wife and I both lost our jobs, the thought of staying away from Christian meetings or reducing our share in the evangelizing work never crossed our minds. That perspective protected us from becoming overly worried about tomorrow." Ryszard shares similar sentiments: "If it were not for the meetings and the ministry, we could never have coped; we would definitely have been eaten up by worry. Spiritual conversations with others are uplifting, for they turn our attention to their needs and away from our own."—Philippians 2:4.

Yes, instead of worrying about employment, try to use the extra time for spiritual activities, engaging in personal study, sharing in congregational activities, or expanding your ministry. Rather than living the life of the unemployed, you will have "plenty to do in the work of the Lord"—which will bring joy both to you and to any sincere individuals who respond to the Kingdom message you preach.—1 Corinthians 15:58.

Providing for Your Family Materially

However, spiritual nourishment will not fill an empty stomach. We do well to keep in mind the following principle: "Certainly if anyone does not provide for those who are his own, and especially for those who are members of his household, he has disowned the faith and is worse than a person without faith." (1 Timothy 5:8) "Even though the brothers in the congregation are quick to respond to our physical needs," Adam admits, "as Christians, we have an obligation to work at searching for employment." We can count on Jehovah's support and that of his people, but we should never forget that we need to take the initiative to find a job.

What initiative? "Do not wait with folded arms for God to act, hoping for a miracle," explains Adam. "When you are looking for work, do not hesitate to identify yourself as one of Jehovah's Witnesses. Employers usually value that." Ryszard gives this advice: "Ask anyone you know about job opportunities, keep checking at the employment agency, read advertisements, such as: 'Wanted, woman to care for a disabled person'; or, 'Temporary employment: Strawberry picking.' Keep on searching! Do not be too choosy, even if you have to do something menial or something that does not fulfill your ambitions."

Yes, "Jehovah is [your] helper." He will "by no means leave you nor by any means forsake you." (Hebrews 13:5, 6) You do not have to be overly anxious. The psalmist David wrote: "Roll upon Jehovah your way, and rely upon him, and he himself will act." (Psalm 37:5) 'Rolling our way upon Jehovah' means that we rely on him and do things his way, even when circumstances may not look favorable to us.

Adam and Irena managed to support themselves by window washing and stairwell cleaning and by being thrifty when purchasing things. They also visited the employment agency regularly. "Help always came just when we needed it," notes Irena. Her husband adds: "Time has shown that the matters we brought up in our prayers were not necessarily in line with God's will. This has taught us to rely on his wisdom and not to act according to our own understanding. It is better to wait calmly for the solution God will provide."—James 1:4.

Ryszard and Mariola took various odd jobs but at the same time became involved in witnessing in territories where the need was greater. "We got needed jobs right at the times when we had nothing left to eat," says Ryszard. "We refused well-paying jobs that would interfere with our theocratic responsibilities. We preferred to wait on Jehovah." They believe that Jehovah maneuvered matters so that they were able to rent a flat very cheaply and Ryszard finally found a job.

Losing one's livelihood can be very painful, but why not view it as an opportunity to see for yourself that Jehovah will never forsake you? Jehovah looks after you. (1 Peter 5: 6, 7) He has promised through the prophet Isaiah: "Do not gaze about, for I am your God. I will fortify you. I will really help you." (Isaiah 41:10) Never allow an unexpected incident, including job loss, to paralyze you. Do everything you can, and then leave the rest in Jehovah's hands. Wait on Jehovah, "even silently." (Lamentations 3:26) Rich blessings will be yours.—Jeremiah 17:7.

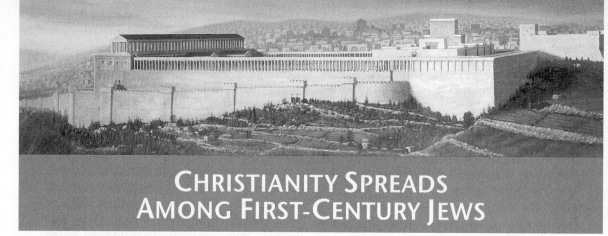

CHRISTIANITY SPREADS AMONG FIRST-CENTURY JEWS

AN IMPORTANT meeting took place in Jerusalem about 49 C.E. "The ones who seemed to be pillars" of the first-century Christian congregation—John, Peter, and Jesus' half brother James—were there. The other two named as attending the meeting were the apostle Paul and his companion Barnabas. On the agenda was how to divide the vast territory for the preaching work. Paul explained: "[They] gave me and Barnabas the right hand of sharing together, that we should go to the nations, but they to those who are circumcised."—Galatians 2:1, 9.*

How should we understand this agreement? Was the territory in which the good news should be preached divided into Jews and proselytes on the one hand and Gentiles on the other? Or was the agreement rather a geographical division of the territory? To find a possible answer, we need some historical information about the Diaspora, Jews living outside of Palestine.

The Jewish World in the First Century

How many Jews were in the Diaspora in the first century? Many scholars seem to agree with the publication *Atlas of the Jewish World:* "Absolute figures are hard to ar-

rive at, but it has been plausibly estimated that shortly before 70 there were two and a half million Jews in Judaea and well over four million in the Roman diaspora. . . . It is likely that the Jews represented something like a tenth of the whole population of the empire, and in the places where they were most concentrated, in the cities of the eastern provinces, they may have been a quarter or more of the inhabitants."

The main centers were in Syria, Asia Minor, Babylon, and Egypt, in the East, with smaller communities in Europe. Some well-known early Jewish Christians had a Diaspora background, such as Barnabas from Cyprus, Prisca and Aquila from Pontus and then Rome, Apollos from Alexandria, and Paul from Tarsus.—Acts 4:36; 18:2, 24; 22:3.

The Diaspora communities had many links with their homeland. One was the annual tax sent to the temple in Jerusalem, a way to participate in temple life and worship. Regarding this, scholar John Barclay observes: "There is good evidence that the collection of this money, supplemented by extra donations from the wealthy, was scrupulously undertaken by Diaspora communities."

Another link was the tens of thousands of pilgrims who went to Jerusalem every year for the festivals. The account at Acts 2:9-11

---

* This meeting was probably held at the time of or in connection with the discussion of the first-century governing body on the matter of circumcision.—Acts 15: 6-29.

about Pentecost 33 C.E. illustrates this. The Jewish pilgrims present came from Parthia, Media, Elam, Mesopotamia, Cappadocia, Pontus, Asia, Phrygia, Pamphylia, Egypt, Libya, Rome, Crete, and Arabia.

The temple administration in Jerusalem communicated with Jews in the Diaspora in writing. It is known that Gamaliel, the law teacher mentioned at Acts 5:34, sent letters to Babylon and other parts of the world. When the apostle Paul arrived as a prisoner in Rome about 59 C.E., "the principal men of the Jews" told him that "neither have we received letters concerning you from Judea, nor has anyone of the brothers that has arrived reported or spoken anything wicked about you." This indicates that letters and reports were frequently sent from the homeland to Rome.—Acts 28:17, 21.

The Bible of the Diaspora Jews was a Greek translation of the Hebrew Scriptures known as the *Septuagint.* A reference work notes: "It is plausible to conclude that the LXX [*Septuagint*] was read and received throughout the diaspora as the diaspora Jewish Bible or 'holy writ.'" The same translation was extensively used by the early Christians in their teaching.

The members of the Christian governing body in Jerusalem were familiar with these circumstances. The good news had already reached Diaspora Jews in Syria and beyond, including Damascus and Antioch. (Acts 9: 19, 20; 11:19; 15:23, 41; Galatians 1:21) At the meeting in 49 C.E., the ones present were evidently planning for future work. Let us consider the Biblical references to the expansion among the Jews and proselytes.

Paul's Travels and Jews in the Diaspora

The apostle Paul's original assignment was "to bear [Jesus Christ's] name to the nations as well as to kings and *the sons of Israel.*"* (Acts 9:15) After the Jerusalem meeting, Paul continued to reach out to the Diaspora Jews wherever he traveled. (See the box on page 14.) This indicates that the territorial agreement likely became a geographical one. Paul and Barnabas expanded their missionary work to the west, and the others served the Jewish homeland and the large Jewish communities in the Eastern world.

When Paul and his companions started the second missionary trip from Antioch in Syria, they were guided westward through Asia Minor up to Troas. From there they crossed over to Macedonia because they concluded that "God had summoned [them] to declare the good news to [the Macedonians]." Later, Christian congregations were started in other European cities, including Athens and Corinth.—Acts 15:40, 41; 16:6-10; 17:1–18:18.

About 56 C.E., at the end of his third missionary trip, Paul planned to move even farther westward and expand the territory that he had been assigned at the Jerusalem meeting. He wrote: "There is eagerness on my part to declare the good news also to you there in Rome," and, "I shall depart by way of you for Spain." (Romans 1:15; 15:24, 28) But what about the large Diaspora communities in the East?

Jewish Communities in the East

During the first century C.E., Egypt had the largest Diaspora community, especially in its capital, Alexandria. This center of trade and culture had a Jewish population numbering into the hundreds of thousands, with synagogues scattered all over the city. Philo, an Alexandrian Jew, claimed that in all of Egypt, there were at least a million Jews at that time. A considerable

---

* This article focuses on Paul's witnessing to the Jews, not on his activities as "an apostle to the nations."—Romans 11:13.

number had also settled in nearby Libya, in the city of Cyrene and vicinity.

Some Jews who became Christians were from these areas. We read of "Apollos, a native of Alexandria," "some men of Cyprus and Cyrene," and "Lucius of Cyrene," who supported the congregation in Syrian Antioch. (Acts 2:10; 11:19, 20; 13:1; 18:24) Otherwise the Bible is silent about the early Christian work in Egypt and its vicinity, except for the Christian evangelizer Philip's witnessing to the Ethiopian eunuch.—Acts 8:26-39.

Babylon, with extensions into Parthia, Media, and Elam, was another major center. One historian says that "every territory in the plain of the Tigris and Euphrates, from Armenia to the Persian gulf, as well as northeastward to the Caspian Sea, and eastward to Media, contained Jewish populations." The *Encyclopaedia Judaica* estimates their number at 800,000 or more. The first-century Jewish historian Josephus tells us that tens of thousands of Babylonian Jews traveled to Jerusalem for the annual festivals.

Were some of the Babylonian pilgrims baptized at Pentecost 33 C.E.? We do not know, but among those who heard the apostle Peter on that day were ones from Mesopotamia. (Acts 2:9) We do know that the apostle Peter was in Babylon about 62-64 C.E. While there, he wrote his first letter and possibly the second one as well. (1 Peter 5:13) Babylon with its large population of Jews was obviously considered part of the territory assigned to Peter, John, and James at the meeting referred to in the letter to the Galatians.

Jerusalem Congregation and Jews in the Diaspora

James, who also attended the meeting where territories were mentioned, served as an overseer in the Jerusalem congregation. (Acts 12:12, 17; 15:13; Galatians 1:18, 19) He was an eyewitness at Pentecost 33 C.E. when thousands of visiting Jews in the Diaspora

THE APOSTLE PAUL'S CONCERN FOR JEWS IN THE DIASPORA

BEFORE THE MEETING IN JERUSALEM IN 49 C.E.

Acts 9:19, 20	**Damascus** — "in the synagogues he began to preach"	
Acts 9:29	**Jerusalem** — "talking . . . with the Greek-speaking Jews"	
Acts 13:5	**Salamis, Cyprus** — "publishing the word of God in the synagogues of the Jews"	
Acts 13:14	**Antioch in Pisidia** — "going into the synagogue"	
Acts 14:1	**Iconium** — "entered . . . into the synagogue of the Jews"	

AFTER THE MEETING IN JERUSALEM IN 49 C.E.

Acts 16:14	**Philippi** — "Lydia, . . . a worshiper of God"	
Acts 17:1	**Thessalonica** — "a synagogue of the Jews"	
Acts 17:10	**Beroea** — "the synagogue of the Jews"	
Acts 17:17	**Athens** — "reason in the synagogue with the Jews"	
Acts 18:4	**Corinth** — "give a talk in the synagogue"	
Acts 18:19	**Ephesus** — "entered into the synagogue and reasoned with the Jews"	
Acts 19:8	**Ephesus** — "entering into the synagogue, he spoke with boldness for three months"	
Acts 28:17	**Rome** — "called together . . . the principal men of the Jews"	

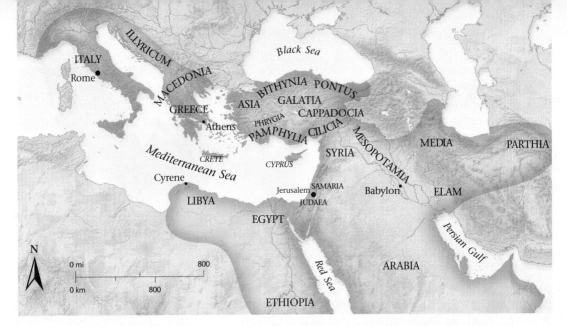

Those who heard the good news at Pentecost 33 C.E. came from a wide area

responded to the good news and were baptized.—Acts 1:14; 2:1, 41.

Then and thereafter tens of thousands of Jews came for the annual festivals. The city became overcrowded, and visitors had to stay in the neighboring villages or encamp in tents. Besides their meeting friends, *Encyclopaedia Judaica* explains, the pilgrims entered the temple to worship, offer sacrifices, and engage in the study of the Torah.

No doubt, James and the other members of the Jerusalem congregation used these opportunities to witness to Diaspora Jews. Perhaps the apostles did so with great discretion during the period when the "great persecution arose against the congregation that was in Jerusalem" as a result of Stephen's death. (Acts 8:1) Before and after this event, the record indicates, the zeal of these Christians for preaching resulted in continued increase.—Acts 5:42; 8:4; 9:31.

What Can We Learn?

Yes, the early Christians made sincere efforts to contact the Jews wherever they lived. At the same time, Paul and others reached out to the Gentiles in the European field. They observed Jesus' parting command to his followers to make disciples "of people of all the nations."—Matthew 28: 19, 20.

From their example, we can learn the importance of preaching in an organized way in order to have the support of Jehovah's spirit. We can also see the advantages of contacting those who have respect for God's Word, especially in territories with few of Jehovah's Witnesses. Are some areas of the territory assigned to your congregation more productive than others? It might be beneficial to cover these more frequently. Are there public events in the neighborhood suitable for special efforts of informal and street witnessing?

It is enriching for us not only to read in the Bible about the early Christians but also to acquaint ourselves with some of the historical and geographic details. One tool that we can use to expand our understanding is the brochure *"See the Good Land,"* with its many maps and photographs.

Eagle: © Brian K. Wheeler/VIREO

Jehovah's Word Soars in "the Land of the Eagle"

"THE Land of the Eagle." That is what the Albanians call their country in their language. This country facing the Adriatic Sea lies on the Balkan Peninsula, snuggled between Greece and the former Yugoslavia. Although there are many theories about the origin of Albanians, most historians agree that Albanians and their language descend from the ancient Illyrians, whose culture, according to *The Encyclopædia Britannica,* dates back to 2000 B.C.E.

Albania's natural beauty ranges from jagged mountains in the far north to long, white sandy beaches in the south on the Adriatic. The greatest beauty, however, lies in the people. They are warm and hospitable, lively and expressive, quick learners who passionately express their opinions with animated gestures.

A Visit by a Renowned Missionary

The attractive personality of the people and the beautiful scenery no doubt caught

ITALY

ALBANIA

GREECE

Mediterranean Sea

the attention of one unique traveler centuries ago. About 56 C.E., the well-traveled apostle Paul wrote: "As far as Illyricum I have thoroughly preached the good news about the Christ." (Romans 15:19) The southern part of Illyricum corresponds to modern-day central and northern Albania. Paul was writing from Corinth, Greece, south of Illyricum. Saying that he thoroughly preached "as far as Illyricum" indicates that he went either up to the border or right into the region. In either case, he would have preached in what is now southern Albania. So the earliest known Kingdom-preaching work in Albania can be attributed to Paul.

Centuries passed. Empires rose and fell. Foreign powers came and went in this little corner of Europe until Albania became an independent state in 1912. About a decade later, the word about Jehovah's Kingdom was again heard in Albania.

An Exciting Modern Beginning

In the 1920's, a few Albanian immigrants to the United States who were associated with the International Bible Students, as Jehovah's Witnesses were then known, returned to Albania to share what they had learned. Among these was Nasho Idrizi. Some people responded favorably. To care for the increased interest, in 1924 the Romanian office was assigned oversight of the preaching work in Albania.

Thanas Duli (Athan Doulis) was among those who learned about Jehovah in Albania during those years. He recalled: "In 1925 there were three organized congregations in Albania, as well as isolated Bible Students and interested persons here and there throughout the land. Their love among themselves was so much in contrast with . . . the people around them!"*

The lack of a road system made travel extremely difficult. Yet, zealous publishers took up the challenge. For example, on the southern coast in Vlorë, Areti Pina got baptized in 1928, when she was 18. She climbed up and down rugged mountains, preaching with Bible in hand. She was part of a strong congregation in Vlorë in the early 1930's.

---

* For the life story of Thanas Duli, see *The Watchtower,* December 1, 1968.

Young Witnesses imitate the zeal of older ones

troops invaded the country. As World War II ended, a charismatic military leader, Enver Hoxha, emerged. His Communist Party won the 1946 elections, and he became prime minister. The years that followed came to be called the time of liberation, but they meant just the opposite for Jehovah's people.

Gradually, the government became less and less tolerant of religion. True to their Christian neutrality, Jehovah's Witnesses in Albania refused to take up arms and to get involved in politics. (Isaiah 2:2-4; John 15:17-19) Many were thrown in prison, without food or the bare necessities of life. In many cases, their spiritual sisters on the outside washed their clothes and cooked for them.

By 1930 the preaching work in Albania was directed by the branch office in Athens, Greece. In 1932 a traveling overseer from Greece visited Albania to encourage and strengthen the brothers. Most of those learning Bible truth back then had the heavenly hope. Their reputation for being clean and upright people earned them deep respect far and wide. The work of these faithful brothers bore much fruit. In each of the years 1935 and 1936, some 6,500 pieces of Bible literature were placed in Albania.

Areti Pina served faithfully from 1928 until her death in 1994

One day, in the center of Vlorë, Nasho Idrizi played one of J. F. Rutherford's discourses on the gramophone. People closed their businesses and came to listen as Brother Idrizi interpreted in Albanian. The zeal of those early, untiring Bible educators was blessed. By 1940 there were 50 Witnesses in Albania.

An Atheistic State

In 1939, Italian Fascists occupied the country. The legal recognition of Jehovah's Witnesses was revoked, and their preaching work was banned. Soon afterward, German

Fearless in the Face of Persecution

In the early 1940's, Frosina Xheka, then a teenager in a village near Përmet, heard what her older fleshly brothers were learning from a Witness shoemaker named Nasho Dori.* The authorities were cracking down on Jehovah's Witnesses, but to her parents' displeasure, Frosina's faith grew stronger. "They would hide my shoes and beat me if I went to Christian meetings. They tried to arrange for me to marry an unbeliever. When I refused, they kicked me out of the house. It was snowing that day. Nasho Dori asked Brother Gole Flloko in Gjirokastër to help me. They arranged for me to live with his family. My brothers were in prison for two years because of their neutral stand. After they were released, I moved to Vlorë to live with them.

---

* For the life story of Nasho Dori, see *The Watchtower,* January 1, 1996.

The first group of foreign pioneers attending a language course

"The police tried to force me to take part in political activities. I refused. They arrested me, took me to a room, and surrounded me. One of them threatened me: 'Do you know what we can do to you?' I answered: 'You can only do what Jehovah lets you do.' He retorted: 'You must be crazy! Get out of here!' "

That same loyal spirit characterized the Albanian brothers throughout those years. By 1957 a peak of 75 Kingdom publishers was reached. In the early 1960's, the headquarters of Jehovah's Witnesses arranged for John Marks, an Albanian immigrant in the United States, to visit Tiranë to help organize the Christian work.* Soon, though, Luçi Xheka, Mihal Sveci, Leonidha Pope, and other responsible brothers were sent to labor camps.

Light at the End of the Tunnel

Until 1967 all religion was frowned upon in Albania. Then it was no longer tolerated. No Catholic, Orthodox, or Muslim priests could officiate at rituals. Churches and mosques were closed or converted into gymnasiums, museums, or markets. No one was supposed to have a Bible. The very thought of belief in God was not to be expressed.

Preaching and meeting together were next to impossible. Individual Witnesses did their best to serve Jehovah, despite being separated from one another. From the 1960's through the 1980's, the number of Witnesses dwindled to a handful. Yet they were spiritually strong.

In the late 1980's, political changes in Albania inched forward. Food and clothing were scarce. People were not happy. The

___
* For the life story of John Marks' wife, Helen, see *The Watchtower,* January 1, 2002.

reforms sweeping through Eastern Europe reached Albania in the early 1990's. After 45 years of the totalitarian regime, a new government allowed religious freedom once again.

At the direction of the Governing Body of Jehovah's Witnesses, the branch offices in Austria and Greece quickly set out to contact local Albanian brothers. Greek brothers who knew Albanian brought some newly translated Bible literature to Tiranë and Berat. Joy filled the hearts of the formerly dispersed local brothers as they met Witnesses from abroad for the first time in years.

Zealous Foreign Pioneers Spearhead the Work

In early 1992, the Governing Body arranged for Michael and Linda DiGregorio, a missionary couple with an Albanian background, to transfer to Albania. They contacted the elderly faithful ones, helping them come together once again as part of an international spiritual family. A group of 16 hardworking Italian special pioneers, or full-time evangelizers, arrived in November, along with four Greek pioneers. To help them learn the local tongue, a language course was organized.

Daily life was rough for these foreign pioneers. Electricity was erratic. Winter was cold and damp. People stood in line for hours to get food and other necessities of life. Yet, the biggest problem the brothers faced was how to find buildings large enough to hold the throngs of interested ones responding to the truth!

Pioneers struggling to speak Albanian learned that a language is only a means to an end. An experienced Bible teacher told them: "We don't need to conjugate verbs perfectly to smile warmly or to hug our brothers. Albanians will respond to love from your heart, not perfect grammar. Don't worry, they'll understand."

After the first language course, the pioneers got down to work in Berat, Durres, Gjirokastër, Shkodër, Tiranë, and Vlorë. Soon congregations mushroomed in those cities. Areti Pina, now in her 80's and in poor health, was still in Vlorë. Two special pioneers were sent there to preach with Areti. People were amazed that foreigners were speaking Albanian: "Missionaries from other religious groups make us learn English or Italian if we want to learn anything. You must really love us and have something important to say, for you've actually learned Albanian!" Areti faithfully finished her earthly course in January 1994, active in preaching down to the very last month. The zeal that she and the pioneers showed was blessed. A congregation was reestablished in Vlorë in 1995. Today, three thriving congregations are busy preaching in that seaport.

Throughout the country, people were starving spiritually and had little religious prejudice. They devoured any and all Bible-based literature they received from the Witnesses. Many young ones began to study and quickly made progress.

Over 90 congregations and groups continue "to be made firm in the faith and to increase in number from day to day" throughout the country. (Acts 16:5) The 3,513 Witnesses in Albania still have much work to do. In March 2005, the Memorial of Christ's death was attended by 10,144. Discussions with the hospitable people in the preaching work have led to over 6,000 Bible studies. Clearly, thousands will be benefiting from the recently released *New World Translation* in Albanian. Indeed, Jehovah's word soars in "the Land of the Eagle" to Jehovah's praise.

ETHNIC STRIFE MELTS AWAY IN KOSOVO!

Kosovo became a household name in the late 1990's when territorial disputes and deep-seated ethnic hatred led to war and international intervention.

During the war in the Balkans, many Witnesses had to flee to neighboring lands. After the war subsided, a small band of them returned to Kosovo, ready for work. Albanian and Italian special pioneers offered to move to Kosovo to help the 2,350,000 inhabitants there. Four congregations and six active groups, totaling about 130 publishers, are serving Jehovah in this territory.

A special assembly day was held in Priština in the spring of 2003, and 252 were present. Among them were individuals of Albanian, German, Gypsy, Italian, and Serbian backgrounds. At the end of the baptism talk, the speaker asked two questions. Three individuals stood to answer affirmatively: an ethnic Albanian, a Gypsy, and a Serbian.

Thunderous applause broke out after the audience heard the loud simultaneous: "Va!," "Da!," and "Po!" from the three baptismal candidates. They hugged one another. They have found the answer to the deeply rooted ethnic problems that have plagued their land.

BEWARE OF DEVELOPING A HAUGHTY HEART

"God opposes the haughty ones."—JAMES 4:6.

HAS some event ever caused your heart to swell with pride? Most of us have experienced that pleasurable sensation. Our capacity for feeling a measure of pride is not bad. For example, when a Christian couple read a school report about their daughter's good behavior and hard work, their faces likely glow with warm satisfaction over her accomplishments. The apostle Paul and his companions took pride in a new congregation that they had helped to establish, for the brothers faithfully endured persecution.—1 Thessalonians 1: 1, 6; 2:19, 20; 2 Thessalonians 1:1, 4.

² From the foregoing examples, we can see that pride may imply a sense of delight that comes from some act or possession. Frequently, though, pride reflects unseemly self-esteem, a feeling of superiority because of one's abilities, appearance, wealth, or rank. It is often displayed in arrogance of demeanor, a haughty bearing. Such pride is definitely something that we as Christians should guard against. Why? Because we have an inborn tendency to selfishness that we inherited from our forefather Adam. (Genesis 8:21) As a result, our hearts can easily mislead us into feeling proud for the wrong reasons.

For instance, Christians must resist feeling pride over race, wealth, education, natural abilities, or work performance in comparison with others. Pride that arises from such things is improper and is displeasing to Jehovah.—Jeremiah 9:23; Acts 10:34, 35; 1 Corinthians 4:7; Galatians 5:26; 6:3, 4.

³ There is another reason for rejecting improper pride. If we allow such to grow in our heart, it can develop into a very despicable form of pride called haughtiness. What is haughtiness? In addition to feeling superior, a haughty person looks down on others, those whom he or she views as inferior. (Luke 18:9; John 7:47-49) Jesus listed "haughtiness" along with other wicked traits that come "out of the heart" and "defile a man." (Mark 7:20-23) Christians can see how vital it is to avoid developing a haughty heart.

⁴ You can be helped to avoid haughtiness by considering some Bible accounts of haughty ones. You will thus be in a better position to detect improper feelings of pride that might reside within you or that may develop in time. This will help you to reject thoughts or feelings that could lead to a haughty heart. As a result, you will not be

---

1. Give an example of appropriate feelings of pride.
2. Why are feelings of pride usually undesirable?

3. What is haughtiness, and what did Jesus say about it?
4. How can a consideration of Bible examples of haughtiness help us?

affected negatively when God acts in line with his warning: "I shall remove from the midst of you your haughtily exultant ones; and you will never again be haughty in my holy mountain."—Zephaniah 3:11.

God Deals With Haughty Ones

⁵ You can also see Jehovah's view of haughtiness in the way he dealt with such powerful rulers as Pharaoh. There can be no doubt that Pharaoh had a haughty heart. Viewing himself as a god to be worshipped, he despised his slaves, the Israelites. Consider his reaction to the request that Israel be allowed to go into the wilderness to "celebrate a festival" to Jehovah. "Who is Jehovah, so that I should obey his voice to send Israel away?" was Pharaoh's haughty reply.—Exodus 5:1, 2.

⁶ After Pharaoh had experienced six plagues, Jehovah told Moses to ask Egypt's ruler: "Are you still behaving haughtily against my people in not sending them away?" (Exodus 9:17) Moses now announced the seventh plague—hail that devastated the land. Once the Israelites were free to leave after the tenth plague, Pharaoh changed his mind and pursued them. Finally, Pharaoh and his armies were trapped in the Red Sea. Imagine what they must have thought as the waters closed in upon them! What was the fruitage of Pharaoh's haughtiness? His elite troops said: "Let us flee from any contact with Israel, because Jehovah certainly fights for them against the Egyptians."—Exodus 14:25.

⁷ Humiliation at Jehovah's hand also came to other haughty rulers. One was Sennacherib, king of Assyria. (Isaiah 36:1-4, 20; 37:36-38) Eventually, Assyria was conquered by the Babylonians, but two haughty Babylonian kings were humiliated too. Recall the feast that King Belshazzar had during which he and his royal guests drank wine out of vessels taken from Jehovah's temple, praising Babylon's gods. Suddenly, the fingers of a man's hand appeared and wrote a message on the wall. Asked to explain the mysterious writing, the prophet Daniel reminded Belshazzar: "The Most High God himself gave to Nebuchadnezzar your father the kingdom . . . But when his heart became haughty . . . , he was brought down from the throne of his kingdom, and his own dignity was taken away from him. . . . As for you, his son Belshazzar, you have not humbled your heart, although you knew all this." (Daniel 5:3, 18, 20, 22) That very night, the Medo-Persian army conquered Babylon, and Belshazzar was killed.—Daniel 5:30, 31.

⁸ Think, too, of other haughty men who despised Jehovah's people: the Philistine giant Goliath, the Persian Prime Minister Haman, and King Herod Agrippa, who ruled the province of Judaea. Because of their haughtiness, those three men suffered a humiliating death at God's hand. (1 Samuel 17:42-51; Esther 3:5, 6; 7:10; Acts 12:1-3, 21-23) How Jehovah dealt with those haughty men underlines this truth: "Pride is before a crash, and a haughty spirit before stumbling." (Proverbs 16:18) Indeed, there can be no doubt that "God opposes the haughty ones."—James 4:6.

⁹ In contrast with the haughty rulers of Egypt, Assyria, and Babylon, the king of Tyre at one time proved helpful to God's people. During the reigns of Kings David and Solomon, he provided skilled craftsmen and materials for royal buildings and for God's temple. (2 Samuel 5:11; 2 Chronicles 2:11-16) Sadly, in time, the Tyrians turned against Jehovah's people. What caused that development?—Psalm 83:3-7; Joel 3:4-6; Amos 1:9, 10.

5, 6. How did Pharaoh show haughtiness, and with what result?

7. How did rulers of Babylon show haughtiness?

8. How did Jehovah deal with various haughty ones?

9. How did the kings of Tyre prove to be traitors?

"Your Heart Became Haughty"

¹⁰ Jehovah inspired his prophet Ezekiel to expose and condemn Tyre's dynasty of kings. That message addressed to "the king of Tyre" contains expressions that fit both the Tyrian dynasty and the original traitor, Satan, who "did not stand fast in the truth." (Ezekiel 28:12; John 8:44) Satan was once a loyal spirit creature in Jehovah's organization of heavenly sons. Jehovah God gave indication through Ezekiel of the basic cause of the defection of both the Tyrian dynasty and Satan:

¹¹ "In Eden, the garden of God, you proved to be. Every precious stone was your covering . . . You are the anointed cherub that is covering . . . You were faultless in your ways from the day of your being created until unrighteousness was found in you. Because of the abundance of your sales goods they filled the midst of you with violence, and you began to sin. And I shall . . . destroy you, O cherub that is covering . . . Your heart became haughty because of your beauty. You brought your wisdom to ruin on account of your beaming splendor." (Ezekiel 28:13-17) Yes, haughtiness moved Tyre's kings to violence against Jehovah's people. Tyre became exceedingly wealthy as a commercial center and famous for its beautiful products. (Isaiah 23:8, 9) Tyre's kings came to think too much of themselves, and they began to oppress God's people.

¹² Similarly, the spirit creature who became Satan once had the wisdom needed to fulfill any assignment God gave him. Instead of being thankful, he became "puffed up with pride" and began to despise God's way

Pharaoh's haughtiness led to his humiliation

of ruling. (1 Timothy 3:6) He thought so much of himself that he began to crave the worship of Adam and Eve. This wicked desire became fertile and gave birth to sin. (James 1:14, 15) Satan seduced Eve into eating the fruit of the only tree that God had ruled out. Then, Satan used her to get Adam to eat of the forbidden fruit. (Genesis 3:1-6) Thus the first human pair rejected God's right to rule over them and, in effect, became worshippers of Satan. His haughtiness knows no bounds. He has tried to seduce all intelligent creatures in heaven and on earth, including Jesus Christ, into worshipping him in rejection of Jehovah's sovereignty.—Matthew 4:8-10; Revelation 12:3, 4, 9.

¹³ You can thus see that haughtiness originates with Satan; it is the basic cause of sin, suffering, and corruption in the world today. As "god of this system of things," Satan continues to promote improper feelings of

---

10, 11. (a) Who might be compared to the kings of Tyre? (b) What changed the Tyrians' attitude toward Israel?

12. What led to Satan's course of treachery, and what has he continued to do?

13. What fruitage has haughtiness produced?

pride and haughtiness. (2 Corinthians 4:4) He knows that his time is short, so he wages war against true Christians. His goal is to turn them away from God, to become lovers of themselves, self-assuming, and haughty. The Bible foretold that such selfish traits would be common in these "last days." —2 Timothy 3:1, 2, footnote; Revelation 12: 12, 17.

¹⁴ For his part, Jesus Christ boldly exposed the rotten fruitage caused by Satan's haughtiness. On at least three occasions and in the

---

14. According to what rule does Jehovah deal with his intelligent creatures?

Hagar's improved status caused her to become haughty

presence of self-righteous enemies, Jesus laid down the rule by which Jehovah deals with mankind: "Everyone that exalts himself will be humiliated, but he that humbles himself will be exalted."—Luke 14:11; 18:14; Matthew 23:12.

Guard Your Heart Against Haughtiness

¹⁵ You may have noted that the examples of haughtiness mentioned above involved prominent men. Does that mean that ordinary people are not prone to becoming haughty? Definitely not. Consider an incident that occurred in Abraham's household. The patriarch had no son to be his heir, and his wife, Sarah, was beyond the age of childbearing. It was customary for a man in Abraham's situation to take a second wife and have children. God tolerated such marriages because it was not yet his time to reestablish his original standard of marriage among true worshippers.—Matthew 19:3-9.

¹⁶ At his wife's urging, Abraham agreed to produce a potential heir through Sarah's Egyptian maidservant, Hagar. As a secondary wife of Abraham, Hagar became pregnant. She should have been deeply grateful for her honored status. Instead, she allowed her heart to become haughty. The Bible relates: "When she became aware that she was pregnant, then her mistress began to be despised in her eyes." That attitude caused such strife in Abraham's household that Sarah chased Hagar away. But there was a solution to the problem. God's angel counseled Hagar: "Return to your mistress and humble yourself under her hand." (Genesis 16:4, 9) Evidently, Hagar followed this counsel, adjusted her attitude toward Sarah, and became ancestress to a multitude.

15, 16. What caused Hagar to become haughty?

¹⁷ The case of Hagar illustrates that when someone's situation changes for the better, haughtiness may result. The lesson is that even a Christian who has shown a good heart in serving God can become haughty upon gaining wealth or authority. That attitude can also develop if others praise him for his success, wisdom, or ability. Yes, a Christian should be alert to keep haughtiness out of his heart. That is especially true if he achieves success or receives more responsibility.

¹⁸ The most powerful reason for avoiding haughtiness is God's view of this trait. His Word states: "Haughty eyes and an arrogant heart, the lamp of the wicked ones, are sin." (Proverbs 21:4) Interestingly, the Bible in particular warns Christians "who are rich in the present system of things" not to be "high-minded," or "haughty." (1 Timothy 6: 17, footnote; Deuteronomy 8:11-17) Those Christians who are not rich should avoid having "an envious eye," and they should remember that haughtiness can develop in anyone—rich or poor.—Mark 7:21-23; James 4:5.

¹⁹ Haughtiness along with other wicked traits can ruin a good relationship with Jehovah. Consider, for example, the first part of King Uzziah's reign: "He kept doing what was right in Jehovah's eyes . . . And he continually tended to search for God . . . ; and, in the days of his searching for Jehovah, the true God made him prosperous." (2 Chronicles 26:4, 5) Sadly, though, King Uzziah spoiled his good record, for "his heart became haughty even to the point of causing ruin." He came to think so much of himself that he entered the temple to offer up incense. When the priests warned him not to commit this presumptuous act, "Uzziah became enraged." As a result, Jehovah struck

Hezekiah humbled himself and regained God's favor

him with leprosy, and he died in God's disfavor.—2 Chronicles 26:16-21.

²⁰ You can contrast that with the example of King Hezekiah. On one occasion, that king's excellent record was in danger of being spoiled because "his heart became haughty." Happily, "Hezekiah humbled himself for the haughtiness of his heart" and regained God's favor. (2 Chronicles 32:25, 26) Notice that the cure for Hezekiah's haughtiness was humility. Yes, humility is the opposite of haughtiness. Therefore, in the next article, we will consider how we can cultivate and maintain Christian humility.

²¹ May we not forget, though, all the bad fruitage that has been produced by

---

17, 18. Why do all of us need to guard against haughtiness?

19. In what way did Uzziah ruin his good record?

20. (a) How was King Hezekiah's good record endangered? (b) What will be considered in the next article?

21. To what can humble Christians look forward?

haughtiness. Since "God opposes the haughty ones," let us be firmly resolved to reject feelings of improper pride. As we strive to be humble Christians, we can look forward to surviving God's great day, when haughty ones and their fruitage will be removed from the earth. Then "the haughtiness of the earthling man must bow down, and the loftiness of men must become low; and Jehovah alone must be put on high in that day."—Isaiah 2:17.

Points for Meditation

- How would you describe a haughty person?
- What is the origin of haughtiness?
- What can cause a person to become haughty?
- Why must we guard against haughtiness?

CULTIVATE GENUINE HUMILITY

"The humble people you will save."—2 SAMUEL 22:28.

THE pyramids of Egypt bear testimony to men who once ruled that land. Others who left their mark on history were Sennacherib of Assyria, Alexander the Great of Greece, and Julius Caesar of Rome. All such rulers had one thing in common. They did not leave a record of being genuinely humble.—Matthew 20:25, 26.

² Could you imagine any of the above-mentioned rulers being in the habit of searching their realm to find lowly subjects in need of comfort? Of course not! Nor could you imagine that they would go to the humble dwell-

Jesus was genuinely humble

ings of crushed citizens to uplift the spirits of such ones. How different their attitude toward lowly human creatures is from that of the Supreme Ruler of the universe, Jehovah God!

The Greatest Example of Humility

³ Jehovah is unsearchably great and lofty, yet "his eyes are roving about through all the earth to show his strength in behalf of those whose heart is complete toward him." (2 Chronicles 16:9) And what does Jehovah do when he finds lowly worshippers who are crushed in spirit as a result of various trials?

1, 2. What have many world rulers had in common?

3. How does the Supreme Ruler treat his human subjects?

In a sense, he "is residing" with such ones by means of his holy spirit "to revive the spirit of the lowly ones and to revive the heart of the ones being crushed." (Isaiah 57:15) Thus, his revived worshippers are better able to resume serving him with rejoicing. What humility on God's part!

⁴ No one else in the universe has humbled himself to the same extent as the Sovereign Lord in order to help sinful humans. The psalmist could write: "Jehovah has become high above all the nations; his glory is above the heavens. Who is like Jehovah our God, him who is making his dwelling on high? He is condescending to look on heaven and earth, raising up the lowly one from the very dust; he exalts the poor one from the ashpit itself."—Psalm 113:4-7.

⁵ Note the word "condescending." When referring to humans, that word can have a bad connotation, 'to assume an air of superiority to one inferior or less fortunate.' Such a haughty attitude could never describe Jehovah God, who is pure and holy and thus devoid of "haughtiness." (Mark 7:22, 23) But "condescend" can also carry the sense of coming down to the level of one socially lower or descending from one's rank or dignity in dealings with an inferior. Thus, some Bibles render Psalm 113:6 as saying that God humbles himself. How well that conveys the image of our humble God giving loving attention to the needs of his imperfect human worshippers!—2 Samuel 22:36.

Why Jesus Was Humble

⁶ God's greatest act of humility and love was that of sending his beloved firstborn Son to be born on earth and raised as a human for the salvation of mankind. (John 3: 16) Jesus taught us the truth about his heavenly Father and then gave up his perfect human life to take away "the sin of the world." (John 1:29; 18:37) Perfectly reflecting his Father, including Jehovah's humility, Jesus was willing to do what God asked of him. That was the greatest example of humility and love ever set by one of God's creatures. Not all appreciated Jesus' humility, his enemies even considering him to be "the lowliest one of mankind." (Daniel 4:17) Nonetheless, the apostle Paul realized that his fellow believers should imitate Jesus and thus be humble in their dealings with one another. —1 Corinthians 11:1; Philippians 2:3, 4.

⁷ Paul highlighted Jesus' outstanding example, writing: "Keep this mental attitude in you that was also in Christ Jesus, who, although he was existing in God's form, gave no consideration to a seizure, namely, that he should be equal to God. No, but he emptied himself and took a slave's form and came to be in the likeness of men. More than that, when he found himself in fashion as a man, he humbled himself and became obedient as far as death, yes, death on a torture stake."—Philippians 2:5-8.

7, 8. (a) How did Jesus learn to be humble? (b) What appeal does Jesus make to potential disciples?

IN OUR NEXT ISSUE

Can Anyone Really Change the World?

The Ransom Magnifies God's Righteousness

Jehovah Is Our Shepherd

4, 5. (a) How did the psalmist feel about God's way of ruling? (b) What does God's "condescending" to help "the lowly one" mean?

6. What was Jehovah's greatest act of humility?

⁸ Some might wonder, 'How did Jesus learn to be humble?' It was a marvelous benefit of his close association with his heavenly Father for aeons of time, during which he served as God's "master worker" in the creation of all things. (Proverbs 8:30) After the rebellion in Eden, God's First-born was in a position to note his Father's humble dealings with human sinners. Accordingly, when on earth, Jesus reflected his Father's humility and made the appeal: "Take my yoke upon me and learn from me, for I am mild-tempered and lowly in heart, and you will find refreshment for your souls."—Matthew 11:29; John 14:9.

⁹ Because Jesus was genuinely humble, little children were not afraid of him. Rather, they felt drawn to him. He for his part showed fondness for children and gave attention to them. (Mark 10:13-16) What was it about children that Jesus found so appealing? Certainly, they had desirable qualities that some of his adult disciples did not always display. It is a simple fact that little children view adults as being superior. You can see this by the many questions they ask. Yes, compared with many adults, children are more teachable and not as prone to pride. On one occasion, Jesus singled out a young child and said to His followers: "Unless you turn around and become as young children, you will by no means enter into the kingdom of the heavens." He continued:

The world encourages people to strive to be superior to others

WHO photo by L. Almasi/K. Hemző

"Whoever will humble himself like this young child is the one that is the greatest in the kingdom of the heavens." (Matthew 18:3, 4) Jesus stated the rule: "Everyone that exalts himself will be humbled and he that humbles himself will be exalted."—Luke 14:11; 18:14; Matthew 23:12.

¹⁰ That truth raises important questions. Our prospect of gaining everlasting life is in part dependent on our cultivating genuine humility, but why do Christians sometimes find it difficult to be humble? Why is it a challenge for us to swallow our pride, so to speak, and react to trials with humility? And what will help us to succeed in cultivating genuine humility?—James 4:6, 10.

Why It Is Difficult to Be Humble

¹¹ If you have found yourself struggling to be humble, you are not alone. Back in 1920, this journal discussed the Bible's counsel on the need for humility, commenting: "As we thus see how great a value the Lord places upon humility it should encourage all true disciples to cultivate this quality daily." Then came this frank admission: "Notwithstanding all these exhortations of the Scriptures the perversity of human nature seems to be such that those who become the Lord's people and who engage to run in this way seem to find more trouble, more to contend against, in this matter than in any other." That highlights one reason why true Christians have to

---

9. (a) What did Jesus find appealing in children? (b) Using a young child, what lesson did Jesus teach?

10. What questions will we consider?
11. Why is it not surprising that we struggle to be humble?

struggle to be humble—our sinful human nature craves undue glory. This is because we are the descendants of a sinful couple, Adam and Eve, who gave in to selfish cravings.—Romans 5:12.

¹² Another reason we may find it difficult to display humility is that we are surrounded by a world that encourages people to strive to be superior to others. Among this world's common goals is a craving for satisfying "the desire of the [sinful] flesh and the desire of the eyes and the showy display of one's means of life." (1 John 2:16) Rather than being dominated by such worldly desires, Jesus' disciples are to keep their eye simple and to focus on doing God's will. —Matthew 6:22-24, 31-33; 1 John 2:17.

¹³ A third reason why cultivating and displaying humility is difficult is that the originator of haughtiness, Satan the Devil, rules this world. (2 Corinthians 4:4; 1 Timothy 3:6) Satan promotes his wicked traits. For example, he sought worship from Jesus in exchange for giving him "all the kingdoms of the world and their glory." Ever humble, Jesus flatly rejected the Devil's offer. (Matthew 4:8, 10) Likewise, Satan tempts Christians to seek glory for themselves. Instead, humble Christians strive to follow Jesus' example, directing praise and honor to God. —Mark 10:17, 18.

Humility helps us to approach strangers in our ministry

Cultivating and Displaying Genuine Humility

¹⁴ In his letter to the Colossians, the apostle Paul warned against the outward pretense of humility to impress men. Paul described this as "a mock humility." Those who make a mere pretense of being humble are not spiritual people. Rather, they betray that they are really "puffed up" with pride. (Colossians 2:18, 23) Jesus pointed to examples of such false humility. He condemned the Pharisees for their showy prayers and for the way they fasted with sad and disfigured faces to be observed by men. In contrast, for our private prayers to have value before God, they should be uttered humbly.—Matthew 6:5, 6, 16.

¹⁵ Christians are helped to maintain genuine lowliness of mind by focusing on the best examples of humility, Jehovah God and Jesus Christ. Doing this involves a regular study of the Bible and Bible study aids provided through "the faithful and discreet slave." (Matthew 24:45) Such a study is vital for Christian overseers, "that [their] heart may not exalt itself above [their] brothers." (Deuteronomy 17:19, 20; 1 Peter 5:1-3) Reflect on the numerous examples of ones who were blessed for their humble attitude, such as Ruth, Hannah, Elizabeth, and many others. (Ruth 1:16, 17; 1 Samuel 1:11, 20; Luke 1:41-43) Think, too, of the many fine examples of prominent

12, 13. (a) How is the world an obstacle to Christian humility? (b) Who makes our struggle to cultivate humility even more difficult?

14. What is "mock humility"?
15. (a) What can we do to maintain lowliness of mind? (b) What are some good examples of humility?

men who remained humble in Jehovah's service, such as David, Josiah, John the Baptizer, and the apostle Paul. (2 Chronicles 34:1, 2, 19, 26-28; Psalm 131:1; John 1:26, 27; 3:26-30; Acts 21:20-26; 1 Corinthians 15:9) And what about the many modern-day examples of humility that we find in the Christian congregation? By meditating on these examples, true Christians will be helped to have "lowliness of mind toward one another."—1 Peter 5:5.

¹⁶ Having a regular share in the Christian ministry can also help us to be humble. Lowliness of mind can make us effective when we approach strangers we find from house to house and in other places. This is especially true when householders initially respond to the Kingdom message with apathy or rudeness. Our beliefs are often challenged, and humility can help the Christian to keep answering questions "with a mild temper and deep respect." (1 Peter 3:15) Humble servants of God have moved to new territories and have helped people with different cultures and standards of living. Such ministers may humbly have to cope with the difficult task of learning a new language in order to be of better service to those with whom they want to share the good news. How commendable! —Matthew 28:19, 20.

---

16. How does the Christian ministry help us to be humble?

Points for Meditation

- Who are the best examples of humility?

- Why is humility difficult to cultivate?

- What can help us to be humble?

- Why is it so important to remain humble?

---

¹⁷ With humility, many have fulfilled their Christian duties, putting the interests of others ahead of their own. For example, it takes humility for a Christian father to set aside time from his own pursuits to prepare and conduct an effective Bible study with his children. Humility also helps children to honor and be obedient to their parents, who are imperfect. (Ephesians 6:1-4) Wives who have unbelieving husbands often face humbling situations as they try to win over their mates by "chaste conduct together with deep respect." (1 Peter 3:1, 2) Humility and self-sacrificing love are assets too when we lovingly care for the needs of sick and aging parents.—1 Timothy 5:4.

Humility Solves Problems

¹⁸ All of God's human servants are imperfect. (James 3:2) At times, differences or misunderstandings may develop between two Christians. One may have a valid cause for complaint against another. Usually, such situations can be solved by applying this coun-

---

17. What Christian responsibilities require humility?

18. How can humility help us to resolve problems?

Differences can often be solved by our humbly covering over the matter in love

There are many ways in which Christians show humility

sel: "Continue putting up with one another and forgiving one another freely if anyone has a cause for complaint against another. Even as Jehovah freely forgave you, so do you also." (Colossians 3:13) Admittedly, following this advice is not easy, but humility will help one put it into practice.

¹⁹ Sometimes a Christian may feel that a valid cause for complaint is too serious to be covered over. Then, humility will help him to approach the alleged offender with a view to restoring peace. (Matthew 18:15) One reason that problems between Christians sometimes persist is that one or perhaps both parties are too proud to admit being at fault. Or the one who takes the initiative to approach the other may do so in a self-righteous, critical manner. In contrast, a genuinely humble attitude will go a long way toward solving many differences.

²⁰ A key step in developing humility is to pray for God's help and spirit. But remember,

"God . . . gives undeserved kindness [including his holy spirit] to the humble ones." (James 4:6) So if you have a difference with a fellow believer, pray to Jehovah to help you humbly to admit any minor or major blame on your part. If you have been hurt and the offender says a sincere, "I'm sorry," then humbly forgive. If doing this is difficult, prayerfully seek Jehovah's help to rid your heart of any lingering haughtiness.

²¹ Understanding the many benefits that humility brings should move us to cultivate and maintain this precious quality. To that end, what wonderful examples we have in Jehovah God and Jesus Christ! Never forget the divine assurance: "The result of humility and the fear of Jehovah is riches and glory and life."—Proverbs 22:4.

19. What must we remember when we speak to someone who has upset us?
20, 21. What is one of the greatest helps to being humble?

"They That Go Down to the Sea in Ships"

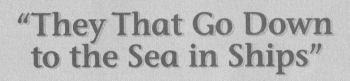

FACING the outer harbor of Gloucester, Massachusetts, U.S.A., stands a bronze statue depicting a helmsman, intent on steering his ship through a storm. The statue commemorates the thousands of Gloucester fishermen known to have died at sea. On the statue's base and a nearby plaque are the words of Psalm 107:23, 24: "They that go down to the sea in ships, that do business in great waters; These see the works of the Lord, and his wonders in the deep." —*King James Version.*

Working on the rich undersea banks of the Atlantic is perilous business. Over the years, as many as 5,368 men from Gloucester, which now has a population of some 30,000, are known to have lost their lives while fishing at sea. Says the memorial: "Some were overtaken by the howling winds and mountainous seas of a catastrophic northeaster. Some met their fate in the solitude of a small dory gone astray from the schooner that brought them to the banks. Some ships collided in storms and tragically sank. Others were run down by steamers in shipping lanes."

The memorial stands as a sad witness to the toil and dangers that fishermen have faced over the centuries. Imagine the tears of desperation shed for lost husbands, fathers, brothers, and sons. Yet, Jehovah God does not forget the widows, the orphans, or those who lost their lives at sea. The apostle John pointed to this future development: "The sea gave up those dead in it, and death and Hades gave up those dead in them." (Revelation 20:13) At the time of their resurrection, those who went "down to the sea in ships" will see wonderful "works of the Lord" indeed.

NOVEMBER 1, 2005

THE WATCHTOWER

ANNOUNCING JEHOVAH'S KINGDOM

CAN ANYONE
CHANGE THE WORLD?

THE WATCHTOWER®

ANNOUNCING JEHOVAH'S KINGDOM

November 1, 2005   Average Printing Each Issue: 26,439,000   Vol. 126, No. 21

THE PURPOSE OF *THE WATCHTOWER* is to exalt Jehovah God as Sovereign Lord of the universe. It keeps watch on world events as these fulfill Bible prophecy. It comforts all peoples with the good news that God's Kingdom will soon destroy those who oppress their fellowmen and that it will turn the earth into a paradise. It encourages faith in God's now-reigning King, Jesus Christ, whose shed blood opens the way for mankind to gain eternal life. *The Watchtower,* published by Jehovah's Witnesses continuously since 1879, is nonpolitical. It adheres to the Bible as its authority.

IN THIS ISSUE

3 An Unfair World

4 Can Anyone Really Change the World?

8 I Received 'the Requests of My Heart'

13 The Ransom Magnifies God's Righteousness

14 Good Conduct Bears Fruit

15 "One of the Best Days of My Life"

16 Jehovah Is Our Shepherd

21 Will You Walk With God?

26 Contributions That Warm God's Heart

31 Questions From Readers

32 They Share Good News With the Deaf

WATCHTOWER STUDIES

NOVEMBER 28–DECEMBER 4:
Jehovah Is Our Shepherd.
Page 16. Songs to be used: 77, 58.

DECEMBER 5-11:
Will You Walk With God?
Page 21. Songs to be used: 138, 42.

Publication of *The Watchtower* is part of a worldwide Bible educational work supported by voluntary donations.

Unless otherwise indicated, Scripture quotations are from the modern-language *New World Translation of the Holy Scriptures—With References.*

The Watchtower (ISSN 0043-1087) is published semimonthly by Watchtower Bible and Tract Society of New York, Inc.; M. H. Larson, President; G. F. Simonis, Secretary-Treasurer; 25 Columbia Heights, Brooklyn, NY 11201-2483. Periodicals Postage Paid at Brooklyn, NY, and at additional mailing offices. **POSTMASTER:** Send address changes to Watchtower, **Wallkill, NY 12589.**

Changes of address should reach us 30 days before your moving date. Give us your old and new address (if possible, your old address label).

Semimonthly   ENGLISH

Would you welcome more information or a free home Bible study? Please send your request to Jehovah's Witnesses, using the appropriate address below.

America, United States of: Wallkill, NY 12589. *Antigua:* Box 119, St. Johns. *Australia:* Box 280, Ingleburn, NSW 1890. *Bahamas:* Box N-1247, Nassau, N.P. *Barbados, W.I.:* Crusher Site Road, Prospect, St. James. *Britain:* The Ridgeway, London NW7 1RN. *Canada:* Box 4100, Halton Hills (Georgetown), Ontario L7G 4Y4. *Germany:* Niederselters, Am Steinfels, D-65618 Selters. *Ghana:* P. O. Box GP 760, Accra. *Guyana:* 352-360 Tyrell St., Republic Park Phase 2 EBD. *Hawaii 96819:* 2055 Kam IV Rd., Honolulu. *Hong Kong:* 4 Kent Road, Kowloon Tong. *India:* Post Box 6440, Yelahanka, Bangalore 560 064, KAR. *Ireland:* Newcastle, Greystones, Co. Wicklow. *Jamaica:* P. O. Box 103, Old Harbour, St. Catherine. *Japan:* 1271 Nakashinden, Ebina City, Kanagawa Pref., 243-0496. *Kenya:* P.O. Box 47788, GPO Nairobi 00100. *New Zealand:* P.O. Box 75-142, Manurewa. *Nigeria:* P.M.B. 1090, Benin City 300001, Edo State. *Philippines, Republic of:* P. O. Box 2044, 1060 Manila. *South Africa:* Private Bag X2067, Krugersdorp, 1740. *Trinidad and Tobago, Republic of:* Lower Rapsey Street & Laxmi Lane, Curepe. *Zambia:* Box 33459, Lusaka 10101. *Zimbabwe:* Private Bag WG-5001, Westgate.

NOW PUBLISHED IN 151 LANGUAGES. SEMIMONTHLY: Afrikaans, Albanian,* Amharic, Arabic, Bengali, Bicol, Bislama, Bulgarian, Cebuano,* Chichewa,* Chinese, Chinese (Simplified),* Cibemba,* Croatian,* Czech,*# Danish,*# Dutch,*# East Armenian, Efik,* English*#+◎ (also Braille), Estonian, Ewe, Fijian, Finnish,*# French*# (also Braille), Ga, Georgian,* German,*# Greek,* Gujarati, Gun, Hebrew, Hiligaynon, Hindi, Hungarian,*# Igbo,* Iloko,* Indonesian, Italian,*# Japanese*# (also Braille), Kannada, Kinyarwanda, Kirundi, Korean*# (also Braille), Latvian, Lingala, Lithuanian, Luvale, Macedonian, Malagasy,* Malayalam, Maltese, Myanmar, Nepali, Norwegian,*# Pangasinan, Papiamento (Aruba), Papiamento (Curaçao), Polish,*# Portuguese*# (also Braille), Punjabi, Rarotongan, Romanian,* Russian,* Samar-Leyte, Samoan, Sango, Sepedi, Serbian, Sesotho, Shona,* Silozi, Sinhala, Slovak,* Slovenian, Solomon Islands Pidgin, Spanish*# (also Braille), Sranantongo, Swahili,* Swedish,*# Tagalog,* Tamil, Telugu, Thai, Tigrinya, Tok Pisin, Tongan, Tshiluba, Tsonga, Tswana, Turkish, Twi, Ukrainian,* Urdu, Vietnamese, Wallisian, Xhosa, Yoruba,* Zulu*

MONTHLY: American Sign Language,◎□ Armenian, Assamese, Azerbaijani (roman script), Brazilian Sign Language,△ Cambodian, Chitonga, Gilbertese, Greenlandic, Haitian Creole, Hausa, Hiri Motu, Icelandic, Isoko, Kaonde, Kazakh, Kikongo, Kiluba, Kirghiz, Kosraean, Kwanyama/Ndonga, Luganda, Marathi, Marshallese, Mauritian Creole, Maya, Mizo, Monokutuba, Moore, Niuean, Ossetian, Otetela, Palauan, Persian, Ponapean, Seychelles Creole, Tahitian, Tatar, Tiv, Trukese, Tumbuka, Tuvaluan, Umbundu, Uruund, Venda, Yapese, Zande

* Study articles also available in large-print edition.
# Audiocassettes also available.
+ CD also available.
◎ MP3 CD-ROM also available.
△ Videocassette
□ DVD

COVER: Man with a child: UN PHOTO 148426/McCurry/Stockbower

AN **UNFAIR WORLD**

DO YOU agree that we live in an unfair world? No doubt you do. After all, whatever our talents are and however wisely we plan our lives, we are guaranteed neither wealth nor success nor even food. It often turns out as wise King Solomon of old said: "Bread does not belong to the wise, nor wealth to the intelligent, nor success to the skilful." Why? Because, Solomon continues, "time and chance govern all."—Ecclesiastes 9:11, *The New English Bible.*

"When Bad Times Come Suddenly"

Yes, "time and chance," which often means being in the wrong place at the wrong time, often wrecks our carefully laid plans and fondest hopes. According to Solomon, we are "like fish caught in a net, like a bird taken in a snare, . . . when bad times come suddenly." (Ecclesiastes 9:12, *NE*) Millions of people, for example, work tirelessly to cultivate the ground to get food for their families, only to find themselves trapped in "bad times" when the rains fail and drought destroys their crops.

Others try to help, but even the help given to victims of "bad times" by the rest of the world community often seems unfair. In the fight against famine, for example, in one recent year, "the whole continent [of Africa] received in aid just one-fifth of the money that was allocated to the Gulf war," according to one leading relief agency. Was it fair that those with the resources spent five times as much money fighting a war in one country as they spent on alleviating the pain and suffering caused by famine on a whole continent? And is it fair in a time of material prosperity for many that 1 in 4 of earth's inhabitants still lives in absolute poverty or that millions of children die each year of preventable diseases? Surely not!

Of course, more than "time and chance" are involved when "bad times come suddenly." Powerful forces completely beyond our control also dominate our lives and dictate what happens to us. That was certainly true in Beslan, Alania, in the autumn of 2004, when hundreds of people, many of them young children on their first day at school, were killed in a brutal conflict between terrorists and security forces. True, exactly who died and who survived in that tragedy was largely a matter of chance—but the fundamental cause of those "bad times" was human conflict.

Will It Always Be This Way?

"But that is the way life is," some say when speaking about injustices. "It has always been that way, and it will always be." According to them, the strong will always oppress the weak, and the rich will always exploit the poor. That combined with "time and chance," they say, will affect us as long as the human family exists.

Does it really have to be this way? Will it ever be possible for those who use their abilities intelligently and wisely to reap a just reward for all their hard work? Can anyone do anything to bring permanent, lasting change to an unfair world? Consider what the next article has to say on this subject.

CAN ANYONE REALLY CHANGE THE WORLD?

The Star, Johannesburg, S.A.

"Poor people tell us that, above all, they want peace and security —and then opportunities to make their lives better. They want fair national and international systems so that their efforts are not thwarted by the overriding power of rich countries and rich companies."

THAT is how the director of one international relief agency described the hopes and aspirations of poor people. In fact, her words could well describe the desire of all victims of the world's tragedies and injustices. All of them long for a world of true peace and security. Will such a world ever become a reality? Does anyone really have the power and ability to change what is fundamentally an unfair world?

Efforts at Change

Many people have tried. For example, Florence Nightingale, a 19th-century Englishwoman, devoted her life to the cause of providing clean, compassionate nursing care for the sick. In her day—before antiseptics and antibiotics—hospital care was not what we have come to expect today. "Nurses," says one account, were "uneducated, unclean, and notorious for their drunkenness and immorality." Did Florence Nightingale have any success in her efforts to change the world of nursing? She did. Similarly, countless caring, altruistic people have had outstanding success in many areas of life—literacy, education, medicine, housing, feeding programs, to name a few. As a result, significant improvements have been made to the quality of life of millions of disadvantaged people.

Still, we cannot ignore this harsh reality: Hundreds of millions still find their lives blighted by war, crime, disease, famine, and other calamitous events. "Poverty," says Irish aid agency Concern, "kills 30,000 people every day." Even slavery, the target of so many reformers over the centuries, is still with us. "There are more slaves alive today than all the people stolen from Africa in the time of the transatlantic slave trade," states *Disposable People—New Slavery in the Global Economy.*

What has thwarted the efforts of people to bring about complete, lasting change? Is it simply the overriding power of the rich and the powerful, or is more involved?

Barriers to Change

According to God's Word, *the* overriding barrier to any of man's efforts to bring about a truly fair world is Satan the Devil. The apostle John tells us that "the whole world is lying in the power of the wicked one." (1 John 5:19) Right now, in fact, Satan is "misleading the entire inhabited earth."

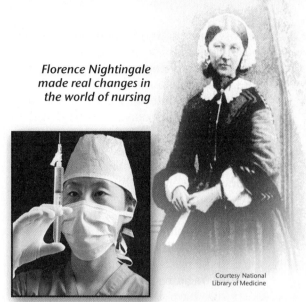

Florence Nightingale made real changes in the world of nursing

(Revelation 12:9) Until his malign influence is removed, there will be victims of evil and injustice. What brought about this sad situation?

Our original parents, Adam and Eve, were gifted with an earth that was designed to be a perfect paradise home for the whole human family—a world that was "very good." (Genesis 1:31) What changed things? Satan did. He challenged God's right to make the rules by which men and women should live. God's way of ruling, he insinuated, was unfair. He induced Adam and Eve to opt for a course of independence so that they could decide for themselves what was good and what was bad. (Genesis 3:1-6) This resulted in a second barrier to man's efforts to produce a fair, just world—sin and imperfection. —Romans 5:12.

Why Allow It?

'But why did God let sin and imperfection develop?' some may ask. 'Why did he not use his limitless power to get rid of the rebels and start over again?' That sounds like a simple solution. However, the use of power raises serious questions. Is it not true that abuse of power is one of the main grievances of the poor and oppressed of the world? Does it not raise questions in the minds of righthearted people when some despot uses power to eliminate anyone who disagrees with his policies?

To assure honesthearted ones that He is not a tyrannical abuser of power, God chose to allow Satan and the human rebels to act independently of divine laws and principles —*for a limited period of time only.* Time would prove that God's way of ruling is the only right way. It would show that any restrictions he places on us are for our good. In fact, the tragic results of rebellion against God's rule have already shown that to be true. And they have proved that God is fully justified in using his great power to eliminate all wickedness when he chooses to do so. That will be very soon.—Genesis 18:23-32; Deuteronomy 32:4; Psalm 37:9, 10, 38.

Until God acts, we are trapped in an unfair system, "groaning together and being in pain together." (Romans 8:22) Whatever we do to change things, we cannot get rid of Satan, nor can we completely eradicate the basic imperfection that is at the root of all the suffering we experience. It is simply beyond us to remedy the effects of sin inherited from Adam.—Psalm 49:7-9.

Jesus Christ Will Produce Lasting Change

Does this mean that the situation is completely hopeless? Certainly not. Someone far more powerful than mere mortal man has been charged with the responsibility of bringing about permanent change. Who is that? It is Jesus Christ. He is described in the Bible as God's Chief Agent for the salvation of the human family.—Acts 5:31.

He is now waiting for God's "appointed time" to act. (Revelation 11:18) What exactly will he do? He will bring about the "restoration of all things of which God spoke through the mouth of his holy prophets of old time." (Acts 3:21) Jesus will, for example, "deliver the poor one crying for help, also the afflicted one and whoever has no helper. . . . From oppression and from violence he will redeem their soul." (Psalm 72:12-16) Through Jesus Christ, God promises to make "wars to cease to the extremity of the earth." (Psalm 46:9) "No resident [of his cleansed earth] will say: 'I am sick,'" he promises. The blind, the deaf, the lame—all those affected by sickness and disease—will be restored to perfect health. (Isaiah 33:24; 35:5, 6; Revelation 21:3, 4) Even those who died in past centuries will benefit. He promises to bring back to life victims of injustice and oppression.—John 5:28, 29.

Jesus Christ will not bring about a partial, temporary change. He will totally eliminate all barriers to a truly fair world. He will remove sin and imperfection and destroy Satan the Devil and all those who follow his rebellious course. (Revelation 19:19, 20; 20: 1-3, 10) The distress and suffering that God has temporarily permitted "will not rise up a second time." (Nahum 1:9) This is what Jesus had in mind when he taught us to pray for God's Kingdom to come and for God's will to take place "as in heaven, *also upon earth.*"—Matthew 6:10.

'But,' you may object, 'did not Jesus himself say that we "will always have the poor with us"? Does that not mean that there will always be injustice and poverty?' (Matthew 26:11) Yes, Jesus did say that there would always be poor people. However, the context of his words along with the promises of God's Word shows that he meant that there would always be poor people *as long as this system of things lasts.* He knew that no human would ever be able to rid the world of

Christ's followers do good to others

poverty and injustice. He also knew that he would change all of that. He will soon bring about a totally new system of things—"new heavens and a new earth" in which pain, sickness, poverty, and death will cease to exist.—2 Peter 3:13; Revelation 21:1.

"Do Not Forget the Doing of Good"

Does this mean that it is pointless to do whatever we can to help other people? By no means. The Bible encourages us to help others when they face trials and distressing circumstances. "Do not hold back good from those to whom it is owing, when it happens to be in the power of your hand to do it," writes ancient King Solomon. (Proverbs 3:27) "Do not forget the doing of good and the sharing of things with others," urges the apostle Paul.—Hebrews 13:16.

Jesus Christ himself encouraged us to do whatever we can to help others. He told the illustration of a Samaritan who came across a man who had been beaten and robbed. The Samaritan man, said Jesus, was "moved with pity" to use his own resources to bind up the wounds of the beaten man and to help him recover from the assault. (Luke 10:29-37) That compassionate Samaritan did not change the world, but he did make a huge difference to another man's life. We can do the same.

However, Jesus Christ can do more than help individuals. He really can bring about change, and he will do so very soon. When he does, victims of today's unjust conditions will be able to better their lives and enjoy true peace and security.—Psalm 4:8; 37:10, 11.

While we wait for that to happen, let us never hesitate to do anything we can, both spiritually and materially, to "work what is good" toward all those who are victims of an unfair world.—Galatians 6:10.

I RECEIVED 'THE REQUESTS OF MY HEART'

AS TOLD BY
DOMINIQUE MORGOU

At last, in December 1998, I was in Africa! A childhood dream
was now a reality. I had always been thrilled by the thought of Africa's
wide-open spaces and fascinating wildlife. Now I was actually there!
At the same time, another dream had come true. I was a full-time evangelizer
serving in a foreign land. To many, this might have seemed impossible. My
sight is severely limited, and I walk the sandy streets of African villages with
the help of a guide dog trained for the streets of European cities. Let me
tell you how serving in Africa became possible for me and how
Jehovah gave me 'the requests of my heart.'—Psalm 37:4.

I WAS born on June 9, 1966, in southern France. I was the youngest of seven children—two boys and five girls—all of us cared for by loving parents. However, there was one dark spot in my young life. Like my grandmother, my mother, and one of my sisters, I suffer from a hereditary disease that eventually leads to total blindness.

As a teenager, I was confronted with racism, prejudice, and hypocrisy, which made me rebel against society. It was during this difficult time that we moved to the region of Hérault. There, something wonderful happened.

One Sunday morning, two of Jehovah's Witnesses came to our door. My mother knew them and invited them in. One of the women asked Mother if she remembered that she once promised that someday she would accept a Bible study. Mother remembered and asked, "When do we start?" They agreed to meet every Sunday morning, and in this way my mother began learning "the truth of the good news."—Galatians 2:14.

Gaining Insight

Mother spared no effort to understand and remember what she learned. Being blind, she had to memorize everything. The Witnesses were very patient with her. As for me, whenever the Witnesses came, I hid in my room and only came out when they left. One afternoon, however, Eugénie, one of the Witnesses, met me and spoke to me. She told me that God's Kingdom would end all hypocrisy, hatred, and prejudice in the world. "Only God holds the key to the solution," she said. Did I want to know more? The next day, I started my Bible study.

Everything I learned was new to me. I now understood that God is temporarily permitting wickedness on earth for good reasons. (Genesis 3:15; John 3:16; Romans 9:17) I further learned that Jehovah does not leave us without hope. He has given us his wonderful promise of everlasting life on a paradise earth. (Psalm 37:29; 96:11, 12; Isaiah 35:1, 2; 45:18) In that Paradise, I would recover the gift of sight, which I was losing gradually. —Isaiah 35:5.

Taking Up Full-Time Service

On December 12, 1985, I symbolized my dedication to Jehovah by water baptism, joining my sister Marie-Claire, who had already taken this step. My brother Jean-Pierre soon followed suit, as did my dear mother.

In the congregation with which I was associated, there were several regular pioneers,

or full-time evangelizers. I warmed to their joy and enthusiasm for the ministry. Even Marie-Claire, suffering from an eye affliction and wearing an orthopedic device on one leg, entered the full-time service. To this day she continues to give me spiritual encouragement. Being surrounded by pioneers in the congregation and in the family helped me to develop a keen desire to share in full-time service myself. So in November 1990, I began serving in Béziers as a pioneer.—Psalm 94:17-19.

Coping With Discouragement

In the ministry, I was helped by the watchful care of other pioneers. Even so, from time to time, I felt discouraged because of my limitations and wished that I could do more. However, Jehovah sustained me through those periods of discouragement. I did research in the *Watch Tower Publications Index,* looking for life stories of pioneers who like me suffered from impaired vision. I was amazed how many there were! These practical and encouraging accounts taught me to appreciate what I was able to do and to accept my limitations.

To care for my needs, I did cleaning work at shopping malls together with other Witnesses. One day I noticed that my coworkers were going back over the areas that I had just cleaned. Obviously, I was missing a lot of dirt. I went to see Valérie, who was the pioneer in charge of our cleaning team, and I asked her to be frank with me and to tell me if I was making things difficult for everyone else. She kindly left it to me to decide when I felt I could no longer do the job. In March 1994, I gave up my cleaning job.

Again, I was overwhelmed by a feeling of uselessness. I prayed fervently to Jehovah, and I know that he heard my petitions. Once more, studying the Bible and Christian

I had always been thrilled by the thought of Africa's wide-open spaces and fascinating wildlife

publications was a great help. Even so, while my eyesight was weakening, my desire to serve Jehovah was growing stronger. What could I do?

First a Waiting List, Then a Quick Decision

I applied for training at the Rehabilitation Center for the Blind and Visually Impaired in Nîmes and eventually was admitted for

Océane came along on return visits

three months. It was time well spent. I came to understand the extent of my handicap and learned to adapt to it. Mixing with people who suffered from all kinds of infirmities helped me to realize how precious my Christian hope is. I at least had a goal and could do something productive. In addition, I learned French Braille.

When I returned home, my family noticed how much the training had helped me. One thing, though, that I really did not like was the white cane I had to use. I had a hard time coming to terms with that "stick." It would be nice to have another aid—perhaps a guide dog.

I filed a request for a dog but was told that there was a long waiting list. Also, the agency would have to conduct an investigation. A guide dog is not given to just anybody. One day a woman who helps run an association for the blind told me that a local tennis club was going to donate a guide dog to a blind or partially sighted person living in our area. She said that she had thought of me. Would I accept? I discerned Jehovah's hand in the matter and accepted the kind offer. Nevertheless, I had to wait for the dog.

Still Thinking About Africa

While waiting, I turned my attention in another direction. As mentioned earlier, since childhood I have had a deep interest in

Africa. Despite my deteriorating eyesight, that interest was stronger than ever, especially since I had learned that so many people in Africa are interested in the Bible and in serving Jehovah. Some time earlier, I had casually mentioned to Valérie that I would like to go to Africa for a visit. Would she like to come with me? She agreed, and we wrote to several French-speaking branches of Jehovah's Witnesses in Africa.

A reply came from Togo. Thrilled, I asked Valérie to read it to me. The letter was encouraging, so Valérie said: "Well, why not?" After corresponding with the brothers at the branch, I was put in touch with Sandra, a pioneer in Lomé, the capital city. We set our departure date for December 1, 1998.

What a contrast, but what a delight! After landing in Lomé, we exited the plane and felt the African heat engulf us like a blanket. Sandra met us. We had never seen one another before, but right away we felt like old friends. Shortly before our arrival, Sandra and her partner, Christine, had been appointed as special pioneers in Tabligbo, a small town in the interior. We now had the privilege of accompanying them to their new assignment. We stayed about two months, and when we left, I knew that I would return.

A Delight to Be Back

In France, I immediately began preparing for my second trip to Togo. With my family's support, I was able to make arrangements to stay there for six months. So in September 1999, I was again on a plane bound for Togo. This time, however, I was alone. Imagine the feelings of my family when they saw me leave on my own in spite of my disability! But there was no reason to worry. I assured my parents that my friends, who had already become like family to me, would be waiting for me in Lomé.

What a delight it was to be back in an area where so many people show an interest in the Bible! It is not unusual to see people reading the Bible on the street. In Tabligbo people call you over just to have a Bible discussion. And what a privilege it was to share modest accommodations with two special pioneer sisters! I came to know another culture, a different way of looking at things. First and foremost, I noticed that our Christian brothers and sisters in Africa put Kingdom interests first in their lives. For example, having to walk many miles to the Kingdom Hall does not prevent them from attending meetings. I also learned many lessons from their warmth and hospitality.

One day when returning from field service, I confided to Sandra that I was afraid of returning to France. My eyesight had deteriorated further. I thought of the crowded and noisy streets in Béziers, of the stairs in apartment buildings, and of so many other things

The elders agreed that I should bring Océane to meetings

that make life difficult for someone with limited vision. In contrast, the streets in Tabligbo, although not paved, were quiet—no large crowds and not much traffic. How would I manage in France now that I was used to Tabligbo?

Two days later my mother called to let me know that the school for guide dogs was waiting for me. A young Labrador retriever named Océane was ready to become my "eyes." Once again, my needs were cared for and my anxieties dispelled. After six months of happy service in Tabligbo, I was on my way back to France to meet Océane.

After several months of training, Océane was entrusted to my care. Initially, it was not easy. We had to learn to understand each other. Gradually, though, I came to realize how much I needed Océane. In reality, Océane is now a part of me. How did people in Béziers react when they saw me coming to their door with a dog? I met with much respect and kindness. Océane became the "hero" of the neighborhood. Since many people are uncomfortable in the presence of a disabled person, having the dog enabled me to speak of my infirmity in a natural way. People relaxed and listened to me. Indeed, Océane became the best possible conversation opener.

In Africa With Océane

I had not forgotten Africa, and I now set about preparing for my third journey. This time, Océane came along. I was also accompanied by a young couple, Anthony and Aurore, and my friend Caroline—all pioneers like me. On September 10, 2000, we arrived in Lomé.

At first, many were afraid of Océane. Few people in Lomé had ever seen such a big dog, since most dogs in Togo are small. When they saw her harness, some thought that she was a vicious animal that needed to be restrained. For her part, Océane adopted a defensive attitude, ready to protect me against anything she perceived as a threat. Still, Océane soon felt at home in the new environment. When she wears the harness, she is on the job—disciplined, responsible, staying by my side. When she is released, she is playful, sometimes naughty. We have a lot of fun together.

All of us were invited to stay with Sandra and Christine in Tabligbo. To help the local brothers and sisters get used to Océane, we invited them to visit us and explained the role of a guide dog, why I needed one, and how they should act around her. The elders agreed that Océane should come along with me to the Kingdom Hall. Since this arrangement was so unusual in Togo, an announcement explaining the matter was made to the congregation. As for the ministry, Océane came along only when I was making return visits and conducting Bible studies—situations where her presence would be more easily understood.

Preaching in this territory continues to be delightful. I was always touched by the thoughtfulness of the gentle people, demonstrated by kind actions, such as their eagerness to provide me with a chair. In October 2001, my mother came with me on my fourth trip to Togo. After three weeks she returned to France, reassured and happy.

I am deeply grateful to Jehovah that I have been able to serve in Togo. I am confident that Jehovah will continue to give me 'the requests of my heart' as I continue to use all I have in his service.*

---

* Sister Morgou returned to France and was able to make a fifth trip to Togo from October 6, 2003, to February 6, 2004. Sadly, because of medical complications, that trip might be her last to Togo in this system of things. Nevertheless, her strongest desire continues to be to serve Jehovah.

THE
RANSOM
Magnifies God's Righteousness

AFTER the rebellion of Adam and Eve, Jehovah stated his purpose to raise up a Seed who would be bruised in the heel. (Genesis 3:15) This was fulfilled when God's enemies caused Jesus Christ's death on a torture stake. (Galatians 3:13, 16) Jesus was without sin, being miraculously conceived in the womb of a virgin by the power of holy spirit. Therefore, his shed blood could be used as the ransom price to free humans, who inherited sin and death from Adam.—Romans 5:12, 19.

Nothing can stop the almighty God, Jehovah, from fulfilling what he purposes. Thus, after man's fall into sin, the ransom price was as good as paid from Jehovah's viewpoint and he could have dealings with those who exercised faith in the fulfillment of his promises. This enabled sinful descendants of Adam, such as Enoch, Noah, and Abraham, to walk with and even be befriended by God without tarnishing his holiness.—Genesis 5:24; 6:9; James 2:23.

Some individuals who had faith in Jehovah committed serious sins. King David is one example. 'How,' you may ask, 'could Jehovah continue to bless King David after David committed adultery with Bath-sheba and then caused the death of her husband, Uriah?' An important factor was David's genuine repentance and faith. (2 Samuel 11:1-17; 12:1-14) Based on the future sacrifice of Jesus Christ, God could pardon the sins of the repentant David and yet maintain His own justice and righteousness. (Psalm 32:1, 2) In proof of this, the Bible explains what the most wonderful accomplishment of Jesus' ransom is, namely "to exhibit [God's] own righteousness, because he was forgiving the sins that occurred in the past" and "in this present season."—Romans 3:25, 26.

Yes, great benefits flow to mankind because of the value of Jesus' blood. On the basis of the ransom, repentant human sinners can enjoy a close relationship with God. In addition, the ransom opens the way for a resurrection of the dead into God's new world. That will include faithful servants of God who died before Jesus paid the ransom and even many who died in ignorance and did not worship Him. The Bible says: "There is going to be a resurrection of both the righteous and the unrighteous." (Acts 24:15) At that time, based on the ransom, Jehovah will grant all obedient humans everlasting life. (John 3:36) Jesus himself explained: "God loved the world so much that he gave his only-begotten Son, in order that everyone exercising faith in him might not be destroyed but have *everlasting life*." (John 3:16) All these benefits will flow to mankind because of God's provision of the ransom sacrifice.

The outstanding thing about the ransom, however, is not the benefits that we receive from it. Of greater importance is what Christ's ransom does for Jehovah's name. It proves that Jehovah is a God of perfect justice who can deal with sinful humans and still remain pure and holy. If God had not purposed to provide the ransom, no descendant of Adam, not even Enoch, Noah, and Abraham, could have walked with Jehovah or been his friend. The psalmist realized this and wrote: "If errors were what you watch, O Jah, O Jehovah, who could stand?" (Psalm 130:3) How thankful we should be both to Jehovah for sending his beloved Son to earth and to Jesus for willingly giving his life as a ransom for us!—Mark 10:45.

Good Conduct Bears Fruit

ON A small island off the coast of southern Japan, a mother and her three young children began to study the Bible with Jehovah's Witnesses. Seeing this, the neighbors in that isolated and very conservative area began to ignore the mother whenever they saw her. "What hurt more than their ignoring me was that they gave my husband and children the cold shoulder," she relates. Nevertheless, she told her children: "We must continue to greet our neighbors for Jehovah's sake."—Matthew 5:47, 48.

At home, she taught her children to be polite despite rejection. On the way to their regular visits to the local hot springs, the children practiced their greetings in the car. Upon entering the building, the children always called out cheerily, *"Konnichiwa!"*—"Good day!" The family patiently continued to greet all whom they met, even though the neighbors' re-

sponse remained chilly. Still, people could not help but notice the children's good manners.

Finally, one neighbor and then another responded with *"Konnichiwa."* At the end of two years, almost everyone in town was returning the family's greetings. They had also begun greeting one another and had become friendlier. The deputy mayor wanted to honor the children for their role in this change. But their mother assured him that they were only doing what Christians should do. Later, in an island-wide speech contest, one son related how his mother had trained the family to greet others politely regardless of the reaction. His talk won first prize and was printed in the town newspaper. Today, the family is very happy that following Christian principles produced such good results. Sharing the good news with others is much easier when people are friendly.

"One of the Best Days of My Life"

"DEPRESSION is the most frequently reported, and arguably the most important mental health problem for young people," claims Beyondblue, a government-funded agency in Australia. Studies reveal that about 100,000 young Australians suffer from depression each year.

Young Christians are not immune to depression. Faith in Jehovah, however, has helped many of them to overcome negative feelings and to make a success of their youth. In doing so, they make a fine impression on others. How?

Consider the experience of 18-year-old Claire. She and her mother attend a congregation of Jehovah's Witnesses in Melbourne. When Claire's father abandoned the family, she became depressed. But her faith in her heavenly Father, Jehovah, remained strong. One day, the family doctor, Lydia, called at Claire's home to check up on Claire's mother, who was ill. Afterward, she kindly offered to drive Claire to the shopping center. Along the way, she asked Claire whether she had a boyfriend. Claire explained that as one of Jehovah's Witnesses, she did not casually date boys. This surprised the doctor. Claire then explained how the Bible had helped her to make wise decisions in life. Finally, she offered to bring the doctor a copy of a Bible-based publication that had greatly helped Claire. The book was entitled *Questions Young People Ask—Answers That Work.*

Three days after receiving the book, Lydia telephoned Claire's mother to say how much she had enjoyed reading it. She then requested six more books for her colleagues. When Claire delivered the books, the doctor explained how impressed she was by Claire's faith. Claire offered to study the Bible with her, and the doctor accepted.

For several months, Claire conducted the study during the doctor's lunch break. Then Lydia asked Claire if she would speak at a seminar on the subject of depression in youths. Although apprehensive, Claire agreed. Over 60 people attended the seminar. Four mental-health professionals—all adults—addressed the audience. Then it was Claire's turn to speak. She highlighted how important it is for young people to have a relationship with God. She explained that Jehovah God cares deeply for young people and helps all those who turn to him for support and comfort. Additionally, she expressed her conviction that Jehovah will soon do away with all forms of physical and mental illness. (Isaiah 33:24) What resulted from this fine witness?

"Many came up to me after the session to say how impressed they were to hear a young person talk about God," said Claire. "I placed 23 copies of the *Young People Ask* book. Three girls in the audience gave me their telephone numbers. One of these girls is now studying the Bible. It was one of the best days of my life."

JEHOVAH IS OUR SHEPHERD

"Jehovah is my Shepherd. I shall lack nothing."
—PSALM 23:1.

IF YOU were asked to describe the way Jehovah cares for his people, what would you say? What comparison could you draw that would convey the tender care that he gives his faithful servants? Over 3,000 years ago, the royal psalmist David put in writing a beautiful description of Jehovah, using an analogy drawn from the occupation of David's early life.

2 As a young man, David had been a shepherd, so he knew about caring for sheep. He was well-aware that sheep, if left to themselves, easily get lost and become prey for robbers or wild beasts. (1 Samuel 17:34-36) Without a caring shepherd, they may not find their pasture and their food. In his later years, David no doubt had fond memories of the many hours he had spent leading, protecting, and feeding sheep.

3 It is not surprising that the work of a shepherd came to mind when David was inspired to describe the care that Jehovah shows for his people. The 23rd Psalm, penned by David, begins with the words: "Jehovah is my Shepherd. I shall lack nothing." Let us consider why this is a fitting statement. Then, with the help of Psalm 23, we will see in what ways Jehovah cares for his worshippers as a shepherd cares for his sheep. —1 Peter 2:25.

A Fitting Comparison

4 Jehovah bears many titles in the Scriptures, but the designation "Shepherd" is among the most tender. (Psalm 80:1) To understand better why Jehovah is fittingly called a Shepherd, it is helpful for us to know two things: first, the disposition of sheep and second, the duties and qualities of a good shepherd.

5 The Bible often alludes to the traits of sheep, describing them as readily responding to a shepherd's affection (2 Samuel 12:3), unaggressive (Isaiah 53:7), and defenseless. (Micah 5:8) One writer who raised sheep for a number of years noted: "Sheep do not 'just take care of themselves' as some might suppose. They require, more

1-3. Why is it not surprising that David compared Jehovah to a shepherd?

4, 5. How does the Bible describe the traits of sheep?

than any other class of livestock, endless attention and meticulous care." To survive, these helpless creatures need a caring shepherd.—Ezekiel 34:5.

⁶ What was a typical day like for the ancient shepherd? One Bible dictionary explains: "In early morning he led forth the flock from the fold, marching at its head to the spot where they were to be pastured. Here he watched them all day, taking care that none of the sheep strayed, and if any for a time eluded his watch and wandered away from the rest, seeking diligently till he found and brought it back. . . . At night he brought the flock home to the fold, counting them as they passed under the rod at the door to assure himself that none were missing. . . . Often he had to guard the fold through the dark hours from the attack of wild beasts, or the wily attempts of the prowling thief."*

⁷ There were times when sheep, especially the pregnant ewes and the young, required extra patience and tenderness. (Genesis 33: 13) One Bible reference work states: "The birth of offspring in a flock often occurs far off on the mountain side. The shepherd solicitously guards the mother during her helpless moments and picks up the lamb and carries it to the fold. For the few days, until it is able to walk, he may carry it in his arms or in the loose folds of his coat." (Isaiah 40:10, 11) Clearly, a good shepherd needed a blend of strong and tender qualities.

⁸ "Jehovah is my Shepherd"—is that not a

---

* See Genesis 29:7; Job 30:1; Jeremiah 33:13; Luke 15:4; John 10:3, 4.

6. How does one Bible dictionary explain a typical day in the life of an ancient shepherd?
7. Why did a shepherd at times need to show extra patience and tenderness?
8. David cites what reasons for his confidence in Jehovah?

fitting description of our heavenly Father? As we examine Psalm 23, we will see how God cares for us with the strength and tenderness of a shepherd. In verse 1, David expresses his confidence that God will make all necessary provisions for His sheep so that they will "lack nothing." In the verses that follow, David cites three reasons for this confidence: Jehovah leads, protects, and feeds His sheep. Let us discuss these one at a time.

"He Leads Me"

⁹ First, Jehovah *leads* his people. David writes: "In grassy pastures he makes me lie down; by well-watered resting-places he conducts me. My soul he refreshes. He leads me in the tracks of righteousness for his name's sake." (Psalm 23:2, 3) A flock lying down peacefully in the midst of abundance —David here paints a scene of contentment, refreshment, and security. The Hebrew word rendered "pastures" can mean "pleasant place." Likely, on their own, the sheep would not find a refreshing spot to lie down in peace. Their shepherd must lead them to such a "pleasant place."

¹⁰ How does Jehovah lead us today? One way he does so is by example. His Word urges us to "become imitators of God." (Ephesians 5:1) The context of those words mentions compassion, forgiveness, and love. (Ephesians 4:32; 5:2) Certainly, Jehovah sets the finest example in displaying such warm qualities. Is he being unrealistic in asking us to imitate him? No. That inspired counsel is actually a marvelous expression of his confidence in us. In what way? We are made in God's image, meaning that we are endowed with moral qualities

---

9. What peaceful scene does David describe, and how would sheep come to be in such a setting?
10. How does God show his confidence in us?

and the capacity for spirituality. (Genesis 1: 26) Hence, Jehovah knows that despite our imperfections, we have within us the potential for cultivating the same qualities that he exemplifies. Just think—our loving God is confident that we can be like him. If we follow his example, he will lead us, as it were, to a pleasant 'resting-place.' In the midst of this violent world, we will "dwell in security," experiencing the peace that comes from knowing that we have God's approval.—Psalm 4:8; 29:11.

[11] In leading us, Jehovah is tender and patient. A shepherd considers the limitations of his sheep, so he leads "according to the pace of the livestock." (Genesis 33:14) Jehovah likewise leads "according to the pace of" his sheep. He considers our abilities and circumstances. In effect, he adjusts the pace, never asking more than we can give. What he does ask is that we be whole-souled. (Colossians 3:23) But what if you are older and cannot do what you used to? Or what if you have a serious illness that limits you? Therein lies the beauty of the requirement that we be whole-souled. No two souls are exactly alike. Serving whole-souled means using all your strength and energy to the fullest extent possible *for you* in God's service. Despite the frailties that may affect our pace, Jehovah values our wholehearted worship. —Mark 12:29, 30.

[12] To illustrate that Jehovah leads "according to the pace of" his sheep, consider what is said about certain guilt offerings in the Mosaic Law. Jehovah wanted fine offerings that were prompted by grateful hearts. At the same time, the offerings were graded according to the offerer's ability. The Law said: "If . . . he cannot afford enough for a sheep, then he must bring . . . two turtledoves or two young pigeons." And if he could not afford even two pigeons? Then he could bring some "fine flour." (Leviticus 5:7, 11) This shows that God did not demand what was beyond the offerer's reach. Since God does not change, we can find comfort in knowing that he never asks more than we can give; rather, he is pleased to accept what is within our reach. (Malachi 3:6) What a pleasure it is to be led by such an understanding Shepherd!

"I Fear Nothing Bad, for You Are With Me"

[13] David gives a second reason for his confidence: Jehovah *protects* his sheep. We read: "Even though I walk in the valley of deep shadow, I fear nothing bad, for you are with me; your rod and your staff are the things that comfort me." (Psalm 23:4) David now speaks more intimately, addressing Jeho-

---

11. In leading his sheep, what does Jehovah consider, and how is this reflected in what he asks of us?

12. What example from the Mosaic Law illustrates that Jehovah leads "according to the pace of" his sheep?

13. At Psalm 23:4, how does David speak more intimately, and why is this not surprising?

Like a shepherd in Israel, Jehovah leads His sheep

vah with the pronoun "you." This is not surprising, for David is talking about how God helped him to endure adversity. David had been through many dark valleys—times when his very life was in danger. But he did not allow fear to dominate him, for he sensed that God—with His "rod" and "staff" at the ready—was with him. This awareness of protection comforted David and no doubt drew him closer to Jehovah.*

14 How does Jehovah protect his sheep today? The Bible assures us that no opposers —demon or human—will ever succeed in eliminating his sheep from the earth. Jehovah would never allow that. (Isaiah 54:17; 2 Peter 2:9) However, this does not mean that our Shepherd will shield us from all calamity. We experience the trials that are common to humans, and we face the opposition that befalls all true Christians. (2 Timothy 3:12; James 1:2) There are times when we may, so to speak, "walk in the valley of deep shadow." For example, we may come close to death as a result of persecution or some health crisis. Or it may be that someone dear to us comes close to or even succumbs to death. During what seem to be the darkest moments, our Shepherd is with us, and he will safeguard us. How?

15 Jehovah does not promise miraculous intervention.# But of this we can be sure: Jehovah will help us to get through whatever

obstacles we may face. He can grant us the wisdom to cope "with various trials." (James 1:2-5) A shepherd uses his rod or staff not only to ward off predators but also to nudge his sheep in the right direction. Jehovah can "nudge" us, perhaps by means of a fellow worshipper, to apply Bible-based counsel that may make a big difference in our situation. In addition, Jehovah can give us the strength to endure. (Philippians 4:13) By means of his holy spirit, he can equip us with "power beyond what is normal." (2 Corinthians 4:7) God's spirit can enable us to endure any test that Satan might bring upon us. (1 Corinthians 10:13) Is it not comforting to know that Jehovah is ever ready to help us?

16 Yes, no matter what dark valley we may find ourselves in, we do not have to walk through it alone. Our Shepherd is with us, helping us in ways that we may not fully perceive at first. Consider the experience of a Christian elder who was diagnosed with a malignant brain tumor. "I must admit that at first I found myself wondering if Jehovah was angry at me or even if he loved me. But I was determined not to pull away from Jehovah. Instead, I voiced my concerns to him. And Jehovah helped me, often comforting me through my brothers and sisters. Many shared helpful insights based on their own experience of coping with serious illness. Their balanced comments reminded me that there was nothing unusual about what I was going through. Practical assistance, including some touching offers of kindness, reassured me that Jehovah was not displeased with me. Of course, I must continue to battle my illness, and I do not know what the outcome will be. But I am convinced that Jehovah is with me and that he will continue to help me through this trial."

---

* David composed a number of psalms in which he praised Jehovah for delivering him out of danger.—See, for example, the superscriptions of Psalms 18, 34, 56, 57, 59, and 63.

See the article "Divine Intervention—What Can We Expect?" in the October 1, 2003, issue of The Watchtower.

---

14. What assurance does the Bible give us regarding Jehovah's protection, but what does this not mean? 15, 16. (a) In what ways does Jehovah help us to handle the obstacles we may face? (b) Relate an experience to show how Jehovah helps us in times of trial.

"You Arrange Before Me a Table"

[17] David now cites a third reason for his confidence in his Shepherd: Jehovah *feeds* his sheep, and he does so in abundance. David writes: "You arrange before me a table in front of those showing hostility to me. With oil you have greased my head; my cup is well filled." (Psalm 23:5) In this verse, David describes his Shepherd as a generous host who provides food and drink in abundance. The two illustrations—a caring shepherd and a generous host—are not at odds. After all, a good shepherd must know where to find rich pasture grounds and sufficient drinking water so that his flock will "lack nothing." —Psalm 23:1, 2.

[18] Is our Shepherd also a generous host? There is no question about that! Just think of the quality, quantity, and variety of spiritual food that we now enjoy. Through the faithful and discreet slave class, Jehovah has provided us with helpful publications and rich programs at meetings, assemblies, and conventions—all of which fill our spiritual needs. (Matthew 24:45-47) There is certainly no shortage of spiritual food. "The faithful and discreet slave" has produced millions of

---

17. How does David describe Jehovah at Psalm 23:5, and why is this not at odds with the illustration of a shepherd?
18. What shows that Jehovah is a generous host?

Do You Recall?

- Why is it fitting that David compared Jehovah to a shepherd?

- How does Jehovah lead us with understanding?

- In what ways does Jehovah help us to endure trials?

- What shows that Jehovah is a generous host?

Bibles and Bible study aids, and such publications are now available in 413 languages. Jehovah has provided this spiritual food in great variety—from "milk," basic Bible teachings, to "solid food," deeper spiritual information. (Hebrews 5:11-14) As a result, when we face problems or decisions, we can usually find just what we need. Where would we be without such spiritual food? Our Shepherd is truly a most generous provider!—Isaiah 25:6; 65:13.

"I Will Dwell in the House of Jehovah"

[19] After contemplating the ways of his Shepherd and Provider, David concludes: "Surely goodness and loving-kindness themselves will pursue me all the days of my life; and I will dwell in the house of Jehovah to the length of days." (Psalm 23:6) David speaks from a heart filled with gratitude and faith—gratitude in recalling the past and faith in looking to the future. This former shepherd is secure, knowing that as long as he stays close to his heavenly Shepherd, as if dwelling in His house, he will always be the object of Jehovah's loving care.

[20] How thankful we are for the beautiful words recorded in the 23rd Psalm! David could hardly have found a more fitting way to describe how Jehovah leads, protects, and feeds his sheep. David's warm expressions have been preserved to give us confidence that we too can look to Jehovah as our Shepherd. Yes, as long as we stay close to Jehovah, he will care for us as a loving Shepherd "to the length of days," even to all eternity. However, as his sheep, we have the responsibility to walk with our great Shepherd, Jehovah. What this involves will be discussed in the next article.

19, 20. (a) At Psalm 23:6, what confidence does David express, and how may we share that confidence? (b) What will be discussed in the next article?

WILL YOU
WALK WITH GOD?

"Be modest in walking with your God."
—MICAH 6:8.

A BABY, standing on wobbly legs, reaches toward a parent's outstretched arms and takes its first few steps. It may seem a small thing, but to the mother and father, it is a milestone, a moment full of promise for the future. The parents eagerly look forward to walking with their child, hand in hand, in the months and years to come. In many ways, they hope to provide the child with guidance and support far into the future.

2 Jehovah God has similar feelings toward his earthly children. He once said regarding his people Israel, or Ephraim: "I taught Ephraim to walk, taking them upon my arms . . . With the ropes of earthling man I kept drawing them, with the cords of love." (Hosea 11:3, 4) Jehovah here describes himself as a loving parent who is patiently teaching a child to walk, perhaps taking him into His arms when he falls. Jehovah, the ultimate Parent, is eager to teach us how to walk. He also delights in accompanying us as we continue to make progress. As our theme text shows, we can walk with God! (Micah 6:8) But what does it mean to walk with God? Why do we need to do so? How is it possible? And what blessings come from walking with God? Let us consider these four questions one at a time.

What Does It Mean to Walk With God?

3 Of course, a flesh-and-blood human cannot literally take a walk with Jehovah, a spirit being. (Exodus 33:20; John 4:24) So when the Bible speaks of humans walking with God, it uses figurative language. It paints a remarkable word picture, one that rises above national and cultural boundaries and that even transcends time. After all, in what place or era would people be unable to grasp the concept of one person walking in company with another? This word picture conveys warmth and closeness, does it not? Such feelings give us some insight into what it means to walk with God. Let us be more specific, though.

4 Remember the faithful men Enoch and Noah. Why are they described as walking

---

1, 2. How might Jehovah's feelings toward us be compared to those of a parent teaching a child to walk?

3, 4. (a) What is remarkable about the word picture of walking with God? (b) What does it mean to walk with God?

with God? (Genesis 5:24; 6:9) In the Bible, the term "to walk" often means to follow a certain course of action. Enoch and Noah chose a course in life that was in harmony with the will of Jehovah God. Unlike those in the world around them, they looked to Jehovah for guidance and obeyed his direction. They trusted in him. Does this mean that Jehovah made their decisions for them? No. Jehovah has given humans free will, and he wants us to use that gift along with our own "power of reason." (Romans 12:1) As we make decisions, however, we humbly allow our power of reason to be guided by Jehovah's infinitely superior mind. (Proverbs 3: 5, 6; Isaiah 55:8, 9) In effect, as we walk through life, we take that journey in close company with Jehovah.

5 The Bible often likens life to a journey or a walk. In some cases, that comparison is direct, but in other cases, it is implied. For instance, Jesus said: "Who of you by being anxious can add one cubit to his life span?" (Matthew 6:27) Something about those words may strike you as puzzling. Why would Jesus speak of adding "one cubit," which is a measure of distance, to a person's "life span," which is measured in terms of time?* Jesus was evidently picturing life as a journey. In effect, he taught that worrying will not help you to add even a small step to the walk of your life. Should we conclude, though, that there is nothing we can do about the length of that walk? Far from it! That brings us to our second question, Why do we need to walk with God?

---

* Some Bible translations change the "cubit" in this verse to a measurement of time, as in "one moment" (*The Emphatic Diaglott*) or "a single minute" (*A Translation in the Language of the People,* by Charles B. Williams). However, the word used in the original text definitely means a cubit, which was about 18 inches in length.

---

5. Why did Jesus speak of adding a cubit to one's life span?

Why Do We Need to Walk With God?

6 One reason why we need to walk with Jehovah God is explained at Jeremiah 10:23: "I well know, O Jehovah, that to earthling man his way does not belong. It does not belong to man who is walking even to direct his step." So we humans have neither the ability nor the right to direct our own life course. We are in desperate need of guidance. Those who insist on going their own way, independent of God, make the same mistake that Adam and Eve made. The first pair assumed the right to determine for themselves what is good and what is bad. (Genesis 3:1-6) That right simply "does not *belong"* to us.

7 Do you not feel the need for guidance on life's journey? Every day, we face decisions small and great. Some of these are difficult and can affect our future—as well as that of our loved ones. Just think, though, that someone infinitely older and wiser than we are is happy to give us loving guidance in making those decisions! Sadly, most people today prefer to trust their own judgment and guide their own steps. They ignore the truth stated at Proverbs 28:26: "He that is trusting in his own heart is stupid, but he that is walking in wisdom is the one that will escape." Jehovah wants us to escape the disasters that result from trusting the treacherous human heart. (Jeremiah 17:9) He wants us to walk in wisdom, to trust in him as our wise Guide and Instructor. When we do, our walk in life is secure, satisfying, and fulfilling.

8 Another reason why we need to walk with God involves the length of the walk we want to take. The Bible states a grim truth. In a sense, all imperfect humans are walking toward the same destination. In describing the

---

6, 7. Imperfect humans have what desperate need, and why do we do well to turn to Jehovah to fill that need?
8. Sin and imperfection naturally lead humans to what destination, yet what does Jehovah want for us?

trials that come with old age, Ecclesiastes 12:5 says: "Man is walking to his long-lasting house and the wailers have marched around in the street." What is this "long-lasting house"? The grave, where sin and imperfection naturally take us. (Romans 6:23) However, Jehovah wants more for us than a short, troubled walk from cradle to grave. (Job 14:1) Only by walking with God can we hope to walk for as long as we were meant to walk —forever. Is that not what you want? Clearly, then, you need to walk with your Father.

How Can We Walk With God?

⁹ The third question in our consideration deserves our most careful attention. It is, How can we walk with God? We find the answer at Isaiah 30:20, 21: "Your Grand Instructor will no longer hide himself, and your eyes must become eyes seeing your Grand Instructor. And your own ears will hear a word behind you saying: 'This is the way. Walk in it, you people,' in case you people should go to the right or in case you should go to the left." In this encouraging passage, Jehovah's words recorded in verse 20 may have reminded his people that when they rebelled against him, he was, in effect, hidden from them. (Isaiah 1:15; 59:2) Here, though, Jehovah is

represented, not as hiding, but as standing openly before his faithful people. We might think of an instructor standing before his students, demonstrating what he wants them to learn.

¹⁰ In verse 21, a different word picture is painted. Jehovah is depicted as walking behind his people, issuing directions on the right way to walk. Bible scholars have noted that this expression might be based on the way a shepherd sometimes follows his sheep, calling out to guide them and to keep them from going the wrong way. How does this word picture apply to us? Well, when we turn to God's Word for guidance, we are reading words that were recorded thousands of years ago. They are coming from behind us, as it were, in the stream of time. Yet, they are just as relevant today as they were the day they were written. Bible counsel can guide us in our day-to-day decisions, and it can help us to map out the course of our life over the years to come. (Psalm 119:105) When we earnestly seek out such counsel and apply it, then Jehovah is our Guide. We are walking with God.

¹¹ Are we really allowing God's Word to

---

9. Why was Jehovah at times hidden from his people, yet what assurance did he provide according to Isaiah 30:20?

10. In what sense may you "hear a word behind you" from your Grand Instructor?

11. According to Jeremiah 6:16, Jehovah painted what inviting word picture for his people, but how did they respond?

Through the pages of the Bible, we hear Jehovah's voice behind us say, "This is the way"

guide us that closely? It is worthwhile to pause at times and examine ourselves honestly. Consider a verse that will help us to do so: "This is what Jehovah has said: 'Stand still in the ways, you people, and see, and ask for the roadways of long ago, where, now, the good way is; and walk in it, and find ease for your souls.'" (Jeremiah 6:16) These words might remind us of a traveler who pauses at a crossroads to ask for directions. In a spiritual sense, Jehovah's rebellious people in Israel needed to do something similar. They needed to find their way back to "the roadways of long ago." That "good way" was the way in which their faithful forefathers had walked, the way from which the nation had foolishly strayed. Sadly, Israel responded stubbornly to this loving reminder from Jehovah. The same verse continues: "But they kept saying: 'We are not going to walk.'" In modern times, though, God's people have responded differently to such counsel.

¹² Since late in the 19th century, Christ's anointed followers have applied the counsel of Jeremiah 6:16 to themselves. As a class, they have led the way in a wholehearted return to "the roadways of long ago." Unlike apostate Christendom, they have faithfully adhered to "the pattern of healthful words" that was established by Jesus Christ and up-

12, 13. (a) How have Christ's anointed followers responded to the counsel of Jeremiah 6:16? (b) How might we examine ourselves regarding the way we are walking today?

How Would You Answer?

- What does it mean to walk with God?
- Why do you feel a need to walk with God?
- What will help you to walk with God?
- What blessings come to those who walk with God?

---

held by his faithful followers back in the first century C.E. (2 Timothy 1:13) To this day, the anointed help one another as well as their "other sheep" companions to pursue the healthful, happy way of life that Christendom has abandoned.—John 10:16.

¹³ By providing spiritual food at the proper time, the faithful slave class has helped millions to find "the roadways of long ago" and to walk with God. (Matthew 24:45-47) Are you among those millions? If so, what can you do to avoid drifting away, turning to follow your own course? It is wise to stop periodically and examine the way you are walking in life. If you faithfully read the Bible and Bible-based publications and attend the programs of instruction sponsored by the anointed today, then you are being trained to walk with God. And when you humbly apply the counsel you are given, you are indeed walking with God, following "the roadways of long ago."

Walk as Though "Seeing the One Who Is Invisible"

¹⁴ For us to walk with Jehovah, he must be real to us. Remember, Jehovah assured faithful ones in ancient Israel that he was not hidden from them. Today, he likewise reveals himself to his people as the Grand Instructor. Is Jehovah that real to you, as though he were standing before you to instruct you? That is the kind of faith we need if we are to walk with God. Moses had such faith, "for he continued steadfast as seeing the One who is invisible." (Hebrews 11:27) If Jehovah is real to us, then we will take his feelings into account when we make decisions. For example, we would not even consider engaging in wrongdoing and then try to hide our sins from Christian elders or family members. Rather, we endeavor to walk with God even when no

14. If Jehovah is real to us, how will that be reflected in the personal decisions that we make?

At meetings, we receive spiritual food at the proper time

fellow human can see us. Like King David of old, we resolve: "I shall walk about in the integrity of my heart inside my house."—Psalm 101:2.

¹⁵ Jehovah understands that we are imperfect, fleshly creatures and that we may at times find it a challenge to believe in what we cannot see. (Psalm 103:14) He does much to help us overcome such weakness. For example, he has gathered together "a people for his name" from all the nations of the earth. (Acts 15:14) As we unitedly serve together, we draw strength from one another. Hearing how Jehovah has helped a spiritual brother or sister overcome some weakness or pass some difficult test makes our God even more real to us.—1 Peter 5:9.

¹⁶ Above all, Jehovah has given us the example of his Son. Jesus said: "I am the way and the truth and the life. No one comes to the Father except through me." (John 14:6) Studying Jesus' life course on earth is one of the best ways to make Jehovah more real to us. Everything that Jesus said or did was a perfect reflection of his heavenly Father's personality and ways. (John 14:9) As we make decisions, we need to think carefully about how Jesus would handle matters. When our decisions reflect such careful and prayerful thought, then we are following in Christ's footsteps. (1 Peter 2:21) As a result, we are walking with God.

What Blessings Result?

¹⁷ To walk with Jehovah God is to lead a blessed life. Remember what Jehovah promised his people about seeking out "the good way." He said: "Walk in it, and find ease for your souls." (Jeremiah 6:16) What does that "ease" mean? An easy life that is filled with pleasures and luxuries? No. Jehovah provides something far better, something that the wealthiest among mankind rarely find. To find ease for your soul is to find inner peace, joy, satisfaction, and spiritual fulfillment. Such ease means that you can be confident that you have chosen the best path in life. Such peace of mind is a rare blessing in this hard world!

¹⁸ Of course, life itself is a great blessing. Even a short walk is better than no walk at all. However, Jehovah never meant for your walk to consist of merely a brief trip from the vigor of youth to the pain of old age. No, Jehovah wants you to have the greatest blessing of all. He wants you to walk with him forever! This is well-expressed at Micah 4:5: "All the peoples, for their part, will walk each one in the name of its god; but we, for our part, shall walk in the name of Jehovah our God to time indefinite, even forever." Will you take hold of that blessing? Will you live what Jehovah invitingly calls "the real life"? (1 Timothy 6:19) By all means, then, make it your resolve to walk with Jehovah today, tomorrow, and every day thereafter on into eternity!

---

15. How will associating with our Christian brothers and sisters help us to see Jehovah as real?
16. How will learning about Jesus help us to walk with God?
17. If we walk in Jehovah's way, what "ease" will we find for our souls?

---

18. What blessing does Jehovah want to bestow upon you, and what is your resolve?

CONTRIBUTIONS
That Warm God's Heart

THE story is not a pretty one. Queen Athaliah had seized the throne of Judah by means of subterfuge and murder. Wrongly assuming that all the natural heirs had been slain, she installed herself as queen. Another woman, the princess Jehosheba, who dearly loved Jehovah and his Law, courageously hid a royal offspring, the baby Jehoash. Jehosheba and her husband, High Priest Jehoiada, concealed the heir for six years in their temple quarters. —2 Kings 11:1-3.

By the time Jehoash reached seven years of age, High Priest Jehoiada was ready to launch his plan to dislodge the usurping queen from her ill-gotten throne. He brought the boy out of hiding and crowned him rightful heir to the kingdom. Wicked Queen Athaliah was then hauled outside the temple grounds by the royal guards and executed, to the relief and joy of the people. By their actions, Jehoiada and Jehosheba contributed greatly to the restoration of true worship in the land of Judah. But more important, they contributed to the continuation of the royal line of David, which would lead to the Messiah. —2 Kings 11:4-21.

The newly installed king was also to make a contribution that would warm God's heart. The house of Jehovah was badly in need of repairs. Athaliah's unbridled ambition to be sole ruler of Judah resulted not only in the neglecting of the temple but also in the pillaging of it. So Jehoash set his heart on rebuilding and restoring the temple. Without delay, he issued an edict to gather needed funds for the rehabilitation of Jehovah's house. He said: "All the money for the holy offerings that is brought to the house of Jehovah, the money at which each one is assessed, the money for the souls according to individual valuation, all the money that it comes up on the heart of each one to bring to the house of Jehovah, let the priests take for themselves, each one from his acquaintance; and let them, for their part, repair the cracks of the house wherever any crack is found." —2 Kings 12:4, 5.

The people contributed willingly. The priests, however, were not wholehearted in fulfilling their duty to repair the temple. Hence, the king decided to take matters into his own hands and ordered that all contributions go directly into a special box. He put Jehoiada in charge, and the account states: "Jehoiada the priest now took a chest and bored a hole in its lid and put it beside the altar on the right as a person comes into the house of Jehovah, and there the priests, the doorkeepers, put all the money that was being brought into the house of Jehovah. And it came about that as soon as they saw that there was a great deal of money in the chest, the secretary of the king and the high priest would come up, and they would bind it up and count the money that was being found at the house of Jehovah. And they gave the money that had been counted off over to the hands of doers of the work that were appointed to the house of Jehovah. In turn they paid it out to the workers in wood and to the builders that were working at the house of Jehovah, and to the masons and to the hewers of stone, and to buy timbers and hewn stones for repairing the cracks of the house of Jehovah and for all that was expended upon the house to repair it." —2 Kings 12:9-12.

The people's response was wholehearted. Jehovah's house of worship was restored so that his worship could continue in a dignified manner. Thus, all contributed funds were used appropriately. King Jehoash made sure of that!

Today, Jehovah's visible organization watches carefully that all donated funds are properly used to advance the worship of Jehovah, and true Christians have responded as those ancient Israelites did—in a wholehearted way. Perhaps you are among those who contributed toward the furtherance of Kingdom interests during the past service year. Let us take note of some of the ways your contributions have been used.

PUBLISHING

Worldwide, the following publications were printed for study and distribution:

- Books: 47,490,247
- Booklets: 6,834,740
- Brochures: 167,854,462
- Calendars: 5,405,955
- Magazines: 1,179,266,348
- Tracts: 440,995,740
- Videos: 3,168,611

Printing is done in Africa, North, Central, and South America, Asia, Europe, and island nations of the Pacific—a total of 19 countries.

"My name is Katelyn May. I am eight years old. I have $28, and I would like you to have it to help pay for the printing presses. Your little sister, Katelyn."

"We had a family meeting about the new presses. Our children, ages 11 and 9, decided to take money from their savings and do their part. We are happy to send their contribution along with ours."

Faithful video: Stalin: U.S. Army photo

CONSTRUCTION

Following are some of the building projects undertaken to support the activities of Jehovah's Witnesses:

- Kingdom Halls in lands with limited resources: 2,180
- Assembly Halls: 15
- Branches: 10
- International volunteers in full-time service: 2,342

"This weekend we had the first meeting in our new Kingdom Hall. We are so happy to have a proper place to give praise to our Father, Jehovah God. We thank Jehovah and you for giving attention to our needs by building more Kingdom Halls. Indeed, our Kingdom Hall is a real asset to the neighborhood."—Chile.

"The brothers and sisters appreciate very much the help that is given by Jehovah's organization. To this day, we continue to talk about the wonderful time we spent with the construction crew."
—Moldova.

"My wife and I recently celebrated our 35th wedding anniversary. We were trying to decide what to get each other for the occasion, and we decided to give something back to Jehovah and his organization, for without their help, we probably wouldn't have succeeded in our marriage. We would like the money enclosed to be used in assisting in the building of a Kingdom Hall in one of the less privileged countries."

"I recently received an inheritance, and since my 'wants' are few and my 'needs' are even fewer, I would like you to have the money enclosed to help build Kingdom Halls, which are so badly needed in many countries."

Ways in Which Some Choose to Give

CONTRIBUTIONS TO THE WORLDWIDE WORK

Many set aside, or budget, an amount that they place in the contribution boxes labeled "Contributions for the Worldwide Work—Matthew 24:14."

Each month, congregations forward these amounts to the office of Jehovah's Witnesses that serves their respective countries. Voluntary donations of money may also be sent directly to **Watch Tower Bible and Tract Society of Pennsylvania, Attention Treasurer's Office, 25 Columbia Heights, Brooklyn, New York 11201-2483,** or to the branch office of Jehovah's Witnesses that serves your country. Checks sent to the above address should be made payable to "Watch Tower." Jewelry or other valuables may be donated as well. A brief letter stating that such is an outright gift should accompany these contributions.

CONDITIONAL-DONATION TRUST ARRANGEMENT

Money may be placed in trust with Watch Tower for use worldwide. However, upon request the funds will be returned. For more information, please contact the Treasurer's Office at the address noted above.

CHARITABLE PLANNING

In addition to outright gifts of money, there are other methods of giving to benefit Kingdom service worldwide. These include:

DISASTER RELIEF

In these last days, disasters often strike without warning. Many of Jehovah's Witnesses make extra contributions so that their brothers in stricken areas can be helped. As a reminder, contributions for disaster relief are administered as part of the worldwide work. Following are some of the places where Jehovah's Witnesses have helped disaster victims:

- Africa
- Asia
- Caribbean region
- Islands of the Pacific

"My husband and I would like to thank you very much for sending supplies for the relief efforts for the damage incurred during the hurricanes. We were able to put a new roof on our house. We truly appreciate that you responded so quickly."

"My name is Connor, and I am 11. When I saw what happened when the tsunami hit, I wanted to help. I hope this will help my brothers and sisters."

Insurance: Watch Tower may be named as the beneficiary of a life insurance policy or a retirement/pension plan.

Bank Accounts: Bank accounts, certificates of deposit, or individual retirement accounts may be placed in trust for or made payable on death to Watch Tower, in accord with local bank requirements.

Stocks and Bonds: Stocks and bonds may be donated to Watch Tower as an outright gift.

Real Estate: Salable real estate may be donated either by making an outright gift or, in the case of residential property, by reserving a life estate to the donor, who can continue to live therein during his or her lifetime. Contact the branch office in your country before deeding any real estate.

Gift Annuity: A gift annuity is an arrangement whereby one transfers money or securities to a designated corporation that is used by Jehovah's Witnesses. In exchange, the donor, or someone designated by the donor, receives a specified annuity payment every year for life. The donor receives an income-tax deduction for the year in which the gift annuity is established.

Wills and Trusts: Property or money may be bequeathed to Watch Tower by means of a legally executed will, or Watch Tower may be named as beneficiary of a trust agreement. A trust benefiting a religious organization may provide certain tax advantages.   ▶

SPECIAL FULL-TIME SERVANTS

A number of Christians serve in the evangelizing work or in Bethel homes full-time. Some full-time volunteers are supported by voluntary contributions. Among these are the following:

- Missionaries: 2,635
- Traveling overseers: 5,325
- Bethelites: 20,092

"Since I cannot go to serve at Bethel now [five-year-old boy], I want to send this contribution with much love. When I grow up, I am going to go to Bethel to work hard."

Promoting Bible Education

Jesus Christ commissioned his followers to "make disciples of people of all the nations." (Matthew 28:19) In obedience to his words, Jehovah's Witnesses are busy preaching and teaching the Bible's message in 235 lands. They publish and distribute Bible literature in 413 languages.

Indeed, the most valuable contribution a Christian can make to help more people learn about God and His purposes is his time. Jehovah's Witnesses have given of their time and strength in abundance to help their neighbors. They have also generously contributed in a financial way, and all their contributions, in one form or another, have helped to make Jehovah's name and purposes known throughout the earth. May Jehovah continue to bless these efforts to help others to learn more about him. (Proverbs 19:17) Such willingness to help warms Jehovah's heart!—Hebrews 13:15, 16.

As the term "charitable planning" implies, these types of donations typically require some planning on the part of the donor. To assist individuals desiring to benefit the worldwide work of Jehovah's Witnesses through some form of charitable planning, a brochure has been prepared in English and Spanish entitled **Charitable Planning to Benefit Kingdom Service Worldwide.** The brochure was written to provide information on a variety of ways that gifts may be made either now or through a bequest at death. After reading the brochure and conferring with their own legal or tax advisers, many have been able to help support the religious and humanitarian activities of Jehovah's Witnesses worldwide and maximize their tax benefits while doing so. This brochure may be obtained by requesting a copy directly from the Charitable Planning Office.

For more information, you may contact the Charitable Planning Office, either in writing or by telephone, at the address listed below or you may contact the branch office of Jehovah's Witnesses that serves your country.

Charitable Planning Office
Watch Tower Bible and Tract Society
  of Pennsylvania
100 Watchtower Drive
Patterson, New York 12563-9204
Telephone: (845) 306-0707

Questions From Readers

Can a Christian maintain a good conscience if he accepts employment that involves being armed?

Jehovah's Witnesses the world over take seriously their God-given responsibility to provide materially for their families. (1 Timothy 5:8) However, certain forms of employment are in clear violation of Bible principles and should be avoided. These include employment connected with gambling, the misuse of blood, and the promoting of tobacco products. (Isaiah 65:11; Acts 15:29; 2 Corinthians 7:1; Colossians 3:5) Other types of work, though not directly condemned in the Bible, could violate one's conscience or the conscience of others.

Engaging in secular work that requires carrying a firearm or another weapon is a personal decision. However, armed employment exposes one to the possibility of becoming bloodguilty if called upon to use one's weapon. Hence, a Christian needs to consider prayerfully whether he is willing to accept the burden of making a snap decision where human life is involved. Carrying a weapon also exposes a person to the danger of injury or death from an attack or reprisal.

Others may be affected by one's decision as well. For instance, a Christian's primary responsibility is preaching the good news of God's Kingdom. (Matthew 24:14) Would it be possible to teach others to "be peaceable with all men," while at the same time earning a living by carrying a weapon? (Romans 12:18) What about children or other family members? Would having a handgun in the house put their lives in danger? Moreover, could others be stumbled by one's stand on the matter?—Philippians 1:10.

In these "last days," more and more people are "fierce, without love of goodness." (2 Timothy 3:1, 3) Knowing this, could a person remain "free from accusation" were he to choose armed employment that might bring him into conflict with such individuals? (1 Timothy 3:10) Hardly. For this reason, the congregation would not regard such a person as "irreprehensible" if he continued to carry a weapon after being kindly given Bible counsel. (1 Timothy 3:2; Titus 1:5, 6) Thus, such a man or woman would not qualify for any special privileges in the congregation.

Jesus assured his disciples that if they put Kingdom interests first in their lives, they need not be overly concerned about having the necessities of life. (Matthew 6:25, 33) Indeed, if we place our full trust in Jehovah, "he himself will sustain [us]. Never will he allow the righteous one to totter."—Psalm 55:22.

IN OUR NEXT ISSUE

Is the Devil Real?

———

Wonders of Creation Exalt Jehovah

———

Hosea's Prophecy Helps Us to Walk With God

They Share Good News
With the Deaf

"THEY bring you spirituality!" That was how the director of a home for senior citizens in Navalcarnero, Madrid, Spain, recently described the visits of Jehovah's Witnesses to his center. What prompted him to say that?

Several of the residents of the Rosas del Camino center are deaf. However, since the Witnesses have made the effort to learn Spanish Sign Language, they can communicate with these residents. The director praised the Witnesses for freely offering their time to teach spiritual values to those in need. He observed the favorable effect the teaching of the good news of the Kingdom has had on the residents. And the residents—especially those with hearing or visual impediments—also greatly value the visits of the Witnesses.

Eulogio, one of the residents who is blind and deaf, is now studying the Bible with Jehovah's Witnesses. One day while the study was in progress, an elderly man approached and offered the Witness a poem that the residents had composed as a token of their gratitude. The poem was entitled "To Be a Witness." In part, it said: "They live a good, well-disciplined life, and from Jehovah they obtain joyful wisdom. They go back and forth to the houses because they trust in Jehovah."

It is precisely this trust in Jehovah that has led many Witnesses all over the world to learn the sign language of the deaf people in their country. In this way they share with such ones the encouraging message of hope found in the Bible.

NOVEMBER 15, 2005

THE WATCHTOWER
ANNOUNCING JEHOVAH'S KINGDOM

Is the
DEVIL
Real?

THE WATCHTOWER®
ANNOUNCING JEHOVAH'S KINGDOM

November 15, 2005   Average Printing Each Issue: 26,439,000   Vol. 126, No. 22

THE PURPOSE OF *THE WATCHTOWER* is to exalt Jehovah God as Sovereign Lord of the universe. It keeps watch on world events as these fulfill Bible prophecy. It comforts all peoples with the good news that God's Kingdom will soon destroy those who oppress their fellowmen and that it will turn the earth into a paradise. It encourages faith in God's now-reigning King, Jesus Christ, whose shed blood opens the way for mankind to gain eternal life. *The Watchtower,* published by Jehovah's Witnesses continuously since 1879, is nonpolitical. It adheres to the Bible as its authority.

IN THIS ISSUE

3   Is the Devil Real?

4   How Real Is the Devil to You?

8   Self-Sacrifice Brings Jehovah's Blessing

10   The Art of Listening With Love

13   Wonders of Creation Exalt Jehovah

17   Hosea's Prophecy Helps Us to Walk With God

22   Walk With God, and Reap What Is Good

27   "The Ways of Jehovah Are Upright"

32   'The Love of All of You Is Increasing'

WATCHTOWER STUDIES

DECEMBER 12-18:
Hosea's Prophecy Helps Us to Walk With God.
Page 17. Songs to be used: 85, 81.

DECEMBER 19-25:
Walk With God, and Reap What Is Good.
Page 22. Songs to be used: 135, 143.

DECEMBER 26–JANUARY 1:
"The Ways of Jehovah Are Upright."
Page 27. Songs to be used: 33, 148.

Publication of *The Watchtower* is part of a worldwide Bible educational work supported by voluntary donations.

Unless otherwise indicated, Scripture quotations are from the modern-language *New World Translation of the Holy Scriptures—With References.*

The Watchtower (ISSN 0043-1087) is published semimonthly by Watchtower Bible and Tract Society of New York, Inc.; M. H. Larson, President; G. F. Simonis, Secretary-Treasurer; 25 Columbia Heights, Brooklyn, NY 11201-2483. Periodicals Postage Paid at Brooklyn, NY, and at additional mailing offices. **POSTMASTER:** Send address changes to Watchtower, **Wallkill, NY 12589.**

Changes of address should reach us 30 days before your moving date. Give us your old and new address (if possible, your old address label).

© 2005 Watch Tower Bible and Tract Society of Pennsylvania. All rights reserved. Printed in U.S.A.

Semimonthly   ENGLISH

Would you welcome more information or a free home Bible study? Please send your request to Jehovah's Witnesses, using the appropriate address below.

America, United States of: Wallkill, NY 12589. *Antigua:* Box 119, St. Johns. *Australia:* Box 280, Ingleburn, NSW 1890. *Bahamas:* Box N-1247, Nassau, N.P. *Barbados, W.I.:* Crusher Site Road, Prospect, St. James. *Britain:* The Ridgeway, London NW7 1RN. *Canada:* Box 4100, Halton Hills (Georgetown), Ontario L7G 4Y4. *Germany:* Niederselters, Am Steinfels, D-65618 Selters. *Ghana:* P. O. Box GP 760, Accra. *Guyana:* 352-360 Tyrell St., Republic Park Phase 2 EBD. *Hawaii 96819:* 2055 Kam IV Rd., Honolulu. *Hong Kong:* 4 Kent Road, Kowloon Tong. *India:* Post Box 6440, Yelahanka, Bangalore 560 064, KAR. *Ireland:* Newcastle, Greystones, Co. Wicklow. *Jamaica:* P. O. Box 103, Old Harbour, St. Catherine. *Japan:* 1271 Nakashinden, Ebina City, Kanagawa Pref., 243-0496. *Kenya:* P.O. Box 47788, GPO Nairobi 00100. *New Zealand:* P.O. Box 75-142, Manurewa. *Nigeria:* P.M.B. 1090, Benin City 300001, Edo State. *Philippines, Republic of:* P. O. Box 2044, 1060 Manila. *South Africa:* Private Bag X2067, Krugersdorp, 1740. *Trinidad and Tobago, Republic of:* Lower Rapsey Street & Laxmi Lane, Curepe. *Zambia:* Box 33459, Lusaka 10101. *Zimbabwe:* Private Bag WG-5001, Westgate.

NOW PUBLISHED IN 151 LANGUAGES. SEMIMONTHLY: Afrikaans, Albanian,* Amharic, Arabic, Bengali, Bicol, Bislama, Bulgarian, Cebuano,* Chichewa,* Chinese, Chinese (Simplified),* Cibemba,* Croatian,* Czech,*# Danish,*# Dutch,*# East Armenian, Efik,* English*#+⊙ (also Braille), Estonian, Ewe, Fijian, Finnish,*# French*# (also Braille), Ga, Georgian,* German,*# Greek,* Gujarati, Gun, Hebrew, Hiligaynon, Hindi, Hungarian,*# Igbo,* Iloko,* Indonesian, Italian,*# Japanese*# (also Braille), Kannada, Kinyarwanda, Kirundi, Korean*# (also Braille), Latvian, Lingala, Lithuanian, Luvale, Macedonian, Malagasy,* Malayalam, Maltese, Myanmar, Nepali, Norwegian,*# Pangasinan, Papiamento (Aruba), Papiamento (Curaçao), Polish,*# Portuguese*# (also Braille), Punjabi, Rarotongan, Romanian,* Russian,* Samar-Leyte, Samoan, Sango, Sepedi, Serbian, Sesotho, Shona,* Silozi, Sinhala, Slovak,* Slovenian, Solomon Islands Pidgin, Spanish*# (also Braille), Sranantongo, Swahili,* Swedish,*# Tagalog,* Tamil, Telugu, Thai, Tigrinya, Tok Pisin, Tongan, Tshiluba, Tsonga, Tswana, Turkish, Twi, Ukrainian,* Urdu, Vietnamese, Wallisian, Xhosa, Yoruba,* Zulu*

MONTHLY: American Sign Language,△□ Armenian, Assamese, Azerbaijani (roman script), Brazilian Sign Language,△ Cambodian, Chitonga, Gilbertese, Greenlandic, Haitian Creole, Hausa, Hiri Motu, Icelandic, Isoko, Kaonde, Kazakh, Kikongo, Kiluba, Kirghiz, Kosraean, Kwanyama/Ndonga, Luganda, Marathi, Marshallese, Mauritian Creole, Maya, Mizo, Monokutuba, Moore, Niuean, Ossetian, Otetela, Palauan, Persian, Ponapean, Seychelles Creole, Tahitian, Tatar, Tiv, Trukese, Tumbuka, Tuvaluan, Umbundu, Uruund, Venda, Yapese, Zande

* Study articles also available in large-print edition.
# Audiocassettes also available.
+ CD also available.
⊙ MP3 CD-ROM also available.
△ Videocassette
□ DVD

Is the DEVIL Real?

How difficult it can be to identify someone who is determined to remain concealed behind a mask!

H OW do you view the Devil? Do you think of him as a real person who tempts people to do wicked things, or does he merely represent the principle of evil? Is the Devil someone to be feared, or should he be dismissed as nothing more than a superstitious notion or a mythological unreality? Does the word "devil" refer to some abstract destructive force in the universe? Could the term simply be a symbol of the evil traits in humans, as many modern theologians claim?

It is not surprising that mankind is divided on the question of who the Devil is. Imagine how difficult it can be to discover the true identity of someone who is a master of disguise! Particularly is that so if he is determined to remain concealed behind a mask. The Bible describes the Devil as such a personality. Referring to him as Satan, it says: "Satan himself keeps transforming himself into an angel of light." (2 Corinthians 11:14) Though he is evil, the Devil presents himself as good in order to misguide others. And if he gets people to believe that he simply does not exist, that suits his purpose even better.

Really, then, who is the Devil? When and how did he come into existence? How does he influence mankind today? What, if anything, can we do to resist that influence? The Bible contains the accurate history of the Devil from his very beginning and provides truthful answers to these questions.

How Real Is the DEVIL to You?

THE Scriptures portray the Devil as a real person. He is invisible to humans for the same reason that God is invisible to human eyes. "God is a Spirit," says the Bible. (John 4:24) The Devil is a spirit creature. Unlike the Creator, however, the Devil had a beginning.

Long before Jehovah God created humans, he made a multitude of spirit creatures. (Job 38:4, 7) In the Bible these spirits are called angels. (Hebrews 1:13, 14) God created all of them perfect—not a single one was a devil or had any evil trait. How, then, did the Devil come to be? The word "devil" means "slanderer" and thus refers to someone who tells malicious lies about others. "Satan" means "Resister," or opposer. Just as a formerly honest man makes himself a thief by stealing, one of the perfect spirit sons of God acted upon an improper desire and made himself Satan the Devil. The Bible explains the process of self-corruption this way: "Each one is tried by being drawn out and enticed by his own desire. Then the desire, when it has become fertile, gives birth to sin; in turn, sin, when it has been accomplished, brings forth death."—James 1:14, 15.

This is apparently what happened. When Jehovah God created the first human pair, Adam and Eve, the angel who was about to rebel against God took note. He knew that Jehovah commanded Adam and Eve to fill the earth with righteous people, who would worship the Creator. (Genesis 1:28) This angel saw that there was a possibility that he could gain honor and importance. Motivated by greed, he coveted what rightly belongs only to the Creator—worship from humans. Instead of rejecting such an improper desire, this spirit son of God nurtured it until it gave birth to a lie and then to rebellion. Consider what he did.

The rebellious angel used a serpent to speak to the first woman, Eve. "Is it really so that God said you must not eat from every tree of the garden?" the serpent asked Eve. When Eve cited God's command and the penalty for disobeying it, the serpent declared: "You positively will not die. For God knows that in the very day of your eating from [the tree that is in the middle of the garden] your eyes are bound to be opened and you are bound to be like God, knowing good and bad." (Genesis 3:1-5) The assertion was that God had not told Adam and Eve the truth. By eating the fruit of that tree, Eve would supposedly become like God, having the authority to decide what was good and what was bad. That was the first lie ever spoken. Telling it made that angel a slanderer. He also became an opposer of God. The Bible thus identifies this enemy of God as "the original serpent, the one called Devil and Satan."—Revelation 12:9.

"Be Watchful"

The lie that the Devil told Eve worked just as he had planned. The Bible says: "Consequently the woman saw that the tree was good for food and that it was something to be longed for to the eyes, yes, the tree was desirable to look upon. So she began taking of its fruit and eating it. Afterward she gave some also to her husband when with her and he began eating it." (Genesis 3:6) Eve believed Satan and disobeyed God. She was able to get Adam to break God's law too. The Devil thus succeeded in setting the first human couple on a course of rebellion against God. Ever since then, Satan has exercised unseen influence over human affairs. His goal? To turn people away from worshipping the true God and gain their worship for himself. (Matthew 4:8, 9) With good rea-

son, then, the Scriptures warn: "Keep your senses, be watchful. Your adversary, the Devil, walks about like a roaring lion, seeking to devour someone."—1 Peter 5:8.

How clearly the Bible portrays the Devil as a real spirit person—an angel that became corrupt and dangerous! The first essential step in our keeping watchful is to recognize that he really exists. But keeping our senses and remaining watchful involves more. It is also important not to be ignorant of Satan's "designs" and of his methods of misleading people. (2 Corinthians 2:11) What are his schemes? And how can we stand firm against them?

The Devil Exploits Man's Inherent Need

The Devil has observed humans since the creation of mankind. He knows man's makeup—his needs, his interests, and his desires. Satan is well-aware that man was created with a spiritual need, and the Devil has cleverly exploited this need. How? By feeding mankind religious untruths. (John 8:44) Many religious teachings about God are contradictory and confusing. Whose purpose do you think this serves? Contradictory teachings cannot all be true. Is it not possible, then, that many religious teachings are expressly designed and used by Satan to misguide people? In fact, the Bible refers to him as "the god of this system of things," who has blinded people's minds.—2 Corinthians 4:4.

Divine truth provides protection against religious deceptions. The Bible likens the truth of God's Word to the girdle that a soldier of ancient times wore to help protect his loins. (Ephesians 6:14) If you take in knowledge of the Bible and keep its message close to you, as if you were girded with it, God's Word will safeguard you from being misled by religious lies and errors.

Man's spiritual inclination has led him to explore the unknown. This has exposed him to another of Satan's deceptive devices. Exploiting man's curiosity about what is strange and mysterious, Satan has used spiritism to bring many under his control. As a hunter uses bait to attract his prey, Satan employs such devices as fortune-telling, astrology, hypnotism, witchcraft, palmistry, and magic to attract and entrap people around the world.—Leviticus 19:31; Psalm 119:110.

How can you protect yourself from being ensnared by spiritism? Deuteronomy 18:10-12 states: "There should not be found in you anyone who makes his son or his daughter pass through the fire, anyone who employs divination, a practicer of magic or anyone who looks for omens or a sorcerer, or one who binds others with a spell or anyone who consults a spirit medium or a professional foreteller of events or anyone who inquires of the dead. For everybody doing these things is something detestable to Jehovah, and on account of these detestable things Jehovah your God is driving them away from before you."

The Scriptural advice is direct: Have nothing to do with spiritism. What if you have been sharing in some practice of spiritism and now want to break free? You can follow the example of early Christians in the city of Ephesus. When they accepted "the word of Jehovah," the Bible says, "quite a number of those who practiced magical arts brought their books together and burned them up before everybody." Those books were costly. They were worth 50,000 pieces of silver. (Acts 19:19, 20) Yet, Christians in Ephesus did not hesitate to destroy them.

Satan Preys on Human Weaknesses

A perfect angel became Satan the Devil because he gave in to the desire for self-exaltation. He also awakened in Eve a proud, selfish longing to be like God. Today, Satan keeps many in his grip by arousing in them the feeling of pride. For example, some feel that their race, ethnic group, or nationality is better than that of others. How contrary this is to what the Bible teaches! (Acts 10:34, 35) The Bible clearly states: "[God] made out of one man every nation of men."—Acts 17:26.

An effective defense against Satan's appeal to pride is humility. The Bible admonishes us "not to think more of [ourselves] than it is necessary to think." (Romans 12:3) "God opposes the haughty ones," it states, "but he gives undeserved kindness to the humble

Those who became Christians burned their books on spiritism

6

ones." (James 4:6) One sure way to resist Satan's efforts is to manifest in your personal life humility and other qualities approved by God.

The Devil is also eager to exploit the human weakness of yielding to improper sensual desires. Jehovah God intended for humans to enjoy life. When desires are fulfilled within the limits of God's will, the result is genuine happiness. But Satan tempts humans to satisfy their cravings in immoral ways. (1 Corinthians 6:9, 10) It is much better to keep the mind focused on things that are chaste and virtuous. (Philippians 4:8) This will help you to exercise firm control over your thoughts and emotions.

Keep Resisting the Devil

Can you succeed in resisting the Devil? Yes, you can. The Bible assures us: "Oppose the Devil, and he will flee from you." (James 4:7) Even if you oppose Satan, he will not give up immediately and refrain from causing you any further trouble as you take in knowledge of God. No, the Devil will try again at "another convenient time." (Luke 4:13) However, you need not be afraid of the Devil. If you continue to resist him, he will not be able to turn you away from the true God.

Resisting the Devil, however, requires knowledge of who he is and how he misleads people as well as of the protective measures you can take against his schemes. There is only one accurate source of that knowledge —God's Word, the Bible. So be firm in your determination to study the inspired Scriptures, and apply in your life what you learn from them. Jehovah's Witnesses in your area will be happy to assist you free of charge with such a study at a time convenient to you. Please do not hesitate to contact them or to write the publishers of this magazine.

As you undertake a study of the Bible, you need to realize that Satan may use opposition or persecution to get you to stop learning the truth from God's Word. Some of your loved ones may become angry with you because you study the Bible. This may happen because they do not know the wonderful truths found in it. Others may make fun of you. But would succumbing to such pressures really please God? The Devil wants to discourage you so that you will stop learning about the true God. Why should you let Satan win? (Matthew 10:34-39) You owe him nothing. You owe Jehovah your very life. So, then, be determined to resist the Devil and 'make Jehovah's heart rejoice.'—Proverbs 27:11.

Make a firm decision to study the Bible

Self-Sacrifice Brings Jehovah's Blessing

A MAN travels by bicycle in the deep forest of Cameroon. For hours, he cycles along flooded roads and through mud, facing danger in order to strengthen others. To teach an isolated group, some in Zimbabwe walk nine miles through flooding rivers, balancing their clothes and shoes on their head to keep them dry. Elsewhere, a woman gets up at four o'clock in the morning to visit and teach a nurse who can spare an hour only early in the day.

What do the people making such efforts have in common? They are all full-time ministers of Jehovah's Witnesses engaging in the work of teaching Bible truth. They include regular and special pioneers, missionaries, traveling overseers, and thousands of volunteers at Bethel homes around the world. And self-sacrifice is their hallmark.*

Proper Motive

Jehovah's Witnesses are heeding the apostle Paul's admonition to Timothy: "Do your utmost to present yourself approved to God, a workman with nothing to be ashamed of, handling the word of the truth aright." (2 Timothy 2:15) But what motivates hundreds of thousands of Witnesses to serve as full-time ministers?

When full-time servants are asked why they are exerting themselves in Jehovah's service, their answer involves love for God and for fellow humans. (Matthew 22:37-39) This is most appropriate, for without love as the motive, any amount of effort would be in vain.—1 Corinthians 13:1-3.

_____
* See *2005 Calendar of Jehovah's Witnesses,* November/December.

Self-Sacrificing Service

All dedicated Christians have accepted Jesus' call: "If anyone wants to come after me, let him disown himself and pick up his torture stake and continually follow me." (Matthew 16:24) To disown ourselves means to submit willingly to being owned and directed by Jehovah God and Jesus Christ. For many, this has led to self-sacrificing service in the full-time ministry.

Many Witnesses make great efforts to expand their service to Jehovah. Consider 56-year-old Júlia, a regular pioneer in São Paulo, Brazil. "A Chinese brother telephoned to ask me if I was willing to learn Chinese," she recalls. "Because of my age, I had not considered learning a new language. But after some days, I accepted the challenge. Today, I am able to give Scriptural presentations in Chinese."

The branch office of Jehovah's Witnesses in Peru reports: "In recent years, hundreds of regular pioneers have moved to un-

---

JEHOVAH CHERISHES HIS DEVOTED SERVANTS

"Become steadfast, unmovable, always having plenty to do in the work of the Lord, knowing that your labor is not in vain in connection with the Lord."
—1 Corinthians 15:58.

"God is not unrighteous so as to forget your work and the love you showed for his name."
—Hebrews 6:10.

"Your people will offer themselves willingly on the day of your military force."
—PSALM 110:3

assigned territories, displaying a courageous and self-sacrificing spirit. They move to distant towns where there are no basic services and work opportunities are limited. These brothers and sisters are willing to do whatever it takes to remain in their assignments. But most important, their activity in the ministry is a blessing in one place after another. Traveling overseers report that new groups have been formed with the help of these self-sacrificing regular pioneers."

Some Christians have risked their lives in order to help fellow believers. (Romans 16:3, 4) A circuit overseer in a war-torn area of Africa reports: "Before reaching the last roadblock between the territories occupied by the rebels and that controlled by the government, my wife and I were surrounded by four rebel military commanders and their bodyguards, who inquired about our identity. While checking our identity cards, they saw that we were from the government-controlled area, so they became nervous. I was accused of being a spy. Therefore, they decided to throw me into a pit. I explained who we were, and they eventually let us go." How grateful the congregations were that this self-sacrificing couple succeeded in visiting them!

Despite the difficulties encountered, the ranks of such full-time ministers are swelling worldwide. (Isaiah 6:8) These diligent workers cherish their privilege of serving Jehovah. With a similar spirit of self-sacrifice, millions of others are now praising Jehovah. In turn, he blesses them abundantly. (Proverbs 10:22) Confident of continued blessing and support, such hard workers reflect the attitude of the psalmist who sang: "My help is from Jehovah."—Psalm 121:2.

The Art of
Listening With Love

"THANKS for listening." Has anyone said that to you lately? What a compliment that is! A good listener is appreciated by just about everyone. By listening well, we can refresh people who are distressed or loaded down with problems. And does not being a good listener help us to enjoy people? In the Christian congregation, listening with love is an essential part of 'considering one another to incite to love and fine works.' —Hebrews 10:24.

Many people, however, are poor listeners. They like to give advice, relate their own experiences, or present their viewpoint instead of giving a listening ear to what others have to say. Listening really is an art. How can we learn to listen with love?

A Vital Key

Jehovah is our "Grand Instructor." (Isaiah 30:20) He can teach us much about listening. Consider how Jehovah helped the prophet Elijah. Frightened by Queen Jezebel's threats, Elijah ran away into the wilderness and expressed a wish to die. There God's angel spoke to him. As the prophet explained his fears, Jehovah listened and then displayed His great power. The result? No longer afraid, Elijah returned to his assignment. (1 Kings 19:2-15) Why does Jehovah take time to listen to the concerns of his servants? Because he cares for them. (1 Peter 5:7) Here is a key to becoming a good listener: Care for others, and show genuine concern for them.

When a man in Bolivia committed a serious wrong, he appreciated receiving such care from a fellow believer. The man explains: "I was then at one of the lowest points in my life. I might easily have given up trying to serve Jehovah if it hadn't been for a brother who took time to listen to me. He didn't say much, but knowing that he cared enough to listen really strengthened me. I didn't need a solution; I knew what I had to do. I just needed to know that someone cared about how I felt. His listening saved me from being swallowed up by despair."

A great Exemplar in the art of listening with love is Jesus Christ. Shortly after Jesus' death, two of his disciples were journeying from Jerusalem to a village some seven miles away. No doubt they were discouraged. So the resurrected Jesus Christ began walking with them. He asked carefully phrased questions to draw them out, and the disciples responded. They expressed the hopes they had entertained and the disappointment and confusion they now felt. Jesus cared for them, and his listening with love prepared the two disciples to listen. Then Jesus "interpreted to them things pertaining to himself in all the Scriptures."—Luke 24:13-27.

Listening first is a loving way to get others to listen to us. "My parents and my in-laws began objecting to the way I was raising my children," says a Bolivian woman. "I resented their comments, but I felt unsure of myself as a parent. About that time, one of Jehovah's Witnesses called on me. She spoke to me about God's promises. However, it was the way she asked my opinion that told me that this person was willing to listen. I invited her in, and soon I was explaining my problem to her. She listened with patience. She asked what I wanted for my children and how my husband felt about it. It was a relief to be with someone who was willing to try to understand me. When she began showing me what the Bible says about family life, I knew I was speaking to someone who cared about my situation."

"Love . . . does not look for its own interests," says the Bible. (1 Corinthians 13:4, 5) Listening with love, then, implies that we put our own interests aside. This may call for switching off the television, putting down the newspaper, or turning off the cell phone when others are speaking to us about a serious matter. Listening with love means becoming intensely interested in the other person's thoughts. It requires that we refrain from starting to talk about ourselves by saying something like, "That reminds me of what happened to me some time ago." While such an exchange is acceptable in a friendly conversation, we need to put personal interests aside when someone is discussing a serious problem. Genuine interest in others can be manifested in yet another way.

Listen to Discern Feelings

Companions of the man Job heard no fewer than ten of his discourses. Still, Job exclaimed: "O that I had someone listening to me!" (Job 31:35) Why? Because their listening provided no comfort. They neither cared about Job nor wanted to understand his feelings. They surely did not have fellow feeling as sympathetic listeners. But the apostle Peter counsels: "All of you be like-minded, showing fellow feeling, having brotherly affection, tenderly compassionate, humble in mind." (1 Peter 3:8) How can we show fellow feeling? One way is by showing concern for the other person's feelings and trying to understand them. Making such sympathetic comments as "that must have been upsetting" or "you must have felt misunderstood" is one way to show that we are concerned. Another way is to put what the person is saying in our own words, thus showing that we understood what he said. Listening with love means paying attention not only to the words but also to the emotions subtly expressed.

Robert* is an experienced full-time minister of Jehovah's Witnesses. He relates: "I became frustrated with my ministry at one point. So I asked to speak with the traveling overseer. He really listened and tried to understand my feelings. He even seemed to

---

* Name has been changed.

When listening, we must put our own interests aside

comprehend my fear that he would criticize me for my attitude. The brother assured me that my feelings were understandable, for he himself had experienced similar feelings. This really helped me to carry on."

Can we listen without agreeing with what is being said? Can we say to someone that we appreciate being told how he feels? Yes. What if a young son gets into a fight at school or a teenage daughter comes home and says that she is in love? Is it not better for a parent to listen and try to understand what is going on in the mind of the youth before explaining what is proper and improper behavior?

"Counsel in the heart of a man is as deep waters," says Proverbs 20:5, "but the man of discernment is one that will draw it up." If a wise and experienced person is not inclined to give unsolicited advice, we may have to draw him out to get his counsel. The situation is similar when we listen with love. It takes discernment to draw a person out. Asking questions helps, but we must be careful that our questions do not pry into private matters. It may be helpful to suggest that the one speaking start with matters he feels comfortable mentioning. For example, a wife who wants to talk about problems in her marriage may find it easier to start by talking about how she and her husband met and got married. A person who has become inactive in the Christian ministry may find it easier to begin by explaining how he learned the truth.

Listening With Love—A Challenge

Listening when someone is upset with us can be challenging, for our natural inclination is to defend ourselves. How can we meet the challenge? "An answer, when mild, turns away rage," says Proverbs 15:1. Kindly inviting the person to talk and then patiently listening as he expresses his grievance is one way to reply with mildness.

Heated arguments often consist of two people merely repeating what they have already said. Each one feels that the other individual is not listening. How good it would be if one of them would stop and really listen! Of course, it is important to exercise self-control and express oneself in a discreet and loving way. The Bible tells us: "The one keeping his lips in check is acting discreetly."—Proverbs 10:19.

The ability to listen with love does not come naturally. However, it is an art that can be learned through effort and discipline. It certainly is a skill worth acquiring. Really listening when others speak is an expression of our love. It also contributes to our happiness. How wise it is, then, to cultivate the art of listening with love!

Listening when someone is upset can be a challenge

Wonders
of
Creation
EXALT JEHOVAH

JEHOVAH GOD is more exalted than imperfect humans can imagine. His creative works on earth and in the heavens bring him praise and fill us with awe.—Psalm 19:1-4.

As the Creator and Universal Sovereign, Jehovah certainly deserves to be heard when he speaks. But how amazed we would be if he were to speak to us mere humans here on earth! Suppose he spoke to you, perhaps through an angel. Surely you would pay attention. The upright man Job must have listened very attentively when God addressed him some 3,500 years ago. What can we learn from God's words to Job regarding the earth and the material heavens?

Who Founded the Earth, and Who Controls the Sea?

Out of a windstorm, God asks Job about the earth and the sea. (Job 38:1-11) No human architect decided how big the earth should be and then helped to form it. Comparing the earth to a building, God asks Job: "Who laid its cornerstone?" Not man! God's angelic sons looked on and rejoiced as Jehovah created this planet.

The sea is an infant in relation to God, who figuratively clothes it with garments. It "began to go forth as when it burst out from the womb." God confines the sea as if by bars and bolted doors, and tides are regulated by lunar and solar attractions.

Says *The World Book Encyclopedia:* "The wind causes most ocean waves, from small ripples to giant hurricane waves more than 100 feet (30 meters) high. . . . After the wind stops, the waves continue to move over the ocean surface and can travel great distances from where they originated. They become smoother and longer. Finally, the waves reach the shoreline, where they break and form the surf." The sea obeys God's command: "This far you may come, and no farther; and here your proud waves are limited."

Who Makes the Dawn Ascend?

God next asks Job about the effects of light and other matters. (Job 38:12-18) No human can command the succession of night and day. Morning light figuratively lays hold of the ends of the earth and shakes out the wicked. Sinners may perform unrighteous acts in "evening darkness." (Job 24:15, 16) But dawn disperses many evildoers.

In God's hand, morning light is as a seal from which the earth gets a beautiful impression. Sunlight brings to view many colors, so that the globe seems to be arrayed in splendid garments. Job had nothing to do with this and had not walked about in the watery deep to take inventory of its treasures. Why, to this day researchers have only limited knowledge of oceanic life!

Who Has Storehouses of Snow and Hail?

No man has escorted either light or darkness to its home or has entered the storehouses of snow and hail that God keeps back for "the day of fight and war." (Job 38:19-23) When Jehovah used hail against his foes at Gibeon, "there were more who died from the hailstones than those whom the sons of Israel killed with the sword." (Joshua 10:11) He may use hailstones of undisclosed size to destroy wicked humans led by Gog, or Satan. —Ezekiel 38:18, 22.

IN OUR NEXT ISSUE

Armageddon—A Catastrophic End?

———

A Testimony to Love, Faith, and Obedience

———

Becoming Progressive and Adaptable Ministers

Egg-size hailstones killed 25 people and injured 200 others in central Henan Province, China, in July 2002. Regarding a hailstorm in 1545, Italian sculptor Benvenuto Cellini wrote: "We were one day distant from Lyons . . . when the heavens began to thunder with sharp rattling claps. . . . After the thunder the heavens made a noise so great and horrible that I thought the last day had come; so I reined in for a moment, while a shower of hail began to fall without a drop of water. . . . The hail now grew to the size of big lemons. . . . The storm raged for some while, but at last it stopped . . . We showed our scratches and bruises to each other; but about a mile farther on we came upon a scene of devastation which surpassed what we had suffered, and defies description. All the trees were stripped of their leaves and shattered; the beasts in the field lay dead; many of the herdsmen had also been killed; we observed large quantities of hailstones which could not have been grasped with two hands."—*Autobiography* (Book II, 50), *Harvard Classics,* Volume 31, pages 352-3.

What will happen when Jehovah opens his storehouses of snow and hail against his enemies? They cannot possibly survive when snow or hail is used to carry out his will.

Whose Handiwork Are Rain, Dew, Frost, and Ice?

Jehovah next asks Job about rain, dew, frost, and ice. (Job 38:24-30) God is the great Rainmaker, and even "the wilderness in which there is no earthling man" enjoys his blessing. Rain, ice, and frost have no human father or originator.

The *Nature Bulletin* states: "The strangest and perhaps the most important property [of ice] is that water expands as it freezes . . . The blanket of ice that forms and floats on a pond in winter makes it possible for aquatic plants and animals (fish, etc.) to remain alive in the water underneath. If . . . water contracted and became denser as it solidified, ice would be heavier than water and sink to the bottom. More ice would form on the surface until the pond was frozen solid. . . . In the cooler parts of the world the rivers, ponds, lakes, and even the oceans would all be permanently frozen."

How thankful we can be that bodies of water do not freeze solid! And we certainly are grateful that as Jehovah's handiwork, rain and dew invigorate the earth's vegetation.

Who Set the Statutes of the Heavens?

God next asks Job about the heavens. (Job 38:31-33) The Kimah constellation is usually identified as the Pleiades, a group consisting of seven large stars and a number of smaller ones some 380 light-years from the sun. Man cannot "tie fast the bonds of the Kimah constellation," binding that group in a cluster. No human can "loosen the very cords of the Kesil constellation," generally identified as the stellar group called Orion. Whatever may be the present identification of the Mazzaroth and Ash constellations, man cannot control and guide them. Humans cannot alter "the statutes of the heavens," the laws governing the universe.

God established the laws that guide the heavenly bodies, which influence earth's weather, tides, atmosphere, and the very existence of life on this planet. Consider the sun. Concerning it, *The Encyclopedia Americana* (1996 Edition) states: "The sun's rays supply the earth with heat and light, contribute to the growth of plant life, evaporate water from the ocean and other bodies of water, play a role in the production of winds, and perform many other functions that are vital to the existence of life on earth." The same reference work says: "To appreciate the vastness of the power that is inherent in sunlight, one need only reflect that all the

Pleiades: NASA, ESA and AURA/Caltech; fish: U.S. Fish & Wildlife Service, Washington, D.C./William W. Hartley

power represented in the winds and in dams and rivers and all the power contained in natural fuels such as wood, coal, and oil is nothing more than sunlight that has been stored up by a tiny planet [the earth] 93 million miles away from the sun."

Who Put Wisdom in the Clouds?

Jehovah tells Job to consider the clouds. (Job 38:34-38) Man cannot order a single cloud to appear and release its water. But how dependent humans are on the water cycle that the Creator has established!

What is the water cycle? One reference work states: "The water cycle consists of four distinct stages: storage, evaporation, precipitation, and runoff. Water may be stored temporarily in the ground; in oceans, lakes, and rivers; and in ice caps and glaciers. It evaporates from the earth's surface, condenses in clouds, falls back to the earth as precipitation (rain or snow), and eventually either runs into the seas or reevaporates into the atmosphere. Almost all the water on the earth has passed through the water cycle countless times."—*Microsoft Encarta Reference Library 2005.*

Rain-filled clouds are like water jars of heaven. When Jehovah tips them, they may pour down so much rain that the dust becomes mire and the clods cleave togeth-er. God can produce rain or hold it back. —James 5:17, 18.

Rain is often accompanied by lightning, but man cannot cause it to fulfill his wishes. Lightnings are represented as reporting to God and saying, "Here we are!" *Compton's Encyclopedia* states: "Lightning produces significant chemical changes in the atmosphere. As a stroke moves through the air, it generates tremendous heat that unites nitrogen and oxygen to form nitrates and other compounds. These compounds fall to the Earth with the rain. In this way, the atmosphere is able continually to help replenish the supply of nutrients that soil needs to produce plants." Full knowledge of lightning remains a mystery to man but not to God.

Wonders of Creation Bring God Praise

Creation's wonders truly do exalt the Creator of all things. (Revelation 4:11) How Job must have been impressed by Jehovah's words regarding the earth and celestial bodies in space!

The wonders of creation we have just considered are not the only questions and descriptions presented to Job. Yet, even those we have considered move us to exclaim: "Behold! God is more exalted than we can know."—Job 36:26.

HOSEA'S PROPHECY HELPS US TO WALK WITH GOD

"After Jehovah they will walk."—HOSEA 11:10.

DO YOU enjoy dramas with fascinating characters and intriguing plots? The Bible book of Hosea contains a symbolic drama.* That drama deals with the family affairs of God's prophet Hosea and is related to the figurative marriage that Jehovah contracted with ancient Israel by means of the Mosaic Law covenant.

2 The setting for this drama is found in Hosea chapter 1. Hosea apparently lived in the territory of the ten-tribe kingdom of Israel (also called Ephraim, for its dominant tribe). He prophesied during the reigns of Israel's last seven rulers and of Kings Uzziah, Jotham, Ahaz, and Hezekiah of Judah. (Hosea 1:1) So Hosea prophesied for at least 59 years. Though the book bearing his name was completed not long after 745 B.C.E., it is relevant today, when millions are pursuing a course like that foretold in the words: "After Jehovah they will walk."—Hosea 11:10.

What an Overview Reveals

3 A brief overview of Hosea chapters 1 through 5 will strengthen our resolve to walk with God by exercising faith and pursuing a course in harmony with his will. Although inhabitants of the kingdom of Israel became guilty of spiritual adultery, God would be merciful to them if they repented. This was illustrated by the way Hosea dealt with his wife, Gomer. After she bore one child to him, she apparently had two illegitimate children. Yet, Hosea took her back, just as Jehovah was willing to show mercy to repentant Israelites.—Hosea 1:1–3:5.

4 Jehovah had a legal case against Israel because there was no truth, loving-kindness, or knowledge of God in the land. He would hold an accounting against both idolatrous Israel and the wayward kingdom of Judah. When God's people were "in sore straits," however, they would seek Jehovah.—Hosea 4:1–5:15.

The Drama Unfolds

5 "Go," God commanded Hosea, "take to yourself a wife of fornication and children of fornication, because by fornication the land positively turns from following Jehovah." (Hosea 1:2) How widespread was fornication in Israel? We are told: "The very spirit of fornication has caused [the people of the ten-tribe kingdom] to wander off, and by fornication they go out from under their God. . . .

---

* A symbolic drama is presented at Galatians 4:21-26. Concerning it, see Volume 2, pages 693-4, of *Insight on the Scriptures*, published by Jehovah's Witnesses.

1. What symbolic drama is found in the book of Hosea?
2. What is known about Hosea?
3, 4. Briefly explain what is covered in Hosea chapters 1 through 5.

5, 6. (a) How widespread was fornication in the ten-tribe kingdom of Israel? (b) Why is the warning given to ancient Israel significant for us?

Your daughters commit fornication and your own daughters-in-law commit adultery. . . . As to the men, it is with the harlots that they get off to themselves, and with the female temple prostitutes that they sacrifice."—Hosea 4:12-14.

⁶ Fornication was rampant in Israel in both a physical and a spiritual sense. Jehovah would therefore hold "an accounting" against the Israelites. (Hosea 1:4; 4:9) This warning has significance for us because Jehovah will hold an accounting against those practicing immorality and engaging in unclean worship today. But those walking with God meet his standards for clean worship and are aware that "no fornicator . . . has any inheritance in the kingdom of the Christ and of God." —Ephesians 5:5; James 1:27.

⁷ When Hosea married Gomer, she evidently was a virgin, and she was a faithful wife at the time she "bore to him a son." (Hosea 1:3) As portrayed in the symbolic drama, shortly after freeing the Israelites from Egyptian bondage in 1513 B.C.E., God similarly made a covenant with them that was like a contract for a clean marriage. By agreeing to the covenant, Israel promised to be faithful to her "husbandly owner," Jehovah. (Isaiah 54:5) Yes, this figurative marriage of Israel to God was symbolized by Hosea's clean marriage to Gomer. But how things changed!

⁸ Hosea's wife "proceeded to become pregnant another time and to give birth to a

Do you know whom Hosea's wife represents?

daughter." That girl and a later child were probably conceived by Gomer in adultery. (Hosea 1:6, 8) Since Gomer represented Israel, you might ask, 'How did Israel come to prostitute herself?' In 997 B.C.E., ten of Israel's tribes separated from the southern tribes of Judah and Benjamin. Calf worship was set up in the northern ten-tribe kingdom of Israel so that its people would not go to Judah to worship Jehovah at his temple in Jerusalem. Worship of the false god Baal, with its sex orgies, became entrenched in Israel.

⁹ At the birth of Gomer's likely illegitimate second child, God told Hosea: "Call her name Lo-ruhamah [meaning "She Was Not Shown Mercy"], for I shall no more show mercy again to the house of Israel, because I shall positively take them away." (Hosea 1:6) Jehovah 'took them away' when the Assyrians carried the Israelites into captivity in 740 B.C.E. However, God showed mercy to the two-tribe kingdom of Judah and saved her but not by bow, sword, war, horses, or horsemen. (Hosea 1:7) During a single night in 732 B.C.E., just one angel killed 185,000 Assyrian soldiers who were threatening Judah's capital city, Jerusalem.—2 Kings 19:35.

Jehovah's Legal Case Against Israel

¹⁰ Gomer left Hosea and became "a wife of fornication," living adulterously with another man. This illustrated how the kingdom of Israel entered into political alliances with idolatrous nations and began to depend upon them. Instead of crediting Jehovah

7. What was symbolized by Hosea's marriage to Gomer?
8. How did the ten-tribe kingdom of Israel come into existence, and what can you say about its worship?

9. As foretold at Hosea 1:6, what happened to Israel?
10. Gomer's adulterous conduct illustrated what?

with her material blessings, Israel attributed these to the gods of such nations and violated her marriage covenant with God by engaging in false worship. No wonder Jehovah had a legal case against the spiritually adulterous nation!—Hosea 1:2; 2:2, 12, 13.

¹¹ What penalty did Israel pay for leaving her Husbandly Owner? God caused her "to go into the wilderness" of Babylonia, the nation that conquered Assyria, where the Israelites had been exiled in 740 B.C.E. (Hosea 2:14) When Jehovah thus caused the 10-tribe kingdom to end, he did not cancel his marriage covenant with the original 12-tribe nation of Israel. In fact, when God let Jerusalem be destroyed by the Babylonians in 607 B.C.E. and allowed the people of Judah to become captives, he did not abolish the Mosaic Law covenant by which 12-tribe Israel had entered into a figurative marriage with him. That relationship was done away with only after Jewish leaders rejected Jesus Christ and had him put to death in 33 C.E.—Colossians 2:14.

Jehovah Admonishes Israel

¹² God admonished Israel to "put away her fornication," but she wanted to go after those passionately loving her. (Hosea 2:2, 5) "Therefore," said Jehovah, "here I am hedging your way about with thorns; and I will heap up a stone wall against her, so that her

own roadways she will not find. And she will actually chase after her passionate lovers, but she will not overtake them; and she will certainly look for them, but she will not find them. And she will have to say, 'I want to go and return to my husband, the first one, for I had it better at that time than now.' But she herself did not recognize that it was I who had given to her the grain and the sweet wine and the oil, and that I had made silver itself abound for her, and gold, which they made use of for Baal [or, which "they made into a Baal image," footnote]."—Hosea 2:6-8.

¹³ Although Israel sought the help of nations that had been her "passionate lovers," none of them were able to assist her. She was hedged about as if by an impenetrable thicket, so that they were unable to get any help to her. After a three-year Assyrian siege, her capital city, Samaria, fell in 740 B.C.E., and the ten-tribe kingdom was never reestablished. Only some individuals among the captive Israelites would realize how good things had been when their forefathers had served Jehovah. That remnant would reject Baal worship and seek a renewed covenant relationship with Jehovah.

Another Look at the Drama

¹⁴ To understand more fully the connection between Hosea's domestic affairs and Israel's relationship with Jehovah, consider these words: "Jehovah went on to say to me:

---

11. What happened to the Law covenant when Jehovah allowed Israel and Judah to go into exile?
12, 13. What is the substance of Hosea 2:6-8, and how did those words apply to Israel?

---

14. How did it come about that Hosea renewed marital relations with Gomer?

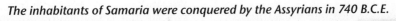

The inhabitants of Samaria were conquered by the Assyrians in 740 B.C.E.

Joyful people return to their homeland

'Go once again, love a woman loved by a companion and committing adultery.'" (Hosea 3:1) Hosea complied with this command by repurchasing Gomer from the man with whom she had been living. Afterward, Hosea firmly admonished his wife: "For many days you will dwell as mine. You must not commit fornication, and you must not come to belong to another man." (Hosea 3:2, 3) Gomer responded to the discipline, and Hosea renewed marital relations with her. How did this apply to God's dealings with the people of Israel and Judah?

¹⁵ While exiles from Israel and Judah were captives in Babylon, God used his prophets to

'speak to their heart.' To receive divine mercy, his people had to manifest repentance and go back to their Husbandly Owner, as Gomer had returned to her husband. Then Jehovah would take his disciplined wifelike nation out of the Babylonian "wilderness" and bring her back to Judah and Jerusalem. (Hosea 2:14, 15) He fulfilled that promise in 537 B.C.E.

¹⁶ God also fulfilled this promise: "I shall certainly conclude a covenant in that day in connection with the wild beast of the field and with the flying creature of the heavens and the creeping thing of the ground, and the bow and the sword and war I shall break out of the land, and I will make them lie down in security." (Hosea 2:18) The Jewish remnant who returned to their homeland lived in security, with nothing to fear from animals. This prophecy also had a fulfillment in 1919 C.E., when the remnant of spiritual Israel was freed from "Babylon the Great," the world empire of false religion. They now dwell in security and enjoy life in a spiritual paradise with their companions, who hope to live forever on earth. Animalistic traits do not exist among these true Christians.—Revelation 14:8; Isaiah 11:6-9; Galatians 6:16.

Take the Lessons to Heart

¹⁷ *God is merciful and compassionate, and that is how we should be.* That is one lesson taught by the early chapters of Hosea. (Hosea 1:6, 7; 2:23) God's willingness to extend mercy to repentant Israelites is in harmony with the inspired proverb: "He that is covering over his transgressions will not succeed, but he that is confessing and leaving them will be shown mercy." (Proverbs 28:13) Also comforting to repentant wrongdoers are the psalmist's words: "The sacrifices to God are a

---

15, 16. (a) Under what circumstances could God's disciplined nation receive his mercy? (b) How has Hosea 2:18 been fulfilled?

17-19. (a) What qualities of God are we here urged to imitate? (b) How should we be affected by Jehovah's mercy and compassion?

broken spirit; a heart broken and crushed, O God, you will not despise."—Psalm 51:17.

¹⁸ Hosea's prophecy highlights the compassion and mercy of the God we worship. Even if some deviate from his righteous ways, they can repent and turn around. If they do, Jehovah welcomes them. He showed mercy to repentant members of the nation of Israel, with which he had entered a figurative marriage. Though they disobeyed Jehovah and 'pained the Holy One of Israel, he was merciful and kept remembering that they were flesh.' (Psalm 78:38-41) Such mercy should move us to keep walking with our compassionate God, Jehovah.

¹⁹ Even though such sins as murder, stealing, and the committing of adultery were rampant in Israel, Jehovah 'spoke to her heart.' (Hosea 2:14; 4:2) Our own hearts should be stirred and our personal attachment to Jehovah strengthened as we reflect on his mercy and compassion. Let us therefore ask ourselves: 'How can I better imitate Jehovah's mercy and compassion in my dealings with others? If a fellow Christian who has offended me asks for forgiveness, am I as ready to forgive as God is?'—Psalm 86:5.

²⁰ *God gives true hope.* For example, he promised: "I will give her . . . the low plain of Achor as an entrance to hope." (Hosea 2:15) Jehovah's ancient wifelike organization had the sure hope of being restored to her homeland, where "the low plain of Achor" was located. Fulfillment of that promise, in 537 B.C.E., gives us sound reason to rejoice in the sure hope that Jehovah sets before us.

²¹ *To continue walking with God, we need to keep on taking in knowledge of him and applying it in our life.* Knowledge of Jehovah was sorely lacking in Israel. (Hosea 4:1, 6) Yet,

some prized divine teaching highly, acted in harmony with it, and were greatly blessed. Hosea was one of them. So were the 7,000 who in Elijah's day had not bent the knee to Baal. (1 Kings 19:18; Romans 11:1-4) Our own gratitude for divine instruction will help us to keep on walking with God.—Psalm 119:66; Isaiah 30:20, 21.

²² *Jehovah expects men taking the lead among his people to reject apostasy.* However, Hosea 5:1 says: "Hear this, O priests, and pay attention, O house of Israel, and you, O house of the king, give ear, for with you people the judgment has to do; because a trap is what you have become to Mizpah and as a net spread over Tabor." Apostate leaders were a trap and a net for the Israelites, enticing them to practice idolatry. Mount Tabor and a place named Mizpah likely were centers of such false worship.

²³ So far, Hosea's prophecy has shown us that Jehovah is a merciful God who gives hope and blesses those applying his instruction and rejecting apostasy. Like repentant Israelites of the past, let us therefore seek Jehovah and always endeavor to please him. (Hosea 5:15) By doing so, we will reap what is good and have the incomparable joy and peace experienced by all who faithfully walk with God.—Psalm 100:2; Philippians 4:6, 7.

---

22. How is apostasy to be viewed?
23. How have you benefited from a study of Hosea chapters 1 through 5?

How Would You Answer?

- What did Hosea's marriage to Gomer symbolize?

- Why did Jehovah have a legal case against Israel?

- Which lesson in Hosea chapters 1 to 5 impressed you?

---

20. Give an example to show that we should have confidence in God-given hope.
21. What role does knowledge play in our walking with God?

WALK WITH GOD, AND REAP WHAT IS GOOD

"It is wind that they keep sowing, and a storm wind is what they will reap."—HOSEA 8:7.

A TRIP through a dangerous region would be safer if an experienced guide led the way. It would be wise to walk with such a guide rather than heading off on our own. In some respects, this illustrates the situation that we are in. Jehovah has, in effect, offered to guide us through the vast desert of the present wicked world. We are wise to walk with him rather than trying to direct our own steps. How can we walk with God? By following the guidance he provides in his Word.

² The preceding article discussed the symbolic drama found in Hosea chapters 1 to 5. As we have seen, that drama contains lessons that can help us to walk with God. Let us now discuss some highlights of chapters 6 through 9. It would be helpful to begin with an overview of these four chapters.

A Brief Overview

³ Jehovah sent Hosea to prophesy primarily to the northern ten-tribe kingdom of Israel. That nation, also known as Ephraim after the name of its dominant tribe, had turned away from God. Hosea chapters 6 through 9 show that the people displayed disloyalty by overstepping Jehovah's covenant and practicing wickedness. (Hosea 6:7) They trusted in worldly alliances rather than returning to Jehovah. Because they kept sowing what was bad, they would reap what was bad. In oth-

er words, adverse judgment was coming. But Hosea's prophecy also contains a heartwarming message. The people were assured that they could return to Jehovah and would be shown mercy if they gave evidence of heartfelt repentance.

⁴ From these four chapters of Hosea's prophecy, we can obtain further guidance that will help us to walk with God. Let us consider four practical lessons: (1) True repentance is manifested by deeds, not just words; (2) sacrifices alone do not please God; (3) Jehovah feels hurt when his worshippers turn away from him; and (4) to reap what is good, we must sow what is good.

How True Repentance Is Manifested

⁵ Hosea's prophecy teaches us much about repentance and mercy. At Hosea 6:1-3, we read: "Come, you people, and do let us return to Jehovah, for he himself has torn in pieces but he will heal us. He kept striking, but he will bind us up. He will make us alive after two days. On the third day he will make us get up, and we shall live before him. And we will know, we will pursue to know Jehovah. Like dawn, his going forth is firmly established. And he will come in like a pouring rain to us; like a spring rain that saturates the earth."

⁶ Who spoke the words recorded in these

---

1. How can we walk with Jehovah?
2. What will be discussed in this article?
3. Briefly relate the contents of Hosea chapters 6 through 9.

4. What practical lessons from Hosea's prophecy will we consider?
5. Give the essence of what is said at Hosea 6:1-3.
6-8. What was wrong with Israel's repentance?

verses? Some ascribe these statements to the unfaithful Israelites and say that the disobedient people were feigning repentance and presuming upon God's mercy. Others, however, say that the prophet Hosea was speaking, begging the people to come back to Jehovah. Regardless of who made these statements, the crucial question is, Did the people of the ten-tribe kingdom of Israel in general return to Jehovah, manifesting genuine repentance? The answer is no. Jehovah says through Hosea: "What shall I do to you, O Ephraim? What shall I do to you, O Judah, when the loving-kindness of you people is like the morning clouds and like the dew that early goes away?" (Hosea 6:4) What a testimony to the deplorable spiritual condition of God's people! Loving-kindness, or loyal love, had almost disappeared—like the morning mist that quickly vanishes with the rising of the sun. Although the people apparently pretended to repent, Jehovah found no basis for extending mercy. What was the problem?

⁷ Israel's repentance was not truly from the heart. Hosea 7:14 says this about Jehovah's displeasure with his people: "They did not call to me for aid with their heart, although they kept howling on their beds." Verse 16 adds: "They proceeded to return, not to any-thing higher"—that is, "not to an elevated form of worship." (Footnote) The people were not willing to return to Jehovah's exalted worship by making the changes that were needed to restore their relationship with him. Indeed, they did not really want to walk with God.

⁸ There was another problem with Israel's repentance. The people were continuing to practice sin—actually, a great variety of sins, including fraud, murder, stealing, idolatry, and forming unwise alliances with other nations. At Hosea 7:4, the people are likened to "a furnace," or baker's oven, evidently because evil desires were burning within them. In view of such a deplorable spiritual condition, did the people deserve mercy? Certainly not! Hosea tells the rebellious people that Jehovah will "remember their error" and "give attention to their sins." (Hosea 9:9) No mercy for them!

⁹ As we read Hosea's words, what do we learn about repentance and mercy? The warning example of the faithless Israelites teaches us that in order to benefit from Jehovah's mercy, we must demonstrate heartfelt repentance. How is such repentance manifested? Jehovah is not deceived by tears or

---

9. Hosea's words teach us what about repentance and mercy?

Like morning clouds,
Israel's loyal love vanished

Israel's evil desires
burned like a furnace

mere words. Genuine repentance is made apparent by actions. In order to receive mercy, a wrongdoer must completely abandon his sinful course and bring his life into harmony with the high standards of Jehovah's elevated worship.

Sacrifices Alone Do Not Please Jehovah

¹⁰ Now let us discuss a second lesson that can help us to walk with Jehovah. It is this: Sacrifices alone do not please God. Hosea 6:6 says: "In loving-kindness I [Jehovah] have taken delight, and not in sacrifice; and in the knowledge of God rather than in whole burnt offerings." Notice that Jehovah takes delight in loving-kindness, or loyal love—a quality of the heart—and in knowledge about him. But you may be wondering: 'Why does this verse say that Jehovah does *not* take delight in "sacrifice" and in "whole burnt offerings"? Were those not required under the Mosaic Law?'

¹¹ Sacrifices and offerings were required under the Law, but there was a serious problem with Hosea's contemporaries. Evidently, there were Israelites who dutifully made such offerings in a showy display of devotion. At the same time, they were practicing sin. By their sinfulness they indicated that their hearts were devoid of loyal love. They also showed that they had rejected knowledge of God, for they were not living in harmony with it. If the people did not have the proper heart condition and were not pursuing the right way of life, of what value were their sacrifices? Their sacrifices were offensive to Jehovah God.

¹² Hosea's words contain a warning for many churchgoers today. They make offerings to God in the form of religious practices.

Why did Jehovah reject the sacrifices of his people?

But their worship has little, if any, real influence on their daily conduct. Are such people really pleasing to God if their hearts do not motivate them to take in accurate knowledge of him and to apply that knowledge by turning away from sinful practices? Let no one imagine that religious works alone please God. Jehovah finds no delight in humans who try to earn his favor by a mere form of worship instead of truly living by his Word. —2 Timothy 3:5.

¹³ As true Christians, we bear in mind that sacrifices alone do not please God. It is true that we do not offer animal sacrifices to Jehovah. Nevertheless, we do "offer to God a sacrifice of praise, that is, the fruit of lips which make public declaration to his name." (Hebrews 13:15) It is vital that we do not become like the sinful Israelites of Hosea's day, thinking that we can compensate for wrongdoing by offering such spiritual sacrifices to God. Consider the example of one youth who secretly engaged in sexual immorality. She later admitted: "I increased my field ministry, thinking that this would somehow cover up the wrong." That was similar to what the

---

10, 11. As illustrated in the case of Israel, why do sacrifices alone not please Jehovah?

12. Hosea 6:6 contains what warning for people living today?

---

13. What kind of sacrifices do we offer, but what should be borne in mind about their value?

wayward Israelites tried to do. However, our sacrifice of praise is acceptable to Jehovah only if it is accompanied by the proper heart motivation and godly conduct.

Jehovah Is Hurt When His Worshippers Leave Him

¹⁴ A third lesson we learn from Hosea chapters 6 to 9 is regarding how Jehovah feels when his worshippers turn away from him. God has both strong and tender feelings. He has tender feelings of joy and compassion toward those who repent of their sins. When his people are unrepentant, though, he takes strong, decisive action. Because God has deep concern for our welfare, he rejoices when we faithfully walk with him. "Jehovah is taking pleasure in his people," says Psalm 149:4. Yet, how does God feel when his servants are unfaithful?

¹⁵ Referring to the unfaithful Israelites, Je-

_____
14. Hosea's prophecy reveals what about God's feelings?
15. According to Hosea 6:7, how were some Israelites acting?

hovah says: "They themselves, like earthling man, have overstepped the covenant. There is where they have dealt treacherously with me." (Hosea 6:7) The Hebrew word rendered 'deal treacherously' also means "deal deceitfully, (deal) unfaithfully." At Malachi 2:10-16, the same Hebrew word is used to describe the disloyal conduct of those Israelites who were unfaithful to their marriage partner. Regarding the use of this term at Hosea 6:7, one reference work says that it is "a marriage metaphor that infuses personal qualities into the relationship . . . The situation is a personal one in which love has been violated."

¹⁶ Jehovah viewed Israel as his figurative wife by reason of his covenant with the nation. So when his people violated the terms of that covenant, it was as if they were committing adultery. God was like a faithful husband, but his people deserted him!

¹⁷ What about us? God cares about whether we walk with him or not. We do well to

_____
16, 17. (a) How did Israel act with respect to God's covenant with that nation? (b) What should we remember regarding our actions?

To reap what is good, we must sow what is good

remember that "God is love" and that our actions affect him. (1 John 4:16) If we pursue a wrong course, we may cause Jehovah pain and will certainly displease him. Our keeping this in mind can be a powerful deterrent to yielding to temptation.

How We Can Reap What Is Good

¹⁸ Let us consider a fourth lesson from Hosea's prophecy—how we can reap what is good. Regarding the Israelites and the folly and vanity of their faithless course, Hosea writes: "It is wind that they keep sowing, and a storm wind is what they will reap." (Hosea 8:7) Here we find a principle that we do well to keep in mind: There is a direct relationship between what we do now and what happens to us later. How did this principle prove true in the case of the unfaithful Israelites?

¹⁹ By practicing sin, those Israelites were sowing what was bad. Would they be able to continue doing so without reaping bad consequences? They surely would not escape adverse judgment. Hosea 8:13 states: "He [Jehovah] will remember their error and hold an accounting for their sins." And at Hosea 9:17, we read: "My God will reject them, for they have not listened to him, and they will be-

come fugitives among the nations." Jehovah would hold the Israelites accountable for their sins. Because they sowed what was bad, they would reap what was bad. God's judgment against them was carried out in 740 B.C.E., when the Assyrians overthrew the ten-tribe kingdom of Israel and led its inhabitants into captivity.

²⁰ The experience of those Israelites teaches us a basic truth: We reap what we sow. God's Word warns us: "Do not be misled: God is not one to be mocked. For whatever a man is sowing, this he will also reap." (Galatians 6:7) If we sow what is bad, we will reap what is bad. For example, those who pursue an immoral way of life will reap bitter consequences. There will be an unhappy outcome for an unrepentant wrongdoer.

²¹ How, then, can we reap what is good? That question can be answered with a simple illustration. If a farmer wants to harvest wheat, would he plant barley? Of course not! He must plant what he wants to reap. Similarly, if we want to reap what is good, we must sow what is good. Do you want to continue reaping what is good—a satisfying life now with the prospect of everlasting life in God's new world? If so, you must continue to sow what is good by walking with God and living in harmony with his righteous standards.

²² From Hosea chapters 6 through 9, we have learned four lessons that can help us to walk with God: (1) True repentance is manifested by actions; (2) sacrifices alone do not please God; (3) Jehovah feels hurt when his worshippers turn away from him; and (4) to reap what is good, we must sow what is good. How can the final five chapters of this Bible book help us to walk with God?

18, 19. What principle do we find at Hosea 8:7, and how did that principle work out for the Israelites?

---

20. The experience of the Israelites teaches us what?
21. How can we reap what is good?
22. What lessons have we learned from Hosea chapters 6 through 9?

How Would You Answer?

- How is genuine repentance manifested?

- Why do sacrifices alone not please our heavenly Father?

- How does God feel when his worshippers leave him?

- What must we sow if we are to reap what is good?

"THE WAYS OF JEHOVAH ARE UPRIGHT"

"The ways of Jehovah are upright, and the righteous are the ones who will walk in them."—HOSEA 14:9.

JEHOVAH gave the Israelites an upright start in the days of the prophet Moses. By the early eighth century B.C.E., however, their situation had become so bad that God found them guilty of gross wrongdoing. This is evident from Hosea chapters 10 through 14.

² Israel's heart had become hypocritical. The people of that ten-tribe kingdom had "plowed wickedness" and reaped unrighteousness. (Hosea 10:1, 13) "When Israel was a boy, then I loved him," said Jehovah, "and out of Egypt I called my son." (Hosea 11:1) Although God had delivered the Israelites from Egyptian bondage, they repaid him with lying and deception. (Hosea 11:12) Jehovah therefore gave them this counsel: "To your God you should return, keeping lovingkindness and justice."—Hosea 12:6.

³ Rebellious Samaria and its king would have a disastrous end. (Hosea 13:11, 16) But the final chapter of Hosea's prophecy opens with the plea: "Do come back, O Israel, to Jehovah your God." If the Israelites repentantly sought forgiveness, God would extend mercy. Of course, they would have to acknowledge that "the ways of Jehovah are upright" and walk in them.—Hosea 14:1-6, 9.

⁴ This section of Hosea's prophecy contains many principles that can help us to walk with God. We will consider these: (1) Jehovah requires unhypocritical worship, (2) God shows his people loyal love, (3) we need to hope in Jehovah constantly, (4) Jehovah's ways are always upright, and (5) sinners can return to Jehovah.

Jehovah Requires Unhypocritical Worship

⁵ *Jehovah expects us to render sacred service to him in a clean, unhypocritical manner.* However, Israel had become an unproductive "degenerating vine." Israel's inhabitants had 'multiplied altars' for use in false worship. These apostates had even put up pillars —perhaps obelisks designed for use in unclean worship. Jehovah was going to break down these altars and destroy such pillars. —Hosea 10:1, 2.

⁶ Hypocrisy has no place among Jehovah's servants. Yet, what had happened to the Israelites? Why, 'their heart had become hypocritical'! Although they had once entered a covenant with Jehovah as a people dedicated to him, he found them guilty of hypocrisy. What can we learn from this? If we have dedicated ourselves to God, we must not be hypocrites. Proverbs 3:32 warns: "The devious person is a detestable thing to Jehovah, but His intimacy is with the upright ones." In order to walk with God, we must display love "out of a clean heart and out of a

---

1, 2. Jehovah gave the Israelites what kind of start, but what happened to them?
3. What was to happen to rebellious Samaria, but how could the Israelites receive mercy?
4. We will consider what principles from Hosea's prophecy?

---

5. What kind of service does God expect from us?
6. To walk with God, we must be free of what trait?

Accept spiritual help from Christian elders

good conscience and out of faith without hypocrisy."—1 Timothy 1:5.

God Shows His People Loyal Love

⁷ *If we worship Jehovah in an unhypocritical and upright way, we will be recipients of his loving-kindness, or loyal love.* The wayward Israelites were told: "Sow seed for yourselves in righteousness; reap in accord with loving-kindness. Till for yourselves arable land, when there is time for searching for Jehovah until he comes and gives instruction in righteousness to you."—Hosea 10:12.

⁸ If only the Israelites would repentantly search for Jehovah! Then he would gladly 'give them instruction in righteousness.' If we have personally sinned seriously, let us search for Jehovah, praying to him for forgiveness and seeking spiritual help from Christian elders. (James 5:13-16) May we also seek the guidance of God's holy spirit, for "he who is sowing with a view to his flesh will reap corruption from his flesh, but he who is sowing with a view to the spirit will reap everlasting life from the spirit." (Galatians 6:8) If we 'sow with a view to the spirit,' we will continue to enjoy God's loyal love.

⁹ We can have confidence that Jehovah always deals with his people in a loving way.

Evidence of this is found at Hosea 11:1-4, where we read: "When Israel was a boy, then I loved him, and out of Egypt I called my son. . . . To the Baal images they took up sacrificing, and to the graven images they began making sacrificial smoke. But as for me, I taught Ephraim [the Israelites] to walk, taking them upon my arms; and they did not recognize that I had healed them. With the ropes of earthling man I kept drawing them, with the cords of love, so that I became to them as those lifting off a yoke on their jaws, and gently I brought food to each one."

¹⁰ Here Israel is compared to a small child. Jehovah lovingly taught the Israelites to walk, taking them upon his arms. And he kept drawing them with "the cords of love." What a touching picture! Imagine that you are a parent helping your child to take his first steps. Your arms are outstretched. You may be using cords for your little one to hold on to so that he does not fall. Well, Jehovah's love for you is just as tender. He is delighted to lead you with "the cords of love."

¹¹ In dealing with the Israelites, Jehovah "became to them as those lifting off a yoke on their jaws, and gently [he] brought food to each one." God acted as one who lifts off or pushes back a yoke far enough to enable an animal to eat comfortably. Only when the people of Israel broke their yoke of submission to Jehovah did they come under the oppressive yoke of their enemies. (Deuteronomy 28:45, 48; Jeremiah 28:14) May we never fall into the clutches of our archenemy, Satan, and suffer the pains of his oppressive yoke. Instead, let us continue loyally walking with our loving God.

7, 8. (a) Under what circumstances can we enjoy God's loyal love? (b) What should we do if we have sinned seriously?

9, 10. How does Hosea 11:1-4 apply to Israel?

11. In what way did God 'become as one lifting off a yoke'?

Hope in Jehovah Constantly

¹² *To go on walking with God, we must hope in him constantly.* The Israelites were told: "As respects you, to your God you should return, keeping loving-kindness and justice; and let there be a hoping in your God constantly." (Hosea 12:6) Israel's inhabitants could provide evidence of a repentant return to Jehovah by displaying loving-kindness, by exercising justice, and by 'hoping in God constantly.' Regardless of how long we have walked with God, we must be determined to display loving-kindness, exercise justice, and hope in God constantly. —Psalm 27:14.

¹³ Hosea's prophecy involving the Israelites gives us a special reason to hope in God. "From the hand of Sheol I shall redeem them," said Jehovah. "From death I shall recover them. Where are your stings, O Death? Where is your destructiveness, O Sheol?" (Hosea 13:14) Jehovah was not going to rescue the Israelites from physical death at that time, but he would eventually swallow up death forever and nullify its victory.

¹⁴ Addressing fellow anointed Christians, Paul quoted from Hosea's prophecy and wrote: "When this which is corruptible puts on incorruption and this which is mortal puts on immortality, then the saying will take place that is written: 'Death is swallowed up forever.' 'Death, where is your victory? Death, where is your sting?' The sting producing death is sin, but the power for sin is the Law. But thanks to God, for he gives us the victory through our Lord Jesus Christ!" (1 Corinthians 15:54-57) Jehovah raised Jesus from death, providing a comforting guarantee that people in God's memory will be resurrected. (John 5:28, 29) What a blessed reason to hope in Jehovah! Yet, something in addition to the resurrection hope motivates us to walk with God.

Hosea's prophecy gives us reason to hope in Jehovah's resurrection promises

Jehovah's Ways Are Always Upright

¹⁵ *Our conviction that "the ways of Jehovah are upright" helps us to continue walking with God.* The inhabitants of Samaria did not walk in God's righteous ways. Consequently, they would have to pay a price for their sin and lack of faith in Jehovah. It was foretold: "Samaria will be held guilty, for she is actually rebellious against her God. By the sword they will fall. Their own children will be dashed to pieces, and their pregnant women themselves will be ripped up." (Hosea 13:16) Historical records show that the Assyrians, who conquered Samaria, were capable of such dreadful atrocities.

¹⁶ Samaria was the capital city of the ten-tribe kingdom of Israel. Here, though, the name Samaria may apply to the entire territory of that kingdom. (1 Kings 21:1) Assyrian King Shalmaneser V laid siege to the city of Samaria in 742 B.C.E. When Samaria finally fell in 740 B.C.E., many of its leading residents were exiled to Mesopotamia and

---

12. According to Hosea 12:6, what is required in order for us to go on walking with God?

13, 14. How does Paul apply Hosea 13:14, giving us what reason to hope in Jehovah?

15, 16. What was foretold regarding Samaria, and how was the prophecy fulfilled?

Media. Whether Samaria was captured by Shalmaneser V or by his successor, Sargon II, remains uncertain. (2 Kings 17:1-6, 22, 23; 18:9-12) Nevertheless, Sargon's records refer to the deportation of 27,290 Israelites to places in the Upper Euphrates and Media.

¹⁷ Samaria's inhabitants paid dearly for their failure to comply with Jehovah's upright ways. As dedicated Christians, we too would suffer tragic consequences if we were to become practicers of sin, treating God's righteous standards with contempt. May we never pursue such a wicked course! Rather, let each of us apply the apostle Peter's counsel: "Let none of you suffer as a murderer or a thief or an evildoer or as a busybody in other people's matters. But if he suffers as a Christian, let him not feel shame, but let him keep on glorifying God in this name."—1 Peter 4: 15, 16.

¹⁸ We "keep on glorifying God" by walking in his upright ways instead of doing things our own way. Cain committed murder because he went his own way and failed to heed Jehovah's warning that sin was about to pounce on him. (Genesis 4:1-8) Balaam accepted payment from Moab's king but tried in vain to curse Israel. (Numbers 24:10) And God put the Levite Korah and others to death

---

17. Rather than treating God's standards with contempt, what should we do?
18. How can we "keep on glorifying God"?

How Would You Answer?

- If we render clean worship to God, how will he deal with us?
- Why should we hope in Jehovah constantly?
- Why are you convinced that Jehovah's ways are upright?
- How can we continue to walk in Jehovah's upright ways?

---

for rebelling against the authority of Moses and Aaron. (Numbers 16:1-3, 31-33) Surely we do not want to go in the murderous "path of Cain," rush into "the erroneous course of Balaam," or perish in "the rebellious talk of Korah." (Jude 11) If we should err, however, Hosea's prophecy gives us comfort.

Sinners Can Return to Jehovah

¹⁹ *Even those who have stumbled by committing serious sin can return to Jehovah.* At Hosea 14:1, 2, we find this entreaty: "Do come back, O Israel, to Jehovah your God, for you have stumbled in your error. Take with yourselves words and come back to Jehovah. Say to him, all you people, 'May you pardon error; and accept what is good, and we will offer in return the young bulls of our lips.'"

²⁰ Repentant Israelites were able to offer God 'the young bulls of their lips.' These were sacrifices of sincere praise. Paul alluded to this prophecy when he urged Christians to "offer to God a sacrifice of praise, that is, the fruit of lips which make public declaration to his name." (Hebrews 13:15) What a privilege it is to walk with God and offer such sacrifices today!

²¹ Israelites who abandoned their wayward course and turned back to God offered him 'the young bulls of their lips.' They thus experienced spiritual restoration, even as God had promised. Hosea 14:4-7 says: "I [Jehovah] shall heal their unfaithfulness. I shall love them of my own free will, because my anger has turned back from him. I shall become like the dew to Israel. He will blossom like the lily, and will strike his roots like Lebanon. His twigs will go forth, and his dignity will become like that of the olive tree, and his fragrance will be like that of Lebanon. They

---

19, 20. Repentant Israelites were able to offer what sacrifices?
21, 22. What restoration would repentant Israelites experience?

*Keep on walking with God
with everlasting life in view*

will again be dwellers in his shadow. They will grow grain, and will bud like the vine. His memorial will be like the wine of Lebanon."

²² Repentant Israelites would be healed spiritually and would again enjoy God's love. Jehovah would become like refreshing dew to them in that he would bless them abundantly. His restored people would have dignity "like that of the olive tree," and they would walk in God's ways. Since we ourselves are determined to walk with Jehovah God, what is required of us?

Keep Walking in Jehovah's Upright Ways

²³ If we are to continue walking with God, we must exercise "the wisdom from above" and always act in harmony with his upright ways. (James 3:17, 18) The last verse of Hosea's prophecy reads: "Who is wise, that he may understand these things? Discreet, that he may know them? For the ways of Jehovah are upright, and the righteous are the

ones who will walk in them; but the transgressors are the ones who will stumble in them."—Hosea 14:9.

²⁴ Instead of being guided by the wisdom and standards of this world, let us be determined to walk in God's upright ways. (Deuteronomy 32:4) Hosea did that for 59 years or more. He faithfully delivered divine messages, knowing that those who were wise and discreet would understand such words. What about us? As long as Jehovah allows us to give a witness, we will keep on looking for those who will wisely accept his undeserved kindness. And we are delighted to do this in full cooperation with "the faithful and discreet slave."—Matthew 24:45-47.

²⁵ Our consideration of Hosea's prophecy should help us to go on walking with God with everlasting life in his promised new world in view. (2 Peter 3:13; Jude 20, 21) What a splendid hope! That hope will become a personal reality if we prove by word and deed that we mean it when we say: "The ways of Jehovah are upright."

23, 24. The book of Hosea concludes with what encouraging prophecy, and how does it affect us?

25. Our consideration of Hosea's prophecy should help us to do what?

'The Love of All of You Is Increasing'

A NUMBER of natural disasters struck Japan in 2004. Among these were typhoons, floods, and earthquakes. They drastically affected the lives of many, including Jehovah's Witnesses. (Ecclesiastes 9: 11) These adversities, though, provided opportunities for Witnesses to show brotherly affection for one another.—1 Peter 1:22.

For example, because of heavy rains in July, a river in central Japan overflowed its banks. Flooding damaged more than 20 homes of Jehovah's Witnesses. In one Kingdom Hall, the water rose some three feet above the floor. Immediately, Witnesses from neighboring congregations pitched in to help. Hundreds of volunteers cleaned the mud-soaked houses. The Kingdom Hall was fully cleaned up and repaired within just two weeks.

On October 23, an earthquake measuring 6.8 on the Richter scale struck the same area. At least 40 lives were lost, and over 100,000 people had to be evacuated from their homes. Water, gas, and electricity were cut off. Although the epicenter of the quake was just 30 miles away, the renovated Kingdom Hall was not damaged. It immediately became a temporary relief center. Christian overseers quickly checked on the safety of their fellow believers and were relieved to learn that none had been hurt or killed. Early the next morning, six Witnesses who had been victims of the July flood eagerly volunteered to deliver food and water to the affected area. Within hours of the earthquake, relief goods were made available.

"Those who were victims of the floods considered the relief work for those affected by the earthquake to be an opportunity to express their appreciation for the help they themselves had received," relates one overseer. "They worked hard from early morning till late night. And how their faces shone with happiness!"

Neither floods nor earthquakes are threats to the bond of love that binds the Christian brotherhood of Jehovah's Witnesses. On the contrary, when such disasters strike, Christians experience what the apostle Paul told fellow believers in Thessalonica: "The love of each and all of you is increasing one toward the other."—2 Thessalonians 1:3.

DECEMBER 1, 2005

THE WATCHTOWER

ANNOUNCING JEHOVAH'S KINGDOM

Do You Know the Truth About ARMAGEDDON?

THE WATCHTOWER®

ANNOUNCING JEHOVAH'S KINGDOM

December 1, 2005   Average Printing Each Issue: 26,439,000   Vol. 126, No. 23

THE PURPOSE OF *THE WATCHTOWER* is to exalt Jehovah God as Sovereign Lord of the universe. It keeps watch on world events as these fulfill Bible prophecy. It comforts all peoples with the good news that God's Kingdom will soon destroy those who oppress their fellowmen and that it will turn the earth into a paradise. It encourages faith in God's now-reigning King, Jesus Christ, whose shed blood opens the way for mankind to gain eternal life. *The Watchtower,* published by Jehovah's Witnesses continuously since 1879, is nonpolitical. It adheres to the Bible as its authority.

IN THIS ISSUE

3   Armageddon—A Catastrophic End?

4   Armageddon—A Happy Beginning

8   A Testimony to Love, Faith, and Obedience

13   Determined to Continue Serving My Creator

18   Jehovah's Word Is Alive—Highlights From the Book of Second Chronicles

22   People "out of All the Languages" Hear the Good News

27   Becoming Progressive and Adaptable Ministers

32   "Good News for People of All Nations"

WATCHTOWER STUDIES

JANUARY 2-8:
People "out of All the Languages" Hear the Good News.
Page 22. Songs to be used: 6, 151.

JANUARY 9-15:
Becoming Progressive and Adaptable Ministers.
Page 27. Songs to be used: 193, 156.

Publication of *The Watchtower* is part of a worldwide Bible educational work supported by voluntary donations.

Unless otherwise indicated, Scripture quotations are from the modern-language *New World Translation of the Holy Scriptures—With References.*

The Watchtower (ISSN 0043-1087) is published semimonthly by Watchtower Bible and Tract Society of New York, Inc.; M. H. Larson, President; G. F. Simonis, Secretary-Treasurer; 25 Columbia Heights, Brooklyn, NY 11201-2483. Periodicals Postage Paid at Brooklyn, NY, and at additional mailing offices. **POSTMASTER:** Send address changes to Watchtower, **Wallkill, NY 12589.**

Changes of address should reach us 30 days before your moving date. Give us your old and new address (if possible, your old address label).

Semimonthly   ENGLISH

Would you welcome more information or a free home Bible study? Please send your request to Jehovah's Witnesses, using the appropriate address below.

America, United States of: Wallkill, NY 12589. *Antigua:* Box 119, St. Johns. *Australia:* Box 280, Ingleburn, NSW 1890. *Bahamas:* Box N-1247, Nassau, N.P. *Barbados, W.I.:* Crusher Site Road, Prospect, St. James. *Britain:* The Ridgeway, London NW7 1RN. *Canada:* Box 4100, Halton Hills (Georgetown), Ontario L7G 4Y4. *Germany:* Niederselters, Am Steinfels, D-65618 Selters. *Ghana:* P. O. Box GP 760, Accra. *Guyana:* 352-360 Tyrell St., Republic Park Phase 2 EBD. *Hawaii 96819:* 2055 Kam IV Rd., Honolulu. *Hong Kong:* 4 Kent Road, Kowloon Tong. *India:* Post Box 6440, Yelahanka, Bangalore 560 064, KAR. *Ireland:* Newcastle, Greystones, Co. Wicklow. *Jamaica:* P. O. Box 103, Old Harbour, St. Catherine. *Japan:* 1271 Nakashinden, Ebina City, Kanagawa Pref., 243-0496. *Kenya:* P.O. Box 47788, GPO Nairobi 00100. *New Zealand:* P.O. Box 75-142, Manurewa. *Nigeria:* P.M.B. 1090, Benin City 300001, Edo State. *Philippines, Republic of:* P. O. Box 2044, 1060 Manila. *South Africa:* Private Bag X2067, Krugersdorp, 1740. *Trinidad and Tobago, Republic of:* Lower Rapsey Street & Laxmi Lane, Curepe. *Zambia:* Box 33459, Lusaka 10101. *Zimbabwe:* Private Bag WG-5001, Westgate.

NOW PUBLISHED IN 151 LANGUAGES. SEMIMONTHLY: Afrikaans, Albanian,* Amharic, Arabic, Bengali, Bicol, Bislama, Bulgarian, Cebuano,* Chichewa,* Chinese, Chinese (Simplified),* Cibemba,* Croatian,* Czech,*# Danish,*# Dutch,*# East Armenian, Efik,* English**#+◉ (also Braille), Estonian, Ewe, Fijian, Finnish,*# French*# (also Braille), Ga, Georgian,*# German,*# Greek,* Gujarati, Gun, Hebrew, Hiligaynon, Hindi, Hungarian,*# Igbo,* Iloko,* Indonesian, Italian,*# Japanese*# (also Braille), Kannada, Kinyarwanda, Kirundi, Korean*# (also Braille), Latvian, Lingala, Lithuanian, Luvale, Macedonian, Malagasy,* Malayalam, Maltese, Myanmar, Nepali, Norwegian,*# Pangasinan, Papiamento (Aruba), Papiamento (Curaçao), Polish,*# Portuguese*# (also Braille), Punjabi, Rarotongan, Romanian,* Russian,* Samar-Leyte, Samoan, Sango, Sepedi, Serbian, Sesotho, Shona,* Silozi, Sinhala, Slovak,* Slovenian, Solomon Islands Pidgin, Spanish*# (also Braille), Sranantongo, Swahili,* Swedish,*# Tagalog,* Tamil, Telugu, Thai, Tigrinya, Tok Pisin, Tongan, Tshiluba, Tsonga, Tswana, Turkish, Twi, Ukrainian,* Urdu, Vietnamese, Wallisian, Xhosa, Yoruba,* Zulu*.

MONTHLY: American Sign Language,△◻ Armenian, Assamese, Azerbaijani (roman script), Brazilian Sign Language,△ Cambodian, Chitonga, Gilbertese, Greenlandic, Haitian Creole, Hausa, Hiri Motu, Icelandic, Isoko, Kaonde, Kazakh, Kikongo, Kiluba, Kirghiz, Kosraean, Kwanyama/Ndonga, Luganda, Marathi, Marshallese, Mauritian Creole, Maya, Mizo, Monokutuba, Moore, Niuean, Ossetian, Otetela, Palauan, Persian, Ponapean, Seychelles Creole, Tahitian, Tatar, Tiv, Trukese, Tumbuka, Tuvaluan, Umbundu, Uruund, Venda, Yapese, Zande

* Study articles also available in large-print edition.
# Audiocassettes also available.
+ CD also available.
◉ MP3 CD-ROM also available.
△ Videocassette
◻ DVD

ARMAGEDDON
A Catastrophic End?

ARMAGEDDON! Does this word conjure up images of mass destruction or a cosmic conflagration? Few Bible expressions have become as much a part of everyday speech as "Armageddon" has. The term has been widely used to describe the gloomy prospects facing humans. The entertainment industry has fed people's imagination with horrific scenes of a coming "Armageddon." The word is shrouded in mystery and misconceptions. While ideas as to its meaning abound, most of them are not in line with what the Bible—the source of the expression—teaches about Armageddon.

Since the Bible links Armageddon with "the end of the world," would you not agree that it is vital to have a clear understanding of what the word really signifies? (Matthew 24:3, *King James Version*) And would it not be reasonable to turn to the ultimate source of truth, God's Word, to find answers about the nature of Armageddon and what it will mean for you and your family?

Such an examination will show that instead of bringing a cataclysmic end, Armageddon will introduce a happy beginning for people who desire to live and thrive in a righteous new world. You will be rewarded with a clear understanding of this vital Scriptural truth as you consider the discussion of Armageddon's real meaning in the next article.

WHAT DO YOU THINK ARMAGEDDON IS?

- A nuclear holocaust
- An environmental disaster
- A collision of a celestial body with the earth
- Divine destruction of the wicked

ARMAGEDDON
A Happy Beginning

THE word "Armageddon" has its origin in the Hebrew expression "Har–Magedon," or "Mountain of Megiddo." It is found at Revelation 16:16, which states: "They gathered them together to the place that is called in Hebrew Har–Magedon." Who are assembled to Armageddon, and why? Just two verses earlier, at Revelation 16:14, we read: "The *kings* of the entire inhabited earth" are gathered together "to the *war* of the great day of God the Almighty." Naturally, those statements raise additional intriguing questions. Where do these "kings" fight? Over what issue do they battle, and with whom? Will they, as many believe, use weapons of mass destruction? Will there be survivors of Armageddon? Let the Bible provide the answers.

Does the reference to the "Mountain of Megiddo" mean that Armageddon will be fought at a certain mountain in the Middle East? No. For one thing, no such mountain really exists—at the site of ancient Megiddo, there is only a mound rising about 70 feet above the adjacent valley plain. In addition, the area around Megiddo could not begin to hold all "the kings of the earth and their armies." (Revelation 19:19) However, Megiddo was the site of some of the fiercest and most decisive battles in Middle Eastern history. Thus, the name Armageddon stands as a symbol of a decisive conflict, with only one clear victor.—See the box "Megiddo—A Fitting Symbol," on page 5.

Armageddon cannot be just a conflict among earthly nations, since Revelation 16:14 states that "the kings of the entire inhabited earth" form a united front at "the war of the great day of God the Almighty." In his inspired prophecy, Jeremiah stated that "those slain by Jehovah" will be scattered "from one end of the earth clear to the other end of the earth." (Jeremiah 25:33) Thus, Armageddon is not a human war confined to a particular location in the Middle East. It is Jehovah's war, and it is global.

Note, however, that at Revelation 16:16, Armageddon is called a "place." In the Bible, "place" may signify a condition or a situation—in this case, that the entire world will be united in its opposition to Jehovah. (Revelation 12:6, 14) At Armageddon all earthly nations ally themselves against "the armies that were in heaven" under the military command of the "King of kings and Lord of lords," Jesus Christ.—Revelation 19:14, 16.

What about the claim that Armageddon will be a holocaust involving weapons of mass destruction or a collision with a celestial body? Would a loving God allow such a horrific end to humankind and their home, the earth? No. He expressly states that he did not create the earth "simply for nothing" but "formed it even to be inhabited." (Isaiah 45:18; Psalm 96:10) At Armageddon, Jehovah will not ruin our globe in a cataclysmic conflagration. Rather, he will "bring to ruin those ruining the earth."—Revelation 11:18.

Armageddon—When?

Over the centuries, a pressing question that has generated endless speculation has been, When will Armageddon come? Examining the book of Revelation in the light of other parts of the Bible can help us determine the timing of this crucial battle. Revelation 16:15 links Armageddon with Jesus' coming as a thief. That word picture is also used by Jesus in describing his coming to execute judgment on this system of things. —Matthew 24:43, 44; 1 Thessalonians 5:2.

As shown by the fulfillment of Bible prophecies, since 1914 we have been living in the last days of this system of things.* Marking the final part of the last days will be the period that Jesus called the "great tribula-

---

* See *Knowledge That Leads to Everlasting Life,* chapter 11, published by Jehovah's Witnesses.

tion." The Bible does not say how long that period will be, but the calamities associated with it will be worse than anything the world has ever seen. That great tribulation will culminate at Armageddon.—Matthew 24:21, 29.

Since Armageddon is "the war of the great day of *God the Almighty,*" there is nothing that humans can do to postpone it. Jehovah has set an "appointed time" for that war to start. "It will not be late."—Habakkuk 2:3.

A God of Righteousness Wages a Just War

Why, though, would God wage a global war? Armageddon is closely related to one of

---

MEGIDDO—A FITTING SYMBOL

Ancient Megiddo was strategically situated, overlooking the western section of the fertile Jezreel Valley, in northern Israel. It controlled the international trade and military routes that intersected there. Thus, Megiddo became a place of decisive battles. Professor Graham Davies writes in his book *Cities of the Biblical World—Megiddo:* "The city of Megiddo . . . was easily accessible to traders and migrants from all directions; but at the same time it could, if powerful enough, control access by means of these routes and so direct the course of both trade and

war. It is not surprising therefore that it was . . . a prize often fought over and when secured strongly defended."

The long history of Megiddo began in the second millennium B.C.E. when the Egyptian ruler Thutmose III defeated the Canaanite rulers there. It continued through the centuries to 1918 when British General Edmund Allenby inflicted a stinging defeat on the Turkish army. It was at Megiddo that God enabled Judge Barak to inflict a smashing blow upon Canaanite King Jabin. (Judges 4:12-24; 5:19, 20) In that vi-

Pictorial Archive (Near Eastern History) Est.

cinity Judge Gideon routed the Midianites. (Judges 7: 1-22) It was there, too, that Kings Ahaziah and Josiah were killed.—2 Kings 9:27; 23:29, 30.

Associating Armageddon with that vicinity is thus appropriate, since it was the site of numerous decisive battles. It is a fitting symbol of God's complete victory over all opposing forces.

his cardinal qualities, justice. The Bible declares: "Jehovah is a lover of justice." (Psalm 37:28) He has seen all the acts of injustice perpetrated during man's history. This naturally provokes his righteous displeasure. Thus, he has appointed his Son to wage a just war in order to do away with this entire wicked system.

Only Jehovah is capable of waging a truly just and truly selective war during which righthearted individuals, wherever they may be on earth, will be preserved. (Matthew 24: 40, 41; Revelation 7:9, 10, 13, 14) And only he has the right to impose his sovereignty over all the earth, for it is his creation.—Revelation 4:11.

What forces will Jehovah use against his enemies? We simply do not know. What we do know is that he has at his disposal the means to devastate the wicked nations completely. (Job 38:22, 23; Zephaniah 1:15-18) However, God's earthly worshippers will not participate in the battle. The vision in Revelation chapter 19 indicates that only heavenly armies will share with Jesus Christ in the warfare. None of Jehovah's Christian servants on earth will take part.—2 Chronicles 20:15, 17.

A God of Wisdom Gives Ample Warning

What about survivors? Indeed, no one needs to perish at Armageddon. The apostle Peter observed: "Jehovah . . . does not desire any to be destroyed but desires all to attain to repentance." (2 Peter 3:9) And the apostle Paul stated that God's "will is that all sorts of men should be saved and come to an accurate knowledge of truth."—1 Timothy 2:4.

To that end, Jehovah has wisely made sure that the "good news of the kingdom" is proclaimed far and wide, in hundreds of languages. People everywhere are being given the opportunity for survival and salvation.

(Matthew 24:14; Psalm 37:34; Philippians 2: 12) Those who respond favorably to the good news can survive Armageddon and live forever in perfection on a paradise earth. (Ezekiel 18:23, 32; Zephaniah 2:3; Romans 10:13) Is this not what one would expect from a God who is love?—1 John 4:8.

Can a God of Love Fight?

Many wonder, however, why a God who is the very embodiment of love would inflict death and destruction on much of humankind. The situation might be compared to that of a pest-infested house. Would you not agree that a conscientious homeowner should safeguard the health and well-being of his family by exterminating the pests?

Similarly, it is because of Jehovah's deep affection for humans that the battle of Armageddon has to be fought. God's purpose is to make the earth a paradise and to elevate mankind to perfection and peace, with "no one making them tremble." (Micah 4:3, 4; Revelation 21:4) What, then, is to be done with those who threaten the peace and security of their fellow humans? God must eliminate such "pests"—the incorrigibly wicked—for the sake of the righteous ones.—2 Thessalonians 1:8, 9; Revelation 21:8.

Much of the strife and bloodshed today is caused by imperfect human rulership and the selfish striving for nationalistic interests. (Ecclesiastes 8:9) Seeking to expand their influence, human governments totally disregard God's established Kingdom. There is no indication that they will relinquish their sovereignty to God and Christ. (Psalm 2: 1-9) Such governments must therefore be removed to pave the way for the righteous rule of Jehovah's Kingdom under Christ. (Daniel 2:44) Armageddon must be fought in order to resolve once and for all the issue of who has the right to rule this planet and humankind.

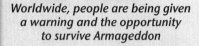

Worldwide, people are being given a warning and the opportunity to survive Armageddon

Jehovah's active intervention at Armageddon will be with mankind's best interests at heart. In the face of worsening world conditions, only God's perfect rulership will completely satisfy mankind's needs. Only by means of his Kingdom will true peace and prosperity prevail. What would world conditions be like if God forever refrained from taking action? Would not hatred, violence, and wars continue to plague mankind as they have throughout the centuries of human rulership? The battle of Armageddon is actually one of the best things that could happen to us!—Luke 18:7, 8; 2 Peter 3:13.

The War to End All Wars

Armageddon will accomplish something that no other war has ever accomplished—the end of all wars. Who does not yearn for the day when warfare will be a thing of the past? However, the end of war has eluded all human efforts. Such repeated failure of human attempts to end war merely emphasizes the truth of Jeremiah's words: "I well know, O Jehovah, that to earthling man his way does

not belong. It does not belong to man who is walking even to direct his step." (Jeremiah 10: 23) Regarding what Jehovah will accomplish, the Bible promises: "He is making wars to cease to the extremity of the earth. The bow he breaks apart and does cut the spear in pieces; the wagons he burns in the fire."—Psalm 46:8, 9.

As the nations use their deadly weapons on one another and threaten to destroy the environment, the Maker of the earth will take action—at the Biblical Armageddon! (Revelation 11:18) This war, therefore, will accomplish what God-fearing men throughout the ages could only hope for. It will vindicate the rightful rulership of earth's Owner, Jehovah God, over all his creation.

Thus, Armageddon is not to be feared by people who love righteousness. Rather, it provides a basis for hope. The war of Armageddon will cleanse the earth of all corruption and wickedness and open the way for a righteous new system of things under the rule of God's Messianic Kingdom. (Isaiah 11: 4, 5) Instead of being a frightening cataclysmic end, Armageddon will signal a happy beginning for righteous individuals, who will live forever on a paradise earth.—Psalm 37:29.

Armageddon will signal a happy beginning

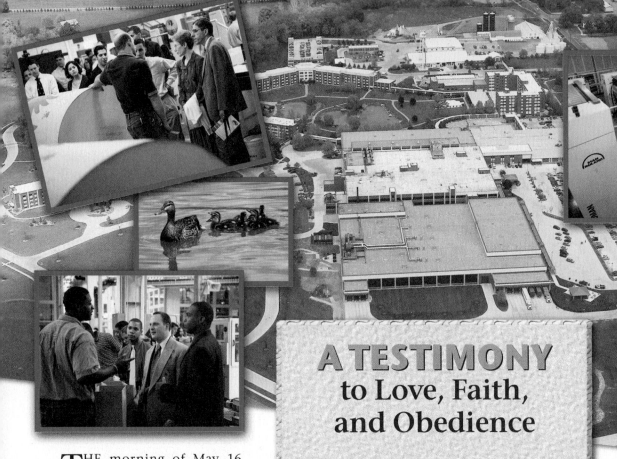

A TESTIMONY
to Love, Faith, and Obedience

THE morning of May 16, 2005, was pleasantly cool and bright at Watchtower Farms in Wallkill, New York. The manicured lawns and flower beds glistened from a predawn rain. A duck with eight ducklings glided quietly on the calm water near the edge of the pond. Visitors marveled at the beauty. They spoke softly, as if not wanting to spoil the tranquillity of the morning.

The visitors were Jehovah's Witnesses who had come from 48 countries around the world. But they had not come to see the scenery. They were interested in what was happening inside an expansive red-brick building, the most recent addition to the United States Bethel complex at Wallkill. Inside that building, they marveled again, though the scene was neither quiet nor tranquil.

From a mezzanine, the visitors gazed down upon a maze of machinery. Five massive presses spread over a polished concrete floor larger than nine football fields. It is here that Bibles, books, and magazines are printed. Huge rolls of paper, weighing 3,800 pounds each, spin like the wheels of a fast-moving truck. Each 14-mile roll of paper unwinds and passes through the press in just 25 minutes. In that time, the press applies and dries the ink and cools the paper so that it can be folded into magazines that speed along overhead conveyors to be boxed and shipped to congregations. Other presses are busy printing book signatures, which are swiftly moved to a floor-to-ceiling storage area until they

are sent to the bindery. The operation is a computer-directed symphony of precise movements.

Leaving the pressroom, the visitors toured the bindery. Here machines produce hardcover books and deluxe Bibles at a rate of up to 50,000 copies per day. Book signatures are collated, bound, and trimmed. Covers are then attached. Cartons are slipped over stacks of finished books. The cartons are automatically sealed, labeled, and stacked on a pallet. Additionally, a paperback-book line assembles and packs as many as 100,000 books per day. This too is a world of machinery—countless motors, conveyors, gears, wheels, and belts—all moving at astounding speed to produce Bible literature.

Operating with the precision of a well-made watch, the printery's high-speed, state-of-the-art machinery is a marvel of modern technology. As we will see, it is also a testimony to the love, faith, and obedience of God's people. Why, though, were the printing operations moved from Brooklyn, New York, to Wallkill?

A major reason was to simplify printing and shipping by centralizing operations at one location. For years, books were printed and shipped from Brooklyn, and magazines were printed and shipped from Wallkill. Combining operations would reduce personnel and make better use of dedicated funds. Furthermore, since the presses in Brooklyn were getting old, two new MAN Roland Lithoman printing presses were ordered from Germany. These presses were too large to fit into the printery in Brooklyn.

Jehovah Backs the Work

The purpose of the printing has always been to further the good news of God's Kingdom. It has been evident that Jehovah's blessing has been on the work from the very beginning. From 1879 to 1922, the books were printed by commercial printing establishments. In 1922, a six-story building at 18 Concord Street in Brooklyn was rented and equipment purchased for the printing of books. At that time, some doubted whether the brothers could handle the task.

One of those doubters was the president of the company that had printed most of our books. When visiting Concord Street, he said: "Here you are with a first-class printing establishment on your hands, and nobody around the place that knows a thing about what to do with it. In six months the whole thing will be a lot of junk; and you will find out that the people to do your printing are those that have always done it, and make it their business."

The printery overseer at the time, Robert J. Martin, observed: "That sounded logical enough, but it left out the Lord; and he has always been with us. . . . It was not long before we were making books." During the next 80 years, Jehovah's Witnesses printed billions of pieces of literature on their own printing presses.

Then on October 5, 2002, at the annual meeting of the Watch Tower Bible and Tract Society of Pennsylvania, it was announced that the Governing Body had approved the moving of printing operations of the United States branch to Wallkill. Two new presses had been ordered, with a delivery date of February 2004. The brothers would need to design and expand the printery and be ready

within 15 months to receive the new presses. Then, the installation of new bindery and shipping operations would have to be completed within the following nine months. Some may have had doubts when they heard the timetable—the task seemed daunting. Yet, the brothers knew that with Jehovah's blessing, it could be done.

"A Happy Spirit of Cooperation"

Knowing that Jehovah's people would offer themselves willingly, the brothers started the project. (Psalm 110:3) Its magnitude required more workers than were available from within the Bethel construction departments. From the United States and Canada, over 1,000 brothers and sisters with construction skills volunteered to serve from one week to three months as part of a temporary volunteer program. Others from the international servant and volunteer programs were invited to share in the project. Regional Building Committees also contributed greatly.

For many, volunteering for the Wallkill project meant a significant expenditure on travel and time away from secular employment. Yet, they joyfully made these sacrifices. Housing and feeding these many additional volunteers provided opportunities for the Bethel family to exert themselves in support of the project. Over 535 Bethel family members from Brooklyn, Patterson, and Wallkill volunteered to work on the project on Saturdays, in addition to their normal weekday assignments. The overwhelming support that God's people gave to this historic endeavor was possible only because Jehovah was backing the project.

Others contributed financially. For example, the brothers received a letter from nine-year-old Abby. She wrote: "I am so grateful for all the work you do—making all the wonderful books. I might be coming over soon. My daddy said next year! I'll wear a badge so you know who I am. Here's 20 dollars for the new printing press! It's my allowance money, but I want to give it to you brothers."

A sister wrote: "Please accept my gift of crocheted hats that I made with my own two little hands. I would like these hats to be given to the workers who are working on the Wallkill project. An almanac said it's going to be a very bad winter. Whether they're right or not, I don't know. But I know that much of the work at Wallkill will be done outside, and I want to make sure that my brothers and sisters will keep their head warm. I don't have any of the skills that the brothers are looking for, but I can crochet, so I decided to use this skill to contribute what I could." Enclosed were 106 crocheted hats!

The printery was completed on schedule. John Larson, printery overseer, said: "There was such a happy spirit of cooperation. Who could doubt that Jehovah was blessing the work? Things moved so quickly. I recall standing in the mud in May 2003 watching the brothers lay the foundation of the building. Less than a year later, I stood on the same spot observing a printing press in operation."

Dedication Program

The program to dedicate the new printery, along with three residence buildings, was held at Wallkill on Monday, May 16, 2005. The Bethel complexes at Patterson and Brooklyn, as well as Canada Bethel, were tied in by video line. In all, 6,049 enjoyed the program. Theodore Jaracz, a member of the Governing Body of Jehovah's Witnesses, served as chairman and gave a brief overview of the history of the printing work. By means of interviews and video presentations, Branch Committee members John Larson and John Kikot reviewed the history of both the construction project and the printing operations in the United States. John Barr of the Governing Body delivered the final talk, dedicating the new printery and three residence complexes to Jehovah God.

During the week that followed, Bethelites from Patterson and Brooklyn were given the opportunity to tour the new facilities. In all, 5,920 visited during that time.

How Do We View the Printery?

In the dedication talk, Brother Barr reminded his listeners that the printery, impressive though it may be, is not about machinery. It is about people. The literature we print has a profound impact on people's life.

EXPANSION OF PRINTING IN THE UNITED STATES

◄ **1920:** Magazines printed with first rotary press, at 35 Myrtle Avenue, Brooklyn.

▲ **1922:** The printery relocated to a six-story building at 18 Concord Street. Books now printed.

▼ **1927:** Printery moved to a new building erected at 117 Adams Street.

◄ **1949:** A nine-story addition doubled printery size.

▲ **1956:** Adams Street printery doubled again when new building is erected at 77 Sands Street.

◄ **1967:** Ten-story building erected, making possible an interconnected printery ten times larger than original building.

◄ **1973:** Subsidiary printery at Wallkill built, primarily for magazine production.

2004: All printing, binding, and shipping operations in the United States consolidated at Wallkill.

Each of the new presses can print a million tracts in just over an hour! Yet, a single tract can have a far-reaching effect on someone's life. For example, in 1921 a team of railroad-maintenance men in South Africa worked their way along a stretch of railway track. One of them, a man named Christiaan, noticed a piece of paper wedged under a rail. It was one of our tracts. Christiaan read it with intense interest. He ran to meet his son-in-law and announced excitedly: "Today I have found the truth!" Shortly afterward, they wrote for more information. The South Africa branch sent additional Bible literature. The two men studied, got baptized, and shared Bible truth with others. As a result, many accepted the truth. In fact, by the early 1990's, more than a hundred of their descendants were Witnesses of Jehovah—all the result of one man's discovering a single tract on a railroad track!

The literature that we print, Brother Barr said, brings people into the truth, keeps them in the truth, motivates them to greater zeal, and unifies the brotherhood. And most of all, the literature, which we all have a share in distributing, glorifies our God, Jehovah!

How Does Jehovah View the Printery?

Brother Barr also asked the audience to consider how Jehovah views the printery. He certainly does not depend on it. He could make the stones preach the good news! (Luke 19:40) Furthermore, he is not impressed by the complexity, size, speed, or capabilities of machinery. Why, he created the universe! (Psalm 147:10, 11) Jehovah knows more advanced ways to produce literature, ways that have been neither devised nor even imagined by humans. So, what does Jehovah see that he truly values? Surely he sees in this printery the precious qualities of his people—their love, faith, and obedience.

The aspect of love was illustrated. A girl bakes a cake for her parents. Likely, the parents will be touched. Yes, however the cake turns out, what touches the parents is their child's love, as shown by her generous act. Similarly, when Jehovah looks at this new printery, he sees beyond the building and the machinery. Primarily, he sees it as an expression of love for his name.—Hebrews 6:10.

Furthermore, just as Jehovah viewed the ark as an expression of Noah's faith, he sees this printery as tangible evidence of our faith. Faith in what? Noah had faith that what Jehovah foretold would come true. We have faith that we are living in the last days, that the good news is the most important message being sounded on earth, and that it is vital for people to hear it. We know that the Bible's message can save lives.—Romans 10: 13, 14.

Doubtless, Jehovah also sees in this printery an expression of our obedience. As we know, it is his will that the good news be preached worldwide before the end comes. (Matthew 24:14) This printery, along with those in other regions of the globe, will play a role in fulfilling that commission.

Yes, the love, faith, and obedience shown in the financing, construction, and operation of these facilities is also reflected in the zealous activity of Jehovah's people everywhere as they continue to proclaim the truth to all who will listen.

IN OUR NEXT ISSUE

Christmastime—What Is Its Focus?

———

The Bible in Italian
—A Troubled History

———

Now Is the Time for Decisive Action

DETERMINED TO CONTINUE SERVING MY CREATOR

AS TOLD BY
CONSTANCE BENANTI

It all happened so quickly! Within a span of six days, Camille, our 22-month-old daughter, developed a high fever and died. My grief was unbearable. I wanted to die too. Why did God permit such a thing? I was confused.

MY PARENTS were immigrants from Castellammare del Golfo, a town in Sicily, Italy. They came to New York City, where I was born on December 8, 1908. Our family consisted of my father and mother and their eight children, five boys and three girls.*

In 1927 my father, Santo Catanzaro, started attending the meetings of a small group of Bible Stu-

Camille

dents, as Jehovah's Witnesses were then called. Giovanni De Cecca, an Italian brother serving at the Brooklyn, New York, headquarters (called Bethel), held meetings where we lived, in nearby New Jersey. In time, Father began preaching and took up the full-time ministry, continuing in that work until his death in 1953.

When Mother was young, she wanted to be a nun, but her parents would not permit it. At first, I was influenced by Mother not to share with Father in

---

* The experience of my brother Angelo Catanzaro was published in the April 1, 1975, issue of *The Watchtower*, pages 205-7.

the talk at Camille's funeral. "Do you really believe in the resurrection?" I asked.

"I do!" he answered. "Why don't we find out more about what the Bible has to say?"

That night I couldn't sleep. At six in the morning, before Father left for work, I went to him and told him that Charles and I wanted to study the Bible. He was delighted and hugged me. Mother, who was still in bed, overheard us talking. She asked me what had happened. "Nothing," I said. "Charles and I have simply decided to study the Bible."

"We all need to study the Bible," was her answer. So all of us, including my brothers and sisters—11 in total—began to study together as a family.

The Bible study gave me comfort, and slowly my mental confusion and grief gave way to hope. A year later, in 1935, Charles and I began to share Bible truths with others. In February 1937, after hearing a talk at headquarters in Brooklyn that explained the Scriptural significance of water baptism, we were baptized at a nearby hotel along with many others. I took this step not only because I hoped to see my daughter again someday but also because I desired to serve our Creator, whom I had come to know and love.

Bible study. Soon, though, I noticed changes in him. He became calmer, milder, and there was more peace in the family. I liked that.

Meanwhile, I met Charles, a man my age who was born in Brooklyn. His family, like mine, came from Sicily. We soon became engaged, and following Father's return from the 1931 convention of Jehovah's Witnesses in Columbus, Ohio, we were married. Within a year, our daughter Camille was born. When she died, I was inconsolable. One day Charles, who was crying, said to me: "Camille was as much my daughter as she was yours. Why can't we just go ahead with our lives, comforting each other?"

Not interested at first, Mother agreed that we all should study the Bible

We Accept Bible Truth

Charles reminded me that Father had spoken of the resurrection hope when he gave

Entering the Full-Time Ministry

Speaking to others about what I had learned was exciting and rewarding, especially since many at that time responded to the Kingdom message and shared in proclaiming it. (Matthew 9:37) In 1941, Charles and I be-

With Brother Knorr at Gilead graduation, 1946

came pioneers, as Jehovah's Witnesses call their full-time ministers. Not long afterward, we bought a trailer, and Charles left our family's pants factory in the hands of my brother Frank. In time, we were excited to receive a letter informing us that we had been assigned as special pioneers. Initially, we served in New Jersey, and later we were sent to New York State.

In 1946, while attending a convention in Baltimore, Maryland, we were asked to report to a meeting with special representatives of Jehovah's Witnesses. There we met Nathan H. Knorr and Milton G. Henschel. They spoke to us about the missionary work and, in particular, about the preaching work in Italy. They invited us to consider the possibility of attending the Watchtower Bible School of Gilead.

"Think about it," we were told, "and then give us your answer." After leaving the office, Charles and I exchanged glances, turned around, and went right back in. "We thought about it," we said. "We're ready for Gilead." Ten days later, we were attending the seventh class of Gilead.

Our months of training were unforgettable. What particularly impressed us was the patience and love of the instructors, preparing us to face difficulties in the foreign field. After graduating in July 1946, we were assigned to preach for a while in New York City, where there was a sizable Italian population. Then came the great day! On June 25, 1947, we left for Italy, our missionary assignment.

Getting Settled in Our Assignment

We made the crossing in a ship that had previously been used for military purposes. After 14 days at sea, we docked at the Italian port of Genoa. The city bore the scars of World War II, which had ended only two years earlier. The train station, for example, did not have any windowpanes because of the bombings. From Genoa we proceeded by freight train to Milan, where the branch office and a missionary home were located.

The living conditions in postwar Italy were very poor. Reconstruction efforts were under way, but poverty was rampant. Soon, I developed a serious health problem. According to one doctor, my heart was in such bad condition that he thought it would be best for me to return to the United States. I am glad that he got it all wrong. After 58 years, I'm still in my assignment in Italy.

We had been in our assignment only a few years when my brothers in the United States wanted to provide us with a car. But Charles turned their offer down, a decision I appreciated. To our knowledge, no Witness in Italy had a car then, and Charles felt that it was best for us to maintain a standard of living comparable to that of our Christian brothers. Not until 1961 did we get a small car.

Our first Kingdom Hall in Milan was in a basement with an earthen floor. There was no bathroom, and the only water was under our feet when it rained. We also had the company of little mice that darted here and there. Two light bulbs provided illumination for our meetings. Despite such inconveniences, it was encouraging to see sincere ones come to our meetings and eventually join us in the ministry.

Missionary Experiences

We once left the booklet *Peace—Can It Last?* with a man. As we were leaving, his wife, Santina, arrived laden with grocery bags. She was a little irritated, saying that she had eight daughters to care for and did not have any time to spare. When I called on Santina again, her husband was not at home, and she was knitting. "I don't have time to listen," she said. "Besides, I don't know how to read."

I prayed silently to Jehovah and then asked if I could pay her to knit a sweater for my husband. Two weeks later, I had the sweater, and Santina and I began to study the Bible regularly with the aid of the book *"The Truth Shall Make You Free."* Santina learned to read, and despite her husband's opposition, she made progress and was baptized. Five of her daughters became Witnesses, and Santina has also helped many others to accept Bible truth.

In March 1951, along with two other missionaries—Ruth Cannon* and Loyce Callahan, who later married Bill Wengert—we were transferred to Brescia, where there were no Witnesses. We found a furnished apartment, but two months later, the landlord asked us to leave the house within 24 hours. Since there were no other Witnesses in the area, we had no choice but to go to a hotel, where we stayed for almost two months.

Our diet was limited: cappuccino and croissants for breakfast, fruit and bread sticks with cheese for lunch, and fruit and bread sticks with cheese for supper. Despite the

---

* For her life story, see *The Watchtower,* May 1, 1971, pages 277-80.

inconveniences, we were really blessed. In time, we found a small apartment, and at the Memorial of Christ's death in 1952, 35 were present in the small room that we used as a Kingdom Hall.

Coping With Challenges

During that time, the clergy still wielded great power over the people. For example, while we were preaching in Brescia, some boys were encouraged by the priest to throw rocks at us. In time, however, 16 persons started studying the Bible with us, and within a short time, they became Witnesses. And who was among them? One of the boys who had threatened to throw rocks at us! He now serves as an elder in one of the congregations in Brescia. In 1955 when we left Brescia, 40 Kingdom publishers were sharing in the preaching work.

After that, we served for three years in Leghorn (Livorno), where most of the Witnesses were women. This meant that we sisters had to take care of congregation duties that are usually assigned to brothers. We next moved to Genoa, where we started out 11 years earlier. By now, there was a congregation. The Kingdom Hall was on the first floor in the building where our apartment was located.

Upon our arrival in Genoa, I started a study with a lady whose husband was a former boxer and the manager of a boxing gym. The lady made spiritual progress and soon became our Christian sister. Her husband, however, was opposed and remained so for a long time. Then he started to accompany his wife to the meetings. Rather than enter the hall, he sat outside and listened. Later on, after we had left Genoa, we learned that he had asked for a Bible study. In time, he was baptized and became a loving Christian overseer. He remained faithful till his death.

With Charles shortly before his death

I also studied the Bible with a woman who was engaged to a policeman. Initially, he showed some interest, but after the wedding, his attitude changed. He opposed her, and she stopped studying. When she later resumed the Bible study, her husband threatened her, saying that if he ever found us studying, he would shoot us both. Well, she made spiritual progress and became a baptized Witness. Needless to say, he never shot us. In fact, years later when I was attending an assembly in Genoa, someone came up to me from behind, covered my eyes with his hands, and asked if I could guess who he was. I could not hold back the tears when I saw the husband of that woman. After giving me a hug, he told me that he had symbolized his dedication to Jehovah by getting baptized that very day!

From 1964 to 1972, I had the privilege of accompanying Charles when he visited congregations to strengthen them spiritually. We served in almost all of northern Italy—in Piedmont, Lombardy, and Liguria. Then we resumed pioneer service near Florence and later in Vercelli. In 1977, there was only one congregation in Vercelli, but when we left in 1999, there were three. That year, I turned 91, and we were encouraged to move to the missionary home in Rome, a beautiful little building in a comparatively peaceful area.

Another Sad Occasion

In March 2002, Charles, who had always enjoyed good health, suffered a collapse. His health deteriorated until he died on May 11, 2002. For 71 years, we cried together during sad times and rejoiced together when blessings came our way. His death was an immense and grievous loss for me.

I often picture Charles in my mind, with his double-breasted suit and his 1930's hat. I imagine his smile, or I seem to hear his familiar laugh. With Jehovah's help and thanks to the love of many dear Christian brothers and sisters, I have been able to endure over this sad period. I eagerly await the time when I will see Charles again.

Continuing My Service

Serving my Creator has been the most wonderful thing in my life. Over the years, 'I have tasted and seen that Jehovah is good.' (Psalm 34:8) I have felt his love and experienced his care. Even though I lost my baby, Jehovah has given me many spiritual sons and daughters—scattered throughout Italy—who have brought joy to my heart and to his.

Speaking to others about my Creator is what I have always loved to do the most. That is why I continue to preach and conduct Bible studies. Sometimes I regret that I cannot do more because of my health. But I realize that Jehovah knows my limitations and that he loves me and appreciates what I am able to do. (Mark 12:42) I strive to make mine the words of Psalm 146:2: "I will praise Jehovah during my lifetime. I will make melody to my God as long as I am."*

---

* Sister Benanti passed away on July 16, 2005, as this article was being prepared. She was 96.

Jehovah's Word Is Alive
Highlights From the Book of Second Chronicles

AS THE Bible book of Second Chronicles opens, Solomon is ruling as king over Israel. The book ends with these words of Persian King Cyrus to the exiled Jews in Babylonia: "[Jehovah] himself has commissioned me to build him a house in Jerusalem, which is in Judah. Whoever there is among you of all his people, Jehovah his God be with him. So let him go up [to Jerusalem]." (2 Chronicles 36:23) Completed by the priest Ezra in 460 B.C.E., the book covers 500 years—from 1037 B.C.E. to 537 B.C.E.

Cyrus' decree makes it possible for the Jews to return to Jerusalem and reestablish Jehovah's worship there. However, the long years of Babylonian captivity have taken their toll. The returned exiles lack knowledge of their national history. Second Chronicles provides them with a vivid summary of events under kings of the royal line of David. The narrative is also of interest to us because it highlights the blessings that come from obedience to the true God and the consequences of disobedience to him.

A KING BUILDS A HOUSE TO JEHOVAH
(2 Chronicles 1:1–9:31)

Jehovah gives King Solomon the request of his heart—wisdom and knowledge—along with riches and honor. The king builds a magnificent house to Jehovah in Jerusalem, and the people are "joyful and feeling good at heart." (2 Chronicles 7:10) Solomon comes to be "greater than all the other kings of the earth in riches and wisdom." —2 Chronicles 9:22.

After ruling over Israel for 40 years, Solomon 'lies down with his forefathers, and Rehoboam his son begins to rule in his place.' (2 Chronicles 9:31) Ezra does not record Solomon's deviation from true worship. The only negative points mentioned about the king are his unwise acquisition of many horses from Egypt and his marriage to the daughter of Pharaoh. The chronicler thus presents the account from a positive standpoint.

Do you know why bulls were a fitting representation in the base of the molten sea?

Scriptural Questions Answered:

2:14—Why is the lineage of the craftsman described here different from the one found at 1 Kings 7:14? First Kings refers to the craftsman's mother as "a widowed woman from the tribe of Naphtali" because she had married a man of that tribe. She herself, though, was from the tribe of Dan. After her husband's death, she married a man of Tyre, and the artisan was an offspring of that marriage.

2:18; 8:10—These verses state that the number of deputies serving as overseers and as foremen over the labor force was 3,600 plus 250, whereas according to 1 Kings 5:16; 9:23, they numbered 3,300 plus 550. Why do the numbers differ? The difference seems to be in the way the deputies are classified. It may be that Second Chronicles differentiates between 3,600 non-Israelites and 250 Israelite deputies, while First Kings distinguishes 3,300 foremen from 550 chief supervisors of higher rank. In any case, the total number of those serving as deputies was 3,850.

4:2-4—Why was the representation of bulls used in the construction of the base of the molten sea? In the Scriptures, bulls are a symbol of strength. (Ezekiel 1:10; Revelation 4:6, 7) The choice of bulls as a representation was fitting because the 12 copper bulls supported the huge "sea," which weighed some 30 tons. The making of bulls for this purpose did not in any way violate the second commandment, which prohibited the making of objects for worship.—Exodus 20:4, 5.

4:5—What was the total capacity of the molten sea? When filled, the sea could hold three thousand bath measures, or about 17,400 gallons. The normal level, however, was probably about two thirds of its capacity. First Kings 7:26 states: "Two thousand bath measures [11,600 gallons] were what [the sea] would contain."

5:4, 5, 10—What furniture from the original tabernacle became part of Solomon's temple? The only item from the original tent of meeting that was kept in Solomon's temple was the Ark. After the construction of the temple, the tabernacle was taken from Gibeon to Jerusalem and was apparently stored there.—2 Chronicles 1:3, 4.

Lessons for Us:

1:11, 12. Solomon's request showed Jehovah that gaining wisdom and knowledge was close to the king's heart. Our prayers to God indeed reveal what is close to our heart. We are wise to analyze their content.

6:4. Heartfelt appreciation for Jehovah's loving-kindness and goodness should move us to bless Jehovah—that is, praise him with affection and gratitude.

6:18-21. Though God cannot be contained in any building, the temple was to serve as the center of Jehovah's worship. Today, Kingdom Halls of Jehovah's Witnesses are centers of true worship in the community.

6:19, 22, 32. Jehovah was accessible to all —from the king to the least ones in the nation—even to a foreigner who came to him in earnest.*—Psalm 65:2.

SUCCESSION OF KINGS IN THE LINE OF DAVID
(2 Chronicles 10:1–36:23)

The united kingdom of Israel is divided in two—the northern ten-tribe kingdom and the southern two-tribe kingdom of Judah and Benjamin. The priests and the Levites in all Israel place loyalty to the Kingdom covenant above nationalism and take their stand with Solomon's son Rehoboam. In a little

* For questions pertaining to the inauguration of the temple and other lessons from Solomon's prayer on that occasion, see *The Watchtower,* July 1, 2005, pages 28-31.

over 30 years after its completion, the temple is robbed of its treasures.

Of the 19 kings who follow Rehoboam, 5 are faithful, 3 start out well but become unfaithful, and one turns around from his wrong course. The rest of the rulers do what is bad in Jehovah's eyes.* The activities of the five kings who place their confidence in Jehovah are emphasized. The accounts of Hezekiah reviving temple services and Josiah arranging for a great Passover must have been of great encouragement to the Jews interested in reestablishing Jehovah's worship in Jerusalem.

Scriptural Questions Answered:

13:5—What is meant by the expression "a covenant of salt"? Because of its preserving properties, salt became a symbol of permanence and immutability. "A covenant of salt," then, denotes a binding agreement.

14:2-5; 15:17—Did King Asa remove all "the high places"? Apparently, he did not. It may be that Asa removed only the high places associated with the worship of false gods but not those where people worshipped Jehovah. It could also be that high places were built again in the latter part of Asa's reign. These his son Jehoshaphat removed. Actually, the high places did not disappear completely, even during Jehoshaphat's reign.—2 Chronicles 17:5, 6; 20:31-33.

15:9; 34:6—What was the standing of the tribe of Simeon with respect to the division of the kingdom of Israel? Having received as an inheritance various enclaves in Judah, the tribe of Simeon was geographically within the kingdom of Judah and Benjamin. (Joshua 19:1) Religiously and politically, however, the tribe aligned itself with the northern kingdom. (1 Kings 11:30-33; 12:20-24)

---

* For a chronological list of Judah's kings, see *The Watchtower,* August 1, 2005, page 12.

Hence, Simeon was counted with the ten-tribe kingdom.

16:13, 14—Was Asa cremated? No, the "extraordinarily great funeral burning" refers, not to the cremation of Asa, but to the burning of spices.—Footnote.

35:3—From where did Josiah have the holy Ark brought into the temple? Whether the Ark was removed earlier by one of the wicked kings or was relocated by Josiah for safekeeping during the extensive repair work of the temple, the Bible does not say. The only historical reference to the Ark after Solomon's day is when Josiah brought it into the temple.

Lessons for Us:

13:13-18; 14:11, 12; 32:9-23. What a lesson we can learn about the importance of leaning on Jehovah!

16:1-5, 7; 18:1-3, 28-32; 21:4-6; 22:10-12; 28:16-22. Alliances with foreigners or nonbelievers have tragic consequences. We are wise to avoid any unnecessary involvement with the world.—John 17:14, 16; James 4:4.

16:7-12; 26:16-21; 32:25, 26. Haughtiness caused King Asa to behave badly during the last years of his life. A haughty spirit led to Uzziah's downfall. Hezekiah acted unwisely and perhaps proudly when he showed Babylonian emissaries his treasury. (Isaiah 39:1-7) "Pride is before a crash," warns the Bible, "and a haughty spirit before stumbling." —Proverbs 16:18.

16:9. Jehovah helps those whose heart is complete toward him, and he is eager to use his power in their behalf.

18:12, 13, 23, 24, 27. Like Micaiah, we should be courageous and bold in speaking about Jehovah and his purposes.

19:1-3. Jehovah looks for the good in us even when we give him reasons to be angry with us.

Though he had limited help as a child, Josiah grew up to be faithful to Jehovah

20:1-28. We can be confident that Jehovah will let himself be found by us when we humbly turn to him for direction.—Proverbs 15:29.

20:17. To "see the salvation of Jehovah," we need to "take [our] position" in active support of God's Kingdom. Rather than take matters into our own hands, we must "stand still," placing our implicit trust in Jehovah.

24:17-19; 25:14. Idolatry proved to be a snare for Jehoash and his son Amaziah. Today, idolatry can be equally seductive, particularly when it comes in the subtle form of covetousness or nationalism.—Colossians 3:5; Revelation 13:4.

32:6, 7. We too must be courageous and strong as we "put on the complete suit of armor from God" and carry on spiritual warfare.—Ephesians 6:11-18.

33:2-9, 12, 13, 15, 16. A person shows true repentance by abandoning a wrong course and putting forth a determined effort to do what is right. On the basis of genuine repentance, even a person who has acted as wickedly as King Manasseh can receive Jehovah's mercy.

34:1-3. Any negative circumstances of childhood need not prevent us from coming to know God and serving him. A positive influence Josiah may have had during his early years could have come from his repentant grandfather, Manasseh. Whatever positive influences Josiah might have had eventually produced fine results. So it can be with us.

36:15-17. Jehovah is compassionate and patient. However, his compassion and patience are not limitless. People must respond favorably to the Kingdom-preaching work if they are to survive when Jehovah brings an end to this wicked system of things.

36:17, 22, 23. Jehovah's word always comes true.—1 Kings 9:7, 8; Jeremiah 25:9-11.

Moved to Action by a Book

"Josiah removed all the detestable things out of all the lands that belonged to the sons of Israel," states 2 Chronicles 34:33, "and he had all who were found in Israel take up service, to serve Jehovah their God." What moved Josiah to do this? When Shaphan the secretary brought the newly discovered book of Jehovah's Law to King Josiah, the king had it read aloud. So touched was Josiah by what he heard that he zealously promoted pure worship throughout his life.

Reading God's Word and meditating on what we read can affect us profoundly. Does not reflecting on the account of the kings in the Davidic line encourage us to imitate the examples of those who made Jehovah their confidence and avoid the conduct of those who did not? Second Chronicles stimulates us to give our exclusive devotion to the true God and remain faithful to him. Its message certainly is alive and exerts power.—Hebrews 4:12.

PEOPLE
"OUT OF ALL THE LANGUAGES"
HEAR THE GOOD NEWS

"Ten men out of all the languages of the nations will [say]:
'We will go with you people, for we have heard that God is with you people.'"
—ZECHARIAH 8:23.

THE timing and the setting could not have been better. It was the day of Pentecost 33 C.E. Weeks earlier, Jews and proselytes from at least 15 regions of the far-flung Roman Empire and beyond had packed Jerusalem to celebrate the Passover. On that day, thousands of them heard—not in confusion, as those at ancient Babel did, but with understanding—ordinary people filled with holy spirit proclaim the good news in numerous languages spoken in the empire. (Acts 2:1-12) That occasion marked the birth of the Christian congregation and the start of a multilingual, international educational work that has continued down to this day.

2 Jesus' disciples could probably speak common Greek, the popular language of the day. They also used Hebrew, the language spoken at the temple. However, on that Pentecost day, they "astonished" their diverse audience by speaking in the native languages of those people. What was the result? The hearts of the listeners were touched by the vital truths that they heard in their mother tongue. By the end of the day, the small group of disciples had grown to be a vast company of more than 3,000!—Acts 2:37-42.

3 Soon after that momentous event, a wave of persecution broke out in Jerusalem, and "those who had been scattered went through the land declaring the good news of the word." (Acts 8:1-4) For example, we read in Acts chapter 8 about Philip, apparently a Greek-speaking evangelizer. Philip preached to the Samaritans. He also preached to an Ethiopian official who responded to the message about Christ.—Acts 6:1-5; 8:5-13, 26-40; 21:8, 9.

4 As the Christians moved and searched for places to rebuild their lives outside the confines of Jerusalem, Judaea, and Galilee, they encountered new ethnic and language barriers. Some of them might have witnessed only to Jews. But the disciple Luke reports: "There were some men of Cyprus and Cyrene that came to Antioch and began talking to the Greek-speaking people, declaring the good news of the Lord Jesus."—Acts 11:19-21.

An Impartial God—A Message for All

5 Such developments are in keeping with God's ways; favoritism is alien to him. After the apostle Peter was helped by Jehovah to

---

1. How did Jehovah provide the best timing and setting for the multilingual and international launch of Christianity?
2. How did the disciples of Jesus 'astonish' their diverse audience at Pentecost 33 C.E.?

3, 4. How did the preaching work expand as the disciples moved out from Jerusalem, Judaea, and Galilee?
5. How is Jehovah's impartiality seen in connection with the good news?

adjust his view of people of the nations, he appreciatively noted: "For a certainty I perceive that God is not partial, but in every nation the man that fears him and works righteousness is acceptable to him." (Acts 10:34, 35; Psalm 145:9) When the apostle Paul, formerly a persecutor of Christians, declared that God's "will is that all sorts of men should be saved," he reaffirmed that God is free from bias. (1 Timothy 2:4) The Creator's impartiality is seen in that the Kingdom hope is open to people of any gender, race, nationality, or language.

At Pentecost 33 C.E., people from 15 regions of the Roman Empire and beyond heard the good news in their native languages

⁶ This international expansion was foretold centuries earlier. According to Daniel's prophecy, "there were given [to Jesus] rulership and dignity and kingdom, that the peoples, national groups and languages should all serve even him." (Daniel 7:14) The fact that this magazine is published in 151 languages and distributed worldwide, enabling you to read about Jehovah's Kingdom, reflects the fulfillment of that Bible prophecy.

⁷ The Bible foretold a time when people of diverse languages would hear its life-giving message. Describing how true worship would attract many, Zechariah prophesied: "It will be in those days that ten men *out of all the languages of the nations* will take hold, yes, they will actually take hold of the skirt of a man who is a Jew [spirit-anointed Christian, part of "the Israel of God"], saying: 'We will go with you people, for we have heard that God is with you people.'" (Zechariah 8:23; Galatians 6:16) And relating what he saw in a vision, the apostle John said: "Look! a great crowd, which no man was

6, 7. What Bible prophecies foretold the international, multilingual spread of the good news?

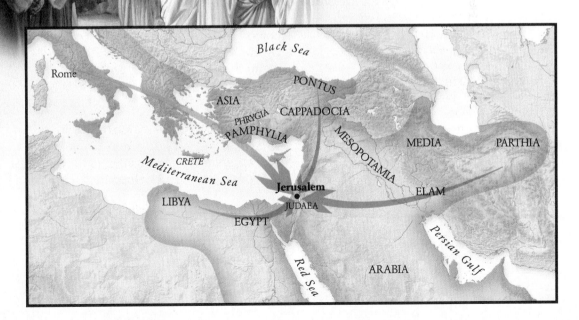

able to number, *out of all nations and tribes and peoples and tongues,* standing before the throne and before the Lamb." (Revelation 7:9) We have seen such prophecies coming true!

Reaching People of All Sorts

8 Today, people have become increasingly mobile. Globalization has opened a new era of migration. Droves of people from war zones and economically depressed areas have moved to more stable places, seeking a materially secure way of life. In many lands, an influx of immigrants and refugees has resulted in the formation of foreign-speaking enclaves. For instance, in Finland more than 120 languages are spoken; in Australia the number is over 200. In just one city in the United States—San Diego—over 100 languages can be heard!

---

8. What modern-day reality has called for adjustments in our witnessing work?

9 Do we as Christian ministers view the presence of such people who speak different languages as an impediment to our ministry? Not at all! Rather, we see this as a welcome expansion of our ministerial territory —'fields white for harvesting.' (John 4:35) We endeavor to care for people who are conscious of their spiritual need, regardless of their nationality or language. (Matthew 5:3) As a result, each year a growing number of people of 'every tongue' are becoming disciples of Christ. (Revelation 14:6) For example, as of August 2004, the preaching work in Germany was being carried out in about 40 languages. At the same time, the good news was preached in Australia in close to 30 languages, up from 18 just ten years ago. In Greece, Jehovah's Witnesses were reaching people in almost 20 different languages. Worldwide, about 80 percent of Jehovah's Witnesses speak a language other than English, the prevalent international language.

---

9. What view should we take of the presence in our territory of people who speak different languages?

Many foreigners respond well to Bible truth

¹⁰ Indeed, Jesus' command to "make disciples of people of *all the nations*" is being carried out! (Matthew 28:19) Eagerly embracing that commission, Jehovah's Witnesses are active in 235 lands, distributing literature in more than 400 languages. While Jehovah's organization provides the material needed to reach the people, the individual Kingdom publisher must take the initiative to convey the Bible's message to "people of all sorts" in the language they can best understand. (John 1:7) This united effort enables millions of people of various language groups to benefit from the good news. (Romans 10:14, 15) Yes, each one of us plays a vital role!

Rising to the Challenge

¹¹ Today, many Kingdom publishers would like to learn another language, but they cannot depend on or expect miraculous gifts of God's spirit. (1 Corinthians 13:8) Learning a new language is a major undertaking. Even those who already speak a second language may have to adjust their thinking and approach in order to make the Bible's message appealing to people who speak that language but have different backgrounds and cultures. Then, too, new immigrants are often shy and timid; to understand their way of thinking takes hard work.

¹² Nonetheless, the holy spirit is still operative among Jehovah's servants in their efforts to help people who speak other languages. (Luke 11:13) Rather than imparting miraculous linguistic abilities, the spirit can heighten our desire to communicate with people who do not speak our language. (Psalm 143:

Kingdom Hall of Jehovah's Witnesses
Salón del Reino de los Testigos de Jehová
Salão do Reino das Testemunhas de Jeová
Αίθουσα Βασιλείας των Μαρτύρων του Ιεχωβά
यहोवा के साक्षियों का राज्यगृह

*A Kingdom Hall sign
in five languages*

10) Preaching or teaching the Bible's message to people in a language they are not familiar with may reach their mind. However, in order to touch the heart of our listeners, it is often better to use their mother tongue—the language that speaks to their deepest aspirations, motives, and hopes.—Luke 24:32.

¹³ Many Kingdom publishers have taken up the ministry in a foreign-language field when they observe the fine response to Bible truth. Others feel invigorated when their service becomes more challenging and interesting. "Many of those who come from Eastern Europe are thirsting for the truth," states a branch office of Jehovah's Witnesses in southern Europe. How satisfying it is to help such receptive individuals!—Isaiah 55:1, 2.

¹⁴ To have a meaningful share in this work, however, we need determination and self-sacrifice. (Psalm 110:3) For instance, a number of Japanese Witness families have given up comfortable homes in large cities and have moved to remote areas to help groups of Chinese immigrants understand the Bible. On the west coast of the United States, publishers regularly drive from one to two hours to conduct Bible studies with people in the Filipino field. In Norway, a couple studies

10. What is the individual publisher's role in making disciples of people of "all the nations"?
11, 12. (a) What challenges must be met, and how does the holy spirit help? (b) Why is preaching to people in their mother tongue often helpful?

13, 14. (a) What motivates some to take up the ministry in another language? (b) How is the spirit of self-sacrifice seen?

with a family from Afghanistan. The Witness couple uses the English and Norwegian editions of the brochure *What Does God Require of Us?** The family read the paragraphs in Persian, a language closely related to their native Dari. They converse in English and Norwegian. Such a spirit of self-sacrifice and adaptability is richly rewarded when foreigners respond to the good news.#

¹⁵ Can you have a share in this multilingual activity? Why not start by noting which foreign languages are commonly spoken in your territory? Then you might carry some tracts or brochures in those languages. The booklet *Good News for People of All Nations,* released in 2004, has already been instrumental in spreading the Kingdom hope by its simple, positive message in numerous languages.—See the article "Good News for People of All Nations," on page 32.

"Loving the Alien Resident"

¹⁶ Whether we learn another language or not, we can all help with the spiritual

---

* Published by Jehovah's Witnesses.
# For further examples, see "Small Sacrifices Brought Us Great Blessings," in *The Watchtower,* April 1, 2004, pages 24-8.

15. How can all of us share in the multilingual preaching effort?
16. How can responsible brothers manifest selfless interest in helping foreign-speaking people?

Can You Explain?

- How can we imitate Jehovah in showing impartiality to all people?
- How should we view people in our territory who do not speak our language?
- Why is it helpful to preach to people in their mother tongue?
- How can we show concern for the foreigners among us?

education of foreigners in our area. Jehovah instructed his people to "love the alien resident." (Deuteronomy 10:18, 19) For example, in one large city in North America, five congregations meet in the same Kingdom Hall. As in many halls, there is a yearly rotation of meeting times that would have moved the Chinese meetings there to a later hour on Sunday. However, this would mean that many of the immigrants who work at restaurant-related jobs would not be able to attend. The elders in the other congregations graciously made adjustments so that the Chinese meetings could be held earlier on Sunday.

¹⁷ Loving overseers commend qualified and skilled brothers and sisters who want to move to assist other language groups. Such experienced Bible teachers may be missed locally, but the overseers feel as did the elders in Lystra and Iconium. Those elders did not hold Timothy back from traveling with Paul, even though Timothy was an asset to their own congregations. (Acts 16:1-4) In addition, those who take the lead in the preaching work are not deterred by the different mentality, customs, or manners of foreigners. Instead, they embrace the diversity and seek ways to cultivate good relations for the sake of the good news.—1 Corinthians 9:22, 23.

¹⁸ As prophesied, the good news is being preached in "all the languages of the nations." Wonderful potential for increase still exists in foreign-language fields. Thousands of resourceful publishers have entered this "large door that leads to activity." (1 Corinthians 16:9) Yet, more is needed in order to cultivate such territories, as the next article will show.

---

17. How should we feel when some decide to move to help another language group?
18. What large door of activity is open to all?

BECOMING PROGRESSIVE AND ADAPTABLE MINISTERS

"I have become all things to people of all sorts, that I might by all means save some."—1 CORINTHIANS 9:22.

HE WAS at ease with sophisticated intellectuals and with humble tentmakers. He was persuasive to Roman dignitaries and to Phrygian peasants. His writings were motivating to liberal Greeks and to conservative Jews. His logic was as unassailable as his emotional appeal was powerful. He tried to find common ground with everyone so that he might bring some to Christ.—Acts 20:21.

² The man was the apostle Paul, without a doubt an effective and progressive minister. (1 Timothy 1:12) He received from Jesus the commission to "bear [Christ's] name to the nations as well as to kings and the sons of Israel." (Acts 9:15) What was his attitude toward this assignment? He declared: "I have become all things to people of all sorts, that I might by all means save some. But I do all things for the sake of the good news, that I may become a sharer of it with others." (1 Corinthians 9:19-23) What can we learn from Paul's example that can help us to be more effective in our preaching and teaching?

A Changed Man Met the Challenge

³ Had Paul always been a long-suffering, considerate person, fit for the assignment he received? By no means! Religious fanaticism had made Saul (as Paul was formerly known) a violent persecutor of Christ's followers. As a young man, he approved the murder of Stephen. Afterward, Paul ruthlessly hunted down Christians. (Acts 7:58; 8:1, 3; 1 Timothy 1:13) He continued to breathe "threat and murder against the disciples of the Lord." Not being content to pursue believers in Jerusalem only, he began spreading his hate campaign as far north as Damascus.—Acts 9:1, 2.

⁴ At the root of Paul's intense hatred of Christianity might well have been the conviction that the new faith would corrupt Judaism by mixing it with foreign, undesirable ideas. After all, Paul had been "a Pharisee," the very name meaning "separated one." (Acts 23:6) Imagine how shocked Paul must have been when he learned that God had chosen him to preach Christ to—of all people—the Gentiles! (Acts 22:14, 15; 26:16-18) Why, Pharisees refused even to eat with those whom they considered to be sinners! (Luke 7:36-39) No doubt it required great effort on his part to reevaluate his viewpoint and to bring it into harmony with God's will that all sorts of people should be saved.—Galatians 1:13-17.

⁵ We might have to do the same. As we meet an increasing variety of people in our international, multilingual field, we need to make a conscious effort to check our attitude and rid ourselves of any prejudice. (Ephesians 4:22-24) Whether we realize it or not, we are shaped by our social and educational upbringing. This can instill in us views

---

1, 2. (a) In what ways was the apostle Paul an effective minister? (b) How did Paul describe his own attitude toward his assignment?

3. What was Paul's feeling toward Christians before his conversion?

4. What adjustment did Paul have to make to fulfill his assignment?

5. How can we imitate Paul in our ministry?

and attitudes that are biased, prejudiced, inflexible. We must overcome such sentiments if we are to have success in finding and helping sheeplike ones. (Romans 15:7) That is what Paul did. He accepted the challenge to expand his ministry. Motivated by love, he developed teaching skills that are worthy of imitation. Indeed, a study of the ministry of the "apostle to the nations" shows that he was attentive, flexible, and resourceful in preaching and teaching.*—Romans 11:13.

* For examples of such qualities in Paul's ministry, consider Acts 13:9, 16-42; 17:2-4; 18:1-4; 19:11-20; 20:34; Romans 10:11-15; 2 Corinthians 6:11-13.

A Progressive Minister in Action

⁶ Paul was attentive to the beliefs and background of his listeners. When addressing King Agrippa II, Paul acknowledged that the king was an "expert on all the customs as well as the controversies among Jews." Then Paul skillfully used his knowledge of Agrippa's beliefs and discussed with him matters that the king understood very well. The clarity and conviction of Paul's reasoning was such that Agrippa said: "In a short time you would persuade me to become a Christian."—Acts 26:2, 3, 27, 28.

⁷ Paul was also flexible. Note how different his approach was when he tried to dissuade a crowd in the city of Lystra from worshipping him and Barnabas as gods. It has been said that these people, who spoke Lycaonian, were among the less educated and more superstitious of the population. According to Acts 14:14-18, Paul pointed to the creation and its natural bounties as evidence of the su-

6. How was Paul attentive to the background of his listeners, and with what result?
7. How did Paul show flexibility when preaching to a crowd in Lystra?

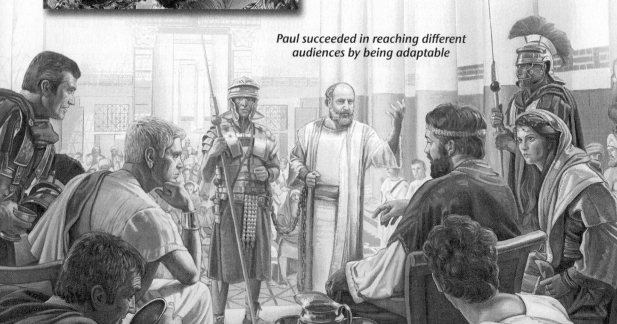

Paul succeeded in reaching different audiences by being adaptable

periority of the true God. The argument was easy to follow, and it apparently "restrained the crowds from sacrificing" to Paul and Barnabas.

8 Of course, Paul was not perfect, and at times, he had strong feelings about certain things. For example, on one occasion when he was attacked in a humiliating and unjust way, he lashed out against a Jew named Ananias. But when Paul was told that he had unknowingly insulted the high priest, he immediately apologized. (Acts 23:1-5) In Athens, he was at first "irritated at beholding that the city was full of idols." Yet, in his speech on Mars' Hill, Paul betrayed no such irritation. Instead, he addressed the Athenians at their forum, building on common ground by referring to their altar "To an Unknown God" and citing one of their poets.—Acts 17:16-28.

9 In dealing with different audiences, Paul manifested remarkable resourcefulness. He took into account the culture and environment that shaped the thinking of his audience. When he wrote to the Christians in Rome, he was well-aware that they lived in the capital of the greatest power of the day. A major point of Paul's letter to Christians in Rome was that the power of Adam's sin to corrupt is conquered by Christ's power to redeem. He spoke to the Roman Christians and those around them in language that would appeal to their heart.—Romans 1:4; 5:14, 15.

10 What did Paul do when he wanted to explain deep Bible truths to his listeners? The apostle was adept at using common, easily understood illustrations to clarify complex spiritual ideas. For example, Paul knew that the people in Rome were acquainted with the

system of slavery throughout the Roman Empire. In fact, many of the people to whom he was writing were probably slaves. Paul therefore used slavery as an illustration to bolster his powerful argument about a person's choice of submission either to sin or to righteousness.—Romans 6:16-20.

11 "Among the Romans," says one reference work, "an owner could free a slave outright, or the slave could purchase his freedom by paying his owner. Freedom could also be arranged if ownership was transferred to a god." A freed slave could continue to work for his master for wages. Paul evidently alluded to this practice when he wrote of the individual's choice of which master to obey—sin or righteousness. Christians in Rome had been

The apostle Paul was attentive, flexible, and resourceful in preaching and teaching

freed from sin and were now owned by God. They were free to serve God, yet they could still choose to serve sin—the former master—if they so desired. That simple but familiar illustration would prompt those Christians in Rome to ask themselves, 'Which master am I serving?'*

Learning From Paul's Example

12 Like Paul, we must be attentive, flexible, and resourceful in order to reach the heart of

---

* Similarly, in explaining the new relationship between God and his spirit-anointed "sons," Paul used a legal concept quite familiar to his readers in the Roman Empire. (Romans 8:14-17) "Adoption was essentially a Roman usage, and was closely connected with the Roman ideas of family," says the book St. Paul at Rome.

---

8. In what ways did Paul show that he was flexible in spite of his strong feelings at times?
9. How did Paul demonstrate resourcefulness when dealing with different audiences?
10, 11. How did Paul tailor his illustrations to his listeners? (See also footnote.)

12, 13. (a) What effort is needed today in order to reach the heart of our diverse audience? (b) What have you found to be effective when preaching to people from different backgrounds?

Effective ministers consider the cultural background of their listeners

our diverse audience. To help our listeners get the sense of the good news, we desire to do more than make superficial contact, deliver a prepared message, or leave some Bible literature. We endeavor to discern their needs and concerns, their likes and dislikes, and their fears and prejudices. Though this requires a great deal of thought and effort, Kingdom publishers around the world are eagerly doing so. For example, the branch office of Jehovah's Witnesses in Hungary reports: "The brothers show respect for the customs and lifestyle of people of other nations and

do not expect them to adapt to local customs." Witnesses elsewhere endeavor to do the same.

¹³ In one country in the Far East, most people are concerned with health, child training, and education. Kingdom publishers there try to highlight these subjects instead of discussing such matters as deteriorating global conditions or complex social issues. Similarly, publishers in a large city in the United States noticed that people in a particular neighborhood in their territory are concerned with such matters as corruption, traffic congestion, and crime. The Witnesses successfully use these subjects to start Bible discussions. Effective Bible teachers make sure that regardless of the topic they choose, they remain positive and encouraging, stressing the practical value of applying Bible principles now and the bright prospects that God offers for the future.—Isaiah 48:17, 18; 52:7.

¹⁴ It is also helpful to vary our approach in the ministry, since people have vastly different cultural, educational, and religious backgrounds. Our approach to people who believe in a Creator but not in the Bible will differ from that used to talk to those who believe that God does not exist. With someone who feels that all religious literature is an indoctrination tool, the presentation we use will be different from the one we use for a person who accepts what the Bible teaches. Flexibility is also needed in dealing with the wide variety of educational levels of the people we talk to. Skillful teachers will use reasoning and illustrations appropriate to the situation at hand.—1 John 5:20.

---

14. Describe ways in which we can adapt to people's differing needs and circumstances.

Do You Remember?

- In what ways can we imitate Paul in our ministry?

- What changes in our thinking are likely needed?

- How can we keep our message positive?

- What do new ministers need in order to develop confidence?

*Progressive ministers help
new ones prepare for the ministry*

Help for New Ministers

15 Paul was not concerned with improving only his own teaching methods. He saw the need for training and preparing those of a younger generation, such as Timothy and Titus, to become effective ministers. (2 Timothy 2:2; 3:10, 14; Titus 1:4) Similarly, a pressing need to provide and receive training exists today.

16 In 1914, there were approximately 5,000 Kingdom publishers earth wide; today, *each week* about 5,000 new ones are baptized! (Isaiah 54:2, 3; Acts 11:21) When new ones begin to associate with the Christian congregation and wish to share in the ministry, they need training and direction. (Galatians 6:6) It is vital that we use the methods of the Master, Jesus, in teaching and training disciples.*

17 Jesus did not just find a crowd and tell his apostles to start talking. He first emphasized the need for the preaching work and encouraged a prayerful attitude. Then he made three basic provisions: a partner, a territory assignment, and a message. (Matthew 9:35-

---

* Currently, the Pioneers Assist Others program is available in all congregations of Jehovah's Witnesses. The program utilizes the experience and training of full-time ministers in assisting less-experienced publishers.

15, 16. Why is there a need for training new ministers?

17, 18. How can we help new ones gain confidence in the ministry?

38; 10:5-7; Mark 6:7; Luke 9:2, 6) We can do the same. Whether we are helping our own child, a new student, or someone who has not shared in the preaching activity for a while, it is appropriate to make an effort to provide training in this way.

18 New ones need considerable help to gain confidence in presenting the Kingdom message. Can you assist them to prepare and practice a simple, appealing presentation? In the field, let them learn from your example as you take the first few calls. You can follow the pattern of Gideon, who said to his fellow fighters: "You should learn from watching me, and that is how you should do." (Judges 7:17) Then give the new one the opportunity

> **Jesus made three basic provisions for his disciples: a partner, a territory assignment, and a message**

to participate. Warmly commend new ones for their efforts, and when appropriate, offer brief suggestions for improvement.

19 In order to 'accomplish our ministry fully,' we are determined to become more flexible in our approach, and we want to train new ministers to do the same. When we consider the importance of our goal—to impart the very knowledge of God that leads to salvation—we are convinced that it is worth all the effort it takes to become "all things to people of all sorts, that [we] might by all means save some."—2 Timothy 4:5; 1 Corinthians 9:22.

---

19. What is your determination as you strive to 'accomplish your ministry fully'?

Good News for People of All Nations

SHOWN above is a booklet released at the 2004/05 "Walk With God" District Conventions of Jehovah's Witnesses. One edition of it is a 96-page booklet that contains a brief message in 92 languages, ranging from Afrikaans to Zulu, and is designed to help spread the Kingdom good news to as many people as possible. (Matthew 24:14) The following are typical of the results when the booklet is used.

• After receiving the booklet at the convention, a Witness family visited three national parks. There they met people from India, the Netherlands, Pakistan, and the Philippines. The husband noted: "Though all these people spoke some English, they were impressed when we showed them the message in their own language, since they were thousands of miles from home. The worldwide nature of our work as well as our unity became clear to them."

• A Witness showed the booklet to a coworker from India. He was excited to see all the languages in it and read the message in his own language. This led to more discussions about the Bible. A coworker from the Philippines was amazed to find her native language in the booklet and became interested in learning more about Jehovah's Witnesses.

• In Canada, a lady from Nepal agreed to study the Bible with a Witness over the phone but was reluctant to invite the sister to her home. However, when the Witness told the lady about the booklet with a message in Nepali, she excitedly invited the sister to come over. She just had to see for herself the message in her mother tongue! The Bible study has been held at the lady's home ever since.

DECEMBER 15, 2005

THE WATCHTOWER

ANNOUNCING JEHOVAH'S KINGDOM

The Holiday Season

Will It Be All You Want?

THE WATCHTOWER®
ANNOUNCING JEHOVAH'S KINGDOM

December 15, 2005   Average Printing Each Issue: 26,439,000   Vol. 126, No. 24

THE PURPOSE OF *THE WATCHTOWER* is to exalt Jehovah God as Sovereign Lord of the universe. It keeps watch on world events as these fulfill Bible prophecy. It comforts all peoples with the good news that God's Kingdom will soon destroy those who oppress their fellowmen and that it will turn the earth into a paradise. It encourages faith in God's now-reigning King, Jesus Christ, whose shed blood opens the way for mankind to gain eternal life. *The Watchtower*, published by Jehovah's Witnesses continuously since 1879, is nonpolitical. It adheres to the Bible as its authority.

IN THIS ISSUE

3 The Holiday Season—Will It Be All You Want It to Be?

4 Christmastime—What Is Its Focus?

9 "Preach a Release to the Captives"

13 The Bible in Italian—A Troubled History

17 Helping Chinese People in Mexico

19 Whom Do You Obey—God or Men?

24 Now Is the Time for Decisive Action

30 Do You Remember?

31 Subject Index for *The Watchtower* 2005

32 New Year's Tree—Is It Russian? Is It Christian?

WATCHTOWER STUDIES

JANUARY 16-22:
Whom Do You Obey—God or Men?
Page 19. Songs to be used: 2, 47.

JANUARY 23-29:
Now Is the Time for Decisive Action.
Page 24. Songs to be used: 129, 146.

Publication of *The Watchtower* is part of a worldwide Bible educational work supported by voluntary donations.

Unless otherwise indicated, Scripture quotations are from the modern-language *New World Translation of the Holy Scriptures—With References.*

The Watchtower (ISSN 0043-1087) is published semimonthly by Watchtower Bible and Tract Society of New York, Inc.; M. H. Larson, President; G. F. Simonis, Secretary-Treasurer; 25 Columbia Heights, Brooklyn, NY 11201-2483. Periodicals Postage Paid at Brooklyn, NY, and at additional mailing offices. **POSTMASTER:** Send address changes to Watchtower, **Wallkill, NY 12589.**

Changes of address should reach us 30 days before your moving date. Give us your old and new address (if possible, your old address label).

Semimonthly   ENGLISH

Would you welcome more information or a free home Bible study? Please send your request to Jehovah's Witnesses, using the appropriate address below.

America, United States of: Wallkill, NY 12589. *Antigua:* Box 119, St. Johns. *Australia:* Box 280, Ingleburn, NSW 1890. *Bahamas:* Box N-1247, Nassau, N.P. *Barbados, W.I.:* Crusher Site Road, Prospect, St. James. *Britain:* The Ridgeway, London NW7 1RN. *Canada:* Box 4100, Halton Hills (Georgetown), Ontario L7G 4Y4. *Germany:* Niederselters, Am Steinfels, D-65618 Selters. *Ghana:* P. O. Box GP 760, Accra. *Guyana:* 352-360 Tyrell St., Republic Park Phase 2 EBD. *Hawaii 96819:* 2055 Kam IV Rd., Honolulu. *Hong Kong:* 4 Kent Road, Kowloon Tong. *India:* Post Box 6440, Yelahanka, Bangalore 560 064, KAR. *Ireland:* Newcastle, Greystones, Co. Wicklow. *Jamaica:* P. O. Box 103, Old Harbour, St. Catherine. *Japan:* 1271 Nakashinden, Ebina City, Kanagawa Pref., 243-0496. *Kenya:* P.O. Box 47788, GPO Nairobi 00100. *New Zealand:* P.O. Box 75-142, Manurewa. *Nigeria:* P.M.B. 1090, Benin City 300001, Edo State. *Philippines, Republic of:* P. O. Box 2044, 1060 Manila. *South Africa:* Private Bag X2067, Krugersdorp, 1740. *Trinidad and Tobago, Republic of:* Lower Rapsey Street & Laxmi Lane, Curepe. *Zambia:* Box 33459, Lusaka 10101. *Zimbabwe:* Private Bag WG-5001, Westgate.

NOW PUBLISHED IN 151 LANGUAGES. SEMIMONTHLY: Afrikaans, Albanian,* Amharic, Arabic, Bengali, Bicol, Bislama, Bulgarian, Cebuano,* Chichewa,* Chinese, Chinese (Simplified),* Cibemba,* Croatian,* Czech,*# Danish,*# Dutch,*# East Armenian, Efik,* English*#+◉ (also Braille), Estonian, Ewe, Fijian, Finnish,*# French*# (also Braille), Ga, Georgian,* German,*# Greek,* Gujarati, Gun, Hebrew, Hiligaynon, Hindi, Hungarian,*# Igbo,* Iloko,* Indonesian, Italian,*# Japanese*# (also Braille), Kannada, Kinyarwanda, Kirundi, Korean*# (also Braille), Latvian, Lingala, Lithuanian, Luvale, Macedonian, Malagasy,* Malayalam, Maltese, Myanmar, Nepali, Norwegian,*# Pangasinan, Papiamento (Aruba), Papiamento (Curaçao), Polish,*# Portuguese*# (also Braille), Punjabi, Rarotongan, Romanian,* Russian,* Samar-Leyte, Samoan, Sango, Sepedi, Serbian, Sesotho, Shona,* Silozi, Sinhala, Slovak,* Slovenian, Solomon Islands Pidgin, Spanish*# (also Braille), Sranantongo, Swahili,* Swedish,*# Tagalog,* Tamil, Telugu, Thai, Tigrinya, Tok Pisin, Tongan, Tshiluba, Tsonga, Tswana, Turkish, Twi, Ukrainian,* Urdu, Vietnamese, Wallisian, Xhosa, Yoruba,* Zulu*

MONTHLY: American Sign Language,△◻ Armenian, Assamese, Azerbaijani (roman script), Brazilian Sign Language,△ Cambodian, Chitonga, Gilbertese, Greenlandic, Haitian Creole, Hausa, Hiri Motu, Icelandic, Isoko, Kaonde, Kazakh, Kikongo, Kiluba, Kirghiz, Kosraean, Kwanyama/Ndonga, Luganda, Marathi, Marshallese, Mauritian Creole, Maya, Mizo, Monokutuba, Moore, Niuean, Ossetian, Otetela, Palauan, Persian, Ponapean, Seychelles Creole, Tahitian, Tatar, Tiv, Trukese, Tumbuka, Tuvaluan, Umbundu, Uruund, Venda, Yapese, Zande

* Study articles also available in large-print edition.
# Audiocassettes also available.
+ CD also available.
◉ MP3 CD-ROM also available.
△ Videocassette
◻ DVD

The Holiday Season
Will It Be All You Want It to Be?

"Peter [the Great] ordered special New Year's services held in all the churches on January 1. Further, he instructed that festive evergreen branches be used to decorate the doorposts in interiors of houses, and he commanded that all citizens of Moscow should 'display their happiness by loudly congratulating' one another on the New Year."
—*Peter the Great—His Life and World.*

WHAT are you looking forward to during what many call the holiday season? People around the globe say that this season centers on Christmas, the traditional day of Christ's birth, but it also includes the New Year's celebration. So it is an extended holiday period. Both parents and children may be on vacation during this time, so it would seem to be an ideal occasion for families to spend time together. Others, though, refer to this season as "the Christmas season," since they wish to honor Christ at this time of year. Perhaps you too feel that this is the most important aspect of the season.

Whether it be to honor Christ, enjoy one's family, or both, millions of husbands, wives, and children worldwide await this time with keen anticipation. What about this year? Will it turn out to be that special time for the family, and is it special for God? If there is a family gathering, will it be all you want it to be, or will you be disappointed?

Many who look forward to the religious aspect notice that both Christmas and New Year's are often celebrated with anything but the spirit of Christ. Rather, the holiday season becomes merely a time for receiving gifts, an excuse for a party that may include conduct that dishonors Christ, or primarily a reason for a family reunion. Many times, such a gathering is marred by one or more members overindulging in food and alcohol, sparking arguments that all too often provoke domestic violence. You may have noted that, or it may even have been your experience.

If so, it may seem to you that very little has changed since the time of the Russian Czar Peter the Great, described at the outset. Disturbed by the current trend, many wish that the holiday season could be a time for deep religious reflection and wholesome family association. Some even campaign for a change, employing such slogans as, Jesus is the reason for the season. But can a change be effected? And would this truly bring honor to Christ? Are there reasons for taking a different view of the holiday season?

To find satisfying answers, let us view the situation through the eyes of people of one nation who should have special reason to appreciate this time of year.

Christmastime
What Is Its Focus?

FOR millions the holiday season is a time to be with family and friends, a time to renew bonds of affection. Many others consider it a time to reflect on the birth of Jesus Christ and his role in the salvation of humankind. In Russia, unlike in many other lands, celebrating Christmas was not always something that people were free to do. Though for centuries those of the Russian Orthodox Church had openly celebrated Christmas, they were not allowed to do so for most of the 20th century. What was behind the change?

On the heels of the 1917 Bolshevik Communist revolution, Soviet authorities pursued an aggressive policy of statewide atheism. The entire Christmas holiday season with its religious overtones fell into disfavor. The State began waging a campaign against both Christmas and New Year's celebrations. There was even open condemnation of the local symbols of the season—the Christmas tree and Ded Moroz, or Grandfather Frost, the Russian equivalent of Santa Claus.

In 1935, a change occurred that profoundly altered the way Russians marked the holiday season.

The Soviets reinstated Grandfather Frost, the seasonal tree, and the New Year's celebration—but with a significant twist. Grandfather Frost, it was said, would bring presents, not at Christmas, but on New Year's Day. Similarly, no longer would there be a Christmas tree. It would be a New Year's tree! Thus, there was a major change of focus in the Soviet Union. The New Year's celebration, in effect, supplanted Christmas.

The Christmas season became a wholly secular festive occasion, officially bereft of any religious meaning. The New Year's tree was decorated, not with religious ornaments, but with secular ones depicting the progress of the Soviet Union. The Russian journal *Vokrug Sveta* (Around the World) explains: "It is possible to retrace the history of the establishing of a Communist society by the New Year's tree decorations of various years of the Soviet era. Along with commonplace bunnies, icicles, and round loaves of bread, decorations in the shape of sickles, hammers, and tractors were released. These were later replaced by figurines of miners and cosmonauts, oil rigs, rockets, and moon buggies."

What about Christmas Day itself? It certainly was not recognized. Rather, the Soviet authority relegated it to the status of an ordinary workday. Those who wished to hold the religious celebration of Christmas could do so only very discreetly, risking the State's disfavor and unpleasant consequences. Yes, in 20th-century Russia, there was a shift in the focus of the holiday season, from religious observance to secular celebration.

A More Recent Shift

In 1991 the Soviet Union fell and greater freedoms were realized. Gone was the State policy of atheism. Various newly formed sovereign states were largely secular, with a separation of Church and State. Many religiously inclined people felt that they could now pursue their religious convictions. They reasoned that one way to do this would be to celebrate the religious holiday of Christmas. However, deep disappointment soon set in for many such ones. Why?

With each passing year, the holiday has become more commercialized. Yes, as in the West, the Christmas season has become one of the best ways for manufacturers, wholesalers, and merchants to make money. Christmas decorations are prominently displayed on storefronts. Western-style Christmas music and carols, hitherto unknown in Russia, emanate from shops. Salesmen carrying large bags of Christmas knickknacks ply their wares on commuter trains and other public transportation. That is what you find now.

Even those who see nothing wrong with this rank commercialism may be bothered by another disturbing element of the season —alcohol abuse with all its negative consequences. An emergency-room physician in a Moscow hospital explained: "For doctors, it's a given that the New Year's celebration will mean a slew of injuries ranging from bumps and bruises to knife and bullet wounds, most having been caused by domestic violence, drunken brawls, and car accidents." A senior staff scientist of a branch of the Russian Academy of Sciences said: "There is a surge in the number of alcohol-related deaths. It was particularly high in the year 2000. The number of suicides and murders jumped as well."

Unfortunately, any such behavior during the holiday season in Russia is aggravated by another factor. Under the headline "Russians Celebrate Christmas Twice," the newspaper *Izvestiya* reports: "Almost 1 in 10 Russians celebrates Christmas twice. As witnessed by the survey of the ROMIR monitoring center, 8 percent of respondents admitted that they celebrate Christmas both on December 25, according to the Catholic Christmas calendar, and on January 7, according to Orthodoxy . . . For some, it is evidently not the religious essence of Christmas that is important as much as it is the opportunity to celebrate."*

---

* Before the October 1917 revolution, Russia employed the older Julian calendar, but most countries had switched to the Gregorian calendar. In 1917 the Julian calendar was 13 days behind its Gregorian counterpart. After the revolution, the Soviets switched to the Gregorian calendar, bringing Russia into line with the rest of the world. The Orthodox Church, however, retained the Julian calendar for its celebrations, designating it the "Old Style" calendar. You may hear of Christmas in Russia being celebrated on January 7. Keep in mind, however, that January 7 on the Gregorian calendar is December 25 on the Julian calendar. Thus, many Russians organize their holiday season this way: December 25, Western Christmas; January 1, secular New Year's; January 7, Orthodox Christmas; January 14, Old Style New Year's.

Does the Current Focus Really Honor Christ?

Clearly, much ungodly conduct accompanies the holiday season. As disturbing as this is, some may feel that they should observe the celebrations out of respect for God and Christ. A desire to please God is commendable. But are God and Christ actually pleased with the Christmas season? Consider its roots.

For instance, whatever one's view of the Soviet stance on Christmas, it would be hard to argue with the following historical facts set out in the *Great Soviet Encyclopedia:* "Christmas . . . was borrowed from the pre-Christian worship of gods 'dying and rising from the dead,' which was especially prevalent among agricultural peoples who, in a period usually confined to the winter solstice from December 21-25, annually celebrated the 'birth' of the God-Savior, who wakens nature to new life."

You may find significant what that encyclopedia accurately points out: "Christianity of the first centuries did not know the celebration of Christmas. . . . From the middle of the fourth century, Christianity assimilated the celebration of the winter solstice from the worship of Mithra, turning it into the Christmas celebration. The first to celebrate Christmas were the religious communities of Rome. In the tenth century, Christmas, along with Christianity, spread to Russia, where it became fused with the winter celebration of the ancient Slavs, honoring the spirits of the ancestors."

'What does God's Word, the Bible, say about Jesus' being born on December 25?' you may ask. Actually, the Bible specifies no date for Jesus' birth, and there is no record that Jesus himself spoke of it, much less directed that it be celebrated. However, the Bi-

Museum Wiesbaden

Christendom assimilated the worship of Mithra

ble does help us to determine the time of year when Jesus was born.

According to Matthew's Gospel, chapters 26 and 27, Jesus was executed on Nisan 14, late in the day of the Jewish Passover that had begun on March 31, 33 C.E. We learn from Luke's Gospel that Jesus was about 30 years old when he was baptized and began his ministry. (Luke 3:21-23) That ministry lasted three and a half years. Therefore, Jesus was about 33 1/2 years old when he died. He would have turned 34 about October 1, 33 C.E. Luke reports that at the time of Jesus' birth, shepherds were "living out of doors and keeping watches in the night over their flocks." (Luke 2:8) Shepherds would not have been out with their flocks in the cold of December, when it may even snow in the vicinity of Bethlehem. But they could have been there with their flocks about October 1, which according to the evidence is when Jesus was born.

Shepherds would not have been out with their flocks in the cold of December

Incidentally, what about the New Year's celebration? As we have seen, it is marked by debauched behavior. Despite attempts to secularize it, it too has dubious roots.

Clearly, in the light of the facts surrounding the holiday season, such slogans as, Jesus is the reason for the season ring hollow. If you are upset by the commercialism and disturbing conduct associated with the Christmas season, as well as its unsavory pagan origins, do not be discouraged. There is a fitting way in which we can show due

Roots of the New Year's Celebration
A Georgian Orthodox Monk Speaks Out

"The New Year's holiday originates with a number of pagan holidays from ancient Rome. The 1st of January was a holiday dedicated to the pagan god Janus, and the name of the month comes from his name. Images of Janus had two faces on opposite sides, which meant that he saw both the past and the present. There was a saying that whoever greeted January 1st with fun, laughter, and plenty would pass the entire year in happiness and well-being. The very same superstition accompanies the celebrating of the new year for many of our compatriots . . . During certain pagan holidays, people would directly bring sacrifices to an idol. Some were notorious for immoral orgies, adultery, and fornication. On other occasions, for example during the Janus holiday, there were excesses in eating and drinking, drunkenness, and every sort of uncleanness that accompanies them. If we remember how we ourselves in times past have celebrated New Year's, then we must admit that all of us have participated in this pagan celebration."—A Georgian newspaper.

reverence for God and honor Christ, at the same time strengthening family ties.

A Better Way to Honor God and Christ

The Bible tells us that Jesus Christ came "to give his soul a ransom in exchange for many." (Matthew 20:28) He allowed himself to be executed, willingly dying for our sins. Some might like to honor Christ, feeling that they can do this during the Christmas season. But as we have seen, Christmas and New Year's have little to do with Christ and have their roots in pagan celebrations. Also, the Christmas season, however attractive it is to some, is marked by crass commercialism. Furthermore, it must be admitted that the Christmas holiday is associated with shameful conduct that displeases God and Christ.

How should one who is seeking to please God react? Rather than clinging to human traditions that may soothe feelings of religiosity but that are contrary to the Scriptures, a sincere person would seek the true way to honor God and Christ. What is that true way, and what should we do?

Christ himself tells us: "This means everlasting life, their taking in knowledge of you, the only true God, and of the one whom you sent forth, Jesus Christ." (John 17:3) Yes, the truly sincere person seeks to take in accurate knowledge of how to honor God and Christ. He then applies this knowledge not just during a certain time of the year but in everyday life. God is well-pleased with such sincere efforts, which can lead to everlasting life.

Would you like your family to be among those who truly honor God and Christ in harmony with the Scriptures? Jehovah's Witnesses have helped millions of families worldwide to take in vital knowledge from the Bible. We warmly invite you to contact Jehovah's Witnesses in your area or to write to them at the appropriate address found on page 2 of this magazine.

A T THE beginning of his ministry, Jesus declared that part of his commission was "to preach a release to the captives." (Luke 4:18) Following the example of their Master, true Christians preach the Kingdom good news to "all sorts of men," bringing them release from spiritual captivity and helping them to improve their life.—1 Timothy 2:4.

Today, this work includes preaching to literal captives—people who are imprisoned for various crimes and who appreciate a spiritual release. Enjoy this encouraging report about the preaching activities of Jehovah's Witnesses in the prisons of Ukraine and elsewhere in Europe.

From Drug Addicts to Christians

Of the 38 years of Serhii's* life, 20 have been spent behind bars. He even finished school in prison. He says: "Years ago, I was imprisoned for murder, and I still have time to serve. In prison I acted like a tyrant, and other prisoners were afraid of me." Did this make him feel liberated? No. For many years, Serhii was enslaved to drugs, alcohol, and tobacco.

Then a fellow prisoner shared Bible truth with him. It was like a beam of light in the dark. Within a few months, he freed himself from his addictions, became a preacher of the good news, and was baptized. Serhii now leads a busy life in prison, serving as a full-time minister of Jehovah. He has helped sev-

---
* Some names have been changed.

"Preach a Release to the Captives"

en criminals to change their ways and become his spiritual brothers. Six of them have been released, but Serhii remains behind bars. He is not upset at this because he is happy that he can help others to receive a release from spiritual captivity.—Acts 20:35.

One of Serhii's students in prison was Victor, a former drug dealer and addict. After his release from prison, Victor continued to make spiritual progress and eventually graduated from the Ministerial Training School

*Prison wall,
L'viv, Ukraine*

in Ukraine. Now he serves as a special pioneer minister in Moldova. Victor says: "I began smoking when I was 8, abusing alcohol at 12, and using drugs when I was 14. I wanted to change my life, but all my attempts failed. Then in 1995, just as my wife and I were planning to move away from my bad associates, she was stabbed to death by a homicidal maniac. My life became absolutely dismal. 'Where is my wife now? What happens when a person dies?' I kept asking questions but could find no answers. I took more and more drugs to fill the void. I was arrested for dealing drugs and was sentenced to five years in prison. There, Serhii helped me to find the answers. I had tried to break free from drugs many times, but only now with help from the Bible did I succeed. God's Word is so powerful!"—Hebrews 4:12.

Hardened Criminals Change

Vasyl never used drugs, but he did not escape captivity. "Kickboxing was my addiction," he explains. "I trained myself to beat up people without leaving any marks." Vasyl used his violent ways to rob people. "I was in prison three times, which led my wife to divorce me. During the last five-year term, I got acquainted with the literature of Jehovah's Witnesses. This motivated me to read the Bible, but I was still involved in what I really loved—fights without rules.

"After six months of Bible reading, however, something changed within

me. Winning a fight no longer brought me the satisfaction it once did. So I started to analyze my life in the light of Isaiah 2:4 and realized that unless I adjusted my thinking, I would spend the rest of my life in prison. So I threw out all my fighting gear and began to work on my personality. It was not easy, but meditation and prayer gradually helped me to kick my bad habits. At times, I tearfully begged Jehovah to give me the strength to break free from my addiction. Finally, I succeeded.

"After release from prison, I was reunited with my family. Now I work in a coal mine. This gives me enough time to share in the preaching work along with my wife and to

Vasyl with his wife, Iryna

Mykola

Victor

fulfill my responsibilities in the congregation."

Mykola and his friends robbed several banks in Ukraine. This resulted in a ten-year prison term for him. Before his incarceration, he had been to church only once—to prepare to rob that church. Things did not work out, but that visit made Mykola believe that the Bible must be full of boring stories about Orthodox priests, candles, and religious holidays. He says: "I do not know exactly why, but I began reading the Bible. I was amazed to discover that it was nothing like what I had imagined!" He asked for a Bible study and was baptized in 1999. Looking at him now, it is hard to believe that this humble ministerial servant was once a malicious armed bank robber!

Vladimir was given a death sentence. While awaiting execution, he prayed to God and promised to serve Him if he was spared. Meanwhile, the law was changed, and his death penalty was commuted to life imprisonment. To keep his promise, Vladimir began looking for the true religion. He enrolled in a correspondence course and received a diploma from an Adventist church, but he was not satisfied.

However, after reading the *Watchtower* and *Awake!* magazines in the prison library, Vladimir wrote to the branch office of Jehovah's Witnesses in Ukraine, asking for a visit. When local brothers visited him, he already considered himself a Witness and was preaching in the prison. He was helped to qualify as a Kingdom publisher. As of this writing, Vladimir and seven others in that prison are awaiting baptism. But they have a problem. Since inmates with life sentences are kept in cells according to their religious beliefs, Vladimir and his cell mates are of the same faith. So to whom can they preach? They share the good news with prison guards and by writing letters.

Nazar moved from Ukraine to the Czech Republic, where he joined a gang of thieves. This led to three and a half years of imprisonment. While in prison, he responded to the visits of Jehovah's Witnesses from the city of Karlovy Vary, learned the truth, and was fully rehabilitated. Seeing this, one of the security guards said to Nazar's cell mates: "If all of you would be like that Ukrainian, I could finally change my profession." Another said: "These Jehovah's Witnesses are real experts. Into prison comes a criminal; out goes a decent man." Now Nazar is back home. He learned carpentry and got married, and he and his wife are in the full-time ministry. How thankful he is for the prison visits of the Witnesses!

Official Recognition

Prisoners are not the only ones who are grateful for the service provided by Jehovah's Witnesses. Miroslaw Kowalski, a spokesman for one of the prisons in Poland, said: "We appreciate their visits very much. Some prisoners have sad backgrounds. Probably they were never treated as human beings. . . . The help [of the Witnesses] is very valuable because we have a shortage of personnel and educators."

The warden of another prison in Poland wrote to the branch office, asking the Witnesses to increase their activity in his prison. Why? He explained: "More frequent visits by Watchtower representatives may help the prisoners to develop socially desirable qualities, suppressing aggression among them."

A Ukrainian newspaper reported on a depressed prisoner who attempted to commit suicide but then received help from Jehovah's Witnesses. "Presently, this man is on the way to emotional recovery," says the report. "He sticks to the prison routine and is an example to other prisoners."

Benefits Beyond Prison Gates

The benefits of the work done by Jehovah's Witnesses do not stop at the prison gate. They continue after the prisoners are released. Two Christians, Brigitte and Renate, have been helping people in this way for some years. A German newspaper, *Main-Echo Aschaffenburg,* reports about them: "They look after prisoners for three to five months after their release, encouraging them to find a purpose in life.... They have been officially recognized as volunteer probation officers. ... They also have constructive and positive dealings with the prison personnel." A number of people have dedicated their life to Jehovah as a result of this kind of help.

Even prison officials benefit from the Bible education work of Jehovah's Witnesses. For example, Roman was a military major and a psychologist in a Ukrainian prison. When the Witnesses visited his home, he agreed to a Bible study. Then he learned that the Witnesses were not permitted to contact the inmates where he worked. So he asked the warden for permission to use the Bible in his work with the prisoners. His request was granted, and

about ten prisoners showed interest. Roman regularly shared his growing Bible knowledge with these prisoners, and his efforts produced excellent results. After being released, some continued to make progress and became baptized Christians. Seeing the power of God's Word, Roman took his study more seriously. He left the military and continued in his Bible education activities. Now he shares in the preaching work with a former prisoner.

"Here we live on the Bible, Bible publications, and Bible study," wrote one prisoner. These words well describe the need that exists in some prisons for Bible literature. One congregation in Ukraine reports about the Bible education work in a local prison: "The administration is thankful for the literature we provide. We supply them with 60 copies of each issue of *The Watchtower* and *Awake!*" Another congregation writes: "We care for a correctional facility that has 20 small libraries. We provided each library with our main publications. This amounted to 20 boxes of literature." In one prison, the guards maintain a file of our magazines in the library so that prisoners can benefit from every issue.

In 2002 the branch office in Ukraine established a Prison Desk. Thus far, the desk has contacted about 120 correctional facilities and has assigned congregations to care for them. Every month about 50 letters from prisoners are received, most of them requesting literature or asking for a Bible study. The branch sends books, magazines, and brochures to them until local brothers can contact them.

"Keep in mind those in prison bonds," wrote the apostle Paul to his fellow Christians. (Hebrews 13:3) He was referring to those who were imprisoned for their faith. Today, Jehovah's Witnesses keep in mind those who are incarcerated, visit prisons, and "preach a release to the captives."—Luke 4:18.

THE BIBLE IN ITALIAN

A Troubled History

Bible title page: Biblioteca Nazionale Centrale di Roma

"THE Bible is among the most widely circulated books in our country [Italy], but it is perhaps among the least read as well. The faithful still receive little encouragement to get acquainted with the Bible and little help to read it as the Word of God. There are those who want to know the Bible, but often there is no one to break the bread of the Word for them."

This statement, made in 1995 by a body of the Italian Bishops' Conference, raises a number of questions. How widely read was the Bible in Italy in centuries past? Why did its circulation lag behind that in other countries? Why is it still among the least read books in Italy? An examination of the history of Italian-language versions of the Bible offers some answers.

It took centuries for Romance languages —French, Italian, Portuguese, Spanish, and so on—to develop from Latin. In various European countries with a Latin background, the vernacular, the tongue of the common people, gradually acquired a new dignity and was even used in literary works. Development of the vernacular had a direct bearing on Bible translation. How? At a certain point, the gulf between Latin, the sacred ecclesiastical language, and the vernacular, with its dialects and local variants, became so wide that Latin was no longer understood by those who had no formal education.

By the year 1000, most inhabitants of the Italian peninsula would have found it difficult to read the Latin *Vulgate,* even if they could obtain a copy. For centuries, the ecclesiastical hierarchy monopolized education, including that at the few universities that existed. Only a privileged few benefited from it. Hence, the Bible eventually became "an unknown book." Yet, many desired to gain access to the Word of God and understand it in their own language.

In general, the clergy opposed Bible translation, fearing that it would encourage the spread of so-called heresies. According to historian Massimo Firpo, "use of the vernacular [would mean] demolition of a language barrier [the use of Latin] that safeguarded the clergy's exclusive dominion over religious matters." Hence, a combination of cultural, religious, and social factors lie at the root of the general lack of Biblical education that still prevails in Italy.

First Partial Translations of the Bible

The 13th century saw the first translations of Bible books from Latin into the vernacular. Such partial translations were hand-copied and very costly. With an increasing number of translations in the 14th century, almost the entire Bible was available in the vernacular, although its books were translated by different people at different times and places. Most of these translations, produced by anonymous translators, were acquired by the wealthy or the learned, the only ones who had the means to procure them. Even when printing considerably reduced the cost of books, Bibles, according to historian Gigliola Fragnito, were "accessible to few."

For centuries, the vast majority of the population remained illiterate. Even at the time of the unification of Italy in 1861, 74.7 percent of the population were illiterate. Incidentally, when the new Italian government prepared to make free and mandatory public education available for all, Pope Pius IX wrote to the king in 1870 urging him to oppose the law, which the pope described as a "plague" aimed at "totally destroying Catholic schools."

The First Bible in Italian

The first complete Bible in Italian was printed in Venice in 1471, some 16 years after movable type was first used in Europe. Nicolò Malerbi, a Camaldolese monk, produced his translation in eight months. He drew heavily on the existing translations, edited them on the basis of the Latin *Vulgate,* and replaced some words with those typical of his area, Venetia. His translation was the first printed edition of the Bible in Italian to attain a significant circulation.

Another man who published a version of the Bible in Venice was Antonio Brucioli. He was a humanist with Protestant leanings, but he never broke away from the Catholic Church. In 1532, Brucioli translated the Bible from the original Hebrew and Greek. This was the first Bible to be translated from the original texts into Italian. Though not in fine literary Italian, the translation's faithfulness to the original texts is remarkable, given the knowledge of ancient languages in those days. In some places and editions, Brucioli restored God's name in the form "Ieova." For nearly a century, his Bible was very popular among Italian Protestants and religious dissidents.

Other Italian translations—in reality revisions of Brucioli's Bible—were published, some by Catholics. None of them achieved any notable circulation. In 1607, Giovanni Diodati, a Calvinist pastor whose parents had fled to Switzerland to avoid religious persecution, published in Geneva another translation into Italian from the original languages. His version became the Bible of Italian Protestants for centuries. For the period in which it was produced, it is considered an excellent Italian translation. Diodati's Bible helped Italians to grasp the Bible's teachings. But clerical censorship stood in the way of this and other translations.

The Bible—"An Unknown Book"

"The Church has always fulfilled its duty to keep books under surveillance, but until the invention of printing, it did not feel the need to compile a catalog of prohibited books because those writings considered dangerous were burned," states the *Enciclopedia Cattolica.* Even af-

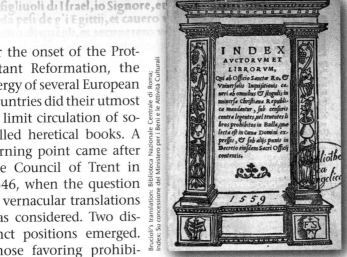

Brucioli's translation used the divine name Ieova in its text

only legitimate form of the Bible." Ensuing developments bore this out.

In 1559, Pope Paul IV published the first index of prohibited books, a list of works that Catholics were forbidden to read, sell, translate, or possess. These volumes were considered evil and dangerous to faith and moral integrity. The index forbade the reading of vernacular translations of the Bible, including Brucioli's. Transgressors were excommunicated. The 1596 index was even more restrictive. Authorization was no longer to be given to translate or print Bibles in the vernacular. Such Bibles were to be destroyed.

As a result, Bible burnings in church squares multiplied after the end of the 16th century. In the minds of the people in general, the Scriptures became a book of the heretics, and that image is still very much alive. Almost all Bibles and Bible commentaries in public and private libraries were destroyed, and for the next 200 years, no Catholic would translate a Bible into Italian. The only Bibles that circulated on the Italian peninsula—in secret, for fear of confiscation—were those translated by Protestant scholars. Thus, historian Mario Cignoni states: "In practice, Bible reading by laymen ceased completely for centuries. The Bible became virtually an unknown book, and millions of Italians lived their lives without ever reading a page of it."

ter the onset of the Protestant Reformation, the clergy of several European countries did their utmost to limit circulation of so-called heretical books. A turning point came after the Council of Trent in 1546, when the question of vernacular translations was considered. Two distinct positions emerged. Those favoring prohibition held that the Bible in the common tongue was "the mother and origin of all heresies." Those against the prohibition stated that their "adversaries," the Protestants, would argue that the church prohibited the Bible in the vernacular to hide "fraud and deceit."

Lack of agreement meant that the Council took no definite stand on the issue but limited itself to sanctioning the authenticity of the *Vulgate,* which became the standard text for the Catholic Church. However, Carlo Buzzetti, teacher at the Pontifical University Salesianum, Rome, notes that pronouncing the *Vulgate* "authentic" "favored the idea that, in practice, it was to be the

The index of prohibited books listed translations of the Bible into the vernacular as dangerous

Prohibition Relaxed

Later, Pope Benedict XIV, in a decree on the index dated June 13, 1757, modified the previous rule, "permitting readings of vernacular versions approved by the Holy See and published under the direction of bishops." As a consequence, Antonio Martini, who later became archbishop of Florence, prepared to translate the *Vulgate.* The first part was published in 1769, and the work was completed in 1781. According to one Catholic source, Martini's translation was "the first truly worthy of particular mention." Until then, Catholics who did not understand Latin were unable to read a Bible authorized by the church. For the next 150 years, Martini's was the only version approved for Italian Catholics.

A turning point was reached at the ecumenical council Vatican II. In 1965 the document *Dei Verbum* for the first time encouraged "suitable and correct translations . . . into various languages, especially from the original texts of the sacred books." Shortly before, in 1958, the Pontificio istituto biblico (Pontifical Biblical Institute) published "the first complete Catholic translation from the original texts." This version restored a few occurrences of the divine name in the form "Jahve."

Opposition to Bibles in the vernacular has been devastating, and its effects are still felt. As stated by Gigliola Fragnito, it has had the effect of "inculcating in believers distrust of their own freedom of intellect and conscience." In addition, there has been an imposition of religious traditions, which many Catholics view as more important than the Bible. All of this has caused people to become estranged from the Scriptures, even though illiteracy has virtually disappeared.

The evangelizing work of Jehovah's Witnesses, however, has aroused new interest in the Bible in Italian. In 1963 the Witnesses published the *New World Translation of the Christian Greek Scriptures* in Italian. In 1967 the whole Bible became available. More than 4,000,000 copies of this version have been distributed in Italy alone. The *New World Translation,* which restores the divine name, Jehovah, in its text, distinguishes itself for its scrupulous adherence to the sense of the original texts.

Jehovah's Witnesses go from house to house, reading and explaining the Scriptural message of hope to all who will listen. (Acts 20:20) The next time you meet Jehovah's Witnesses, why not ask them to show you what your own Bible says concerning God's marvelous promise that soon he will establish "a new earth" in which "righteousness is to dwell"?—2 Peter 3:13.

HELPING CHINESE PEOPLE IN MEXICO

"TEN men out of all the languages of the nations will take hold, yes, they will actually take hold of the skirt of a man who is a Jew, saying: 'We will go with you people, for we have heard that God is with you people.'" (Zechariah 8:23) Today, this beautiful prophecy is being fulfilled throughout the world. People "out of all the languages of the nations" are clinging to the spiritual Israelites in order to worship Jehovah God. Jehovah's Witnesses are keenly interested in the fulfillment of this prophecy. Many of them are learning another language in order to share in the worldwide preaching work.

Jehovah's Witnesses in Mexico are no exception. An estimated 30,000 Chinese-speaking people live in Mexico. In 2003, 15 of them attended the Memorial of Christ's death held in Mexico City. Thus Witnesses in Mexico became aware of the potential for spiritual growth in the Chinese field. In order to have more preachers to care for these Chinese-speaking people, a three-month course was established to teach Mexican Witnesses simple presentations in Mandarin Chinese. Altogether, 25 Witnesses took the course. At its completion, an official from the Mandarin-speaking community in Mexico City attended the graduation, showing the impact of the class on the Chinese-speaking populace. A local Chinese institution offered three of the students scholarships to go abroad to polish up their Chinese.

The language course involved practical training. After learning some very basic phrases, the students immediately began preaching in Chinese in the business district of Mexico City. The zealous students started 21 Bible studies. The brochure *What Does God Require of Us?* in Chinese with text rendered in the Roman alphabet, called Pinyin, was of great help.

How did the Witnesses who had just started to take the course in Chinese conduct Bible studies? At first, they could say only, *"Qing Du* [Please read]" and point to a paragraph and then to the question. After the person read and answered in Chinese, they would say, *"Shei shei* [Thank you]" and, *"Hen Hao* [Very good]."

One such Bible study was started with a woman who was a nominal Christian. After the third study, the Witness wondered if the

A Chinese language class in Mexico City

woman really understood the information. So the Witness took along a brother whose native tongue was Chinese. When he asked the woman if she had any questions, the woman asked: "To get baptized, do I have to be able to swim?"

Before long, a Congregation Book Study was established with an average attendance of 9 Chinese-speaking persons and 23 local Mexican Witnesses. Among those attending was a Chinese doctor, who had received the *Watchtower* and *Awake!* magazines in Spanish from one of his patients. Since he did not read Spanish, he had someone translate a few lines for him. Realizing that the magazines dealt with the Bible, he asked the patient if she could obtain the magazines in Chinese. She did, and through the branch office of Jehovah's Witnesses in Mexico, arrangements were made for a Chinese-speaking Witness to call on him. His mother in China had a Bible, and the doctor had enjoyed reading it. When he decided to go to Mexico, his mother told him not to stop reading the Bible. So he had been praying for someone who could help him learn more about the God of the Bible. He exclaimed: "God has listened to my prayer!"

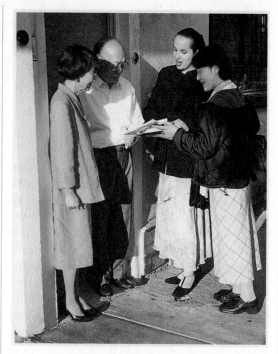

Door-to-door ministry in Chinese, Mexico City

Also attending the book study was a Chinese family who rented living quarters from a Mexican woman who was studying the Bible with Jehovah's Witnesses. Although the Chinese family understood very little Spanish, they would sit in on the Bible discussions. In time, the family asked the Witness conducting the study if she had any publications in Chinese. Soon a Bible study in Chinese was conducted with them. Before long, the family expressed a desire to preach to their fellow countrymen and to dedicate their lives to Jehovah.

True, Chinese is a difficult language to learn. As seen in the foregoing experiences, however, with Jehovah's help people of many languages, including Chinese, are learning God's will in Mexico, as well as in other parts of the earth.

A Mexican Witness conducting a Bible study in Chinese

WHOM DO *YOU* OBEY —GOD OR MEN?

"We must obey God as ruler rather than men."—ACTS 5:29.

THE judges of the Jewish supreme court must have been furious. The prisoners were missing. They were apostles of Jesus Christ, a man the high court had condemned to death a few weeks earlier. Now the court was ready to deal with his closest followers. But when the guards went to fetch them, they discovered that their cells were empty, although the doors had been locked. The guards soon learned that the apostles were at the temple in Jerusalem, fearlessly teaching the people about Jesus Christ—the very activity for which they had been arrest-

___
1. (a) What is the theme text for this study? (b) Why were the apostles taken into custody?

ed! The guards went straightaway to the temple, took the apostles back into custody, and brought them to court.—Acts 5:17-27.

² An angel had released the apostles from prison. Was this to spare them further persecution? No. It was in order that the inhabitants of Jerusalem should hear the good news about Jesus Christ. The angel's instruction to the apostles was that they "keep on speaking to the people all the sayings about this life." (Acts 5:19, 20) So it was that when the temple guards caught up with them, they found the apostles obediently carrying out that command.

___
2. What did an angel command the apostles to do?

"We must obey God as ruler rather than men"

19

³ Two of those tenacious preachers, the apostles Peter and John, had been in court before, as the chief justice, Joseph Caiaphas, sternly reminded them. He said: "We positively ordered you not to keep teaching upon the basis of [the name of Jesus], and yet, look! you have filled Jerusalem with your teaching." (Acts 5:28) Caiaphas should not have been surprised to see Peter and John back in court. When ordered to stop preaching the first time, the two apostles answered: "Whether it is righteous in the sight of God to listen to you rather than to God, judge for yourselves. But as for us, we *cannot* stop speaking about the things we have seen and heard." Like the ancient prophet Jeremiah, Peter and John could not hold back from carrying out their commission to preach. —Acts 4:18-20; Jeremiah 20:9.

⁴ Now, not only Peter and John but all the apostles—including the newly selected Matthias—had the opportunity to go on record with the court. (Acts 1:21-26) When ordered to stop preaching, they too boldly replied: "We *must* obey God as ruler rather than men."—Acts 5:29.

God as Ruler Versus Man as Ruler

⁵ The apostles were law-abiding men who would not normally disobey a court order. However, no human, no matter how powerful, is authorized to order another to disobey one of God's commands. Jehovah is "the Most High over all the earth." (Psalm 83:18) Not only is he "the Judge of all the earth" but he is also the Supreme Lawgiver, as well as the King of eternity. Any court order that attempts to override one of God's commands is invalid from God's standpoint.—Genesis 18:25; Isaiah 33:22.

⁶ This fact has been acknowledged by some of the finest legal minds. For example, the noted 18th-century English jurist William Blackstone wrote that no human law should be allowed to contradict "the law of revelation" as found in the Bible. Thus, the Sanhedrin crossed the line when it ordered the apostles to stop preaching. The apostles simply could not comply with that order.

⁷ The apostles' determination to keep preaching angered the chief priests. Certain members of the priesthood, including Caiaphas himself, were Sadducees, who did not believe in the resurrection. (Acts 4:1, 2; 5:17) Yet, the apostles kept insisting that Jesus had been resurrected from the dead. In addition, some of the chief priests had gone to great lengths to curry favor with the Roman authorities. At Jesus' trial, when offered the opportunity to accept Jesus as their king, the chief priests went so far as to cry out: "We have no king but Caesar." (John 19:15)* Not only were the apostles affirming that Jesus had been resurrected but they were teaching that apart from the name of Jesus, "there is not another name under heaven that has been given among men by which we must get saved." (Acts 2:36; 4:12) If the people began to look to the resurrected Jesus as their Leader, the priests feared, the Romans might come and the Jewish leaders might lose 'both their place and their nation.'—John 11:48.

⁸ The future looked grim for the apostles of Jesus Christ. The judges of the Sanhedrin

---

* The "Caesar" whom the chief priests publicly embraced on that occasion was the despised Roman Emperor Tiberius, a hypocrite and a murderer. Tiberius was also known for his debased sexual practices.—Daniel 11: 15, 21.

3, 4. (a) When ordered to stop preaching, how did Peter and John respond? (b) How did the other apostles respond?

5, 6. Why did the apostles not obey the order of the court?

7. Why did the preaching work anger the chief priests?

8. What wise counsel did Gamaliel give to the Sanhedrin?

Caiaphas put his trust in men rather than in God

were determined to have them put to death. (Acts 5:33) However, events took an unexpected turn. Gamaliel, an expert in the Law, stood up and warned his colleagues not to act hastily. He wisely observed: "If this scheme or this work is from men, it will be overthrown; but if it is from God, you will not be able to overthrow them." Then, significantly, Gamaliel added: "Otherwise, you may perhaps be found fighters actually against God."—Acts 5:34, 38, 39.

9 Amazingly, the court accepted Gamaliel's advice. The Sanhedrin "summoned the apostles, flogged them, and ordered them to stop speaking upon the basis of Jesus' name, and let them go." Far from being intimidated, however, the apostles were determined to obey the angelic command to preach. Thus, after their release, "every day in the temple and from house to house [the apostles] continued without letup teaching and declaring

the good news about the Christ, Jesus." (Acts 5:40, 42) Jehovah blessed their efforts. To what extent? "The word of God went on growing, and the number of the disciples kept multiplying in Jerusalem very much." In fact, "a great crowd of priests began to be obedient to the faith." (Acts 6:7) How devastating that must have been for the chief priests! The evidence was piling up: The work of the apostles was indeed from God!

Fighters Against God Cannot Succeed

10 In the first century, the Jewish high priests were appointed by the Roman authorities. Wealthy Joseph Caiaphas was placed in his position by Valerius Gratus, and he held that post longer than many of his predecessors. Caiaphas likely attributed this accomplishment to his skill as a diplomat and his personal friendship with Pilate rather than

---

9. What proves that the apostles' work was from God?

10. From a human standpoint, why might Caiaphas have felt secure in his position, but why was his confidence misplaced?

to divine providence. In any case, his confidence in men proved to be misplaced. Just three years after the apostles appeared before the Sanhedrin, Caiaphas fell out of favor with the Roman authorities and was removed as high priest.

¹¹ The order to strip Caiaphas of his office came from Pilate's immediate superior, Lucius Vitellius, governor of Syria, and Caiaphas' close friend Pilate was unable to prevent it. In fact, just one year after Caiaphas' downfall, Pilate himself was removed from office and was recalled to Rome to answer serious charges. As for the Jewish leaders who put their trust in Caesar, the Romans did take away 'both their place and their nation.' This occurred in the year 70 C.E. when the Roman armies completely destroyed the city of Jerusalem, including the temple and the Sanhedrin hall. How true the words of the psalmist proved to be in this case: "Do not put your trust in nobles, nor in the son of earthling man, to whom no salvation belongs"!—John 11:48; Psalm 146:3.

¹² In contrast, God appointed the resurrected Jesus Christ as High Priest of a great spiritual temple. No man can cancel that appointment. Indeed, Jesus "has his priesthood without any successors." (Hebrews 2:9; 7:17, 24; 9:11) God also appointed Jesus as Judge of the living and the dead. (1 Peter 4:5) In that capacity, Jesus will determine whether Joseph Caiaphas and Pontius Pilate have any possibility of future life.—Matthew 23:33; Acts 24:15.

Fearless Modern-Day Kingdom Preachers

¹³ In our day, as in the first century, there has been no shortage of 'fighters against God.' (Acts 5:39) For example, when Jehovah's Witnesses in Germany refused to heil Adolf Hitler as their Führer, Hitler vowed to exterminate them. (Matthew 23:10) His efficient death machine seemed more than equal to the task. The Nazis did succeed in rounding up thousands of Witnesses and sending them off to concentration camps. They even managed to kill some Witnesses. But the Nazis failed to break the Witnesses' resolve to worship God alone, and they failed to eliminate God's servants as a group. The work of these Christians was from God, not man, and the work of God cannot be overthrown. Sixty years later, faithful survivors of Hitler's concentration camps are still serving Jehovah 'with their whole heart and soul and mind,' whereas Hitler and his Nazi party live only in infamy.—Matthew 22:37.

¹⁴ In the years since the Nazis' efforts, others have joined the losing battle against Jehovah and his people. In a number of countries in Europe, crafty religious and political elements have endeavored to brand Jeho-

---

11. What end came to Pontius Pilate and the Jewish system of things, and what conclusion do you draw from this?
12. How does the case of Jesus prove that obedience to God is the course of wisdom?

Can You Answer?

- What encouraging example did the apostles set for us by the way they faced opposition?

- Why should we always obey God as ruler rather than men?

- Our opposers are really fighting against whom?

- What outcome can we expect for those who endure persecution?

---

13. In modern times, what work proved to be from men, and what work proved to be from God? How do you know?
14. (a) What efforts have opposers made to slander God's servants, and with what results? (b) Will such efforts bring any lasting harm to God's people? (Hebrews 13:5, 6)

vah's Witnesses a 'dangerous sect,' the same charge that was leveled against first-century Christians. (Acts 28:22) The fact is, the European Court of Human Rights has recognized Jehovah's Witnesses as a religion, not a sect. Opposers must know that. Still, they persist in slandering the Witnesses. As a direct result of this mischaracterization, some of these Christians have been discharged from their employment. Witness children have been harassed in schools. Fearful landlords have canceled contracts for buildings that the Witnesses have long used as meeting places. In a few cases, government agencies have even denied citizenship to individuals solely on the grounds that they are Jehovah's Witnesses! Still, the Witnesses are undeterred.

15 In France, for example, people are generally reasonable and fair-minded. However, a few opposers have promoted laws aimed at crippling the Kingdom work. How have Jehovah's Witnesses there reacted? They have intensified their activity in the field as never before and with thrilling results. (James 4:7) Why, in just one six-month period, the number of home Bible studies increased by an amazing 33 percent in that country! It must infuriate the Devil to see honesthearted ones in France respond to the good news. (Revelation 12:17) Our fellow Christians in France are confident that the words of the prophet Isaiah will prove true in their case: "Any weapon whatever that will be formed against you will have no success, and any tongue at all that will rise up against you in the judgment you will condemn."—Isaiah 54:17.

16 Jehovah's Witnesses do not enjoy being persecuted. However, in obedience to God's command to all Christians, they cannot and

---

The yeartext for 2006 will be: "We must obey God as ruler rather than men." —Acts 5:29

will not stop speaking about the things they have heard. They endeavor to be good citizens. Where there is a conflict between God's law and man's law, however, they must obey God as ruler.

Fear Them Not

17 Our enemies are in a very precarious position. They are fighting against God. Thus, in harmony with Jesus' command, rather than fear them, we pray for those persecuting us. (Matthew 5:44) We pray that if any are opposing God out of ignorance, as Saul of Tarsus was, Jehovah will graciously open their eyes to the truth. (2 Corinthians 4:4) Saul became the Christian apostle Paul and suffered greatly at the hands of the authorities of his day. Still, he kept reminding fellow believers "to be in subjection and be obedient to governments and authorities as rulers, to be ready for every good work, to speak injuriously of no one [no, not even of their most ardent persecutors], not to be belligerent, to be reasonable, exhibiting all mildness toward all men." (Titus 3:1, 2) Jehovah's Witnesses in France and elsewhere endeavor to take this counsel to heart.

18 God told the prophet Jeremiah: "I am

15, 16. How have Jehovah's Witnesses in France reacted to opposition to their Christian work, and why do they keep on preaching?

17. (a) Why are our enemies not to be feared? (b) What should be our attitude toward persecutors? 18. (a) In what ways might Jehovah deliver his people? (b) What will be the final outcome?

with you to deliver you." (Jeremiah 1:8) How might Jehovah deliver us from persecution today? He might raise up a fair-minded judge like Gamaliel. Or he may see to it that a corrupt or antagonistic official is unexpectedly replaced by a more reasonable one. At times, though, Jehovah may permit the persecution of his people to run its course. (2 Timothy 3:12) If God allows us to be persecuted, he will always give us the strength to endure persecution. (1 Corinthians 10:13) And no matter what God permits, we have no doubt as to the final outcome: Those who fight against God's people are fighting against God, and fighters against God will not prevail.

¹⁹ Jesus told his disciples to expect tribulation. (John 16:33) In view of this, the words recorded at Acts 5:29 have never been more timely: *"We must obey God as ruler rather than men."* For that reason, these thrilling words have been selected as the yeartext of Jehovah's Witnesses for 2006. May it be our resolve during the coming year and throughout eternity to obey God as Ruler at all costs!

---

19. What is the yeartext for 2006, and why is it appropriate?

NOW IS THE TIME FOR DECISIVE ACTION

"How long will you be limping upon two different opinions?"—1 KINGS 18:21.

DO YOU believe that Jehovah is the only true God? Do you also believe that Bible prophecies point to our time as "the last days" of Satan's wicked system? (2 Timothy 3:1) If so, you will surely agree that now, of all times, there is a need for decisive action. Never before in human history have so many lives been at stake.

² In the tenth century B.C.E., the nation of Israel needed to make a very serious decision. Whom would they serve? King Ahab, under the influence of his pagan wife, Jezebel, promoted Baal worship in the ten-tribe kingdom of Israel. Baal was a fertility god who was supposed to provide rain and fruitful crops.

Many Baal worshippers may have blown a kiss or bowed down to an idol of their god. To induce Baal to bless their crops and livestock, his worshippers took part in sex orgies with temple prostitutes. They also had the custom of cutting themselves to make blood flow. —1 Kings 18:28.

³ A remnant of some 7,000 Israelites refused to take part in this idolatrous, immoral, violent form of worship. (1 Kings 19:18) They loyally stuck to their covenant relationship with Jehovah God, and for this they were persecuted. For example, Queen Jezebel murdered many prophets of Jehovah. (1 Kings 18:4, 13) Because of these trying conditions, the majority of the Israel-

---

1. What makes our time so different from the past?
2. What happened in the ten-tribe kingdom of Israel during the reign of King Ahab?

3. What effect did Baal worship have on God's people?

ites practiced interfaith, trying to please both Jehovah and Baal. But it was apostasy for an Israelite to turn away from Jehovah and worship a false god. Jehovah promised to bless the Israelites if they loved him and obeyed his commandments. However, he warned them that if they failed to give him "exclusive devotion," they would be annihilated. —Deuteronomy 5:6-10; 28:15, 63.

⁴ A similar situation exists in Christendom today. Church members claim to be Christians, but their holidays, behavior, and beliefs conflict with Bible teachings. Like Jezebel, Christendom's clergy spearhead the persecution of Jehovah's Witnesses. Christendom's clergy also have a long record of supporting wars and are thus responsible for the deaths of countless millions of church members. Such religious support of worldly

governments is identified in the Bible as spiritual fornication. (Revelation 18:2, 3) In addition, Christendom has become increasingly tolerant of literal fornication, even among its clergy. Jesus Christ and his apostles foretold this great apostasy. (Matthew 13:36-43; Acts 20:29, 30; 2 Peter 2:1, 2) What will be the final outcome for the more than one billion adherents of Christendom? And what responsibility do true worshippers of Jehovah have toward these and all others who have been misled by false religion? We get a clear answer to such questions by examining the dramatic events that led to the 'annihilation of Baal out of Israel.'—2 Kings 10:28.

God's Love for His Wayward People

⁵ Jehovah God takes no delight in punishing those who become unfaithful to him. As a loving Father, he desires that wicked ones

---

4. What did Jesus and his apostles foretell would happen among Christians, and how has it been fulfilled?

5. How did Jehovah show loving concern for his wayward people?

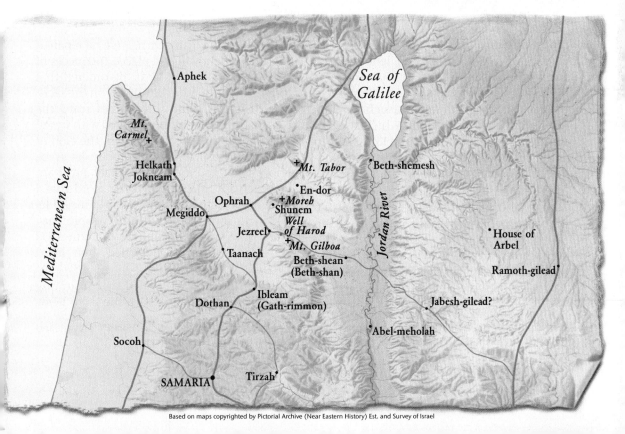

Regularly sharing in Kingdom preaching and attending Christian meetings are vital aspects of true worship

as Elijah was the only prophet representing Jehovah. Getting to the root of their problem, Elijah asked the people: "How long will you be limping upon two different opinions?" Then, in even plainer words, he placed the issue before them: "If Jehovah is the true God, go following him; but if Baal is, go following him." To move the indecisive Israelites to render exclusive devotion to Jehovah, Elijah proposed a test of Godship. Two bulls were to be slaughtered as a sacrifice, one for Jehovah and the other for Baal. The true God would consume his sacrifice with fire. The Baal prophets got their sacrifice ready, and then for hours they kept calling: "O Baal, answer us!" When Elijah began to mock them, they cut themselves until blood flowed, and they shouted at the top of their voice. But there was no answer. —1 Kings 18:21, 26-29.

repent and turn back to him. (Ezekiel 18:32; 2 Peter 3:9) As evidence of this, Jehovah used many prophets in the days of Ahab and Jezebel to warn His people of the consequences of Baal worship. Elijah was one such prophet. After a devastating drought, which was announced in advance, Elijah told King Ahab to gather the Israelites and Baal prophets together on Mount Carmel.—1 Kings 18:1, 19.

⁶ The meeting took place at the site of an altar of Jehovah that had been "torn down," probably to please Jezebel. (1 Kings 18:30) Sadly, the Israelites in attendance were not sure who—Jehovah or Baal—was in the best position to produce the much-needed rain. Baal was represented by 450 prophets, where-

⁷ Now came Elijah's turn. First, he repaired the altar of Jehovah and placed the pieces of the young bull on it. Next, he ordered that four large jars of water be poured on the sacrifice. This was done three times until the trench around the altar was filled with water. Then Elijah prayed: "O Jehovah, the God of Abraham, Isaac and Israel, today let it be known that you are God in Israel and I am your servant and it is by your word that I have done all these things. Answer me, O Jehovah, answer me, that this people may know that you, Jehovah, are the true God and you yourself have turned their heart back."—1 Kings 18:30-37.

⁸ The true God responded by consuming both sacrifice and altar with fire from heav-

6, 7. (a) How did Elijah expose the root cause of Israel's apostasy? (b) What did the Baal prophets do? (c) What did Elijah do?

8. How did God respond to Elijah's prayer, and what action did the prophet take?

en. That fire consumed even the water in the trench around the altar! Imagine the effect on the Israelites. "They immediately fell upon their faces and said: 'Jehovah is the true God! Jehovah is the true God!'" Elijah now took further decisive action, ordering the Israelites: "Seize the prophets of Baal! Do not let a single one of them escape!" All 450 Baal prophets were then executed at the foot of Mount Carmel.—1 Kings 18:38-40.

⁹ On that same unforgettable day, Jehovah caused rain to fall upon the land for the first time in three and a half years! (James 5:17, 18) You can imagine all the talk among the Israelites as they returned home; Jehovah had vindicated his Godship. The Baal worshippers, however, did not give up. Jezebel continued her campaign of persecuting Jehovah's servants. (1 Kings 19:1, 2; 21:11-16) Thus the integrity of God's people was again tested. Would they be giving exclusive devotion to Jehovah when his day of judgment against Baal worshippers came?

Act Decisively Now

¹⁰ In modern times, anointed Christians have done a work like that of Elijah. By word of mouth and by the printed page, they have warned people of all nations inside and outside of Christendom about the danger of false religion. As a result, millions have taken decisive action to end their membership in false religion. They have dedicated their lives to Jehovah and have become baptized disciples of Jesus Christ. Yes, they have heeded God's urgent appeal respecting false religion: "Get out of her, my people, if you do not want to share with her in her sins, and if you do not want to receive part of her plagues."—Revelation 18:4.

---

9. How were true worshippers still tested?
10. (a) In modern times, what have anointed Christians been doing? (b) What does it mean to obey the command found at Revelation 18:4?

¹¹ Other millions, while attracted to the Bible-based message spread by Jehovah's Witnesses, are still unsure about what they should do. Some of these occasionally come to Christian meetings, such as the observance of the Lord's Evening Meal or sessions of a district convention. We urge all such ones to consider carefully Elijah's words: "How long will you sit on the fence?" (1 Kings 18:21, *New English Bible*) Instead of delaying, they need to take decisive action now and zealously work toward the goal of becoming dedicated, baptized worshippers of Jehovah. Their prospects for everlasting life are at stake!—2 Thessalonians 1:6-9.

¹² Sadly, some baptized Christians have become irregular or inactive in their worship. (Hebrews 10:23-25; 13:15, 16) Some have lost their zeal because of fear of persecution, the anxieties of making a living, efforts to get rich, or the pursuit of selfish pleasures. Jesus warned that these very things would stumble, choke, and ensnare some of his followers. (Matthew 10:28-33; 13:20-22; Luke 12:22-31; 21:34-36) Instead of 'limping on two opinions,' as it were, such ones should "be zealous and repent" by taking decisive action to carry out their dedication to God.—Revelation 3:15-19.

False Religion's Sudden End

¹³ The reason why it is urgent for humans to take decisive action now is seen in what happened in Israel about 18 years after the issue of Godship was settled on Mount Carmel. Jehovah's day of judgment against Baal worship came suddenly and unexpectedly during the ministry of Elijah's successor, Elisha. King Ahab's son Jehoram was ruling

---

11. What is needed to have Jehovah's approval?
12. Into what dangerous condition have some baptized Christians slipped, and what should they do?
13. Describe the situation in Israel when Jehu was anointed as king.

Like Jehu, all who want to survive Jehovah's day must take decisive action

Israel, and Jezebel was still alive as queen mother. Quietly, Elisha sent his attendant to anoint Israel's army chief, Jehu, as the new king. At the time, Jehu was on the east side of the Jordan at Ramoth-gilead, directing a war against Israel's enemies. King Jehoram was at Jezreel in the valley plain near Megiddo, recovering from a battle wound.—2 Kings 8:29–9:4.

¹⁴ This is what Jehovah commanded Jehu to do: "You must strike down the house of

---

14, 15. What commission did Jehu receive, and how did he respond?

Ahab your lord, and I must avenge the blood of my servants the prophets and the blood of all the servants of Jehovah at the hand of Jezebel. And the whole house of Ahab must perish; . . . Jezebel the dogs will eat up in the tract of land at Jezreel, and there will be no one burying her."—2 Kings 9:7-10.

¹⁵ Jehu was a decisive man. Without delay, he got into his chariot and sped toward Jezreel. A watchman at Jezreel recognized the driving of Jehu and reported to King Jehoram, whereupon Jehoram got into his chariot and went out to meet his army chief. When they met, Jehoram asked: "Is there peace, Jehu?" Jehu replied: "What peace could there be as long as there are the fornications of Jezebel your mother and her many sorceries?" Then, before King Jehoram could flee, Jehu drew his bow and killed Jehoram with an arrow that pierced his heart.—2 Kings 9:20-24.

¹⁶ Wasting no time, Jehu raced to the city in his chariot. Looking down from a window, the heavily made-up Jezebel greeted Jehu with a challenging threat. Ignoring her, Jehu called for support: "Who is with me? Who?" Jezebel's attendants now had to act decisively. Two or three court officials stuck their heads out of the window. Immediately, their loyalty was put to the test. "Let her drop!" ordered Jehu. The officials let Jezebel

---

16. (a) What situation did Jezebel's court officials suddenly face? (b) How was Jehovah's word about Jezebel fulfilled?

Questions for Meditation

- How did ancient Israel become guilty of Baal worship?
- What great apostasy did the Bible foretell, and how has that prophecy been fulfilled?
- How did Jehu eradicate Baal worship?
- What must we do to survive God's day of judgment?

drop to the street below, where she was trampled by Jehu's horses and chariot. Thus the instigator of Baal worship in Israel came to her deserved end. Before there was time to bury her, dogs had eaten up her fleshy parts, just as foretold.—2 Kings 9:30-37.

¹⁷ A similar shocking end will come to the symbolic harlot who has the name "Babylon the Great." The harlot represents the false religions of Satan's world, which have their origin in the ancient city of Babylon. After false religion's end, Jehovah God will turn his attention to all humans who make up the secular parts of Satan's world. These will also be destroyed, preparing the way for a righteous new world.—Revelation 17:3-6; 19:19-21; 21:1-4.

¹⁸ After Jezebel's death, King Jehu wasted no time in executing all Ahab's descendants and key supporters. (2 Kings 10:11) But many Baal-worshipping Israelites remained in the land. Concerning these, Jehu took decisive action to show his "toleration of no rivalry toward Jehovah." (2 Kings 10:16) Pretending to be a Baal worshipper himself, Jehu organized a great festival at the temple of Baal that Ahab had built in Samaria. All Baal worshippers in Israel came to the festival. Trapped inside the temple, they were all

slaughtered by Jehu's men. The Bible concludes the account with the words: "Thus Jehu annihilated Baal out of Israel."—2 Kings 10:18-28.

¹⁹ Baal worship was eradicated from Israel. Just as surely, this world's false religions will come to a sudden, shocking end. On whose side will you be during that great day of judgment? Act decisively now, and you may be privileged to be included among the "great crowd" of human survivors of "the great tribulation." Then you will be able to look back with joy, and you will praise God for executing judgment on "the great harlot who corrupted the earth with her fornication." United with other true worshippers, you will be in agreement with the thrilling words that heavenly voices sing: "Praise Jah, you people, because Jehovah our God, the Almighty, has begun to rule as king."—Revelation 7:9, 10, 14; 19:1, 2, 6.

---

19. What grand prospect awaits the "great crowd" of Jehovah's loyal worshippers?

---

17. God's judgment upon Jezebel should strengthen our faith in what future event?
18. After Jezebel's death, what happened to Baal worshippers in Israel?

Do You Remember?

Have you appreciated reading the recent issues of *The Watchtower?*
See if you can answer the following questions:

● **Why can the first sin—Adam's disobedience—be likened to a hereditary disease?**
It is like a disease because Adam transmitted sin to his offspring. We have thus inherited the defect of sin, just as some children inherit a disease from their parents.—8/15, page 5.

● **What are basic causes of the increased violence today?**
Satan is trying to estrange people from Jehovah by sowing a spirit of violence in hearts, such as through movies, music, and computer games that incite players to simulate brutality and slaughter. Media violence has contributed to many acts of violence.—9/1, page 29.

● **Who was Pontius Pilate?**
He was a Roman of the lower nobility who had likely been in the military. Roman Emperor Tiberius appointed Pilate governor of the province of Judaea in 26 C.E. At Jesus' trial, Pilate heard charges made by the Jewish leaders. To please the crowd, he sanctioned Jesus' execution.—9/15, pages 10-12.

● **What is "the sign" mentioned at Matthew 24:3?**
This sign is composed of several facets that make up a composite identifying mark, or signal. The sign includes war, famine, pestilence, and earthquakes, and it would enable Jesus' followers to recognize his "presence" as well as "the conclusion of the system of things."—10/1, pages 4-5.

● **What was the Diaspora, and what locations were involved?**
The term applies to the Jews living outside Palestine. In the first century, the main Jewish centers were in Syria, Asia Minor, Babylonia, and Egypt, and there were smaller communities in the European part of the Roman Empire.—10/15, page 12.

● **Can a Christian maintain a good conscience if he accepts armed employment?**
Engaging in secular work that requires carrying a firearm or another weapon is a personal decision. But armed employment exposes one to possible bloodguilt if one uses the weapon and to the danger of injury or death from an attack or reprisal. A Christian carrying such a weapon would not qualify for special privileges in the congregation. (1 Timothy 3:3, 10)—11/1, page 31.

● **Since the word "Armageddon" is drawn from the expression "Mountain of Megiddo," will the battle of Armageddon be fought at a mountain in the Middle East?**
No. There is no Mountain of Megiddo, only a mound, or tell, rising above the adjacent valley plain in Israel. That area could not hold all "the kings of the earth and their armies." God's great war will be fought earth wide, and it will end all wars. (Revelation 16:14, 16; 19:19; Psalm 46:8, 9)—12/1, pages 4-7.

IN OUR NEXT ISSUE

How Good Will Conquer Evil

———

How Firm Is Your Trust in God?

———

Seeking Righteousness Will Protect Us

SUBJECT INDEX FOR *THE WATCHTOWER* 2005

Indicating date of issue in which article appears

BIBLE

Berleburg Bible, 2/15
Can Help You Find Joy, 8/1
"Clear Light" From Russia's Oldest Library, 7/15
Early German, Uses God's Name, 9/1
Highlights From Judges, 1/15
Highlights From Ruth, 3/1
Highlights From 1 Samuel, 3/15
Highlights From 2 Samuel, 5/15
Highlights From 1 Kings, 7/1
Highlights From 2 Kings, 8/1
Highlights From 1 Chronicles, 10/1
Highlights From 2 Chronicles, 12/1
History—How Accurate? 4/15
Italian—Troubled History, 12/15
"It Is Finished" (*New World Translation of the Christian Greek Scriptures* in Lingala), 7/1
"Pim" Testifies to Historicity, 3/15
Royal Bible, 8/15
Science and, Contradict? 4/1
Sea of Galilee (ancient boat), 8/15
Translation Aid, 4/15
True Teachings, 7/15

CALENDAR

Families Fortified, 5/15
Multitudes Embrace Jehovah's Worship, 9/15
Old Age "a Crown of Beauty," 1/15
Self-Sacrifice, 11/15
Single and Contented, 7/15
Youths Praise Jehovah, 3/15

CHRISTIAN LIFE AND QUALITIES

Basis for Taking Offense? 8/1
"Be Hospitable," 1/15
Can Cope With Any Trial! 6/15
Common Sense, 5/15
Conscience Well Trained? 10/1
Converse With Those You Love, 6/1
Courage in Face of Opposition, 5/1
Customs That Displease God, 1/1
Faith Move You to Action? 4/15
'Fear of Jehovah Is Wisdom' (Pr 14), 9/15
Listening With Love, 11/15
Loyalty, 9/1
Make Each Day Count, 5/1
Making Jehovah Your God, 4/1
Making Peace, 3/1
Marital Disagreements, 6/1
Mealtime, 1/1
Measure Yourself Against Others? 2/15
Not Give Up in What Is Fine, 6/1
On What Foundation Building? 5/15
Protect Children by Godly Wisdom, 1/1
Resist Wrong Thinking! 9/15
"Rich Toward God"? 10/1
'Shrewd One Considers Steps' (Pr 14), 7/15
Truth Bearing Fruit in Those You Teach? 2/1
What Others Think of Us, 9/15

JEHOVAH

Always Does What Is Right, 2/1
Jehovah's "Saying" Safeguard You, 9/1
Jehovah Will Not Leave You, 10/15

JEHOVAH'S WITNESSES

Assembly in Refugee Camp (Kenya), 4/15
Australia's Outback, 4/1
Contributions, 11/1
'Could Have Been Freed,' 8/15
"Did Not Compromise," 7/15
"Faithful Under Trials" (video), 3/1
Gilead Graduation, 2/1
"Godly Obedience" Conventions, 3/1
Good Conduct Bears Fruit (Japan), 11/1
"Good News for People of All Nations" (booklet), 12/1

Helping Chinese in Mexico, 12/15
Honest People, 6/1
"Land of the Eagle" (Albania), 10/15
'Love of All Is Increasing' (Japan), 11/15
Macedonia, 4/15
Mennonites Search for Truth (Bolivia), 9/1
'One of Best Days of My Life' (Australia), 11/1
"Persecuted for His Faith" (N. Riet), 6/15
Power of God's Word, 2/15
Praising Jehovah at School, 6/15
'Preach Release to Captives' (prison work), 12/15
Saba, 2/15
Share Good News With Deaf (Spain), 11/1
Testimony to Love, Faith, Obedience (Watchtower Farms printery), 12/1
Where Early Christianity Flourished (Italy), 6/15

JESUS CHRIST

What Influence on You? 3/15
Who Is Jesus Christ? 9/15

LIFE STORIES

Determined to Continue Serving (C. Benanti), 12/1
Enduring as Soldier of Christ (Y. Kaptola), 9/1
Happy for Share in Bible Education (A. Matheakis), 7/1
I Received 'Requests of My Heart' (D. Morgou), 11/1
Jehovah Richly Rewards (R. Stawski), 8/1
Learned to Trust Completely in Jehovah (N. Holtorf), 1/1
Orphan Finds a Loving Father (D. Sidiropoulos), 4/1
Parents' Example Strengthened Me (J. Rekelj), 10/1
"The Life Now"—Enjoying It Fully! (T. Buckingham), 6/1
Though Weak, I Am Powerful (L. Engleitner), 5/1
Triumphant in Special Way (E. Ludolph), 5/1
Used Circumstances to Witness Far and Wide (R. Malicsi), 3/1

MISCELLANEOUS

Armageddon, 12/1
Best Education, 10/15
Change the World? 11/1
Christianity Among First-Century Jews, 10/15
Christmastime, 12/15
Control Your Future? 1/15
Death, 8/15
Devil Real? 11/15
Holiday Season, 12/15
'Impressed Into Service" (Mt 5:41), 2/15
"Jehovah's Sword and Gideon's!" 7/15
Mari—Queen of Desert, 5/15
Miracles, 2/15
Philo of Alexandria, 6/15
Pontius Pilate, 9/15
Poverty, 6/15
'Precious Red-Colored Stone' (Re 4:3), 3/15
Ransom Magnifies God's Righteousness, 11/1
Religion Unite Mankind? 1/1
Resurrection, 5/1
Samson Triumphs, 3/15
Saul's Preaching Excites Hostility, 1/15
Search for Inner Peace, 7/1
Sign of Jesus' Presence, 10/1
Taking in Knowledge—Now and Forever, 4/15
'They That Go Down to Sea in Ships,' 10/15
True Teachings, 7/15
What Is Life Worth? 2/1
Wonders of Creation Exalt Jehovah, 11/15
Work—Blessing or Curse? 6/15
World Unity, 6/1

QUESTIONS FROM READERS

Armed employment, 11/1
Contradiction about eating dead bodies? (Le 11:40; De 14:21), 7/1

David and men eat showbread, 3/15
David treat captives savagely? 2/15
"One alone having immortality" and "not one of men has seen" apply to Jesus? (1Ti 6:15, 16), 9/1
Paul: "I am a Pharisee" (Ac 23:6), 4/15
Peter's "Angel" (Ac 12:15), 6/1
"Probably" (Zep 2:3), 8/1
Samson rips lion apart as if kid? 1/15
Samson touch corpses as Nazirite? 1/15
Shechinah's significance, 8/15
Solomon to be resurrected? 7/15
Stephen pray to Jesus? 4/1
Tip government employee? 4/1
Violent computer games, 9/15
Why David and Bath-sheba not executed? 5/15
Women "kept safe through childbearing" (1Ti 2:15), 5/1

STUDY ARTICLES

Are You Faithful in All Things? 7/15
Becoming Progressive and Adaptable Ministers, 12/1
Beware of Developing Haughty Heart, 10/15
"Bringing Good News of Something Better," 7/1
Christ—Focus of Prophecy, 1/15
Christians—Be Proud of Who You Are! 2/15
Christians Reflect Glory of Jehovah, 8/15
Coming to Know Jehovah's Ways, 5/15
Cultivate Genuine Humility, 10/15
"Finding One Pearl of High Value," 2/1
Foregleams of God's Kingdom Become Reality, 1/15
Good News for People of All Nations, 7/1
Go On Walking as Jesus Christ Walked, 9/15
Hold to Pattern Jesus Set, 1/1
Hosea's Prophecy Helps Us Walk With God, 11/15
Jehovah Has Numbered "Very Hairs of Your Head," 8/1
Jehovah Is Our Shepherd, 11/1
Jehovah Is "Rewarder of Those Earnestly Seeking Him," 8/1
Jehovah Safeguards Those Who Hope in Him, 6/1
"Keep on the Watch"—Hour of Judgment Has Arrived! 10/1
"Keep Proving What You Yourselves Are," 7/15
'Keep Yourself Restrained Under Evil,' 5/15
Law of Love in Hearts, 8/15
Let God's Word Light Your Roadway, 4/15
Living No Longer for Ourselves, 3/15
Marriage Can Succeed in Today's World, 3/1
Now Is Time for Decisive Action, 12/15
Our Children—Precious Inheritance, 4/1
Parents, Protect Your Precious Inheritance, 4/1
Parents, Provide for Needs of Your Family, 6/15
Parents—What Future Do You Want for Your Children? 10/1
People 'of All Languages' Hear Good News, 12/1
Pursuing "Pearl of High Value" Today, 2/1
Resurrection Hope—What Does It Mean for You? 5/1
Resurrection—Teaching That Affects You, 5/1
Safeguarding Our Christian Identity, 2/15
Saved, Not by Works Alone, But by Undeserved Kindness, 6/1
Trained to Give Thorough Witness, 1/1
Trust in Jehovah's Word, 4/15
Walk by Faith, Not by Sight! 9/15
Walk With God in These Turbulent Times, 9/1
Walk With God, Reap What Is Good, 11/15
"Ways of Jehovah Are Upright," 11/15
We Shall Walk in Name of Jehovah Our God, 9/1
Whom Do You Obey—God or Men? 12/15
Who Will Be Resurrected? 5/1
Will You Reflect God's Glory? 8/15
Will You Walk With God? 11/1
Wise Guidance for Married Couples, 3/1
Young People, Praise Jehovah! 6/15
"You Were Bought With a Price," 3/15

NEW YEAR'S TREE
Is It Russian?
Is It Christian?

"**A**T THE beginning of the 1830's, the evergreen tree was still being referred to as a 'fetching German notion.' At the end of that decade, it had 'become a custom' in homes of the St. Petersburg elite. . . . Only in the homes of the clergy and in peasant huts did the evergreen tree fail to take root in the 19th century. . . .

"Before, the tree . . . was not especially favored. Its association as a death-symbol and its link with 'the underworld' according to Russian tradition, as well as the tradition of setting the tree on the roofs of taverns, contrasted with the changes in attitudes that occurred in the middle of the 19th century. . . . It is fully understandable that in the process of acceptance, the foreign tradition would take on the same meaning that was attributed to the Christmas tree in the West, its link to the Christmas theme. . . .

"The process of the tree's Christianization was not very smooth in Russia. It met opposition from the Orthodox Church. The clergy saw in the new celebration 'demonic action,' a pagan tradition, which had nothing to do with the birth of the Savior, and furthermore, it was a tradition from the West."—Professor Yelena V. Dushechkina, doctor of philological sciences at the St. Petersburg State University.

*w*05-E 12/15